Color-Coded Accounting Equation

This color-coded accounting equation is a tool you will use throughout your first accounting course. This tool is so important that we have to put it here for quick reference. You may find this helpful when preparing your homework assignments. Each financial statement is identified by a unique color. You will see these colors throughout the chapters when we present a financial statement.

1 The **income statement**, enclosed in the red box, provides the details of revenues earned and expenses incurred.

2 The revenue and expense transactions are then condensed into one number—net income—that becomes part of the **statement of owner's equity**, which appears in the yellow box.

3 Information from the statement of owner's equity flows into the **balance sheet**, shown in the blue box.

4 The **statement of cash flows**, as indicated by the green box, will provide details of how a company got its cash and how it spent cash during the accounting period.

accounting

7e

Charles T. Horngren Series in Accounting

Auditing and Assurance Services: An Integrated Approach, 11th ed.
Arens/Elder/Beasley

Governmental and Nonprofit Accounting: Theory and Practice, 8th ed.
Freeman/Shoulders

Financial Accounting, 6th ed.
Harrison/Horngren

Cases in Financial Reporting, 5th ed.
Hirst/McAnally

Cost Accounting: A Managerial Emphasis, 12th ed.
Horngren/Datar/Foster

Accounting, 7th ed.
Horngren/Harrison

Introduction to Financial Accounting, 9th ed.
Horngren/Sundem/Elliott

Introduction to Management Accounting, 13th ed.
Horngren/Sundem/Stratton

accounting

7e

Charles T. Horngren
Stanford University

Walter T. Harrison Jr.
Baylor University

Upper Saddle River, New Jersey 07458

Library of Congress Cataloging-in-Publication Data
Horngren, Charles T.
    Accounting / Charles T. Horngren, Walter T. Harrison, Jr. — 7th ed.
    p. cm.
    Includes bibliographical references and index.
    ISBN 0-13-243960-3 (hardback : alk. paper)
    1. Accounting.   I. Harrison, Walter T.   II. Title
HF5635.H8   2007
657—dc22   2006029536

Executive Editor: Jodi McPherson
VP/Editorial Director: Jeff Shelstad
Developmental Editors: Claire Hunter, Ralph Moore
Executive Marketing Manager: Sharon Koch
Marketing Assistant: Patrick Barbera
Associate Director, Production Editorial: Judy Leale
Production Editor: Michael Reynolds
Permissions Supervisor: Charles Morris
Manufacturing Manager: Arnold Vila
Creative Director: Maria Lange
Cover Design: Solid State Graphics
Director, Image Resource Center: Melinda Patelli
Manager, Rights and Permissions: Zina Arabia
Manager, Visual Research: Beth Brenzel
Manager, Cover Visual Research & Permissions: Karen Sanatar
Image Permission Coordinator: Nancy Seise
Photo Researcher: Diane Austin
Manager, Print Production: Christy Mahon
Composition/Full-Service Project Management: BookMasters, Inc.
Printer/Binder: RR Donnelley–Willard
Typeface: 10/12 Sabon

Credits and acknowledgments borrowed from other sources and reproduced, with permission, in this textbook appear on page PC-1.

Pearson Education LTD.
Pearson Education Singapore, Pte. Ltd
Pearson Education, Canada, Ltd
Pearson Education–Japan

Pearson Education Australia PTY, Limited
Pearson Education North Asia Ltd
Pearson Educación de Mexico, S.A. de C.V.
Pearson Education Malaysia, Pte. Ltd

10 9 8 7 6 5 4 3 2 1
ISBN 0-13-243960-3

Brief Contents

Contents

5 **Merchandising Operations** 252

21 Cost-Volume-Profit Analysis   1050

22 The Master Budget and Responsibility Accounting   1100

To Billie Harrison, who taught me excellence

The *Accounting, 7e*, Demo Doc System: For professors whose greatest joy is hearing students say "I get it!"

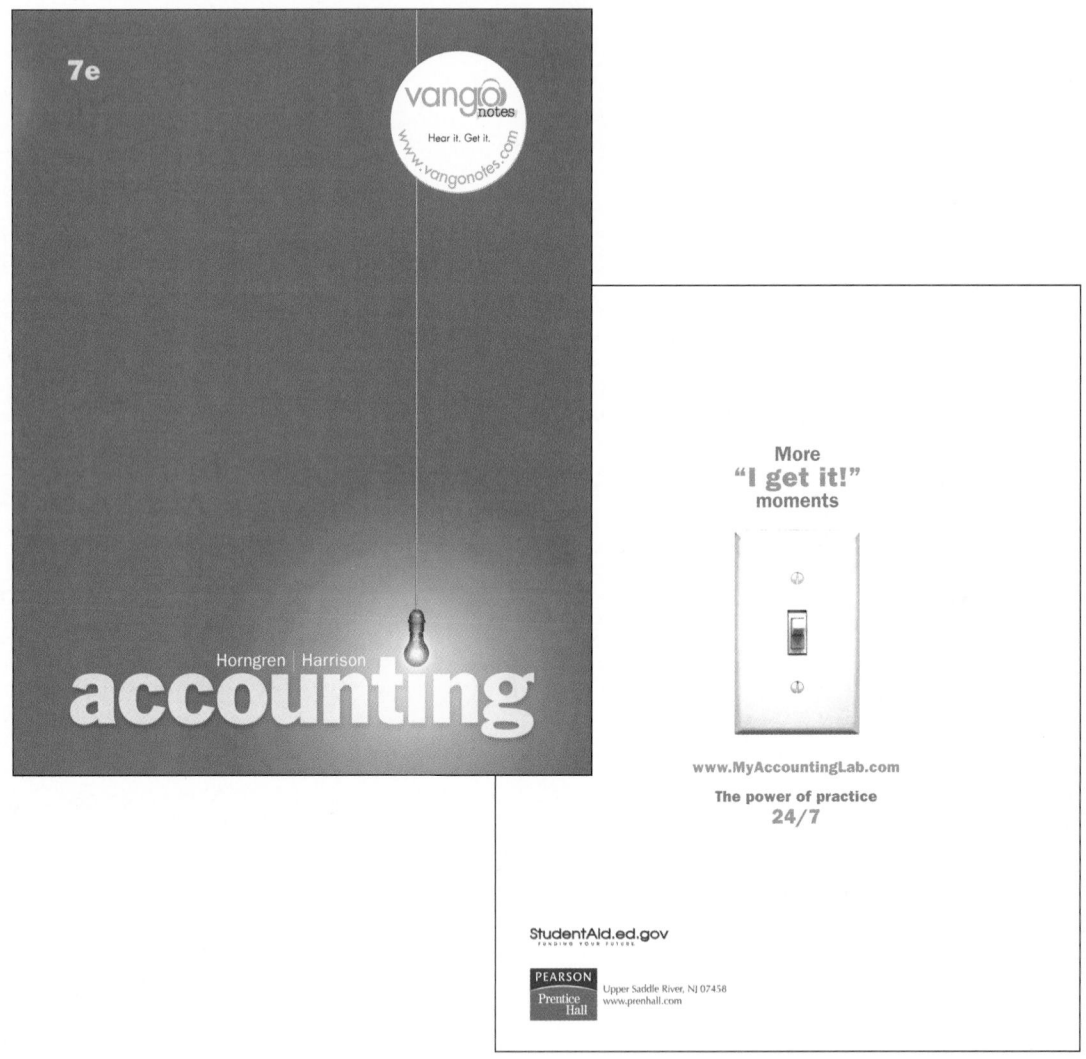

Help your students achieve "I get it!" moments when you're with them AND when you're NOT.

When you're there showing how to solve a problem in class, students "get it." When you're not there, they get stuck—it's only natural.

Our system is designed to help you deliver the best "I get it!" moments. (Instructor's Edition, Instructor Demo Docs)

But it's the really tricky situations that no one else has zeroed in on—the 2 A.M. outside-of-class moments, when you're not there—that present the greatest challenge.

That's where we come in, at these "they have the book, but they don't have you" moments. *Accounting 7e*'s Demo Doc System will help in those critical times. That's what makes this package different from all other textbooks.

The *Accounting 7e,* Demo Doc System provides the vehicle for you and your students to have more "I get it!" moments inside and outside of class.

Duplicate the classroom experience anytime, anywhere with Horngren & Harrison's *Accounting, Seventh Edition*

How The System Works

- The Demo Docs are entire problems worked through step-by-step, from start to finish, with the kind of comments around them that YOU would say in class. They exist in the first four chapters of this text to support the critical accounting cycle chapters, in the Study Guide both in print and in FLASH versions, and as a part of the instructor package for instructors to use in class.

- The authors have created a "no clutter" layout so that critical content is clear and easily referenced.

- Consistency is stressed across all mediums: text, student, and instructor supplements.

- MyAccountingLab is an online homework system that combines "I get it!" moments with the power of practice.

The System's Backbone

Demo Docs in the Text, the Study Guide, and MyAccountingLab.

▶ *NEW* **DEMO DOCS** – Introductory accounting students consistently tell us, "When doing homework, I get stuck trying to solve problems the way they were demonstrated in class." Instructors consistently tell us, "I have so much to cover in so little time; I can't afford to go backward and review homework in class." Those challenges inspired us to develop Demo Docs. Demo Docs are comprehensive worked-through problems, available for nearly every chapter of our introductory accounting text, to help students when they are trying to solve exercises and problems on their own. The idea is to help students duplicate the classroom experience outside of class. Entire problems that mirror end-of-chapter material are shown solved and annotated with explanations written in a conversational style, essentially imitating what an instructor might say if standing over a student's shoulder. All Demo Docs will be available online in Flash and in print so students can easily refer to them when and where they need them.

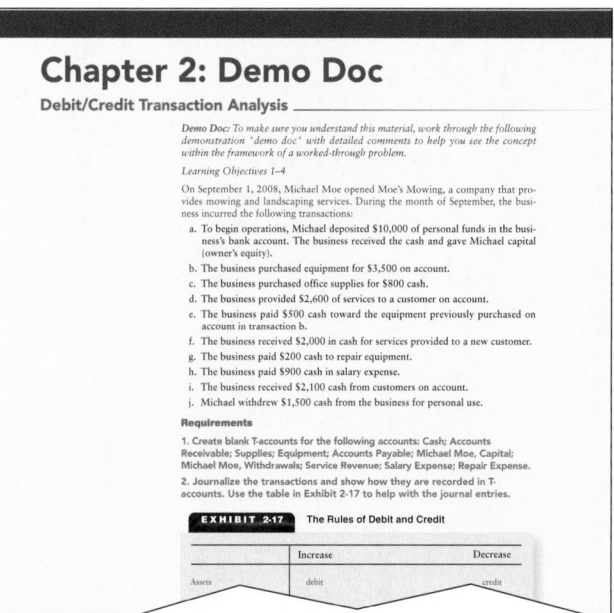

MyAccountingLab – This online homework and assessment tool supports the same theme as the text and resources by providing "I get it!" moments inside and outside of class. It is in MyAccountingLab where "I get it!" moments meet the power of practice. MyAccountingLab is about helping students at their teachable moment, whether that is 1 P.M. or 1 A.M. MyAccountingLab is packed with algorithmic problems because practice makes perfect. It is also packed with the exact same end-of-chapter material in the text that you are used to assigning for homework. MyAccountingLab features the same look and feel for exercises and problems in journal entries and financial statements so that students are familiar and comfortable working in it. Because it includes a Demo Doc for each of the end-of-chapter exercises and problems that students can refer to as they work through the question, it extends The System just one step further by providing students with the help they need to succeed when you are not with them.

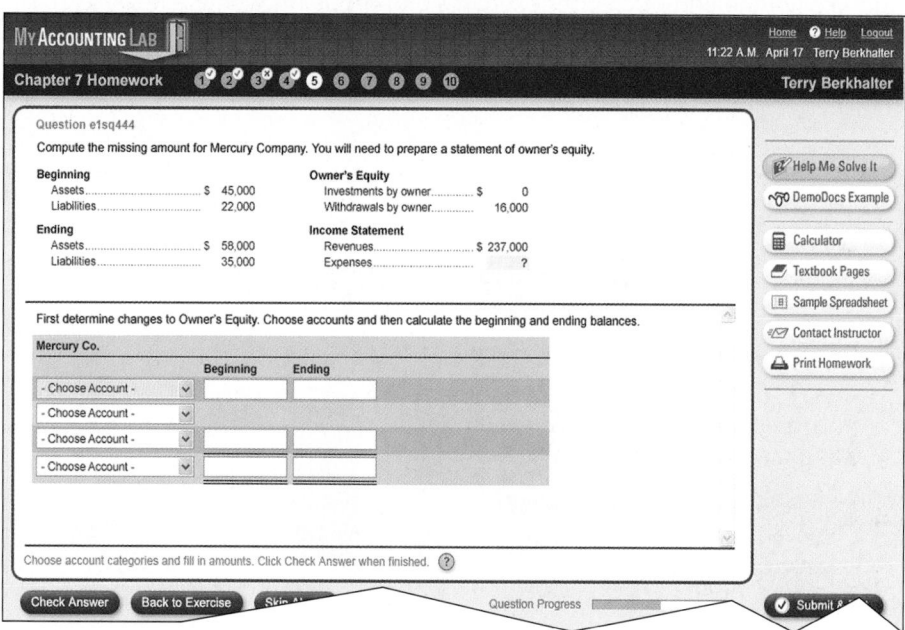

The System's Details

CHAPTERS 1–4 We know it's critical that students have a solid understanding of the fundamentals and language surrounding the accounting cycle before they can move to practice. To that end, we're spending extra time developing the accounting cycle chapters (Chs 1–4) to make sure they will help students succeed. We're adding extra visuals, additional comprehensive problems, and a Demo Doc per chapter to give students additional support to move on through the material successfully. You'll be able to stay on schedule in the syllabus because students understand the accounting cycle.

CONSISTENCY – The entire package matters. Consistency in terminology and problem set-ups from one medium to another—test bank to study guide to MyAccountingLab—is critical to your success in the classroom. So when students ask "Where do the numbers come from?," they can go to our text **or** go online and see what to do. If it's worded one way in the text, you can count on it being worded the same way in the supplements.

CLUTTER-FREE – This edition is built on the premise of "Less is More." Extraneous boxes and features, non-essential bells and whistles—they are all gone. The authors know that excess crowds out what really matters—the concepts, the problems, and the learning objectives. Instructors asked for fewer "features" in favor of less clutter and better cross-referencing, and Horngren/Harrison, *Accounting, 7e,* is delivering on that wish. And we've redone all of the end-of-chapter exercises and problems with a renewed focus on the critical core concepts.

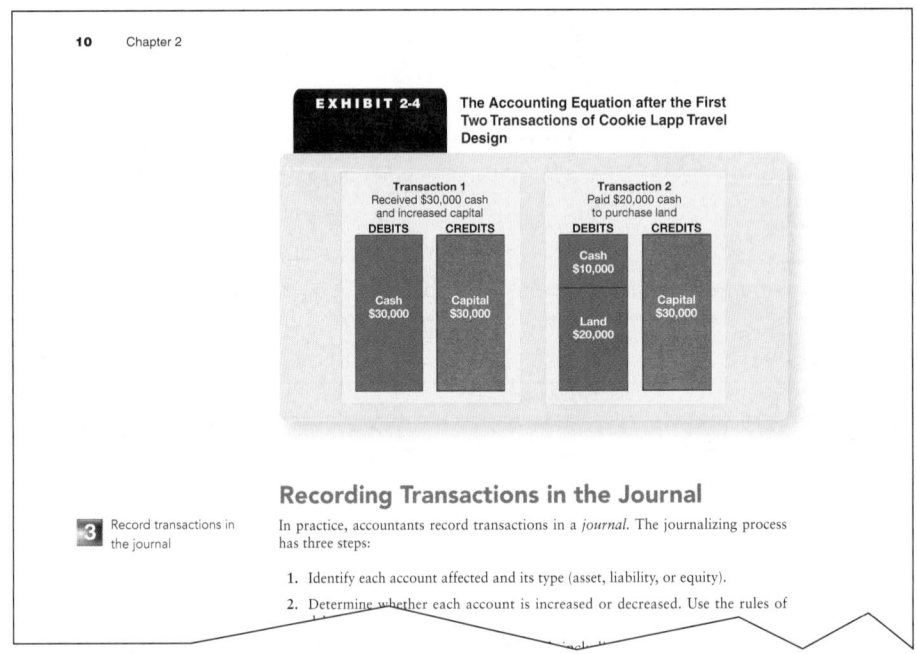

EXHIBIT 2-4   The Accounting Equation after the First Two Transactions of Cookie Lapp Travel Design

Recording Transactions in the Journal

3 Record transactions in the journal

In practice, accountants record transactions in a *journal.* The journalizing process has three steps:

1. Identify each account affected and its type (asset, liability, or equity).

2. Determine whether each account is increased or decreased. Use the rules of

INSTRUCTOR SUPPLEMENTS

Instructor's Edition Featuring *Instructor Demo Docs*

▶ **The New Look of the Instructor's Edition**

We've asked a lot of instructors how we can help them successfully implement new course-delivery methods (e.g. online) while maintaining their regular campus schedule of classes and academic responsibilities. In response, we developed a system of instruction for those of you who are long on commitment and expertise—but short on time and assistance.

The primary goal of the Instructor's Edition is **ease of implementation, using any delivery method**—traditional, self-paced, or online. That is, the Instructor's Edition quickly answers for you, the professor, the question "What must the student do?" Likewise, the Instructor's Edition quickly answers for the student "What must I do?," offers time-saving tips with "best of" categories for in class discussion, and strong examples to illustrate difficult concepts to a wide variety of students. The Instructor's Edition also offers a quick one-shot cross-reference at the exact point of importance with key additional teaching resources, so everything is in one place. The Instructor's Edition includes summaries and teaching tips, pitfalls for new students, and "best of" practices from instructors from across the world.

▶ **The Instructor's Edition also includes *Instructor Demo Docs***

In *Instructor Demo Docs*, we walk the students through how to solve a problem as if it were the first time they've seen it. There are no lengthy passages of text. Instead, bits of expository text are woven into the steps needed to solve the problem, in the exact sequence—for you to provide at the teachable *"I get it!"* moment. This is the point at which the student has a context within which he or she can understand the concept. We provide conversational text around each of the steps so the student stays engaged in solving the problem. We provide notes to the instructor for key teaching points around the Demo Docs, and "best of" practice tid-bits before each *Instructor Demo Doc*.

The *Instructor Demo Docs* are written with all of your everyday classroom realities in mind—and trying to save your time in prepping new examples each time your book changes. Additionally, algorithmic versions of these Demo Docs are provided to students in their student guide. We keep the terminology consistent with the text, so there are no surprises for students as they try and work through a problem the first time.

Solutions Transparencies

These transparency masters are the **Solutions Manual** in an easy-to-use format for class lectures.

Instructor's Resource Center CD or www.prenhall.com/horngren

The password-protected site and resource CD includes the following:

- **The Instructor's Edition with *Instructor Demo Docs***
- **Problem Set C**

- **Solutions Manual with Interactive Excel Solutions**

  The Solutions Manual contains solutions to all end-of-chapter questions, multiple-choice questions, short exercises, exercise sets, problems sets, and Internet exercises. The Solutions Manual is available in Microsoft Excel, Microsoft Word, and in print. You can access the solutions in MS Excel and MS Word formats by visiting the Instructor's Resource Center on the Prentice Hall catalog site at www.prenhall.com/horngren or on the Instructor's CD. You will need a Pearson Educator username and password to retrieve materials from the Web site.

  Solutions to select end-of-chapter exercises and problems are available in **interactive MS Excel format** so that instructors can present material in dynamic, step-by-step sequences in class. The interactive solutions were prepared by Kathleen O'Donnell of the State University of New York, Onondaga Community College.

- **Test Bank**

The test item file includes more than 2,000 questions:
  - Multiple Choice
  - Matching
  - True/False
  - Computational Problems
  - Essay

- **Test Bank** is formatted for use with WebCT, Blackboard, and Course Compass.

- **PowerPoints (instructor and student)** summarize and reinforce key text materials. They capture classroom attention with original problems and solved step-by-step exercises. These walk-throughs are designed to help facilitate classroom discussion and demonstrate where the numbers come from and what they mean to the concept at hand. There are approximately 35 slides per chapter. PowerPoints are available on the Instructor's CD and can be downloaded from www.prenhall.com/horngren.

New *MyAccountingLab* Online Homework and Assessment Manager

The **"I get it!"** moment meets *the power of practice*. The power of repetition when you "get it" means learning happens. **MyAccountingLab** is about helping students at their teachable moments, whether it's 1 P.M. or 1 A.M.

MyAccountingLab is an online homework and assessment tool, packed with algorithmic versions of every text problem, because practice makes perfect. It's also packed with the exact same end-of-chapter material that you're used to assigning for homework. Additionally, **MyAccountingLab** includes:

1. A **Demo Doc** for each of the end-of-chapter exercises and problems that students can refer to as they work through the questions.

2. A **Guided Solution** to the exact problem they are working on. It helps students when they're trying to solve a problem the way it was demonstrated in class.

3. A full **e-book** so the students can reference the book at the point of practice.

4. New **topic specific videos** that walk students through difficult concepts.

Companion Web Site–www.prenhall.com/Horngren

The book's Web site at www.prenhall.com/horngren—contains the following:

- Self-study quizzes—interactive study guide for each chapter
- MS Excel templates that students can use to complete homework assignments for each chapter (e-working papers)
- Samples of the Flash Demo Docs for students to work through the accounting cycle

Online Courses with WebCT/BlackBoard/Course Compass

Prentice Hall offers a link to MyAccountingLab through the Bb and WebCT Course Management Systems.

Classroom Response Systems (CRS)

CRS is an exciting new wireless polling technology that makes large and small classrooms even more interactive, because it enables instructors to pose questions to their students, record results, and display those results instantly. Students can easily answer questions using compact remote-control–type transmitters. Prentice Hall has partnerships with leading classroom response-systems providers and can show you everything you need to know about setting up and using a CRS system. Prentice Hall will provide the classroom hardware, text-specific PowerPoint slides, software, and support.

Visit **www.prenhall.com/crs** to learn more.

STUDENT SUPPLEMENTS

Runners Corporation PT Lab Manual

Containing numerous simulated real-world examples, the **Runners Corporation** practice set is available complete with data files for Peachtree, QuickBooks, and PH General Ledger. Each practice set also includes business stationery for manual entry work.

A-1 Photography-Manual PT Lab Manual

Containing numerous simulated real-world examples, the **A-1 Photography** practice set is available complete with data files for Peachtree, QuickBooks, and PH General Ledger. Each set includes business stationery for manual entry work.

Study Guide including Demo Docs and e-Working Papers

Introductory accounting students consistently tell us, "When doing homework, I get stuck trying to solve problems the way they were demonstrated in class." Instructors consistently tell us, "I have so much to cover in so little time; I can't afford to go backwards and review homework in class." Those challenges inspired us to develop Demo Docs. Demo Docs are comprehensive worked-through problems available for nearly every chapter of our introductory accounting text to help students when they are trying to solve exercises and problems on their own. The idea is to help students duplicate the classroom experience outside of class. Entire problems that mirror end-of-chapter material are shown solved and annotated with explanations written in a conversational style, essentially imitating what an instructor might say if standing over a student's shoulder. All Demo Docs will be available in the Study Guide—in print and on CD in Flash, so students can easily refer to them when they need them. The Study Guide also includes a summary overview of key topics and multiple-choice and short-answer questions for students to test their knowledge. Free electronic working papers are included on the accompanying CD.

MyAccountingLab Online Homework and Assessment Manager

The **"I get it!"** moment meets **power of practice**. The power of repetition when you "get it" means that learning happens. **MyAccountingLab** is about helping students at their teachable moment, whether that is 1 P.M. or 1 A.M.

MyAccountingLab is an online homework and assessment tool, packed with algorithmic versions of every text problem because practice makes perfect. It's also packed with the exact same end-of-chapter that you're used to assigning for homework. Additionally, **MyAccountingLab** includes:

1. A **Demo Doc** for each of the end-of-chapter exercises and problems that students can refer to as they work through the question.

2. A **Guided Solution** to the exact problem they are working on. It helps students when they're trying to solve a problem the way it was demonstrated in class.

3. A full **e-book** so the students can reference the book at the point of practice.

4. New **topic specific videos** that walk students through difficult concepts.

PowerPoints

For student use as a study aide or note-taking guide, these PowerPoint slides may be downloaded at the companion Web site at www.prenhall.com/horngren.

Companion Web Site–www.prenhall.com/Horngren

The book's Web site at www.prenhall.com/horngren—contains the following:

- Self-study quizzes—interactive study guide for each chapter
- MS Excel templates that students can use to complete homework assignments for each chapter (e-working papers)
- Samples of the Flash Demo Docs for students to work through the accounting cycle.

Classroom Response Systems (CRS)

CRS is an exciting new wireless polling technology that makes large and small classrooms even more interactive because it enables instructors to pose questions to their students, record results, and display those results instantly. Students can easily answer questions using compact remote-control-type transmitters. Prentice Hall has partnerships with leading classroom response-systems providers and can show you everything you need to know about setting up and using a CRS system. Prentice Hall will provide the classroom hardware, text-specific PowerPoint slides, software, and support.

Visit **www.prenhall.com/crs** to learn more.

- **VangoNotes in MP3 Format**

  Students can study on the go with VangoNotes, chapter reviews in downloadable MP3 format that offer brief audio segments for each chapter:

  - Big Ideas: the vital ideas in each chapter
  - Practice Test: lets students know if they need to keep studying
  - Key Terms: audio "flashcards" that review key concepts and terms
  - Rapid Review: a quick drill session—helpful right before tests

  Students can learn more at **www.vangonotes.com**

vango notes
In partnership with **Audible** Education

Hear it. Get It.

Study on the go with VangoNotes.

Just download chapter reviews from your text and listen to them on any mp3 player. Now wherever you are-- whatever you're doing--you can study by listening to the following for each chapter of your textbook:

Big Ideas: Your "need to know" for each chapter

Practice Test: A gut check for the Big Ideas--tells you if you need to keep studying

Key Terms: Audio "flashcards" to help you review key concepts and terms

Rapid Review: A quick drill session--use it right before your test

VangoNotes.com

Acknowledgments

We'd like to thank the following contributors:

Florence McGovern *Bergen Community College*
Sherry Mills *New Mexico State University*

Suzanne Oliver *Okaloosa Walton Junior College*
Helen Brubeck *San Jose State University*

We'd like to extend a special thank you to the following members of our advisory panel:

Jim Ellis *Bay State College, Boston*
Mary Ann Swindlehurst *Carroll Community College*
Andy Williams *Edmonds Community College*
Donnie Kristof-Nelson *Edmonds Community College*
Joan Cezair *Fayetteville State University*
David Baglia *Grove City College*

Anita Ellzey *Harford Community College*
Cheryl McKay *Monroe County Community College*
Todd Jackson *Northeastern State University*
Margaret Costello Lambert *Oakland Community College*
Al Fagan *University of Richmond*

We'd also like to thank the following reviewers:

Shi-Mu (Simon) Yang *Adelphi University*
Thomas Stolberg *Alfred State University*
Thomas Branton *Alvin Community College*
Maria Lehoczky *American Intercontinental University*
Suzanne Bradford *Angelina College*
Judy Lewis *Angelo State University*
Roy Carson *Anne Arundel Community College*
Paulette Ratliff-Miller *Arkansas State University*
Joseph Foley *Assumption College*
Jennifer Niece *Assumption College*
Bill Whitley *Athens State University*
Shelly Gardner *Augustana College*

Becky Jones *Baylor University*
Betsy Willis *Baylor University*
Michael Robinson *Baylor University*
Kay Walker-Hauser *Beaufort County Community College, Washington*
Joe Aubert *Bemidji State University*
Calvin Fink *Bethune Cookman College*
Michael Blue *Bloomsburg University*
Scott Wallace *Blue Mountain College*
Lloyd Carroll *Borough Manhattan Community College*
Ken Duffe *Brookdale Community College*
Chuck Heuser *Brookdale Community College*
Shafi Ullah *Broward Community College South*
Lois Slutsky *Broward Community College South*
Ken Koerber *Bucks County Community College*

Julie Browning *California Baptist University*
Richard Savich *California State University—San Bernardino*
David Bland *Cape Fear Community College*
Robert Porter *Cape Fear Community College*
Vickie Campbell *Cape Fear Community College*
Cynthia Thompson *Carl Sandburg College—Carthage*

Liz Ott *Casper College*
Joseph Adamo *Cazenovia College*
Julie Dailey *Central Virginia Community College*
Jeannie Folk *College of DuPage*
Lawrence Steiner *College of Marin*
Dennis Kovach *Community College Allegheny County—Allegheny*
Norma Montague *Central Carolina Community College*
Debbie Schmidt *Cerritos College*
Janet Grange *Chicago State University*
Bruce Leung *City College of San Francisco*
Pamela Legner *College of DuPage*
Bruce McMurrey *Community College of Denver*
Martin Sabo *Community College of Denver*
Jeffrey Jones *Community College of Southern Nevada*
Tom Nohl *Community College of Southern Nevada*
Christopher Kelly *Community College of Southern Nevada*
Patrick Rogan *Cosumnes River College*
Kimberly Smith *County College of Morris*

Jerold Braun *Daytona Beach Community College*
Greg Carlton *Davidson County Community College*
Irene Bembenista *Davenport University*
Thomas Szczurek *Delaware County Community College*
Charles Betts *Delaware Technical and Community College*
Patty Holmes *Des Moines Area Community College—Ankeny*
Tim Murphy *Diablo Valley College*

Phillipe Sammour *Eastern Michigan University*
Saturnino (Nino) Gonzales *El Paso Community College*
Lee Cannell *El Paso Community College*
John Eagan *Erie Community College*

Ron O'Brien *Fayetteville Technical Community College*
Patrick McNabb *Ferris State University*
John Stancil *Florida Southern College*
Lynn Clements *Florida Southern College*
Alice Sineath *Forsyth Technical Community College*
James Makofske *Fresno City College*
Marc Haskell *Fresno City College*
James Kelly *Ft. Lauderdale City College*

Christine Jonick *Gainesville State College*
Bruce Lindsey *Genesee Community College*
Constance Hylton *George Mason University*
Cody King *Georgia Southwestern State University*
Lolita Keck *Globe College*
Kay Carnes *Gonzaga University, Spokane*
Carol Pace *Grayson County College*
Rebecca Floor *Greenville Technical College*
Geoffrey Heriot *Greenville Technical College*
Jeffrey Patterson *Grove City College*
Lanny Nelms *Gwinnet Technical College*
Chris Cusatis *Gwynedd Mercy College*

Tim Griffin *Hillsborough Community College*
Clair Helms *Hinds Community College*
Michelle Powell *Holmes Community College*
Greg Bischoff *Houston Community College*
Donald Bond *Houston Community College*
Marina Grau *Houston Community College*
Carolyn Fitzmorris *Hutchinson Community College*

Susan Koepke *Illinois Valley Community College*
William Alexander *Indian Hills Community College—
Ottumwa*
Dale Bolduc *Intercoast College*
Thomas Carr *International College of Naples*
Lecia Berven *Iowa Lakes Community College*
Nancy Schendel *Iowa Lakes Community College*
Michelle Cannon *Ivy Tech*
Vicki White *Ivy Tech*
Chuck Smith *Iowa Western Community College*

Stephen Christian *Jackson Community College*
DeeDee Daughtry *Johnston Community College*
Richard Bedwell *Jones County Junior College*

Ken Mark *Kansas City Kansas Community College*
Ken Snow *Kaplan Education Centers*
Charles Evans *Keiser College*
Bunney Schmidt *Keiser College*
Amy Haas *Kingsborough Community College*

Jim Racic *Lakeland Community College*
Doug Clouse *Lakeland Community College*

Patrick Haggerty *Lansing Community College*
Patricia Walczak *Lansing Community College*
Humberto M. Herrera *Laredo Community College*
Christie Comunale *Long Island University*
Ariel Markelevich *Long Island University*
Randy Kidd *Longview Community College*
Kathy Heltzel *Luzerne County Community College*
Lori Major *Luzerne County Community College*

Fred Jex *Macomb Community College*
Glenn Owen *Marymount College*
Behnaz Quigley *Marymount College*
Penny Hanes *Mercyhurst College, Erie*
John Miller *Metropolitan Community College*
Denise Leggett *Middle Tennessee State University*
William Huffman *Missouri Southern State College*
Ted Crosby *Montgomery County Community College*
Beth Engle *Montgomery County Community College*
David Candelaria *Mount San Jacinto College*
Linda Bolduc *Mount Wachusett Community College*

Barbara Gregorio *Nassau Community College*
James Hurat *National College of Business and Technology*
Denver Riffe *National College of Business and
Technology*
Asokan Anandarajan *New Jersey Institute of Technology*
Robert Schoener *New Mexico State University*
Stanley Carroll *New York City Technical College of
CUNY*
Audrey Agnello *Niagara County Community College*
Catherine Chiang *North Carolina Central University*
Karen Russom *North Harris College*
Dan Bayak *Northampton Community College*
Elizabeth Lynn Locke *Northern Virginia Community
College*
Debra Prendergast *Northwestern Business College*
Nat Briscoe *Northwestern State University*
Tony Scott *Norwalk Community College*

Deborah Niemer *Oakland Community College*
John Boyd *Oklahoma City Community College*
Kathleen O'Donnell *Onondaga Community College*
J.T. Ryan *Onondaga Community College*

Toni Clegg *Palm Beach Atlantic College*
David Forsyth *Palomar College*
John Graves *PCDI*
Carla Rich *Pensacola Junior College*
Judy Grotrian *Peru State College*
Judy Daulton *Piedmont Technical College*
John Stone *Potomac State College*
Betty Habershon *Prince George's Community College*

Kathi Villani *Queensborough Community College*

William Black *Raritan Valley Community College*
Verne Ingram *Red Rocks Community College*
Paul Juriga *Richland Community College*
Patty Worsham *Riverside Community College*
Margaret Berezewski *Robert Morris College*
Phil Harder *Robert Morris College*
Shifei Chung *Rowan University of New Jersey*

Charles Fazzi *Saint Vincent College*
Lynnette Yerbuy *Salt Lake Community College*
Susan Blizzard *San Antonio College*
Hector Martinez *San Antonio College*
Audrey Voyles *San Diego Miramar College*
Margaret Black *San Jacinto College*
Merrily Hoffman *San Jacinto College*
Randall Whitmore *San Jacinto College*
Carroll Buck *San Jose State University*
Cynthia Coleman *Sandhills Community College*
Barbara Crouteau *Santa Rosa Junior College*
Pat Novak *Southeast Community College*
Susan Pallas *Southeast Community College*
Al Case *Southern Oregon University*
Gloria Worthy *Southwest Tennessee Community College*
Melody Ashenfelter *Southwestern Oklahoma State University*
Douglas Ward *Southwestern Community College*
Brandi Shay *Southwestern Community College*
John May *Southwestern Oklahoma State University*
Jeffrey Waybright *Spokane Community College*
Renee Goffinet *Spokane Community College*
Susan Anders *ST Bonaventure University*
John Olsavsky *SUNY at Fredonia*
Peter Van Brunt *SUNY College of Technology at Delhi*

David L. Davis *Tallahassee Community College*
Kathy Crusto-Way *Tarrant County Community College*
Sally Cook *Texas Lutheran University*
Bea Chiang *The College of New Jersey*
Matt Hightower *Three Rivers Community College*

Susan Pope *University of Akron*
Joe Woods *University of Arkansas*
Allen Blay *University of California, Riverside*

Barry Mishra *University of California, Riverside*
Laura Young *University of Central Arkansas*
Jane Calvert *University of Central Oklahoma*
Bambi Hora *University of Central Oklahoma*
Joan Stone *University of Central Oklahoma*
Kathy Terrell *University of Central Oklahoma*
Harlan Etheridge *University of Louisiana*
Pam Meyer *University of Louisiana*
Sandra Scheuermann *University of Louisiana*
Tom Wilson *University of Louisiana*
Lawrence Leaman *University of Michigan*
Larry Huus *University of Minnesota*
Brian Carpenter *University of Scranton*
Ashraf Khallaf *University of Southern Indiana*
Tony Zordan *University of St. Francis*
Gene Elrod *University of Texas, Arlington*
Cheryl Prachyl *University of Texas, El Paso*
Karl Putnam *University of Texas, El Paso*
Stephen Rockwell *University of Tulsa*
Chula King *University of West Florida*
Charles Baird *University of Wisconsin – Stout*

Mary Hollars *Vincennes University*
Lisa Nash *Vincennes University*
Elaine Dessouki *Virginia Wesleyan College*

Sueann Hely *West Kentucky Community and Technical College*
Darlene Pulliam *West Texas A&M University, Canyon*
Judy Beebe *Western Oregon University*
Michelle Maggio *Westfield State College*
Kathy Pellegrino *Westfield State College*
Nora McCarthy *Wharton County Junior College*
Sally Stokes *Wilmington College*
Maggie Houston *Wright State University*

Gerald Caton *Yavapai College*
Chris Crosby *York Technical College*
Harold Gellis *York College of CUNY*

About the Authors

Charles T. Horngren is the Edmund W. Littlefield Professor of Accounting, Emeritus, at Stanford University. A graduate of Marquette University, he received his M.B.A. from Harvard University and his Ph.D. from the University of Chicago. He is also the recipient of honorary doctorates from Marquette University and DePaul University.

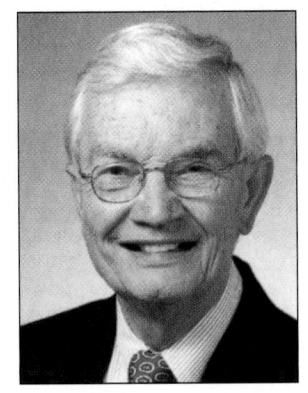

A Certified Public Accountant, Horngren served on the Accounting Principles Board for six years, the Financial Accounting Standards Board Advisory Council for five years, and the Council of the American Institute of Certified Public Accountants for three years. For six years, he served as a trustee of the Financial Accounting Foundation, which oversees the Financial Accounting Standards Board and the Government Accounting Standards Board.

Horngren is a member of the Accounting Hall of Fame.

A member of the American Accounting Association, Horngren has been its President and its Director of Research. He received its first annual Outstanding Accounting Educator Award.

The California Certified Public Accountants Foundation gave Horngren its Faculty Excellence Award and its Distinguished Professor Award. He is the first person to have received both awards.

The American Institute of Certified Public Accountants presented its first Outstanding Educator Award to Horngren.

Horngren was named Accountant of the Year, Education, by the national professional accounting fraternity, Beta Alpha Psi.

Professor Horngren is also a member of the Institute of Management Accountants, from whom he has received its Distinguished Service Award. He was a member of the Institute's Board of Regents, which administers the Certified Management Accountant examinations.

Horngren is the author of other accounting books published by Prentice-Hall: *Cost Accounting: A Managerial Emphasis*, Twelfth Edition, 2006 (with Srikant Datar and George Foster*); Introduction to Financial Accounting*, Ninth Edition, 2006 (with Gary L. Sundem and John A. Elliott*); Introduction to Management Accounting*, Thirteenth Edition, 2005 (with Gary L. Sundem and William Stratton); *Financial Accounting*, Sixth Edition, 2006 (with Walter T. Harrison, Jr.).

Horngren is the Consulting Editor for Prentice-Hall's Charles T. Horngren Series in Accounting.

Walter T. Harrison, Jr. is Professor Emeritus of Accounting at the Hankamer School of Business, Baylor University. He received his B.B.A. degree from Baylor University, his M.S. from Oklahoma State University, and his Ph.D. from Michigan State University.

Professor Harrison, recipient of numerous teaching awards from student groups as well as from university administrators, has also taught at Cleveland State Community College, Michigan State University, the University of Texas, and Stanford University.

A member of the American Accounting Association and the American Institute of Certified Public Accountants, Professor Harrison has served as Chairman of the Financial Accounting Standards Committee of the American Accounting Association, on the Teaching/Curriculum Development Award Committee, on the Program Advisory

Committee for Accounting Education and Teaching, and on the Notable Contributions to Accounting Literature Committee.

Professor Harrison has lectured in several foreign countries and published articles in numerous journals, including *Journal of Accounting Research*, *Journal of Accountancy*, *Journal of Accounting and Public Policy*, *Economic Consequences of Financial Accounting Standards*, *Accounting Horizons*, *Issues in Accounting Education*, and *Journal of Law and Commerce*.

He is co-author of *Financial Accounting*, Sixth Edition, 2006 (with Charles T. Horngren), published by Prentice Hall. Professor Harrison has received scholarships, fellowships, and research grants or awards from PriceWaterhouse Coopers, Deloitte & Touche, the Ernst & Young Foundation, and the KPMG Foundation.

accounting

7e

1 Accounting and the Business Environment

Learning Objectives

1 Use accounting vocabulary

2 Apply accounting concepts and principles

3 Use the accounting equation

4 Analyze business transactions

5 Prepare the financial statements

6 Evaluate business performance

You may dream of running your own business. Where do you begin? How much money does it take? How will you measure success or failure?

Haig Sherman operated a lawn-service business while in college and graduated with thousands in the bank. Julie DeFilippo started a successful catering business. How did they do it? By following their dreams, treating people fairly, and having realistic expectations. It didn't hurt that Sherman majored in accounting. His accounting knowledge gave him a leg up on organizing the business and keeping track of important details. ■

We'll start with a small business such as Sherman Lawn Service or DeFilippo Catering. A business with a single owner is called a proprietorship. What role does accounting play for Sherman Lawn Service or DeFilippo Catering?

Accounting: The Language of Business

Accounting is the information system that measures business activity, processes the data into reports, and communicates the results to decision makers. Accounting is "the language of business." The better you understand the language, the better you can manage the business. For example, how will you decide whether to borrow money? You need to consider your income: The concept of income comes straight from accounting.

A key product of accounting is a set of documents called the financial statements. **Financial statements** report on a business in monetary terms. Is Sherman Lawn Service making a profit? Should DeFilippo Catering expand? Answering these questions requires the financial statements.

Exhibit 1-1 illustrates the role of accounting in business. The process shows people making decisions.

1 Use accounting vocabulary

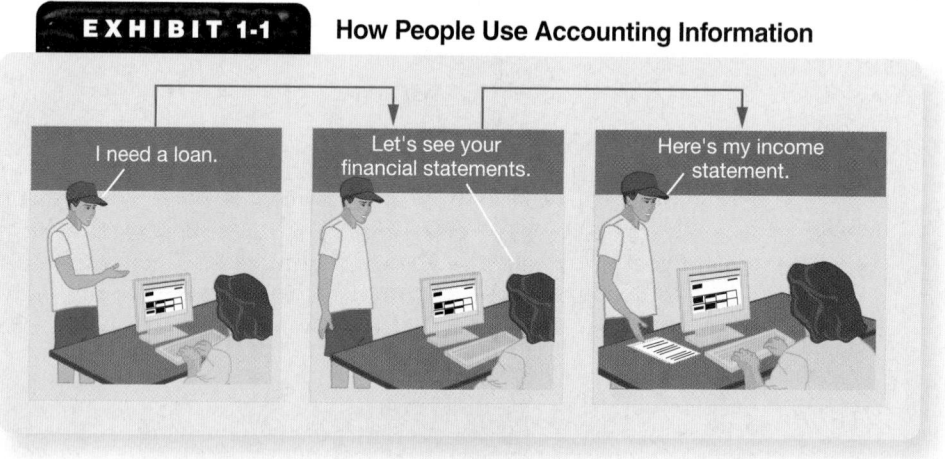

EXHIBIT 1-1 How People Use Accounting Information

I need a loan.

Let's see your financial statements.

Here's my income statement.

Decision Makers: The Users of Accounting Information

Decision makers need information. The bigger the decision, the greater the need. Here are some of the ways people use accounting information.

Individuals

You use accounting information to manage your bank account, evaluate a new job, and decide whether you can afford a new car. Haig Sherman and Julie DeFilippo make the same decisions that you do.

Businesses

Business owners use accounting information to set goals. They evaluate progress toward those goals and take corrective action when needed. For example, Julie DeFilippo must decide how many heaters she'll need to keep food warm on a catering job. Accounting provides this information.

Investors

Outside investors often provide the money to get a business going. To decide whether to invest, a person predicts the amount of income to be earned on the investment. The investor analyzes the financial statements and keeps up with the company. For large public companies, log onto www.yahoo.com (click on Finance), www.hoovers.com (click on Companies), and the SEC's EDGAR database.

Creditors

Before lending money to Haig Sherman, a bank evaluates Sherman's ability to make the loan payments. This requires a report on Sherman's predicted income. To borrow money before striking it rich, Michael Dell, who founded Dell Inc., the computer company, probably had to document his income and financial position.

Taxing Authorities

Local, state, and federal governments levy taxes. Income tax is figured using accounting information. Sales tax depends upon a company's sales.

Financial Accounting and Management Accounting

Accounting can be divided into two fields—financial accounting and management accounting.

Financial accounting provides information for people outside the company. Outside investors and lenders are not part of day-to-day management. These outsiders use the company's financial statements. Chapters 2–17 of this book deal primarily with financial accounting.

Management accounting focuses on information for internal decision making by the company's managers. Chapters 18 through 25 cover management accounting. Exhibit 1-2 illustrates the difference between financial accounting and management accounting.

EXHIBIT 1-2   **Financial Accounting and Management Accounting**

Outside Investors:
Should we invest in DeFilippo Catering?
Is the business profitable?
Investors use financial accounting information to measure profitability.

DeFilippo Catering:
Julie DeFilippo uses management accounting information to operate her business.

Creditors:
Should we lend money to DeFilippo Catering?
Can DeFilippo pay us back?
Creditors use financial accounting information to decide whether to make a loan.

The Accounting Profession

There are several learned professions, including accounting, architecture, engineering, law, and medicine. To be certified in a profession, one must pass a qualifying exam, and professionals are paid quite well. For example, the starting salary for a college graduate with a bachelor's degree in accounting can range from $35,000 to $50,000. A graduate with a master's degree earns about $2,000 more to start. After five years you may be earning as much as $75,000.

Many accounting firms are organized as partnerships, and the partners are the owners. It usually takes 10 to 15 years to rise to the rank of partner. The partners of the large accounting firms earn from $150,000 to $500,000 per year. In private accounting, the top position is called the chief financial officer (CFO), and a CFO earns about as much as a partner in an accounting firm.

What do businesses such as Sherman Lawn Service, DeFilippo Catering, General Motors, and Coca-Cola have in common? They all need accountants! That's why accounting opens so many doors to a job upon graduation.

Accountants get to the top of organizations as often as anyone else. Why? Because the accountants must deal with everything in the company in order to account for all of its activities. Accountants often have the broadest view of what's going on in the company. People sometimes complain that the accountants control the purse strings, but they must admit that accountants often keep companies on the straight and narrow path to success.

As you move through this book, observe that you will learn to account for everything that affects the business—all the income, all the expenses, all the cash, all the inventory, and all the debts. Accounting requires you to consider everything, and that's why it's so valuable to an organization.

All professions have regulations. Let's see the organizations that govern the accounting profession.

Governing Organizations

In the United States the **Financial Accounting Standards Board (FASB)**, a private organization, formulates accounting standards. The FASB works with governmental agencies, the Securities and Exchange Commission (SEC) and the Public Companies Accounting Oversight Board (PCAOB), and private groups, the American Institute of Certified Public Accountants (AICPA) and the Institute of Management Accountants (IMA). **Certified public accountants**, or **CPAs**, are professional accountants who are licensed to serve the general public. **Certified management accountants**, or **CMAs**, are licensed professionals who work for a single company.

The rules for public information are called *generally accepted accounting principles (GAAP)*. Exhibit 1-3 diagrams the relationships among the various accounting organizations.

Ethics in Accounting and Business

Ethical considerations affect accounting. Investors and creditors need relevant and reliable information about a company such as Amazon.com or General Motors. Companies want to make themselves look good to attract investors, so there is a conflict of interest here. To provide reliable information, the SEC requires companies to have their financial statements audited by independent accountants. An **audit** is a financial examination. The independent accountants then tell whether the financial statements give a true picture of the company's situation.

The vast majority of accountants do their jobs professionally and ethically. We never hear about them. Unfortunately, only those who cheat make the headlines. In recent years we've seen more accounting scandals than at any time since the 1920s.

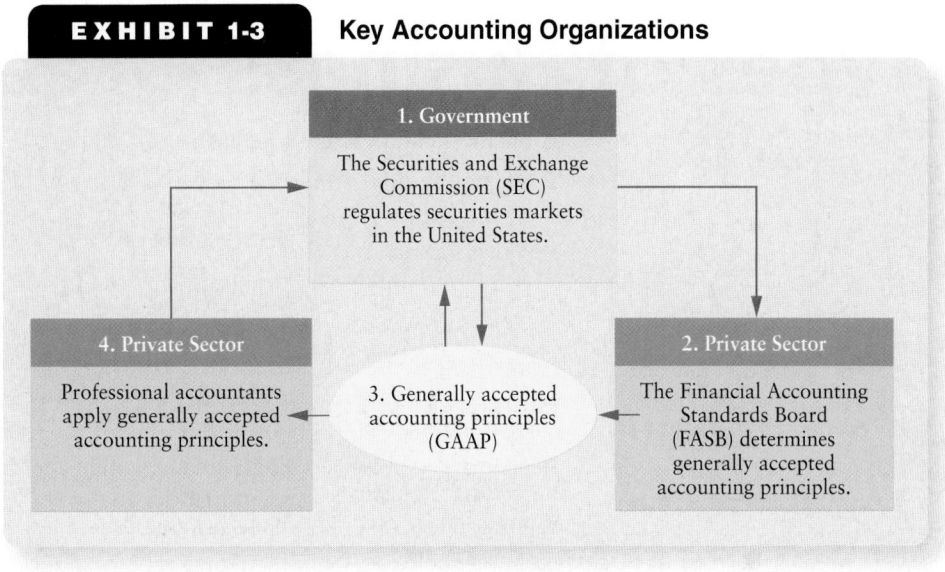

EXHIBIT 1-3 Key Accounting Organizations

1. Government

The Securities and Exchange Commission (SEC) regulates securities markets in the United States.

4. Private Sector

Professional accountants apply generally accepted accounting principles.

3. Generally accepted accounting principles (GAAP)

2. Private Sector

The Financial Accounting Standards Board (FASB) determines generally accepted accounting principles.

Enron Corp., for example, was one of the largest companies in the United States before reporting misleading data. WorldCom, a major long-distance telephone provider, admitted accounting for expenses as though they were assets (resources). These and other scandals rocked the business community and hurt investor confidence. Innocent people lost their jobs, and the stock market suffered. The U.S. government took swift action. It passed the Sarbanes-Oxley Act that made it a criminal offense to falsify financial statements. It also created a new watchdog agency, the Public Companies Accounting Oversight Board, to monitor the work of accountants.

Standards of Professional Conduct

The AICPA's Code of Professional Conduct for Accountants provides guidance to CPAs in their work. Ethical standards are designed to produce relevant and reliable information for decision making. The preamble to the Code states:

> "[A] certified public accountant assumes an obligation of self-discipline above and beyond the requirements of laws and regulations . . . [and] an unswerving commitment to honorable behavior. . . ."

The opening paragraph of the Standards of Ethical Conduct of the Institute of Management Accountants (IMA) states:

> "Management accountants have an obligation to the organizations they serve, their profession, the public, and themselves to maintain the highest standards of ethical conduct."

Most companies also set standards of ethical conduct for employees. DeFilippo Catering must comply with state health standards in order to serve customers ethically. The Boeing Company, a leading manufacturer of aircraft, has a highly developed set of business conduct guidelines. A business's or an individual's reputation is fragile and can easily be lost. As one chief executive has stated, "Ethical practice is simply good business." Truth is always better than dishonesty—in accounting, in business, and in life.

Types of Business Organizations

A business can be organized as a:

- Proprietorship
- Partnership
- Corporation
- Limited-liability partnership (LLP) and limited-liability company (LLC)

You should understand the differences among the four.

Proprietorships

A **proprietorship** has a single owner, called the proprietor, who often manages the business. Proprietorships tend to be small retail stores or professional businesses, such as physicians, attorneys, and accountants. As to its accounting, each proprietorship is distinct from its owner: The accounting records of the proprietorship do *not* include the proprietor's personal records. However, from a legal perspective, the business *is* the proprietor. In this book, we start with a proprietorship because many students will organize their first business that way.

Partnerships

A **partnership** joins two or more individuals as co-owners. Each owner is a partner. Many retail stores and professional organizations of physicians, attorneys, and accountants are partnerships. Most partnerships are small or medium-sized, but some are gigantic, with 1,000 or more partners. As to its accounting the partnership is a separate organization, distinct from the partners. But from a legal perspective, a partnership *is* the partners in a manner similar to a proprietorship.

Corporations

A **corporation** is a business owned by **stockholders**, or **shareholders**. These are the people who own shares of ownership in the business. A business becomes a corporation when the state approves its articles of incorporation. Unlike a proprietorship and a partnership, a corporation is a legal entity distinct from its owners.

Corporations differ from traditional proprietorships and partnerships in another way. If a proprietorship or a partnership cannot pay its debts, lenders can take the owners' personal assets to satisfy the obligations. But if a corporation goes bankrupt, lenders cannot take the personal assets of the stockholders. This *limited liability* of stockholders for corporate debts is one reason corporations are so popular: People can invest in corporations with limited personal risk.

Another factor for corporations is the division of ownership into individual shares. The Coca-Cola Company, for example, has billions of shares of stock owned by many stockholders. An investor with no personal relationship to Coca-Cola can become a stockholder by buying 50, 100, 5,000, or any number of shares of its stock.

Limited-Liability Partnerships (LLPs) and Limited-Liability Companies (LLCs)

A *limited-liability partnership* is one in which a wayward partner cannot create a large liability for the other partners. Each partner is liable only for his or her own actions and those under his or her control. And a proprietorship can be organized as a *limited-liability company*. In an LLC the business, and not the proprietor, is liable for the company's debts. Today most proprietorships and partnerships are organized as LLCs and LLPs. The limited-liability aspect gives these organizations one of the chief advantages of a corporation.

Exhibit 1-4 summarizes the differences among the four types of business organization.

EXHIBIT 1-4   **Comparison of the Four Forms of Business Organization**

	Proprietorship	Partnership	Corporation	LLC
1. Owner(s)	Proprietorship—only one	Partners—two or more owners	Stockholders—generally many owners	Members
2. Life of the organization	Limited by the owner's choice, or death	Limited by the owner's choice, or death	Indefinite	Indefinite
3. Personal liability of the owner(s) for the business's debts	Proprietor is personally liable	Partners are personally liable*	Stockholders are not personally liable	Members are not personally liable

*unless it's a limited-liability partnership (LLP)

Accounting Concepts and Principles

The rules that govern accounting fall under the heading **GAAP,** which stands for **generally accepted accounting principles.** GAAP rests on a conceptual framework.

> The primary objective of financial reporting is to provide information useful for making investment and lending decisions.

2 Apply accounting concepts and principles

To be useful, information must be relevant, reliable, and comparable. We begin the discussion of GAAP by introducing basic accounting concepts and principles.

The Entity Concept

The most basic concept in accounting is that of the **entity.** An accounting entity is an organization that stands apart as a separate economic unit. We draw boundaries around each entity so as not to confuse its affairs with those of other entities.

Consider Sherman Lawn Service. Assume Haig Sherman started the business with $500 obtained from a bank loan. Following the entity concept, Sherman would account for the $500 separately from his personal assets, such as his clothing and automobile. To mix the $500 of business cash with his personal assets would make it difficult to measure the success or failure of Sherman Lawn Service.

Consider Toyota, a huge organization with several divisions. Toyota management evaluates each division as a separate entity. If Lexus sales are dropping, Toyota can find out why. But if sales figures from all divisions of the company are combined, management can't tell that Lexus sales are going down. Thus, *the entity concept applies to any economic unit that needs to be evaluated separately.*

The Reliability (Objectivity) Principle

Accounting information is based on the most reliable data available. This guideline is the *reliability principle,* also called the *objectivity principle.* Reliable data are verifiable, which means they may be confirmed by any independent observer. For example, a bank loan is supported by a promissory note. This is objective evidence of the loan. Without the reliability principle, accounting data might be based on whims and opinions.

Suppose you want to open an electronics store. For a store location, you transfer a small building to the business. You believe the building is worth $50,000. A real estate appraiser values the building at $40,000. Which is the more reliable estimate of the building's value, your estimate of $50,000 or the $40,000 professional appraisal? The appraisal of $40,000 is more reliable because it is supported by a professional appraisal. The business should record the building at $40,000.

The Cost Principle

The *cost principle* states that acquired assets and services should be recorded at their actual cost (also called *historical cost*). Even though the purchaser may believe the price is a bargain, the item is recorded at the price actually paid and not at the "expected" cost. Suppose your electronics store purchases TV equipment from a supplier who is going out of business. Assume that you get a good deal and pay only $2,000 for equipment that would have cost you $3,000 elsewhere. The cost principle requires you to record the equipment at its actual cost of $2,000, not the $3,000 that you believe the equipment is worth.

The cost principle also holds that the accounting records should continue reporting the historical cost of an asset over its useful life. Why? Because cost is a reliable measure. Suppose your store holds the TV equipment for six months. During that time TV prices rise, and the equipment can be sold for $3,500. Should its accounting value—the figure on the books—be the actual cost of $2,000 or the current market value of $3,500? By the cost principle, the accounting value of the equipment remains at actual cost of $2,000.

The Going-Concern Concept

Another reason for measuring assets at historical cost is the *going-concern concept.* This concept assumes that the entity will remain in operation for the foreseeable future. Under the going-concern concept, accountants assume that the business will remain in operation long enough to use existing resources for their intended purpose.

To understand the going-concern concept better, consider the alternative—which is to go out of business. A store holding a going-out-of-business sale is trying to sell everything. In that case, the relevant measure is current market value. But going out of business is the exception rather than the rule.

The Stable-Monetary-Unit Concept

In the United States, we record transactions in dollars because the dollar is the medium of exchange. The value of a dollar changes over time, and a rise in the price level is called *inflation.* During inflation, a dollar will purchase less food and less gas for your car. But accountants assume that the dollar's purchasing power is stable.

The Accounting Equation

3 Use the accounting equation

The basic tool of accounting is the **accounting equation**. It measures the resources of a business and the claims to those resources.

Assets and Liabilities

Assets are economic resources that are expected to benefit the business in the future. Cash, merchandise inventory, furniture, and land are assets.

Claims to those assets come from two sources. **Liabilities** are debts payable to outsiders. These outside parties are called *creditors*. For example, a creditor who has loaned money to DeFilippo Catering has a claim to some of DeFilippo's assets until DeFilippo pays the debt. Many liabilities have the word *payable* in their titles. Examples include Accounts Payable, Notes Payable and Salary Payable.

The owner's claims to the assets of the business are called **owner's equity**, or **capital**. These insider claims begin when the owner, Julie DeFilippo, invests assets in the business.

The accounting equation shows how assets, liabilities, and owner's equity are related. Assets appear on the left side of the equation, and the liabilities and owner's equity appear on the right side. Exhibit 1-5 diagrams how the two sides must always be equal:

$$\underset{\text{(Economic Resources)}}{\text{ASSETS}} = \underset{\text{(Claims to Economic Resources)}}{\text{LIABILITIES} + \text{OWNER'S EQUITY}}$$

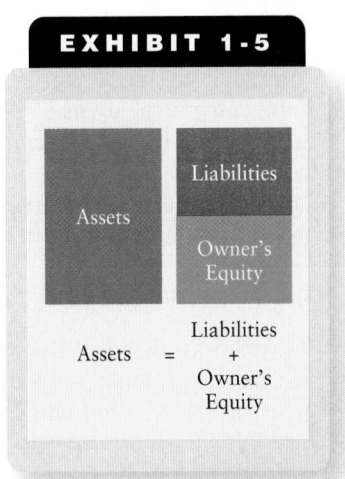

EXHIBIT 1-5

Liabilities

Assets

Owner's Equity

Assets = Liabilities + Owner's Equity

The Accounting Equation

Owner's Equity

Owner's equity is the amount of an entity's assets that remain after its liabilities are subtracted (amounts are assumed for the illustration).

$$\text{ASSETS} - \text{LIABILITIES} = \text{OWNER'S EQUITY}$$
$$\$5,000 - \$2,000 = \$3,000$$

The purpose of business is to increase owner's equity. Exhibit 1-6 shows the two ways to increase the owner's equity of a business:

- Owner investments increase the business's equity when the owner invests assets in the business. For example, Julie DeFilippo invested $1,000 of kitchen equipment to start DeFilippo Catering. Owner's equity of the business increased by $1,000.
- **Revenues** increase owner's equity from delivering goods or services to customers. For example, DeFilippo catering served a banquet and earned $1,500 of revenue. Owner's equity of the business increased by $1,500.

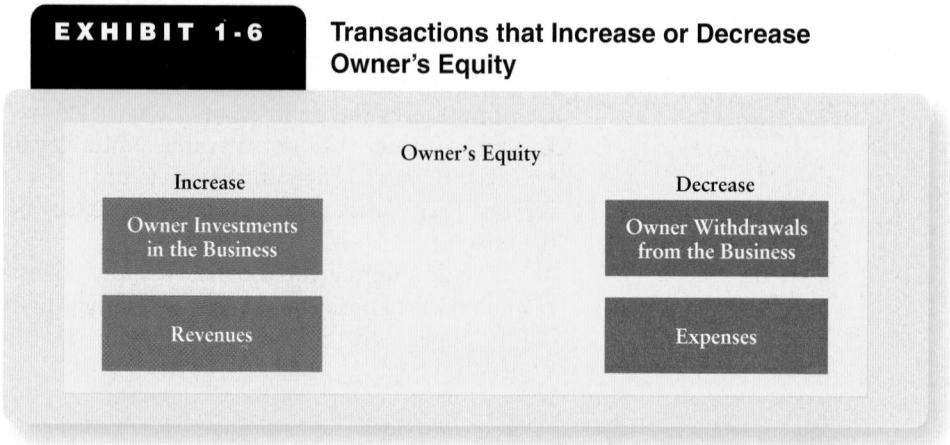

EXHIBIT 1-6   **Transactions that Increase or Decrease Owner's Equity**

There are relatively few types of revenue, including:

- **Sales revenue.** DeFilippo Catering earns sales revenue by selling food to customers.
- **Service revenue.** Sherman Lawn Service earns service revenue by mowing and trimming customers' lawns.
- **Interest revenue.** Interest revenue is earned on bank deposits and on money lent out to others.
- **Dividend revenue.** Dividend revenue is earned on investments in the stock of corporations.

Exhibit 1-6 also shows the two ways to decrease owner's equity:

- **Owner withdrawals** decrease owner's equity when the owner takes assets out of the business for personal use. For example, Julie DeFilippo withdrew $800 cash for personal use. This owner withdrawal decreased the owner's equity of DeFilippo Catering by $800. Withdrawals are the opposite of owner investments.
- **Expenses** decrease owner's equity by using up assets or increasing liabilities in order to deliver goods or services to customers. For example, DeFilippo Catering paid its chef a salary of $1,200, and that's an expense of the business. You can see that expenses are the opposite of revenues. Unfortunately, businesses have lots of expenses, including:
  - Store (or office) rent expense
  - Salary expense for employees
  - Advertising expense
  - Utilities expense for water, electricity, and gas
  - Insurance expense
  - Supplies expense for supplies used up
  - Interest expense on loans payable
  - Property tax expense

Accounting for Business Transactions

Accounting is based on actual transactions, not opinions or desires. A **transaction** is any event that affects the financial position of the business *and* can be measured reliably. Many events affect a company, including economic booms and recessions. Accountants do not record the effects of those events because they can't be measured reliably. An accountant records only those events that can be measured reliably, such as the purchase of a building, a sale of merchandise, and the payment of rent. The dollar amounts of these events can be measured reliably, so accountants record these transactions.

What are some of your personal transactions? You may have bought a car. Your purchase was a transaction. If you are making payments on an auto loan, your payments are also transactions. You need to record all your business transactions just as DeFilippo catering does in order to manage your personal affairs.

To illustrate accounting for a business, let's use Cookie Lapp Travel Design, a travel agency organized as a proprietorship. Online customers can plan and pay for their trips through the business's Web site. The Web site is linked to airlines, hotels, and cruise lines, so clients can obtain the latest information 24/7. The Web site allows the agency to transact more business. Now let's account for the transactions of Cookie Lapp Travel Design.

4 Analyze business transactions

Transaction 1: Starting the Business

Cookie Lapp invests $30,000 of her own money to start the business. She deposits $30,000 in a bank account titled Cookie Lapp Travel Design. The effect of this transaction on the accounting equation of the business is:

ASSETS	=	LIABILITIES	+	OWNER'S EQUITY	TYPE OF OWNER'S EQUITY TRANSACTION
Cash				Cookie Lapp, Capital	
(1) +30,000				+30,000	*Owner investment*

For each transaction, the amount on the left side of the equation must equal the amount on the right side. The first transaction increases both the assets (in this case, Cash) and the owner's equity (Cookie Lapp, Capital) of the business. To the right of the transaction, we write "Owner investment" to keep track of the source of the owner's equity.

Transaction 2: Purchase of Land

Lapp purchases land for an office location, paying cash of $20,000. This transaction affects the accounting equation as follows:

	ASSETS		=	LIABILITIES	+	OWNER'S EQUITY	TYPE OF OWNER'S EQUITY TRANSACTION
	Cash	+ Land				Cookie Lapp, Capital	
(1)	30,000					30,000	*Owner investment*
(2)	−20,000	+ 20,000					
Bal.	10,000	20,000				30,000	
	30,000					30,000	

The cash purchase of land increases one asset, Land, and decreases another asset, Cash. After the transaction is completed, the travel agency has cash of $10,000, land of $20,000, no liabilities, and owner's equity of $30,000. Note that the total balances (abbreviated Bal.) on both sides of the equation must always be equal—in this case $30,000.

With software, such as QuickBooks and Peachtree, a business can print a balance sheet to see where it stands financially. After we move through a sequence of transactions, we will prepare the balance sheet of Cookie Lapp Travel Design. Now let's account for additional transactions of the travel agency.

Transaction 3: Purchase of Office Supplies

Cookie Lapp buys stationery and other office supplies, agreeing to pay $500 within 30 days. This transaction increases both the assets and the liabilities of the business, as follows:

	ASSETS				LIABILITIES	+	OWNER'S EQUITY
	Cash	+	Office Supplies	+ Land	Accounts Payable	+	Cookie Lapp, Capital
Bal.	10,000			20,000			30,000
(3)	____		+500	____	+500		____
Bal.	10,000		500	20,000	500		30,000
			30,500				30,500

Office Supplies is an asset, not an expense, because the supplies can be used in the future. The liability created by this transaction is an account payable. **A payable is always a liability.**

Transaction 4: Earning of Service Revenue

Cookie Lapp Travel Design earns service revenue by providing travel services for clients. She earns $5,500 revenue and collects this amount in cash. The effect on the accounting equation is an increase in Cash and an increase in Cookie Lapp, Capital, as follows:

	ASSETS			LIABILITIES +	OWNER'S EQUITY	TYPE OF OWNER'S EQUITY TRANSACTION
	Cash	+ Office Supplies +	Land	Accounts Payable +	Cookie Lapp, Capital	
Bal.	10,000	500	20,000	500	30,000	
(4)	+5,500	____	____	____	+5,500	*Service revenue*
Bal.	15,500	500	20,000	500	35,500	
		36,000			36,000	

A revenue transaction grows the business, as shown by the increases in assets and owner's equity.

Transaction 5: Earning of Service Revenue on Account

Cookie Lapp performs service for clients who do not pay immediately. Lapp receives the clients' promises to pay $3,000 within one month. This promise is an asset, an account receivable, because Lapp expects to collect the cash in the future. In accounting, we say that Lapp performed this service *on account*. It's performing the service, not collecting the cash, that earns the revenue. Lapp records earning $3,000 of revenue on account as follows:

	Cash	+	Accounts Receivable	+	Office Supplies	+	Land	=	Accounts Payable	+	Cookie Lapp, Capital	TYPE OF OWNER'S EQUITY TRANSACTION
											ASSETS / **LIABILITIES + OWNER'S EQUITY**	
Bal.	15,500				500		20,000		500		35,500	
(5)	_____		+3,000		___		_____		___		+3,000	*Service revenue*
Bal.	15,500		3,000		500		20,000		500		38,500	
			39,000								39,000	

Transaction 6: Payment of Expenses

During the month, Cookie Lapp pays $3,300 in cash expenses: rent expense on a computer, $600; office rent, $1,100; employee salary, $1,200; and utilities, $400. The effects on the accounting equation are:

	Cash	+	Accounts Receivable	+	Office Supplies	+	Land	=	Accounts Payable	+	Cookie Lapp, Capital	TYPE OF OWNER'S EQUITY TRANSACTION
Bal.	15,500		3,000		500		20,000		500		38,500	
(6)	–600										–600	*Rent expense, computer*
(6)	–1,100										–1,100	*Rent expense, office*
(6)	–1,200										–1,200	*Salary expense*
(6)	–400		___		___		___		___		–400	*Utilities expense*
Bal.	12,200		3,000		500		20,000		500		35,200	
			35,700								35,700	

Expenses have the opposite effect of revenues. Expenses shrink the business, as shown by the decreased balances of assets and owner's equity.

Each expense should be recorded separately. The expenses are listed together here for simplicity. We could record the cash payment in a single amount for the sum of the four expenses: $3,300 ($600 + $1,100 + $1,200 + $400). In all cases, the accounting equation must balance.

Transaction 7: Payment on Account

Cookie Lapp pays $300 to the store from which she purchased supplies in transaction 3. In accounting, we say that she pays $300 *on account*. The effect on the accounting equation is a decrease in Cash and a decrease in Accounts Payable, as shown here:

	Cash	+	Accounts Receivable	+	Office Supplies	+	Land	=	Accounts Payable	+	Cookie Lapp, Capital
Bal.	12,200		3,000		500		20,000		500		35,200
(7)	–300		___		___		___		–300		___
Bal.	11,900		3,000		500		20,000		200		35,200
			35,400								35,400

The payment of cash on account has no effect on office supplies or expenses. Lapp was paying off a liability, not an expense.

Transaction 8: Personal Transaction

Cookie Lapp remodels her home at a cost of $40,000, paying cash from personal funds. This event is *not* a transaction of Cookie Lapp Travel Design. It has no effect on the travel agency and, therefore, is not recorded by the business. It is a transaction of the Cookie Lapp *personal* entity, not the travel agency. This transaction illustrates the *entity concept*.

Transaction 9: Collection on Account

In transaction 5, Lapp performed services for a client on account. The business now collects $1,000 from the client. We say that Lapp collects the cash *on account*. She will record an increase in Cash. Should she also record an increase in service revenue? No, because she already recorded the revenue when she earned the revenue in transaction 5. The phrase "collect cash on account" means to record an increase in Cash and a decrease in Accounts Receivable. The effect on the accounting equation is:

		ASSETS				LIABILITIES	+	OWNER'S EQUITY
	Cash	+ Accounts Receivable	+ Office Supplies	+ Land		Accounts Payable	+	Cookie Lapp, Capital
Bal.	11,900	3,000	500	20,000	=	200		35,200
(9)	+1,000	−1,000	___	___		___		___
Bal.	12,900	2,000	500	20,000		200		35,200
			35,400				35,400	

Total assets are unchanged from the preceding total. Why? Because Lapp merely exchanged one asset for another.

Transaction 10: Sale of Land

Lapp sells some land owned by the travel agency. The sale price of $9,000 is equal to Lapp's cost of the land. The business receives $9,000 cash, and the effect on the accounting equation of the travel agency follows:

		ASSETS				LIABILITIES	+	OWNER'S EQUITY
	Cash	+ Accounts Receivable	+ Office Supplies	+ Land		Accounts Payable	+	Cookie Lapp, Capital
Bal.	12,900	2,000	500	20,000	=	200		35,200
(10)	+9,000	___	___	−9,000		___		___
Bal.	21,900	2,000	500	11,000		200		35,200
			35,400				35,400	

Transaction 11: Withdrawal of Cash

Cookie Lapp withdraws $2,000 cash from the business for personal use. The effect on the accounting equation is:

		ASSETS				LIABILITIES	+	OWNER'S EQUITY	TYPE OF OWNER'S EQUITY TRANSACTION
	Cash	+ Accounts Receivable	+ Office Supplies	+ Land		Accounts Payable	+	Cookie Lapp, Capital	
Bal.	21,900	2,000	500	11,000	=	200		35,200	
(11)	−2,000	___	___	___		___		−2,000	*Owner withdrawal*
Bal.	19,900	2,000	500	11,000		200		33,200	
			33,400				33,400		

The owner's withdrawal of $2,000 cash decreases Cash and also the owner's equity of the business. *Owner withdrawals do not represent an expense because the cash is used for the owner's personal transactions.* We record this decrease in owner's equity as Withdrawals or as Drawings. The double underlines below each column indicate a final total after the last transaction.

Evaluating Business Transactions—The User Perspective of Accounting

We have now recorded Cookie Lapp Travel Design's transactions, and they are summarized in Exhibit 1-7. Note that every transaction maintains the equation

$$\text{Assets} = \text{Liabilities} + \text{Owner's Equity}$$

But a basic question remains: How will people actually use this information? The mass of data in Exhibit 1-7 won't tell a lender whether Cookie Lapp can pay off a loan. The data in the exhibit don't tell whether the travel agency is profitable.

To address these important questions, we need financial statements. The **financial statements** are business documents that report on a business in monetary terms. People use the financial statements to make business decisions. Before launching into the nuts and bolts of accounting, let's see how people actually use accounting information. Here we're giving only a thumbnail sketch of each financial statement; we'll explain them in more detail in the next section. First, the decisions:

- Cookie Lapp wants to know whether her travel agency is profitable. Is the business earning a net income—is it profitable—or is it experiencing a net loss? The **income statement** answers this question by reporting the net income or net loss of the business.
- Suppose Cookie Lapp needs $200,000 to buy an office building. She calls her banker and requests a loan. The banker wants to know how much in assets Lapp has and how much she already owes. The **balance sheet** answers this question by reporting the business's assets and liabilities. The banker asks what Lapp did with any profits the business earned. Did Lapp withdraw a lot for personal use, or did she leave the money in the travel agency? The **statement of owner's equity** answers this question.
- The banker wants to know if the travel agency generates enough cash to pay its bills. The **statement of cash flows** answers this question by reporting cash receipts and cash payments and whether cash increased or decreased.
- Outside investors also use financial statements. Cookie Lapp may decide to sell her business. Suppose you are considering buying the travel agency. In making this important decision—and in deciding how much to pay for the business—you would ask the same questions that Lapp and her banker have been asking:
  - Is the business profitable? See the **income statement**.
  - What did the owner do with any profits? See the **statement of owner's equity**.
  - How much in assets, liabilities, and owner's equity does the business have? See the **balance sheet**.
  - Does the business generate enough cash flow to succeed? See the **statement of cash flows**.

In summary, the main users of financial statements are:

- Business owners and managers
- Lenders
- Outside investors

EXHIBIT 1-7	Analysis of Transactions, Cookie Lapp Travel Design

PANEL A—Details of Transactions

1. Lapp, the owner, invested $30,000 cash in the business.
2. Paid $20,000 cash for land.
3. Bought $500 of office supplies on account.
4. Received $5,500 cash from clients for service revenue earned.
5. Performed travel service for clients on account, $3,000.
6. Paid cash expenses: computer rent, $600; office rent, $1,100; employee salary, $1,200; utilities, $400.
7. Paid $300 on the account payable created in transaction 3.
8. Remodeled Lapp's personal residence. This is *not* a transaction of the business.
9. Collected $1,000 on the account receivable created in transaction 5.
10. Sold land for cash at its cost of $9,000.
11. Withdrew $2,000 cash for personal use.

PANEL B—Analysis of Transactions

		Assets				Liabilities	+	Owner's Equity		Type of Owner's Equity Transaction
	Cash	+ Accounts Receivable	+ Office Supplies	+ Land		Accounts Payable	+	Cookie Lapp, Capital		
1.	+30,000							+30,000		*Owner investment*
Bal.	30,000							30,000		
2.	−20,000			+20,000						
Bal.	10,000			20,000				30,000		
3.			+500			+500				
Bal.	10,000		500	20,000		500		30,000		
4.	+5,500							+5,500		*Service revenue*
Bal.	15,500		500	20,000		500		35,500		
5.		+3,000						+3,000		*Service revenue*
Bal.	15,500	3,000	500	20,000		500		38,500		
6.	−600							−600		*Rent expense, computer*
6.	−1,100							−1,100		*Rent expense, office*
6.	−1,200							−1,200		*Salary expense*
6.	−400							−400		*Utilities expense*
Bal.	12,200	3,000	500	20,000		500		35,200		
7.	−300					−300				
Bal.	11,900	3,000	500	20,000		200		35,200		
8.	Not a transaction of the business									
9.	+1,000	−1,000								
Bal.	12,900	2,000	500	20,000		200		35,200		
10.	+9,000			−9,000						
Bal.	21,900	2,000	500	11,000		200		35,200		
11.	−2,000							−2,000		*Owner withdrawal*
Bal.	19,900	2,000	500	11,000		200		33,200		

(=)

33,400   33,400

Others also use the financial statements, but these groups are paramount, and we will be referring to them throughout this book. Now let's examine the financial statements in detail.

The Financial Statements

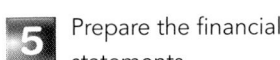

5 Prepare the financial statements

After analyzing transactions, we want to see the overall results. We look now at the financial statements discussed in the preceding section. The financial statements summarize the transaction data into a form that's useful for decision making. The financial statements are the:

- Income statement
- Statement of owner's equity
- Balance sheet
- Statement of cash flows

Income Statement

The **income statement** presents a summary of an entity's revenues and expenses for a period of time, such as a month or a year. The income statement, also called the **statement of earnings** or **statement of operations**, is like a video—a moving picture of operations during the period. The income statement holds one of the most important pieces of information about a business:

- *Net income* (total revenues greater than total expenses) or
- *Net loss* (total expenses greater than total revenues)

Net income is good news, and a net loss is bad news. What was the result of Cookie Lapp Travel Design's operations during April? Good news—the business earned net income (see the top part of Exhibit 1-8, page 20). The income statement is very important!

Statement of Owner's Equity

The **statement of owner's equity** shows the changes in *owner's equity* during a time period, such as a month or a year.
Increases in owner's equity come from:

- Owner investments
- Net income (revenues exceed expenses)

Decreases in owner's equity result from:

- Owner withdrawals
- Net loss (expenses exceed revenues)

Balance Sheet

The *balance sheet* lists the entity's assets, liabilities, and owner's equity as of a specific date, usually the end of a month or a year. The balance sheet is like a snapshot of the entity. For this reason, it is also called the *statement of financial position* (see the middle of Exhibit 1-8, page 20). The balance sheet is very important!

Statement of Cash Flows

The **statement of cash flows** reports the cash coming in (cash receipts) and the cash going out (*cash payments*) during a period. Business activities result in a net cash inflow or a net cash outflow. The statement reports the net increase or decrease in cash during the period and the ending cash balance.

In the first part of this book, we focus on the:

- Income statement
- Balance sheet
- Statement of owner's equity

COOKIE LAPP TRAVEL DESIGN
Income Statement
Month Ended April 30, 2008

Revenue:		
Service revenue		$8,500

The income statement and the balance sheet are more important than the statement of owner's equity. In Chapter 16 we cover the statement of cash flows in detail.

Financial Statement Headings

Each financial statement has a heading giving three pieces of data:

- Name of the business (such as Cookie Lapp Travel Design)
- Name of the financial statement (income statement, balance sheet, and so on)
- Date or time period covered by the statement (April 30, 2008, for the balance sheet; month ended April 30, 2008, for the other statements)

An income statement (or a statement of owner's equity) that covers a year ended in December 2008 is dated "Year Ended December 31, 2008." A monthly income statement (or statement of owner's equity) for September 2008 shows "Month Ended September 30, 2008." Income must be identified with a particular time period.

Relationships Among the Financial Statements

6 Evaluate business performance

Exhibit 1-8 illustrates all four financial statements. Their data come from the transaction analysis in Exhibit 1-7 that covers the month of April 2008. Study the exhibit carefully. Specifically, observe the following in Exhibit 1-8:

1. The *income statement* for the month ended April 30, 2008:
   a. Reports April's revenues and expenses. Expenses are listed in decreasing order of their amount, with the largest expense first.
   b. Reports *net income* of the period if total revenues exceed total expenses. If total expenses exceed total revenues, a *net loss* is reported instead.

2. The *statement of owner's equity* for the month ended April 30, 2008:
   a. Opens with the owner's capital balance at the beginning of the period.
   b. Adds *investments by the owner* and also adds *net income* (or subtracts *net loss*, as the case may be). Net income or net loss come directly from the income statement (see arrow **1** in Exhibit 1-8).
   c. Subtracts *withdrawals* by the owner. Parentheses indicate a subtraction.
   d. Ends with the owner's capital balance at the end of the period.

3. The *balance sheet* at April 30, 2008:
   a. Reports all *assets*, all *liabilities*, and *owner's equity* at the end of the period. Assets are listed in the order of their liquidity (closeness to cash) with cash coming first because it is the most liquid asset.
   Liabilities are reported similarly. That is, list first the liability that must be paid first, usually Accounts Payable.
   b. Reports that total assets equal total liabilities plus total owner's equity.
   c. Reports the owner's ending capital balance, taken directly from the statement of owner's equity (see arrow **2**).

4. The *statement of cash flows* for the month ended April 30, 2008:
   a. Reports cash flows from three types of business activities (*operating, investing,* and *financing activities*) during the month. Each category of cash-flow activities includes both cash receipts (positive amounts), and cash payments (negative amounts denoted by parentheses).
   b. Reports a net increase in cash during the month and ends with the cash balance at April 30, 2008. This is the amount of cash to report on the balance sheet (see arrow **3**).

As we conclude this chapter, we return to our opening question: Have you ever thought of having your own business? The Decision Guidelines feature on the next page shows how to make some of the decisions that you will face if you start a business. Decision Guidelines appear in each chapter.

Decision Guidelines

Suppose you open a business to take photos at parties at your college. You hire a professional photographer and line up suppliers for party favors and photo albums.

Here are some factors you must consider if you expect to be profitable.

Decision	Guidelines
How to organize the business?	If a single owner—a *proprietorship*.
	If two or more owners, but not incorporated—a *partnership*.
	If the business issues stock to stockholders—a *corporation*.
What to account for?	Account for the business, a separate entity apart from its owner (*entity concept*).
	Account for transactions and events that affect the business and can be measured reliably.
How much to record for assets and liabilities?	Actual historical amount (*cost principle*).
How to analyze a transaction?	The accounting equation:
	$$\text{Assets} = \text{Liabilities} + \text{Owner's Equity}$$
How to measure profits and losses?	Income statement:
	$$\text{Revenues} - \text{Expenses} = \text{Net Income (or Net Loss)}$$
Did owner's equity increase or decrease?	Statement of owner's equity:
	Beginning capital + Owner investments + Net income (or – Net loss) – Owner withdrawals = Ending capital
Where does the business stand financially?	Balance sheet (accounting equation):
	$$\text{Assets} = \text{Liabilities} + \text{Owner's Equity}$$

Summary Problem

Ron Smith opens an apartment-locator business near a college campus. He is the sole owner of the proprietorship, which he names Campus Apartment Locators. During the first month of operations, July 2007, the business completes the following transactions:

   a. Smith invests $35,000 of personal funds to start the business.

   b. Purchases on account office supplies costing $350.

   c. Pays cash of $30,000 to acquire a lot next to the campus. He intends to use the land as a future building site for the business office.

   d. Locates apartments for clients and receives cash of $1,900.

   e. Pays $100 on the account payable he created in transaction b.

   f. Pays $2,000 of personal funds for a vacation.

   g. Pays cash expenses for office rent, $400, and utilities, $100.

   h. Sells office supplies to another business for its cost of $150.

   i. Withdraws cash of $1,200 for personal use.

Requirements

1. Analyze the preceding transactions in terms of their effects on the accounting equation of Campus Apartment Locators. Use Exhibit 1-7 as a guide but show balances only after the last transaction.

2. Prepare the income statement, statement of owner's equity, and balance sheet of the business after recording the transactions. Use Exhibit 1-8 as a guide.

Solution

Requirement 1
PANEL A—Details of transactions

   a. Smith invested $35,000 cash to start the business.

   b. Purchased $350 of office supplies on account.

   c. Paid $30,000 to acquire land as a future building site.

   d. Earned service revenue and received cash of $1,900.

   e. Paid $100 on account.

   f. Paid for a personal vacation, which is not a transaction of the business.

   g. Paid cash expenses for rent, $400, and utilities, $100.

   h. Sold office supplies for cost of $150.

   i. Withdrew $1,200 cash for personal use.

PANEL B—Analysis of transactions

	ASSETS							LIABILITIES	+	OWNER'S EQUITY	TYPE OF OWNER'S EQUITY TRANSACTION
	Cash	+	Office Supplies	+	Land			Accounts Payable	+	Ron Smith, Capital	
(a)	+35,000									+35,000	*Owner investment*
(b)			+ 350					+ 350			
(c)	−30,000				+30,000						
(d)	+ 1,900									+ 1,900	*Service revenue*
(e)	− 100							− 100			
(f)	Not a transaction of the business										
(g)	− 400									− 400	*Rent expense*
	− 100									− 100	*Utilities expense*
(h)	+ 150		− 150								
(i)	− 1,200									− 1,200	*Owner withdrawal*
Bal.	5,250		200		30,000			250		35,200	

$=$

35,450

35,450

Requirement 2
Financial Statements of Campus Apartment Locators

CAMPUS APARTMENT LOCATORS
Income Statement
Month Ended July 31, 2007

Revenue:		
Service revenue		$1,900
Expenses:		
Rent expense	$400	
Utilities expense	100	
Total expenses		500
Net income		$1,400

CAMPUS APARTMENT LOCATORS
Statement of Owner's Equity
Month Ended July 31, 2007

Ron Smith, capital, July 1, 2007	$ 0
Add: Investment by owner	35,000
Net income for the month	1,400
	36,400
Less: Withdrawals by owner	(1,200)
Ron Smith, capital, July 31, 2007	$35,200

CAMPUS APARTMENT LOCATORS
Balance Sheet
July 31, 2007

Assets		Liabilities	
Cash	$ 5,250	Accounts payable	$ 250
Office supplies	200		
Land	30,000	**Owner's Equity**	
		Ron Smith, capital	35,200
		Total liabilities and	
Total assets	$35,450	owner's equity	$35,450

Accounting Vocabulary _____

Account Payable
A liability backed by the general reputation and credit standing of the debtor.

Account Receivable
A promise to receive cash from customers to whom the business has sold goods or for whom the business has performed services.

Accounting
The information system that measures business activities, processes that information into reports, and communicates the results to decision makers.

Accounting Equation
The basic tool of accounting, measuring the resources of the business and the claims to those resources: Assets = Liabilities + Owner's Equity

Asset
An economic resource that is expected to be of benefit in the future.

Audit
An examination of a company's financial situation.

Balance Sheet
An entity's assets, liabilities, and owner's equity as of a specific date. Also called the **statement of financial position**.

Capital
The claim of a business owner to the assets of the business.

Certified Management Accountant (CMA)
A licensed accountant who works for a single company.

Certified Public Accountant (CPA)
A licensed accountant who serves the general public rather than one particular company.

Corporation
A business owned by stockholders; it begins when the state approves its articles of incorporation. A corporation is a legal entity, an "artificial person," in the eyes of the law.

Entity
An organization or a section of an organization that, for accounting purposes, stands apart from other organizations and individuals as a separate economic unit.

Expense
Decrease in owner's equity that occurs from using assets or increasing liabilities in the course of delivering goods or services to customers.

Financial Accounting
The branch of accounting that focuses on information for people outside the firm.

Financial Accounting Standards Board (FASB)
The private organization that determines how accounting is practiced in the United States.

Financial Statements
Documents that report on a business in monetary amounts, providing information to help people make informed business decisions.

Generally Accepted Accounting Principles (GAAP)
Accounting guidelines, formulated by the Financial Accounting Standards Board, that govern how accountants measure, process, and communicate financial information.

Income Statement
Summary of an entity's revenues, expenses, and net income or net loss for a specific period. Also called the **statement of earnings** or the **statement of operations**.

Liability
An economic obligation (a debt) payable to an individual or an organization outside the business.

Management Accounting
The branch of accounting that focuses on information for internal decision makers of a business.

Net Income
Excess of total revenues over total expenses. Also called **net earnings** or **net profit**.

Net Loss
Excess of total expenses over total revenues.

Note Payable
A written promise of future payment.

Owner's Equity
The claim of a business owner to the assets of the business. Also called **capital**.

Owner's Withdrawals
Amounts removed from the business by an owner.

Partnership
A business with two or more owners.

Proprietorship
A business with a single owner.

Revenue
Amounts earned by delivering goods or services to customers. Revenues increase owner's equity.

Shareholder
A person who owns stock in a corporation.

Statement of Cash Flows
Report of cash receipts and cash payments during a period.

Statement of Earnings
Summary of an entity's revenues, expenses, and net income or net loss for a specific period.

Also called the **income statement** or the **statement of operations**.

Statement of Operations
Summary of an entity's revenues, expenses, and net income or net loss for a specific period. Also called the **income statement** or **statement of earnings**.

Statement of Owner's Equity
Summary of the changes in an entity's owner's equity during a specific period.

Stockholder
A person who owns stock in a corporation. Also called a **shareholder**.

Transaction
An event that affects the financial position of a particular entity and can be recorded reliably.

Review Accounting and the Business Environment

Quick Check

1. Generally accepted accounting principles (GAAP) are formulated by the
   a. Institute of Management Accountants (IMA)
   b. American Institute of Certified Public Accountants (AICPA)
   c. Securities and Exchange Commission (SEC)
   d. Financial Accounting Standards Board (FASB)

2. Which type of business organization is owned by its stockholders?
   a. Corporation
   b. Partnership
   c. Proprietorship
   d. All the above are owned by stockholders

3. Which accounting concept or principle specifically states that we should record transactions at amounts that can be verified?
   a. Entity concept
   b. Going-concern concept
   c. Cost principle
   d. Reliability principle

4. Fossil is famous for fashion wristwatches and leather goods. At the end of a recent year, Fossil's total assets added up to $381 million, and owners' equity was $264 million. How much were Fossil's liabilities?
   a. Cannot determine from the data given
   b. $381 million
   c. $117 million
   d. $264 million

5. Assume that Fossil sold watches to a department store on account for $50,000. How would this transaction affect Fossil's accounting equation?
   a. Increase both liabilities and owners' equity by $50,000
   b. Increase both assets and liabilities by $50,000
   c. Increase both assets and owners' equity by $50,000
   d. No effect on the accounting equation because the effects cancel out

6. Which parts of the accounting equation does a sale on account affect?
   a. Accounts Receivable and Accounts Payable
   b. Accounts Receivable and Owner, Capital
   c. Accounts Payable and Owner, Capital
   d. Accounts Payable and Cash

7. Assume that Fossil paid expenses totaling $35,000. How does this transaction affect Fossil's accounting equation?
   a. Increases assets and decreases liabilities
   b. Increases both assets and owners' equity
   c. Decreases assets and increases liabilities
   d. Decreases both assets and owners' equity

8. Consider the overall effects of transactions 5 and 7 on Fossil. What is Fossil's net income or net loss?

   a. Net income of $15,000

   b. Net loss of $35,000

   c. Net income of $50,000

   d. Cannot determine from the data given

9. The balance sheet reports

   a. Results of operations on a specific date

   b. Financial position on a specific date

   c. Financial position for a specific period

   d. Results of operations for a specific period

10. The income statement reports

   a. Financial position on a specific date

   b. Results of operations on a specific date

   c. Results of operations for a specific period

   d. Financial position for a specific period

Answers are given after Apply Your Knowledge (p. 48).

Assess Your Progress

Short Exercises

Explaining revenues, expenses

S1-1 Sherman Lawn Service has been open for one year, and Haig Sherman, the owner, wants to know whether the business earned a net income or a net loss for the year. First, he must identify the revenues earned and the expenses incurred during the year. What are *revenues* and *expenses?* (pp. 11, 12)

Explaining assets, liabilities, owner's equity

S1-2 Suppose you need a bank loan in order to purchase food-service equipment for DeFilippo Catering, which you own. In evaluating your loan request, the banker asks about the assets and liabilities of your business. In particular, the banker wants to know the amount of your owner's equity. In your own words, explain the meanings of *assets, liabilities,* and *owner's equity.* Also show the relationship among assets, liabilities, and owner's equity. (pp. 11, 12)

Applying accounting concepts and principles

S1-3 Suppose you are starting a business, T-Shirts Plus, to imprint logos on T-shirts. In organizing the business and setting up its accounting records, consider the following:

1. Should you combine your personal assets and personal liabilities with the assets and the liabilities of the business, or should you keep the two sets of records separate? Why? Which accounting concept or principle provides guidance? (pp. 9, 10)

2. In keeping the books of T-Shirts Plus, you must decide the amount to record for assets and liabilities. At what amount should you record assets and liabilities? Which accounting concept or principle provides guidance? (pp. 9, 10)

Applying accounting concepts and principles

S1-4 Claire Hunter owns and operates Claire Hunter Floral Designs. She proposes to account for flowers at current market value in order to have realistic amounts on the books if the business liquidates. Which accounting concept or principle is Hunter violating? How should Hunter account for the assets of the business? Which concept or principle governs this decision? (pp. 9, 10)

Using the accounting equation

S1-5 You begin A-1 Accounting Service by investing $2,000 of your own money in a business bank account. Before starting operations, you borrow $1,000 cash by signing a note payable to Summit Bank. Write the business's accounting equation after it has completed these transactions (Exhibit 1-5, page 11).

Using the accounting equation

S1-6 Wendy Craven owns a travel agency near the campus of Prince George's Community College. The business has cash of $2,000 and furniture that cost $8,000. Debts include accounts payable of $6,000. Using Craven's figures, write the accounting equation of the travel agency. How much equity does Craven have in the business? (pp. 11, 12)

Analyzing transactions

S1-7 Monte Jackson paid $20,000 cash to purchase land. To buy the land, Jackson was obligated to pay for it. Why, then, did Jackson record no liability in this transaction? (pp. 13, 14)

Analyzing transactions

S1-8 Air & Sea Travel recorded revenues of $3,000 earned on account by providing travel service for clients. How much are the business's cash and total assets after the transaction? Name the business's asset. (pp. 14, 15)

S1-9 Brad Polson collected cash on account from a client for whom he had provided delivery services one month earlier. Why didn't Polson record revenue when he collected the cash on account? (p. 16)

S1-10 Quail Creek Kennel earns service revenue by caring for the pets of customers. Quail Creek's main expense is the salary paid to an employee. Write two accounting equations to show the effects of:

a. Receiving cash of $300 for service revenue earned

b. Payment of $200 for salary expense.

Show all appropriate headings, starting with the accounting equation. Also list the appropriate item under each heading. (p. 14)

S1-11 Examine Exhibit 1-7 on page 18. The exhibit summarizes the transactions of Cookie Lapp Travel Design for the month of April 2008. Suppose Cookie has completed only the first seven transactions and needs a bank loan on April 21. The vice president of the bank requires financial statements to support all loan requests. Prepare the balance sheet that Cookie Lapp would present to the banker after completing the first seven transactions on April 21, 2008. Exhibit 1-8, page 20, shows the format of the balance sheet.

S1-12 Cookie Lapp wishes to know how well her business performed during April. The income statement in Exhibit 1-8, page 20, helps answer this question. Write the formula for measuring net income or net loss on the income statement. (p. 20)

S1-13 Advanced Automotive has just completed operations for the year ended December 31, 2008. This is the third year of operations for the company. As the proprietor, you want to know how well the business performed during the year. To address this question, you have assembled the following data:

Insurance expense	$ 4,000	Salary expense	$42,000
Service revenue	90,000	Accounts payable	8,000
Supplies expense	1,000	Supplies	2,000
Rent expense	13,000	Withdrawals by owner	36,000

Prepare the income statement of Advanced Automotive for the year ended December 31, 2008. Follow the format in Exhibit 1-8, page 20.

Exercises

E1-14 Suppose you have saved some money and you are investing in eBay stock. What accounting information will you use to decide whether to invest in eBay? Which accounting principle do you hope eBay's accountants follow closely? Explain your answer. (pp. 4, 9)

E1-15 Terry Maness publishes a travel magazine. In need of cash, Maness asks Metro Bank for a loan. The bank requires borrowers to submit financial statements. With little knowledge of accounting, Maness doesn't know

continued . . .

how to proceed. Explain to him the information provided by the balance sheet and the income statement. Indicate why a lender would require this information. (pp. 4, 19)

Business transactions

E1-16 As the manager of a Wendy's restaurant, you must deal with a variety of business transactions. Give an example of a transaction that has each of the following effects on the accounting equation: (pp. 13–17)

a. Increase one asset and decrease another asset.

b. Decrease an asset and decrease owner's equity.

c. Decrease an asset and decrease a liability.

d. Increase an asset and increase owner's equity.

e. Increase an asset and increase a liability.

Transaction analysis

E1-17 Jake's Roasted Peanuts, a proprietorship, supplies snack foods. The business experienced the following events. State whether each event (1) increased, (2) decreased, or (3) had no effect on the *total assets* of the business. Identify any specific asset affected. (pp. 13–17)

a. Jake's Roasted Peanuts received a cash investment from the owner.

b. Cash purchase of land for a building site.

c. Paid cash on accounts payable.

d. Purchased equipment; signed a note payable in payment.

e. Performed service for a customer on account.

f. The owner withdrew cash from the business for personal use.

g. Received cash from a customer on account receivable.

h. Borrowed money from the bank.

Accounting equation

E1-18 Compute the missing amount in the accounting equation for each entity: (p. 11)

	Assets	Liabilities	Owner's Equity
Pep Boys	$?	$60,000	$21,000
Eddie Bauer	72,000	?	40,000
Benbrook Exxon	100,000	79,000	?

Accounting equation

E1-19 Allison Landscaping started 2006 with total assets of $22,000 and total liabilities of $10,000. At the end of 2006, Allison's total assets stood at $30,000, and total liabilities were $14,000.

Requirements

1. Did the owner's equity of Allison Landscaping increase or decrease during 2006? By how much? (pp. 11, 12)

2. Identify two possible reasons for the change in owner's equity during the year. (p. 20)

Accounting equation

E1-20 A-1 Rentals' balance sheet data at May 31, 2009, and June 30, 2009, follow.

	May 31, 2009	June 30, 2009
Total assets	$150,000	$195,000
Total liabilities	100,000	130,000

continued . . .

Following are three situations about investments and withdrawals by the owner of the business during June. For each situation, compute the amount of net income or net loss during June 2009.

1. The owner invested $2,000 in the business and made no withdrawals. (p. 20)

2. The owner made no additional investments in the business but withdrew $5,000 for personal use. (p. 20)

3. The owner invested $6,000 in the business and withdrew $10,000 for personal use. (p. 20)

Transaction analysis
4

E1-21 Indicate the effects of the following business transactions on the accounting equation of a Blockbuster Video location. Transaction (a) is answered as a guide. (pp. 13–17)

a. Received cash of $10,000 from the owner, who was investing in the business.

    Answer: Increase asset (Cash)

                Increase owner's equity (Capital)

b. Earned video rental revenue on account, $1,200.

c. Purchased office furniture on account, $600.

d. Received cash on account, $300.

e. Paid cash on account, $250.

f. Sold land for $12,000, which was the cost of the land.

g. Rented videos and received cash of $600.

h. Paid monthly office rent of $800.

i. Paid $100 cash to purchase supplies.

Transaction analysis;
accounting equation
3 **4**

E1-22 Maria Lange opened a medical practice. During July, the first month of operation, the business, titled Maria Lange, M.D., experienced the following events.

July 6	Lange invested $45,000 in the business by opening a bank account in the name of M. Lange, M.D.
9	Paid $35,000 cash for land.
12	Purchased medical supplies for $2,000 on account.
15	Officially opened for business.
15–31	During the rest of the month, Lange treated patients and earned service revenue of $7,000, receiving cash.
15–31	Paid cash expenses: employees' salaries, $1,700; office rent, $1,000; utilities, $300.
28	Sold supplies to another physician for the cost of those supplies, $500.
31	Paid $1,500 on account.

continued . . .

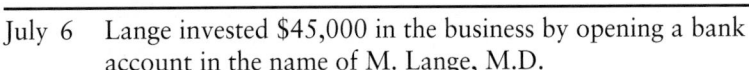

Requirement

Analyze the effects of these events on the accounting equation of the medical practice of M. Lange, M.D. Use a format similar to that of Exhibit 1-7 (p. 18), with headings for Cash; Medical Supplies; Land; Accounts Payable; and M. Lange, Capital.

Business transactions and net income

E1-23 The analysis of Rountree TV Service's first eight transactions follows. The owner made only one investment to start the business and made no withdrawals.

	Cash	+	Accounts Receivable	+	Equipment	=	Accounts Payable	+	Owner Capital
1.	+25,000								+25,000
2.			+2,400						+2,400
3.					+10,000		+10,000		
4.	+150		−150						
5.	−400				+400				
6.	−8,000						−8,000		
7.	+900								+900
8.	−2,000								−2,000

Requirements

1. Describe each transaction. (pp. 13–17)
2. If these transactions fully describe the operations of Rountree TV Service during the month, what was the amount of net income or net loss? (p. 20)

Business organization, balance sheet

5

E1-24 The account balances of Allen Samuel Road Service at November 30, 2009, follow.

Equipment	$15,500	Service revenue	$12,000
Supplies	500	Accounts receivable	6,000
Note payable	5,000	Accounts payable	3,500
Rent expense	800	Allen Samuel, capital	?
Cash	2,000	Salary expense	2,000

Requirements

1. Prepare the balance sheet of the business at November 30, 2009. (p. 20)
2. What does the balance sheet report—financial position or operating results? Which financial statement reports the other information? (p. 19)

Income Statement

5

E1-25 The assets, liabilities, owner's equity, revenues, and expenses of Ciliotta Design Studio at December 31, 2006, the end of its first year of operation, have the following balances. During the year, J. Ciliotta, the owner, invested $15,000 in the business.

continued . . .

Note payable	$41,000	Office furniture	$ 45,000
Rent expense	24,000	Utilities expense	6,800
Cash	3,600	Accounts payable	3,300
Office supplies	4,800	J. Ciliotta, capital	27,100
Salary expense	60,000	Service revenue	158,100
Salaries payable	2,000	Accounts receivable	9,000
Property tax expense	1,200	Supplies expense	4,000

Requirements

1. Prepare the income statement of Ciliotta Design Studio for the year ended December 31, 2006. What is the result of operations for 2006? (p. 20)

2. What was the amount of the proprietor's withdrawals during the year? (p. 20)

Evaluating the performance of a real company

E1-26 In this exercise you will practice using the data of a well-known company with the amounts rounded. The 2004 annual report of UPS, the overnight shipping company, reported revenue of $32 billion. Total expenses for the year were $29 billion. UPS ended the year with total assets of $33 billion, and it owed debts totaling $17 billion. At year-end 2003, UPS reported total assets of $30 billion and total liabilities of $17 billion.

Requirements

1. Compute UPS's net income for 2004. (p. 20)

2. Did UPS's owners' equity increase or decrease during 2004? By how much? (p. 20)

3. How would you rate UPS's performance for 2004—good or bad? Give your reason. (Challenge)

Using the financial statements
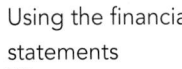
E1-27 Compute the missing amount for Jupiter Company. You will need to prepare a statement of owner's equity.

Jupiter Company	
Beginning:	
Assets	$ 50,000
Liabilities	20,000
Ending:	
Assets	$ 70,000
Liabilities	30,000
Owner's Equity:	
Investments by owner	$ 0
Withdrawals by owner	45,000
Income Statement:	
Revenues	$230,000
Expenses	?

Did Jupiter earn a net income or suffer a net loss for the year? Compute the amount. (pp. 11, 20)

Problems (Group A)

Entity concept, transaction
analysis, accounting
equation

P1-28A Abraham Woody practiced accounting with a partnership for five years. Recently he opened his own accounting firm, which he operates as a proprietorship. The name of the new entity is Abraham Woody, CPA. Woody experienced the following events during the organizing phase of his new business and its first month of operations. Some of the events were personal and did not affect the business.

Feb. 4	Received $75,000 cash from former accounting partners.
5	Deposited $60,000 cash in a new business bank account titled Abraham Woody, CPA.
6	Paid $300 cash for letterhead stationery for the new office.
7	Purchased office furniture for the office. Woody agreed to pay the account payable, $7,000, within 3 months.
10	Sold personal investment in Amazon.com stock, which he had owned for several years, receiving $50,000 cash.
11	Deposited the $50,000 cash from sale of the Amazon stock in his personal bank account.
12	A representative of a large company telephoned Woody and told him of the company's intention to transfer its accounting business to Woody.
18	Finished tax hearings on behalf of a client and submitted a bill for accounting services, $5,000. Woody expected to collect from this client within two weeks.
25	Paid office rent, $1,000.
28	Withdrew $3,000 cash from the business for personal use.

Requirements

1. Analyze the effects of the events on the accounting equation of the proprietorship of Abraham Woody, CPA. Use a format similar to Exhibit 1-7 on page 18.
2. At February 28, compute:
   a. Total assets (p. 18)
   b. Total liabilities (p. 18)
   c. Total owner's equity (p. 18)
   d. Net income or net loss for February (p. 20)

Transaction analysis,
accounting equation,
financial statements

P1-29A Marilyn Crone owns and operates a public relations firm called Best Foot Forward. The following amounts summarize her business on August 31, 2007:

	Assets				Liabilities +	Owner's Equity
		Accounts			Accounts	Marilyn Crone,
	Cash +	Receivable +	Supplies +	Land	Payable +	Capital
Bal.	2,200	1,500		12,000	8,000	7,700

During September 2007, the following events occurred.

a. Crone inherited $20,000 and deposited the cash in the business bank account.
b. Performed service for a client and received cash of $700.

continued . . .

c. Paid off the beginning balance of accounts payable.

d. Purchased supplies on account, $1,000.

e. Collected cash from a customer on account, $1,000.

f. Invested personal cash of $1,000 in the business.

g. Consulted for a Senate candidate and billed the client for services rendered, $3,000.

h. Recorded the following business expenses for the month:

　1. Paid office rent, $900.

　2. Paid advertising, $100.

i. Sold supplies to another business for $100 cash, which was the cost of the supplies.

j. Withdrew cash of $1,500 for personal use.

Requirements

1. Analyze the effects of the preceding transactions on the accounting equation of Best Foot Forward. Adapt the format of Exhibit 1-7, page 18.

2. Prepare the income statement of Best Foot Forward for the month ended September 30, 2007. List expenses in decreasing order by amount. (p. 20)

3. Prepare the entity's statement of owner's equity for the month ended September 30, 2007. (p. 20)

4. Prepare the balance sheet at September 30, 2007 (p. 20)

Business transactions and analysis

P1-30A Carolina Sports Consulting was recently formed as a proprietorship. The balance of each item in the company's accounting equation is shown for June 1 and for each of the following business days.

	Cash	Accounts Receivable	Supplies	Land	Accounts Payable	Owner's Equity
June 1	$ 4,000	$4,000	$1,000	$ 8,000	$4,000	$13,000
4	13,000	4,000	1,000	8,000	4,000	22,000
9	6,000	4,000	1,000	15,000	4,000	22,000
13	6,000	4,000	3,000	15,000	6,000	22,000
16	5,000	4,000	3,000	15,000	5,000	22,000
19	7,000	2,000	3,000	15,000	5,000	22,000
22	15,000	2,000	3,000	15,000	5,000	30,000
25	12,000	2,000	3,000	15,000	2,000	30,000
27	11,000	2,000	4,000	15,000	2,000	30,000
30	3,000	2,000	4,000	15,000	2,000	22,000

Requirements

A single transaction took place on each day. Briefly describe the transaction that most likely occurred on each day, beginning with June 4. Indicate which accounts were increased or decreased and by what amounts. No revenue or expense transactions occurred on these dates. (pp. 13–17)

P1-31A Accent Photography works weddings and prom-type parties. The capital balance of M.A. Thomas, the proprietor, was $56,000 at December 31, 2006. During 2007 he withdrew $46,000 for personal use. At December 31, 2007, the business's accounting records show these balances:

Insurance expense	$ 2,000	Accounts receivable	$ 3,000
Cash	14,000	Note payable	35,000
Accounts payable	1,000	M. A. Thomas, capital	?
Advertising expense	4,000	Salary expense	14,000
Service revenue	71,000	Equipment	80,000

Prepare the following financial statements for Accent Photography:

a. Income statement for the year ended December 31, 2007 (p. 20)

b. Statement of owner's equity for the year ended December 31, 2007 (p. 20)

c. Balance sheet at December 31, 2007 (p. 20)

P1-32A Presented here are (a) the assets and liabilities of Gotcha Covered Security Systems at December 31, 2007, and (b) the revenues and expenses of the company for the year ended on that date.

Land	$ 60,000	Accounts payable	$ 19,000
Note payable	35,000	Accounts receivable	13,000
Property tax expense	4,000	Advertising expense	12,000
Rent expense	23,000	Building	131,000
Salary expense	63,000	Cash	14,000
Salary payable	1,000	Equipment	20,000
Service revenue	189,000	Insurance expense	2,000
Supplies	3,000	Interest expense	9,000

The capital balance of Andrew Stryker, the owner, was $150,000 one year ago, at December 31, 2006. During 2007, Stryker withdrew $40,000 for personal use.

Requirements

1. Prepare Gotcha Covered's income statement for the year ended December 31, 2007. (p. 20)

2. Prepare the statement of owner's equity for the year ended December 31, 2007. (p. 20)

3. Prepare the balance sheet at December 31, 2007. (p. 20)

4. Answer these questions about the company:

   a. Was the result of operations for the year a profit or a loss? How much? (p. 20)

   b. How much in total economic resources does the company have as it moves into the new year? How much does the company owe? What is the dollar amount of the owner's equity interest in the business at the end of the year? (p. 20)

P1-33A Jan Featherston is a realtor. She organized her business as a proprietorship on November 1, 2006. Consider the following facts at November 30, 2006.

a. Featherston owes $55,000 on a note payable for land that her business acquired for a total price of $80,000.

b. The business spent $20,000 for a Coldwell Banker real estate franchise, which entitles Featherston to represent herself as a Coldwell Banker agent. This franchise is a business asset.

c. Featherston owes $60,000 on a personal mortgage for her personal residence, which she acquired in 2003 for a total price of $150,000.

d. Featherston has $4,000 in her personal bank account and $7,000 in her business bank account.

e. Featherston owes $3,000 on a personal charge account with Nordstrom.

f. Featherston acquired business furniture for $14,000 on November 25. Of this amount, her business owes $5,000 on account at November 30.

g. Office supplies on hand at the real estate office total $1,000.

1. Prepare the balance sheet of the real estate business of Jan Featherston, Realtor, at November 30, 2006. (p. 20)

2. Identify the personal items that would not be reported on the balance sheet of the business. (pp. 9, 20)

P1-34A The bookkeeper of Lone Star Landscaping prepared the company's balance sheet while the accountant was ill. The balance sheet contains numerous errors. In particular, the bookkeeper knew that the balance sheet should balance, so he plugged in the owner's equity amount needed to achieve this balance. The owner's equity amount, therefore, is incorrect. All other amounts are accurate, but some are out of place.

LONE STAR LANDSCAPING
Balance Sheet
Month Ended July 31, 2008

Assets		Liabilities	
Cash	$ 4,000	Accounts receivable	$ 23,000
Office supplies	1,000	Service revenue	73,500
Land	50,000	Property tax expense	800
Salary expense	2,500	Accounts payable	8,000
Office furniture	16,000		
Note payable	36,000	**Owner's Equity**	
Rent expense	2,500	Lynn Woodward, capital	6,700
Total assets	$112,000	Total liabilities	$112,000

Requirement
Prepare the correct balance sheet, and date it correctly. Compute total assets, total liabilities, and owner's equity. (p. 20)

Problems (Group B)

Entity concept, transaction analysis, accounting equation

P1-35B Amy Fisk practiced law with a partnership for 10 years. Recently she opened her own law office, which she operates as a proprietorship. The name of the new entity is Amy Fisk, Attorney. Fisk experienced the following events during the organizing phase of the new business and its first month of operation. Some of the events were personal and did not affect the law practice. Others were business transactions and should be accounted for by the business.

July 1	Sold personal investment in eBay stock, which she had owned for several years, receiving $29,000 cash.
2	Deposited the $29,000 cash from sale of the eBay stock in her personal bank account.
3	Received $150,000 cash from former law partners.
5	Deposited $100,000 cash in a new business bank account titled Amy Fisk, Attorney.
6	A representative of a large company telephoned Fisk and told her of the company's intention to transfer its legal business to Amy Fisk, Attorney.
7	Paid $500 cash for letterhead stationery for the new law office.
9	Purchased office furniture for the law office, agreeing to pay the account, $9,500, within 3 months.
23	Finished court hearings on behalf of a client and submitted a bill for legal services, $3,000, on account.
30	Paid office rent, $1,500.
31	Withdrew $5,000 cash from the business for personal use.

Requirements

1. Analyze the effects of the preceding events on the accounting equation of the proprietorship of Amy Fisk, Attorney. Use a format similar to Exhibit 1-7, page 18.

2. At July 31, compute the business's
   a. Total assets (p. 18)
   b. Total liabilities (p. 18)
   c. Total owner's equity (p. 18)
   d. Net income or net loss for the month (p. 20)

Transaction analysis, accounting equation, financial statements

P1-36B Bob Grayson owns and operates an architectural firm called Grayson Architecture. The following amounts summarize his business on April 30, 2007.

		Assets				Liabilities +	Owner's Equity
	Cash	+ Accounts Receivable	+ Supplies	+ Land	=	Accounts Payable +	Bob Grayson, Capital
Bal.	1,720	3,240		24,100		5,400	23,660

During May 2007, the following events occurred.

a. Grayson received $12,000 as a gift and deposited the cash in the business bank account.

continued . . .

b. Paid off the beginning balance of accounts payable.

c. Performed services for a client and received cash of $1,100.

d. Collected cash from a customer on account, $750.

e. Purchased supplies on account, $720.

f. Consulted on the interior design of a building and billed the client for services rendered, $5,000 on account.

g. Invested personal cash of $1,700 in the business.

h. Recorded the following business expenses for the month:

    1. Paid office rent, $1,200.

    2. Paid advertising, $600.

i. Sold supplies to an interior designer for $80 cash, which was the cost of the supplies.

j. Withdrew cash of $2,400 for personal use.

Requirements

1. Analyze the effects of the preceding transactions on the accounting equation of Grayson Architecture. Adapt the format of Exhibit 1-7, page 18.

2. Prepare the income statement of Grayson Architecture for the month ended May 31, 2007. List expenses in decreasing order by amount. (p. 20)

3. Prepare the statement of owner's equity of Grayson Architecture for the month ended May 31, 2007. (p. 20)

4. Prepare the balance sheet of Grayson Architecture at May 31, 2007. (p. 20)

Business transactions and analysis

P1-37B Pellegrini Electronics was recently formed. The balance of each item in the company's accounting equation follows for May 4 and for each of the following days:

		Cash	Accounts Receivable	Supplies	Land	Accounts Payable	Owner's Equity
May	4	$2,000	$7,000	$ 800	$11,000	$3,800	$17,000
	7	6,000	3,000	800	11,000	3,800	17,000
	12	4,000	3,000	800	11,000	1,800	17,000
	17	4,000	3,000	1,100	11,000	2,100	17,000
	19	5,000	3,000	1,100	11,000	2,100	18,000
	20	3,900	3,000	1,100	11,000	1,000	18,000
	22	9,900	3,000	1,100	5,000	1,000	18,000
	25	9,900	3,700	400	5,000	1,000	18,000
	26	9,300	3,700	1,000	5,000	1,000	18,000
	30	4,200	3,700	1,000	5,000	1,000	12,900

Requirement

A single transaction took place on each day. Describe briefly the transaction that most likely occurred on each day, beginning with May 7. Indicate which accounts were increased or decreased and by what amount. No revenue or expense transactions occurred on these dates. (pp. 13–17)

Preparing the financial
statements—simple
situation

P1-38B Studio Gallery provides pictures for high school yearbooks. During 2009 Mike Magid, the owner, withdrew $16,000 for personal use. At December 31, 2009, the business's accounting records show these balances:

Rent expense	$ 7,000	Accounts receivable	$ 8,000
Cash	20,000	Note payable	12,000
Accounts payable	6,000	Mike Magid, capital	?
Advertising expense	4,000	Salary expense	22,000
Service revenue	74,000	Equipment	65,000

Prepare the following financial statements for Studio Gallery:

a. Income statement for the year ended December 31, 2009 (p. 20)

b. Statement of owner's equity for the year ended December 31, 2009. Mike Magid, Capital had a balance of $50,000 on December 31, 2008. (p. 20)

c. Balance sheet at December 31, 2009 (p. 20)

Income statement,
statement of owner's equity,
balance sheet

P1-39B The amounts of (a) the assets and liabilities of Town & Country Realty at December 31, 2007, and (b) the revenues and expenses of the company for the year ended on that date follow.

Note payable	$ 31,000	Accounts payable	$ 12,000
Property tax expense	2,000	Accounts receivable	3,000
Rent expense	14,000	Building	56,000
Salary expense	38,000	Cash	7,000
Service revenue	100,000	Equipment	13,000
Supplies	7,000	Interest expense	4,000
Utilities expense	3,000	Interest payable	1,000
Land	8,000		

The capital balance of Kevin Kobelsky, the owner, was $43,000 one year ago, at December 31, 2006. During 2007, Kobelsky withdrew $32,000 for personal use.

Requirements

1. Prepare the income statement of Town & Country Realty for the year ended December 31, 2007. (p. 20)

2. Prepare the statement of owner's equity for the year ended December 31, 2007. (p. 20)

3. Prepare the balance sheet at December 31, 2007. (p. 20)

4. Answer these questions about the company.

   a. Was the result of operations for the year a profit or a loss? How much? (p. 20)

   b. Did Kobelsky drain off all the earnings for the year, or did he increase the company's capital during the period? How would his actions affect the company's ability to borrow? (p. 20)

Balance sheet, entity concept

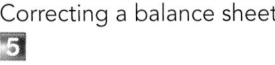

P1-40B Martha Agee operates a Kinko's store. Agee organized the business as a proprietorship on March 1, 2006. Consider the following facts at March 31, 2006:

   a. Agee has $3,000 in her personal bank account and $17,000 in her business bank account.

   b. Office supplies on hand at the store total $1,000.

   c. The business spent $15,000 for a Kinko's franchise, which entitles the business to operate as a Kinko's store. This franchise is an asset.

   d. Agee owes $34,000 on a note payable for some land acquired by the business for a total price of $60,000.

   e. Agee owes $60,000 on a personal mortgage on her personal residence, which she acquired in 2001 for a total price of $100,000.

   f. Agee owes $950 on her personal MasterCard.

   g. Agee acquired business furniture for $22,000 on March 26. Of this amount, the business owes $15,000 on account at March 31.

Requirements

1. Prepare the balance sheet of Kinko's of Santa Rosa at March 31, 2006. (p. 20)

2. Identify the personal items that would not be reported on the balance sheet of the business. (pp. 9, 20)

Correcting a balance sheet

5

P1-41B The bookkeeper of Dave Lundy Tax Service prepared the balance sheet of the company while the accountant was ill. The balance sheet contains numerous errors. In particular, the bookkeeper knew that the balance sheet should balance, so he plugged in the owner's equity amount to achieve this balance. The owner's equity amount, however, is not correct. All other amounts are accurate, but some are out of place.

DAVE LUNDY TAX SERVICE
Balance Sheet
Month Ended Ocober 31, 2007

Assets		Liabilities	
Cash	$ 5,400	Notes receivable	$ 3,000
Insurance expense	300	Interest expense	600
Land	31,500	Office supplies	800
Salary expense	3,300	Accounts receivable	2,600
Office furniture	6,000	Note payable	21,000
Accounts payable	2,300		
Utilities expense	2,100	**Owner's Equity**	
		Dave Lundy, capital	22,900
Total assets	$50,900	Total liabilities	$50,900

Requirement

Prepare the correct balance sheet, and date it correctly. Compute total assets, total liabilities, and owner's equity. (p. 20)

For 24/7 practice, visit
www.MyAccountingLab.com

Continuing Problem

Problem 1-42 is the first problem in a sequence that begins an accounting cycle. The cycle is continued in Chapter 2 and completed in Chapter 5.

Recording transactions and preparing a trial balance

P1-42 Carl Redmon completed these transactions during the first half of December:

Dec. 2	Invested $10,000 to start a consulting practice titled Redmon Consulting.
2	Paid monthly office rent, $500.
3	Paid cash for a Dell computer, $2,000. This equipment is expected to remain in service for five years.
4	Purchased office furniture on account, $3,600. The furniture should last for five years.
5	Purchased supplies on account, $300.
9	Performed consulting service for a client on account, $1,700.
12	Paid utility expenses, $200.
18	Performed service for a client and received cash of $800.

Requirements

1. Analyze the effects of Redmon's transactions on the accounting equation. Use the format of Exhibit 1-7, page 18, and include these headings: Cash, Accounts Receivable, Supplies, Equipment, Furniture, Accounts Payable, and Carl Redmon, Capital.

2. Prepare the income statement of Redmon Consulting for the month ended December 31, 2007. List expenses in decreasing order by amount. (p. 20)

3. Prepare the statement of owner's equity for the month ended December 31, 2007. (p. 20)

4. Prepare the balance sheet at December 31, 2007. (p. 20)

In Chapter 2, we will account for these same transactions a different way—as the accounting is actually performed in practice.

Apply Your Knowledge
Decision Cases

Accounting equation, evaluating performance

Case 1. This case follows up on the chapter-opening story about Sherman Lawn Service and DeFilippo Catering. It is now the end of the first year of operations, and both owners—Haig Sherman and Julie DeFilippo—want to know how well they came out at the end of the year. Neither business kept complete accounting records (even though Haig Sherman majored in accounting). Sherman and DeFilippo throw together the following data at year end:

Sherman Lawn Service:	
Total assets	$12,000
Haig Sherman, capital	8,000
Total revenues	35,000
Total expenses	22,000
DeFilippo Catering:	
Total liabilities	$ 7,000
Julie DeFilippo, capital	6,000
Total expenses	44,000
Net income	9,000

Working in the lawn-service business, Sherman has forgotten all the accounting he learned in college. DeFilippo majored in dietetics, so she never learned any accounting. To gain information for evaluating their businesses, they ask you several questions. For each answer, you must show your work to convince Sherman and DeFilippo that you know what you are talking about.

1. Which business has more assets? (pp. 11, 20)

2. Which business owes more to creditors? (pp. 11, 20)

3. Which owner has more invested in the business? (pp. 11, 20)

4. Which business brought in more revenue? (pp. 11, 20)

5. Which business is more profitable? (p. 20)

6. Which of the foregoing questions do you think is most important for evaluating these two businesses? Why? (Challenge)

7. Which business looks better from a financial standpoint? (Challenge)

Measuring net income

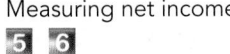

Case 2. Dave and Reba Guerrera saved all their married life to open a bed and breakfast (B&B) in Tucson, Arizona. They invested $100,000 of their own money and also got a $100,000 bank loan for the $200,000 needed to get started. The Guerreras bought a beautiful old Spanish colonial home in Tucson for $80,000. It cost another $50,000 to renovate. They found most of the furniture at antique shops and flea markets—total cost was $20,000. Kitchen equipment cost $10,000, and a Dell computer set them back another $2,000.

continued . . .

Prior to the grand opening, the banker requests a report on their activities thus far. Dave and Reba's bank statement shows a cash balance of $38,000. They feel pretty good with that much net income in only six months. To better understand how well they are doing, they prepare the following income statement for presentation to the bank:

TRES AMIGOS BED AND BREAKFAST
Income Statement
Six Months Ended June 30, 2007

Revenues:	
Investments by owner	$100,000
Bank loan	100,000
Total revenues	200,000
Expenses:	
Cost of the house	$ 80,000
Repairs to the house	50,000
Furniture expense	20,000
Kitchen equipment expense	10,000
Computer expense	2,000
Total expenses	162,000
Net income	38,000

1. Suppose you are the Guerreras' banker, and they have given you this income statement. Would you congratulate them on their net income? If so, explain why. If not, how would you advise them to measure the net income of the business? Does the amount of cash in the bank measure net income? Explain. (Challenge)

2. Prepare Tres Amigos' balance sheet from their data. (p. 20)

Ethical Issues

Ethical Issue 1. The board of directors of Xiaping Trading Company is meeting to discuss the past year's results before releasing financial statements to the public. The discussion includes this exchange:

Wai Lee, company president: "This has not been a good year! Revenue is down and expenses are way up. If we're not careful, we'll report a loss for the third year in a row. I can temporarily transfer some land that I own into the company's name, and that will beef up our balance sheet. Brent, can you shave $500,000 from expenses? Then we can probably get the bank loan that we need."

Brent Ray, company chief accountant: "Wai Lee, you are asking too much. Generally accepted accounting principles are designed to keep this sort of thing from happening."

Requirements

1. What is the fundamental ethical issue in this situation? (Challenge)

2. Discuss how Wai Lee's proposals violate generally accepted accounting principles. Identify each specific concept or principle involved. (pp. 9–10)

Ethical Issue 2. The tobacco companies have paid billions because of smoking-related illnesses. In particular, **Philip Morris**, a leading cigarette manufacturer, paid over $3 billion in one year.

Requirements

1. Suppose you are the chief financial officer (CFO) responsible for the financial statements of Philip Morris. What ethical issue would you face as you consider what to report in your company's annual report about the cash payments? What is the ethical course of action for you to take in this situation? (Challenge)

2. What are some of the negative consequences to Philip Morris for not telling the truth? What are some of the negative consequences to Philip Morris for telling the truth? (Challenge)

Financial Statement Case

Identifying items from a company's financial statements

This and similar cases in later chapters focus on the financial statement of a real company—**Amazon.com, Inc.**, the Internet shopping leader. As you work each case, you will gain confidence in your ability to use the financial statements of real companies.

Refer to Amazon.com's financial statements in Appendix A at the end of the book.

Requirements

1. How much in cash (including cash equivalents) did Amazon have on December 31, 2005?

2. What were the company's total assets at December 31, 2005? At December 31, 2004?

3. Write the company's accounting equation at December 31, 2005, by filling in the dollar amounts:

$$\text{ASSETS} = \text{LIABILITIES} + \text{STOCKHOLDERS' EQUITY}$$

4. Identify net sales (revenue) for the year ended December 31, 2005. How much did total revenue increase or decrease from 2004 to 2005?

5. How much net income or net loss did Amazon earn for 2005 and for 2004? Based on net income, was 2005 better or worse than 2004?

Team Projects

Project I. You are opening Quail Creek Pet Kennel. Your purpose is to earn a profit, and you organize as a proprietorship.

1. Make a detailed list of 10 factors you must consider to establish the business.

2. Identify 10 or more transactions that your business will undertake to open and operate the kennel.

continued . . .

3. Prepare Quail Creek Pet Kennel's income statement, statement of owner's equity, and balance sheet at the end of the first month of operations before you have had time to pay all the business's bills. Use made-up figures and include a complete heading for each financial statement. Date the balance sheet as of January 31, 20XX.

4. Discuss how you will evaluate the success of your business and how you will decide whether to continue its operation.

Project 2. You are promoting a rock concert in your area. Your purpose is to earn a profit, and you organize Concert Enterprises as a proprietorship.

Requirements

1. Make a detailed list of 10 factors you must consider to establish the business.

2. Describe 10 of the items your business must arrange in order to promote and stage the rock concert.

3. Prepare your business's income statement, statement of owner's equity, and balance sheet on June 30, 20XX, immediately after the rock concert and before you have had time to pay all the business's bills and to collect all receivables. Use made-up amounts, and include a complete heading for each financial statement. For the income statement and the statement of owner's equity, assume the period is the three months ended June 30, 20XX.

4. Assume that you will continue to promote rock concerts if the venture is successful. If it is unsuccessful, you will terminate the business within three months after the concert. Discuss how you will evaluate the success of your venture and how you will decide whether to continue in business.

For Internet Exercises, Excel in Practice, and additional online activities, go to the Web site www.prenhall.com/horngren

---

Quick Check Answers

1. *d*   2. *a*   3. *d*   4. *c*   5. *c*   6. *b*   7. *d*   8. *a*   9. *b*   10. *c*

Chapter 1: Demo Doc

Transaction Analysis Using Accounting Equation/Financial Statement Preparation

Demo Doc: To make sure you understand this material, work through the following demonstration "demo doc" with detailed comments to help you see the concept within the framework of a worked-through problem.

Learning Objectives 4–5

On March 1, 2008, David Richardson opened a painting business near a historical housing district. David was the sole owner of the proprietorship, which he named DR Painting. During March 2008, David engaged in the following transactions:

- a. **David invested $40,000 of personal cash to start the business.**

- b. **The business paid $20,000 cash to acquire a truck.**

- c. **The business purchased supplies costing $1,800 on account.**

- d. **The business painted a house for a customer and received $3,000 cash.**

- e. **The business painted a house for a customer for $4,000. The customer agreed to pay next week.**

- f. **The business paid $800 cash toward the supplies purchased in transaction c.**

- g. **The business paid employee salaries of $1,000 cash.**

- h. **David withdrew $1,500 cash from the business for personal use.**

- i. **The business collected $2,600 from the customer in transaction e.**

- j. **David paid $100 cash for personal groceries.**

Requirements

1. Analyze the preceding transactions in terms of their effects on the accounting equation of DR Painting. Use Exhibit 1-7 (p. 18) as a guide.

2. Prepare the income statement, statement of owner's equity, and balance sheet of the business after recording the transactions. Use Exhibit 1-8 (p. 20) in the text as a guide.

Chapter 1: Demo Doc Solutions

Requirement 1

Analyze the preceding transactions in terms of their effects on the accounting equation of DR Painting. Use Exhibit 1-7 (p. 18) as a guide.

Part 1	Part 2	Part 3	Part 4	Demo Doc Complete

a. David invested $40,000 of personal cash to start the business.

David is giving his own money *to the business*, so it is a recordable transaction for the business.

From the business's perspective, Cash (an asset) is increased by $40,000 and David Richardson, Capital (owner's equity) is also increased by $40,000.

The effect of this transaction on the accounting equation is:

	ASSETS		LIABILITIES	+	OWNER'S EQUITY	TYPE OF OWNER'S EQUITY TRANSACTION
	Cash	=		+	David Richardson, Capital	
a.	+40,000				+40,000	*Owner investment*
Bal.	40,000				40,000	

To record this in the table, we add $40,000 under Assets: Cash. We also add $40,000 under Owner's Equity. To the right of the transaction, we write "Owner investment" to help us keep track of changes in the equity account. This will be helpful again when we prepare the financial statements. Before we move on, we should double-check to see that the left side of the equation equals the right side. Remember: The equation must always balance after each transaction.

b. The business paid $20,000 cash to acquire a truck.

The Truck account (an asset) is increased by $20,000, while Cash (an asset) is decreased by $20,000.

The effect of this transaction on the accounting equation is:

	ASSETS				LIABILITIES	+	OWNER'S EQUITY	TYPE OF OWNER'S EQUITY TRANSACTION
	Cash	+	Truck	=			David Richardson, Capital	
a.	40,000						40,000	*Owner investment*
b.	−20,000	+	20,000					
Bal.	20,000		20,000				40,000	
			40,000				40,000	

Note that transactions do not have to affect both sides of the equation. However, the accounting equation *always* holds, so *both sides must always balance*. It helps to check that this is true after every transaction.

c. The business purchased supplies costing $1,800 on account.

The supplies are an asset that is increased by $1,800. However, the supplies were not paid for in cash but were purchased *on account*. This relates to accounts *pay*able (because it will have to be *paid* later). Because this debt must be paid later, it is an increase to Accounts Payable (a liability) of $1,800.

The effect of this transaction on the accounting equation is:

		ASSETS				LIABILITIES +	OWNER'S EQUITY	TYPE OF OWNER'S EQUITY TRANSACTION
	Cash	+ Supplies +	Truck	=		Accounts Payable +	David Richardson, Capital	
Bal.	20,000		20,000				40,000	
c.	____	+1,800	____			+1,800	____	
Bal.	20,000	1,800	20,000			1,800	40,000	
			41,800			**41,800**		

Remember that the supplies will be recorded as an asset until they are used by the business (the adjustment will be addressed in a later chapter). The obligation to pay the $1,800 will remain in Accounts Payable until it is paid.

d. The business painted a house for a customer and received $3,000 cash.

When the business paints houses, it means that it is doing work, or performing services, for customers, which is the way that the business makes money. By performing services, the business is earning service revenue (as opposed to *sales* revenue).

This means that Service Revenues is increased (which increases owner's equity) by $3,000. Because the customer paid in cash, Cash (an asset) is increased by $3,000.

Remember: Revenues *increase* net income, which increases owner's equity.

The effect of this transaction on the accounting equation is:

		ASSETS				LIABILITIES +	OWNER'S EQUITY	TYPE OF OWNER'S EQUITY TRANSACTION
	Cash	+ Supplies +	Truck	=		Accounts Payable +	David Richardson, Capital	
Bal.	20,000	1,800	20,000			1,800 +	40,000	
d.	+3,000	____	____			____	+3,000	*Service revenue*
Bal.	23,000	1,800	20,000			1,800	43,000	
			44,800			**44,800**		

Note that we write "Service revenue" to the right of the owner's equity column to record why equity increased.

e. The business painted a house for a customer for $4,000. The customer agreed to pay next week.

This transaction is similar to transaction **d**, except that the business is not receiving the cash immediately. Does this mean that we should wait to record the revenue when the cash is received? No, DR Painting should recognize the revenue when the service is performed, regardless of whether it has received the cash.

Again, the business is performing services for customers, which means that it is earning service revenues. This results in an increase to Service Revenue (owner's equity) of $4,000.

However, this time the customer did not pay in cash so Richardson will collect cash later. This is the same as charging the services *on account*. This is money that the business will *receive* in the future (when the customers eventually pay), so it is called accounts *receiv*able. Accounts Receivable (an asset) is increased by $4,000. The Accounts Receivable account represents amounts the business expects to collect. Accounts Receivable will decrease when a customer pays us.

The effect of this transaction on the accounting equation is:

	Cash	+	Accounts Receivable	+	Supplies	+	Truck	=	Accounts Payable	+	David Richardson, Capital	Type of Owner's Equity Transaction
Bal.	23,000				1,800		20,000		1,800		43,000	
e.	____		+4,000		____		____		____		+4,000	*Service revenue*
Bal.	23,000		4,000		1,800		20,000		1,800		47,000	
							48,800		48,800			

f. The business paid $800 cash toward the supplies purchased in transaction c.

Think of Accounts Payable (a liability) as a list of companies to which the business will *pay* money at some point in the future. In this particular problem, the business owes money to the company from which it purchased supplies on account in transaction **c**. When we *pay* the money in full, we can cross this company off of the list. Right now, we are paying only *part* of the money owed.

This is a decrease to Accounts Payable (a liability) of $800 and a decrease to Cash (an asset) of $800. Because we are only paying part of the money we owe to the supply store, our balance of Accounts Payable is $1,800 − $800 = $1,000.

You should note that this transaction does not affect Office Supplies because the business is not buying more supplies. It is simply paying off a liability, not acquiring more assets or incurring a new expense.

The effect of this transaction on the accounting equation is:

	Cash	+	Accounts Receivable	+	Supplies	+	Truck	=	Accounts Payable	+	David Richardson, Capital	Type of Owner's Equity Transaction
Bal.	23,000		4,000		1,800		20,000		1,800		47,000	
f.	−800		____		____		____		−800		____	
Bal.	22,200		4,000		1,800		20,000		1,000		47,000	
							48,000		48,000			

g. The business paid employee salaries of $1,000 cash.

The work the employees have given to the business has *already been used*. By the end of March, DR Painting has had the employees working and painting for customers for the entire month. The *benefit* of the work has already been received. This means that it is a salary *expense*. So, Salary Expense is increased by $1,000, and all expenses decrease owner's equity.

Remember: Expenses *decrease* net income, which decreases owner's equity.

The salaries were paid in cash, so Cash (an asset) is also decreased by $1,000.

The effect of this transaction on the accounting equation is:

		ASSETS				=	LIABILITIES +	OWNER'S EQUITY	TYPE OF OWNER'S EQUITY TRANSACTION
	Cash	+ Accounts Receivable	+ Supplies	+ Truck		=	Accounts Payable +	David Richardson, Capital	
Bal.	22,200	4,000	1,800	20,000			1,000	47,000	
g.	–1,000	____	____	____			____	–1,000	*Salary expense*
Bal.	21,200	4,000	1,800	20,000			1,000	46,000	
				47,000			47,000		

h. David withdrew $1,500 cash from the business for personal use.

When an owner makes a withdrawal from the business, it is a recordable transaction for the business. In this case, there is a decrease of $1,500 to Cash (an asset). Because David is the owner, this results in an increase of $1,500 to Owner Withdrawals, which is a decrease to owner's equity.

You should note that *the withdrawal is not an expense* because the transaction was unrelated to revenue-producing activities. The cash withdrawn is for the owner's personal use rather than to earn revenue for the business.

The effect of this transaction on the accounting equation is:

		ASSETS				=	LIABILITIES +	OWNER'S EQUITY	TYPE OF OWNER'S EQUITY TRANSACTION
	Cash	+ Accounts Receivable	+ Supplies	+ Truck		=	Accounts Payable +	David Richardson, Capital	
Bal.	21,200	4,000	1,800	20,000			1,000	46,000	
h.	–1,500	____	____	____			____	–1,500	*Owner withdrawal*
Bal.	19,700	4,000	1,800	20,000			1,000	44,500	
				45,500			45,500		

i. The business collected $2,600 from the customer in transaction e.

Think of Accounts Receivable (an asset) as a list of customers from whom the business will *receive* money at some point in the future. Later, when the business collects (*receives*) the cash in full from any particular customer, it can cross that customer off the list.

In transaction e, DR Painting performed services for a customer on account. Now DR is receiving part of that money. This is a collection that decreases Accounts Receivable (an asset) by $2,600.

Because the cash is received, Cash (an asset) is increased by $2,600.

The effect of this transaction on the accounting equation is:

		ASSETS					LIABILITIES +	OWNER'S EQUITY	TYPE OF OWNER'S EQUITY TRANSACTION
	Cash	+ Accounts Receivable	+ Supplies	+ Truck	=		Accounts Payable	+ David Richardson, Capital	
Bal.	+19,700	4,000	1,800	20,000			1,000	44,500	
i.	+ 2,600	+2,600							
Bal.	22,300	1,400	1,800	20,000			1,000	44,500	
				45,500			45,500		

j. David paid $100 cash for personal groceries.

David is using $100 of *his own cash* for groceries. This is a *personal* expense for David's *personal* use that does not relate to the business and, therefore, is not a recordable transaction for the business. This transaction has no effect on the business's accounting equation. Had David used the *business's cash* to purchase groceries, *then* the business would record the transaction.

All of the recorded transactions are summarized as follows:

	ASSETS						LIABILITIES +	OWNER'S EQUITY	TYPE OF OWNER'S EQUITY TRANSACTION
	Cash	+ Accounts Receivable	+ Supplies	+ Truck			Accounts Payable	David Richardson, Capital	
a.	+$40,000							+$40,000	*Owner investment*
b.	–$20,000			+$20,000					
c.			+$1,800				+1,800		
d.	+$3,000				=			+$3,000	*Service revenue*
e.		+$4,000						+$4,000	*Service revenue*
f.	–$800						–$800		
g.	–$1,000							–$1,000	*Salary expense*
h.	–$1,500							–$1,500	*Owner withdrawal*
i.	+$2,600	–$2,600							
j.	Not a transaction of the business.								
	$22,300	$1,400	$1,800	$20,000			$1,000	$44,500	
		$45,500					$45,500		

Requirement 2

Prepare the income statement, statement of owner's equity, and balance sheet of the business after recording the transactions. Use Exhibit 1-8 (p. 20) in the text as a guide.

Part 1	**Part 2**	Part 3	Part 4	Demo Doc Complete

Income Statement

The income statement is the first statement that can be prepared because the other financial statements rely on the net income number calculated on the income statement.

The income statement reports the profitability of the business. To prepare an income statement, begin with the proper heading. A proper heading includes the name of the company (DR Painting), the name of the statement (Income Statement), and the time period covered (Month Ended March 31, 2008). Notice that the income statement reports income for a period of time rather than on a single date.

The income statement lists all revenues and expenses. It uses the following formula to calculate net income:

$$\text{Revenues} - \text{Expenses} = \text{Net Income}$$

First, you should list revenues. Second, list the expenses. Having trouble finding the revenues and expenses? Look in the equity column of the accounting equation. After you list and total the revenues and expenses, subtract the total expenses from total revenues to determine net income or net loss. If you have a positive number, then you report net income. A negative number indicates that expenses exceeded revenues, and you report this as a net loss.

In the case of DR Painting, transactions **d** and **e** increased Service Revenue (by $3,000 and $4,000, respectively). This means that total Service Revenue for the month was $3,000 + $4,000 = $7,000.

The only expenses incurred were in transaction **g**, which resulted in a Salary Expense of $1,000. On the income statement these would be reported as follows:

DR PAINTING Income Statement Month Ended March 31, 2008		
Revenue:		
Service revenue		$ 7,000
Expenses:		
Salary expense	$ 1,000	
Total expenses		1,000
Net income		$ 6,000

Note the result is a net income of $6,000 ($7,000 − $1,000 = $6,000). You will use this amount on the statement of owner's equity.

Statement of Owner's Equity

Part 1	Part 2	**Part 3**	Part 4	Demo Doc Complete

The statement of owner's equity shows the changes in owner's equity over a period of time. To prepare a statement of owner's equity, begin with the proper heading. A proper heading includes the name of the company (DR Painting), the name of the statement (Statement of Owner's Equity), and the time period covered (Month Ended March 31, 2008). As with the income statement, the statement of owner's equity reports changes in equity for a period of time rather than on a single date.

Net income is used on the statement of owner's equity to calculate the new balance in the Capital account. This calculation uses the following formula:

> Beginning capital amount
>
> + Owner investments
>
> + Net income
>
> – Owner withdrawals
>
> = Ending capital amount

You will begin the statement of owner's equity with the owner's capital at the beginning of the period (March 1). List the owner's name, capital, and beginning date to the left, and enter the dollar amount of capital to the right. Then you will list additions to capital, such as additional investment by the owner or net income. You should notice that the amount of net income comes directly from the income statement. Following additions, you will report deductions from equity, such as withdrawals made by the owner or a net loss. After reporting the additions and deductions, you then compute the owner's capital balance at the end of the period.

In this case, because this is a new company, the beginning capital is zero. Additions to capital include the initial investment by the owner ($40,000 from transaction **a**), plus the net income as reported on the income statement ($6,000) for a subtotal of $46,000. A deduction from equity occurred in transaction **h**, when David withdrew $1,500 from the business for personal use. On the statement of owner's equity, these would be reported as follows:

DR PAINTING Statement of Owner's Equity Month Ended March 31, 2008	
D. Richardson, capital, March 1, 2008	$ 0
Add: Investment by owner	40,000
Net income for the month	6,000
	46,000
Less: Withdrawals by owner	(1,500)
D. Richardson, capital, March 31, 2008	$44,500

Note the result is an ending capital amount of $44,500 ($46,000 – $1,500 = $44,500). You will use this amount on the balance sheet.

Balance Sheet

| Part 1 | Part 2 | Part 3 | **Part 4** | Demo Doc Complete |

The balance sheet reports the financial position of the business. To prepare a balance sheet, begin with the proper heading. A proper heading includes the name of the company (DR Painting), the name of the statement (Balance Sheet), and the date covered (March 31, 2008). Unlike the income statement and statement of owner's equity, we are reporting the financial position of the company for a specific date rather than for a period of time.

The balance sheet is a listing of all assets, liabilities, and equity, with the accounting equation verified at the bottom.

To prepare the body of the balance sheet, begin by listing assets. Then list the liabilities and owner's equity. Notice that the balance sheet is organized in the same order as the accounting equation. You should note that the amount of owner's equity comes directly from the ending capital on your statement of owner's equity. Now total both sides of the balance sheet to make sure that they are equal. If they are not equal, then you will need to correct the error.

In this case, assets include the total cash balance of $22,300; accounts receivable of $1,400; $1,800 worth of supplies; and the truck's value of $20,000, for a total of $45,500 in assets. Liabilities total $1,000: the balance of Accounts Payable. The figures for assets and liabilities come directly from the accounting equation worksheet. From the statement of owner's equity, we have an ending capital amount of $44,500. This gives us a total for liabilities and owner's equity of $1,000 + $44,500 = $45,500, confirming that Assets = Liabilities + Owner's Equity.

DR PAINTING
Balance Sheet
March 31, 2008

Assets		Liabilities	
Cash	$22,300	Accounts payable	$ 1,000
Accounts receivable	1,400		
Supplies	1,800	**Owner's Equity**	
Truck	20,000	D. Richardson, capital	44,500
		Total liabilities and	
Total assets	$45,500	owner's equity	$45,500

| Part 1 | Part 2 | Part 3 | Part 4 | **Demo Doc Complete** |

2 Recording Business Transactions

Learning Objectives

1 Use accounting terms

2 Apply the rules of debit and credit

3 Record transactions in the journal

4 Post from the journal to the ledger

5 Prepare and use a trial balance

Sherman Lawn Service and DeFilippo Catering are now up and running. Both businesses are buying supplies, earning revenues, collecting cash, and paying expenses. The proprietors, Haig Sherman and Julie DeFilippo, naturally want to know how they're doing.

In Chapter 1 Sherman and DeFilippo learned about the income statement and the balance sheet—two financial statements that help them measure progress. Sherman and DeFilippo also learned to record transactions in terms of the accounting equation. That procedure works well for a handful of transactions. But even Sherman Lawn Service or DeFilippo Catering would need a huge Excel spreadsheet to record all their transactions with the accounting equation. Fortunately, there's a better way.

In this chapter we show how accounting is actually done in business. This may be the most important chapter of the whole book. After you master this material, you'll have a foundation for learning accounting. But if you miss this, well, let's just say the picture won't be very pretty. Therefore, make sure you learn this material before you go on. ■

The following diagram summarizes the accounting process covered in this chapter.

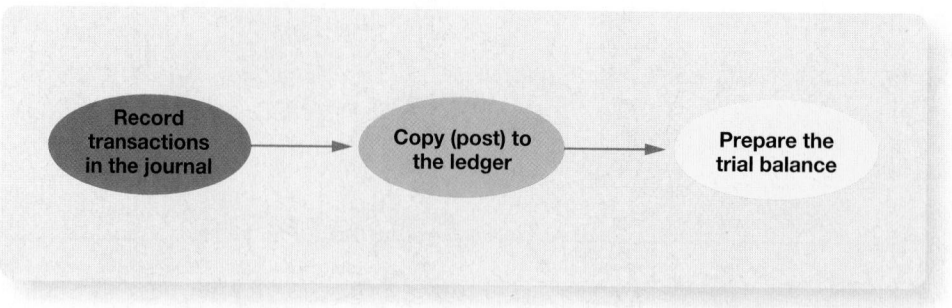

The Account, the Ledger, and the Journal

The basic summary device of accounting is the account. An **account** is the detailed record of all the changes that have occurred in a particular asset, liability, or owner's equity during a period. As we saw in Chapter 1, business transactions cause the changes.

Accountants record transactions first in a **journal**, which is the chronological record of transactions. Accountants then copy (post) the data to the book (or print-out) of accounts called the **ledger**. A list of all the ledger accounts and their balances is called a **trial balance**.

Take a moment to memorize these important terms. You will be using them over and over again.

- **Account**—the detailed record of the changes in a particular asset, liability, or owner's equity
- **Ledger**—the book (or printout) holding all the accounts
- **Journal**—the chronological record of transactions
- **Trial balance**—the list of all the accounts with their balances

Accounts are grouped in three broad categories, according to the accounting equation:

$$\text{Assets} = \text{Liabilities} + \text{Owner's Equity}$$

Assets

Assets are economic resources that will benefit the business in the future. Most firms use the following asset accounts.

Cash

The Cash account is a record of the cash effects of transactions. Cash includes money, such as a bank balance, paper currency, coins, and checks. Cash is the most pressing need of start-up businesses such as Sherman Lawn Service and DeFilippo Catering.

Accounts Receivable

Most businesses sell goods or services in exchange for a promise of future cash receipt. Such sales are made on credit ("on account"), and Accounts Receivable is

1 Use accounting terms

the account that holds these amounts. Most sales in the United States and in other developed countries are made on account.

Notes Receivable

A business may sell goods or services and receive a *promissory note*. A note receivable is a written pledge that the customer will pay a fixed amount of money by a certain date.

Prepaid Expenses

A business often pays certain expenses, such as rent and insurance, in advance. A *prepaid expense* is an asset because the prepayment provides a future benefit. Prepaid Rent, Prepaid Insurance, and Office Supplies are separate prepaid expense accounts. Your prepaid rent on your apartment or dorm room is an asset to you.

Land

The Land account shows the cost of land a business holds for use in operations. Land held for sale is different. Its cost is an investment.

Building

The cost of buildings—an office or a warehouse—appears in the Buildings account. Frito-Lay and The Coca-Cola Company own buildings around the world, where they make chips and drinks.

Equipment, Furniture, and Fixtures

A business has a separate asset account for each type of equipment—Computer Equipment, Office Equipment, and Store Equipment, for example. The Furniture account shows the cost of this asset.

Liabilities

Recall that a *liability* is a debt. A business generally has fewer liability accounts than asset accounts because the liabilities are summarized in a handful of accounts.

Accounts Payable

Accounts Payable are the opposite of Accounts Receivable. The promise to pay a debt arising from a credit purchase is an Account Payable. Such a purchase is said to be made on account. All companies from DeFilippo Catering to Coca-Cola to eBay, have Accounts Payable.

Notes Payable

Notes Payable are the opposite of Notes Receivable. Notes Payable represent debts the business owes because it signed promissory notes to borrow money or to purchase something.

Accrued Liabilities

An *accrued liability* is a liability for an expense that has not been paid. Taxes Payable, Interest Payable, and Salary Payable are accrued liability accounts.

Owner's Equity

The owner's claim to the assets of the business is called *owner's equity*. A proprietorship or a partnership has a separate capital account and a separate withdrawal account for each owner.

Capital

The Capital account shows the owner's claim to the assets of the business. Consider Cookie Lapp Travel Design. The balance of Cookie Lapp, Capital equals Lapp's investments in the business plus net income minus net losses and minus her withdrawals.

Withdrawals

When Cookie Lapp withdraws cash from the business for personal use, both its assets and owner's equity decrease. The amounts taken out of the business appear in a separate account Cookie Lapp, Withdrawals, or Cookie Lapp, Drawing. If withdrawals were recorded directly in the Capital account, the amount of owner withdrawals would not show up and the data would be lost. The Withdrawals account *decreases* owner's equity.

Revenues

The increase in owner's equity created by delivering goods or services to customers is called *revenue*. The ledger contains as many revenue accounts as needed. Cookie Lapp Travel Design needs a Service Revenue account for amounts earned by providing travel services. If Cookie Lapp Travel lends money to an outsider, it needs an Interest Revenue account for the interest earned on the loan. If the business rents out a building to a tenant, it needs a Rent Revenue account.

Expenses

Expenses use up assets or create liabilities in the course of operating a business. Expenses have the opposite effect of revenues; expenses *decrease* owner's equity. A business needs a separate account for each type of expense, such as Salary Expense, Rent Expense, Advertising Expense, and Utilities Expense. Businesses strive to minimize their expenses in order to maximize net income—whether it's General Electric, Cookie Lapp Travel, or Sherman Lawn Service.

Exhibit 2-1 shows how asset, liability, and owner's equity accounts can be grouped in the ledger.

Chart of Accounts

The ledger contains the accounts grouped under these headings:

- Assets, Liabilities, and Owner's Equity
- Revenues and Expenses

Organizations use a **chart of accounts** to list all their accounts along with the account numbers.

Account numbers usually have two or more digits. Assets are often numbered beginning with 1, liabilities with 2, owner's equity with 3, revenues with 4, and expenses with 5. The second and third digits in an account number indicate where the account fits within the category. For example, Cash may be account number 101, the first asset account. Accounts Receivable may be account number 111, the second asset. Accounts Payable may be number 201, the first liability. All accounts are numbered by this system.

The chart of accounts for Cookie Lapp Travel Design appears in Exhibit 2-2. Notice the gap in account numbers between 121 and 141. Lapp may need to add

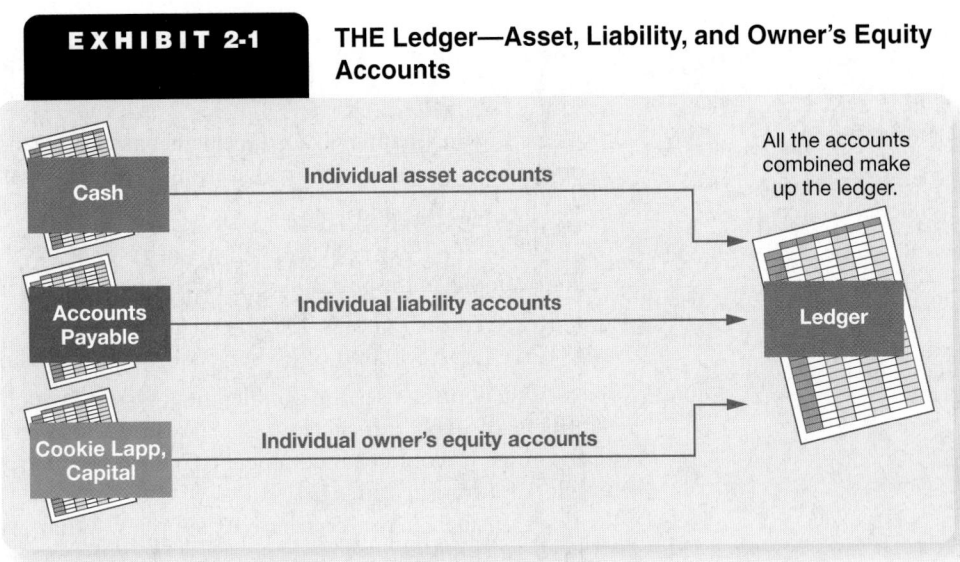

EXHIBIT 2-1 THE Ledger—Asset, Liability, and Owner's Equity Accounts

another asset account. For example, she may start selling some type of inventory, account number 131.

The inside covers of this book give expanded charts of accounts that you will find helpful throughout this course. The first chart lists the typical accounts of a *service* proprietorship, such as Cookie Lapp Travel Design. The second chart is for a *merchandising* business, which sells a product rather than a service. The third chart lists the accounts for a *manufacturing* company. You will use the manufacturing accounts in Chapters 18 through 25. Study the service proprietorship now, and refer to the other charts of accounts as needed later.

EXHIBIT 2-2 Chart of Accounts—Cookie Lapp Travel Design

Balance Sheet Accounts

Assets	Liabilities	Owner's Equity
101 Cash	201 Accounts Payable	301 Cookie Lapp, Capital
111 Accounts Receivable	211 Salary Payable	311 Cookie Lapp, Withdrawals
121 Notes Receivable	221 Interest Payable	
141 Supplies	231 Notes Payable	
151 Furniture		
171 Building		
191 Land		

Income Statement Accounts
(Part of Owner's Equity)

Revenues	Expenses
401 Service Revenue	501 Rent Expense, Computer
411 Interest Revenue	502 Rent Expense, Office
	505 Salary Expense
	510 Depreciation Expense
	520 Utilities Expense
	530 Advertising Expense
	540 Supplies Expense

Double-Entry Accounting

As we saw in Chapter 1, accounting is based on transaction data, not on mere whim or opinion. Each business transaction has dual effects:

- The receiving side
- The giving side

For example, in the $30,000 cash receipt by Cookie Lapp Travel Design, the business:

- Received cash of $30,000
- Gave Lapp $30,000 of owner's equity in the business

Accounting uses the double-entry system, which means that we record the dual effects of each transaction. As a result, every transaction affects at least two accounts. It would be incomplete to record only the giving side, or only the receiving side, of a transaction.

Consider a cash purchase of supplies. What are the dual effects? A cash purchase of supplies:

1. Increases supplies (you received supplies)
2. Decreases cash (you gave cash)

A credit purchase of equipment (a purchase on account):

1. Increases equipment (you received equipment)
2. Increases accounts payable (you gave your promise to pay in the future)

The T-Account

The most widely used form of account is called the *T-account* because it takes the form of the capital letter *T*. The vertical line divides the account into its left and right sides, with the title at the top. For example, the Cash account appears as follows.

Cash	
(Left side)	(Right side)
Debit	Credit

The left side of the account is called the **Debit** side, and the right side is called the **Credit** side. The words *debit* and *credit* are new. To become comfortable using them, remember that:

Debit = Left	Credit = Right

The terms *debit* and *credit* are deeply entrenched in business.[1] They are abbreviated as follows:

DR = Debit	CR = Credit

Increases and Decreases in the Accounts

2 Apply the rules of debit and credit

The account category (asset, liability, equity) governs how we record increases and decreases. For any given account, increases are recorded on one side, and decreases are recorded on the opposite side. The following T-accounts provide a summary.

---

[1]The words *debit* and *credit* abbreviate the Latin terms *debitum* and *creditum*. Luca Pacioli, the Italian monk who wrote about accounting in the 15th century, popularized these terms.

Assets		Liabilities and Owner's Equity	
Increase = Debit	Decrease = Credit	Decrease = Debit	Increase = Credit

These are the *rules of debit and credit*. In your study of accounting, forget the general usage of credit and debit because accounting uses these terms in a specialized way.

Remember that *debit means left* and *credit means right*. Whether an account is increased or decreased by a debit or a credit depends on the type of account.

In a computerized accounting system, the computer interprets debits and credits as increases or decreases. For example, a computer reads a debit to Cash as an increase. The computer reads a debit to Accounts Payable as a decrease.

Exhibit 2-3 shows the relationship between the accounting equation and the rules of debit and credit.

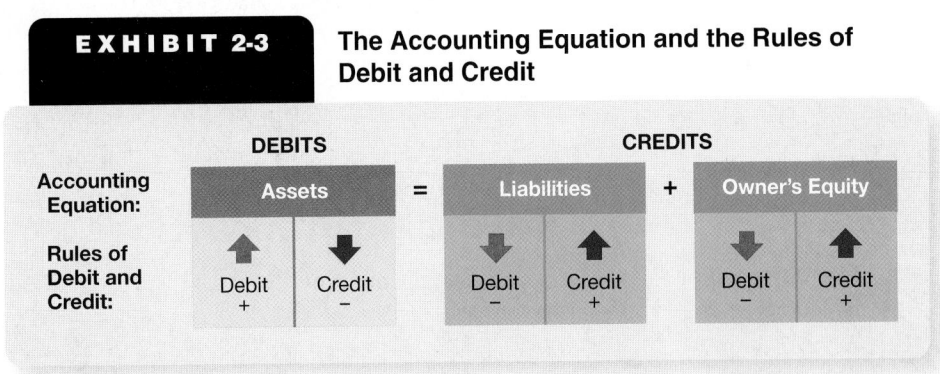

EXHIBIT 2-3 **The Accounting Equation and the Rules of Debit and Credit**

To illustrate the ideas diagrammed in Exhibit 2-3, reconsider the first transaction from Chapter 1. Cookie Lapp Travel Design received $30,000 cash and gave Lapp equity in the business. Which accounts of the business are affected?

The answer: The business's assets and capital would increase by $30,000, as the T-accounts show.

ASSETS	=	LIABILITIES	+	OWNER'S EQUITY

Cash		Cookie Lapp, Capital	
Debit for increase, 30,000			Credit for increase, 30,000

The amount remaining in an account is called its *balance*. The first transaction gives Cash a $30,000 debit balance and Cookie Lapp, Capital a $30,000 credit balance. Exhibit 2-4 illustrates the accounting equation after Cookie Lapp Travel Design's first two transactions.

The second transaction is a $20,000 purchase of land. After transaction 2, Cash has a $10,000 debit balance, Land has a debit balance of $20,000, and Cookie Lapp, Capital has a $30,000 credit balance.

We create accounts as needed. The process of creating a new account is called *opening the account*. For transaction 1, we opened the Cash account and the Cookie Lapp, Capital account. For transaction 2, we opened the Land account.

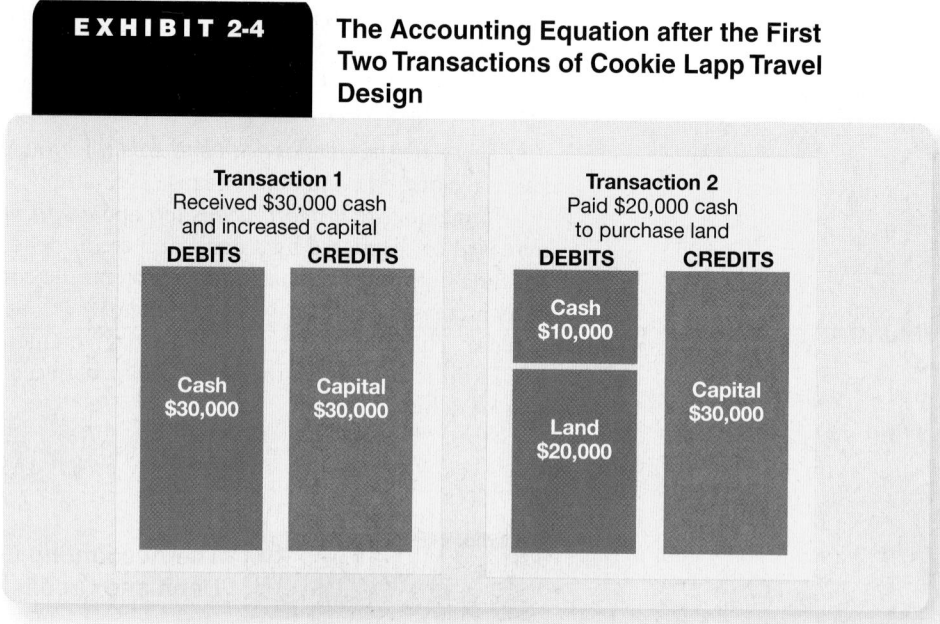

EXHIBIT 2-4   The Accounting Equation after the First Two Transactions of Cookie Lapp Travel Design

Recording Transactions in the Journal

3 | Record transactions in the journal

In practice, accountants record transactions in a *journal*. The journalizing process has three steps:

1. Identify each account affected and its type (asset, liability, or equity).

2. Determine whether each account is increased or decreased. Use the rules of debit and credit.

3. Record the transaction in the journal, including a brief explanation. The debit side of the entry is entered first. Total debits should always equal total credits. This step is also called "making the journal entry" or "journalizing the transaction."

These steps are the same whether computerized or manual.

Let's journalize the first transaction of Cookie Lapp Travel Design—the receipt of $30,000 cash invested by the owner.

STEP 1 The accounts affected by the receipt of cash from the owner are *Cash* and *Cookie Lapp, Capital*. Cash is an asset. Cookie Lapp, Capital is equity.

STEP 2 Both accounts increase by $30,000. Therefore, we debit Cash, the asset, and we credit Cookie Lapp, Capital, the owner's equity.

STEP 3 The journal entry is:

Journal				Page 1
Date	Accounts and Explanation		Debit	Credit
Apr. 1[a]	Cash[b]		30,000[b]	
	Cookie Lapp, Capital[c]			30,000[c]
	Received investment from owner.[d]			

Footnotes a, b, c, d, are explained as follows. The journal entry includes four parts:

a. Date of the transaction

b. Title of the account debited, along with the dollar amount

c. Title of the account credited, along with the dollar amount

d. Brief explanation of the transaction

Dollar signs are omitted because it's understood that the amounts are in dollars.

The journal entry presents the full story for each transaction. Exhibit 2-5 shows how Journal Page 1 looks after Cookie Lapp has recorded the first transaction.

EXHIBIT 2-5   **The Journal**

Journal				Page 1
Date	Accounts and Explanation		Debit	Credit
Apr. 1	Cash		30,000	
		Cookie Lapp, Capital		30,000
	Received investment from owner.			

Posting (Copying Information) from the Journal to the Ledger

Journalizing a transaction records the data only in the journal—but not in the ledger. The data must also show up in the ledger and, therefore, must be copied to the ledger. The process of copying from the journal to the ledger is called **posting**. We *post* from the journal to the ledger.

4 Post from the journal to the ledger

Debits in the journal are posted as debits in the ledger and credits as credits—no exceptions. The first transaction of Cookie Lapp Travel Design is posted to the ledger in Exhibit 2-6.

Expanding the Rules of Debit and Credit: Revenues and Expenses

As we have noted, *revenues* are increases in owner's equity by providing goods or services for customers. *Expenses* are decreases in equity from using up assets or increasing liabilities in the course of operations. Therefore, we must expand the accounting equation.

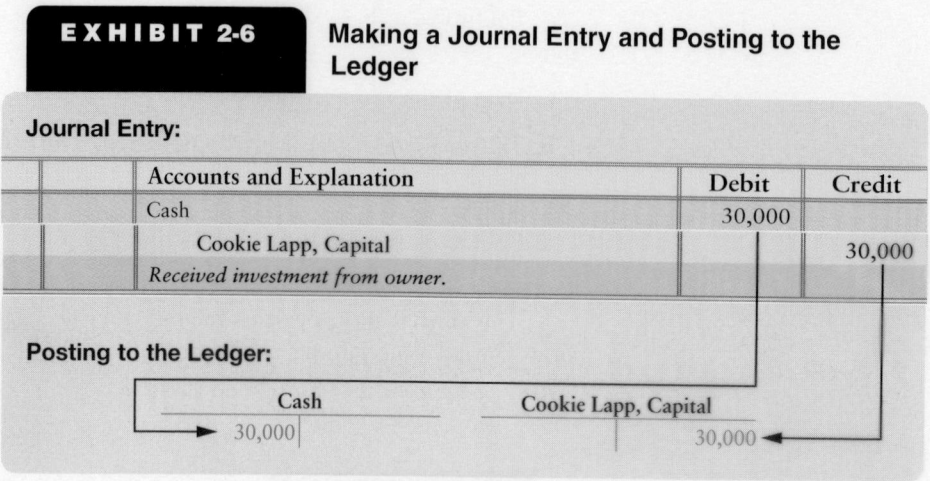

EXHIBIT 2-6 Making a Journal Entry and Posting to the Ledger

Journal Entry:

		Accounts and Explanation	Debit	Credit
		Cash	30,000	
		Cookie Lapp, Capital		30,000
		Received investment from owner.		

Posting to the Ledger:

Cash	Cookie Lapp, Capital
30,000	30,000

Exhibit 2-7 shows revenues and expenses under equity because they directly affect owner's equity.

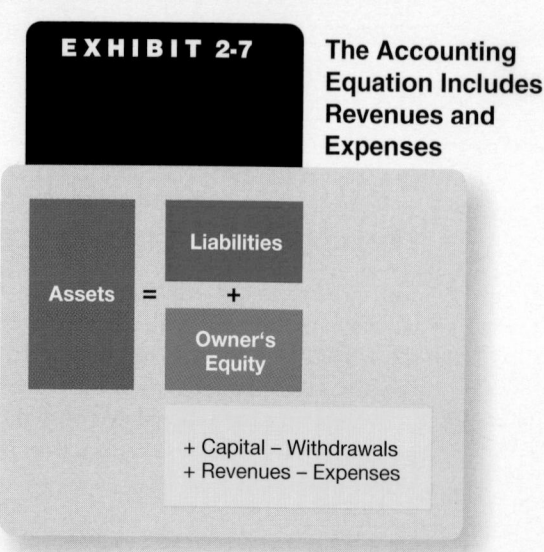

EXHIBIT 2-7 The Accounting Equation Includes Revenues and Expenses

Assets = Liabilities + Owner's Equity

+ Capital – Withdrawals
+ Revenues – Expenses

We can now express the rules of debit and credit in final form as shown in Exhibit 2-8. The accounting equation now includes revenues and expenses.

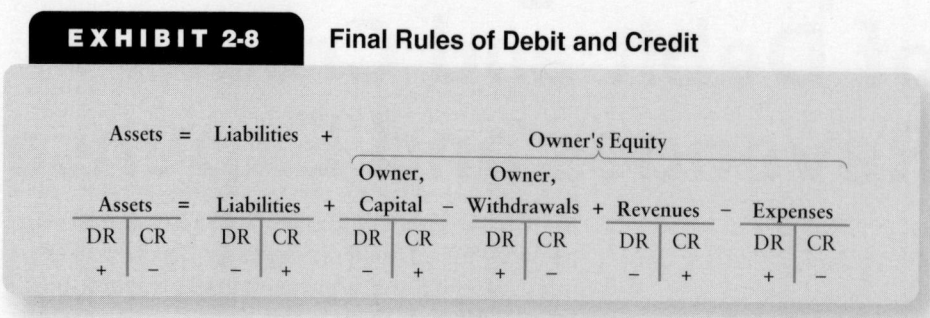

EXHIBIT 2-8 Final Rules of Debit and Credit

Assets	=	Liabilities	+	Owner's Equity							

	Assets	=	Liabilities	+	Owner, Capital	–	Owner, Withdrawals	+	Revenues	–	Expenses
DR	CR		DR	CR		DR	CR		DR	CR		DR	CR		DR	CR
+	–		–	+		–	+		+	–		–	+		+	–

The Normal Balance of an Account

An account's **normal balance** appears on the side—debit or credit—where we record an *increase*. For example, assets normally have a debit balance, so assets are *debit-balance accounts*. Liabilities and equity accounts normally have the opposite balance, so they are *credit-balance accounts*. Exhibit 2-9 illustrates the normal balances of assets, liabilities, and equity accounts.

EXHIBIT 2-9   **Normal Balances of the Accounts**

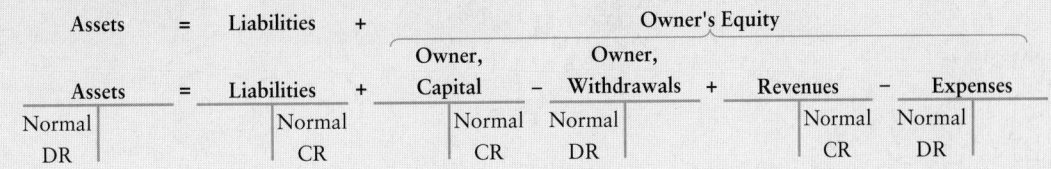

Revenues increase equity, so a revenue's normal balance is a credit. Expenses decrease equity, so an expense normally has a debit balance.

As we have seen, owner's equity includes:

Cookie Lapp, Capital—a credit-balance account

Cookie Lapp, Withdrawals—a debit-balance account

The sum of these two accounts should be a credit; for example,

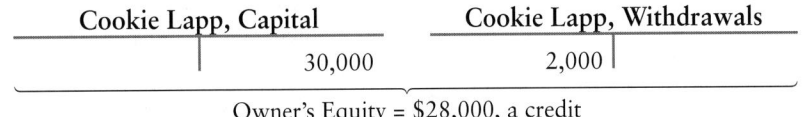

Owner's Equity = $28,000, a credit

A debit account may occasionally have a credit balance. That indicates a negative amount of the item. For example, Cash will have a credit balance if the business overdraws its bank account. Similarly, the liability Accounts Payable—a credit balance account—will have a debit balance if the entity overpays its account. In other instances, an odd balance indicates an error. For example, a credit balance in Office Supplies, Furniture, or Buildings is an error because negative amounts of these assets make no sense.

Now let's put your new learning to practice. Let's account for the early transactions of Cookie Lapp Travel Design.

The Flow of Accounting Data

Exhibit 2-10 summarizes the flow of data through the accounting system. In the pages that follow, we record Cookie Lapp Travel Design's early transactions. Keep

| EXHIBIT 2-10 | Flow of Accounting Data from the Journal to the Ledger |

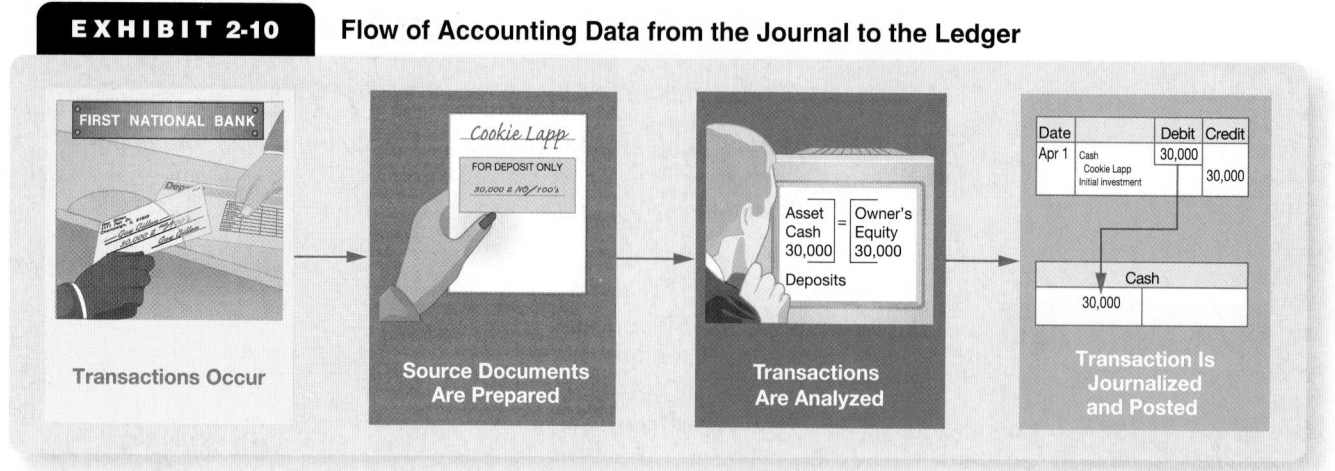

in mind that we are accounting for the travel agency. We are *not* accounting for Cookie Lapp's *personal* transactions.

Source Documents

Accounting data come from source documents, as shown in the second segment of Exhibit 2-10. There Cookie Lapp Travel Design received $30,000 from the owner and deposited the money in the business bank account. The *bank deposit ticket* is the document that shows the amount of cash received by the business. Based on this source document, Lapp can see how to record this transaction in the journal.

When Lapp buys supplies on account, the vendor sends Lapp an invoice requesting payment. The *purchase invoice* is the source document that tells Lapp to pay the vendor. The invoice shows what Lapp purchased and how much it cost—telling Lapp how to record the transaction.

Lapp may pay the account payable with a *bank check,* another source document. The check and the purchase invoice give Lapp the information she needs to record the cash payment accurately.

When Lapp provides travel service for a client, Lapp faxes a sales invoice to the client. Lapp's *sales invoice* is the source document that tells Lapp how much revenue to record.

There are many different types of source documents in business. In the transactions that follow, we illustrate some of the more common types of documents that Cookie Lapp Travel Design uses in its business.

Journalizing Transactions and Posting to the Ledger
Transaction 1

Cookie Lapp Travel Design received $30,000 cash that the owner invested to begin her travel agency. Lapp deposits the money in the business bank account, as proved by this deposit ticket.

```
┌─────────────────────────────────────────────────────────────────────┐
│                                                                       │
│       ──┤ DEPOSIT TICKET ├──                                          │
│                                            ┌──────┬──────────┬──────┐ │
│                                            │      │ CURRENCY │      │ │
│       Cookie Lapp Travel Design            │ CASH ├──────────┼──────┤ │
│       9000 CLARE BLVD.                     │      │   COIN   │      │ │
│       Austin, TX 78702                     ├──────┴──────────┼──────┼───┤
│                                            │ LIST CHECKS SINGLY │ 30,000 │ 00 │
│                                            ├─────────────────┼──────┼───┤
│                                            │                 │      │   │
│                                            ├─────────────────┼──────┼───┤
│       DATE ____April 1____ , 2008          │                 │      │   │
│                                            ├─────────────────┼──────┼───┤
│                                            │ TOTAL FROM OTHER SIDE │ │ │
│                                            ├─────────────────┼──────┼───┤
│                                            │     TOTAL       │ 30,000 │ 00 │
│       TEXAS FIRST STATE BANK               ├─────────────────┼──────┼───┤
│       Box 1739 Terminal Annex              │ LESS CASH RECEIVED │  │   │
│       Austin, TX 78713                     ├─────────────────┼──────┼───┤
│                                            │  NET DEPOSIT    │ 30,000 │ 00 │
│                                            └─────────────────┴──────┴───┘
│       ⑈⑆122000661⑆1400⑈03857                                          │
└─────────────────────────────────────────────────────────────────────┘
```

The business increased cash, which is an asset, so we debit Cash. The business also increased owner's equity, so we credit Cookie Lapp, Capital.

Journal Entry		Cash		30,000	
		Cookie Lapp, Capital			30,000
		Received investment from owner.			

Ledger Accounts	Cash		Cookie Lapp, Capital
	(1) 30,000		(1) 30,000

Transaction 2

Lapp paid $20,000 cash for land. The purchase decreased cash; therefore, credit Cash. The asset, land, increased, so we debit the Land account.

Journal Entry		Land		20,000	
		Cash			20,000
		Paid cash for land.			

Ledger Accounts	Cash		Land
	(1) 30,000 |(2) 20,000		(2) 20,000

Transaction 3

Lapp purchased $500 of office supplies on account, as shown on this purchase invoice.

INVOICE (purchase)

WHOLESALE OFFICE SUPPLY, INC.
500 HENDERSON ROAD
AUSTIN, TX 78722

Date: April 3, 2008
Terms: 30 days
Sold to: **COOKIE LAPP TRAVEL DESIGN**
             9000 CLARE BLVD.
             AUSTIN, TX 78702

Quantity	Item	Price	Total
38	Laser paper	$10	$380.00
8	Desk calendars	15	120.00

Total amount due: **$500.00**

The asset office supplies increased, so we debit Office Supplies. The liability accounts payable increased, so we credit Accounts Payable.

Journal Entry	Office Supplies		500	
	Accounts Payable			500
	Purchased supplies on account.			

Ledger Accounts	Office Supplies		Accounts Payable	
	(3) 500		(3) 500	

Transaction 4

Lapp collected cash of $5,500 for service revenue that she earned by providing travel services for clients. The source document is Lapp's sales invoice.

```
                    INVOICE  (sale)

              COOKIE LAPP TRAVEL DESIGN
                    9000 CLARE BLVD.
                    Austin, TX 78702


     Date:           April 8, 2008
     Sold to:        Allied Energy, Inc.
                     325 Brooks Street
                                            PAID
     Invoice No:     15
     Service:        Trip to Greece


     Total amount due:  $5,500

     All accounts are due and payable within 30 days.
```

The asset cash increased, so debit Cash. Revenue increased, so credit Service Revenue.

Journal Entry	Cash	5,500	
	Service Revenue		5,500
	Performed service and received cash.		

Ledger Accounts	Cash				Service Revenue	
(1)	30,000	(2)	20,000		(4)	5,500
(4)	5,500					

Transaction 5

Lapp performs service for clients and lets then pay later. She earned $3,000 of service revenue or account. This transaction increased Accounts Receivable, so we debit this asset. Service Revenue is increased with a credit.

Journal Entry	Accounts Receivable	3,000	
	Service Revenue		3,000
	Performed service on account.		

Ledger Accounts	Accounts Receivable		Service Revenue	
(5)	3,000	(4)	5,500
		(5)	3,000

Transaction 6

Lapp paid the following cash expenses: Rent expense on a computer, $600; Office rent, $1,000; Salary expense, $1,200; Utilities expense, $400. Debit each expense account to record its increase. Credit Cash for its decrease.

Journal Entry			
	Rent Expense, Computer	600	
	Rent Expense, Office	1,000	
	Salary Expense	1,200	
	Utilities Expense	400	
	Cash		3,200
	Paid cash expenses.		

Note: In practice, the business would record these expenses in four separate journal entries. Here we show them together to illustrate a *compound journal entry.*

Ledger Accounts

Cash			
(1)	30,000	(2)	20,000
(4)	5,500	(6)	3,200

Rent Expense, Computer		Rent Expense, Office	
(6)	600	(6)	1,000

Salary Expense		Utilities Expense	
(6)	1,200	(6)	400

Transaction 7

Lapp paid $300 on the account payable created in transaction 3. The paid check is Lapp's source document for this transaction.

The payment decreased cash; therefore, credit Cash. The payment decreased accounts payable, so we debit that liability.

Journal Entry			
	Accounts Payable	300	
	Cash		300
	Paid cash on account.		

Ledger Accounts	Cash				Accounts Payable			
	(1)	30,000	(2)	20,000	(7)	300	(3)	500
	(4)	5,500	(6)	3,200				
			(7)	300				

Transaction 8

Cookie Lapp remodeled her home with personal funds. This is not a transaction of the travel agency, so there's no entry on the business's books.

Transaction 9

Lapp collected $2,000 cash from the client in transaction 5. Cash is increased, so debit Cash. Accounts receivable is decreased; credit Accounts Receivable.

Journal Entry	Cash	2,000	
	Accounts Receivable		2,000
	Received cash on account.		

Note: This transaction has no effect on revenue; the related revenue was recorded in transaction 5.

Ledger Accounts	Cash				Accounts Receivable			
	(1)	30,000	(2)	20,000	(5)	3,000	(9)	2,000
	(4)	5,500	(6)	3,200				
	(9)	2,000	(7)	300				

Transaction 10

Lapp sells a parcel of land owned by the travel agency. The sale price, $9,000, equals her cost. Cash increased, so debit Cash. Land decreased; credit Land.

Journal Entry	Cash	9,000	
	Land		9,000
	Sold land at cost.		

Ledger Accounts	Cash				Land			
	(1)	30,000	(2)	20,000	(2)	20,000	(10)	9,000
	(4)	5,500	(6)	3,200				
	(9)	2,000	(7)	300				
	(10)	9,000						

Transaction 11

Lapp received a telephone bill for $100 and will pay this expense next month. There is no cash payment now. Utilities expense increased, so debit this expense. The liability accounts payable increased, so credit Accounts Payable.

Journal Entry		Utilities Expense	100	
		Accounts Payable		100
		Received utility bill.		

Ledger Accounts		**Accounts Payable**				**Utilities Expense**	
	(7)	300	(3)	500	(6)	400	
			(11)	100	(11)	100	

Transaction 12

Lapp withdrew $2,000 cash for personal living expenses. The withdrawal decreased the entity's cash; therefore, credit Cash. The transaction also decreased owner's equity. Decreases in equity that result from owner withdrawals are debited to a separate account, Withdrawals. Therefore, debit Cookie Lapp, Withdrawals.

Journal Entry		Cookie Lapp, Withdrawals	2,000	
		Cash		2,000
		Withdrawal by owner.		

Ledger Accounts		**Cash**				**Cookie Lapp, Withdrawals**	
	(1)	30,000	(2)	20,000	(12)	2,000	
	(4)	5,500	(6)	3,200			
	(9)	2,000	(7)	300			
	(10)	9,000	(12)	2,000			

Each journal entry posted to the ledger is keyed by date or by transaction number. In this way, any transaction can be traced back and forth between the journal and the ledger. This helps locate any information you may need.

The Ledger Accounts After Posting

We next show the accounts of Cookie Lapp Travel Design after posting. The accounts are grouped under their headings in Exhibit 2-11.

Each account has a balance, denoted *Bal.* An account balance is the difference between the account's total debits and its total credits. For example, the $21,000 balance in the Cash account is the difference between:

- Total debits, $46,500 ($30,000 + $5,500 + $2,000 + $9,000)
- Total credits, $25,500 ($20,000 + $3,200 + $300 + $2,000)

We set a balance apart from the transaction amounts by a horizontal line. The final figure, below the horizontal line, is denoted as the balance (Bal.).

The Trial Balance

5 Prepare and use a trial balance

A **trial balance** summarizes the ledger by listing all the accounts with their balances—assets first, followed by liabilities and then owner's equity. In a manual accounting

EXHIBIT 2-11	Ledger Accounts After Posting

ASSETS		LIABILITIES			OWNER'S EQUITY		REVENUE		EXPENSES	
Cash		**Accounts Payable**			**Cookie Lapp, Capital**		**Service Revenue**		**Rent Expense, Computer**	
(1) 30,000	(2) 20,000	(7) 300	(3) 500			(1) 30,000		(4) 5,500	(6) 600	
(4) 5,500	(6) 3,200		(11) 100			Bal. 30,000		(5) 3,000	Bal. 600	
(9) 2,000	(7) 300		Bal. 300					Bal. 8,500		
(10) 9,000	(12) 2,000				**Cookie Lapp, Withdrawals**				**Rent Expense, Office**	
Bal. 21,000					(12) 2,000				(6) 1,000	
					Bal. 2,000				Bal. 1,000	
Accounts Receivable										
(5) 3,000	(9) 2,000								**Salary Expense**	
Bal. 1,000									(6) 1,200	
									Bal. 1,200	
Office Supplies										
(3) 500									**Utilities Expense**	
Bal. 500									(6) 400	
									(11) 100	
Land									Bal. 500	
(2) 20,000	(10) 9,000									
Bal. 11,000										

system, the trial balance provides an accuracy check by showing whether total debits equal total credits. In all types of systems, the trial balance is a useful summary of the accounts and their balances. Exhibit 2-12 is the trial balance of Cookie Lapp Travel Design at April 30, 2008, end of the first month of operations.

A warning: Do not confuse the trial balance with the balance sheet. A trial balance is an internal document used only by company insiders. The public never sees a trial balance. Outsiders get only the company's financial statements.

EXHIBIT 2-12	Trial Balance

COOKIE LAPP TRAVEL DESIGN
Trial Balance
April 30, 2008

			Balance	
	Account Title		Debit	
	Cash		$21,000	
	Accounts receivable		1,000	
	Office supplies		500	
	Land		11,000	
	Accounts payable			$ 300
	Cookie Lapp, capital			30,000
	Cookie Lapp, withdrawals		2,000	
	Service revenue			8,500
	Rent expense, computer		600	
	Rent expense, office		1,000	
	Salary expense		1,200	
	Utilities expense		500	
	Total		$38,800	$38,800

Correcting Trial Balance Errors

Throughout the accounting process, total debits should always equal total credits. If not, there is an error. Computerized accounting systems eliminate many errors because most software won't let you make a journal entry that doesn't balance. But computers cannot *eliminate* all errors because humans can input the wrong data.

Errors can be detected by computing the difference between total debits and total credits on the trial balance. Then perform one or more of the following actions:

1. Search the trial balance for a missing account. For example suppose the accountant omitted Cookie Lapp, Withdrawals, from the trial balance in Exhibit 2-12. Total debits would then be $36,800 ($38,800 − $2,000). Trace each account from the ledger to the trial balance, and you will locate the missing account.

2. Divide the difference between total debits and total credits by 2. A debit treated as a credit, or vice versa, doubles the amount of error. Suppose the accountant posted a $500 credit as a debit. Total debits contain the $500, and total credits omit the $500. The out-of-balance amount is $1,000. Dividing the difference by 2 identifies the $500 amount of the transaction. Then search the trial balance for a $500 transaction and trace to the account affected.

3. Divide the out-of-balance amount by 9. If the result is evenly divisible by 9, the error may be a *slide* (example: writing $1,000 as $100) or a *transposition* (example: treating $1,200 as $2,100). Suppose Cookie Lapp printed her $2,000 Withdrawal as $20,000 on the trial balance—a slide-type error. Total debits would differ from total credits by $18,000 ($20,000 − $2,000 = $18,000). Dividing $18,000 by 9 yields $2,000, the correct amount of withdrawals. Trace $2,000 through the ledger until you reach the Cookie Lapp, Withdrawals account. You have then found the error.

Details of Journals and Ledgers

In practice, the journal and the ledger provide details to create a "trail" through the records. Suppose a supplier bills us twice for an item that we purchased. To show we've already paid the bill, we must prove our payment. That requires us to use the journal and the ledger.

Details in the Journal

Exhibit 2-13 illustrates a transaction and then shows the journal with these details:

• The *transaction date*, April 1, 2008.
• The *accounts* debited and credited, along with their dollar amounts.
• The *posting reference*, abbreviated Post. Ref. Use of this column will become clear when we discuss details in the ledger, which come next.

| EXHIBIT 2-13 | Details of Journalizing and Posting |

Journal Entry

Page 1

Date	Accounts and Explanation	Post Ref.	Debit	Credit
2008				
Apr. 1	Cash	101	30,000	
	Cookie Lapp, Capital	301		30,000
	Received investment from owner.			

1

2

3

4

Ledger

CASH   Account No. 101

Date	Item	Jrnl. Ref.	Debit	Date	Item	Jrnl. Ref.	Credit
2008							
Apr. 1		J.1.	30,000				

COOKIE LAPP, CAPITAL   Account No. 301

Date	Item	Jrnl. Ref.	Debit	Date	Item	Jrnl. Ref.	Credit
				2008			
				Apr. 1		J.1.	30,000

Details in the Ledger

Posting means copying information from the journal to the ledger. But how do we handle the details? Exhibit 2-13 illustrates the steps, denoted by arrows:

Arrow **1**—Post the transaction **date** from the journal to the ledger.

Arrow **2**—Post the debit (**$30,000**) from the journal as a debit to the Cash account in the ledger. Likewise, post the credit (also **$30,000**) from the journal to the Cookie Lapp, Capital account in the ledger. Now the ledger accounts have correct amounts.

Arrow **3**—Post the account numbers (**101** and **301**) from the ledger back to the journal. This step shows that the debit and the credit have both been posted to the ledger. **Post. Ref.** is the abbreviation for Posting Reference.

Arrow **4**—Post the page number from the journal to the ledger. **Jrnl. Ref.** means Journal Reference, and **J.1** refers to Journal Page 1. This step shows where the data came from: Journal Page 1.

The Four-Column Account: An Alternative to the T-Account

The ledger accounts illustrated thus far appear as T-accounts, with the debit on the left and the credit on the right. The T-account clearly separates debits from credits and is used for teaching, where there isn't much detail. Another account format has four amount columns, as illustrated in Exhibit 2-14.

The first pair of Debit/Credit columns are for transaction amounts posted to the account, such as the $30,000 debit. The second pair of amount columns show the running balance of the account. For this reason, the four-column format is used more often in practice than the T-account. In Exhibit 2-14, Cash has a debit balance of $30,000 after the first transaction and a $10,000 balance after the second transaction.

EXHIBIT 2-14   **Account in Four-Column Format**

CASH						Account No. 101
					Balance	
Date	Item	Jrnl. Ref.	Debit	Credit	Debit	Credit
2008						
Apr. 1		J.1	30,000		30,000	
Apr. 3		J.1		20,000	10,000	

Recording Transactions from Actual Business Documents

In practice, businesses record transactions from the data of their actual documents such as bank deposit receipts and purchase invoices. When Cookie Lapp Travel Design collects cash for revenue earned, Lapp deposits the cash in the bank and gets a deposit receipt as shown in Exhibit 2-15.

EXHIBIT 2-15   **Actual Bank Deposit Receipt**

Thank You
FOR YOUR BUSINESS

TEXAS FIRST STATE BANK
Box 1739 Terminal Annex
Austin, TX 78702

CHECKING DEPOSIT RECEIPT UNLESS MARKED BELOW

☐ SAVINGS ☐ LOANS ☐ _____

015 TFB 6-10-08 $225.00   4190-637-2

DEPOSITS MAY NOT BE AVAILABLE FOR IMMEDIATE WITHDRAWAL. BANK SYMBOL, TRANSACTION NUMBER AND AMOUNT OF DEPOSIT ARE SHOWN ABOVE.

Lapp's journal entry to record this cash receipt and revenue earned is

June 10	Cash	225.00	
	Service Revenue		225.00
	Performed service and received cash.		

To promote its business, Cookie Lapp Travel Design held a party and ordered flowers for table arrangements. Exhibit 2-16 shows the actual purchase invoice.

EXHIBIT 2-16 Actual Purchase Invoice

Rosetree Flower & Gift Shop · INVOICE

P.O. BOX 76708
AUSTIN, TX 76708

Date	Invoice #
6/13/2008	193690

Bill to:	Ship to:	Delivered on:
Cookie Lapp Travel Design 9000 Clare Blvd. Austin, TX 78702	Cookie Lapp Travel 9000 Clare Blvd. Austin, TX 78702	6/11/08

Quantity	Item Code	Description	Price Each	Amount
14	ARRANGEMENT	ARRANGEMENT - TABLES	9.00	126.00
	ARRANGEMENT	ARRANGEMENT - BLUE HYDRANGEA	100.00	100.00
		Sales Tax	8.25%	18.65

THANK YOU FOR YOUR BUSINESS	TOTAL	244.65

In this purchase transaction, Cookie Lapp Travel Design purchased flowers costing $244.65 on account. Lapp recorded this promotion expense with the following journal entry:

June 13	Promotion Expense	244.65	
	Accounts Payable		244.65
	Purchased flowers on account.		

Lapp would record payment on June 30 as follows:

June 30	Accounts Payable	244.65	
	Cash		244.65
	Paid on account.		

Decision Guidelines

Suppose Julie De Fillippo in the chapter-opening story opens a small office and hires a helper to keep her books. QuickBooks software is used for the accounting.

De Fillippo offers you a job as accountant for this small business. The pay is good. Can you answer the manager's questions, which are outlined in the Decision Guidelines? If so, you may get the job.

Decision	Guidelines
• Has a transaction occurred?	If the event affects the entity's financial position and can be recorded reliably —*Yes* If either condition is absent—*No*
• Where to record the transaction?	In the *journal*, the chronological record of transactions
• What to record for each transaction?	Increases and/or decreases in all the accounts affected by the transaction
• How to record an increase/decrease in a (an)	Rules of debit and credit:

	Increase	Decrease
Asset	Debit	Credit
Liability	Credit	Debit
Owner's Equity	Credit	Debit
Revenue	Credit	Debit
Expense	Debit	Credit

Decision	Guidelines
• Where to store all the information for each account?	In the *ledger*, the record holding all the accounts
• Where to list all the accounts and their balances?	In the *trial balance*
• Where to report the results of operations?	In the income statement (Revenues − Expenses = Net income or Net loss)
• Where to report financial position?	In the balance sheet (Assets = Liabilities + Owner's equity)

Summary Problem

The trial balance of Reitmeier Service Center on March 1, 2007, lists the entity's assets, liabilities, and owner's equity on that date.

		Balance	
Account Title		Debit	Credit
Cash		$ 26,000	
Accounts receivable		4,500	
Accounts payable			$ 2,000
Mike Reitmeier, capital			28,500
Total		$30,500	$30,500

During March, the business engaged in the following transactions:

a. Borrowed $45,000 from the bank and signed a note payable in the name of the business.

b. Paid cash of $40,000 to acquire land.

c. Performed service for a customer and received cash of $5,000.

d. Purchased supplies on credit, $300.

e. Performed customer service and earned revenue on account, $2,600.

f. Paid $1,200 on account.

g. Paid the following cash expenses: salaries, $3,000; rent, $1,500; and interest, $400.

h. Received $3,100 on account.

i. Received a $200 utility bill that will be paid next week.

j. Withdrew $1,800 for personal use.

Requirements

1. Open the following accounts, with the balances indicated, in the ledger of Reitmeier Service Center. Use the T-account format.
   - **Assets**—Cash, $26,000; Accounts Receivable, $4,500; Supplies, no balance; Land, no balance
   - **Liabilities**—Accounts Payable, $2,000; Note Payable, no balance
   - **Owner's Equity**—Mike Reitmeier, Capital, $28,500; Mike Reitmeier, Withdrawals, no balance
   - **Revenues**—Service Revenue, no balance
   - **Expenses**—(none have balances) Salary Expense, Rent Expense, Utilities Expense, Interest Expense

2. Journalize each transaction. Key journal entries by transaction letter.

3. Post to the ledger.

4. Prepare the trial balance of Reitmeier Service Center at March 31, 2007.

Solution

Requirement 1

ASSETS	LIABILITIES	OWNER'S EQUITY	EXPENSES
Cash	**Accounts Payable**	**Mike Reitmeier, Capital**	**Salary Expense**
Bal. 26,000	Bal. 2,000	Bal. 28,500	
Accounts Receivable	**Note Payable**	**Mike Reitmeier, Withdrawals**	**Rent Expense**
Bal. 4,500			
Supplies		**REVENUE**	**Utilities Expense**
		Service Revenue	
Land			**Interest Expense**

Requirement 2

a. Journal Entry		Cash	45,000	
		Note Payable		45,000
		Borrowed cash on note payable.		
b. Journal Entry		Land	40,000	
		Cash		40,000
		Purchased land.		
c. Journal Entry		Cash	5,000	
		Service Revenue		5,000
		Preformed service and received cash.		
d. Journal Entry		Supplies	300	
		Accounts Payable		300
		Purchased supplies on account.		
e. Journal Entry		Accounts Receivable	2,600	
		Service Revenue		2,600
		Performed service on account.		
f. Journal Entry		Accounts Payable	1,200	
		Cash		1,200
		Paid on account.		
g. Journal Entry		Salary Expense	3,000	
		Rent Expense	1,500	
		Interest Expense	400	
		Cash		4,900
		Paid expenses.		
h. Journal Entry		Cash	3,100	
		Accounts Receivable		3,100
		Received cash on account.		
i. Journal Entry		Utilities Expense	200	
		Accounts Payable		200
		Received utility bill.		
j. Journal Entry		Mike Reitmeier, Withdrawals	1,800	
		Cash		1,800
		Owner withdrawal.		

Requirement 3

ASSETS

Cash

Bal.	26,000	(b)	40,000
(a)	45,000	(f)	1,200
(c)	5,000	(g)	4,900
(h)	3,100	(j)	1,800
Bal.	31,200		

Accounts Receivable

Bal.	4,500	(h)	3,100
(e)	2,600		
Bal.	4,000		

Supplies

(d)	300		
Bal.	300		

Land

(b)	40,000		
Bal.	40,000		

LIABILITIES

Accounts Payable

(f)	1,200	Bal.	2,000
		(d)	300
		(i)	200
		Bal.	1,300

Note Payable

		(a)	45,000
		Bal.	45,000

OWNER'S EQUITY

Mike Reitmeier, Capital

		Bal.	28,500

Mike Reitmeier, Withdrawals

(j)	1,800		
Bal.	1,800		

REVENUE

Service Revenue

		(c)	5,000
		(e)	2,600
		Bal.	7,600

EXPENSES

Salary Expense

(g)	3,000		
Bal.	3,000		

Rent Expense

(g)	1,500		
Bal.	1,500		

Interest Expense

(g)	400		
Bal.	400		

Utilities Expense

(i)	200		
Bal.	200		

Requirement 4

REITMEIER SERVICE CENTER
Trial Balance
March 31, 2007

	Account Title	Balance	
		Debit	Credit
	Cash	$31,200	
	Accounts receivable	4,000	
	Supplies	300	
	Land	40,000	
	Accounts payable		$ 1,300
	Note payable		45,000
	Mike Reitmeier, capital		28,500
	Mike Reitmeier, withdrawals	1,800	
	Service revenue		7,600
	Salary expense	3,000	
	Rent expense	1,500	
	Interest expense	400	
	Utilities expense	200	
	Total	$82,400	$82,400

Review Recording Business Transactions

Accounting Vocabulary

Account
The detailed record of the changes in a particular asset, liability, or owner's equity during a period. The basic summary device of accounting.

Chart of Accounts
List of all the accounts with their account numbers.

Credit
The right side of an account.

Debit
The left side of an account.

Journal
The chronological accounting record of an entity's transactions.

Ledger
The record holding all the accounts.

Normal Balance
The balance that appears on the side of an account—debit or credit—where we record increases.

Note Receivable
A written promise for future collection of cash.

Posting
Copying amounts from the journal to the ledger.

Trial Balance
A list of all the accounts with their balances.

1. Which sequence correctly summarizes the accounting process?

    a. Journalize transactions, post to the accounts, prepare a trial balance

    b. Post to the accounts, journalize transactions, prepare a trial balance

    c. Prepare a trial balance, journalize transactions, post to the accounts

    d. Journalize transactions, prepare a trial balance, post to the accounts

2. The left side of an account is used to record:

    a. Debit or credit, depending on the type of account

    b. Credits

    c. Debits

    d. Increases

3. Suppose your business has cash of $50,000, receivables of $60,000, and furniture totaling $200,000. The store owes $80,000 on account and has a $100,000 note payable. How much is your equity?

    a. $20,000

    b. $130,000

    c. $180,000

    d. $310,000

4. Your business purchased supplies of $1,000 on account. The journal entry to record this transaction is:

    a. Inventory 1,000
        Accounts Payable 1,000

    b. Accounts Payable 1,000
        Supplies 1,000

    c. Supplies 1,000
        Accounts Payable 1,000

    d. Supplies 1,000
        Accounts Receivable 1,000

5. Which journal entry records your payment for the supplies purchased in transaction 4?

    a. Accounts Payable 1,000
        Accounts Receivable 1,000

    b. Supplies 1,000
        Cash 1,000

    c. Cash 1,000
        Accounts Payable 1,000

    d. Accounts Payable 1,000
        Cash 1,000

6. Posting a $1,000 purchase of supplies on account appears as follows:

    a.

Supplies	Accounts Payable
1,000	1,000

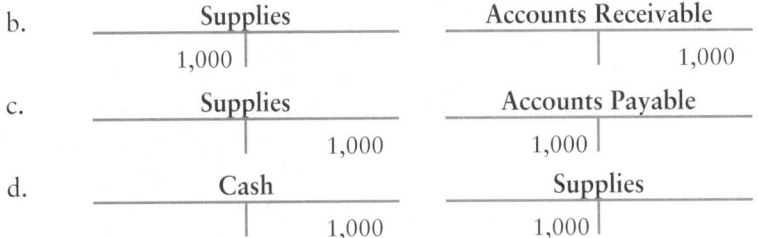

b.

Supplies		Accounts Receivable	
1,000			1,000

c.

Supplies		Accounts Payable	
	1,000	1,000	

d.

Cash		Supplies	
	1,000	1,000	

7. You paid $500 for supplies and purchased additional supplies on account for $700. Later you paid $300 of the accounts payable. What is the balance in your Supplies account?

   a. $500

   b. $900

   c. $1,500

   d. $1,200

8. **Kinko's Copies** recorded a cash collection on account by debiting Cash and crediting Accounts Payable. What will the trial balance show for this error?

   a. Too much for liabilities

   b. Too much for expenses

   c. The trial balance will not balance

   d. Too much for cash

9. Brett Wilkinson, Attorney, began the year with total assets of $120,000, liabilities of $70,000, and owner's equity of $50,000. During the year he earned revenue of $110,000 and paid expenses of $30,000. He also withdrew $60,000 for living expenses. How much is Wilkinson's equity at year-end?

   a. $90,000

   b. $120,000

   c. $70,000

   d. $160,000

10. How would Brett Wilkinson record his expenses for the year in question 9?

   a. Expenses 30,000

      Accounts Payable   30,000

   b. Expenses 30,000

      Cash   30,000

   c. Cash 30,000

      Expenses   30,000

   d. Accounts Payable 30,000

      Cash   30,000

   Answers are given after Apply Your Knowledge (p. 113).

Assess Your Progress

Short Exercises

Explaining the rules of debit and credit

2

S2-1 Aretha Franklin is tutoring Blaine McCormick, who is taking introductory accounting. Aretha explains to Blaine that *debits* are used to record increases in accounts and *credits* record decreases. Blaine is confused and seeks your advice.

- When are debits increases? When are debits decreases?
- When are credits increases? When are credits decreases?

Exhibit 2-8, page 68, gives the rules of debit and credit.

Using accounting terms

1

S2-2 Tighten your grip by filling in the blanks to review some key accounting definitions.

Rita Bowden is describing the accounting process for a friend who is a philosophy major. Rita states, "The basic summary device in accounting is the _____. The left side is called the _____ side, and the right side is called the _____ side. We record transactions first in a _____. Then we post (copy the data) to the _____. It is helpful to list all the accounts with their balances on a _____." (pp. 60–63)

Using accounting terms

1

S2-3 Accounting has its own vocabulary and basic relationships. Match the accounting terms at left with the corresponding definitions at right. (challenge)

_____ 1. Capital	A. Record of transactions
_____ 2. Debit	B. An asset
_____ 3. Expense	C. Left side of an account
_____ 4. Net income	D. Side of an account where increases
_____ 5. Ledger	are recorded
_____ 6. Posting	E. Copying data from the journal to the
_____ 7. Normal balance	ledger
_____ 8. Payable	F. Using up assets in the course of
_____ 9. Journal	operating a business
_____ 10. Receivable	G. Always a liability
	H. Revenues − Expenses = _____
	I. Book of accounts
	J. Owner's equity

Normal account balances

2

S2-4 Accounting records include three basic categories of accounts: assets, liabilities, and owner's equity. In turn, owner's equity holds the following categories: capital, withdrawals, revenues, and expenses. Identify which categories of the accounts have a normal debit balance and which categories have a normal credit balance. (p. 67)

Recording transactions

3

S2-5 Mark Brown opened a medical practice in Alexandria, Virginia. Record the following transactions in the journal of Mark Brown, M.D. Include an explanation with each entry. (pp. 70–76)

continued . . .

June 1	Brown invested $25,000 cash in a business bank account to start his medical practice. The business received the cash and gave Brown owner's equity in the business.
2	Purchased medical supplies on account, $10,000.
2	Paid monthly office rent of $4,000.
3	Recorded $12,000 revenue for service rendered to patients on account.

Journalizing transactions; posting

S2-6 Rick Spinn Optical Dispensary purchased supplies on account for $1,000. Two weeks later, Spinn paid half on account.

1. Journalize the two transactions for Rick Spinn Optical Dispensary. Include an explanation for each entry. (pp. 70–75)
2. Open the Accounts Payable T-account and post to Accounts Payable. Compute the balance, and denote it as *Bal.* (pp. 70–75)

Recording transactions

S2-7 Merry-Go-Round Sales Consultants completed the following transactions during the latter part of October:

October 22	Performed service for customers on account, $6,000.
30	Received cash on account from customers, $2,000.
31	Received a utility bill, $200, which will be paid during November.
31	Paid monthly salary to salesman, $3,000.
31	Paid advertising expense of $900.

Journalize the transactions of Merry-Go-Round Sales Consultants. Include an explanation with each journal entry.

Journalizing transactions; posting

S2-8 Hughes Law Firm performed legal service for a client who could not pay immediately. Hughes expected to collect the $5,000 the following month. Later, Hughes received $3,500 cash from the client.

1. Record the two transactions for Laura Hughes, Attorney. Include an explanation for each transaction. (pp. 70–75)
2. Open these T-accounts: Cash; Accounts Receivable; Service Revenue. Post to all three accounts. Compute each account's balance, and denote as *Bal.* (pp. 70–75)
3. Answer these questions based on your analysis:
   a. How much did Hughes earn? Which account shows this amount? (p. 70)
   b. How much in total assets did Hughes acquire as a result of the two transactions? Identify each asset and show its amount. (p. 75)

Posting; preparing a trial balance

S2-9 Use the June transaction data for Mark Brown, M.D., given in Short Exercise 2-5.

1. Open the following T-accounts: Cash; Accounts Receivable; Medical Supplies; Accounts Payable; Mark Brown, Capital; Service Revenue; and Rent Expense. (pp. 70–75)

2. After making the journal entries in Short Exercise 2-5, post to the ledger. No dates or posting references are required. Compute the balance of each account, and denote it as *Bal.*

3. Prepare the trial balance, complete with a proper heading, at June 3, 2008. Use the trial balance in Exhibit 2-12, page 77, as a guide. (pp. 70–76)

Preparing a trial balance

S2-10 Redbird Floor Coverings reported the following summarized data at December 31, 2007. Accounts appear in no particular order.

Revenues	$ 29,000	Other liabilities	$ 19,000
Equipment	40,000	Cash	12,000
Accounts payable	1,000	Expenses	22,000
Capital	25,000		

Prepare the trial balance of Redbird Floor Coverings at December 31, 2007. List the accounts in proper order, as on page 77.

Correcting a trial balance

S2-11 Cookie Lapp Travel Design prepared its trial balance on page 77. Suppose Lapp made an error: She erroneously listed her capital balance of $30,000 as a debit rather than a credit.

Compute the incorrect trial balance totals for debits and credits. Then refer to the discussion of correcting errors on page 78, and show how to correct this error. (pp. 77, 78)

Correcting a trial balance

S2-12 Return to Cookie Lapp Travel Design's trial balance on page 77. Assume that Lapp accidentally listed her withdrawals as $200 instead of the correct amount of $2,000. Compute the incorrect trial balance totals for debits and credits. Then show how to correct this error, which is called a *slide*. (pp. 77, 78)

Exercises

Using accounting terms

E2-13 Review basic accounting definitions by completing the following crossword puzzle. (pp. 60–63)

continued . . .

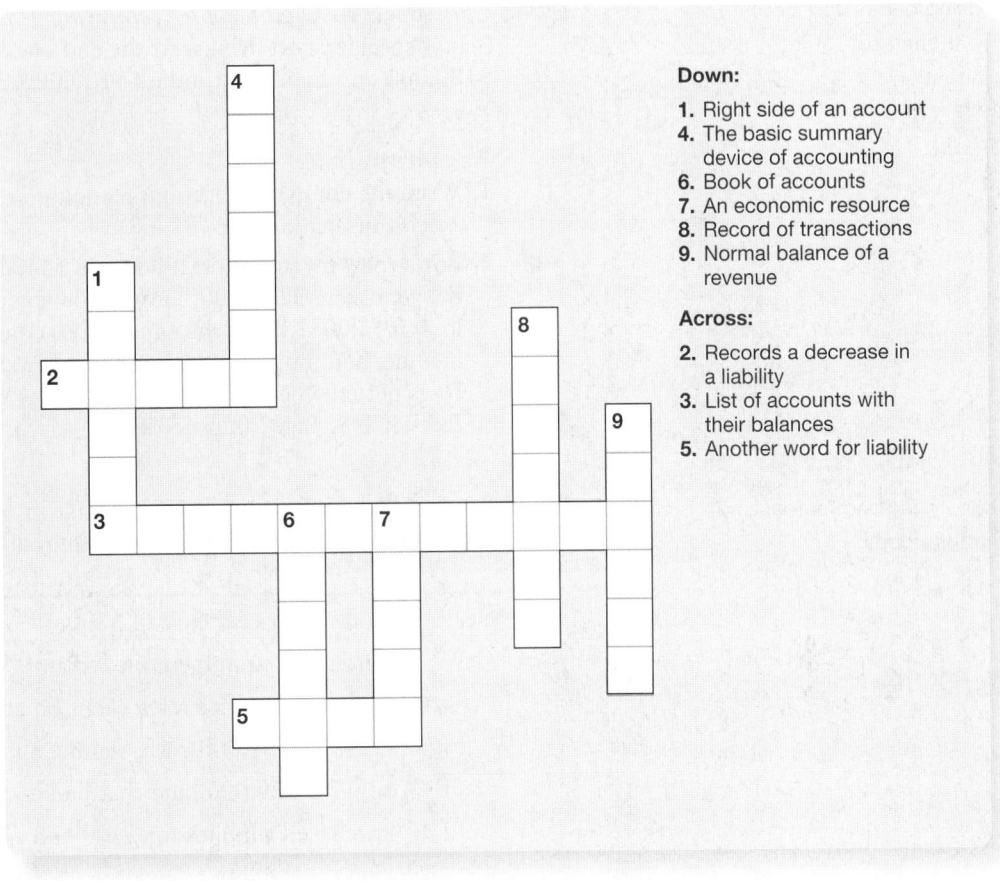

Down:

1. Right side of an account
4. The basic summary device of accounting
6. Book of accounts
7. An economic resource
8. Record of transactions
9. Normal balance of a revenue

Across:

2. Records a decrease in a liability
3. List of accounts with their balances
5. Another word for liability

Using accounting terms

E2-14 Sharpen your use of accounting terms by working this crossword puzzle. (pp. 67–70)

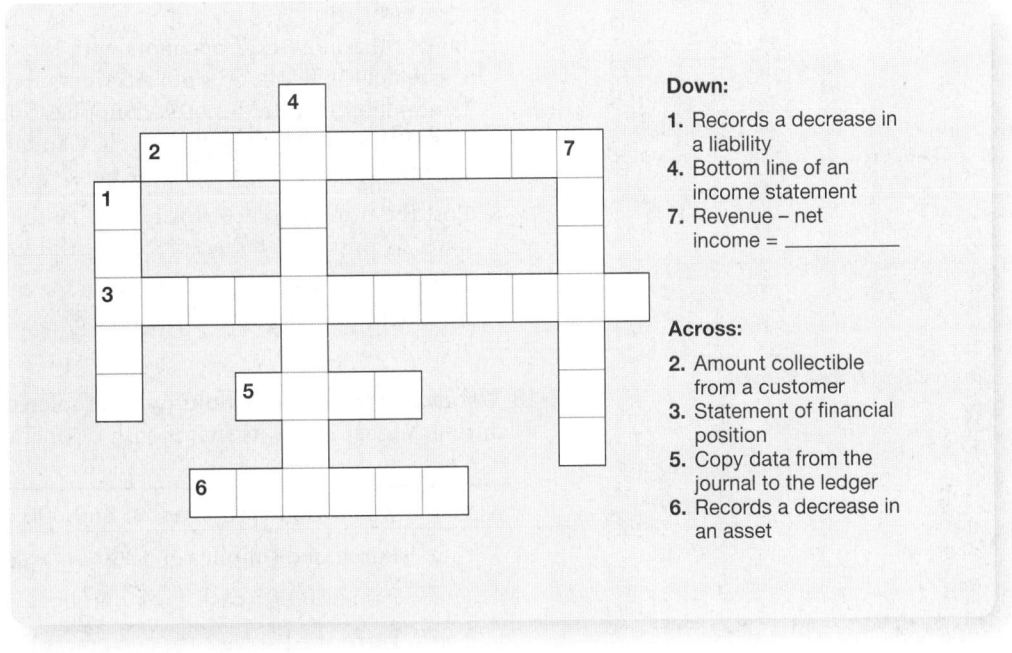

Down:

1. Records a decrease in a liability
4. Bottom line of an income statement
7. Revenue – net income = _____

Across:

2. Amount collectible from a customer
3. Statement of financial position
5. Copy data from the journal to the ledger
6. Records a decrease in an asset

Using debits and credits
with the accounting
equation

E2-15 *Link Back to Chapter 1 (Accounting Equation).* Bob's Cream Soda makes specialty soft drinks. At the end of 2008, Bob's had total assets of $180,000 and liabilities totaling $100,000.

Requirements

1. Write the company's accounting equation, and label each amount as a debit or a credit. (pp. 67–68)

2. Bob's total revenues for 2006 were $240,000, and total expenses for the year were $200,000. How much was Bob's net income (or net loss) for 2008? Write the equation to compute the company's net income, and indicate which element is a debit and which is a credit. Does net income represent a net debit or a net credit? Review Exhibit 1-8, page 20, if needed.

E2-16 Record the following transactions in the journal of Blackwell Engineering. Explanations are not required. (pp. 70–76)

Dec. 2	Paid utilities expense of $300.
5	Purchased equipment on account, $2,000.
10	Performed service for a client on account, $1,600.
12	Borrowed $7,000 cash, signing a note payable.
19	Sold for $29,000 land that had cost this same amount.
21	Purchased supplies for $600 and paid cash.
27	Paid the liability from December 5.

E2-17 This exercise should be used only in connection with Exercise 2-16. Refer to the transactions of Blackwell Engineering in Exercise 2-16.

Requirements

1. Open the following T-accounts with their December 1 balances: Cash, debit balance $3,000; Accounts Receivable $0; Equipment $0; Land, debit balance $29,000; Supplies $0; Accounts Payable $0; Notes Payable $0; Rex Blackwell, Capital, credit balance $32,000; Service Revenue $0; Utilities Expense $0. (pp. 70–76)

2. Post the transactions of Exercise 2-16 to the T-accounts. Use the dates as posting references. Start with December 2. (pp. 70–76)

3. Compute the December 31 balance for each account, and prove that total debits equal total credits. (p. 77)

E2-18 Woodward Technology Solutions completed the following transactions during August 2007, its first month of operations:

Aug. 1	Ron Woodward invested $60,000 of cash to start the business.
2	Purchased supplies of $200 on account.
4	Paid $50,000 cash for a building.
6	Performed service for customers and received cash, $3,000.

continued . . .

9   Paid $100 on accounts payable.

17   Performed service for customers on account, $2,100.

23   Received $1,200 cash from a customer on account.

31   Paid the following expenses: salary, $1,200; rent, $500.

Requirement

Record the preceding transactions in the journal of Woodward Technology Solutions. Key transactions by date and include an explanation for each entry, as illustrated in the chapter. Use the following accounts: Cash; Accounts Receivable; Supplies; Building; Accounts Payable; Ron Woodward, Capital; Service Revenue; Salary Expense; Rent Expense. (pp. 70–76)

Posting to the ledger and preparing a trial balance

E2-19 Refer to Exercise 2-18 for the transactions of Woodward Technology Solutions.

Requirements

1. After journalizing the transactions of Exercise 2-18, post to the ledger, using T-account format. Key transactions by date. Date the ending balance of each account Aug. 31. (pp. 70–76).

2. Prepare the trial balance of Woodward Technology Solutions at August 31, 2007. (p. 77)

Describing transactions and posting

E2-20 The journal of Alert Defensive Driving includes the following entries for May 2006.

Journal Entry:

| | | | | Page 5 |
Date	Accounts and Explanation	Post Ref.	Debit	Credit
May 2	Cash		20,000	
	Betty Sawyer, Capital			20,000
9	Supplies		200	
	Accounts Payable			200
11	Accounts Receivable		2,600	
	Service Revenue			2,600
14	Rent Expense		3,200	
	Cash			3,200
22	Accounts Payable		300	
	Cash			300
25	Advertising Expense		400	
	Cash			400
27	Cash		1,400	
	Accounts Receivable			1,400
31	Fuel		100	
	Fuel Expense			100

Requirements

1. Describe each transaction. (pp. 70–76)

2. Set up T-accounts using the following account numbers: Cash, 110; Accounts Receivable, 120; Supplies, 130; Accounts Payable, 210; Betty Sawyer, Capital, 310; Service Revenue, 410; Rent Expense, 510; Advertising Expense, 520; Fuel Expense, 530. (p. 79)

3. Post to the accounts. Write dates and journal references in the accounts, as illustrated in Exhibit 2-13, page 79. Compute the balance of each account after posting. (p. 79)

4. Prepare the trial balance of Alert Defensive Driving at May 31, 2006. (p. 77)

Journalizing transactions

3

E2-21 The first five transactions of Reed's Home Care, have been posted to the accounts as follows:

Cash				Supplies		Equipment		Building	
(1)	12,000	(3)	40,000	(2) 400		(5) 6,000		(3) 40,000	
(4)	37,000	(5)	6,000						

Accounts Payable		Note Payable		Harry Reed, Capital	
	(2) 400		(4) 37,000		(1) 12,000

Requirement

Prepare the journal entries that served as the sources for the five transactions. Include an explanation for each entry as illustrated in the chapter. (pp. 70–76)

Preparing a trial balance

5

E2-22 Prepare the trial balance of Reed's Home Care at October 31, 2007, using the accounts from Exercise 2-21. (p. 77)

Preparing a trial balance

5

E2-23 The accounts of Mayflower Moving Company follow with their normal balances at December 31, 2006. The accounts are listed in no particular order.

Joe Mayflower, capital	$ 48,700	Trucks	$125,000
Insurance expense	700	Fuel expense	2,000
Accounts payable	4,300	Joe Mayflower, withdrawals	6,000
Service revenue	86,000	Utilities expense	400
Building	44,000	Accounts receivable	9,400
Supplies expense	300	Note payable	60,000
Cash	5,000	Supplies	200
Salary expense	6,000		

Requirement

Prepare Mayflower's trial balance at December 31, 2006, listing accounts in proper sequence, as illustrated in the chapter. For example, Supplies comes before Trucks and Building. List the largest expense first, the second-largest expense next, and so on. (p. 77)

Recording transactions and
using four-column accounts

E2-24 Open the following four-column accounts of Lee Bivona, CPA: Cash; Accounts Receivable; Office Supplies; Office Furniture; Accounts Payable; Lee Bivona, Capital; Lee Bivona, Withdrawals; Service Revenue; Salary Expense; Rent Expense.

Journalize the following transactions and then post to the four-column accounts. Use the letters to identify the transactions. Keep a running balance in each account.

a. Bivona opened an accounting firm by investing $15,000 cash and office furniture valued at $5,400.

b. Paid monthly rent of $1,500.

c. Purchased office supplies on account, $700.

d. Paid employee's salary, $1,800.

e. Paid $400 of the account payable created in transaction (c).

f. Performed accounting service on account, $5,600.

g. Withdrew $7,000 for personal use.

Preparing a trial balance

E2-25 After recording and posting the transactions in Exercise 2-24, prepare the trial balance of Lee Bivona, CPA, at December 31, 2007.

Correcting errors in a trial balance

E2-26 The trial balance of Joy McDowell Tutoring Service at March 31, 2009, does not balance:

		Balance	
Account Title		**Debit**	
Cash		$ 3,000	
Accounts receivable		2,000	
Supplies		600	
Computer equipment		26,000	
Accounts payable			$11,500
Joy McDowell, capital			11,600
Service revenue			9,700
Salary expense		1,700	
Rent expense		800	
Utilities expense		300	
Total		$34,400	$32,800

Investigation of the accounting records reveals that the bookkeeper:

a. Recorded a $400 cash revenue transaction by debiting Accounts Receivable. The credit entry was correct.

b. Posted a $1,000 credit to Accounts Payable as $100.

c. Did not record utilities expense or the related account payable in the amount of $200.

d. Understated Joy McDowell, Capital, by $700.

Requirement

Prepare the correct trial balance at March 31, complete with a heading; journal entries are not required. (pp. 77, 78)

E2-27 Blenda Lozano has trouble keeping her debits and credits equal. During a recent month, Blenda made the following accounting errors:

   a. In preparing the trial balance, Blenda omitted a $5,000 note payable. (p. 78)

   b. Blenda posted a $700 utility expense as $70. The credit to Cash was correct.

   c. In recording a $400 payment on account, Blenda debited Supplies instead of Accounts Payable. (p. 78)

   d. In journalizing a receipt of cash for service revenue, Blenda debited Cash for $80 instead of the correct amount of $800. The credit was correct. (p. 78)

   e. Blenda recorded a $120 purchase of supplies on account by debiting Supplies and crediting Accounts Payable for $210. (p. 78)

Requirements

1. For each of these errors, state whether total debits equal total credits on the trial balance.

2. Identify each account that has an incorrect balance, and indicate the amount and direction of the error (such as "Accounts Receivable $500 too high").

E2-28 The owner of Jackson Lighting Company needs to compute the following summary information from the accounting records:

   a. Net income for the month of July

   b. Total cash paid during July

   c. Cash collections from customers during July

   d. Payments on account during July

The quickest way to compute these amounts is to analyze the following accounts:

Account	Balance June 30	Balance July 31	Additional Information for the Month of July
a. Owner, Capital	$ 9,000	$22,000	Withdrawals, $4,000
b. Cash	7,000	2,000	Cash receipts, $50,000
c. Accounts Receivable	24,000	26,000	Revenues on account, $75,000
d. Accounts Payable	11,000	20,000	Purchases on account, $40,000

The net income for July can be computed as follows:

Owner, Capital

		June 30 Bal.	9,000
July Withdrawals	4,000	July Net Income	X = $17,000
		July 31 Bal.	22,000

Use a similar approach to compute the other three items. (Challenge)

Using actual business
documents

E2-29 Suppose your name is Grant Schaeffer, and Advanced Automotive repaired your car. You settled the bill as noted on the following invoice. To you this is a purchase invoice. To Advanced Automotive, it's a sales invoice.

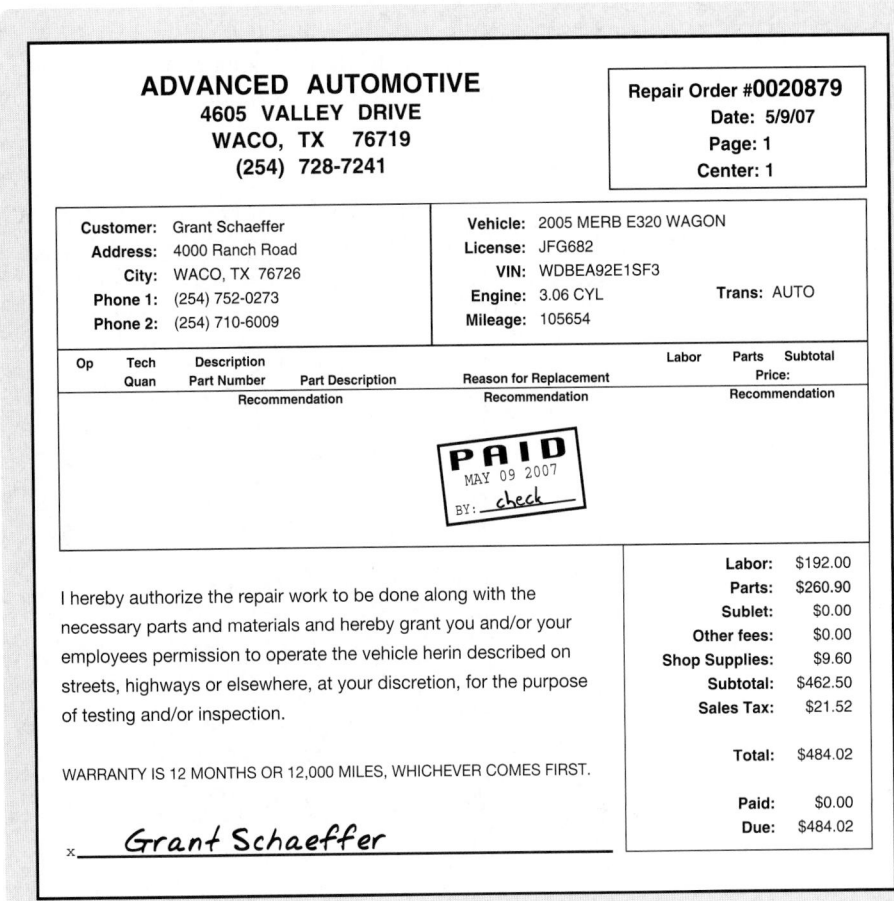

Journalize:

a. Your repair expense transaction. (pp. 80–81)

b. Advanced Automotive's service revenue transaction. (pp. 80–81)

Problems (Group A)

Using accounting terms and
analyzing a trial balance

P2-30A →*Link Back to Chapter 1 (Balance Sheet, Income Statement).* Amber Shea, owner of the Shea Law Firm, is considering adding another lawyer. Courtney Martinez is considering joining Shea and asks to see Shea's financial information. Shea gives Martinez the firm's trial balance, which follows. Help Martinez decide whether to join the firm by answering these questions for her.

1. How much are the firm's total assets? total liabilities? net income or net loss? (pp. 60–62)

continued . . .

2. Suppose Shea earned all the service revenue on account. Make a single journal entry to record the revenue, set up the two T-accounts affected, and post to those accounts. (p. 70)

3. In your own words, describe the accounting process that results in Shea's $12,000 balance for Cash. Use the following terms in your explanation: account, balance, journal ledger, post, and trial balance. (pp. 66–77)

4. If Martinez joins Shea as a co-owner of the law firm, what form of business organization will the firm take? If necessary, review Chapter 1.

SHEA LAW FIRM
Trial Balance
December 31, 2008

		Account Title	Balance	
			Debit	Credit
		Cash	$ 12,000	
		Accounts receivable	27,000	
		Prepaid expenses	4,000	
		Furniture	31,000	
		Accounts payable		$ 35,000
		Amber Shea, capital		
		Amber Shea, withdrawals	53,000	30,000
		Service revenue		121,000
		Rent expense	26,000	
		Utilities expense	3,000	
		Wage expense	23,000	
		Supplies expense	7,000	
		Total	$186,000	$186,000

Analyzing and journalizing transactions

P2-31A Showtime Amusements owns movie theaters. Showtime engaged in the following business transactions:

July 1	Darrell Palusky invested $350,000 personal cash in the business by depositing that amount in a bank account titled Showtime Amusements. The business gave Palusky owner's equity in the company.
2	Paid $300,000 cash to purchase a theater building.
5	Borrowed $220,000 from the bank. Palusky signed a note payable to the bank in the name of Showtime Amusements.
10	Purchased theater supplies on account, $1,700.
15	Paid $800 on account.
15	Paid property tax expense on theater building, $1,200.
16	Paid employee salaries, $2,800, and rent on equipment, $1,800. Make a single compound entry.

continued . . .

28   Withdrew $6,000 from the business for personal use.

31   Received $20,000 cash from service revenue and deposited that amount in the bank.

Showtime Amusements uses the following accounts: Cash; Supplies; Building; Accounts Payable; Notes Payable; Darrel Palusky, Capital; Darrel Palusky, Withdrawals; Service Revenue; Salary Expense; Rent Expense; Property Tax Expense.

Requirement

Journalize each transaction of Showtime Amusements as shown for July 1. Explanations are not required. (pp. 70–76)

July 1	Cash	350,000	
	Darrel Palusky, Capital		350,000

Journalizing transactions, posting to T-accounts, and preparing a trial balance

P2-32A Doris Higgins started her practice as a design consultant on September 1 of the current year. During the first month of operations, the business completed the following transactions:

Sep. 1   Higgins transferred $25,000 cash from her personal bank account to a business account titled Doris Higgins, Designer. The business gave Higgins owner's equity in the firm.

4   Purchased supplies, $200, and furniture, $1,800, on account.

6   Performed services for a law firm and received $4,000 cash.

7   Paid $20,000 cash to acquire land for a future office site.

10   Performed service for a hotel and received its promise to pay the $800 within one week.

14   Paid for the furniture purchased September 4 on account.

15   Paid secretary's salary, $600.

17   Received cash on account, $500.

20   Prepared a design for a school on account, $800.

28   Received $1,500 cash for consulting with **Procter & Gamble.**

30   Paid secretary's salary, $600.

30   Paid rent expense, $500.

30   Withdrew $2,000 for personal use.

Requirement

Open the following T-accounts: Cash; Accounts Receivable; Supplies; Furniture; Land; Accounts Payable; Doris Higgins, Capital; Doris Higgins, Withdrawals; Service Revenue; Salary Expense; Rent Expense.

continued . . .

1. Record each transaction in the journal, using the account titles given. Key each transaction by date. Explanations are not required. (pp. 70–76)

2. Post the transactions to the T-accounts, using transaction dates as posting references in the ledger accounts. Label the balance of each account *Bal.*, as shown in the chapter. (pp. 70–76)

3. Prepare the trial balance of Doris Higgins, Designer, at September 30 of the current year. (p. 77)

Journalizing transactions, posting to accounts in four-column format, and preparing a trial balance

2, 3, 4, 5

P2-33A The trial balance of John Hilton, CPA, is dated January 31, 2007:

JOHN HILTON, CPA
Trial Balance
January 31, 2007

Account Number	Account Title	Balance	
		Debit	Credit
11	Cash	$ 2,000	
12	Accounts receivable	9,500	
13	Supplies	800	
14	Land	18,600	
21	Accounts payable		$ 3,000
31	John Hilton, capital		27,900
32	John Hilton, withdrawals		
41	Service revenue		
51	Salary expense		
52	Rent expense		
	Total	$30,900	$30,900

During February, Hilton completed the following transactions:

Feb. 4	Hilton collected $3,500 cash from a client on account.
8	Performed tax services for a client on account, $7,000.
13	Paid on account, $1,000.
18	Purchased supplies on account, $100.
20	Withdrew $1,200 for personal use.
21	Paid for a deck for private residence, using personal funds, $9,000.
22	Received cash of $5,500 for consulting work just completed.
28	Paid rent, $800.
28	Paid employee salary, $1,800.

Requirements

1. Record the February transactions on page 3 of the journal. Include an explanation for each entry. (pp. 70–76)

continued . . .

2. Post the transactions to four-column accounts in the ledger, using dates, account numbers, journal references, and posting references. Open the ledger accounts listed in the trial balance, together with their balances at January 31. Enter *Bal.* (for January 31 balance) in the Item column, and place a check mark (✔) in the journal reference column for the January 31 balance in each account. (pp. 78–79)

3. Prepare the trial balance of John Hilton, CPA, at February 28, 2007.

Recording transactions;
using four-column accounts;
preparing a trial balance

P2-34A Maury Wills started an environmental consulting business and during the first month of operations (June 2008) completed the following transactions:

a. Wills began the business with an investment of $25,000 cash and a building valued at $30,000. The business gave Wills the owner's equity in the firm.

b. Purchased office supplies on account, $2,100.

c. Paid $18,000 for office furniture.

d. Paid employee's salary, $2,200.

e. Performed consulting service on account, $5,100.

f. Paid $800 of the account payable created in transaction (b).

g. Received a $600 bill for advertising expense that will be paid in the near future.

h. Performed consulting service for customers and received cash, $1,600.

i. Received cash on account, $1,200.

j. Paid the following cash expenses and made a single compound entry:
   (1) Rent on equipment, $700.
   (2) Utilities, $400.

k. Withdrew $5,000 for personal use.

Requirements

1. Open the following four-column accounts: Cash; Accounts Receivable; Office Supplies; Office Furniture; Building; Accounts Payable; Maury Wills, Capital; Maury Wills, Withdrawals; Service Revenue; Salary Expense; Rent Expense; Advertising Expense; Utilities Expense.

2. Record each transaction in the journal. Use the letters to identify the transactions. (pp. 70–76)

3. Post to the accounts and keep a running balance for each account. (p. 78)

4. Prepare the trial balance of Wills Environmental Consulting at June 30, 2008. (p. 77)

Note: Problem 2-35A should be used in conjunction with Problem 2-34A.

Preparing the financial
statements

P2-35A → *Link Back to Chapter 1 (Income Statement, Statement of Owner's Equity, Balance Sheet).* Refer to Problem 2-34A. After completing the trial

continued . . .

balance in Problem 2-34A, prepare the following financial statements for Wills Consulting:

1. Income statement for the month ended June 30, 2008. (p. 20)
2. Statement of owner's equity for the month ended June 30, 2008. (p. 20)
3. Balance sheet at June 30, 2008. (p. 20)

Draw arrows to link the statements. If needed, use Exhibit 1-8, page 20, as a guide for preparing the financial statements.

Correcting errors in a trial balance
2 5

P2-36A The trial balance of URNO.1 Child Care does not balance. The following errors are detected:

a. Cash is understated by $1,000.

b. A $2,000 debit to Accounts Receivable was posted as a credit.

c. A $1,000 purchase of supplies on account was neither journalized nor posted.

d. Equipment's cost is $75,000, not $85,000.

e. Salary expense is overstated by $100.

URNO.1 CHILD CARE
Trial Balance
June 30, 2008

Account Title	Balance Debit	Balance Credit
Cash	$ 3,000	
Accounts receivable	10,000	
Supplies	900	
Equipment	85,000	
Accounts payable		$ 55,000
Mary Hulse, capital		38,500
Mary Hulse, withdrawals	2,100	
Service revenue		6,500
Salary expense	3,100	
Rent expense	1,000	
Total	$105,100	$100,000

Requirements

Prepare the correct trial balance at June 30. Journal entries are not required. (pp. 77, 79)

Problems (Group B)

Using accounting terms and analyzing a trial balance
1

P2-37B → *Link Back to Chapter 1 (Balance Sheet, Income Statement).* Judy Kroll, owner of A+ Fire & Safety, is selling the business. Kroll offers the following trial balance to prospective buyers. Your best friend is considering buying the company. He seeks your advice in interpreting this information.

continued . . .

A+ FIRE & SAFETY
Trial Balance
December 31, 2007

Account Title	Balance Debit	Credit
Cash	$ 7,000	
Accounts receivable	6,000	
Prepaid expenses	4,000	
Equipment	130,000	
Accounts payable		$ 31,000
Note payable		45,000
Judy Kroll, capital		33,000
Judy Kroll, withdrawals	21,000	
Service revenue		112,000
Wage expense	38,000	
Rent expense	8,000	
Supplies expense	7,000	
Total	$221,000	$221,000

Requirements

Help your friend decide whether to buy A+ Fire & Safety by answering the following questions.

1. How much are the firm's total assets? total liabilities? net income or net loss? (pp. 60–62)

2. Suppose A+ earned all the service revenue on account. Make a single journal entry to record the revenue, set up the two T-accounts affected, and post to those accounts. (p. 70)

3. In your own words, describe the accounting process that results in A+'s $7,000 balance for Cash. Use the following terms in your explanation: account, balance, journal, ledger, post, and trial balance. (pp. 66–77)

4. If your friend were to join Judy Kroll as a co-owner of A+ Fire & Safety, what form of business organization would the firm then take? If necessary, review Chapter 1.

Analyzing and journalizing transactions
 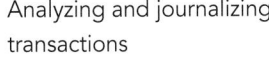

P2-38B Dan Bell practices medicine under the business title Dan Bell, M.D. During April, his medical practice engaged in the following transactions:

April 1 Bell deposited $70,000 cash in the business bank account. The business gave Bell owner's equity in the firm.

5 Paid monthly rent on medical equipment, $700.

9 Paid $22,000 cash to purchase land for an office site.

10 Purchased supplies on account, $1,200.

19 Borrowed $20,000 from the bank for business use. Bell signed a note payable to the bank in the name of the business.

22 Paid $1,000 on account.

continued . . .

30	Revenues earned during the month included $6,000 cash and $5,000 on account.
30	Paid employees' salaries ($2,400), office rent ($1,500), and utilities ($400). Make a single compound entry.
30	Withdrew $10,000 from the business for personal use.

Bell's business uses the following accounts: Cash; Accounts Receivable; Supplies; Land; Accounts Payable; Notes Payable; Dan Bell, Capital; Dan Bell, Withdrawals; Service Revenue; Salary Expense; Rent Expense; Utilities Expense.

Requirement
Journalize each transaction, as shown for April 1. Explanations are not required. (pp. 70–76)

| April 1 | Cash | 70,000 | |
| | Dan Bell, Capital | | 70,000 |

Journalizing transactions, posting to T-accounts, and preparing a trial balance

P2-39B Laura Knipper opened a law office on January 2 of the current year. During the first month of operations, the business completed the following transactions:

January 2	Knipper deposited $36,000 cash in the business bank account Laura Knipper, Attorney.
3	Purchased supplies, $500, and furniture, $2,600, on account.
4	Performed legal service for a client and received cash, $1,500.
7	Paid cash to acquire land for a future office site, $22,000.
11	Prepared legal documents for a client on account, $900.
15	Paid secretary's salary, $570.
16	Paid for the furniture purchased January 3 on account.
18	Received $1,800 cash for helping a client sell real estate.
19	Defended a client in court and billed the client for $800.
29	Received cash on account, $400.
31	Paid secretary's salary, $570.
31	Paid rent expense, $700.
31	Withdrew $2,200 for personal use.

Requirements
Open the following T-accounts: Cash; Accounts Receivable; Supplies; Furniture; Land; Accounts Payable; Laura Knipper, Capital; Laura Knipper, Withdrawals; Service Revenue; Salary Expense; Rent Expense.

1. Record each transaction in the journal, using the account titles given. Key each transaction by date. Explanations are not required. (pp. 70–76)

continued . . .

2. Post the transactions to T-accounts, using transaction dates as posting references in the ledger. Label the balance of each account *Bal.*, as shown in the chapter. (pp. 70–76)

3. Prepare the trial balance of Laura Knipper, Attorney, at January 31 of the current year. (p. 77)

Journalizing transactions, posting to accounts in four-column format, and preparing a trial balance

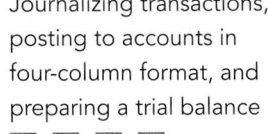

P2-40B The trial balance of Stephanie Stouse, Registered Dietician, at October 31, 2007, follows.

STEPHANIE STOUSE, REGISTERED DIETICIAN
Trial Balance
October 31, 2007

		Balance	
Account Number	Account Title	Debit	Credit
11	Cash	$ 3,000	
12	Accounts receivable	8,000	
13	Supplies	600	
14	Equipment	15,000	
21	Accounts payable		$ 4,600
31	Stephanie Stouse, capital		22,000
32	Stephanie Stouse, withdrawals		
41	Service revenue		
51	Salary expense		
52	Rent expense		
	Total	$26,600	$26,600

During November, Stouse completed the following transactions:

Nov. 4	Collected $6,000 cash from a client on account.
7	Performed a nutritional analysis for a hospital on account, $5,700.
12	Used personal funds to pay for the renovation of private residence, $55,000.
16	Purchased supplies on account, $800.
19	Withdrew $2,100 for personal use.
20	Paid on account, $2,600.
24	Received $1,900 cash for consulting with **Kraft Foods**.
30	Paid rent, $700.
30	Paid employee salary, $2,000.

Requirements

1. Record the November transactions on page 6 of the journal. Include an explanation for each entry. (pp. 70–76)

continued . . .

2. Post the transactions to four-column accounts in the ledger, using dates, account numbers, journal references, and posting references. Open the ledger accounts listed in the trial balance together with their balances at October 31. Enter *Bal.* (for October 31 balance) in the Item column, and place a check mark (✔) in the journal reference column for the October 31 balance of each account. (pp. 78–79)

3. Prepare the trial balance of Stephanie Stouse, Registered Dietician, at November 30, 2007.

Recording transactions; using four-column accounts; preparing a trial balance

P2-41B Vince Serrano started Serrano Carpet Installers, and during the first month of operations (January 2007) he completed the following selected transactions:

a. Serrano began the business with an investment of $40,000 cash and a van (automobile) valued at $20,000. The business gave Serrano owner's equity in the firm.

b. Paid $32,000 for equipment.

c. Purchased supplies on account, $400.

d. Paid employee's salary, $1,300.

e. Received $800 for a carpet installation job.

f. Received a $500 bill for advertising expense that will be paid in the near future.

g. Paid the account payable created in transaction (c).

h. Installed carpet for a hotel on account, $3,300.

i. Received cash on account, $1,100.

j. Paid the following cash expenses and made a single compound entry:
   (1) Rent, $1,000.
   (2) Insurance, $600.

k. Withdrew $2,600 for personal use.

Requirements
1. Open the following four-column accounts: Cash; Accounts Receivable; Supplies; Equipment; Automobile; Accounts Payable; Vince Serrano, Capital; Vince Serrano, Withdrawals; Service Revenue; Salary Expense; Rent Expense; Advertising Expense; Insurance Expense.

2. Record the transactions in the journal. Use the letters to identify the transactions. (pp 70–76).

3. Post to the accounts and keep a running balance for each account. (p. 77)

4. Prepare the trial balance of Serrano Carpet Installers at January 31, 2007. (p. 77)

Note: Problem 2-42B should be used in conjunction with Problem 2-41B.

Preparing the financial statements

5

P2-42B → *Link Back to Chapter 1 (Income Statement, Statement of Owner's Equity, Balance Sheet).* Refer to Problem 2-41B. After completing the

continued . . .

trial balance in Problem 2-41B, prepare the following financial statements for Serrano Carpet Installers:

1. Income statement for the month ended January 31, 2007. (p. 20)

2. Statement of owner's equity for the month ended January 31, 2007. (p. 20)

3. Balance sheet at January 31, 2007. (p. 20)

Draw arrows to link the statements. If needed, use Exhibit 1-8, page 20, as a guide for preparing the financial statements.

Correcting errors in a trial balance
2 5

P2-43B The trial balance for Missing Link Exploration Company does not balance.

| | | MISSING LINK EXPLORATION COMPANY Trial Balance March 31, 2007 | Balance | |
		Account Title	Debit	Credit
		Cash	$ 6,200	
		Accounts receivable	2,000	
		Supplies	500	
		Exploration equipment	22,300	
		Computers	46,000	
		Accounts payable		$ 2,700
		Note payable		18,300
		Jack Ballard, capital		50,800
		Jack Ballard, withdrawals	5,000	
		Service revenue		4,900
		Salary expense	1,300	
		Rent expense	500	
		Advertising expense	300	
		Utilities expense	200	
		Total	$84,300	$76,700

The following errors were detected:

a. The cash balance is overstated by $1,000.

b. Rent expense of $350 was erroneously posted as a credit rather than a debit.

c. A $6,900 credit to Service Revenue was not posted.

d. A $600 debit to Accounts Receivable was posted as $60.

e. The balance of Utilities Expense is understated by $60.

f. A $100 purchase of supplies on account was neither journalized nor posted.

g. Exploration equipment should be listed in the amount of $21,300.

Requirement

Prepare the correct trial balance at March 31. Journal entries are not required. (pp. 77, 79)

Continuing Problem

Problem 2-44 continues with the consulting business of Carl Redmon, begun in Problem 1-42, page 44. Here you will account for Redmon's transactions as it's actually done in practice.

Recording transactions and preparing a trial balance

P2-44 Carl Redmon completed these transactions during the first half of December:

Dec. 2	Invested $10,000 to start a consulting practice titled Redmon Consulting.
2	Paid monthly office rent, $500.
3	Paid cash for a Dell computer, $2,000. This equipment is expected to remain in service for five years.
4	Purchased office furniture on account, $3,600. The furniture should last for five years.
5	Purchased supplies on account, $300.
9	Performed consulting service for a client on account, $1,700.
12	Paid utility expenses, $200.
18	Performed service for a client and received cash of $800.

Requirements

1. Open T-accounts in the ledger: Cash; Accounts Receivable; Supplies; Equipment; Furniture; Accounts Payable; Carl Redmon, Capital; Carl Redmon, Withdrawals; Service Revenue; Rent Expense; Utilities Expense; and Salary Expense.

2. Journalize the transactions. Explanations are not required.

3. Post to the T-accounts. Key all items by date, and denote an account balance as *Bal.* Formal posting references are not required.

4. Prepare a trial balance at December 18. In the Continuing Problem of Chapter 3, we will add transactions for the remainder of December and prepare a trial balance at December 31.

Apply Your Knowledge

Decision Cases

Recording transactions directly in T-accounts, preparing a trial balance, and measuring net income or loss

Case 1. You have been requested by a friend named Dean McChesney to advise him on the effects that certain transactions will have on his business. Time is short, so you cannot journalize the transactions. Instead, you must analyze the transactions without a journal. McChesney will continue the business only if he can expect to earn monthly net income of $6,000. The business completed the following transactions during June:

   a. McChesney deposited $10,000 cash in a business bank account to start the company.

   b. Paid $300 cash for supplies.

   c. Incurred advertising expense on account, $700.

   d. Paid the following cash expenses: secretary's salary, $1,400; office rent, $1,100.

   e. Earned service revenue on account, $8,800.

   f. Collected cash from customers on account, $1,200.

Requirements

1. Open the following T-accounts: Cash; Accounts Receivable; Supplies; Accounts Payable; Dean McChesney, Capital; Service Revenue; Salary Expense; Rent Expense; Advertising Expense. (pp. 70–76)

2. Post the transactions directly to the accounts without using a journal. Key each transaction by letter. Follow the format illustrated here for the first transaction.

Cash		Dean McChesney, Capital	
(a) 10,000			(a) 10,000

3. Prepare a trial balance at June 30, 2009. List the largest expense first, the next largest second, and so on. The business name is A-Plus Travel Planners. (p. 77)

4. Compute the amount of net income or net loss for this first month of operations. Would you recommend that McChesney continue in business? (p. 20)

Using the accounting equation

Case 2. Answer the following questions. Consider each question separately. (Challenge)

1. Explain the advantages of double-entry bookkeeping over single-entry bookkeeping to a friend who is opening a used book store.

2. When you deposit money in your bank account, the bank credits your account. Is the bank misusing the word *credit* in this context? Why does the bank use the term *credit* to refer to your deposit, and not *debit*?

Ethical Issue

Better Days Ahead, a charitable organization, has a standing agreement with First National Bank. The agreement allows Better Days Ahead to overdraw its cash balance at the bank when donations are running low. In the past, Better Days Ahead managed funds wisely and rarely used this privilege. Jacob Henson has recently become the president of Better Days. To expand operations, Henson acquired office equipment and spent large amounts on fundraising. During Henson's presidency, Better Days Ahead has maintained a negative bank balance of approximately $10,000.

Requirement

What is the ethical issue in this situation? State why you approve or disapprove of Henson's management of Better Days Ahead's funds.

Financial Statement Case

Journalizing transactions for a company

This problem helps you develop skill in recording transactions by using a company's actual account titles. Refer to the **Amazon.com** financial statements in Appendix A. Assume that Amazon completed the following selected transactions during December 2005:

Dec. 1	Earned sales revenue and collected cash, $60,000.
9	Borrowed $200,000 by signing a note payable.
12	Purchased equipment on account, $10,000.
22	Paid half the account payable from December 12.
28	Paid electricity bill for $3,000 (this is an administrative expense)
31	Paid $100,000 of the note payable, plus interest expense of $1,000.

Requirement

Journalize these transactions, using the following account titles taken from the Amazon.com financial statements: Cash; Equipment; Accounts Payable; Note Payable; Sales Revenue; Administrative Expense; and Interest Expense. Explanations are not required.

Team Project

Contact a local business and arrange with the owner to learn what accounts the business uses.

Requirements

1. Obtain a copy of the business's chart of accounts.

2. Prepare the company's financial statements for the most recent month, quarter, or year. You may use either made-up account balances or balances supplied by the owner.

continued . . .

If the business has a large number of accounts within a category, combine related accounts and report a single amount on the financial statements. For example, the company may have several cash accounts. Combine all cash amounts and report a single Cash amount on the balance sheet.

You will probably encounter numerous accounts that you have not yet learned. Deal with these as best you can. The chart of accounts given in the inside covers of this book will be helpful.

Keep in mind that the financial statements report the balances of the accounts listed in the company's chart of accounts. Therefore, the financial statements must be consistent with the chart of accounts.

For Internet Exercises, Excel in Practice, and additional online activities, go to the Web site www.prenhall.com/horngren.

Quick Check Answers

1. *a*   2. *c*   3. *b*   4. *c*   5. *d*   6. *a*   7. *d*   8. *a*   9. *c*   10. *b*

Chapter 2: Demo Doc

Debit/Credit Transaction Analysis

Demo Doc: To make sure you understand this material, work through the following demonstration "demo doc" with detailed comments to help you see the concept within the framework of a worked-through problem.

Learning Objectives 1–4

On September 1, 2008, Michael Moe opened Moe's Mowing, a company that provides mowing and landscaping services. During the month of September, the business incurred the following transactions:

a. **To begin operations, Michael deposited $10,000 of personal funds in the business's bank account. The business received the cash and gave Michael capital (owner's equity).**

b. **The business purchased equipment for $3,500 on account.**

c. **The business purchased office supplies for $800 cash.**

d. **The business provided $2,600 of services to a customer on account.**

e. **The business paid $500 cash toward the equipment previously purchased on account in transaction b.**

f. **The business received $2,000 in cash for services provided to a new customer.**

g. **The business paid $200 cash to repair equipment.**

h. **The business paid $900 cash in salary expense.**

i. **The business received $2,100 cash from customers on account.**

j. **Michael withdrew $1,500 cash from the business for personal use.**

Requirements

1. Create blank T-accounts for the following accounts: Cash; Accounts Receivable; Supplies; Equipment; Accounts Payable; Michael Moe, Capital; Michael Moe, Withdrawals; Service Revenue; Salary Expense; Repair Expense.

2. Journalize the transactions and show how they are recorded in T-accounts. Use the table in Exhibit 2-17 to help with the journal entries.

EXHIBIT 2-17	The Rules of Debit and Credit	
	Increase	Decrease
Assets	debit	credit
Liabilities	credit	debit
Capital/Owner's Equity	credit	debit
Revenues	credit	debit
	like an increase in capital/owner's equity	
Expenses and Withdrawals	debit	credit
	like a decrease in capital/owner's equity	

3. Total all of the T-accounts to determine their balances at the end of the month.

Demo Doc Solutions

Requirement 1

Create blank T-accounts for the following accounts: Cash; Accounts Receivable; Supplies; Equipment; Accounts Payable; Michael Moe, Capital; Michael Moe, Withdrawals; Service Revenue; Salary Expense; Repairs Expense.

Part 1	Part 2	Part 3	Demo Doc Complete

Opening a T-account means drawing a blank account that looks like a capital "T" and putting the account title across the top. T-accounts give you a diagram of the additions and subtractions made to the accounts. For easy reference, they are usually organized into assets, liabilities, owner's equity, revenue, and expenses (in that order).

Draw empty T-accounts for every account listed in the question.

ASSETS	=	LIABILITIES	+	OWNER'S EQUITY

Cash

Supplies

Accounts Payable

Michael Moe, Capital

Equipment

Michael Moe, Withdrawals

Accounts Receivable

Service Revenue

Salary Expense

Repairs Expense

Requirement 2

Journalize the transactions and show how they are posted to T-accounts.

Part 1	**Part 2**	Part 3	Demo Doc Complete

a. To begin operations, Michael deposited $10,000 of personal funds in the business's bank account. The business received the cash and gave Michael capital (owner's equity).

First, we must determine which accounts are affected.

The business received $10,000 cash from its owner (Michael Moe). In exchange, Michael received an equity interest in the business. So the accounts involved are Cash and Michael Moe, Capital.

The next step is to determine what type of accounts these are. Cash is an asset, whereas Capital accounts are part of equity.

Next, we must determine if these accounts increased or decreased. From *the business's* point of view, Cash (an asset) has increased. Michael Moe, Capital (equity) has also increased.

Now we must determine if these accounts should be debited or credited. According to the rules of debit and credit (see Exhibit 2-17 on p. 114), an increase in assets is a debit, whereas an increase in capital (equity) is a credit.

So, Cash (an asset) is increased by a debit. Michael Moe, Capital (equity) is also increased—by a credit.

The journal entry would be as follows:

a.	Cash (Asset, ↑; debit)	10,000	
	Michael Moe, Capital (Equity, ↑; credit)		10,000
	Received investment from owner.		

The total dollar amounts of the debits must always equal the total dollar amounts of the credits.

Remember to use the transaction letters as references. This will help as we post this entry to the T-accounts.

Each T-account has two sides for recording debits and credits. To post the transaction to the T-account, simply transfer the amount of the debit(s) to the correct account(s) as a debit (left-side) entry, and transfer the amount of the credit(s) to the correct account(s) as a credit (right-side) entry.

For this transaction, there is a debit of $10,000 to Cash. This means that $10,000 is posted to the left side of the Cash T-account. There is also a credit of $10,000 to Michael Moe, Capital. This means that $10,000 is posted to the right side of the Michael Moe, Capital account.

Cash		Michael Moe, Capital	
a. 10,000			a. 10,000

b. The business purchased equipment for $3,500 on account.

The business received equipment in exchange for a promise to pay for the cost ($3,500) at a future date. So the accounts involved in the transaction are Equipment and Accounts Payable.

Equipment is an asset and Accounts Payable is a liability.

The asset Equipment is increased. The liability Accounts Payable is also increased.

Looking at Exhibit 2-17 (p. 114), an increase in assets (in this case, the increase in Equipment) is a debit, whereas an increase in liabilities (in this case, Accounts Payable) is a credit.

The journal entry would be as follows:

b.		Equipment (Asset, ↑; debit)	3,500	
		Accounts Payable (Liability, ↑; credit)		3,500
		Purchase of equipment on account.		

The amount $3,500 is posted to the debit (left) side of the Equipment T-account. The amount $3,500 is posted to the credit (right) side of the Accounts Payable account.

Equipment			Accounts Payable	
b.	3,500		b.	3,500

c. The business purchased office supplies for $800 cash.

The business purchased supplies and paid cash ($800). So the accounts involved in the transaction are Supplies and Cash.

Supplies and Cash are both assets.

Supplies (an asset) is increased. Cash (an asset) is decreased.

Looking at Exhibit 2-17 (p. 114), an increase in assets is a debit, whereas a decrease in assets is a credit.

So the increase to Supplies (an asset) is a debit, whereas the decrease to Cash (an asset) is a credit.

The journal entry would be as follows:

c.		Supplies (Asset, ↑; debit)	800	
		Cash (Asset, ↓; credit)		800
		Purchase of supplies for cash.		

The amount $800 is posted to the debit (left) side of the Supplies T-account. The amount $800 is posted to the credit (right) side of the Cash T-account.

Cash				Supplies	
a.	10,000		c.	800	
		c.	800		

Notice the $10,000 already on the debit side of the Cash account. This came from transaction **a**.

d. The business provided $2,600 of services to a customer on account.

The business received promises from a customer to send cash ($2,600) on some future date in exchange for services rendered. So the accounts involved in the transaction are Accounts Receivable and Service Revenue.

Accounts Receivable is an asset and Service Revenue is revenue.

Accounts Receivable (an asset) has increased. Service Revenue (revenue) has also increased.

Looking at Exhibit 2-17 (p. 114), an increase in assets is a debit, whereas an increase in revenue is a credit.

So the increase to Accounts Receivable (an asset) is a debit, whereas the increase to Service Revenue (revenue) is a credit.

The journal entry is as follows:

d.	Accounts Receivable (Asset, ↑; debit)	2,600	
	Service Revenue (Revenue, ↑; credit)		2,600
	Provided services on credit.		

The amount $2,600 is posted to the debit (left) side of the Accounts Receivable T-account. The amount $2,600 is posted to the credit (right) side of the Service Revenue account.

Accounts Receivable		Service Revenue	
d. 2,600			d. 2,600

e. The business paid $500 cash toward the equipment previously purchased on account in transaction b.

The business paid *some* of the money that was owed on the purchase of equipment in transaction **b.** The accounts involved in the transaction are Accounts Payable and Cash.

Accounts Payable is a liability that has decreased. Cash is an asset that has also decreased.

Remember, the Accounts Payable account is a list of creditors to whom the business will have to make payments in the future (a liability). When the business makes these payments to the creditors, Accounts Payable decrease because the business now owes less (in this case, it reduces from $3,500—in transaction **b**—to $3,000).

Looking at Exhibit 2-17 (p. 114), a decrease in liabilities is a debit, whereas a decrease in assets is a credit.

So Accounts Payable (a liability) is decreased, by a debit. Cash (an asset) is decreased, by a credit.

e.	Accounts Payable (Liability, ↓; debit)	500	
	Cash (Asset, ↓; credit)		500
	Partial payment on account.		

The amount $500 is posted to the debit (left) side of the Accounts Payable T-account. The amount $500 is posted to the credit (right) side of the Cash account.

Cash		Accounts Payable	
a. 10,000			b. 3,500
	c. 800	e. 500	
	e. 500		

Again notice the amounts already in the T-accounts from previous transactions. We can tell which transaction caused each amount from the reference letter next to each number.

f. The business received $2,000 in cash for services provided to a new customer.

The business received cash ($2,000) in exchange for services that Michael Moe rendered to clients. The accounts involved in the transaction are Cash and Service Revenue.

Cash is an asset that has increased and Service Revenue is revenue, which has also increased.

Looking at Exhibit 2-17 (p. 114), an increase in assets is a debit, whereas an increase in revenue is a credit.

So the increase to Cash (an asset) is a debit. The increase to Service Revenue (revenue) is a credit.

f.	Cash (Asset, ↑; debit)	2,000	
	Service Revenue (Equity, ↑; credit)		2,000
	Provided services for cash.		

The amount $2,000 is posted to the debit (left) side of the Accounts Receivable T-account. The amount $2,000 is posted to the credit (right) side of the Service Revenue account.

	Cash					Service Revenue	
a.	10,000				d.		2,600
		c.	800		f.		2,000
		e.	500				
f.	2,000						

Notice how we keep adding onto the T-accounts. The values from previous transactions remain in their respective places.

g. The business paid $200 cash to repair equipment.

Because the benefit of the repairs has already been used, the repairs are recorded as Repair Expense. Because the repairs were paid in cash, the Cash account is also affected.

Repair Expense is an expense that has increased and Cash is an asset that has decreased.

Looking at Exhibit 2-17 (p. 114), an increase in expenses is a debit, whereas a decrease in an asset is a credit.

So Repair Expense (an expense) is increased, by a debit. Cash (an asset) is decreased, by a credit.

g.	Repair Expense (Expense, ↑; debit)	200	
	Cash (Asset, ↓; credit)		200
	Payment for repairs.		

The amount $200 is posted to the debit (left) side of the Repair Expense T-account. The amount $200 is posted to the credit (right) side of the Cash account.

Cash				Repair Expense	
a.	10,000			g.	200
		c.	800		
		e.	500		
f.	2,000				
		g.	200		

h. The business paid $900 cash for salary expense.

The business paid salaries of $900 in cash. Because the benefit of the employees' work has already been used, their salaries are recorded as Salary Expense. Because the salaries were paid in cash, the Cash account is also affected.

Salary Expense is an expense that has increased and Cash is an asset that has decreased.

Looking at Exhibit 2-17 (p. 114), an increase in expenses is a debit, whereas a decrease in an asset is a credit.

In this case, Salary Expense (an expense) is increased, by a debit. Cash (an asset) is decreased, by a credit.

h.	Salary Expense (Expense, ↑; debit)	900	
	Cash (Asset, ↓; credit)		900
	Payment of salary.		

The amount $900 is posted to the debit (left) side of the Salary Expense T-account. The amount $900 is posted to the credit (right) side of the Cash account.

Cash				Salary Expense	
a.	10,000			h.	900
		c.	800		
		e.	500		
f.	2,000				
		g.	200		
		h.	900		

i. The business received $2,100 cash from customers on account.

The business received cash ($2,100) from customers for services previously recorded in transaction d. The accounts involved in this transaction are Cash and Accounts Receivable.

Cash and Accounts Receivable are both assets.

The asset Cash has increased, and the asset Accounts Receivable has decreased.

Remember, Accounts Receivable is a list of customers from whom the business will receive money. When the business receives cash from its customers, the account receivable decreases because the business now has less to receive in the future (in this case, it reduces from $2,600—in transaction d—to $500).

Looking at Exhibit 2-17 (p. 114), an increase in assets is a debit, and a decrease in an asset is a credit.

So Cash (an asset) is increased, by a debit. Accounts Receivable (an asset) is decreased by a credit.

i.		Cash (Asset, ↑; debit)	2,100	
		Accounts Receivable (Asset, ↓; credit)		2,100
		Receipt of cash from customer on account.		

The amount $2,100 is entered on the debit (left) side of the Cash T-account. The amount $2,100 is entered on the credit (right) side of the Accounts Receivable account.

	Cash					Accounts Receivable	
a.	10,000				d.	2,600	
		c.	800				i.	2,100
		e.	500				
f.	2,000						
		g.	200				
		h.	900				
i.	2,100						

j. Michael withdrew $1,500 cash from the business for personal use.

Michael Moe (the owner of the business) withdrew cash from the business. The business paid cash to Michael, whose ownership interest (equity) decreased. The accounts involved in this transaction are Michael Moe, Withdrawals and Cash.

Michael Moe, Withdrawals is a withdrawal that has increased and Cash is an asset that has decreased.

Looking at Exhibit 2-17 (p. 114), an increase in withdrawals is a debit, whereas a decrease in an asset is a credit.

So in this case Michael Moe, Withdrawals (withdrawal) is increased by a debit. Cash (an asset) is decreased by a credit.

j.		Michael Moe, Withdrawals (Equity, ↓; debit)	1,500	
		Cash (Asset, ↓; credit)		1,500
		Cash withdrawal by owner.		

The amount $1,500 is posted to the debit (left) side of the Michael Moe, Withdrawals T-account. The amount $1,500 is posted to the credit (right) side of the Cash account.

	Cash					Michael Moe, Withdrawals	
a.	10,000				j.	1,500	
		c.	800				
		e.	500				
f.	2,000						
		g.	200				
		h.	900				
i.	2,100						
		j.	1,500				

Now we can summarize all of the journal entries during the month:

Ref.		Accounts and Explanation	Debit	Credit
a.		Cash	10,000	
		Michael Moe, Capital		10,000
		Investment by owner.		
b.		Equipment	3,500	
		Accounts Payable		3,500
		Purchase of equipment on account.		
c.		Supplies	800	
		Cash		800
		Purchase of supplies for cash.		
d.		Accounts Receivable	2,600	
		Service Revenue		2,600
		Provide services on credit.		
e.		Accounts Payable	500	
		Cash		500
		Partial payment on Accounts Payable.		
f.		Cash	2,000	
		Service Revenue		2,000
		Provide services for cash.		
g.		Repair Expense	200	
		Cash		200
		Payment for repairs.		
h.		Salary Expense	900	
		Cash		900
		Payment of salary.		
i.		Cash	2,100	
		Accounts Receivable		2,100
		Receipt of cash from customer on account.		
j.		Michael Moe, Withdrawals	1,500	
		Cash		1,500
		Cash withdrawal by owner.		

Requirement 3

Compute the balance in each T-account to determine its balance at the end of the month.

Part 1	Part 2	**Part 3**	Demo Doc Complete

To compute the balance in a T-account (total the T-account), add up the numbers on the debit/left side of the account, and (separately) add up the numbers on the credit/right side of the account. The difference between the total debits and the total credits is the account's balance, which is placed on the side of the account with the larger number (that is, the side with a balance). This gives the balance in the T-account (the net total of both sides combined).

For example, for the Cash account, the numbers on the left side total $10,000 + $2,000 + $2,100 = $14,100. The credit/right side = $800 + $500 + $200 + $900 + $1,500 = $3,900. The difference is $14,100 − $3,900 = $10,200. We put the $10,200 on the debit side because that side holds the bigger number. This $10,200 is called Cash's debit balance.

An easy way to think of computing a T-account's balance is as follows:

> Beginning balance in the T-account
> + Increases to the T-account
> − Decreases to the T-account
> _____
> T-account balance (total)

T-accounts after posting all transactions and computing each account's balance:

ASSETS	=	LIABILITIES	+	OWNER'S EQUITY

Cash

a.	10,000		
		c.	800
		e.	500
f.	2,000		
		g.	200
		h.	900
i.	2,100		
		j.	1,500
Bal.	10,200		

Accounts Receivable

d.	2,600		
		i.	2,100
Bal.	500		

Supplies

c.	800		
Bal.	800		

Equipment

b.	3,500		
Bal.	3,500		

Accounts Payable

		b.	3,500
e.	500		
		Bal.	3,000

Michael Moe, Capital

		a.	10,000
		Bal.	10,000

Michael Moe, Withdrawals

j.	1,500		
Bal.	1,500		

Service Revenue

		d.	2,600
		f.	2,000
		Bal.	4,600

Salary Expense

h.	900		
Bal.	900		

Repair Expense

g.	200		
Bal.	200		

Part 1	Part 2	Part 3	**Demo Doc Complete**

3 The Adjusting Process

Learning Objectives

1 Distinguish accrual accounting from cash-basis accounting

2 Apply the revenue and matching principles

3 Make adjusting entries

4 Prepare an adjusted trial balance

5 Prepare the financial statements from the adjusted trial balance

Chapter 1 introduced you to the accounting equation and the financial statements. Chapter 2 brought T-accounts, debits, credits, and the trial balance. You're now ready for the next step in the accounting cycle.

Sherman Lawn Service and DeFilippo Catering have good businesses and well-oiled accounting systems. At the end of each period Haig Sherman and Julie DeFilippo need to measure their:

- net income
- financial position

Chapter 3 continues the accounting cycle by showing how to update the accounts at the end of the period. The process is called *adjusting the books*, and it requires special journal entries called *adjusting entries*.

Study this material carefully. It applies to small businesses like DeFilippo Catering and Cookie Lapp Travel Design and to giant companies such as eBay and PepsiCo. It also applies to the business you may operate some day.

Accounting Concepts and Principles

Accountants have concepts and principles to guide their work. Chief among these are:

- Accrual accounting versus cash-basis accounting
- The accounting period
- The revenue principle
- The matching principle

In this chapter, we apply these principles to Cookie Lapp Travel Design for the month of April. Coca-Cola, Toyota, and all other companies follow the same principles.

Accrual Accounting Versus Cash-Basis Accounting

1 Distinguish accrual accounting from cash-basis accounting

There are two ways to do accounting:

- **Accrual accounting** records the effect of each transaction as it occurs. Most businesses use the accrual basis as covered in this book.
- **Cash-basis accounting** records only cash receipts and cash payments. It ignores receivables, payables, and depreciation. Only very small businesses use the cash basis of accounting.

Suppose Cookie Lapp Travel purchased $2,000 of office supplies on account. On the accrual basis, Lapp records this transaction as follows:

Office Supplies	2,000	
Accounts Payable		2,000
Purchased supplies on account.		

In contrast, cash-basis accounting ignores this transaction because the business paid no cash. The cash basis records only cash receipts and cash payments. **In the cash basis,**

- Cash receipts are treated as revenues.
- Cash payments are treated as expenses.

Under the cash basis, Cookie Lapp Travel would record each cash payment as an expense. This is faulty accounting because Lapp acquired supplies, which are assets.

Now let's see how differently the accrual basis and the cash basis account for a revenue. Suppose Cookie Lapp Travel performed service and earned revenue but collected no cash. Under the accrual basis, Lapp records $10,000 of revenue on account as follows:

Accounts Receivable	10,000	
Service Revenue		10,000
Earned revenue on account.		

Under the cash basis, the business would record no revenue because there is no cash receipt. Instead, Lapp would wait until she receives the cash. Then she would record the cash receipt as revenue. As a result, cash-basis accounting never reports accounts receivable from customers. In this case, cash-basis accounting shows the revenue in the wrong accounting period. Revenue should be recorded when it is earned, and that is how the accrual basis operates.

Exhibit 3-1 illustrates the difference between the accrual basis and the cash basis for a florist. Keep in mind that the accrual basis is the correct way to do accounting.

EXHIBIT 3-1   Accrual Accounting Versus Cash-Basis Accounting

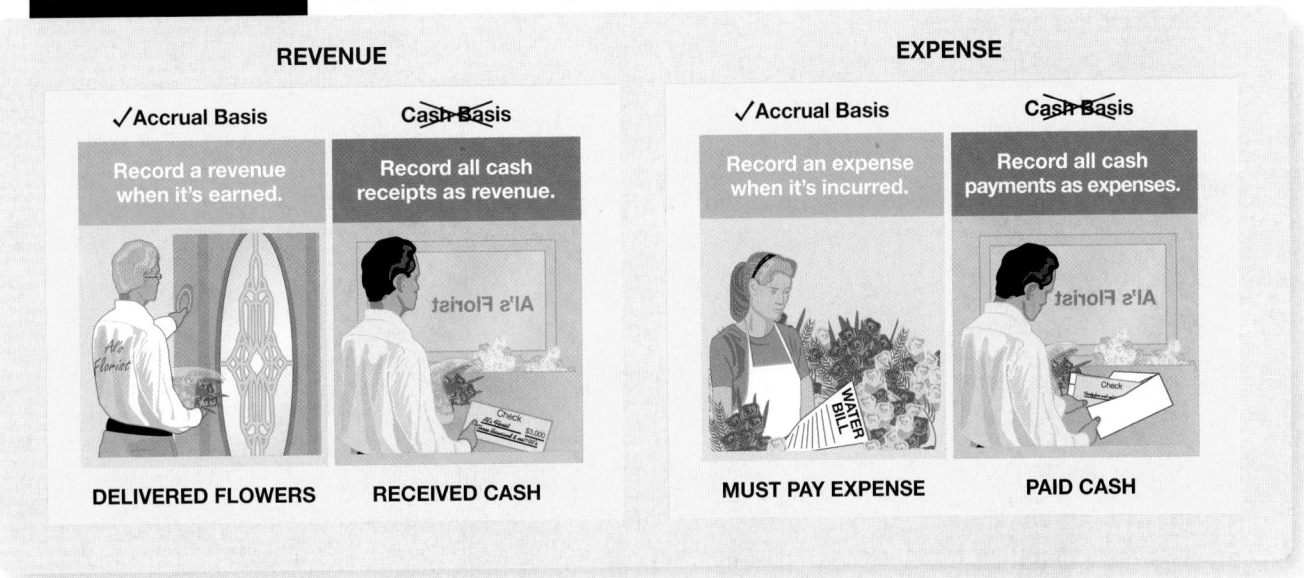

The Accounting Period

Cookie Lapp Travel Design will know for certain how well it has operated only after Lapp sells the assets, pays the liabilities, and gives any leftover cash to the owners. This process of going out of business is called *liquidation*. It is not practical to measure income this way because businesses need periodic reports on their affairs. Accountants slice time into small segments and prepare financial statements for specific periods.

The basic accounting period is one year, and all businesses prepare annual financial statements. For most companies, the annual accounting period runs the calendar year from January 1 through December 31. Other companies use a *fiscal year*, which ends on a date other than December 31. The year-end date is usually the low point in business activity for the year. Retailers are a notable example. For instance, Wal-Mart, JCPenney, and most other retailers use a fiscal year that ends on January 31 because their low point comes about a month after Christmas.

Companies also prepare financial statements for *interim* periods, such as monthly, quarterly, and semiannually. Most of our discussions are based on an annual accounting period, but everything can be applied to interim periods as well.

The Revenue Principle

The **revenue principle** tells accountants:

- *When* to record revenue—that is, when to make a journal entry for a revenue
- The *amount* of revenue to record.

"Recording" something in accounting means to make an entry in the journal. That's where the process starts.

When to Record Revenue

The revenue principle says to record revenue when it has been earned—but not before. This occurs when the business has delivered a good or service to the customer. The company has done everything required by the sale agreement.

Exhibit 3-2 shows two situations that provide guidance on when to record revenue for Cookie Lapp Travel Design. The first situation illustrates when *not* to record revenue—because the client merely states his plan. Situation 2 illustrates when revenue should be recorded—after the travel agency has performed a service for the client.

EXHIBIT 3-2   **Recording Revenue: The Revenue Principle**

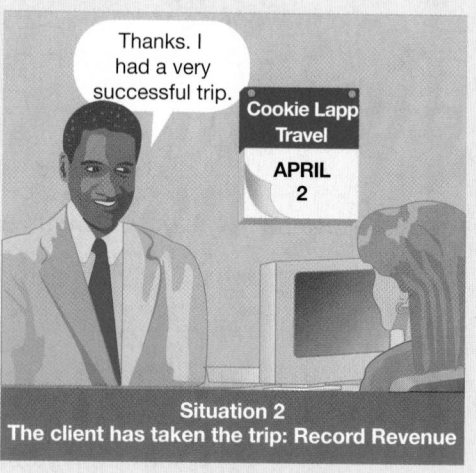

The Amount of Revenue to Record

Record revenue for the cash value of the item transferred to the customer. Suppose that to obtain a new client, Cookie Lapp performs travel service for the cut-rate price of $100. Ordinarily, Lapp would have charged $200 for this service. How much revenue should Lapp record? The answer is $100 because that was the value of the transaction. Lapp will not receive $200, so that is not the amount of revenue. She will receive only $100 cash, so she records that amount of revenue.

The Matching Principle

The **matching principle** guides accounting for expenses. Recall that expenses—such as salaries, rent, utilities, and advertising—are assets used up and liabilities created in order to earn revenue. The matching principle directs accountants to:

1. Measure all the expenses incurred during the period.

2. Match the expenses against the revenues of the period.

To match expenses against revenues means to subtract expenses from revenues. The goal is to compute net income or net loss. Exhibit 3-3 illustrates the matching principle.

EXHIBIT 3-3   **Recording Expenses: The Matching Principle**

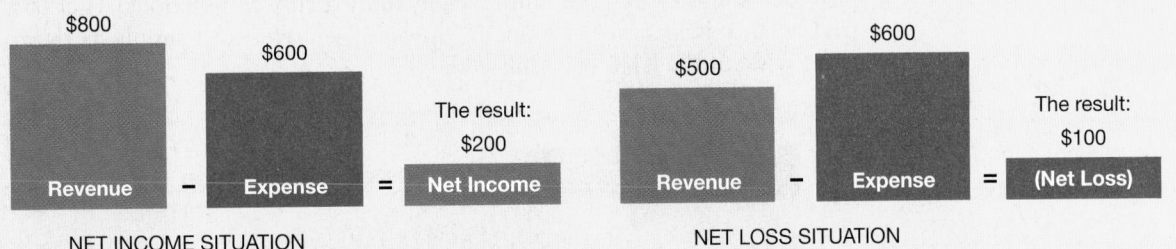

Matching expense against revenue means to subtract the expense from the revenue. The goal is to measure net income.

NET INCOME SITUATION   NET LOSS SITUATION

There is a natural link between some expenses and revenues. For example, Cookie Lapp Travel pays a commission to employees who sell the travel agency's services. *Cost of goods sold* is another example. If Toyota sells no automobiles, Toyota has no cost of goods sold.

Other expenses are not so easy to link to sales. For example, Cookie Lapp Travel Design's monthly rent expense occurs regardless of the revenues earned that month. The matching principle says to identify those expenses with a particular period, such as a month or a year. Lapp will record rent expense each month based on the lease agreement. Lapp also pays monthly salaries to her employee.

How does Cookie Lapp Travel Design bring its accounts up-to-date for the financial statements? To address this question, accountants use the time-period concept.

The Time-Period Concept

Owners need periodic readings on their business. The **time-period concept** ensures that information is reported often. To measure income, companies update their accounts at the end of each period. Cookie Lapp Travel provides an example of an expense accrual. At April 30, Lapp recorded salary expense of $900 that she owed her employee at the end of the month. Lapp's accrual entry was

Apr. 30	Salary Expense		900	
	Salary Payable			900
	Accrued salary expense.			

This entry assigns the salary expense to April because that was the month when the employee worked for the company. Without this entry, April's expenses would be understated, and net income would be overstated. The accrual entry also records the liability owed at April 30. Without this entry, total liabilities would be understated. The remainder of the chapter shows how to adjust the accounts and bring the books up-to-date.

Adjusting the Accounts

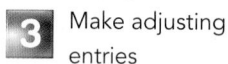

Make adjusting entries

At the end of the period, the accountant prepares the financial statements. The end-of-period process begins with the trial balance. Exhibit 3-4 is the trial balance of Cookie Lapp Travel Design at April 30, 2008. This *unadjusted trial balance* lists the revenues and expenses of the travel agency for April. But these amounts are incomplete because they omit certain revenue and expense transactions. That is why the trial balance is *unadjusted*. Usually, however, we refer to it simply as the trial balance, without the label "unadjusted."

EXHIBIT 3-4   Unadjusted Trial Balance

COOKIE LAPP TRAVEL DESIGN
Unadjusted Trial Balance
April 30, 2008

Cash	$24,800	
Accounts receivable	2,200	
Supplies	700	
Prepaid rent	3,000	
Furniture	18,000	
Accounts payable		$13,000
Unearned service revenue		600
Cookie Lapp, capital		32,600
Cookie Lapp, withdrawals	3,200	
Service revenue		7,000
Salary expense	900	
Utilities expense	400	
Total	$53,200	$53,200

Accrual accounting requires adjusting entries at the end of the period. We must have correct balances for the financial statements. To see why, consider the Supplies account in Exhibit 3-4.

Cookie Lapp Travel uses supplies during the month. This reduces the supplies on hand and creates an expense. It is a waste of time to record supplies expense every time it's used. But by the end of the month, the $700 of Supplies on the unadjusted trial balance (Exhibit 3-4) is out of date. So how does Lapp account for supplies expense? She must adjust the accounts at April 30.

Adjusting entries assign revenues to the period when they are earned and expenses to the period when they are incurred. Adjusting entries also update the asset and liability accounts. Adjustments are needed to properly measure two things:

1. Net income on the income statement and

2. Assets and liabilities on the balance sheet.

This end-of-period process is called *making the adjustments* or *adjusting the books.*

Prepaids and Accruals

The two basic categories of adjustments are *prepaids* and *accruals.* In a *prepaid* adjustment, the cash payment occurs before an expense is recorded. *Accrual* adjustments are the opposite. An accrual records an expense before the cash payment.

Adjusting entries fall into five categories:

1. Prepaid expenses

2. Depreciation

3. Accrued expenses

4. Accrued revenues

5. Unearned revenues

The core of this chapter shows how to account for these five types of adjusting entries.

Prepaid Expenses

Prepaid expenses are advance payments of expenses. Prepaid rent and prepaid insurance are examples. For example, McDonald's, the restaurant chain, makes prepayments for rent, insurance, and supplies. Keep in mind that prepaid expenses are assets, not expenses.

Prepaid Rent

Landlords require tenants to pay rent in advance. This prepayment creates an asset for the renter. Suppose Cookie Lapp Travel Design prepays three months' office rent on April 1, 2008. If the lease specifies a monthly rental of $1,000, the entry to record the payment is:

Apr. 1	Prepaid Rent ($1,000 × 3)	3,000	
	Cash		3,000
	Paid rent in advance.		

After posting, Prepaid Rent has a $3,000 debit balance.

ASSETS

Prepaid Rent

Apr. 1   3,000

The trial balance at April 30, 2008, lists Prepaid Rent with a debit balance of $3,000 (Exhibit 3-4). Throughout April, Prepaid Rent maintains this balance. But $3,000 is *not* the amount of Prepaid Rent for the balance sheet at April 30. Why?

At April 30, Prepaid Rent should be decreased for the amount that has been used up. The used-up portion is one-third of the prepayment. Recall that an asset that has expired is an *expense*. The adjusting entry transfers $1,000 ($3,000 × 1/3) of the Prepaid Rent to Rent Expense. The adjusting entry is:

Apr. 30	Rent Expense ($3,000 × 1/3)	1,000	
	Prepaid Rent		1,000
	To record rent expense.		

After posting, Prepaid Rent and Rent Expense show correct ending balances:

	ASSETS				EXPENSES	
	Prepaid Rent				**Rent Expense**	
Apr. 1	3,000	Apr. 30	1,000	Apr. 30	1,000	
Bal.	2,000			Bal.	1,000	

Correct asset amount: $2,000 → Total accounted for: $3,000 ← Correct expense amount: $1,000

The same analysis applies to the prepayment of three months of insurance. The only difference is in the account titles, which would be Prepaid Insurance instead of Prepaid Rent and Insurance Expense instead of Rent Expense. In a computerized system, the adjusting entry is programmed to recur automatically each accounting period.

The chapter Appendix 3A shows an alternative treatment of prepaid expenses. The end result on the financial statements is the same as illustrated here.

Supplies

Supplies are accounted for as prepaid expenses. On April 2, Cookie Lapp paid $700 for office supplies:

Apr. 2	Supplies	700	
	Cash		700
	Paid cash for supplies.		

The April 30 trial balance, therefore, lists Supplies with a $700 debit balance, as shown in Exhibit 3-4. But Lapp's April 30 balance sheet should *not* report supplies of $700. Why?

During April, the travel agency used supplies to conduct business. The cost of the supplies used becomes *supplies expense*. To measure supplies expense, Lapp counts the supplies on hand at the end of April. This is the amount of the asset still available to the business. Assume that supplies costing $600 remain at April 30. Supplies available minus supplies on hand measures supplies expense for the month ($100).

Asset available	−	Asset on hand at the end of the period	=	Expense (asset used during the period)
$700	−	$600	=	$100

The April 30 adjusting entry updates Supplies and records Supplies Expense for April as follows:

Apr. 30	Supplies Expense ($700 – $600)	100	
	Supplies		100
	To record supplies expense.		

After posting, Supplies and Supplies Expense hold correct ending balances:

ASSETS				EXPENSES		
Supplies				**Supplies Expense**		
Apr. 2	700	Apr. 30	100	Apr. 30	100	
Bal.	600			Bal.	100	

Correct asset amount: $600 $\rightarrow$ Total accounted for: $700 $\leftarrow$ Correct expense amount: $100

The Supplies account then enters May with a $600 balance, and the adjustment process is repeated each month.

Depreciation

Accrual accounting is clearly illustrated by depreciation. **Plant assets** are long-lived tangible assets used in the operation of a business. Examples include land, buildings, equipment, and furniture. As one accountant said, "All assets but land are on a march to the junkyard" because they decline in usefulness. This decline in usefulness of a plant asset is an expense, and accountants systematically spread its cost over its useful life. The allocation of a plant asset's cost to expense is called **depreciation**. Land is the exception. We record no depreciation for land.

Similarity to Prepaid Expenses

The concept of accounting for plant assets is the same as for a prepaid expense. The major difference is the length of time it takes for the asset to wear out. Prepaid expenses expire within a year, while plant assets remain useful for several years. On April 3 Cookie Lapp Travel purchased furniture for $18,000 and made this journal entry:

Apr. 3	Furniture	18,000	
	Cash		18,000
	Purchased furniture.		

After posting, the Furniture account has an $18,000 balance:

ASSETS	
Furniture	
Apr. 3	18,000

Cookie Lapp believes the furniture will remain useful for 5 years and then be worthless. One way to compute depreciation is to divide the cost of the asset

($18,000) by its expected useful life (5 years). This procedure—called the straight-line method—computes depreciation of $3,600 per year ($18,000/5 years). Depreciation for each month is $300 ($3,600/12 months = $300 per month). Depreciation expense for April is recorded by this entry:

Apr. 30	Depreciation Expense—Furniture	300	
	Accumulated Depreciation—Furniture		300
	To record depreciation on furniture.		

The Accumulated Depreciation Account

Accumulated Depreciation is credited—not Furniture—because it's helpful to keep the original cost in the Furniture account. Managers can then refer to the Furniture account to see how much the asset cost. This information may help decide how much to pay for new furniture. The Accumulated Depreciation account holds the sum of all the depreciation recorded for the asset and the total increases over time.

Accumulated Depreciation is a contra asset, which means an asset account with a normal credit balance. A **contra account** has two main characteristics:

* A contra account follows a companion account.
* A contra account's normal balance (debit or credit) is opposite that of the companion.

Accumulated Depreciation is the contra account that follows Furniture. Furniture has a debit balance, so Accumulated Depreciation, a contra asset, has a credit balance. *All contra assets have credit balances.*

A business carries an accumulated depreciation account for each depreciable asset. If Cookie Lapp Travel has both a building and furniture, it will carry two accounts: Accumulated Depreciation—Building and Accumulated Depreciation—Furniture.

After posting the depreciation, Lapp's accounts appear as follows:

	ASSETS			EXPENSES
NORMAL ASSET		**CONTRA ASSET**		
Furniture		Accumulated Depreciation—Furniture		Depreciation Expense—Furniture
Apr. 3 18,000			Apr. 30 300	Apr. 30 300
Bal. 18,000			Bal. 300	Bal. 300

Book Value

The balance sheet reports both Furniture and Accumulated Depreciation. Because it's a contra account, Accumulated Depreciation is subtracted from Furniture. The resulting net amount (cost minus accumulated depreciation) of a plant asset is called its **book value**, as follows for Furniture:

Book value of plant assets:	
Furniture	$18,000
Less: Accumulated depreciation	(300)
Book value of the furniture	$17,700

Suppose the travel agency also owns a building that cost $48,000, with annual depreciation of $2,400. The amount of depreciation for one month would be $200 ($2,400/12), and the following entry records depreciation for April:

Apr. 30	Depreciation Expense—Building	200	
	Accumulated Depreciation—Building		200
	To record depreciation on building.		

The April 30 balance sheet would report plant assets as shown in Exhibit 3-5.

EXHIBIT 3-5 Plant Assets on the Balance Sheet of Cookie Lapp Travel (April 30)

Plant Assets		
Furniture	$18,000	
Less: Accumulated depreciation	(300)	$17,700
Building	$48,000	
Less: Accumulated depreciation	(200)	47,800
Plant assets, net		$65,500

Exhibit 3-6 shows how Fossil, the fashion watch company, reported Property, Plant, and Equipment as adapted from its annual report. The only new items are the last two. Leasehold improvements show Fossil's cost of changes made to the assets that Fossil leases. An example would be the cost to paint the Fossil logo on delivery trucks. The last item reports the cost of Fossil's plant assets that are under construction.

EXHIBIT 3-6 Fossil Reports Property, Plant, and Equipment (Adapted)

	(in millions)	
Land	$ 8	
Buildings	16	
Furniture and fixtures	33	
Computer equipment	19	
Leasehold improvements	20	
Construction in progress	27	
	123	
Less: Accumulated depreciation	(33)	
Property, plant, and equipment, net	$ 90	

Fossil's total cost of plant assets was $123 million, and Fossil has depreciated $33 million. The book value of the plant assets is, therefore, $90 million.

Now let's return to Cookie Lapp Travel Design.

Accrued Expenses

Businesses often have expenses before paying them. Consider an employee's salary. Lapp's salary expense grows as the employee works, so the expense is said to *accrue*. Another accrued expense is interest expense on a note payable. Interest accrues as the clock ticks. The term **accrued expense** refers to an expense the business has incurred but not yet paid. An accrued expense always creates a liability.

Companies don't make weekly journal entries to accrue expenses. That would waste time and money. Instead they wait until the end of the period. They make an adjusting entry to bring each expense (and the related liability) up-to-date for the financial statements.

Remember that prepaids and accruals are opposites.

- A *prepaid expense* is paid first and expensed later.
- An *accrued expense* is expensed first and paid later.

Now let's see how to account for accrued expenses.

Accruing Salary Expense

Suppose Cookie Lapp pays her employee a monthly salary of $1,800, half on the 15th and half on the last day of the month. Here is a calendar for April with the two paydays circled:

April						
S	M	T	W	T	F	S
					1	2
3	4	5	6	7	8	9
10	11	12	13	14	(15)	16
17	18	19	20	21	22	23
24	25	26	27	28	29	(30)

To illustrate a salary accrual, assume that if either payday falls on a weekend, Lapp pays the following Monday. During April, Lapp paid the first half-month salary on Friday, April 15, and made this entry:

Apr. 15	Salary Expense	900	
	Cash		900
	To pay salary.		

After posting, Salary Expense shows this balance:

EXPENSES

Salary Expense

Apr. 15	900	

The trial balance at April 30 (Exhibit 3-4) includes Salary Expense, with a debit balance of $900. This is Lapp's salary expense for the first half of April. The second payment of $900 will occur in May, so Lapp must accrue salary expense for the second half of April. At April 30, Lapp makes this adjusting entry:

Apr. 30	Salary Expense	900	
	Salary Payable		900
	To accrue salary expense.		

After posting, Salary Expense and Salary Payable are up-to-date:

EXPENSES		LIABILITIES	
Salary Expense		**Salary Payable**	
Apr. 15 900			Apr. 30 900
Apr. 30 900			Bal. 900
Bal. 1,800			

Salary Expense holds a full month's salary, and Salary Payable shows the liability owed at April 30.

Accruing Interest Expense

Borrowing money creates a liability for a Note Payable. The entry to borrow $20,000 after signing a one-year note payable on December 1, 2008, is:

2008			
Dec. 1	Cash	20,000	
	Note Payable		20,000
	Borrowed money.		

Your interest on this note is payable one year later, on December 1, 2009. At December 31, 2008, the company must make an adjusting entry to record the interest expense that has accrued for the month of December. Assume one month's interest expense on this note is $100. Your December 31 adjusting entry to accrue interest expense is:

2008			
Dec. 31	Interest Expense	100	
	Interest Payable		100
	To acccrue interest expense.		

After posting, Interest Expense and Interest Payable have these balances:

EXPENSES		LIABILITIES	
Interest Expense		**Interest Payable**	
Dec. 31 100			Dec. 31 100
Bal. 100			Bal. 100

Accrued Revenues

As we have just seen, expenses can occur before the cash payment, and that creates an accrued expense. Likewise, businesses also earn revenue before they receive the cash. This calls for an **accrued revenue**, which is a revenue that has been earned but not yet collected in cash.

Assume that Cookie Lapp Travel is hired on April 15 to perform travel services for San Jacinto College. Under this agreement, Lapp will earn $800 monthly. During April, Lapp will earn half a month's fee, $400, for work April 16 through April 30. On April 30, Lapp makes the following adjusting entry to accrue the revenue earned during April 16 through 30:

Apr. 30	Accounts Receivable ($800 × 1/2)	400	
	Service Revenue		400
	To accrue service revenue.		

The unadjusted trial balance in Exhibit 3-4 shows that Accounts Receivable has an unadjusted balance of $2,200. Service Revenue's unadjusted balance is $7,000. The adjustment updates both accounts.

	ASSETS		**REVENUES**	
	Accounts Receivable		**Service Revenue**	
	2,200			7,000
Apr. 30	400		Apr. 30	400
Bal.	2,600		Bal.	7,400

Without the adjustment, Lapp's financial statements would understate both Accounts Receivable and Service Revenue. All accrued revenues are accounted for similarly: Debit a receivable and credit a revenue.

Now we turn to the final category of adjusting entries.

Unearned Revenues

Some businesses collect cash from customers in advance. Receiving cash before earning it creates a liability called **unearned revenue**; the company owes a product or a service to the customer. Only after completing the job will the business *earn* the revenue.

Suppose a law firm engages Cookie Lapp Travel to provide travel services, agreeing to pay her $600 monthly, beginning immediately. Lapp collects the first amount on April 20. Lapp records the cash receipt and a liability as follows:

Apr. 20	Cash	600	
	Unearned Service Revenue		600
	Collected revenue in advance.		

Now the liability account Unearned Service Revenue shows that Lapp owes $600.

LIABILITIES

Unearned Service Revenue

| | Apr. 20 | 600 |

Unearned Service Revenue is a liability because it represents Lapp's obligation to perform service for a client.

The April 30 trial balance (Exhibit 3-4) lists Unearned Service Revenue with a $600 credit balance. During the last 10 days of the month—April 21 through April 30—Lapp will *earn* one-third (10 days divided by April's 30 days) of the $600, or $200. Therefore, Lapp makes the following adjustment to record earning $200 of revenue:

Apr. 30	Unearned Service Revenue ($600 × 1/3)	200	
	Service Revenue		200
	To record service revenue that was collected in advance.		

This adjusting entry shifts $200 from liability to revenue. Service Revenue increases by $200, and Unearned Service Revenue decreases by $200. Now both accounts are up-to-date at April 30:

LIABILITIES

Unearned Service Revenue

Apr. 30	200	Apr. 20	600
		Bal.	400

REVENUES

Service Revenue

			7,000
		Apr. 30	400
		Apr. 30	200
		Bal.	7,600

Correct liability amount: $400 → Total accounted for: $600 ← Correct revenue amount: $200

Remember this key point:

An unearned revenue is a liability, not a revenue.

An unearned revenue to one company is a prepaid expense to the company that paid in advance. Consider the law firm in the preceding example. The law firm had prepaid travel expense—an asset. Cookie Lapp Travel had unearned service revenue—a liability.

Exhibit 3-7 summarizes the timing of prepaid and accrual adjustments. Study the exhibit from left to right, and then move down. The chapter Appendix 3A shows an alternative treatment for unearned revenues.

Summary of the Adjusting Process

The adjusting process has two purposes:

1. Measure net income or net loss on the *income statement*. Every adjustment affects a *revenue* or an *expense*.

2. Update the *balance sheet*. Every adjustment affects an *asset* or a *liability*.

Exhibit 3-8 summarizes the effects of the various adjusting entries.

Exhibit 3-9 summarizes the adjusting entries of Cookie Lapp Travel Design at April 30. The adjustments are keyed by letter.

- Panel A gives the data for each adjustment.
- Panel B shows the adjusting entries.
- Panel C gives the accounts after posting.

EXHIBIT 3-7 Prepaid and Accrual Adjustments

PREPAIDS—Cash transaction comes *first*.

Prepaid Expenses

Pay expense in advance and record an asset.

| Prepaid Rent | XXX | |
| Cash | | XXX |

Record the expense later.

| Rent Expense | XXX | |
| Prepaid Rent | | XXX |

Unearned Revenues

Receive cash in advance and record a liability.

| Cash | XXX | |
| Unearned Service Revenue | | XXX |

Record the revenue later.

| Unearned Service Revenue | XXX | |
| Service Revenue | | XXX |

ACCRUALS—Cash transaction comes *later*.

Accrued Expenses

Accrue an expense first.

| Salary Expense | XXX | |
| Salary Payable | | XXX |

Pay the liability later.

| Salary Payable | XXX | |
| Cash | | XXX |

Accrued Revenues

Accrue a revenue first.

| Interest Receivable | XXX | |
| Interest Revenue | | XXX |

Collect cash later.

| Cash | XXX | |
| Interest Receivable | | XXX |

Source: The authors thank Darrel Davis and Alfonso Oddo for suggesting this exhibit.

EXHIBIT 3-8 Summary of Adjusting Entries

Category of Adjusting Entry	Debit	Credit
Prepaid expense	Expense	Asset
Depreciation	Expense	Contra asset
Accrued expense	Expense	Liability
Accrued revenue	Asset	Revenue
Unearned revenue	Liability	Revenue

Source: Adapted from material provided by Beverly Terry.

EXHIBIT 3-9 Journalizing and Posting the Adjusting Entries of Cookie Lapp Travel Design

PANEL A—Information for Adjustments at April 30, 2008

a. Prepaid rent expired, $1,000.
b. Supplies expense, $100.
c. Depreciation on furniture, $300.
d. Accrued salary expense, $900.

e. Accrued service revenue, $400.
f. Service revenue that was collected in advance and now has been earned, $200.

PANEL B—Adjusting Entries

a.	Rent Expense	1,000	
	Prepaid Rent		1,000
	To record rent expense.		
b.	Supplies Expense	100	
	Supplies		100
	To record supplies used.		
c.	Depreciation Expense—Furniture	300	
	Accumulated Depreciation—Furniture		300
	To record depreciation on furniture.		
d.	Salary Expense	900	
	Salary Payable		900
	To accrue salary expense.		
e.	Accounts Receivable	400	
	Service Revenue		400
	To accrue service revenue.		
f.	Unearned Service Revenue	200	
	Service Revenue		200
	To record revenue that was collected in advance.		

EXHIBIT 3-9 continued

PANEL C—Ledger Accounts

Assets

Cash

Bal. 24,800	

Accounts Receivable

2,200	
(e) 400	
Bal. 2,600	

Supplies

700	(b) 100
Bal. 600	

Prepaid Rent

3,000	(a) 1,000
Bal. 2,000	

Furniture

18,000	
Bal. 18,000	

Accumulated Depreciation—Furniture

	(c) 300
	Bal. 300

Liabilities

Accounts Payable

	Bal. 13,000

Salary Payable

	(d) 900
	Bal. 900

Unearned Service Revenue

(f) 200	600
	Bal. 400

Owner's Equity

Cookie Lapp, Capital

	Bal. 32,600

Cookie Lapp, Withdrawals

(a) 3,200	

Revenue

Service Revenue

	7,000
	(e) 400
	(f) 200
	Bal. 7,600

Expenses

Rent Expense

(a) 1,000	
Bal. 1,000	

Salary Expense

900	
(d) 900	
Bal. 1,800	

Supplies Expense

(b) 100	
Bal. 100	

Depreciation Expense—Furniture

(c) 300	
Bal. 300	

Utilities Expense

Bal. 400	

The Adjusted Trial Balance

This chapter began with the *unadjusted* trial balance (Exhibit 3-4). After the adjustments, the accounts appear as shown in Exhibit 3-9, Panel C. A useful step in preparing the financial statements is to list the accounts, along with their adjusted balances, on an **adjusted trial balance**. Exhibit 3-10 shows how to prepare the adjusted trial balance.

Exhibit 3-10 is a *work sheet*. We will continue this work sheet into Chapter 4. For now, simply note how clear this format is. The Account Titles and the Trial Balance are copied directly from the trial balance. The two Adjustments columns show the adjustment Debits and Credits. Each debit is identified by a letter keyed to Exhibit 3-9.

4 Prepare an adjusted trial balance

EXHIBIT 3-10 Preparation of Adjusted Trial Balance

COOKIE LAPP TRAVEL DESIGN
Preparation of Adjusted Trial Balance
April 30, 2008

Account Title	Trial Balance Debit	Trial Balance Credit	Adjustments Debit	Adjustments Credit	Adjusted Trial Balance Debit	Adjusted Trial Balance Credit	
Cash	24,800				24,800		
Accounts receivable	2,200		(e) 400		2,600		
Supplies	700			(b) 100	600		
Prepaid rent	3,000			(a) 1,000	2,000		
Furniture	18,000				18,000		Balance Sheet *(Exhibit 3-13)*
Accumulated depreciation				(c) 300		300	
Accounts payable		13,000				13,000	
Salary payable				(d) 900		900	
Unearned service revenue		600	(f) 200			400	
Cookie Lapp, capital		32,600				32,600	Statement of Owner's Equity *(Exhibit 3-12)*
Cookie Lapp, withdrawals	3,200				3,200		
Service revenue		7,000		(e) 400			
				(f) 200		7,600	
Rent expense			(a) 1,000		1,000		Income Statement *(Exhibit 3-11)*
Salary expense	900		(d) 900		1,800		
Supplies expense			(b) 100		100		
Depreciation expense			(c) 300		300		
Utilities expense	400				400		
Total	53,200	53,200	2,900	2,900	54,800	54,800	

The Adjusted Trial Balance columns give the adjusted account balances. Each amount in these columns is computed by combining the trial balance amounts plus or minus the adjustments. For example, Accounts Receivable starts with a debit balance of $2,200. Adding the $400 debit from adjustment (e) gives Accounts Receivable an adjusted balance of $2,600. Supplies begins with a debit balance of $700. After the $100 credit adjustment, Supplies has a $600 balance. More than one entry may affect a single account, such as for Service Revenue.

The Financial Statements

The April financial statements of Cookie Lapp Travel Design can be prepared from the adjusted trial balance in Exhibit 3-10. In the right margin, we see how the accounts are distributed to the financial statements. As always,

- the income statement (Exhibit 3-11) reports revenues and expenses.
- the statement of owner's equity (Exhibit 3-12) shows why owner's capital changed during the period.
- the balance sheet (Exhibit 3-13) reports assets, liabilities, and owner's equity.

Preparing the Statements

The financial statements should be prepared in this order:

1. Income statement—to determine net income

2. Statement of owner's equity—to compute ending capital

5 Prepare the financial statements from the adjusted trial balance

3. Balance sheet—which needs the amount of ending capital to achieve its balancing feature

All financial statements include these elements:

Heading

- Name of the entity—such as Cookie Lapp Travel Design
- Title of the statement—income statement, balance sheet, and so on
- Date, or period, covered by the statement—April 30, 2008, or Month Ended April 30, 2008

Body of the statement

The income statement should list expenses in descending order by amount, as shown in Exhibit 3-11. But Miscellaneous Expense, a catchall category, usually comes last.

Relationships Among the Financial Statements

The arrows in Exhibits 3-11, 3-12, and 3-13 show how the financial statements relate to each other.

1. Net income from the income statement increases owner's equity. A net loss decreases owner's equity.

2. Ending capital from the statement of owner's equity goes to the balance sheet and makes total liabilities plus owner's equity equal total assets.

To solidify your understanding of these relationships, trace net income from the income statement to the statement of owner's equity. Then trace ending capital to the balance sheet.

EXHIBIT 3-11 **The Income Statement Reports the Results of Operations**

COOKIE LAPP TRAVEL DESIGN
Income Statement
Month Ended April 30, 2008

Revenue:		
Service revenue		$7,600
Expenses:		
Salary expense	$1,800	
Rent expense	1,000	
Utilities expense	400	
Depreciation expense	300	
Supplies expense	100	
Total expenses		3,600
Net income		$4,000

EXHIBIT 3-12 **Statement of Owner's Equity**

COOKIE LAPP TRAVEL DESIGN
Statement of Owner's Equity
Month Ended April 30, 2008

Cookie Lapp, capital, April 1, 2008	$32,600
Add: Net income	4,000
	36,600
Less: Withdrawals	(3,200)
Cookie Lapp, capital, April 30, 2008	$33,400

EXHIBIT 3-13 **The Balance Sheet Reports Financial Position**

COOKIE LAPP TRAVEL DESIGN
Balance Sheet
April 30, 2008

Assets			Liabilities	
Cash		$24,800	Accounts payable	$13,000
Accounts receivable		2,600	Salary payable	900
Supplies		600	Unearned service revenue	400
Prepaid rent		2,000	Total liabilities	14,300
Furniture	$18,000		**Owner's Equity**	
Less: Accumulated			Cookie Lapp, capital	33,400
depreciation	(300)	17,700	Total liabilities and	
Total assets		$47,700	owner's equity	$47,700

Ethical Issues in Accrual Accounting

Like all areas of business, accounting poses ethical challenges. Accountants must be honest in their work. Only with complete and accurate information can people make wise decisions. An example will illustrate.

Cookie Lapp Travel has done well as a business and wishes to open another office. Assume the company needs to borrow $30,000.

Suppose the travel agency understated expenses in order to inflate net income on the income statement. A banker could be tricked into lending the company money. Then if Lapp couldn't pay the loan, the bank would lose—all because the banker relied on incorrect accounting information.

Accrual accounting provides opportunities for unethical accounting. It would be easy for a dishonest businessperson to overlook depreciation expense at the end of the year. Failing to record depreciation would overstate net income and paint a rosy picture of the company's financial position. It is important for accountants to prepare accurate and complete financial statements because people rely on the data for their decisions.

Decision Guidelines

THE ACCOUNTING PROCESS

Take the role of Haig Sherman, who owns Sherman Lawn Service. Assume it's now the end of the first year, and Sherman wants to know where the business stands financially. The Decision Guidelines give a map of the accounting process to help Sherman manage the business.

Decision	Guidelines
Which basis of accounting better measures business income?	*Accrual basis,* because it provides more complete reports of operating performance and financial position
How to measure revenues?	Revenue principle—Record revenues only after they're earned
How to measure expenses?	Matching principle—Subtract expenses from revenues in order to measure net income
Where to start with the measurement of income at the end of the period?	Unadjusted trial balance, usually referred to simply as the *trial balance*
How to update the accounts for the financial statements? What are the categories of adjusting entries?	*Adjusting entries* at the end of the period

Prepaid expenses — Accrued revenues
Depreciation of plant assets — Unearned revenues
Accrued expenses

How do the adjusting entries differ from other journal entries?	1. Adjusting entries are made only at the end of the period.
	2. Adjusting entries never affect cash.
	3. All adjusting entries debit or credit
	• At least one *income statement* account (a revenue or an expense), and
	• At least one *balance sheet* account (an asset or a liability)
Where are the accounts with their adjusted balances summarized?	*Adjusted trial balance,* which aids preparation of the financial statements

Summary Problem

The trial balance of Clay Employment Services pertains to December 31, 2009, which is the end of Clay's annual accounting period. Data needed for the adjusting entries include:

a. Supplies on hand at year-end, $200.

b. Depreciation on furniture, $2,000.

c. Depreciation on building, $1,000.

d. Salaries owed but not yet paid, $500.

e. Accrued service revenue, $1,300.

f. $3,000 of the unearned service revenue has been earned.

Requirements

1. Open the ledger accounts with their unadjusted balances as for Accounts Receivable:

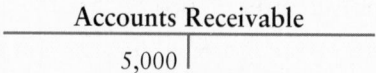

Accounts Receivable	
5,000	

2. Journalize Clay's adjusting entries at December 31, 2009. Key entries by letter, as in Exhibit 3-9.

3. Post the adjusting entries.

4. Write the trial balance on a work sheet, enter the adjusting entries, and prepare an adjusted trial balance, as shown in Exhibit 3-10.

5. Prepare the income statement, the statement of owner's equity, and the balance sheet. Draw arrows linking the three financial statements.

CLAY EMPLOYMENT SERVICES
Trial Balance
December 31, 2009

Account Title	Balance Debit	Balance Credit
Cash	$ 6,000	
Accounts receivable	5,000	
Supplies	1,000	
Furniture	10,000	
Accumulated depreciation—furniture		$ 4,000
Building	50,000	
Accumulated depreciation—building		30,000
Accounts payable		2,000
Salary payable		
Unearned service revenue		8,000
Jay Clay, capital		12,000
Jay Clay, withdrawals	25,000	
Service revenue		60,000
Salary expense	16,000	
Supplies expense		
Depreciation expense—furniture and fixtures		
Depreciation expense—building		
Miscellaneous expense	3,000	
Total	$116,000	$116,000

Solution

Requirements 1 and 3

ASSETS

Cash

Bal. 6,000	

Accounts Receivable

5,000	
(e) 1,300	
Bal. 6,300	

Supplies

1,000	(a) 800
Bal. 200	

Furniture

Bal. 10,000	

Accumulated Depreciation—Furniture

	4,000
	(b) 2,000
	Bal. 6,000

Building

Bal. 50,000	

Accumulated Depreciation—Building

	30,000
	(c) 1,000
	Bal. 31,000

LIABILITIES

Accounts Payable

	Bal. 2,000

Salary Payable

	(d) 500
	Bal. 500

Unearned Service Revenue

(f) 3,000	8,000
	Bal. 5,000

OWNER'S EQUITY

Jay Clay, Capital

	Bal. 12,000

Jay Clay, Withdrawals

Bal. 25,000	

REVENUE

Service Revenue

	60,000
	(e) 1,300
	(f) 3,000
	Bal. 64,300

EXPENSES

Salary Expense

16,000	
(d) 500	
Bal. 16,500	

Supplies Expense

(a) 800	
Bal. 800	

Depreciation Expense—Furniture

(b) 2,000	
Bal. 2,000	

Depreciation Expense—Building

(c) 1,000	
Bal. 1,000	

Miscellaneous Expense

Bal. 3,000	

Requirement 2

	2009			
a.	Dec. 31	Supplies Expense ($1,000 – $200)	800	
		Supplies		800
		To record supplies used.		
b.	31	Depreciation Expense—Furniture	2,000	
		Accumulated Depreciation—Furniture		2,000
		To record depreciation expense on furniture.		
c.	31	Depreciation Expense—Building	1,000	
		Accumulated Depreciation—Building		1,000
		To record depreciation expense on building.		
d.	31	Salary Expense	500	
		Salary Payable		500
		To accrue salary expense.		
e.	31	Accounts Receivable	1,300	
		Service Revenue		1,300
		To accrue service revenue.		
f.	31	Unearned Service Revenue	3,000	
		Service Revenue		3,000
		To record service revenue that was collected in advance.		

Requirement 4

CLAY EMPLOYMENT SERVICES
Preparation of Adjusted Trial Balance
December 31, 2009

Account Title	Trial Balance Debit	Trial Balance Credit	Adjustments Debit	Adjustments Credit	Adjusted Trial Balance Debit	Adjusted Trial Balance Credit
Cash	6,000				6,000	
Accounts receivable	5,000		(e) 1,300		6,300	
Supplies	1,000			(a) 800	200	
Furniture	10,000				10,000	
Accumulated depreciation—furniture		4,000		(b) 2,000		6,000
Building	50,000				50,000	
Accumulated depreciation—building		30,000		(c) 1,000		31,000
Accounts payable		2,000				2,000
Salary payable				(d) 500		500
Unearned service revenue		8,000	(f) 3,000			5,000
Jay Clay, capital		12,000				12,000
Jay Clay, withdrawals	25,000				25,000	
Service revenue		60,000		(e) 1,300		
				(f) 3,000		64,300
Salary expense	16,000		(d) 500		16,500	
Supplies expense			(a) 800		800	
Depreciation expense—furniture			(b) 2,000		2,000	
Depreciation expense—building			(c) 1,000		1,000	
Miscellaneous expense	3,000				3,000	
Total	116,000	116,000	8,600	8,600	120,800	120,800

Requirement 5

CLAY EMPLOYMENT SERVICES
Income Statement
Year Ended December 31, 2009

Revenue:		
Service revenue		$64,300
Expenses:		
Salary expense	$16,500	
Depreciation expense—furniture	2,000	
Depreciation expense—building	1,000	
Supplies expense	800	
Miscellaneous expense	3,000	
Total expenses		23,300
Net income		$41,000

CLAY EMPLOYMENT SERVICES
Statement of Owner's Equity
Year Ended December 31, 2009

Jay Clay, capital, January 1, 2009	$12,000
Add: Net income	41,000
	53,000
Less: Withdrawals	(25,000)
Jay Clay, capital, December 31, 2009	$28,000

CLAY EMPLOYMENT SERVICES
Balance Sheet
December 31, 2009

Assets			Liabilities	
Cash		$ 6,000	Accounts payable	$ 2,000
Accounts receivable		6,300	Salary payable	500
Supplies		200	Unearned service revenue	5,000
Furniture	$10,000		Total liabilities	7,500
Less: Accumulated				
depreciation	(6,000)	4,000		
Building	$50,000		**Owner's Equity**	
Less: Accumulated			Jay Clay, capital	28,000
depreciation	(31,000)	19,000	Total liabilities and	
Total assets		$35,500	owner's equity	$35,500

Review The Adjusting Process

Accounting Vocabulary

Accrual Accounting
Accounting that records the impact of a business event as it occurs regardless of whether the transaction affected cash.

Accrued Expense
An expense that the business has incurred but not yet paid.

Accrued Revenue
A revenue that has been earned but not yet collected in cash.

Accumulated Depreciation
The cumulative sum of all depreciation expense recorded for an asset.

Adjusted Trial Balance
A list of all the accounts with their adjusted balances.

Adjusting Entry
Entry made at the end of the period to assign revenues to the period in which they are earned and expenses to the period in which they are incurred. Adjusting entries help measure the period's income and bring the related asset and liability accounts to correct balances for the financial statements.

Book Value (of a plant asset)
The asset's cost minus accumulated depreciation.

Cash-Basis Accounting
Accounting that records transactions only when cash is received or paid.

Contra Account
An account that always has a companion account and whose normal balance is opposite that of the companion account.

Deferred Revenue
A liability created when a business collects cash from customers in advance of doing work. Also called **unearned revenue**.

Depreciation
The allocation of a plant asset's cost to expense over its useful life.

Matching Principle
Guide to accounting for expenses. Identify all expenses incurred during the period, measure the expenses, and match them against the revenues earned during that same time period.

Plant Asset
Long-lived tangible assets—such as land, buildings, and equipment—used in the operation of a business.

Prepaid Expense
Advance payments of expenses. Examples include prepaid rent, prepaid insurance, and supplies.

Revenue Principle
The basis for recording revenues; tells accountants when to record revenue and the amount of revenue to record.

Time-Period Concept
Ensures that information is reported at regular intervals.

Unearned Revenue
A liability created when a business collects cash from customers in advance of doing work. Also called **deferred revenue**.

Quick Check

1. What are the distinctive features of accrual accounting and cash-basis accounting?
   a. Cash-basis accounting records all transactions.
   b. Accrual accounting records only receivables, payables, and depreciation.
   c. Accrual accounting is superior because it provides more information.
   d. All the above are true.

2. The revenue principle says
   a. Divide time into annual periods to measure revenue properly.
   b. Record revenue after you receive cash.
   c. Measure revenues and expenses in order to compute net income.
   d. Record revenue only after you have earned it.

3. Adjusting the accounts is the process of
   a. Zeroing out account balances to prepare for the next period
   b. Subtracting expenses from revenues to measure net income
   c. Recording transactions as they occur during the period
   d. Updating the accounts at the end of the period

4. Which types of adjusting entries are natural opposites?
   a. Prepaids and accruals
   b. Expenses and revenues
   c. Prepaids and depreciation
   d. Net income and net loss

5. Assume that the weekly payroll of Cookie Lapp Travel Design is $300. December 31, end of the year, falls on Monday, and Lapp will pay her employee on Friday for the full week. What adjusting entry will Lapp make on Monday, December 31?

a. Salary Expense	240	
Cash		240
b. Salary Expense	60	
Salary Payable................................		60
c. Salary Payable	300	
Salary Expense..............................		300

   d. No adjustment is needed because the company will pay the payroll on Friday.

6. Body Studio gains a client who prepays $600 for a package of six physical training sessions. Body Studio collects the $600 in advance and will provide the training later. After two training sessions, what should Body Studio report on its income statement?
   a. Cash of $400
   b. Service revenue of $200
   c. Service revenue of $600
   d. Unearned service revenue of $200

7. Unearned revenue is always a (an)

   a. Asset

   b. Revenue

   c. Liability

   d. Owner's equity because you collected the cash in advance

8. Assume you prepay Body Studio for a package of six physical training sessions. Which type of account should you have in your records?

   a. Prepaid expense

   b. Accrued expense

   c. Accrued revenue

   d. Unearned revenue

9. The adjusted trial balance shows

   a. Amounts that may be out of balance

   b. Revenues and expenses only

   c. Amounts ready for the financial statements

   d. Assets, liabilities, and owner's equity only

10. Accounting data flow from the

    a. Balance sheet to the income statement

    b. Income statement to the statement of owner's equity

    c. Statement of owner's equity to the balance sheet

    d. Both b and c are correct

    Answers are given after Apply Your Knowledge (p. 178).

Assess Your Progress

Short Exercises

Comparing accrual accounting and cash-basis accounting

1

S3-1 Suppose you work summers house-sitting for people while they're away on vacation. Most of your customers pay you immediately after you finish a job. A few ask you to send them a bill. It is now June 30 and you have collected $600 from cash-paying customers. Your remaining customers owe you $500. How much service revenue would you have under the (a) cash basis and (b) accrual basis? Which method of accounting provides more information about your house-sitting business? Explain your answer. (pp. 126–127)

Accrual accounting versus cash-basis accounting for expenses

1

S3-2 The **Naman Howell Law Firm** uses a client database. Suppose Naman Howell paid $5,000 for a **Dell** computer. Describe how Naman Howell would account for the $5,000 expenditure under (a) the cash basis and (b) the accrual basis. State in your own words why the accrual basis is more realistic for this situation. (pp. 126–127)

Applying the revenue principle

2

S3-3 *Phoenix Magazine* sells annual subscriptions for the 12 monthly magazines mailed out each year. The company collects cash in advance and then mails out the magazines to subscribers each month.

Apply the revenue principle to determine (a) when Phoenix Magazine should record revenue for this situation and (b) the amount of revenue Phoenix should record for the magazines mailed out January through March. (pp. 128–129)

Applying the matching principle

2

S3-4 Suppose on January 1 you prepaid apartment rent of $3,600 for the full year. At September 30, what are your two account balances for this situation? Identify the two accounts and give their balances at September 30. (pp. 131–132)

Adjusting prepaid expenses

3

S3-5 On April 1 you prepaid six months of rent, $3,000. Give your adjusting entry to record rent expense at April 30. Include the date of the entry and an explanation. Then post to the two accounts involved, and show their balances at April 30. (pp. 131–132)

Recording depreciation

3

S3-6 On May 1 your company paid cash of $36,000 for computers that are expected to remain useful for three years. At the end of three years, the value of the computers is expected to be zero.

Make journal entries to record (a) purchase of the computers on May 1 and (b) depreciation on May 31. Include dates and explanations, and use the following accounts: Computer Equipment; Accumulated Depreciation—Computer Equipment; and Depreciation Expense—Computer Equipment. (pp. 133–134)

Adjusting entry; posting

3

S3-7 Refer to the data in Short Exercise 3-6.

1. Post to the accounts listed in Short Exercise 3-6, and show their balances at May 31. (p. 134)
2. What is the computer equipment's book value at May 31? (pp. 135–136)

Accruing interest expense

S3-8 Cookie Lapp Travel borrowed $50,000 on October 1 by signing a one-year note payable to Community One Bank. Lapp's interest expense for the remainder of the year (October through December) is $700.

1. Make Cookie Lapp's adjusting entry to accrue interest expense at December 31. Date the entry and include its explanation. (p. 137)

2. Post to the two accounts affected by the adjustment. (p. 137)

Accounting for unearned revenues

S3-9 **People Magazine** collects cash from subscribers in advance and then mails the magazines to subscribers over a one-year period. Give the adjusting entry that People Magazine makes to record the earning of $5,000 of Subscription Revenue that was collected in advance. Include an explanation for the entry, as illustrated in the chapter. (p. 139)

Preparing an adjusted trial balance

S3-10 Scissors Hair Stylists has begun the preparation of its adjusted trial balance as follows:

SCISSORS HAIR STYLISTS
Preparation of Adjusted Trial Balance
December 31, 2006

Account Title	Trial Balance Debit	Trial Balance Credit	Adjustments Debit	Adjustments Credit	Adjusted Trial Balance Debit	Adjusted Trial Balance Credit
Cash	400					
Supplies	700					
Equipment	17,000					
Accumulated depreciation		1,000				
Accounts payable		200				
Interest payable						
Note payable		3,000				
Suzanne Byrd, capital		6,000				
Service revenue		12,000				
Rent expense	4,000					
Supplies expense						
Depreciation expense						
Interest expense	100					
Total	22,200	22,200				

Year-end data:

a. Supplies on hand, $200

b. Depreciation, $1,000

c. Accrued interest expense, $100

Complete Scissors' adjusted trial balance. Key each adjustment by letter. To save time, you may write your answers in the spaces provided on the adjusted trial balance given here.

Note: Short Exercises 3-11 and 3-12 should be used only after completing Short Exercise 3-10.

Computing net income

S3-11 Refer to the data in Short Exercise 3-10. Compute Scissors' net income for the year ended December 31, 2006. (pp. 144–145)

Computing total assets

S3-12 Refer to the data in Short Exercise 3-10. Compute Scissors' total assets at December 31, 2006. Remember that Accumulated Depreciation is a contra asset. (pp. 144–145)

Exercises

Cash basis versus accrual basis

E3-13 Best Yet Catering completed the following selected transactions during April:

Apr. 1	Prepaid rent for three months, $900.
5	Paid electricity expenses, $300.
9	Received cash for meals served to customers, $2,000.
14	Paid cash for kitchen equipment, $3,000.
23	Served a banquet on account, $3,000.
30	Made the adjusting entry for rent (from April 1).
30	Accrued salary expense, $900.

Show whether each transaction would be handled as a revenue or an expense using the accrual basis. Give the amount of revenue or expense for April. Journal entries are not required. Use the following format for your answer, and show your computations: (pp. 125–127)

Amount of Revenue (Expense) for April		
Date	Revenue (Expense)	Accrual-Basis Amount of Revenue (Expense)

Accrual accounting concepts and principles

E3-14 Identify the accounting concept or principle (there may be more than one) that gives the most direction on how to account for each of the following situations: (pp. 128–130)

a. The owner of a business desires *monthly* financial statements to measure the progress of the entity on an ongoing basis.

b. Expenses of the period total $5,500. This amount should be subtracted from revenue to compute the period's net income.

c. Expenses of $1,200 must be accrued in order to measure net income properly.

d. A customer states her intention to switch health clubs. Should the new health club record revenue based on this intention? Give the reason for your answer.

Cash versus accrual; applying the revenue principle

E3-15 Suppose you start up your own photography business to shoot videos at college parties. The freshman class pays you $100 in advance just to guarantee your services for its party. The sophomore class promises you a minimum of $250 for filming its formal, and you end up collecting cash of $400 for this party. Answer the following questions about the correct way to account for your revenue under the accrual basis.

continued . . .

a. When did you earn your revenue for both parties? What caused you to earn the revenue? Did you earn the revenue at the moment you received cash? (pp. 127–128)

b. In addition to cash, what type of account was created when you received $100 from the freshman class? Name the new account. (pp. 137–138)

Allocating prepaid expense to the asset and the expense

E3-16 Compute the amounts indicated by question marks for each of the following Prepaid Rent situations. For situations A and B, make the needed journal entry. Consider each situation separately. (pp. 131–132)

	Situation			
	A	B	C	D
Beginning Prepaid Rent................	$ 800	$ 600	$ 400	$500
Payments for Prepaid Rent during the year.........................	1,100	?	1,400	?
Total amount to account for.........	1,900	1,500	?	?
Ending Prepaid Rent....................	700	700	?	400
Rent Expense...............................	$?	$ 800	$1,500	$900

Journalizing adjusting entries

E3-17 Journalize the adjusting entries for the following adjustments at January 31, end of the accounting period. (pp. 132–133, 141–142)

a. Depreciation, $700.

b. Prepaid rent expired, $300.

c. Interest expense accrued, $800.

d. Employee salaries owed for Monday through Thursday of a five-day workweek; weekly payroll, $10,000.

e. Unearned service revenue earned, $500.

Analyzing the effects of adjustments on net income

E3-18 Suppose the adjustments required in Exercise 3-17 were not made. Compute the overall overstatement or understatement of net income as a result of the omission of these adjustments. (Challenge)

Journalizing adjusting entries

E3-19 Journalize the adjusting entry needed at December 31 for each of the following independent situations. (pp. 131–132, 139)

a. On October 1, we collected $4,000 rent in advance, debiting Cash and crediting Unearned Rent Revenue. The tenant was paying one year's rent in advance. At December 31, we must account for the amount of rent we've earned.

b. Salary expense is $1,500 per day—Monday through Friday—and the business pays employees each Friday. This year December 31 falls on a Tuesday.

c. The unadjusted balance of the Supplies account is $3,100. Supplies on hand total $1,200.

d. Equipment was purchased last year at a cost of $10,000. The equipment's useful life is four years. Record the year's depreciation.

e. On September 1, when we prepaid $1,200 for a two-year insurance policy, we debited Prepaid Insurance and credited Cash.

Recording adjustments in T-accounts

E3-20 The accounting records of Meg Grayson, Architect, include the following unadjusted balances at March 31: Accounts Receivable, $1,000; Supplies, $600; Salary Payable, $0; Unearned Service Revenue, $400; Service Revenue, $4,700; Salary Expense, $1,200; Supplies Expense, $0. Grayson's accountant develops the following data for the March 31 adjusting entries:

a. Service revenue accrued, $600.

b. Unearned service revenue that has been earned, $200.

c. Supplies on hand, $500.

d. Salary owed to employee, $400.

Open a T-account for each account and record the adjustments directly in the accounts, keying each adjustment by letter. Show each account's adjusted balance. Journal entries are not required. (pp. 141–142)

Preparing an adjusted trial balance

E3-21 Merry Maids, the cleaning service, started the preparation of its adjusted trial balance as follows:

MERRY MAIDS
Preparation of Adjusted Trial Balance
June 30, 2007

Account Title	Trial Balance		Adjustments		Adjusted Trial Balance	
	Debit	Credit	Debit	Credit	Debit	Credit
Cash	800					
Supplies	2,000					
Prepaid insurance	900					
Equipment	20,000					
Accumulated depreciation		3,000				
Accounts payable		2,100				
Salary payable						
Unearned service revenue		600				
Lou Smith, capital		8,000				
Lou Smith, withdrawals	4,000					
Service revenue		22,000				
Salary expense	8,000					
Supplies expense						
Depreciation expense						
Insurance expense						
Total	35,700	35,700				

During the six months ended June 30, 2007, Merry Maids:

a. Used supplies of $1,500.

b. Used up prepaid insurance of $600.

c. Used up $500 of the equipment through depreciation.

d. Accrued salary expense of $300 that Merry Maids hasn't paid yet.

e. Earned $400 of the unearned service revenue.

continued . . .

Complete the adjusted trial balance. Key each adjustment by letter. To save time, you may write your answers directly in the spaces given here. (p. 143)

Using an adjusted trial balance

E3-22 Refer to the data is Exercise 3-21. Journalize the five adjustments, all dated June 30, 2007. Explanations are not required. (pp. 141–142)

Note: Exercise 3-23 should be used only in conjunction with Exercise 3-21.

Using an adjusted trial balance

E3-23 Refer to the data in Exercise 3-21.
   a. Compute Merry Maids' net income for the period ended June 30, 2007. (pp. 144–145)
   b. Compute Merry Maids' total assets at June 30, 2007. (pp. 144–145)

Adjusting the accounts

E3-24 The adjusted trial balance of Job Link Employment Service is incomplete. Enter the adjustment amounts directly in the Adjustments columns below. (p. 143)

JOB LINK EMPLOYMENT SERVICE
Preparation of Adjusted Trial Balance
January 31, 2008

Account Title	Trial Balance Debit	Trial Balance Credit	Adjustments Debit	Adjustments Credit	Adjusted Trial Balance Debit	Adjusted Trial Balance Credit
Cash	900				900	
Accounts receivable	4,500				5,600	
Supplies	1,000				700	
Equipment	32,300				32,300	
Accumulated depreciation		14,000				14,600
Salary payable						900
L. Teagarden, capital		24,300				24,300
L. Teagarden, withdrawals	5,100				5,100	
Service revenue		9,600				10,700
Salary expense	2,700				3,600	
Rent expense	1,400				1,400	
Depreciation expense					600	
Supplies expense					300	
Total	47,900	47,900			50,500	50,500

Journalizing adjustments

E3-25 Make the journal entry for each adjustment needed to complete the adjusted trial balance in Exercise 3-24. Date the entries and include explanations. (pp. 141–143)

Preparing the financial statements

E3-26 Refer to the adjusted trial balance in Exercise 3-24. Prepare the Job Link Employment Service income statement and statement of owner's equity for the month ended January 31, 2008, and its balance sheet on that date. Draw arrows linking the three statements. (pp. 144–145)

Preparing the income
statement

E3-27 The accountant for John Eagle, CPA, has posted adjusting entries (a) through (e) to the accounts at December 31, 2007. Selected balance sheet accounts and all the revenues and expenses of the entity follow in T-account form.

Accounts Receivable	
23,000	
(e) 1,000	

Supplies	
1,000	(a) 400

Accumulated Depreciation—Equipment	
	5,000
	(b) 2,000

Accumulated Depreciation—Building	
	30,000
	(c) 5,000

Salary Payable	
	(d) 600

Service Revenue	
	105,000
	(e) 1,000

Salary Expense	
28,000	
(d) 600	

Supplies Expense	
(a) 400	

Depreciation Expense—Equipment	
(b) 2,000	

Depreciation Expense—Building	
(c) 5,000	

Requirements

1. Prepare the income statement of John Eagle, CPA, for the year ended December 31, 2007. List expenses in order from the largest to the smallest. (pp. 144–145)

2. Were 2007 operations successful? Give the reason for your answer. (Challenge)

Preparing the statement of owner's equity

5

E3-28 Lake Air Interiors began the year with capital of $20,000. On July 12, Cynthia Norcross (the owner) invested $12,000 cash in the business. On September 26, Norcross transferred to the company land valued at $70,000. The income statement for the year ended December 31, 2005, reported net income of $65,000. During this fiscal year, Norcross withdrew $4,000 each month for personal use.

Requirements

Prepare Lake Air Interiors' statement of owner's equity for the year ended December 31, 2005. (pp. 144–145)

Computing financial statement amounts

5

E3-29 The adjusted trial balances of Pacific International at December 31, 2007, and December 31, 2006, include these amounts:

	2007	2006
Supplies	$ 2,000	$ 1,000
Salary payable	2,500	4,000
Unearned service revenue........	13,000	16,000

continued . . .

Analysis of the accounts at December 31, 2007, reveals these transactions for 2007:

Cash payment for supplies.................................	$ 6,000
Cash payments for salaries	47,000
Cash receipts in advance for service revenue.....	80,000

Compute the amount of supplies expense, salary expense, and service revenue to report on the Pacific International income statement for 2007. (pp. 131–139, 141–142)

Problems (Group A)

Applying accounting principles

P3-30A As the controller of Highland Academy, a private high school, you have hired a new bookkeeper, whom you must train. He objects to making an adjusting entry for accrued salaries at the end of the period. He reasons, "We will pay the salaries within a week or two. Why not wait until payment to record the expense? In the end, the result will be the same." Write a business memo to explain to the bookkeeper why the adjusting entry for accrued salary expense is needed. The format of a business memo follows. (pp. 125–127)

Date: _____

To: New Bookkeeper

From: (Student Name) _____

Subject: Why the adjusting entry for salary expense is needed

---

Cash basis versus accrual basis

P3-31A Tee's Golf School completed the following transactions during January:

Jan. 1 Prepaid insurance for January through March, $300.

4 Performed service (gave golf lessons) on account, $2,200.

5 Purchased equipment on account, $1,900.

8 Paid property tax expense, $450.

11 Purchased office equipment for cash, $800.

19 Performed service and received cash, $700.

24 Collected $400 on account.

26 Paid account payable from January 5.

continued . . .

29   Paid salary expense, $900.

31   Recorded adjusting entry for January insurance expense (see Jan. 1).

31   Debited unearned revenue and credited revenue to adjust the accounts, $600.

Requirements

1. Show how each transaction would be handled using the accrual basis of accounting. Give the amount of revenue or expense for January. Journal entries are not required. Use the following format for your answer, and show your computations: (pp. 125–127)

Amount of Revenue (Expense) for January		
Date	Revenue (Expense)	Accrual-Basis Amount of Revenue (Expense)

2. Compute January net income or net loss under the accrual basis of accounting. (Challenge)

3. State why the accrual basis of accounting is preferable to the cash basis. (pp. 125–127)

Journalizing adjusting entries
3

P3-32A Journalize the adjusting entry needed on December 31, the end of the current year, for each of the following independent cases affecting Lindsey Landscaping. (pp. 131–132, 139)

a. Each Friday, Lindsey pays employees for the current week's work. The amount of the payroll is $5,000 for a five-day workweek. This year December 31 falls on a Monday. (p. 136)

b. Details of Prepaid Insurance are shown in the account:

Lindsey prepays a full year's insurance each year on January 1. Record insurance expense for the year ended December 31. (pp. 131–132)

Prepaid Insurance	
January 1 3,000	

c. The beginning balance of Supplies was $3,800. During the year, Lindsey purchased supplies costing $5,000, and at December 31, the supplies on hand total $2,400. (p. 132)

d. Lindsey designed a landscape plan, and the client paid Lindsey $4,000 at the start of the project. Lindsey recorded this amount as Unearned Service Revenue. The job will take several months to complete, and Lindsey estimates that the company has earned three-fourths of the total revenue during the current year. (p. 139)

e. Depreciation for the current year includes: Equipment, $5,500; and Trucks, $3,000. Make a compound entry, as illustrated in Chapter 2. (pp. 131–134, 72–73)

Journalizing and posting
adjustments to T-accounts;
preparing the adjusted trial
balance

P3-33A The trial balance of Dynaclean Air Purification Systems at November 30, 2007, and the data needed for the month-end adjustments follow.

DYNACLEAN AIR PURIFICATION SYSTEMS
Trial Balance
November 30, 2007

Account Title	Balance Debit	Balance Credit
Cash	$ 7,100	
Accounts receivable	19,800	
Prepaid rent	2,400	
Supplies	1,200	
Equipment	19,700	
Accumulated depreciation		$ 3,600
Accounts payable		3,300
Salary payable		
Unearned service revenue		2,800
Dinah Klein, capital		40,000
Dinah Klein, withdrawals	9,800	
Service revenue		15,600
Salary expense	3,800	
Rent expense		
Depreciation expense		
Advertising expense	1,500	
Supplies expense		
Total	$65,300	$65,300

Adjustment data at November 30:

a. Unearned service revenue still unearned, $1,100.

b. Prepaid rent still in force, $400.

c. Supplies used during the month, $1,000.

d. Depreciation for the month, $400.

e. Accrued advertising expense, $600. (Credit Accounts Payable.)

f. Accrued salary expense, $500.

Requirements

1. As directed by your instructor, open T-accounts (or four-column accounts) for the accounts listed in the trial balance, inserting their November 30 unadjusted balances. (pp. 141–142, 80)

2. Journalize the adjusting entries and post to the T-accounts. Key the journal entries and the posted amounts by letter. Show the ending balance of each account. (pp. 141–142)

continued . . .

If you are instructed to use four-column accounts, then post to the accounts and write "Balance" in the Item column for the November 30 unadjusted balance, as shown here for the Cash account:

ACCOUNT CASH

Date	Item	Jrnl. Ref.	Debit	Credit	Balance Debit	Balance Credit
Nov. 30	Balance				7,100	

Use the actual date (Nov. 30) for each posted amount. (pp. 141–142, 80)

3. Prepare the adjusted trial balance. (p. 143)
4. How will Dynaclean use the adjusted trial balance? (pp. 143–145)

Analyzing and journalizing adjustments

3

P3-34A Galaxy Theater Productions' unadjusted and adjusted trial balances at December 31, 2007, follow.

GALAXY THEATER PRODUCTIONS
Adjusted Trial Balance
December 31, 2007

Account Title	Trial Balance Debit	Trial Balance Credit	Adjusted Trial Balance Debit	Adjusted Trial Balance Credit
Cash	3,200		3,200	
Accounts receivable	5,200		11,200	
Supplies	1,200		300	
Prepaid insurance	2,600		2,300	
Equipment	21,600		21,600	
Accumulated depreciation		8,200		9,800
Accounts payable		4,400		4,400
Salary payable				1,000
Paul Lombardy, capital		14,400		14,400
Paul Lombardy, withdrawals	29,600		29,600	
Service revenue		68,000		74,000
Depreciation expense			1,600	
Supplies expense			900	
Utilities expense	5,000		5,000	
Salary expense	26,600		27,600	
Insurance expense			300	
Total	95,000	95,000	103,600	103,600

Requirements

Journalize the adjusting entries that account for the differences between the two trial balances. (pp. 141–142).

Preparing the financial
statements from an
adjusted trial balance
5

P3-35A The adjusted trial balance of Festive Occasions Party Planners at December 31, 2008, follows.

	FESTIVE OCCASIONS PARTY PLANNERS Adjusted Trial Balance December 31, 2008		
		Balance	
Account Title		**Debit**	**Credit**
Cash		$ 12,300	
Accounts receivable		10,400	
Supplies		900	
Equipment		25,600	
Accumulated depreciation			$ 12,200
Accounts payable			3,600
Unearned service revenue			4,500
Salary payable			900
Note payable			15,000
D. Brooks, capital			10,000
D. Brooks, withdrawals		38,000	
Service revenue			63,700
Depreciation expense		5,300	
Salary expense		9,000	
Utilities expense		3,700	
Insurance expense		3,100	
Supplies expense		1,600	
Total		$109,900	$109,900

Requirements

1. Prepare Festive Occasions' 2008 income statement and statement of owner's equity and year-end balance sheet. List expenses in decreasing order on the income statement and show total liabilities on the balance sheet. Draw arrows linking the three financial statements. (pp. 144–145)

2. a. Which financial statement reports Festive Occasions' results of operations? Were 2008 operations successful? Cite specifics from the financial statements to support your evaluation. (pp. 144–145)

   b. Which statement reports the company's financial position? Does Festive Occasions' financial position look strong or weak? Give the reason for your evaluation. (pp. 144–145)

Preparing an adjusted trial
balance and the financial
statements
3 4 5

P3-36A Consider the unadjusted trial balance of Hummer Limo Service at October 31, 2007, and the related month-end adjustment data.

continued . . .

HUMMER LIMO SERVICE
Trial Balance
October 31, 2007

Account Title	Balance Debit	Balance Credit
Cash	$ 6,300	
Accounts receivable	1,000	
Prepaid rent	3,000	
Supplies	600	
Automobile	72,000	
Accumulated depreciation		$ 3,000
Accounts payable		2,800
Salary payable		
Ben Hummer, capital		73,000
Ben Hummer, withdrawals	3,600	
Service revenue		9,400
Salary expense	1,400	
Rent expense		
Fuel expense	300	
Depreciation expense		
Supplies expense		
Total	$88,200	$88,200

Adjustment data:

a. Accrued service revenue at October 31, $2,000.

b. One-fifth of the prepaid rent expired during the month.

c. Supplies on hand October 31, $200.

d. Depreciation on automobile for the month. The auto's expected useful life is six years.

e. Accrued salary expense at October 31 for one day only. The five-day weekly payroll is $1,000.

Requirements

1. Write the trial balance on a work sheet, using Exhibit 3-10 as an example, and prepare the adjusted trial balance of Hummer Limo Service at October 31, 2007. Key each adjusting entry by letter. (p. 143)

2. Prepare the income statement and the statement of owner's equity for the month ended October 31, 2007, and the balance sheet at that date. Draw arrows linking the three financial statements. (pp. 144–145)

Problems (Group B)

Applying accounting principles

P3-37B Assume you own Bowen Electric Company, and you employ 10 people. Write a business memo to your assistant manager to explain the difference between the cash basis of accounting and the accrual basis. Mention

continued . . .

the roles of the revenue principle and the matching principle in accrual accounting. The format of a business memo follows. (pp. 125–127)

```
Date: _____

  To: Assistant Manager

From: (Student Name) _____

 Subject: Difference between the cash basis and the accrual basis of accounting
```

Cash basis versus accrual basis

P3-38B Multiplex Medical Clinic completed these transactions during October:

Oct. 2	Prepaid insurance for October through December, $900.
4	Paid water bill, $200.
5	Performed services on account, $8,000.
9	Purchased medical equipment for cash, $1,400.
12	Received cash for services performed, $7,400.
14	Purchased office equipment on account, $300.
28	Collected $500 on account from October 5.
29	Paid salary expense, $1,100.
30	Paid account payable from October 14.
31	Recorded adjusting entry for October insurance expense (see October 2).
31	Debited unearned revenue and credited revenue in an adjusting entry, $700.

Requirements

1. Show how each transaction would be handled using the accrual basis of accounting. Give the amount of revenue or expense for October. Journal entries are not required. Use the following format for your answer, and show your computations: (pp. 125–127)

AMOUNT OF REVENUE (EXPENSE) FOR OCTOBER

Date	Revenue (Expense)	Accrual-Basis Amount of Revenue (Expense)

2. Compute October net income or net loss under the accrual basis of accounting. (Challenge)
3. Why is the accrual basis of accounting preferable to the cash basis? (pp. 125–127)

Journalizing adjusting entries

P3-39B Journalize the adjusting entry needed on December 31, end of the current year, for each of the following independent cases affecting Mid-America Water Park. (pp. 131–139)

a. Details of Prepaid Insurance are shown in the account:

Prepaid Insurance	
June 30 5,000	

continued . . .

Mid-America prepays a full year's liability insurance each year on June 30. Record insurance expense for the year ended December 31. (p. 136)

b. Mid-America pays employees each Friday. The amount of the weekly payroll is $2,000 for a five-day workweek. December 31 falls on a Wednesday. (p. 136)

c. Mid-America has borrowed money, signing a note payable. At December 31 Mid-America accrues interest expense of $300 that it will pay next year. (p. 138)

d. The beginning balance of Supplies was $1,000. During the year, Mid-America purchased supplies for $6,100, and at December 31 the supplies on hand total $2,100. (p. 132)

e. Mid-America is hosting a church group from Chicago. The tour operator paid Mid-America $12,000 as the service fee and Mid-America recorded this amount as Unearned Service Revenue. By December 31 Mid-America earned 60% of the total fee. (p. 139)

f. Depreciation for the current year includes Canoe Equipment, $3,800; and Trucks, $1,300. Make a compound entry, as illustrated in Chapter 2. (pp. 133–134, 72–73)

Journalizing and posting adjustments to T-accounts; preparing the adjusted trial balance

3 **4**

P3-40B The trial balance of Lexington Inn at December 31, 2008, and the data needed for the month-end adjustments follow.

LEXINGTON INN
Trial Balance
December 31, 2008

		Balance	
Account Title		**Debit**	**Credit**
Cash		$ 12,200	
Accounts receivable		14,100	
Prepaid insurance		3,100	
Supplies		800	
Building		412,000	
Accumulated depreciation			$311,000
Accounts payable			1,900
Salary payable			
Unearned service revenue			2,300
Paul Revere, capital			115,000
Paul Revere, withdrawals		2,900	
Service revenue			17,800
Salary expense		2,100	
Insurance expense			
Depreciation expense			
Advertising expense		800	
Supplies expense			
Total		$448,000	$448,000

Adjustment data at December 31:

a. Prepaid insurance still in force, $600.

b. Supplies used during the month, $600.

continued . . .

c. Depreciation for the month, $900.

d. Accrued salary expense, $100.

e. Unearned service revenue still unearned, $1,100.

Requirements

1. As directed by your instructor, open T-accounts (or four-column accounts) for the accounts listed in the trial balance, inserting their December 31 unadjusted balances. (pp. 141–142, 80)

2. Journalize the adjusting entries and post to the T-accounts. Key the journal entries and the posted amounts by letter. Show the ending balance of each account. (pp. 141–142)

   If you are instructed to use four-column accounts, then post to the accounts and write "Balance" in the Item column for the December 31 unadjusted balance, as shown here for the Cash account:

ACCOUNT CASH

Date	Item	Jrnl. Ref.	Debit	Credit	Balance Debit	Balance Credit
Dec. 31	Balance				12,200	

Use the actual date (Dec. 31) for each posted amount. (pp. 141–142, 80)

3. Prepare the adjusted trial balance. (p. 143)

4. How will Lexington Inn use the adjusted trial balance? (pp. 143–145)

Analyzing and journalizing adjustments

3

P3-41B Assume that a **Kinko's** store had the following unadjusted and adjusted trial balances at April 30, 2007.

KINKO'S
Adjusted Trial Balance
April 30, 2007

Account Title	Trial Balance Debit	Trial Balance Credit	Adjusted Trial Balance Debit	Adjusted Trial Balance Credit
Cash	6,200		6,200	
Accounts receivable	6,000		6,900	
Supplies	1,000		300	
Prepaid rent	2,400		1,600	
Equipment	66,400		66,400	
Accumulated depreciation		16,000		17,200
Accounts payable		6,900		6,900
Salary payable				300
Mel Kinko, capital		55,000		55,000
Mel Kinko, withdrawals	3,600		3,600	
Service revenue		9,500		10,400
Salary expense	1,600		1,900	
Rent expense			800	
Depreciation expense			1,200	
Supplies expense			700	
Utilities expense	200		200	
Total	87,400	87,400	89,800	89,800

continued . . .

Requirements

Journalize the adjusting entries that account for the differences between the two trial balances. (pp. 131–138, 141–143)

Preparing the financial statements from an adjusted trial balance

5

P3-42B The adjusted trial balance of Snyder Piano Tuning Service at December 31, 2007, follows.

SNYDER PIANO TUNING SERVICE		
Adjusted Trial Balance		
December 31, 2007		
	Adjusted Trial Balance	
Account Title	Debit	Credit
Cash	$ 8,300	
Accounts receivable	4,900	
Supplies	2,300	
Prepaid rent	1,600	
Equipment	7,700	
Accumulated depreciation		$ 4,900
Accounts payable		4,500
Unearned service revenue		600
Dot Snyder, capital		3,000
Dot Snyder, withdrawals	29,000	
Service revenue		66,000
Depreciation expense	2,300	
Rent expense	17,400	
Utilities expense	2,600	
Supplies expense	2,900	
Total	$79,000	$79,000

Requirements

1. Prepare the 2007 income statement, statement of owner's equity, and year-end balance sheet of Snyder Piano Tuning Service. List expenses in decreasing order on the income statement and show total liabilities on the balance sheet. Draw arrows linking the three financial statements. (pp. 144–145)

2. a. Which financial statement reports the company's results of operations? Were operations successful during 2007? Cite specifics from the financial statements to support your evaluation. (pp. 144–145)

   b. Which statement reports the company's financial position? Does its financial position look strong or weak? Give the reason for your evaluation. (pp. 144–145)

P3-43B The unadjusted trial balance of Solar Energy Consulting at July 31, 2007, and the related month-end adjustment data follow.

			Balance	
	Account Title		**Debit**	**Credit**
	Cash		$ 8,900	
	Accounts receivable		11,600	
	Prepaid rent		4,000	
	Supplies		800	
	Equipment		28,800	
	Accumulated depreciation			$ 3,500
	Accounts payable			3,400
	Salary payable			
	Spike Martin, capital			39,100
	Spike Martin, withdrawals		4,000	
	Service revenue			15,000
	Salary expense		2,400	
	Rent expense			
	Utilities expense		500	
	Depreciation expense			
	Supplies expense			
	Total		$61,000	$61,000

SOLAR ENERGY CONSULTING
Trial Balance
July 31, 2007

Adjustment data:
a. Accrued service revenue at July 31, $2,000.
b. Prepaid rent expired during the month, $1,000.
c. Supplies on hand at July 31, $400.
d. Depreciation on equipment for the month, $300.
e. Accrued salary expense at July 31 for one day only. The five-day weekly payroll is $1,000.

Requirements
1. Using Exhibit 3-10 as an example, write the trial balance on a work sheet and prepare the adjusted trial balance of Solar Energy Consulting at July 31, 2007. Key each adjusting entry by letter. (p. 143)
2. Prepare the income statement and the statement of owner's equity for the month ended July 31, 2007, and the balance sheet at that date. Draw arrows linking the three statements. (pp. 144–145)

for 24/7 practice, visit
www.MyAccountingLab.com

Continuing Problem

Problem 3-44 continues the Carl Redmon Consulting situation from Problem 2-44 of Chapter 2.

Adjusting the accounts, preparing an adjusted trial balance, and preparing the financial statements

3 **4** **5**

P3-44 Refer to Problem 2-44 of Chapter 2. Start from the trial balance and the posted T-accounts that Carl Redmon Consulting prepared at December 18, as follows:

			Balance	
	Account Title		Debit	Credit
	Cash		$ 8,100	
	Accounts receivable		1,700	
	Supplies		300	
	Equipment		2,000	
	Accumulated depreciation			
	Furniture		3,600	
	Accumulated depreciation			
	Accounts payable			$ 3,900
	Salary payable			
	Unearned service revenue			
	Carl Redmon, capital			10,000
	Carl Redmon, withdrawals			
	Service revenue			2,500
	Rent expense		500	
	Utilities expense		200	
	Salary expense			
	Depreciation expense—equipment			
	Depreciation expense—furniture			
	Supplies expense			
	Total		$16,400	$16,400

CARL REDMON CONSULTING
Trial Balance
December 18, 2008

Later in December, the business completed these transactions, as follows:

Dec. 21	Received $900 in advance for client service to be performed evenly over the next 30 days.
21	Hired a secretary to be paid $1,500 on the 20th day of each month. The secretary begins work immediately.
26	Paid $300 on account.
28	Collected $600 on account.
30	Withdrew $1,600 for personal use.

continued . . .

Requirements

1. Open these additional T-accounts: Accumulated Depreciation—Equipment; Accumulated Depreciation—Furniture; Salary Payable; Unearned Service Revenue; Depreciation Expense—Equipment; Depreciation Expense—Furniture; Supplies Expense. (pp. 141–142)

2. Journalize the transactions of December 21 through 30. (pp. 70–76)

3. Post to the T-accounts, keying all items by date. (pp. 72–76)

4. Prepare a trial balance at December 31. Also set up columns for the adjustments and for the adjusted trial balance, as illustrated in Exhibit 3-10, page 143.

5. At December 31, Redmon gathers the following information for the adjusting entries:

   a. Accrued service revenue, $400.

   b. Earned $300 of the service revenue collected in advance on December 21.

   c. Supplies on hand, $100.

   d. Depreciation expense—equipment, $50; furniture, $60.

   e. Accrued $500 expense for secretary's salary.

   On your work sheet make these adjustments directly in the adjustments columns, and complete the adjusted trial balance at December 31. Throughout the book, to avoid rounding errors, we base adjusting entries on 30-day months and 360-day years. (p. 143)

6. Journalize and post the adjusting entries. In the accounts denote each adjusting amount as *Adj.* and an account balance as *Bal.* (pp. 141–142)

7. Prepare the income statement and the statement of owner's equity of Carl Redmon Consulting for the month ended December 31, and prepare the balance sheet at that date. Draw arrows linking the statements. (pp. 144–145)

Apply Your Knowledge

Decision Cases

Valuing a business on the basis of its net income

Case 1. Lee Nicholas has owned and operated World.com Advertising since its beginning 10 years ago. The company has prospered. Recently, Nicholas mentioned that he would sell the business for the right price.

Assume that you are interested in buying World.com Advertising. You obtain the most recent monthly trial balance, which follows. Revenues and expenses vary little from month to month, and January is a typical month. Your investigation reveals that the trial balance does *not* include monthly revenues of $3,800 and expenses of $1,100. Also, if you were to buy World.com Advertising, you would hire a manager so you could devote your time to other duties. Assume that this person would require a monthly salary of $5,000.

		WORLD.COM ADVERTISING Trial Balance January 31, 2008		
			Balance	
	Account Title		Debit	Credit
	Cash		$ 9,700	
	Accounts receivable		14,100	
	Prepaid expenses		2,600	
	Building		221,300	
	Accumulated depreciation			$ 68,600
	Accounts payable			13,000
	Salary payable			
	Unearned service revenue			56,700
	Lee Nicholas, capital			110,400
	Lee Nicholas, withdrawals		9,000	
	Service revenue			12,300
	Rent expense			
	Salary expense		3,400	
	Utilities expense		900	
	Depreciation expense			
	Supplies expense			
	Total		$261,000	$261,000

Requirements

1. Assume that the most you would pay for the business is 20 times the monthly net income *you could expect to earn* from it. Compute this possible price. (pp. 143–145)

2. Nicholas states that the least he will take for the business is his capital balance on January 31. Compute this amount. (pp. 144–145)

3. Under these conditions, how much should you offer Nicholas? Give your reason. (Challenge)

Completing the
accounting cycle to
compute net income

3 5

Case 2. One year ago, Tyler Stasney founded Swift Classified Ads. Stasney remembers that you took an accounting course while in college and comes to you for advice. He wishes to know how much net income his business earned during the past year in order to decide whether to keep the company going. His accounting records consist of the T-accounts from his ledger, which were prepared by an accountant who moved to another city. The ledger at December 31 follows. The accounts have *not* been adjusted.

Cash		Accounts Receivable		Prepaid Rent		Supplies	
Dec. 31 5,800		Dec. 31 12,000		Jan. 2 2,800		Jan. 2 2,600	

Equipment		Accumulated Depreciation				Accounts Payable	
Jan. 2 36,000							Dec. 31 21,500

Unearned Service Revenue		Salary Payable	
	Dec. 31 4,000		

Tyler Stasney, Capital		Tyler Stasney, Withdrawals				Service Revenue	
	Dec. 31 20,000	Dec. 31 28,000					Dec. 31 59,500

Salary Expense		Depreciation Expense		Rent Expense		Utilities Expense	
Dec. 31 17,000						Dec. 31 800	

Supplies Expense	

Stasney indicates that at year-end, customers owe him $1,600 for accrued service revenue. These revenues have not been recorded. During the year, Stasney collected $4,000 service revenue in advance from customers, but he earned only $900 of that amount. Rent expense for the year was $2,400, and he used up $1,700 of the supplies. Stasney determines that depreciation on his equipment was $5,000 for the year. At December 31, he owes his employee $1,200 accrued salary.

Requirements

Help Stasney compute his net income for the year. Advise him whether to continue operating Swift Classified Ads. (pp. 141–145)

Ethical Issue

The net income of Steinbach & Sons, a department store, decreased sharply during 2007. Mort Steinbach, owner of the store, anticipates the need for a bank loan in 2008. Late in 2007, Steinbach instructs the store's accountant to record a $2,000 sale of furniture to the Steinbach family, even though the goods will not be shipped from the manufacturer until January 2008. Steinbach also tells the accountant *not* to make the following December 31, 2007, adjusting entries:

Salaries owed to employees	$900
Prepaid insurance that has expired	400

continued . . .

Requirements

1. Compute the overall effects of these transactions on the store's reported income for 2007. (pp. 141–145)

2. Why is Steinbach taking this action? Is his action ethical? Give your reason, identifying the parties helped and the parties harmed by Steinbach's action. (Challenge)

3. As a personal friend, what advice would you give the accountant? (Challenge)

Financial Statement Case

Journalizing and posting transactions and tracing account balances to the financial statements

Amazon.com—like all other businesses—makes adjusting entries prior to year-end in order to measure assets, liabilities, revenues, and expenses properly. Examine Amazon's balance sheet and Note 3. Pay particular attention to Accumulated Depreciation.

1. Open T-accounts for the following accounts with their balances at December 31, 2004 (amounts in millions, as in the Amazon.com financial statements):

Accumulated Depreciation	$ 177
Accounts Payable	1,142
Other Assets	42

2. Assume that during 2005 Amazon.com completed the following transactions (amounts in billions). Journalize each transaction (explanations are not required).

   a. Recorded depreciation expense, $46.

   b. Paid the December 31, 2004, balance of accounts payable.

   c. Purchased inventory on account, $1,366.

   d. Sold other assets and received cash of $5.

3. Post to the three T-accounts. Then the balance of each account should agree with the corresponding amount reported in Amazon's December 31, 2005, balance sheet. Check to make sure they do agree with Amazon's actual balances. You can find Accumulated Depreciation in Note 3.

Team Project

It's Just Lunch is a nationwide service company that arranges lunch dates for clients. It's Just Lunch collects cash up front for a package of dates. Suppose your group is opening an It's Just Lunch office in your area. You must make some important decisions—where to locate, how to advertise, and so on—and you must also make some accounting decisions. For example, what will be the end of your business's accounting year? How often will you need financial statements to evaluate operating performance and financial position? Will you use the cash basis or the accrual basis? When will you account for the revenue that the business earns? How will you account for the expenses?

continued . . .

Requirements

Write a report (or prepare an oral presentation, as directed by your professor) to address the following considerations:

1. Will you use the cash basis or the accrual basis of accounting? Give a complete explanation of your reasoning.

2. How often do you want financial statements? Why? Discuss how you will use each financial statement.

3. What kind of revenue will you earn? When will you record it as revenue? How will you decide when to record the revenue?

4. Prepare a made-up income statement for It's Just Lunch for the year ended December 31, 2008. List all the business's expenses, starting with the most important (largest dollar amount) and working through the least important (smallest dollar amount). Merely list the accounts. Dollar amounts are not required.

For Internet Exercises, Excel in Practice, and additional online activities, go to the Web site www.prenhall.com/horngren.

Quick Check Answers

1. *c* 2. *d* 3. *d* 4. *a* 5. *b* 6. *b* 7. *c* 8. *a* 9. *c* 10. *d*

Alternative Treatment of Prepaid Expenses and Unearned Revenues

Chapters 1 through 3 illustrate the most popular way to account for prepaid expenses and unearned revenues. This appendix illustrates an alternative approach.

Prepaid Expenses

Prepaid expenses are advance payments of expenses such as Prepaid Insurance, Prepaid Rent, and Prepaid Advertising. Supplies are also accounted for as prepaid expenses.

When a business prepays an expense—rent, for example—it can debit an *asset* account (Prepaid Rent), as illustrated on page 131.

Aug. 1	Prepaid Rent	XXX	
	Cash		XXX

Alternatively, it can debit an *expense* account to record this cash payment:

Aug. 1	Rent Expense	XXX	
	Cash		XXX

Either way, the business must adjust the accounts at the end of the period to report the correct amounts of the expense and the asset.

Prepaid Expense Recorded Initially as an Expense

Prepaying an expense creates an asset. However, the asset may be so short-lived that it will expire in the current accounting period—within one year or less. Thus, the accountant may decide to debit the prepayment to an expense account at the time of payment. A $6,000 cash payment for rent (one year, in advance) on August 1 may be debited to Rent Expense:

2006				
Aug. 1	Rent Expense		6,000	
	Cash			6,000

At December 31, only five months' prepayment has expired (for August through December), leaving seven months' rent still prepaid. In this case, the accountant must transfer 7/12 of the original prepayment of $6,000, or $3,500, to the asset account Prepaid Rent. At December 31, 2006, the business still has the benefit of the prepayment for January through July of 2007. The adjusting entry at December 31 is:

2006	Adjusting Entries		
Dec. 31	Prepaid Rent ($6,000 × 7/12)	3,500	
	Rent Expense		3,500

After posting, the two accounts appear as follows:

Prepaid Rent			
2006			
Dec. 31 Adjusting	3,500		
Dec. 31 Balance	3,500		

Rent Expense			
2006		2006	
Aug. 1 Payment	6,000	Dec. 31 Adjusting	3,500
Dec. 31 Balance	2,500		

The balance sheet at the end of 2006 reports Prepaid Rent of $3,500, and the income statement for 2006 reports Rent Expense of $2,500, regardless of whether the business initially debits the prepayment to an asset account or to an expense account.

Unearned (Deferred) Revenues

Unearned (deferred) revenues arise when a business collects cash before earning the revenue. Unearned revenues are liabilities because the business that receives cash owes the other party goods or services to be delivered later.

Unearned (Deferred) Revenue Recorded Initially as a Revenue

Receipt of cash in advance creates a liability, as discussed on page 000. Another way to account for the receipt of cash is to credit a *revenue account* when it receives the cash. If the business then earns all the revenue within the same period, no adjusting entry is needed at the end. However, if the business earns only part of the revenue that period, it must make an adjusting entry.

Suppose on October 1, 2006, a law firm records as service revenue the receipt of $9,000 cash for service revenue to be earned over nine months. The cash receipt entry is:

2006			
Oct. 1	Cash	9,000	
	Service Revenue		9,000

At December 31, the attorney has earned only 3/9 of the $9,000, or $3,000, for the months of October, November, and December. Accordingly, the law firm makes an adjusting entry to transfer the unearned portion (6/9 of $9,000, or $6,000) from the revenue account to a liability, as follows:

2006			
Dec. 31	Service Revenue ($9,000 × 6/9)	6,000	
	Unearned Service Revenue		6,000

The adjusting entry transfers the unearned portion to the liability account because the law firm still owes legal service to the client for January through June of 2007. After posting, the total amount ($9,000) is properly divided between the liability account ($6,000) and the revenue account ($3,000), as follows.

Unearned Service Revenue		
	2006	
	Dec. 31 Adjusting	6,000
	Dec. 31 Balance	6,000

Service Revenue			
2006		2006	
Dec. 31 Adjusting	6,000	Oct. 1 Receipt	9,000
		Dec. 31 Balance	3,000

The attorney's 2006 income statement reports service revenue of $3,000, and the balance sheet reports the unearned revenue of $6,000 as a liability. The result is the same whether the business initially credits a liability account or a revenue account.

Appendix 3A Assignments

Exercises

Recording supplies transactions two ways

E3A-1 At the beginning of the year, supplies of $1,100 were on hand. During the year, Damon Air Conditioning Service paid $5,400 for more supplies. At the end of the year, Damon has $800 of supplies on hand.

Requirements

1. Assume that Damon records supplies by initially debiting an *asset* account. Therefore, place the beginning balance in the Supplies T-account, and record the preceding entries directly in the accounts without using a journal.

2. Assume that Damon records supplies by initially debiting an *expense* account. Therefore, place the beginning balance in the Supplies Expense T-account, and record the preceding entries directly in the accounts without using a journal.

3. Compare the ending account balances under both approaches. Are they the same?

Recording unearned revenues two ways

E3A-2 At the beginning of the year, Avant Garde Advertising owed customers $2,700 for unearned service revenue collected in advance. During the year, Avant Garde received advance cash receipts of $7,000. At year-end, the liability for unearned revenue is $3,700.

Requirements

1. Assume that Avant Garde records unearned revenues by initially crediting a *liability* account. Open T-accounts for Unearned Service Revenue and Service Revenue, and place the beginning balance in Unearned Service Revenue. Journalize the cash collection and adjusting entries, and post their dollar amounts. As references in the T-accounts, denote a balance by *Bal.*, a cash receipt by *CR*, and an adjustment by *Adj.*

2. Assume that Avant Garde records unearned revenues by initially crediting a *revenue* account. Open T-accounts for Unearned Service

Revenue and Service Revenue, and place the beginning balance in Service Revenue. Journalize the cash collection and adjusting entries, and post their dollar amounts. As references in the T-accounts, denote a balance by *Bal.*, a cash receipt by *CR*, and an adjustment by *Adj.*

3. Compare the ending balances in the two accounts.

Problem

Recording prepaid rent and rent revenue collected in advance two ways

1

P3A-1 Smart Pages Pack'n Mail completed the following transactions during 2008:

Nov. 1	Paid $4,500 store rent covering the three-month period ending January 31, 2009.
Dec. 1	Collected $3,200 cash in advance from customers. The service revenue will be earned $800 monthly over the four-month period ending March 31, 2009.

Requirements

1. Journalize these entries by debiting an asset account for Prepaid Rent and by crediting a liability account for Unearned Service Revenue. Explanations are unnecessary.

2. Journalize the related adjustments at December 31, 2008.

3. Post the entries to the ledger accounts, and show their balances at December 31, 2008. Posting references are unnecessary.

4. Repeat requirements 1 through 3. This time, debit Rent Expense for the rent payment and credit Service Revenue for the collection of revenue in advance.

5. Compare the account balances in requirements 3 and 4. They should be equal.

Chapter 3: Demo Doc

Preparation of Adjusting Entries, Adjusted Trial Balance, and Financial Statements

Demo Doc: To make sure you understand this material, work through the following demonstration "demo doc" with detailed comments to help you see the concept within the framework of a worked-through problem.

Learning Objectives 3–5

Cloud Break Consulting has the following information at June 30, 2008:

CLOUD BREAK CONSULTING
Unadjusted Trial Balance
December 31, 2008

			Balance	
	Account Title		Debit	Credit
	Cash		$131,000	
	Accounts receivable		104,000	
	Supplies		4,000	
	Prepaid rent		27,000	
	Land		45,000	
	Building		300,000	
	Accumulated depreciation—building			$155,000
	Accounts payable			159,000
	Unearned service revenue			40,000
	Susan Cloud, capital			152,000
	Susan Cloud, withdrawals		57,000	
	Service revenue			450,000
	Salary expense		255,000	
	Rent expense		25,000	
	Miscellaneous expense		8,000	
	Total		$956,000	$956,000

Cloud must make adjusting entries for the following items:

a. **Supplies on hand at year-end, $1,000.**

b. **Nine months of rent ($27,000) was paid in advance on October 1, 2008. No rent expense has been recorded since that date.**

c. **Depreciation expense has not been recorded on the building for 2008. The building has a useful life of 25 years.**

d. **Employees work Monday through Friday. The five-day weekly payroll is $5,000 and is paid every Friday. December 31, 2008, is a Thursday.**

e. **Service revenue of $15,000 must be accrued.**

f. **A client paid $40,000 in advance for consulting services to be provided evenly from July 1, 2008, through February 28, 2009. None of the revenue from this client has been recorded.**

Requirements

1. Open the ledger T-accounts with their unadjusted balances.

2. Journalize Cloud's adjusting entries at December 31, 2008, and post the entries to the T-accounts.

3. Total all of the T-accounts in the ledger.

4. Write the trial balance on a work sheet, enter the adjusting entries, and prepare an adjusted trial balance.

5. Prepare the income statement, the statement of owner's equity, and the balance sheet. Draw arrows linking the three financial statements.

Demo Doc Solution

Requirement 1

Open the ledger T-accounts with their unadjusted balances.

Part 1	Part 2	Part 3	Part 4	Part 5	Demo Doc Complete

Remember from Chapter 2 that opening a T-account means drawing a blank account that looks like a capital "T" and putting the account title across the top. To help find the accounts later, they are usually organized into assets, liabilities, owner's equity, revenue, and expenses (in that order). If the account has a starting balance, it *must* be put in on the correct side.

Remember that debits are always on the left side of the T-account and credits are always on the right side. This is true for *every* account.

The correct side to enter each account's starting balance is the side of *increase* in the account. This is because we expect all accounts to have a *positive* balance (that is, more increases than decreases).

For assets, an increase is a debit, so we would expect all assets except Accumulated Depreciation, a contra asset, to have a debit balance. For liabilities and owner's equity, an increase is a credit, so we would expect all of these accounts to have a credit balance. By the same reasoning, we expect revenues to have a credit balance and expenses and withdrawals to have a debit balance.

The unadjusted balances to be posted into the T-accounts are simply the amounts from the starting trial balance.

ASSETS

Cash
Bal. 131,000 |

Accounts Receivable
104,000 |

Supplies
4,000 |

Prepaid Rent
Bal. 27,000 |

Land
Bal. 45,000 |

Building
Bal. 300,000 |

Accumulated Depreciation—Building
| 155,000

LIABILITIES

Accounts Payable
| Bal. 159,000

Unearned Service Revenue
| 40,000

OWNER'S EQUITY

Susan Cloud, Capital
| Bal. 152,000

Susan Cloud, Withdrawals
Bal. 57,000 |

REVENUE

Service Revenue
| 450,000

EXPENSES

Salary Expense
255,000 |

Rent Expense
Bal. 25,000 |

Miscellaneous Expense
Bal. 8,000 |

Requirement 2

Journalize Cloud's adjusting entries at December 31, 2008, and post the entries to the T-accounts.

Part 1	**Part 2**	Part 3	Part 4	Part 5	Demo Doc Complete

a. Supplies on hand at year-end, $1,000.

On December 31, the unadjusted balance in supplies was $4,000. However, a count shows that only $1,000 of supplies actually remains on hand. The supplies that are no longer there have been used. When assets/benefits are used, an expense is created.

Cloud will need to make an adjusting journal entry to show the correct amount of supplies on the balance sheet.

Looking at the Supplies T-account:

Supplies			
Bal.	4,000		X
Bal.	1,000		

The supplies have decreased because they have been used up. The amount of the decrease is **X**, and **X** = $4,000 − $1,000 = $3,000.

Supplies Expense of $3,000 must be recorded to show the value of supplies that have been used.

Dec. 31	Supplies Expense ($4,000 − $1,000) (Expense,↑; debit)	3,000	
	Supplies (Asset,↓; credit)		3,000
	To record supplies expense.		

After posting, Supplies and Supplies Expense hold correct ending balances:

ASSETS				EXPENSES		
Supplies				Supplies Expense		
Bal	4,000	a.	3,000	a.	3,000	
Bal.	1,000			Bal.	3,000	

b. Nine months of rent ($27,000) was paid in advance on October 1, 2008. No rent expense has been recorded since that date.

When something is prepaid, such as is common with rent or insurance, it is a *future* benefit (an asset) because the business is now entitled to receive goods or services for the period covered by the prepayment. Once those goods or services are received (in this case, once Cloud has occupied the building being rented), this becomes a *past* benefit and, therefore, an expense.

Cloud prepaid $27,000 for nine months of rent on October 1. This means that Cloud pays $27,000/9 = $3,000 a month for rent. At December 31, Prepaid Rent is adjusted for the amount of the asset that has been used up. Because Cloud has occupied the building being rented for three months, three months of the prepayment have been used. The amount of rent used is $3 \times \$3,000 = \$9,000$. Because that portion of the past benefit (asset) has expired, it becomes an expense (in this case, the adjustment transfers $9,000 from Prepaid Rent to Rent Expense).

This means that Rent Expense must be increased (a debit) and Prepaid Rent (an asset) must be decreased (a credit).

Dec. 31	Rent Expense (Expense,↑; debit)	9,000	
	Prepaid Rent (Asset, ; credit)↓		9,000
	To record rent expense.		

ASSETS				**EXPENSES**		
Prepaid Rent				**Rent Expense**		
Bal.	27,000			Bal.	25,000	
		b.	9,000	b.	9,000	
Bal.	18,000			Bal.	34,000	

c. Depreciation expense has not been recorded on the building for 2008. The building has a useful life of 25 years.

Depreciation expense per year is calculated as:

$$\text{Depreciation expense per year} = \frac{\text{Original cost of asset}}{\text{Useful life of asset (in years)}}$$

The cost principle compels us to keep the original cost of a plant asset in that asset account. Because there is $300,000 in the Building account, we know that this is the original cost of the building. We are told in the question that the building's useful life is 25 years.

$$\text{Depreciation expense per year} = \$300,000/25 \text{ years} = \$12,000 \text{ per year}$$

We will record depreciation of $12,000 in the adjusting journal entry.

The journal entry to record depreciation expense is *always* the same. It is only the *number* (dollar amount) in the entry that changes. There is always an increase to Depreciation Expense (a debit) and an increase to the contra-asset account of Accumulated Depreciation (a credit).

Dec. 31	Depreciation Expense—Building (Expense,↑; debit)	12,000	
	Accumulated Depreciation—Building		
	(Contra Asset,↑; credit)		12,000
	To record depreciation on building.		

ASSETS				EXPENSES	
ASSET		**CONTRA ASSET**			
Building		**Accumulated Depreciation—Building**		**Depreciation Expense—Building**	
Bal.	300,000		Bal. 155,000	c.	12,000
			c. 12,000		
Bal.	300,000		Bal. 167,000	Bal.	12,000

The book value of the building is its original cost (the amount in the Building T-account) minus the accumulated depreciation on the building.

Book value of plant assets:	
Building	$300,000
Less: Accumulated depreciation	(167,000)
Book value of the building	$133,000

d. Employees work Monday through Friday. The weekly payroll is $5,000 and is paid every Friday. December 31, 2008, is a Thursday.

Salary is an accrued expense. That is, it is an *expense* that hasn't been paid yet. Most employers pay their employees *after* the work has been done, so the work is a past benefit. This expense (Salary Expense, in this case) grows until payday.

Cloud's employees are paid $5,000 for five days of work. That means they earn $5,000/5 = $1,000 per day. By the end of the day on Thursday, June 30, they have earned $1,000/day × 4 days = $4,000 of salary.

If the salaries have not been paid, then they are pay*able* (or in other words, they are *owed*) and must be recorded as some kind of payable account. You might be tempted to use Accounts Payable, but this account is usually reserved for *bills* received for things like utilities and inventory purchases. Employees do not typically bill employers for their paychecks. They simply expect to be paid. The payable account for salaries is Salary Payable.

There is an increase to Salary Expense (a debit) and an increase to the liability Salary Payable (a credit) of $4,000.

Dec. 31	Salary Expense (Expense,↑; debit)		4,000	
	Salary Payable (Liability, ↑; credit)			4,000
	To accrue salary expense.			

EXPENSES			LIABILITIES		
Salary Expense			**Salary Payable**		
Bal.	255,000			d.	4,000
d.	4,000				
Bal.	259,000			Bal.	4,000

e. Service revenue of $15,000 must be accrued.

Accrued revenue is another way of saying "we have a receivable" (or receipt in the future). When *accrued* service revenue is recorded, accounts receivable are recorded because your customers received service from the business, but you have not yet received the cash. The business is entitled to these receivables because the revenue has been earned.

Service Revenue must be increased by $15,000 (a credit) and the Accounts Receivable asset must be increased by $15,000 (a debit).

Dec. 31	Accounts Receivable (Asset,↑; debit)	15,000	
	Service Revenue (Revenue,↑; credit)		15,000
	To accrue service revenue.		

ASSETS			REVENUES		
Accounts Receivable			**Service Revenue**		
	104,000				450,000
e.	15,000			e.	15,000
Bal.	119,000			Bal.	465,000

f. A client paid $40,000 in advance for consulting services to be provided evenly from July 1, 2008, through February 28, 2009. None of the revenue from this client has been recorded.

Cloud received cash in advance for work not yet performed for the client. By accepting the cash, Cloud also accepted the obligation to perform that work (or provide a refund if not performed). In accounting, an obligation is a liability. We call this liability "unearned revenue" because it *will* be revenue (after the work is performed) but it is not revenue *yet*.

The $40,000 collected in advance is still in the Unearned Revenue account. However, some of the revenue has been earned as of December 31. Six months of the earnings period have passed (July 1 through December 31), so six months worth of the revenue has been earned.

The entire revenue earnings period is eight months (July 1 through the following February), so the revenue earned per month is $40,000/8 = $5,000. The six months of revenue that have been earned are 6 × $5,000 = $30,000.

Unearned Service Revenue, a liability, must be decreased by $30,000 (a debit). Because that portion of the revenue is now earned, it can be recorded as service revenue. Therefore, Service Revenue also increases by $30,000 (a credit).

Dec. 31	Unearned Service Revenue (Liability, ↓; debit)	30,000	
	Service Revenue (Revenue,↑; credit)		30,000
	To record service revenue that was collected in advance.		

Essentially, the $30,000 has been shifted from "unearned" to "earned" revenue.

LIABILITIES			REVENUES		
Unearned Service Revenue			**Service Revenue**		
f.	30,000	Bal.	40,000	Bal.	450,000
				e.	15,000
				f.	30,000
		Bal.	10,000	Bal.	495,000

Now we will summarize all of the adjusting journal entries:

Ref.	Date	Accounts and Explanation	Debit	Credit
	2008			
a.	Dec. 31	Supplies Expense ($4,000 – $3,000)	1,000	
		Supplies		1,000
		To record supplies used.		
b.	31	Rent Expense	9,000	
		Prepaid Rent		9,000
		To record rent expense.		
c.	31	Depreciation Expense—Building	12,000	
		Accumulated Depreciation—Building		12,000
		To record depreciation expense on building.		
d.	31	Salary Expense	4,000	
		Salary Payable		4,000
		To accrue salary expense.		
e.	31	Accounts Receivable	15,000	
		Service Revenue		15,000
		To accrue service revenue.		
f.	31	Unearned Service Revenue	30,000	
		Service Revenue		30,000
		To record service revenue that was collected in advance.		

Requirement 3

Total all of the T-accounts in the ledger.

| Part 1 | Part 2 | **Part 3** | Part 4 | Part 5 | Demo Doc Complete |

After posting all of these entries and totaling all of the T-accounts, we have:

ASSETS

Cash

Bal. 131,000	

Accounts Receivable

104,000	
e. 15,000	
Bal. 119,000	

Supplies

4,000	a. 3,000
Bal. 1,000	

Prepaid Rent

Bal. 27,000	
	b. 9,000
Bal. 18,000	

Land

Bal. 45,000	

Building

Bal. 300,000	

Accumulated Depreciation—Building

	155,000
	c. 12,000
	Bal. 167,000

LIABILITIES

Accounts Payable

	Bal. 159,000

Salary Payable

	d. 4,000
	Bal. 4,000

Unearned Service Revenue

f. 30,000	40,000
	Bal. 10,000

OWNER'S EQUITY

Susan Cloud, Capital

	Bal. 152,000

Susan Cloud, Withdrawals

Bal. 57,000	

REVENUE

Service Revenue

	450,000
	e. 15,000
	f. 30,000
	Bal. 495,000

EXPENSES

Salary Expense

255,000	
d. 4,000	
Bal. 259,000	

Supplies Expense

a. 3,000	
Bal. 3,000	

Rent Expense

Bal. 25,000	
b. 9,000	
Bal. 34,000	

Depreciation Expense—Building

c. 12,000	
Bal. 12,000	

Miscellaneous Expense

Bal. 8,000	

Requirement 4

Write the trial balance on a work sheet, enter the adjusting entries, and prepare an adjusted trial balance.

| Part 1 | Part 2 | Part 3 | **Part 4** | Part 5 | Demo Doc Complete |

First, we must copy the account titles and trial balance amounts directly from the trial balance (shown at the beginning of the question) into the Trial Balance section (columns). Place the amounts in the correct debit or credit column.

Next, we must record the adjusting journal entries in the correct debit or credit columns of the Adjustments section (columns) of the work sheet. Each entry should include a letter identifying the adjusting entry recorded.

Now calculate the new balances for each account by adding the debits and credits across. These should be the same balances that you calculated for the T-accounts in Requirement 3. Place these amounts into the Adjusted Trial Balance columns to give the adjusted account balances.

CLOUD BREAK CONSULTING
Work Sheet
December 31, 2008

Account Title	Trial Balance Debit	Trial Balance Credit	Adjustments Debit	Adjustments Credit	Adjusted Trial Balance Debit	Adjusted Trial Balance Credit
Cash	131,000				131,000	
Accounts receivable	104,000		(e)15,000		119,000	
Supplies	4,000			(a) 3,000	1,000	
Prepaid rent	27,000			(b) 9,000	18,000	
Land	45,000				45,000	
Building	300,000				300,000	
Accumulated depreciation—building		155,000		(c) 12,000		167,000
Accounts payable		159,000				159,000
Salary payable				(d) 4,000		4,000
Unearned service revenue		40,000	(f) 30,000			10,000
Susan Cloud, capital		152,000				152,000
Susan Cloud, withdrawals	57,000				57,000	
Service revenue		450,000		(e) 15,000		
				(f) 30,000		495,000
Salary expense	255,000		(d) 4,000		259,000	
Supplies expense			(a) 3,000		3,000	
Rent expense	25,000		(b) 9,000		34,000	
Depreciation expense—building			(c)12,000		12,000	
Miscellaneous expense	8,000				8,000	
Totals	956,000	956,000	73,000	73,000	987,000	987,000

You should be sure that the debit and credit columns equal before moving on to the next section.

Requirement 5

Prepare the income statement, the statement of owner's equity, and the balance sheet. Draw arrows linking the three financial statements.

Part 1	Part 2	Part 3	Part 4	**Part 5**	Demo Doc Complete

CLOUD BREAK CONSULTING
Income Statement
Year Ended December 31, 2008

Revenue:		
Service revenue		$495,000
Expenses:		
Salary expense	$259,000	
Rent expense	34,000	
Depreciation expense—building	12,000	
Supplies expense	3,000	
Miscellaneous expense	8,000	
Total expenses		316,000
Net income		$179,000

CLOUD BREAK CONSULTING
Statement of Owner's Equity
Year Ended December 31, 2008

Susan Cloud, capital, January 1, 2008	$152,000
Add: Net income	179,000
	331,000
Less: Withdrawals	(57,000)
Susan Cloud, capital, December 31, 2008	$274,000

CLOUD BREAK CONSULTING
Balance Sheet
December 31, 2008

Assets			Liabilities	
Cash		$131,000	Accounts payable	$159,000
Accounts receivable		119,000	Salary payable	4,000
Supplies		1,000	Unearned service revenue	10,000
Prepaid rent		18,000	Total liabilities	173,000
Land		45,000		
Building	$300,000		**Owner's Equity**	
Less: Accumulated			Susan Cloud, capital	274,000
depreciation	(167,000)	133,000	Total liabilities and	
Total assets		$447,000	owner's equity	$447,000

Part 1	Part 2	Part 3	Part 4	Part 5	**Demo Doc Complete**

4 Completing the Accounting Cycle

Learning Objectives

1 Prepare an accounting work sheet

2 Use the work sheet

3 Close the revenue, expense, and withdrawal accounts

4 Classify assets and liabilities as current or long-term

5 Use the current ratio and the debt ratio to evaluate a company

What do football, baseball, basketball, and accounting have in common? They all start the first period with a score of zero.

Haig Sherman and Julie DeFilippo have operated Sherman Lawn Service and DeFilippo Catering, respectively, for a year. They took in revenue, incurred expenses, and earned net income during year 1. It's time to look ahead to the next period.

Should Sherman Lawn Service start year 2 with the net income that the business earned last year? No, Sherman must start from zero in order to measure its business performance in year 2. That requires Sherman to set his accounting scoreboard back to zero.

This process is called closing the books, and it's the last step in the accounting cycle. The **accounting cycle** is the process by which companies produce their financial statements. ■

Chapter 4 completes the accounting cycle by showing how to close the books. It begins with the adjusted trial balance, which you learned in Chapter 3. Here we extend to a more complete document called the accounting work sheet. Work sheets help by summarizing lots of data.

The Accounting Cycle

The accounting cycle starts with the beginning asset, liability, and owner's equity account balances left over from the preceding period. Exhibit 4-1 outlines the complete accounting cycle of Cookie Lapp Travel Design and every other business. Start with item **1** and move clockwise.

EXHIBIT 4-1   **The Accounting Cycle**

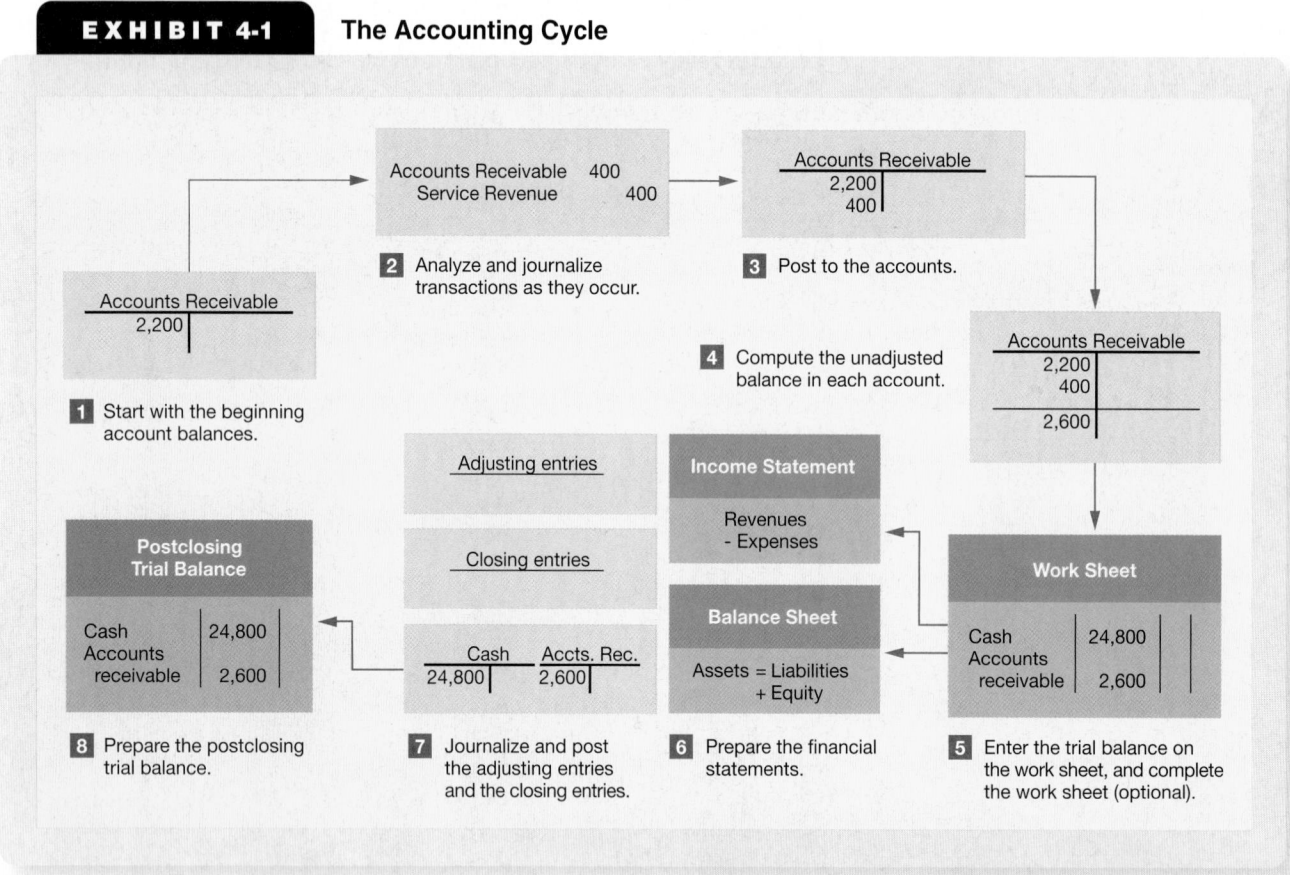

Accounting takes place at two different times:

- During the period—Journalizing transactions
  Posting to the accounts
- End of the period—Adjusting the accounts
  Closing the accounts
  Preparing the financial statements

The end-of-period work also readies the accounts for the next period. In Chapters 3 and 4, we cover the end-of-period accounting for a service business such as Sherman Lawn Service and Cookie Lapp Travel Design. Chapter 5 shows how a merchandising entity such as Wal-Mart or McDonald's adjusts and closes its books.

The Work Sheet

1 Prepare an accounting work sheet

Accountants often use a **work sheet**—a document with several columns—to summarize data for the financial statements. The work sheet is neither a journal, a ledger, nor a financial statement. It is merely a summary device that helps identify the accounts needing adjustment. An Excel spreadsheet works well for an accounting work sheet.

Exhibits 4-2 through 4-6 illustrate the development of a typical work sheet for Cookie Lapp Travel Design. The heading at the top displays the:

- Name of the business (Cookie Lapp Travel Design)
- Title of the document (Accounting Work Sheet)
- Period covered by the work sheet (Month ended April 30, 2008)

A step-by-step description of the work sheet follows, with all amounts given in Exhibits 4-2 through 4-6. Simply turn the acetate pages to follow from exhibit to exhibit.

Exhibit 4-2

1. **Enter the account titles and their unadjusted balances in the Trial Balance columns of the work sheet, and total the amounts.** The data come from the ledger accounts before any adjustments. Accounts are listed in proper order (Cash first, Accounts Receivable second, and so on). Total debits must equal total credits.

   An account with a zero balance (for example, Depreciation Expense) needs to be adjusted.

Exhibit 4-3

2. **Enter the adjusting entries in the Adjustments columns, and total the amounts.** Exhibit 4-3 includes the April adjusting entries that we made in Chapter 3.

   We can identify the accounts needing adjustment from the trial balance. Cash needs no adjustment because all cash transactions are recorded during the period. Consequently, Cash's balance is up-to-date.

   Accounts Receivable comes next. Has Cookie Lapp earned any revenue that she hasn't recorded? The answer is yes. At April 30, Lapp has earned $400 and will receive the cash later. For service revenue earned but not collected, Lapp debits Accounts Receivable and credits Service Revenue on the work sheet. A letter links the debit and the credit of each adjustment.

   By moving down the trial balance, Lapp identifies other accounts needing adjustment, such as Supplies. The business has used supplies during April, so Lapp debits Supplies Expense and credits Supplies. The other adjustments are analyzed and entered on the work sheet as we did in Chapter 3. After the adjustments are entered on the work sheet, the amount columns are totaled. Total debits must equal total credits.

Exhibit 4-4

3. **Compute each account's adjusted balance by combining the trial balance and adjustment figures. Enter each account's adjusted amount in the Adjusted Trial Balance columns.** Exhibit 4-4 shows the work sheet with the adjusted trial balance completed. For example, Cash is up-to-date, so it receives no adjustment. Accounts Receivable's adjusted balance of $2,600 is computed by adding the unadjusted amount of $2,200 to the $400 adjustment. For Supplies we subtract the $100 credit adjustment from the unadjusted balance of $700. An account may receive more than one adjustment, as for Service Revenue. On the adjusted trial balance, total debits must equal total credits.

Exhibit 4-5

4. **Extend (that is, copy) the asset, liability, and owner's equity amounts from the Adjusted Trial Balance to the Balance Sheet columns. Copy the revenue and expense amounts to the Income Statement columns. Total the statement columns.** Each account's balance should appear in only one column, as shown in Exhibit 4-5.

EXHIBIT 4-2 Trial Balance

COOKIE LAPP TRAVEL DESIGN
Accounting Work Sheet
Month Ended April 30, 2008

Account Title	Trial Balance Dr.	Trial Balance Cr.	Adjustments Dr.	Adjustments Cr.	Adjusted Trial Balance Dr.	Adjusted Trial Balance Cr.	Income Statement Dr.	Income Statement Cr.	Balance Sheet Dr.	Balance Sheet Cr.
Cash	24,800									
Accounts receivable	2,200									
Supplies	700									
Prepaid rent	3,000									
Furniture	18,000									
Accumulated depreciation										
Accounts payable		13,000								
Salary payable										
Unearned service revenue		600								
Cookie Lapp, capital		32,600								
Cookie Lapp, withdrawals	3,200									
Service revenue		7,000								
Rent expense										
Salary expense	900									
Supplies expense										
Depreciation expense										
Utilities expense	400									
	53,200	53,200								
Net income										

Write the account titles and their unadjusted balances in the Trial Balance columns of the work sheet. Total the amounts.

First, total the *income statement columns,* as follows:

Income Statement

■ Debits (Dr.) ⟶ Total expenses = $3,600 ⎱ Difference = $4,000, a net income
■ Credits (Cr.) ⟶ Total revenues = $7,600 ⎰ because total credits (revenues) exceed total debits (expenses)

Then total the *balance sheet* columns:

Balance Sheet

■ Debits (Dr.) ⟶ Total assets and withdrawals   = $51,200 ⎫ Difference = $4,000,
■ Credits (Cr.) ⟶ Total liabilities, owner's equity, ⎬ a net income because
    and accumulated depreciation = $47,200 ⎭ total debits are greater

Exhibit 4-6

5. **On the income statement, compute net income or net loss as total revenues minus total expenses. Enter net income as the balancing amount on the income statement. Also enter net income as the balancing amount on the balance sheet. Then total the financial statement columns.** Exhibit 4-6 presents the completed work sheet.

Revenue (total **credits** on the income statement)...............................	$7,600
Less: Expenses (total **debits** on the income statement)	(3,600)
Net income...	$4,000

Net Income

Net income of $4,000 is entered as a "plug figure" in the debit column of the income statement. This brings total debits up to total credits on the income statement. Net income is also entered as a "plug figure" in the credit column of the balance sheet. Net income brings the balance sheet into balance.

Net Loss

If expenses exceed revenues, the result is a net loss. In that event, print Net Loss on the work sheet. The net loss amount should be entered in the *credit* column of the income statement (to balance out) and in the *debit* column of the balance sheet (to balance out). After completion, total debits should equal total credits in the Income Statement columns and in the Balance Sheet columns.

Now practice what you've learned by working Summary Problem 1.

Summary Problem 1

The trial balance of Clay Employment Services at December 31, 2009, follows.

CLAY EMPLOYMENT SERVICES
Trial Balance
December 31, 2009

Account Title	Balance Debit	Balance Credit
Cash	$ 6,000	
Accounts receivable	5,000	
Supplies	1,000	
Furniture	10,000	
Accumulated depreciation—furniture		$ 4,000
Building	50,000	
Accumulated depreciation—building		30,000
Accounts payable		2,000
Salary payable		
Unearned service revenue		8,000
Jay Clay, capital		12,000
Jay Clay, withdrawals	25,000	
Service revenue		60,000
Salary expense	16,000	
Supplies expense		
Depreciation expense—furniture		
Depreciation expense—building		
Miscellaneous expense	3,000	
Total	$116,000	$116,000

Data needed for the adjusting entries include:

   a. Supplies on hand at year-end, $200.

   b. Depreciation on furniture, $2,000.

   c. Depreciation on building, $1,000.

   d. Salaries owed but not yet paid, $500.

   e. Accrued service revenue, $1,300.

   f. $3,000 of the unearned service revenue was earned during 2009.

Requirements

Prepare the accounting work sheet of Clay Employment Services for the year ended December 31, 2009. Key each adjusting entry by the letter corresponding to the data given.

Solution

CLAY EMPLOYMENT SERVICES
Work Sheet
Year Ended December 31, 2009

Account Title	Trial Balance Dr.	Trial Balance Cr.	Adjustments Dr.	Adjustments Cr.	Adjusted Trial Balance Dr.	Adjusted Trial Balance Cr.	Income Statement Dr.	Income Statement Cr.	Balance Sheet Dr.	Balance Sheet Cr.
Cash	6,000				6,000				6,000	
Accounts receivable	5,000		(e) 1,300		6,300				6,300	
Supplies	1,000			(a) 800	200				200	
Furniture	10,000				10,000				10,000	
Accumulated depreciation— furniture		4,000		(b) 2,000		6,000				6,000
Building	50,000				50,000				50,000	
Accumulated depreciation—building		30,000		(c) 1,000		31,000				31,000
Accounts payable		2,000				2,000				2,000
Salary payable				(d) 500		500				500
Unearned service revenue		8,000	(f) 3,000			5,000				5,000
Jay Clay, capital		12,000				12,000				12,000
Jay Clay, withdrawals	25,000				25,000				25,000	
Service revenue		60,000		(e) 1,300 (f) 3,000		64,300		64,300		
Salary expense	16,000		(d) 500		16,500		16,500			
Supplies expense			(a) 800		800		800			
Depreciation expense—furniture			(b) 2,000		2,000		2,000			
Depreciation expense—building			(c) 1,000		1,000		1,000			
Miscellaneous expense	3,000				3,000		3,000			
	116,000	116,000	8,600	8,600	120,800	120,800	23,300	64,300	97,500	56,500
Net income							41,000			41,000
							64,300	64,300	97,500	97,500

Completing the Accounting Cycle

2 Use the work sheet

The work sheet helps accountants prepare the financial statements, make the adjusting entries, and close the accounts. First, let's prepare the financial statements. We return to the running example of Cookie Lapp Travel Design, whose financial statements are given in Exhibit 4-7.

EXHIBIT 4-7   **April Financial Statements of Cookie Lapp Travel Design**

COOKIE LAPP TRAVEL DESIGN
Income Statement
Month Ended April 30, 2008

Revenue:		
Service revenue		$7,600
Expenses:		
Salary expense	$1,800	
Rent expense	1,000	
Utilities expense	400	
Depreciation expense	300	
Supplies expense	100	
Total expensees		3,600
Net income		$4,000

COOKIE LAPP TRAVEL DESIGN
Statement of Owner's Equity
Month Ended April 30, 2008

Cookie Lapp, capital, April 1, 2008	$32,600
Add: Net income	4,000
	36,600
Less: Withdrawals	(3,200)
Cookie Lapp, capital, April 30, 2008	$33,400

COOKIE LAPP TRAVEL DESIGN
Balance Sheet
April 30, 2008

Assets			Liabilities	
Cash		$24,800	Accounts payable	$13,000
Accounts receivable		2,600	Salary payable	900
Supplies		600	Unearned service revenue	400
Prepaid rent		2,000	Total liabilities	14,300
Furniture	$18,000			
Less: Accumulated			**Owner's Equity**	
depreciation	(300)	17,700	Cookie Lapp, capital	33,400
			Total liabilities and	
Total assets		$47,700	owner's equity	$47,700

Preparing the Financial Statements

The work sheet shows the amount of net income or net loss for the period, but we still must prepare the financial statements. Exhibit 4-7 shows the April financial statements for Cookie Lapp Travel Design (based on data from the work sheet in Exhibit 4-6). We can prepare Lapp's financial statements immediately after completing the work sheet.

Recording the Adjusting Entries

Adjusting the accounts requires journalizing entries and posting to the accounts. The adjustments should be journalized after they are entered on the work sheet. Panel A of Exhibit 4-8 repeats Cookie Lapp's adjusting entries that we journalized in Chapter 3. Panel B shows the revenue and the expense accounts after all adjustments have been posted. Only the revenue and expense accounts are presented here to focus on the closing process. *Adj.* denotes an amount posted from an adjusting entry.

| EXHIBIT 4-8 | Journalizing and Posting the Adjusting Entries |

PANEL A—Journalizing:

		Adjusting Entries		
Apr. 30	Accounts Receivable		400	
	Service Revenue			400
30	Supplies Expense		100	
	Supplies			100
30	Rent Expense		1,000	
	Prepaid Rent			1,000
30	Depreciation Expense		300	
	Accumulated Depreciation			300
30	Salary Expense		900	
	Salary Payable			900
30	Unearned Service Revenue		200	
	Service Revenue			200

PANEL B—Posting the Adjustments to the Revenue and Expense Accounts:

REVENUE

Service Revenue
	7,000
Adj.	400
Adj.	200
Bal.	7,600

EXPENSES

Rent Expense
| Adj. 1,000 | |
| Bal. 1,000 | |

Salary Expense
	900
Adj.	900
Bal. 1,800	

Supplies Expense
| Adj. 100 | |
| Bal. 100 | |

Depreciation Expense
| Adj. 300 | |
| Bal. 300 | |

Utilities Expense
| 400 | |
| Bal. 400 | |

Accountants can use the work sheet to prepare monthly or quarterly statements without journalizing and posting the adjusting entries. Many companies journalize and post the adjusting entries (as in Exhibit 4-8) only at the end of the year.

Now we are ready to move to the last step—closing the accounts.

Closing the Accounts

3 Close the revenue, expense, and withdrawal accounts

Closing the accounts occurs at the end of the period. Closing gets the accounts ready for the next period and consists of journalizing and posting the closing entries. The closing process zeroes out all the revenues and all the expenses in order to measure each period's net income separately from all other periods.

Recall that the income statement reports net income for a specific period. For example, Cookie Lapp's net income for 2008 relates exclusively to 2008. At December 31, 2008, Lapp closes her revenue and expense accounts for the year. For this reason, revenues and expenses are called **temporary accounts**. For example, Lapp's balance of Service Revenue at April 30, 2008, is $7,600. This balance relates exclusively to April and must be zeroed out before Lapp records revenue for May.

The owner's Withdrawal account is also temporary because it measures the owner's withdrawals for only one period. The Withdrawals account is also closed at the end of the period.

To better understand the closing process, contrast the temporary accounts with the **permanent accounts**—the assets, liabilities, and owner capital. These accounts are *not* closed at the end of the period because their balances are not used to measure income.

Consider Cash, Accounts Receivable, Accounts Payable, and Cookie Lapp, Capital. These accounts carry over to the next period. For example, the Cash balance at December 31, 2008, becomes the beginning balance for 2009. Accounts Receivable at December 31, 2008, becomes the beginning balance for 2009. The same is true for all the other assets, all the liabilities, and the owner's capital account.

Closing entries transfer the revenue, expense, and owner withdrawal balances to the capital account.

As an intermediate step the revenues and the expenses are transferred first to an account titled **Income Summary**. This temporary account collects the sum of all the expenses (a debit) and the sum of all the revenues (a credit). The Income Summary account is like a "holding tank." Its balance is then transferred (closed) to capital. Exhibit 4-9 summarizes the closing process.

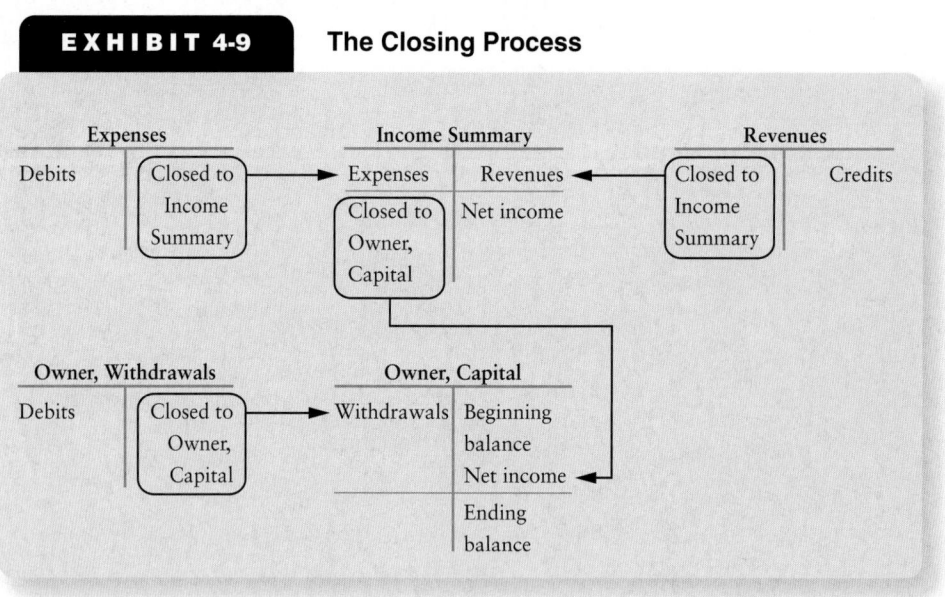

EXHIBIT 4-9   **The Closing Process**

Start with Revenues at the far right and Expenses at the left. Then work toward the middle and down. Owner, Capital is the final account in the closing process.

Closing a Net Income

The steps in closing the books follow for a net income (the circled numbers are keyed to Exhibit 4-10).

1 Debit each *revenue* account for the amount of its credit balance. Credit Income Summary for the total of the revenues. This closing entry transfers total revenues to the *credit* side of Income Summary.

EXHIBIT 4-10	Journalizing and Posting the Closing Entries

PANEL A—Journalizing:

			Closing Entries		
1	Apr. 30	Service Revenue		7,600	
		Income Summary			7,600
2	30	Income Summary		3,600	
		Rent Expense			1,000
		Salary Expense			1,800
		Supplies Expense			100
		Depreciation Expense			300
		Utilities Expense			400
3	30	Income Summary ($7,600– $3,600)		4,000	
		Cookie Lapp, Capital			4,000
4	30	Cookie Lapp, Capital		3,200	
		Cookie Lapp, Withdrawals			3,200

PANEL B—Posting:

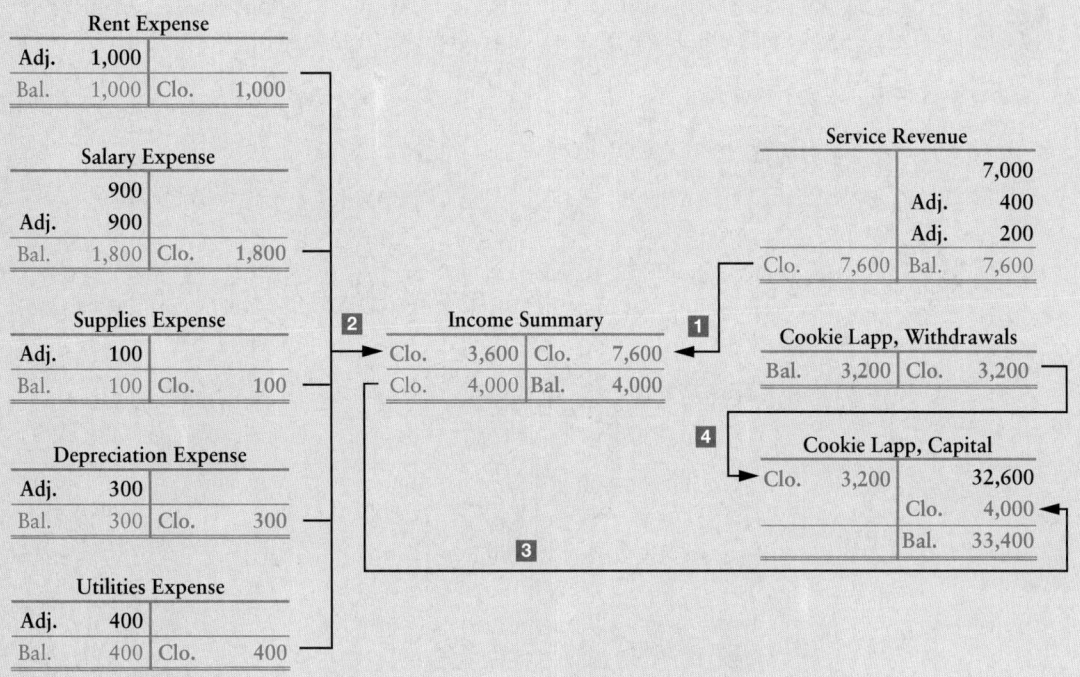

Adj. = Amount posted from an adjusting entry

Clo. = Amount posted from a closing entry

Bal. = Balance

2 Credit each *expense* account for the amount of its debit balance. Debit Income Summary for the total of the expenses. This closing entry transfers total expenses to the *debit* side of Income Summary.

3 The Income Summary account now holds the net income of the period, but only for a moment. To close net income, we debit Income Summary for the amount of its *credit balance*, and credit the Capital account. This closing entry transfers net income to the owner's Capital account.

4 Credit the *Withdrawals* account for the amount of its debit balance. Debit the owner's Capital account. This entry transfers the owner's withdrawals to the *debit* side of the Capital account.

These steps are best illustrated with an example. Suppose Cookie Lapp closes the books at the end of April. Exhibit 4-10 shows the complete closing process for Lapp's travel agency. Panel A gives the closing entries, and Panel B shows the accounts after posting.

After the closing entries, Cookie Lapp, Capital ends with a balance of $33,400. Trace this balance to the statement of owner's equity and then to the balance sheet in Exhibit 4-7.

Closing a Net Loss

What would the closing entries be if Lapp's travel agency had suffered a net *loss* during April? Suppose expenses totaled $8,100 and revenues remained $7,600. In that case, the business suffered a net loss of $500 for April. The loss shows up as a debit balance in Income Summary, as follows:

Income Summary			
Expenses	8,100	Revenue	7,600
Net loss	500		

Closing entry **3** would then credit Income Summary for $500 and debit Cookie Lapp, Capital, as follows:

3	Apr. 30	Cookie Lapp, Capital		500	
		Income Summary			500

Then Income Summary is closed out and Cookie Lapp, Capital has its ending balance, as follows:

Income Summary					Cookie Lapp, Capital			
Expenses	8,100	Revenue	7,600		Clo.	500		32,600
Net loss	500	Clo.	500				Bal.	32,100

Finally, the Withdrawals balance would be closed to Capital, as before. Double underlines mean the account has a zero balance.

Postclosing Trial Balance

The accounting cycle can end with a **postclosing trial balance** (Exhibit 4-11). This optional step lists the accounts and their adjusted balances after closing.

Only assets, liabilities, and capital appear on the postclosing trial balance. No temporary accounts—revenues, expenses, or withdrawals—are included because they've been closed. The ledger is up-to-date and ready for the next period.

EXHIBIT 4-11   Postclosing Trial Balance

COOKIE LAPP TRAVEL DESIGN
Postclosing Trial Balance
April 30, 2008

Cash	$24,800	
Accounts receivable	2,600	
Supplies	600	
Prepaid rent	2,000	
Furniture	18,000	
Accumulated depreciation		$ 300
Accounts payable		13,000
Salary payable		900
Unearned service revenue		400
Cookie Lapp, capital		33,400
Total	$48,000	$48,000

Reversing entries are special journal entries that key off the adjustments at the end of the period. Reversing entries ease the accounting of the next period. They are optional, and we cover them in Appendix 4A at the end of this chapter.

Classifying Assets and Liabilities

 Classify assets and liabilities as current or long-term

Assets and liabilities are classified as either *current* or *long-term* to show their relative liquidity. **Liquidity** measures closeness to cash, and cash is the most liquid asset. Accounts receivable are relatively liquid because receivables are collected quickly. Supplies are less liquid, and furniture and buildings are even less liquid because of their long lives. A classified balance sheet lists assets in the order of their liquidity.

Assets
Current Assets

Current assets will be converted to cash, sold, or used up during the next 12 months or within the business's operating cycle if the cycle is longer than a year. The **operating cycle** is the time span when:

1. Cash is used to acquire goods and services.

2. These goods and services are sold to customers.

3. The business collects cash from customers.

For most businesses the operating cycle is a few months. Cash, Accounts Receivable, Supplies, and Prepaid Expenses are current assets. Merchandising entities such as

Home Depot, Sears, and Coca-Cola have another current asset: inventory. Inventory shows the cost of the goods the company holds for sale to customers.

Long-Term Assets

Long-term assets are all the assets other than current assets. One category of long-term assets is **plant assets** (also called **fixed assets** or property, plant, and equipment). Land, Buildings, Furniture, and Equipment are plant assets. Of these, Cookie Lapp Travel Design has only Furniture.

Other categories of long-term assets include Long-Term Investments and Other Assets (a catchall category). We discuss these categories in later chapters.

Liabilities

Owners need to know when they must pay each liability. Liabilities that are payable immediately create pressure, so the balance sheet lists liabilities in the order they must be paid. Balance sheets report two liability categories: *current liabilities* and *long-term liabilities.*

Current Liabilities

Current liabilities must be paid with cash or with goods and services within one year or within the entity's operating cycle if the cycle is longer than a year. Accounts Payable, Notes Payable due within one year, Salary Payable, Interest Payable, and Unearned Revenue are current liabilities.

Long-Term Liabilities

All liabilities that are not current are classified as **long-term liabilities.** Many notes payable are long-term. Some notes are payable in installments, with the first installment due within one year, the second due the second year, and so on. The first installment is a current liability, and the remaining amounts are long-term. A $100,000 note payable to be paid $10,000 per year over 10 years would include:

- A current liability of $10,000 for next year's payment, and
- A long-term liability of $90,000.

The Classified Balance Sheet

Thus far we have presented the *unclassified* balance sheet of Cookie Lapp Travel Design. We are now ready for the balance sheet that's actually used in practice—called a classified balance sheet. Exhibit 4-12 presents Cookie Lapp's classified balance sheet.

Cookie Lapp classifies each asset and each liability as current or long-term. She could have labeled plant assets as *fixed assets.*

Balance Sheet Forms

The balance sheet of Cookie Lapp Travel Design in Exhibit 4-13 lists the assets at the top and the liabilities and owner equity below. This arrangement is known as the *report form.* Lapp's balance sheet in Exhibit 4-12 lists the assets at the left and the liabilities and the equity at the right. That arrangement is known as the *account form.* Either form is acceptable; the report form is more popular.

EXHIBIT 4-12   **Classified Balance Sheet in** Account Form

COOKIE LAPP TRAVEL DESIGN
Balance Sheet
April 30, 2008

Assets			Liabilities	
Current assets:			Current liabilities:	
Cash		$24,800	Accounts payable	$13,000
Accounts receivable		2,600	Salary payable	900
Supplies		600	Unearned service revenue	400
Prepaid rent		2,000	Total current liabilities	14,300
Total current assets		30,000	Long-term liabilities (None)	0
Plant assets:			Total liabilities	14,300
Furniture	$18,000			
Less: Accumulated			**Owner's Equity**	
depreciation	(300)	17,700	Cookie Lapp, capital	33,400
			Total liabilities and	
Total assets		$47,700	owner's equity	$47,700

EXHIBIT 4-13   **Classified Balance Sheet in** Report Form

COOKIE LAPP TRAVEL DESIGN
Balance Sheet
April 30, 2008

Assets		
Current assets:		
Cash		$24,800
Accounts receivable		2,600
Supplies		600
Prepaid rent		2,000
Total current assets		30,000
Plant assets:		
Furniture	$18,000	
Less: Accumulated		
depreciation	(300)	17,700
Total assets		$47,700
Liabilities		
Current liabilities:		
Accounts payable		$13,000
Salary payable		900
Unearned service revenue		400
Total current liabilities		14,300
Long-term liabilities (None)		0
Owner's Equity		
Cookie Lapp, capital		33,400
Total liabilities and owner's equity		47,700

Accounting Ratios

5 Use the current ratio and the debt ratio to evaluate a company

Accounting is designed to provide information for decision making by business owners, managers, and lenders. A bank considering lending money to Cookie Lapp must predict whether she can repay the loan. If Lapp already has a lot of debt, repayment is less certain than if she doesn't owe much money. To measure Cookie Lapp's financial position, decision makers use ratios that they compute from the company's financial statements. Two of the most widely used decision aids in business are the current ratio and the debt ratio.

Current Ratio

The **current ratio** measures a company's ability to pay its current liabilities. This ratio is computed as follows:

$$\text{Current ratio} = \frac{\text{Total current assets}}{\text{Total current liabilities}}$$

A company prefers to have a high current ratio because that means it has plenty of current assets to pay current liabilities. An increasing current ratio indicates improvement in ability to pay current debts. A decreasing current ratio signals deterioration in the ability to pay current liabilities.

A RULE OF THUMB   A strong current ratio is 1.50, which indicates that the company has $1.50 in current assets for every $1.00 in current liabilities. A current ratio of 1.00 is considered low and somewhat risky.

Debt Ratio

A second decision aid is the **debt ratio**, which measures overall ability to pay debts. The debt ratio is computed as follows:

$$\text{Debt ratio} = \frac{\text{Total liabilities}}{\text{Total assets}}$$

The debt ratio indicates the proportion of a company's assets that are financed with debt. A *low* debt ratio is safer than a high debt ratio. Why? Because a company with low liabilities has low required payments. This company is unlikely to get into financial difficulty.

A RULE OF THUMB   A debt ratio below 0.60, or 60%, is considered safe for most businesses. A debt ratio above 0.80, or 80%, borders on high risk.

Now study the Decision Guidelines feature, which summarizes what you have learned in this chapter.

Decision Guidelines

Suppose you own Sherman Lawn Service, DeFilippo Catering, or Cookie Lapp Travel Design. How can you measure the success of your business? The Decision

Guidelines describe the accounting process you will use to provide the information for your decisions.

Decision	Guidelines
What document summarizes the effects of all the entity's transactions and adjustments throughout the period?	Accountant's *work sheet* with columns for • Trial balance • Adjustments • Adjusted trial balance • Income statement • Balance sheet
What is the last *major* step in the accounting cycle?	*Closing entries for the temporary accounts:* • Revenues } • Expenses } Income statement accounts • Owner's withdrawals
Why close out the revenues, expenses, and owner withdrawals?	Because these *temporary accounts* have balances that relate only to one accounting period and *do not* carry over to the next period.
Which accounts do *not* get closed out?	*Permanent (balance sheet) accounts:* • Assets • Liabilities • Owner's capital The balances of these accounts *do* carry over to the next period.
How do businesses classify their assets and liabilities for reporting on the balance sheet?	*Current* (within one year or the entity's operating cycle if longer than a year), or *Long-term* (not current)
How do Haig Sherman, Julie DeFilippo, and Cookie Lapp evaluate their companies?	There are many ways, such as the company's net income (or net loss) on the income statement and the trend of net income from year to year. Another way to evaluate a company is based on the company's *financial ratios*. Two key ratios:

$$\text{Current ratio} = \frac{\text{Total current assets}}{\text{Total current liabilities}}$$

The *current ratio* measures the ability to pay current liabilities with current assets.

$$\text{Debt ratio} = \frac{\text{Total liabilities}}{\text{Total assets}}$$

The *debt ratio* measures the overall ability to pay liabilities. The debt ratio shows the proportion of the entity's assets that are financed with debt.

Summary Problem 2

Refer to the data in Problem 1 (Clay Employment Services, page 200–201).

Requirements

1. Journalize and post the adjusting entries. (Before posting to the accounts, enter into each account its balance as shown in the trial balance. For example, enter the $5,000 balance in the Accounts Receivable account before posting its adjusting entry.) Key adjusting entries by *letter,* as shown in the work sheet solution to Summary Problem 1. You can take the adjusting entries straight from the work sheet on page 201.

2. Journalize and post the closing entries. (Each account should carry its balance as shown in the adjusted trial balance.) To distinguish closing entries from adjusting entries, key the closing entries by *number.* Draw arrows to illustrate the flow of data, as shown in Exhibit 4-10. Indicate the balance of the Capital account after the closing entries are posted.

3. Prepare the income statement for the year ended December 31, 2009. List Miscellaneous Expense last among the expenses, a common practice.

4. Prepare the statement of owner's equity for the year ended December 31, 2009. Draw an arrow linking the income statement to the statement of owner's equity.

5. Prepare the classified balance sheet at December 31, 2009. Use the report form. All liabilities are current. Draw an arrow linking the statement of owner's equity to the balance sheet.

Solution

Requirement 1

		Adjusting Entries		
a.	Dec. 31	Supplies Expense	800	
		Supplies		800
b.	31	Depreciation Expense—Furniture	2,000	
		Accumulated Depreciation—Furniture		2,000
c.	31	Depreciation Expense—Building	1,000	
		Accumulated Depreciation—Building		1,000
d.	31	Salary Expense	500	
		Salary Payable		500
e.	31	Accounts Receivable	1,300	
		Service Revenue		1,300
f.	31	Unearned Service Revenue	3,000	
		Service Revenue		3,000

Accounts Receivable

	5,000	
(e)	1,300	
Bal.	6,300	

Supplies

	1,000	(a)	800
Bal.	200		

Accumulated Depreciation—Furniture

	4,000
(b)	2,000
Bal.	6,000

Accumulated Depreciation—Building

	30,000
(c)	1,000
Bal.	31,000

Salary Payable

(d)	500
Bal.	500

Unearned Service Revenue

(f)	3,000		8,000
		Bal.	5,000

Service Revenue

	60,000
(e)	1,300
(f)	3,000
Bal.	64,300

Salary Expense

	16,000
(d)	500
Bal.	16,500

Supplies Expense

(a)	800
Bal.	800

Depreciation Expense—Furniture

(b)	2,000
Bal.	2,000

Depreciation Expense—Building

(c)	1,000
Bal.	1,000

Requirement 2

Closing Entries				
1.	Dec. 31	Service Revenue	64,300	
		Income Summary		64,300
2.	31	Income Summary	23,300	
		Salary Expense		16,500
		Supplies Expense		800
		Accumulated Depreciation—Furniture		2,000
		Accumulated Depreciation—Building		1,000
		Miscellaneous Expense		3,000
3.	31	Income Summary ($64,300 – $23,300)	41,000	
		Jay Clay, Capital		41,000
4.	31	Jay Clay, Capital	25,000	
		Jay Clay, Withdrawals		25,000

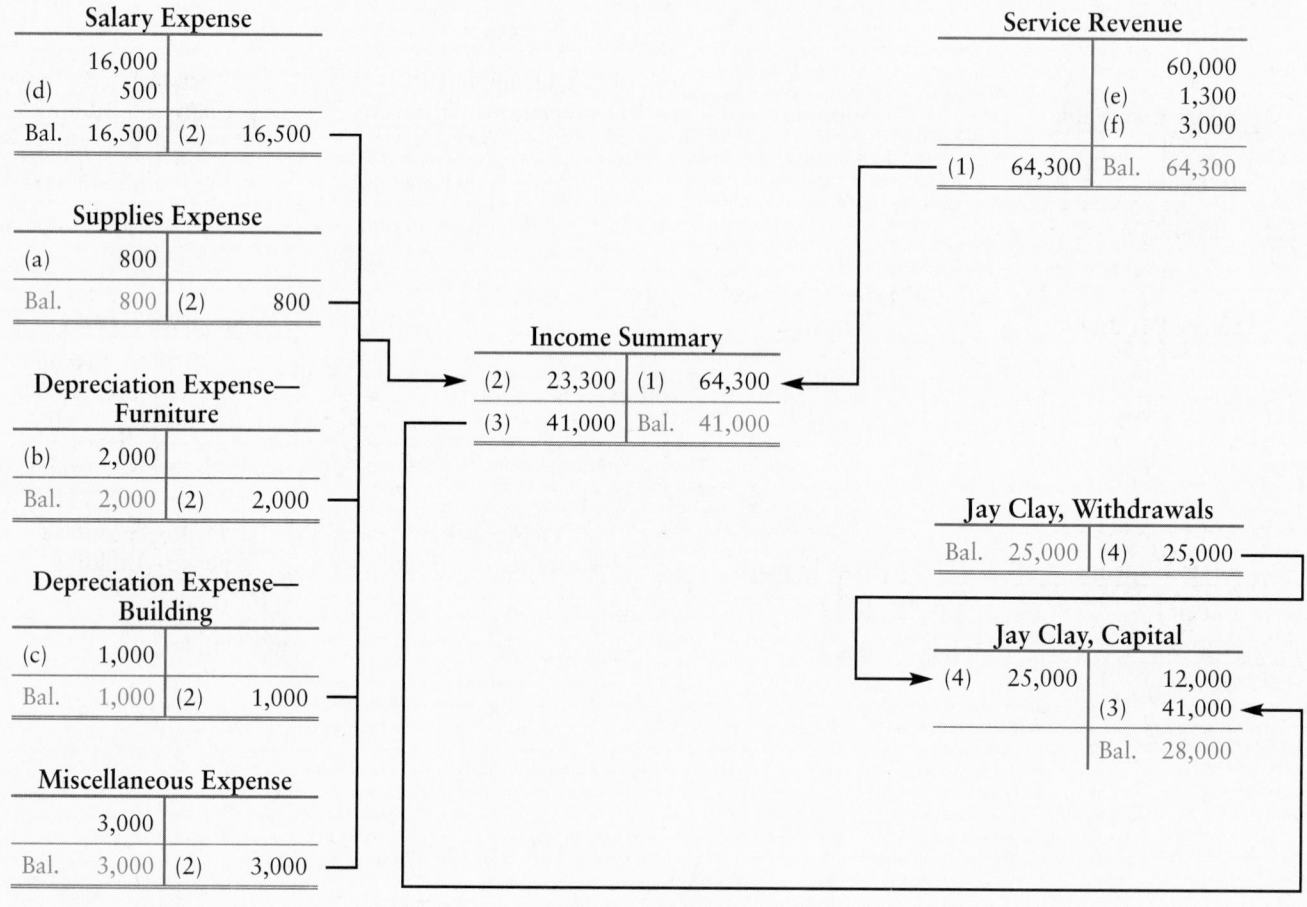

Requirement 3

CLAY EMPLOYMENT SERVICES
Income Statement
Year Ended December 31, 2009

Revenue:		
Service revenue		$64,300
Expenses:		
Salary expense	$16,500	
Depreciation expense—furniture	2,000	
Depreciation expense—building	1,000	
Supplies expense	800	
Miscellaneous expense	3,000	
Total expenses		23,300
Net income		$41,000

Requirement 4

CLAY EMPLOYMENT SERVICES
Statement of Owner's Equity
Year Ended December 31, 2009

Jay Clay, capital, January 1, 2009	$12,000
Add: Net income	41,000
	53,000
Less: Withdrawals	(25,000)
Jay Clay, capital, December 31, 2009	$28,000

Requirement 5

CLAY EMPLOYMENT SERVICES
Balance Sheet
December 31, 2009

Assets			Liabilities	
Current assets:			Current liabilities:	
Cash		$ 6,000	Accounts payable	$ 2,000
Accounts receivable		6,300	Salary payable	500
Supplies		200	Unearned service	
Total current assets		12,500	revenue	5,000
Long-term assets:			Total current liabilities	7,500
Furniture	$10,000			
Less: Accumulated				
depreciation	(6,000)	4,000		
Building	$50,000		**Owner's Equity**	
Less: Accumulated			Jay Clay, capital	28,000
depreciation	(31,000)	19,000	Total liabilities and	
Total assets		$35,500	owner's equity	$35,500

Review Completing the Accounting Cycle

Accounting Vocabulary

Accounting Cycle
Process by which companies produce their financial statements for a specific period.

Closing the Accounts
Step in the accounting cycle at the end of the period. Closing the accounts consists of journalizing and posting the closing entries to set the balances of the revenue, expense, and withdrawal accounts to zero for the next period.

Closing Entries
Entries that transfer the revenue, expense, and owner withdrawal balances to the capital account.

Current Asset
An asset that is expected to be converted to cash, sold, or consumed during the next 12 months, or within the business's normal operating cycle if the cycle is longer than a year.

Current Liability
A debt due to be paid with cash or with goods and services within one year or within the entity's operating cycle if the cycle is longer than a year.

Current Ratio
Current assets divided by current liabilities. Measures the company's ability to pay current liabilities from current assets.

Debt Ratio
Ratio of total liabilities to total assets. Tells the proportion of a company's assets that it has financed with debt.

Fixed Asset
Another name for property, plant, and equipment.

Income Summary
A temporary "holding tank" account into which revenues and expenses are transferred prior to their final transfer to the capital account.

Liquidity
Measure of how quickly an item can be converted to cash.

Long-Term Asset
An asset other than a current asset.

Long-Term Liability
A liability other than a current liability.

Operating Cycle
Time span during which cash is paid for goods and services, which are then sold to customers from whom the business collects cash.

Permanent Accounts
Accounts that are *not* closed at the end of the period—the asset, liability, and capital accounts.

Plant Asset
Another name for property, plant, and equipment.

Postclosing Trial Balance
List of the accounts and their balances at the end of the period after journalizing and posting the closing entries. This last step of the accounting cycle ensures that the ledger is in balance to start the next accounting period.

Reversing Entries
Special journal entries that ease the burden of accounting for transactions in the next period.

Temporary Accounts
The revenue and expense accounts that relate to a particular accounting period and are closed at the end of the period. For a proprietorship, the owner withdrawal account is also temporary.

Work Sheet
A columnar document designed to help move data from the trial balance to their financial statements.

Quick Check

1. Consider the steps in the accounting cycle in Exhibit 4-1, page 196. Which part of the accounting cycle provides information to help a business decide whether to expand its operations?
   a. Postclosing trial balance
   b. Adjusting entries
   c. Closing entries
   d. Financial statements

2. Which columns of the accounting work sheet show unadjusted amounts?
   a. Trial balance
   b. Adjustments
   c. Income Statement
   d. Balance Sheet

3. Which columns of the work sheet show net income?
   a. Trial Balance
   b. Adjustments
   c. Income Statement
   d. Both b and c

4. Which situation indicates a net loss on the income statement?
   a. Total debits equal total credits
   b. Total credits exceed total debits
   c. Total debits exceed total credits
   d. None of the above

5. Supplies has a $6,000 unadjusted balance on your trial balance. At year-end you count supplies of $2,000. What adjustment will appear on your work sheet?
   a. Supplies 4,000
      Supplies Expense.........................   4,000
   b. Supplies Expense 2,000
      Supplies......................................   2,000
   c. Supplies Expense 4,000
      Supplies......................................   4,000
   d. No adjustment is needed because the Supplies account already has a correct balance.

6. Which of the following accounts is not closed?
   a. Accumulated Depreciation
   b. Service Revenue
   c. Depreciation Expense
   d. Owner, Withdrawals

7. What do closing entries accomplish?
   a. Transfer revenues, expenses, and owner withdrawals to the capital account
   b. Zero out the revenues, expenses, and owner withdrawals

continued . . .

c. Bring the capital account to its correct ending balance

d. All of the above

8. Which of the following is not a closing entry?

a. Income Summary.................................... XXX

    Rent Expense....................................   XXX

b. Owner, Capital.................................... XXX

    Owner, Withdrawals..........................   XXX

c. Service Revenue.................................... XXX

    Income Summary..............................   XXX

d. Salary Payable.................................... XXX

    Income Summary..............................   XXX

9. Assets and liabilities are listed on the balance sheet in order of their

a. Purchase date

b. Liquidity

c. Balance

d. Adjustments

10. Sherman Lawn Service has cash of $300, receivables of $800, and supplies of $400. Sherman owes $500 on accounts payable and salary payable of $100. Sherman's current ratio is

a. 3.00

b. 0.31

c. 2.07

d. 2.50

Answers are given after Apply Your Knowledge (p. 238).

Assess Your Progress

Short Exercises

Explaining items on the
work sheet

1

S4-1 ← *Link Back to Chapter 3 (Adjusting Entries).* Explain why the following accounts must be adjusted (pp. 131–132, 139):

a. Prepaid rent   d. Salary payable

b. Unearned service revenue   e. Accumulated depreciation

c. Supplies

Explaining items on the
work sheet

1

S4-2 ← *Link Back to Chapters 2 and 3 (Definitions of Accounts).* Explain
what the following terms mean (pp. 60–64, 134, 137–139):

a. Accounts receivable   f. Accounts payable

b. Supplies   g. Unearned service revenue

c. Prepaid rent   h. Service revenue

d. Furniture   i. Rent expense

e. Accumulated depreciation

Using the work sheet

1 **2**

S4-3 Answer the following questions:

1. What type of balance does the Owner's Capital account have—debit
   or credit? (pp. 67–69)

2. Which Income Statement account has the same type of balance as the
   Capital account? (pp. 67–69)

3. Which type of Income Statement account has the opposite type of
   balance as the Capital account? (pp. 67–69)

4. What do we call the difference between total debits and total credits
   on the Income Statement? Into what account is the difference figure
   closed at the end of the period? (pp. 202–203, 205)

Making closing entries

3

S4-4 It is December 31 and time for you to close the books.

Journalize the closing entries for Brett Kaufman Enterprises (p. 205):

a. Owner's withdrawals, $6,000

b. Service revenue, $22,000

c. Make a single closing entry for all the expenses: Salary, $7,000; Rent,
   $4,000; Advertising, $3,000.

d. Income Summary

Analyzing the overall effect
of the closing entries on the
owner's capital account

3

S4-5 This exercise should be used in conjunction with Short Exercise 4-4.

1. Set up each T-account given in Short Exercise 4-4 and insert its adjusted
   balance as given (denote as *Bal.*) at December 31. Also set up a T-account
   for Brett Kaufman, Capital, $25,000; and for Income Summary. Post the
   closing entries to the accounts, denoting posted amounts as *Clo.* (p. 205)

2. Compute the ending balance of Brett Kaufman, Capital. (p. 205)

Making closing entries

3

S4-6 Riley Insurance Agency reported the following items at May 31:

Sales and marketing expense	$2,000	Cash	$1,000
Other assets	500	Service revenue	5,000
Depreciation expense	800	Accounts payable	300
Long-term liabilities	400	Accounts receivable	1,200

Make Riley's closing entries, as needed, for these accounts. (p. 205)

Posting closing entries

S4-7 This exercise should be used in conjunction with Short Exercise 4-6. Use the data in Short Exercise 4-6 to set up T-accounts for those accounts that Riley Insurance Agency closed out at May 31. Insert their account balances prior to closing, post the closing entries to these accounts, and show each account's ending balance after closing. Also show the Income Summary T-account. Denote a balance as *Bal.* and a closing entry amount as *Clo.* (p. 205)

Preparing a postclosing trial balance

S4-8 After closing its accounts at May 31, 2008, Hueske Electric Company had the following account balances:

Long-term liabilities	$ 500	Equipment	$4,000
Other assets	800	Cash	300
Accounts receivable	2,000	Service revenue	0
Total expenses	0	Will Hueske, capital	4,400
Accounts payable	900	Supplies	100
Unearned service revenue	400	Accumulated depreciation	1,000

Prepare Hueske's postclosing trial balance at May 31, 2008. List accounts in proper order, as shown in Exhibit 4-11, p. 207.

Classifying assets and liabilities as current or long-term

S4-9 Ink Jet Printing reported the following (amounts in thousands).

Buildings	$4,000	Service revenue	$1,300
Accounts payable	400	Cash	200
Total expenses	1,050	Receivables	500
Accumulated depreciation	2,800	Interest expense	90
Accrued liabilities (such as		Equipment	800
Salary payable)	300	Prepaid expenses	100

1. Identify the assets (including contra assets) and liabilities. (p. 203)
2. Classify each asset and each liability as current or long-term. (pp. 208–209)

Classifying assets and liabilities as current or long-term

S4-10 ← *Link Back to Chapter 3 (Book Value).* Examine Ink Jet Printing's account balances in Short Exercise 4-9. Identify or compute the following amounts for Ink Jet:

a. Total current assets (p. 208–209) c. Book value of plant assets (p. 134)
b. Total current liabilities (p. 208–209) d. Total long-term liabilities (pp. 207–208)

Computing the current ratio and the debt ratio

S4-11 Heart of Texas Telecom had these account balances at December 31, 2007.

Note payable, long-term	$ 9,000	Accounts payable	$ 4,000
Prepaid rent	2,000	Accounts receivable	6,000
Salary payable	2,000	Cash	3,000
Service revenue	31,000	Depreciation expense	4,000
Supplies	1,000	Equipment	12,000

Compute Heart of Texas' current ratio and debt ratio. (p. 210)

Computing and using the
current ratio and the
debt ratio

S4-12 This exercise should be used in conjunction with Short Exercise 4-11.

1. How much in *current* assets does Heart of Texas Telecom have for every dollar of *current* liabilities that it owes? What ratio measures this relationship? (p. 210)

2. What percentage of Heart of Texas Telecom's total assets are financed with debt? What is the name of this ratio? (p. 210)

3. What percentage of Heart of Texas's total assets does the owner of the company actually own? (Challenge)

Exercises _____

Preparing a work sheet

E4-13 The trial balance of Wireless Solutions follows.

			Balance	
		Account Title	**Debit**	**Credit**
		Cash	$ 3,500	
		Accounts receivable	3,400	
		Prepaid rent	1,200	
		Supplies	3,300	
		Equipment	34,100	
		Accumulated depreciation		$ 1,800
		Accounts payable		5,100
		Salary payable		
		Charles Voss, capital		36,000
		Charles Voss, withdrawals	2,000	
		Service revenue		7,100
		Depreciation expense		
		Salary expense	1,800	
		Rent expense		
		Utilities expense	700	
		Supplies expense		
		Total	$50,000	$50,000

WIRELESS SOLUTIONS
Trial Balance
November 30, 2007

Additional information at November 30, 2007:

a. Accrued service revenue, $300   d. Prepaid rent expired, $800

b. Depreciation, $100   e. Supplies used, $1,600

c. Accrued salary expense, $500

Requirements
Complete Wireless Solutions' work sheet for the month ended November 30, 2007. How much was net income for November? (pp. 197–198)

Journalizing adjusting and
closing entries

E4-14 Journalize Wireless Solutions' adjusting and closing entries in Exercise 4-13. (pp. 204–205)

E4-15 Set up T-accounts for those accounts affected by the adjusting and closing entries in Exercise 4-14. Post the adjusting and closing entries to the accounts; denote adjustment amounts by *Adj.,* closing amounts by *Clo.,* and balances by *Bal.* Double underline the accounts with zero balances after you close them, and show the ending balance in each account. (pp. 204–205)

Preparing a postclosing trial
balance

E4-16 After completing Exercises 4-14 and 4-15, prepare the postclosing trial balance of Wireless Solutions at November 30, 2007. (p. 206)

Adjusting the accounts

E4-17 ← *Link Back to Chapter 3 (Adjusting Entries).* Todd McKinney Magic Shows' records include the following account balances:

	December 31,	
	2006	**2007**
Prepaid rent	$400	$600
Unearned service revenue	800	300

During 2007, McKinney recorded the following:

a. Prepaid annual rent of $6,000. (pp. 131–132)

b. Made the year-end adjustment to record rent expense of $5,800 for the year. (pp. 131–132)

c. Collected $4,000 cash in advance for service revenue to be earned later. (p. 138)

d. Made the year-end adjustment to record the earning of $4,500 service revenue that had been collected in advance. (p. 139)

Requirements

1. As directed by your instructor, set up T-accounts (p. 204) or four-column accounts (p. 80) for Prepaid Rent, Rent Expense, Unearned Service Revenue, and Service Revenue. Insert beginning and ending balances for Prepaid Rent and Unearned Service Revenue.

2. Journalize entries a through d above, and post to the accounts. Explanations are not required. Ensure that the ending balances for Prepaid Rent and Unearned Service Revenue agree with the December 31, 2007, balances given above. (pp. 131–132, 204)

Closing the books

E4-18 Refer to the Todd McKinney data in Exercise 4-17. After making the adjusting entries in Exercise 4-17, journalize McKinney's closing entries at the end of 2007. Also set up T-accounts (p. 204) or four-column accounts (p. 80) for Rent Expense and Service Revenue and post the closing entries to these accounts. What are their balances after closing? (p. 205)

Identifying and journalizing entries

3

E4-19 From the following selected accounts of Pikasso Party Planning at June 30, 2008, prepare the entity's closing entries (p. 205):

Accounts receivable	$14,000	Pablo Pikasso, capital	$21,600
Depreciation expense	10,200	Service revenue	89,000
Rent expense	5,900	Unearned revenues	1,300
Pablo Pikasso, withdrawals	40,000	Salary expense	12,500
Supplies	1,400	Supplies expense	3,900

Prepare a T-account for Pablo Pikasso, Capital. What is Pikasso's ending capital balance at June 30, 2008? (p. 205)

Identifying and journalizing closing entries

3

E4-20 The accountant for Passport Photography has posted adjusting entries (a) through (e) to the following selected accounts at December 31, 2008.

Accounts Receivable	
41,000	
(a) 3,000	

Supplies	
4,000	(b) 2,000

Accumulated Depreciation—Furniture	
	5,000
	(c) 1,100

Accumulated Depreciation—Building	
	33,000
	(d) 6,000

Salary Payable	
	(e) 700

Roland Poe, Capital	
	52,000

Roland Poe, Withdrawals	
61,000	

Service Revenue	
	108,000
	(a) 3,000

Salary Expense	
26,200	
(e) 700	

Supplies Expense	
(b) 2,000	

Depreciation Expense—Furniture	
(c) 1,100	

Depreciation Expense—Building	
(d) 6,000	

Requirements

1. Journalize Passport Photography's closing entries at December 31, 2008. (p. 205)

2. Determine Roland Poe's ending capital balance at December 31, 2008. (p. 205)

Preparing a statement of owner's equity

3

E4-21 From the following accounts of Fleet Truck Wash, prepare the company's statement of owner's equity for the year ended December 31, 2007. (p. 203)

Rhonda Fleet, Capital			
Clo.	32,000	Jan. 1	164,000
		Clo.	140,000
		Bal.	272,000

Rhonda Fleet, Withdrawals			
Mar. 31	9,000		
Jun. 30	7,000		
Sep. 30	9,000		
Dec. 31	7,000		
Bal.	32,000	Clo.	32,000

Income Summary			
Clo.	88,000	Clo.	228,000
Clo.	140,000	Bal.	140,000

E4-22 The adjusted trial balance and the income statement amounts from the April work sheet of Swift Sign Company follow:

Account Title	Adjusted Trial Balance		Income Statement	
Cash	$14,200			
Supplies	2,400			
Prepaid rent	1,100			
Equipment	52,000			
Accumulated depreciation		$ 6,000		
Accounts payable		4,600		
Salary payable		400		
Unearned service revenue		4,200		
Long-term note payable		5,000		
Rob Swift, capital		39,800		
Rob Swift, withdrawals	1,000			
Service revenue		17,400		17,400
Salary expense	3,800		$ 3,800	
Rent expense	1,400		1,400	
Depreciation expense	300		300	
Supplies expense	400		400	
Utilities expense	800		800	
	$77,400	$77,400	6,700	17,400
Net income or net loss			?	?
			$17,400	$17,400

Requirements

1. Journalize Swift's closing entries at April 30. (p. 205)
2. How much net income or net loss did Swift earn for April? How can you tell? (pp. 198, 205)

E4-23 Refer to Exercise 4-22.

Requirements

1. After solving Exercise 4-22, use the data in that exercise to prepare the classified balance sheet of Swift Sign Company at April 30 of the current year. Use the report form. You must compute the ending balance of Rob Swift, Capital. (pp. 203, 209)
2. Compute Swift's current ratio and debt ratio at April 30. One year ago, the current ratio was 1.50 and the debt ratio was 0.30. Indicate whether Swift's ability to pay current and total debts has improved, deteriorated, or remained the same during the current year. (p. 210)

E4-24 Data for the unadjusted trial balance of Planet Beach Tanning Salon at December 31, 2007 follow.

Cash	$ 3,000	Service revenue	$93,600
Equipment	66,200	Salary expense	42,700
Accumulated depreciation	21,800	Depreciation expense	
Accounts payable	6,100	Supplies expense	

Adjusting data for 2007 are:

a. Accrued service revenue, $3,100. c. Accrued salary expense, $1,400.

b. Supplies used in operations, $600. d. Depreciation expense, $4,000.

Lex Noonan, the owner, has received an offer to sell the company. He needs to know the net income for the year covered by these data.

Requirements

Without opening accounts, making journal entries, or using a work sheet, give Noonan the requested information. Prepare an income statement, and show all computations. (pp. 109, 203)

Problems (Group A)

Preparing a work sheet

1

P4-25A The trial balance of Victoria Motors at June 30, 2008, follows.

VICTORIA MOTORS
Trial Balance
June 30, 2008

Account Title	Balance Debit	Balance Credit
Cash	$ 21,200	
Accounts receivable	37,800	
Supplies	17,600	
Prepaid insurance	2,300	
Equipment	32,600	
Accumulated depreciation		$ 26,200
Accounts payable		22,600
Wages payable		
Unearned service revenue		10,500
Victoria Mann, capital		46,600
Victoria Mann, withdrawals	4,200	
Service revenue		20,100
Depreciation expense		
Wage expense	3,200	
Insurance expense		
Rent expense	6,000	
Utilities expense	1,100	
Supplies expense		
Total	$126,000	$126,000

continued . . .

Additional data at June 30, 2008:

a. Depreciation on equipment, $600.

b. Accrued wage expense, $200.

c. Supplies on hand, $14,300.

d. Prepaid insurance expired during June, $500.

e. Unearned service revenue earned during June, $4,900.

f. Accrued service revenue, $1,100.

Requirements

Complete Victoria Motors' work sheet for June. Key adjusting entries by letter. (p. 198)

Preparing a work sheet and the financial statements

1 **2**

P4-26A The unadjusted T-accounts of Paladdin Investment Advisers, at December 31, 2007, and the related year-end adjustment data follow.

Cash	Accounts Receivable	Supplies	Equipment
Bal. 15,000	Bal. 36,000	Bal. 9,000	Bal. 99,000

Accumulated Depreciation	Accounts Payable	Salary Payable	Unearned Service Revenue
Bal. 13,000	Bal. 6,000		Bal. 5,000

Note Payable, Long-Term		S. Paladdin, Capital	S. Paladdin, Withdrawals
Bal. 60,000		Bal. 36,000	Bal. 62,000

Service Revenue		Salary Expense	Supplies Expense
Bal. 182,000		Bal. 53,000	

Depreciation Expense	Interest Expense	Rent Expense	Insurance Expense
	Bal. 6,000	Bal. 15,000	Bal. 7,000

Adjustment data at December 31, 2007:

a. Unearned service revenue earned during the year, $1,000.

b. Supplies on hand, $1,000.

c. Depreciation for the year, $9,000.

d. Accrued salary expense, $1,000.

e. Accrued service revenue, $2,000.

Requirements

1. Enter the account data in the Trial Balance columns of a work sheet, and complete the work sheet. Key each adjusting entry by the letter corresponding to the data given. List all the accounts, including those with zero balances. Leave a blank line under Service Revenue. (p. 198)

2. Prepare the income statement, the statement of owner's equity, and the classified balance sheet in account format. (p. 203)

3. Did Paladdin have a good or a bad year during 2007? Give the reason for your answer. (Challenge)

P4-27A The *unadjusted* trial balance of Glenn Real Estate Appraisal at June 30, 2009 follows.

GLENN REAL ESTATE APPRAISAL
Trial Balance
June 30, 2009

Account Title	Balance Debit	Balance Credit
Cash	$ 12,300	
Accounts receivable	26,400	
Supplies	1,200	
Prepaid insurance	3,200	
Building	70,700	
Accumulated depreciation		$ 33,200
Land	30,000	
Accounts payable		39,100
Interest payable		1,400
Salary payable		
Maggie Glenn, capital		37,900
Maggie Glenn, withdrawals	45,300	
Service revenue		109,800
Salary expense	21,400	
Depreciation expense		
Insurance expense	3,100	
Utilities expense	4,300	
Supplies expense	3,500	
Total	$221,400	$221,400

Adjustment data at June 30, 2009:

a. Prepaid insurance expired, $3,000.

b. Accrued service revenue, $900.

c. Accrued salary expense, $700.

d. Depreciation for the year, $11,200.

e. Supplies used during the year, $200.

Requirements

1. Open T-accounts for Maggie Glenn, Capital and all the accounts that follow. Insert their unadjusted balances. Also open a T-account for Income Summary, which has a zero balance. (p. 204)

2. Journalize the adjusting entries and post to the accounts that you opened. Show the balance of each revenue account and each expense account. (p. 204)

3. Journalize the closing entries and post to the accounts that you opened. Draw double underlines under each account balance that you close to zero. (p. 205)

4. Compute the ending balance of Maggie Glenn, Capital. (p. 205)

P4-28A Refer to the data for Glenn Real Estate Appraisal in Problem 4-27A. After journalizing and posting Glenn's adjusting and closing entries, prepare the company's income statement for the year ended June 30, 2009. List expenses in descending order—largest first, second-largest next, and so on. (p. 203)

4-29A The trial balance of Road Runner Internet at August 31, 2009, and the data for the month-end adjustments follow.

ROAD RUNNER INTERNET Trial Balance August 31, 2009		
	Balance	
Account Title	Debit	Credit
Cash	$ 3,000	
Accounts receivable	6,500	
Prepaid rent	1,200	
Supplies	900	
Equipment	35,300	
Accumulated depreciation		$12,800
Accounts payable		4,200
Salary payable		
Unearned service revenue		8,900
Speedy Rhodes, capital		10,400
Speedy Rhodes, withdrawals	4,800	
Service revenue		27,300
Salary expense	2,100	
Rent expense	9,800	
Depreciation expense		
Supplies expense		
Total	$63,600	$63,600

Adjustment data:

a. Unearned service revenue still unearned at August 31, $6,500.

b. Prepaid rent still in force at August 31, $1,000.

c. Supplies used during the month, $500.

d. Depreciation for the month, $300.

e. Accrued salary expense at August 31, $400.

Requirements

1. Open the accounts listed in the trial balance and insert their August 31 unadjusted balances. Also open the Income Summary account. Use four-column accounts. Date the balances of the following accounts as of August 1: Prepaid Rent; Supplies; Equipment; Accumulated Depreciation; Unearned Service Revenue; and Speedy Rhodes, Capital. (p. 80)

   If your instructor so directs, use T-accounts. Date the balances of the following accounts as of August 1: Prepaid Rent; Supplies;

continued . . .

Equipment; Accumulated Depreciation; Unearned Service Revenue; and Speedy Rhodes, Capital. (p. 205)

2. Enter the trial balance on a work sheet and complete the work sheet of Road Runner Internet for the month ended August 31, 2009. (p. 198)

3. Prepare the income statement, the statement of owner's equity, and the classified balance sheet in report form. (p. 203)

4. Using the work sheet data that you prepare, journalize and post the adjusting and closing entries. Use dates and show the ending balance of each account (pp. 80, 204–205)

5. Prepare a postclosing trial balance. (p. 206)

Preparing a classified balance sheet in report form

P4-30A Selected accounts of Blume Irrigation Systems at December 31, 2007, follow:

Cotton Blume, capital	$97,100	Accounts payable	$ 19,800
Note payable, long-term	37,800	Accounts receivable	26,600
Other assets	3,600	Accumulated depreciation—	
Prepaid insurance	7,700	equipment	7,800
Insurance expense	6,600	Accumulated depreciation—	
Salary expense	24,600	building	11,600
Salary payable	3,900	Equipment	14,400
Supplies	2,500	Cash	6,500
Unearned service revenue	5,400	Service revenue	93,500
Interest payable	600	Building	122,700

Requirements

1. Prepare Blume's classified balance sheet in report form at December 31, 2007. Show totals for total assets, total liabilities, and total liabilities and owner's equity. (p. 209)

2. Compute Blume's current ratio and debt ratio at December 31, 2007. At December 31, 2006, the current ratio was 1.60 and the debt ratio was 0.35. Did the company's ability to pay both current and total debts improve or deteriorate during 2007? (p. 210)

Analyzing errors and journalizing adjusting entries

P4-31A ← *Link Back to Chapter 2 (Accounting Errors).* The accountant for William Smith, M.D., encountered the following situations while adjusting and closing the books at December 31. Consider each situation independently.

a. The accountant failed to make the following adjusting entries at December 31:

1. Accrued salary expense, $600.

2. Supplies expense, $1,100.

3. Accrued interest expense on a note payable, $1,600.

4. Depreciation of equipment, $400.

5. Earned service revenue that had been collected in advance, $200.

Compute the overall net income effect of these omissions. (p. 204, Challenge)

continued . . .

b. Record each adjusting entry identified in item a. (p. 204)

c. The $16,000 balance of Equipment was entered as $1,600 on the trial balance.

1. What is the name of this type of error? (p. 78)

2. Assume that this is the only error in the trial balance. Which will be greater, the total debits or the total credits, and by how much? (p. 78)

3. How can this type of error be identified? (p. 78)

d. A $500 credit to Accounts Receivable was posted as a debit.

1. At what stage of the accounting cycle will this error be detected? (p. 78)

2. Describe the technique for identifying the amount of the error. (p. 78)

Problems (Group B)

Preparing a work sheet

1

P4-32B The trial balance of Jane's Preschool at May 31, 2008, follows.

JANE'S PRESCHOOL
Trial Balance
May 31, 2008

	Balance	
Account Title	Debit	Credit
Cash	$ 4,300	
Supplies	500	
Prepaid insurance	1,700	
Furniture	27,400	
Accumulated depreciation—furniture		$ 1,400
Building	53,900	
Accumulated depreciation—building		34,500
Accounts payable		13,300
Salary payable		
Unearned service revenue		8,800
Jane King, capital		20,000
Jane King, withdrawals	3,800	
Service revenue		16,800
Depreciation expense—furniture		
Depreciation expense—building		
Salary expense	2,100	
Insurance expense		
Utilities expense	1,100	
Supplies expense		
Total	$94,800	$94,800

Additional data at May 31, 2008.

a. Depreciation: furniture, $500; building, $400.

b. Accrued salary expense, $600.

continued . . .

c. Supplies on hand, $400.

d. Prepaid insurance expired, $300.

e. Unearned service revenue earned during May, $4,400.

Requirements

Complete Jane's work sheet for May. Key adjusting entries by letter. (p. 198)

Preparing a work sheet and
the financial statements

1 **2**

P4-33B The unadjusted T-accounts of Investors Brokerage at December 31, 2007, and the related year-end adjustment data follow.

Cash	
Bal. 29,000	

Accounts Receivable	
Bal. 44,000	

Supplies	
Bal. 6,000	

Computers	
Bal. 22,000	

Accumulated Depreciation	
	Bal. 12,000

Accounts Payable	
	Bal. 16,000

Salary Payable	

Unearned Service Revenue	
	Bal. 2,000

Note Payable, Long-Term	
	Bal. 40,000

Tom Fritz, Capital	
	Bal. 41,000

Tom Fritz, Withdrawals	
Bal. 54,000	

Service Revenue	
	Bal. 95,000

Salary Expense	
Bal. 36,000	

Supplies Expense	

Depreciation Expense	

Interest Expense	
Bal. 5,000	

Advertising Expense	
Bal. 10,000	

Adjustment data at December 31, 2007.

a. Depreciation for the year, $5,000.

b. Supplies on hand, $2,000.

c. Accrued service revenue, $4,000.

d. Unearned service revenue earned during the year, $2,000.

e. Accrued salary expense, $1,000.

Requirements

1. Enter the account data in the trial balance columns of a work sheet, and complete the work sheet. Key each adjusting entry by the letter corresponding to the data given. List all the accounts, including those with zero balances. Leave a blank line under Service Revenue. (p. 198)

2. Prepare the income statement, the statement of owner's equity, and the classified balance sheet in account form. (p. 203)

3. Did Investors Brokerage have a good or a bad year during 2007? Give the reason for your answer. (Challenge)

Journalizing adjusting and
closing entries

2 **3**

P4-34B The *unadjusted* trial balance of Jen Weaver Insurance at April 30, 2008, follows on the next page. Adjustment data at April 30, 2008, consist of

a. Accrued service revenue, $1,600.

b. Depreciation for the year: equipment, $1,000; building, $3,000.

c. Accrued salary expense, $800.

continued . . .

d. Unearned service revenue earned during the year, $1,100.

e. Supplies used during the year, $500.

f. Prepaid insurance expired, $700.

			Balance	
JEN WEAVER INSURANCE Adjusted Trial Balance April 30, 2008				
		Account Title	Debit	Credit
		Cash	$ 4,500	
		Accounts receivable	3,700	
		Supplies	3,600	
		Prepaid insurance	2,200	
		Equipment	13,900	
		Accumulated depreciation—equipment		$ 8,400
		Building	74,300	
		Accumulated depreciation—building		18,200
		Accounts payable		19,500
		Salary payable		800
		Unearned service revenue		3,600
		Jen Weaver, capital		30,300
		Jen Weaver, withdrawals	27,500	
		Service revenue		98,500
		Salary expense	32,800	
		Depreciation expense—equipment		
		Depreciation expense—building		
		Insurance expense	5,100	
		Utilities expense	4,900	
		Supplies expense	6,800	
		Total	$179,300	$179,300

Requirements

1. Open T-accounts for Jen Weaver, Capital and all the accounts that follow. Insert their unadjusted balances. Also open a T-account for Income Summary, which has a zero balance. (p. 204)

2. Journalize the adjusting entries and post to the accounts that you opened. Show the balance of each revenue account and each expense account. (p. 204)

3. Journalize the closing entries and post to the accounts that you opened. Draw double underlines under each account balance that you close to zero. (p. 205)

4. Compute the ending balance of Jen Weaver, Capital. (p. 205)

Preparing an income statement

3

P4-35B Refer to the data for Jen Weaver Insurance in Problem 4-34B. After journalizing and posting Weaver's adjusting and closing entries, prepare the company's income statement for the year ended April 30, 2008. List expenses in descending order—that is, largest first, second-largest next, and so on. (p. 203)

P4-36B The trial balance of Alpha Graphics at October 31, 2007, follows, along with the data for the month-end adjustments.

	ALPHA GRAPHICS Trial Balance October 31, 2007		
		Balance	
Account Title		**Debit**	**Credit**
Cash		$ 4,900	
Accounts receivable		15,310	
Prepaid rent		2,200	
Supplies		840	
Equipment		31,370	
Accumulated depreciation			$ 3,400
Accounts payable			7,290
Salary payable			
Unearned service revenue			5,300
Courtney Rolfe, capital			28,290
Courtney Rolfe, withdrawals		3,900	
Service revenue			17,100
Salary expense		2,860	
Rent expense			
Depreciation expense			
Supplies expense			
Total		$61,380	$61,380

Adjusting data at October 31:

a. Unearned service revenue still unearned, $800.

b. Prepaid rent still in force, $2,000.

c. Supplies used, $770.

d. Depreciation for the month, $250.

e. Accrued salary expense, $310.

Requirements

1. Open the accounts listed in the trial balance, inserting their October 31 unadjusted balances. Also open the Income Summary account. Use four-column accounts. Date the balances of the following accounts October 1: Prepaid Rent; Supplies; Equipment; Accumulated Depreciation; Unearned Service Revenue; and Courtney Rolfe, Capital. (p. 211)

   If your instructor so directs, use T-accounts. Date the balances of the following accounts as of October 1: Prepaid Rent; Supplies; Equipment; Accumulated Depreciation; Unearned Service Revenue; and Courtney Rolfe, Capital. (p. 204)

2. Enter the trial balance on a work sheet and complete the work sheet of Alpha Graphics for the month ended October 31, 2007. (p. 198)

3. Prepare the income statement, statement of owner's equity, and classified balance sheet in report form. (p. 203)

continued . . .

4. Using the work sheet data that you prepare, journalize and post the adjusting and closing entries. Use dates and show the ending balance of each account. (pp. 80, 204–205)

5. Prepare a postclosing trial balance. (p. 206)

Preparing a classified balance sheet in report form

P4-37B Selected accounts of Elevator Service Company, at December 31, 2008, follow.

Insurance expense	$ 600	Accounts payable	$34,700
Note payable, long-term	3,200	Accounts receivable	42,100
Other assets	2,300	Accumulated depreciation—	
Building	55,900	building	47,300
Prepaid rent	4,700	Accumulated depreciation—	
Salary expense	17,800	equipment	7,700
Salary payable	3,500	Cash	12,000
Service revenue	71,100	Depreciation expense	1,900
Supplies	3,800	Leah Jacobs, capital	46,900
Unearned service revenue	1,700	Equipment	24,200

Requirements

1. Prepare the company's classified balance sheet in report form at December 31, 2008. Show totals for total assets, total liabilities, and owner's equity. (p. 209)

2. Compute the company's current ratio and debt ratio at December 31, 2008. At December 31, 2007, the current ratio was 1.30 and the debt ratio was 0.55. Did the company's ability to pay debts improve, deteriorate, or remain the same during 2008? (p. 210)

Analyzing errors and journalizing adjusting entries

P4-38B ← *Link Back to Chapter 2 (Accounting Errors).* The accountant of Lancer Copy Center encountered the following situations while adjusting and closing the books at February 28. Consider each situation independently.

a. The accountant failed to make the following adjusting entries at February 28:

1. Depreciation of equipment, $700.

2. Earned service revenue that had been collected in advance, $2,000.

3. Accrued service revenue, $1,400.

4. Insurance expense, $300.

5. Accrued interest expense on a note payable, $500.

Compute the overall net income effect of these omissions. (p. 204, Challenge)

b. Record each of the adjusting entries identified in item a. (p. 148)

c. The $1,300 balance of Computer Software was entered as $13,000 on the trial balance.

1. What is the name of this type of error? (p. 78)

2. Assume that this is the only error in the trial balance. Which will be greater, the total debits or the total credits, and by how much? (p. 78)

3. How can this type of error be identified? (p. 78)

for 24-7 practice, visit www.MyAccountingLab.com

continued . . .

d. A $1,400 debit to Supplies was posted as $4,100.

    1. At what stage of the accounting cycle will this error be detected? (p. 78)

    2. What is the name of this type of error? Explain how to identify the error. (p. 78)

Continuing Problem

This problem continues the Carl Redmon Consulting situation begun in Problem 1-42 of Chapter 1 and continued from Problem 3-44 of Chapter 3.

Closing the books and preparing a classified balance sheet

P4-39 Refer to Problem 3-44 of Chapter 3. Start from the posted T-accounts and the *adjusted* trial balance that Carl Redmon Consulting prepared for his business at December 31:

CARL REDMON CONSULTING Adjusted Trial Balance December 31, 2008		
	Balance	
Account Title	**Debit**	**Credit**
Cash	$ 7,700	
Accounts receivable	1,500	
Supplies	100	
Equipment	2,000	
Accumulated depreciation—equipment		$ 50
Furniture	3,600	
Accumulated depreciation—furniture		60
Accounts payable		3,600
Salary payable		500
Unearned service revenue		600
Carl Redmon, capital		10,000
Carl Redmon, withdrawals	1,600	
Service revenue		3,200
Rent expense	500	
Utilities expense	200	
Salary expense	500	
Depreciation expense—equipment	50	
Depreciation expense—furniture	60	
Supplies expense	200	
Total	$18,010	$18,010

Requirements

1. Journalize and post the closing entries at December 31. Denote each closing amount as *Clo.* and an account balance as *Bal.*

2. Prepare a classified balance sheet at December 31.

3. If your instructor assigns it, complete the accounting work sheet at December 31.

Apply Your Knowledge

Decision Case

Completing the accounting cycle to develop the information for a bank loan

3 **4**

One year ago, Ralph Collins founded Collins Consignment Sales, and the business has prospered. Collins comes to you for advice. He wishes to know how much net income the business earned during the past year. He also wants to know what his capital balance is. The accounting records consist of the T-accounts in the ledger, which were prepared by an accountant who has moved. The accounts at December 31 are shown below.

Collins indicates that, at year-end, customers owe him $1,000 accrued service revenue, which he expects to collect early next year. These revenues have not been recorded. During the year, he collected $4,100 service revenue in advance from customers, but the business has earned only $800 of that amount. Advertising expense for the year was $2,400, and he used up $2,100 of the supplies. Collins estimates that depreciation on equipment was $7,000 for the year. At December 31, he owes his employee $1,200 accrued salary.

Collins expresses concern that his withdrawals during the year might have exceeded the business's net income. To get a loan to expand the business, Collins must show the bank that his capital account has grown from its original $50,000 balance. Has it? You and Collins agree that you will meet again in one week.

Requirements

Prepare the financial statement that helps answer Collins's question. Can he expect to get the loan? Give your reason.

Cash	
Dec. 31 5,800	

Accounts Receivable	
Dec. 31 12,300	

Prepaid Rent	
Jan. 2 2,800	

Supplies	
Jan. 2 2,600	

Equipment	
Jan. 2 62,000	

Accumulated Depreciation	

Accounts Payable	
	Dec. 31 18,500

Salary Payable	

Unearned Service Revenue	
	Dec. 31 4,100

Ralph Collins, Capital	
	Jan. 2 50,000

Ralph Collins, Withdrawals	
Dec. 31 50,000	

Service Revenue	
	Dec. 31 80,700

Salary Expense	
Dec. 31 17,000	

Depreciation Expense	

Advertising Expense	

Utilities Expense	
Dec. 31 800	

Supplies Expense	

Ethical Issue

← *Link Back to Chapter 3 (Revenue Principle).* Grant Film Productions wishes to expand and has borrowed $100,000. As a condition for making this loan, the bank requires that the store maintain a current ratio of at least 1.50.

Business has been good but not great. Expansion costs have brought the current ratio down to 1.40 at December 15. Rita Grant, owner of the business, is considering what might happen if she reports a current ratio of 1.40 to the bank. One course of action for Grant is to record in December $10,000 of revenue that the business will earn in January of next year. The contract for this job has been signed.

Requirements

1. Journalize the revenue transaction, and indicate how recording this revenue in December would affect the current ratio.

2. Discuss whether it is ethical to record the revenue transaction in December. Identify the accounting principle relevant to this situation, and give the reasons underlying your conclusion.

Financial Statement Case

Using a balance sheet

This case, based on the balance sheet of **Amazon.com** in Appendix A at the end of the book, will familiarize you with some of the assets and liabilities of that company. Use the Amazon balance sheet to answer the following questions.

Requirements

1. Which balance sheet format does Amazon.com use?

2. Name the company's largest current asset and largest current liability at December 31, 2005.

3. Compute Amazon's current ratios at December 31, 2005 and 2004. Did the current ratio improve, worsen, or hold steady during 2005?

4. Under what category does Amazon report furniture, fixtures, and equipment?

5. What was the cost of the company's fixed assets at December 31, 2005? What was the amount of accumulated depreciation? What was the book value of the fixed assets? See Note 3 for the data.

Team Project

Haig Sherman formed a lawn service business as a summer job. To start the business on May 1, he deposited $1,000 in a new bank account in the name of the proprietorship. The $1,000 consisted of a $600 loan from his father and $400 of his own money. Sherman rented lawn equipment, purchased supplies, and hired other students to mow and trim customers' lawns.

At the end of each month, Sherman mailed bills to his customers. On August 31, he was ready to dissolve the business and return to college. Because he was so busy, he kept few records other than his checkbook and a list of receivables from customers.

At August 31, Sherman's checkbook shows a balance of $2,000, and customers still owe him $750. During the summer, he collected $5,500 from customers. His checkbook lists payments for supplies totaling $400, and he still has gasoline, weedeater cord, and other supplies that cost a total of $50. He paid his employees $1,800, and he still owes them $300 for the final week of the summer.

Sherman rented some equipment from Ludwig's Machine Shop. On May 1, he signed a six-month lease on mowers and paid $600 for the full lease period. Ludwig's will refund the unused portion of the prepayment if the equipment is in good shape. In order to get the refund, Sherman has kept the mowers in excellent condition. In fact, he had to pay $300 to repair a mower.

continued . . .

To transport employees and equipment to jobs, Sherman used a trailer that he bought for $300. He figures that the summer's work used up one-third of the trailer's service potential. The business checkbook lists a payment of $500 for cash withdrawals by Sherman during the summer. Sherman paid his father back during August.

Requirements

1. Prepare the income statement of Sherman Lawn Service for the four months May through August.

2. Prepare the classified balance sheet of Sherman Lawn Service at August 31.

3. Was Sherman's summer work successful? Give the reason for your answer.

For Internet Exercises, Excel in Practice, and additional online activities, go to the Web site www.prenhall.com/horngren.

Quick Check Answers

1. *d*   2. *a*   3. *c*   4. *c*   5. *c*   6. *a*   7. *d*   8. *d*   9. *b*   10. *d*

Reversing Entries: An Optional Step

Reversing entries are special journal entries that ease the burden of accounting for transactions in a later period. Reversing entries are the exact opposites of certain adjusting entries at the end of the prior period. Reversing entries are used most often in conjunction with accrual-type adjustments, such as accrued salary expense and accrued service revenue. *Generally accepted accounting principles do not require reversing entries. They are used only for convenience and to save time.*

Accounting for Accrued Expenses

To see how reversing entries work, return to Cookie Lapp's unadjusted trial balance at April 30 (Exhibit 4-2, page 198). Salary Expense has a debit balance of $900 for salaries paid during April. At April 30, the business still owes its employee an additional $900 for the last half of the month, so Lapp makes this adjusting entry:

Adjusting Entries			
Apr. 30	Salary Expense	900	
	Salary Payable		900

After posting, the accounts are updated at April 30.[1]

Salary Payable		
	Apr. 30 Adj.	900
	Apr. 30 Bal.	900

Salary Expense		
Paid during April, CP	900	
Apr. 30 Adj.	900	
Apr. 30 Bal.	1,800	

After the adjusting entry,

- The April income statement reports salary expense of $1,800.
- The April 30 balance sheet reports salary payable of $900.

The $1,800 debit balance of Salary Expense is closed at April 30, 2007, with this closing entry:

Closing Entries			
Apr. 30	Income Summary	1,800	
	Salary Expense		1,800

---

[1]Entry explanations used throughout this discussion are

Adj. = Adjusting entry
Bal. = Balance
Clo. = Closing entry
CP = Cash payment entry—a credit to Cash
CR = Cash receipt entry—a debit to Cash
Rev. = Reversing entry

After posting, Salary Expense has a zero balance as follows:

Salary Expense

Paid during April, CP	900		
Apr. 30 Adj.	900		
Apr. 30 Bal.	1,800	Apr. 30 Clo.	1,800

Zero balance

Assume for this illustration that on May 5, the next payday, Lapp will pay the $900 of salary payable left over from April 30 plus $100 of salary expense for the first few days of May. Lapp's next payroll payment will be $1,000 ($900 + $100).

Accounting Without a Reversing Entry

On May 5, the next payday, Lapp pays the payroll of $1,000 and makes this journal entry:

May 5	Salary Payable	900	
	Salary Expense	100	
	Cash		1,000

This method of recording the cash payment is correct. However, it wastes time because Lapp must refer back to the April 30 adjustments. Otherwise, she does not know the amount of the debit to Salary Payable (in this example, $900). Searching April's adjusting entries wastes time and money. To save time, accountants can use reversing entries.

Making a Reversing Entry

A **reversing entry** switches the debit and the credit of a previous adjusting entry. *A reversing entry, then, is the exact opposite of a prior adjusting entry.* The reversing entry is dated the first day of the new period.

To illustrate reversing entries, recall that on April 30, Lapp made the following adjusting entry to accrue Salary Payable:

Adjusting Entries			
Apr. 30	Salary Expense	900	
	Salary Payable		900

The reversing entry simply reverses the debit and the credit of the adjustment:

Reversing Entries			
May 1	Salary Payable	900	
	Salary Expense		900

Observe that the reversing entry is dated the first day of the new period. It is the exact opposite of the April 30 adjusting entry. Ordinarily, the accountant who makes the adjusting entry also prepares the reversing entry at the same time. Lapp dates the reversing entry as of May 1 so that it affects only the new period. Note how the accounts appear after Lapp posts the reversing entry:

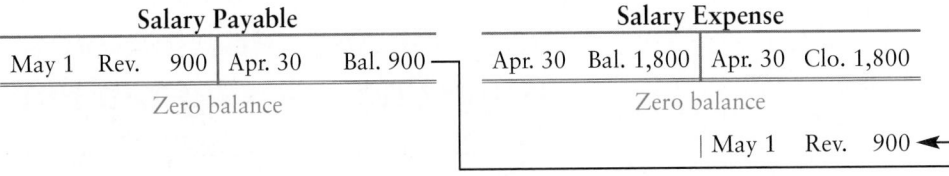

Salary Payable				Salary Expense			
May 1	Rev.	900	Apr. 30 Bal. 900	Apr. 30 Bal. 1,800	Apr. 30	Clo. 1,800
	Zero balance				Zero balance	
					May 1	Rev.	900

The arrow shows the transfer of the $900 credit balance from Salary Payable to Salary Expense. This credit balance in Salary Expense does not mean that the entity has negative salary expense, as you might think. Instead, the odd credit balance in the Salary Expense account is merely a temporary result of the reversing entry. The credit balance is eliminated on May 5, when Lapp pays the payroll and debits Salary Expense in the customary manner:

May 5	Salary Expense		1,000	
	Cash			1,000

This cash payment entry is posted as follows:

Salary Expense					
May 5	CP	1,000	May 1	Rev.	900
May 5	Bal.	100			

Now Salary Expense has its correct debit balance of $100, which is the amount of salary expense incurred in May. The $1,000 cash payment also pays the liability for Salary Payable so that Salary Payable has a zero balance, which is correct.

Appendix 4A Assignment

Problem

P4A-1 Refer to the data in Problem 4-29A, page 228.

Requirements
1. Open accounts for Salary Payable and Salary Expense. Insert their unadjusted balances at August 31, 2009.
2. Journalize adjusting entry (e) and the closing entry for Salary Expense at August 31. Post to the accounts.
3. On September 5, Road Runner Internet paid the next payroll amount of $500. This payment included the accrued amount at August 31, plus $100 for the first few days of September. Journalize this cash payment, and post to the accounts. Show the balance in each account.
4. Using a reversing entry, repeat requirements 1 through 3. Compare the balances of Salary Payable and Salary Expense after using a reversing entry with those balances computed without the reversing entry (as they appear in your answer to requirement 3).

Comprehensive Problem for Chapters 1–4

Journalizing, Posting, Work Sheet, Adjusting, Closing the Financial Statements

Dwyer Delivery Service completed the following transactions during its first month of operations, January 2009.

a. **Dwyer Delivery Service, a proprietorship, began operations by receiving from the owner $5,000 cash and a truck valued at $10,000. The business gave Paul Dwyer, the owner, capital in the business.**

b. **Paid $200 cash for supplies.**

c. **Prepaid insurance, $600.**

d. **Performed delivery services for a customer and received $700 cash.**

e. **Completed a large delivery job, billed the customer $2,000, and received a promise to collect the $2,000 within one week.**

f. **Paid employee salary, $800.**

g. **Received $900 cash for performing delivery services.**

h. **Collected $500 in advance for delivery service to be performed later.**

i. **Collected $2,000 cash from a customer on account.**

j. **Purchased fuel for the truck, paying $100 with a company credit card. Credit Accounts Payable.**

k. **Performed delivery services on account, $800.**

l. **Paid office rent, $500. This rent is not paid in advance.**

m. **Paid $100 on account.**

n. **Dwyer withdrew $1,900 for personal use.**

Requirements

1. Record each transaction in the journal, using the account titles given below. Key each transaction by its letter. Explanations are not required. (pp. 70–76, 131–133, 138–139)

2. Open the following T-accounts in this sequence:

Cash	Service Revenue
Accounts Receivable	Salary Expense
Supplies	Depreciation Expense
Prepaid Insurance	Insurance Expense
Delivery Truck	Fuel Expense
Accumulated Depreciation	Rent Expense
Accounts Payable	Supplies Expense
Salary Payable	
Unearned Service Revenue	
Paul Dwyer, Capital	
Paul Dwyer, Withdrawals	
Income Summary	

Then post the transactions that you recorded in requirement 1. (pp. 70–76)

3. Prepare the trial balance of Dwyer Delivery Service at the end of the month. Enter the trial balance on a 10-column accounting work sheet for the month ended January 31, 2009, listing all accounts in the sequence given above, including those accounts with zero balances. Then complete the work sheet using the following adjustment data at January 31. (p. 198)

   o. Accrued salary expense, $800

   p. Depreciation expense, $50

   q. Prepaid insurance expired, $150

   r. Supplies on hand, $100

   s. Unearned service revenue earned during January, $400

4. Prepare Dwyer Delivery Service's income statement and statement of owner's equity for the month ended January 31, 2009 (page 202), and the classified balance sheet (page 209) on that date. On the income statement list expenses in decreasing order by amount—that is, the largest expense first, the smallest expense last. On the balance sheet, report assets at the left and liabilities and owner's equity at the right, as on page 202. Draw the arrows linking the three financial statements.

5. Journalize and post the adjusting entries. (p. 203)

6. Journalize and post the closing entries. Draw double underlines under the Withdrawals account, the Income Summary account, all the revenue accounts, and all the expense accounts to indicate their zero balances. (p. 205)

7. Prepare a post-closing trial balance at January 31, 2009. (pp. 206–207)

Chapter 4: Demo Doc

Accounting Work Sheets and Closing Entries

Demo Doc: To make sure you understand this material, work through the following demonstration "demo doc" with detailed comments to help you see the concept within the framework of a worked through problem.

Learning Objectives 1–3

This question continues on from the Cloud Break Consulting demo doc in Chapter 3 (pp. 183–184).

Use the data from the adjusted trial balance of Cloud Break Consulting at December 31, 2008:

		Account Title	Adjusted Trial Balance	
			Debit	Credit
		Cash	$131,000	
		Accounts receivable	119,000	
		Supplies	1,000	
		Prepaid rent	18,000	
		Land	45,000	
		Building	300,000	
		Accumulated depreciation		$167,000
		Accounts payable		159,000
		Salary payable		4,000
		Unearned service revenue		10,000
		Susan Cloud, capital		152,000
		Susan Cloud, withdrawals	57,000	
		Service revenue		495,000
		Salary expense	259,000	
		Supplies expense	3,000	
		Rent expense	34,000	
		Depreciation expense	12,000	
		Miscellaneous expense	8,000	
		Totals	$987,000	$987,000

CLOUD BREAK CONSULTING
Adjusted Trial Balance
December 31, 2008

Requirements

1. Prepare Cloud's accounting work sheet showing the adjusted trial balance, the income statement accounts, and the balance sheet accounts.

2. Journalize and post Cloud's closing entries.

Chapter 4: Demo Doc Solution

Requirement 1

Prepare Cloud's accounting work sheet showing the adjusted trial balance, the income statement accounts, and the balance sheet accounts.

Part 1	Part 2	Part 3	Part 4	Part 5	Demo Doc Complete

The accounting work sheet is very similar to the adjusted trial balance; however, it has additional debit and credit columns for the income statement and balance sheet.

CLOUD BREAK CONSULTING
Work Sheet
December 31, 2008

Account Title	Adjusted Trial Balance		Income Statement		Balance Sheet	
	Debit	Credit	Debit	Credit	Debit	Credit
Cash	131,000					
Accounts receivable	119,000					
Supplies	1,000					
Prepaid rent expense	18,000					
Land	45,000					
Building	300,000					
Accumulated depreciation		167,000				
Accounts payable		159,000				
Salary payable		4,000				
Unearned service revenue		10,000				
Susan Cloud, capital		152,000				
Susan Cloud, withdrawals	57,000					
Service revenue		495,000				
Salary expense	259,000					
Supplies expense	3,000					
Rent expense	34,000					
Depreciation expense	12,000					
Miscellaneous expense	8,000					
	987,000	987,000				

The accounts that belong on the income statement are sorted to the income statement columns and all other accounts are sorted to the balance sheet columns.

The income statement lists revenues and expenses. So Cloud's revenue (service revenue) and expenses (salary expense, supplies expense, rent expense, depreciation

continued . . .

expense, and miscellaneous expense) are copied over to the income statement columns:

CLOUD BREAK CONSULTING
Work Sheet
December 31, 2008

Account Title	Adjusted Trial Balance Debit	Adjusted Trial Balance Credit	Income Statement Debit	Income Statement Credit	Balance Sheet Debit	Balance Sheet Credit
Cash	131,000					
Accounts receivable	119,000					
Supplies	1,000					
Prepaid rent expense	18,000					
Land	45,000					
Building	300,000					
Accumulated depreciation		167,000				
Accounts payable		159,000				
Salary payable		4,000				
Unearned service revenue		10,000				
Susan Cloud, capital		152,000				
Susan Cloud, withdrawals	57,000					
Service revenue		495,000		495,000		
Salary expense	259,000		259,000			
Supplies expense	3,000		3,000			
Rent expense	34,000		34,000			
Depreciation expense	12,000		12,000			
Miscellaneous expense	8,000		8,000			
	987,000	987,000	316,000	495,000		
Net income			179,000			
			495,000	495,000		

Net income is calculated by subtracting the expenses from the revenues, $495,000 − $316,000 = $179,000. We add net income to the debit side of the income statement. This makes total debits equal total credits. Notice that this $179,000 is the same as net income from the income statement prepared in the Chapter 3 Demo Doc (p. 193).

The other accounts (assets, liabilities, and equity) are now copied over to the balance sheet columns.

CLOUD BREAK CONSULTING
Work Sheet
December 31, 2008

Account Title	Adjusted Trial Balance		Income Statement		Balance Sheet	
	Debit	Credit	Debit	Credit	Debit	Credit
Cash	131,000				131,000	
Accounts receivable	119,000				119,000	
Supplies	1,000				1,000	
Prepaid rent expense	18,000				18,000	
Land	45,000				45,000	
Building	300,000				300,000	
Accumulated depreciation		167,000				167,000
Accounts payable		159,000				159,000
Salary payable		4,000				4,000
Unearned service revenue		10,000				10,000
Susan Cloud, capital		152,000				152,000
Susan Cloud, withdrawals	57,000				57,000	
Service revenue		495,000		495,000		
Salary expense	259,000		259,000			
Supplies expense	3,000		3,000			
Rent expense	34,000		34,000			
Depreciation expense	12,000		12,000			
Miscellaneous expense	8,000		8,000			
	987,000	987,000	316,000	495,000	671,000	492,000
Net income			179,000			179,000
			495,000	495,000	671,000	671,000

Net income is added to the credit side of the balance sheet to make total debits equal total credits. This is because net income increases the Capital account (as seen in Requirement 2 of this question, in which the closing entries are journalized).

Requirement 2

Journalize and post Cloud's closing entries.

Part 1	**Part 2**	Part 3	Part 4	Part 5	Demo Doc Complete

We prepare closing entries to (1) clear out the revenue, expense, and withdrawal accounts to a zero balance. This gets them ready for the next period; that is, they must begin the next period empty so that we can evaluate each period's income separately from other periods. We also need to (2) update the Capital account by transferring all revenues, expenses, and withdrawals into it.

continued . . .

The Capital account balance is calculated each year using the following formula:

Beginning capital balance
+ Owner investments
———————————————
Adjusted capital balance
+ Net income (or − Net loss)
− Owner withdrawals
———————————————
= Ending capital balance

You can see this in the Capital T-account as well:

Capital	
	Beginning Capital Balance **Investments**
	Adjusted Capital Balance **Net Income**
Withdrawals	
	Ending Capital Balance

This formula is the key to preparing the closing entries. We will use this formula, but we will do it *inside* the Capital T-account.

From the adjusted trial balance, we know that the adjusted Capital balance is $152,000. This is the *adjusted* Capital balance because any capital investments during the year were already credited to this account before the trial balance was prepared. Therefore, the adjusted Capital amount is already in the T-account.

The next component is net income, which is *not* already in the Capital account. There is no T-account with net income in it, but we can *create* one.

We will create a new T-account called Income Summary. We will place in the Income Summary account all the components of net income and come out with the net income number at the bottom. Remember:

Revenues − Expenses = Net income

This means that we need to get all of the revenues and expenses into the Income Summary account.

Let's look at the Service Revenue T-account:

Service Revenue	
	Bal. 495,000

In order to clear out the Income Statement accounts so that they are empty to begin the next year, the first step is to debit each revenue account for the amount of its credit balance. Service Revenue has a *credit* balance of $495,000, so to bring that to zero, we need to *debit* $495,000.

This means that we have part of our first closing entry:

1.	Service Revenue	495,000	
	???		495,000

What is the credit side of this entry? The reason we started with Service Revenue was to help calculate net income using the Income Summary account. So the other side of the entry must go to the Income Summary:

| 1. | Service Revenue | 495,000 | |
| | Income Summary | | 495,000 |

Part 1	Part 2	**Part 3**	Part 4	Part 5	Demo Doc Complete

The second step is to *credit* each expense account for the amount of its *debit* balance to bring these accounts to zero. In this case, we have five different expenses:

Salary Expense		Supplies Expense	
Bal.	259,000	Bal.	3,000

Rent Expense		Depreciation Expense	
Bal.	34,000	Bal.	12,000

Miscellaneous Expense	
Bal.	8,000

The balancing debit for each expense will go to the debit side of the Income Summary account:

2.	Income Summary	316,000	
	Salary Expense		259,000
	Supplies Expense		3,000
	Rent Expense		34,000
	Depreciation Expense		12,000
	Miscellaneous Expense		8,000

Part 1	Part 2	Part 3	**Part 4**	Part 5	Demo Doc Complete

Now the Income Summary account holds all the revenues (1), all the expenses (2), and, therefore, net income (Bal.).

Income Summary			
		1.	495,000
2.	316,000		
		Bal.	179,000

Remember that the credit of $495,000 is from the first closing entry prepared at the beginning of this requirement.

The purpose of creating this account was to get a net income number. Notice that this balance is the same net income number that appears on the income statement and in the accounting work sheet in Requirement 1.

Income Summary now has a *credit* balance of $179,000. The third step in the closing process is to transfer net income to the Capital account. To remove it from the Income Summary, we must *debit* the Income Summary for $179,000:

3.	Income Summary	179,000	
	???		179,000

What is the credit side of this entry? The reason we created the (temporary) Income Summary account was to help calculate net income or net loss for the Capital account. So the credit side of the entry must go to Susan Cloud, Capital:

3.	Income Summary	179,000	
	Susan Cloud, Capital		179,000

This adds the net income to the Capital account. Notice that it also brings the Income Summary account to a zero balance.

Part 1	Part 2	Part 3	Part 4	**Part 5**	Demo Doc Complete

The last component of the Capital account formula is withdrawals. There is already a Withdrawals account that exists:

Susan Cloud, Withdrawals

Bal.	57,000	

The final step in the closing process is to transfer the owner's withdrawals to the debit side of the Capital account. The Withdrawals account has a *debit* balance of $57,000, so to bring that to zero, we need to *credit* the Withdrawals account for $57,000. The balancing debit will go to the Susan Cloud, Capital account:

4.	Susan Cloud, Capital	57,000	
	Susan Cloud, Withdrawals		57,000

This subtracts the withdrawals from the Capital account.
The Capital account now holds the following transactions:

Susan Cloud, Capital

			152,000	**Adjusted Capital Balance**
		3.	179,000	**Net Income**
Withdrawals 4.		57,000		
		Bal.	274,000	**Ending Capital Balance**

The formula to update the Capital amount has now been recreated inside the Capital T-account.

The following accounts are used in the closing process:

Service Revenue		
		495,000
1.	495,000	
	Bal.	0

Income Summary		
	1.	495,000
2.	316,000	
	Bal.	179,000
3.	179,000	
	Bal.	0

Salary Expense		
259,000		
	2.	259,000
Bal.	0	

Susan Cloud, Withdrawals		
57,000		
	4.	57,000
Bal.	0	

Supplies Expense		
3,000		
	2.	3,000
Bal.	0	

Rent Expense		
34,000		
	2.	34,000
Bal.	0	

Susan Cloud, Capital		
		152,000
	3.	179,000
4.	57,000	
	Bal.	274,000

Depreciation Expense		
12,000		
	2.	12,000
Bal.	0	

Miscellaneous Expense		
8,000		
	2.	8,000
Bal.	0	

Notice that all temporary accounts (the revenue, the expense, the withdrawals, and the Income Summary accounts) now have a zero balance.

Part 1	Part 2	Part 3	Part 4	Part 5	Demo Doc Complete

5 Merchandising Operations

Learning Objectives

1 Account for the purchase of inventory

2 Account for the sale of inventory

3 Adjust and close the accounts of a merchandising business

4 Prepare a merchandiser's financial statements

5 Use gross profit percentage and inventory turnover to evaluate a business

6 Compute cost of goods sold in a periodic inventory system

hapters 1–4 began with Sherman Lawn Service and DeFilippo Catering. You can identify with these businesses because you might operate a lawn service, a catering operation, or other small business. Sherman Lawn Service and DeFilippo Catering are similar. Both are proprietorships, and they follow the same accounting procedures.

Julie DeFilippo's catering business differs from the lawn service of Haig Sherman. Sherman provides a service for customers, whereas DeFilippo sells a product—food. Businesses that sell a product are called merchandisers because they sell merchandise, or goods, to customers.

In the early going we accounted for service companies, such as Sherman Lawn Service and Cookie Lapp Travel Design. That enabled us to focus on basic accounting:

- recording transactions
- adjusting and closing the books
- preparing the financial statements

These aspects of accounting are the same for service and merchandising entities.

Merchandisers have an additional asset—merchandise inventory—that service companies don't need. (We usually drop the term *merchandise* and refer simply to *inventory*). **Inventory** is defined as the merchandise that a company holds for sale to customers. For example, DeFilippo Catering must hold some food inventory in order to operate. Wal-Mart carries food inventory in addition to clothing, housewares, and school supplies. A Chevy dealer holds inventories of automobiles and auto parts. ■

Chapter 5 introduces merchandising. In this chapter we show how to account for the purchase and sale of inventory. We feature a small music store, and we use an actual business document to illustrate transactions.

Before launching into merchandising, let's compare service entities, with which you are familiar, to merchandising companies. Exhibit 5-1 shows how a service entity (on the left) differs from a merchandiser (on the right).

EXHIBIT 5-1	Financial Statements of a Service Company and a Merchandiser

SERVICE CO.* Balance Sheet June 30, 2008		MERCHANDISING CO.** Balance Sheet June 30, 2008	
Assets		**Assets**	
Current assets:		Current assets:	
Cash	$X	Cash	$X
Short-term investments	X	Short-term investments	X
Accounts receivable, net	X	Accounts receivable, net	X
Prepaid expenses	X	Inventory	X
		Prepaid expenses	X
*Such as Cookie Lapp Travel Design		**Such as Austin Sound, a music store in Austin, Texas	

SERVICE CO. Income Statement Year Ended June 30, 2008		MERCHANDISING CO. Income Statement Year Ended June 30, 2008	
Service revenue	$XXX	Sales revenue	$X,XXX
Expenses:		Cost of goods sold	X
Salary expense	X	Gross profit	XXX
Depreciation expense	X	Operating expenses:	
Rent expense	X	Salary expense	X
Net income	$ X	Depreciation expense	X
		Rent expense	X
		Net income	$ X

What Are Merchandising Operations?

Merchandising consists of buying and selling products rather than services. Merchandisers have some new balance sheet and income statement items.

BALANCE SHEET:

- Inventory, an asset

INCOME STATEMENT:

- Sales revenue (often abbreviated as Sales)
- Cost of goods sold, an expense

These items are highlighted in Exhibit 5-1 for Merchandising Co. Let's examine the operating cycle of a merchandising business.

The Operating Cycle of a Merchandising Business

The operating cycle of a merchandiser (see Exhibit 5-2):

1. Begins when the company purchases inventory
2. Then sells the inventory
3. And, last, collects cash from customers

EXHIBIT 5-2   Operating Cycle of a Merchandiser

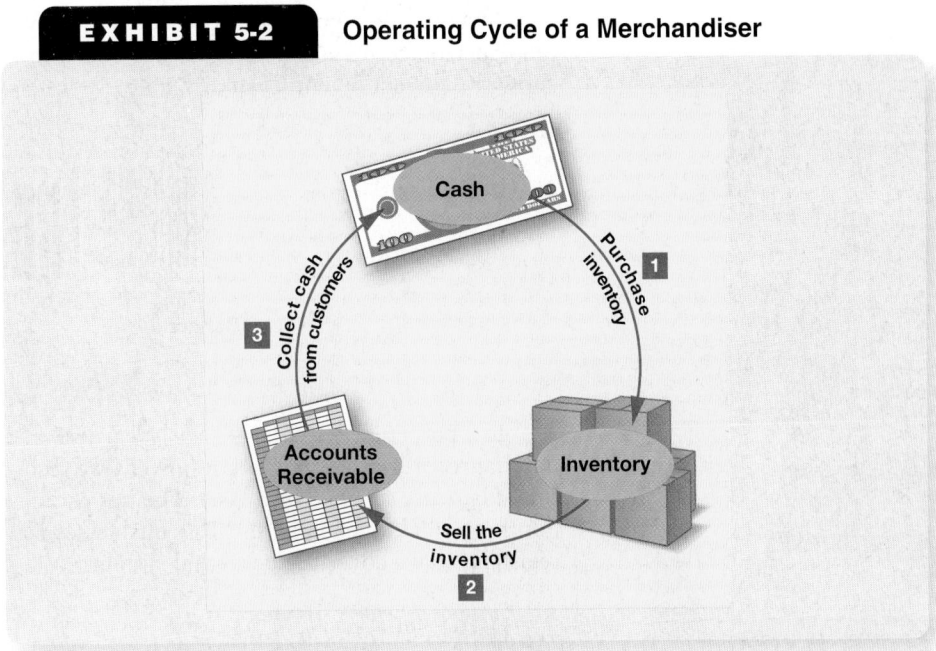

Now let's see how companies account for their inventory. We begin with journal entries. Then we post to the ledger accounts and, finally, prepare the financial statements.

Inventory Systems: Perpetual and Periodic

There are two main types of inventory accounting systems:

- Periodic system
- Perpetual system

The **periodic inventory system** is used for relatively inexpensive goods. A convenience store without optical-scanning cash registers doesn't keep a running record of every loaf of bread and every key chain that it sells. Instead, the business counts its inventory periodically to determine the quantities on hand. Restaurants and small retail stores also use the periodic system. Appendix 5B to this chapter (page 304) covers the periodic system, which is becoming less and less popular with the use of computers.

The **perpetual inventory system** keeps a running record of inventory and cost of goods sold. This system achieves control over the inventory. Even in a perpetual system, the business counts inventory at least once a year. The physical count establishes the correct amount of ending inventory for the financial statements and also serves as a check on the perpetual records.

The following chart compares the perpetual and periodic systems:

Perpetual Inventory System	Periodic Inventory System
• Keeps a running record of all inventory as it is bought and sold.	• Does *not* keep a running record of inventory on hand.

In both systems the inventory on hand is counted at least once each year.

Perpetual Inventory Systems

A modern perpetual inventory system records

- units purchased
- units sold
- the quantity of inventory on hand

Inventory systems are integrated with accounts receivable and sales. For example, Amazon.com's computers use bar codes to keep up-to-the-minute records and show the current inventory at any time.

Bar code

In a perpetual system, the "cash register" at a Target store is a computer terminal that records sales and updates inventory records. Bar codes such as the one illustrated here are scanned by a laser. The bar coding represents inventory and cost data that keep track of each item. Most businesses use bar codes and computerized cash registers, so we cover the perpetual system.

Accounting for Inventory in the Perpetual System

The cycle of a merchandising entity begins with the purchase of inventory. In this section, we trace the steps that Austin Sound Center, a music store in Austin, Texas, takes to account for inventory. Austin Sound sells DVD players that it purchases from JDC.

1. JDC ships the inventory to Austin Sound and sends an invoice the same day. The **invoice** is the seller's request for payment from the buyer. An invoice is also called a *bill*. Exhibit 5-3 is the purchase invoice that Austin Sound received from JDC.

2. After the inventory is received, Austin Sound pays JDC.

EXHIBIT 5-3 Purchase Invoice

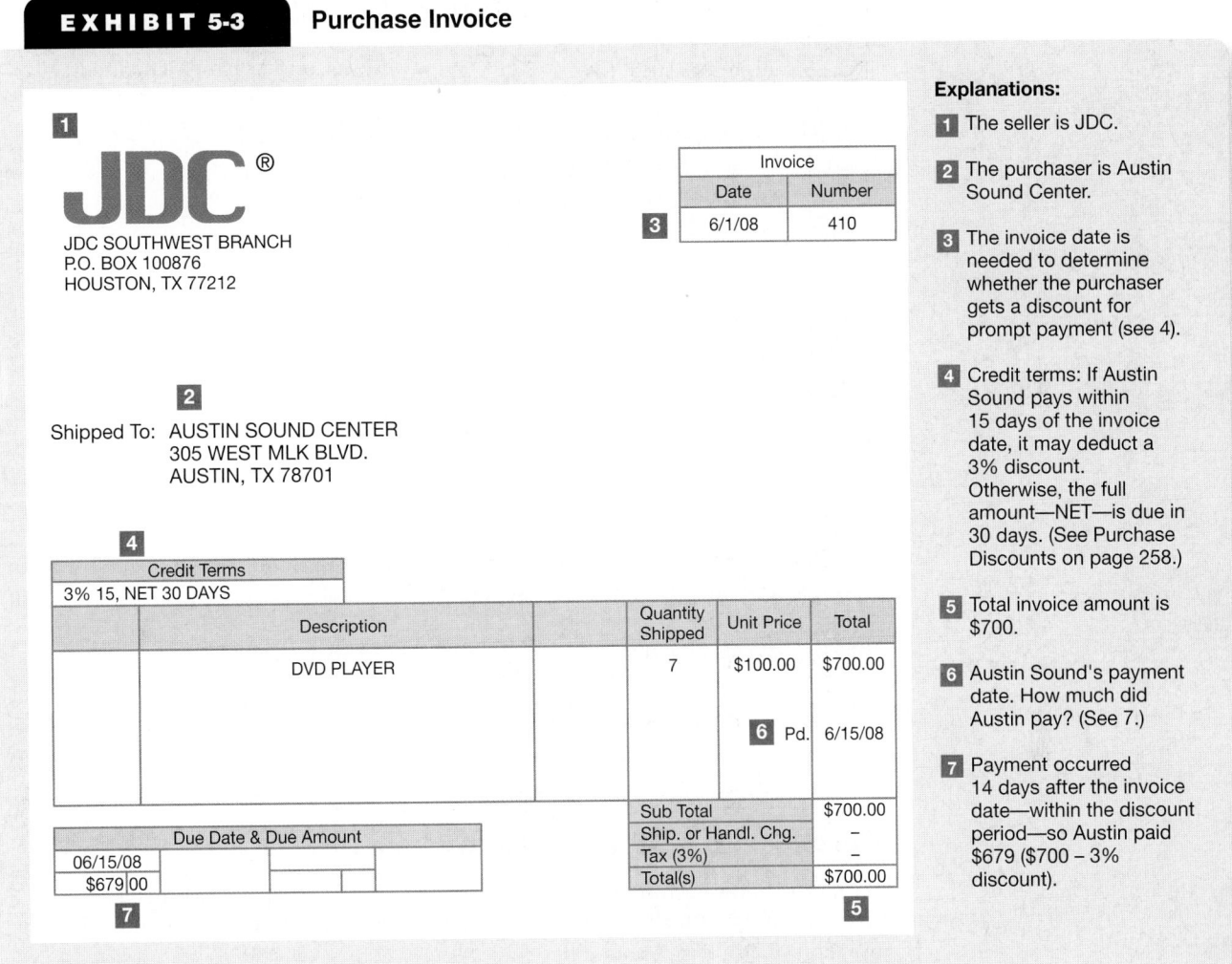

Explanations:

1. The seller is JDC.

2. The purchaser is Austin Sound Center.

3. The invoice date is needed to determine whether the purchaser gets a discount for prompt payment (see 4).

4. Credit terms: If Austin Sound pays within 15 days of the invoice date, it may deduct a 3% discount. Otherwise, the full amount—NET—is due in 30 days. (See Purchase Discounts on page 258.)

5. Total invoice amount is $700.

6. Austin Sound's payment date. How much did Austin pay? (See 7.)

7. Payment occurred 14 days after the invoice date—within the discount period—so Austin paid $679 ($700 – 3% discount).

Purchase of Inventory

1. Account for the purchase of inventory

Here we use the actual invoice in Exhibit 5-3 to illustrate the purchasing process. Suppose Austin Sound receives the goods on June 3. Austin Sound records this purchase on account as follows:

June 3	Inventory	700	
	Accounts Payable		700
	Purchased inventory on account.		

The Inventory account is used only for goods purchased for resale. Supplies, equipment, and other assets are recorded in their own accounts. Inventory is an asset until it's sold.

Purchase Discounts

Many businesses offer customers a purchase discount for early payment. JDC's credit terms of "3% 15, NET 30 DAYS" mean that Austin Sound may deduct 3% if Austin pays within 15 days of the invoice date. Otherwise, the full amount—NET—is due in 30 days. These credit terms can also be expressed as "3/15, n/30."

Terms of "n/30" mean that no discount is offered and payment is due 30 days after the invoice date. Terms of *eom* mean that payment is due at the end of the current month.

Austin Sound paid within the discount period, so the cash payment entry is

June 15	Accounts Payable	700	
	Cash ($700 × 0.97)		679
	Inventory ($700 × 0.03)		21
	Paid within discount period.		

The discount is credited to Inventory because the discount decreases the cost, as shown in the Inventory account:

Inventory			
June 3	700	June 15	21
Bal.	679		

But if Austin Sound pays this invoice after the discount period, Austin Sound must pay the full $700. In that case, the payment entry is:

June 24	Accounts Payable	700	
	Cash		700
	Paid after discount period.		

Purchase Returns and Allowances

Businesses allow customers to *return* merchandise that is defective, damaged, or otherwise unsuitable. Or the seller may deduct an *allowance* from the amount the buyer owes. Purchase returns and allowances decrease the buyer's cost of the inventory.

Suppose a DVD player purchased by Austin Sound (Exhibit 5-3) was damaged in shipment. Austin returns the goods to JDC and records the purchase return as follows:

June 4	Accounts Payable	100	
	Inventory		100
	Returned inventory to seller.		

Transportation Costs

Someone must pay the transportation cost of shipping inventory from seller to buyer. The purchase agreement specifies FOB terms (*free on board*) to indicate who pays the freight. Exhibit 5-4 shows that:

- FOB shipping point means buyer pays the freight.
- FOB destination means seller pays the freight.

| EXHIBIT 5-4 | FOB Terms Determine Who Pays the Freight |

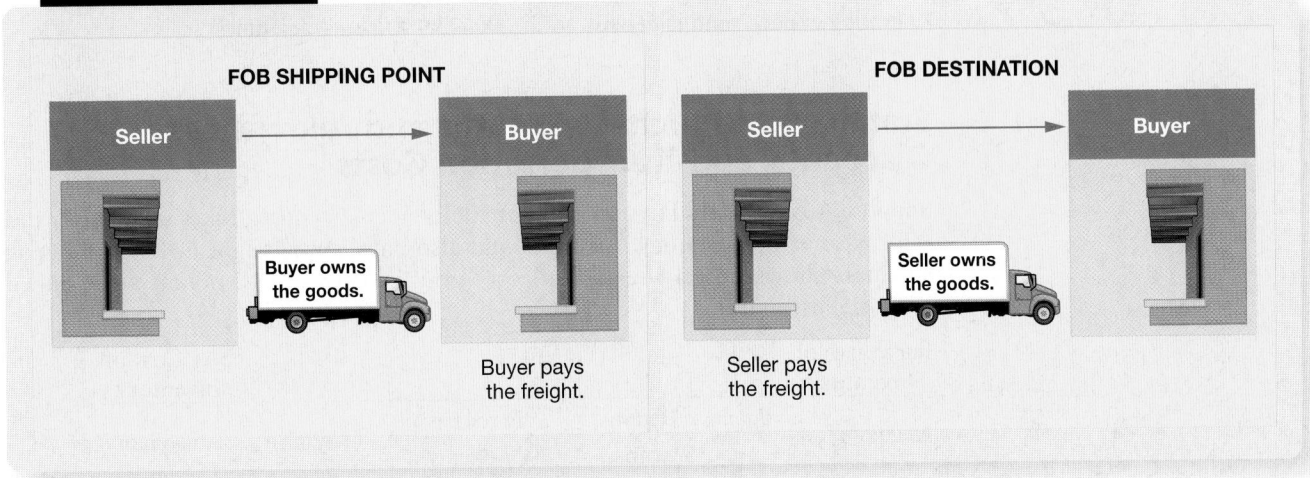

Freight costs are either freight in or freight out.

- *Freight in* is the transportation cost on *purchased goods.*
- *Freight out* is the transportation cost on *goods sold.*

FREIGHT IN FOB shipping point is most common. The buyer owns the goods while they are in transit, so the buyer pays the freight. Freight in becomes part of the cost of inventory and is, therefore, debited to the Inventory account. Suppose Austin Sound pays a $60 freight charge and makes this entry:

June 3	Inventory	60	
	Cash		60
	Paid a freight bill.		

The freight charge increases the net cost of the inventory to $660, as follows:

		Inventory			
June 3	Purchase	700	June 4	Return	100
June 3	Freight in	60			
Bal.	Net cost	660			

Discounts are computed only on the account payable to the seller ($600), not on the transportation costs, because there is no discount on freight.

Under FOB shipping point, the seller sometimes prepays the transportation cost as a convenience and lists this cost on the invoice. A $5,000 purchase of goods, coupled with a related freight charge of $400, would be recorded as follows:

June 20	Inventory ($5,000 + $400)	5,400	
	Accounts Payable		5,400
	Purchased inventory on account, including freight.		

If the buyer pays within the discount period, the discount will be computed on the $5,000 merchandise cost, not on the $5,400. For example, a 2% discount would be $100 ($5,000 × 0.02).

FREIGHT OUT   The seller may pay freight charges to ship goods to customers. This is called *freight out*. Freight out is delivery expense to the seller. Delivery expense is an operating expense and is debited to the Delivery Expense account.

Summary of Purchase Returns and Allowances, Discounts, and Transportation Costs

Suppose Austin Sound buys $35,000 of audio/video inventory, takes a discount, and returns some of the goods. Austin Sound also pays some freight in. The following summary shows Austin Sound's net cost of this inventory. All amounts are assumed for this illustration.

Purchases of Inventory				Net Cost of Inventory
Inventory −	Purchase Returns and Allowances −	Purchase Discounts +	Freight in =	Inventory
$35,000 −	$700 −	$800 +	$2,100 =	$35,600

Inventory			
Purchases of inventory	35,000	Purchase returns & allow.	700
Freight in	2,100	Purchase discount	800
Balance	35,600		

Sale of Inventory

2   Account for the sale of inventory

After a company buys inventory, the next step is to sell the goods. We shift now to the selling side and follow Austin Sound Center through a sequence of selling transactions.

The amount a business earns from selling merchandise inventory is called **sales revenue** (often abbreviated as **sales**). A sale also creates an expense, Cost of Goods Sold, as the seller gives up the asset Inventory. **Cost of goods sold** is the cost of inventory that has been sold to customers. Cost of goods sold (often abbreviated as **cost of sales**) is the merchandiser's major expense.

After making a sale on account, Austin Sound may experience any of the following:

- *A sales return:* The customer may return goods to Austin Sound.
- *A sales allowance:* Austin Sound may grant a sales allowance to reduce the cash to be collected from the customer.
- *A sales discount:* If the customer pays within the discount period—under terms such as 2/10, n/30—Austin Sound collects the discounted amount.
- *Freight out:* Austin Sound may have to pay delivery expense to transport the goods to the buyer.

Let's begin with a cash sale.

Cash Sale

Sales of retailers, such as Austin Sound, grocery stores, and Old Navy, are often for cash. Suppose Austin Sound made a $3,000 cash sale and issued the sales invoice in Exhibit 5-5.

| EXHIBIT 5-5 | Sales Invoice |

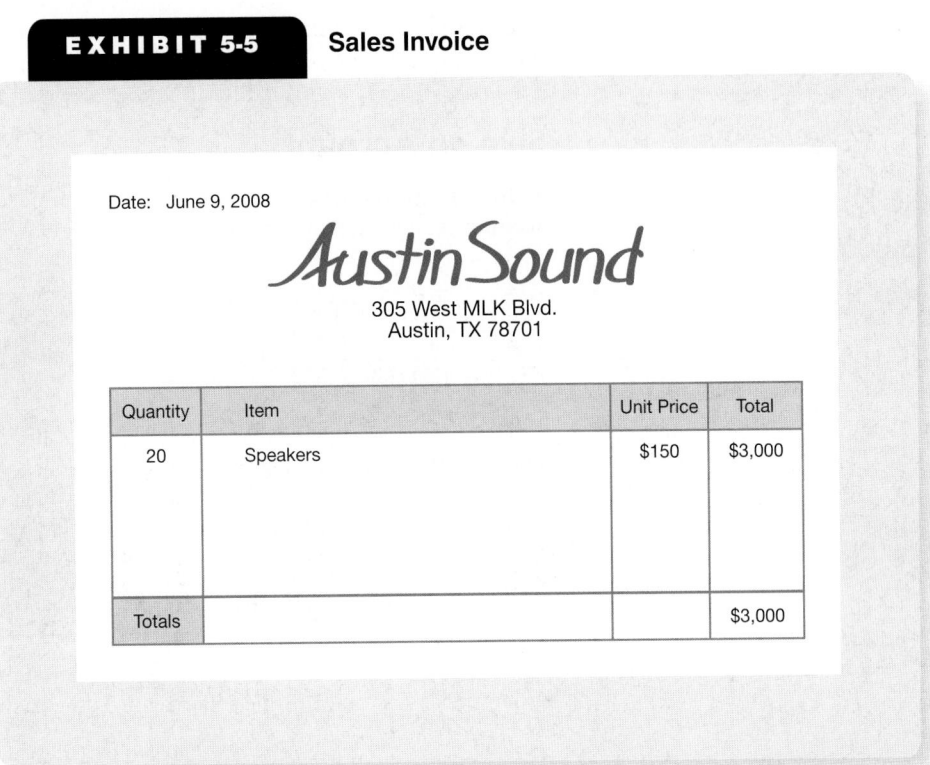

Date: June 9, 2008

AustinSound
305 West MLK Blvd.
Austin, TX 78701

Quantity	Item	Unit Price	Total
20	Speakers	$150	$3,000
Totals			$3,000

Cash sales of $3,000 are recorded by debiting Cash and crediting Sales Revenue as follows:

June 9	Cash	3,000	
	Sales Revenue		3,000
	Cash sale.		

Austin Sound sold goods and, therefore, must decrease the Inventory balance. Suppose these goods cost Austin $1,900. A second journal entry is needed to transfer the $1,900 cost of the goods from the Inventory account to Cost of Goods Sold, as follows:

June 9	Cost of Goods Sold	1,900	
	Inventory		1,900
	Recorded the cost of goods sold.		

The Cost of Goods Sold account keeps a current balance throughout the period. In this example, cost of goods sold is not $3,000, because that's the selling price of the goods. *Cost of goods sold is always based on the entity's cost, not the selling price.*

After posting, the Cost of Goods Sold account holds the cost of the inventory sold ($1,900 in this case):

Inventory			Cost of Goods Sold	
Purchases 50,000	Cost of sales 1,900 ⟵⟶	June 9	1,900	
(amount assumed)				

The computer automatically records the cost of goods sold entry. The cashier scans the bar code on the product and the computer performs this task.

Sale on Account

Most sales in the United States are made on account (on credit). A $5,000 sale on account is recorded as follows:

June 11	Accounts Receivable	5,000	
	Sales Revenue		5,000
	Sale on account.		

These goods cost the seller $2,900, so the related cost of goods sold entry is:

June 11	Cost of Goods Sold	2,900	
	Inventory		2,900
	Recorded the cost of goods sold.		

When the cash comes in, the seller records the cash receipt on account as follows:

June 19	Cash	5,000	
	Accounts Receivable		5,000
	Collection on account.		

Sales Discounts and Sales Returns and Allowances

We saw that purchase returns and allowances and purchase discounts decrease the cost of inventory purchases. In the same way, **sales returns and allowances** and **sales discounts** decrease the net amount of revenue earned on sales. Sales Returns and Allowances and Sales Discounts are contra accounts to Sales Revenue.

$$\frac{\text{Sales}}{\text{Revenue}} - \frac{\text{Sales Returns}}{\text{and Allowances}} - \frac{\text{Sales}}{\text{Discounts}} = \frac{\text{Net Sales}}{\text{Revenue}}[1]$$

Companies maintain separate accounts for Sales Discounts and Sales Returns and Allowances. Now let's examine a sequence of JDC sale transactions. Assume JDC is selling to Austin Sound Center.

On July 7, JDC sells stereo components for $7,200 on credit terms of 2/10, n/30. These goods cost JDC $4,700. JDC's entries to record this credit sale and the related cost of goods sold are:

July 7	Accounts Receivable	7,200	
	Sales Revenue		7,200
	Sale on account.		

7	Cost of Goods Sold	4,700	
	Inventory		4,700
	Recorded cost of goods sold.		

---

[1]Often abbreviated as Net sales.

SALES RETURNS Assume that the buyer returns $600 of the goods. JDC, the seller, records the sales return as follows:

July 12	Sales Returns and Allowances	600	
	Accounts Receivable		600
	Received returned goods.		

Accounts Receivable decreases because JDC will not collect cash for the returned goods.

JDC receives the returned merchandise and updates its inventory records. JDC must also decrease Cost of Goods Sold as follows (the returned goods cost JDC $400):

July 12	Inventory	400	
	Cost of Goods Sold		400
	Placed goods back in inventory.		

SALES ALLOWANCES Suppose JDC grants a $100 sales allowance for damaged goods. A sales allowance is recorded as follows:

July 15	Sales Returns and Allowances	100	
	Accounts Receivable		100
	Granted a sales allowance for damaged goods.		

There is no inventory entry for a sales allowance because the seller receives no returned goods from the customer.

After these entries are posted, Accounts Receivable has a $6,500 debit balance, as follows:

Accounts Receivable					
July 7	Sale	7,200	July 12	Return	600
			15	Allowance	100
Bal.		6,500			

SALES DISCOUNTS On July 17, the last day of the discount period, JDC collects this receivable. JDC's cash receipt is $6,370 [$6,500 − ($6,500 × 0.02)], and the collection entry is:

July 17	Cash	6,370	
	Sales Discounts ($6,500 × 0.02)	130	
	Accounts Receivable		6,500
	Cash collection within the discount period.		

Now, JDC's Accounts Receivable balance is zero:

Accounts Receivable					
July 7	Sale	7,200	July 12	Return	600
			15	Allowance	100
			17	Collection	6,500
Bal.		–0–			

Sales Revenue, Cost of Goods Sold, and Gross Profit

Net sales, cost of goods sold, and gross profit are key elements of profitability. Net sales revenue minus cost of goods sold is called **gross profit**, or **gross margin**.

Net sales − Cost of goods sold = Gross profit

Gross profit, along with net income, is a measure of business success. A sufficiently high gross profit is vital to a merchandiser.

The following example will clarify the nature of gross profit. Suppose JDC's cost to purchase a DVD is $15 and JDC sells the DVD for $20. JDC's gross profit per unit is $5, computed as follows:

Sales revenue earned by selling one DVD	$20
Less: Cost of goods sold for the DVD (what the DVD cost JDC)	(15)
Gross profit on the sale of one DVD	$ 5

The gross profit reported on JDC's income statement is the sum of the gross profits on the DVDs and all the other products the company sold during the year.

Let's put into practice what you've learned in the first half of this chapter.

Summary Problem 1

Suppose Liberty Sales Co. engaged in the following transactions during June of the current year:

June 3	Purchased inventory on credit terms of 1/10 net eom (end of month), $1,600.
9	Returned 40% of the inventory purchased on June 3. It was defective.
12	Sold goods for cash, $920 (cost, $550).
15	Purchased goods for $5,000. Credit terms were 3/15, net 30.
16	Paid a $260 freight bill on goods purchased.
18	Sold inventory for $2,000 on credit terms of 2/10, n/30 (cost, $1,180).
22	Received returned goods from the customer of the June 18 sale, $800 (cost, $480).
24	Borrowed money from the bank to take advantage of the discount offered on the June 15 purchase. Signed a note payable to the bank for the net amount, $4,850.
24	Paid supplier for goods purchased on June 15, less the discount.
28	Received cash in full settlement of the account from the customer who purchased inventory on June 18, less the return on June 22, and less the discount.
29	Paid the amount owed on account from the purchase of June 3, less the June 9 return.

Requirements

1. Journalize the preceding transactions for Liberty. Explanations are not required.

2. Set up T-accounts and post the journal entries to show the ending balances in the Inventory and the Cost of Goods Sold accounts.

3. Assume that the note payable signed on June 24 requires the payment of $90 interest expense. Was borrowing funds to take the cash discount a wise or unwise decision?

Solution

Requirement 1

June	3	Inventory	1,600	
		Accounts Payable		1,600
	9	Accounts Payable ($1,600 × 0.40)	640	
		Inventory		640
	12	Cash	920	
		Sales Revenue		920
	12	Cost of Goods Sold	550	
		Inventory		550
	15	Inventory	5,000	
		Accounts Payable		5,000
	16	Inventory	260	
		Cash		260
	18	Accounts Receivable	2,000	
		Sales Revenue		2,000
	18	Cost of Goods Sold	1,180	
		Inventory		1,180
	22	Sales Returns and Allowances	800	
		Accounts Receivable		800
	22	Inventory	480	
		Cost of Goods Sold		480
	24	Cash	4,850	
		Note Payable		4,850
	24	Accounts Payable	5,000	
		Inventory ($5,000 × 0.03)		150
		Cash ($5,000 × 0.97)		4,850
	28	Cash [($2,000 − $800) × 0.98]	1,176	
		Sales Discounts [($2,000 − $800) × 0.02]	24	
		Accounts Receivable ($2,000 − $800)		1,200
	29	Accounts Payable ($1,600 − $640)	960	
		Cash		960

Requirement 2

Inventory					Cost of Goods Sold			
June 3	1,600	June 9	640		June 12	550	June 22	480
15	5,000	12	550		18	1,180		
16	260	18	1,180					
22	480	24	150		Bal.	1,250		
Bal.	4,820							

Requirement 3

Liberty's decision to borrow funds was wise because the discount received ($150) exceeded the interest paid ($90). Thus Liberty was $60 better off.

Adjusting and Closing the Accounts of a Merchandiser

3 Adjust and close the accounts of a merchandising business

A merchandiser adjusts and closes accounts the same way a service entity does. If a work sheet is used, the trial balance is entered, and the work sheet is completed to determine net income or net loss.

Adjusting Inventory Based on a Physical Count

The inventory account should stay current at all times. However, the actual amount of inventory on hand may differ from what the books show. Theft, damage, and errors occur. For this reason, businesses take a physical count of inventory at least once a year. The most common time to count inventory is at the end of the year. The business then adjusts the Inventory account based on the physical count.

At year end Austin Sound's Inventory account shows an unadjusted balance of $40,500.

Inventory	
Dec. 31 40,500	

With no shrinkage—due to theft or error—the business should have inventory costing $40,500. But on December 31, Austin Sound counts the inventory on hand, and the total cost comes to only $40,200.

INVENTORY BALANCE BEFORE ADJUSTMENT	–	ACTUAL INVENTORY ON HAND	=	ADJUSTING ENTRY TO INVENTORY
$40,500	–	$40,200	=	Credit of $300

Austin Sound records this adjusting entry for inventory shrinkage:

Dec. 31	Cost of Goods Sold	300	
	Inventory ($40,500 – $40,200)		300
	Adjustment for inventory shrinkage.		

This entry brings Inventory to its correct balance.

Inventory			
Dec. 31	40,500	Dec. 31 Adj.	300
Dec. 31 Bal.	40,200		

Austin Sound's other adjustments, plus a complete merchandising work sheet, are covered in Appendix 5A, pages 279–280, at the end of this chapter.

Closing the Accounts of a Merchandiser

Exhibit 5-6 presents Austin Sound's closing entries, which are similar to those in Chapter 4, except for the new accounts (highlighted in color). All amounts are assumed for this illustration. C. Ernest is the owner of Austin Sound Center.

EXHIBIT 5-6	Closing Entries for a Merchandiser

Journal

		Closing Entries		
1.	Dec. 31	Sales Revenue	169,300	
		Income Summary		169,300
2.	31	Income Summary	116,200	
		Sales Discounts		1,400
		Sales Returns and Allowances		2,000
		Cost of Goods Sold		90,800
		Wage Expense		10,200
		Rent Expense		8,400
		Depreciation Expense		600
		Insurance Expense		1,000
		Supplies Expense		500
		Interest Expense		1,300
3.	31	Income Summary ($169,300 – $116,200)	53,100	
		C. Ernest, Capital		53,100
4.	31	C. Ernest, Capital	54,100	
		C. Ernest, Withdrawals		54,100

Income Summary			
Closing	116,200	Closing	169,300
Closing	53,100	Bal.	53,100

C. Ernest, Capital			
Closing	54,100	Bal.	25,900
		Closing	53,100
		Bal.	24,900

C. Ernest, Withdrawals			
Bal.	54,100	Closing	54,100

The first closing entry:

- debits all revenue accounts for their credit balances.
- credits Income Summary for total revenues ($169,300).

The second closing entry:

- debits Income Summary for total expenses plus the contra revenues ($116,200).
- credits the contra revenues (Sales Discounts and Sales Returns and Allowances) and all the expenses for their debit balances.

The last two closing entries:

- close net income from Income Summary to the Capital account.
- close Withdrawals into the Capital account.

Preparing a Merchandiser's Financial Statements

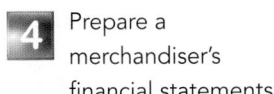

Prepare a merchandiser's financial statements

Exhibit 5-7 shows Austin Sound's financial statements for 2008.

INCOME STATEMENT The income statement begins with sales, cost of goods sold, and gross profit. Then come the **operating expenses**, which are those expenses (other than cost of goods sold) that occur in the entity's major line of business.

Many companies report operating expenses in two categories:

- **Selling expenses** are expenses related to marketing the company's products—sales salaries; sales commissions; advertising; depreciation, rent, and utilities on store buildings; and delivery expense.
- **General expenses** include office expenses, such as the salaries of the executives and office employees; depreciation; rent; utilities; and property taxes on the home office building.

Gross profit minus operating expenses equals **operating income**, or **income from operations**. Operating income measures the results of the entity's major ongoing activities.

The last section of Austin Sound's income statement is **other revenue and expense**. This category reports revenues and expenses that fall outside its main operations. Examples include interest revenue, interest expense, and gains and losses on the sale of plant assets.

The bottom line of the income statement is net income:

Net income = Total revenues and gains − Total expenses and losses

We often hear the term *bottom line* to refer to a final result. The *bottom line* is net income on the income statement.

STATEMENT OF OWNER'S EQUITY A merchandiser's statement of owner's equity looks exactly like that of a service business.

BALANCE SHEET If the business is a merchandiser, the balance sheet shows inventory as a current asset. Service businesses have no inventory.

Income Statement Formats: Multi-Step and Single-Step

As we saw in Chapter 4, the balance sheet appears in two formats:

- The report format (assets on top, . . . , owner's equity at bottom)
- The account format (assets at left, liabilities and owner's equity at right)

continued on page 271 . . .

EXHIBIT 5-7   Financial Statements of Austin Sound Center

AUSTIN SOUND CENTER
Income Statement
Year Ended December 31, 2008

Sales revenue		$169,300
Less: Sales discounts	$(1,400)	
Sales returns and allowances	(2,000)	(3,400)
Net sales revenue		165,900
Cost of goods sold		90,800
Gross profit		75,100
Operating expenses:		
Wage expense	$10,200	
Rent expense	8,400	
Insurance expense	1,000	
Depreciation expense	600	
Supplies expense	500	20,700
Operating income		54,400
Other revenue and (expense):		
Interest expense		(1,300)
Net income		$ 53,100

AUSTIN SOUND CENTER
Statement of Owner's Equity
Year Ended December 31, 2008

C. Ernest, capital, Dec. 31, 2007	$25,900
Add: Net income	53,100
	79,000
Less: Withdrawals	(54,100)
C. Ernest, capital, Dec. 31, 2008	$24,900

AUSTIN SOUND CENTER
Balance Sheet
December 31, 2008

Assets			Liabilities	
Current Assets:			Current Liabilities:	
Cash		$ 2,800	Accounts payable	$39,500
Accounts receivable		4,600	Unearned sales revenue	700
Inventory		40,200	Wages payable	400
Prepaid insurance		200	Total current liabilities	40,600
Supplies		100	Long-term Liabilities:	
Total current assets		47,900	Note payable	12,600
Plant Assets:			Total liabilities	53,200
Furniture	$33,200			
Less: Accumulated			**Owner's Equity**	
depreciation	(3,000)	30,200	C. Ernest, capital	24,900
			Total liabilities and	
Total assets		$78,100	owner's equity	$78,100

There are also two formats for the income statement:

- The multi-step format
- The single-step format

The multi-step format is more popular.

Multi-Step Income Statement

A **multi-step income statement** lists several important subtotals. In addition to net income, it also reports gross profit and income from operations. The income statements presented thus far in this chapter have been multi-step. Austin Sound's multi-step income statement appears in Exhibit 5-7.

Single-Step Income Statement

The **single-step income statement** groups all revenues together and all expenses together without drawing other subtotals. Many companies use this format. The single-step format clearly distinguishes revenues from expenses and works well for service entities because they have no gross profit to report. Exhibit 5-8 shows a single-step income statement for Austin Sound.

EXHIBIT 5-8	Single-Step Income Statement

AUSTIN SOUND CENTER
Income Statement
Year Ended December 31, 2008

Revenues:			
Sales revenue			$169,300
Less: Sales discounts		$ 1,400	
Sales returns and allowances		2,000	(3,400)
Net sales revenue			165,900
Interest revenue			1,000*
Total revenues			166,900
Expenses:			
Cost of goods sold		$90,800	
Wage expense		11,200*	
Rent expense		8,400	
Interest expense		1,300	
Insurance expense		1,000	
Depreciation expense		600	
Supplies expenses		500	
Total expenses			113,800
Net income			$ 53,100

*Added or modified for this illustration.

Two Ratios for Decision Making

Inventory is the most important asset for a merchandiser. Business owners use several ratios to evaluate their operations, among them the gross profit percentage and the rate of inventory turnover.

5 Use gross profit
percentage and
inventory turnover to
evaluate a business

The Gross Profit Percentage

Gross profit (gross margin) is net sales minus cost of goods sold. Merchandisers strive to increase the **gross profit percentage**, which is computed as follows:

For Austin Sound Center
(Exhibit 5-7)

$$\text{Gross profit percentage} = \frac{\text{Gross profit}}{\text{Net sales revenue}} = \frac{\$75,100}{\$165,900} = 0.453 = 45.3\%$$

The gross profit percentage (also called the *gross margin percentage*) is one of the most carefully watched measures of profitability. A small increase may signal an important rise in income, and vice versa for a decrease.

Exhibit 5-9 compares Austin Sound's gross margin to that of Target and Amazon.com.

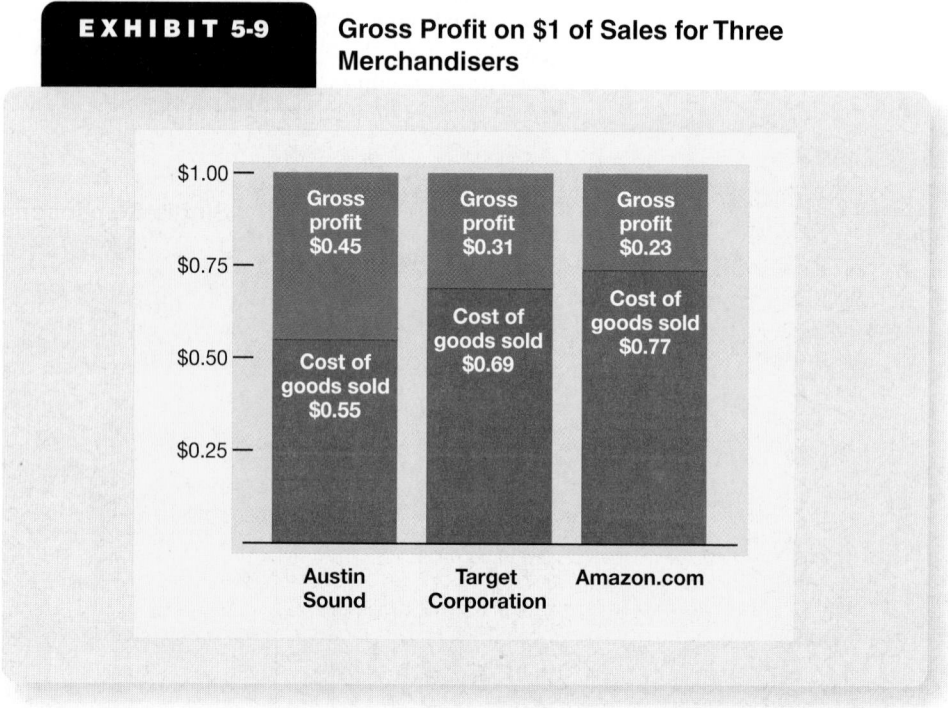

EXHIBIT 5-9 Gross Profit on $1 of Sales for Three Merchandisers

The Rate of Inventory Turnover

Owners and managers strive to sell inventory quickly because the inventory generates no profit until it is sold. The faster the sales, the higher the income. **Inventory turnover** measures how rapidly inventory is sold. It is computed as follows:

For Austin Sound Center
(Exhibit 5-7)

$$\frac{\text{Inventory}}{\text{turnover}} = \frac{\text{Cost of goods sold}}{\text{Average inventory}} = \frac{\text{Cost of goods sold}}{(\text{Beginning inventory}^* + \text{Ending inventory}) / 2}$$

$$= \frac{\$90,800}{(\$38,600^* + \$40,200) / 2} = 2.3 \text{ times per year}$$

---

*Ending inventory from the preceding period. Amount assumed for this illustration.

A high turnover rate is desirable, and an increase in the turnover rate usually means higher profits. Exhibit 5-10 tells an interesting story. Amazon.com moves its merchandise much faster than Austin Sound.

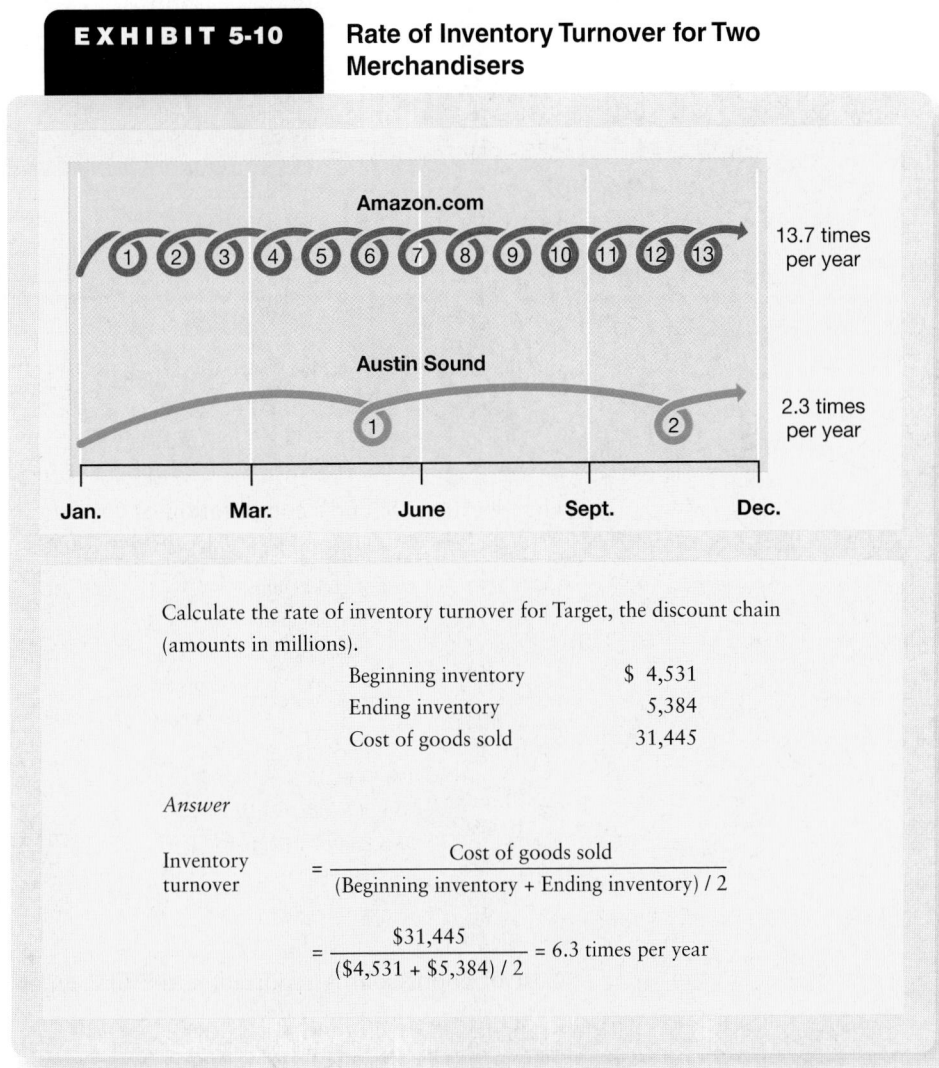

EXHIBIT 5-10 Rate of Inventory Turnover for Two Merchandisers

Calculate the rate of inventory turnover for Target, the discount chain (amounts in millions).

Beginning inventory	$ 4,531
Ending inventory	5,384
Cost of goods sold	31,445

Answer

$$\text{Inventory turnover} = \frac{\text{Cost of goods sold}}{(\text{Beginning inventory} + \text{Ending inventory}) / 2}$$

$$= \frac{\$31,445}{(\$4,531 + \$5,384) / 2} = 6.3 \text{ times per year}$$

Cost of Goods Sold in a Periodic Inventory System

6 Compute cost of goods sold in a periodic inventory system

The amount of cost of goods sold is the same regardless of the inventory system—perpetual or periodic. As we have seen under the perpetual system, cost of goods sold is simply the sum of the amounts posted to that account.

Cost of goods sold is computed differently under the periodic system. At the end of each period the company combines a number of accounts to compute cost of goods sold for the period. Exhibit 5-11 shows how to make the computation.

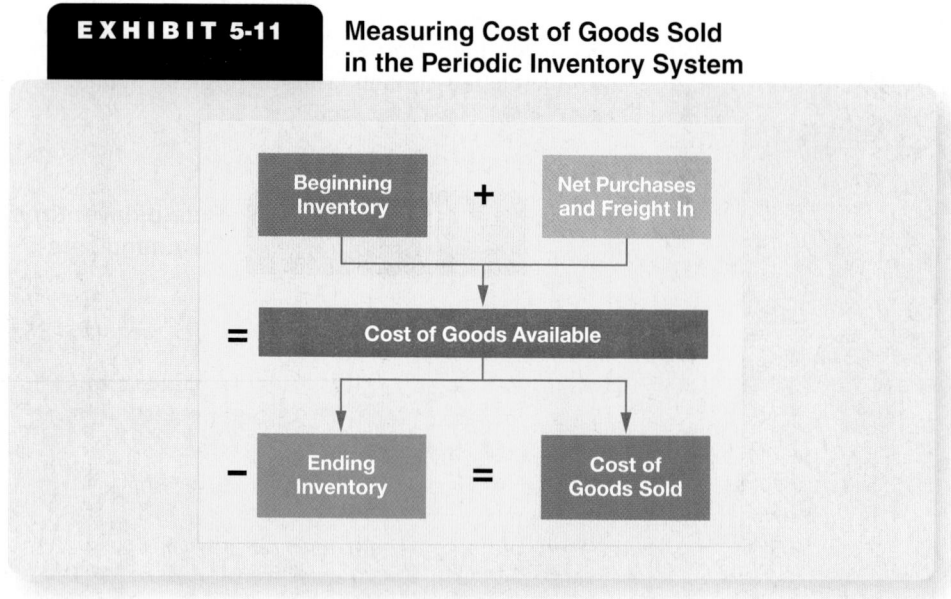

EXHIBIT 5-11 Measuring Cost of Goods Sold in the Periodic Inventory System

Here is Austin Sound's computation of cost of goods sold for 2008:

Cost of goods sold:		
Beginning inventory		$ 38,600
Purchases	$91,400	
Less: Purchase discounts	(3,000)	
Purchase returns and allowances	(1,200)	
Net purchases		87,200
Freight in		5,200
Cost of goods available		131,000
Less: Ending inventory		(40,200)
Cost of goods sold		$ 90,800

Cost of goods sold is reported as the first expense on the merchandiser's income statement.

Appendix 5B, pages 304–307, shows how to account for the purchase and the sale of inventory in the periodic inventory system.

Decision Guidelines

Austin Sound and Cookie Lapp Travel Design are two very different companies. How do these two businesses differ? How are they similar? The Decision Guidelines answer these questions.

Decision	Guidelines
1. How do merchandisers differ from service entities?	• Merchandisers, such as Austin Sound, buy and sell *merchandise inventory*. • Service entities, such as Cookie Lapp Travel Design, perform a *service*.
2. How do a merchandiser's financial statements differ from the statements of a service business? **Balance Sheet:** Merchandiser has *Inventory,* an asset.	Service business has *no* inventory.

Income Statement:

Merchandiser		*Service Business*	
Sales revenue	$XXX	Service revenue	$XX
– Cost of goods sold	(X)	– Operating expenses.......................	(X)
= Gross profit..................................	XX	= Net income	$ X
– Operating expenses.......................	(X)		
= Net income..................................	$ X		

Statements of Owner's Equity:

No difference

3. Which type of inventory system to use?

• At all times the *perpetual system* shows the amount of *inventory* on hand (the asset) and the cost of goods sold (the expense).
• *Periodic system* shows the correct balances of inventory and cost of goods sold only after a count of the inventory, which occurs at least once each year.

4. How to format the merchandiser's income statement?

Multi-Step Format		**Single-Step Format**	
Sales revenue...............................	$XXX	*Revenues:* Sales revenue	$ XXX
– Cost of goods sold.......................	(X)	Other revenues	X
= Gross profit..................................	XX	Total revenues	XXXX
– Operating expenses	(X)	*Expenses:* Cost of goods sold.......................	(X)
= Operating income	X	Operating expenses	(X)
+ Other revenues...........................	X	Other expenses...........................	(X)
– Other expenses...........................	(X)	Total expenses	XXX
= Net income	$ X	Net income..................................	$ X

5. How to evaluate merchandising operations?

Two key ratios

$$\text{Gross profit percentage}^* = \frac{\text{Gross profit}}{\text{Net sales revenue}}$$

$$\text{Inventory turnover}^* = \frac{\text{Cost of goods sold}}{\text{Average inventory}}$$

*In most cases—the higher, the better.

Summary Problem 2

The adjusted trial balance of Jan King Distributing Company follows.

JAN KING DISTRIBUTING COMPANY		
Adjusted Trial Balance		
December 31, 2007		
Cash	$ 5,600	
Accounts receivable	37,100	
Inventory	25,800	
Supplies	1,300	
Prepaid rent	1,000	
Furniture	26,500	
Accumulated depreciation		$ 23,800
Accounts payable		6,300
Salary payable		2,000
Interest payable		600
Unearned sales revenue		2,400
Note payable, long-term		35,000
Jan King, capital		22,200
Jan King, withdrawals	48,000	
Sales revenue		244,000
Interest revenue		2,000
Sales discounts	10,000	
Sales returns and allowances	8,000	
Cost of goods sold	81,000	
Salary expense	72,700	
Rent expense	7,700	
Depreciation expense	2,700	
Utilities expense	5,800	
Supplies expense	2,200	
Interest expense	2,900	
Total	$338,300	$338,300

Requirements

1. Journalize the closing entries at December 31. Post to the Income Summary account as an accuracy check on net income. The credit balance closed out of Income Summary should equal net income computed on the income statement. Also post to Jan King, Capital. Her ending capital balance should agree with the amount reported on the balance sheet.

2. Prepare the company's single-step income statement, statement of owner's equity, and balance sheet in account form. Draw arrows linking the statements.

3. Compute the inventory turnover for 2007. Inventory at December 31, 2006, was $21,000. Turnover for 2006 was 3.0 times. Would you expect Jan King Distributing Company to be more profitable or less profitable in 2007 than in 2006? Give your reason.

Requirement 1

		Closing Entries		
2007				
Dec. 31		Sales Revenue	244,000	
		Interest Revenue	2,000	
		Income Summary		246,000
	31	Income Summary	193,000	
		Sales Discounts		10,000
		Sales Returns and Allowances		8,000
		Cost of Goods Sold		81,000
		Salary Expense		72,700
		Rent Expense		7,700
		Depreciation Expense		2,700
		Utilities Expense		5,800
		Supplies Expense		2,200
		Interest Expense		2,900
	31	Income Summary ($246,000 – $193,000)	53,000	
		Jan King, Capital		53,000
	31	Jan King, Capital	48,000	
		Jan King, Withdrawals		48,000

Income Summary					Jan King, Capital			
Clo.	193,000	Clo.	246,000	Withdrawals	48,000			22,200
Clo.	53,000	Bal.	53,000			Net inc.		53,000
						Bal.		27,200

Requirement 2

JAN KING DISTRIBUTING COMPANY
Income Statement
Year Ended December 31, 2007

Revenues:			
Sales revenue			$244,000
Less: Sales discounts		$ (10,000)	
Sales returns and allowances		(8,000)	(18,000)
Net sales revenue			226,000
Interest revenue			2,000
Total revenue			228,000
Expenses:			
Cost of goods sold		$81,000	
Salary expense		72,700	
Rent expense		7,700	
Utilities expense		5,800	
Interest expense		2,900	
Depreciation expense		2,700	
Supplies expense		2,200	
Total expenses			175,000
Net income			$ 53,000

continued. . .

JAN KING DISTRIBUTING COMPANY
Statement of Owner's Equity
Year Ended December 31, 2007

Jan King, capital, Dec. 31, 2006	$22,200
Add: Net income	53,000
	75,200
Less: Withdrawals	(48,000)
Jan King, capital, Dec. 31, 2007	$27,200

JAN KING DISTRIBUTING COMPANY
Balance Sheet
December 31, 2007

Assets			Liabilities	
Current:			Current:	
Cash		$ 5,600	Accounts payable	$ 6,300
Accounts receivable		37,100	Salary payable	2,000
Inventory		25,800	Interest payable	600
Supplies		1,300	Unearned sales revenue	2,400
Prepaid rent		1,000	Total current liabilities	11,300
Total current assets		70,800	Long-term:	
Plant:			Note payable	35,000
Furniture	$26,500		Total liabilities	46,300
Less: Accumulated				
depreciation	(23,800)	2,700	**Owner's Equity**	
			Jan King, capital	27,200
			Total liabilities and	
Total assets		$73,500	owner's equity	$73,500

Requirement 3

$$\frac{\text{Inventory}}{\text{turnover}} = \frac{\text{Cost of goods sold}}{\text{Average inventory}} = \frac{\$81,000}{(\$21,000 + \$25,800) / 2} = 3.5 \text{ times}$$

The increase in the rate of inventory turnover from 3.0 to 3.5 suggests higher profits.

Work Sheet for a Merchandising Business

The work sheet of a merchandiser is similar to the work sheet for a service business. The main new account is the Inventory account, which must be adjusted based on a physical count, as discussed on page 267. Also, the merchandiser's work sheet carries the other new merchandising accounts (Sales Revenue, Cost of Goods Sold, and so on). Work sheet procedures are the same as for a service business. The sum of the Trial Balance amounts, plus or minus the adjustments, equal the Adjusted Trial Balance amounts. Then take the revenues and the expenses to the income statement and the assets, liabilities, and equity amounts to the balance sheet.

Exhibit 5A-1 is the work sheet of Austin Sound Center for the year ended December 31, 2008.

EXHIBIT 5A-1 Accounting Work Sheet for a Merchandising Business

AUSTIN SOUND CENTER
Accounting Work Sheet
Year Ended December 31, 2008

Account Title	Trial Balance Debit	Trial Balance Credit	Adjustments Debit	Adjustments Credit	Adjusted Trial Balance Debit	Adjusted Trial Balance Credit	Income Statement Debit	Income Statement Credit	Balance Sheet Debit	Balance Sheet Credit
Cash	2,800				2,800				2,800	
Accounts receivable	4,600				4,600				4,600	
Inventory	40,500			(a) 300	40,200				40,200	
Supplies	600			(e) 500	100				100	
Prepaid insurance	1,200			(c)1,000	200				200	
Furniture	33,200				33,200				33,200	
Accumulated depreciation		2,400		(d) 600		3,000				3,000
Accounts payable		39,500				39,500				39,500
Unearned sales revenue		2,000	(b)1,300			700				700
Wages payable				(f) 400		400				400
Note payable, long-term		12,600				12,600				12,600
C. Ernest, capital		25,900				25,900				25,900
C. Ernest, withdrawals	54,100				54,100				54,100	
Sales revenue		168,000		(b)1,300		169,300		169,300		
Sales discounts	1,400				1,400		1,400			
Sales returns and allowances	2,000				2,000		2,000			
Cost of goods sold	90,500		(a) 300		90,800		90,800			
Wage expense	9,800		(f) 400		10,200		10,200			
Rent expense	8,400				8,400		8,400			
Depreciation expense			(d) 600		600		600			
Insurance expense			(c)1,000		1,000		1,000			
Supplies expense			(e) 500		500		500			
Interest expense	1,300				1,300		1,300			
	250,400	250,400	4,100	4,100	251,400	251,400	116,200	169,300	135,200	82,100
Net income							53,100			53,100
							169,300	169,300	135,200	135,200

Adjustment data at December 31, 2008:

a. Actual inventory on hand, based on the physical count, $40,200. The unadjusted Inventory balance is $40,500, so we must adjust Inventory and Cost of Goods Sold by $300.

b. Unearned sales revenue that has been earned, $1,300.

c. Prepaid insurance expired, $1,000.

d. Depreciation, $600.

e. Supplies on hand, $100.

f. Accrued wages payable, $400.

A work sheet will aid the preparation of the closing entries (Exhibit 5-6, page 265) and the financial statements (Exhibit 5-7, page 270). However, the work sheet is optional.

Review *Merchandising Operations*

Accounting Vocabulary

Cost of Goods Sold
The cost of the inventory that the business has sold to customers. Also called **cost of sales**.

Cost of Sales
The cost of the inventory that the business has sold to customers. Also called **cost of goods sold**.

Gross Margin
Excess of net sales revenue over cost of goods sold. Also called **gross profit**.

Gross Margin Percentage
Gross profit divided by net sales revenue. A measure of profitability. Also called **gross profit percentage**.

Gross Profit
Excess of net sales revenue over cost of goods sold. Also called **gross margin**.

Gross Profit Percentage
Gross profit divided by net sales revenue. A measure of profitability. Also called **gross margin percentage**.

Income from Operations
Gross profit minus operating expenses plus any other operating revenues. Also called **operating income**.

Inventory
All the goods that the company owns and expects to sell in the normal course of operations.

Inventory Turnover
Ratio of cost of goods sold to average inventory. Measures the number of times a company sells its average level of inventory during a year.

Invoice
A seller's request for cash from the purchaser.

Multi-Step Income Statement
Format that contains subtotals to highlight significant relationships. In addition to net income, it reports gross profit and operating income.

Net Purchases
Purchases less purchase discounts and purchase returns and allowances.

Net Sales Revenue
Sales revenue less sales discounts and sales returns and allowances.

Operating Expenses
Expenses, other than cost of goods sold, that are incurred in the entity's major line of business. Examples include rent, depreciation, salaries, wages, utilities, and supplies expense.

Operating Income
Gross profit minus operating expenses plus any other operating revenues. Also called **income from operations**.

Other Expense
Expense that is outside the main operations of a business, such as a loss on the sale of plant assets.

Other Revenue
Revenue that is outside the main operations of a business, such as gain on the sale of plant assets.

Periodic Inventory System
A system in which the business does not keep a continuous record of inventory on hand. At the end of the period, it makes a physical count of on-hand inventory and uses this information to prepare the financial statements.

Perpetual Inventory System
The accounting inventory system in which the business keeps a running record of inventory and cost of goods sold.

Sales
The amount that a merchandiser earns from selling its inventory.

Sales Discount
Reduction in the amount receivable from a customer, offered by the seller as an incentive for the customer to pay promptly. A contra account to Sales Revenue.

Sales Returns and Allowances
Decreases in the seller's receivable from a customer's return of merchandise or from granting the customer an allowance from the amount owed to the seller. A contra account to Sales Revenue.

Sales Revenue
The amount that a merchandiser earns from selling its inventory. Also called **sales**.

Single-Step Income Statement
Format that groups all revenues together and then lists and deducts all expenses together without drawing any subtotals.

Quick Check

1. Which account does a merchandiser, but not a service company, use?
   a. Sales revenue
   b. Inventory
   c. Cost of goods sold
   d. All of the above

2. The two main inventory accounting systems are the:
   a. Purchase and sale
   b. Returns and allowances
   c. Cash and accrual
   d. Perpetual and periodic

3. The journal entry for the purchase of inventory on account is:

   a. Inventory XXX
           Accounts Payable   XXX

   b. Accounts Payable.................... XXX
           Inventory.............................   XXX

   c. Inventory XXX
           Accounts Receivable.............   XXX

   d. Inventory XXX
           Cash.....................................   XXX

4. JDC purchased inventory for $5,000 and also paid a $300 freight bill. JDC returned half the goods to the seller and later took a 2% purchase discount. What is JDC's cost of the inventory that it kept?
   a. $2,700
   b. $2,800
   c. $2,750
   d. $2,500

5. Suppose Austin Sound had sales of $300,000 and sales returns of $40,000. Cost of goods sold was $160,000. How much gross profit did Austin Sound report?
   a. $160,000
   b. $180,000
   c. $100,000
   d. $260,000

6. Suppose DeFilippo Catering's Inventory account showed a balance of $10,000 before the year-end adjustments. The physical count of goods on hand totaled $9,700. To adjust the accounts, DeFilippo would make this entry:

   a. Inventory 300
           Accounts Receivable.............   300

   b. Cost of Goods Sold.................. 300
           Inventory.............................   300

   c. Inventory 300
           Cost of Goods Sold   300

   d. Accounts Payable..................... 300
           Inventory.............................   300

7. Which account in question 6 would DeFilippo close at the end of the year?

   a. Cost of Goods Sold

   b. Accounts Receivable

   c. Accounts Payable

   d. Inventory

8. The final closing entry for a proprietorship is:

   a. Owner, Withdrawals................ XXX
       Owner, Capital...................... XXX

   b. Owner, Capital XXX
       Owner, Withdrawals XXX

   c. Sales Revenue XXX
       Income Summary XXX

   d. Income Summary..................... XXX
       Expenses XXX

9. Which subtotals appear on a multi-step income statement but not on a single-step income statement?

   a. Net sales and Cost of goods sold

   b. Operating expenses and Net income

   c. Cost of good sold and Net income

   d. Gross profit and Income from operations

10. Austin Sound made net sales of $85,000, and cost of goods sold totaled $51,000. Average inventory was $17,000. What was Austin Sound's gross profit percentage for this period?

    a. 34%

    b. 40%

    c. 60%

    d. 3.0 times

Answers are given after Apply Your Knowledge (p. 303).

Assess Your Progress

Short Exercises

Recording purchase and cash payment transactions

S5-1 You may have shopped at a Gap store. Suppose Gap purchased T-shirts on account for $10,000. Credit terms are 2/10, n/30. Gap paid within the discount period. Journalize the following transactions for Gap. (pp. 256–258)

a. Purchase of inventory.

b. Payment on account.

Accounting for the purchase of inventory—purchase discount

S5-2 Suppose Toys "Я" Us buys $100,000 worth of Lego toys on credit terms of 3/15, n/45. Some of the goods are damaged in shipment, so Toys "Я" Us returns $10,000 of the merchandise to Lego.

How much must Toys "Я" Us pay Lego

a. After the discount period? (p. 258)

b. Within the discount period? (p. 258)

Recording purchase, purchase return, and cash payment transactions

S5-3 Refer to the Toys "Я" Us situation in Short Exercise 5-2 and journalize the following transactions on the books of Toys "Я" Us. Explanations are not required. (pp. 256–258)

a. Purchase of the goods on May 6, 2005.

b. Return of the damaged goods on May 13.

c. Payment on May 15.

d. In the final analysis, how much did the inventory cost Toys "Я" Us?

Recording purchase transactions

S5-4 Suppose a Target store purchases $60,000 of women's sportswear on account from Tommy. Credit terms are 2/10, net 30. Target pays electronically, and Tommy receives the money on the tenth day.

Journalize Target's (a) purchase and (b) payment transactions. What was Target's net cost of this inventory? (pp. 256–258)

Note: Short Exercise 5-5 covers this same situation for the seller.

Recording sales, cost of goods sold, and cash collections

S5-5 Tommy sells $60,000 of women's sportswear to a Target store under credit terms of 2/10, net 30. Tommy's cost of the goods is $32,000, and Tommy collects cash from Target on the tenth day.

Journalize Tommy's (a) sale, (b) cost of goods sold, and (c) cash receipt. (pp. 261–264)

Note: Short Exercise 5-4 covers the same situation for the buyer.

Recording sales, sales return, and collection entries

S5-6 Suppose Amazon.com sells 1,000 books on account for $10 each (cost of these books is $6,000). One hundred of these books (cost, $600) were damaged in shipment, so Amazon later received the damaged goods as sales returns. Then the customer paid the balance within the discount period. Credit terms were 2/15, net 30.

Journalize Amazon's (a) sale, (b) sale return, and (c) cash collection transactions. (pp. 261–264)

Computing net sales and gross profit

S5-7 Use the data in Short Exercise 5-6 to compute Amazon.com's (a) net sales revenue and (b) gross profit. (p. 264)

S5-8 Patio Furniture's Inventory account at year-end appeared as follows:

Inventory	
Unadjusted balance 65,000	

The physical count of inventory came up with a total of $63,900. Journalize the adjusting entry. (pp. 267–269)

S5-9 Hayes RV Center accounting records include the following accounts at December 31:

Cost of goods sold	$385,000	Accumulated depreciation	$ 38,000
Accounts payable	16,000	Cash	40,000
Rent expense	20,000	Sales revenue	700,000
Building	110,000	Depreciation expense	10,000
J. Hayes, capital	140,000	J. Hayes, withdrawals	60,000
Inventory	260,000	Sales discounts	9,000

Journalize closing entries for Hayes': (p. 268)

a. Revenues

b. Expenses

c. Income Summary account

d. Withdrawals

S5-10 Carolina Communications reported these figures in its financial statements:

Cash...	$ 3,800
Total operating expenses.............	3,500
Accounts payable........................	4,000
Owner capital	4,200
Long-term notes payable.............	900
Inventory	400
Cost of goods sold	20,000
Equipment, net............................	3,700
Accrued liabilities........................	1,600
Net sales revenue	25,000
Accounts receivable......................	2,800

Prepare Carolina's multi-step income statement for the year ended January 31, 2007. (p. 270)

S5-11 Use the data in Short Exercise 5-10 to prepare Carolina Communications' classified balance sheet at January 31, 2007. Use the report form with all headings, and list accounts in proper order. (p. 270)

Computing the gross profit
percentage and the rate of
inventory turnover

S5-12 Refer to the Carolina Communications situation in Short Exercises 5-10
and 5-11. Compute the gross profit percentage and rate of inventory
turnover for 2007. One year earlier, at January 31, 2006, Carolina's
inventory balance was $300. (pp. 256–258, 272)

Computing cost of goods
sold in a periodic inventory
system

6

S5-13 T Wholesale Company began the year with inventory of $8,000. During
the year, T purchased $90,000 of goods and returned $6,000 due to
damage. T also paid freight charges of $1,000 on inventory purchases.
At year-end T's adjusted inventory balance stood at $11,000. T uses the
periodic inventory system.

Compute T's cost of goods sold for the year. (pp. 273–274)

Exercises

E5-14 As the proprietor of Discount Tire Co., you received the following
invoice from a supplier:

 **WHOLESALE DISTRIBUTORS, INC.**
2600 Commonwealth Avenue
Boston, Massachusetts 02215

Invoice date: May 14, 2007

Sold to: Discount Tire Co.
4219 Crestwood Parkway
Lexington, Mass. 02173

Payment terms: 3/10 n/30

Description	Quantity Shipped	Price	Amount
P135–X4 Radials.....................................	1	$37.24	$ 37.24
L912 Belted-bias....................................	8	41.32	330.56
R39 Truck tires.....................................	10	60.02	600.20
Total...			$968.00

Due date:	**Amount:**
May 24, 2007	$938.96
May 25 through June 13, 2007	$968.00

Requirements

1. Discount received the invoice on May 15. Record the May 15
purchase on account. Carry amounts to the nearest cent throughout. (p. 256)
2. The P135–X4 Radial was ordered by mistake and was, therefore,
returned to Wholesale Distributors. Journalize the return on May 19.
(p. 258)
3. Record the May 22 payment of the net amount owed. (p. 258)

Journalizing purchase
transactions

E5-15 On April 30, Boozer Jewelers purchased inventory of $6,000 on account from Van Dyke Diamonds, a jewelry importer. Terms were 3/15, net 45. The same day Boozer paid freight charges of $300. On receiving the goods, Boozer checked the order and found $1,000 of unsuitable merchandise. Boozer returned the unsuitable merchandise to Van Dyke on May 4. Then, on May 14, Boozer paid Van Dyke.

Requirements
Record the indicated transactions in the journal of Boozer Jewelers. Explanations are not required. (pp. 256–260)

Journalizing sales
transactions

E5-16 Refer to the business situation in Exercise 5-15. Journalize the transactions of Van Dyke Diamonds. Van Dyke's cost of goods sold runs 60% of sales. Explanations are not required. (pp. 261–264)

Journalizing purchase and
sales transactions

E5-17 Journalize, without explanations, the following transactions of Soul Art Gift Shop during the month of February: (pp. 256–264)

Feb. 3	Purchased $2,000 of inventory on account under terms of 2/10, n/eom (end of month) and FOB shipping point.
7	Returned $300 of defective merchandise purchased on February 3.
9	Paid freight bill of $50 on February 3 purchase.
10	Sold inventory on account for $3,100. Payment terms were 3/15 n/30. These goods cost Soul Art $1,700.
12	Paid amount owed on credit purchase of February 3, less the return and the discount.
16	Granted a sales allowance of $500 on the February 10 sale.
23	Received cash from February 10 customer in full settlement of her debt, less the allowance and the discount.

Adjusting and closing;
computing gross profit

E5-18 Candy Creations' accounts at June 30 included these unadjusted balances:

Inventory	$ 5,600
Cost of goods sold	41,200
Sales revenue	86,900
Sales discounts	900
Sales returns and allowances	1,400

The physical count of inventory on hand added up to $5,400. This is the only adjustment needed.

a. Journalize the adjustment for inventory shrinkage. Include an explanation. (p. 268)

b. Journalize the closing entries for the appropriate accounts. (p. 268)

c. Compute the gross profit. (p. 270)

E5-19 Supply the missing income statement amounts in each of the following situations: (p. 270)

Sales	Sales Discounts	Net Sales	Cost of Goods Sold	Gross Profit
$91,500	$1,800	$89,700	$59,400	(a)
98,300	(b)	92,800	(c)	$33,000
62,400	2,100	(d)	44,100	(e)
(f)	3,000	(g)	72,500	39,600

E5-20 Jackson Auto Glass's accounting records carried the following accounts at January 31, 2008.

Inventory	$ 5,500	Selling expense	$ 6,800
Interest revenue	40	Sales revenue	38,400
Accounts payable	2,000	Interest expense	30
Cost of goods sold	27,000	Accounts receivable	600
Other expense	1,600	General and administrative	
Jackson, withdrawals	300	expense	700

Requirements

1. Journalize all of Jackson's closing entries at January 31, 2008. Use a Jackson, Capital account. (p. 270)

2. Set up T-accounts for Income Summary and the Jackson, Capital account. Post to these accounts and take their ending balances. One year earlier, at January 31, 2007, the Jackson, Capital balance was $8,740. (p. 268)

E5-21 This exercise uses Appendix 5A, page 279. The trial balance and adjustments columns of the work sheet of Budget Business Systems at March 31, 2007 follow.

Account Title	Trial Balance Debit	Trial Balance Credit	Adjustments Debit	Adjustments Credit
Cash	2,100			
Accounts receivable	8,500		(a) 1,000	
Inventory	36,100			(b) 4,200
Supplies	13,000			(c) 7,600
Equipment	42,400			
Accumulated depreciation		11,200		(d) 2,200
Accounts payable		9,300		

continued. . .

Account Title	Trial Balance Debit	Trial Balance Credit	Adjustments Debit	Adjustments Credit
Salary payable				(e) 1,200
Note payable, long-term		7,500		
Pat Thompson, capital		33,900		
Pat Thompson, withdrawals	45,000			
Sales revenue		233,000		(a) 1,000
Sales discounts	2,000			
Cost of goods sold	111,600		(b) 4,200	
Selling expense	21,000		(c) 5,200	
			(e) 1,200	
General expense	10,500		(c) 2,400	
			(d) 2,200	
Interest expense	2,700			
Total	294,900	294,900	16,200	16,200

Compute the adjusted balance for each account that must be closed. Then journalize Budget's closing entries at March 31, 2007. How much was Budget's net income or net loss? (pp. 268, 279)

Preparing a multi-step income statement

E5-22 Use the data in Exercise 5-21 to prepare the multi-step income statement of Budget Business Systems for the year ended March 31, 2007. (p. 269–271)

Preparing a merchandiser's multi-step income statement to evaluate the business

E5-23 Selected amounts from the accounting records of Azalea Technology follow.

Accounts payable	$16,200	Owner's equity,	
Accumulated depreciation	18,700	December 31, 2008	$126,070
Cost of goods sold	99,400	Sales discounts	9,000
General expenses	23,500	Sales returns	4,600
Interest revenue	1,300	Sales revenue	241,000
Inventory, December 31, 2008	21,000	Selling expenses	37,800
Inventory, December 31, 2007	26,400	Unearned sales revenue	6,500

Requirements

1. Prepare Azalea's *multi-step* income statement for the year ended December 31, 2008. (p. 270)

2. Compute the rate of inventory turnover for 2008. Last year the turnover rate was 3.8 times. Does this trend suggest improvement or deterioration in inventory turnover? (p. 272)

Preparing a single-step
income statement to
evaluate the business

E5-24 Prepare Azalea Technology's *single-step* income statement for 2008, using the data from Exercise 5-23. Compute the gross profit percentage, and compare it with last year's gross profit percentage of 50%. Does the trend in the gross profit percentage suggest better or worse profitability during the current year? (pp. 271, 272)

Computing gross profit
percentage and inventory
turnover

E5-25 Networking Systems earned sales revenue of $65 million in 2009. Cost of goods sold was $33 million, and net income reached $8 million, the company's highest ever. Total current assets included inventory of $3 million at December 31, 2009. Last year's ending inventory was $4 million. The managers of Networking Systems need to know the company's gross profit percentage and rate of inventory turnover for 2009. Compute these amounts. (p. 272)

E5-26 Baker Electric Co. uses the periodic inventory system. Baker reported these amounts at May 31, 2007:

Inventory, May 31, 2006	$19,000	Freight in	$ 4,000
Inventory, May 31, 2007	21,000	Sales revenue	170,000
Purchases (of inventory)	82,000	Sales discounts	3,000
Purchase discounts	2,000	Sales returns	15,000
Purchase returns	8,000		

Compute Baker's:

a. Net sales revenue (p. 270)

b. Cost of goods sold (p. 273)

c. Gross profit (p. 270)

Problems (Group A)

P5-27A Home Depot operates home-improvement stores across the country. Home Depot has a sophisticated perpetual inventory accounting system.

Requirements

You are the manager of a Home Depot store in Fort Lauderdale, Florida. Write a one-paragraph business memo to a new employee explaining how the company accounts for the purchase and sale of merchandise inventory. Use the following heading for your memo. (pp. 256–264)

Date: _____

To: New Employee

From: Store Manager

Subject: Home Depot's perpetual inventory accounting system

Accounting for the purchase
and sale of inventory

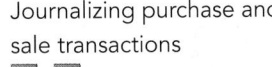

P5-28A The following transactions occurred between BMS Pharmaceuticals and VIP, the pharmacy chain, during October of the current year:

Oct. 6	VIP purchased $5,000 of merchandise from BMS on credit terms of 3/10, n/30, FOB shipping point. Separately, VIP paid a $500 bill for freight in. These goods cost BMS $2,100.
10	VIP returned $900 of the merchandise purchased on October 6. BMS accounted for the $900 sales return and placed the goods back in inventory (BMS's cost, $590).
15	VIP paid $3,000 of the invoice amount owed to BMS for the October 6 purchase, less the discount. This payment included none of the freight charge.
27	VIP paid the remaining amount owed to BMS for the October 6 purchase.

Requirements

Journalize these transactions, first on the books of VIP and second on the books of BMS Pharmaceuticals. (pp. 256–264)

Journalizing purchase and
sale transactions

P5-29A Terry's Amusements completed in the following transactions during May:

May 1	Purchased supplies for cash, $300.
4	Purchased inventory on credit terms of 3/10 net eom, $6,000.
8	Returned half the inventory purchased on May 4. It was not the inventory ordered.
10	Sold goods for cash, $450 (cost, $250).
13	Sold inventory on credit terms of 2/15, n/45, $3,900 (cost, $1,800).
14	Paid the amount owed on account from May 4, less the return (May 8) and the discount.
17	Received defective inventory as a sales return from the May 13 sale, $900. Terry's cost of the inventory received was $600.
18	Purchased inventory of $5,000 on account. Payment terms were 2/10 net 30.
26	Paid the net amount owed for the May 18 purchase.
28	Received cash in full settlement of the account from the customer who purchased inventory on May 13, less the return and the discount.
29	Purchased inventory for cash, $2,000, plus freight charges of $160.

Requirements

Journalize the preceding transactions on the books of Terry's Amusements. (pp. 256–264)

P5-30A The accounting records of A-1 Publishers list the following at November 30, 2007:

Selling expenses	$ 18,800	Inventory	$41,500
Furniture	37,000	Cash	36,000
Sales returns and allowances	3,200	Notes payable	21,600
Salary payable	800	Accumulated depreciation	23,600
M. Nolen, capital	27,000	Cost of goods sold	52,000
Sales revenue	113,700	Sales discounts	2,100
Accounts payable	13,200	General expenses	9,300

Requirements

1. Prepare a multi-step income statement to show the computation of A-1 Publishers' net sales, gross profit, and net income for the month ended November 30, 2007. (p. 270)

2. M. Nolen, owner of the company, strives to earn gross profit of $50,000 and net income of $25,000 each month. Did he achieve these goals? Write a sentence to explain. (Challenge)

Preparing a multi-step
income statement and a
classified balance sheet

4

P5-31A ← *Link Back to Chapter 4 (Classified Balance Sheet).* The accounts of Northeast Electronics are listed along with their balances before closing at May 31, 2009.

Interest revenue	$ 400	Accounts payable	$ 16,900
Inventory	45,500	Accounts receivable	33,700
Note payable, long-term	45,000	Accumulated depreciation	38,000
Salary payable	2,800	Lou Colgin, capital,	
Sales discounts	2,400	April 30, 2009	53,900
Sales returns and allowances	8,000	Lou Colgin, withdrawals	19,000
Sales revenue	296,600	Cash	7,800
Selling expenses	37,900	Cost of goods sold	162,000
Supplies	5,900	Equipment	129,600
Unearned sales revenue	13,800	General expenses	16,700
Interest payable	1,100		

Requirements

1. Prepare Northeast Electronics' *multi-step* income statement for the month ended May 31, 2009: (p. 270)

2. Prepare Northeast Electronics' classified balance sheet in *report form* at May 31, 2009. Show your computation of the May 31 balance of Lou Colgin, Capital. (p. 270)

Preparing a single-step
income statement and a
classified balance sheet

P5-32A ← *Link Back to Chapter 4 (Classified Balance Sheet).*

Requirements

1. Use the data of Problem 5-31A to prepare a *single-step* income statement for the month ended May 31, 2009. (p. 271)

2. Prepare Northeast Electronics' classified balance sheet in *report format* at May 31, 2009. Show your computation of the May 31 balance of Lou Colgin, Capital. (p. 270)

Making closing entries;
computing gross profit
percentage, inventory
turnover, and cost of
goods sold

P5-33A The adjusted trial balance of Big Daddy Music Company at December 31, 2008, follows:

Account Title	Adjusted Trial Balance	
	Debit	Credit
Cash	4,000	
Accounts receivable	38,500	
Inventory	17,400	
Supplies	400	
Furniture	39,600	
Accumulated depreciation		8,700
Accounts payable		13,600
Salary payable		900
Unearned sales revenue		6,800
Note payable, long-term		15,000
Big Daddy, capital		36,400
Big Daddy, withdrawals	42,000	
Sales revenue		185,000
Sales returns	7,000	
Cost of goods sold	82,000	
Selling expense	19,000	
General expense	15,000	
Interest expense	1,500	
Total	266,400	266,400

Requirements

1. Journalize Big Daddy's closing entries. (p. 268)

2. Compute the gross profit percentage and the rate of inventory turnover for 2008. Inventory on hand one year ago, at December 31, 2007, was $12,600. For 2007, Big Daddy's gross profit percentage was 50%, and inventory turnover was 4.9 times. Do the trends in these ratios suggest improvement or deterioration in profitability? (p. 272)

continued. . .

3. Additional inventory data:

| Purchases | $84,800 | Purchase returns | $3,000 |
| Purchase discounts | 1,000 | Freight in | 6,000 |

Compute Big Daddy's cost of goods sold under the periodic inventory system. Does your computed amount agree with Big Daddy's adjusted balance of cost of goods sold? It should. (p. 273)

Preparing a merchandiser's work sheet

P5-34A This problem is based on Appendix 5A, page 279. Harley's of Chicago's trial balance pertains to December 31, 2009.

HARLEY'S OF CHICAGO Trial Balance December 31, 2009		
Cash	$ 7,000	
Accounts receivable	4,000	
Inventory	73,000	
Prepaid rent	5,000	
Equipment	22,000	
Accumulated depreciation		$ 8,000
Accounts payable		6,000
Salary payable		
Note payable, long-term		18,000
J. Harley, capital		50,000
J. Harley, withdrawals	39,000	
Sales revenue		170,000
Cost of goods sold	67,000	
Salary expense	24,000	
Rent expense	7,000	
Utilities expense	3,000	
Depreciation expense		
Interest expense	1,000	
Total	$252,000	$252,000

Adjustment data at December 31, 2009:
a. Prepaid rent expired, $3,000.

b. Depreciation, $5,000.

c. Accrued salaries, $1,000.

d. Inventory on hand, $71,000.

Requirements
Complete Harley's accounting work sheet for the year ended December 31, 2009. Key adjusting entries by letter. (p. 279)

Journalizing the adjusting
and closing entries of a
merchandising business

P5-35A Refer to the data in Problem 5-34A.

1. Journalize Harley's adjusting and closing entries. (pp. 268–279)

2. Determine the December 31, 2009, balance of J. Harley, Capital. (pp. 268–270)

Problems (Group B)

Explaining the perpetual
inventory system

P5-36B Scooter Mike sells pocket rockets, mini choppers, and all-terrain vehicles. The company has launched a new advertising campaign to introduce its products to the public.

Requirements

Scooter Mike expects to grow rapidly and to increase its level of inventory. As the chief accountant of this company, you wish to install a perpetual inventory system. Write a one-paragraph business memo to the company president to explain how that system would work for the purchase and sale of inventory. Use the following heading for your memo: (pp. 255–257)

> **Date:** _____
>
> **To:** Company President
>
> **From:** Chief Accountant
>
> **Subject:** How a perpetual inventory system works for purchases and sales

Accounting for the purchase
and sale of inventory

P5-37B Assume the following transactions occurred between Heights Pharmacy and Procter & Gamble (P&G), the consumer products company, during August of the current year.

Aug. 8	Heights Pharmacy purchased $3,000 of merchandise from P&G on credit terms of 2/10, n/30, FOB shipping point. Separately, Heights paid a $100 bill for freight in. These goods cost P&G $900).
11	Heights returned $1,000 of the merchandise purchased on August 8. P&G accounted for the sales return and placed the goods back in inventory (P&G's cost, $400).
17	Heights paid $1,500 of the invoice amount owed to P&G for the August 8 purchase, less the discount. This payment included none of the freight charge.
26	Heights paid the remaining amount owed to P&G for the August 8 purchase.

continued. . .

Requirements

Journalize these transactions, first on the books of Heights Pharmacy and second on the books of Procter & Gamble. (pp. 256–264)

Journalizing purchase and sale transactions

P5-38B Alpha Graphics completed in the following transactions during September:

Sept. 2	Purchased inventory for cash, $740.
5	Purchased store supplies on credit terms of net eom, $600.
8	Purchased inventory of $3,000, plus freight charges of $200. Credit terms are 3/15, n/30.
9	Sold goods for cash, $1,200. Alpha Graphics' cost of these goods was $700.
11	Returned $1,000 of the inventory purchased on September 8. It was damaged.
12	Purchased inventory on credit terms of 3/10, n/30, $3,800.
14	Sold inventory on credit terms of 2/10, n/30, $9,600 (cost $5,000).
16	Paid utilities expense, $275.
20	Received returned inventory from the September 14 sale, $400. Alpha Graphics shipped the wrong goods by mistake. Alpha Graphics' cost of the inventory received was $250.
21	Paid supplier for goods purchased on September 8 less the return (September 11) and the discount.
23	Received $6,860 cash in partial settlement of his account from the customer who purchased inventory on September 14. Granted the customer a 2% discount and credited his account receivable for $7,000.
30	Paid for the store supplies purchased on September 5.

Requirements

Journalize the preceding transactions on the books of Alpha Graphics. (pp. 256–264)

Preparing a multi-step income statement

P5-39B The accounting records of Steubs Environmental Solutions at June 30, 2008, list the following:

Cash	$ 22,300	Inventory	$28,500
Note payable	4,300	Equipment	51,600
Sales revenue	206,000	Cost of goods sold	95,000
Salary payable	1,800	Accumulated depreciation	6,900
Marty Steubs, capital	5,600	Sales discounts	3,400
Sales returns and allowances	11,500	General expenses	16,300
Selling expenses	19,800	Accounts payable	23,800

continued. . .

Requirements

1. Prepare a multi-step income statement to show the computation of Steubs Environmental Solutions' net sales, gross profit, and net income for the year ended June 30, 2008. (p. 270)

2. Marty Steubs, owner of the business, strives to earn gross profit of $90,000 and net income of $50,000. Did he achieve these goals? Write a sentence or two to explain. (Challenge)

Preparing a multi-step income statement and a classified balance sheet

P5-40B ← *Link Back to Chapter 4 (Classified Balance Sheet).* The accounts of Mackey Home Center are listed along with their balances before closing at July 31, 2008.

Accounts payable	$ 27,300	Inventory	$ 87,300
Accounts receivable	48,600	Note payable, long-term	60,000
Accumulated depreciation	116,400	Salary payable	6,100
Len Mackey, capital,		Sales discounts	1,100
June 30	19,400	Sales returns and allowances	7,000
Len Mackey, withdrawals	11,000	Sales revenue	268,200
Cash	4,300	Selling expense	34,600
Cost of goods sold	160,900	Building	126,000
General expense	25,800	Supplies	4,300
Interest payable	3,000	Unearned sales revenue	9,300
Interest revenue	1,200		

Requirements

1. Prepare Mackey Home Center's *multi-step* income statement for the month ended July 31, 2008. (p. 270)

2. Prepare Mackey's classified balance sheet in *report form* at July 31, 2008. Show your computation of the July 31 balance of Len Mackey, Capital. (p. 270)

Preparing a single-step income statement and a classified balance sheet

P5-41B ← *Link Back to Chapter 4 (Classified Balance Sheet).*

Requirements

1. Use the data of Problem 5-40B to prepare Mackey Home Center's *single-step* income statement for the month ended July 31, 2008. (p. 271)

2. Prepare Mackey's classified balance sheet in *report form* at July 31, 2008. Show your computation of the July 31 balance of Len Mackey, Capital. (p. 271)

Making closing entries; computing gross profit percentage, inventory turnover, and cost of goods sold

P5-42B The adjusted trial balance of Arctic Cat RVs at December 31, 2009, follows.

	Adjusted Trial Balance	
Account Title	**Debit**	**Credit**
Cash	7,000	
Accounts receivable	4,500	
Inventory	42,000	

continued...

Account Title	Adjusted Trial Balance	
	Debit	Credit
Supplies	1,500	
Building	140,000	
Accumulated depreciation		29,000
Accounts payable		11,000
Salary payable		200
Unearned sales revenue		1,600
Note payable, long-term		30,000
B. Bonds, capital		111,600
B. Bonds, withdrawals	45,000	
Sales revenue		201,400
Sales returns	14,000	
Cost of goods sold	101,000	
Selling expense	17,900	
General expense	9,900	
Interest expense	2,000	
Total	384,800	384,800

Requirements

1. Journalize Arctic Cat's closing entries. (p. 268)
2. Compute the gross profit percentage and the rate of inventory turnover for 2009. Inventory on hand at December 31, 2008, was $40,000. For 2008 Arctic Cat's gross profit percentage was 50% and the inventory turnover rate was 3.0 times. Do the trends in these ratios suggest improvement or deterioration in profitability? (p. 272)
3. Additional inventory data:

Purchases	$108,000	Purchase returns	$6,000
Purchase discounts	3,000	Freight in	4,000

Compute Arctic Cat's cost of goods sold under the periodic inventory system. Does your computed amount agree with Arctic Cat's adjusted balance of cost of goods sold? It should. (p. 273)

P5-43B This problem is based on Appendix 5A, page 279. The trial balance of Rustic Elegance pertains to December 31, 2007.

RUSTIC ELEGANCE Trial Balance December 31, 2007		
Cash	$ 2,900	
Accounts receivable	10,100	
Inventory	71,000	
Prepaid insurance	3,200	
Furniture	23,900	
Accumulated depreciation		$ 7,000
Accounts payable		9,000
Salary payable		
Note payable, long-term		20,000
Andrea Sulak, capital		58,000
Andrea Sulak, withdrawals	36,300	
Sales revenue		190,000
Cost of goods sold	61,000	
Salary expense	46,500	
Rent expense	14,000	
Utilities expense	6,700	
Depreciation expense		
Insurance expense	5,300	
Interest expense	3,100	
Total	$284,000	$284,000

Adjustment data at December 31, 2007:

a. Prepaid insurance expired, $2,000.

b. Depreciation, $4,000.

c. Accrued salaries, $1,000.

d. Inventory on hand, $68,000.

Requirement

Complete the accounting work sheet of Rustic Elegance for the year ended December 31, 2007. Key adjusting entries by letter. (p. 279)

Journalizing the adjusting
and closing entries of a
merchandising business

P5-44B Refer to the data in Problem 5-43B.

Requirements

1. Journalize the adjusting and closing entries of Rustic Elegance. (pp. 268, 279)

2. Determine the December 31, 2007, balance of Andrea Sulak, Capital. (pp. 268, 279)

Continuing Problem

This problem completes the Carl Redmon Consulting situation, begun in Problem 1-42 of Chapter 1 and continued through Chapters 2–4.

Accounting for both merchandising and service operations

P5-45 Carl Redmon performs systems consulting. Redmon has also begun selling accounting software. During January, Carl Redmon Consulting completed these transactions:

Jan. 2	Completed a consulting engagement and received cash of $7,200.
2	Prepaid three months' office rent, $1,500.
7	Purchased software inventory on account, $3,900, plus freight in, $100.
16	Paid employee salary, $1,400.
18	Sold software on account, $1,100 (cost $700).
19	Consulted with a client for a fee of $900 on account.
21	Paid on account, $2,000.
24	Paid utilities, $300.
28	Sold software for cash, $600 (cost $400).
31	Recorded these adjusting entries:
	Accrued salary expense, $1,400.
	Depreciation, $200.
	Expiration of prepaid rent, $500.
	Physical count of inventory, $2,800.

Requirements

1. Open the following selected T-accounts in the ledger: Cash; Accounts Receivable; Software Inventory; Prepaid Rent; Accumulated Depreciation; Accounts Payable; Salary Payable; Carl Redmon, Capital; Income Summary; Service Revenue; Sales Revenue; Cost of Goods Sold; Salary Expense; Rent Expense; Utilities Expense; and Depreciation Expense.

2. Journalize and post the January transactions. Key all items by date. Compute each account balance, and denote the balance as *Bal*.

3. Journalize and post the closing entries. Denote each closing amount as *Clo*. After posting all closing entries, prove the equality of debits and credits in the ledger.

4. Prepare the January income statement of Carl Redmon Consulting. Use the single-step format.

Apply Your Knowledge

Decision Cases

Using the financial statements to decide on a business expansion

Case 1. ← *Link Back to Chapter 4 (Classified Balance Sheet. Current Ratio. Debt Ratio).* Jan Louis owns Poppa Rollo's Pizza, which has prospered during its second year of operation. Deciding whether to open another pizzeria, Louis has prepared the current income statement of the business. Louis read in an industry trade journal that a successful two-year-old pizzeria meets these criteria:

a. Gross profit percentage is at least 60%.

b. Net income is at least $90,000.

Louis believes the business meets both criteria. She intends to go ahead with the expansion plan and asks your advice on preparing the income statement in accordance with generally accepted accounting principles. When you point out that the statement includes errors, Louis assures you that all amounts are correct. But some items are listed in the wrong place.

Requirements

Prepare a multi-step income statement and make a recommendation about whether Louis should undertake the expansion. (p. 270)

POPPA ROLLO'S PIZZA	
Income Statement	
Year Ended December 31, 2008	
Sales revenue	$195,000
Gain on sale of land	24,600
Total revenue	219,600
Cost of goods sold	85,200
Gross profit	134,400
Operating expenses:	
Salary expense	35,600
Interest expense	6,000
Depreciation expense	4,800
Utilities expense	3,700
Total operating expense	50,100
Income from operations	84,300
Other revenue:	
Sales returns	10,700
Net income	$ 95,000

Expanding a business

Case 2. Bill Hildebrand and Melissa Nordhaus opened Party-Time T-Shirts to sell T-shirts for parties at their college. The company completed the first year of operations, and the owners are generally pleased with operating results, as shown by the following income statement:

continued...

PARTY-TIME T-SHIRTS
Income Statement
Year Ended December 31, 2007

Net sales revenue	$350,000
Cost of goods sold	210,000
Gross margin	140,000
Operating expenses:	
Selling expense	40,000
General expense	25,000
Net income	$ 75,000

Hildebrand and Nordhaus are considering how to expand the business. They each propose a way to increase profits to $100,000 during 2008.

a. Hildebrand believes they should advertise more heavily. He believes additional advertising costing $20,000 will increase net sales by 30% and leave general expense unchanged.

b. Nordhaus proposes selling higher-margin merchandise, such as party dresses. An importer can supply a minimum of 1,000 dresses for $40 each; Party-Time can mark these dresses up 100% and sell them for $80. Nordhaus realizes they will have to advertise the new merchandise, and this advertising will cost $5,000. Party-Time can expect to sell only 80% of these dresses during the coming year.

Requirements
Help Hildebrand and Nordhaus determine which plan to pursue. Prepare a single-step income statement for 2008 to show the expected net income under each plan. (p. 269–271)

Ethical Issue

Dobbs Wholesale Antiques makes all sales under terms of FOB shipping point. The company usually receives orders for sales approximately one week before shipping inventory to customers. For orders received late in December, Kathy Dobbs, the owner, decides when to ship the goods. If profits are already at an acceptable level, Dobbs delays shipment until January. If profits for the current year are lagging behind expectations, Dobbs ships the goods during December.

Requirements
1. Under Dobbs' FOB policy, when should the company record a sale?

2. Do you approve or disapprove of Dobbs' manner of deciding when to ship goods to customers and record the sales revenue? If you approve, give your reason. If you disapprove, identify a better way to decide when to ship goods. (There is no accounting rule against Dobbs' practice.)

Financial Statement Case

Closing entries for a well-known company

This case uses both the income statement (statement of operations) and the balance sheet of Amazon.com in Appendix A at the end of the book. It will help you understand the closing process of a business.

Requirements

1. Journalize Amazon.com's closing entries for the revenues and expenses of 2005. Show all amounts in millions as in the Amazon financial statements. You may be unfamiliar with certain revenues and expenses, but treat each item on the income statement as either a revenue or an expense. For example, Net Sales is the first revenue, and Interest Income is also a revenue. The last revenue is Cumulative Effect of Change in Accounting Principle. A loss is like an expense. In your closing entries ignore all subtotals such as Gross Profit, Total Operating Expenses, and Net Loss.

2. Create a T-account for Income Summary, post to that account, and then close Income Summary (debit Income Summary and credit Retained Earnings for $359). For this purpose, Retained Earnings is similar to the Owner's Capital account. How much was closed to Retained Earnings? How is the amount that was closed to Retained Earnings labeled on the income statement?

Team Project

With a small team of classmates, visit one or more merchandising businesses in your area. Interview a responsible official of the company to learn about its inventory policies and accounting system. Obtain answers to the following questions, write a report, and be prepared to make a presentation to the class if your instructor so directs:

Requirements

1. What merchandise inventory does the business sell?

2. From whom does the business buy its inventory? Is the relationship with the supplier new or longstanding?

3. What are the FOB terms on inventory purchases? Who pays the freight, the buyer or the seller? Is freight a significant amount? What percentage of total inventory cost is the freight?

4. What are the credit terms on inventory purchases—2/10, n/30, or other? Does the business pay early to get purchase discounts? If so, why? If not, why not?

5. How does the business actually pay its suppliers? Does it mail a check or pay electronically? What is the actual payment procedure?

6. Which type of inventory accounting system does the business use—perpetual or periodic? Is this system computerized?

7. How often does the business take a physical count of its inventory? When during the year is the count taken? Describe the count procedures followed by the company.

8. Does the owner or manager use the gross profit percentage and the rate of inventory turnover to evaluate the business? If not, show the manager how to use these ratios in decision making.

9. Ask any other questions your group considers appropriate.

For Internet Exercises, Excel in Practice, and additional online activities, go to the Web site www.prenhall.com/horngren

---

Quick Check Answers

1. *d*   2. *d*   3. *a*   4. *c*   5. *c*   6. *b*   7. *a*   8. *b*   9. *d*   10. *b*

Appendix 5B

Accounting for Merchandise in a Periodic Inventory System

Some businesses find it too expensive to invest in a perpetual inventory system. These businesses use a periodic system.

Recording the Purchase of Inventory

All inventory systems use the Inventory account. But in a periodic system, purchases, purchase discounts, purchase returns and allowances, and transportation costs are recorded in separate accounts. Let's account for Austin Sound Center's purchase of the JDC goods in Exhibit 5B-1.

EXHIBIT 5B-1   Purchase Invoice

1

JDC SOUTHWEST BRANCH
P.O. BOX 100876
HOUSTON, TX 77212

	Invoice	
	Date	Number
3	6/1/08	410

2

Shipped To: AUSTIN SOUND CENTER
305 WEST MLK BLVD.
AUSTIN, TX 78701

4

Credit Terms
3% 15, NET 30 DAYS

Description		Quantity Shipped	Unit Price	Total
DVD PLAYER		7	$100.00	$700.00
		6 Pd.	6/15/08	

Due Date & Due Amount			
06/15/08			
$679 00			

7

Sub Total	$700.00
Ship. or Handl. Chg.	–
Tax (3%)	–
Total(s)	$700.00

5

Explanations:

1   The seller is JDC.

2   The purchaser is Austin Sound Center.

3   The invoice date is needed to determine whether the purchaser gets a discount for prompt payment (see 4).

4   Credit terms: If Austin Sound pays within 15 days of the invoice date, it may deduct a 3% discount. Otherwise, the full amount—NET—is due in 30 days. (See Purchase Discounts on page 305.)

5   Total invoice amount is $700.

6   Austin Sound's payment date. How much did Austin pay? (See 7.)

7   Payment occurred 14 days after the invoice date—within the discount period—so Austin paid $679 ($700 – 3% discount).

Recording Purchases and Purchase Discounts

The following entries record the purchase and payment on account within the discount period. Austin Sound received the goods on June 3 and paid within the discount period.

June 3	Purchases	700	
	Accounts Payable		700
	Purchased inventory on account.		
June 15	Accounts Payable	700	
	Cash ($700 × 0.97)		679
	Purchase Discounts ($700 × 0.03)		21
	Paid within discount period.		

Recording Purchase Returns and Allowances

Suppose that, prior to payment, Austin Sound returned to JDC goods costing $100 and also received from JDC a purchase allowance of $10. Austin Sound would record these transactions as follows:

June 4	Accounts Payable	100	
	Purchase Returns and Allowances		100
	Returned inventory to seller.		
4	Accounts Payable	10	
	Purchase Returns and Allowances		10
	Received a purchase allowance.		

During the period, the business records the cost of all inventory bought in the Purchases account. The balance of Purchases is a *gross* amount because it does not include subtractions for discounts, returns, or allowances. **Net purchases** is the remainder after subtracting the contra accounts from Purchases:

> Purchases (*debit*)
>
> − Purchase Discounts (*credit*)
>
> − Purchase Returns and Allowances (*credit*)
> ---
> = Net purchases (a *debit* subtotal, not a separate account)

Recording Transportation Costs

Under the periodic system, costs to transport purchased inventory from seller to buyer are debited to a separate Freight In account, as shown for a $60 freight bill:

June 3	Freight In	60	
	Cash		60
	Paid a freight bill.		

Recording the Sale of Inventory

Recording sales is streamlined in the periodic system. With no running record of inventory to maintain, we can record a $3,000 sale as follows:

June 9	Accounts Receivable	3,000	
	Sales Revenue		3,000
	Sale on account.		

There is no accompanying entry to Inventory and Cost of Goods Sold in the periodic system.

Accounting for sales discounts and sales returns and allowances is the same as in a perpetual inventory system (pages 000–000), except that there are no entries to Inventory or Cost of Goods Sold.

Cost of goods sold (also called *cost of sales*) is the largest single expense of most businesses that sell merchandise, such as Austin Sound and Gap Inc. It is the cost of the inventory the business has sold to customers. In a periodic system, cost of goods sold must be computed as shown in Exhibit 5-11, page 274.

Exhibit 5B-2 summarizes this appendix by showing Austin Sound's net sales revenue, cost of goods sold, and gross profit on the income statement for the periodic system. (All amounts are assumed.)

EXHIBIT 5B-2 · Partial Income Statement—Periodic Inventory System

AUSTIN SOUND CENTER Income Statement Year Ended December 31, 2008			
Sales revenue			$169,300
Less: Sales discounts			(1,400)
Sales returns and allowances			(2,000)
Net sales revenue			$165,900
Cost of goods sold:			
Beginning inventory		$38,600	
Purchases	$91,400		
Less: Purchase discounts	(3,000)		
Purchase returns and allowances	(1,200)		
Net purchases		87,200	
Freight in		5,200	
Cost of goods available		131,000	
Less: Ending inventory		(40,200)	
Cost of goods sold			90,800
Gross profit			$ 75,100

Appendix 5B Assignments

Exercises

Journalizing purchase
transactions

E5B-1 On April 30, Stanley & Weaver Jewelers purchased inventory of $8,000 on account from Intergem Jewels, a jewelry importer. Terms were 3/15, net 45. On receiving the goods, Stanley & Weaver checked the order and found $1,000 of unsuitable merchandise. Therefore, Stanley & Weaver returned $1,000 of merchandise to Intergem on May 4.

On May 14, Stanley & Weaver paid the net amount owed from April 30, less the return.

Requirements
Record the indicated transactions in the journal of Stanley & Weaver Jewelers. Use the periodic inventory system. Explanations are not required. (pp. 305–306)

Journalizing sale
transactions

E5B-2 Refer to the business situation in Exercise 5B-1. Journalize the transactions of Intergem Jewels. Explanations are not required. (pp. 305–306, 262–264)

Problem

Journalizing purchase and
sale transactions

P5B-1 Assume that the following transactions occurred between Providence Medical Supply and a Walgreen's drug store during November of the current year.

Nov. 6	Walgreen's purchased $6,200 of merchandise from Providence Medical Supply on credit terms 2/10, n/30, FOB shipping point. Separately, Walgreen's paid freight in of $300.
10	Walgreen's returned $900 of the merchandise to Providence.
15	Walgreen's paid $3,000 of the invoice amount owed to Providence for the November 6 purchase, less the discount.
27	Walgreen's paid the remaining amount owed to Providence for the November 6 purchase.

Requirements
Journalize these transactions, first on the books of the Walgreen's drug store and second on the books of Providence Medical Supply. Use the periodic inventory system.

Comprehensive Problem for Chapters 1–5

Completing a Merchandiser's Accounting Cycle

The end-of-month trial balance of St. James Technology at January 31, 2009, follows. Additional data at January 31, 2009:

a. Supplies consumed during the month, $1,500. Half is selling expense, and the other half is general expense.

b. Depreciation for the month: building, $4,000; furniture, $4,800. One-fourth of depreciation is selling expense, and three-fourths is general expense.

c. Unearned sales revenue earned during January, $4,580.

d. Accrued salaries, a general expense, $1,150.

e. Inventory on hand, $63,720. St. James uses the perpetual inventory system.

Requirements

1. Using four-column accounts, open the accounts listed on the trial balance, inserting their unadjusted balances. Date the balances of the following accounts January 1: Supplies; Building; Accumulated Depreciation—Building; Furniture; Accumulated Depreciation—Furniture; Unearned Sales Revenue; and Dirk St. James, Capital. Date the balance of Dirk St. James, Withdrawals, January 31. Also open the Income Summary account. (p. 80)

2. Enter the trial balance on an accounting work sheet, and complete the work sheet for the month ended January 31, 2009. St. James Technology groups all operating expenses under two accounts, Selling Expense and General Expense. Leave two blank lines under Selling Expense and three blank lines under General Expense. (p. 279)

ST. JAMES TECHNOLOGY Trial Balance January 31, 2009		
Cash	$ 16,430	
Accounts receivable	19,090	
Inventory	65,400	
Supplies	2,700	
Building	188,170	
Accumulated depreciation—building		$ 36,000
Furniture	45,600	
Accumulated depreciation—furniture		5,800
Accounts payable		28,300
Salary payable		
Unearned sales revenue		6,560
Note payable, long-term		87,000
Dirk St. James, capital		144,980
Dirk St. James, withdrawals	9,200	
Sales revenue		187,970
Sales discounts	7,300	
Sales returns and allowances	8,140	
Cost of goods sold	103,000	
Selling expense	21,520	
General expense	10,060	
Total	$496,610	$496,610

3. Prepare the company's *multi-step* income statement and statement of owner's equity for the month ended January 31, 2009. Also prepare the balance sheet at that date in *report* form. (p. 270)
4. Journalize the adjusting and closing entries at January 31. (pp. 204, 268)
5. Post the adjusting and closing entries, using dates. (pp. 204, 205)

6 Merchandise Inventory

Learning Objectives

1 Account for inventory by the FIFO, LIFO, and average-cost methods

2 Compare the effects of FIFO, LIFO, and average cost

3 Apply the lower-of-cost-or-market rule to inventory

4 Measure the effects of inventory errors

5 Estimate ending inventory by the gross profit method

hapter 5 introduced the accounting for merchandise inventory. It showed how Austin Sound Center, a music store, recorded the purchase and sale of its inventory. Amazon.com, Wal-Mart, and Rocky Mountain Sportswear are other merchandising companies. The current chapter completes the accounting for merchandise inventory.

Rocky Mountain Sportswear (RMS) makes ski parkas for men, women, and children. RMS, like all other companies, may select from several different methods to account for its inventory. Inventory is the first area in which you must pick the accounting method you will use. In this chapter we use Rocky Mountain Sportswear to illustrate the different inventory accounting methods.

Get ready to learn a new vocabulary. By the time you complete this chapter, you'll be able to use new terms including *FIFO* and *LIFO*. You'll also be prepared to decide which accounting method is best for you if you ever start your own business. ■

First let's review how merchandise inventory affects a company. Exhibit 6-1 gives the merchandising section of Rocky Mountain Sportswear's balance sheet and income statement. Inventories, cost of goods sold, and gross profit are highlighted. These amounts (X, Y, and Z) are left blank to indicate that throughout the chapter we will be computing them using various accounting methods.

EXHIBIT 6-1 Rocky Mountain Sportswear: Merchandising Sections of the Financial Statements

ROCKY MOUNTAIN SPORTSWEAR COMPANY
Balance Sheet (partial)
December 31, 2008

Assets	
Current assets:	
Cash	$ 6,000
Short-term investments	3,000
Accounts receivable	12,000
Inventories	X
Prepaid expenses	4,000

ROCKY MOUNTAIN SPORTSWEAR COMPANY
Income Statement (partial)
Year Ended December 31, 2008

	(Millions)
Net sales	$80,000
Cost of goods sold	Y
Gross profit	Z

The remainder of the chapter explores how to compute these amounts in Exhibit 6-1:

- Ending inventory (X) on the balance sheet
- Cost of goods sold (Y) and gross profit (Z) on the income statement

We turn now to the different inventory costing methods.

Inventory Costing Methods

As we saw in Chapter 5,

$$\text{Ending inventory} = \begin{array}{c}\text{Number of units}\\ \textit{on hand}\end{array} \times \text{Unit cost}$$

$$\text{Cost of goods sold} = \begin{array}{c}\text{Number of units}\\ \textit{sold}\end{array} \times \text{Unit cost}$$

Companies determine the number of units from perpetual inventory records backed up by a physical count. The cost of each unit of inventory is:

$$\text{Unit cost} = \text{Purchase price} - \text{Purchase discounts}$$

Exhibit 6-2 gives the inventory data for a line of Rocky Mountain Sportswear (RMS) ski parkas.

EXHIBIT 6-2	Perpetual Inventory Record— Quantities Only

Item: Ski Parkas

Date	Quantity Purchased	Quantity Sold	Quantity on Hand
Nov. 1			1
5	6		7
15		4	3
26	7		10
30		8	2
Totals	13	12	2

In this illustration, RMS began November with 1 ski parka on hand. RMS had 2 parkas at the end of the month. Assume that RMS's unit cost of each ski parka is $40. In this case,

$$\text{Ending inventory} = \underset{2}{\text{Number of units } \textit{on hand} \text{ (Exhibit 6-2)}} \quad \underset{\times \quad \$40}{\text{Unit Cost}} \quad = \$80$$

$$\text{Cost of goods sold} = \underset{12}{\text{Number of units } \textit{sold} \text{ (Exhibit 6-2)}} \quad \underset{\times \quad \$40}{\text{Unit cost}} \quad = \$480$$

What would ending inventory and cost of goods sold be if the cost of a ski parka increased from $40 to $50? Companies face price increases like this all the time. To determine inventory costs, the accounting profession has developed several costing methods.

Measuring inventory cost is easy when prices are constant. But unit cost often changes. A ski parka that cost RMS $40 in January may cost $45 in April. Suppose RMS sells 10,000 ski parkas in November. How many of the parkas cost $40? How many cost $45? To compute ending inventory and cost of goods sold, RMS must assign a specific unit cost to each item. The four costing methods GAAP allows are:

1. Specific unit cost
2. Average cost
3. First-in, first-out (FIFO) cost
4. Last-in, first-out (LIFO) cost

A company can use any of these methods to account for its inventory.

The **specific-unit-cost method** is also called the **specific-identification method**. This method uses the specific cost of each unit of inventory. Some businesses deal in unique inventory items, such as automobiles, jewels, and real estate. For instance, a

Chevrolet dealer may have two vehicles—a "stripped-down" model that costs $16,000 and a "loaded" model that costs $19,000. If the dealer sells the loaded model, cost of goods sold is $19,000. Suppose the stripped-down auto is the only unit left in inventory at the end of the period; ending inventory is $16,000.

Amazon.com uses the specific-unit-cost method to account for its inventory. But very few other companies use this method, so we shift to the more popular inventory costing methods. Exhibit 6-3 illustrates how each method works.

- Under FIFO, the cost of goods sold is based on the oldest purchases. In Exhibit 6-3, this is illustrated by the Cost of goods sold coming from the *bottom* of the container.
- Under LIFO, the cost of goods sold is based on the most recent purchases (new costs). This is illustrated by the Cost of goods sold coming from the *top* of the container.
- Under the average-cost method, the cost of goods sold is based on an average cost for the period. This is illustrated by the cost of goods sold coming from the *middle* of the container.

EXHIBIT 6-3 **Cost Flows for the Three Most Popular Inventory Methods**

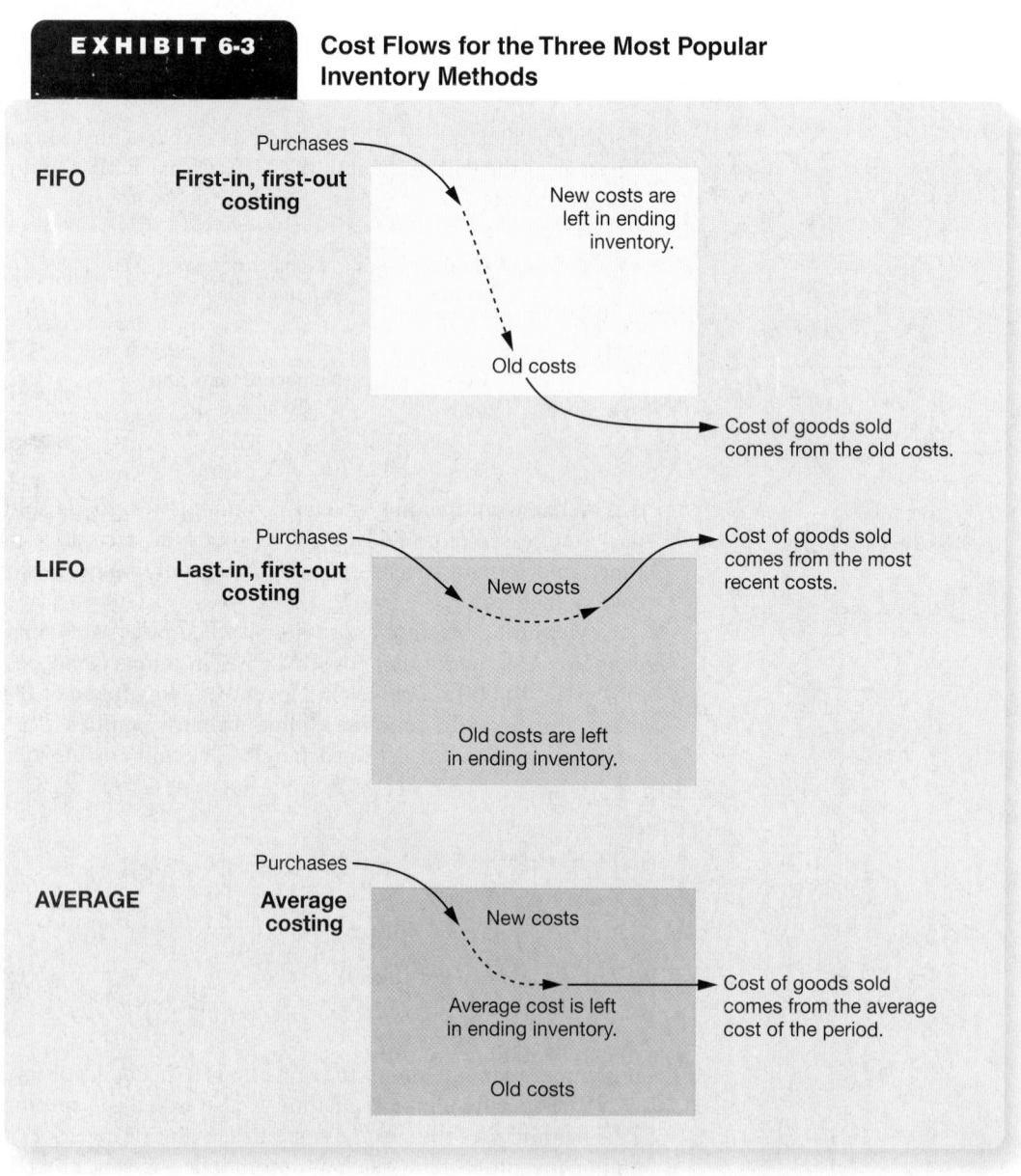

Now let's see how Rocky Mountain Sportswear would compute inventory amounts under FIFO, LIFO, and average costing. We use the following transaction data for all the illustrations:

ROCKY MOUNTAIN SPORTSWEAR SKI PARKA		Number of Units	Unit Cost
Nov. 1	Beginning inventory	1	$40
5	Purchase	6	45
15	Sale	4	
26	Purchase	7	50
30	Sale	8	

In the body of the chapter, we show inventory costing in a perpetual system. The chapter Appendix 6A (page 346) shows inventory costing in a periodic system.

Inventory Costing in a Perpetual System

The different inventory costing methods produce different amounts for:

- Ending inventory
- Cost of goods sold

Let's begin with the FIFO method.

First-In, First-Out (FIFO) Method

1 Account for inventory by the FIFO, LIFO, and average-cost methods

Rocky Mountain Sportswear (RMS) uses the **FIFO method** to account for its inventory. FIFO costing is consistent with the physical movement of inventory for most companies. That is, they sell their oldest inventory first. Under FIFO, the first costs incurred by RMS are the first costs assigned to cost of goods sold. FIFO leaves in ending inventory the last—the newest—costs. This is illustrated in the FIFO inventory record in Exhibit 6-4.

RMS began November with 1 ski parka that cost $40. After the November 5 purchase, the inventory on hand consists of 7 units.

$$7 \text{ units on hand} \begin{cases} 1 @ \$40 & = \$\ 40 \\ 6 @ \$45 & = \ \underline{270} \end{cases}$$
$$\text{Inventory on hand} = \$310$$

On November 15, RMS sold 4 units. Under FIFO, the first unit sold has the oldest cost ($40 per unit). The next 3 units sold cost $45 each. That leaves 3 units in inventory on hand at $45 each. The remainder of the inventory record follows the same pattern.

The FIFO monthly summary at November 30 is:

- Cost of goods sold: 12 units that cost a total of $560
- Ending inventory: 2 units that cost a total of $100

RMS measures cost of goods sold and inventory in this manner to prepare its financial statements.

EXHIBIT 6-4   Perpetual Inventory Record: FIFO

	Purchases			Cost of Goods Sold			Inventory on Hand		
Date	Quantity	Unit Cost	Total Cost	Quantity	Unit Cost	Total Cost	Quantity	Unit Cost	Total Cost
Nov. 1							1	$40	$40
5	6	$45	$270				1	40	40
							6	45	270
15				1	$40	$ 40			
				3	45	135	3	45	135
26	7	50	350				3	45	135
							7	50	350
30				3	45	135			
				5	50	250	2	50	100
30	13		$620	12		$560	2		$100

Journal Entries Under FIFO

The journal entries under FIFO follow the data in Exhibit 6-4. For example, on November 5, RMS purchased $270 of inventory and made the first journal entry. On November 15, RMS sold 4 ski parkas for the sale price of $80 each. RMS recorded the sale ($320) and the cost of goods sold ($175). The remaining journal entries (November 26 and 30) follow the inventory data in Exhibit 6-4.

The amounts unique to FIFO are highlighted for emphasis. All other amounts are the same for all three inventory methods.

FIFO Journal Entries:	(All purchases and sales on account. The sale price of a ski parka is $80 per unit.)		
Nov. 5	Inventory (6 × $45)...	270	
	Accounts Payable...		270
	Purchased inventory on account.		
15	Accounts Receivable (4 × $80)..............................	320	
	Sales Revenue		320
	Sale on account.		
15	Cost of Goods Sold ($40 + $135)............................	175	
	Inventory		175
	Cost of goods sold.		
26	Inventory (7 × $50)...	350	
	Accounts Payable...		350
	Purchased inventory on account.		
30	Accounts Receivable (8 × $80)..............................	640	
	Sales Revenue		640
	Sale on account.		
30	Cost of Goods Sold ($135 + $250).........................	385	
	Inventory		385
	Cost of goods sold.		

Last-In, First-Out (LIFO) Method

LIFO is the opposite of FIFO. Under **LIFO**, cost of goods sold comes from the newest—the most recent—purchases. Ending inventory comes from the oldest costs of the period. Exhibit 6-5 shows how LIFO works. Exhibit 6-5 gives a perpetual inventory record for the LIFO method.

EXHIBIT 6-5 Perpetual Inventory Record: LIFO

Ski Parkas									
	Purchases			**Cost of Goods Sold**			**Inventory on Hand**		
Date	**Quantity**	**Unit Cost**	**Total Cost**	**Quantity**	**Unit Cost**	**Total Cost**	**Quantity**	**Unit Cost**	**Total Cost**
Nov. 1							1	$40	$40
5	6	$45	$270				1	40	40
							6	45	270
15				4	$45	$180	1	40	40
							2	45	90
26	7	50	350				1	40	40
							2	45	90
							7	50	350
30				7	50	350			
				1	45	45	1	40	40
							1	45	45
30	13		$620	12		$575	2		$85

Again, RMS had 1 ski parka at the beginning. After the purchase on November 5, RMS holds 7 units of inventory (1 @ $40 plus 6 @ $45). On November 15, RMS sells 4 units. Under LIFO, the cost of goods sold always comes from the newest purchase. That leaves 3 ski parkas in inventory on November 15.

$$3 \text{ units on hand} \begin{cases} 1 @ \$40 & = & \$ 40 \\ 2 @ \$45 & = & \underline{\quad 90} \end{cases}$$
$$\text{Inventory on hand} \quad = \quad \$130$$

The purchase of 7 units on November 26 adds a new $50 layer to inventory. Now inventory holds 10 units.

$$10 \text{ units on hand} \begin{cases} 1 @ \$40 & = & \$ 40 \\ 2 @ \$45 & = & 90 \\ 7 @ \$50 & = & \underline{\quad 350} \end{cases}$$
$$\text{Inventory on hand} \quad = \quad \$480$$

Then the sale of 8 units on November 30 peels back units in LIFO order. The LIFO monthly summary at November 30 is:

- Cost of goods sold: 12 units that cost a total of $575
- Ending inventory: 2 units that cost a total of $85

Under LIFO, RMS could measure cost of goods sold and inventory in this manner to prepare its financial statements.

Journal Entries Under LIFO

The journal entries under LIFO follow the data in Exhibit 6-5. On November 5, RMS purchased inventory of $270. The November 15 sale brought in sales revenue (4 units @ $80 = $320) and cost of goods sold ($180). The November 26 and 30 entries also come from the data in Exhibit 6-5. Amounts unique to LIFO are shown in color.

LIFO Journal Entries:	(All purchases and sales on account. The sale price of a ski parka is $80 per unit.)		
Nov. 5	Inventory (6 × $45)	270	
	Accounts Payable		270
	Purchased inventory on account.		
15	Accounts Receivable (4 × $80)	320	
	Sales Revenue		320
	Sale on account.		
15	Cost of Goods Sold	180	
	Inventory		180
	Cost of goods sold.		
26	Inventory (7 × $50)	350	
	Accounts Payable		350
	Purchased inventory on account.		
30	Accounts Receivable (8 × $80)	640	
	Sales Revenue		640
	Sale on account.		
30	Cost of Goods Sold ($350 + $45)	395	
	Inventory		395
	Cost of goods sold.		

Average-Cost Method

Suppose RMS uses the **average-cost method** to account for its inventory of ski parkas. With this method, the business computes a new average cost per unit after each purchase. Ending inventory and cost of goods sold are then based on the same average cost per unit. Exhibit 6-6 shows a perpetual inventory record for the

EXHIBIT 6-6   Perpetual Inventory Record: Average Cost

	Ski Parkas								
	Purchases			Cost of Goods Sold			Inventory on Hand		
Date	Quantity	Unit Cost	Total Cost	Quantity	Unit Cost	Total Cost	Quantity	Unit Cost	Total Cost
Nov. 1							1	$40.00	$ 40
5	6	$45	$270				7	44.29	310
15				4	$44.29	$177	3	44.29	133
26	7	50	350				10	48.30	483
30				8	48.30	386	2	48.30	97
30	13		$620	12		$563	2		$ 97

average-cost method. We round average unit cost to the nearest cent and total cost to the nearest dollar.

After each purchase, RMS computes a new average cost per unit. For example, on November 5, the new average unit cost is:

	Total cost of inventory on hand		Number of units on hand		Average cost per unit
Nov. 5	$40 + $270 = $310	÷	7 units	=	$44.29

The goods sold on November 15 are then costed out at $44.29 per unit. After each purchase, RMS computes a new average cost.

The average-cost summary at November 30 is:

- Cost of goods sold: 12 units that cost a total of $563
- Ending inventory: 2 units that cost a total of $97

Under the average-cost method, RMS could use these amounts to prepare its financial statements.

Journal Entries Under Average Costing

2 Compare the effects of FIFO, LIFO, and average cost

The journal entries under average costing follow the data in Exhibit 6-6. On November 5, RMS purchased $270 of inventory and made the first journal entry. On November 15, RMS sold 4 ski parkas for $80 each. RMS recorded the sale ($320) and the cost of goods sold ($177). The remaining journal entries (November 26 and 30) follow the data in Exhibit 6-6. Amounts unique to the average cost method are highlighted.

Average-Cost Journal Entries:	(All purchases and sales on account. The sale price of a ski parka is $80 per unit.)	
Nov. 5	Inventory 270	
	Accounts Payable	270
	Purchased inventory on account.	
15	Accounts Receivable (4 × $80) 320	
	Sale Revenue	320
	Sale on account.	
15	Cost of Goods Sold 177	
	Inventory	177
	Cost of goods sold.	
26	Inventory 350	
	Accounts Payable	350
	Purchased inventory on account.	
30	Accounts Receivable (8 × $80) 640	
	Sales Revenue	640
	Sale on account.	
30	Cost of Goods Sold 386	
	Inventory	386
	Cost of goods sold.	

Comparing FIFO, LIFO, and Average Cost

Exhibit 6-7 shows that FIFO is the most popular inventory costing method. LIFO is next most popular and average cost ranks third.

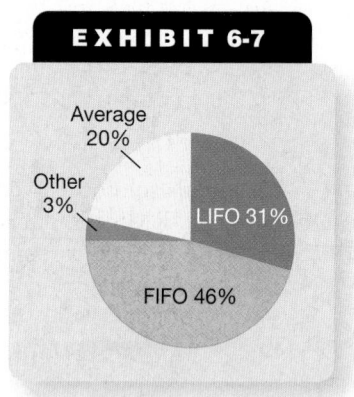

EXHIBIT 6-7

Average 20%

Other 3%

LIFO 31%

FIFO 46%

Use of the Various Inventory Methods

What leads Rocky Mountain Sportswear to select the FIFO method, General Electric to use LIFO, and Fossil (the watch company) to use average cost? The different methods have different benefits.

Exhibit 6-8 summarizes the results for the three inventory methods for RMS. It shows sales revenue, cost of goods sold, and gross profit for FIFO, LIFO, and average cost.

EXHIBIT 6-8   **Comparative Results for FIFO, LIFO, and Average Cost**

	FIFO	LIFO	Average
Sales revenue	$960	$960	$960
Cost of goods sold	560	575	563
Gross profit	$400	$385	$397

Exhibit 6-8 shows that FIFO produces the lowest cost of goods sold and the highest gross profit. Net income is also the highest under FIFO when inventory costs are rising. Many companies prefer high income in order to attract investors and borrow on good terms. FIFO offers this benefit.

LIFO results in the highest cost of goods sold and the lowest gross profit. That lets companies pay the lowest income taxes when inventory costs are rising. Low tax payments conserve cash and that's the main benefit of LIFO. The downside of LIFO is that the company reports low net income.

The average-cost method generates amounts that fall between the extremes of FIFO and LIFO. Companies that seek a "middle-ground" solution, therefore, use the average-cost method for inventory.

Summary Problem 1

Fossil specializes in designer watches and leather goods. Assume Fossil began June holding 10 wristwatches that cost $50 each. Fossil sells these watches for $100 each. During June, Fossil bought and sold inventory as follows:

June 3	Sold 8 units for $100 each
16	Purchased 10 units @ $55 each
23	Sold 8 units for $100 each

Requirements

1. Prepare a perpetual inventory record for Fossil under:
   - FIFO
   - LIFO
   - Average Cost

   Round unit cost to the nearest cent and all other amounts to the nearest dollar.

2. Journalize all of Fossil's inventory transactions for June under all three costing methods.

3. Show the computation of gross profit for each method.

4. Which method maximizes net income? Which method minimizes income taxes?

continued...

Solution

1. Perpetual inventory records:

FIFO

Wristwatches	Purchases			Cost of Goods Sold			Inventory on Hand		
Date	Quantity	Unit Cost	Total Cost	Quantity	Unit Cost	Total Cost	Quantity	Unit Cost	Total Cost
June 1							10	$50	$500
3				8	$50	$400	2	50	100
16	10	$55	$550				2	50	100
							10	55	550
23				2	50	100			
				6	55	330	4	55	220
30				16		$830	4		$220

LIFO

Wristwatches	Purchases			Cost of Goods Sold			Inventory on Hand		
Date	Quantity	Unit Cost	Total Cost	Quantity	Unit Cost	Total Cost	Quantity	Unit Cost	Total Cost
June 1							10	$50	$500
3				8	$50	$400	2	50	100
16	10	$55	$550				2	50	100
							10	55	550
23				8	55	440	2	50	100
							2	55	110
30				16		$840	4		$210

AVERAGE COST

Wristwatches	Purchases			Cost of Goods Sold			Inventory on Hand		
Date	Quantity	Unit Cost	Total Cost	Quantity	Unit Cost	Total Cost	Quantity	Unit Cost	Total Cost
June 1							10	$50.00	$500
3				8	$50.00	$400	2	50.00	100
16	10	$55	$550				12	54.17	650
23				8	54.17	433	4	54.17	217
30				16		$833	4		217

2. Journal Entries:

			FIFO		LIFO		Average	
June 3	Accounts Receivable		800		800		800	
	Sales Revenue			800		800		800
3	Cost of Goods Sold		400		400		400	
	Inventory			400		400		400
16	Inventory		550		550		550	
	Accounts Payable			550		550		550
23	Accounts Receivable		800		800		800	
	Sales Revenue			800		800		800
30	Cost of Goods Sold		430		440		433	
	Inventory			430		440		433

3. Gross Profit:

	FIFO	LIFO	Average
Sales revenue ($800 + $800)............................	$1,600	$1,600	$1,600
Cost of goods sold ($400 + $430)	830		
($400 + $440)		840	
($400 + $433)			833
Gross profit...	$ 770	$ 760	$ 767

4. FIFO maximizes net income.
LIFO minimizes income taxes.

Accounting Principles and Inventories

Several accounting principles affect inventories. Among them are consistency, disclosure, materiality, and accounting conservatism.

Consistency Principle

The **consistency principle** states that businesses should use the same accounting methods from period to period. Consistency helps investors compare a company's financial statements from one period to the next.

Suppose you are analyzing a company's net income over a two-year period. The company switched from LIFO to FIFO. Its net income increased dramatically but only as a result of the change in inventory method. If you did not know of the change, you might believe that the company's income really increased. Therefore, companies must report any changes in the accounting methods they use. Investors need this information to make wise decisions about the company.

Disclosure Principle

The **disclosure principle** holds that a company should report enough information for outsiders to make wise decisions about the company. In short, the company should report *relevant, reliable,* and *comparable* information about itself. This means disclosing the method being used to account for inventories. Suppose a banker is comparing two companies—one using LIFO and the other FIFO. The FIFO company reports higher net income, but only because it uses the FIFO method. Without knowledge of these accounting methods, the banker could lend money to the wrong business.

Materiality Concept

The **materiality concept** states that a company must perform strictly proper accounting *only* for significant items. Information is significant—or, in accounting terms, *material*—when it would cause someone to change a decision. The materiality concept frees accountants from having to report every last item in strict accordance with GAAP.

Accounting Conservatism

Conservatism in accounting means exercising caution in reporting items in the financial statements. Conservatism says,

- "Anticipate no gains, but provide for all probable losses."
- "If in doubt, record an asset at the lowest reasonable amount and a liability at the highest reasonable amount."
- "When there's a question, record an expense rather than an asset."

The goal of conservatism is to report realistic figures.

Other Inventory Issues

In addition to the FIFO, LIFO, and average cost methods, accountants face other inventory issues. This section covers:

- The lower-of-cost-or-market rule
- Effects of inventory errors
- Ethical issues
- Estimating ending inventory

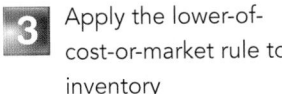

Apply the lower-of-cost-or-market rule to inventory

Lower-of-Cost-or-Market Rule

The **lower-of-cost-or-market rule** (abbreviated as **LCM**) shows accounting conservatism in action. LCM requires that inventory be reported in the financial statements at whichever is lower—

- the historical cost of the inventory or
- the market value of the inventory

For inventories, *market value* generally means *current replacement cost* (that is, the cost to replace the inventory on hand). If the replacement cost of inventory falls below its historical cost, the business must write down the inventory value. On the balance sheet the business reports ending inventory at its LCM value.

Suppose Rocky Mountain Sportswear paid $3,000 for inventory. By December 31, the inventory can now be replaced for $2,200, and the decline in value appears permanent. Market value is below cost, and the entry to write down the inventory to LCM follows:

Cost of Goods Sold (cost, $3,000 – market, $2,200)	800	
Inventory		800
To write inventory down to market value.		

In this case, Rocky Mountain Sportswear's balance sheet would report this inventory as follows:

Balance Sheet

Current assets:
   Inventory, at market
      (which is lower than FIFO cost) $2,200

Companies often disclose LCM in notes to their financial statements, as shown here for Rocky Mountain Sportswear:

NOTE 2: STATEMENT OF SIGNIFICANT ACCOUNTING POLICIES

Inventories. Inventories are carried at the *lower of cost or market*. Cost is determined using the first-in, first-out method.

Effects of Inventory Errors

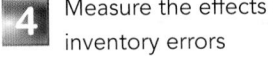

Measure the effects of inventory errors

Businesses count their inventory at the end of the period. For the financial statements to be accurate, it's important to get a correct count of ending inventory. This can be difficult for a company with far-flung operations.

An error in ending inventory creates a whole string of errors. To illustrate, suppose Rocky Mountain Sportswear accidentally counted too much ending inventory. Therefore, ending inventory is overstated on the balance sheet. The following diagram shows how an overstatement of ending inventory affects cost of goods sold, gross profit, and net income:

	Ending Inventory Overstated
Sales revenue	Correct
Cost of goods sold:	
Beginning inventory	Correct
Net purchases	Correct
Cost of goods available	Correct
Ending inventory	ERROR: Overstated
Cost of goods sold	Understated
Gross profit	Overstated
Operating expenses	Correct
Net income	Overstated

Understating the ending inventory—reporting the inventory too low—has the opposite effect, as shown here:

	Ending Inventory Understated
Sales revenue	Correct
Cost of goods sold:	
Beginning inventory	Correct
Net purchases	Correct
Cost of goods available	Correct
Ending inventory	ERROR: Understated
Cost of goods sold	Overstated
Gross profit	Understated
Operating expenses	Correct
Net income	Understated

Recall that one period's ending inventory becomes the next period's beginning inventory. Thus, an error in ending inventory carries over into the next period. Exhibit 6-9 illustrates the effect of an inventory error. Period 1's ending inventory is overstated by $5,000; period 1's ending inventory should be $10,000. The error carries over to period 2. Period 3 is correct. In fact, both Period 1 and Period 2 should look like Period 3.

Ending inventory is *subtracted* to compute cost of goods sold in one period and the same amount is *added* as beginning inventory the next period. Therefore, an inventory error cancels out after two periods. The overstatement of cost of goods sold in period 2 counterbalances the understatement for period 1. Thus, total gross profit for the two periods combined is correct. These effects are summarized in Exhibit 6-10.

Ethical Issues

No area of accounting has a deeper ethical dimension than inventory. Companies whose profits are lagging can be tempted to "cook the books." An increase in reported income will make the business look more successful than it really is.

There are two main schemes for cooking the books. The easiest way is to overstate ending inventory. In Exhibit 6-10, we saw how an inventory error affects net income.

continued after the exhibits on page 327...

EXHIBIT 6-9 Inventory Errors: An Example

	Period 1		Period 2		Period 3	
	Ending Inventory Overstated by $5,000		*Beginning* Inventory Overstated by $5,000		Correct	
Sales revenue		$100,000		$100,000		$100,000
Cost of goods sold:						
Beginning inventory	$10,000		$ 15,000		$ 10,000	
Net purchases	50,000		50,000		50,000	
Cost of goods available	60,000		65,000		60,000	
Ending inventory	(15,000)		(10,000)		(10,000)	
Cost of goods sold		45,000		55,000		50,000
Gross profit		$ 55,000		$ 45,000		$ 50,000

The correct gross profit is $50,000 for each period. $100,000

Source: The authors thank Carl High for this example.

EXHIBIT 6-10 Effects of Inventory Errors

	Period 1		Period 2	
	Cost of Goods Sold	Gross Profit and Net Income	Cost of Goods Sold	Gross Profit and Net Income
Period 1 Ending inventory *overstated*	Understated	Overstated	Overstated	Understated
Period 1 Ending inventory *understated*	Overstated	Understated	Understated	Overstated

The second way to cook the books involves sales. Datapoint Corporation and MiniScribe, both computer-related concerns, were charged with creating fictitious sales to boost reported profits.

Datapoint is alleged to have hired drivers to transport its inventory around the city so that the goods could *not* be counted. Datapoint's plan seemed to create the impression that the inventory must have been sold. The scheme broke down when the trucks returned the goods to Datapoint. The sales returns were much too high to be realistic, and the sales proved to be phony.

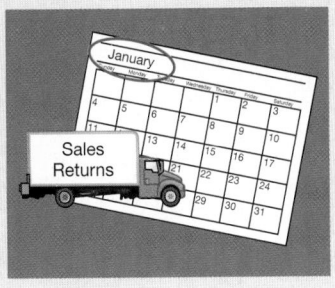

MiniScribe is alleged to have cooked its books by shipping boxes of bricks labeled as computer parts. The scheme boomeranged when MiniScribe had to record the sales returns. In virtually every area, accounting imposes a discipline that brings out the facts sooner or later.

Estimating Ending Inventory

5 Estimate ending inventory by the gross profit method

Often a business must *estimate* the value of its ending inventory. Suppose Rocky Mountain Sportswear suffers a fire loss and must estimate the value of the inventory destroyed. Or a company needs monthly financial statements.

The **gross profit method** provides a way to estimate inventory as follows:

> Beginning inventory
> + Net purchases
> = Cost of goods available
> − Ending inventory
> = Cost of goods sold

Rearranging *ending inventory* and *cost of goods sold* helps to estimate ending inventory:

> Beginning inventory
> + Net purchases
> = Cost of goods available
> − Cost of goods sold (Sales − Gross profit = COGS)
> = Ending inventory

Suppose a fire destroys your inventory. To collect insurance, you must estimate the cost of the inventory destroyed. Using your normal *gross profit percent* (that is, gross profit divided by net sales revenue), you can estimate cost of goods sold. Then subtract cost of goods sold from goods available to estimate ending inventory. Exhibit 6-11 illustrates the gross profit method (amounts assumed for this illustration):

EXHIBIT 6-11 | **Gross Profit Method of Estimating Inventory (amounts assumed)**

Beginning inventory		$14,000
Net purchases		66,000
Cost of goods available		80,000
Estimated cost of goods sold:		
Sales revenue	$100,000	
Less: Estimated gross profit of 40%	(40,000)	
Estimated cost of goods sold		(60,000)
Estimated cost of *ending inventory*		$20,000

Decision Guidelines

Assume you are starting a business to sell school supplies to your college friends. You'll need to stock computer disks, notebooks, and other inventory items. To manage the business, you'll also need some accounting records. Here are some of the decisions you'll face.

Decision	Guidelines	System or Method
Which inventory system to use?	• Expensive merchandise • Cannot control inventory by visual inspection	Perpetual system
	• Can control inventory by visual inspection	Periodic system
Which costing method to use?	• Unique inventory items	Specific unit cost
	• The most current cost of ending inventory • Maximizes reported income when costs are rising	FIFO
	• The most current measure of cost of goods sold and net income • Minimizes income tax when costs are rising	LIFO
	• Middle-of-the-road approach for income tax and net income	Average-cost method
How to estimate the cost of ending inventory?	• The cost-of-goods-sold model provides the framework	Gross profit method

Summary Problem 2

Suppose a division of IBM that handles computer parts has these inventory records for January 2008:

Date	Item	Quantity	Unit Cost	Sale Price
Jan. 1	Beginning inventory..............	100 units	$ 8	
10	Purchase	60 units	9	
15	Sale......................................	70 units		$20
21	Purchase	100 units	10	
30	Sale......................................	90 units		25

Operating expense for January was $1,900.

Requirement

Prepare the January income statement in multi-step format. Show amounts for FIFO, LIFO, and average cost. Label the bottom line "Operating income." (Round the average cost per unit to three decimal places and all other figures to whole-dollar amounts.) Show your computations, and use the cost-of-goods-sold model from pages 325 and 326 to compute cost of goods sold.

Solution

IBM
Income Statement for Computer Parts
Month Ended January 31, 2008

	FIFO		LIFO		Average Cost	
Sales revenue		$3,650		$3,650		$3,650
Cost of goods sold:						
Beginning inventory	$ 800		$ 800		$ 800	
Net purchases	1,540		1,540		1,540	
Cost of goods available	2,340		2,340		2,340	
Ending inventory	(1,000)		(800)		(900)	
Cost of goods sold		1,340		1,540		1,440
Gross profit		2,310		2,110		2,210
Operating expenses		1,900		1,900		1,900
Operating income		$ 410		$ 210		$ 310

Computations

Sales revenue:	(70 × $20) + (90 × $25)	= $3,650
Beginning inventory:	100 × $8	= $800
Purchases:	(60 × $9) + (100 × $10)	= $1,540
Ending inventory:		
FIFO	100* × $10	= $1,000
LIFO	100 × $8	= $800
Average cost:	100 × $9**	= $900

**Number of units in ending inventory = 100 + 60 − 70 + 100 − 90 =100
**Average cost per unit = $2,340/260 units† = $9
†Number of units available = 100 + 60 + 100 = 260.

Review *Merchandise Inventory*

Accounting Vocabulary

Average-Cost Method
Inventory costing method based on the average cost of inventory during the period. Average cost is determined by dividing the cost of goods available for sale by the number of units available.

Conservatism
Reporting the least favorable figures in the financial statements.

Consistency Principle
A business should use the same accounting methods and procedures from period to period.

Disclosure Principle
A business's financial statements must report enough information for outsiders to make knowledgeable decisions about the company.

First-In, First-Out (FIFO) Inventory Costing Method
Inventory costing method: The first costs into inventory are the first costs out to cost of goods sold. Ending inventory is based on the costs of the most recent purchases.

Gross Profit Method
A way to estimate inventory on the basis of the cost-of-goods-sold model: Beginning inventory + Net purchases = Cost of goods available for sale. Cost of goods available for sale – Cost of goods sold = Ending inventory.

Last-In, First-Out (LIFO) Inventory Costing Method
Inventory costing method: The last costs into inventory are the first costs out to cost of goods sold. Leaves the oldest costs—those of beginning inventory and the earliest purchases of the period—in ending inventory.

Lower-of-Cost-or-Market (LCM) Rule
Rule that an asset should be reported in the financial statements at whichever is lower—its historical cost or its market value.

Materiality Concept
A company must perform strictly proper accounting only for items that are significant to the business's financial situations.

Specific-Identification Method
Inventory costing method based on the specific cost of particular units of inventory. Also called the **specific-identification method**.

Specific-Unit-Cost Method
Inventory costing method based on the specific cost of particular units of inventory. Also called the **specific-identification method**.

Quick Check

1. T. J. Bronson made sales of $9,300 and ended April with inventories totaling $900. Cost of goods sold was $6,000. Total operating expenses were $2,700. How much net income did Bronson earn for the month?
   a. $600
   b. $900
   c. $3,300
   d. $6,600

2. Which inventory costing method assigns to ending inventory the newest—the most recent—costs incurred during the period?
   a. Specific unit cost
   b. Last-in, first-out (LIFO)
   c. First-in, first-out (FIFO)
   d. Average cost

3. Assume Amazon.com began June with 10 units of inventory that cost a total of $190. During June, Amazon purchased and sold goods as follows:

June 8	Purchase............................	30 units @ $20
14	Sale	25 units @ $40
22	Purchase............................	20 units @ $22
27	Sale	30 units @ $40

   Under the FIFO inventory method, how much is Amazon's cost of goods sold for the sale on June 14?
   a. $490
   b. $500
   c. $790
   d. $1,000

4. After the purchase on June 22, what is Amazon's cost of the inventory on hand? Amazon uses FIFO.
   a. $300
   b. $740
   c. $440
   d. $720

5. Under the FIFO method, Amazon's journal entry (entries) on June 14 is (are):
   a. Accounts Receivable 490
          Inventory....................................... 490
   b. Accounts Receivable 1,000
          Sales Revenue 1,000
   c. Cost of Goods Sold 490
          Inventory....................................... 490
   d. Both b and c are correct.

6. Which inventory costing method results in the lowest net income during a period of rising inventory costs?

   a. Specific unit cost

   b. First-in, first-out (FIFO)

   c. Last-in, first-out (LIFO)

   d. Average cost

7. Suppose Amazon.com used the average-cost method and the perpetual inventory system. Use the Amazon data in question 3 to compute the average unit cost of the company's inventory on hand at June 8. Round unit cost to the nearest cent.

   a. $19.00

   b. $19.75

   c. $20.00

   d. Cannot be determined from the data given

8. Which of the following is most closely linked to accounting conservatism?

   a. Consistency principle

   b. Disclosure principle

   c. Lower-of-cost-or-market rule

   d. Materiality concept

9. At December 31, 2008, McAdam Company overstated ending inventory by $40,000. How does this error affect cost of goods sold and net income for 2008?

   a. Understates costs of goods sold
      Overstates net income

   b. Overstates cost of goods sold
      Understates net income

   c. Overstates both cost of goods sold and net income

   d. Leaves both cost of goods sold and net income correct because the errors cancel each other

10. Suppose Rockey Mountain Sportswear (RMS) suffered a fire loss and needs to estimate the cost of the goods destroyed. Beginning inventory was $100,000, net purchases totaled $600,000, and sales came to $1,000,000. RMS's normal gross profit percentage is 50%. Use the gross profit method to estimate the cost of the inventory lost in the fire.

   a. $350,000

   b. $300,000

   c. $250,000

   d. $200,000

Answers are given after Apply Your Knowledge (p. 345)

Assess Your Progress

Short Exercises

Perpetual inventory record—FIFO

S6-1 Shepherd Cycles uses the FIFO inventory method. Shepherd started June with 10 bicycles that cost $70 each. On June 16, Shepherd bought 20 bicycles at $80 each. On June 30, Shepherd sold 25 bicycles. Prepare Shepherd's perpetual inventory record. (pp. 315–317)

Perpetual inventory record—LIFO

S6-2 Use the Shepherd Cycles data in Short Exercise 6-1 to prepare a perpetual inventory record for the LIFO method. (p. 317)

Perpetual inventory record—average cost

S6-3 Use the Shepherd Cycles data in Short Exercise 6-1 to prepare a perpetual inventory record for the average-cost method. Round average cost per unit to the nearest cent and all other amounts to the nearest dollar. (pp. 318–319)

Recording inventory transactions—FIFO

S6-4 Use the Shepherd Cycles data in Short Exercise 6-1 to journalize
1. The June 16 purchase of inventory on account. (pp. 315–317)
2. The June 30 sale of inventory on account. Shepherd sold each bicycle for $140. (pp. 315–317)
3. Cost of goods sold under FIFO. (pp. 315–317)

S6-5 Answer these questions in your own words:
1. Why does FIFO produce the lowest cost of goods sold during a period of rising prices? (pp. 320–321)
2. Why does LIFO produce the highest cost of goods sold during a period of rising prices? (pp. 320–321)

Comparing cost of goods sold under FIFO and LIFO

Comparing ending inventory under FIFO and LIFO

S6-6 Explain in your own words which inventory method results in the highest, and the lowest, cost of ending inventory. Prices are rising. Exhibits 6-4, page 316, and 6-5, page 317, provide the needed information.

Applying the lower-of-cost-or-market rule

3

S6-7 Assume that a King Burger restaurant has the following perpetual inventory record for hamburger patties:

HAMBURGER PATTIES

Date	Purchases	Cost of Goods Sold	Inventory on Hand
May 9	$500		$500
22		$300	$200
31	$200		$400

At May 31, the accountant for the restaurant determines that the current replacement cost of the ending inventory is $450. Make any adjusting entry needed to apply the lower-of-cost-or-market rule. Then report inventory on the balance sheet. King Burger uses the average-cost method. (p. 325)

Applying the lower-of-cost-or-market rule

3

S6-8 Use the perpetual inventory record given in Short Exercise 6-7. Assume that the accountant determines that the current replacement cost of the ending inventory is $360. Make any adjusting entry needed to apply the lower-of-cost-or-market rule. Then report inventory on the balance sheet. King Burger uses the average-cost method. (p. 325)

Effect of an inventory error—one year only

4

S6-9 Van Dyke Copier inventory data for the year ended December 31, 2008, follow.

Sales revenue...................................	$50,000
Cost of goods sold:	
Beginning inventory......................	$ 4,200
Net purchases.............................	27,400
Cost of goods available	31,600
Less: Ending inventory	(4,600)
Cost of goods sold.......................	27,000
Gross profit....................................	$23,000

Assume that the ending inventory was accidentally overstated by $1,000. What are the correct amounts of cost of goods sold and gross profit? (p. 327)

Next year's effect of an inventory error

4

S6-10 Refer back to the Van Dyke Copier inventory data in Short Exercise 6-9. How would the inventory error affect Van Dyke's cost of goods sold and gross profit for the year ended December 31, 2009? (p. 327)

Estimating ending inventory by the gross profit method

5

S6-11 Carpetmaster began the year with inventory of $350,000. Inventory purchases for the year total $1,600,000, and cost of goods sold will be $1,750,000. How much is Carpetmaster's estimated cost of ending inventory? Use the gross profit method. (p. 328)

Estimating ending inventory by the gross profit method

5

S6-12 Leather Goods Company began the year with inventory of $50,000 and purchased $250,000 of goods during the year. Sales for the year are $500,000, and Leather Goods' gross profit percentage is 55% of sales. Compute the estimated cost of ending inventory by the gross profit method. (p. 328)

Exercises

Measuring ending inventory and cost of goods sold in a perpetual system—FIFO

1

E6-13 Hyatt Magic carries an inventory of putters and other golf clubs. Hyatt uses the FIFO method and a perpetual inventory system. Company records indicate the following for a particular line of Hyatt Magic putters:

Date	Item	Quantity	Unit Cost
Nov. 1	Balance..........................	5	$70
6	Sale	3	
8	Purchase........................	10	79
17	Sale	4	
30	Sale	5	

Requirement

Prepare a perpetual inventory record for the putters. Then determine the amounts Hyatt Magic should report for ending inventory and cost of goods sold by the FIFO method. (pp. 315–317)

Recording perpetual inventory transactions

E6-14 After preparing the FIFO perpetual inventory record in Exercise 6-13, journalize Hyatt Magic's November 8 purchase of inventory on account and November 17 cash sale (sale price of each putter was $120). (pp. 315–317)

Measuring ending inventory and cost of goods sold in a perpetual system—LIFO

E6-15 Refer to the Hyatt Magic inventory data in Exercise 6-13. Assume that Hyatt Magic uses the LIFO cost method. Prepare Hyatt's perpetual inventory record for the putters on the LIFO basis. Then identify the cost of ending inventory and cost of goods sold for the month. (p. 317)

Applying the average-cost method in a perpetual inventory system

E6-16 Refer to the Hyatt Magic inventory data in Exercise 6-13. Assume that Hyatt Magic uses the average-cost method. Prepare Hyatt's perpetual inventory record for the putters on the average-cost basis. Round average cost per unit to the nearest cent and all other amounts to the nearest dollar. Then identify the cost of ending inventory and cost of goods sold for the month (pp. 318–319)

Recording perpetual inventory transactions

E6-17 Accounting records for Jim's Shopping Bags yield the following data for the year ended December 31, 2008.

Inventory, December 31, 2007	$ 8,000
Purchases of inventory (on account)	49,000
Sales of inventory—80% on account; 20% for cash (cost $41,000)...	75,000
Inventory, December 31, 2008	?

Requirements

1. Journalize Jim's inventory transactions in the perpetual system. (pp. 315–317)

2. Report ending inventory on the balance sheet, and sales, cost of goods sold, and gross profit on the income statement. (p. 312)

Comparing FIFO and LIFO amounts for ending inventory

E6-18 Assume that a Toys "Я" Us store bought and sold a line of dolls for inventory during December as follows:

Beginning inventory	10 units @ $9
Sale	6 units
Purchase	15 units @ $12
Sale	14 units

Toys "Я" Us uses the perpetual inventory system. Compute the cost of ending inventory under (a) FIFO and (b) LIFO. You will need to prepare a perpetual inventory record for LIFO.

Which method results in higher cost of ending inventory? (pp. 315, 317)

Comparing FIFO and LIFO amounts for cost of goods sold

E6-19 Use the data in Exercise 6-18 to compute the cost of goods sold under (a) FIFO and (b) LIFO. You will need a complete perpetual inventory record for LIFO. Which method results in the higher cost of goods sold? (pp. 315, 317)

E6-20 Assume that a Goodyear Tire store completed the following perpetual inventory transactions for a line of tires.

Beginning inventory	20 tires @ $60
Purchase..	8 tires @ $75
Sale	15 tires @ $110

Compute cost of goods sold and gross profit under (a) FIFO, (b) LIFO, and (c) average cost (round average cost per unit to the nearest cent and all other amounts to the nearest dollar). (pp. 315–319)

Determining amounts for the
income statement; periodic
system

1

E6-21 This exercise is based on the Appendix 6A. Supply the missing amounts for each of the following companies (p. 346):

Company	Net Sales	Beginning Inventory	Net Purchases	Ending Inventory	Cost of Goods Sold	Gross Profit
Ash	$101,000	$21,000	$62,000	$19,000	(a)	$37,000
Elm	(b)	25,000	93,000	(c)	$94,000	43,000
Fir	94,000	(d)	54,000	22,000	62,000	(e)
Oak	84,000	10,000	(f)	8,000	(g)	47,000

Prepare the income statement for Ash Company, which uses the periodic inventory system. Include a complete heading and show the full computation of cost of goods sold. Ash's operating expenses for the year were $11,000. (p. 247)

E6-22 Eagle Resources, which uses the FIFO method, has these account balances at December 31, 2008, prior to releasing the financial statements for the year:

Inventory	
Beg. bal. 12,000	
End bal. 14,000	

Cost of Goods Sold	
Bal. 72,000	

Sales Revenue	
	Bal. 118,000

Eagle has determined that the replacement cost (current market value) of the December 31, 2008, ending inventory is $13,000.

Requirement

Prepare Eagle Resources' balance sheet at December 31, 2008, to show how Eagle would apply the lower-of-cost-or-market rule to inventories. Include a complete heading for the statement. (p. 325)

E6-23 Nutriset Foods reports inventory at the lower of average cost or market. Prior to releasing its March 2008 financial statements, Nutriset's *preliminary* income statement, before the year-end adjustments, appears as follows:

NUTRISET FOODS
Income Statement (partial)

Sales revenue	$118,000
Cost of goods sold	48,000
Gross profit	$ 70,000

Nutriset has determined that the replacement cost of ending inventory is $18,000. Cost is $21,000.

Requirement
Show how Nutriset should report sales, cost of goods sold, and gross profit. (pp. 320–321)

E6-24 Poiláne Bakery reported sales revenue of $28,000 and cost of goods sold of $12,000. Compute Poiláne's correct gross profit if the company made each of the following accounting errors. Show your work.

a. Ending inventory is overstated by $3,000. (pp. 325–326)

b. Ending inventory is understated by $3,000. (pp. 325–326)

E6-25 Whole Foods Grocery reported the following comparative income statement for the years ended September 30, 2008 and 2007.

WHOLE FOODS GROCERY
Income Statements
Years Ended September 30, 2008 and 2007

	2008		2007	
Sales revenue		$137,000		$120,000
Cost of goods sold:				
Beginning inventory	$14,000		$12,000	
Net purchases	72,000		66,000	
Cost of goods available	86,000		78,000	
Ending inventory	(16,000)		(14,000)	
Cost of goods sold		70,000		64,000
Gross profit		67,000		56,000
Operating expenses		25,000		20,000
Net income		$ 42,000		$ 36,000

continued...

During 2008, Whole Foods discovered that ending 2007 inventory, as previously reported, was overstated by $3,000. Prepare the corrected comparative income statement for the two-year period, complete with a heading for the statement. What was the effect of the error on net income for the two years combined? Explain your answer. (pp. 326–327)

Estimating ending inventory by the gross profit method
5

E6-26 Toyota holds inventory all over the world. Assume that the records for an auto part show the following:

Beginning inventory..................................	$ 150,000
Net purchases..	800,000
Net sales...	1,000,000
Gross profit rate	40%

Suppose this inventory, stored in the United States, was lost in a fire. Estimate the amount of the loss to Toyota. Use the gross profit method. (p. 328)

Estimating ending inventory by the gross profit method
5

E6-27 Chick Landscaping and Nursery began January with inventory of $47,000. During January, Chick made net purchases of $33,000 and had net sales of $60,000. For the past several years, Chick's gross profit has been 35% of sales. Use the gross profit method to estimate the cost of the ending inventory for the monthly financial statements. (p. 328)

Problems (Group A)

Using the perpetual inventory system—FIFO
1

P6-28A Ornamental Iron Works, which uses the FIFO method, began August with 50 units of iron inventory that cost $40 each. During August, the company completed these inventory transactions:

		Units	Unit Cost	Unit Sale Price
Aug. 3	Sale.......................	40		$70
8	Purchase	80	$44	
21	Sale.......................	70		75
30	Purchase	10	48	

Requirements
1. Prepare a perpetual inventory record for the inventory. (pp. 315–317)
2. Determine the company's cost of goods sold for August. (pp. 315–317)
3. Compute gross profit for August. (pp. 315–317)

Accounting for inventory using the perpetual system—LIFO
1

P6-29A Toy World began January with an inventory of 20 crates of toys that cost a total of $1,100. During the month, Toy World purchased and sold merchandise on account as follows:

Purchase 1	30 crates @ $65	Purchase 2	70 crates @ $70
Sale 1	40 crates @ sale price of $100	Sale 2	75 crates @ sale price of $110

Toy World uses the LIFO method.

continued. . .

Cash payments on account totaled $6,300. Operating expenses for the month were $3,600, with two-thirds paid in cash and the rest accrued as Accounts Payable.

Requirements

1. Prepare a perpetual inventory record, at LIFO cost, for this merchandise. (p. 317)
2. Make journal entries to record Toy World's transactions. (p. 317)

Accounting for inventory in a perpetual system— average-cost

P6-30A Refer to the Toy World situation in Problem 6-29A. Keep all the data unchanged, except that Toy World now uses the average-cost method.

Requirements

1. Prepare a perpetual inventory record at average cost. Round average unit cost to the nearest cent and all other amounts to the nearest dollar. (pp. 318–319)
2. Prepare a multi-step income statement for Toy World for the month ended January 31, 2007. (p. 312)

Applying the lower-of-cost-or-market rule to inventories

3

P6-31A Some of L&M Electronics' merchandise is gathering dust. It is now December 31, 2008, and the current replacement cost of the ending inventory is $25,000 below L&M's cost of the goods, which was $100,000. Before any adjustments at the end of the period, the company's Cost of Goods Sold account has a balance of $600,000.

What action should L&M Electronics take in this situation, if any? Give any journal entry required. At what amount should L&M report Inventory on the balance sheet? At what amount should the company report Cost of Goods Sold on the income statement? Discuss the accounting principle or concept that is most relevant to this situation. (p. 325)

Correcting inventory errors over a three-year period

4

P6-32A Lake Air Carpets' books show the following data (in thousands). In early 2009, auditors found that the ending inventory for 2006 was understated by $8 thousand and that the ending inventory for 2008 was overstated by $4 thousand. The ending inventory at December 31, 2007, was correct.

(Thousands)	2008	2007	2006
Net sales revenue	$360	$285	$244
Cost of goods sold:			
Beginning inventory	$ 65	$ 55	$ 70
Net purchases	195	135	130
Cost of goods available	260	190	200
Less: Ending inventory	(70)	(65)	(55)
Cost of goods sold	190	125	145
Gross profit	170	160	99
Operating expenses	113	109	76
Net income	$ 57	$ 51	$ 23

continued. . .

Requirements

1. Show corrected income statements for the three years. (pp. 326–327)

2. State whether each year's net income—before your corrections—is understated or overstated. For each incorrect figure, indicate the amount of the understatement or overstatement. (pp. 326–327)

Estimating ending inventory by the gross profit method; preparing the income statement

5

P6-33A Party Time Costumes estimates its inventory by the gross profit method. The gross profit has averaged 50% of net sales. The company's inventory records reveal the following data (amounts in thousands):

Inventory, July 1...	$ 360
Transactions during July:	
Purchases..	3,700
Purchase discounts.....................................	20
Purchase returns	10
Sales	6,430
Sales returns	30

Requirements

1. Estimate the July 31 inventory, using the gross profit method. (p. 328)

2. Prepare the July income statement through gross profit for Party Time Costumes. (pp. 270, 330)

Problems (Group B)

Accounting for inventory in a perpetual system—FIFO

1

P6-34B Hobart Sign Company began with an inventory of 50 signs that cost a total of $1,500. Hobart purchased and sold merchandise on account as follows:

Purchase 1...............................	60 signs @ $35
Sale 1	100 signs @ $60
Purchase 2...............................	90 signs @ $40
Sale 2	70 signs @ $70

Hobart uses the FIFO cost method. Cash payments on account totaled $5,000. Operating expenses were $2,700; Hobart paid two-thirds in cash and accrued the rest as Accounts Payable.

Requirements

1. Prepare a perpetual inventory record, at FIFO cost, for this merchandise. (pp. 315–317)

2. Make journal entries to record the company's transactions. (pp. 315–317)

Accounting for inventory in a perpetual system—average cost

P6-35B Refer to the Hobart Sign Company situation in Problem 6-34B. Keep all the data unchanged, except that Hobart now uses the average-cost method.

continued. . .

Requirements

1. Prepare a perpetual inventory record at average cost. Round average unit cost to the nearest cent and all other amounts to the nearest dollar. (pp. 318–319)

2. Prepare a multi-step income statement for Hobart Sign Company for the month ended February 28, 2008. (p. 270)

Using the perpetual inventory system—LIFO
1

P6-36B La Tapatía Mexican Foods, which uses the LIFO method, began March with 50 units of food inventory that cost $15 each. During March, LaTapatía completed these inventory transactions:

		Units	Unit Cost	Unit Sale Price
March 2	Purchase	12	$20	
8	Sale	40		$36
17	Purchase	30	25	
22	Sale	31		40

Requirements

1. Prepare a perpetual inventory record for the inventory. (p. 317)

2. Determine LaTapatía's cost of goods sold for March. (p. 317)

3. Compute gross profit for March. (p. 312)

Applying the lower-of-cost-or-market rule to inventories
3

P6-37B Some of Lamar Scuba Center's merchandise is gathering dust. It is now December 31, 2009. The current replacement cost of Lamar's ending inventory is $15,000 below Lamar's cost of the goods, which was $90,000. Before any adjustments at the end of the period, the Cost of Goods Sold account has a balance of $400,000.

What action should Lamar take in this situation, if any? Give any journal entry required. At what amount should Lamar report Inventory on the balance sheet? At what amount should the company report Cost of Goods Sold on the income statement? Discuss the accounting principle or concept that is most relevant to this situation. (p. 325)

Correcting inventory errors over a three-year period
4

P6-38B The accounting records of Juniper Cove Music Store show these data (in thousands):

	2008	2007	2006
Net sales revenue	$210	$165	$170
Cost of goods sold:			
Beginning inventory	$ 20	$ 25	$ 40
Net purchases	135	100	90
Cost of goods available	155	125	130
Less: Ending inventory	(30)	(20)	(25)
Cost of goods sold	125	105	105
Gross profit	85	60	65
Operating expenses	58	32	29
Net income	$ 27	$ 28	$ 36

continued. . .

In early 2009, auditors discovered that the ending inventory for 2006, as reported here, was understated by $6 thousand and that the ending inventory for 2008 was overstated by $7 thousand. The ending inventory at December 31, 2007, was correct.

Requirements

1. Show corrected income statements for the three years. (pp. 326–327)

2. State whether each year's net income as reported here is understated or overstated. For each incorrect net income figure, indicate the amount of the understatement or overstatement. (pp. 325–327)

Estimating ending inventory by the gross profit method; preparing the income statement

for 24/7 practice, visit www.MyAccountingLab.com

P6-39B Audio-Video estimates its inventory by the gross profit method when preparing monthly financial statements. For the past two years, gross profit has averaged 22% of net sales. The company's inventory records reveal the following data (amounts in thousands):

Inventory, March 1...	$ 690
Transactions during March:	
Purchases..	6,500
Purchase discounts.......................................	150
Purchase returns	10
Sales...	8,610
Sales returns..	110

Requirements

1. Estimate the March 31 inventory using the gross profit method. (p. 328)

2. Prepare the March income statement through gross profit for Audio Video. (p. 312)

Apply Your Knowledge

Decision Cases

Making inventory decisions
2

Case 1. Assume you are opening a Bed Bath & Beyond store. To finance the business, you need a $500,000 loan, and your banker requires a set of forecasted financial statements. Assume you are preparing the statements and must make some decisions about how to do the accounting for the business. Answer the following questions (refer back to Chapter 5 if necessary):

1. Which type of inventory system will you use? Give your reason. (p. 255)

2. Show how to compute net purchases and net sales. How will you treat the cost of transportation-in? (pp. 260–263)

3. How often do you plan to do a physical count of inventory on hand? What will the physical count accomplish? (pp. 266–267)

4. Inventory costs are rising. Which inventory costing method will you use in order to:
   a. Maximize net income? (pp. 320–321)
   b. Pay the least amount of income tax? (pp. 320–321)

Increasing net income
2

Case 2. Suppose you own Campbell Appliance. The store's summarized financial statements for 2008, the most recent year, follow:

CAMPBELL APPLIANCE
Income Statement
Year Ended December 31, 2008

	(Thousands)
Sales	$800
Cost of goods sold	660
Gross profit	140
Operating expenses	100
Net income	$ 40

CAMPBELL APPLIANCE
Balance Sheet
December 31, 2008

(Thousands)	Assets	Liabilities and Capital	
Cash	$ 30	Accounts payable	$ 35
Inventories	75	Note payable	280
Land and buildings, net	360	Total liabilities	315
		Owner, capital	150
Total assets	$465	Total liabilities and capital	$465

Assume that you need to double net income. To accomplish your goal, it will be very difficult to raise the prices you charge because there is a Best Buy nearby. Also, you have little control over your cost of goods sold because the appliance manufacturers set the price you must pay.

Identify several strategies for doubling net income. (Challenge)

Ethical Issue

During 2008, Crop-Paper-Scissors, a craft store, changed to the LIFO method of accounting for inventory. Suppose that during 2009, Crop-Paper-Scissors switched back to the FIFO method and the following year switches back to LIFO again.

Requirements

1. What would you think of a company's ethics if it changed accounting methods every year?

2. What accounting principle would changing methods every year violate?

3. Who can be harmed when a company changes its accounting methods too often? How?

Financial Statement Case

Analyzing inventories

3 4 5

The notes are an important part of a company's financial statements, giving valuable details that would clutter the tabular data presented in the statements. This case will help you learn to use a company's inventory notes. Refer to the Amazon.com financial statements and related notes in Appendix A at the end of the book, and answer the following questions:

Requirements

1. How much was the Amazon.com merchandise inventory at December 31, 2005? At December 31, 2004?

2. Which cost method does Amazon use for inventories? How does Amazon value its inventories? See Note 1.

3. By rearranging the cost-of-goods-sold formula, you can compute purchases, which are not reported in the Amazon statements. How much were Amazon's inventory purchases during 2005?

Team Project

Link Back to Chapter 5 (Gross Profit Percentage and Inventory Turnover). Obtain the annual reports of as many companies as you have team members—one company per team member. Most companies post their financial statements on their Web sites.

Requirements

1. Identify the inventory method used by each company.

2. Compute each company's gross profit percentage and rate of inventory turnover for the most recent two years.

3. For the industries of the companies you are analyzing, obtain the industry averages for gross profit percentage and inventory turnover from Robert Morris Associates, *Annual Statement Studies;* Dun and Bradstreet, *Industry Norms and Key Business Ratios;* or Leo Troy, *Almanac of Business and Industrial Financial Ratios.*

4. How well does each of your companies compare to the average for its industry? What insight about your companies can you glean from these ratios?

For Internet Exercises, Excel in Practice, and additional online activities, go to the Web site www.prenhall.com/horngren.

Quick Check Answers

1. *a*   2. *c*   3. *a*   4. *b*   5. *d*   6. *c*   7. *b*   8. *c*   9. *a*   10. *d*

Appendix 6A

Accounting for Inventory in a Periodic System

We described the periodic inventory system briefly in Chapter 5. Accounting is simpler in a periodic system because the company keeps no daily running record of inventory on hand. The only way to determine the ending inventory and cost of goods sold in a periodic system is to count the goods—usually at the end of the year. The periodic system works well for a small business, in which the owner can control inventory by visual inspection.

This appendix illustrates how the periodic system works. The accounting in a periodic system is similar to a perpetual system, except:

1. The periodic system uses four additional accounts:
   - **Purchases**—this account holds the cost of inventory as it's purchased. Purchases carries a debit balance.
   - **Purchase Discounts**—this contra account carries a credit balance.
   - **Purchase Returns and Allowances**—this contra account carries a credit balance.
   - **Transportation-in**—this account holds the transportation cost paid on inventory purchases. It carries a debit balance.

   In the perpetual system, all these costs go into the Inventory account.

2. The end-of-period entries are more extensive in the periodic system because we must close out the beginning inventory balance and set up the cost of the ending inventory. This appendix illustrates the closing process for the periodic system.

3. Cost of goods sold in a periodic system is computed by the following formula (using assumed amounts for this illustration):

Beginning inventory (ending inventory from the preceding period)	$ 5,000
Net purchases (often abbreviated as Purchases)	20,000*
Cost of goods available	25,000
Less: Ending inventory (on hand at the end of the current period)	(7,000)
Cost of goods sold	$18,000

*Net purchases is determined as follows (all amounts assumed):	
Purchases	$21,000
Less: Purchase discounts	(2,000)
Purchase returns and allowances	(5,000)
Add: Transportation-in	6,000
Net purchases	$20,000

Inventory Costing in the Periodic System

The various costing methods (FIFO, LIFO, and average) in a periodic inventory system follow the pattern illustrated earlier for the perpetual system. To show how the periodic system works, we use the same Rocky Mountain Sportswear data that we used for the perpetual system, as follows:

ROCKY MOUNTAIN SPORTSWEAR SKI PARKA

		Number of Units	Unit Cost
Nov. 1	Beginning inventory	1	$40
5	Purchase	6	45
26	Purchase	7	50
30	Ending inventory	2	?

We use these data to illustrate:

- FIFO
- LIFO
- Average cost

For all three methods cost of goods available is always the sum of beginning inventory plus net purchases:

Beginning inventory (1 unit @ $40)..	$ 40
Net purchases (6 units @ $45) + (7 units @ $50)........................	620
Cost of goods available (14 units)	$660

The different methods—FIFO, LIFO, and average cost—compute different amounts for ending inventory and cost of goods sold.

First-In, First-Out (FIFO) Method

Under FIFO, the ending inventory comes from the newest—the most recent—purchases, which cost $50 per unit. FIFO is illustrated in the box that follows on the next page.

Last-In, First-Out (LIFO) Method

Under LIFO, the ending inventory comes from the oldest cost of the period—in this case the beginning inventory that cost $40 per unit, plus the first purchase at $45. The LIFO illustration follows on the next page.

Average-Cost Method

In the average-cost method, we compute a single average cost per unit for the entire period:

Cost of goods available	÷	Number of units available	=	Average cost per unit
$660	÷	14 units	=	$47.14

Then apply this average cost to compute ending inventory and cost of goods sold, as shown in the far right column:

	FIFO	LIFO	Average
Cost of goods available	$660	$660	$660
Less: Ending inventory			
FIFO (2 units @ $50).............................	(100)		
LIFO (1 unit @ $40			
1 unit @ $45).............................		(85)	
Average (2 units @ $47.14)....................			(94)
Cost of goods sold	$560	$575	$566

Comparing the Perpetual and Periodic Inventory Systems

Exhibit 6A-1 provides a side-by-side comparison of the perpetual and the periodic inventory systems. It gives the:

- Journal entries
- Ledger accounts
- Reporting in the financial statements

EXHIBIT 6A-1 Comparing the Perpetual and Periodic Inventory Systems (all amounts assumed for this illustration)

JOURNAL ENTRIES

Perpetual System			Periodic System		
Inventory	$570,000		Purchases	$570,000	
Accounts Payable		570,000	Accounts Payable		$570,000
Purchased on account.			*Purchased inventory on account.*		
Accounts Payable	20,000		Accounts Payable	20,000	
Inventory		20,000	Purchase Returns and Allowances		20,000
Returned damaged goods to seller.			*Returned damaged goods to seller.*		
Accounts Receivable	900,000		Accounts Receivable	900,000	
Sales Revenue		900,000	Sales Revenue		900,000
Sale on account.			*Sale on account.*		
Cost of Goods Sold	530,000		No entry for cost of goods sold.		
Inventory		530,000			
Cost of goods sold.					

CLOSING ENTRIES

End of the Period			End of the Period		
			1. Cost of Goods Sold	$100,000	
			Inventory (beginning)		$100,000
			Transfer beginning inventory to		
			cost of goods sold.		
			2. Inventory (ending)	120,000	
			Cost of Goods Sold		120,000
			Record ending inventory based on a		
			physical count.		
			3. Cost of Goods Sold	550,000	
			Purchase Returns and Allowances	20,000	
			Purchases		570,000
			Transfer net purchases to cost of		
			goods sold.		
1. Income Summary	530,000		4. Income Summary	530,000	
Cost of Goods Sold		530,000	Cost of Goods Sold		530,000
Close cost of goods sold.			*Close cost of goods sold.*		
			($100,000 − $120,000 + $550,000 = $530,000)		

LEDGER ACCOUNTS

Perpetual System				Periodic System			
Inventory		**Cost of Goods Sold**		**Inventory**		**Cost of Goods Sold**	
100,000	20,000	530,000	530,000	100,000*	100,000	100,000	120,000
570,000	530,000			120,000		550,000	530,000
120,000							

*Beginning inventory was $100,000.

REPORTING IN THE FINANCIAL STATEMENTS

Perpetual System		Periodic System		
Income Statement		**Income Statement**		
Sales revenue.....................................	$900,000	Sales revenue..		$900,000
Cost of goods sold............................	530,000 ◄───	Cost of goods sold:		
Gross profit.......................................	$370,000 ◄──	Beginning inventory.............................	$ 100,000	
		Purchases.........................	$570,000	
		Less: Purchase returns		
		and allowances........	(20,000)	550,000
		Cost of goods available.........................		650,000
		Less: Ending inventory..........................		(120,000)
	└──►	Cost of goods sold...		530,000
	└──►	Gross profit...		$370,000

Perpetual System			Periodic System		
Balance Sheet			**Balance Sheet**		
Current assets:			Current assets:		
Cash..$	XXX		Cash... $	XXX	
Accounts receivable............................	XXX		Accounts receivable..............................	XXX	
Inventory..	120,000 ◄──────►		Inventory...	120,000	

Appendix 6A Assignments

Exercises

Determining ending inventory and cost of goods sold by four methods—periodic system.

1

E6A-1 The periodic inventory records of Flexon Prosthetics indicate the following at October 31:

Oct. 1	Beginning inventory	9 units @ $60
8	Purchase.....................................	4 units @ 60
15	Purchase.....................................	10 units @ 70
26	Purchase.....................................	3 units @ 80

At October 31 Flexon counts 8 units of inventory on hand.

continued...

Requirements

Compute ending inventory and cost of goods sold, using each of the following methods.

1. Average cost (round average unit cost to the nearest cent) (pp. 346–347)
2. First-in, first-out (pp. 346–347)
3. Last-in, first-out (pp. 346–347)

Journalizing purchase, sale, and closing entries—periodic system

E6A-2 Flexon Prosthetics uses the periodic inventory system. Journalize Flexon Prosthetics'

a. Purchase of inventory on account, $1,180. (pp. 349–350)
b. Sale of inventory for $3,000. (pp. 349–350)
c. Closing entries: (pp. 349–350)
   (1) Beginning inventory, $540.
   (2) Ending inventory at FIFO cost, $590.
   (3) Purchases, $1,180.
   (4) Cost of goods sold at FIFO cost, $1,130.

Include an explanation for each entry.

Problem

Computing inventory by three methods—periodic system

P6A-1 A Best Yet Electronic Center began December with 100 units of inventory that cost $75 each. During December, the store made the following purchases:

Dec. 3	20 @ $80
12	50 @ 82
18	80 @ 85

Best Yet uses the periodic inventory system, and the physical count at December 31 indicates that 110 units of inventory are on hand.

Requirements

1. Determine the ending inventory and cost-of-goods-sold amounts for the December financial statements under the average cost, FIFO, and LIFO methods. (pp. 346–347)
2. Sales revenue for December totaled $25,000. Compute Best Yet's gross profit for December under each method. (pp. 349–350)
3. Which method will result in the lowest income taxes for Best Yet? Why? Which method will result in the highest net income for Best Yet? Why? (pp. 349–350, 320–321)

7 Accounting Information Systems

Learning Objectives

1 Describe an effective accounting information system

2 Understand both computerized and manual accounting systems

3 Understand how spreadsheets are used in accounting

4 Use the sales journal, the cash receipts journal, and the accounts receivable ledger

5 Use the purchases journal, the cash payments journal, and the accounts payable ledger

You've just started a small business, In Motion, to print T-shirts with club and party logos at your college. With everyone wearing T-shirts, you can make a little money while in school. You've lined up a supplier of Hanes Beefy Tee T-shirts, and a local printer can imprint the logos. It's early in the semester and parties are in full swing. With an order for 100 T-shirts you're ready to go. What's your next step?

At some point you'll need to keep track of your cash and other assets. You'll want to measure In Motion's performance. That brings us back to accounting. The early chapters of this book have shown how to:

- set up your ledger
- record transactions
- adjust and close the books
- prepare the financial statements

Think of handling all this accounting manually—one journal entry at a time. Even for your small business, that would be quite a task. ◼

In this chapter we describe the features of an effective information system. This background will help you design an accounting system for your business. The second half of the chapter covers special journals that can be used for repetitive transactions. They can save you lots of time, and that will enable you to hustle more business. Let's begin by seeing what makes for a good accounting system.

An Effective Accounting Information System

1 Describe an effective accounting information system

Good design features make an accounting system run smoothly. An effective system provides:

- Control
- Compatibility
- Flexibility
- A good cost/benefit relationship

Control

An owner must *control* the business. Internal controls can safeguard your assets and eliminate waste. For example, you need procedures for making cash payments. Designate a trusted employee to review incoming bills before writing checks. If you extend credit to customers, you'll need accounts receivable records to ensure that you collect cash on time.

Compatibility

A *compatible* system works smoothly with your personnel and organizational structure. Your small T-shirt business doesn't need a big accounting system. You can probably do your accounting with software such as QuickBooks or Peachtree. But a large company needs a different system. For example, Bank of America has hundreds of branch offices. Managers track revenues in each region where the bank operates. If revenues in Texas are lagging, managers can focus on the Texas banks.

Flexibility

Your accounting system must be *flexible* to accommodate changes in your business over time. In Motion may start selling some new products, such as baseball caps. You may expand to other colleges and universities. That will require a more complicated accounting system.

A Good Cost/Benefit Relationship

Control, compatibility, and flexibility cost money. You need a system that gives the *most benefit for the least cost*. QuickBooks may be the most economical way to do your accounting. Or it may be cheaper to hire a CPA firm. Most CPAs will process your data at a reasonable cost. Simply give your business documents—incoming bills, sales invoices, and so on—to your CPA each month, and let him or her do your accounting.

All these features are needed whether the accounting system is computerized or manual. Let's start with a computerized system.

Components of a Computerized System

A computerized accounting system has two basic components:

- Hardware
- Software

Hardware is the electronic equipment: computers, monitors, printers, and the network that connects them. Most systems require a **network** to link computers. In a networked system, the **server** stores the program and the data. With a network, a PriceWaterhouseCoopers auditor in London can work on the data of a client in Sydney, Australia. The result is a speedier audit for the client.

Software is the set of programs that drives the computer. Accounting software reads, edits, and stores transaction data. It also generates the reports you can use to run the business. Many software packages are flexible. For example, a chain of gas stations may be only partly computerized. This small business may use the computer for employee payrolls. Other parts of the accounting system may be manual.

How Computerized and Manual Systems Work

2 Understand both computerized and manual accounting systems

Data processing includes three steps—inputs, processing, and outputs—as shown in Exhibit 7-1.

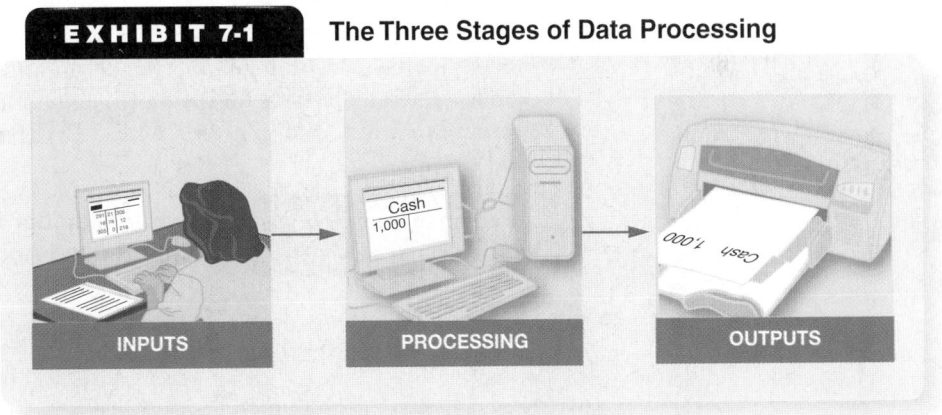

EXHIBIT 7-1   The Three Stages of Data Processing

INPUTS · PROCESSING · OUTPUTS

Inputs

Inputs come from source documents, such as orders received from customers and sales invoices faxed to customers. Inputs are usually grouped by type. For example, you would enter cash sales separately from sales on account.

Processing

In a manual system, *processing* includes journalizing transactions, posting to the accounts, and preparing the financial statements. A computerized system can process transactions without the intermediate steps (journal, ledger, and trial balance).

Outputs

Outputs are the reports used for decision making, including the financial statements. You can make better decisions with the reports produced by a good accounting system. Exhibit 7-2 diagrams a computerized system. Start with data inputs in the lower left corner.

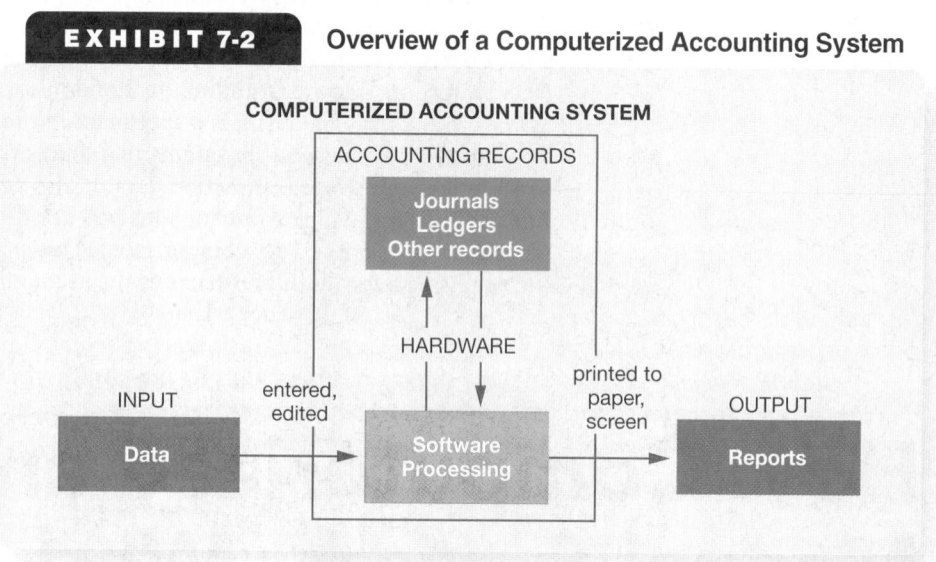

EXHIBIT 7-2 Overview of a Computerized Accounting System

COMPUTERIZED ACCOUNTING SYSTEM

ACCOUNTING RECORDS

Journals
Ledgers
Other records

HARDWARE

INPUT — entered, edited — Software Processing — printed to paper, screen — OUTPUT

Data

Reports

Data are processed into accounting records and printed out as reports.

Designing a System: The Chart of Accounts

As we saw in Chapter 2, an accounting system begins with the chart of accounts. In most companies, account *numbers* take on added importance. Recall that asset accounts generally begin with the digit 1, liabilities with a 2, owner's equity with a 3, revenues with 4, and expenses with 5. Exhibit 7-3 diagrams one structure for

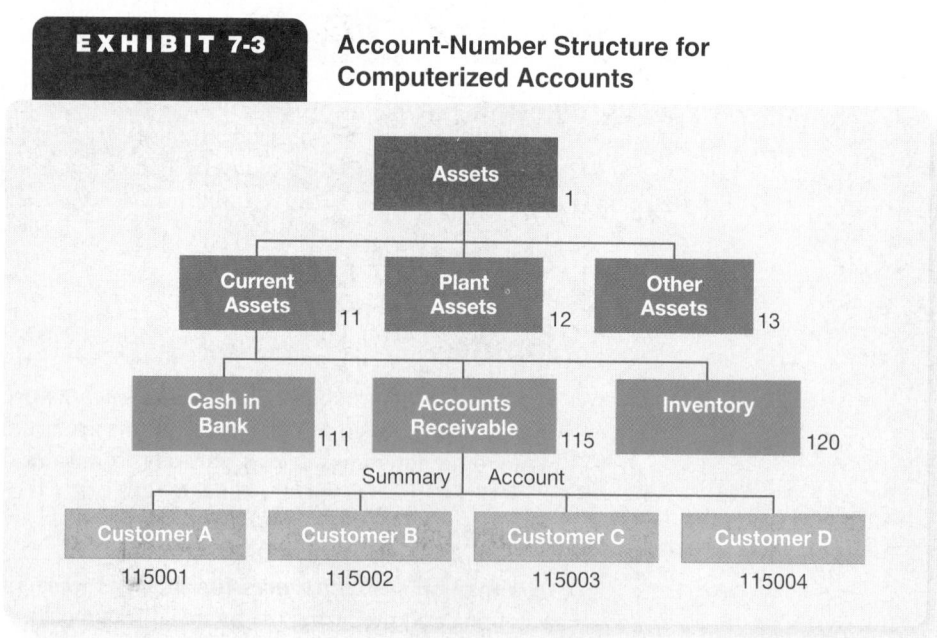

EXHIBIT 7-3 Account-Number Structure for Computerized Accounts

Assets — 1

Current Assets — 11   Plant Assets — 12   Other Assets — 13

Cash in Bank — 111   Accounts Receivable — 115   Inventory — 120

Summary | Account

Customer A — 115001   Customer B — 115002   Customer C — 115003   Customer D — 115004

computerized accounts. Assets are divided into current assets, plant assets (property, plant, and equipment), and other assets. Among the current assets, we illustrate only three accounts: Cash in Bank (Account No. 111), Accounts Receivable (No. 115), and Inventory (No. 120).

The account numbers in Exhibit 7-3 get longer and more detailed as you move from top to bottom. For example, Customer A's account number is 115001: 115 represents Accounts Receivable, and 001 refers to Customer A.

Processing Transactions: Manual and Menu-Driven Systems

Recording transactions in an actual accounting system requires an additional step that we have skipped thus far. A business of any size classifies transactions by type for efficient handling. In a manual system, credit sales, cash receipts, purchases on account, and cash payments are treated as four separate categories. Each category of transactions has its own special journal. For example:

- Credit sales are recorded in a *sales journal*.
- Cash receipts are recorded in a *cash receipts journal*.
- Purchases of inventory and other assets on account are recorded in a *purchases journal*.
- Cash payments are recorded in a *cash payments journal*.
- Transactions that do not fit any of the special journals, such as adjusting entries, are recorded in the *general journal*, which serves as the "journal of last resort."

Computerized systems are organized by function, or task. You can select a functions, such as recording sales on account, from a menu. A **menu** is a list of options for choosing computer functions. In a *menu-driven* system, you first access the *main menu*. Then choose from a submenu until you reach the function you want.

Exhibit 7-4 illustrates one type of menu structure. The menu bar at the top gives the main menu. In the diagram the accountant has chosen the ledger option highlighted by the cursor. This action opened a submenu of four items: Transactions,

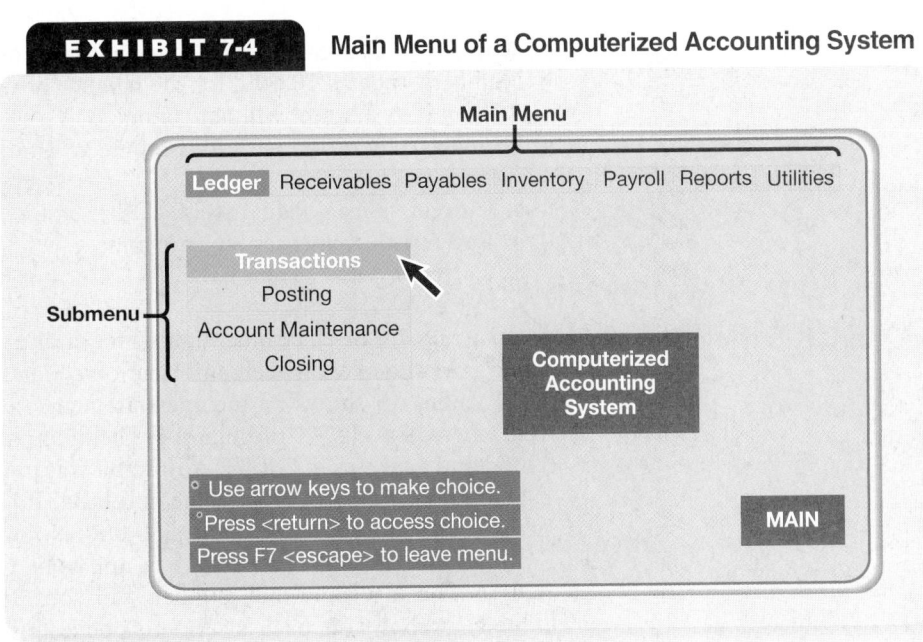

EXHIBIT 7-4   **Main Menu of a Computerized Accounting System**

Posting, Account Maintenance, and Closing. The Transactions option was then chosen (highlighted).

Posting in a computerized system can be performed continuously (**online processing**) or later for a group of similar transactions (**batch processing**). The posting then updates the account balances.

Enterprise Resource Planning (ERP) Systems

Many small businesses use QuickBooks or Peachtree. But larger companies are using **ERP** (**enterprise resource planning**) systems to manage their data. ERP systems such as SAP, Oracle, and PeopleSoft can integrate all company data into a single **data warehouse**. ERP feeds the data into software for all company activities—from purchasing to production and customer service.

Advantages of ERP systems include:

- A centralized ERP system can save lots of money.
- ERP helps companies adjust to changes. A change in sales ripples through the purchasing, shipping, and accounting systems.
- An ERP system can replace separate software systems, such as sales and payroll.

ERP is expensive. Major installations can cost millions. Implementation also requires a large commitment of time and people. For example, Hershey Foods tried to shrink a four-year ERP project into two and a half years. The result? The software did not map into Hershey's operations, and disrupted deliveries hurt profits in the Halloween candy-buying season.

Integrated Accounting Software: Spreadsheets

3 Understand how spreadsheets are used in accounting

Spreadsheets are computer programs that link data by means of formulas and functions. Spreadsheets are organized by *cells*, each defined by a row and a column. A cell can contain:

- Words (labels), such as Assets, Current assets, or Sales revenue, to identify an item.
- Numbers, such as 10,000, for the balance of Cash or Accounts receivable. Use a *number* if its amount will not change.
- Formulas, where you need to compute an amount that may change. Examples of formulas include:
  a. Current assets + Plant assets + Other assets = Total assets
  b. Revenues − Expenses = Net income
  c. Current assets/Current liabilities = Current ratio

The *cursor,* or electronic highlighter, indicates which cell is active. When the cursor is placed over any cell, information can be entered there for processing.

Exhibit 7-5 shows an income statement on a spreadsheet screen. The labels were entered in cells A1 through A4. The dollar amount of revenues was entered in cell B2 and expenses in cell B3. A formula was placed in cell B4 as follows: =B2−B3. This formula computes net income in cell B4. If revenues increase to $170,000, net income automatically increases to $80,000. No other cells will change.

The power of a spreadsheet is apparent when large amounts of data are analyzed. Change only one number, and you save hours of manual calculations. Exhibit 7-6 shows the basic arithmetic operations in Excel.

EXHIBIT 7-5   A Spreadsheet Screen

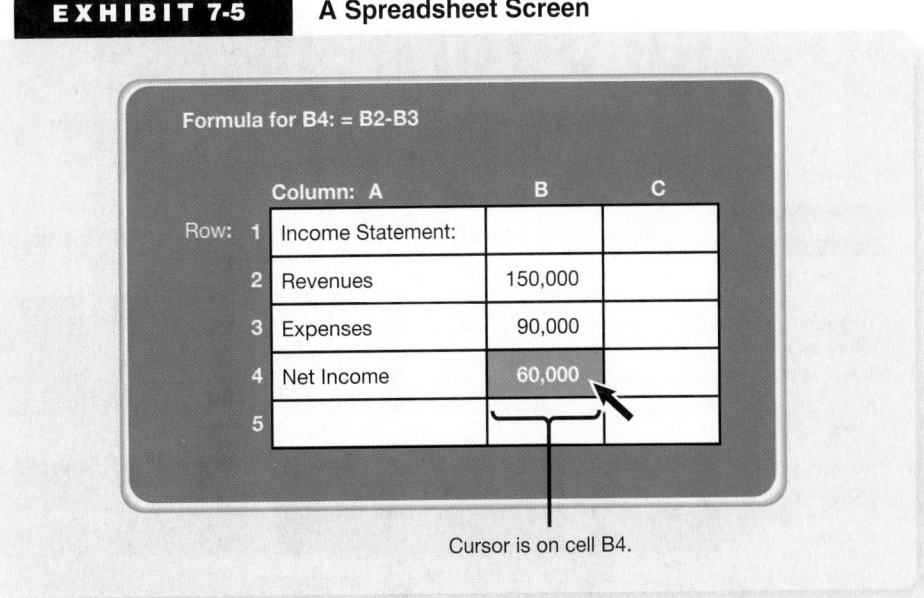

Cursor is on cell B4.

EXHIBIT 7-6   Basic Arithmetic Operations in Excel Spreadsheets

Operation	Symbol
Addition	+
Subtraction	−
Multiplication	*
Division	/
Addition of a range of cells	=SUM (beginning cell:ending cell)
Examples:	
Add cells A2 through A9	=SUM (A2:A9)
Divide cell C2 by cell D1	=C2/D1

Special Journals

Exhibit 7-7 diagrams an accounting system for In Motion, your T-shirt business. The remainder of this chapter describes how this system works.

EXHIBIT 7-7   **Overview of an Accounting System with Special Journals**

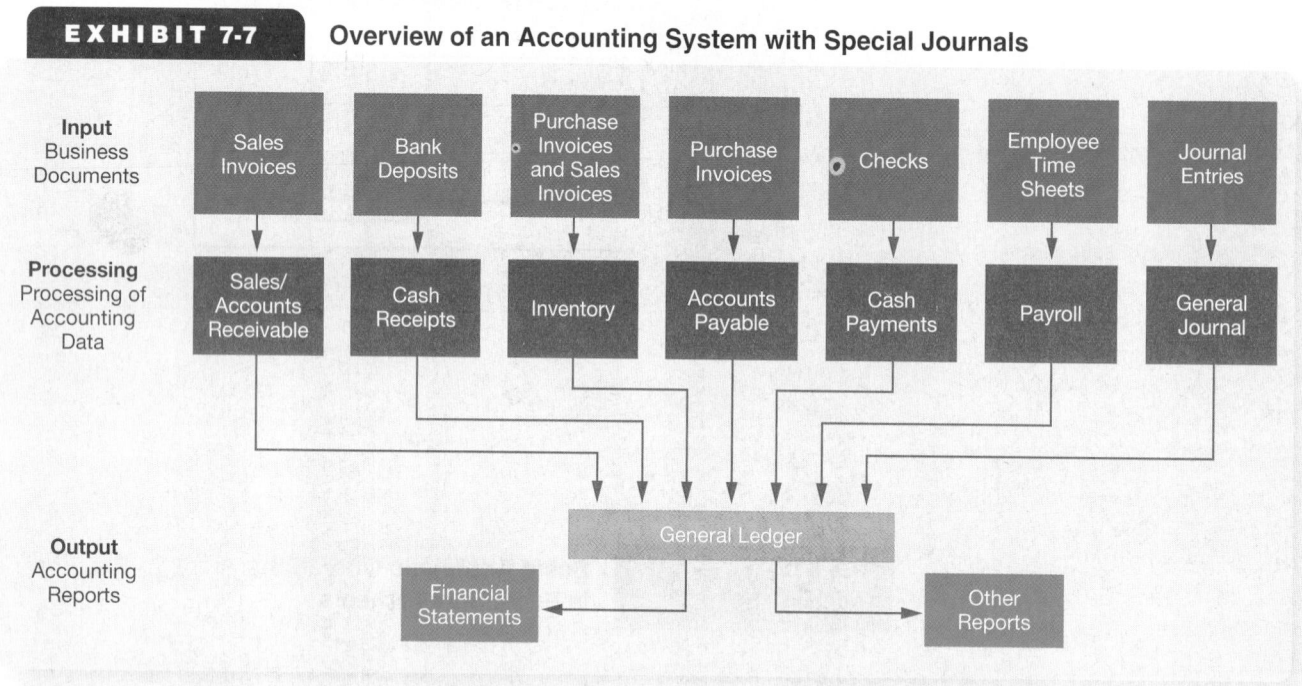

Special Journals in a Manual System

The journal entries illustrated so far have used the **general journal**. It is inefficient to record all transactions in the general journal, so we use special journals. A **special journal** is an accounting journal designed to record a specific type of transaction.

Most transactions fall into one of five categories, so accountants use five different journals. This system saves time and money. The five types of transactions, the related special journal, and the posting abbreviation follow.

Transaction	Special Journal	Posting Abbreviation
1. Sale on account	Sales journal	S
2. Cash receipt	Cash receipts journal	CR
3. Purchase on account	Purchases journal	P
4. Cash payment	Cash payments journal	CP
5. All others	General journal	J

Transactions are recorded in either a special journal or the general journal, but not in both. You may be wondering why we cover manual accounting systems, since many businesses have computerized. There are three main reasons:

1. Learning a manual system will equip you to work with both manual and electronic systems. The accounting is the same regardless of the system.

---

4   Use the sales journal, the cash receipts journal, and the accounts receivable ledger

2. Few small businesses have computerized all their accounting. Even companies that use QuickBooks or Peachtree keep some manual accounting records.

3. Learning a manual system will help you master accounting. One of the authors of this book has a friend who uses QuickBooks for his business. This man knows only which keys to punch. If he knew the accounting, he could better manage his business.

The Sales Journal

Most merchandisers sell inventory on account. These credit sales are entered in the **sales journal**. Credit sales of assets other than inventory—for example, buildings—occur infrequently and are recorded in the general journal.

Exhibit 7-8 illustrates a sales journal (Panel A) and the related posting to the ledgers (Panel B) of In Motion, your T-shirt business. Each entry in the Accounts Receivable Dr./Sales Revenue Cr. column of the sales journal in Exhibit 7-8 debits (Dr.) Accounts Receivable and credits (Cr.) Sales Revenue, as the heading indicates. For each transaction, the accountant enters the:

- date
- invoice number
- customer name
- transaction amount

This streamlined way of recording sales saves time.

In previous chapters, we did not record the names of our customers. In practice, the business must know the amount receivable from each customer. How else can the company ensure that it collects its receivables?

Consider the first transaction in Panel A. On November 2, you sold goods on account to Maria Galvez for $935. The invoice number is 422. All this information appears on a single line in the sales journal. No explanation is necessary. The transaction debits Accounts Receivable—Maria Galvez and credits Sales Revenue.

In Motion, like most other companies, uses a *perpetual* inventory system. Throughout this chapter we illustrate the perpetual system. When recording a sale, you also must record the cost of the goods sold and the decrease in your T-shirt inventory.

Computerized accounting systems can read both the sales amount and the cost of goods sold from the bar code on the package. The far right column of the sales journal records the cost of goods sold and inventory entry—$505 for the goods sold to Maria Galvez. If In Motion used a *periodic* inventory system, you would not record cost of goods sold or the decrease in inventory at the time of sale. The sales journal would need only one column to debit Accounts Receivable and credit Sales Revenue.

Posting to the General Ledger

The only ledger we've used so far is the **general ledger**, which holds the financial statement accounts. We will soon introduce other ledgers.

Posting from the sales journal to the general ledger can be done only at the end of the month. In Exhibit 7-8 (Panel A), November's credit sales total $4,319. When the $4,319 is posted to Accounts Receivable and Sales Revenue, you can print their account numbers beneath the total in the sales journal. In Panel B of Exhibit 7-8, the account number for Accounts Receivable is 115 and the account number for Sales Revenue is 410. Printing these account numbers in the sales journal shows that the $4,319 has been posted to the two accounts.

The debit to Cost of Goods Sold and the credit to Inventory for the monthly total of $1,814 is also posted at the end of the month. After posting, these accounts'

EXHIBIT 7-8   Sales Journal (Panel A) and Posting to the Ledgers (Panel B)

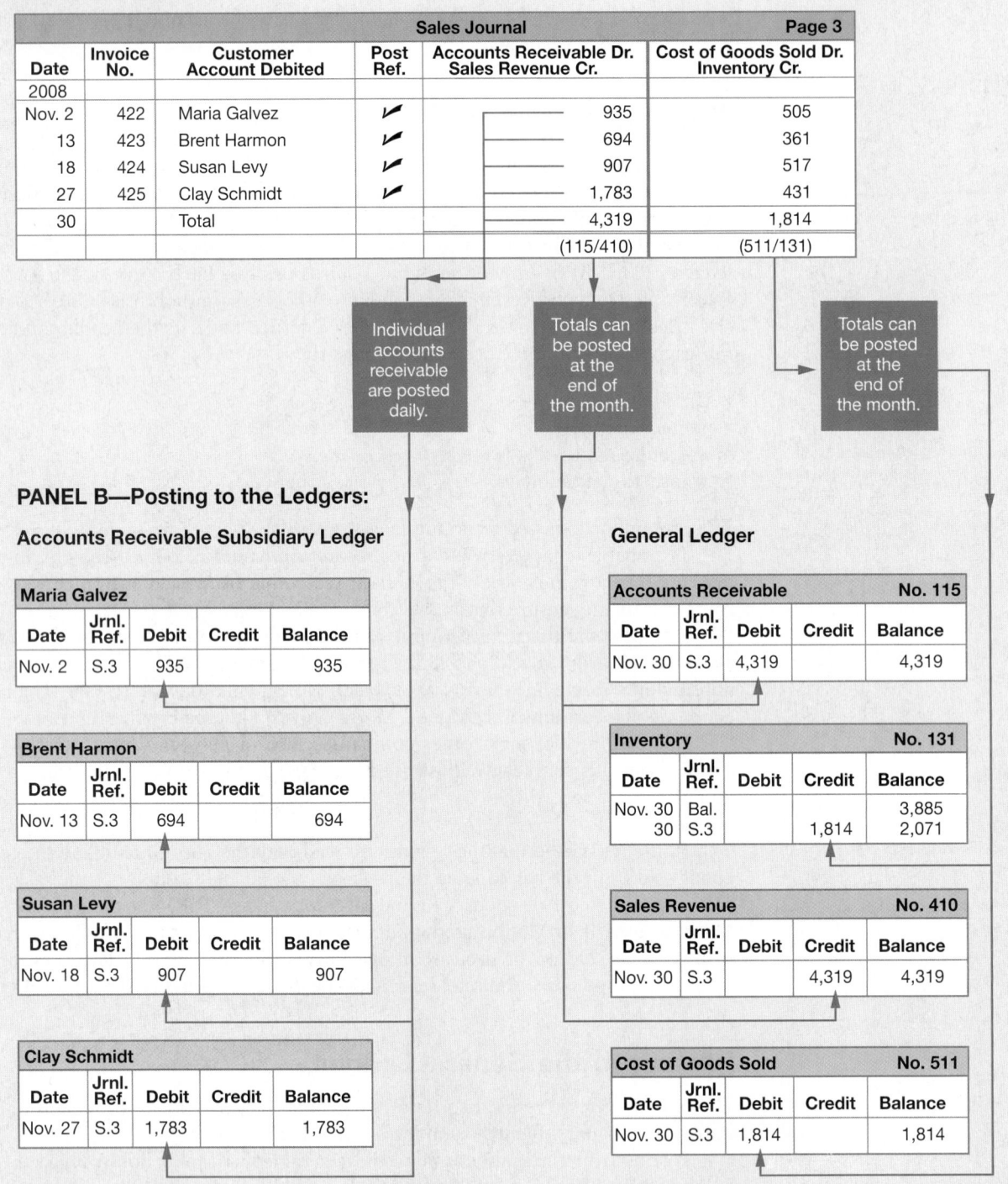

PANEL A—Sales Journal:

				Sales Journal		Page 3
Date	Invoice No.	Customer Account Debited	Post Ref.	Accounts Receivable Dr. Sales Revenue Cr.		Cost of Goods Sold Dr. Inventory Cr.
2008						
Nov. 2	422	Maria Galvez	✔		935	505
13	423	Brent Harmon	✔		694	361
18	424	Susan Levy	✔		907	517
27	425	Clay Schmidt	✔		1,783	431
30		Total			4,319	1,814
					(115/410)	(511/131)

> Individual accounts receivable are posted daily.

> Totals can be posted at the end of the month.

> Totals can be posted at the end of the month.

PANEL B—Posting to the Ledgers:

Accounts Receivable Subsidiary Ledger

Maria Galvez

Date	Jrnl. Ref.	Debit	Credit	Balance
Nov. 2	S.3	935		935

Brent Harmon

Date	Jrnl. Ref.	Debit	Credit	Balance
Nov. 13	S.3	694		694

Susan Levy

Date	Jrnl. Ref.	Debit	Credit	Balance
Nov. 18	S.3	907		907

Clay Schmidt

Date	Jrnl. Ref.	Debit	Credit	Balance
Nov. 27	S.3	1,783		1,783

General Ledger

Accounts Receivable   No. 115

Date	Jrnl. Ref.	Debit	Credit	Balance
Nov. 30	S.3	4,319		4,319

Inventory   No. 131

Date	Jrnl. Ref.	Debit	Credit	Balance
Nov. 30	Bal.			3,885
30	S.3		1,814	2,071

Sales Revenue   No. 410

Date	Jrnl. Ref.	Debit	Credit	Balance
Nov. 30	S.3		4,319	4,319

Cost of Goods Sold   No. 511

Date	Jrnl. Ref.	Debit	Credit	Balance
Nov. 30	S.3	1,814		1,814

numbers are entered beneath the total to show that Cost of Goods Sold and Inventory have been updated.

Posting to the Accounts Receivable Subsidiary Ledger

The $4,319 debit to Accounts Receivable does not identify the amount receivable from each customer. A business may have many customers.

You must create an account for each customer in a subsidiary ledger called the Accounts Receivable ledger. A **subsidiary ledger** holds individual accounts that support a general ledger account. The customer accounts in the subsidiary ledger are arranged in alphabetical order (Galvez, then Harmon, then Levy, and so on).

Amounts in the sales journal are posted to the subsidiary ledger *daily* to keep a current record of the amount receivable from each customer. Suppose Maria Galvez telephones In Motion to ask how much she owes. The subsidiary ledger shows that Galvez owes $935.

After posting to the subsidiary ledger, print a check mark in the posting reference column of the sales journal (see Exhibit 7-8). That lets you know you've posted $935 to Galvez's account.

Journal References in the Ledgers

As you post to the ledgers, print the journal page number in the account to show the source of the data. All transaction data in Exhibit 7-8 originated on page 3 of the sales journal, so all journal references are S.3. "S" indicates sales journal.

Trace all the postings in Exhibit 7-8. The way to learn an accounting system is to study the flow of data. The arrows indicate the direction of the information.

Balancing the Ledgers

The Accounts Receivable balance in the general ledger should equal the sum of the individual customer balances in the subsidiary ledger, as follows. This is called balancing the ledgers.

GENERAL LEDGER

Accounts Receivable debit balance	$4,319

SUBSIDIARY LEDGER: CUSTOMER ACCOUNTS RECEIVABLE

Customer	Balance
Maria Galvez...	$ 935
Brent Harmon	694
Susan Levy	907
Clay Schmidt..	1,783
Total accounts receivable..................................	$4,319

Accounts Receivable in the general ledger is called a **control account**. A control account's balance equals the sum of the balances of accounts in a subsidiary ledger.

Using Documents as Journals

You can streamline your accounting even further. Simply use your business documents as journals. This saves time and money. For example, In Motion could keep sales invoices in a loose-leaf binder and let the invoices serve as the sales journal. At the end of the period, simply total your sales on account and post the total as a debit to Accounts Receivable and a credit to Sales Revenue. You can also post directly from the invoices to the customer accounts in the accounts receivable ledger.

The Cash Receipts Journal

All businesses have lots of cash transactions, and a **cash receipts journal** comes in handy.

Exhibit 7-9 illustrates the cash receipts journal of In Motion T-Shirts. Posting to the ledgers is shown in Panel B.

Every transaction recorded in this journal is a cash receipt, so there's a column for debits to Cash. The next column is for debits to Sales Discounts. The main sources of cash are cash sales and collections on account.

The cash receipts journal has credit columns for Accounts Receivable, Sales Revenue, and Other Accounts. This Other Accounts column is also used to record the names of customers from whom cash is collected on account.

In Exhibit 7-9, the first cash sale occurred on November 6. Observe the debit to Cash and the credit to Sales Revenue ($517). Each sale entry is accompanied by a separate entry that debits Cost of Goods Sold and credits Inventory for the cost of the merchandise sold. The column for this entry is at the far right of the journal.

On November 11, In Motion borrowed $1,000 from First Bank. Cash is debited, and Note Payable to First Bank is credited. We use the Other Accounts column because there is no specific credit column for borrowings. For this transaction, we print the account title, Note Payable to First Bank, in the Other Accounts/Account Title column.

The November 11 and 25 transactions illustrate a key fact. Different companies have different types of transactions, and they adapt special journals to their needs. In this case, the Other Accounts column is the catchall used to record all non-routine cash receipts.

On November 14, In Motion collected $900 from Maria Galvez. Back on November 2, we sold $935 of merchandise to Galvez. This credit sale allowed a $35 discount for prompt payment, and Galvez paid within the discount period. In Motion records this cash receipt by debiting Cash and Sales Discounts and by crediting Accounts Receivable for $935. The customer's name appears in the Other Accounts/Account Title column.

In the cash receipts journal, as in all the journals, total debits should equal total credits. For the month, total debits ($6,169 = $6,134 + $35) equal total credits ($6,169 = $1,235 + $3,172 + $1,762). The debit to Cost of Goods Sold and the credit to Inventory are completely separate.

Posting to the General Ledger

Column totals can be posted monthly. After posting, print the account number below the column total in the cash receipts journal. The account number for Cash (101) appears below the column total, and likewise for the other column totals. Follow the arrows, which track the posted amounts.

The column total for *Other Accounts* is *not* posted. Instead, these credits are posted individually. In Exhibit 7-9, the November 11 transaction reads "Note Payable to First Bank." This account's number (221) in the Post. Ref. column shows that the transaction amount was posted individually. The letter x below the column means that the column total was *not* posted.

Posting to the Subsidiary Ledger

Amounts from the cash receipts journal are posted to the accounts receivable ledger daily. The postings are credits. Trace the $935 credit to Maria Galvez's account. It reduces her balance to zero. The $300 receipt from Brent Harmon reduces his balance to $394.

EXHIBIT 7-9 Cash Receipts Journal (Panel A) and Posting to the Ledgers (Panel B)

PANEL A—Cash Receipts Journal:

Cash Receipts Journal								Page 5
	Debits		Credits					
					Other Accounts			
Date	Cash	Sales Discounts	Accounts Receivable	Sales Revenue	Account Title	Post Ref.	Amount	Cost of Goods Sold Dr. Inventory Cr.
2008								
Nov. 6	517			517				290
11	1,000				Note Payable to First Bank	221	1,000	
14	900	35	935		Maria Galvez	✔		
19	853			853				426
22	300		300		Brent Harmon	✔		
25	762				Interest Revenue	460	762	
28	1,802			1,802				991
30	6,134	35	1,235	3,172	Totals		1,762	1,707
	(101)	(420)	(115)	(410)			(X)	(511/131)

Totals can be posted at the end of the month.

Individual accounts receivable are posted daily.

Individual amounts can be posted at the end of the month.

Total is not posted.

Totals can be posted at the end of the month.

PANEL B—Posting to the Ledgers:

Accounts Receivable Subsidiary Ledger

Maria Galvez

Date	Jrnl. Ref.	Debit	Credit	Balance
Nov. 2	S.3	935		935
14	CR.5		935	-0-

Brent Harmon

Date	Jrnl. Ref.	Debit	Credit	Balance
Nov. 13	S.3	694		694
22	CR.5		300	394

Susan Levy

Date	Jrnl. Ref.	Debit	Credit	Balance
Nov. 18	S.3	907		907

Clay Schmidt

Date	Jrnl. Ref.	Debit	Credit	Balance
Nov. 27	S.3	1,783		1,783

General Ledger

Cash No. 101

Date	Jrnl. Ref.	Debit	Credit	Debit Balance
Nov. 30	CR.5	6,134		6,134

Accounts Receivable No. 115

Date	Jrnl. Ref.	Debit	Credit	Debit Balance
Nov. 30	S.3	4,319		4,319
30	CR.5		1,235	3,084

Inventory No. 131

Date	Jrnl. Ref.	Debit	Credit	Debit Balance
Nov. 30	Bal.			3,885
30	S.3		1,814	2,071
30	CR.5		1,707	364

Note Payable to First Bank No. 221

Date	Jrnl. Ref.	Debit	Credit	Credit Balance
Nov. 11	CR.5		1,000	1,000

Sales Revenue No. 410

Date	Jrnl. Ref.	Debit	Credit	Credit Balance
Nov. 30	S.3		4,319	4,319
30	CR.5		3,172	7,491

Sales Discounts No. 420

Date	Jrnl. Ref.	Debit	Credit	Debit Balance
Nov. 30	CR.5	35		35

Interest Revenue No. 460

Date	Jrnl. Ref.	Debit	Credit	Credit Balance
Nov. 25	CR.5		762	762

Cost of Goods Sold No. 511

Date	Jrnl. Ref.	Debit	Credit	Debit Balance
Nov. 30	S.3	1,814		1,814
30	CR.5	1,707		3,521

Balancing the Ledgers

After posting, the sum of the individual balances in the accounts receivable ledger equals the balance of Accounts Receivable in the general ledger, as follows:

GENERAL LEDGER

Accounts Receivable debit balance	$3,084

SUBSIDIARY LEDGER: CUSTOMER ACCOUNTS RECEIVABLE

Customer	Balance
Brent Harmon	$ 394
Susan Levy	907
Clay Schmidt...	1,783
Total accounts receivable....................................	$3,084

The Purchases Journal

5 Use the purchases journal, the cash payments journal, and the accounts payable ledger

A merchandising business such as In Motion T-Shirts purchases inventory and supplies on account. The **purchases journal** handles these transactions plus expenses incurred *on account*. Cash purchases are recorded in the cash payments journal.

Exhibit 7-10 illustrates In Motion's purchases journal (Panel A) and posting to the ledgers (Panel B).[1] This purchases journal has special columns for:

- Credits to Accounts Payable
- Debits to Inventory, Supplies, and Other Accounts

A periodic inventory system would replace the Inventory column with a column titled "Purchases." The Other Accounts columns hold purchases of items other than inventory and supplies. Accounts Payable is credited for all transactions recorded in the purchases journal.

On November 2, In Motion purchased inventory costing $700 from Hanes Textiles. The supplier's name (Hanes) is entered in the Supplier Account Credited column. The purchase terms of 3/15, n/30 are also entered to show the due date and the discount available. Accounts Payable is credited for the transaction amount, and Inventory is debited.

Note the November 9 purchase of equipment from City Office Supply. The purchases journal holds no column for equipment, so we use the Other Accounts debit column. Because this was a credit purchase, the accountant prints the supplier name (City Office Supply) in the Supplier Account Credited column and Equipment in the Other Accounts/Account Title column. The total credits in the purchases journal ($2,876) must equal the total debits ($2,876 = $1,706 + $103 + $1,067).

Accounts Payable Subsidiary Ledger

To pay debts on time, a company must know how much it owes each supplier. Accounts Payable in the general ledger shows only a single total for the amount

---

[1]This is the only special journal with the credit column placed to the left and the debit columns to the right. The focus is on Accounts Payable (which is credited for each entry to this journal).

EXHIBIT 7-10   Purchases Journal (Panel A) and Posting to the Ledgers (Panel B)

PANEL A—Purchases Journal:

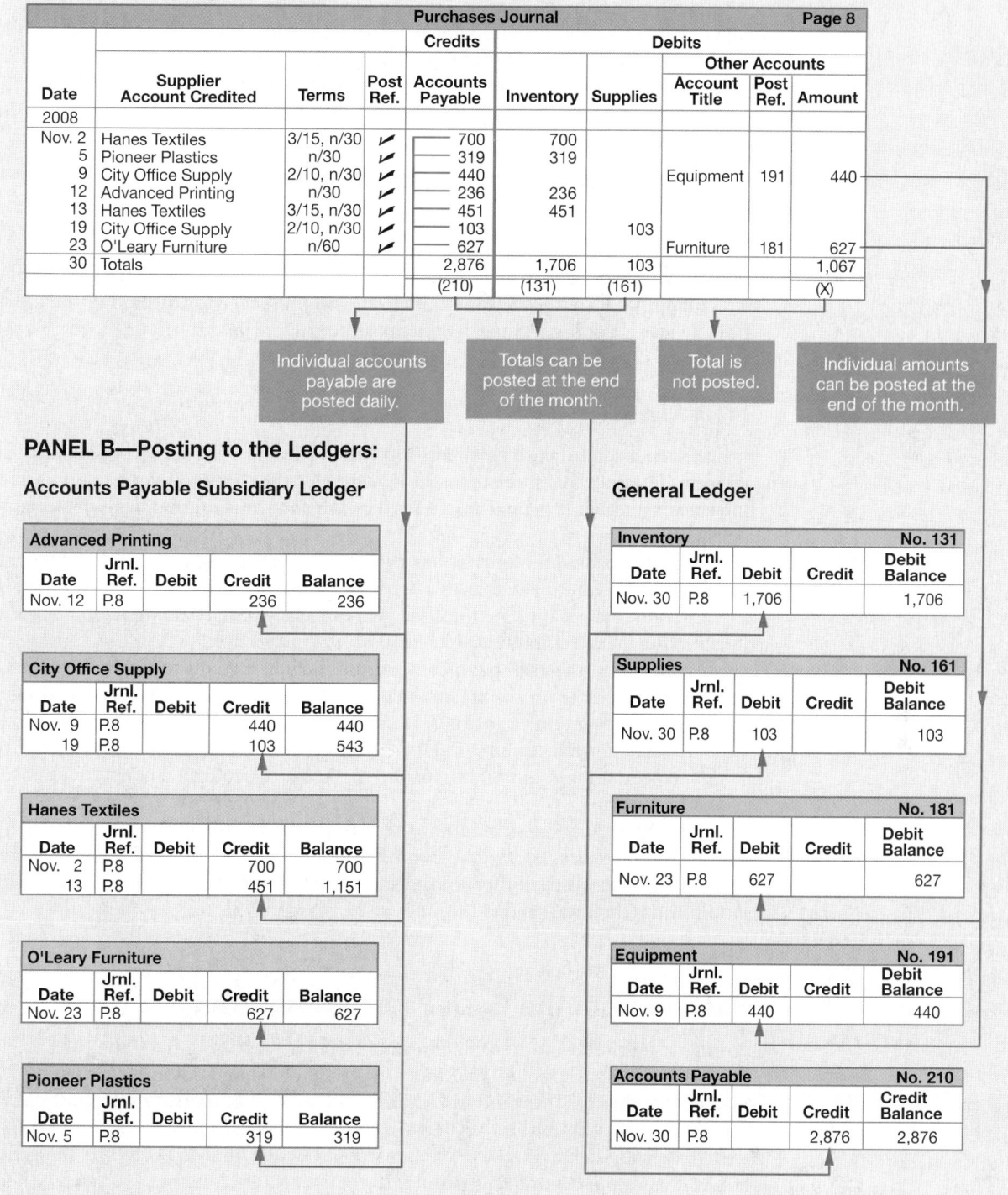

							Other Accounts		
Purchases Journal									Page 8
				Credits	Debits				
Date	Supplier Account Credited	Terms	Post Ref.	Accounts Payable	Inventory	Supplies	Account Title	Post Ref.	Amount
2008									
Nov. 2	Hanes Textiles	3/15, n/30	✔	700	700				
5	Pioneer Plastics	n/30	✔	319	319				
9	City Office Supply	2/10, n/30	✔	440			Equipment	191	440
12	Advanced Printing	n/30	✔	236	236				
13	Hanes Textiles	3/15, n/30	✔	451	451				
19	City Office Supply	2/10, n/30	✔	103		103			
23	O'Leary Furniture	n/60	✔	627			Furniture	181	627
30	Totals			2,876	1,706	103			1,067
				(210)	(131)	(161)			(X)

Individual accounts payable are posted daily.

Totals can be posted at the end of the month.

Total is not posted.

Individual amounts can be posted at the end of the month.

PANEL B—Posting to the Ledgers:

Accounts Payable Subsidiary Ledger

Advanced Printing

Date	Jrnl. Ref.	Debit	Credit	Balance
Nov. 12	P.8		236	236

City Office Supply

Date	Jrnl. Ref.	Debit	Credit	Balance
Nov. 9	P.8		440	440
19	P.8		103	543

Hanes Textiles

Date	Jrnl. Ref.	Debit	Credit	Balance
Nov. 2	P.8		700	700
13	P.8		451	1,151

O'Leary Furniture

Date	Jrnl. Ref.	Debit	Credit	Balance
Nov. 23	P.8		627	627

Pioneer Plastics

Date	Jrnl. Ref.	Debit	Credit	Balance
Nov. 5	P.8		319	319

General Ledger

Inventory   No. 131

Date	Jrnl. Ref.	Debit	Credit	Debit Balance
Nov. 30	P.8	1,706		1,706

Supplies   No. 161

Date	Jrnl. Ref.	Debit	Credit	Debit Balance
Nov. 30	P.8	103		103

Furniture   No. 181

Date	Jrnl. Ref.	Debit	Credit	Debit Balance
Nov. 23	P.8	627		627

Equipment   No. 191

Date	Jrnl. Ref.	Debit	Credit	Debit Balance
Nov. 9	P.8	440		440

Accounts Payable   No. 210

Date	Jrnl. Ref.	Debit	Credit	Credit Balance
Nov. 30	P.8		2,876	2,876

owed on account. It does not indicate the amount owed to each supplier. Companies keep an accounts payable ledger that is similar to the accounts receivable ledger.

The accounts payable ledger lists suppliers in alphabetical order, along with amounts owed to them. Exhibit 7-10, Panel B, shows In Motion's accounts payable ledger, which includes accounts for Advanced Printing, City Office Supply, and others. After all the posting, the total of the individual balances in the subsidiary ledger equals the Accounts Payable balance in the general ledger.

Posting from the Purchases Journal

Posting from the purchases journal is similar to posting from the other special journals. Exhibit 7-10, Panel B, illustrates the posting process.

Individual accounts payable in the *accounts payable ledger* are posted daily, and column totals and other amounts to the *general ledger* at the end of the month. In the ledger accounts, P.8 means purchases journal page 8.

The Cash Payments Journal

Businesses make most cash payments by check, and all checks are recorded in the **cash payments journal**. This special journal is also called the **check register** and the **cash disbursements journal**. Exhibit 7-11 shows the cash payments journal, with the ledgers in Panel B.

The cash payments journal has two debit columns—one for Other Accounts and one for Accounts Payable. It has two credit columns—one for Inventory (for purchases discounts) and one for Cash. This special journal also has columns for the date and for the check number of each cash payment.

All entries in the cash payments journal include a credit to Cash. Payments on account are debits to Accounts Payable. On November 15, In Motion paid Hanes on account, with credit terms of 3/15, n/30 (for details, see the first transaction in the purchases journal, Exhibit 7-10). Paying within the discount period, you took the 3% discount and paid $679 ($700 less the $21 discount). The discount is credited to Inventory.

The Other Accounts column is used to record debits to accounts for which no special column exists. For example, on November 3, In Motion paid rent expense of $1,200. As with all the other journals, the total debits ($4,280 = $3,461 + $819) should equal the total credits ($4,280 = $21 + $4,259).

Posting from the Cash Payments Journal

Posting from the cash payments journal is similar to posting from the cash receipts journal. Individual supplier amounts are posted daily, and column totals and Other Accounts at the end of the month. (Exhibit 7-11, Panel B, illustrates the posting).

Amounts in the Other Accounts column are posted individually (for example, Rent Expense—debit $1,200). When each Other Account is posted to the general ledger, the account number is printed in the Post. Ref. column. The letter x below the column signifies that the total is *not* posted.

Balancing the Ledgers

To review accounts payable, companies list individual supplier balances in the accounts payable ledger. The general ledger and subsidiary totals should agree.

EXHIBIT 7-11 Cash Payments Journal (Panel A) and Posting to the Ledgers (Panel B)

PANEL A—Cash Payments Journal:

Cash Payments Journal							Page 6
				Debits		**Credits**	
Date	Ck. No.	Account Debited	Post. Ref.	Other Accounts	Accounts Payable	Inventory	Cash
2008							
Nov. 3	101	Rent Expense	541	1,200			1,200
8	102	Supplies	161	61			61
15	103	Hanes Textiles	✓		700	21	679
20	104	Pioneer Plastics	✓		119		119
26	105	Inventory	131	2,200			2,200
30		Totals		3,461	819	21	4,259
				(X)	(210)	(131)	(101)

> Total is not posted.

> Totals can be posted at the end of the month.

> Individual accounts payable are posted daily.

PANEL B—Posting to the Ledgers:

> Individual accounts can be posted at the end of the month.

Accounts Payable Subsidiary Ledger

Advanced Printing

Date	Jrnl. Ref.	Debit	Credit	Balance
Nov. 12	P.8		236	236

City Office Supply

Date	Jrnl. Ref.	Debit	Credit	Balance
Nov. 9	P.8		440	440
19	P.8		103	543

Hanes Textiles

Date	Jrnl. Ref.	Debit	Credit	Balance
Nov. 2	P.8		700	700
13	P.8		451	1,151
15	CP. 6	700		451

O'Leary Furniture Co.

Date	Jrnl. Ref.	Debit	Credit	Balance
Nov. 23	P.8		627	627

Pioneer Plastics

Date	Jrnl. Ref.	Debit	Credit	Balance
Nov. 5	P.8		319	319
20	CP. 6	119		200

General Ledger

Cash   No. 101

Date	Jrnl. Ref.	Debit	Credit	Debit Balance
Nov. 30	CR. 5	6,134		6,134
30	CP. 6		4,259	1,875

Inventory   No. 131

Date	Jrnl. Ref.	Debit	Credit	Debit Balance
Nov. 30	P.8	1,706		1,706
26	CP. 6	2,200		3,906
30	CP. 6		21	3,885

Supplies   No. 161

Date	Jrnl. Ref.	Debit	Credit	Debit Balance
Nov. 30	P.8	103		103
8	CP. 6	61		164

Accounts Payable   No. 210

Date	Jrnl. Ref.	Debit	Credit	Credit Balance
Nov. 30	P.8		2,876	2,876
30	CP. 6	819		2,057

Rent Expense   No. 541

Date	Jrnl. Ref.	Debit	Credit	Debit Balance
Nov. 3	CP. 6	1,200		1,200

GENERAL LEDGER

Accounts Payable credit balance.........................	$2,057

SUBSIDIARY LEDGER: ACCOUNTS PAYABLE

Supplier	Balance
Advanced Printing..	$ 236
City Office Supply...	543
Hanes Textiles...	451
O'Leary Furniture	627
Pioneer Plastics..	200
Total accounts payable	$2,057

The Role of the General Journal

Special journals save time recording repetitive transactions. But some transactions don't fit a special journal. Examples include depreciation, the expiration of prepaid insurance, and the accrual of salary payable at the end of the period.

> All accounting systems need a general journal. The adjusting entries and the closing entries are recorded in the general journal, along with other nonroutine transactions.

Many companies use the general journal for sales returns and allowances and purchase returns and allowances. Let's turn now to sales returns and allowances. The related business document is called a *credit memo*.

The Credit Memo—Recording Sales Returns and Allowances

As we've seen, customers sometimes return merchandise to the seller. And sellers sometimes grant allowances to customers because of product defects. The effect of sales returns and sales allowances is the same—they decrease net sales and accounts receivable. The document issued by the seller for a sales return is called a **credit memo** because the company gives the customer credit for the returned merchandise. When a company issues a credit memo, it debits Sales Returns and Allowances and credits Accounts Receivable.

On November 27, In Motion sold T-shirts to Clay Schmidt for $1,783 on account. Later, Schmidt discovered a defect and returned the inventory. In Motion then issued to Schmidt a credit memo like the one in Exhibit 7-12.

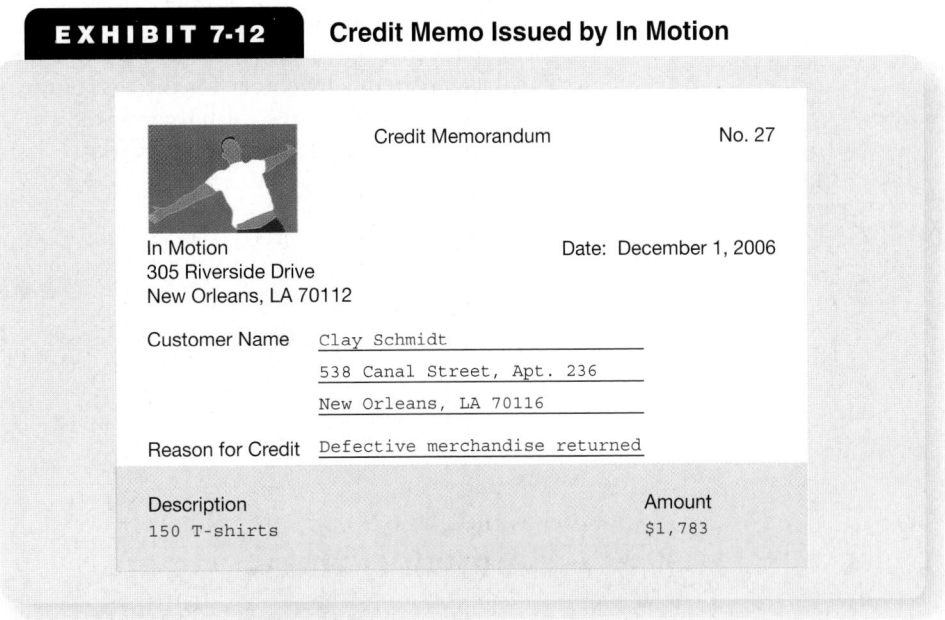

EXHIBIT 7-12   **Credit Memo Issued by In Motion**

Credit Memorandum   No. 27

In Motion   Date: December 1, 2006
305 Riverside Drive
New Orleans, LA 70112

Customer Name   Clay Schmidt
                 538 Canal Street, Apt. 236
                 New Orleans, LA 70116

Reason for Credit   Defective merchandise returned

Description	Amount
150 T-shirts	$1,783

To record the *sale return* and the receipt of the defective merchandise, In Motion would make these entries in the general journal:

General Journal					Page 9
Date	**Accounts**	**Post Ref.**	**Debit**	**Credit**
Dec. 1	Sales Returns and Allowances	430	1,783	
	Accounts Receivable—Clay Schmidt	115/✔		1,783
	Credit memo no. 27.			
Dec. 1	Inventory	131	431	
	Cost of Goods Sold	511		431
	Received defective goods from customer.			

Focus on the first entry. Sales Returns and Allowances is debited. After posting, its account number (430) is written in the posting reference column. The credit entry requires two postings: one to Accounts Receivable in the general ledger (account number 115) and the other to Clay Schmidt in the accounts receivable ledger, denoted by the check mark (✔).

The second entry records In Motion's receipt of the defective inventory from Schmidt. Now let's see how In Motion records its purchase return of these defective T-shirts to Hanes Textiles.

The Debit Memo—Recording Purchase Returns and Allowances

A purchase return occurs when a business returns goods to the seller. The purchaser receives a cash refund or replacement goods.

The purchaser may also send a document known as a **debit memo**. This document states that the buyer no longer owes for the goods. The buyer debits Accounts Payable and credits Inventory for the cost of the goods returned to the seller.

Many businesses record purchase returns in the general journal. In Motion would record its purchase return of defective T-shirts to Hanes Textiles as follows:

	Date	Accounts	Post Ref.	Debit	Credit
	Dec. 2	Accounts Payable—Hanes Textiles	210/✔	431	
		Inventory	131		431
		Debit memo no. 16.			

General Journal Page 9

Balancing the Ledgers

At the end of the period, after all postings, equality should exist as follows:

1. **General ledger:** Total debits = Total credits

2. **General ledger and Accounts Receivable subsidiary ledger:**

$$
\begin{array}{ccc}
\text{Balance of the} & & \text{Sum of all the} \\
\text{Accounts Receivable} & = & \text{customer balances in the} \\
\text{control account} & & \text{Accounts Receivable ledger}
\end{array}
$$

3. **General ledger and Accounts Payable subsidiary ledger:**

$$
\begin{array}{ccc}
\text{Balance of the} & & \text{Sum of all the} \\
\text{Accounts Payable} & = & \text{supplier balances in the} \\
\text{control account} & & \text{Accounts Payable ledger}
\end{array}
$$

This process is called *balancing the ledgers*. It maintains the accuracy of the accounting records.

Blending Computers and Special Journals

Computerizing special journals requires no drastic change. Systems designers can create a special screen for each accounting module—credit sales, cash receipts, purchases on account, and cash payments.

The special screen for credit sales would ask the computer operator to enter the following information:

- Date
- Customer number
- Customer name
- Invoice number
- Dollar amount of the sale
- Cost of the goods sold

These data can generate the sales journal and the monthly statements for customers.

The Decision Guidelines feature focuses on major decisions accountants make as they use an information system.

Decision Guidelines

Using Special Journals and Control Accounts

Let's continue with In Motion, your T-shirt business. Suppose it's not economical to computerize, so you set up a manual accounting system. How do you get started? The Decision Guidelines point you in the right direction.

Decision

What are the main components of an accounting system?

Where to record
- Sales on account?
- Cash receipts?
- Purchases on account?
- Cash payments?
- All other transactions?

How does the general ledger relate to the subsidiary ledgers?

When to post from the journals to the
- General ledger?
- Subsidiary ledgers?

How to achieve control over
- Accounts receivable?
- Accounts payable?

Guidelines

Journals
- General journal
- Special journals

Ledgers
- General ledger
- Subsidiary ledgers:
  Accounts receivable
  Accounts payable

Journals
- Sales journal
- Cash receipts journal
- Purchases journal
- Cash payments journal
- General journal

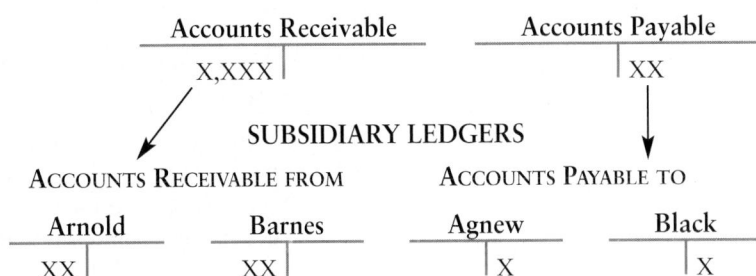

—Monthly (or more often, if needed)
—Daily

Balance the ledgers, as follows:

General Ledger		Subsidiary Ledger
Accounts receivable	=	Sum of individual *customer* accounts receivable
Accounts payable	=	Sum of individual *supplier* accounts payable

Summary Problem

Houlihan Company completed the following selected transactions during March:

Mar. 4	Received $500 for a cash sale to a customer (cost, $319).
6	Received $60 on account from Brady Lee. The full invoice amount was $65, but Lee paid within the discount period to gain the $5 discount.
9	Received $1,080 on a note receivable from Beverly Mann. This amount includes the $1,000 note receivable plus interest revenue.
15	Received $800 for a cash sale to a customer (cost, $522).
24	Borrowed $2,200 by signing a note payable to Interstate Bank.
27	Received $1,200 on account from Lance Albert. Collection was received after the discount period, as there was no discount.

Requirements

The general ledger showed the following balances at February 28: Cash, $1,117; Accounts Receivable, $2,790; Note Receivable—Beverly Mann, $1,000; and Inventory, $1,819. The accounts receivable subsidiary ledger at February 28 contained debit balances as follows: Lance Albert, $1,840; Melinda Fultz, $885; Brady Lee, $65.

1. Record the transactions in the cash receipts journal, page 7.

2. Compute column totals at March 31. Show that total debits equal total credits in the cash receipts journal.

3. Post to the general ledger and the accounts receivable subsidiary ledger. Use complete posting references, including the following account numbers: Cash, 11; Accounts Receivable, 12; Note Receivable—Beverly Mann, 13; Inventory, 14; Note Payable—Interstate Bank, 22; Sales Revenue, 41; Sales Discounts, 42; Interest Revenue, 46; and Cost of Goods Sold, 51. Insert a check mark (✔) in the posting reference column for each February 28 account balance.

4. Balance the Accounts Receivable subsidiary ledger with the Accounts Receivable account in the general ledger.

Solution

Requirements 1 and 2

Date	Cash (Debits)	Sales Discounts (Debits)	Accounts Receivable (Credits)	Sales Revenue (Credits)	Account Title (Other Accounts)	Post. Ref.	Amount	Cost of Goods Sold Debit Inventory Credit
Mar. 4	500			500				319
6	60	5	65		Brady Lee	✔		
9	1,080				Note Receivable—Beverly Mann	13	1,000	
					Interest Revenue	46	80	
15	800			800				522
24	2,200				Note Payable—Interstate Bank	22	2,200	
27	1,200		1,200		Lance Albert	✔		
31	5,840	5	1,265	1,300	Total		3,280	841
	(11)	(42)	(12)	(41)			(X)	(51/14)

Total Dr. = 5,845   Total Cr. = 5,845

Requirement 3

ACCOUNTS RECEIVABLE LEDGER

Lance Albert

Date	Jrnl. Ref.	Debit	Credit	Balance
Feb. 28	✔			1,840
Mar. 27	CR.7		1,200	640

Melinda Fultz

Date	Jrnl. Ref.	Debit	Credit	Balance
Feb. 28	✔			885

Brady Lee

Date	Jrnl. Ref.	Debit	Credit	Balance
Feb. 28	✔			65
Mar. 6	CR.7		65	—

GENERAL LEDGER

Cash   No. 11

Date	Jrnl. Ref.	Debit	Credit	Balance
Feb. 28	✔			1,117
Mar. 31	CR.7	5,840		6,957

Accounts Receivable   No. 12

Date	Jrnl. Ref.	Debit	Credit	Balance
Feb. 28	✔			2,790
Mar. 31	CR.7		1,265	1,525

Note Receivable—Beverly Mann   No. 13

Date	Jrnl. Ref.	Debit	Credit	Balance
Feb. 28	✔			1,000
Mar. 9	CR.7		1,000	—

Inventory   No. 14

Date	Jrnl. Ref.	Debit	Credit	Balance
Feb. 28	✔			1,819
Mar. 31	CR.7		841	978

Note Payable—Interstate Bank   No. 22

Date	Jrnl. Ref.	Debit	Credit	Balance
Mar. 24	CR.7		2,200	2,200

Sales Revenue   No. 41

Date	Jrnl. Ref.	Debit	Credit	Balance
Mar. 31	CR.7		1,300	1,300

Sales Discounts   No. 42

Date	Jrnl. Ref.	Debit	Credit	Balance
Mar. 31	CR.7	5		5

Interest Revenue   No. 46

Date	Jrnl. Ref.	Debit	Credit	Balance
Mar. 9	CR.7		80	80

Cost of Goods Sold   No. 51

Date	Jrnl. Ref.	Debit	Credit	Balance
Mar. 31	CR.7	841		841

Requirement 4

General Ledger

Accounts Receivable debit balance .... $1,525 ◄─┐

Accounts Receivable Subsidiary Ledger

Customer	Balance
Lance Albert	$ 640
Melinda Fultz	885
Total accounts receivable	$1,525 ◄─┘

Review *Accounting Information Systems*

Accounting Vocabulary

Batch Processing
Computerized accounting for similar transactions in a group or batch.

Cash Disbursements Journal
Special journal used to record cash payments by check. Also called the **check register** or **cash payments journal**.

Cash Payments Journal
Special journal used to record cash payments by check. Also called the **check register** or **cash disbursements journal**.

Cash Receipts Journal
Special journal used to record cash receipts.

Check Register
Special journal used to record cash payments by check. Also called the **cash disbursements journal** or **cash payments journal**.

Control Account
An account whose balance equals the sum of the balances in a group of related accounts in a subsidiary ledger.

Credit Memo
A document issued by a seller to credit a customer account for returned merchandise.

Data Warehouse
A very large database holding data for a number of years and used for analysis rather than for transaction processing.

Debit Memo
A document issued by a buyer when returning merchandise. The memo informs the seller that the buyer no longer owes the seller for the amount of the returned purchases.

Enterprise Resource Planning (ERP)
Software that can integrate all of a company's worldwide functions, departments, and data into a single system.

General Journal
Journal used to record all transactions that do not fit one of the special journals.

General Ledger
Ledger of accounts that are reported in the financial statements.

Hardware
Electronic equipment that includes computers, disk drives, monitors, printers, and the network that connects them.

Menu
A list of options for choosing computer functions.

Network
The system of electronic linkages that allows different computers to share the same information.

Online Processing
Computerized processing of related functions, such as the recording and posting of transactions on a continuous basis.

Purchases Journal
Special journal used to record all purchases of inventory, supplies, and other assets on account.

Sales Journal
Special journal used to record credit sales.

Server
The main computer in a network where the program and data are stored.

Software
Set of programs or instructions that drives the computer to perform the work desired.

Special Journal
An accounting journal designed to record one specific type of transaction.

Spreadsheet
A computer program that links data by means of formulas and functions; an electronic work sheet.

Subsidiary Ledger
Record of accounts that provides supporting details on individual balances, the total of which appears in a general ledger account.

Quick Check

1. The outputs of a computerized accounting system are called
   a. Reports
   b. Software
   c. Processing
   d. Trial balance

2. Account number 411 is most likely a (an)
   a. Asset
   b. Liability
   c. Owner equity
   d. Revenue
   e. Expense

3. The Excel formula to compute net income's percentage of sales in Exhibit 7-5, page 359, is
   a. =B4*B2
   b. =B4/B2
   c. =B2−B3
   d. =B4+B3

4. Centex Sound Systems purchased inventory costing $8,000 from Sony on account. Where should Centex record this transaction, and what account is credited?
   a. Cash payments journal; credit Cash
   b. Sales journal; credit Sales Revenue
   c. Purchases journal; credit Accounts Payable
   d. General journal; credit Inventory

5. Examine In Motion's sales journal in Exhibit 7-8, page 362. Based on these data, how much gross profit did In Motion earn during November?
   a. $1,814
   b. $2,505
   c. $4,319
   d. Cannot tell from the data given

6. Every transaction recorded in the cash receipts journal includes a
   a. Credit to Cash
   b. Debit to Accounts Receivable
   c. Debit to Sales Discounts
   d. Debit to Cash

7. The purchases journal is used to record all
   a. Purchases of assets
   b. Payments of purchases on account
   c. Purchases of inventory
   d. Purchases on account

8. The individual accounts in the accounts receivable subsidiary ledger identify
   a. Customers
   b. Creditors
   c. Amounts to be paid
   d. Suppliers

9. Which of the following is *not* a general ledger account?
   a. Sales Discounts
   b. Accounts Receivable
   c. Jackson Company
   d. Supplies Expense

10. A debit memo is a (an)
    a. Report of all the debits to the Cash account
    b. Document for a purchase return
    c. Document for a sales return
    d. Entry to the Accounts Receivable account

Answers are given after Apply Your Knowledge (p. 402).

Assess Your Progress

Short Exercises

Features of an effective information system

S7-1 In Motion, your T-shirt business, is growing fast, and you need a better accounting system. Consider the features of an effective system, as discussed on pages 353–355. Which features are most important? Why? Which feature must you consider if your financial resources are limited? (pp. 353–355)

Components of a computerized accounting system

S7-2 Match each component of a computerized accounting system with its meaning. (p. 355)

Meaning	Component
_____ Electronic linkages that allow different computers to share the same information	A. Server
_____ Electronic equipment	B. Software
_____ Programs that drive a computer	C. Hardware
_____ Main computer in a networked system	D. Network

Accounting system vocabulary

S7-3 Complete the crossword puzzle that follows. (pp. 353–356)

Down:

1. Managers need_____over operations in order to authorize transactions and safeguard assets
3. Programs that drive a computer
4. Electronic computer equipment
5. A_____ible information system accommodates changes as the organization evolves
6. The opposite of debits

Across:

2. Electronic linkage that allows different computers to share the same information
3. Main computer in a networked system
7. Cost-_____relationship must be favorable

Assigning account numbers

S7-4 Assign account numbers (from the list that follows) to the accounts of Clarke Logistics. (p. 356)

Jan Marks, Withdrawals   Inventory

Service Revenue   Accounts Payable

Depreciation Expense   Jan Marks, Capital

Numbers from which to choose:

151	301
191	311
201	411
281	531

Using a spreadsheet

3

S7-5 The spreadsheet screen in Exhibit 7-5, page 359, is your income statement. Suppose you are developing your financial plan for the coming year. Revenues should increase by 8% and expenses by 6%. Write the formulas in cells C2 through C4 to compute expected revenues, expenses, and net income for the coming year. (pp. 358–360)

Using the journals

4 **5**

S7-6 Use the following abbreviations to indicate the journal in which you would record transactions a through n. (pp. 361–371)

> J = General journal
> S = Sales journal
> CR = Cash receipts journal
> P = Purchases journal
> CP = Cash payments journal

Transactions:

_____ a. Cash purchase of inventory

_____ b. Collection of dividend revenue earned on an investment

_____ c. Prepayment of insurance

_____ d. Borrowing money on a long-term note payable

_____ e. Purchase of equipment on account

_____ f. Cost of goods sold along with a credit sale

_____ g. Cash sale of inventory

_____ h. Payment of rent

_____ i. Depreciation of computer equipment

_____ j. Purchase of inventory on account

_____ k. Collection of accounts receivable

_____ l. Expiration of prepaid insurance

_____ m. Sale on account

_____ n. Payment on account

Using the sales journal and the related ledgers

4

S7-7 Use the sales journal and the related ledger accounts in Exhibit 7-8, page 362, to answer these questions about In Motion, your T-shirt business. (pp. 361–362)

1. How much inventory did In Motion have on hand at the end of November? Where can you get this information? Be specific.

2. What amount did In Motion post to the Sales Revenue account? When did In Motion post to the Sales Revenue account? Assume a manual accounting system.

3. After these transactions, how much does Susan Levy owe In Motion? Where do you obtain this information? Be specific.

4. If there were no discounts, how much would In Motion hope to collect from all its customers? Where is this amount stored in a single figure? Be specific.

Using accounts receivable records

S7-8 1. In Motion, your T-shirt business, needs good accounts receivable records to ensure collection from customers. What is the name of the detailed record of amounts collectible from individual customers? (pp. 361–362)

2. A key control feature of your accounting system lies in the agreement between the detailed customer receivable records and the summary total in the general ledger. Use the data in Exhibit 7-8, page 362, to prove that In Motion's accounts receivable records are accurate. (pp. 361–362, 363–364)

Using cash receipts data

S7-9 The cash receipts journal of In Motion appears in Exhibit 7-9, page 365, along with the company's various ledger accounts. Use the data in Exhibit 7-9 to answer the following questions about your cash receipts.

1. How much were total cash receipts during November? (p. 365)

2. How much cash did In Motion collect on account from customers? How much in total discounts did customers earn by paying quickly? How much did your accounts receivable decrease because of collections from customers during November? (p. 365)

3. How much were cash sales during November? (p. 365)

Using the purchases journal

S7-10 Use In Motion's purchases journal (Exhibit 7-10, page 367) to address these questions about your purchases on account.

1. How much were In Motion's purchases of inventory on account during November? (p. 367)

2. Suppose it is December 1 and you wish to pay the full amount that you owe on account. Examine only the purchases journal (page 367). Then make a general journal entry to record payment of the correct amount on December 1. Include an explanation. (pp. 367, 70–76)

Using the purchases journal and the cash payments journal

S7-11 Refer to In Motion's purchases journal (Exhibit 7-10, page 367) and cash payments journal (Exhibit 7-11, page 369). Answer the following questions about your business.

1. How much in total credit purchases of inventory, supplies, equipment, and furniture did you make during November? (p. 367)

2. How much of the accounts payable did you pay off during November? (pp. 368–369)

3. At November 30, after all purchases and all cash payments, how much does In Motion owe Hanes Textiles? How much in total does In Motion owe on account? (pp. 368–369)

Using all the journals

S7-12 Answer the following questions about the November transactions of In Motion, your T-shirt business. You will need to refer to Exhibits 7-8 through 7-11, which begin on page 362.

1. How much cash does In Motion have on hand at November 30? (pp. 368–369)

2. Compute In Motion's gross sales revenue and net sales revenue for November. (p. 365)

3. How did In Motion purchase furniture—for cash or on account? Indicate the basis for your answer. (pp. 367, 368–369)

4. From whom did In Motion purchase supplies on account? How much in total does In Motion owe this company on November 30? (pp. 367, 368–369)

Exercises

Setting up a chart of accounts

E7-13 Use account numbers 101 through 106, 201, 221, 301, 321, 401, 501 and 521 to correspond to the following selected accounts from the general ledger of Mobile Technology Company. List the accounts and their account numbers in proper order, starting with the most liquid current asset. (p. 356)

Jerry Mobile, capital	Depreciation expense	Accounts receivable
Cost of goods sold	Cash	Note payable, long-term
Accounts payable	Jerry Mobile, withdrawals	Computer equipment
Inventory	Supplies	
Sales revenue	Accumulated depreciation	

Using a trial balance

E7-14 The accounts of Lake Onondaga Steakhouse show some of these amounts before closing:

Total assets	$?	Larry Nolan, capital	$ 8,600
Current assets	18,100	Larry Nolan, withdrawals	2,000
Plant assets	63,400	Total revenues	40,000
Total liabilities	?	Total expenses	21,000

Compute the missing amounts. You must also compute ending owner's equity. (p. 203)

Using a spreadsheet to compute depreciation

E7-15 Equipment listed on a spreadsheet has a cost of $60,000; this amount is located in cell B9. The years of the asset's useful life (20) are found in cell C8. Write the spreadsheet formula to express annual depreciation expense for the equipment. How much is annual depreciation? (pp. 358–360)

Computing financial statement amounts with a spreadsheet

E7-16 The following items appear in the cells of a Witt Furniture Store spreadsheet:

Item	Cell
Total assets	B22
Current assets	B8
Fixed assets	B11
Total liabilities	C11
Current liabilities	C6
Long-term liabilities	C10

Write the spreadsheet formula to calculate Witt's (pp. 358–360)

a. Current ratio (p. 210)

b. Total owner's equity (p. 11)

c. Debt ratio (p. 210)

E7-17 The sales and cash receipts journals of Kincaid Office Products include the following entries:

SALES JOURNAL

Date	Account Debited	Post. Ref.	Accounts Receivable Dr. Sales Revenue Cr.	Cost of Goods Sold Dr. Inventory Cr.
May 7	L. Ewald	✔	110	76
10	T. Ross	✔	60	29
10	E. Lovell	✔	60	35
12	B. Goebel	✔	120	60
31	Total		350	200

CASH RECEIPTS JOURNAL

	Debits		Credits					Cost of Goods Sold Dr. Inventory Cr.
					Other Accounts			
Date	Cash	Sales Discounts	Accounts Receivable	Sales Revenue	Account Title	Post. Ref.	Amount	
May 16					L. Ewald	✔		
19					E. Lovell	✔		
24	300			300				190
30					T. Ross	✔		

Complete the cash receipts journal for those transactions indicated. There are no sales discounts. Also, total the journal and show that total debits equal total credits. (pp. 361–362, 365)

E7-18 The cash receipts journal of Sironia Plastics follows.

CASH RECEIPTS JOURNAL   PAGE 7

	Debits				Credits		
					Other Accounts		
Date	Cash	Sales Discounts	Accounts Receivable	Sales Revenue	Account Title	Post. Ref.	Amount
Jan. 2	790	20	810		Annan Corp.	(e)	
9	490		490		Kamm, Inc.	(f)	
19	4,480				Note Receivable	(g)	4,000
					Interest Revenue	(h)	480
30	310	10	320		J. T. Franz	(i)	
31	4,230			4,230			
31	10,300	30	1,620	4,230	Totals		4,480
	(a)	(b)	(c)	(d)			(j)

continued. . .

Sironia's general ledger includes the following selected accounts, along with their account numbers:

Number	Account	Number	Account
110	Cash	510	Sales revenue
120	Accounts receivable	512	Sales discounts
125	Note receivable	515	Sales returns
140	Land	520	Interest revenue

Requirements

Indicate whether each posting reference (a) through (j) should be a (p. 365)

- Check mark (✔) for a posting to a customer account in the accounts receivable subsidiary ledger.
- Account number for a posting to an account in the general ledger. If so, give the account number.
- Letter (x) for an amount not posted.

Identifying transactions from postings to the accounts receivable ledger

E7-19 A customer account in the accounts receivable subsidiary ledger of Lyndon Olson Company follows.

JOHN WATERS

Date	Jrnl. Ref.	Dr.	Cr.	Balance Dr.	Balance Cr.
Nov. 1				400	
9	S.5	1,180		1,580	
18	J.8		190	1,390	
30	CR.9		700	690	

Requirement

Describe the three posted transactions. (pp. 361–362, 365)

Recording transactions in the general journal and in the purchases journal

E7-20 During April, Shannon Donut Distributors completed these *credit purchase* transactions:

April 5	Purchased supplies, $400, from Sudan, Inc.
11	Purchased inventory, $1,200, from Greenbrier Corp. Shannon uses a perpetual inventory system.
19	Purchased equipment, $4,300, from Saturn Co.
22	Purchased inventory, $2,210, from Milan, Inc.

Record these transactions first in the general journal—with explanations—and then in the purchases journal. Omit credit terms and posting references. Which procedure for recording transactions is quicker? Why? (pp. 315–317, 367)

E7-21 The purchases journal of TransEastern Publishing Company follows.

PURCHASES JOURNAL   PAGE 7

Date	Account Credited	Terms	Post. Ref.	Account Payable Cr.	Inventory Dr.	Supplies Dr.	Other Accounts Dr.		
							Acct. Title	Post. Ref.	Amount Dr.
Sep. 2	Lancer Tech	n/30		800	800				
5	Jupiter Supply	n/30		170		170			
13	Lancer Tech	2/10 n/30		1,400	1,400				
26	Faver Equipment	n/30		900			Equipment		900
30	Totals			3,270	2,200	170			900

Requirements

1. Open four-column ledger accounts for Inventory, Supplies, Equipment, and Accounts Payable. Post to these accounts from the purchases journal. Use dates and posting references in the accounts. (pp. 80, 367)

2. Open accounts in the accounts payable subsidiary ledger for Faver Equipment, Lancer Tech, and Jupiter Supply. Post from the purchases journal. Use dates and journal references in the ledger accounts. (p. 367)

3. Balance the Accounts Payable control account in the general ledger with the total of the balances in the accounts payable subsidiary ledger. (p. 370)

E7-22 During August, Berryhill Stamp Company had the following transactions:

Aug. 1	Paid $490 on account to Rabin Associates, net of a $10 discount for an earlier purchase of inventory.
5	Purchased inventory for cash, $1,100.
9	Paid $300 for supplies.
16	Paid $4,060 on account to LaGrange Company; there was no discount.
21	Purchased furniture for cash, $900.
26	Paid $3,900 on account to Hallmark for an earlier purchase of inventory. The discount was $100.
30	Made a semiannual interest payment of $800 on a long-term note payable. The entire payment was for interest.

Requirements

1. Prepare a cash payments journal similar to the one illustrated in this chapter. Omit the check number (Ck. No.) and posting reference (Post. Ref.) columns. (p. 369)

2. Record the transactions in the cash payments journal. (p. 369)

3. Total the amount columns of the journal. Determine that total debits equal total credits. (p. 369)

Using business documents
to record transactions

E7-23 The following documents describe two business transactions.

Invoice		
Date: Dec. 12, 2007		
Sold to: Jerry Stevens Bridgestone		
Sold by: Bridgestone Tire Co.		
Terms: 2/10 n/30		

Items Purchased	Tires	
Quantity	**Price**	**Total**
8	$95	$ 760
4	70	280
5	60	300
Total		**$1,340**

Debit Memo		
Date: Dec. 18, 2007		
Sent to: Bridgestone Tire Co.		
Sent by: Jerry Stevens Bridgestone		

Items Returned	Tires	
Quantity	**Price**	**Total**
2	$95	$190
1	70	70
Total		**$260**

Reason: Damaged in shipment

Requirements

Use the general journal to record these transactions and Jerry Stevens' cash payment on December 19. Record the transactions first on the books of Jerry Stevens, Bridgestone and, second, on the books of Bridgestone Tire Company, which manufactures auto tires. Both Stevens and Bridgestone use a perpetual inventory system as illustrated in Chapter 5. Bridgestone's cost of the tires sold to Stevens was $690. Bridgestone's cost of the returned merchandise was $140.

Round amounts to the nearest dollar. Explanations are not required. Set up your answer in the following format. (pp. 315–317, 371)

Date	Stevens Journal Entries	Bridgestone Journal Entries

Using the special journals

E7-24 In Motion's special journals in Exhibits 7-8 through 7-11 (pages 362–369) provide much of the data needed to prepare the financial statements. In Motion uses the *perpetual* inventory system. As the owner, you need to know the business's gross profit for November. Compute the gross profit. (pp. 365, 320–321)

Problems (Group A)

Using a spreadsheet to prepare an income statement

P7-25A The following spreadsheet shows the income statement of Bates Performance Auto:

Row Number	Column A	B
3	Revenues:	
4	Service revenue ⟶	number
5	Rent revenue ⟶	number
6		———
7	Total revenue ⟶	
8		
9	Expenses:	
10	Salary expense ⟶	number
11	Supplies expense ⟶	number
12	Rent expense ⟶	number
13	Depreciation expense ⟶	number
14		———
15	Total expenses ⟶	
16		———
17	Net income ⟶	
18		══════

Requirement
Write the appropriate formula in each cell that will need a formula. Choose from these symbols: (pp. 358–360)

+ add

– subtract

= SUM (beginning cell:ending cell)

* multiply

/ divide

Using the sales, cash receipts, and general journals

P7-26A The general ledger of Barton Springs Glass Company includes the following selected accounts, along with their account numbers:

Cash	11	Equipment	18
Accounts Receivable	12	Sales Revenue	41
Inventory	13	Sales Discounts	42
Notes Receivable	15	Sales Returns and Allowances	43
Supplies	16	Cost of Goods Sold	51

continued...

All credit sales are on Barton Springs' standard terms of 2/10 n/30. Sales and cash receipts transactions in July were as follows:

July 2	Sold inventory on credit to Intelysis, Inc., $1,750. Barton Springs' cost of these goods was $600.
3	As an accommodation to a competitor, sold supplies at cost, $85, receiving cash.
7	Cash sales for the week totaled $1,890 (cost, $1,640).
9	Sold merchandise on account to A. L. Prince, $7,320 (cost, $5,110).
10	Sold land that cost $10,000 for cash of the same amount.
11	Sold goods on account to Sloan Electric, $5,100 (cost, $3,520).
12	Received cash from Intelysis in full settlement of its account receivable from July 2.
14	Cash sales for the week were $2,106 (cost, $1,530).
15	Sold inventory on credit to the partnership of Wilkie & Blinn, $3,650 (cost, $2,260).
18	Received inventory sold on July 9 to A. L. Prince for $600. The goods shipped were unsatisfactory. These goods cost Barton Springs $440.
20	Sold merchandise on account to Sloan Electric, $620 (cost, $450).
21	Cash sales for the week were $990 (cost, $690).
22	Received $4,000 cash from A. L. Prince in partial settlement of his account receivable.
25	Received cash from Wilkie & Blinn for its account receivable from July 15.
25	Sold goods on account to Olsen Co., $1,520 (cost, $1,050).
27	Collected $5,125 on a note receivable. There is no interest.
28	Cash sales for the week totaled $3,774 (cost, $2,460).
29	Sold inventory on account to R. O. Bankston, $240 (cost, $170).
30	Received goods sold on July 25 to Olsen Co. for $40. The cost of these goods was $10.
31	Received $2,720 cash on account from A. L. Prince.

Requirements

1. Use the appropriate journal to record the preceding transactions in a sales journal (omit the Invoice No. column), a cash receipts journal, and a general journal. Barton Springs Glass Company records sales returns and allowances in the general journal. (pp. 361–362, 365, 371)

2. Total each column of the sales journal and the cash receipts journal. Show that total debits equal total credits. (p. 365)

3. Show how postings would be made by writing the account numbers and check marks in the appropriate places in the journals. (pp. 361–362, 365, 371).

Correcting errors in the cash
receipts journal
4

P7-27A The following cash receipts journal of Bernina Sewing Machines contains 5 entries. All 5 entries are for legitimate cash receipt transactions, but the journal has some errors from recording the transactions incorrectly. In fact, only 1 entry is correct, and each of the other 4 entries contains 1 error. Ignore posting references.

CASH RECEIPTS JOURNAL

	Debits				Credits			Cost of Goods
						Other Accounts		Sold Debit
Date	Cash	Sales Discounts	Accounts Receivable	Sales Revenue	Account Title	Post. Ref.	Amount	Inventory Credit
Jan. 4		1,200		1,200				500
7	430	20			Paul Dalton		450	
13	4,100				Note Receivable		4,000	
					Interest Revenue		100	
20				300				150
30		700	700		Jaclyn Webb			
31	4,530	1,920	700	1,500	Totals		4,550	650

Total Dr. = $6,450   Total Cr. = $6,750

Requirements

1. Identify the correct entry. (p. 365)
2. Identify the error in each of the other 4 entries. Cost of Goods Sold and Inventory are correct. (p. 365)
3. Prepare a corrected cash receipts journal using the following format. All column totals are correct in the cash receipts journal that follows. (p. 365)

CASH RECEIPTS JOURNAL

	Debits				Credits			Cost of Goods
						Other Accounts		Sold Debit
Date	Cash	Sales Discounts	Accounts Receivable	Sales Revenue	Account Title	Post. Ref.	Amount	Inventory Credit
Jan. 4								500
7					Paul Dalton			
13	4,100				Note Receivable		4,000	
					Interest Revenue		100	
20								150
30					Jaclyn Webb			
31	6,730	20	1,150	1,500	Totals		4,100	650

Total Dr. = $6,750   Total Cr. = $6,750

Using the purchases, cash
payments, and general
journals

5

P7-28A The general ledger of Crystal Lake Golf Shop includes these accounts,
along with their account numbers:

Cash	111	Equipment	187
Inventory	131	Accounts Payable	211
Prepaid Insurance	161	Rent Expense	564
Supplies	171	Utilities Expense	583

Transactions in December that affected purchases and cash payments follow.

Dec. 2	Purchased inventory on credit from Titleist, $4,000. Terms were 2/10 n/30.
3	Paid monthly rent, debiting Rent Expense for $2,000.
5	Purchased supplies on credit terms of 2/10 n/30 from Ross Supply, $450.
8	Paid electricity utility bill, $580.
9	Purchased equipment on account from A-1 Equipment, $6,100. Payment terms were net 30.
10	Returned the equipment to A-1 Equipment. It was damaged.
11	Paid Titleist the amount owed on the purchase of December 2.
12	Purchased inventory on account from Callaway Golf, $4,400. Terms were 3/10 n/30.
13	Purchased inventory for cash, $650.
14	Paid a semiannual insurance premium, debiting Prepaid Insurance, $1,200.
16	Paid our account payable to Ross Supply, from December 5.
18	Paid gas and water utility bills, $190.
21	Purchased inventory on credit terms of 1/10 n/45 from Dunlop, Inc., $3,900.
21	Paid account payable to Callaway Golf from December 12.
22	Purchased supplies on account from Office Sales, Inc., $100. Terms were net 30.
26	Returned to Dunlop, Inc., $1,200 of the inventory purchased on December 21.
31	Paid Dunlop, Inc., the net amount owed from December 21 less the return on December 26.

Requirements

1. Crystal Lake Golf Shop records purchase returns in the general journal. Use the appropriate journal to record the transactions in a purchase journal, a cash payments journal (omit the Check No. column), and a general journal. (pp. 367, 368–369, 371)

2. Total each column of the special journals. Show that total debits equal total credits in each special journal. (pp. 367, 368–369)

3. Show how postings would be made from the journals by writing the account numbers and check marks in the appropriate places in the journals. (pp. 367, 368–369, 371)

P7-29A Crestview Computer Security uses the perpetual inventory system and makes all credit sales on terms of 2/10 n/30. Crestview completed the following transactions during May:

May 2	Issued invoice no. 913 for sale on account to K. D. Forbes, $2,000. Crestview's cost of this inventory was $900.
3	Purchased inventory on credit terms of 3/10 n/60 from Chicosky Co., $2,467.
5	Sold inventory for cash, $1,077 (cost, $480).
5	Issued check no. 532 to purchase furniture for cash, $2,185.
8	Collected interest revenue of $1,775.
9	Issued invoice no. 914 for sale on account to Bell Co., $5,550 (cost, $2,310).
10	Purchased inventory for cash, $1,143, issuing check no. 533.
12	Received cash from K. D. Forbes in full settlement of her account receivable from the sale on May 2.
13	Issued check no. 534 to pay Chicosky Co. the net amount owed from May 3. Round to the nearest dollar.
13	Purchased supplies on account from Manley, Inc., $441. Terms were net end-of-month.
15	Sold inventory on account to M. O. Brown, issuing invoice no. 915 for $665 (cost, $240).
17	Issued credit memo to M. O. Brown for $665 for merchandise returned to us by Brown. Also accounted for receipt of the inventory at cost.
18	Issued invoice no. 916 for credit sale to K. D. Forbes, $357 (cost, $127).
19	Received $5,439 from Bell Co. in full settlement of its account receivable from May 9. Bell earned a discount by paying early.
20	Purchased inventory on credit terms of net 30 from Sims Distributing, $2,047.
22	Purchased furniture on credit terms of 3/10 n/60 from Chicosky Co., $645.
22	Issued check no. 535 to pay for insurance coverage, debiting Prepaid Insurance for $1,000.
24	Sold supplies to an employee for cash of $54, which was Crestview's cost.
25	Issued check no. 536 to pay utilities, $453.
28	Purchased inventory on credit terms of 2/10 n/30 from Manley, Inc., $675.
29	Returned damaged inventory to Manley, Inc., issuing a debit memo for $675.
29	Sold goods on account to Bell Co., issuing invoice no. 917 for $2,900 (cost, $800).
30	Issued check no. 537 to pay Manley, Inc., in full on account from May 13.

continued. . .

| May 31 | Received cash in full from K. D. Forbes on credit sale of May 18. There was no discount. |
| 31 | Issued check no. 538 to pay monthly salaries of $1,950. |

Requirements

1. Open the following four-column general ledger accounts using the Crestview Computer Security account numbers as follows: (pp. 361–369)

Cash	111	Sales Revenue	411
Accounts Receivable	112	Sales Discounts	412
Supplies	116	Sales Returns and Allowances	413
Prepaid Insurance	117	Interest Revenue	419
Inventory	118	Cost of Goods Sold	511
Furniture	151	Salary Expense	531
Accounts Payable	211	Utilities Expense	541

2. Open these accounts in the subsidiary ledgers: Accounts receivable ledger—Bell Co., M. O. Brown, and K. D. Forbes. Accounts payable ledger—Chicosky Co.; Manley, Inc.; and Sims Distributing. (pp. 361, 367)

3. Enter the transactions in a sales journal (page 7), a cash receipts journal (page 5), a purchases journal (page 10), a cash payments journal (page 8), and a general journal (page 6), as appropriate. (pp. 361, 365, 367, 368–369, 371)

4. Post daily to the accounts receivable ledger and to the accounts payable ledger. On May 31, post to the general ledger. (pp. 361, 365, 367, 368–369, 371)

5. Total each column of the special journals. Show that total debits equal total credits in each special journal. (pp. 361, 365, 367, 368–369)

6. Balance the total of the customer balances in the accounts receivable ledger against Accounts Receivable in the general ledger. Do the same for the accounts payable ledger and Accounts Payable in the general ledger. (pp. 364, 366, 370)

Problems (Group B)

Using a spreadsheet to prepare a balance sheet

3

P7-30B The spreadsheet on the next page shows the assets of the Pandera Pizzeria balance sheet.

Requirement

Write the appropriate formula in each cell that will need a formula. Choose from these symbols (pp. 358–360):

+ add	* multiply
– subtract	/ divide
= SUM (beginning cell:ending cell)	

continued. . .

	Column	
Row Number	A	B
3	Assets:	
4	Current assets:	
5	Cash ⟶	number
6	Receivables ⟶	number
7	Inventory ⟶	number
8		_____
9	Total current assets ⟶	
10		
11	Equipment ⟶	number
12	Accumulated depreciation ⟶	number
13		_____
14	Equipment, net ⟶	
15		_____
16	Total assets ⟶	
17		══════

Using the sales, cash receipts, and general journals

4

P7-31B The general ledger of Suds Soap Company includes the following selected accounts, along with their account numbers:

Cash	111	Land	142
Accounts Receivable	112	Sales Revenue	411
Notes Receivable	115	Sales Discounts	412
Inventory	131	Sales Returns and Allowances	413
Equipment	141	Cost of Goods Sold	511

All credit sales are on Suds' standard terms of 2/10 n/30. Sales and cash receipts transactions in November were as follows:

Nov. 2	Sold inventory on credit to Grant Thornton, $800. Suds' cost of these goods was $310.
6	As an accommodation to another company, sold new equipment for its cost of $770, receiving cash for this amount.
6	Cash sales for the week totaled $2,100 (cost, $1,360).
8	Sold goods to McNair Co. on account, $2,830 (cost, $1,780).
9	Sold land that cost $22,000 for cash of $22,000.

continued. . .

Nov. 11	Sold goods on account to Nickerson Supply, $1,500 (cost, $800).
11	Received cash from Grant Thornton in full settlement of his account receivable from November 2.
13	Cash sales for the week were $1,900 (cost, $1,200).
15	Sold inventory on credit to Montez and Montez, $900 (cost, $500).
18	Received inventory from McNair Co. as a sales return, $120. The goods we shipped were unsatisfactory. These goods cost Suds $70.
19	Sold inventory to Nickerson supply on account, $3,900 (cost, $2,610).
20	Cash sales for the week were $2,330 (cost, $1,570).
21	Received $1,200 cash from McNair Co. in partial settlement of its account receivable. There was no discount.
22	Received cash from Montez and Montez for its account receivable from November 15.
22	Sold goods on account to Diamond Co., $2,000 (cost, $1,300).
25	Collected $4,200 on a note receivable. There was no interest.
27	Cash sales for the week totaled $2,900 (cost, $1,900).
27	Sold inventory on account to Littleton Corporation, $600 (cost, $230).
28	Received goods from Diamond Co. as a sales return, $680. The cost of these goods was $390.
30	Received $1,510 cash on account from McNair Co. There was no discount.

Requirements

1. Use the appropriate journal to record the preceding transactions in a sales journal (omit the Invoice No. column), a cash receipts journal, and a general journal. Record sales returns and allowances in the general journal. (pp. 361, 365, 371)

2. Total each column of the sales journal and the cash receipts journal. Determine that total debits equal total credits. (p. 365)

3. Show how postings would be made from the journals by writing the account numbers and check marks in the appropriate places in the journals. (pp. 361, 365, 371)

Correcting errors in the cash receipts journal

4

P7-32B The following cash receipts journal shows 5 entries. All 5 entries are for legitimate cash receipt transactions, but the journal has some errors due to recording the transactions incorrectly. In fact, only 1 entry is correct, and each of the other 4 entries contains 1 error. Ignore posting references.

continued...

CASH RECEIPTS JOURNAL

CASH RECEIPTS JOURNAL

| | Debits | | Credits | | | | | Cost of Goods Sold Debit Inventory Credit |
| | | | | | Other Accounts | | | |
Date	Cash	3% Sales Discounts	Accounts Receivable	Sales Revenue	Account Title	Post. Ref.	Amount	
May 1	582	18	600		Alliance Chemicals			
9			650	650	Carl Ryther			
10	8,000			8,000	Land			
19				70				44
30		1,000		1,000				631
31	8,582	1,018	1,250	9,720	Totals			675

Total Dr. = $9,600 Total Cr. = $10,970

Requirements

1. Identify the correct entry. (p. 365)
2. Identify the error in each of the other four entries. Cost of Goods Sold and Inventory are correct. (p. 365)
3. Prepare a corrected cash receipts journal using the following format. All column totals are correct in the cash receipts journal that follows. (p. 365)

CASH RECEIPTS JOURNAL

| | Debits | | Credits | | | | | Cost of Goods Sold Debit Inventory Credit |
| | | | | | Other Accounts | | | |
Date	Cash	3% Sales Discounts	Accounts Receivable	Sales Revenue	Account Title	Post. Ref.	Amount	
May 1	582	18	600		Alliance Chemicals			
9					Carl Ryther			
10					Land			
19								
30								
31	10,302	18	1,250	1,070	Totals		8,000	675

Total Dr. = $10,320 Total Cr. = $10,320

Using the purchases, cash payments, and general journals

5

P7-33B The general ledger of British Car Specialists includes the following accounts, along with their account numbers:

Cash	111	Equipment	189
Inventory	131	Accounts Payable	211
Prepaid Insurance	161	Rent Expense	562
Supplies	171	Utilities Expense	565

continued. . .

Transactions in January that affected purchases and cash payments were as follows:

Jan. 2	Paid monthly rent, debiting Rent Expense for $900.
5	Purchased inventory on credit from Sylvania Co., $5,000. Terms were 2/15 n/45.
6	Purchased supplies on credit terms of 2/10 n/30 from Harmon Sales, $800.
7	Paid utility bills, $400.
10	Purchased equipment on account from Lancer Co., $1,050. Payment terms were 2/10 n/30.
11	Returned the equipment to Lancer Co. It was defective.
12	Paid Sylvania Co. the amount owed on the purchase of January 5.
12	Purchased inventory on account from Lancer Co., $1,100. Terms were 2/10 n/30.
14	Purchased inventory for cash, $1,585.
15	Paid an insurance premium, debiting Prepaid Insurance, $2,410.
17	Paid electricity utility bill, $165.
19	Paid our account payable to Harmon Sales, from January 6.
20	Paid account payable to Lancer Co., from January 12.
21	Purchased supplies on account from Master Supply, $110. Terms were net 30.
22	Purchased inventory on credit terms of 1/10 n/30 from Linz Brothers, $900.
26	Returned inventory purchased for $500 on January 22, to Linz Brothers.
31	Paid Linz Brothers the net amount owed from January 22, less the return on January 26.

Requirements

1. Use the appropriate journal to record the preceding transactions in a purchases journal, a cash payments journal (omit the Check No. column), and a general journal. British Car Specialists records purchase returns in the general journal. (pp. 367, 369, 371)

2. Total each column of the special journals. Show that total debits equal total credits in each special journal. (pp. 367, 369)

3. Show how postings would be made from the journals by writing the account numbers and check marks in the appropriate places in the journals. (pp. 367, 369, 371)

Using all the journals,
posting, and balancing the
ledgers

P7-34B Prudhoe Bay Co. uses the perpetual inventory system and makes all credit sales on terms of 2/10 n/30. During March, Prudhoe Bay Co. completed these transactions:

Mar. 2   Issued invoice no. 191 for sale on account to L. E. Wooten, $2,350. Prudhoe Bay's cost of this inventory was $1,390.

3   Purchased inventory on credit terms of 3/10 n/60 from Delwood Plaza, $5,900.

4   Sold inventory for cash, $3,410 (cost, $1,820).

5   Issued check no. 473 to purchase furniture for cash $1,080.

8   Collected interest revenue of $120.

9   Issued invoice no. 192 for sale on account to Cortez Co., $6,250 (cost, $3,300).

10   Purchased inventory for cash, $770, issuing check no. 474.

12   Received $2,303 cash from L. E. Wooten in full settlement of her account receivable, net of the discount, from the sale of March 2.

13   Issued check no. 475 to pay Delwood Plaza net amount owed from March 3.

13   Purchased supplies on account from Havrilla Corp., $680. Terms were net end-of-month.

15   Sold inventory on account to J. R. Wakeland, issuing invoice no. 193 for $740 (cost, $410).

17   Issued credit memo to J. R. Wakeland for $740 for defective merchandise returned to us by Wakeland. Also accounted for receipt of the inventory at cost.

18   Issued invoice no. 194 for credit sale to L. E. Wooten, $1,825 (cost, $970).

19   Received $6,125 from Cortez Co. in full settlement of its account receivable from March 9.

20   Purchased inventory on credit terms of net 30 from Jasper Sales, $2,150.

22   Purchased furniture on credit terms of 3/10 n/60 from Delwood Plaza, $775.

22   Issued check no. 476 to pay for insurance coverage, debiting Prepaid Insurance for $1,345.

24   Sold supplies to an employee for cash of $80, which was Prudhoe Bay's cost.

25   Issued check no. 477 to pay utilities, $380.

28   Purchased inventory on credit terms of 2/10 n/30 from Havrilla Corp., $420.

29   Returned damaged inventory to Havrilla Corp., issuing a debit memo for $420.

29   Sold goods on account to Cortez Co., issuing invoice no. 195 for $1,800 (cost, $1,000).

continued. . .

	30	Issued check no. 478 to pay Havrilla Corp. on account from March 13.
	31	Received cash in full from L. E. Wooten on credit sale of March 18. There was no discount.
	31	Issued check no. 479 to pay monthly salaries of $1,100.

Requirements

1. Open four-column general ledger accounts using Prudhoe Bay Co.'s account numbers that follow. (pp. 361–369)

Cash	111	Sales Revenue	411
Accounts Receivable	112	Sales Discounts	412
Supplies	116	Sales Returns and Allowances	413
Prepaid Insurance	117	Interest Revenue	419
Inventory	118	Cost of Goods Sold	511
Furniture	151	Salary Expense	531
Accounts Payable	211	Utilities Expense	541

2. Open these accounts in the subsidiary ledgers. Accounts receivable ledger: Cortez Co., J. R. Wakeland, and L. E. Wooten. Accounts payable ledger: Delwood Plaza, Havrilla Corp., and Jasper Sales. (pp. 361, 367)

3. Enter the transactions in a sales journal (page 8), a cash receipts journal (page 3), a purchases journal (page 6), a cash payments journal (page 9), and a general journal (page 4), as appropriate. (pp. 361, 365, 367, 368–369, 371)

4. Post daily to the accounts receivable ledger and to the accounts payable ledger. On March 31, post to the general ledger. (pp. 361, 365, 367, 368–369, 371)

5. Total each column of the special journals. Show that total debits equal total credits in each special journal. (pp. 361, 365, 367, 368–369)

6. Balance the total of the customer account balances in the accounts receivable ledger against Accounts Receivable in the general ledger. Do the same for the accounts payable ledger and Accounts Payable in the general ledger. (pp. 366, 370)

for 24-7 practice, visit www.MyAccountingLab.com

Apply Your Knowledge

Decision Cases

Reconstructing transactions from amounts posted to the accounts receivable subsidiary ledger

4

Case 1. A fire destroyed certain accounting records of Golden Books. The owner, Marilyn Golden, asks your help in reconstructing the records. *She needs to know (1) the beginning and ending balances of Accounts Receivable, (2) the sales on account and (3) total cash receipts on account from customers during April.* All of the sales are on account, with credit terms of 2/10 n/30. All cash receipts on account reached the store within the 10-day discount period, except as noted. The only accounting record preserved from the fire is the accounts receivable subsidiary ledger, which follows. (p. 365)

Garcia Sales

Date	Item	Jrnl. Ref.	Debit	Credit	Balance
Apr. 1	Balance				450
3		CR.8		450	-0-
25		S.6	3,600		3,600
29		S.6	1,100		4,700

Leewright, Inc.

Date	Item	Jrnl. Ref.	Debit	Credit	Balance
Apr. 1	Balance				2,800
15		S.6	2,600		5,400
29		CR.8		1,500*	3,900

*Cash receipt did not occur within the discount period.

Sally Jones

Date	Item	Jrnl. Ref.	Debit	Credit	Balance
Apr. 1	Balance				1,100
5		CR.8		1,100	-0-
11		S.6	400		400
21		CR.8		400	-0-
24		S.6	2,000		2,000

Jacques LeHavre

Date	Item	Jrnl. Ref.	Debit	Credit	Balance
Apr. 1	Balance				-0-
8		S.6	2,400		2,400
16		S.6	900		3,300
18		CR.8		2,400	900
19		J.5		200	700
27		CR.8		700	-0-

Designing a special journal

4 **5**

Case 2. MicroData Solutions sells cutting-edge networking software. MicroData's quality control officer estimates that 20% of the company's sales and purchases of inventory are returned for additional debugging. MicroData needs special journals for:

- Sales returns and allowances

- Purchase returns and allowances

Requirements

1. Design the two special journals. For each special journal, include a column for the appropriate business document (credit memo or debit memo). (pp. 371, Challenge)

2. Enter one transaction in each journal, using the In Motion transaction data illustrated on pages 361–371. Show all posting references, including those for column totals.

Ethical Issue

On a recent trip to Africa, J. T. Brown, sales manager of Prompt Technology, took his wife along at company expense. Linda White, vice president of sales and Brown's boss, thought his travel and entertainment expenses seemed excessive. But White approved the reimbursement because she owed Brown a favor. White was aware that the company president reviews all expenses recorded in the cash payments journal, so White recorded Brown's wife's expenses in the *general* journal as follows:

Sales Promotion Expense		9,100	
Cash			9,100

Requirements

1. Does recording the transaction in the *general* journal rather than in the cash payments journal affect the amounts of cash and total expenses reported in the financial statements?

2. Why did White record these expenses in the *general* journal?

3. What is the ethical issue in this situation? What role does accounting play in this issue?

Team Projects

Project 1. Preparing a Business Plan for a Merchandising Entity. As you work through Chapters 6 through 12, you will be examining in detail the current assets, current liabilities, and plant assets of a business. Most of the organizations that form the context for business activity in the remainder of the book are merchandising entities. Therefore, in a group or individually—as directed by your instructor—develop a plan for beginning and operating an audio/video store or other type of business. Develop your plan in as much detail as you can. Remember that the business manager who attends to the most details delivers the best product at the lowest price for customers!

Project 2. Preparing a Business Plan for a Service Entity. List what you have learned thus far in the course. On the basis of what you have learned, refine your plan for promoting a rock concert (from Team Project 2 in Chapter 1) to include everything you believe you must do to succeed in this business venture.

For Internet Exercises, Excel in Practice, and additional online activities, go to the Web site www.prenhall.com/horngren.

Quick Check Answers

1. *a*   2. *d*   3. *b*   4. *c*   5. *b*   6. *d*   7. *d*   8. *a*   9. *c*   10. *b*

Comprehensive Problem for Chapters 1–7

Completing The Accounting Cycle for a Merchandising Entity—Using Special Journals

A-1 Networking Systems closes its books and prepares financial statements monthly. A-1 uses the perpetual inventory system. The company completed the following transactions during August:

Aug. 1	Issued check no. 682 for August office rent of $1,000. (Debit Rent Expense.)
2	Issued check no. 683 to pay the salary payable of $1,250 from July 31.
2	Issued invoice no. 503 for sale on account to R. T. Loeb, $600. A-1's cost of this merchandise was $190.
3	Purchased inventory on credit terms of 1/15 n/60 from Grant, Inc., $1,400.
4	Received net amount of cash on account from Fullam Company, $2,156, within the discount period.
4	Sold inventory for cash, $330 (cost, $104).
5	Received from Park-Hee, Inc., merchandise that had been sold earlier for $550 (cost, $174). (Record this sales return in the general journal.)
5	Issued check no. 684 to purchase supplies for cash, $780.
7	Issued invoice no. 504 for sale on account to K. D. Skipper, $2,400 (cost, $759).
8	Issued check no. 685 to pay Federal Company $2,600 of the amount owed at July 31. This payment occurred after the end of the discount period.
11	Issued check no. 686 to pay Grant, Inc., the net amount owed from August 3.
12	Received cash from R. T. Loeb in full settlement of her account receivable from August 2.
16	Issued check no. 687 to pay salary expense of $1,240.
19	Purchased inventory for cash, $850, issuing check no. 688.
22	Purchased furniture on credit terms of 3/15 n/60 from Beaver Corporation, $510.
23	Sold inventory on account to Fullam Company, issuing invoice no. 505 for $9,966 (cost, $3,152).
24	Received half the July 31 amount receivable from K. D. Skipper—after the end of the discount period.
26	Purchased supplies on credit terms of 2/10 n/30 from Federal Company, $180.
30	Returned damaged inventory to company from whom A-1 made the cash purchase on August 19, receiving cash of $850.
31	Purchased inventory on credit terms of 1/10 n/30 from Suncrest Supply, $8,330.
31	Issued check no. 689 to Lester Mednick, owner of the business, for personal withdrawal, $1,700.

continued. . .

Requirements

1. Open these four-column accounts with their account numbers and July 31 balances in the various ledgers. (p. 80)

GENERAL LEDGER

101	Cash	$ 4,490	
102	Accounts Receivable	22,560	
105	Inventory	41,800	
109	Supplies	1,340	
117	Prepaid Insurance	2,200	
160	Furniture	37,270	
161	Accumulated Depreciation		$10,550
201	Accounts Payable		12,600
204	Salary Payable		1,250
208	Unearned Sales Revenue		
220	Note Payable, Long-term		31,000
301	Lester Mednick, Capital		54,260
302	Lester Mednick, Withdrawals		
400	Income Summary		
401	Sales Revenue		
402	Sales Discounts		
403	Sales Returns and Allowances		
501	Cost of Goods Sold		
510	Salary Expense		
513	Rent Expense		
514	Depreciation Expense		
516	Insurance Expense		
519	Supplies Expense		

Accounts Receivable Subsidiary Ledger: Fullam Company $2,200; R. T. Loeb, $0; Park-Hee, Inc., $11,590; K. D. Skipper, $8,770. (pp. 80, 362)

Accounts Payable Subsidiary Ledger: Beaver Corporation, $0; Federal Company, $12,600; Grant, Inc., $0; Suncrest Supply, $0. (pp. 80, 362)

2. Journalize the August transactions in a series of special journals: a sales journal (page 4), a cash receipts journal (page 11), a purchases journal (page 8), a cash payments journal (page 5), and a general journal (page 9). A-1 makes all credit sales on terms of 2/10 n/30. (pp. 361–371)

3. Post daily to the accounts receivable subsidiary ledger and the accounts payable subsidiary ledger. On August 31, post to the general ledger. (pp. 361–371)

4. If required by your instructor, prepare a trial balance in the Trial Balance columns of a work sheet, and use the following information to complete the work sheet for the month ended August 31: (p. 279)

continued...

a. Supplies on hand, $990.

b. Prepaid insurance expired, $550.

c. Depreciation expense, $230.

d. Accrued salary expense, $1,030.

e. Unearned sales revenue, $450.*

f. Inventory on hand, $46,700.

5. Journalize and post the adjusting and closing entries. (pp. 141–142, 268)

---

*At August 31, $450 of unearned sales revenue needs to be recorded as a credit to Unearned Sales Revenue. Debit Sales Revenue. Also, the cost of this merchandise ($142) needs to be debited to Inventory and credited to Cost of Goods Sold.

8 Internal Control and Cash

Learning Objectives

1. Define internal control

2. Describe good internal control procedures

3. Prepare a bank reconciliation and the related journal entries

4. Apply internal controls to cash receipts

5. Apply internal controls to cash payments

6. Make ethical business judgments

n the preceding chapter your business, In Motion, imprinted logos on T-shirts for groups around your campus. Operating out of your apartment, the business has been successful. Last year sales totaled $100,000, and your net income was $25,000. Not bad for a college student.

Suppose you are graduating and you want to expand the business. A college buddy wants into the action and has agreed to join In Motion. He can sell T-shirts around neighboring colleges and also help with the handling and delivery of inventory. In addition, he made an A in ACC 110, so you'll let him do the accounting.

With boxes of T-shirts crammed into every corner, your apartment is a bit cozy. You will need to rent warehouse space or possibly buy a building. Expansion will bring a new set of challenges:

- How will you safeguard In Motion's assets?
- How will you ensure that your friend follows policies that are best for the business?

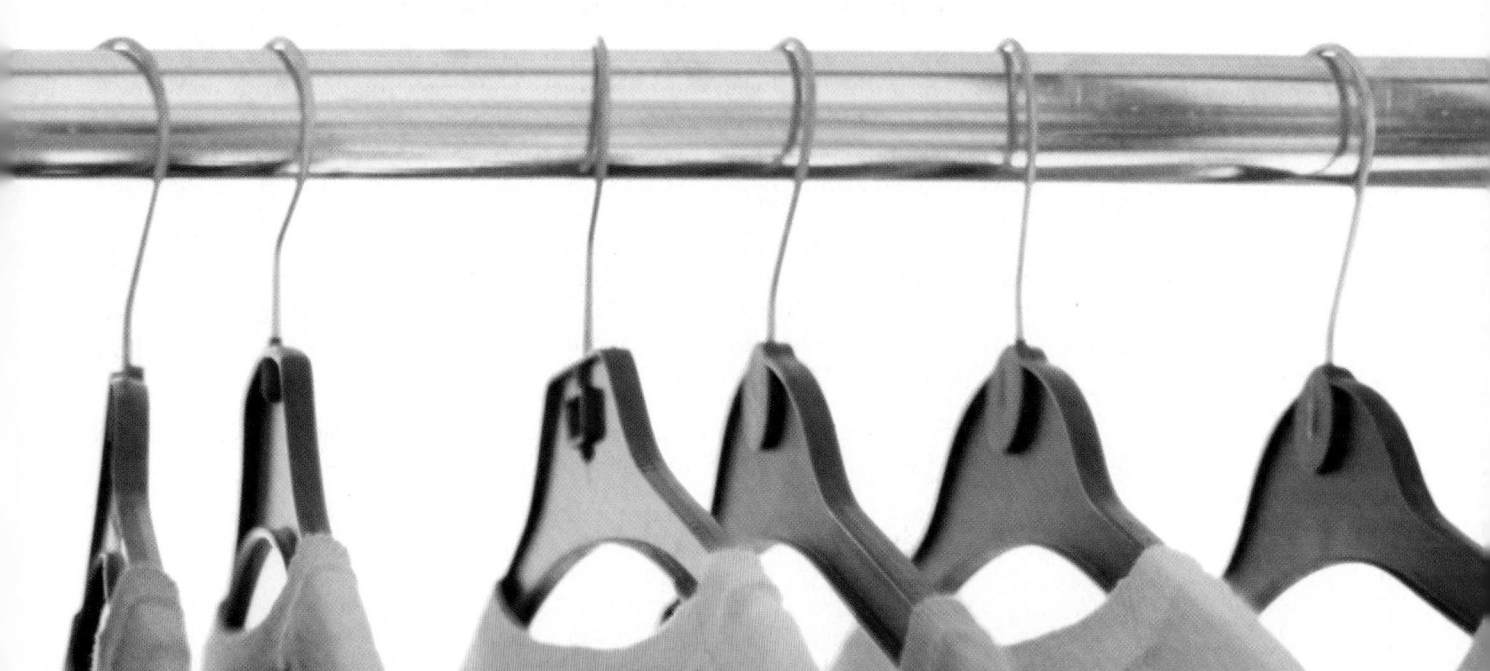

Thic chapter presents a framework for dealing with these issues. It also shows how to account for cash, the most liquid of all assets.

Internal Control

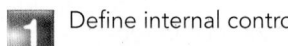 Define internal control

A key responsibility of a business owner is to control operations. Owners set goals, they hire managers to lead the way, and employees carry out the plan. **Internal control** is the organizational plan and all the related measures designed to:

1. **Safeguard assets.** A company must safeguard its assets; otherwise it's throwing away resources. If you fail to safeguard your cash, it will slip away.

2. **Encourage employees to follow company policy.** Everyone in an organization needs to work toward the same goal. With a friend operating part of In Motion, it's important for both of you to pursue the same goal. It's also important for you to develop policies so that you treat all customers similarly.

3. **Promote operational efficiency.** You cannot afford to waste resources. You work hard to make a sale, and you don't want to waste any of the benefits. If you can buy a T-shirt for $3, why pay $3.50? Eliminate waste, and increase your profits.

4. **Ensure accurate, reliable accounting records.** Good records are essential. Without reliable records, you cannot tell which part of the business is profitable and which part needs improvement. You could be losing money on every T-shirt you sell—unless you keep good records for the cost of your products.

How critical are internal controls? They're so important that the U.S. Congress passed a law that requires public companies—those that sell their stock to the public—to maintain a system of internal controls.

The Sarbanes-Oxley Act (SOX)

The Enron and WorldCom accounting scandals rocked the United States. Enron overstated profits and went out of business almost overnight. WorldCom (now MCI) reported expenses as assets and overstated both profits and assets. The company is just now emerging from bankruptcy. Sadly, the same accounting firm, Arthur Andersen, had audited both companies' financial statements. Arthur Andersen then closed its doors.

As the scandals unfolded, many people asked, "How can these things happen? Where were the auditors?" To address public concern, Congress passed the Sarbanes-Oxley Act, abbreviated as SOX. SOX revamped corporate governance in the United States and affected the accounting profession. Here are some of the SOX provisions:

1. Public companies must issue an internal control report, and the outside auditor must evaluate the client's internal controls.

2. A new body, the Public Company Accounting Oversight Board, oversees the work of auditors of public companies.

3. Accounting firms may not both audit a public client and also provide certain consulting services for the same client.

4. Stiff penalties await violators—25 years in prison for securities fraud; 20 years for an executive making false sworn statements.

Recently, the former chief executive of WorldCom was convicted of securities fraud and sentenced to 25 years in prison. The top executives of Enron were also sent to prison. You can see that internal controls and related matters can have serious consequences.

Exhibit 8-1 diagrams the shield that internal controls provide for an organization. Protected by the wall, people do business securely. How does a business achieve good internal control? The next section identifies the components of internal control.

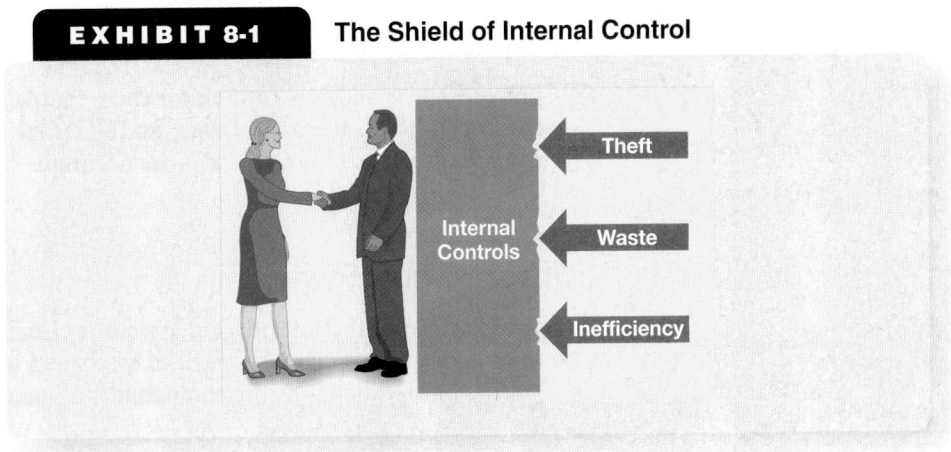

EXHIBIT 8-1   The Shield of Internal Control

The Components of Internal Control

A business can achieve its internal control objectives by applying five components:

- Control environment
- Risk assessment
- Control procedures
- Monitoring of controls
- Information system

Control Environment

The control environment is the "tone at the top" of the business. It starts with the owner and the top managers. They must behave honorably to set a good example for company employees. The owner must demonstrate the importance of internal controls if he or she expects the employees to take the controls seriously. Former executives of Enron, WorldCom, and Tyco failed to establish a good control environment and are in prison as a result.

Risk Assessment

A company must identify its risks. For example, Kraft Foods faces the risk that its food products may harm people. American Airlines planes may go down, and all companies face the risk of bankruptcy. Companies facing difficulties are tempted to falsify the financial statements to make themselves look better than they really are.

Control Procedures

These are the procedures designed to ensure that the business's goals are achieved. Examples include assigning responsibilities, separating duties, and using security devices to protect inventory from theft. The next section discusses internal control procedures.

Monitoring of Controls

Companies hire auditors to monitor their controls. Internal auditors monitor company controls to safeguard assets, and external auditors monitor the controls to ensure that the accounting records are accurate.

Information System

As we have seen, the information system is critical. The owner of a business needs accurate information to keep track of assets and measure profits and losses.

Exhibit 8-2 diagrams the components of internal control.

EXHIBIT 8-2   The Components of Internal Control

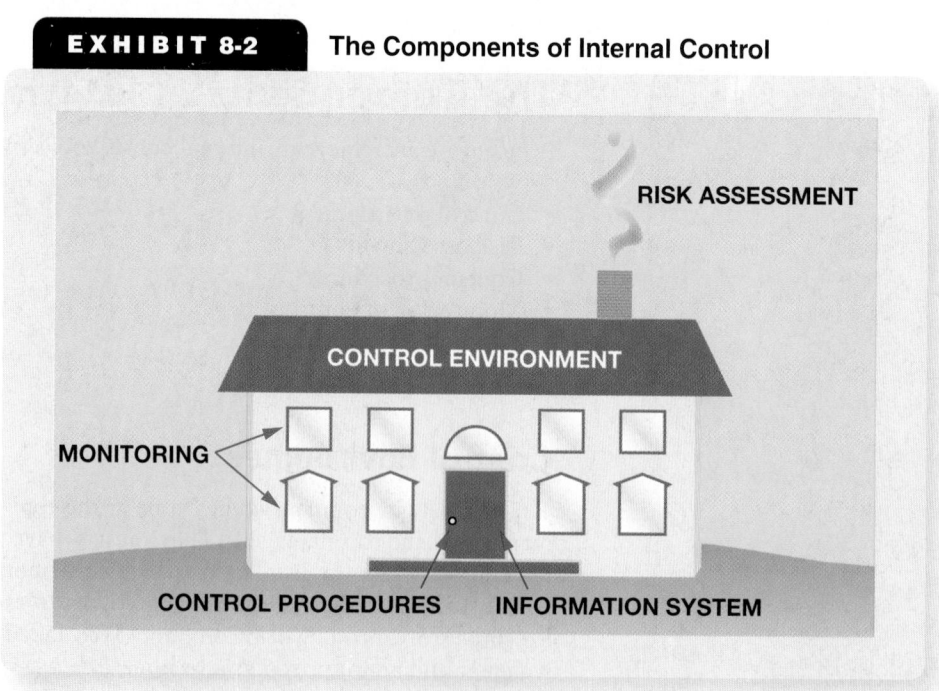

Internal Control Procedures

2 Describe good internal control procedures

Whether the business is In Motion (your T-shirt business), Microsoft, or an Exxon gas station, you need the following internal control procedures.

Competent, Reliable, and Ethical Personnel

Employees should be *competent, reliable,* and *ethical.* Paying good salaries will attract high-quality employees. You also must train them to do the job and supervise their work. This will build a competent staff.

Assignment of Responsibilities

In a business with good internal controls, no important duty is overlooked. Each employee has certain responsibilities. At In Motion, you'll be the boss because you own the business. Suppose you write the checks in order to control cash payments. You may let your friend do the accounting. In a large company the person in charge of writing checks is called the **treasurer.** The chief accounting officer is called the **controller.** With clearly assigned responsibilities, all important jobs get done.

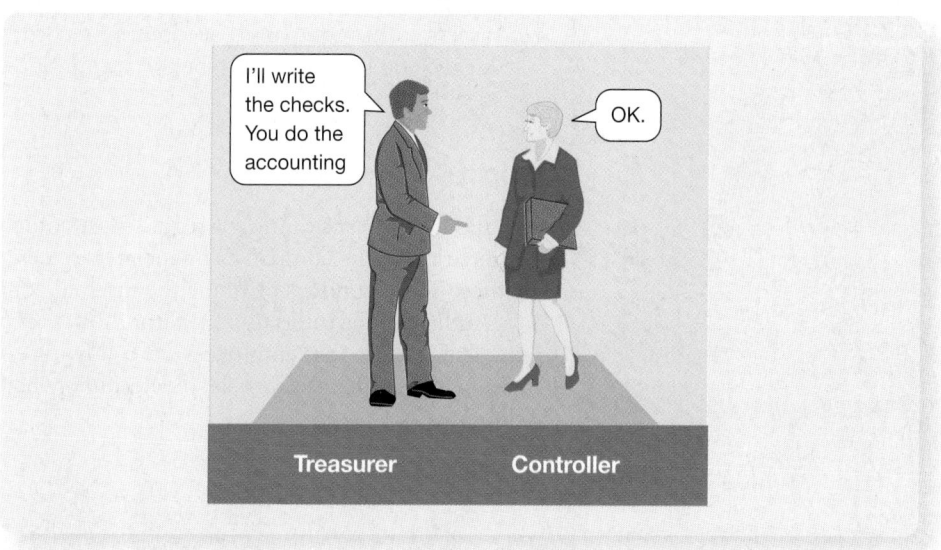

Separation of Duties

Smart management divides responsibility between two or more people. *Separation of duties* limits fraud and promotes the accuracy of the accounting records. Separation of duties can be divided into two parts:

1. **Separate operations from accounting.** Accounting should be completely separate from the operating departments, such as production and sales. What would happen if sales personnel recorded the company's revenue? Sales figures would be inflated, and top managers wouldn't know how much the company actually sold. This is why you should separate accounting and sales duties.

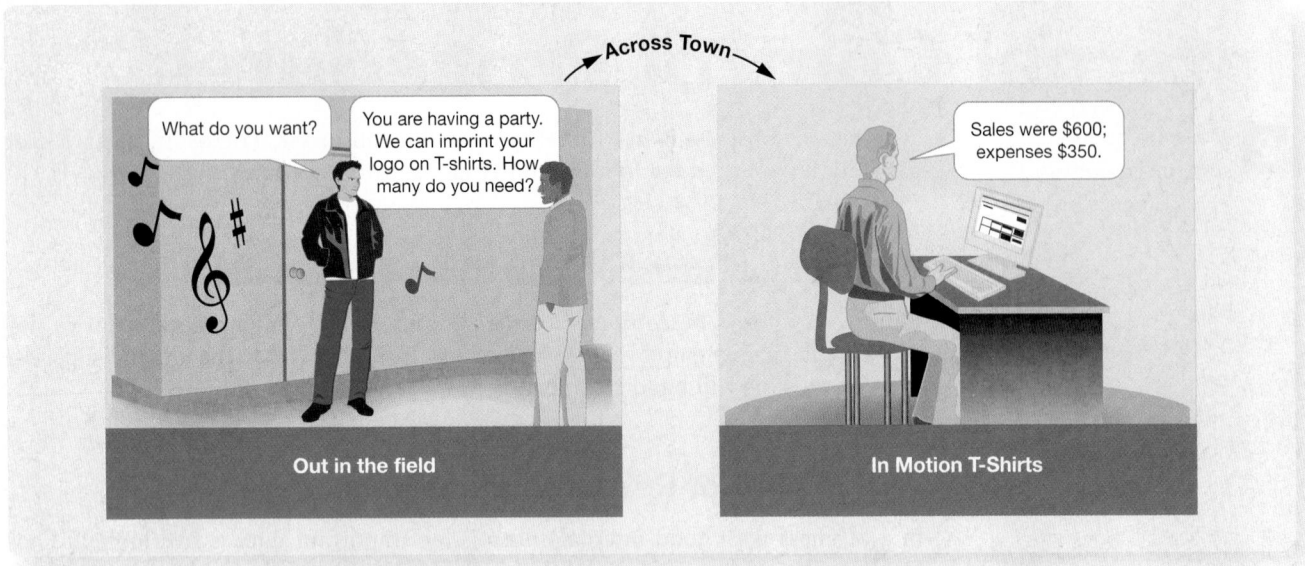

2. **Separate the custody of assets from accounting.** Accountants must not handle cash, and cashiers must not have access to the accounting records. If one employee has both duties, that person can steal cash and conceal the theft. The treasurer of a company handles cash, and the controller accounts for the cash. Neither person has both responsibilities. In an actual case, the cashier had access to his company's accounting records. With both duties, he was able to steal $600,000 and make bogus accounting entries to cover the theft.

Audits

To validate their accounting records, most companies have an audit. An **audit** is an examination of the company's financial statements and accounting system. To evaluate the system, auditors examine the internal controls.

Audits can be internal or external. *Internal auditors* are employees of the business. They ensure that employees are following company policies and operations are running efficiently. Auditors also determine whether the company is following legal requirements.

External auditors are completely independent of the business. They are hired to determine that the company's financial statements agree with generally accepted accounting principles. Auditors also suggest improvements that help the business run smoothly.

Documents

Documents provide the details of business transactions. Documents include invoices and fax orders. Documents should be prenumbered to prevent theft and inefficiency. A gap in the numbered sequence draws attention.

In a bowling alley a key document is the score sheet. The manager can compare the number of games scored with the amount of cash received. Multiply the number of games by the charge per game and compare the revenue with cash receipts. You can see whether the business is collecting all the revenue.

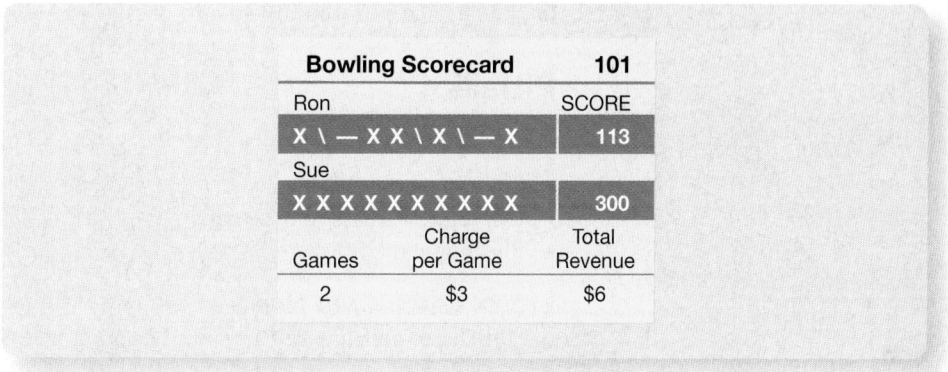

Electronic Devices

Accounting systems are relying less on documents and more on digital storage devices. For example, retailers such as Target Stores and Macy's control inventory by attaching an electronic sensor to merchandise. The cashier removes the sensor. If a customer tries to leave the store with the sensor attached, an alarm sounds. According to Checkpoint Systems, these devices reduce theft by as much as 50%.

Other Controls

Businesses keep important documents in *fireproof vaults*. *Burglar alarms* protect buildings, and *security cameras* protect other property. *Loss-prevention specialists* train employees to spot suspicious activity.

Employees who handle cash are in a tempting position. Many businesses purchase *fidelity bonds* on cashiers. The bond is an insurance policy that reimburses the company for any losses due to employee theft. Before issuing a fidelity bond, the insurance company investigates the employee's record.

Mandatory vacations and *job rotation* improve internal control. Companies move employees from job to job. This improves morale by giving employees a broad view of the business. Also, knowing someone else will do your job next month keeps you honest.

Internal Controls for E-Commerce

E-commerce creates its own risks. Hackers may gain access to confidential information such as account numbers and passwords.

Pitfalls

E-commerce pitfalls include:

- Stolen credit-card numbers
- Computer viruses and Trojans
- Phishing expeditions

STOLEN CREDIT-CARD NUMBERS   Suppose you buy CDs from EMusic.com. To make the purchase, your credit-card number must travel through cyberspace. Wireless networks (Wi-Fi) are creating new security hazards.

Amateur hacker Carlos Salgado, Jr., used his home computer to steal 100,000 credit-card numbers with a combined limit exceeding $1 billion. Salgado was caught when he tried to sell the numbers to an undercover FBI agent.

COMPUTER VIRUSES AND TROJANS   A **computer virus** is a malicious program that (a) enters program code without consent and (b) performs destructive actions. A **Trojan** hides inside a legitimate program and works like a virus. Viruses can destroy or alter data, make bogus calculations, and infect files. Most firms have found a virus in their system.

Suppose the U.S. Department of Defense takes bids for a missile system. Raytheon and Lockheed-Martin are competing for the contract. A hacker infects Raytheon's system and alters Raytheon's design. Then the government labels the Raytheon design as flawed and awards the contract to Lockheed.

PHISHING EXPEDITIONS   Thieves phish by creating bogus Web sites, such as AOL4Free.com. The neat-sounding Web site attracts lots of visitors, and the thieves obtain account numbers and passwords from unsuspecting people. They then use the data for illicit purposes.

Security Measures

To address the risks posed by e-commerce, companies have devised a number of security measures, including

- Encryption
- Firewalls

ENCRYPTION The server holding confidential information may not be secure. One technique for protecting customer data is encryption. **Encryption** rearranges messages by a mathematical process. The encrypted message can't be read by those who don't know the code. An accounting example uses check-sum digits for account numbers. Each account number has its last digit equal to the sum of the previous digits. For example, consider Customer Number 2237, where $2 + 2 + 3 = 7$. Any account number that fails this test triggers an error message.

FIREWALLS **Firewalls** limit access into a local network. Members can access the network but nonmembers can't. Usually several firewalls are built into the system. Think of a fortress with multiple walls protecting the king's chamber in the center. At the point of entry, passwords, PINs (personal identification numbers), and signatures are used. More sophisticated firewalls are used deeper in the network. Start with Firewall 3, and work toward the center.

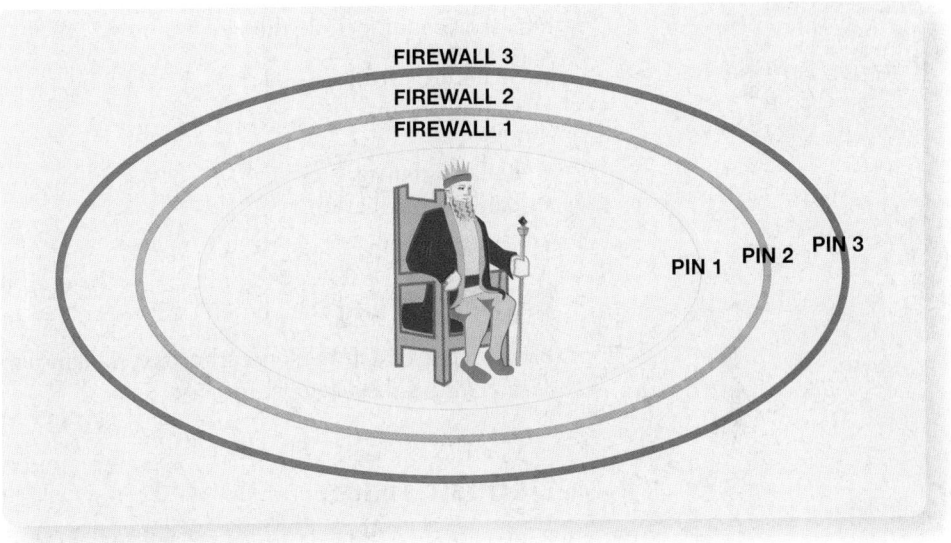

The Limitations of Internal Control— Costs and Benefits

Unfortunately, most internal controls can be overcome. Collusion—two or more people working together—can beat internal controls. Consider Galaxy Theater. Ralph and Lana can design a scheme in which Ralph sells tickets and pockets the cash from 10 customers. Lana, the ticket taker, admits 10 customers without tickets. Ralph and Lana split the cash. To prevent this situation, the manager must take additional steps, such as matching the number of people in the theater against the number of ticket stubs retained. But that takes time away from other duties.

The stricter the internal control system, the more it costs. A complex system of internal control can strangle the business with red tape. How tight should the controls be? Internal controls must be judged in light of their costs and benefits. An example of a good cost/benefit relationship: A security guard at a Wal-Mart store costs about $28,000 a year. On average, each guard prevents about $50,000 of theft. The net savings to Wal-Mart is $22,000.

The Bank Account as a Control Device

Cash is the most liquid asset because it's the medium of exchange. Cash is easy to conceal and relatively easy to steal. As a result, most businesses create specific controls for cash.

Keeping cash in a *bank account* helps control cash because banks have established practices for safeguarding customers' money. The documents used to control a bank account include the:

- Signature card
- Deposit ticket
- Check
- Bank statement
- Bank reconciliation

Signature Card

Banks require each person authorized to sign on an account to provide a *signature card*. This protects against forgery.

Deposit Ticket

Banks supply standard forms such as *deposit tickets*. The customer fills in the amount of each deposit. As proof of the transaction, the customer keeps a deposit receipt.

Check

To pay cash, the depositor writes a **check**, which tells the bank to pay the designated party a specified amount. There are three parties to a check:

- the *maker*, who signs the check
- the *payee*, to whom the check is paid
- the *bank* on which the check is drawn

Exhibit 8-3 shows a check drawn by In Motion T-Shirts, the maker. The check has two parts, the check itself and the *remittance advice* below. This optional attachment tells the payee the reason for the payment.

Bank Statement

Banks send monthly statements to customers. A **bank statement** reports what the bank did with the customer's cash. The statement shows the account's beginning and ending balances, cash receipts, and payments. Included with the statement are

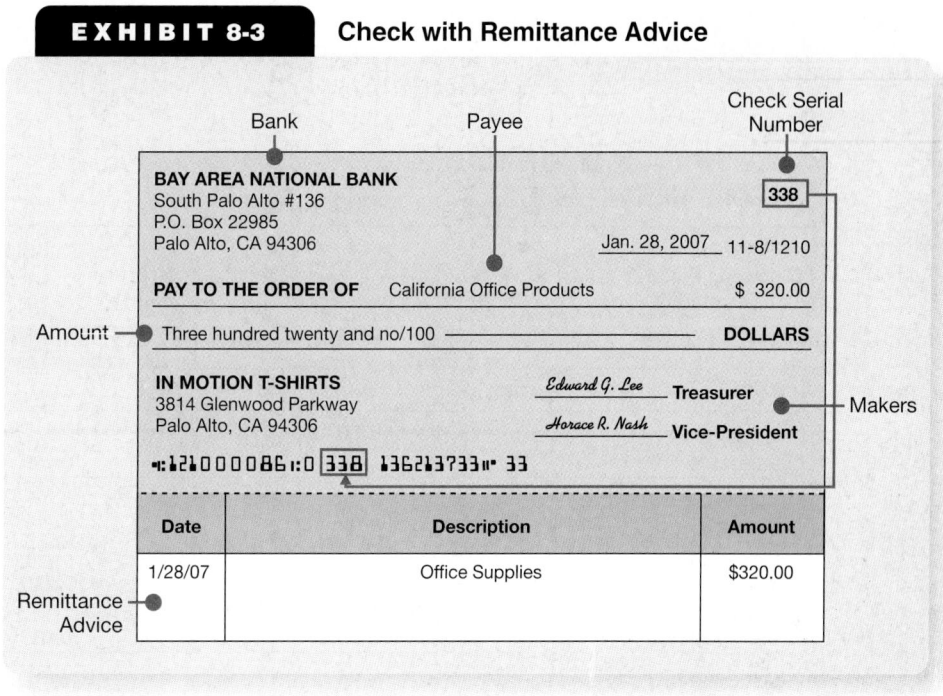

EXHIBIT 8-3 **Check with Remittance Advice**

copies of the maker's *canceled checks* (or the actual paid checks). Exhibit 8-4 is the January bank statement of In Motion T-shirts.

Electronic funds transfer (EFT) moves cash by electronic communication. It is cheaper to pay without having to mail a check, so many people pay their mortgage, rent, and insurance by EFT.

The Bank Reconciliation

There are two records of a business's cash:

1. The Cash account in the company's general ledger. Exhibit 8-5 (page 419) shows that In Motion's ending cash balance is $3,340.

2. The bank statement, which shows the cash receipts and payments transacted through the bank. In Exhibit 8-4 (page 418), the bank shows an ending balance of $5,900 for In Motion T-shirts.

The books and the bank statement usually show different cash balances. Differences arise because of a time lag in recording transactions—two examples:

- When you write a check, you immediately deduct it in your checkbook. But the bank does not subtract the check from your account until it pays the check—a few days later. Likewise, you immediately add the cash receipt for all your deposits. But it may take a day or two for the bank to add deposits to your balance.
- Your EFT payments and cash receipts are recorded by the bank before you learn of them.

To ensure accurate cash records, you need to update your checkbook—either online or after you receive your bank statement. The result of this updating process creates a **bank reconciliation**, which you must prepare. The bank reconciliation explains all differences between your cash records and your bank balance. The person who prepares the bank reconciliation should have no other cash duties. Otherwise, he or she can steal cash and manipulate the reconciliation to conceal the theft.

EXHIBIT 8-4   Bank Statement

BANK STATEMENT

BAY AREA NATIONAL BANK

SOUTH PALO ALTO #136 P.O. BOX 22985 PALO ALTO, CA 94306

In Motion T-Shirts
3814 Glenwood Parkway
Palo Alto, CA 94306

CHECKING ACCOUNT 136–213733

JANUARY 31, 2007

BEGINNING BALANCE	TOTAL DEPOSITS	TOTAL WITHDRAWALS	SERVICE CHARGES	ENDING BALANCE
6,550	4,370	5,000	20	5,900

TRANSACTIONS

DEPOSITS	DATE	AMOUNT
Deposit	01/04	1,150
Deposit	01/08	190
EFT—Collection of rent	01/17	900
Bank Collection	01/26	2,100
Interest	01/31	30

CHARGES	DATE	AMOUNT
Service Charge	01/31	20

CHECKS

Number	Amount	Number	Amount	Number	Amount
307	100	333	150	335	100
332	3,000	334	100	336	1,100

OTHER DEDUCTIONS	DATE	AMOUNT
NSF	01/04	50
EFT—Insurance	01/20	400

Preparing the Bank Reconciliation

 Prepare a bank reconciliation and the related journal entries

Here are the items that appear on a bank reconciliation. They all cause differences between the bank balance and the book balance. (We call your checkbook record the "Books.")

Bank Side of the Reconciliation

1. Items to show on the *Bank* side:
   a. **Deposits in transit** (outstanding deposits). You have recorded these deposits, but the bank has not. Add deposits in transit.
   b. **Outstanding checks**. You have recorded these checks, but the bank has not yet paid them. Subtract outstanding checks.
   c. **Bank errors**. Correct all bank errors on the Bank side of the reconciliation.

EXHIBIT 8-5 · Cash Records of In Motion T-Shirts

General Ledger:

ACCOUNT Cash

Date	Item	Debit	Credit	Balance
2007				
Jan. 1	Balance			6,550
2	Cash receipt	1,150		7,700
7	Cash receipt	190		7,890
31	Cash payments		6,150	1,740
31	Cash receipt	1,600		3,340

Cash Payments:

Check No.	Amount	Check No.	Amount
332	$3,000	337	$ 280
333	510	338	320
334	100	339	250
335	100	340	490
336	1,100	Total	$6,150

Book Side of the Reconciliation

2. Items to show on the *Book* side:
   a. **Bank collections.** Bank collections are cash receipts that the bank has recorded for your account. But you haven't recorded the cash receipt yet. Many businesses have their customers pay directly to their bank. This is called a *lock-box system* and reduces theft. An example is a bank's collecting a note receivable for you. Add bank collections.
   b. **Electronic funds transfers.** The bank may receive or pay cash on your behalf. An EFT may be a cash receipt or a cash payment. Add EFT receipts and subtract EFT payments.
   c. **Service charge.** This cash payment is the bank's fee for processing your transactions. Subtract service charges.
   d. **Interest revenue on your checking account.** You earn interest if you keep enough cash in your account. The bank statement tells you of this cash receipt. Add interest revenue.
   e. **Nonsufficient funds (NSF) checks** are your earlier cash receipts that have turned out to be worthless. NSF checks (sometimes called *hot checks*) are treated as cash payments on your bank reconciliation. Subtract NSF checks.
   f. **The cost of printed checks.** This cash payment is handled like a service charge. Subtract this cost.
   g. **Book errors.** Correct all book errors on the Book side of the reconciliation.

Bank Reconciliation Illustrated

The bank statement in Exhibit 8-4 shows that the January 31 bank balance of In Motion T-shirts is $5,900 (upper right corner). However, the company's Cash account has a balance of $3,340, as shown in Exhibit 8-5. This situation calls for a bank reconciliation. Exhibit 8-6, panel A, lists the reconciling items for your easy reference, and panel B shows the completed reconciliation.

EXHIBIT 8-6 Bank Reconciliation

PANEL A—Reconciling Items

Bank side:

1. Deposit in transit, $1,600.
2. Bank error: The bank deducted $100 for a check written by another company. Add $100 to the bank balance.
3. Outstanding checks—total of $1,340.

Check No.	Amount
337	$280
338	320
339	250
340	490

Book side:

4. EFT receipt of your rent revenue, $900.
5. Bank collection of your note receivable, $2,100.
6. Interest revenue earned on your bank balance, $30.
7. Book error: You recorded check no. 333 for $510. The amount you actually paid Brown Company on account was $150. Add $360 to your book balance.
8. Bank service charge, $20.
9. NSF check from L. Ross, $50. Subtract $50 from your book balance.
10. EFT payment of insurance expense, $400.

PANEL B—Bank Reconciliation

IN MOTION T-SHIRTS
Bank Reconciliation
January 31, 2007

Bank			Books		
Balance, January 31		$5,900	Balance, January 31		$3,340
Add:			Add:		
1. Deposit in transit		1,600	4. EFT receipt of rent revenue		900
2. Correction of bank error		100	5. Bank collection of note		
		7,600	receivable		2,100
			6. Interest revenue earned on		
			bank balance		30
			7. Correction of book error—		
			overstated our check no. 333		360
Less:					6,730
3. Outstanding checks					
No. 337	$280		Less:		
No. 338	320		8. Service charge	$ 20	
No. 339	250		9. NSF check	50	
No. 340	490	(1,340)	10. EFT payment of insurance expense	400	(470)
Adjusted bank balance		$6,260	Adjusted bank balance		$6,260

These amounts should agree.

SUMMARY OF THE VARIOUS RECONCILING ITEMS:

BANK BALANCE—ALWAYS

- *Add* deposits in transit.
- *Subtract* outstanding checks.
- *Add* or *subtract* corrections of bank errors.

BOOK BALANCE—ALWAYS

- *Add* bank collections, interest revenue, and EFT receipts.
- *Subtract* service charges, NSF checks, and EFT payments.
- *Add* or *subtract* corrections of book errors.

Journalizing Transactions from the Reconciliation

The bank reconciliation is an accountant's tool separate from the journals and ledgers. It does *not* account for transactions in the journal. To get the transactions into the accounts, we must make journal entries and post to the ledger. All items on the Book side of the bank reconciliation require journal entries.

The bank reconciliation in Exhibit 8-6 requires In Motion to make journal entries to bring the Cash account up-to-date. Numbers in parentheses correspond to the reconciling items listed in Exhibit 8-6, Panel A.

4.	Jan. 31	Cash	900	
		Rent Revenue		900
		Receipt of monthly rent.		
5.	31	Cash	2,100	
		Notes Receivable		2,100
		Note receivable collected by bank.		
6.	31	Cash	30	
		Interest Revenue		30
		Interest earned on bank balance.		
7.	31	Cash	360	
		Accounts Payable—Brown Co.		360
		Correction of check no. 333.		
8.	31	Miscellaneous Expense[1]	20	
		Cash		20
		Bank service charge.		
9.	31	Accounts Receivable—L. Ross	50	
		Cash		50
		NSF check returned by bank.		
10.	31	Insurance Expense		
		Cash	400	
		Payment of monthly insurance.		400

[1]Miscellaneous Expense is debited for the bank service charge because the service charge pertains to no particular expense category.

The entry for the NSF check (entry 9) needs explanation. Upon learning that L. Ross's $50 check to us was not good, we must credit Cash to update the Cash account. Unfortunately, we still have a receivable from Ross, so we must debit Accounts Receivable—L. Ross to reinstate our receivable from Ross.

Online Banking

Online banking allows you to pay bills and view your account electronically. You don't have to wait until the end of the month to get a bank statement. With online banking you can reconcile transactions at any time and keep your account current whenever you wish. Exhibit 8-7 shows a page from the account history of Toni Anderson's bank account.

The account history—like a bank statement—lists deposits, checks, EFT payments, ATM withdrawals, and interest earned on your bank balance.

EXHIBIT 8-7 Online Banking—Account History (like a Bank Statement)

Account History for Toni Anderson Checking # 5401-632-9 as of Close of Business 07/27/2007

Account Details

Current Balance $4,136.08

Date ↓	Description	Withdrawals	Deposits	Balance
	Current Balance			**$4,136.08**
07/27/07	DEPOSIT		1,170.35	
07/26/07	28 DAYS-INTEREST		2.26	
07/25/07	Check #6131 View Image	443.83		
07/24/07	Check #6130 View Image	401.52		
07/23/07	EFT PYMT CINGULAR	61.15		
07/22/07	EFT PYMT CITICARD PAYMENT	3,172.85		
07/20/07	Check #6127 View Image	550.00		
07/19/07	Check #6122 View Image	50.00		
07/16/07	Check #6116 View Image	2,056.75		
07/15/07	Check #6123 View Image	830.00		
07/13/07	Check #6124 View Image	150.00		
07/11/07	ATM 4900 SANGER AVE	200.00		
07/09/07	Check #6119 View Image	30.00		
07/05/07	Check #6125 View Image	2,500.00		
07/04/07	ATM 4900 SANGER AVE	100.00		
07/01/07	DEPOSIT		9,026.37	

FDIC Each depositor insured to $100,000.00 FEDERAL DEPOSIT INSURANCE CORPORATION · EQUAL HOUSING LENDER · E-Mail

But the account history doesn't show your beginning balance, so you can't work from your beginning balance to your ending balance.

Summary Problem 1

The cash account of Baylor Associates at February 28, 2007, follows.

Cash

Feb. 1	Bal. 3,995	Feb. 3	400
6	800	12	3,100
15	1,800	19	1,100
23	1,100	25	500
28	2,400	27	900
Feb. 28	Bal. 4,095		

Baylor Associates received the bank statement on February 28, 2007 (negative amounts are in parentheses):

Bank Statement for February 2007

Beginning balance		$3,995
Deposits:		
Feb. 7	$ 800	
15	1,800	
24	1,100	3,700
Checks (total per day):		
Feb. 8	$ 400	
16	3,100	
23	1,100	(4,600)
Other items:		
Service charge		(10)
NSF check from M. E. Crown		(700)
Bank collection of note receivable for the company		1,000
EFT—monthly rent expense		(330)
Interest revenue earned on account balance		15
Ending balance		$3,070

Additional data:
Baylor deposits all cash receipts in the bank and makes all payments by check.

Requirements

1. Prepare the bank reconciliation of Baylor Associates at February 28, 2007.

2. Journalize the entries based on the bank reconciliation.

Solution

Requirement 1

<table>
<tr><td colspan="4" align="center">**BAYLOR ASSOCIATES**
Bank Reconciliation
February 28, 2007</td></tr>
<tr><td colspan="4">**Bank:**</td></tr>
<tr><td colspan="2">Balance, February 28, 2007</td><td></td><td>$3,070</td></tr>
<tr><td colspan="2">Add: Deposit of February 28 in transit</td><td></td><td>2,400</td></tr>
<tr><td colspan="2"></td><td></td><td>5,470</td></tr>
<tr><td colspan="2">Less: Outstanding checks issued on Feb. 25 ($500)</td><td></td><td></td></tr>
<tr><td colspan="2">and Feb. 27 ($900)</td><td></td><td>(1,400)</td></tr>
<tr><td colspan="2">Adjusted bank balance, February 28, 2007</td><td></td><td>$4,070</td></tr>
<tr><td colspan="4">**Books:**</td></tr>
<tr><td colspan="2">Balance, February 28, 2007</td><td></td><td>$4,095</td></tr>
<tr><td colspan="2">Add: Bank collection of note receivable</td><td></td><td>1,000</td></tr>
<tr><td colspan="2">Interest revenue earned on bank balance</td><td></td><td>15</td></tr>
<tr><td colspan="2"></td><td></td><td>5,110</td></tr>
<tr><td colspan="2">Less: Service charge</td><td>$ 10</td><td></td></tr>
<tr><td colspan="2">NSF check</td><td>700</td><td></td></tr>
<tr><td colspan="2">EFT—Rent expense</td><td>330</td><td>(1,040)</td></tr>
<tr><td colspan="2">Adjusted book balance, February 28, 2007</td><td></td><td>$4,070</td></tr>
</table>

Requirement 2

Feb. 28	Cash	1,000	
	Note Receivable		1,000
	Note receivable collected by bank.		
28	Cash	15	
	Interest Revenue		15
	Interest earned on bank balance.		
28	Miscellaneous Expense	10	
	Cash		10
	Bank service charge.		
28	Accounts Receivable—M. E. Crown	700	
	Cash		700
	NSF check returned by bank.		
28	Rent Expense	330	
	Cash		330
	Monthly rent expense.		

Internal Control over Cash Receipts

4 Apply internal controls to cash receipts

All cash receipts should be deposited for safekeeping in the bank—quickly. Companies receive cash over the counter and through the mail. Each source of cash has its own security measures.

Cash Receipts over the Counter

Exhibit 8-8 illustrates a cash receipt over the counter in a department store. The point-of-sale terminal (cash register) provides control over the cash receipts. Consider a Macy's store. For each transaction, Macy's issues a receipt to ensure that each sale is recorded. The cash drawer opens when the clerk enters a transaction, and the machine records it. At the end of the day, a manager proves the cash by comparing the cash in the drawer against the machine's record of sales. This step helps prevent theft by the clerk.

EXHIBIT 8-8 Cash Receipts over the Counter

At the end of the day—or several times a day if business is brisk—the cashier deposits the cash in the bank. The machine tape then goes to the accounting department for the journal entry to record sales revenue. These measures, coupled with oversight by a manager, discourage theft.

Cash Receipts by Mail

Many companies receive cash by mail. Exhibit 8-9 shows how companies control cash received by mail. All incoming mail is opened by a mailroom employee. The mailroom then sends all customer checks to the treasurer, who has the cashier deposit the money in the bank. The remittance advices go to the accounting department for journal entries to Cash and customer accounts. As a final step, the controller compares the following records for the day:

- Bank deposit amount from the treasurer
- Debit to Cash from the accounting department

The debit to Cash should equal the amount deposited in the bank. All cash receipts are safe in the bank, and the company books are up-to-date.

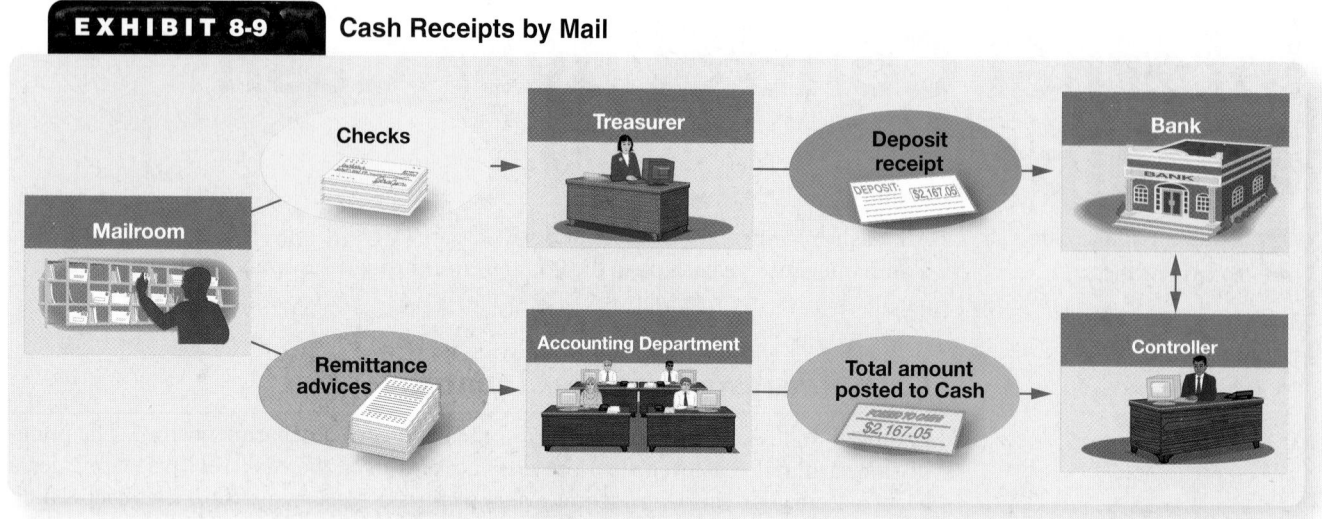

EXHIBIT 8-9 Cash Receipts by Mail

Many companies use a lock-box system. Customers send their checks directly to the company's bank account. Internal control is tight because company personnel never touch incoming cash. The lock-box system puts your cash to work immediately.

Internal Control over Cash Payments

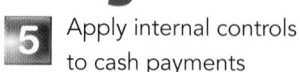 Apply internal controls to cash payments

Companies make most payments by check. They also pay small amounts from a petty cash fund. Let's begin with cash payments by check.

Controls over Payment by Check

As we have seen, you need a good separation of duties between operations and writing checks for cash payments. Payment by check is an important internal control, as follows:

- The check provides a record of the payment.
- The check must be signed by an authorized official.
- Before signing the check, the official should study the evidence supporting the payment.

Controls over Purchase and Payment

To illustrate the internal control over cash payments by check, suppose In Motion T-Shirts buys its inventory from Hanes Textiles. The purchasing and payment process follows these steps, as shown in Exhibit 8-10. Start with the box for In Motion T-Shirts on the left side.

1 In Motion faxes a *purchase order* to Hanes Textiles. In Motion says, "Please send us 100 T-shirts."

2 Hanes Textiles ships the goods and faxes an *invoice* back to In Motion. Hanes sent the goods.

EXHIBIT 8-10 Cash Payments by Check

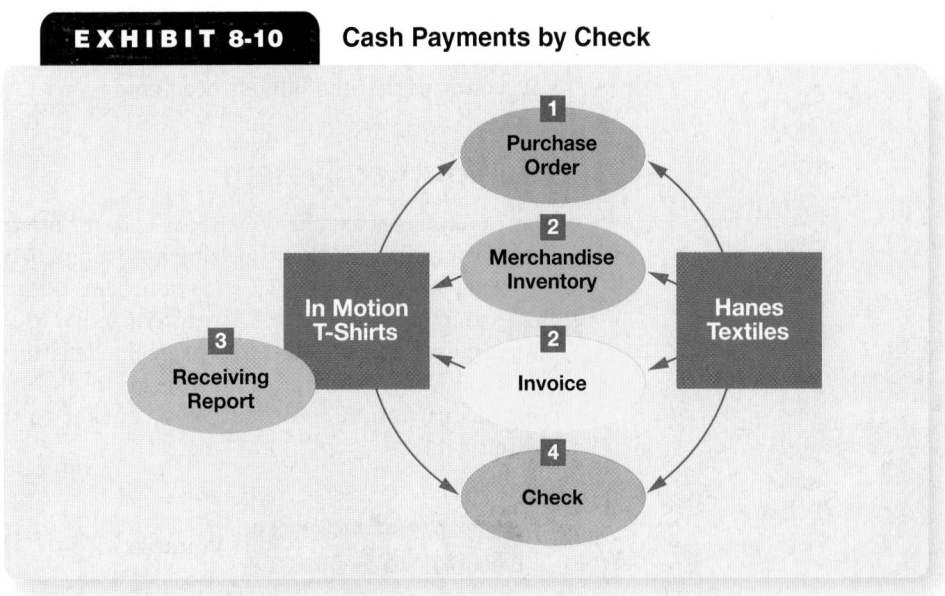

3 In Motion receives the *inventory* and prepares a *receiving report*. In Motion got its T-shirts.

4 After approving all documents, In Motion sends a *check* to Hanes. In Motion says, "Okay, we'll pay you."

For good internal control, the purchasing agent should neither receive the goods nor approve the payment. If these duties aren't separated, a purchasing agent can buy goods and have them shipped to his or her home. Or a purchasing agent can spend too much on purchases, approve the payment, and split the excess with the supplier.

Exhibit 8-11 shows In Motion's payment packet of documents. Before signing the check, the controller or the treasurer should examine the packet to prove that all the documents agree. Only then does the company know that:

1. It received the goods ordered.

2. It is paying only for the goods received.

EXHIBIT 8-11 Payment Packet

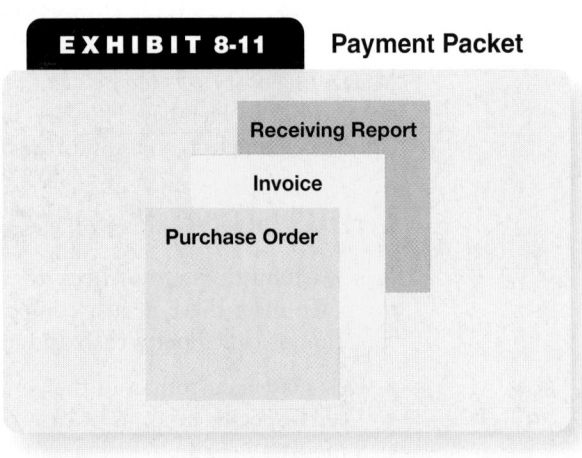

After payment, the check signer punches a hole through the payment packet. Dishonest people have been known to run a bill through twice for payment. This hole confirms that the bill has been paid.

The Voucher System

Many companies use the voucher system for internal control over cash payments. A **voucher** is a document authorizing a cash payment.

The voucher system uses (1) vouchers, (2) a voucher register (similar to a purchases journal), and (3) a check register (similar to a cash payments journal). All expenditures must be approved before payment. This approval takes the form of a voucher.

Exhibit 8-12 illustrates the voucher of In Motion T-Shirts. To enhance internal control, In Motion could add this voucher to the payment packet illustrated in Exhibit 8-11.

EXHIBIT 8-12   Voucher

VOUCHER
In Motion T-Shirts

Payee   Hanes Textiles

Due Date   March 7
Terms   2/10, n/30

Date	Invoice No.	Description	Amount
Mar. 1	620	100 T-shirts	$300

Approved	*Jane Trent*	Approved	*Bob Kraft*
	Controller		Treasurer

Streamlined Procedures

Technology is streamlining payment procedures. Evaluated Receipts Settlement (ERS) compresses the approval process into a single step: compare the receiving report to the purchase order. If those documents match, that proves In Motion got the T-shirts it ordered. Then In Motion pays Hanes Textiles, the supplier.

An even more streamlined process bypasses people and documents altogether. In Electronic Data Interchange (EDI), Wal-Mart's computers communicate directly with the computers of suppliers like Hanes Textiles and Hershey Foods. When Wal-Mart's inventory of Hershey candy reaches a low level, the computer sends a purchase order to Hershey. Hershey ships the candy and invoices Wal-Mart electronically. Then an electronic fund transfer (EFT) sends Wal-Mart's payment to Hershey.

Controlling Petty Cash Payments

It is wasteful to write a check for a taxi fare or the delivery of a package across town. To meet these needs, companies keep cash on hand to pay small amounts. This fund is called **petty cash** and needs controls such as the following:

- Designate a custodian of the petty cash fund.
- Keep a specific amount of cash on hand.
- Support all fund payments with a petty cash ticket.

Setting Up the Petty Cash Fund

The petty cash fund is opened when you write a check for the designated amount. Make the check payable to Petty Cash. On February 28, In Motion creates a petty cash fund of $200. The custodian cashes a $200 check and places the money in the fund. The journal entry is:

Feb. 28	Petty Cash	200	
	Cash in Bank		200
	To open the petty cash fund.		

For each petty cash payment, the custodian prepares a *petty cash ticket* like the one in Exhibit 8-13.

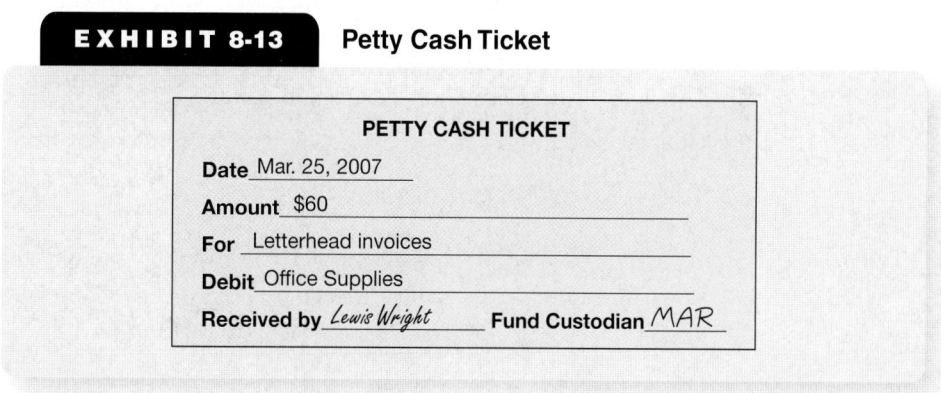

EXHIBIT 8-13   Petty Cash Ticket

> **PETTY CASH TICKET**
>
> Date_Mar. 25, 2007_
>
> Amount_$60_
>
> For _Letterhead invoices_
>
> Debit _Office Supplies_
>
> Received by _Lewis Wright_   Fund Custodian _MAR_

Signatures (or initials) identify the recipient of the cash and the fund custodian. The custodian keeps the petty cash tickets in the fund. The sum of the cash plus the total of the tickets should equal the fund balance ($200) at all times.

Maintaining the Petty Cash account at its designated balance is the nature of an **imprest system**. This clearly identifies the amount of cash for which the custodian is responsible, and that is the system's main internal control feature. Payments deplete the fund, so periodically it must be replenished.

Replenishing the Petty Cash Fund

On March 31 the petty cash fund holds

- $118 in petty cash
- $80 in petty cash tickets

You can see that $2 is missing:

Fund balance	$200
Cash on hand......................................	$118
Petty cash tickets.................................	80
Total accounted for..............................	$198
Amount of cash missing.......................	$ 2

To replenish the petty cash fund, you need to bring the cash on hand up to $200. The company writes a check, payable to Petty Cash, for $82 ($200 − $118). The fund custodian cashes this check and puts $82 back in the fund. Now the fund holds $200 cash as it should.

The petty cash tickets tell you what to debit, as shown in the entry to replenish the fund (items assumed for this illustration):

Mar. 31	Office Supplies	60	
	Delivery Expense	20	
	Cash Short and Over	2	
	Cash in Bank		82
	To replenish the petty cash fund.		

In this case, you lost $2. Losses are debited to a new account, Cash Short & Over.

At times the sum of cash in the petty cash fund ($118) plus the tickets ($90) may exceed the fund balance ($200). That situation creates a gain, which is credited to Cash Short & Over, as follows (using assumed amounts):

Mar. 31	Office Supplies	60	
	Delivery Expense	30	
	Cash		82
	Cash Short and Over		8
	To replenish the petty cash fund.		

Over time the Cash Short & Over account should net out to a zero balance. If not, you need to find a new petty cash custodian.

The Petty Cash account keeps its $200 balance at all times. Petty Cash is debited only when the fund is started (see the February 28 entry) or when its amount is changed. If the business raises the fund amount from $200 to $250, this would require a $50 debit to Petty Cash.

Reporting Cash on the Balance Sheet

Cash is the first asset listed on the balance sheet because it's the most liquid asset. Businesses often have many bank accounts and several petty cash funds. But they combine all cash amounts into a single total called "Cash and Cash Equivalents" for reporting on the balance sheet.

Cash equivalents include liquid assets such as time deposits, which are interest-bearing accounts that can be withdrawn with no penalty. Time deposits are sufficiently liquid to be reported along with cash. The balance sheet of In Motion T-Shirts reported the following current assets:

IN MOTION T-SHIRTS Balance Sheet December 31, 2008	
Assets	
Current assets:	
Cash and cash equivalents	$ 800
Short-term investments	1,000
Accounts receivable	2,000
Inventories	3,200
Prepaid insurance	400
Total current assets	$7,400

In Motion's cash balance means that In Motion has $800 available for immediate use. Cash that is restricted should not be reported as a current asset. For example, the bank may require you to keep a *compensating balance* on deposit in order to borrow from the bank. The compensating balance is not included in the cash amount on the balance sheet because it's not available for immediate use.

Ethics and Accounting

6 Make ethical business judgments

Roger Smith, the former chairman of General Motors, said, "Ethical practice is [. . .] good business." Smith knows that unethical behavior doesn't work. Sooner or later it comes back to haunt you. Moreover, ethical behavior wins out in the long run because it is the right thing to do.

Corporate and Professional Codes of Ethics

Most companies have a code of ethics to encourage employees to behave ethically. But codes of ethics are not enough by themselves. Owners and managers must set a high ethical tone, as we saw in the section on Control Environment. The owner must make it clear that the company will not tolerate unethical conduct.

As professionals, accountants are expected to maintain higher standards than society in general. Their ability to do business depends entirely on their reputation. Most independent accountants are members of the American Institute of Certified Public Accountants and must abide by the *AICPA Code of Professional Conduct*. Accountants who are members of the Institute of Management Accountants are bound by the *Standards of Ethical Conduct for Management Accountants*.

Ethical Issues in Accounting

In many situations, the ethical choice is easy. For example, stealing cash is both unethical and illegal. In other cases, the choices are more difficult. But in every instance, ethical judgments boil down to a personal decision: What should I do in a given situation? Let's consider three ethical issues in accounting.

Situation 1

Grant Busby is preparing the income tax return of a client who has earned more income than expected. On January 2, the client pays for advertising and asks Busby to backdate the expense to the preceding year. Backdating the deduction would lower the client's immediate tax payments. After all, there is a difference of only two days between January 2 and December 31. This client is important to Busby. What should he do?

> Busby should refuse the request because the transaction took place in January of the new year.

What control device could prove that Busby behaved unethically if he backdated the transaction in the accounting records? An IRS audit could prove that the expense occurred in January rather than in December. Falsifying IRS documents is both unethical and illegal.

Situation 2

Diane Scott's software company owes $40,000 to Bank of America. The loan agreement requires Scott's company to maintain a current ratio (current assets divided by current liabilities) of 1.50 or higher. At present, the company's current ratio is 1.40. At this level, Scott is in violation of her loan agreement. She can increase the current ratio to 1.53 by paying off some current liabilities right before year-end. Is it ethical to do so?

> Yes, because the action is a real business transaction.

Scott should be aware that paying off the liabilities is only a delaying tactic. It will hold off the bank for now, but the business must improve in order to keep from violating the agreement in the future.

Situation 3

David Duncan, the lead auditor of Enron Corporation, thinks Enron may be understating the liabilities on its balance sheet. Enron's transactions are very complex, and outsiders may never figure this out. Duncan asks his firm's Standards Committee how he should handle the situation. They reply, "Require Enron to report all its liabilities." Enron is Duncan's most important client, and Enron is pressuring him to certify the liabilities. Duncan can rationalize that Enron's reported amounts are okay. What should Duncan do? To make his decision, Duncan could follow the framework outlined in the following Decision Guidelines feature.

Decision Guidelines

Weighing tough ethical judgments requires a decision framework. Answering these four questions will guide you through tough decisions. Let's apply them to David Duncan's situation.

Question

1. What is the ethical issue?

2. What are Duncan's options?

3. What are the possible consequences?

4. What shall I do?

Decision Guidelines

1. *Identify the ethical issue.* The root word of ethical is *ethics,* which Webster's dictionary defines as "the discipline dealing with what is good and bad and with moral duty and obligation." Duncan's ethical dilemma is to decide what he should do with the information he has uncovered.
2. *Specify the alternatives.* For David Duncan, the alternatives include (a) go along with Enron's liabilities as reported or (b) force Enron to report higher amounts of liabilities.
3. *Assess the possible outcomes.*
   a. If Duncan certifies Enron's present level of liabilities—and if no one ever objects—Duncan will keep this valuable client. But if Enron's actual liabilities turn out to be higher than reported, Enron investors may lose money and take Duncan to court. That would damage his reputation as an auditor and hurt his firm.
   b. If Duncan follows his company policy, he must force Enron to increase its reported liabilities. That will anger the company, and Enron may fire Duncan as its auditor. In that case, Duncan will save his reputation, but it will cost him some business in the short run.
4. *Make the decision.* In the end Duncan went along with Enron and certified the company's liabilities. He went directly against his firm's policies. Enron later admitted understating its liabilities, Duncan had to retract his audit opinion, and Duncan's firm, Arthur Andersen, collapsed quickly. Duncan should have followed company policy. Rarely is one person smarter than a team of experts. Duncan got out from under his firm's umbrella of protection, and it cost him and many others dearly.

Summary Problem 2

Abbey Company established a $300 petty cash fund. James C. Brown (JCB) is the fund custodian. At the end of the week, the petty cash fund contains the following:

a. Cash: $163   **b.** Petty cash tickets, as follows:

No.	Amount	Issued to	Signed by	Account Debited
44	$14	B. Jarvis	B. Jarvis and JCB	Office Supplies
45	39	S. Bell	S. Bell	Delivery Expense
47	43	R. Tate	R. Tate and JCB	—
48	33	L. Blair	L. Blair and JCB	Travel Expense

Requirements

1. Identify three internal control weaknesses revealed in the given data.

2. Prepare the general journal entries to record:
   a. Establishment of the petty cash fund.
   b. Replenishment of the fund. Assume that petty cash ticket no. 47 was issued for the purchase of office supplies.

3. What is the balance in the Petty Cash account immediately before replenishment? Immediately after replenishment?

Solution

Requirement 1
The three internal control weaknesses are

1. Petty cash ticket no. 46 is missing. There is no indication of what happened to this ticket. The company should investigate.

2. The petty cash custodian (JCB) did not sign petty cash ticket no. 45. This omission may have been an oversight on his part. However, it raises the question of whether he authorized the payment. Both the fund custodian and the recipient of cash should sign the ticket.

3. Petty cash ticket no. 47 does not indicate which account to debit. What did Tate do with the money, and what account should be debited? See 2b above.

Requirement 2
Petty cash journal entries:

a. Entry to establish the petty cash fund:

Petty Cash	300	
Cash in Bank		300

b. Entry to replenish the fund:

Office Supplies ($14 + $43)	57	
Delivery Expense	39	
Travel Expense	33	
Cash Short and Over	8	
Cash in Bank		137

Requirement 3
The balance in Petty Cash is *always* its specified balance, in this case $300.

Review *Internal Control and Cash*

Accounting Vocabulary

Audit
An examination of a company s financial statements and the accounting system.

Bank Collection
Collection of money by the bank on behalf of a depositor.

Bank Reconciliation
Document explaining the reasons for the difference between a depositor's cash records and the depositor's cash balance in its bank account.

Bank Statement
Document the bank uses to report what it did with the depositor's cash. Shows the bank account beginning and ending balance and lists the month's cash transactions conducted through the bank.

Check
Document that instructs a bank to pay the designated person or business a specified amount of money.

Computer Virus
A malicious program that (a) reproduces itself, (b) enters program code without consent, and (c) performs destructive actions.

Controller
The chief accounting officer of a company.

Deposit in Transit
A deposit recorded by the company but not yet by its bank.

Electronic Funds Transfer (EFT)
System that transfers cash by electronic communication rather than by paper documents.

Encryption
Rearranging plain-text messages by a mathematical process, the primary method of achieving confidentiality in e-commerce.

Firewalls
Devices that enable members of a local network to access the Internet but keep nonmembers out of the network.

Imprest System
A way to account for petty cash by maintaining a constant balance in the petty cash account, supported by the fund (cash plus payment tickets) totaling the same amount.

Internal Control
Organizational plan and all the related measures adopted by an entity to safeguard assets, encourage employees to follow company policy, promote operational efficiency, and ensure accurate and reliable accounting records.

Nonsufficient Funds (NSF) Check
A "hot" check; one for which the maker's bank account has insufficient money to pay the check.

Outstanding Check
A check issued by the company and recorded on its books but not yet paid by its bank.

Petty Cash
Fund containing a small amount of cash that is used to pay for minor expenditures.

Treasurer
In a large company, the person in charge of writing checks.

Trojan
A malicious program that hides inside a legitimate program and works like a virus.

Voucher
Instrument authorizing a cash payment.

Quick Check _____

1. Which of the following is not part of the definition of internal control?
   a. Safeguard assets
   b. Encourage employees to follow company policy
   c. Separation of duties
   d. Promote operational efficiency

2. Internal auditors focus on _____; external auditors are more concerned with _____. Fill in the blanks.
   a. cash receipts; cash payments
   b. e-commerce; fraud
   c. documents; records
   d. operations; financial statements

3. Darice Goodrich receives cash from customers. Her other assigned job is to post the collections to customer accounts receivable. Her company has weak
   a. Ethics
   b. Assignment of responsibilities
   c. Separation of duties
   d. Computer controls

4. Encryption
   a. Creates firewalls to protect data
   b. Cannot be broken by hackers
   c. Avoids the need for separation of duties
   d. Rearranges messages by a special process

5. The document that explains all differences between the company's cash records and the bank's figures is called a
   a. Bank statement
   b. Bank collection
   c. Bank reconciliation
   d. Electronic fund transfer

6. Which items appear on the Book side of a bank reconciliation?
   a. Outstanding checks
   b. Deposits in transit
   c. Both a and b
   d. None of the above

7. Which items appear on the Bank side of a bank reconciliation?
   a. Outstanding checks
   b. Deposits in transit
   c. Both a and b
   d. None of the above

8. Navarro Company's Cash account shows an ending balance of $770. The bank statement shows a $20 service charge and an NSF check for $100. A $250 deposit is in transit, and outstanding checks total $400. What is Navarro's adjusted cash balance?

   a. $530

   b. $650

   c. $680

   d. $1,050

9. After performing a bank reconciliation, we need to journalize

   a. All items on the Bank side of the reconciliation

   b. All items on the Book side of the reconciliation

   c. All items on the reconciliation

   d. No items from the reconciliation because the cash transactions need no adjustments.

10. Separation of duties is important for internal control of

   a. Cash receipts

   b. Cash payments

   c. Neither of the above

   d. Both a and b

   Answers are given after Apply Your Knowledge (p. 453).

Assess Your Progress

Short Exercises

Definition of internal control

S8-1 Internal controls are designed to safeguard assets, encourage employees to follow company policies, promote operational efficiency, and ensure accurate records. Which objective is most important? Which must the internal controls accomplish for the business to survive? Give your reason. (p. 408)

Applying the definition of internal control

S8-2 How does the Sarbanes-Oxley Act relate to internal controls? Be specific. (p. 408)

Characteristics of an effective system of internal control

S8-3 Explain in your own words why separation of duties is often described as the cornerstone of internal control for safeguarding assets. Describe what can happen if the same person has custody of an asset and also accounts for the asset. (pp. 411–412)

Characteristics of an effective system of internal control

S8-4 How do external auditors differ from internal auditors? How does an external audit differ from an internal audit? How are the two types of audits similar? (pp. 411–412)

Aspects of a bank reconciliation

S8-5 Answer the following questions about the bank reconciliation: (pp. 418–419, 421)

1. Is the bank reconciliation a journal, a ledger, an account, or a financial statement? If none of these, what is it? (pp. 418–419, 421)

2. What is the difference between a bank statement and a bank reconciliation?

Preparing a bank reconciliation

S8-6 The Cash account of Ranger Security Systems reported a balance of $2,480 at May 31. There were outstanding checks totaling $900 and a May 31 deposit in transit of $200. The bank statement, which came from Park Cities Bank, listed a May 31 balance of $3,800. Included in the bank balance was a collection of $630 on account from Kelly Brooks, a Ranger customer who pays the bank directly. The bank statement also shows a $20 service charge and $10 of interest revenue that Ranger earned on its bank balance. *Prepare Ranger's bank reconciliation at May 31.* (p. 420)

Recording transactions from a bank reconciliation

S8-7 After preparing Ranger Security Systems' bank reconciliation in Short Exercise 8-6, journalize the company's transactions that arise from the bank reconciliation. Date each transaction May 31, and include an explanation with each entry. (p. 421)

Control over cash receipts
4

S8-8 Diedre Chevis sells furniture for DuBois Furniture Company. Chevis is having financial problems and takes $500 that she received from a customer. She rang up the sale through the cash register. What will alert Betsy DuBois, the owner, that something is wrong? (p. 425)

Control over cash receipts by mail
4

S8-9 Review the internal controls over cash receipts by mail. Exactly what is accomplished by the final step in the process, performed by the controller? (p. 425)

**Internal control over
payments by check**

S8-10 A purchasing agent for Westgate Wireless receives the goods that he purchases and also approves payment for the goods. How could this purchasing agent cheat his company? How could Westgate avoid this internal control weakness? (p. 426)

Petty cash

S8-11 Record the following petty cash transactions of Lexite Laminated Surfaces in general journal form (explanations are not required): (p. 429)

April 1	Established a petty cash fund with a $200 balance.
30	The petty cash fund has $19 in cash and $187 in petty cash tickets that were issued to pay for Office Supplies ($117) and Entertainment Expense ($70). Replenished the fund with $181 of cash and recorded the expenses.

Making an ethical judgment

S8-12 Gwen O'Malley, an accountant for Ireland Limited, discovers that her supervisor, Blarney Stone, made several errors last year. Overall, the errors overstated the company's net income by 20%. It is not clear whether the errors were deliberate or accidental. What should O'Malley do? (p. 433)

Exercises

**Identifying and correcting
an internal control weakness**

E8-13 Lane & Goble Bookstore has a liberal return policy. A customer can return any product for a full refund within 30 days of purchase. When a customer returns merchandise, Lane & Goble policy specifies:

- Store clerk issues a prenumbered return slip and refunds cash from the cash register. Keep a copy of the return slip for review by the manager.
- Store clerk places the returned goods back on the shelf as soon as possible. Lane & Goble uses a perpetual inventory system.
  1. How can a dishonest store clerk steal from Lane & Goble? What part of company policy enables the store clerk to steal without getting caught? (pp. 411–412)
  2. How can Lane & Goble improve its internal controls to prevent this theft? (pp. 411–412)

**Identifying internal control
strengths and weaknesses**

E8-14 The following situations suggest a strength or a weakness in internal control. Identify each as *strength* or *weakness*, and give the reason for your answer.

  a. Top managers delegate all internal control procedures to the accounting department. (p. 410)
  b. The accounting department orders merchandise and approves invoices for payment. (pp. 411–412)
  c. Cash received over the counter is controlled by the sales clerk, who rings up the sale and places the cash in the register. The sales clerk matches the total recorded by the register to each day's cash sales. (p. 425)
  d. The officer who signs checks need not examine the payment packet because he is confident the amounts are correct. (p. 426)

E8-15 Identify the missing internal control procedure in the following situations. Consider each situation separately. Select from these characteristics:

- Assignment of responsibilities
- Separation of duties
- Audits
- Electronic controls
- Other controls (specify)

  a. While reviewing the records of Discount Pharmacy, you find that the same employee orders merchandise and approves invoices for payment. (pp. 411–412)

  b. Business is slow at Fun City Amusement Park on Tuesday, Wednesday, and Thursday nights. To reduce expenses, the owner decides not to use a ticket taker on those nights. The ticket seller (cashier) is told to keep the tickets as a record of the number sold. (pp. 411–412)

  c. The same trusted employee has served as cashier for 10 years. (p. 414)

  d. When business is brisk, Stop-n-Go deposits cash in the bank several times during the day. The manager at one store wants to reduce the time employees spend delivering cash to the bank, so he starts a new policy. Cash will build up over weekends, and the total will be deposited on Monday. (pp. 424–425)

  e. Grocery stores such as **Safeway** and **Meijer's** purchase most merchandise from a few suppliers. At another grocery store, the manager decides to reduce paperwork. He eliminates the requirement that the receiving department prepare a receiving report listing the goods actually received from the supplier. (p. 426–427)

Classifying bank reconciliation items

E8-16 The following items could appear on a bank reconciliation:

a. Outstanding checks

b. Deposits in transit

c. NSF check

d. Bank collection of our note receivable

e. Interest earned on bank balance

f. Service charge

g. Book error: We credited Cash for $200. The correct amount was $2,000

h. Bank error: The bank decreased our account for a check written by another customer

Requirements
Classify each item as (1) an addition to the book balance, (2) a subtraction from the book balance, (3) an addition to the bank balance, or (4) a subtraction from the bank balance. (p. 420)

Preparing a bank
reconciliation

3

E8-17 D. J. Hunter's checkbook lists the following:

Date	Check No.	Item	Check	Deposit	Balance
9/1					$ 525
4	622	Art Café	$ 19		506
9		Dividends received		$ 116	622
13	623	General Tire Co.	43		579
14	624	ExxonMobil	58		521
18	625	Cash	50		471
26	626	Woodway Baptist Church	75		396
28	627	Bent Tree Apartments	275		121
30		Paycheck		1,209	1,330

Hunter's September bank statement shows the following:

Balance			$525
Add: Deposits			116
Debit checks:	No.	Amount	
	622	$19	
	623	43	
	624	68*	
	625	50	(180)
Other charges:			
Printed checks		$18	
Service charge		12	(30)
Balance			$431

*This is the correct amount for check number 624.

Requirements

Prepare Hunter's bank reconciliation at September 30. How much cash does Hunter actually have on September 30? (p. 420)

Preparing a bank
reconciliation

3

E8-18 Fred Midas operates four bowling alleys. He just received the October 31 bank statement from City National Bank, and the statement shows an ending balance of $900. Listed on the statement are an EFT rent collection of $400, a service charge of $12, NSF checks totaling $74, and a $9 charge for printed checks. In reviewing his cash records, Midas identifies outstanding checks totaling $467 and a deposit in transit of $1,788. During October, he recorded a $290 check by debiting Salary Expense and crediting Cash for $29. Midas's Cash account shows an October 31 balance of $2,177. *Prepare the bank reconciliation at October 31.* (p. 420)

Making journal entries from
a bank reconciliation

3

E8-19 Using the data from Exercise 8-18, make the journal entries Midas should record on October 31. Include an explanation for each entry. (p. 421)

E8-20 Lynn Cavender owns Cavender's Boot City. She fears that a trusted employee has been stealing from the company. This employee receives cash from customers and also prepares the monthly bank reconciliation. To check up on the employee, Cavender prepares her own bank reconciliation, as follows. This reconciliation is both complete and accurate.

CAVENDER'S BOOT CITY
Bank Reconciliation
August 31, 2007

Bank			Books	
Balance, August 31	$ 1,500		Balance, August 31	$1,000
Add: Deposit in transit	400		Add: Bank collection	820
			Interest revenue	10
Less: Outstanding checks	(1,100)		Less: Service charge	(30)
Adjusted bank balance	$ 800		Adjusted book balance	$1,800

Which side of the reconciliation shows the true cash balance? What is Cavender's true cash balance? Does it appear that the employee has stolen from the company? If so, how much? Explain your answer. (p. 420)

E8-21 When you check out at a Target store, the cash register displays the amount of the sale. It also shows the cash received and any change returned to you. Suppose the register also produces a customer receipt but keeps no internal record of the transactions. At the end of the day, the clerk counts the cash in the register and gives it to the cashier for deposit in the company bank account.

Write a memo to the store manager. Identify the internal control weakness over cash receipts, and explain how the weakness gives an employee the opportunity to steal cash. State how to prevent such a theft. (p. 425)

E8-22 Joy's Dance Studio created a $200 imprest petty cash fund. During the month, the fund custodian authorized and signed petty cash tickets as follows:

Petty Cash Ticket No.	Item	Account Debited	Amount
1	Delivery of programs to customers	Delivery Expense	$22
2	Mail package	Postage Expense	42
3	Newsletter	Supplies Expense	34
4	Key to closet	Miscellaneous Expense	16
5	Computer diskettes	Supplies Expense	8

Requirements

Make the general journal entries to (a) create the petty cash fund and (b) record its replenishment. Cash in the fund totals $75, so $3 is missing. Include explanations. (pp. 429–431)

Control over petty cash

E8-23

1. Explain how an *imprest* petty cash system works. (p. 429)

2. Steppin' Out Night Club maintains an imprest petty cash fund of $100, which is under the control of Brenda Montague. At November 30, the fund holds $20 cash and petty cash tickets for office supplies, $60; and delivery expense, $25.

   Journalize (**a**) establishment of the petty cash fund on November 1 and (**b**) replenishment of the fund on November 30. (pp. 429–431)

3. Prepare a T-account for Petty Cash, and post to the account. What is Petty Cash's balance at all times? (pp. 430–431)

Evaluating the ethics of conduct by government legislators

E8-24 Members of the U.S. House of Representatives wrote a quarter million dollars of checks on the House bank without having the cash in their accounts. In effect, these representatives were borrowing money from each other on an interest-free, no-service-charge basis. The House closed its bank after these events were featured on FOX, CNN, ABC, and NBC.

Requirements

Suppose you are a new congressional representative from your state. Apply the ethical judgment framework outlined in the Decision Guidelines to decide whether you would intentionally write NSF checks through the House bank. (p. 433)

Problems (Group A)

Identifying the characteristics of an effective internal control system

P8-25A An employee of Kindler Orthopedics stole thousands of dollars from the company. Suppose Kindler has installed a new system of internal controls. As a consultant for Kindler Orthopedics, write a memo to the board of directors explaining how internal controls safeguard assets. (pp. 411–416)

Correcting internal control weaknesses

P8-26A Each of the following situations has an internal control weakness.

a. Rite-Way Applications sells accounting software. Recently, development of a new program stopped while the programmers redesigned Rite-Way's accounting system. Rite-Way's accountants could have performed this task. (p. 411)

b. Betty Grable has been your trusted employee for 30 years. She performs all cash-handling and accounting duties. Ms. Grable just purchased a new Lexus and a new home in an expensive suburb. As owner of the company you wonder how she can afford these luxuries because you pay her only $35,000 a year and she has no source of outside income.

c. Sanchez Hardwoods, a private company, falsified sales and inventory figures in order to get an important loan. The loan went through, but Sanchez later went bankrupt and couldn't repay the bank. (pp. 411–412)

d. The office supply company where Champs Sporting Goods purchases sales receipts recently notified Champs that its documents were not prenumbered. Alex Champ, the owner, replied that he never uses the receipt numbers. (p. 413)

e. Discount stores such as Target make most of their sales for cash, with the remainder in credit-card sales. To reduce expenses, one store manager ceases purchasing fidelity bonds on the cashiers. (p. 414)

continued . . .

Requirements

1. Identify the missing internal control characteristics in each situation.

2. Identify the possible problem caused by each control weakness.

3. Propose a solution to each internal control problem.

Preparing a bank
reconciliation

3

P8-27A The March cash records of Tru-Value Insurance follow.

	Cash Receipts (CR)		Cash Payments (CP)	
Date	Cash Debit	Check No.	Cash Credit	
Mar. 4	$2,716	1416	$ 8	
9	544	1417	775	
14	896	1418	88	
17	367	1419	126	
31	2,038	1420	970	
		1421	200	
		1422	2,267	

Tru-Value's Cash account shows a balance of $6,172 on March 31. On March 31, Tru-Value received the following bank statement.

Bank Statement for March

				$4,045
Beginning balance				
Deposits and other Credits:				
Mar. 1		EFT	$ 625	
5			2,716	
10			544	
15			896	
18			367	
31		BC	1,000	6,148
Checks and other Debits:				
Mar. 8		NSF	$ 441	
11 (check no. 1416)			8	
19		EFT	340	
22 (check no. 1417)			775	
29 (check no. 1418)			88	
31 (check no. 1419)			216	
31		SC	25	(1,893)
Ending balance				$8,300

Explanations: BC—bank collection; EFT—electronic funds transfer; NSF—nonsufficient funds checks; SC—service charge.

Additional data for the bank reconciliation:

a. The EFT deposit was a receipt of rent revenue. The EFT debit was payment of insurance expense.

b. The NSF check was received from a customer.

continued . . .

c. The $1,000 bank collection was for a note receivable.

d. The correct amount of check 1419 is $216. Tru-Value mistakenly recorded the check for $126.

Requirements

Prepare the bank reconciliation of Tru-Value Insurance at March 31, 2008. (p. 420)

Preparing a bank
reconciliation and the
related journal entries
3

P8-28A The May 31 bank statement of Multi-Plex Healthcare has just arrived from First State Bank. To prepare the bank reconciliation, you gather the following data.

a. The May 31 bank balance is $12,209.

b. The bank statement includes two charges for NSF checks from customers. One is for $67, and the other for $195.

c. The following Multi-Plex checks are outstanding at May 31:

Check No.	Amount
616	$405
802	74
806	36
809	161
810	229
811	48

d. Multi-Plex collects from a few customers by EFT. The May bank statement lists a $200 EFT deposit for a collection on account.

e. The bank statement includes two special deposits that Multi-Plex hasn't recorded yet: $900, for dividend revenue, and $16, the interest revenue Multi-Plex earned on its bank balance during May.

f. The bank statement lists a $7 subtraction for the bank service charge.

g. On May 31, the Multi-Plex treasurer deposited $381, but this deposit does not appear on the bank statement.

h. The bank statement includes a $410 deduction for a check drawn by Multi-State Freight Company. Multi-Plex notified the bank of this bank error.

i. Multi-Plex's Cash account shows a balance of $11,200 on May 31.

Requirements

1. Prepare the bank reconciliation for Multi-Plex Healthcare at May 31. (p. 420)

2. Record the entries called for by the reconciliation. Include an explanation for each entry. (p. 421)

Identifying internal control
weakness in cash receipts
4

P8-29A Pendley Productions makes all sales on credit. Cash receipts arrive by mail. Larry Padgitt in the mailroom opens envelopes and separates the checks from the accompanying remittance advices. Padgitt forwards the checks to another employee, who makes the daily bank deposit but has

continued . . .

no access to the accounting records. Padgitt sends the remittance advices, which show cash received, to the accounting department for entry in the accounts. Padgitt's only other duty is to grant sales allowances to customers. (A *sales allowance* decreases the amount receivable.) When Padgitt receives a customer check for less than the full amount of the invoice, he records the sales allowance and forwards the document to the accounting department.

Requirements

You are a new employee of Pendley Productions. Write a memo to Paulette Pendley, owner of the business, identifying the internal control weakness in this situation. State how to correct the weakness. (pp. 411–412, 425, 262–263)

Accounting for petty cash transactions

P8-30A On April 1, Caesar Salad Dressings creates a petty cash fund with an imprest balance of $400. During April, Elise Nelson, the fund custodian, signs the following petty cash tickets:

Petty Cash Ticket Number	Item	Amount
101	Office supplies	$86
102	Cab fare for executive	25
103	Delivery of package across town	37
104	Dinner money for city manager to entertain the mayor	80
105	Inventory	85

On April 30, prior to replenishment, the fund contains these tickets plus cash of $90. The accounts affected by petty cash payments are Office Supplies Expense, Travel Expense, Delivery Expense, Entertainment Expense, and Inventory.

Requirements

1. Explain the characteristics and the internal control features of an imprest fund. (p. 429)

2. On April 30, how much cash should the petty cash fund hold before it's replenished? (p. 429)

3. Make general journal entries to (a) create the fund and (b) replenish it. Include explanations. (pp. 429–431)

4. Make the May 1 entry to increase the fund balance to $500. Include an explanation, and briefly describe what the custodian does. (p. 429)

Making an ethical judgment

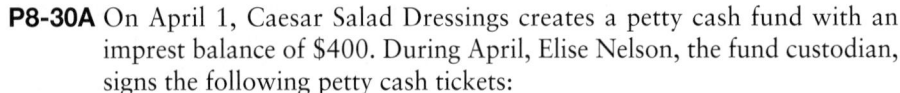

P8-31A Federal Credit Bank has a loan receivable from Subway Construction Company. Subway is late making payments to the bank, and Milton Reed, a Federal Credit Bank vice president, is helping Subway restructure its debt. Reed learns that Subway is depending on landing a contract from Starstruck Theater, another Federal Credit Bank client. Reed also serves as Starstruck's loan officer at the bank. In this capacity, he is aware that Starstruck is considering declaring bankruptcy. Reed has been

continued . . .

a great help to Subway, and Subway's owner is counting on him to carry the company through this difficult restructuring. To help the bank collect on this large loan, Reed has a strong motivation to help Subway survive.

Apply the ethical judgment framework from the chapter to help Reed plan his next action. (p. 433)

Problems (Group B)

Identifying the characteristics of an effective internal control system

P8-32B Sunburst Technology prospered during the recent economic expansion. Business was so good that the company used very few internal controls. A recent decline in the high-tech sector of the economy brought a cash shortage. Adam Klaus, the company owner, is looking for ways to save money.

As a consultant for Sunburst Technology, write a memo to convince Klaus of the company's need for a system of internal control. Be specific in explaining how an internal control system could save the company money. Include the definition of internal control, and briefly discuss the characteristics of an effective internal control system, beginning with competent, reliable, and ethical personnel. (pp. 408–416)

Correcting internal control weaknesses

P8-33B Each of the following situations has an internal control weakness.

a. Architects use paraprofessional employees to perform routine tasks. For example, a draftsman might prepare drawings to assist an architect. In the architecture firm of Lee & Dunham, Joseph Lee, the senior partner, turns over some of his high-level design work to less-qualified draftsmen. (p. 411)

b. Jim Alexander owns Central Forwarding, a storage company. His staff consists of 12 employees, and he manages the office. Often, Alexander's work requires him to travel. When he returns from business trips, the work in the office has not progressed much. In his absence, senior employees take over office management and neglect their regular duties. One employee could manage the office. (p. 411)

c. Aimee Atkins has worked for Michael Riggs, M.D., for many years. Atkins performs all accounting duties, including opening the mail, making the bank deposits, writing checks, and preparing the bank reconciliation. Riggs trusts Atkins completely. (pp. 411–412)

d. Computer programmers for Internet Solutions work under intense pressure. Facing tight deadlines, they sometimes bypass company policies and write programs without securing customer accounts receivable data. (pp. 414–416)

e. In evaluating internal control over cash payments, an auditor learns that the purchasing agent is responsible for purchasing diamonds for use in the company's manufacturing process. The purchasing agent also approves the invoices for payment and signs the checks. (p. 414)

Requirements

1. Identify the missing internal control characteristic in each situation.

2. Identify the possible problem caused by each control weakness.

3. Propose a solution to each internal control problem.

P8-34B The cash records of Dunlap Dollar Stores for April follow.

Cash Receipts (CR)		Cash Payments (CP)	
Date	Cash Debit	Check No.	Cash Credit
Apr. 2	$4,170	3113	$ 890
8	500	3114	140
10	550	3115	1,930
16	2,180	3116	660
22	1,850	3117	1,470
29	1,060	3118	1,000
30	330	3119	630
		3120	1,670
		3121	100
		3122	2,410

Dunlap's Cash account shows a balance of $13,640 at April 30.
On April 30, Dunlap received the following bank statement:

Bank Statement for April

Beginning balance			$13,900
Deposits and other Credits:			
Apr. 1	EFT	$ 300	
4		4,170	
9		500	
12		550	
17		2,180	
22	BC	1,300	
23		1,850	10,850
Checks and other Debits:			
Apr. 7 (check no. 3113)		$ 890	
13 (check no. 3115)		1,390	
14	NSF	900	
15 (check no. 3114)		140	
18 (check no. 3116)		660	
21	EFT	200	
26 (check no. 3117)		1,470	
30 (check no. 3118)		1,000	
30	SC	20	(6,670)
Ending balance			$18,080

Explanations: BC—bank collection; EFT—electronic funds transfer; NSF—nonsufficient funds checks; SC—service charge.

Additional data for the bank reconciliation:
a. The EFT deposit was a receipt of rent. The EFT debit was an insurance payment.
b. The NSF check was received from a customer.
c. The $1,300 bank collection was for a note receivable.
d. The correct amount of check number 3115 is $1,390. (Dunlap mistakenly recorded the check for $1,930.)

continued . . .

Preparing a bank reconciliation and the related journal entries

P8-35B The August 31 bank statement of Ward's Supercenter has just arrived from United Bank. To prepare the Ward's bank reconciliation, you gather the following data:

a. Ward's Cash account shows a balance of $2,420 on August 31.

b. The bank statement includes two NSF checks from customers: $395 and $147.

c. Ward's pays rent expense ($750) and insurance expense ($290) each month by EFT.

d. The Ward checks below are outstanding at August 31.

Check No.	Amount
237	$ 49
288	141
291	578
293	11
294	609
295	8
296	101

e. The bank statement includes a deposit of $1,200, collected on our note receivable by the bank.

f. The bank statement shows that Ward earned $18 of interest on its bank balance during August.

g. The bank statement lists a $10 bank service charge.

h. On August 31, Ward deposited $316, but this deposit does not appear on the bank statement.

i. The bank statement includes a $300 deposit that Ward did not make. The bank erroneously credited Ward's account for another customer's deposit.

j. The August 31 bank balance is $3,527.

Requirements

1. Prepare the bank reconciliation for Ward's Supercenter at August 31. (p. 420)

2. Record the journal entries that bring the book balance of Cash into agreement with the adjusted book balance on the reconciliation. Include an explanation for each entry. (p. 421)

Identifying internal control weakness in cash receipts

P8-36B Advanced Audio Productions makes all sales on account. Cash receipts arrive by mail. James Gilette opens envelopes and separates the checks from the accompanying remittance advices. Gilette forwards the checks to another employee, who makes the daily bank deposit but has no access to the accounting records. Gilette sends the remittance advices, which show the cash received, to the accounting department for entry in the accounts. Gilette's only other duty is to grant sales allowances to customers. (A *sales*

continued . . .

allowance decreases the amount receivable.) When he receives a customer check for less than the full amount of the invoice, he records the sales allowance and forwards the document to the accounting department.

Requirements

You are the new controller of Advanced Audio Productions. Write a memo to the company president identifying the internal control weakness in this situation. State how to correct the weakness. (pp. 411–412, 425, 262–263)

Accounting for petty cash transactions

P8-37B Suppose that on June 1, Cool Gyrations, a disc jockey service, creates a petty cash fund with an imprest balance of $300. During June, Carol McColgin, fund custodian, signs the following petty cash tickets:

Petty Cash Ticket Number	Item	Amount
1	Postage for package received	$18
2	Decorations and refreshments for office party	13
3	Two boxes of stationery	20
4	Printer cartridges	27
5	Dinner money for sales manager entertaining a customer	50

On June 30, prior to replenishment, the fund contains these tickets plus cash of $170. The accounts affected by petty cash payments are Office Supplies Expense, Entertainment Expense, and Postage Expense.

Requirements

1. Explain the characteristics and the internal control features of an imprest fund. (p. 429)

2. On June 30, how much cash should this petty cash fund hold before it's replenished? (p. 429)

3. Make general journal entries to (**a**) create the fund and (**b**) replenish it. Include explanations. (pp. 429–431)

4. Make the entry on July 1 to increase the fund balance to $350. Include an explanation, and briefly describe what the custodian does. (p. 429)

Making an ethical judgment

P8-38B Mike Schoenfeld is vice president of Lancer Bank in Shreveport, Louisiana. Active in community affairs, Schoenfeld serves on the board of directors of Baker Publishing Company. Baker is expanding and relocating its plant. At a recent meeting, board members decided to buy 15 acres of land on the edge of town. The owner of the property, Jack Fletcher, is a customer of Lancer Bank. Fletcher is completing a divorce, and Schoenfeld knows that Fletcher is eager to sell his property. In view of Fletcher's difficult situation, Schoenfeld believes Fletcher would accept almost any offer for the land. Realtors have appraised the property at $5 million.

Apply the ethical judgment framework from the Decision Guidelines (page 433) to help Schoenfeld decide what his role should be in Baker's attempt to buy the land from Fletcher.

for 24-7 practice, visit www.MyAccountingLab.com

Apply Your Knowledge

Decision Cases

Using internal controls

Case 1. Go to sarbox.org, the Web site for the Sarbanes-Oxley Act. Surf around for information on internal control, write a report of your findings, and present it to your class (if required by your instructor).

Correcting an internal control weakness

Case 2. This case is based on an actual situation. Centennial Construction Company, headquartered in Dallas, built a Rodeway Motel 35 miles north of Dallas. The construction foreman, whose name was Slim Chance, hired the 40 workers needed to complete the project. Slim had the construction workers fill out the necessary tax forms, and he sent their documents to the home office.

Work on the motel began on April 1 and ended September 1. Each week, Slim filled out a time card of hours worked by each employee during the week. Slim faxed the time sheets to the home office, which prepared the payroll checks on Friday morning. Slim drove to the home office on Friday, picked up the payroll checks, and returned to the construction site. At 5 P.M. on Friday, Slim distributed payroll checks to the workers.

a. Describe in detail the main internal control weakness in this situation. Specify what negative result(s) could occur because of the internal control weakness. (pp. 411–412, 426)

b. Describe what you would do to correct the internal control weakness. (pp. 411–412, 426)

Using the bank reconciliation to detect a theft

Case 3. San Diego Harbor Tours has poor internal control over cash. Ben Johnson, the owner, suspects the cashier of stealing. Here are some details of company cash at September 30.

a. The Cash account in the ledger shows a balance of $6,450.

b. The September 30 bank statement shows a balance of $4,300. The bank statement lists a $200 bank collection, a $10 service charge, and a $40 NSF check.

c. At September 30, the following checks are outstanding:

Amount
$100
300
600
200

d. There is a $3,000 deposit in transit at September 30.

e. The cashier handles all incoming cash and makes bank deposits. He also writes checks and reconciles the monthly bank statement.

Johnson asks you to determine whether the cashier has stolen cash from the business and, if so, how much. Perform your own bank reconciliation using the format illustrated in the chapter. There are no bank or book errors. Explain how Johnson can improve his internal controls. (pp. 420, 417)

Ethical Issue

Internal control over cash payments; ethical considerations

Mel O'Conner owns rental properties in Michigan. Each property has a manager who collects rent, arranges for repairs, and runs advertisements in the local newspaper. The property managers transfer cash to O'Conner monthly and prepare their own bank reconciliations. The manager in Lansing has been stealing from the company. To cover the theft, he understates the amount of the outstanding checks on the monthly bank reconciliation. As a result, each monthly bank reconciliation appears to balance. However, the balance sheet reports more cash than O'Conner actually has in the bank. In negotiating the sale of the Lansing property, O'Conner is showing the balance sheet to prospective investors.

Requirements

1. Identify two parties other than O'Conner who can be harmed by this theft. In what ways can they be harmed?

2. Discuss the role accounting plays in this situation.

Financial Statement Case

Internal controls and cash

Study the audit opinion (labeled Report of Ernst & Young LLP) of Amazon.com and the Amazon financial statements given in Appendix A at the end of this book. Answer the following questions about the company.

Requirements

1. What is the name of Amazon.com's outside auditing firm (independent registered public accounting firm)? What office of this firm signed the audit report? How long after the Amazon year-end did the auditors issue their opinion?

2. Who bears primary responsibility for the financial statements? How can you tell?

3. Does it appear that the Amazon internal controls are adequate? How can you tell?

4. What standard of auditing did the outside auditors use in examining the Amazon financial statements? By what accounting standards were the statements evaluated?

5. By how much did Amazon's cash balance (including cash equivalents) change during 2005? What were the beginning and ending cash balances?

Team Project

You are promoting a rock concert in your area. Each member of your team will invest $10,000 of their hard-earned money in this venture. It is April 1, and the concert is scheduled for June 30. Your promotional activities begin immediately, and ticket sales start on May 1. You expect to sell all the business's assets, pay all the liabilities, and distribute all remaining cash to the group members by July 31.

Requirements

Write an internal control manual that will help safeguard the assets of the business. The starting point of the manual is to assign responsibilities among the group members. Authorize individuals, including group members and any outsiders that you need to hire, to perform specific jobs. Separate duties among the group and any employees.

For Internet Exercises, Excel in Practice, and additional online activities, go to the Web site www.prenhall.com/horngren.

Quick Check Answers

1. *c*   2. *d*   3. *c*   4. *d*   5. *c*   6. *d*   7. *c*   8. *b*   9. *b*   10. *d*

9 Receivables

Learning Objectives

1 Design internal controls for receivables

2 Use the allowance method to account for uncollectibles

3 Understand the direct write-off method for uncollectibles

4 Account for notes receivable

5 Report receivables on the balance sheet

6 Use the acid-test ratio and days' sales in receivables to evaluate a company

Your business, In Motion T-shirts, is doing well—so well in fact that your college has ordered 50 T-shirts with the college logo on it. The dean will give a T-shirt to all new faculty members. This is quite a vote of confidence, and the free publicity may bring in more business. But there's a hitch.

The college can't pay you immediately. It usually takes around 30 days to clear the paperwork and cut a check. Can you wait 30 days to get your money?

Most businesses face this situation. There are both advantages and disadvantages to extending credit to customers. In the case of your college, the pluses outweigh the minuses so, sure, you'll let them pay you later.

The main advantage of selling on credit (selling on account) is expanding your customer base; you can increase sales that way. The disadvantages are that you have to wait to receive cash and some customers may never pay you. You wind up eating some of the receivables.

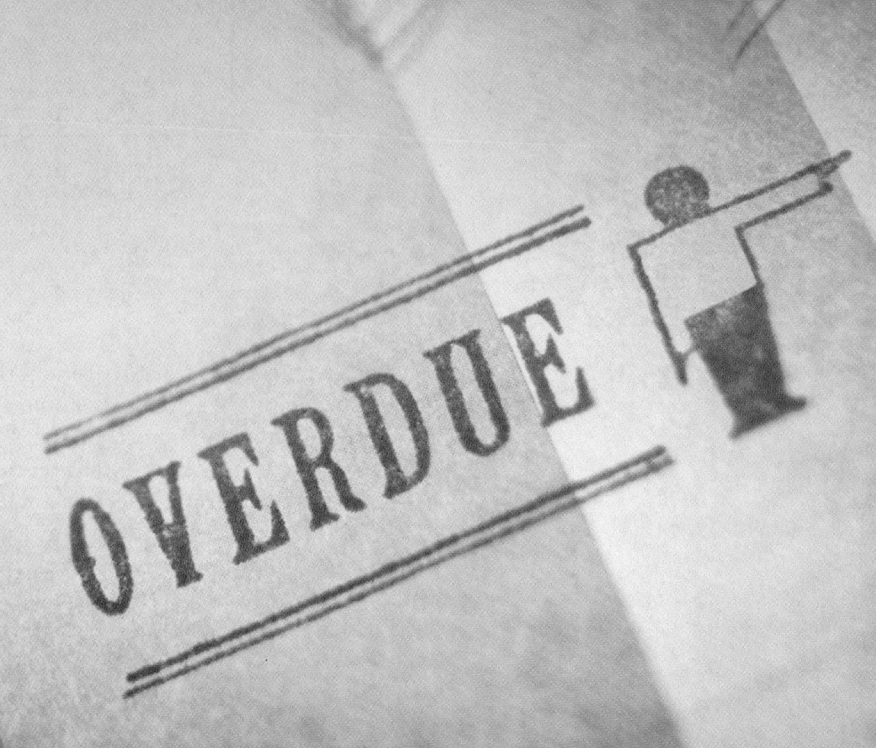

A *receivable* arises when you sell goods or services to another party on credit. The receivable is the seller's claim for the amount of the transaction. A receivable also arises when you loan money to another party. Each credit transaction involves two parties:

- The **creditor**, who obtains a receivable (an asset)
- The **debtor**, who has a payable (a liability)

Your receivable is an asset, just as cash is. But the receivable is slightly different: It's very close to cash, but it's not cash yet. This chapter focuses on accounting for receivables.

Receivables: An Introduction

Types of Receivables

Receivables are monetary claims against others. The two major types of receivables are:

- accounts receivable
- notes receivable

Accounts receivable, also called *trade receivables,* are amounts to be collected from customers. Accounts Receivable serves as a *control account* because it summarizes the total of your receivables. As we saw in Chapter 7, companies also keep a *subsidiary ledger* of the receivable from each customer. This is illustrated as follows:

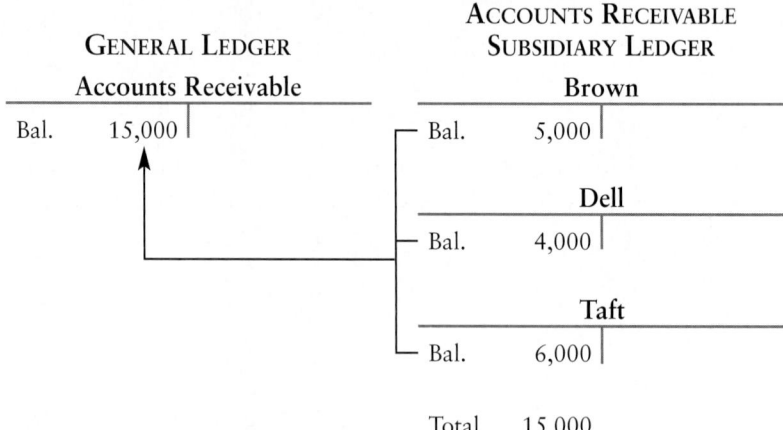

Notes receivable are more formal than accounts receivable, and notes include a charge for interest. The debtor of a note promises to pay the creditor a definite sum at a future date—the *maturity* date. A written document known as a *promissory note* serves as the evidence. Notes receivable due within one year or less are *current assets.* Notes due beyond one year are *long-term.*

Other receivables make up a miscellaneous category that may include loans to employees. Usually, other receivables are long-term, but they're current assets if due within one year or less. Receivables can be reported as shown in Exhibit 9-1. All the receivables are highlighted for emphasis.

| EXHIBIT 9-1 | Receivables on the Balance Sheet |

EXAMPLE COMPANY
Assets
Date

Assets		
Current assets:		
Cash		$X,XXX
Accounts receivable	$X,XXX	
Less: Allowance for uncollectible accounts	(XXX)	X,XXX
Notes receivable, short-term		X,XXX
Inventories		X,XXX
Prepaid expenses		X,XXX
Total		X,XXX
Investments and long-term receivables:		
Investments		X,XXX
Notes receivable, long-term		X,XXX
Other receivables		X,XXX
Total		X,XXX
Plant assets:		
Property, plant, and equipment		X,XXX
Total assets		$X,XXX

Establishing Internal Control over Collection of Receivables

1 Design internal controls for receivables

Businesses that sell on credit receive cash by mail, so internal control over collections is important. A critical element of internal control is the separation of cash-handling and cash-accounting duties. Consider the following case.

> Butler Supply Co. is family-owned and has loyal workers. Most company employees have been with the Butlers for years. The company makes 90% of its sales on account.
>
> The office staff consists of a bookkeeper and a supervisor. The bookkeeper maintains the accounts receivable subsidiary ledger and makes the daily bank deposit. The supervisor manages the office.

Can you spot the internal control weakness here? The bookkeeper has access to the accounts receivable and also handles cash. The bookkeeper could steal a customer check and write off the customer's account as uncollectible.[1] Unless someone reviews the bookkeeper's work, the theft may go undetected.

How can Butler Supply correct this control weakness? *The bookkeeper should not be allowed to handle cash.* The supervisor should make all bank deposits. A bank lock box would achieve the same result. In a lock-box system, customers send cash directly to the bank, and that keeps the bookkeeper's hands off the cash.

---

[1] The bookkeeper would need to forge the endorsement on the check and deposit it in a bank account that he controls.

Managing the Collection of Receivables: The Credit Department

Most companies have a credit department to evaluate customers. The extension of credit requires a balancing act. The company doesn't want to lose sales to good customers, but it also wants to avoid uncollectible receivables.

For good internal control over cash collections, the credit department should have no access to cash. For example, if a credit employee handles cash, he might pocket money received from a customer. He could then label the customer's account as uncollectible, and the company would write off the account receivable, as discussed in the next section. The company would stop billing that customer, and the employee would have covered his theft. For this reason, a sharp separation of duties is important.

The Decision Guidelines feature identifies the main issues in controlling and managing receivables. These guidelines serve as a framework for the remainder of the chapter.

Decision Guidelines

CONTROLLING, MANAGING, AND ACCOUNTING FOR RECEIVABLES

Butler Supply, In Motion T-Shirts, and all other companies that sell on credit face the same accounting challenges.

The main issues in *controlling* and *managing* receivables, plus a plan of action, follow.

Issue	Action
Extend credit only to customers who are most likely to pay.	Run a credit check on prospective customers.
Separate cash-handing, credit, and accounting duties to keep employees from stealing cash collected from customers.	Design the internal control system to separate duties.
Pursue collection from customers to maximize cash flow.	Keep a close eye on collections from customers.

The main issues in *accounting* for receivables, and the related plan of action, are as follows:

Issue	Action
Report receivables at their *net realizable value*, that is, the amount we expect to collect.	Estimate the allowance for uncollectible receivables. The *balance sheet* reports receivables at net realizable value (accounts receivable minus the allowance for uncollectibles).
Report the expense associated with failure to collect your receivables. This expense is called uncollectible-account expense.	The *income statement* reports the expense of failing to collect from customers (uncollectible-account expense).

Accounting for Uncollectibles (Bad Debts)

Selling on credit (on account) creates an account receivable. The revenue—service revenue or sales revenue—is recorded as follows (amounts assumed):

Accounts Receivable	6,000	
Service Revenue		6,000
Performed service on account.		

Accounts Receivable	10,000	
Sales Revenue		10,000
Sold goods on account.		

The business collects cash for most accounts receivable and makes this entry (amount assumed):

Cash	10,000	
Accounts Receivable		10,000
Collected cash on account.		

Selling on credit brings both a benefit and a cost.

- **The benefit:** Increase revenues and profits by making sales to a wider range of customers.
- **The cost:** Some customers don't pay, and that creates an expense. The expense is called **uncollectible-account expense, doubtful-account expense,** or **bad-debt expense.**

To account for uncollectible receivables, you can use the allowance method or, in certain limited cases, the direct write-off method. We begin with the allowance method because it represents GAAP for most companies.

The Allowance Method

Most companies use the **allowance method** to measure bad debts. The key concept is to record uncollectible-account expense in the same period as the sales revenue. The business doesn't wait to see which customers will not pay. Instead, it records an expense on the basis of estimates developed from past experience.

Record Uncollectible-Account Expense for the estimated amount and set up **Allowance for Uncollectible Accounts** (or **Allowance for Doubtful Accounts**), a contra account to Accounts Receivable. The allowance is the amount the business expects *not* to collect. Subtracting the allowance from Accounts Receivable yields the net amount you expect to collect. Here are In Motion's final figures after all adjustments as reported on the balance sheet (amounts assumed):

Balance sheet (partial):	
Accounts receivable	$2,800
Less: Allowance for uncollectible accounts	(400)
Accounts receivable, net	$2,400

Interpretation: Customers owe In Motion $2,800, of which you expect to collect $2,400. You estimate that In Motion will not collect $400 of these receivables.

Another way for In Motion to report receivables follows.

Accounts receivable, net of allowance for uncollectible accounts of $400	$2,400

The income statement reports Uncollectible-Account Expense (Doubtful-Account Expense) among the operating expenses.

In the sections that follow, we show how to arrive at these amounts.

Estimating Uncollectibles

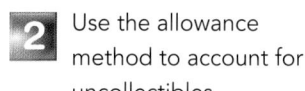 Use the allowance method to account for uncollectibles

How are uncollectible receivables estimated? Companies use their past experience. There are two basic ways to estimate uncollectibles:

- Percent-of-sales
- Aging-of-accounts-receivable

Both approaches work with the allowance method, and both normally require an adjusting entry at the end of the period.

Percent-of-Sales Method

The **percent-of-sales method** computes uncollectible-account expense as a percentage of net credit sales. This method is also called the **income-statement approach** because it focuses on the amount of expense. Assume it is December 31, 2007, and the accounts have these balances *before the year-end adjustments*:

Accounts Receivable	Allowance for Uncollectible Accounts
2,800	100

Interpretation: Accounts Receivable reports the amount that customers owe you. If you were to collect from all customers, you would receive $2,800. Allowance for Uncollectible Accounts should report the amount of the receivables that you expect *not* to collect.

Suppose it's clear to you that In Motion will *fail to collect* more than $100 of the receivables. The allowance is too low, so you need to bring it up to a more realistic credit balance. That requires an adjusting entry at the end of the period.

How the Percent-of-Sales Method Works

Based on prior experience, In Motion's uncollectible-account expense runs 2% of net credit sales, which totaled $15,000 for 2007. The adjusting entry records the following at year end:

2007				
Dec. 31	Uncollectible-Account Expense ($15,000 × 0.02)		300	
	Allowance for Uncollectible Accounts			300
	Recorded expense for the year.			

After posting, the accounts are ready for the balance sheet.

Accounts Receivable		Allowance for Uncollectible Accounts		
2,800				100
		Adj.		300
		End. Bal.		400

Net Accounts Receivable, $2,400

Now the allowance for uncollectible accounts is realistic. The balance sheet will report accounts receivable at the net amount of $2,400. The income statement will report uncollectible-account expense along with the other operating expenses.

Aging-of-Accounts-Receivable Method

The other approach for estimating uncollectible receivables is the **aging-of-accounts method**. This method is also called the **balance-sheet approach** because it focuses on accounts receivable. Assume it is December 31, 2007, and the accounts have these balances *before the year-end adjustments:*

Accounts Receivable		Allowance for Uncollectible Accounts	
2,800			100

Again, the allowance balance is too low. In the aging approach, you group individual accounts (Jones, Smith, etc.) according to how long they've been outstanding. The computer can sort customer accounts by age. Exhibit 9-2 shows how In Motion T-shirts groups its accounts receivable. This is called an aging schedule.

Interpretation: Customers owe you $2,800, but you expect not to collect $400 of this amount. These amounts appear in the lower right corner of the aging schedule that follows. Notice that the percentage uncollectible increases as a customer account gets older.

	Age of Account				
Customer Name	**1–30 Days**	**31–60 Days**	**61–90 Days**	**Over 90 Days**	**Total Balance**
Dean's Office	$ 500				$ 500
Phi Chi Fraternity	700				700
University Ministries	600				600
Drama Department			$340		340
Other accounts	60	$200		$400	660
Totals	$1,860	$200	$340	$400	$2,800
Estimated percentage uncollectible	× 1%	× 2%	× 5%	× 90%	
Allowance for Uncollectible Accounts balance	+ $ 19	+ $ 4	+ $ 17	+ $360	= $ 400

EXHIBIT 9-2 Aging the Accounts Receivable of In Motion T-Shirts

How the Aging Method Works

The aging method tells you what the credit balance of the allowance account needs to be—$400 in this case. The aging method works like this:

Allowance for Uncollectible Accounts:

Credit balance needed $400

Unadjusted balance already in the allowance 100

Adjusting entry for this amount $300

To adjust the allowance, make this entry at year end:

2007			
Dec. 31	Uncollectible-Account Expense	300	
	Allowance for Uncollectible Accounts ($400 – $100)		300
	Adjusted the allowance account.		

After posting, the accounts are up-to-date and ready for the balance sheet.

Accounts Receivable		Allowance for Uncollectible Accounts	
2,800			100
		Adj.	300
		End. Bal.	400

Net Accounts Receivable, $2,400

Report accounts receivable at *net realizable value* ($2,400) because that's the amount In Motion expects to collect in cash.

Using Percent-of-Sales and Aging Methods Together

In practice, companies use the percent-of-sales and the aging-of-accounts methods together.

- For *interim statements* (monthly or quarterly), companies use the percent-of-sales method because it is easier.
- At the end of the year, companies use the aging method to ensure that Accounts Receivable is reported at *net realizable value*.
- Using the two methods together provides good measures of both the expense and the asset. Exhibit 9-3 summarizes and compares the two methods.

EXHIBIT 9-3   **Comparing the Percent-of-Sales and Aging Methods**

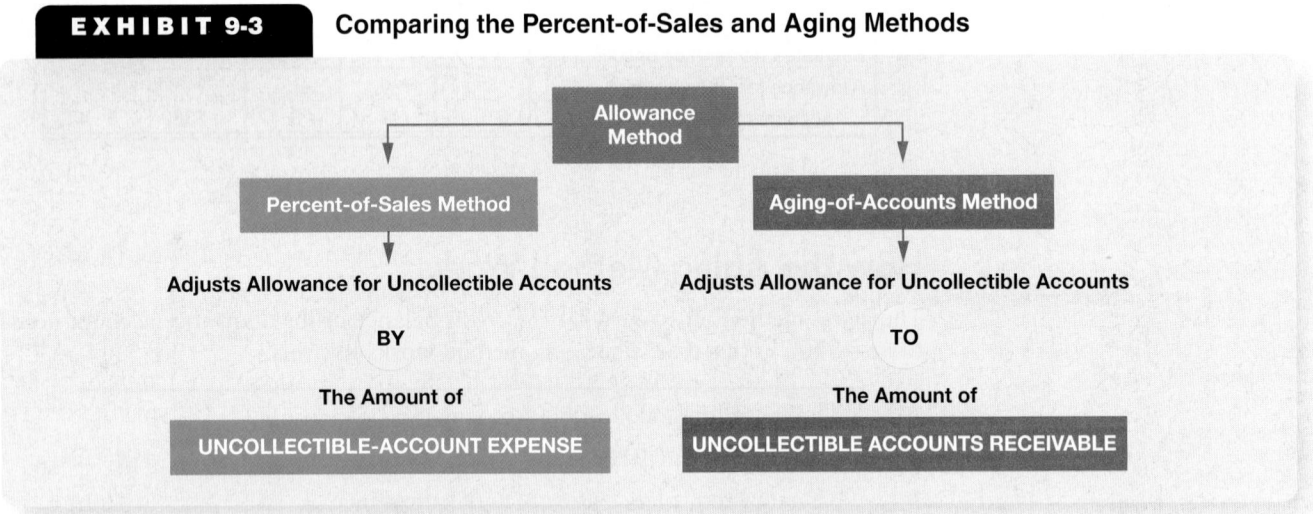

Writing Off Uncollectible Accounts

Early in 2008, In Motion T-shirts collects most of its accounts receivable and records the cash receipts as follows (amount assumed):

2008			
Jan.–Mar.	Cash	2,000	
	Accounts Receivable		2,000
	Collected on account.		

Suppose that, after repeated attempts, you finally decide that In Motion cannot collect a total of $200 from customers Andrews and Jones. You then write off the receivables from these customers, as follows:

2008			
Mar. 31	Allowance for Uncollectible Accounts	200	
	Accounts Receivable—Andrews		80
	Accounts Receivable—Jones		120
	Wrote off uncollectible accounts.		

3   Understand the direct write-off method for uncollectibles

The Direct Write-Off Method

There is another way to account for uncollectible receivables that is unacceptable for most companies. It is called the **direct write-off method**. Under the direct write-off method, you wait until you decide that you'll never collect from the customer. Then you write off the customer's account receivable by debiting Uncollectible-Account Expense and crediting the customer's Account Receivable, as follows (using assumed data):

2008			
Jan. 2	Uncollectible-Account Expense	110	
	Accounts Receivable—Smith		110
	Wrote off a bad account.		

The direct write-off method is defective for two reasons:

1. It does not set up an allowance for uncollectibles. As a result, the direct write-off method always reports the receivables at their full amount. Assets are overstated on the balance sheet.

2. It does not match uncollectible-account expense against revenue very well. In this example, In Motion made the sale to Smith in 2007 and should have recorded the uncollectible-account expense during 2007. That's the only way to measure net income properly. By recording the uncollectible-account expense in 2008, you would *overstate* net income in 2007 and *understate* net income in 2008. Both years' net income amounts are incorrect.

The direct write-off method is acceptable only when uncollectible receivables are very low. It works for retailers such as Wal-Mart, McDonald's, and Gap because those companies carry almost no receivables.

Recovery of Accounts Previously Written Off

When an account receivable is written off as uncollectible, the receivable does not die: The customer still owes the money. However, the company stops pursuing collection and writes off the account as uncollectible.

Some companies turn delinquent receivables over to an attorney and recover some of the cash. This is called *recovery of a bad account*. Let's see how to record the recovery of an account that we wrote off earlier. Recall that In Motion T-shirts wrote off the $80 receivable from customer Andrews (bottom of page 464). It is now January 4, 2009, and In Motion unexpectedly receives $80 from Andrews. To account for this recovery, you make two journal entries to (1) reverse the earlier write-off and (2) record the cash collection, as follows:

1.	Accounts Receivable—Andrews	80	
	Allowance for Uncollectible Accounts		80
	Reinstated Andrews' account receivable.		
2.	Cash	80	
	Accounts Receivable—Andrews		80
	Collected on account.		

Credit-Card, Bankcard, and Debit-Card Sales

Credit-Card Sales

Credit-card sales are common in retailing. Customers present credit cards like American Express and Discover to pay for purchases. The credit-card company pays the seller and then bills the customer.

Credit cards offer the convenience of buying without having to pay cash immediately. An American Express customer receives a monthly statement from American Express, detailing each transaction. The customer can write one check to cover many purchases.

Retailers also benefit. They don't have to check each customer's credit rating. The credit-card company has already done so. Retailers don't have to keep accounts receivable records or pursue collection from customers.

The benefits do not come free. The seller receives less than 100% of the face value of the sale. The credit-card company takes a fee of 1% to 5% on the sale. Suppose you and your family have dinner at a Red Lobster restaurant. You pay the bill—$50—with a Discover card.

Customer pays $50

Seller collects $48

Credit-card company collects $2

Red Lobster's entry to record the $50 sale, subject to the credit-card company's 4% discount, is:

Accounts Receivable—Discover	48	
Credit-Card Discount Expense ($50 × 0.04)	2	
Sales Revenue		50
Recorded credit-card sales.		

On collection of the cash, Red Lobster records the following:

Cash	48	
Accounts Receivable—Discover		48
Collected from Discover.		

Bankcard Sales

Most banks issue their own cards, known as *bankcards,* which operate much like credit cards. VISA and MasterCard are the two main bankcards. When an Exxon station makes a sale and takes a VISA card, the station receives cash at the point of sale. The cash received is less than the full amount of the sale because the bank deducts its fee. Suppose the Exxon station sells $150 of fuel to a family vacationing in its motor home. The station takes a VISA card, and the bank that issued the card charges a 2% fee. The Exxon station records the bankcard sale as follows:

Cash	147	
Bankcard Discount Expense ($150 × 0.02)	3	
Sales Revenue		150
Recorded a bankcard sale.		

Debit-Card Sales

Debit cards are fundamentally different from credit cards and bankcards. Using a debit card is like paying with cash, except that you don't have to carry cash or write a check.

At Target (or Kroger or Wal-Mart), the buyer "swipes" the card through a special terminal, and the buyer's bank balance is automatically decreased. Target's Cash account is increased immediately. Target doesn't have to deposit a check and wonder if it will bounce. With a debit card there is no third party, such as VISA or MasterCard, so there is no Bankcard Discount Expense.

Summary Problem 1

Monarch Map Company's balance sheet at December 31, 2007, reported the following:

Accounts receivable	$60,000
Allowance for uncollectible accounts	2,000

Requirements

1. How much of the receivable did Monarch expect to collect? Stated differently, what was the net realizable value of these receivables?

2. Journalize, without explanations, 2008 entries for Monarch:

   a. Total estimated Uncollectible-Account Expense was $2,400 for the first three quarters of the year, based on the percent-of-sales method.

   b. Write-offs of accounts receivable totaled $2,700.

   c. December 31, 2008, aging of receivables indicates that $2,200 of the receivables is uncollectible.

   Prepare a T-account for Allowance for Uncollectible Accounts, as follows:

Allowance for Uncollectible Accounts

2008 Write-offs	?	Dec. 31, 2007 Bal.	2,000
		2008 Expense	?
		Bal. before Adj.	
		Dec. 31, 2008 Adj.	?
		Dec. 31, 2008 Bal.	2,200

   Post all three transactions to the allowance account.

3. Report Monarch's receivables and related allowance on the December 31, 2008, balance sheet. Accounts receivable total $63,000.
   What is the net realizable value of receivables at December 31, 2008? How much is uncollectible-account expense for 2008?

Solution

Requirement 1

Net realizable value of receivables ($60,000 − $2,000)...........................	$58,000

Requirement 2

(a) Uncollectible-Account Expense...	2,400	
Allowance for Uncollectible Accounts...............................		2,400
(b) Allowance for Uncollectible Accounts	2,700	
Accounts Receivable		2,700
(c) Uncollectible-Account Expense ($2,200 − $1,700)	500	
Allowance for Uncollectible Accounts...............................		500

Allowance for Uncollectible Accounts

		Dec. 31, 2007 Bal.	2,000
2008 Write-offs	2,700	2008 Expense	2,400
		Bal. before Adj.	1,700
		Dec. 31, 2008 Adj.	500
		Dec. 31, 2008 Bal.	2,200

Requirement 3

Accounts receivable..	$63,000
Less: Allowance for uncollectible accounts..	(2,200)
Accounts receivable, net..	$60,800
Uncollectible-account expense for 2008 ($2,400 + $500)......................	$ 2,900

Notes Receivable: An Overview

Notes receivable are more formal than accounts receivable. The debtor signs a promissory note as evidence of the transaction. Before launching into the accounting, let's define the special terms used for notes receivable.

- **Promissory note:** A written promise to pay a specified amount of money at a particular future date.
- **Maker of the note (debtor):** The entity that signs the note and promises to pay the required amount; the maker of the note is the *debtor*.
- **Payee of the note (creditor):** The entity to whom the maker promises future payment; the payee of the note is the *creditor*.
- **Principal:** The amount loaned out by the payee and borrowed by the maker of the note.
- **Interest:** The revenue to the payee for loaning money; interest is expense to the debtor.
- **Interest period:** The period of time during which interest is computed. It extends from the original date of the note to the maturity date. Also called the **note term**, or simply the **time period.**
- **Interest rate:** The percentage rate of interest specified by the note. Interest rates are almost always stated for a period of one year. A 9% note means that the amount of interest for *one year* is 9% of the note's principal.
- **Maturity date:** The date when final payment of the note is due. Also called the **due date.**
- **Maturity value:** The sum of the principal plus interest due at maturity.

Exhibit 9-4 illustrates a promissory note. Study it carefully.

EXHIBIT 9-4   **A Promissory Note**

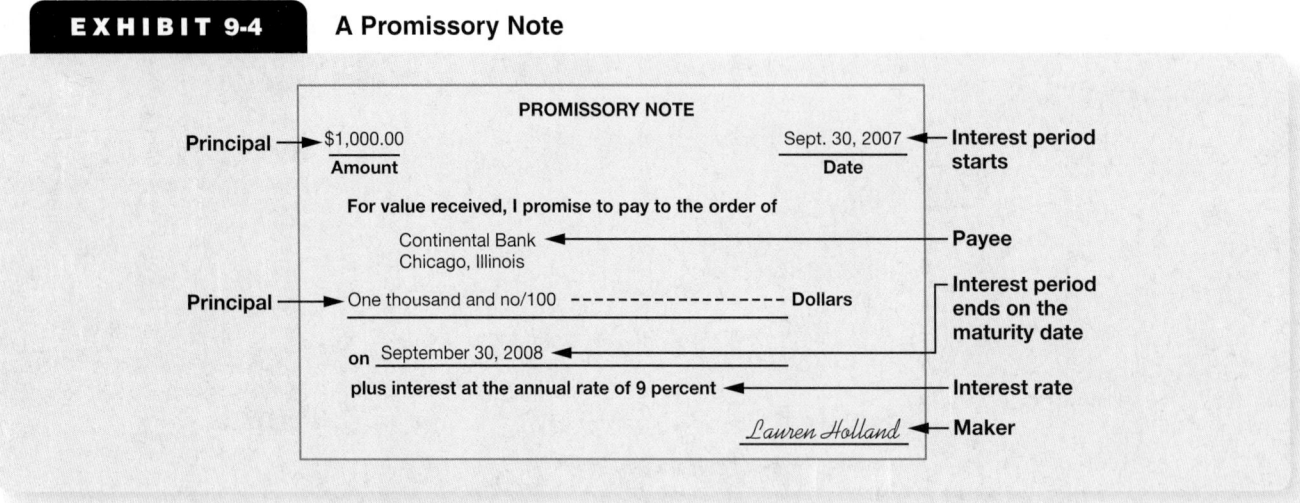

Identifying Maturity Date

Some notes specify the maturity date, as shown in Exhibit 9-4. Other notes state the period of the note in days or months. When the period is given in months, the note's maturity date falls on the same day of the month as the date the note was issued. A six-month note dated February 16 matures on August 16.

When the period is given in days, the maturity date is determined by counting the days from the date of issue. A 120-day note dated September 14, 2007, matures on January 12, 2008, as shown here:

Month	Number of Days	Cumulative Total
Sep. 2007	30 – 14 = 16	16
Oct. 2007	31	47
Nov. 2007	30	77
Dec. 2007	31	108
Jan. 2008	12	120

In counting the days remaining for a note, remember to:

- count the maturity date
- omit the date the note was issued

Computing Interest on a Note

The formula for computing the interest is:

$$\text{AMOUNT OF INTEREST} = \text{PRINCIPAL} \times \text{INTEREST RATE} \times \text{TIME}$$

Using the data in Exhibit 9-4, Continental Bank computes interest revenue for one year as:

AMOUNT OF INTEREST	=	PRINCIPAL	×	INTEREST RATE	×	TIME
$90		$1,000		0.09		1 yr

The maturity value of the note is $1,090 ($1,000 principal + $90 interest). The time element is 1 because the note's term is 1 year.

When the term of a note is stated in months, we compute the interest based on the 12-month year. Interest on a $2,000 note at 10% for three months is computed as:

AMOUNT OF INTEREST	=	PRINCIPAL	×	INTEREST RATE	×	TIME
$50		$2,000		0.10		3 / 12

When the interest period is stated in days, we sometimes compute interest based on a 360-day year rather than on a 365-day year.[2] The interest on a $5,000 note at 12% for 60 days can be computed as:

AMOUNT OF INTEREST	=	PRINCIPAL	×	INTEREST RATE	×	TIME
$100		$5,000		0.12		60 / 360

Keep in mind that interest rates are stated as an annual rate. Therefore, the time in the interest formula should also be expressed in terms of a year.

---

[2] A 360-day year eliminates some rounding, which is consistent with our use of whole-dollar amounts throughout this book.

Accounting for Notes Receivable

Recording Notes Receivable—Three Cases

4 Account for notes receivable

Consider the loan agreement shown in Exhibit 9-4. Lauren Holland signs the note, and Continental Bank gives Holland $1,000 cash. At maturity, Holland pays the bank $1,090 ($1,000 principal plus $90 interest). The bank's entries are:

Loan Out Money	2007			
	Sep. 30	Note Receivable—L. Holland	1,000	
		Cash		1,000
		Loaned out money.		
	2008			
	Sep. 30	Cash	1,090	
		Note Receivable—L. Holland		1,000
		Interest Revenue ($1,000 \times 0.09 \times 1$)		90
		Collected note receivable.		

Some companies sell merchandise in exchange for notes receivable. Assume that on October 20, 2009, General Electric sells household appliances for $15,000 to Dorman Builders. Dorman signs a 90-day promissory note at 10% annual interest. General Electric's entries to record the sale and collection from Dorman are:

Sell On A Note Receivable	2009			
	Oct. 20	Note Receivable—Dorman Builders	15,000	
		Sales Revenue		15,000
		Made a sale.		
	2010			
	Jan. 18	Cash	15,375	
		Note Receivable—Dorman Builders		15,000
		Interest Revenue ($15,000 \times 0.10 \times 90/360$)		375
		Collected note receivable.		

A company may accept a note receivable from a trade customer who fails to pay an account receivable. The customer signs a promissory note and gives it to the creditor. Suppose Sports Club cannot pay Hoffman Supply. Hoffman may accept a one-year, $4,000 note receivable, with 9% interest, from Sports Club. Hoffman's entry is:

Note Receivable On Account	2009			
	Oct. 1	Note Receivable—Sports Club	4,000	
		Accounts Receivable—Sports Club		4,000
		Received a note on account.		

Accruing Interest Revenue

A note receivable may be outstanding at the end of an accounting period. The interest revenue earned on the note up to year-end is part of that year's earnings. Recall that interest revenue is earned over time, not just when cash is received.

Let's continue with the Hoffman Supply note receivable from Sports Club. Hoffman's accounting period ends December 31.

- How much of the total interest revenue does Hoffman earn in 2009 (for October, November, and December)?

$$\$4,000 \times .09 \times 3/12 = \$90$$

Hoffman makes this adjusting entry at December 31, 2009:

2009			
Dec. 31	Interest Receivable ($4,000 × 0.09 × 3/12)	90	
	Interest Revenue		90
	Accrued interest revenue.		

- How much interest revenue does Hoffman earn in 2010 (for January through September)?

$$\$4,000 \times .09 \times 9/12 = \$270$$

On the note's maturity date, Hoffman makes this entry:

2010			
Sep. 30	Cash [$4,000 + ($4,000 × 0.09)]	4,360	
	Note Receivable—Sports Club		4,000
	Interest Receivable ($4,000 × 0.09 × 3/12)		90
	Interest Revenue ($4,000 × 0.09 × 9/12)		270
	Collected note receivable plus interest.		

These entries assign the correct amount of interest to each year.

A company holding a note may need cash before the note matures. A procedure for selling the note, called discounting a note receivable, appears in the chapter Appendix 9A.

Dishonored Notes Receivable

If the maker of a note doesn't pay at maturity, the maker **dishonors** (**defaults on**) the note. Because the note has expired, it is no longer in force. But the debtor still owes the payee. The payee can transfer the note receivable amount to Accounts Receivable. Suppose Rubinstein Jewelers has a 6-month, 10% note receivable for $1,200 from Mark Adair, and Adair defaults. Rubinstein Jewelers will record the default as follows:

Feb. 3	Accounts Receivable—M. Adair	1,260	
	Note Receivable—M. Adair		1,200
	Interest Revenue ($1,200 × 0.10 × 6/12)		60
	Recorded a dishonored note receivable.		

Rubinstein will then bill Adair for the account receivable.

Reporting Receivables on the Balance Sheet

5 Report receivables on the balance sheet

On page 461 we showed two ways In Motion T-Shirts could report its accounts receivable, repeated here:

BALANCE SHEET (PARTIAL):	
Accounts receivable	$2,800
Less: Allowance for uncollectible accounts	(400)
Accounts receivable, net	$2,400
or	
Accounts receivable, net of allowance for doubtful accounts of $400...	$2,400

Most companies use the second approach, but either is acceptable.

Computers and Accounts Receivable

Accounting for receivables by a company like M&M Mars requires thousands of postings for credit sales and cash collections. Manual accounting cannot keep up.

As we saw in Chapter 7, Accounts Receivable can be computerized. At M&M Mars the order entry, shipping, and billing departments work together, as shown in Exhibit 9-5.

EXHIBIT 9-5 Order Entry, Shipping, and Billing Working Together at M&M Mars

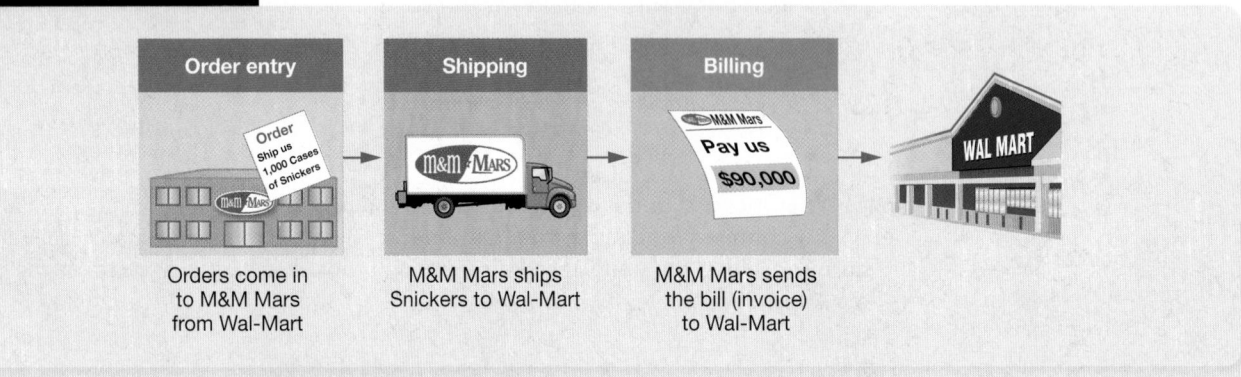

Orders come in to M&M Mars from Wal-Mart

M&M Mars ships Snickers to Wal-Mart

M&M Mars sends the bill (invoice) to Wal-Mart

Using Accounting Information for Decision Making

The balance sheet lists assets in order of liquidity (closeness to cash):

- Cash comes first because it is the liquid asset.
- Short-term investments come next because they are almost as liquid as cash.

- Current receivables are less liquid than short-term investments because the company must collect the receivables.
- Merchandise inventory is less liquid than receivables because the goods must first be sold.

The balance sheet of In Motion T-Shirts provides an example in Exhibit 9-6. Focus on the current assets at December 31, 2007.

EXHIBIT 9-6 **In Motion T-Shirts Balance Sheet**

Assets	December 31, 2007	2006
Current assets:		
Cash	$ 800	$ 400
Short-term investments	1,500	300
Accounts receivable, net of allowance for doubtful accounts of $400 in 2007 and $300 in 2006	2,400	2,600
Inventory	800	600
Total current assets	5,500	3,900
Liabilities		
Current liabilities:		
Total current liabilities	$4,400	$2,900

Balance-sheet data become more useful by showing the relationships among assets, liabilities, and revenues. Let's examine two important ratios.

Acid-Test (or Quick) Ratio

In Chapter 4, we discussed the current ratio, which measures ability to pay current liabilities with current assets. A more stringent measure of ability to pay current liabilities is the **acid-test** (or **quick**) **ratio**. The acid-test ratio reveals whether the entity can pay all its current liabilities if they come due immediately:

For In Motion T-Shirts (Exhibit 9-6)

$$\text{Acid - test ratio} = \frac{\text{Cash} + \begin{array}{c}\text{Short - term}\\\text{investments}\end{array} + \begin{array}{c}\text{Net current}\\\text{receivables}\end{array}}{\text{Total current liabilities}} = \frac{\$800 + \$1,500 + \$2,400}{\$4,400} = 1.07$$

The higher the acid-test ratio, the more able the business is to pay its current liabilities. In Motion's acid-test ratio of 1.07 means that In Motion has $1.07 of quick assets to pay each $1 of current liabilities. This is a strong position.

What is an acceptable acid-test ratio? That depends on the industry. Wal-Mart operates smoothly with an acid-test ratio of less than 0.20. Several things make this possible: Wal-Mart collects cash rapidly and has almost no receivables. The acid-test ratios for most department stores cluster about 0.80, while travel agencies average 1.10. In general, an acid-test ratio of 1.00 is considered safe.

Days' Sales in Receivables

After making a credit sale, the next step is to collect the receivable. **Days' sales in receivables**, also called the **collection period**, indicates how many days it takes to collect the average level of receivables. The shorter the collection period, the more quickly the organization can use its cash. The longer the collection period, the less cash is available for operations. Days' sales in receivables can be computed in two steps, as follows:[3]

For In Motion T-Shirts (Exhibit 9-6)

1. $$\text{One day's sales} = \frac{\substack{\text{Net sales} \\ \text{(or Total revenues)}}}{365 \text{ days}} = \frac{\$22,600^*}{365} = \$62 \text{ per day}$$

2. $$\text{Days' sales in average} \atop \text{accounts receivable} = \frac{\substack{\text{Average net} \\ \text{accounts receivable}}}{\text{One day's sales}} = \frac{\left(\substack{\text{Beginning net} \\ \text{receivables}} + \substack{\text{Ending net} \\ \text{receivables}}\right) \div 2}{\text{One day's sales}}$$

$$= \frac{(\$2,400 + \$2,600) / 2}{\$62} = 40 \text{ days}$$

*From In Motion's 2007 income statement, which is not reproduced here.

On average, it takes In Motion T-Shirts 40 days to collect its accounts receivable. The length of the collection period depends on the credit terms of the sale. For example, sales on net 30 terms should be collected within approximately 30 days. When there is a discount, such as 2/10, net 30, the collection period may be shorter. Credit terms of net 45 result in a longer collection period.

Investors and creditors do not evaluate a company on the basis of one or two ratios. Instead, they analyze all the information available. Then they stand back and ask, "What is our overall impression of this company?" We present all the financial ratios in Chapter 17. By the time you get to that point of your study, you'll have an overall view of the company.

---

[3]Days' sales in average receivables can also be computed in this one step:

$$\text{Days' sales in} \atop \text{average receivables} = \frac{\text{Average net receivables}}{\text{Net sales}} \times 365$$

Decision Guidelines

ACCOUNTING FOR RECEIVABLES

The Decision Guidelines feature summarizes some key decisions for receivables.

Accounting for receivables is the same for In Motion T-Shirts as for a large company like M&M Mars.

Suppose you decide that In Motion will sell on account, as most other companies do. How should you account for your receivables? These guidelines show the way.

Decision

ACCOUNTS RECEIVABLE
How much of our receivables will we collect?

How to report receivables at their net realizable value?

Is there a simpler way to account for uncollectible receivables?

NOTES RECEIVABLE
What two other accounts are related to notes receivable?

How to compute the interest on a note receivable?

RECEIVABLES IN GENERAL
How can you use receivables to evaluate a company's financial position?

How to report receivables on the balance sheet?

Guidelines

Less than the full amount of the receivables because we cannot collect from some customers.

1. Use the *allowance method* to account for uncollectible receivables. Set up the allowance for Uncollectible Accounts.
2. Estimate uncollectibles by the
   a. *Percent-of-sales method* (income-statement approach)
   b. *Aging-of-accounts method* (balance-sheet approach)
3. Write off uncollectible receivables as they prove uncollectible.
4. $$\text{Net accounts receivable} = \text{Accounts Receivable} - \text{Allowance for Uncollectible Accounts}$$

Yes, but it's unacceptable for most companies.

The *direct write-off-method* uses no Allowance for Uncollectibles. It simply debits Uncollectible-Account Expense and credits a customer's Accounts Receivable to write it off when it has proved uncollectible. This method is acceptable only when uncollectibles are insignificant.

Notes receivable are related to:

• Interest Revenue.
• Interest Receivable (Interest revenue earned but not yet collected).

$$\text{Amount of interest} = \text{Principal} \times \text{Interest Rate} \times \text{Time}$$

• $$\text{Acid-test ratio} = \frac{\text{Cash} + \text{Short-term investments} + \text{Net current receivables}}{\text{Total current liabilities}}$$

• $$\text{Day's sales in average receivables} = \frac{\text{Average net accounts receivable}}{\text{One day's sales}}$$

Accounts (or Notes) Receivable .... $XXX
Less: Allowance for uncollectible accounts ..... (X)
Accounts (or notes) receivable, net .... $ XX

Summary Problem 2

Suppose First Fidelity Bank engaged in the following transactions:

2007	
Apr. 1	Loaned out $8,000 to Bland Co. Received a six-month, 10% note.
Oct. 1	Collected the Bland note at maturity.
Dec. 1	Loaned $6,000 to Flores, Inc., on a 180-day, 12% note.
Dec. 31	Accrued interest revenue on the Flores note.
2008	
May 30	Collected the Flores note at maturity.

First Fidelity's accounting period ends on December 31.

Requirements

Explanations are not needed. Use a 360-day year to compute interest.

1. Record the 2007 transactions on April 1 through December 1 on First Fidelity's books.

2. Make the adjusting entry needed on December 31, 2007.

3. Record the May 30, 2008, collection of the Flores note.

Solution

Requirement 1

2007			
Apr. 1	Note Receivable—Bland Co.	8,000	
	Cash		8,000
Oct. 1	Cash ($8,000 + $400)	8,400	
	Note Receivable—Bland Co.		8,000
	Interest Revenue ($8,000 × 0.10 × 6/12)		400

Requirement 2

2007			
Dec. 1	Note Receivable—Flores, Inc.	6,000	
	Cash		6,000
31	Interest Receivable	60	
	Interest Revenue ($6,000 × 0.12 × 30/360)		60

Requirement 3

2008			
May 30	Cash [$6,000 + ($6,000 × .12 × 180/360)]	6,360	
	Note Receivable—Flores, Inc.		6,000
	Interest Receivable		60
	Interest Revenue ($6,000 × 0.12 × 150/360)		300

Review Receivables

Accounting Vocabulary _____

Acid-Test Ratio
Ratio of the sum of cash plus short-term investments plus net current receivables, to total current liabilities. Tells whether the entity could pay all its current liabilities if they came due immediately. Also called the **quick ratio**.

Aging-of-Accounts Methods
A way to estimate bad debts by analyzing individual accounts receivable according to the length of time they have been receivable from the customer. Also called the **balance-sheet approach**.

Allowance for Doubtful Accounts
A contra account, related to accounts receivable, that holds the estimated amount of collection losses. Also called **Allowance for Uncollectible Accounts**.

Allowance for Uncollectible Accounts
A contra account, related to accounts receivable, that holds the estimated amount of collection losses. Also called **Allowance for Doubtful Accounts**.

Allowance Method
A method of recording collection losses on the basis of estimates instead of waiting to see which customers the company will not collect from.

Bad-Debt Expense
Cost to the seller of extending credit. Arises from the failure to collect from credit customers. Also called **doubtful-account expense** or **uncollectible-account expense**.

Balance-Sheet Approach
A way to estimate bad debts by analyzing individual accounts receivable according to the length of time they have been receivable from the customer. Also called the **aging-of-accounts methods**.

Collection Period
Ratio of average net accounts receivable to one day s sales. Tells how many days' sales it takes to collect the average level of receivables. Also called the **days' sales in receivables**.

Creditor
The party to a credit transaction who sells goods or a service and obtains a receivable.

Days' Sales in Receivables
Ratio of average net accounts receivable to one day's sales. Tells how many days' sales it takes to collect the average level of receivables. Also called the **collection period**.

Debtor
The party to a credit transaction who makes a purchase and has a payable.

Default on a Note
Failure of a note's maker to pay a note receivable at maturity. Also called **dishonor of a note**.

Direct Write-Off Method
A method of accounting for uncollectible receivables, in which the company waits until the credit department decides that a customer's account receivable is uncollectible and then debits Uncollectible-Account Expense and credits the customer's Account Receivable.

Discounting a Note Receivable
Selling a note receivable before its maturity date.

Dishonor of a Note
Failure of a note's maker to pay a note receivable at maturity. Also called **default on a note**.

Doubtful-Account Expense
Cost to the seller of extending credit. Arises from the failure to collect from credit customers. Also called **uncollectible-account expense** or **bad-debt expense**.

Due Date
The date when final payment of the note is due. Also called the **maturity date**.

Income-Statement Approach
A method of estimating uncollectible receivables that calculates uncollectible-account expense. Also called the **percent-of-sales method**.

Interest
The revenue to the payee for loaning money; the expense to the debtor.

Interest Period
The period of time during which interest is computed. It extends from the original date of the note to the maturity date. Also called the **note term,** or simply **time period**.

Interest Rate
The percentage rate of interest specified by the note. Interest rates are almost always stated for a period of one year.

Maker of a Note
The person or business that signs the note and promises to pay the amount required by the note agreement: the debtor.

Maturity Date
The date when final payment of the note is due. Also called the **due date**.

Maturity Value
The sum of the principal plus interest due at maturity.

Note Term
The period of time during which interest is computed. It extends from the original date of the note to the maturity date. Also called the **interest period,** or simply **time period**.

Payee of a Note
The person or business to whom the maker of a note promises future payment: the creditor.

Percent-of-Sales Method
A method of estimating uncollectible receivables that calculates uncollectible-account expense. Also called the **income-statement approach**.

Principal
The amount loaned out by the payee and borrowed by the maker of the note.

Principal Amount
The amount loaned out by the payee and borrowed by the maker of the note.

Promissory Note
A written promise to pay a specified amount of money at a particular future date.

Quick Ratio
Ratio of the sum of cash plus short-term investments plus net current receivables, to total current liabilities. Tells whether the entity could pay all its current liabilities if they came due immediately. Also called the **acid-test ratio**.

Receivables
Monetary claims against a business or an individual.

Time Period
The period of time during which interest is computed. It extends from the original date of the note to the maturity date. Also called the **note term** or **interest period**.

Uncollectible-Account Expense
Cost to the seller of extending credit. Arises from the failure to collect from credit customers. Also called **doubtful-account expense** or **bad-debt expense**.

Quick Check

1. With good internal controls, the person who handles cash can also
   a. Account for cash receipts from customers
   b. Account for cash payments
   c. Issue credits to customers for sales returns
   d. None of the above

2. "Bad debts" are the same as
   a. Uncollectible accounts
   b. Doubtful accounts
   c. Neither of the above
   d. Both a and b

3. Which method of estimating uncollectible receivables focuses on Uncollectible-Account Expense for the income statement?
   a. Percent-of-sales approach
   b. Aging-of-accounts approach
   c. Net-realizable-value approach
   d. All of the above.

4. Your company uses the allowance method to account for uncollectible receivables. At the beginning of the year, Allowance for Uncollectibles had a credit balance of $1,100. During the year you recorded Uncollectible-Account Expense of $3,000 and wrote off bad receivables of $2,100. What is your year-end balance in Allowance for Uncollectibles?
   a. $1,000
   b. $2,000
   c. $3,100
   d. $3,200

5. Your ending balance of Accounts Receivable is $20,000. Use the data in the preceding question to compute the net realizable value of Accounts Receivable at year-end.
   a. $18,000
   b. $19,000
   c. $20,000
   d. $21,000

6. What is wrong with the direct write-off method of accounting for uncollectibles?
   a. The direct write-off method does not set up an allowance for uncollectibles.
   b. The direct write-off method overstates assets on the balance sheet.
   c. The direct write-off method does not match expenses against revenue very well.
   d. All of the above.

7. At December 31, you have a $10,000 note receivable from a customer. Interest of 8% has accrued for 6 months on the note. What will your financial statements report for this situation?
   a. Nothing, because you haven't received the cash yet.
   b. Balance sheet will report the note receivable of $10,000.
   c. Balance sheet will report the note receivable of $10,000 and interest receivable of $400.
   d. Income statement will report a note receivable of $10,000.

8. Return to the data in the preceding question. What will the income statement report for this situation?

a. Nothing, because you haven't received the cash yet

b. Interest revenue of $400

c. Note receivable of $10,000

d. Both b and c

9. At year-end, your company has cash of $10,000, receivables of $50,000, inventory of $40,000, and prepaid expenses totaling $5,000. Liabilities of $60,000 must be paid next year. What is your acid-test ratio?

a. 0.83

b. 1.00

c. 1.67

d. Cannot be determined from the data given

10. Return to the data in the preceding question. A year ago receivables stood at $70,000, and sales for the current year total $730,000. How many days did it take you to collect your average level of receivables?

a. 45

b. 35

c. 30

d. 20

Answers are given after Assess Your Progress (p. 501).

Assess Your Progress

Short Exercises

Internal control over the collection of receivables

1

S9-1 Jack Delaney is the accountant responsible for customer accounts in the accounts receivable subsidiary ledger. What duty will a good internal control system withhold from Delaney? Why? (p. 457)

Internal control over the credit department

1

S9-2 What job must be withheld from a company's credit department in order to safeguard its cash? If the credit department does perform this job, what can a credit department employee do to hurt the company? (pp. 458–459)

Applying the allowance method (percent-of-sales) to account for uncollectibles

2

S9-3 During its first year of operations, Signature Lamp Company earned revenue of $350,000 on account. Industry experience suggests that bad debts will amount to 2% of revenues. At December 31, 2008, accounts receivable total $40,000. The company uses the allowance method to account for uncollectibles.

1. Journalize Signature's uncollectible-account expense using the percent-of-sales method. (p. 462)
2. Show how to report accounts receivable on the balance sheet at December 31, 2008. Follow the first reporting format illustrated on page 461.

Applying the allowance method (percent-of-sales) to account for uncollectibles

2

S9-4 During 2009, Signature Lamp Company completed these transactions:

1. Sales revenue on account, $400,000 (ignore cost of goods sold). (p. 460)
2. Collections on account, $420,000. (p. 460)
3. Write-offs of uncollectibles, $6,000. (p. 464)
4. Uncollectible-account expense, 2% of sales revenue. (pp. 461–462)

Journalize Signature's 2009 transactions.

Applying the allowance method (aging-of-accounts) to account for uncollectibles

2

S9-5 Interstate Marble Importers had the following balances at December 31, 2007, before the year-end adjustments:

Accounts Receivable	Allowance for Uncollectible Accounts
74,000	2,000

The aging of accounts receivable yields these data:

	Age of Accounts Receivable		
	0–60 Days	Over 60 Days	Total Receivables
Accounts receivable............	$70,000	$4,000	$74,000
Percent uncollectible	×2%	×20%	

continued . . .

1. Journalize Interstate's entry to adjust the allowance account to its correct balance at December 31, 2007. (pp. 463–464)

2. Prepare a T-account to compute the ending balance of Allowance for Uncollectible Accounts. (p. 463)

Applying the direct write-off method to account for uncollectibles

S9-6 Bob Rassler is an attorney in Los Angeles. Rassler uses the direct write-off method to account for uncollectible receivables.

At May 31, Rassler's accounts receivable totaled $14,000. During June, he earned revenue of $20,000 on account and collected $19,000 on account. He also wrote off uncollectible receivables of $2,000.

1. Use the direct write-off method to journalize Rassler's write-off of the uncollectible receivables. (pp. 465–466)

2. What is Rassler's balance of Accounts Receivable at June 30? Does he expect to collect all of this amount? Explain. (pp. 465–466)

Collecting a receivable previously written off

S9-7 University Cycle Shop had trouble collecting its account receivable from Lance Emmert. On January 19, University finally wrote off Emmert's $600 account receivable. University turned the account over to an attorney, who hounded Emmert for the rest of the year. On December 31, Emmert sent a $600 check to University Cycle Shop with a note that said, "Here's your money. Please call off your bloodhound!"

Journalize for University Cycle Shop:

Jan. 19	Write-off of Emmert's account against Allowance for Uncollectible Accounts. (pp. 465–466)
Dec. 31	Reinstatement of Emmert's account. (pp. 465–466)
31	Collection of cash from Emmert. (pp. 465–466)

Recording credit-card and bankcard sales

S9-8 Restaurants do a large volume of business by credit cards and bankcards. Suppose a Chili's restaurant had these transactions on a Saturday:

American Express credit-card sales...............	$10,000
VISA bankcard sales.....................................	8,000

Suppose American Express charges merchants 2% and VISA charges $1\frac{1}{2}$%. Record these sale transactions for the restaurant. (p. 467)

Computing interest amounts on notes receivable

S9-9 For each of the following notes receivable, compute the amount of interest revenue earned during 2008. Use a 360-day year, and round to the nearest dollar. (pp. 471–472)

	Principal	Interest Rate	Interest Period During 2008
Note 1	$ 50,000	10%	3 months
Note 2	10,000	9%	60 days
Note 3	15,000	12%	75 days
Note 4	100,000	8%	6 months

Accounting for a note receivable

 4

S9-10 Lantana Bank & Trust Company lent $100,000 to Ben Milam on a 90-day, 10% note. Record the following transactions for the bank (explanations are not required):

a. Lending the money on May 6. (pp. 471–472)

b. Collecting the principal and interest at maturity. Specify the date. For the computation of interest, use a 360-day year. (pp. 471–472)

Reporting receivables and other accounts in the financial statements

5

S9-11 Concentra Medical Center included the following items in its financial statements:

Allowance for doubtful accounts	$ 120	Service revenue	$14,400
Cash	1,150	Other assets	350
Accounts receivable	2,580	Cost of services sold and	
Accounts payable	1,020	other expenses	12,800
Notes payable	3,280		

1. How much net income did Concentra earn for the month? (p. 20)

2. Show two ways Concentra can report receivables on its classified balance sheet. (p. 474)

Using the acid-test ratio and days' sales in receivables to evaluate a company

6

S9-12 Avant Garde Clothiers reported the following items at February 28, 2008 (amounts in thousands, with last year's—2007—amounts also given as needed):

Accounts payable	$ 400	Accounts receivable, net:	
Cash	210	February 28, 2008	$ 220
Inventories:		February 28, 2007	150
February 28, 2008	190	Cost of goods sold	1,200
February 28, 2007	160	Short-term investments	160
Net sales revenue	2,190	Other current assets	90
Long-term assets	410	Other current liabilities	140
Long-term liabilities	170		

Compute Avant Garde's (a) acid-test ratio and (b) days' sales in average receivables for 2008. Evaluate each ratio value as strong or weak. Avant Garde sells on terms of net 30. (pp. 475–476)

Computing key ratios for a company

6

S9-13 Use the data in Short Exercise 9-12 to compute the following 2008 ratios for Avant Garde Clothiers. Round decimals to two places.

a. Current ratio (p. 210)

b. Debt ratio (p. 210)

c. Gross profit percentage (p. 272)

d. Rate of inventory turnover (p. 272)

Exercises

Identifying and correcting
an internal control weakness

E9-14 Suppose Toyota is opening a regional office in St. Louis. Lesa Carter, the office manager, is designing the internal control system. Carter proposes the following procedures for credit checks on new customers, sales on account, cash collections, and write-offs of uncollectible receivables.

- The credit department runs a credit check on all customers who apply for credit. When an account proves uncollectible, the credit department authorizes the write-off of the account receivable.

- Cash receipts come into the credit department, which separates the cash received from the customer remittance slips. The credit department lists all cash receipts by customer name and amount of cash received.

- The cash goes to the treasurer for deposit in the bank. The remittance slips go to the accounting department for posting to customer accounts.

- The controller compares the daily deposit slip to the total amount posted to customer accounts. Both amounts must agree.

Identify the internal control weakness in this situation, and propose a way to correct it. (pp. 457–459)

Using the allowance
method for bad debts
(percent-of-sales)

E9-15 At September 30, Eagle Mountain Flagpoles had Accounts Receivable of $28,000 and Allowance for Uncollectible Accounts of $1,000. During October, Eagle Mountain recorded

- Sales of $180,000 ($160,000 on account; $20,000 for cash)
- Collections on account, $130,000
- Uncollectible-account expense, estimated as 2% of credit sales
- Write-offs of uncollectible receivables, $2,400

Requirements
1. Journalize sales, collections, uncollectible-account expense by the allowance method (percent-of-sales method), and write-offs of uncollectibles during October. (pp. 461–462, 465–466)

2. Prepare T-accounts to show the ending balances in Accounts Receivable and Allowance for Uncollectible Accounts. Compute *net* accounts receivable at October 31. How much does Eagle Mountain expect to collect? (pp. 468–470)

Using the direct write-off
method for bad debts

E9-16 Refer to Exercise 9-15.

Requirements
1. Record uncollectible-account expense for October using the direct write-off method. (pp. 465–466)

2. What balance of accounts receivable does Eagle Mountain report on its Oct. 31 balance sheet under the direct write-off method? Does it expect to collect the full amount? (pp. 465–466)

Using the aging method to
estimate bad debts

E9-17 At December 31, 2008, the Accounts Receivable balance of Easy Card is $300,000. The Allowance for Doubtful Accounts has a $8,900 credit balance. Easy Card prepares the following aging schedule for its accounts receivable:

continued . . .

Accounts Receivable	Age of Accounts			
	1–30 Days	31–60 Days	61–90 Days	Over 90 Days
$300,000..........................	$140,000	$80,000	$70,000	$10,000
Estimated percent uncollectible	0.5%	2.0%	6.0%	50%

Requirements

1. Journalize the year-end adjusting entry for doubtful accounts on the basis of the aging schedule. Show the T-account for the Allowance at December 31, 2008. (p. 463)

2. Show how Easy Card will report Accounts Receivable on its December 31, 2008 balance sheet. (pp. 463–464)

Sales, write-offs, and bad-debt recovery

E9-18 High Performance Cell Phones sold $20,000 of merchandise to Avery Trucking Company on account. Avery fell on hard times and paid only $6,000 of the account receivable. After repeated attempts to collect, High Performance finally wrote off its accounts receivable from Avery. Six months later High Performance received Avery's check for $14,000 with a note apologizing for the late payment.

Journalize for High Performance:

- Sale on account, $20,000. (Ignore cost of goods sold.) (p. 460)
- Collection of $6,000 on account. (p. 460)
- Write-off of the remaining portion of the Avery account receivable. High Performance uses the allowance method for uncollectibles. (p. 464)
- Reinstatement of Avery's account receivable. (p. 464)
- Collection in full from Avery, $14,000. (pp. 465–466)

Computing note receivable amounts

E9-19 On April 30, 2007, Synergy Bank loaned $80,000 to Kim Sperry on a one-year, 9% note.

Requirements

1. Compute the interest for the years ended December 31, 2007 and 2008 for the Sperry note. (p. 471)

2. Which party has a (p. 470)

   a. Note receivable?   c. Interest revenue?

   b. Note payable?   d. Interest expense?

3. How much in total would Sperry pay the bank if he pays off the note early—say, on November 30, 2007? (p. 471)

Recording notes receivable and accruing interest revenue

E9-20 Journalize the following transactions of Mediterranean Importers, which ends its accounting year on June 30: (pp. 471–473)

Apr. 1	Loaned $10,000 cash to Carroll Fadal on a one-year, 8% note.
June 6	Sold goods to Turf Masters, receiving a 90-day, 10% note for $9,000.
30	Made a single compound entry to accrue interest revenue on both notes. Use a 360-day year for interest computations.

Recording bankcard sales
and a note receivable, and
accruing interest revenue
4

E9-21 Record the following transactions in the journal of Top Dog Running Shoes: (pp. 471–473)

2008	
Feb. 12	Recorded MasterCard bankcard sales of $100,000, less a 2% discount.
Aug. 1	Loaned $20,000 to Jean Porter, an executive with the company, on a one-year, 12% note.
Dec. 31	Accrued interest revenue on the Porter note.
2009	
Aug. 1	Collected the maturity value of the Porter note.

E9-22 High-Pressure Steam Cleaning performs service on account. When a customer account becomes four months old, High-Pressure converts the account to a note receivable. During 2008, the company completed these transactions:

June 29	Performed service on account for Montclair Club, $15,000. (p. 460)
Nov. 1	Received a $15,000, 60-day, 10% note from Montclair Club in satisfaction of its past-due account receivable. (pp. 472–473)
Dec. 31	Collected the Montclair Club note at maturity. (pp. 472–473)

Requirements

Record the transactions in High-Pressure's journal.

E9-23 Cherokee Carpets reported the following amounts in its 2009 financial statements. The 2008 figures are given for comparison.

		2009		2008
Current assets:				
Cash		$ 3,000		$ 10,000
Short-term investments..............		23,000		11,000
Accounts receivable	$60,000		$74,000	
Less: Allowance for uncollectibles.....................	(7,000)	53,000	(6,000)	68,000
Inventory...................................		192,000		189,000
Prepaid insurance		2,000		2,000
Total current assets....................		$273,000		$280,000
Total current liabilities		$104,000		$107,000
Net sales.....................................		$730,000		$732,000

continued . . .

Requirements

1. Determine whether Cherokee's acid-test ratio improved or deteriorated from 2008 to 2009. How does Cherokee's acid-test ratio compare with the industry average of 0.80? (p. 475)

2. Compare the days' sales in receivables for 2009 with Cherokee's credit terms of net 30. (p. 476)

Collection period for receivables

E9-24 Swift Media Sign Company sells on account. Recently, Swift reported these figures:

	2008	2007
Net sales	$600,060	$570,000
Receivables at end of year	42,800	38,200

Requirements

1. Compute Swift's average collection period on receivables during 2008. (p. 475)

2. Suppose Swift's normal credit terms for a sale on account are "2/10 net 30." How well does Swift's collection period compare to the company's credit terms? Is this good or bad for Swift? Explain. (p. 475)

Problems (Group A)

Controlling cash receipts from customers

P9-25A Mail Plus performs mailing services on account, so virtually all cash receipts arrive in the mail. Gina Star, the owner, has just returned from a meeting with new ideas for the business. Among other things, Star plans to institute stronger internal controls over cash receipts from customers.

Requirement

Assume you are Gina Star. Write a memo to outline procedures that will ensure (1) all cash receipts are deposited in the bank and (2) all cash receipts are posted as credits to customer accounts receivable. Use the following format for your memo. (p. 457)

> **MEMO**
>
> **Date:**
>
> **To:**
>
> **From:**
>
> **Subject:**

Accounting for uncollectibles
by the allowance and direct
write-off methods

P9-26A On February 28, Tradewinds Sailing Supplies had a $75,000 debit balance in Accounts Receivable and a $2,200 credit balance in Allowance for Uncollectible Accounts. During March, Tradewinds made

- Sales on account, $410,000
- Collections on account, $419,000
- Write-offs of uncollectible receivables, $7,000

Requirements

1. Record sales and collections on account. Then record uncollectible-account expense and write-offs of customer accounts using the *allowance* method. Uncollectible-account expense was estimated at 2% of credit sales. Show all March activity in Accounts Receivable, Allowance for Uncollectible Accounts, and Uncollectible-Account Expense (post to these T-accounts). (pp. 460, 461–462, 464)

2. Suppose Tradewinds used a different method to account for uncollectible receivables. Record sales and collections on account. Then record uncollectible-account expense for March using the *direct write-off* method. Post to Accounts Receivable and Uncollectible-Account Expense and show their balances at March 31. (pp. 465–466)

3. What amount of uncollectible-account expense would Tradewinds report on its March income statement under each of the two methods? Which amount better matches expense with revenue? Give your reason. (pp. 461–462, 465–466)

4. What amount of *net* accounts receivable would Tradewinds report on its March 31 balance sheet under each of the two methods? Which amount is more realistic? Give your reason. (pp. 465–466, 469)

Using the percent-of-sales
and aging methods for
uncollectibles

P9-27A At September 30, the accounts of Aguilar Outsourcing Solutions include the following:

Accounts Receivable..	$65,000
Allowance for Uncollectible Accounts (credit balance)...........	1,100

During the last quarter of 2009, Aguilar completed the following selected transactions:

Dec. 22   Wrote off accounts receivable as uncollectible:
Transnet, $300; Webvan, $100; and Alpha Group, $600.

Dec. 31   Recorded uncollectible-account expense based on the aging of receivables, as follows:

Accounts Receivable	Age of Accounts			
	1–30 Days	31–60 Days	61–90 Days	Over 90 Days
$55,000	$30,000	$10,000	$10,000	$5,000
Estimated percent uncollectible	0.5%	1.0%	4%	50%

continued . . .

Requirements

1. Record the transactions in the journal. (p. 463)
2. Open the Allowance for Uncollectible Accounts, and post entries affecting that account. Keep a running balance. (pp. 80, 468)
3. Show how Aguilar should report accounts receivable on its December 31, 2009, balance sheet. Use the first reporting format at the top of page 461.

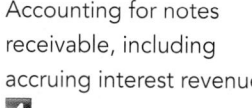

P9-28A Showbiz Sportswear completed the following selected transactions during 2008 and 2009:

2008

Dec. 31   Estimated that uncollectible-account expense for the year was 1% of credit sales of $450,000 and recorded that amount as expense. Use the allowance method.

     31   Made the closing entry for uncollectible-account expense.

2009

Feb.   4   Sold inventory to Marian Holt, $1,500 on account. Ignore cost of goods sold.

July   1   Wrote off Marian Holt's account as uncollectible after repeated efforts to collect from her.

Nov. 19   Received $1,500 from Marian Holt, along with a letter apologizing for being so late. Reinstated Holt's account in full, and recorded the cash receipt.

Dec. 31   Made a compound entry to write off the following accounts as uncollectible: Kaycee Britt, $2,300; Tim Sands, $500; and Anna Chin, $1,200.

     31   Estimated that uncollectible-account expense for the year was 1% on credit sales of $480,000 and recorded the expense.

     31   Made the closing entry for uncollectible-account expense.

Requirements

1. Open general ledger accounts for Allowance for Uncollectible Accounts and Uncollectible-Account Expense. Keep running balances. All accounts begin with a zero balance. (pp. 80, 463)
2. Record the transactions in the general journal, and post to the two ledger accounts. (pp. 460, 464, 203)
3. The December 31, 2009, balance of Accounts Receivable is $164,500. Show how Accounts Receivable would be reported on the balance sheet at that date. Use the first reporting format on page 461.

P9-29A Kelly Realty loaned money and received the following notes during 2008.

Note	Date	Principal Amount	Interest Rate	Term
(1)	Aug. 1	$12,000	9%	1 year
(2)	Oct. 31	11,000	12%	3 months
(3)	Dec. 19	15,000	10%	30 days

continued . . .

Requirements

For each note, compute interest using a 360-day year. Explanations are not required.

1. Determine the due date and maturity value of each note. (p. 470)
2. Journalize a single adjusting entry at December 31, 2008, to record accrued interest revenue on all three notes. (pp. 472–473)
3. For note (1), journalize the collection of principal and interest at maturity. (pp. 472–473)

Accounting for notes receivable, dishonored notes, and accrued interest revenue

P9-30A Record the following transactions in the general journal of Dvorak Interiors. Round all amounts to the nearest dollar. Explanations are not required. (pp. 472–473, 205, 473–474)

2007	
Dec. 21	Received a $4,400, 30-day, 9% note on account from Monica Lee.
31	Made an adjusting entry to accrue interest on the Lee note.
31	Made a closing entry for interest revenue.
2008	
Jan. 20	Collected the maturity value of the Lee note.
Sept. 14	Loaned $6,000 cash to Bullseye Investors, receiving a three-month, 13% note.
30	Received a $1,600, 60-day, 16% note for a sale to Chuck Powers. Ignore cost of goods sold.
Nov. 29	Chuck Powers dishonored his note at maturity; wrote off the note as uncollectible, debiting Allowance for Uncollectible Notes.
Dec. 14	Collected the maturity value of the Bullseye Investors note.

Journalizing uncollectibles, notes receivable, and accrued interest revenue

P9-31A Speedo Paint Company completed the following selected transactions:

2007	
Dec. 1	Sold inventory to Brent Estes, receiving a $16,000, three-month, 12% note. Ignore cost of goods sold.
31	Made an adjusting entry to accrue interest on the Estes note.
31	Made an adjusting entry to record uncollectible-account expense based on an aging of accounts receivable. The aging schedule shows that $12,800 of accounts receivable will not be collected. Prior to this adjustment, the credit balance in Allowance for Uncollectible Accounts is $11,100.
2008	
Mar. 1	Collected the maturity value of the Estes note.
July 21	Sold merchandise to Ann Mellon, receiving a 60-day, 9% note for $22,000. Ignore cost of goods sold.
Sep. 19	Mellon dishonored her note (failed to pay) at maturity; we converted the maturity value of the note to an account receivable.

continued . . .

Nov. 21	Loaned $40,000 cash to Air Control Co., receiving a 90-day, 9% note.
Dec. 2	Collected in full on account from Ann Mellon.
31	Accrued the interest on the Air Control note.

Requirement

Record the transactions in the journal of Speedo Paint Company. Explanations are not required. (pp. 472–473, 463, 473–474)

Using ratio data to evaluate a company's financial position

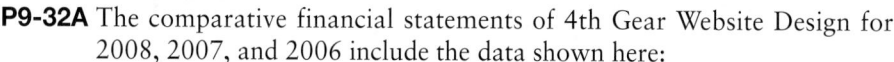

P9-32A The comparative financial statements of 4th Gear Website Design for 2008, 2007, and 2006 include the data shown here:

	(In thousands)		
	2008	**2007**	**2006**
Balance sheet			
Current assets:			
Cash	$ 20	$ 20	$ 10
Short-term investments	70	100	60
Receivables, net	190	150	120
Inventories	420	380	340
Prepaid expenses...............	30	30	20
Total current assets	$ 730	$ 680	$ 550
Total current liabilities..........	$ 480	$ 410	$ 380
Income statement			
Sales revenue	$2,600	$2,500	$1,900

Requirements

1. Compute these ratios for 2008 and 2007:
   a. Current ratio (p. 210)
   b. Acid-test ratio (p. 475)
   c. Days' sales in receivables (p. 476)
2. Write a memo explaining to Les Arnold, the company owner, which ratios improved from 2007 to 2008 and which ratios deteriorated. Discuss whether this trend is favorable or unfavorable for the company. Use the memo format shown for Problem 9-25A, page 489.

Problems (Group B)

Controlling cash receipts from customers

P9-33B Stained Glass Crafters performs all work on account, with regular monthly billing to customers. M. C. Perry, the accountant, opens the mail. Company procedure requires him to separate customer checks from the remittance slips and then post collections to customer accounts. Perry deposits the checks in the bank. He computes each day's total amount posted to

continued . . .

customer accounts and matches this total to the bank deposit slip. This procedure is intended to ensure that all receipts are deposited in the bank.

Requirement

As a consultant hired by Stained Glass Crafters, write a memo to management evaluating the company's internal controls over cash receipts from customers. If the system is effective, identify its strong features. If the system has flaws, propose a way to strengthen the controls. Use the memo format that follows. (p. 457)

MEMO

Date:

To:

From:

Subject:

Accounting for uncollectibles by the allowance and direct write-off methods

P9-34B On May 31, Rosetree Floral Supply had a $160,000 debit balance in Accounts Receivable and a $6,400 credit balance in Allowance for Uncollectible Accounts. During June, Rosetree made:

- Sales on account, $560,000
- Collections on account, $601,000.
- Write-offs of uncollectible receivables, $8,000

Requirements

1. Record sales and collections on account. Then record uncollectible-account expense (2% of credit sales) and write-offs of customer accounts for June using the *allowance* method. Show all June activity in Accounts Receivable, Allowance for Uncollectible Accounts, and Uncollectible-Account Expense (post to these T-accounts). (pp. 460, 461–462, 464)

2. Suppose Rosetree used a different method to account for uncollectible receivables. Record sales and collections on account. Then record uncollectible-account expense for June using the *direct write-off* method. Post to Accounts Receivable and Uncollectible-Account Expense and show their balances at June 30. (pp. 465–466)

3. What amount of uncollectible-account expense would Rosetree report on its June income statement under each of the two methods? Which amount better matches expense with revenue? Give your reason. (pp. 461–462, 465–466)

4. What amount of *net* accounts receivable would Rosetree report on its June 30 balance sheet under each of the two methods? Which amount is more realistic? Give your reason. (pp. 465–466, 469)

Using the percent-of-sales
and aging methods for
uncollectibles

P9-35B At September 30, the accounts of East Terrace Medical Center (ETMC) include the following:

Accounts Receivable	$143,000
Allowance for Uncollectible Accounts (credit balance).........	3,200

During October through December, ETMC completed the following selected transactions:

Dec. 28   Wrote off as uncollectible the $1,500 account receivable from Brown Co. and the $1,100 account receivable from Jacob Weiss.

Dec. 31   Recorded uncollectible-account expense based on the aging of accounts receivable, which follows:

Accounts Receivable	Age of Accounts			
	1–30 Days	31–60 Days	61–90 Days	Over 90 Days
$163,000..........................	$100,000	$40,000	$14,000	$9,000
Estimated percent uncollectible	0.1%	1%	10%	30%

Requirements

1. Record the transactions in the journal. (pp. 463, 464)

2. Open the Allowance for Uncollectible Accounts, and post entries affecting that account. Keep a running balance. (pp. 80, 468)

3. Show how East Terrace Medical Center should report accounts receivable on its balance sheet at December 31, 2007. Use the first reporting format at the top of page 461.

P9-36B Dialex Watches completed the following transactions during 2007 and 2008:

2007

Dec. 31   Estimated that uncollectible-account expense for the year was 1% on credit sales of $400,000, and recorded that amount as expense. Use the allowance method.

31   Made the closing entry for uncollectible-account expense.

2008

Jan. 17   Sold inventory to Mitch Vanez, $600, on account. Ignore cost of goods sold.

June 29   Wrote off the Mitch Vanez account as uncollectible after repeated efforts to collect from him.

Aug. 6   Received $600 from Mitch Vanez, along with a letter stating his apology for paying late. Reinstated Vanez's account in full and recorded the cash collection.

Dec. 31   Made a compound entry to write off the following accounts as uncollectible: Bernard Klaus, $1,700; Marie Monet, $1,300.

continued . . .

2008

Dec. 31 Estimated that uncollectible-account expense for the year was 1% on credit sales of $480,000, and recorded that amount as expense.

31 Made the closing entry for uncollectible-account expense.

Requirements

1. Open general ledger accounts for Allowance for Uncollectible Accounts and Uncollectible-Account Expense. Keep running balances. All accounts begin with a zero balance. (pp. 80, 468)

2. Record the transactions in the general journal, and post to the two ledger accounts. (pp. 460–464, 205)

3. The December 31, 2008, balance of Accounts Receivable is $139,000. Show how Accounts Receivable would be reported on the balance sheet at that date. Use the first reporting format at the top of page 461.

Accounting for notes receivable, including accruing interest revenue

P9-37B Bank of Nashville received the following notes during 2008.

Note	Date	Principal Amount	Interest Rate	Term
(1)	Dec. 11	$13,000	9%	1 year
(2)	Nov. 30	12,000	12%	6 months
(3)	Dec. 7	9,000	10%	60 days

Requirements

For each note compute interest using a 360-day year. Explanations are not required.

1. Determine the due date and maturity value of each note. (p. 470)

2. Journalize a single adjusting entry at December 31, 2008, to record accrued interest revenue on all three notes. (pp. 472–473)

3. For note (1), journalize the collection of principal and interest at maturity. (pp. 472–473)

Accounting for notes receivable, dishonored notes, and accrued interest revenue

P9-38B Record the following transactions in the general journal of Renschler Communication. Explanations are not required. (pp. 472–473, 464, 205)

2007

Dec. 19 Received a $5,000, 60-day, 12% note on account from Video Productions.

31 Made an adjusting entry to accrue interest on the Video Productions note.

31 Made a closing entry for interest revenue.

continued . . .

2008

Feb. 17   Collected the maturity value of the Video Productions note.

June 1   Loaned $10,000 cash to Blues Brothers, receiving a 6-month, 11% note.

Oct. 31   Received a $1,500, 60-day, 12% note for a sale to Mark Phipps. Ignore cost of goods sold.

Dec. 1   Collected the maturity value of the Blues Brothers note.

    30   Mark Phipps dishonored his note at maturity; wrote off the note receivable as uncollectible, debiting Allowance for Uncollectible Notes.

Journalizing uncollectibles, notes receivable, and accrued interest revenue

P9-39B Assume that La-Z Recliner Chairs completed the following selected transactions:

2007

July   1   Sold goods to Wal-Mart, receiving a $40,000, 9-month, 9% note. Ignore cost of goods sold.

Dec. 31   Made an adjusting entry to accrue interest on the Wal-Mart note.

    31   Made an adjusting entry to record uncollectible-account expense based on an aging of accounts receivable. The aging schedule shows that $14,400 of accounts receivable will not be collected. Prior to this adjustment, the credit balance in Allowance for Uncollectible Accounts is $11,300.

2008

Apr. 1   Collected the maturity value of the Wal-Mart note.

June 23   Sold merchandise to Artesian Corp., receiving a 60-day, 10% note for $9,000. Ignore cost of goods sold.

Aug. 22   Artesian Corp. dishonored (failed to pay) its note at maturity; we converted the maturity value of the note to an account receivable.

Nov. 16   Loaned $20,000 cash to Crane, Inc., receiving a 90-day, 12% note.

Dec. 5   Collected in full on account from Artesian Corp.

    31   Accrued the interest on the Crane, Inc., note.

Requirement

Record the transactions in the journal of La-Z Recliner Chairs. Explanations are not required. (pp. 472–473, 463, 473–474)

Using ratio data to evaluate a company's financial position

P9-40B The comparative financial statements of Lomax Cosmetic Supply for 2009, 2008, and 2007 include the following selected data:

continued . . .

	(In thousands)		
	2009	2008	2007
Balance sheet			
Current assets:			
Cash...................................	$ 90	$ 80	$ 60
Short-term investments......	140	170	126
Receivables, net.................	280	260	244
Inventories	360	340	300
Prepaid expenses	50	20	40
Total current assets............	$ 920	$ 870	$ 770
Total current liabilities..........	$ 580	$ 600	$ 660
Income statement			
Sales revenue........................	$5,840	$5,110	$4,200

Requirements

1. Compute these ratios for 2009 and 2008:

    a. Current ratio (p. 210)

    b. Acid-test ratio (p. 475)

    c. Days' sales in receivables (p. 476)

2. Write a memo explaining to Sandra Lomax, the company owner, which ratios improved from 2008 to 2009 and which ratios deteriorated. Discuss whether this trend is favorable or unfavorable for the company. Use the memo format shown for Problem 9-33B, page 493.

for 24/7 practice visit
www.MyAccountingLab.com

Apply Your Knowledge

Decision Cases

Evaluating bankcard sales for profitability

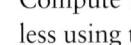

Case 1. Weddings on Demand sells on account and manages its own receivables. Average experience for the past three years has been as follows:

	Total
Sales..	$350,000
Cost of goods sold	210,000
Bad-debt expense.........................	4,000
Other expenses	61,000

Mariel Picasso, the owner, is considering whether to accept bankcards (VISA, MasterCard) from customers because some are slow to pay. Typically, accepting bankcards increases total sales and cost of goods sold by 10%. But VISA and MasterCard charge approximately 2% of bankcard sales. If Picasso switches to bankcards, she'll no longer have bad-debt expense. She can also save $5,000 on other expenses. After the switchover to bankcards, Picasso expects cash sales of $200,000.

Requirement

Should Picasso start accepting bankcards? Show the computations of net income under her present arrangement and under the bankcard plan. (Challenge)

Comparing the allowance and direct write-off methods for uncollectibles

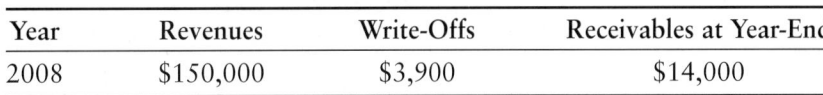

Case 2. Scribbles Stationery has always used the direct write-off method to account for uncollectibles. The company's revenues, bad-debt write-offs, and year-end receivables for the most recent year follow.

Year	Revenues	Write-Offs	Receivables at Year-End
2008	$150,000	$3,900	$14,000

Scribbles is applying for a bank loan, and the loan officer requires figures based on the allowance method of accounting for bad debts. In the past bad debts have run about 4% of revenues.

Requirements

Scribbles must give the banker the following information:

1. How much more or less would net income be for 2008 if Scribbles were to use the allowance method for bad debts? (pp. 461–462, 465–466)

2. How much of the receivables balance at the end of 2008 does Scribbles actually expect to collect? (pp. 461–462)

Compute these amounts, and then explain for Scribbles why net income is more or less using the allowance method versus the direct write-off method for uncollectibles.

Ethical Issue

E-Z Loan Co. makes loans to high-risk borrowers. E-Z borrows from its bank and then lends money to people with bad credit. The bank requires E-Z Loan to submit quarterly financial statements in order to keep its line of credit. E-Z's main asset is Notes Receivable. Therefore, Uncollectible-Note Expense and Allowance for Uncollectible Note are important accounts.

Slade McQueen, the owner of E-Z Loan Co., wants net income to increase in a smooth pattern, rather than increase in some periods and decrease in others. To report smoothly increasing net income, McQueen underestimates Uncollectible-Note Expense in some periods. In other periods, McQueen overestimates the expense. He reasons that over time the income overstatements roughly offset the income understatements.

Requirement

Is McQueen's practice of smoothing income ethical? Why or why not?

Financial Statement Case

Analyzing accounts
receivable and uncollectibles

2 6

Use Amazon.com's balance sheet and the Note 1 data on "Allowance for Doubtful Accounts" in Appendix A at the end of this book.

1. Do accounts receivable appear to be an important asset for Amazon.com? What about Amazon's business affects the importance of accounts receivable?

2. Assume that all of "Accounts Receivable, Net and Other Current Assets" is accounts receivable. Further assume that gross receivables at December 31, 2005, were $317 million. Answer the following questions based on these data, plus what's reported on the balance sheet.

   a. How much did customers owe Amazon.com at December 31, 2005?

   b. How much did Amazon expect to collect from customers after December 31, 2005?

   c. Of the total receivable amount at December 31, 2005, how much did Amazon expect *not* to collect?

3. Compute Amazon.com's acid-test ratio at the end of 2005. Marketable securities are short-term investments. Assume that other current assets are zero. If all the current liabilities came due immediately, could Amazon pay them?

Team Project

Notes Receivable of the Bank. Bob Opper and Denise Shapp worked for several years as sales representatives for Xerox Corporation. During this time, they became close friends as they acquired expertise with the company's full range of copier equipment. Now they see an opportunity to put their experience to work and fulfill lifelong desires to establish their own business. Lakeside College, located in their city, is expanding, and there is no copy center within five miles of the campus. Business in the area is booming, and the population in this section of the city is growing.

continued . . .

Opper and Shapp want to open a copy center, similar to a FedEx Kinko's, near the campus. A small shopping center across the street from the college has a vacancy that would fit their needs. Opper and Shapp each have $20,000 to invest in the business, and they forecast the need for $30,000 to renovate the store. Xerox Corporation will lease two large copiers to them at a total monthly rental of $4,000. With enough cash to see them through the first six months of operation, they are confident they can make the business succeed. The two work very well together, and both have excellent credit ratings. Opper and Shapp must borrow $80,000 to start the business, advertise its opening, and keep it running for its first six months.

Assume the role of Opper and Shapp, the partners who will own Lakeside Copy Center.

1. As a group, visit a copy center to familiarize yourselves with its operations. If possible, interview the manager or another employee. Then write a loan request that Opper and Shapp will submit to a bank with the intent of borrowing $80,000 to be paid back over three years. The loan will be a personal loan to the partnership of Opper and Shapp, not to Lakeside Copy Center. The request should specify all the details of Opper's and Shapp's plan that will motivate the bank to grant the loan. Include a budgeted income statement for the first six months of the copy center's operation.

2. As a group, interview a loan officer in a bank. Have the loan officer evaluate your loan request. Write a report, or make a presentation to your class—as directed by your instructor—to reveal the loan officer's decision.

For Internet Exercises, Excel in Practice, and additional online activies, go to the Web site www.prenhall.com/horngren.

Quick Check Answers

1. *d*   2. *d*   3. *a*   4. *b*   5. *a*   6. *d*   7. *c*   8. *b*   9. *b*   10. *c*

Appendix 9A

Discounting a Note Receivable

A payee of a note receivable may need cash before the maturity date of the note When this occurs, the payee may sell the note, a practice called **discounting a note receivable**. The price to be received for the note is determined by present-value concepts. But the transaction between the seller and the buyer of the note can take any form agreeable to the two parties. Here we illustrate one procedure used for discounting short-term notes receivable. To receive cash immediately, the seller accepts a lower price than the note's maturity value.

To illustrate discounting a note receivable, suppose **General Electric** loaned $15,000 to Dorman Builders on October 20, 2008. GE took a note receivable from Dorman. The maturity date of the 90-day 10% Dorman note is January 18, 2009. Suppose GE discounts the Dorman note at First City Bank on December 9, 2008, when the note is 50 days old. The bank applies a 12% annual interest rate to determine the discounted value of the note. The bank will use a discount rate that is higher than the note's interest rate in order to earn some interest on the transaction. The discounted value, called the *proceeds,* is the amount GE receives from the bank. The proceeds can be computed in five steps, as shown in Exhibit 9A-1.

EXHIBIT 9A-1   Discounting (Selling) a Note Receivable: GE Discounts the Dorman Builders Note

Step	Computation	
1. Compute the original amount of interest on the note receivable.	$15,000 × 0.10 × 90/360	= $375
2. Maturity value of the note = Principal + Interest	$15,000 + $375	= $15,375
3. Determine the period (number of days, months, or years) the *bank* will hold the note (the discount period).	Dec. 9, 2008 to Jan. 18, 2009	= 40 days
4. Compute the bank's discount on the note. This is the bank's interest revenue from holding the note.	$15,375 × 0.12 × 40/360	= $205
5. Seller's proceeds from discounting the note receivable = Maturity value of the note − Bank's discount on the note.	$15,375 − $205	= $15,170

The authors thank Doug Hamilton for suggesting this exhibit.

GE's entry to record discounting (selling) the note on December 9, 2008, is:

2008			
Dec. 9	Cash	15,170	
	Note Receivable—Dorman Builders		15,000
	Interest Revenue ($15,170 − $15,000)		170
	Discounted a note receivable.		

When the proceeds from discounting a note receivable are less than the principal amount of the note, the payee records a debit to Interest Expense for the amount of the difference. For example, GE could discount the note receivable for cash proceeds of $14,980. The entry to record this discounting transaction is:

	2008			
	Dec. 9	Cash	14,980	
		Interest Expense	20	
		Note Receivable—Dorman Builders		15,000
		Discounted a note receivable.		

Appendix 9A Assignments

Exercise

Notes receivable transactions

E9A-1 Big Tex Toys sells on account. When a customer account becomes three months old, Big Tex converts the account to a note receivable and immediately discounts the note to a bank. During 2009, Big Tex completed these transactions:

Aug. 29	Sold goods on account to V. Moyer, $5,000.
Dec. 1	Received a $5,000, 60-day, 10% note from Moyer in satisfaction of his past-due account receivable.
1	Sold the Moyer note by discounting it to a bank for $4,800.

Requirement
Record the transactions in Big Tex's journal.

Problem

Notes receivable transactions

P9A-1 A company received the following notes during 2008. The notes were discounted on the dates and at the rates indicated:

Note	Date	Principal Amount	Interest Rate	Term	Date Discounted	Discount Rate
(1)	Sept. 1	$8,000	9%	120 days	Nov. 2	12%
(2)	Aug. 19	9,000	8%	90 days	Aug. 30	10%
(3)	July 15	6,000	6%	6 months	Oct. 15	8%

Requirements
Identify each note by number, compute interest using a 360-day year, and round all interest amounts to the nearest dollar. Explanations are not required.

1. Determine the due date and maturity value of each note.
2. Determine the discount and proceeds from the sale (discounting) of each note.
3. Journalize the discounting of notes (1) and (2).

10 Plant Assets and Intangibles

Learning Objectives

1 Measure the cost of a plant asset

2 Account for depreciation

3 Select the best depreciation method for tax purposes

4 Account for the disposal of a plant asset

5 Account for natural resources

6 Account for intangible assets

Your business, In Motion T-Shirts, is at a crossroads. Thus far, you've hired outsiders to print logos on the T-shirts that you sell. By letting three printers compete against each other, you've been able to hold costs down. But two of the printers have gone out of business and the only one remaining has jacked up fees. What to do?

One option is to purchase screen-printing equipment and imprint the logos yourself. You'll have to pay $3,000 for the equipment, but the cost savings should recoup your outlay within a year. And you won't have to wait for others to get a job out. Go ahead. Take the plunge and buy the equipment.

Equipment is one type of plant asset. Others include land, buildings, and furniture. Often plant assets are referred to as Property, Plant, and Equipment.

Plant assets have some special characteristics. For example, you hold them for use in the business—not to sell as inventory. Also,

- Plant assets are relatively expensive, and their cost can be a challenge to determine.
- Plant assets last a long time—usually for several years. If plant assets wear out or become obsolete, you need to depreciate them.
- Plant assets may be sold or traded in. Accounting for the disposal of a plant asset is more complicated than selling inventory.

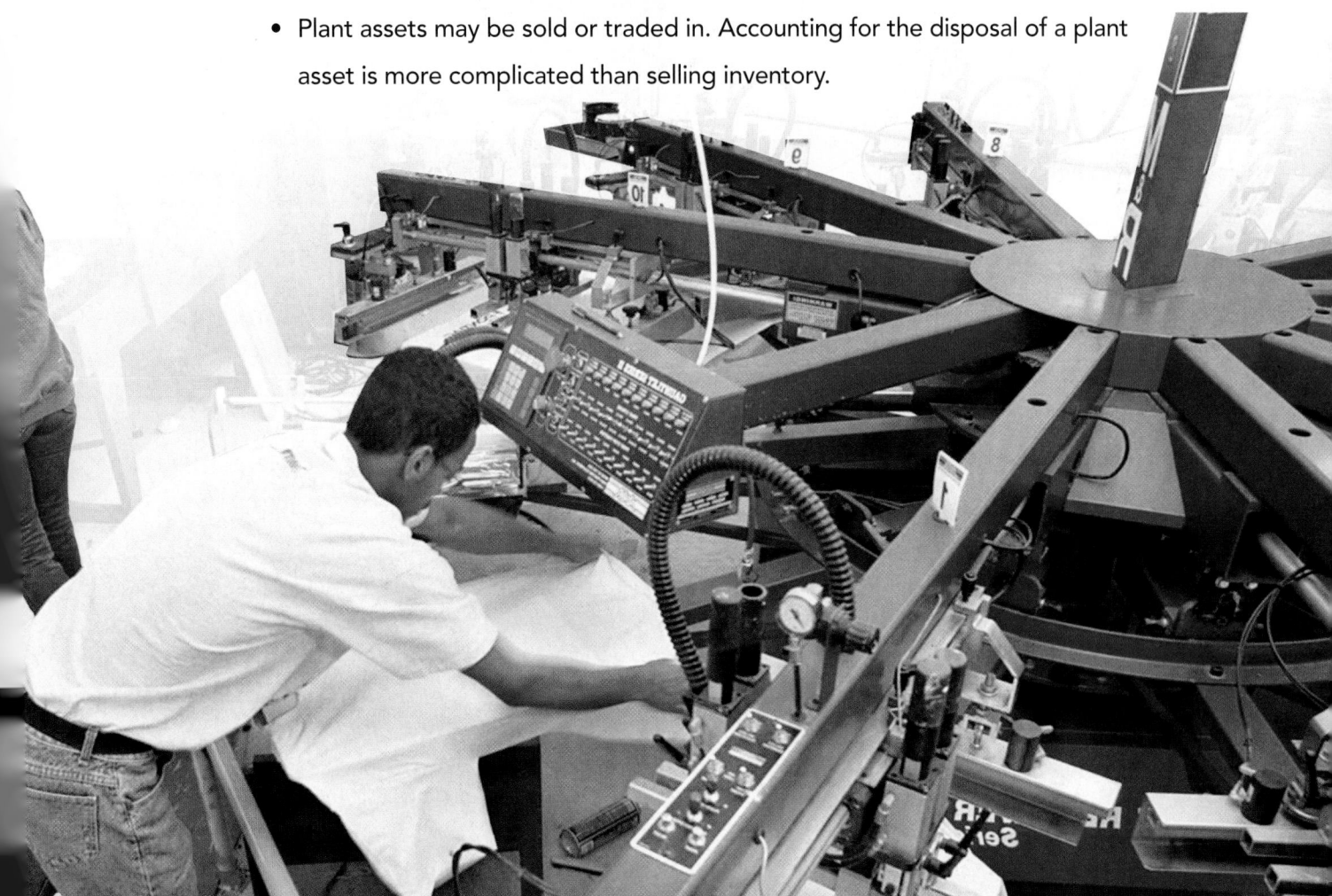

As you can see, plant assets pose some accounting challenges. This chapter addresses these issues and shows how to account for

1. Plant assets, which are useful because of their physical characteristics
2. **Intangible assets**, which have no physical form ■

Chapter 10 concludes our coverage of assets, except for investments. After completing this chapter, you should understand the various assets of a business and how to account for them. Let's begin with an example that is familiar to you.

Plant assets have their own terminology. Exhibit 10-1 shows which expense applies to each category of plant asset.

EXHIBIT 10-1   **Plant Assets and Their Related Expenses**

Plant Asset	Buildings, Machinery, Equipment, Furniture, Fixtures	Natural Resources	Intangible Assets

Related Expense	Depreciation	Depletion	Amortization

Measuring the Cost of a Plant Asset

1 Measure the cost of a plant asset

The *cost principle* says to carry an asset at its cost—the amount paid for the asset. The rule for measuring cost is:

$$\text{Cost of an asset} = \frac{\text{Sum of all the costs incurred to bring the asset}}{\text{to its intended purpose, net of all discounts}}$$

The *cost of a plant asset* is its purchase price plus taxes, purchase commissions, and all other amounts paid to ready the asset for its intended use. In Chapter 6, we applied this principle to inventory. These costs vary, so we discuss each asset individually.

Land and Land Improvements

The cost of land includes the following costs paid by the purchaser:

- purchase price
- brokerage commission
- survey and legal fees
- back property taxes
- cost of clearing the land and removing unwanted buildings

The cost of land is not depreciated.

The cost of land does **not** include the following costs:

- fencing
- paving
- sprinkler systems
- lighting

These separate plant assets—called *land improvements*—are subject to depreciation.

Suppose In Motion T-Shirts needs property and purchases land for $50,000. You also pay $4,000 in back property taxes, $2,000 in transfer taxes, $5,000 to remove an old building, and a $1,000 survey fee. What is your cost of this land? Exhibit 10-2 shows all the costs incurred to bring the land to its intended use, as follows:

EXHIBIT 10-2 **Measuring the Cost of Land**

Purchase price of land		$62,000
Add related costs:		
Back property taxes	$4,000	
Transfer taxes	2,000	
Removal of building	5,000	
Survey fee	1,000	
Total related costs		12,000
Total cost of land		$62,000

Suppose you sign a $50,000 note payable for the land and pay cash for the related costs. Your entry to record purchase of the land is:

Land		62,000	
	Note Payable		50,000
	Cash		12,000

We would say that you *capitalized* the cost of the land at $62,000. This means that In Motion debited the Land account for $62,000.

Suppose you then pay $20,000 for fences, paving, lighting, and signs. The following entry records the cost of these land improvements.

Land Improvements		20,000	
	Cash		20,000

Land and Land Improvements are two entirely separate assets. The cost of land improvements is depreciated over that asset's useful life.

Buildings

The cost of a building includes:

- architectural fees
- building permits
- contractor charges
- payments for material, labor, and overhead

The time to complete a building can be months, even years. If the company constructs its own assets, the cost of the building may include the cost of interest on borrowed money.

You may purchase an existing building. Its cost includes all the usual items, plus the cost to repair and renovate the building for its intended use.

Machinery and Equipment

The cost of machinery and equipment includes its:

- purchase price (less any discounts)
- transportation charges
- insurance while in transit
- sales and other taxes
- purchase commission
- installation costs
- cost of testing the asset before it is used

After the asset is up and running, we no longer capitalize these costs to the Equipment account. Thereafter, insurance, taxes, and maintenance costs are recorded as expenses.

There are many different kinds of equipment. In Motion T-Shirts has screen-printing equipment. American Airlines has airplanes, and Kinko's has copiers. Most businesses have computer equipment.

Furniture and Fixtures

Furniture and fixtures include desks, chairs, file cabinets, and display racks. The cost of furniture and fixtures includes the basic cost of each asset (less any discounts), plus all other costs to ready the asset for use.

A Lump-Sum (Basket) Purchase of Assets

A company may pay a single price for several assets as a group—a "basket purchase." For example, In Motion T-Shirts may pay one price for land and a building. For accounting, you must identify the cost of each asset, as shown in the following diagram. The total cost (100%) is divided among the assets according to their relative sales values. This is called the *relative-sales-value method*.

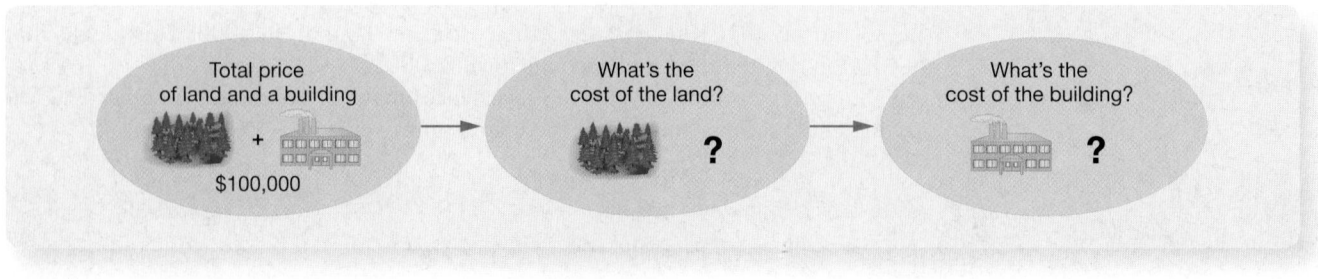

Suppose you purchase land and a building for your plant, and the combined purchase price is $100,000. An appraisal indicates that the land's market (sales) value is $30,000 and the building's market (sales) value is $90,000.

First, figure the ratio of each asset's market value to the total for both assets combined. The total appraised value is $120,000.

	Land		Building		Total Market Value
	$30,000	+	$90,000	=	$120,000

The land makes up 25% of the total market value, and the building 75%, as follows:

Asset	Market (Sales) Value	Percentage of Total Value	Total Purchase Price	Cost of Each Asset
Land	$ 30,000	$30,000/$120,000 = 25% × $100,000 =		$ 25,000
Building	90,000	$90,000/$120,000 = 75% × 100,000 =		75,000
Total	$120,000	100%		$100,000

Suppose you pay cash. The entry to record the purchase of the land and building is:

Land	25,000	
Building	75,000	
Cash		100,000

Capital Expenditures

Accountants divide expenditures on plant assets into two categories:

- Capital expenditures
- Expenses

Capital expenditures are debited to an asset account because they:

- Increase the asset's capacity or efficiency, or
- Extend the asset's useful life

Examples of capital expenditures include the purchase price plus all the other costs to bring an asset to its intended use, as discussed in the preceding sections. Also, an **extraordinary repair** is a capital expenditure because it adds to the asset's capacity or useful life.

Expenses, such as repair or maintenance expense, are *not* debited to an asset account because they merely maintain the asset in working order. Expenses are immediately subtracted from revenue. Examples include the costs of maintaining equipment, repairing a truck, and replacing its tires. These **ordinary repairs** are debited to Repair Expense.

Exhibit 10-3 shows some (a) capital expenditures and (b) expenses for a delivery truck.

Treating a capital expenditure as an expense, or vice versa, creates an accounting error. Suppose American Airlines makes a capital expenditure and expenses this

EXHIBIT 10-3 Delivery-Truck Expenditures— Capital Expenditure or Expense?

CAPITAL EXPENDITURE: Debit an Asset Account	EXPENSE: Debit Repair and Maintenance Expense
Extraordinary repairs:	*Ordinary repairs:*
Major engine overhaul	Repair of transmission or engine
Modification for new use	Oil change, lubrication, and so on
Addition to storage capacity	Replacement of tires or windshield
	Paint job

cost. This is an accounting error because the cost should have been debited to an asset. This error:

- overstates expenses
- understates net income

On the balance sheet, the Equipment account is understated.

Capitalizing an expense creates the opposite error. Expenses are understated, and net income is overstated. The balance sheet overstates assets.

Depreciation

As we've seen, **depreciation** is the allocation of a plant asset's cost to expense over its useful life. Depreciation matches the expense against the revenue to measure net income. Exhibit 10-4 illustrates depreciation for a Boeing 737 jet by American Airlines.

EXHIBIT 10-4

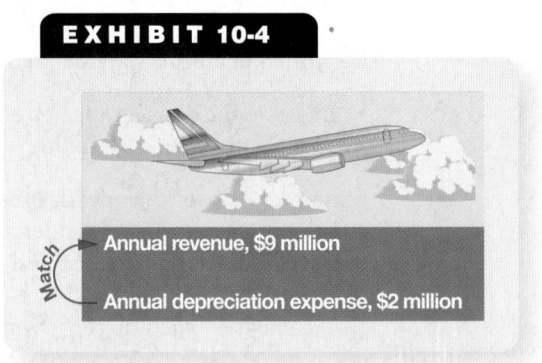

Annual revenue, $9 million

Annual depreciation expense, $2 million

Match

Depreciation and the Matching of Expense with Revenue

Suppose American buys a Boeing 737 jet. American believes it will get 10 years of service from the plane. Using the straight-line depreciation method, American expenses $\frac{1}{10}$ of the asset's cost in each of its 10 years of use.

Let's contrast what depreciation is with what it is *not*.

1. *Depreciation is not a process of valuation.* Businesses do not record depreciation based on the asset's market (sales) value.

2. *Depreciation does not mean that the business sets aside cash to replace an asset when it is used up.* Depreciation has nothing to do with cash.

Causes of Depreciation

All assets except land wear out. For some plant assets, *wear and tear* causes depreciation. For example, physical factors wear out the jets that American, Delta, and United fly. The screen printer you use at In Motion T-Shirts is also subject to physical wear and tear.

Assets such as computers and software may become *obsolete* before they wear out. An asset is obsolete when another asset can do the job more efficiently. Thus, an asset's useful life may be shorter than its physical life. Accountants usually depreciate computers over a short period—perhaps 2 to 4 years—even though they can be used longer. In all cases, the asset's cost is depreciated over its useful life.

Measuring Depreciation

Depreciation of a plant asset is based on three factors:

1. Cost
2. Estimated useful life
3. Estimated residual value

Cost is known. The other two factors are estimates.

Estimated useful life is the length of the service period expected from the asset. Useful life may be expressed in years, output, or miles. For example, a building's life is stated in years, an airplane in the number of miles it can fly, and a Xerox copier in the number of copies it can make.

Estimated residual value—also called **salvage value**—is the asset's expected cash value at the end of its useful life. A delivery truck's useful life may be 100,000 miles. At the end, the company will sell the truck. The expected cash receipt is the truck's estimated residual value. Estimated residual value is *not* depreciated because you expect to receive this amount at the end. If there's no residual value, then depreciate the full cost of the asset. Cost minus residual value is called **depreciable cost**.

Depreciation Methods

2 Account for depreciation

There are three major depreciation methods[1]:

- Straight-line
- Units-of-production
- Declining-balance

These methods work differently, but they all result in the same total depreciation. Exhibit 10-5 gives the data we will use for an American Airlines baggage-handling truck.

---

[1]We omit the sum-of-years'-digits method because only 7 of 600 companies in a recent poll used it.

EXHIBIT 10-5 Data for Recording Depreciation on a Truck

Data Item	Amount
Cost of truck	$41,000
Less: Estimated residual value	(1,000)
Depreciable cost	$40,000
Estimated useful life	
Years	5 years
Units of production	100,000 mi.

Straight-Line Method

The **straight-line (SL) method** allocates an equal amount of depreciation to each year. Depreciable cost is divided by useful life to determine annual depreciation. The equation for SL depreciation, applied to the American Airlines truck, is:

$$\text{Straight-line depreciation} = \frac{\text{Cost } - \text{ Residual value}}{\text{Useful life, in years}} = \frac{\$41,000 - \$1,000}{5}$$
$$= \$8,000 \text{ per year}$$

The entry to record each year's depreciation is:

Depreciation Expense	8,000	
Accumulated Depreciation		8,000

This truck was purchased on January 1, 2008, and a *straight-line depreciation schedule* is given in Exhibit 10-6. The final column shows the asset's *book value*, which is cost less accumulated depreciation.

EXHIBIT 10-6 Straight-Line Depreciation for a Truck

Date	Asset Cost	Depreciation for the Year			Accumulated Depreciation	Book Value
		Depreciation Rate	Depreciable Cost	Depreciation Expense		
1-1-2008	$41,000					$41,000
12-31-2008		0.20* ×	$40,000 =	$8,000	$ 8,000	33,000
12-31-2009		0.20 ×	40,000 =	8,000	16,000	25,000
12-31-2010		0.20 ×	40,000 =	8,000	24,000	17,000
12-31-2011		0.20 ×	40,000 =	8,000	32,000	9,000
12-31-2012		0.20 ×	40,000 =	8,000	40,000	1,000

*1/5 year = 0.20 per year

As an asset is used, accumulated depreciation increases and book value decreases. See the Accumulated Depreciation and Book Value columns in Exhibit 10-6. An asset's final book value is *residual value* ($1,000 in Exhibit 10-6). At the end, the asset is said to be *fully depreciated*.

Units-of-Production (UOP) Method

The **units-of-production (UOP) method** allocates a fixed amount of depreciation to each *unit of output,* as illustrated in Exhibit 10-7:

$$\begin{matrix} \text{Units-of-production} \\ \text{depreciation} \\ \text{per unit of output} \end{matrix} = \frac{\text{Cost} - \text{Residual value}}{\text{Useful life, in units of production}} = \frac{\$41,000 - \$1,000}{100,000 \text{ miles}}$$

$$= \$0.40 \text{ per mile}$$

EXHIBIT 10-7   Units-of-Production Depreciation for a Truck

Date	Asset Cost	Depreciation for the Year				Accumulated Depreciation	Book Value
		Depreciation Per Unit		Number of Units	Depreciation Expense		
1-1-2008	$41,000						$41,000
12-31-2008		$0.40	×	20,000	= $ 8,000	$ 8,000	33,000
12-31-2009		0.40	×	30,000	= 12,000	20,000	21,000
12-31-2010		0.40	×	25,000	= 10,000	30,000	11,000
12-31-2011		0.40	×	15,000	= 6,000	36,000	5,000
12-31-2012		0.40	×	10,000	= 4,000	40,000	1,000

This truck is likely to be driven 20,000 miles the first year, 30,000 the second, 25,000 the third, 15,000 the fourth, and 10,000 during the fifth. The UOP depreciation each period varies with the number of units the asset produces. Exhibit 10-7 shows the *UOP depreciation schedule* for this asset.

Double-Declining Balance Method

Double-declining-balance depreciation is *accelerated.* An **accelerated depreciation method** writes off more depreciation near the start of an asset's life than straight-line does. The main accelerated method is **double-declining-balance (DDB)**. This method multiplies decreasing book value by a constant percentage that is 2 times the straight-line rate. DDB amounts can be computed in two steps:

1. Compute the straight-line depreciation rate per year. A 5-year asset has a straight-line rate of 1/5, or 20% per year. A 10-year asset has a straight-line rate of 1/10, or 10% per year, and so on.

   Multiply the straight-line rate by 2. The DDB rate for a 5-year asset is 40% per year (20% × 2 = 40%). For a 10-year asset, the DDB rate is 20% (10% × 2 = 20%).

2. Compute DDB depreciation for each year. Multiply the asset's book value (cost less accumulated depreciation) at the beginning of each year by the DDB rate.

Ignore residual value, except for the last year. The first-year depreciation for the truck in Exhibit 10-5 is:

$$\text{DDB depreciation for the first year} = \begin{array}{c}\text{Asset book value}\\ \text{at the beginning}\\ \text{of the year}\end{array} \times \text{DDB rate}$$

$$\$16{,}400 = \$41{,}000 \times 0.40$$

The same approach is used to compute DDB depreciation for each year, except for the final year.

Final-year depreciation is the amount needed to bring the asset to residual value. In the DDB schedule (Exhibit 10-8), final-year depreciation is $4,314—book value, $5,314, less the $1,000 residual value.

EXHIBIT 10-8   **Double-Declining-Balance Depreciation for a Truck**

Date	Asset Cost	Depreciation for the Year				Accumulated Depreciation	Book Value
		DDB Rate		Book Value	Depreciation Expense		
1-1-2008	$41,000						$41,000
12-31-2008		0.40	×	$41,000 =	$16,400	$16,400	24,600
12-31-2009		0.40	×	24,600 =	9,840	26,240	14,760
12-31-2010		0.40	×	14,760 =	5,904	32,144	8,856
12-31-2011		0.40	×	8,856 =	3,542	35,686	5,314
12-31-2012				=	4,314*	40,000	1,000

*Last-year depreciation is the "plug figure" needed to reduce book value to the residual amount ($5,314 – $1,000 = $4,314).

The DDB method differs from the other methods in two ways:

- Residual value is ignored at the start. In the first year, depreciation is computed on the asset's full cost.
- Final-year depreciation is the amount needed to bring the asset to residual value. Final-year depreciation is a "plug figure."

SWITCHOVER TO STRAIGHT-LINE   Some companies change to the straight-line method during the next-to-last year of the asset's life. Let's use this plan to compute annual depreciation for 2011 and 2012. In Exhibit 10-8, at the end of 2010:

Book value = $8,856

Depreciable cost = $7,856 ($8,856 − $1,000)

Straight-line depreciation for 2004 and 2005

= $3,928 ($7,856 ÷ 2 years remaining)

Comparing Depreciation Methods

Let's compare the depreciation methods. Annual amounts vary, but total depreciation is $40,000 for all methods.

| | AMOUNT OF DEPRECIATION PER YEAR | | |
| | | | Accelerated Method |
Year	Straight-Line	Units-of-Production	Double-Declining-Balance
1	$ 8,000	$ 8,000	$16,400
2	8,000	12,000	9,840
3	8,000	10,000	5,904
4	8,000	6,000	3,542
5	8,000	4,000	4,314
Total	$40,000	$40,000	$40,000

Which method is best? That depends on the asset. A business should match an asset's expense against the revenue that the asset produces.

Straight-Line

For an asset that generates revenue evenly over time, the straight-line method follows the matching principle. Each period shows an equal amount of depreciation.

Units-of-Production

The UOP method works best for an asset that depreciates due to wear and tear, rather than obsolescence. More use causes greater depreciation.

Double-Declining-Balance

The accelerated method (DDB) works best for assets that produce more revenue in their early years. Higher depreciation in the early years is matched against the greater revenue.

Comparisons

Exhibit 10-9 graphs annual depreciation for the three methods.

- Straight-line is flat because depreciation is the same each period.
- Units-of-production follows no pattern because depreciation varies with asset use.
- Accelerated depreciation is greater in the first year and less in the later years.

EXHIBIT 10-9   **Depreciation Patterns for the Various Methods**

The straight-line depreciation method is most popular, used by the vast majority of companies. Exhibit 10-10 shows the percentages of companies that use each method.

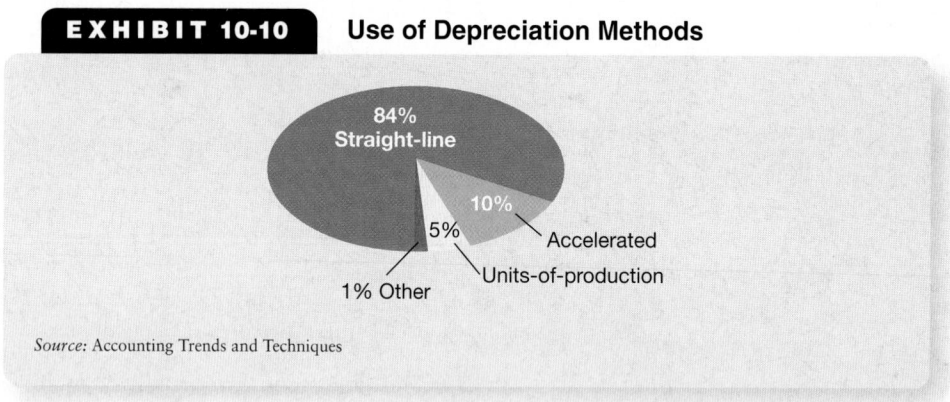

EXHIBIT 10-10 Use of Depreciation Methods

84%
Straight-line

10%
Accelerated

Units-of-production

5%

1% Other

Source: Accounting Trends and Techniques

Summary Problem 1

Latté On Demand purchased a coffee drink machine on January 1, 2007, for $44,000. Expected useful life is 10 years or 100,000 drinks, and residual value is $4,000. Under three depreciation methods, annual depreciation and total accumulated depreciation at the end of 2007 and 2008 are as follows:

	Method A		Method B		Method C	
Year	Annual Depreciation Expense	Accumulated Depreciation	Annual Depreciation Expense	Accumulated Depreciation	Annual Depreciation Expense	Accumulated Depreciation
2007	$1,200	$1,200	$8,800	$ 8,800	$4,000	$4,000
2008	5,600	6,800	7,040	15,840	4,000	8,000

Requirements

1. Identify the depreciation method used in each instance, and show the equation and computation for each method. (Round to the nearest dollar.)

2. Assume use of the same method through 2009. Compute depreciation expense, accumulated depreciation, and asset book value for 2007 through 2009 under each method, assuming 12,000 units of production in 2009.

Solution

Requirement 1

Method A: Units-of-Production

$$\text{Depreciation per unit} = \frac{\$44,000 - \$4,000}{100,000 \text{ units}} = \$0.40$$

2007: $0.40 × 3,000 units = $1,200

2008: $0.40 × 14,000 units = $5,600

Method B: Double-Declining-Balance

$$\text{Rate} = \frac{1}{10 \text{ years}} \times 2 = 20\%$$

2007: 0.20 × $44,000 = $8,800

2008: 0.20 × ($44,000 − $8,800) = $7,040

Method C: Straight-Line

Depreciable cost = $44,000 − $4,000 = $40,000

Each year: $40,000/10 years = $4,000

Requirement 2

Method A: Units-of-Production

Year	Annual Depreciation Expense	Accumulated Depreciation	Book Value
Start			$44,000
2007	$1,200	$ 1,200	42,800
2008	5,600	6,800	37,200
2009	4,800	11,600	32,400

Method B: Double-Declining-Balance

Year	Annual Depreciation Expense	Accumulated Depreciation	Book Value
Start			$44,000
2007	$8,800	$ 8,800	35,200
2008	7,040	15,840	28,160
2009	5,632	21,472	22,528

Method C: Straight-Line

Year	Annual Depreciation Expense	Accumulated Depreciation	Book Value
Start			$44,000
2007	$4,000	$ 4,000	40,000
2008	4,000	8,000	36,000
2009	4,000	12,000	32,000

Computations for 2009:

Units-of-production	$0.40 × 12,000 units = $4,800
Double-declining-balance	0.20 × $28,160 = $5,632
Straight-line	$40,000/10 years = $4,000

Other Issues in Accounting for Plant Assets

Depreciation affects income taxes so you need to select the method that minimizes your taxes. Another issue is that you may have a gain or a loss when you sell a plant asset.

Depreciation and Income Taxes

3 Select the best depreciation method for tax purposes

As we just saw, most companies use straight-line depreciation for their financial statements. But to keep taxes low, they use accelerated depreciation.

Suppose you manage American Airline operations at Chicago O'Hare Airport. The IRS allows DDB depreciation, and you prefer DDB to straight-line. Why? Because DDB provides the fastest tax deductions and conserves cash. You can then invest the cash and earn more income. This is a common strategy.

To see how depreciation affects taxes and cash, recall our earlier depreciation for the American Airlines truck: First-year depreciation is:

- $8,000 under straight-line
- $16,400 under double-declining-balance

Which tax deduction do you prefer? DDB gives you a greater tax deduction and saves cash.

A special depreciation method called the *modified accelerated cost recovery system (MACRS)* is used for income tax purposes. Under MACRS, assets are divided into classes by asset life, as shown in Exhibit 10-11. MACRS depreciation is computed by the DDB method, the 150%-declining-balance method, or the straight-line method. Under 150% DB, the annual depreciation rate is computed by multiplying the straight-line rate by 1.50 (rather than by 2, as for DDB). For a 20-year asset, the straight-line rate is 0.05 (1/20 = 0.05), so the annual MACRS depreciation rate is 0.075 (0.05 × 1.50 = 0.075).

EXHIBIT 10-11 Modified Accelerated Cost Recovery System (MACRS) Depreciation Method

Class Identified by Asset Life (Years)	Representative Assets	Depreciation Method
3	Racehorses	DDB
5	Automobiles, light trucks	DDB
10	Equipment	DDB
20	Certain real estate	150% DB
27 1/2	Residential rental property	SL
39	Nonresidential rental property	SL

Depreciation for Partial Years

Companies purchase plant assets whenever they need them—such as February 8 or August 23. They don't wait until the beginning of a period. Therefore, companies develop policies to compute depreciation for partial years. Suppose In Motion T-Shirts purchases a building on July 1 for $100,000. The building's estimated life is 20 years, with estimated residual value of $40,000. How does In Motion compute depreciation for the year ended December 31?

Many companies compute partial-year depreciation by first calculating a full year's depreciation. They then multiply full-year depreciation by the fraction of the year that they used the asset. In this case you need to record 6 months' depreciation for July through December. Under the straight-line method, the year's depreciation for your building is $1,500, computed as follows:

$$\text{Full-year depreciation:} \quad \frac{\$100,000 - \$40,000}{20 \text{ years}} = \$3,000$$

$$\text{Partial-year depreciation:} \quad \$3,000 \times 6 / 12 = \$1,500$$

Another partial-year depreciation policy:

- Record a full month's depreciation on assets purchased on or before the 15th of the month, and
- Record no depreciation on assets bought after the 15th.

What if you buy an asset for $3,000 on August 22? In that case you record no depreciation for August. The year's depreciation is $1,000 for 4 months—September through December ($3,000 \times \frac{4}{12} = \$1,000$).

Partial-year depreciation is computed under DDB the same way: Apply the percentage of the year that the asset is used. Computers automatically calculate the depreciation expense for each period.

Changing the Useful Life of a Depreciable Asset

Estimating the useful life of a plant asset poses a challenge. As the asset is used, the business may change its estimated useful life. For example, American Airlines may find that its baggage-handling trucks are lasting 8 years instead of 5.

Accounting changes like this are common because no one has perfect foresight. When a company makes an accounting change, generally accepted accounting principles require the business to report the nature, reason, and effect of the accounting change.

For a change in accounting estimate, the asset's remaining depreciable book value is spread over the asset's remaining life. Suppose American Airlines used a truck for two years. Under the straight-line method, accumulated depreciation reached $16,000.

$$\begin{array}{c} \text{Straight-line} \\ \text{depreciation} \\ \text{for 2 years} \end{array} = \frac{\$41,000 - \$1,000}{5 \text{ years}} = \$8,000 \text{ per year} \times 2 \text{ years} = \$16,000$$

Remaining depreciable book value (cost *less* accumulated depreciation *less* residual value) is $24,000 ($41,000 − $16,000 − $1,000). Suppose American believes the truck will remain useful for 6 more years. At the start of year 3, the company would recompute depreciation as follows:

Remaining Depreciable Book Value	÷	(New) Estimated Useful Life Remaining	=	(New) Annual Depreciation
$24,000	÷	6 years	=	$4,000

In years 3 through 8, the yearly depreciation entry based on the new useful life is:

Depreciation Expense—Truck	4,000	
Accumulated Depreciation—Truck		4,000

Revised straight-line depreciation is computed as follows:

$$\frac{\text{Revised}}{\text{SL depreciation}} = \frac{\text{Cost} - \text{Accumulated depreciation} - \text{New residual value}}{\text{Estimated remaining life in years}}$$

Using Fully-Depreciated Assets

A *fully-depreciated asset* is one that has reached the end of its *estimated* useful life. No more depreciation is recorded for the asset. If the asset is no longer useful, it is disposed of. But the asset may still be useful, and the company may continue using it. The asset account and its accumulated depreciation remain on the books, but no additional depreciation is recorded.

Disposing of a Plant Asset

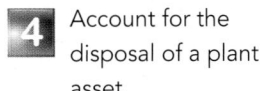
Account for the disposal of a plant asset

Eventually, an asset wears out or becomes obsolete. The owner may sell the asset or exchange it. If not, then it's junked. In all cases, you should bring depreciation up to date and then remove the asset from the books.

To record disposal,
- credit the asset account
- debit its accumulated depreciation

That gets the asset off the books.

Suppose you are disposing of equipment and final-year depreciation has just been recorded. Cost was $6,000, and there is no residual value. Accumulated depreciation, thus, totals $6,000. This asset cannot be sold or exchanged, so you have to junk it. The entry to record disposal is:

Accumulated Depreciation—Equipment	6,000	
Equipment		6,000
To dispose of fully depreciated equipment.		

Now both accounts have a zero balance, as shown in the T-accounts.

Equipment		Accumulated Depreciation—Equipment	
6,000	6,000	6,000	6,000

If assets are junked before being fully depreciated, there's a loss equal to the asset's book value. Suppose store fixtures that cost $4,000 are junked at a loss. Accumulated depreciation is $3,000, and book value is therefore $1,000. Disposal generates a $1,000 loss, as follows:

Accumulated Depreciation—Store Fixtures	3,000	
Loss on Disposal of Store Fixtures	1,000	
Store Fixtures		4,000
To dispose of store fixtures.		

The loss is reported along with expenses on the income statement.

Selling a Plant Asset

Suppose you sell furniture on June 30, 2008, for $5,000 cash. The furniture cost $10,000 when purchased back in 2005. It has been depreciated straight-line over 10 years with no residual value.

First, update depreciation for 6 months—January through June. Your depreciation entry at June 30, 2008, is:

June 30	Depreciation Expense ($10,000/10 years × 6/12)	500	
	Accumulated Depreciation—Furniture		500
	To update depreciation.		

Now Furniture and Accumulated Depreciation are up-to-date.

Furniture		Accumulated Depreciation—Furniture	
Jan. 1, 2005 10,000		Dec. 31, 2005	1,000
		Dec. 31, 2006	1,000
		Dec. 31, 2007	1,000
		June 30, 2008	500
		Balance	3,500

Book Value = $6,500

Book value of the furniture is $6,500. Suppose you sell it for $5,000 cash. The loss on the sale is $1,500, computed as follows:

Cash received from selling the asset		$5,000
Book value of asset sold:		
Cost..	$10,000	
Less: Accumulated depreciation up to date of sale........	(3,500)	6,500
Gain (loss) on sale of the asset		($1,500)

The entry to sell the furniture is:

June 30	Cash	5,000	
	Accumulated Depreciation—Furniture	3,500	
	Loss on Sale of Furniture	1,500	
	Furniture		10,000
	To sell furniture.		

When recording the sale of a plant asset, you must:

- Remove the balances from the asset account (Furniture, in this case) and its accumulated depreciation account.
- Record a gain or loss if the cash received differs from the asset's book value.

In the example we just completed, cash of $5,000 was less than book value of $6,500. The result was a loss of $1,500.

If the sale price had been $7,500, there would have been a gain of $1,000 (Cash, $7,500 − asset book value, $6,500). The entry to record this gain would be:

June 30	Cash	7,500	
	Accumulated Depreciation—Furniture	3,500	
	Furniture		10,000
	Gain on Sale of Furniture		1,000
	To sell furniture.		

Compute gain or loss on the sale of a plant asset as follows:

Gain (credit) = Sale proceeds > Book value

Loss (debit) = Sale proceeds < Book value

All gains and losses are reported on the income statement.

Exchanging Plant Assets

Businesses often trade in old plant assets for new ones. The most common exchange is a trade-in. For example, Domino's Pizza may trade in a five-year-old delivery car for a newer model. To record the exchange, Domino's must write off the old asset and its accumulated depreciation exactly as we just did for the disposal of furniture in the preceding section.

No Gain or Loss on Exchange

For most trade-ins, the business records the cost of the new asset at the book value of the old asset plus any cash payment. For example, assume Domino's old delivery car cost $9,000 and has accumulated depreciation of $8,000. Book value is therefore $1,000. Domino's trades in the old auto and pays cash of $10,000. Domino's records the trade-in with this journal entry:

	Delivery Auto (new)	11,000	
	Accumulated Depreciation (old)	8,000	
	Delivery Auto (old)		9,000
	Cash		10,000
	Traded in old delivery car for new auto.		

Domino's cost of the new car is $11,000 (cash paid $10,000, plus the book value of the old auto, $1,000).

Loss on Exchange

A trade-in can result in a loss. That occurs when the market value of the new asset received is less than the total amount given—book value of old asset plus any cash paid. We never record an asset at more than its *market value*. To illustrate a loss, assume the market value of the new asset received in the preceding example is only $7,000. This situation creates a loss, computed as follows:

Market value of new auto received		$ 7,000
Value given:		
Book value of old auto traded in	$ 1,000	
Cash paid	10,000	11,000
(Loss) on exchange		$(4,000)

You would record this exchange with the following entry:

Delivery Auto (new)	7,000*	
Accumulated Depreciation (old)	8,000	
Loss on Exchange of Assets	4,000	
Delivery Auto (old)		9,000
Cash		10,000
Traded in old delivery car for new auto.		

*Maximum amount is the asset's market value.

Gains on asset exchanges occur less often.

Accounting for Natural Resources

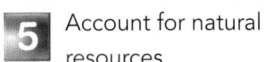

5 Account for natural resources

Natural resources are plant assets. Examples include iron ore, oil, natural gas, and timber. Natural resources are like inventories in the ground (oil) or on top of the ground (timber). Natural resources are expensed through *depletion*. **Depletion expense** is that portion of the cost of natural resources that is used up in a particular period. Depletion expense is computed by the units-of-production formula:

$$\frac{\text{Depletion}}{\text{expense}} = \frac{\text{Cost} - \text{Residual value}}{\text{Estimated total units of natural resource}} \times \text{Number of units removed}$$

An oil well may cost $100,000 and hold 10,000 barrels of oil. Natural resources usually have no residual value. The depletion rate, thus, would be $10 per barrel ($100,000/10,000 barrels). If 3,000 barrels are extracted during the year, then depletion is $30,000 (3,000 barrels × $10 per barrel). The depletion entry is:

Depletion Expense (3,000 barrels × $10)	30,000	
Accumulated Depreciation—Oil		30,000

If 4,500 barrels are removed next year, depletion is $45,000 (4,500 barrels × $10 per barrel).

Accumulated Depletion is a contra account similar to Accumulated Depreciation. Natural resources can be reported on the balance sheet as shown for oil in the following example:

Property, Plant, and Equipment:		
Land		$ 40,000
Buildings	$ 80,000	
Equipment	20,000	
	100,000	
Less: Accumulated depreciation	(30,000)	70,000
Oil	$180,000	
Less: Accumulated depletion	(50,000)	130,000
Property, plant, and equipment, net		$240,000

Accounting for Intangible Assets

6 Account for intangible assets

As we saw earlier, *intangible assets* have no physical form. Instead, these assets convey special rights from patents, copyrights, trademarks, and so on.

In our technology-driven economy, intangibles are very important. Consider online pioneer eBay. The company has no physical products or equipment, but it helps people buy and sell everything from Batman toys to old picture frames. Each month eBay serves millions of customers. In a sense, eBay is a company of intangibles.

The intellectual capital of eBay or Intel is difficult to measure. But when one company buys another, we get a glimpse of the value of the acquired company. For example, America Online (AOL) acquired Time Warner. AOL said it would give $146 billion for Time Warner's net tangible assets of only $9 billion. Why so much for so little? Because Time Warner's intangible assets were worth billions. Intangibles can account for most of a company's market value, so companies must value their intangibles, just as they do inventory and equipment.

A *patent* is an intangible asset that protects a secret process or formula. The acquisition cost of a patent is debited to the Patents account. The intangible is expensed through **amortization**, the systematic reduction of the asset's carrying value on the books. Amortization applies to intangibles exactly as depreciation applies to equipment and depletion to oil and timber.

Amortization is computed over the asset's estimated useful life—usually by the straight-line method. Obsolescence often shortens an intangible's useful life. Amortization expense for an intangible asset can be credited directly to the asset with no accumulated amortization account. The residual value of most intangibles is zero.

Some intangibles have indefinite lives. For them, the company records no systematic amortization each period. Instead, it accounts for any decrease in the value of the intangible, as we shall see for goodwill.

Specific Intangibles

Patents, copyrights, trademarks, and franchises are intangible assets. Their accounting follows the pattern we illustrate for patents.

Patents

A **patent** is a federal government grant conveying an exclusive 20-year right to produce and sell an invention. The invention may be a product or a process—for example, the Dolby noise-reduction process. Like any other asset, a patent may be purchased. Suppose General Electric (GE) pays $200,000 to acquire a patent on January 1. GE believes this patent's useful life is 5 years. Amortization expense is $40,000 per year ($200,000/5 years). Acquisition and amortization entries for this patent are

Jan. 1	Patents		200,000	
	Cash			200,000
	To *acquire a patent.*			
Dec. 31	Amortization Expense—Patents ($200,000/5)		40,000	
	Patents			40,000
	To *amortize the cost of a patent.*			

At the end of the first year, GE will report this patent at $160,000 ($200,000 minus first-year amortization of $40,000), next year at $120,000, and so on.

Copyrights

A **copyright** is the exclusive right to reproduce and sell a book, musical composition, film, or other work of art or intellectual property. Copyrights also protect computer software programs, such as Microsoft Windows® and the Excel spreadsheet. Issued by the federal government, a copyright extends 70 years beyond the author's life.

A company may pay a large sum to purchase an existing copyright. For example, the publisher Simon & Schuster may pay $1 million for the copyright on a popular novel. Most copyrights have short useful lives.

Trademarks, Brand Names

Trademarks and **trade names** (also known as **brand names**) are assets that represent distinctive products or services, such as the CBS "eye" and NBC's peacock. Legally protected slogans include Chevrolet's "Like a Rock" and Avis Rent A Car's "We try harder." The cost of a trademark or trade name is amortized over its useful life.

Franchises, Licenses

Franchises and **licenses** are privileges granted by a private business or a government to sell goods or services under specified conditions. The Green Bay Packers football organization is a franchise granted by the National Football League. McDonald's restaurants and Holiday Inns are well-known business franchises. The acquisition cost of a franchise or license is amortized over its useful life.

Goodwill

Goodwill is truly a unique asset. *Goodwill* in accounting has a different meaning from the everyday phrase "goodwill among men." In accounting, **goodwill** is the excess of the cost to purchase another company over the market value of its net assets (assets minus liabilities).

Wal-Mart has expanded into Mexico. Suppose Wal-Mart acquired Monterrey Company. The sum of the market values of Monterrey's assets was $9 million and its liabilities totaled $1 million, so Monterrey's net assets totaled $8 million. Suppose Wal-Mart paid $10 million to purchase Monterrey Company. In this case, Wal-Mart paid $2 million for goodwill, computed as follows:

Purchase price to acquire Monterrey Company...........		$10 million
Market value of Monterrey Company's assets.............	$9 million	
Less: Monterrey Company's liabilities........................	(1 million)	
Market value of Monterrey Company's net assets.......		8 million
Excess, called *goodwill*...		$ 2 million

Wal-Mart's entry to record the purchase of Monterrey, including the goodwill that Wal-Mart purchased, would be:

Assets (Cash, Receivables, Inventories, Plant Assets, all at market value)	9,000,000	
Goodwill	2,000,000	
Liabilities		1,000,000
Cash		10,000,000
Purchased Monterrey Company.		

Goodwill has some special features:

1. Goodwill is recorded only by the company that purchases another company. An outstanding reputation may create goodwill, but that company never records goodwill for its own business. Instead, goodwill is recorded *only* by the acquiring entity when it buys another company.

2. According to generally accepted accounting principles (GAAP), goodwill is *not* amortized. Instead, the acquiring company measures the current value of its goodwill each year. If the goodwill has increased in value, there is nothing to record. But if goodwill's value has decreased, then the company records a loss and writes the goodwill down. For example, suppose Wal-Mart's goodwill—purchased above—is worth only $1,500,000 at the end of the first year. In that case, Wal-Mart would make this entry:

Loss on Goodwill	500,000	
Goodwill ($2,000,000 – $1,500,000)		500,000
Recorded loss on goodwill.		

Wal-Mart would then report this goodwill at its current value of $1,500,000.

Accounting for Research and Development Costs

Accounting for research and development (R&D) costs is one of the toughest issues the accounting profession has faced. R&D is the lifeblood of companies such as Procter & Gamble, General Electric, Intel, and Boeing. But, in general, companies don't report R&D assets on their balance sheets because GAAP requires companies to expense R&D costs as they incur those costs.

Ethical Issues

The main ethical issue in accounting for plant assets is whether to capitalize or expense a cost. In this area, companies have split personalities. On the one hand, they want to save on taxes. This motivates them to expense all costs and decrease taxable income. But they also want to look as good as possible, with high net income and huge assets.

In most cases, a cost that is capitalized or expensed for tax purposes must be treated the same way in the financial statements. What, then, is the ethical path? Accountants should follow the general guidelines for capitalizing a cost:

Capitalize all costs that provide a future benefit.
Expense all other costs.

Many companies have gotten into trouble by capitalizing costs that were really expenses. They made their financial statements look better than the facts warranted. WorldCom committed this type of accounting fraud, and its former top executives are now in prison as a result. There are very few cases of companies getting into trouble by following the general guidelines, or even by erring on the side of accounting conservatism. It works.

Decision Guidelines

The Decision Guidelines summarize key decisions a company makes in accounting for plant assets. Suppose you buy a T-Shirts Plus or a Curves International franchise and invest in related equipment. You have some decisions to make about how to account for the franchise and the equipment. The Decision Guidelines will help you maximize your cash flow and do the accounting properly.

Decision	Guidelines
Capitalize or expense a cost?	General rule: Capitalize all costs that provide *future benefit*. Expense all costs that provide *no future benefit*.
Capitalize or expense: • Cost associated with a new asset? • Cost associated with an existing asset?	Capitalize all costs that bring the asset to its intended use. Capitalize only those costs that add to the asset's usefulness or its useful life. Expense all other costs as repairs or maintenance.
Which depreciation method to use: • For financial reporting? • For income tax?	Use the method that best matches depreciation expense against the revenues produced by the asset. Use the method that produces the fastest tax deductions (MACRS). A company can use different depreciation methods for the financial statements and for income tax purposes. In the United States, this practice is considered both legal and ethical.

Summary Problem 2

The following figures appear in the Answers to Summary Problem 1, Requirement 2, on page 518.

Year	Method B: Double-Declining-Balance			Method C: Straight-Line		
	Annual Depreciation Expense	Accumulated Depreciation	Book Value	Annual Depreciation Expense	Accumulated Depreciation	Book Value
Start			$44,000			$44,000
2007	$8,800	$ 8,800	35,200	$4,000	$ 4,000	40,000
2008	7,040	15,840	28,160	4,000	8,000	36,000
2009	5,632	21,472	22,528	4,000	12,000	32,000

Latté on Demand purchased equipment on January 1, 2007. Management has depreciated the equipment by using the double-declining-balance method. On July 1, 2009, the company sold the equipment for $27,000 cash.

Requirements

1. Suppose the income tax authorities permit a choice between the two depreciation methods shown. Which method would you select for income tax purposes? Why?

2. Record Latté on Demand's depreciation for 2009 and the sale of the equipment on July 1, 2009.

Solution

Requirement 1

Select the double-declining balance method. For tax purposes, most companies select accelerated depreciation because it results in the fastest write-offs. Accelerated depreciation minimizes taxable income and income tax payments in the early years of the asset's life, thereby conserving cash.

Requirement 2

To record depreciation to date of sale and the sale of the Latté on Demand equipment:

2009				
Jan. 1	Depreciation Expense ($5,632 × 1/2 year)		2,816	
	Accumulated Depreciation			2,816
	To update depreciation.			
July 1	Cash		27,000	
	Accumulated Depreciation ($15,840 + $2,816)		18,656	
	Equipment			44,000
	Gain on Sale of Equipment			1,656
	To record sale of equipment.			

Review Plant Assets and Intangibles

Accounting Vocabulary

Accelerated Depreciation Method
A depreciation method that writes off more of the asset's cost near the start of its useful life than the straight-line method does.

Amortization
Systematic reduction of the asset's carrying value on the books. Expense that applies to intangibles in the same way depreciation applies to plant assets and depletion to natural resources.

Brand Names
Assets that represent distinctive identifications of a product or service.

Capital Expenditure
Expenditure that increases the capacity or efficiency of an asset or extends its useful life. Capital expenditures are debited to an asset account.

Copyright
Exclusive right to reproduce and sell a book, musical composition, film, other work of art, or computer program. Issued by the federal government, copyrights extend 70 years beyond the author's life.

Depletion Expense
Portion of a natural resource's cost used up in a particular period. Computed in the same way as units-of-production depreciation.

Depreciable Cost
The cost of a plant asset minus its estimated residual value.

Depreciation
The allocation of a plant asset's cost to expense over its useful life.

Double-Declining-Balance (DDB) Method
An accelerated depreciation method that computes annual depreciation by multiplying the asset's decreasing book value by a constant percent that is two times the straight-line rate.

Estimated Residual Value
Expected cash value of an asset at the end of its useful life. Also called **salvage value**.

Estimated Useful Life
Length of the service period expected from an asset. May be expressed in years, units of output, miles, or another measure.

Extraordinary Repair
Repair work that generates a capital expenditure.

Franchise
Privileges granted by a private business or a government to sell a product or service under specified conditions.

Goodwill
Excess of the cost of an acquired company over the sum of the market values of its net assets (assets minus liabilities).

Intangibles
Assets with no physical form. Valuable because of the special rights they carry. Examples are patents and copyrights.

Licenses
Privileges granted by a private business or a government to sell a product or service under specified conditions.

Ordinary Repair
Repair work that is debited to an expense account.

Patent
A federal government grant giving the holder the exclusive right to produce and sell an invention for 20 years.

Plant Assets
Long-lived tangible assets, such as land, buildings, and equipment, used to operate a business.

Salvage Value
Expected cash value of an asset at the end of its useful life. Also called **estimated residual value**.

Straight-Line (SL) Depreciation Method
Depreciation method in which an equal amount of depreciation expense is assigned to each year of asset use.

Trademarks
Assets that represent distinctive identifications of a product or service.

Trade Names
Assets that represent distinctive identifications of a product or service.

Units-of-Production (UOP) Depreciation Method
Depreciation method by which a fixed amount of depreciation is assigned to each unit of output produced by an asset.

Quick Check

1. Which cost is not recorded as part of the cost of a building?
    a. Annual building maintenance
    b. Construction materials and labor
    c. Earthmoving for the building's foundation
    d. Real estate commission paid to buy the building

2. FedEx bought two used Boeing airplanes. Each plane was worth $35 million, but the owner sold the combination for $60 million. How much is FedEx's cost of each plane?
    a. $60 million
    b. $70 million
    c. $30 million
    d. $35 million

3. How should you record a capital expenditure?
    a. Debit an asset
    b. Debit an expense
    c. Debit a liability
    d. Debit capital

4. Which method always produces the most depreciation in the first year?
    a. Straight-line
    b. Double-declining-balance
    c. Units-of-production
    d. All produce the same total depreciation

5. A FedEx jet costs $50 million and is expected to fly 500 million miles during its 10-year life. Residual value is expected to be zero because the plane was used when acquired. If the plane travels 20 million miles the first year, how much depreciation should FedEx record under the units-of-production method?
    a. $2 million
    b. $5 million
    c. $10 million
    d. Cannot be determined from the data given

6. Which depreciation method would you prefer to use for income tax purposes? Why?
    a. Straight-line because it is simplest
    b. Units-of-production because it best tracks the asset's use
    c. Double-declining-balance because it gives the fastest tax deductions for depreciation
    d. Double-declining-balance because it gives the most total depreciation over the asset's life

7. A copy machine cost $40,000 when new and has accumulated depreciation of $35,000. Suppose Kinko's junks this machine, receiving nothing. What is the result of the disposal transaction?

a. No gain or loss

b. Gain of $5,000

c. Loss of $35,000

d. Loss of $5,000

8. Suppose Kinko's in the preceding question sold the machine for $5,000. What is the result of this disposal transaction?

a. Gain of $2,000

b. Loss of $2,000

c. Gain of $3,000

d. No gain or loss

9. Which method is used to compute depletion?

a. Depletion method

b. Units-of-production method

c. Straight-line method

d. Double-declining-balance method

10. Which intangible asset is recorded only as part of the acquisition of another company?

a. Patent

b. Copyright

c. Goodwill

d. Franchise

Answers are given after Apply Your Knowledge (p. 547).

Assess Your Progress

Short Exercises

Measuring the cost of a plant asset

S10-1 This chapter lists the costs included for the acquisition of land. First is the purchase price, which is obviously included in the cost of the land. The reasons for including the other costs are not so obvious. For example, removing a building looks more like an expense. State why the costs listed are included as part of the cost of the land. After the land is ready for use, will these costs be capitalized or expensed? (p. 506)

Lump-sum purchase of assets

S10-2 In Motion T-Shirts pays $150,000 for a group purchase of land, building, and equipment. At the time of your acquisition, the land has a market value of $80,000, the building $60,000, and the equipment $20,000. Journalize the lump-sum purchase of the three assets for a total cost of $150,000. You sign a note payable for this amount. (p. 508)

Capitalizing versus expensing plant-asset costs

S10-3 Texas Aero repaired one of its Boeing 737 aircraft at a cost of $250,000. Texas Aero erroneously capitalized this cost as part of the cost of the plane. How will this accounting error affect Texas Aero's net income? Ignore depreciation. (p. 510)

Computing depreciation by three methods—first year only

S10-4 At the beginning of the year, Texas Aero purchased a used Boeing jet for $35,000,000. Texas Aero expects the plane to remain useful for five years (6 million miles) and to have a residual value of $5,000,000. The company expects the plane to be flown 1 million miles the first year.

1. Compute Texas Aero's *first-year* depreciation on the plane using the following methods:
   a. Straight-line (p. 512)
   b. Units-of-production (p. 513)
   c. Double-declining-balance (p. 514)
2. Show the airplane's book value at the end of the first year under the straight-line method. (p. 512)

Computing depreciation by three methods—second year

S10-5 At the beginning of 2007, Texas Aero purchased a used **Boeing** jet at a cost of $35,000,000. Texas Aero expects the plane to remain useful for five years (6 million miles) and to have a residual value of $5,000,000. Texas Aero expects the plane to be flown 1 million miles the first year and 1.5 million miles the second year. Compute *second-year* depreciation on the plane using the following methods:
   a. Straight-line (p. 512)
   b. Units-of-production (p. 513)
   c. Double-declining-balance (p. 514)

Selecting the best depreciation method for income tax purposes

S10-6 This exercise uses the Texas Aero data from Short Exercise 10-4. Texas Aero is deciding which depreciation method to use for income tax purposes.

1. Which depreciation method offers the tax advantage for the first year? Describe the nature of the tax advantage. (pp. 518–519)
2. How much extra depreciation will Texas Aero get to deduct for the first year as compared with the straight-line method? (pp. 512, 514)

Partial-year depreciation

S10-7 On March 31, 2008, FedEx Kinko's purchased a Xerox copy machine for $80,000. FedEx Kinko's expects the machine to last for five years and to have a residual value of $8,000. Compute depreciation on the machine for the year ended December 31, 2008, using the straight-line method. (pp. 519–520)

Computing and recording depreciation after a change in useful life

S10-8 Assume that the Chicago Cubs baseball organization paid $50,000 for a hot dog stand with a 10-year life and zero expected residual value. After using the hot dog stand for four years, the company determines that the asset will remain useful for only two more years. Record depreciation on the hot dog stand for year 5 by the straight-line method. (p. 521)

Recording a gain or loss on disposal of a plant asset

S10-9 Return to the American Airlines baggage-handling truck in Exhibit 10-7, page 513. Suppose American sold the truck on December 31, 2009, for $28,000 cash, after using the truck for two full years. Depreciation for 2009 has been recorded. Make the journal entry to record American's sale of the truck. (p. 523)

Exchanging plant assets

S10-10 Air & Sea Travel purchased a Dell Computer for $3,000, debiting Computer Equipment. During 2007 and 2008, Air & Sea recorded depreciation of $2,200 on the computer. In January 2009, Air & Sea traded in the computer for a new one, paying $2,500 cash. Journalize Air & Sea Travel's exchange of computers. (p. 523)

Accounting for the depletion of natural resources

S10-11 British Petroleum (BP) holds huge reserves of oil and gas assets. Assume that at the end of 2006, BP's cost of oil and gas reserves totaled $24 billion, representing 2.4 billion barrels of oil and gas.

1. Which depreciation method does BP use to compute depletion? (pp. 524–525)

2. Suppose BP removed 0.5 billion barrels of oil during 2007. Record depletion expense for 2007. (pp. 524–525)

Accounting for goodwill

S10-12 When one media company buys another, goodwill is often the most costly asset. Vector Advertising paid $210,000 to acquire *The Thrifty Nickel*, a weekly advertising paper. At the time of the acquisition, *The Thrifty Nickel*'s balance sheet reported total assets of $100,000 and liabilities of $60,000. The fair market value of *Thrifty Nickel* assets was $80,000.

1. How much goodwill did Vector Advertising purchase as part of the acquisition of *The Thrifty Nickel*? (pp. 526–527)

2. Journalize Vector's acquisition of *The Thrifty Nickel*. (pp. 526–527)

Accounting for patents and research and development cost

S10-13 This exercise summarizes the accounting for patents and for research and development.

During 2008, Digital Cable Company paid $50,000 to research and develop a new technology, and also purchased a patent for $10,000. Digital's service revenue for 2008 totaled $700,000, and selling expenses were $400,000. Digital expects the patent to have a useful life of five years. Prepare Digital Cable Company's income statement for the year ended December 31, 2008, complete with a heading. (pp. 525–528, 20)

Exercises

Determining the cost of
plant assets

E10-14 Trautschold Furniture Co. purchased land, paying $80,000 cash plus a $300,000 note payable. In addition, Trautschold paid delinquent property tax of $2,000, title insurance costing $3,000, and $5,000 to level the land and remove an unwanted building. The company then constructed an office building at a cost of $500,000. It also paid $50,000 for a fence around the property, $10,000 for a sign near the entrance, and $6,000 for special lighting of the grounds. Determine the cost of the land, land improvements, and building. Which of these assets will Trautschold depreciate? (pp. 506–508)

Allocating cost to assets
acquired in a lump-sum
purchase

E10-15 Northwood Properties bought three lots in a subdivision for a lump-sum price. An independent appraiser valued the lots as follows:

Lot	Appraised Value
1	$50,000
2	60,000
3	70,000

Northwood paid $150,000 in cash. Record the purchase in the journal, identifying each lot's cost in a separate Land account. Round decimals to three places, and use your computed percentages throughout. (p. 508)

Distinguishing capital
expenditures from expenses

E10-16 Classify each of the following expenditures as a capital expenditure or an expense related to machinery: (a) purchase price; (b) ordinary recurring repairs to keep the machinery in good working order; (c) lubrication before machinery is placed in service; (d) periodic lubrication after machinery is placed in service; (e) major overhaul to extend useful life by three years; (f) sales tax paid on the purchase price; (g) transportation and insurance while machinery is in transit from seller to buyer; (h) installation; (i) training of personnel for initial operation of the machinery; and (j) income tax paid on income earned from the sale of products manufactured by the machinery. (p. 510)

Capitalizing versus
expensing costs; measuring
the effect of an error

E10-17 Amazon.com uses automated shipping equipment. Assume that early in year 1, Amazon purchased equipment at a cost of $500,000. Management expects the equipment to remain in service five years, with zero residual value. Amazon uses straight-line depreciation. Through an accounting error, Amazon accidentally expensed the entire cost of the equipment at the time of purchase.

Requirements

Compute the overstatement or understatement in the following items immediately after purchasing the equipment:

1. Equipment (p. 510)

2. Net income (p. 510)

E10-18 Ron Zander just slept through the class in which Professor Chen explained the concept of depreciation. Because the next test is scheduled for Friday, Zander telephones Sven Svensen to get his notes from the lecture. Svensen's notes are concise: "Depreciation—Sounds like Greek to me." Zander next tries Lisa Lake, who says she thinks depreciation is what happens when an asset wears out. Jason Gerbing is confident that depreciation is the process of creating a cash fund to replace an asset at the end of its useful life. Explain the concept of depreciation for Zander. Evaluate the explanations of Lake and Gerbing. Be specific. (pp. 510–511)

E10-19 Pulley-Bone Fried Chicken bought equipment on January 2, 2007, for $15,000. The equipment was expected to remain in service 4 years and to perform 3,000 fry jobs. At the end of the equipment's useful life, Pulley-Bone estimates that its residual value will be $3,000. The equipment performed 300 jobs the first year, 900 the second year, 1,200 the third, and 600 the fourth year. Prepare a schedule of *depreciation expense* per year for the equipment under the three depreciation methods. After two years under double-declining-balance depreciation, the company switched to the straight-line method. Show your computations. (pp. 512–514)

Which method tracks the wear and tear on the equipment most closely? (p. 515)

E10-20 Flips Gymnastics Center paid $140,000 for fitness equipment that is expected to have a 10-year life. The expected residual value is $40,000.

Select the appropriate MACRS depreciation method for income tax purposes. Then determine the extra amount of depreciation that Flips can deduct by using MACRS depreciation, versus straight-line, during the first two years of the equipment's life. (pp. 519–520, 521)

E10-21 A-1 Security Consultants purchased a building for $500,000 and depreciated it on a straight-line basis over a 40-year period. The estimated residual value was $100,000. After using the building for 15 years, A-1 realized that wear and tear on the building would wear it out before 40 years. Starting with the 16th year A-1 began depreciating the building over a revised total life of 25 years. Record depreciation on the building for years 15 and 16. (pp. 512, 521)

E10-22 On January 2, 2006, Ditto Clothing Consignments purchased showroom fixtures for $10,000 cash, expecting the fixtures to remain in service 5 years. Ditto has depreciated the fixtures on a double-declining-balance basis, with zero residual value. On September 30, 2007, Ditto sold the fixtures for $6,200 cash. Record both depreciation for 2007 and sale of the fixtures on September 30, 2007. (p. 523)

E10-23 Community Bank recently traded in office fixtures. Here are the facts:

Old fixtures:

- Cost, $90,000
- Accumulated depreciation, $75,000

New fixtures:

- Cash paid, $100,000, plus the old fixtures

continued . . .

1. Record Community Bank's trade-in of old fixtures for new ones. (p. 523)

2. Now let's change one fact and see a different outcome. Community Bank feels compelled to do business with Lakeside Furniture, a bank customer, even though the bank can get the fixtures elsewhere at a better price. Community Bank is aware that the new fixtures' market value is only $110,000. Now record the trade-in. (p. 523)

Measuring a plant asset's cost, using UOP depreciation, and trading in an asset

E10-24 Covenant Trucking Company uses the units-of-production (UOP) depreciation method because UOP best measures wear and tear on the trucks. Consider these facts about one Mack truck in the company's fleet.

When acquired in 2006, the rig cost $350,000 and was expected to remain in service for 10 years or 1,000,000 miles. Estimated residual value was $100,000. The truck was driven 80,000 miles in 2006, 120,000 miles in 2007, and 160,000 miles in 2008. After 40,000 miles in 2009, the company traded in the Mack truck for a less-expensive Freightliner. Covenant also paid cash of $20,000. Determine Covenant's cost of the new truck. Journal entries are not required. (pp. 513, 523)

Recording natural resource assets and depletion

E10-25 Sierra Mountain Mining paid $428,500 for the right to extract mineral assets from a 200,000-ton deposit. In addition to the purchase price, Sierra also paid a $500 filing fee, a $1,000 license fee to the state of Nevada, and $70,000 for a geological survey of the property. Because Sierra purchased the rights to the minerals only, it expects the asset to have zero residual value. During the first year, Sierra removed 30,000 tons of the minerals. Make journal entries to record (a) purchase of the minerals (debit Mineral Asset), (b) payment of fees and other costs, and (c) depletion for the first year. (pp. 524–525)

Recording a patent, amortization, and a change in the asset's useful life

E10-26 1. Hewlett Packard (HP) manufactures printers. Assume that HP recently paid $600,000 for a patent on a new laser printer. Although it gives legal protection for 20 years, the patent is expected to provide a competitive advantage for only 8 years. Assuming the straight-line method of amortization, make journal entries to record (a) the purchase of the patent and (b) amortization for year 1. (pp. 525–526)

2. After using the patent for 4 years, HP learns at an industry trade show that another company is designing a more-efficient printer. On the basis of this new information, HP decides, starting with year 5, to amortize the remaining cost of the patent over 2 remaining years, giving the patent a total useful life of 6 years. Record amortization for year 5. (p. 521)

Measuring and recording goodwill

E10-27 PepsiCo, Inc., has acquired several other companies. Assume that PepsiCo purchased Kettle Chips Co. for $8 million cash. The book value of Kettle Chips' assets is $12 million (market value, $15 million), and it has liabilities of $10 million.

Requirements
1. Compute the cost of the goodwill purchased by PepsiCo.
2. Record the purchase of Kettle Chips by PepsiCo.

Problems (Group A) ————————————————————

Identifying the elements of
a plant asset's cost

P10-28A Park and Fly, near an airport, incurred the following costs to acquire land, make land improvements, and construct and furnish a small building:

a. Purchase price of 3 acres of land	$ 60,000
b. Delinquent real estate taxes on the land to be paid by Park and Fly	3,700
c. Additional dirt and earthmoving	5,100
d. Title insurance on the land acquisition	1,000
e. Fence around the boundary of the property	44,200
f. Building permit for the building	200
g. Architect's fee for the design of the building..................	5,000
h. Signs near the approaches to the property	20,900
i. Materials used to construct the building..........................	40,000
j. Labor to construct the building	30,000
k. Interest cost on construction loan for the building...........	3,800
l. Parking lots on the property...	120,000
m. Lights for the parking lot	8,900
n. Salary of construction supervisor (10% to building; 90% to parking lot)	50,000
o. Furniture...	6,000
p. Transportation of furniture from seller to the building....	400
q. Landscaping (shrubs)	9,000

Park and Fly depreciates land improvements over 20 years, buildings over 30 years, and furniture over 8 years, all on a straight-line basis with zero residual value.

Requirements
1. Set up columns for Land, Land Improvements, Building, and Furniture. Show how to account for each cost by listing the cost under the correct account. Determine the total cost of each asset. (pp. 506–508)

2. All construction was complete and the assets were placed in service on March 31. Record partial-year depreciation for the year ended December 31. (pp. 512, 519–520)

Recording plant-asset
transactions, exchange, and
disposal

P10-29A Gretta Chun Associates surveys American eating habits. The company's accounts include Land, Buildings, Office Equipment, and Communication Equipment, with a separate accumulated depreciation account for each asset. During 2007, Chun completed the following transactions:

Jan. 1 Traded in old office equipment with book value of $11,000 (cost of $96,000 and accumulated depreciation of $85,000) for new equipment. Chun also paid $19,000 in cash. (p. 523)

continued . . .

Apr. 1   Acquired land and communication equipment in a group purchase. Total cost was $80,000 paid in cash. An independent appraisal valued the land at $90,000 and the communication equipment at $10,000. (p. 508)

Sep. 1   Sold a building that had cost $128,000 (accumulated depreciation of $100,000 through December 31 of the preceding year). Chun received $60,000 cash from the sale of the building. (p. 523)
Depreciation is computed on a straight-line basis. The building has a 30-year useful life and a residual value of $20,000. (pp. 512–520)

Dec. 31   Recorded depreciations as follows:
Communication equipment is depreciated by the straight-line method over a 5-year life with zero residual value. (pp. 512–520)
Office equipment is depreciated straight-line over 6 years with $3,000 residual value. (pp. 512–520)

Requirement

Record the transactions in the journal of Gretta Chun Associates. Chun ends its accounting year on December 31.

Explaining the concept of depreciation

2

P10-30A The board of directors of Park Place Porsche is having a quarterly meeting. Accounting policies are on the agenda, and depreciation is being discussed. A new board member, an attorney, has some strong opinions about two aspects of depreciation policy. Jennifer Axelrod argues that depreciation must be coupled with a fund to replace company assets. Otherwise, there is no way to guarantee the replacement of worn-out assets, she argues. Axelrod also challenges the 3-year depreciable life of company computers. She states that the computers will last much longer and should be depreciated over at least 5 years.

Requirement

Write a memo to explain the concept of depreciation to Axelrod and to answer her arguments. Format your memo as follows: (pp. 510–511)

MEMO

To: _____

From: _____

Subject: _____

Computing depreciation by three methods and the advantage of accelerated depreciation for tax purposes

P10-31A On January 2, 2006, Speedway Delivery Service purchased a truck at a cost of $63,000. Before placing the truck in service, Speedway spent $2,200 painting it, $800 replacing tires, and $4,000 overhauling the engine. The truck should remain in service for 6 years and have a residual value of $14,200. The truck's annual mileage is expected to be 18,000 miles in each of the first four years and 14,000 miles in each of the next two years—100,000 miles in total. In deciding which depreciation method to use, Jerry Speers, the general manager, requests a depreciation schedule for each of the depreciation methods (straight-line, units-of-production, and double-declining-balance).

Requirements

1. Prepare a depreciation schedule for each depreciation method, showing asset cost, depreciation expense, accumulated depreciation, and asset book value. (pp. 512–514)

2. Speedway prepares financial statements using the depreciation method that reports the highest net income in the early years of asset use. For income-tax purposes, the company uses the depreciation method that minimizes income taxes in the early years. Consider the first year that Speedway uses the truck. Identify the depreciation methods that meet the general manager's objectives, assuming the income tax authorities permit the use of any of the methods. (pp. 515, 518–519)

Accounting for natural resources and the related expenses

P10-32A Conseco Oil Company has an account titled Oil and Gas Properties. Conseco paid $6,000,000 for oil reserves holding an estimated 500,000 barrels of oil. Assume the company paid $550,000 for additional geological tests of the property and $450,000 to prepare for drilling. During the first year, Conseco removed 70,000 barrels of oil, which it sold on account for $30 per barrel. Operating expenses totaled $800,000, all paid in cash.

Requirements

1. Record all of Conseco's transactions, including depletion. (pp. 524–525)

2. Prepare the company's income statement for this oil and gas project for the first year. (p. 20)

Accounting for intangibles

P10-33A Central States Telecom provides communication services in Iowa, Nebraska, the Dakotas, and Montana. Central States purchased goodwill as part of the acquisition of Surety Wireless Company, which had these figures:

Book value of assets............................	$600,000
Market value of assets	900,000
Liabilities...	540,000

continued . . .

Requirements

1. Make the journal entry to record Central States' purchase of Surety Wireless for $300,000 cash plus a $400,000 note payable. (pp. 526–527)

2. What special asset does Central States' acquisition of Surety Wireless identify? How should Central States Telecom account for this asset after acquiring Surety Wireless? Explain in detail. (pp. 526–527)

Reporting plant-asset transactions in the financial statements—a review

P10-34A On May 31, 2004, FedEx, the overnight shipper, had total assets of $19 billion and total liabilities of $11 billion. Included among the assets were property, plant, and equipment with a cost of $20 billion and accumulated depreciation of $11 billion. During the year ended May 31, 2004, FedEx earned total revenues of $25 billion and had total expenses of $24 billion.

Requirements

1. Show how FedEx would report property, plant, and equipment on its balance sheet at May 31, 2004. (pp. 524–525)

2. How much was FedEx's owners' equity at May 31, 2004? (pp. 11–12)

3. Did FedEx report net income or net loss on its 2004 income statement? Compute the amount. (p. 20)

Problems (Group B)

Identifying the elements of a plant asset's cost

P10-35B Vandergiff Jewelry incurred the following costs to acquire land, make land improvements, and construct and furnish a new building.

a. Purchase price of 4 acres of land	$ 85,000
b. Real estate commission	3,400
c. Landscaping (additional dirt and earthmoving)...............	8,100
d. Fence around the boundary of the property	9,900
e. Delinquent real estate taxes on the land to be paid by Vandergriff...	5,900
f. Company signs at front of the property.........................	9,700
g. Building permit for the building	500
h. Architect's fee for the design of the building...................	22,500
i. Labor to construct the building......................................	169,000
j. Materials used to construct the building.........................	215,000
k. Interest cost on construction loan for the building	9,000
l. Landscaping (shrubs)	6,400
m. Parking lot and concrete walks.......................................	29,700
n. Lights for the parking lot and walkways	10,300
o. Salary of construction supervisor (85% to building; 15% to parking lot and concrete walks).........................	40,000
p. Furniture for the building...	117,800
q. Transportation and installation of furniture	2,200

continued . . .

Vandergriff depreciates land improvements over 20 years, buildings over 40 years, and furniture over 8 years, all on a straight-line basis with zero residual value.

Requirements

1. Set up columns for Land, Land Improvements, Building, and Furniture. Show how to account for each cost by listing the cost under the correct account. Determine the total cost of each asset. (pp. 506–508)

2. All construction was complete and the assets were placed in service on May 1. Record partial-year depreciation for the year ended December 31. (pp. 512, 519–520)

Recording plant-asset transactions, exchange, and disposal

P10-36B The accounts of Haley-Davis Printing Company include Land, Buildings, and Equipment. Haley-Davis has a separate accumulated depreciation account for each asset. During 2007, the company completed the following transactions:

Jan.	1	Traded in equipment with accumulated depreciation of $90,000 (cost of $130,000) for similar new equipment. Haley-Davis also paid $80,000 cash. (p. 523)
July	1	Sold a building that cost $550,000 and that had accumulated depreciation of $250,000 through December 31 of the preceding year. Haley-Davis received $100,000 cash and a $200,000 note receivable. (p. 523)
		Depreciation is computed on a straight-line basis. The building has a 40-year useful life and a residual value of $50,000. (pp. 405, 411)
Aug. 31		Purchased land and a building for a lump-sum payment of $300,000. An independent appraisal valued the land at $105,000 and the building at $210,000. (p. 508)
Dec. 31		Recorded depreciation as follows:
		Equipment has an expected useful life of 1,000,000 units of output and estimated residual value of $20,000. Depreciation is units-of-production. During the year, Haley-Davis produced 150,000 units of output. (pp. 513, 519–520)
		Depreciation on buildings is straight-line. The new building has a 40-year useful life and a residual value equal to $50,000. (pp. 512, 519–520)

Requirement

Record the transactions in Haley-Davis's journal.

Explaining the concept of depreciation

P10-37B The board of directors of Computer Solutions is reviewing the 2007 annual report. A new board member—a professor—questions the company accountant about the depreciation. The professor wonders why depreciation has decreased from $200,000 in 2005 to $180,000 in 2006 to $160,000 in 2007. He states that he could understand the decreasing amounts of depreciation if the company had been selling properties, but

continued . . .

that has not occurred. Further, growth in the city is increasing the values of property. He asks why the company is recording depreciation when property values are rising.

Requirement
Write a paragraph or two to explain the concept of depreciation and answer the professor's questions. Which depreciation method does Computer Solutions appear to be using? (pp. 510–514)

Computing depreciation by three methods and the advantage of accelerated depreciation for tax purposes

P10-38B On January 3, 2007, Joe Griffin Photography paid $224,000 for photo equipment. In addition to the purchase price, Griffin paid $700 transportation charges, $100 insurance for the equipment while in transit, $12,100 sales tax, and $3,100 for specialized training to be able to use the equipment. Griffin estimates that the equipment will remain in service 5 years and have a residual value of $20,000. The equipment should produce 50,000 photos the first year, with annual production decreasing by 5,000 photos during each of the next four years (that is, 45,000 photos in year 2; 40,000 in year 3; and so on—a total of 200,000 photos). In trying to decide which depreciation method to use, Griffin has requested a depreciation schedule for each of three depreciation methods (straight-line, units-of-production, and double-declining-balance).

Requirements
1. For each depreciation method, prepare a depreciation schedule showing asset cost, depreciation expense, accumulated depreciation, and asset book value. (pp. 512–514)
2. Griffin prepares financial statements using the depreciation method that reports the highest income in the early years. For income tax purposes, the company uses the method that minimizes income taxes in the early years. Consider the first year of using the equipment. Identify the depreciation methods that meet Griffin's objectives, assuming the income tax authorities permit the use of any of the methods. (pp. 515, 518–519)

Accounting for natural resources and the related expense

P10-39B RKI Properties' balance sheet includes a natural resource asset, Coal. RKI paid $600,000 cash for the right to work a mine with an estimated 100,000 tons of coal. The company paid $60,000 to remove unwanted buildings and $40,000 to prepare the surface for mining. RKI also signed a $50,000 note payable to an environmental company that will return the land to its original condition. During the first year, RKI removed 40,000 tons of coal, which it sold on account for $20 per ton. Operating expenses for the first year totaled $360,000, half paid in cash and half on account.

Requirements
1. Record all of RKI's transactions, including depletion, for the year. (pp. 524–525)
2. Prepare the company's income statement for the year. (p. 20)

P10-40B The balance sheet of MBC Television reports intangible assets. Assume that MBC purchased the intangibles as part of the acquisition of another company, which carried these figures:

Book value of assets.........................	$ 800,000
Market value of assets	1,100,000
Liabilities	400,000

Requirements

1. Make the journal entry to record MBC's purchase of the other company for $1,000,000, half in cash and half for a note payable. (pp. 526–527)

2. What special asset does MBC's acquisition of the other company identify? How should MBC account for this asset after acquiring the other company? Explain in detail. (pp. 526–527)

P10-41B At the end of 2004, PepsiCo had total assets of $28 billion and total liabilities of $14 billion. Included among the assets were property, plant, and equipment with a cost of $16 billion and accumulated depreciation of $8 billion. During 2004, PepsiCo earned total revenues of $29 billion and had total expenses of $25 billion.

Requirements

1. Show how PepsiCo reported property, plant, and equipment on its balance sheet at December 31, 2004. What was the book value of property, plant, and equipment on that date? (pp. 524–525)

2. How much was PepsiCo's owners' equity at December 31, 2004? (pp. 11–12)

3. Did PepsiCo have net income or net loss for 2004? Compute the amount. (p. 20)

Apply Your Knowledge

Decision Case

Measuring profitability based on different inventory and depreciation methods

2 3

Suppose you are considering investing in two businesses, Tiger Woods Enterprises and Phil Mickelson Systems. The two companies are virtually identical, and both began operations at the beginning of the current year. During the year, each company purchased inventory as follows:

Jan.	4	10,000 units at $4 =	$ 40,000
Apr.	6	5,000 units at 5 =	25,000
Aug.	9	7,000 units at 6 =	42,000
Nov.	27	10,000 units at 7 =	70,000
Totals		32,000	$177,000

During the first year, both companies sold 25,000 units of inventory.

In early January, both companies purchased equipment costing $143,000 (10-year estimated useful life and a $20,000 residual value). Woods uses the inventory and depreciation methods that maximize reported income (FIFO and straight-line). By contrast, Mickelson uses the inventory and depreciation methods that minimize income taxes (LIFO and double-declining-balance). Both companies' trial balances at December 31 included the following:

Sales revenue.............................	$270,000
Operating expenses..................	80,700

Requirements

1. Prepare both companies' income statements. (p. 346)

2. Write an investment letter to address the following questions for your clients: Which company appears to be more profitable? Which company has more cash to invest in new projects? Which company would you prefer to invest in? Why? (pp. 320–321) Format your investment letter as follows:

INVESTMENT LETTER

To: Our clients _____

From: Student Name _____

Subject: Selecting Tiger Woods Enterprises or Phil Mickelson Systems for a long-term investment _____

Ethical Issue

Western Bank & Trust purchased land and a building for the lump sum of $3 million. To get the maximum tax deduction, Western allocated 90% of the purchase price to the building and only 10% to the land. A more realistic allocation would have been 70% to the building and 30% to the land.

continued . . .

Requirements

1. Explain the tax advantage of allocating too much to the building and too little to the land.

2. Was Western's allocation ethical? If so, state why. If not, why not? Identify who was harmed.

Financial Statement Case

Plant assets

Refer to the Amazon.com financial statements, including Notes 1 and 3, in Appendix A at the end of this book. Answer the following questions.

Requirements

1. Which depreciation method does Amazon.com use for reporting in the financial statements? What type of depreciation method does the company probably use for income tax purposes? Why is this method preferable for tax purposes?

2. Depreciation expense is embedded in the operating expense amounts listed on the income statement. Note 3 gives the amount of depreciation expense. What was the amount of depreciation for 2005? Record Amazon's depreciation expense for 2005.

3. The statement of cash flows reports the purchases of fixed assets. How much were Amazon's fixed asset purchases during 2005? Journalize the company's cash purchase of fixed assets.

Team Project

Requirements
Visit a local business.

1. List all its plant assets.

2. If possible, interview the manager. Gain as much information as you can about the business's plant assets. For example, try to determine the assets' costs, the depreciation method the company is using, and the estimated useful life of each asset category. If an interview is impossible, then develop your own estimates of the assets' costs, useful lives, and book values, assuming an appropriate depreciation method.

3. Determine whether the business has any intangible assets. If so, list them and learn as much as possible about their nature, cost, and estimated useful lives.

4. Write a detailed report of your findings and be prepared to present it to the class.

For Internet Exercises, Excel in Practice, and additional online activities, go to the Web site www.prenhall.com/horngren.

Quick Check Answers

1. *a*   2. *c*   3. *a*   4. *b*   5. *a*   6. *c*   7. *d*   8. *d*   9. *b*   10. *c*

11 Current Liabilities and Payroll

Learning Objectives

1 Account for current liabilities of known amount

2 Account for current liabilities that must be estimated

3 Compute payroll amounts

4 Record basic payroll transactions

5 Use a payroll system

6 Report current liabilities on the balance sheet

Cameras, computers, and cars carry warranties against defects. Most other new products do too. When you buy a new automobile, the manufacturer agrees to repair the car if something goes wrong. That may motivate you to select a Chevrolet over a Honda.

Product guarantees are called warranties, and warranties are an important liability for General Motors, Sony, and Dell. Warranties pose an accounting challenge because General Motors doesn't know which Chevys will have to be repaired. But it's almost certain that some cars will have problems, so GM goes ahead and records a warranty liability based on estimates.

In this chapter we will see how companies account for product warranties. You also will learn about accounts payable, payroll, and other current liabilities. Recall that *current liabilities* are obligations due within one year or within the company's operating cycle if it's longer than a year. Obligations due beyond that period are *long-term liabilities*.

Current Liabilities of Known Amount

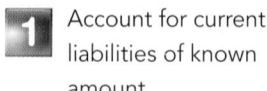 Account for current liabilities of known amount

The amounts of most liabilities are known. A few must be estimated. Let's begin with current liabilities of known amount.

Accounts Payable

Amounts owed for products or services purchased on account are *accounts payable*. We have seen many accounts payable illustrations in preceding chapters. General Motors Corporation (GM) reported accounts payable of $30 billion at December 31, 2005 (see Exhibit 11-1).

EXHIBIT 11-1 How General Motors Reports Its Current Liabilities

GENERAL MOTORS CORPORATION
Balance Sheet (partial; adapted)
December 31, 2005

Liabilities	(*In billions*)
Current Liabilities:	
Accounts payable	$ 30
Notes payable	286
Accrued expenses payable	84

One of GM's common transactions is the credit purchase of inventory. With accounts payable and inventory systems integrated, GM records the purchase of inventory on account as follows (amount assumed):

Oct. 19	Inventory	600	
	Accounts Payable		600
	Purchase on account.		

Then, to pay the liability, GM debits Accounts Payable and credits Cash.

Nov. 12	Accounts Payable	600	
	Cash		600
	Paid on account.		

Short-Term Notes Payable

Short-term notes payable are a common form of financing. Short-term notes payable are promissory notes that must be paid within one year. The following entries are typical for a short-term note used to purchase inventory:

2008			
Sep. 30	Inventory	8,000	
	Note Payable, Short-term		8,000
	Purchased inventory on a one-year, 10% note.		

At year-end it's necessary to accrue interest expense for 3 months as follows:

2008			
Dec. 31	Interest Expense ($8,000 × 0.10 × 3/12)	200	
	Interest Payable		200
	Accrued interest expense at year-end.		

The interest accrual at December 31, 2008, allocated $200 of the interest on this note to 2008. During 2009, the interest on this note is $600, as shown here.

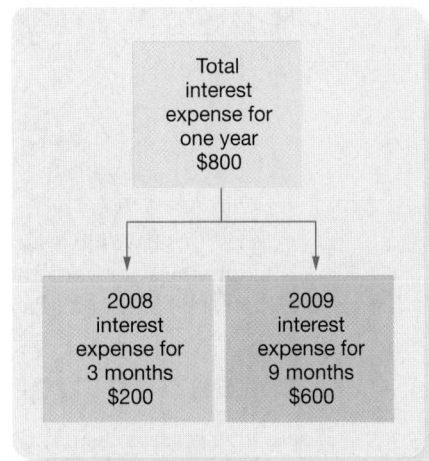

Payment of the note in 2009 is recorded as follows:

2009			
Sep. 30	Note Payable, Short-Term	8,000	
	Interest Payable	200	
	Interest Expense ($8,000 × 0.10 × 9/12)	600	
	Cash [$8,000 + ($8,000 × 0.10)]		8,800
	Paid note and interest at maturity.		

Sales Tax Payable

Most states levy sales tax on retail sales. Retailers collect the sales tax in addition to the price of the item sold. Sales Tax Payable is a current liability because the retailer must pay the state. Consider a McDonald's restaurant.

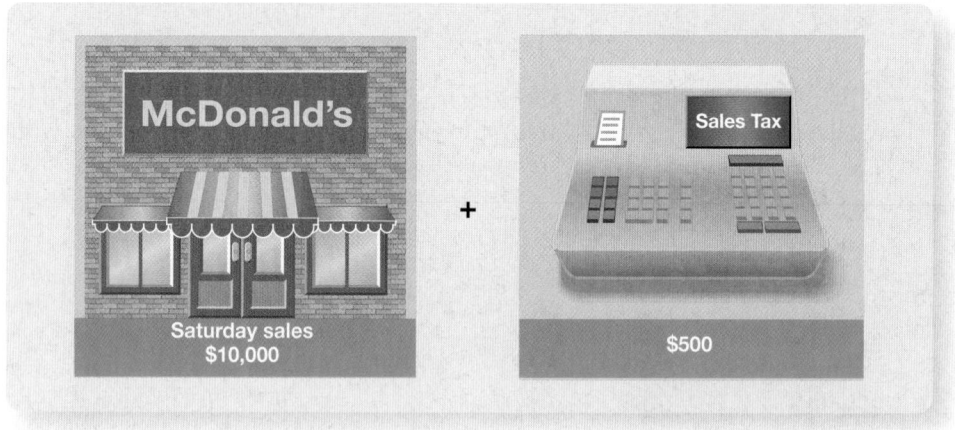

Suppose one Saturday's sales at a McDonald's restaurant totaled $10,000. McDonald's collected an additional 5% sales tax, which would equal $500 ($10,000 × 0.05). McDonald's would record that day's sales as follows:

	Cash ($10,000 × 1.05)	10,500	
	Sales Revenue		10,000
	Sales Tax Payable ($10,000 × 0.05)		500
	To record cash sales and the related sales tax.		

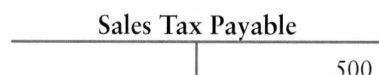

Sales Tax Payable is a current liability.

Companies forward the sales tax to the state at regular intervals. To pay the tax, they debit Sales Tax Payable and credit Cash.

Current Portion of Long-Term Notes Payable

Some long-term notes payable are paid in installments. The **current portion** of **notes payable** (also called **current maturity**) is the principal amount payable within one year—a current liability. The remaining portion is long-term. At the end of the year, the company may make an adjusting entry to shift the current installment of the long-term note payable to a current liability account, as follows (amount assumed):

Dec. 31	Long-Term Note Payable	10,000	
	Current Portion of Note Payable		10,000
	Transferred current portion of note to a current		
	liability account.		

Accrued Expenses (Accrued Liabilities)

An **accrued expense** is an expense that has not yet been paid. That's why accrued expenses are also called **accrued liabilities**. Accrued expenses typically occur with the passage of time, such as interest on a note payable.

Like most other companies, General Motors has accrued liabilities for salaries payable and interest payable. We illustrated accounting for interest payable in the middle of page 551.

Payroll, also called **employee compensation**, also creates accrued expenses. For service organizations—such as CPA firms and travel agencies—payroll is *the* major expense. The second half of this chapter covers payroll liabilities.

Unearned Revenues

Unearned revenue is also called *deferred revenue*. The business has received cash in advance and, therefore, has an obligation to provide goods or services to the customer. Let's consider an example.

Sports Illustrated (SI) sells magazine subscriptions and collects cash in advance. By receiving cash before earning the revenue, SI has a liability for future issues of the magazine. The liability is called Unearned Sales Revenue.

Assume that SI charges $36 for a three-year subscription. SI's entry to record the receipt of cash in advance would be:

2006			
Jan. 1	Cash	36	
	Unearned Sales Revenue		36
	Received cash in advance.		

After receiving the cash on January 1, 2006, SI owes three years of magazines. SI's liability is:

Unearned Sales Revenue	
	36

During 2006, SI delivers one-third of the magazines and earns $12 ($36 × 1/3) of the revenue. At December 31, 2006, SI makes the following adjusting entry to decrease the liability, and increase the revenue, as follows:

2006			
Dec. 31	Unearned Sales Revenue	12	
	Sales Revenue ($36 × 1/3)		12
	Earned revenue that was collected in advance.		

Now SI has earned $12 of the revenue and still owes subscribers $24 of magazines, as follows:

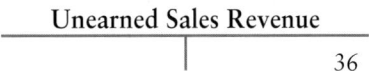

Sales Revenue			Unearned Sales Revenue		
	Dec. 31	12	Dec. 31	12	Jan. 1	36
					Bal.	24

Current Liabilities That Must Be Estimated

2 Account for current liabilities that must be estimated

A business may know that a liability exists but not know the exact amount. It cannot simply ignore the liability. This liability must be reported on the balance sheet. A prime example is Estimated Warranty Payable, which is common for companies like General Motors and Sony.

Estimated Warranty Payable

Many companies guarantee their products against defects under *warranty* agreements. Ninety-day warranties and 1-year warranties are common.

The matching principle says to record the *warranty expense* in the same period that we record the revenue. The expense, therefore, occurs when you make a sale, not when you pay warranty claims. At the time of the sale, the company does not know the exact amount of warranty expense. But the business can estimate its warranty expense and the related liability.

Assume that Whirlpool Corporation, which manufactures appliances, made sales of $200,000 subject to product warranties. Whirlpool estimates that 3% of its products will require warranty payments. The company would record the sales and the warranty expense in the same period, as follows:

June 20	Accounts Receivable	200,000	
	Sales Revenue		200,000
	Sales on account.		
June 20	Warranty Expense ($200,000 × 0.03)	6,000	
	Estimated Warranty Payable		6,000
	To accrue warranty expense.		

Assume that Whirlpool's warranty payments total $5,800. Whirlpool repairs the defective appliances and makes this journal entry:

Dec. 11	Estimated Warranty Payable	5,800	
	Cash		5,800
	To pay warranty claims.		

Whirlpool's expense on the income statement is $6,000, the estimated amount, not the $5,800 actually paid. After paying for these warranties, Whirlpool's liability account has a credit balance of $200.

Estimated Warranty Payable

5,800	6,000
	Bal. 200

Contingent Liabilities

A *contingent liability* is not an actual liability. Instead, it is a potential liability that depends on a *future* event. For example, suppose General Motors is sued because of its GMC trucks. GM thus faces a contingent liability, which may or may not become actual. If this lawsuit's outcome could hurt GM, it would be unethical for GM to withhold knowledge from investors and creditors.

Another contingent liability arises when you *cosign a note payable* for a friend. You have a contingent liability until the note comes due. If your friend pays off the note, the contingent liability vanishes. If not, you must pay the debt, and your liability becomes real.

The accounting profession divides contingent liabilities into three categories, as shown in Exhibit 11-2.

EXHIBIT 11-2   **Contingent Liabilities: Three Categories**

Likelihood of an Actual Loss	How to Report the Contingency
Remote	Ignore. *Example:* A frivolous lawsuit.
Reasonably possible	Describe the situation in a note to the financial statements. *Example:* The company is the defendant in a significant lawsuit and the outcome could go either way.
Probable, and the amount of the loss can be estimated	Record an expense and an actual liability, based on estimated amounts. *Example:* Warranty expense, as illustrated in the preceding section, beginning on page 554.

Stop and review what you have learned by studying the Decision Guidelines.

Decision Guidelines

Suppose you're in charge of accounting for your student service club. The club decides to borrow $1,000 for a Habitat for Humanity project. The bank requires your club's balance sheet. These Decision Guidelines will help you report current liabilities accurately.

Decision	**Guidelines**
What are the two main issues in accounting for current liabilities?	• *Recording* the liability in the journal • *Reporting* the liability on the balance sheet
What are the two basic categories of current liabilities?	• Current liabilities of *known amount:* Accounts payable Accrued expenses Short-term notes payable (accrued liabilities) Sales tax payable Salary, wages, commission, Current portion of notes and bonus payable payable Unearned revenues • Current liabilities that *must be estimated:* Estimated warranty payable

Summary Problem 1

Answer each question independently.

Requirements

1. A **Wendy's** restaurant made cash sales of $4,000 subject to a 5% sales tax. Record the sales and the related sales tax. Also record Wendy's payment of the tax to the state of South Carolina.

2. At December 31, 2006, Head Shapers Hair Salons reported a 6% long-term note payable as follows:

Current Liabilities	
Portion of long-term note payable due within one year.................	$ 10,000
Interest payable ($210,000 × 0.06 × 6/12)	6,300
Long-Term Liabilities	
Long-term note payable	$200,000

Head Shapers pays interest on June 30 each year.

Show how Head Shapers would report its liabilities on the year-end balance sheet one year later—December 31, 2007. The current maturity of the long-term note payable is $10,000 each year until the liability is paid off.

3. How does a contingent liability differ from an actual liability?

Solution

Requirement 1

Cash ($4,000 × 1.05)		4,200	
Sales Revenue			4,000
Sales Tax Payable ($4,000 × 0.05)			200
To record cash sales and sales tax.			
Sales Tax Payable		200	
Cash			200
To pay sales tax.			

Requirement 2

Head Shapers' balance sheet at December 31, 2007:

Current Liabilities	
Portion of long-term note payable due within one year.................	$ 10,000
Interest payable ($200,000 × 0.06 × 6/12)	6,000
Long-Term Liabilities	
Long-term note payable	$190,000

Requirement 3

A contingent liability is a *potential* liability; the contingency may or may not become an actual liability.

Accounting for Payroll

3 Compute payroll amounts

Labor cost is so important that most businesses develop a special payroll system. There are numerous ways to express an employee's pay:

- *Salary* is pay stated at an annual, monthly, or weekly rate, such as $48,000 per year, $4,000 per month, or $1,000 per week.
- *Wages* are pay amounts stated at an hourly rate, such as $10 per hour.
- *Commission* is pay stated as a percentage of a sale amount, such as a 5% commission on a sale. A realtor, thus, earns $5,000 on a $100,000 sale of real estate.
- *Bonus* is pay over and above base salary (wage or commission). A bonus is usually paid for exceptional performance—in a single amount after year-end.
- *Benefits* are extra compensation—items that aren't paid directly to the employee. Benefits cover health, life, and disability insurance. The employer pays the insurance company, which then provides coverage for the employee. Another type of benefit sets aside money for the employee during his or her retirement.

Businesses pay employees at a base rate for a set period—called *straight time*. For additional hours—*overtime*—the employee may get a higher pay rate.

Lucy Childres is an accountant for Bobby Jones Golf Company. Her pay is as follows:

- Lucy earns a salary of $600 per week for straight time (40 hours), so her hourly pay rate is $15 ($600/40).
- The company pays *time-and-a-half* for overtime. That rate is 150% (1.5 times) the straight-time rate. Thus, Lucy earns $22.50 per hour of overtime ($15.00 × 1.5 = $22.50).
- For working 42 hours during a week, she earns gross pay of $645, computed as follows:

Straight-time pay for 40 hours	$600
Overtime pay for 2 overtime hours: 2 × $22.50	45
Gross pay	$645

Gross Pay and Net (Take-Home) Pay

Two pay amounts are important for accounting purposes:

- **Gross pay** is the total amount of salary, wages, commission, and bonus earned by the employee during a pay period. Gross pay is the amount before taxes or any other deductions. Gross pay is the employer's expense. In the preceding illustration, Lucy Childres's gross pay was $645.
- **Net pay**, also called **take-home pay**, is the amount the employee gets to keep. Take-home pay equals gross pay minus all deductions. The employer writes a paycheck to each employee for his or her take-home pay.

The federal government requires employers to deduct taxes from employee paychecks. Insurance companies and investment companies may also get some of the employee's pay. Amounts withheld from paychecks are called *withholding deductions*.

Payroll Withholding Deductions

Payroll withholding deductions are the difference between gross pay and take-home pay. They are withheld from paychecks and sent to the government, to insurance companies, and other entities. Payroll deductions fall into two categories:

- *Required deductions,* such as employee income tax and Social Security tax. Employees pay their income tax and Social Security tax through payroll deductions.
- *Optional deductions,* including insurance premiums, charitable contributions, and other amounts that are withheld at the employee's request.

After being withheld, payroll deductions become the liability of the employer, who then pays the outside party—taxes to the government and contributions to charitable organizations such as United Way.

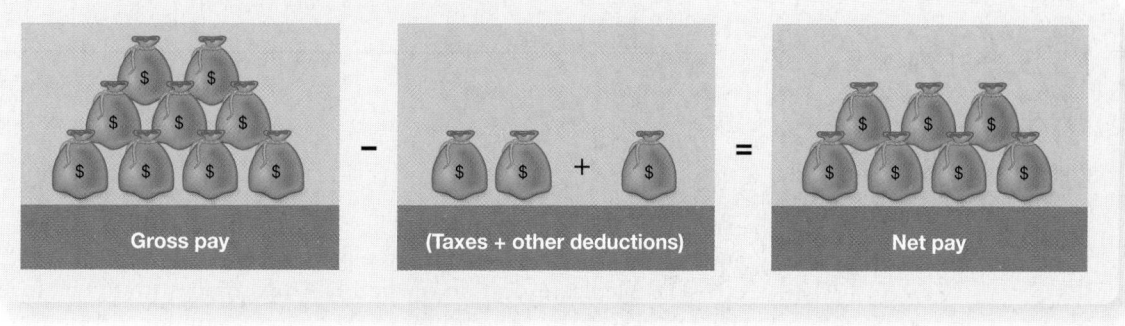

Required Withholding for Employee Income Tax

U.S. law requires companies to withhold income tax from employee paychecks. The income tax deducted from gross pay is called **withheld income tax**. The amount withheld depends on the employee's gross pay and on the number of *withholding allowances* he or she claims.

An employee files Form W-4 with his employer to indicate the number of allowances claimed for income-tax withholding. Each allowance lowers the amount of tax withheld.

- An unmarried taxpayer usually claims one allowance.
- A childless married couple, two allowances.
- A married couple with one child, three allowances, and so on.

Exhibit 11-3 shows a W-4 for R. C. Dean, who claims four allowances (line 5).

Required Withholding for Employee Social Security (FICA) Tax

The *Federal Insurance Contributions Act (FICA),* also known as the Social Security Act, created the Social Security Tax. The Social Security program provides retirement, disability, and medical benefits. The law requires employers to withhold **Social Security (FICA) tax** from employees' paychecks. The FICA tax has two components:

1. Old age, survivors', and disability insurance (OASDI)

2. Health insurance (Medicare)

The amount of tax withheld varies from year to year. For 2008, the OASDI tax applies to the first $90,000 of employee earnings in a year. The taxable amount of

---

EXHIBIT 11-3 **Form W-4**

Cut here and give Form W-4 to your employer. Keep the top part for your records.

| Form **W-4**
Department of the Treasury
Internal Revenue Service | Employee's Withholding Allowance Certificate
For Privacy Act and Paperwork Reduction Act Notice, see page 2. | OMB No. 1545-0010
20**06** |

| 1 | Type or print your first name and middle initial
R.C. | Last name
Dean | Your social security number
344 : 86 :4529 |

Home address (number and street or rural route)
4376 Palm Drive

City or town, state, and ZIP code
Fort Lauderdale, FL 33317

3 ☐ Single ☒ Married ☐ Married, but withhold at higher Single rate.
Note: If married, but legally separated, or spouse is a nonresident alien, check the "Single" box.

4 If your last name differs from that shown on your social security card, check here. You must call 1-800-772-1213 for a new card. ▶ ☐

| 5 | Total number of allowances you are claiming (from line **H** above **or** from the applicable worksheet on page 2) | 5 | 4 |
| 6 | Additional amount, if any, you want withheld from each paycheck | 6 | $ |

7 I claim exemption from withholding for 2003, and I certify that I meet **both** of the following conditions for exemption:
● Last year I had a right to a refund of **all** Federal income tax withheld because I had **no** tax liability **and**
● This year I expect a refund of **all** Federal income tax withheld because I expect to have **no** tax liability.
If you meet both conditions, write "Exempt" here ▶ | 7 |

Under penalties of perjury, I certify that I am entitled to the number of withholding allowances claimed on this certificate, or I am entitled to claim exempt status.

Employee's signature
(Form is not valid
unless you sign it.) ▶ R.C. Dean   Date ▶

| 8 | Employer's name and address (Employer: Complete lines 8 and 10 only if sending to the IRS.)
Blumenthal's
Crescent Square Shopping Center
Fort Lauderdale, FL 33310 | 9 Office code (optional)
14 | 10 Employer identification number
83 : 19475 |

Cat. No. 10220Q

---

earnings is adjusted annually. The OASDI tax rate is 6.2%. Therefore, the maximum OASDI tax that an employee paid in 2008 was $5,580 ($90,000 × 0.062).

The Medicare portion of the FICA tax applies to all employee earnings. This tax rate is 1.45%. An employee thus pays a combined FICA tax rate of 7.65% (6.2% + 1.45%) of the first $90,000 of annual earnings, plus 1.45% of earnings above $90,000.

To ease your computational burden, we assume that the FICA tax is 8% of the first $90,000 of employee earnings each year. (Use these numbers when you complete this chapter's assignments.) For each employee who earns $90,000 or more, we shall assume the employer withholds $7,200 ($90,000 × 0.08) and sends that amount to the federal government.

Assume that Rex Jennings, an employee, earned $85,000 prior to December. Jennings's salary for December is $10,000.

- How much of Jennings' pay is subject to FICA tax? Only $5,000—from $85,000 up to the $90,000 maximum.
- How much FICA tax will be withheld from Jennings's December paycheck? The computation follows.

Employee earnings subject to the tax in one year	$90,000
Employee earnings prior to the current month	−85,000
Current pay subject to FICA tax	$ 5,000
FICA tax rate	×0.08
FICA tax to be withheld from the current paycheck	$ 400

Optional Withholding Deductions

As a convenience to employees, companies withhold payroll deductions and then pay designated organizations according to employee instructions. Insurance premiums, retirement savings, union dues, and gifts to charities such as United Way are examples.

Many employers offer *cafeteria plans* that let workers select from a menu of insurance coverage. Suppose General Motors provides each employee with $500 of insurance coverage each month. One employee may use his $500 to purchase health insurance. Another may select disability coverage. A third worker may choose a combination of health insurance and disability coverage.

Summary of Gross Pay, Withholding Deductions, and Net (Take-Home) Pay

Suppose Rex Jennings has these amounts for his final pay period of the year (amounts assumed):

Gross pay		$10,000
Withholding deductions:		
Employee income tax (20%)	$2,000	
Employee FICA tax	400	
Employee co-pay for health insurance	180	
Employee contribution to United Way	20	
Total withholdings		2,600
Net (take-home) pay		$ 7,400

Employer Payroll Taxes

In addition to income tax and FICA tax, which are withheld from employee paychecks, *employers* must pay at least three payroll taxes. These taxes do *not* come out of employee paychecks.

1. Employer **Social Security (FICA) tax**
2. State **unemployment compensation tax**
3. Federal **unemployment compensation tax**

Employer FICA Tax

In addition to the employee's Social Security tax, the employer must pay an equal amount into the program. The Social Security system is funded by equal contributions from employer and employee. Using our 8% Social Security tax rate, the employer's maximum annual tax is $7,200 ($90,000 × 0.08) for each employee.

State and Federal Unemployment Compensation Taxes

State and federal unemployment taxes finance workers' compensation for people laid off from work. *In recent years, employers have paid a combined tax of 6.2% on the first $7,000 of each employee's annual earnings.* The proportion paid to the state is 5.4%, plus 0.8% to the federal government. For this payroll tax the employer uses two liability accounts:

- Federal Unemployment Tax Payable
- State Unemployment Tax Payable

Exhibit 11-4 shows a typical distribution of payroll costs for one employee. All amounts are assumed.

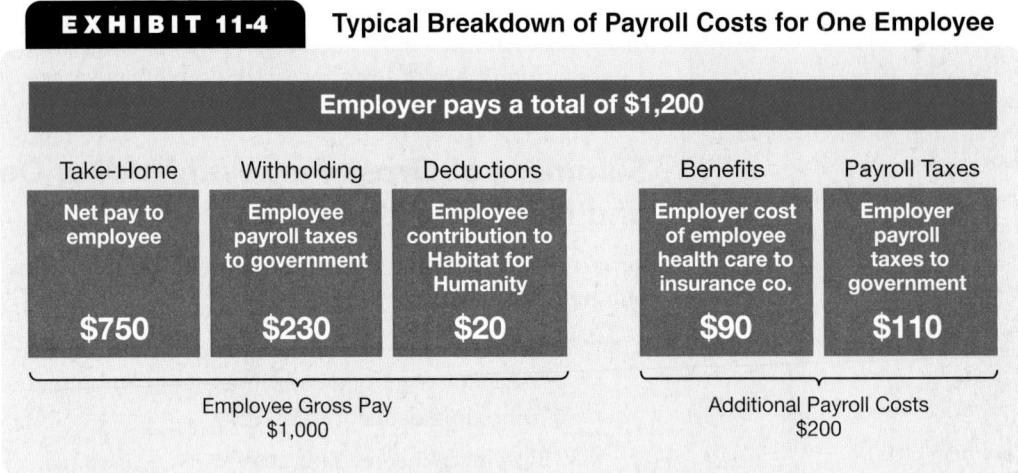

EXHIBIT 11-4 Typical Breakdown of Payroll Costs for One Employee

Employer pays a total of $1,200				
Take-Home	Withholding	Deductions	Benefits	Payroll Taxes
Net pay to employee	Employee payroll taxes to government	Employee contribution to Habitat for Humanity	Employer cost of employee health care to insurance co.	Employer payroll taxes to government
$750	$230	$20	$90	$110
Employee Gross Pay $1,000			Additional Payroll Costs $200	

Payroll Accounting

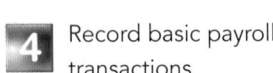 Record basic payroll transactions

Exhibit 11-5 summarizes an employer's entries for a monthly payroll of $10,000. All amounts are assumed for illustration only.

- Entry A records *salary expense. Gross salary* is $10,000, and net (take-home) pay is $7,860. There is a payable to Habitat for Humanity because employees specify this charitable deduction.
- Entry B records *benefits* paid by the employer. This company pays for health and life insurance on its employees, a common practice. The employer also pays cash into retirement plans for the benefit of employees after they retire. 401(k) plans

EXHIBIT 11-5 Payroll Accounting by the Employer

A. Salary Expense		
Salary Expense (or Wage Expense or Commission Expense)	10,000	
Employee Income Tax Payable		1,200
FICA Tax Payable ($10,000 × 0.08)		800
Payable to Habitat to Humanity		140
Salary Payable to Employees (take-home pay)		7,860
To record salary expense.		
B. Benefits Expense		
Health Insurance Expense	800	
Life Insurance Expense	200	
Retirement-Plan Expense	500	
Employee Benefits Payable		1,500
To record employee benefits payable by employer.		
C. Payroll Tax Expense		
Payroll Tax Expense	1,420	
FICA Tax Payable ($10,000 × 0.08)		800
State Unemployment Tax Payable ($10,000 × 0.054)		540
Federal Unemployment Tax Payable ($10,000 × 0.008)		80
To record employer's payroll taxes.		

are popular because they allow workers to specify where their retirement funds are invested.

- Entry C records the employer's *payroll tax expense,* which includes the employer's $800 FICA tax plus state and federal unemployment taxes.

The Payroll System

5 Use a payroll system

Good business requires paying employees accurately and on time. The components of the payroll system are:

- A payroll record
- Payroll checks
- Employee earnings record

Payroll Record

Each pay period the company organizes payroll data in a special journal called the *payroll record.* The payroll record works like a cash payments journal for recording payroll checks.

Exhibit 11-6 is a payroll record for Blumenthal's. The payroll record has sections for each employee's gross pay, withholding deductions, and net pay.

EXHIBIT 11-6   **Blumenthal's Payroll Record (Partial)**

Week Ended December 31, 2007

Employee Name	Hours	Gross Pay			Withholding Deductions				Net Pay	
		Straight-Time	Overtime	Total	Federal Income Tax	FICA Tax	United Way	Total	Amount	Check No.
Chen, W. L.*	40	500		500	71	40	3	114	386	1621
Dean, R. C.	46	400	90	490	59	39	2	100	390	1622
Ellis, M.	41	560	20	580	86	46		132	448	1623
Trimble, E. A.†	40	2,360		2,360	665		15	680	1,680	1641
Total		13,940	685	14,625	3,150	1,170	50	4,370	10,255	

*W. L. Chen earned gross pay of $500. His net pay was $386, paid with check number 1621.
†The business deducted no FICA tax from E. A. Trimble. She has already earned more than $90,000.
Note: For simplicity we combine OASDI and Medicare benefits under a single heading for FICA tax.

The payroll record gives the employer the information needed to record salary expense for the week, as follows:

Dec. 31	Salary Expense (gross pay)		14,625	
	Employee Income Tax Payable			3,150
	FICA Tax Payable			1,170
	Payable to United Way			50
	Salary Payable (net pay)			10,255

Payroll Checks

Most companies pay employees by check or by electronic fund transfer (EFT). A *paycheck* has an attachment that details the payroll amounts. These figures come from the payroll record in Exhibit 11-6. Exhibit 11-7 shows the payroll check to R. C. Dean for take home pay of $390.

EXHIBIT 11-7	**Payroll Check for Take-Home Pay**

Blumenthal's   1622
Payroll Account
Fort Lauderdale, FL   12/31   2007

Pay to the $ 390.00
Order of   R.C. Dean

Three hundred ninety & 00/100   ....   **Dollars**

Republic Bank
Fort Lauderdale
Florida 33310   *Anna Figaro*   **Treasurer**

•A111900031A 0787C50000454C

Pay			Deductions				Net	Check
Straight time	Overtime	Gross	Income tax	FICA	United Way	Total	**Net Pay**	**Check No.**
400	90	490	59	39	2	100	390	1622

Earnings Record

The employer must file a payroll tax return with both federal and state governments. Exhibit 11-8 is the Form 941 that Blumenthal's filed with the Internal Revenue Service for the quarter ended December 31, 2007. These forms must be filed no later than one month after the end of a quarter.

The employer must also provide the employee with a wage and tax statement, Form W-2, at the end of the year. Exhibit 11-9 (on page 566) shows the earnings record of R. C. Dean for the last two weeks of 2007 and his totals for the year.

The employee earnings record is neither a journal nor a ledger, and it is not required by law. It merely helps the employer prepare payroll tax reports.

Exhibit 11-10, page 566, is the Wage and Tax Statement, Form W-2, for employee R. C. Dean. The employer prepares this statement and gives copies to the employee and to the Internal Revenue Service (IRS). Dean uses the W-2 to prepare his income tax return. The IRS uses the W-2 to ensure that Dean is paying income tax on all his income from that job.

Paying the Payroll

Up to this point, we have covered only the *recording* of payroll liabilities. We now turn to the *payment* of these liabilities. Most employers make three cash payments for payrolls:

- Net (take-home) pay to employees
- Employee benefits
- Payroll taxes and other payroll deductions

continued at bottom of page 565 . . .

EXHIBIT 11-8   Payroll Tax Return

Form **941 for 2007:** Employer's Quarterly Federal Tax Return	9901

(Rev. January 2005)   Department of the Treasury — Internal Revenue Service   OMB No. 1545-0029

Employer identification number ☐ ☐ — ☐ ☐ ☐ ☐ ☐ ☐ ☐

Name *(not your trade name)*

Trade name *(if any)*   *Blumenthals*

Address   *Crescent Square Shopping Center*
Number   Street   Suite or room number

Fort Lauderdale   *FL*   *33310-1234*
City   State   ZIP code

Report for this Quarter ...
(Check one.)

☐ **1:** January, February, March
☐ **2:** April, May, June
☐ **3:** July, August, September
☒ **4:** October, November, December

Read the separate instructions before you fill out this form. Please type or print within the boxes.

Part 1: Answer these questions for this quarter.

1	Number of employees who received wages, tips, or other compensation for the pay period including: *Mar. 12 (Quarter 1), June 12 (Quarter 2), Sept. 12 (Quarter 3), Dec. 12 (Quarter 4)*	1	*18*
2	Wages, tips, and other compensation	2	*113,654.*
3	Total income tax withheld from wages, tips, and other compensation	3	*18,168.*
4	If no wages, tips, and other compensation are subject to social security or Medicare tax . . ☐ Check and go to line 6.		
5	Taxable social security and Medicare wages and tips:		

		Column 1		Column 2
5a	Taxable social security wages	*110,774.*	× .124 =	*13,736.*
5b	Taxable social security tips	.	× .124 =	
5c	Taxable Medicare wages & tips	*113,654.*	× .029 =	*3,296.*

5d	Total social security and Medicare taxes (*Column 2, lines 5a + 5b + 5c = line 5d*) . . 5d		*17,032.*
6	Total taxes before adjustments (lines 3 + 5d = line 6) 6		*35,200.*
7	Tax adjustments (If your answer is a negative number, write it in brackets.):		

7a	Current quarter's fractions of cents		.
7b	Current quarter's sick pay		.
7c	Current quarter's adjustments for tips and group-term life insurance		.
7d	Current year's income tax withholding (Attach Form 941c) . .		.
7e	Prior quarters' social security and Medicare taxes (Attach Form 941c)		.
7f	Special additions to federal income tax (reserved use)		.
7g	Special additions to social security and Medicare (reserved use)		.

7h	Total adjustments (Combine all amounts: lines 7a through 7g.) 7h		.
8	Total taxes after adjustments (Combine lines 6 and 7h.) 8		*35,200.*
9	Advance earned income credit (EIC) payments made to employees 9		*—.*
10	Total taxes after adjustment for advance EIC (lines 8 – 9 = line 10) 10		*35,200.*
11	Total deposits for this quarter, including overpayment applied from a prior quarter . . 11		*35,200.*
12	Balance due (lines 10 – 11 = line 12) Make checks payable to the *United States Treasury* . . 12		*—.*
13	Overpayment (If line 11 is more than line 10, write the difference here.) *—.* Check one ☐ Apply to next return. ☐ Send a refund.		

Next ➡

For Privacy Act and Paperwork Reduction Act Notice, see the back of the Payment Voucher.   Cat. No. 17001Z   Form **941** (Rev. 1-2005)

Net (Take-Home) Pay to Employees

To pay employees, the company debits Salary Payable and credits Cash. Using Exhibit 11-6, the company journalizes net pay for the December 31 weekly payroll:

Dec. 31	Salary Payable	10,255	
	Cash		10,255

continued at bottom of page 566 . . .

EXHIBIT 11-9   Employee Earnings Record for 2007

EMPLOYEE NAME AND ADDRESS:	SOCIAL SECURITY NO.: 344-86-4529
DEAN, R. C.	MARITAL STATUS: MARRIED
4376 PALM DRIVE	WITHHOLDING EXEMPTIONS: 4
FORT LAUDERDALE, FL 33317	PAY RATE: $400 PER WEEK
	JOB TITLE: SALESPERSON

		Gross Pay			Withholding Deductions				Net Pay	
Week Ended	Hrs.	Straight-Time	Over-time	Total	Federal Income Tax	FICA Tax	United Way	Total	Amount	Check No.
Dec. 24	48	400	120	520	66	42	2	110	410	1598
Dec. 31	46	400	90	490	59	39	2	100	390	1622
Total		20,800	2,450	23,250	1,940	1,860	100	3,900	19,350	

EXHIBIT 11-10   Employee Wage and Tax Statement, Form W-2

a Control number	2222	Void ☐	For Official Use Only ▶ OMB No. 1545-0008		
b Employer identification number 83-19475				1 Wages, tips, other compensation 23,250.00	2 Federal income tax withheld 1,940
c Employer's name, address, and ZIP code				3 Social security wages 23,250.00	4 Social security tax withheld 1,510
Blumenthal's Crescent Square Shopping Center Fort Lauderdale, FL 33310-1234				5 Medicare wages and tips 23,250.00	6 Medicare tax withheld 350
				7 Social security tips	8 Allocated tips
d Employee's social security number 344-86-4529				9 Advance EIC payment	10 Dependent care benefits
e Employee's name (first, middle initial, last) R.C. Dean				11 Nonqualified plans	12 Benefits included in box 1
4376 Palm Drive Fort Lauderdale, FL 33317				13 See instrs. for box 13	14 Other

15 Statutory employee ☐	Deceased ☐	Pension plan ☐	Legal rep. ☐	Deferred compensation ☐

f Employee's address and ZIP code

16 State Employer's state ID no.	17 Sate wages, tips, etc	18 State income tax	19 Locality name	20 Local wages, tips, etc	21 Local income tax

Form **W-2** Wage and Tax Statement **2007**

Copy A For Social Security Administration—Send this entire page with Form W-3 to the Social Security Administration; photocopies are **not** acceptable.

Cat. No. 10134D

Department of the Treasury—Internal Revenue Service
For Privacy Act and Paperwork Reduction Act Notice, see separate instructions.

Benefits Paid to Insurance Companies and Investment Companies

The employer might pay for employees' insurance coverage and their retirement plans. If the total cash payment for these benefits is $1,500, the entry is:

Dec. 31	Employee Benefits Payable	1,500	
	Cash		1,500

Payroll Taxes and Other Deductions

The employer must send the government two sets of payroll taxes: those withheld from employees and those paid by the employer. From Exhibit 11-6, the business could record these tax payments as follows (the unemployment tax amounts are assumed):

Dec. 31	Employee Income Tax Payable		3,150	
	FICA Tax Payable ($1,170 × 2)		2,340	
	Payable to United Way		50	
	State Unemployment Tax Payable		100	
	Federal Unemployment Tax Payable		10	
	Cash			5,650

Internal Control over Payroll

There are two main controls for payroll:

- controls for efficiency
- controls to safeguard payroll disbursements

Controls for Efficiency

Reconciling the bank account can be time-consuming because there may be many outstanding paychecks. To limit the outstanding checks, a company may use two payroll bank accounts. It pays the payroll from one account one month and from the other account the next month. This way the company can reconcile each account every other month, and that decreases accounting expense.

Payroll transactions are ideal for computer processing. The payroll data are stored in a file, and the computer makes the calculations, prints paychecks, and updates all records electronically.

Controls to Safeguard Payroll Disbursements

The owner of a small business can monitor his or her payroll by personal contact with employees. Large companies cannot. A particular risk is that a paycheck may be written to a fictitious person and cashed by a dishonest employee. To guard against this, large businesses adopt strict internal controls for payrolls.

Hiring and firing employees should be separated from accounting and from passing out paychecks. Photo IDs ensure that only actual employees are paid. Employees clock in at the start and clock out at the end of the workday to prove their attendance and hours worked.

As we saw in Chapter 8, the foundation of internal control is separation of duties. This is why companies have separate departments for the following payroll functions:

- Human Resources hires and fires workers.
- Payroll maintains employee earnings records.
- Accounting records all transactions.
- Treasurer (or bursar) distributes paychecks to employees.

Reporting Current Liabilities

6 Report current liabilities on the balance sheet

At the end of each period, the company reports all of its current liabilities on the balance sheet. Bob May Homes had the current liabilities shown in Exhibit 11-11.

EXHIBIT 11-11   Current Liabilities on the Balance Sheet

Current Liabilities	
Accounts payable	$ 6,400
Current portion of note payable	5,000
Salary payable	3,800
Employee withheld income tax payable	400
Employee FICA tax payable	150*
Employer FICA tax payable	150*
Payable to United Way	100
Unearned revenue	4,500
Interest payable	5,700
Total current liabilities	$26,200
*These amounts can be combined and reported as "FICA Tax Payable"	$ 300

Ethical Issues in Reporting Liabilities

Accounting for liabilities poses an ethical challenge. Businesses like to show high levels of net income because that makes them look successful.

Owners and managers may be tempted to overlook some expenses and liabilities at the end of the accounting period. For example, a company can fail to accrue warranty expense. This will cause total expenses to be understated and net income to be overstated.

Contingent liabilities also pose an ethical challenge. Because contingencies are not real liabilities, they are easy to overlook. But a contingency can turn into a real liability and wreck the company. Successful people don't play games with their accounting. Falsifying financial statements can land a person in prison.

Now let's summarize the accounting for payroll by examining the Decision Guidelines.

Decision Guidelines

What decisions must General Motors make to account for payroll? Whether it's GM or your start-up business, the Decision Guidelines provide an outline for your actions.

Decision	Guidelines
What are the key elements of a payroll accounting system?	• Employee's Withholding Allowance Certificate, Form W-4 • Payroll record • Payroll checks • Employer's quarterly tax returns, Form 941 • Employee earnings record • Employee wage and tax statement, Form W-2

What are the key terms in the payroll area?	*Gross pay* (Total amount earned by the employee)
	
	– *Payroll withholding deductions:*
	  a. Withheld income tax
	  b. Withheld FICA (Social Security) tax—equal amount also paid by employer
	  c. Optional withholding deductions (insurance, retirement, charitable contributions, union dues)
	
	= *Net (take-home) pay*

What is the employer's total payroll expense?	Total payroll expense =
	
	Gross pay
	+ *Employee benefits*
	  a. Insurance (health, life, and disability)
	  b. Retirement benefits
	
	+ *Employer payroll taxes*
	  a. Employer FICA (Social Security) tax—equal amount also paid by employee
	  b. Employer state and federal unemployment taxes

Where to report payroll costs?	• Payroll expenses on the income statement • Payroll liabilities on the balance sheet

Summary Problem 2

Rags-to-Riches, a clothing resale store, employs one salesperson, Dee Hunter. Hunter's straight-time salary is $400 per week, with time-and-a-half pay for hours above 40. Rags-to-Riches withholds income tax (10%) and FICA tax (8%) from Hunter's pay. Rags-to-Riches also pays payroll taxes for FICA (8%) and state and federal unemployment (5.4% and 0.8%, respectively). In addition, Rags-to-Riches contributes 6% of Hunter's gross pay into her retirement plan.

During the week ended December 26, Hunter worked 50 hours. Prior to this week, she had earned $22,000.

Requirements (Round all amounts to the nearest dollar.)

1. Compute Hunter's gross pay and net pay for the week.

2. Record the following payroll entries that Rags-to-Riches would make for:
   a. Hunter's gross pay, including overtime
   b. Expense for employee benefits
   c. Employer payroll taxes
   d. Payment of net pay to Hunter
   e. Payment for employee benefits
   f. Payment of all payroll taxes

3. How much was Rags-to-Riches' total payroll expense for the week?

Solution

Requirement 1

Gross pay:	Straight-time pay for 40 hours.................................		$400
	Overtime pay:		
	Rate per hour ($400/40 × 1.5)	$15	
	Hours (50 − 40)	10	150
	Gross pay		$550
Net pay:	Gross pay		$550
	Less: Withheld income tax ($550 × 0.10)..............	$55	
	Withheld FICA tax ($550 × 0.08).................	44	99
	Net pay..		$451

Requirement 2

a.		Sales Salary Expense	550	
		Employee Income Tax Payable		55
		FICA Tax Payable		44
		Salary Payable		451
b.		Retirement-Plan Expense ($550 × 0.06)	33	
		Employee Benefits Payable		33
c.		Payroll Tax Expense	78	
		FICA Tax Payable ($550 × 0.08)		44
		State Unemployment Tax Payable ($550 × 0.054)		30
		Federal Unemployment Tax Payable ($550 × 0.008)		4
d.		Salary Payable	451	
		Cash		451
e.		Employee Benefits Payable	33	
		Cash		33
f.		Employee Income Tax Payable	55	
		FICA Tax Payable ($44 × 2)	88	
		State Unemployment Tax Payable	30	
		Federal Unemployment Tax Payable	4	
		Cash		177

Requirement 3

Rags-to-Riches incurred *total payroll expense* of $661 (gross pay of $550 + payroll taxes of $78 + benefits of $33). See entries (a) through (c).

Review Current Liabilities and Payroll

Accounting Vocabulary

Accrued Expense
An expense that the business has not yet paid. Also called **accrued liability**.

Accrued Liability
An expense that the business has not yet paid. Also called **accrued expense**.

Current Maturity
Amount of the principal that is payable within one year. Also called **current portion of notes payable**.

Current Portion of Notes Payable
Amount of the principal that is payable within one year. Also called **current maturity**.

Employee Compensation
A major expense. Also called **payroll**.

FICA Tax
Federal Insurance Contributions Act (FICA) tax, which is withheld from employees' pay. Also called **Social Security tax**.

Gross Pay
Total amount of salary, wages, commissions, or any other employee compensation before taxes and other deductions.

Net (Take-Home) Pay
Gross pay minus all deductions. The amount of compensation that the employee actually takes home.

Payroll
A major expense. Also called **employee compensation**.

Short-Term Note Payable
Promissory note payable due within one year, a common form of financing.

Social Security Tax
Federal Insurance Contributions Act (FICA) tax, which is withheld from employees' pay. Also called **FICA tax**.

Unemployment Compensation Tax
Payroll tax paid by employers to the government, which uses the money to pay unemployment benefits to people who are out of work.

Withheld Income Tax
Income tax deducted from employees' gross pay.

Quick Check

1. Known liabilities of uncertain amounts are
   a. Contingent liabilities
   b. Ignored (Record them when paid.)
   c. Reported on the balance sheet
   d. Reported only in the notes to the financial statements

2. On January 1, 2008, you borrowed $10,000 on a five-year, 8% note payable. At December 31, 2009, you should *record*
   a. Interest payable of $800
   b. Nothing (The note is already on the books.)
   c. Note receivable of $10,000
   d. Cash payment of $10,000

3. Your company sells $100,000 of goods and you collect sales tax of 3%. What current liability does the sale create?
   a. None; you collected cash up front.
   b. Unearned revenue of $3,000
   c. Sales tax payable of $3,000
   d. Sales revenue of $103,000

4. At December 31, your company owes employees for three days of the five-day workweek. The total payroll for the week is $8,000. What journal entry should you make at December 31?
   a. Nothing, because you will pay the employees on Friday
   b. Salary Expense 4,800
       Salary Payable 4,800
   c. Salary Expense 8,000
       Salary Payable 8,000
   d. Salary Payable 4,800
       Salary Expense 4,800

5. What is unearned revenue?
   a. Receivable
   b. Current asset
   c. Revenue
   d. Current liability

6. General Electric (GE) owed Estimated Warranty Payable of $1,000 at the end of 2007. During 2008, GE made sales of $100,000 and expects product warranties to cost the company 3% of the sales. During 2008, GE paid $2,500 for warranties. What is GE's Estimated Warranty Payable at the end of 2008?
   a. $3,500
   b. $2,500
   c. $2,000
   d. $1,500

7. Payroll expenses include
   a. Salaries and wages
   b. Employee benefits
   c. Payroll taxes
   d. All of the above

8. What is the most that an employee paid the federal government for old age, survivors', and disability insurance (FICA tax) during 2008?
   a. $5,580.
   b. $90,000.
   c. Nothing. The employer paid it.
   d. There is no upper limit on FICA tax.

9. The document that an employer gives each employee at the end of the year to report annual earnings and taxes paid is the
   a. Form W-2
   b. Form W-4
   c. Payroll record
   d. Form 941

10. The *foundation* of internal control over payroll is
    a. Paying the correct amount of payroll tax
    b. Separating payroll duties
    c. Filing government tax forms on time
    d. Accurately computing gross pay, deductions, and net pay

Answers are given after Apply Your Knowledge (p. 591).

Assess Your Progress

Short Exercises

Accounting for a note payable

S11-1 On June 30, 2006, Cimmaron Co. purchased $8,000 of inventory on a 1-year, 9% note payable. Journalize the company's (a) accrual of interest expense on December 31, 2006, and (b) payment of the note plus interest on June 30, 2007. (pp. 551–552)

Reporting a short-term note payable and the related interest

S11-2 Refer to the data in Short Exercise 11-1. Show what Cimmaron reports for the note payable and related interest payable on its balance sheet at December 31, 2006, and on its income statement for the year ended on that date. (pp. 551–552)

Accounting for warranty expense and warranty payable

S11-3 Sierra Corporation guarantees its snowmobiles for three years. Company experience indicates that warranty costs will add up to 5% of sales.

Assume that the Sierra dealer in Colorado Springs made sales totaling $500,000 during January 2007, its first month of operations. The company received cash for 30% of the sales and notes receivable for the remainder. Warranty payments totaled $21,000 during 2007.

1. Record the sales, warranty expense, and warranty payments for Sierra. (p. 554)
2. Post to the Estimated Warranty Payable T-account. At the end of 2007, how much in estimated warranty payable does Sierra owe? (p. 554)

Applying GAAP; reporting warranties in the financial statements

S11-4 What amount of warranty expense will Sierra (in Short Exercise 11-3) report during 2007? Does the warranty expense for the year equal the year's cash payments for warranties? Which accounting principle addresses this situation? (p. 554)

Interpreting an actual company's contingent liabilities

S11-5 Harley-Davidson, Inc., the motorcycle manufacturer, included the following note (adapted) in its annual report:

> ### Notes to Consolidated Financial Statements
>
> *Commitments and Contingencies (Adapted)*
>
> The Company self-insures its product liability losses in the United States up to $3 million.
>
> Catastrophic coverage is maintained for individual claims in excess of $3 million up to $25 million.

1. Why are these *contingent* (versus real) liabilities? (pp. 555–556)
2. How can a contingent liability become a real liability for Harley-Davidson? What are the limits to the company's product liabilities in the United States? (pp. 555–556)

Short Exercise 11-6 begins a sequence of exercises that ends with Short Exercise 11-8.

Computing an employee's total pay

S11-6 Grant Teiman is paid $640 for a 40-hour workweek and time-and-a-half for hours above 40.

1. Compute Teiman's gross pay for working 50 hours during the first week of February. (pp. 558–559)

2. Teiman is single, and his income tax withholding is 10% of total pay. Teiman's only payroll deductions are payroll taxes. Compute Teiman's net (take-home) pay for the week. Use an 8% FICA tax rate, and carry amounts to the nearest cent. (pp. 559–561)

Computing the payroll expense of an employer

S11-7 Return to the Grant Teiman payroll situation in Short Exercise 11-6. Teiman's employer, College of St. Mary, pays all the standard payroll taxes plus benefits for employee retirement plan (5% of total pay), health insurance ($60 per employee per month), and disability insurance ($8 per employee per month).

Compute College of St. Mary's total expense of employing Grant Teiman for the 50 hours that he worked during the first week of February. Carry amounts to the nearest cent. (pp. 561–562)

Making payroll entries

S11-8 After solving Short Exercises 11-6 and 11-7, journalize for College of St. Mary the following expenses related to the employment of Grant Teiman.

a. Salary expense (pp. 561–562)

b. Benefits (pp. 561–562)

c. Employer payroll taxes (pp. 561–562)

Computing payroll amounts late in the year

S11-9 Suppose you work for KPMG, the accounting firm, all year and earn a monthly salary of $6,000. There is no overtime pay. Your withheld income taxes consume 15% of gross pay. In addition to payroll taxes, you elect to contribute 5% monthly to your retirement plan. KPMG also deducts $200 monthly for your co-pay of the health insurance premium.

Compute your net pay for November. Use an 8% FICA tax rate. (pp. 563–564)

Using a payroll system

S11-10 Refer to Blumenthal's payroll record in Exhibit 11-6, page 563.

1. How much was the company's total salary expense for the week?

2. How much cash did the employees take home for their work?

3. How much did *employees* pay this week for
   a. Federal income tax?
   b. FICA tax?

Internal controls over payroll disbursements

S11-11 What are some of the important elements of good internal control to safeguard payroll disbursements?

S11-12 Citadel Sporting Goods' payroll record for the week ended June 30, 2007, included these totals:

		Withholding Deductions			
Gross Pay	Federal Income Tax	FICA Tax	Habitat for Humanity	Total	Net Pay
$8,000	$790	$640	$110	$1,540	$6,460

In addition to the payroll liabilities shown here, Citadel has the following current liabilities at June 30, 2007:

Accounts payable..................................	$29,000
Employer FICA tax payable.................	640

Prepare the current liabilities section of Citadel's balance sheet at June 30, 2007. List current liabilities in descending order, starting with the largest first, including the payroll liabilities. Show total current liabilities. (p. 568)

Exercises

E11-13 Make general journal entries to record the following transactions of Sagebrush Software. Explanations are not required.

March 31		Recorded cash sales of $200,000, plus sales tax of 8% collected for the state of Texas. (pp. 551–552)
April	6	Sent March sales tax to the state. (pp. 551–552)

E11-14 Journalize the following note payable transactions of Concilio Video Productions. Explanations are not required.

2007		
May	1	Purchased equipment costing $15,000 by issuing a one-year, 8% note payable. (pp. 551–552)
Dec.	31	Accrued interest on the note payable. (pp. 551–552)
2008		
May	1	Paid the note payable at maturity. (pp. 551–552)

E11-15 TransWorld Publishing completed the following transactions during 2008:

Oct.	1	Sold a six-month subscription, collecting cash of $200, plus sales tax of 9%. (pp. 551–552, 553–554)
Nov.	15	Remitted (paid) the sales tax to the state of Tennessee. (pp. 551–552)
Dec.	31	Made the necessary adjustment at year-end to record the amount of sales revenue earned during the year. (pp. 553–554)

continued . . .

Journalize these transactions (explanations are not required). Then report the liability on the company's balance sheet at December 31, 2008.

Accounting for warranty
expense and warranty
payable

E11-16 The accounting records of Durango Ceramics included the following at December 31, 2007:

Estimated Warranty Payable
Balance   3,000

In the past, Durango's warranty expense has been 6% of sales. During 2008, Durango made sales of $100,000 and paid $7,000 to satisfy warranty claims.

Requirements

1. Journalize Durango's warranty expense and warranty payments during 2008. Explanations are not required. (p. 554)

2. What balance of Estimated Warranty Payable will Durango report on its balance sheet at December 31, 2008? (p. 554)

Computing net pay

3

E11-17 Cappy Scanlan manages the women's sportswear department of Parisian Department Store in Seattle. She earns a base monthly salary of $750 plus a 10% commission on her personal sales. Through payroll deductions, Scanlan donates $25 per month to a charitable organization, and she authorizes Parisian to deduct $50 monthly for her co-pay of health insurance. Tax rates on Scanlan's earnings are 12% for income tax and 8% of the first $90,000 for FICA. During the first 11 months of the year, she earned $87,000.

Requirement

Compute Scanlan's gross pay and net (take-home) pay for December, assuming her sales for the month are $80,000. (p. 558)

Computing and recording
gross pay and net pay

3   4   5

E11-18 Harold Sollenberger manages a Dairy Queen drive-in. His straight-time pay is $10 per hour, with time-and-a-half for hours in excess of 40 per week. Sollenberger's payroll deductions include withheld income tax of 9%, FICA tax of 8%, and a weekly deduction of $5 for a charitable contribution to United Fund. Sollenberger worked 50 hours during the week.

Requirements

1. Compute Sollenberger's gross pay and net pay for the week. Carry amounts to the nearest cent. (p. 558)

2. Journalize Dairy Queen's wage expense—including payroll deductions—for Sollenberger's work. An explanation is not required. (pp. 561–562)

Recording a payroll

E11-19 Pablo's Mexican Restaurants incurred salary expense of $65,000 for 2009. The payroll expense includes employer FICA tax of 8% in addition to state unemployment tax of 5.4% and federal unemployment tax

continued . . .

of 0.8%. Of the total salaries, $19,000 is subject to unemployment tax. Also, the company provides the following benefits for employees: health insurance (cost to the company, $2,060), life insurance (cost to the company, $350), and retirement benefits (cost to the company, 6% of salary expense).

Requirement

Record Pablo's expenses for employee benefits and for payroll taxes. Explanations are not required. (pp. 561–562)

Reporting payroll expense and liabilities

E11-20 Saturn Solartech has annual salary expense of $450,000. In addition, Saturn incurs payroll tax expense equal to 10% of the total payroll. At December 31, Saturn owes salaries of $8,000 and payroll taxes of $2,000.

Requirement

Show what Saturn will report for these facts on its income statement and year-end classified balance sheet. (p. 568)

Reporting current and long-term liabilities

E11-21 Optical Dispensary borrowed $300,000 on January 2, 2007, by issuing a 10% note payable that must be paid in three equal annual installments plus interest for the year. The first payment of principal and interest comes due January 2, 2008.

Requirement

Insert the appropriate amounts to show how Optical Dispensary should report its current and long-term liabilities. (pp. 552, 558)

Reporting current and long-term liabilities

	December 31		
	2007	2008	2009
Current liabilities:			
Current portion of note payable	$____	$____	$____
Interest payable................................	____	____	____
Long-term liabilities:			
Long-term note payable...................	____	____	____

E11-22 Oriental Rug Company completed these selected transactions during December 2006, its first month of operations.

a. Sales of $200,000 are subject to estimated warranty cost of 3%. (p. 554)

b. Pier 1 Imports ordered $15,000 of rugs. With its order, Pier 1 sent a check for $15,000 in advance. Oriental Rugs will ship the goods in January 2007. (pp. 553–554)

continued . . .

c. The December payroll of $90,000 is subject to employee withheld income tax of 9% and FICA tax of 8%. Oriental Rugs must also pay FICA tax of 8% plus state unemployment tax of 5.4% and federal unemployment tax of 0.8%. On December 31, Oriental Rugs pays employees their net pay, but accrues all tax amounts. (p. 561)

Requirement

Report each item at its correct amount on Oriental Rugs' balance sheet at December 31, 2006. Show total current liabilities. (p. 568)

Analyzing current liabilities;
using the current ratio
⁌1 ⁌6

E11-23 The comparative balance sheet of Paladin Security Services for two years reported these figures:

	2006	2005
Total current assets	$ 4,600	$ 4,100
Noncurrent assets	14,200	13,000
	$18,800	$17,100
Total current liabilities............	$ 3,700	$ 4,800
Noncurrent liabilities..............	9,500	7,400
Owner's equity	5,600	4,900
	$18,800	$17,100

Compute Paladin's current ratio and debt ratio for both years. Did the ratios improve or deteriorate in 2006? Compute the debt ratio to 3 decimal places. (p. 210)

Recording current liabilities
⁌1 ⁌6

E11-24 Eric O'Neill Associates reported short-term notes payable and salary payable as follows:

	December 31	
	2008	2007
Current liabilities (partial):		
Short-term notes payable.........	$16,500	$15,000
Salary payable	3,300	3,000

During 2008, O'Neill paid off both current liabilities that were left over from 2007. During 2008, O'Neill borrowed money on short-term notes payable and accrued salary expense during 2008.

Requirement

Journalize all four of these transactions for O'Neill during 2008. (pp. 551–552, 561–562, 565–567)

Problems (Group A)

Journalizing liability
transactions

P11-25A The following transactions of Lexington Pharmacies occurred during 2006 and 2007:

2006		
Jan.	9	Purchased computer equipment at a cost of $8,000, signing a six-month, 8% note payable for that amount.
	29	Recorded the week's sales of $60,000, three-fourths on credit, and one-fourth for cash. Sales amounts are subject to a 6% state sales tax.
Feb.	5	Sent the last week's sales tax to the state.
Feb.	28	Borrowed $200,000 on a 4-year, 9% note payable that calls for annual installment payments of $50,000 principal plus interest. Record the short-term and the long-term portions of the note payable in two separate accounts.
July	9	Paid the six-month, 8% note, plus interest, at maturity.
Aug.	31	Purchased inventory for $3,000, signing a six-month, 10% note payable.
Dec.	31	Accrued warranty expense, which is estimated at 3% of sales of $600,000.
	31	Accrued interest on all outstanding notes payable. Make a separate interest accrual entry for each note payable.
2007		
Feb.	28	Paid the first installment and interest for one year on the 4-year note payable.
	28	Paid off the 10% note plus interest at maturity.

Requirement
Record the transactions in Lexington's general journal. Explanations are not required. (pp. 551–552, 554)

Computing and recording a
payroll

P11-26A The records of Georgia Tea & Coffee Company show the following figures:

Employee Earnings	
Straight-time earnings	$16,400
Overtime pay	(a)
Total employee earnings..............	(b)

continued . . .

Deductions and Net Pay	
Withheld income tax...................	$ 2,000
FICA tax.....................................	(c)
Charitable contributions.............	300
Medical insurance.......................	600
Total deductions	5,400
Net pay......................................	18,500
Accounts Debited	
Salary Expense...........................	$ (d)

Requirements

1. Determine missing amounts (a) through (d). (pp. 559–561)

2. Journalize this payroll for the month. No explanation is required. (pp. 561–562)

Computing and recording payroll amounts

P11-27A Felix McKay is general manager of Moonwalk Tanning Salons. During 2008, McKay worked for the company all year at a $6,625 monthly salary. He also earned a year-end bonus equal to 10% of his salary.

McKay's federal income tax withheld during 2008 was $737 per month, plus $924 on his bonus check. State income tax withheld came to $43 per month, plus $67 on the bonus. The FICA tax withheld was 8% of the first $90,000 in annual earnings. McKay authorized the following payroll deductions: United Fund contribution of 1% of total earnings and life insurance of $19 per month.

Moonwalk incurred payroll tax expense on McKay for FICA tax of 8% of the first $90,000 in annual earnings. The company also paid state unemployment tax of 5.4% and federal unemployment tax of 0.8% on the first $7,000 in annual earnings. In addition, Moonwalk provides McKay with health insurance at a cost of $35 per month and retirement benefits. During 2008, Moonwalk paid $7,000 into McKay's retirement plan.

Requirements

1. Compute McKay's gross pay, payroll deductions, and net pay for the full year 2008. Round all amounts to the nearest dollar. (pp. 559–561)

2. Compute Moonwalk's total 2008 payroll expense for McKay. (pp. 561–562)

3. Make the journal entry to record Moonwalk's expense for McKay's total earnings for the year, his payroll deductions, and net pay. Debit Salary Expense and Bonus Expense as appropriate. Credit liability accounts for the payroll deductions and Cash for net pay. An explanation is not required. (pp. 561–562)

Journalizing, posting, and reporting liabilities

P11-28A The general ledger of Pack-N-Ship at June 30, the end of the company's fiscal year, includes the following account balances before adjusting entries.

Accounts Payable	$110,000
Current Portion of Note Payable................	_____
Interest Payable..	_____
Salary Payable...	_____
Employee Payroll Taxes Payable	_____

continued . . .

Employer Payroll Taxes Payable.................	$ _____			
Unearned Rent Revenue...........................	6,000			
Long-Term Note Payable	200,000			

The additional data needed to develop the adjusting entries at June 30 are as follows:

a. The long-term debt is payable in annual installments of $40,000 with the next installment due on July 31. On that date, Pack-N-Ship will also pay one year's interest at 9%. Interest was last paid on July 31 of the preceding year. Make the adjusting entry to shift the current installment of the long-term note payable to a current liability. Also accrue interest expense at year end. (pp. 552–554)

b. Gross salaries for the last payroll of the fiscal year totaled $5,100. Of this amount, employee payroll taxes payable were $1,100, and salary payable was $4,000. (pp. 551–562)

c. Employer payroll taxes payable were $900. (pp. 551–562)

d. On February 1, the company collected one year's rent of $6,000 in advance. (p. 553)

Requirements

1. Using four-column format, open the listed accounts, inserting the unadjusted June 30 balances. (p. 80)

2. Journalize and post the June 30 adjusting entries to the accounts that you opened. Key adjusting entries by letter.

3. Prepare the liabilities section of the balance sheet at June 30, 2008. Show total current liabilities and total liabilities. (p. 568)

Using a payroll record; recording a payroll

5

P11-29A The payroll records of Navasota Video Productions provide the following information for the weekly pay period ended December 29, 2007:

Employee	Hours Worked	Hourly Wage Rate	Federal Income Tax	United Way Contributions	Earnings Through Previous Week
Larry Fisher......	42	$40	$278	$35	$90,474
Felicia Jones......	47	8	87	4	23,154
Joe Opper.........	40	11	64	4	4,880
Sara Tate...........	46	35	288	8	88,600

Employees are paid wages at the rate of time-and-a-half for hours over 40 per week. Round all amounts to the nearest dollar, and show your computations. Explanations are not required for journal entries.

Requirements

1. Enter the appropriate information in a payroll record similar to Exhibit 11-6, page 563. In addition to the deductions listed, the employer also takes out FICA tax: 8% of the first $90,000 of each employee's annual earnings.

continued . . .

2. Record the payroll information in the general journal. (pp. 563–564)

3. The first payroll check is number 319, paid to Larry Fisher. Record the check numbers in the payroll record. Also, prepare the general journal entry to record payment of net wages payable to the employees. (pp. 563–564, 565–567)

4. The employer's payroll taxes include FICA tax of 8% of the first $90,000 of each employee's wages. The employer also pays unemployment taxes of 6.2% (5.4% for the state and 0.8% for the federal government) on the first $7,000 of each employee's annual earnings. Record the employer's payroll taxes in the general journal. (pp. 551–552)

Reporting current liabilities

P11-30A Morrison's Gifts' accounting records provide the following liability data at year-end:

a. Sales of $400,000 were covered by Morrison's product warranty. At January 1, estimated warranty payable was $3,000. During the year, Morrison recorded warranty expense of $12,000 and paid warranty claims of $14,000. (p. 554)

b. December sales totaled $100,000, and Morrison collected an additional state sales tax of 7%. This amount will be sent to the state of Mississippi early in January. (pp. 551–552)

c. Morrison owes $100,000 on a note payable. At December 31, 6% interest on the full note and $20,000 of this principal are payable within one year. (pp. 551–552)

d. On November 30, Morrison received cash of $4,500 in advance for the rent on a building. This rent will be earned evenly over three months. (pp. 553–554)

e. On September 30, Morrison signed a six-month, 8% note payable to purchase equipment costing $30,000. The note requires payment of principal and interest at maturity. (pp. 551–552)

Requirement

For each item, indicate the account and the related amount to be reported as a *current* liability on Morrison's December 31 balance sheet.

Problems (Group B)

Journalizing liability
transactions

P11-31B The following transactions of Pan-American Paper Company occurred during 2006 and 2007.

2006		
Feb.	3	Purchased equipment for $40,000, signing a six-month, 9% note payable.
	28	Recorded the week's sales of $60,000, one-third for cash, and two-thirds on credit. All sales amounts are subject to a 5% sales tax.
Mar.	7	Sent last week's sales tax to the state.

continued . . .

Apr. 30	Borrowed $100,000 on a long-term, 9% note payable that calls for annual payment of interest each April 30.
Aug. 3	Paid the six-month, 9% note at maturity.
Nov. 30	Purchased inventory at a cost of $7,000, signing a three-month, 6% note payable for that amount.
Dec. 31	Accrued warranty expense, which is estimated at 3% of sales of $200,000.
31	Accrued interest on all outstanding notes payable. Make a separate interest accrual entry for each note payable.
2007	
Feb. 28	Paid off the 6% inventory note, plus interest, at maturity.
Apr. 30	Paid the interest for one year on the long-term note payable.

Requirement

Record the transactions in Pan American's general journal. Explanations are not required. (pp. 551–552, 554)

Computing and recording a payroll

P11-32B The records of Lyndon Olson Political Consultants show the following figures:

Employee Earnings	
Straight-time earnings	$ (a)
Overtime pay	5,000
Total employee earnings.............	(b)
Deductions and Net Pay	
Withheld income tax..................	$ 9,000
FICA tax..................................	6,000
Charitable contributions	(c)
Medical insurance......................	1,000
Total deductions	18,000
Net pay.....................................	64,000
Account Debited	
Salary Expense...........................	$ (d)

Requirements

1. Determine missing amounts (a) through (d). (pp. 559–561)
2. Journalize Olson's payroll for the month. No explanation is required. (pp. 561–562)

Computing and recording payroll amounts

P11-33B Louann Winters is a vice president at Crossroads Bank. During 2008, Winters worked for the bank all year at a $6,500 monthly salary. She also earned a year-end bonus equal to 15% of her annual salary.

continued . . .

Winters' federal income tax withheld during 2008 was $820 per month, plus $2,480 on her bonus check. State income tax withheld came to $60 per month, plus $80 on the bonus. The FICA tax withheld was 8% of the first $90,000 of annual earnings. Winters authorized the following payroll deductions: United Fund contribution of 1% of total earnings and life insurance of $20 per month.

Crossroads Bank incurred payroll tax expense on Winters for FICA tax of 8% of the first $90,000 in total annual earnings. The bank also paid state unemployment tax of 5.4% and federal unemployment tax of 0.8% on the first $7,000 of annual earnings. The bank provided Winters with the following benefits: health insurance at a cost of $40 per month, and retirement benefits to be paid during her retirement. During 2008, the bank's cost of Winters's retirement plan was $4,000.

Requirements

1. Compute Winters' gross pay, payroll deductions, and net pay during 2008. Round all amounts to the nearest dollar. (pp. 559–561)

2. Compute the bank's total 2008 payroll expense for Winters. (pp. 561–562)

3. Make the journal entry to record the bank's expense for Winters' total earnings for the year, her payroll deductions, and net pay. Debit Salary Expense and Bonus Expense as appropriate. Credit liability accounts for the payroll deductions and Cash for net pay. An explanation is not required. (pp. 561–562)

Journalizing, posting, and reporting liabilities

P11-34B The Northwood Inn general ledger at September 30, 2008, the end of the company's fiscal year, includes the following account balances before adjusting entries.

Accounts Payable	$ 36,210
Current Portion of Note Payable	_____
Interest Payable	_____
Salary Payable	_____
Employee Payroll Taxes Payable.................	_____
Employer Payroll Taxes Payable	_____
Unearned Rent Revenue	3,900
Long-Term Note Payable.............................	100,000

The additional data needed to develop the adjusting entries at September 30 are as follows:

a. The long-term note payable is payable in annual installments of $50,000, with the next installment due on January 31, 2009. On that date, Northwood will also pay one year's interest at 6%. Interest was last paid on January 31. Make the adjusting entry to shift the current installment of the note payable to a current liability. Also accrue interest expense at year end. (pp. 551–552)

b. Gross salaries for the last payroll of the fiscal year were $4,300. Of this amount, employee payroll taxes payable were $950. (pp. 561–562)

continued . . .

c. Employer payroll taxes payable were $890. (pp. 561–562)

d. On August 1, the company collected six months' rent of $3,900 in advance. (p. 553)

Requirements

1. Using four-column format, open the listed accounts, inserting their unadjusted September 30 balances. (p. 80)

2. Journalize and post the September 30 adjusting entries to the accounts that you opened. Key adjusting entries by letter.

3. Prepare the liabilities section of Northwood Inn's balance sheet at September 30, 2008. Show total current liabilities and total liabilities. (p. 568)

Using a payroll record; recording a payroll

5

P11-35B The payroll records of Carolina Home Improvements provide the following information for the weekly pay period ended December 29, 2007:

Employee	Hours Worked	Weekly Salary	Federal Income Tax	Health Insurance	Earnings Through Previous Week
Cynthia Cooper.......	43	$ 400	$ 74	$16	$17,060
Tim LeMann	46	480	90	10	22,300
Ron Marx	48	1,400	319	46	88,000
Karen York.............	40	240	32	6	3,410

All employees are paid time-and-a-half for hours worked in excess of 40 per week.

Requirements

Round all amounts to the nearest dollar, and show your computations. Explanations are not required for journal entries.

1. Enter the appropriate information in a payroll record similar to Exhibit 11-6, page 563. In addition to the deductions listed, the employer also withholds FICA tax: 8% of the first $90,000 of each employee's annual earnings.

2. Record the payroll information in the general journal. (pp. 563–564)

3. The first payroll check is number 178, paid to Cooper. Record the check numbers in the payroll record. Also, prepare the general journal entry to record payment of net pay to the employees. (pp. 563–564, 565–567)

4. The employer's payroll taxes include FICA of 8% of the first $90,000 of each employee's annual earnings. The employer also pays unemployment taxes of 6.2% (5.4% for the state and 0.8% for the federal government) on the first $7,000 of each employee's annual earnings. Record the employer's payroll taxes in the general journal. (pp. 561–562)

Reporting current liabilities

6

P11-36B Following are pertinent facts about events during the current year at Lafferty Trailers.

a. December sales totaled $300,000, and Lafferty collected sales tax of 5%. The sales tax will be sent to the state of Virginia early in January. (pp. 551–552)

continued . . .

b. Sales are covered by a Lafferty product warranty. At January 1, estimated warranty payable was $1,300. During the year, Lafferty recorded warranty expense of $7,900 and paid warranty claims of $8,100. (p. 554)

c. Lafferty owes $75,000 on a note payable. At December 31, 6% interest for the year plus $25,000 of this principal are payable within one year. (pp. 551–552)

d. On August 31, Lafferty signed a six-month, 6% note payable to purchase equipment costing $80,000. The note requires payment of principal and interest at maturity. (pp. 551–552)

e. On October 31, Lafferty received cash of $2,400 in advance for the rent on a building. This rent will be earned evenly over six months. (pp. 553–554)

Requirement

For each item, indicate the account and the related amount to be reported as a *current* liability on Lafferty's December 31 balance sheet.

For 24/7 practice, visit www.MyAccountingLab.com

Apply Your Knowledge

Decision Cases

Identifying internal control weaknesses and their solution

Case 1. Golden Bear Construction Co. operates throughout California. The owner, Gaylan Beavers, employs 15 work crews. Construction supervisors report directly to Beavers, and the supervisors are trusted employees. The home office staff consists of an accountant and an office manager.

Because employee turnover is high in the construction industry, supervisors hire and fire their own crews. Supervisors notify the office of all personnel changes. Also, supervisors forward to the office the employee W-4 forms. Each Thursday, the supervisors submit weekly time sheets for their crews, and the accountant prepares the payroll. At noon on Friday, the supervisors come to the office to get paychecks for distribution to the workers at 5 p.m.

The company accountant prepares the payroll, including the paychecks. Beavers signs all paychecks. To verify that each construction worker is a bona fide employee, the accountant matches the employee's endorsement signature on the back of the canceled paycheck with the signature on that employee's W-4 form.

Requirements

1. Identify one way that a supervisor can defraud Golden Bear Construction under the present system.

2. Discuss a control feature that the company can use to *safeguard* against the fraud you identified in Requirement 1.

Contingent liabilities

Case 2. Microsoft Corporation is the defendant in numerous lawsuits claiming unfair trade practices. Microsoft has strong incentives not to disclose these contingent liabilities. However, GAAP requires that companies report their contingent liabilities.

Requirements

1. Why would a company prefer *not* to disclose its contingent liabilities?

2. Describe how a bank could be harmed if a company seeking a loan did not disclose its contingent liabilities.

3. What ethical tightrope must companies walk when they report contingent liabilities?

Ethical Issue

Bombadier Industries manufactures aircraft-related electronic devices. Bombadier borrows heavily to finance operations. Often Bombadier is profitable because it can earn operating income much higher than its interest expense. However, when the business cycle has turned down, the company's debt burden has pushed the company to the brink of bankruptcy. Operating income is sometimes less than interest expense.

Requirement

Is it unethical for managers to saddle a company with a high level of debt? Or is it just risky? Who can get hurt when a company takes on too much debt? Discuss.

Financial Statement Case

Details about a company's liabilities appear in a number of places in the annual report. Use Amazon.com's financial statements, including Notes 1 and 4, to answer the following questions. Amazon's financial statements are in Appendix A at the end of this book.

Requirements

1. Give the breakdown of Amazon.com's current liabilities at December 31, 2005. Give the January 2006 entry to record the payment of accrued expenses and other current liabilities that Amazon owed at December 31, 2005.

2. At December 31, 2005, how much did Amazon owe customers for unearned revenue that Amazon had collected in advance? Which account on the balance sheet reports this liability?

3. How much was Amazon's long-term debt at December 31, 2005? Of this amount, how much was due within one year? How much was payable beyond one year in the future?

Team Projects

Project 1. In recent years, the airline industry has dominated headlines. Consumers are shopping Priceline.com and other Internet sites for the lowest rates. The airlines have also lured customers with frequent-flyer programs, which award free flights to passengers who accumulate specified miles of travel. Unredeemed frequent-flyer mileage represents a liability that airlines must report on their balance sheets, usually as Air Traffic Liability.

Southwest Airlines, a profitable, no-frills carrier based in Dallas, has been rated near the top of the industry. Southwest controls costs by flying to smaller, less-expensive airports; using only one model of aircraft; serving no meals; increasing staff efficiency; and having a shorter turnaround time on the ground between flights. The fact that most of the cities served by Southwest have predictable weather maximizes its on-time arrival record.

Requirements

With a partner or group, lead your class in a discussion of the following questions, or write a report as directed by your instructor.

1. Frequent-flyer programs have grown into significant obligations for airlines. Why should a liability be recorded for those programs? Discuss how you might calculate the amount of this liability. Can you think of other industries that offer incentives that create a similar liability?

2. One of Southwest Airlines' strategies for success is shortening stops at airport gates between flights. The company's chairman has stated, "What [you] produce is lower fares for the customers because you generate more revenue from the same fixed cost in that airplane." Look up *fixed cost* in the index of this book. What are some of the "fixed costs" of an airline? How can better utilization of assets improve a company's profits?

Project 2. Consider three different businesses:

a. A bank

b. A magazine publisher

c. A department store

Requirements

For each business, list all of its liabilities—both current and long-term. If necessary, study Chapter 15 on long-term liabilities. Then compare your lists to identify what liabilities the three business have in common. Also identify the liabilities that are unique to each type of business.

For Internet Exercises, Excel in Practice, and additional online activities go to the Web site www.prenhall.com/horngren.

Quick Check Answers

1. *c*   2. *a*   3. *c*   4. *b*   5. *d*   6. *d*   7. *d*   8. *a*   9. *a*   10. *b*

Comprehensive Problem for Chapters 8–11

Comparing Two Businesses

Suppose you created a software package, sold the business, and now are ready to invest in a resort property. Several locations look promising: Monterrey, California; Durango, Colorado; and Mackinac Island, Michigan. Each place has its appeal, but Durango wins out. Two small resorts are available in Durango. The property owners provide the following data:

	Gold Rush Resorts	Mountain Hideaway
Cash	$ 31,000	$ 63,000
Accounts receivable	20,000	18,000
Inventory	64,000	70,000
Land	270,000	669,000
Buildings	1,200,000	1,500,000
Accumulated depreciation—buildings	(20,000)	(100,000)
Furniture	750,000	900,000
Accumulated depreciation—furniture	(75,000)	(180,000)
Total assets	$2,240,000	$2,940,000
Total liabilities	$1,300,000	$1,000,000
Owner's equity	940,000	1,940,000
Total liabilities and owner's equity	$2,240,000	$2,940,000

Income statements for the last year report net income of $500,000 for Gold Rush Resorts and $400,000 for Mountain Hideaway.

Inventories

Gold Rush Resorts uses the FIFO inventory method, and Mountain Hideaway uses LIFO. If Gold Rush had used LIFO, its ending inventory would have been $7,000 lower. (pp. 320–321)

Plant Assets

Gold Rush Resorts uses the straight-line depreciation method and an estimated useful life of 40 years for buildings and 10 years for furniture. Estimated residual values are $400,000 for buildings and $0 for furniture. Gold Rush's buildings are 1 year old. (p. 512)

Mountain Hideaway uses the double-declining-balance method and depreciates buildings over 30 years. The furniture, also 1 year old, is being depreciated over 10 years. (p. 514)

Accounts Receivable

Gold Rush Resorts uses the direct write-off method for uncollectible receivables. Mountain Hideaway uses the allowance method. The Gold Rush owner estimates that $2,000 of the company's receivables are doubtful. Mountain Hideaway receivables are already reported at net realizable value. (pp. 460, 464)

Requirements

1. To compare the two resorts, convert Gold Rush Resorts' net income to the accounting methods and the estimated useful lives used by Mountain Hideaway.

2. Compare the two resorts' net incomes after you have revised Gold Rush's figures. Which resort looked better at the outset? Which looks better when they are placed on equal footing?

12 Partnerships

Learning Objectives

1 Identify the characteristics of a partnership

2 Account for partner investments

3 Allocate profits and losses to the partners

4 Account for the admission of a new partner

5 Account for a partner's withdrawal from the firm

6 Account for the liquidation of a partnership

7 Prepare partnership financial statements

Previous chapters saw you start your own business, In Motion T-Shirts, to imprint logos for groups around your college. Suppose Jonathan Demski, a friend, wants to join In Motion—not as an employee but as a partner. This guy could sell a Ford to General Motors. He can help you double your profits.

What does Jonathan bring to the table besides a good personality? After all, he's joining a business that earned $20,000 last year. Here are some of the issues you will need to address:

- Should you require Jonathan to invest money in your business?
- How will you and Jonathan share profits and losses?
- If Jonathan withdraws from the business, what assets can he take?

If you let Jonathan join you as a co-owner, you will automatically form a partnership. A **partnership** is an association of two or more persons who co-own a business for profit. As you can see, a partnership is more complex than the proprietorships of preceding chapters. ■

Forming a partnership is easy. It requires no permission from the government and no outside legal procedures. A partnership combines the assets and abilities of the partners. New opportunities may open up as you and Jonathan pool your talents and resources. You can offer a fuller range of goods and services than you alone can provide.

Partnerships come in all sizes. Many have one or two owners, but some are quite large. Exhibit 12-1 lists the largest U.S. accounting firms that are organized as partnerships. The largest of these firms have over 2,000 partners.

EXHIBIT 12-1 **The Six Largest Accounting Firms in the United States**

Deloitte & Touche
Ernst & Young
PricewaterhouseCoopers
KPMG
Grant Thornton
RSM/McGladrey & Pullen*

*The RSM unit of the firm is not a partnership.
Source: Adapted from *Accounting Today* (March 14–April 3, 2005).

Characteristics of a Partnership

 Identify the characteristics of a partnership

A partnership is voluntary. You can't be forced to join one, and you can't be forced to accept another person as a partner. Partnerships differ from proprietorships and corporations in the following ways.

The Written Agreement

A partnership is somewhat like a marriage. To be successful, the partners must cooperate. But the partners don't vow to remain together for life. To increase the partners' understanding of how the business is run, they should draw up a **partnership agreement**, also called the **articles of partnership**. This agreement is a contract between the partners and is governed by contract law. The articles of partnership should specify the following:

1. Name, location, and nature of the business

2. Name, investment, and duties of each partner

3. Procedures for admitting a new partner

4. Method of sharing profits and losses among the partners

5. Withdrawals of assets by the partners

6. Procedures for settling up with a partner who withdraws from the firm

7. Procedures for liquidating the partnership—selling the assets, paying the liabilities, and giving any remaining cash to the partners

You'll cover these points as you work through the chapter. A partnership has some special features.

Limited Life

A partnership has a limited life. If a partner withdraws, the old partnership dissolves. **Dissolution** is the ending of a partnership. The addition of a new partner dissolves the old partnership and creates a new one.

Mutual Agency

Mutual agency means that every partner is a mutual agent of the firm. Any partner can bind the business to a contract within the scope of its operations. If Stephanie Jones, a partner in the law firm of Willis & Jones, contracts to pay a debt, then the firm of Willis & Jones—not just Jones—owes the liability. If Jones signs a contract to buy her own car, however, the partnership is not liable because that is a personal matter for Jones.

Unlimited Liability

Each partner has **unlimited personal liability** for the debts of the business. When a partnership can't pay its debts, the partners must pay with their personal assets.

Suppose Willis & Jones can't pay a $20,000 business debit that Jones created. Then Willis and Jones each become personally liable for the $20,000 because each partner has *unlimited liability* for the business's debts. If either partner can't pay his or her part of the debt, the other partner must pay the total. For example, if Jones can pay only $5,000 of the liability, Willis must pay $15,000. If Jones can't pay anything, Willis must pay the full $20,000.

Co-Ownership of Property

Any asset—cash, inventory, computers, and so on—that a partner invests in the partnership becomes the joint property of all the partners. The partner who invested the asset is no longer its sole owner.

No Partnership Income Tax

A partnership pays no business income tax. Instead, the net income of the business flows through and becomes the taxable income of the partners. Suppose the Willis & Jones law firm earned net income of $200,000, shared equally by the partners. The firm pays no income tax *as a business entity*. But Willis and Jones each pay personal income tax on $100,000 of partnership income.

Partners' Capital Accounts

Accounting for a partnership is much like accounting for a proprietorship. But a partnership has more than one owner, so it needs a separate capital account for each partner. For example, the equity account for Blake Willis is Willis, Capital. Similarly, each partner has a withdrawal account such as Blake Willis, Drawing.

Exhibit 12-2 lists the advantages and disadvantages of partnerships (compared with proprietorships and corporations). Most features of a proprietorship also apply to a partnership—most importantly,

- Limited life
- Unlimited liability
- No business income tax

EXHIBIT 12-2 Advantages and Disadvantages of Partnerships

Partnership Advantages	Partnership Disadvantages
Versus Proprietorships:	1. Partnership agreement may be difficult to formulate. Each time a new partner is admitted or a partner withdraws, the business needs a new partnership agreement.
1. Partnership can raise more capital.	
2. Partnership brings together the abilities of more than one person.	
3. Partners working well together can add more value than by working alone. 1 + 1 > 2 in a good partnership.	2. Relations among partners may be fragile.
Versus Corporations:	3. Mutual agency and unlimited liability create personal obligations for each partner.
1. Partnership is less expensive to organize than a corporation, which requires a charter from the state.	
2. There's no double taxation. Partnership income is taxed only to the partners as individuals.	

Types of Partnerships

There are two basic types of partnerships: general and limited.

General Partnership

A **general partnership** is the basic form. Each partner is a co-owner of the business with all the privileges and risks of ownership. The profits and losses of the partnership pass through to the partners, who then pay personal income tax on their income. All the other features we just covered also apply to a general partnership.

Limited Partnership

A **limited partnership** has at least two classes of partners. There must be at least one *general partner,* who takes primary responsibility. The general partner also takes most of the risk if the partnership goes bankrupt. Usually, the general partner is the last owner to receive a share of profits and losses. But the general partner often gets all the excess profit after the limited partners get their share of the income.

The *limited partners* have limited liability for partnership debts. Their liability is limited to their investment in the business. Limited partners usually have first claim to profits and losses, but only up to a certain limit. In exchange for their limited liability, their potential for profits is also limited.

Most accounting firms—including those in Exhibit 12-1—are organized as **limited liability partnerships,** or **LLPs.** That means each partner's personal liability for business debts is limited to a certain amount. The LLP must carry a large insurance policy to protect the public in case the partnership is found guilty of malpractice. Medical, legal, and other professional firms are also organized as LLPs.

Limited-Liability Company (LLC)

A limited-liability company is its own form of business organization—neither a partnership nor a corporation. It combines the advantages of both. The LLC form is perhaps the most flexible way to organize a business because the owners, called *members*, have numerous choices.

The features of a limited-liability company that parallel a *corporation* are:

- The LLC must file articles of organization with the state.
- The business name must include "LLC" or a similar designation to alert the public about the limited liability of the members.
- The members are *not* personally liable for the business's debts. This is one of the chief advantages of an LLC compared to a proprietorship or a partnership.

The features of an LLC similar to a *partnership* are:

- The LLC can elect *not* to pay business income tax. The income of the LLC can be taxed to the members as though they were partners. This is the other big advantage of an LLC, as compared to a corporation. Corporations pay a corporate income tax. Then the stockholders pay personal income tax on any dividends they receive from the corporation. This is why we say that corporations face *double taxation.*
- The members (owners of the LLC) can participate actively in management of the business.
- The accounting for an LLC follows the pattern for a partnership.

S Corporation

An **S corporation** is a corporation taxed as a partnership. This form of business organization comes from Subchapter S of the U.S. Internal Revenue Code. An S corporation offers its owners the benefits of a corporation—no personal liability for business debts—and of a partnership—no double taxation. An ordinary (Subchapter C) corporation is subject to double taxation.

An S corporation pays no corporate income tax. Instead, the corporation's income flows through to the stockholders, who pay personal income tax on their share of the corporation's income, as in a partnership.

Exhibit 12-3 summarizes this section by showing the features of the different types of business organization.

EXHIBIT 12-3 **Features of the Different Types of Business Organization**

Organization	Legal Entity	Personal Liability of the Owners	Pays Business Income Tax
Proprietorship	No	Unlimited	No
Partnership	No		No
General partners		Unlimited	
Limited partners		Limited	
Limited-Liability			
Company (LLC)	Yes	Limited	No*
S Corporation	Yes	Limited	No
C Corporation	Yes	Limited	Yes

*In some states, a limited-liability company can elect to pay corporate income tax.

The Start-Up of a Partnership

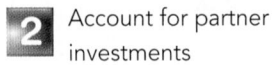 Account for partner investments

Let's examine the start-up of a partnership. The partners may invest both assets and liabilities. These contributions are journalized the same as for a proprietorship—debit the assets and credit the liabilities. The excess—assets minus liabilities—measures each partner's capital.

Suppose Lisa Lane and Don Reed form a partnership to sell computer software. The partners agree on the following values:

Lane's Investment

- Cash, $10,000; inventory, $40,000; and accounts payable, $80,000 (The current market values for these items equal Lane's values.)
- Computer equipment—cost, $800,000; accumulated depreciation, $200,000; *current market value, $450,000*

Reed's Investment

- Cash, $5,000
- Computer software: cost, $20,000; *market value, $100,000*

The partnership records the partners' investments at *current market value*. Why? Because the partnership is buying the assets and assuming the liabilities at their current market values. The partnership entries follow.

	Lane's Investment		
June 1	Cash	10,000	
	Inventory	40,000	
	Computer Equipment	450,000	
	Accounts Payable		80,000
	Lane, Capital		420,000
	To record Lane's investment.		
	Reed's Investment		
June 1	Cash	5,000	
	Computer Software	100,000	
	Reed, Capital		105,000
	To record Reed's investment.		

The initial partnership balance sheet appears in Exhibit 12-4. The assets and liabilities are the same for a proprietorship and a partnership.

EXHIBIT 12-4	Partnership Balance Sheet

L&R SOFTWARE
Balance Sheet
June 1, 2008

Assets			Liabilities		
Cash	$ 15,000		Accounts payable		$ 80,000
Inventory	40,000		**Capital**		
Computer equipment	450,000		Lane, capital		420,000
Computer software	100,000		Reed, capital		105,000
			Total liabilities		
Total assets	$605,000		and capital		$605,000

Sharing Profits and Losses, and Partner Drawings

 Allocate profits and losses to the partners

Allocating profits and losses among partners can be challenging. The partners can agree to any profit-and-loss-sharing method they desire. Typical arrangements include the following:

1. Sharing of profits and losses based on a stated fraction for each partner, such as 50/50 or 2/3 and 1/3 or 4:3:3 (which means 40% to Partner A, 30% to B, and 30% to C)

2. Sharing based on each partner's investment

3. Sharing based on each partner's service

4. Sharing based on a combination of stated fractions, investments, and service

If the partners have no agreement as to how to divide profits and losses, then they share equally. If the agreement specifies a method for sharing profits but not losses, then losses are shared the same way as profits. For example, a partner who gets 75% of the profits will absorb 75% of any losses.

Let's see how some of these profit-and-loss plans work.

Sharing Based on a Stated Fraction

The agreement may state each partner's fraction of the profits and losses. Suppose Jason Cruz and Susan Moore allocate 2/3 of the profits and losses to Cruz and 1/3 to Moore. This sharing rule can also be expressed as 2:1. If their net income for the year is $60,000, the Income Summary account has a credit balance of $60,000 prior to closing.

Income Summary	
	Bal. 60,000

The entry to close net income to the partners' capital accounts is:

Dec. 31	Income Summary	60,000	
	Cruz, Capital ($60,000 × 2/3)		40,000
	Moore, Capital ($60,000 × 1/3)		20,000
	To close net income to the partners.		

Suppose Cruz's beginning capital balance was $50,000 and Moore's $10,000. After posting, the accounts appear as follows:

Income Summary			Cruz, Capital			Moore, Capital	
Clo. 60,000	60,000			Beg. 50,000			Beg. 10,000
				Clo. 40,000			Clo. 20,000
				End. 90,000			End. 30,000

If the partnership had a net loss of $15,000, the Income Summary account would have a debit balance of $15,000, as follows:

Income Summary

Bal. 15,000

In that case Cruz takes a hit for 2/3 of the loss, and the closing entry is:

Dec. 31	Cruz, Capital ($15,000 × 2/3)	10,000	
	Moore, Capital ($15,000 × 1/3)	5,000	
	Income Summary		15,000
	To close net loss to the partners.		

Sharing Based on Capital Balances and on Service

One partner may invest more capital. Another may put more work into the business. Even among partners who log equal time, one person may be worth more to the firm. To reward the more-valuable person, the profits and losses may be divided based on a combination of partner capital balances *and* service.

Chris Hilton and Dana Lee formed a partnership in which Hilton invested $60,000 and Lee $40,000, for total capital of $100,000. But Lee devotes more time to the business and earns more from the firm. Accordingly, the two partners have agreed to share profits as follows:

1. The first $50,000 is allocated based on partner capital balances.

2. The next $60,000 is allocated based on service, with Hilton getting $24,000 and Lee $36,000.

3. Any remaining profit is allocated equally.

The partnership's net income for the first year is $125,000, and the partners share this profit as follows:

		Hilton	Lee	Total
Total net income				$125,000
Sharing of first $50,000 of net income,				
based on capital balances:				
Hilton ($60,000/$100,000 × $50,000)		$30,000		
Lee ($40,000/$100,000 × $50,000)			$20,000	
Total				50,000
Net income remaining for allocation				75,000
Sharing of next $60,000, based on service:				
Hilton		24,000		
Lee			36,000	
Total				60,000
Net income remaining for allocation				15,000
Remainder shared equally:				
Hilton ($15,000 × 1/2)		7,500		
Lee ($15,000 × 1/2)			7,500	
Total				15,000
Net income remaining for allocation				$ 0
Net income remaining for the partners		$61,500	$63,500	$125,000

For this allocation, the closing entry is:

Dec. 31	Income Summary	125,000	
	Hilton, Capital		61,500
	Lee, Capital		63,500
	To close net income to the partners.		

Partner Drawings of Cash and Other Assets

Partners need cash for personal expenses like everyone else. The written agreement usually allows partners to withdraw assets from the business. Drawings (withdrawals) from a partnership are recorded exactly as for a proprietorship. Assume that Kay Neal and Gina Chen each get monthly withdrawals of $3,000. The partnership records the March withdrawals with this entry:

Mar. 31	Neal, Drawing	3,000	
	Chen, Drawing	3,000	
	Cash		6,000
	Partner withdrawals of cash.		

During the year, each partner gets 12 monthly withdrawals, a total of $36,000 ($3,000 × 12). At year-end, the general ledger shows these partner drawing accounts:

Neal, Drawing		Chen, Drawing	
Dec. 31 Bal. 36,000		Dec. 31 Bal. 36,000	

The drawing accounts are closed at the end of the period, exactly as for a proprietorship: Credit each partner's drawing account and debit his or her capital account.

Admission of a Partner

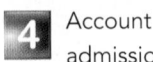

Account for the admission of a new partner

Admitting a new partner dissolves the old partnership and begins a new one. Often, the new partnership continues the old one's business. Let's look at the ways a new owner can be added to a partnership.

Admission by Purchasing a Partner's Interest

A person can become an owner by purchasing an existing partner's interest. First, however, the new person must gain the approval of the other partners.

Jan Fisher and Benny Garcia have a partnership that carries these figures:

Cash	$ 40,000	Total liabilities	$120,000
Other assets	360,000	Fisher, capital	170,000
		Garcia, capital	110,000
Total assets	$400,000	Total liabilities and capital	$400,000

Suppose Fisher wants out and Barry Holt, an outside party, buys Fisher's interest.

Garcia accepts Holt as a partner, and Fisher agrees to accept $150,000. The firm records the transfer of capital interest with this entry:

Apr. 16	Fisher, Capital	170,000	
	Holt, Capital		170,000
	To transfer Fisher's equity to Holt.		

Fisher, Capital		Holt, Capital		Garcia, Capital	
170,000	170,000		170,000		110,000

The debit closes Fisher's capital account, and the credit sets up Holt's capital, as shown in the T-accounts. The entry amount is Fisher's capital balance ($170,000) and not the $150,000 that Holt paid Fisher. Why $170,000?

In this example, the partnership receives no cash because the transaction was between Holt and Fisher, not between Holt and the partnership. The full $150,000 went to Fisher. Suppose Holt pays Fisher more than her capital balance—say, $200,000. The entry on the partnership books is not affected. Fisher's equity is transferred to Holt at book value ($170,000).

The old partnership of Fisher & Garcia has dissolved. Garcia and Holt draw up a new agreement with a new profit-and-loss ratio and continue in business. If Garcia does not accept Holt as a partner, then Holt gets no voice in management. But under the Uniform Partnership Act, Holt shares in the profits and losses of the firm and in its assets at liquidation.

Admission by Investing in the Partnership

A person can enter a partnership by investing directly in the business. (This is different from buying out an existing partner, as in the preceding example.)

Here the new partner invests assets—for example, cash or equipment—in the business. Assume that the partnership of Ingel and Jay has the following:

Cash..................	$ 20,000	Total liabilities	$ 60,000
Other assets	200,000	Ingel, capital	70,000
		Jay, capital	90,000
Total assets........	$220,000	Total liabilities and capital	$220,000

Let's consider several possible investments by a new partner.

Admission by Investing in the Partnership at Book Value—No Bonus to Amy Partner

Cheryl Kaska wants into the Ingel & Jay partnership.

Kaska can invest equipment and land (labeled Other Assets) with a market value of $80,000. Ingel and Jay agree to dissolve their partnership and start up a new one, giving Kaska a 1/3 interest for her $80,000 investment, as follows:

Partnership capital before Kaska is admitted ($70,000 + $90,000)........	$160,000
Kaska's investment in the partnership...	80,000
Partnership capital after Kaska is admitted...	$240,000
Kaska's capital in the new partnership ($240,000 × 1/3)	$ 80,000

Notice that Kaska is buying into the partnership at book value because her 1/3 investment ($80,000) equals 1/3 of the new firm's total capital ($240,000). The partnership's entry to record Kaska's investment is:

July 18	Other Assets	80,000	
	Kaska, Capital		80,000
	To admit Kaska as a partner.		

After this entry, the new partnership's books show:

Cash	$ 20,000		Total liabilities.....................	$ 60,000
Other assets			Ingel, capital........................	70,000
($200,000 + $80,000).	280,000		Jay, capital...........................	90,000
			Kaska, capital......................	80,000
Total assets	$300,000		Total liabilities and capital..	$300,000

Kaska's 1/3 interest does not necessarily entitle her to 1/3 of the profits. Remember: The sharing of profits and losses is a separate element in the partnership agreement.

Admission by Investing in the Partnership—Bonus to the Old Partners

A successful partnership may require a higher payment from a new partner. The old partners may demand a bonus, which will increase their capital accounts.

The Kaga & Opper partnership has earned above-average profits for 10 years. The partners share profits and losses equally. Their balance sheet carries these figures:

Cash.................	$ 40,000		Total liabilities	$100,000
Other assets	210,000		Kaga, capital............................	70,000
			Opper, capital	80,000
Total assets........	$250,000		Total liabilities and capital	$250,000

Kaga and Opper admit Nancy Fry to a 1/4 interest in return for Fry's cash investment of $90,000. Fry's capital balance on the new partnership books is only $60,000, computed as follows:

Partnership capital before Fry is admitted ($70,000 + $80,000)	$150,000
Fry's investment in the partnership	90,000
Partnership capital after Fry is admitted	$240,000
Fry's capital in the partnership ($240,000 × 1/4)	$ 60,000
Bonus to the old partners ($90,000 − $60,000)	$ 30,000

In effect, Fry had to buy into the partnership at a price ($90,000) above the book value of her 1/4 interest ($60,000). Fry's higher-than-book-value investment creates a *bonus* for Kaga and Opper. The partnership entry to record the receipt of Fry's investment is:

Mar. 1	Cash	90,000	
	Fry, Capital		60,000
	Kaga, Capital ($30,000 × 1/2)		15,000
	Opper, Capital ($30,000 × 1/2)		15,000
	To admit Fry as a partner.		

Fry's capital account got credited for her 1/4 interest in the partnership. The *bonus* was allocated to Kaga and Opper based on their profit-and-loss ratio.

The new partnership's balance sheet reports these amounts:

Cash ($40,000 + $90,000).	$130,000	Total liabilities		$100,000
Other assets	210,000	Kaga, capital ($70,000 + $15,000)		85,000
		Opper, capital ($80,000 + $15,000)		95,000
		Fry, capital		60,000
Total assets	$340,000	Total liabilities and capital		$340,000

Admission by Investing in the Partnership—Bonus to the New Partner

A new partner may be so important that the old partners offer a partnership share that includes a bonus to the new person. For example, it's common in big-league cities for a restaurant owner to go into partnership with a sports star.

Suppose Page and Franco have a restaurant. Their partnership balance sheet follows.

Cash	$140,000	Total liabilities	$120,000
Other assets	360,000	Page, capital	230,000
		Franco, capital	150,000
Total assets	$500,000	Total liabilities and capital	$500,000

Page and Franco admit Tiger Jones, a famous golfer, as a partner with a 1/3 interest in exchange for Jones's cash investment of $100,000. Page and Franco share profits and losses in the ratio of 2/3 to Page and 1/3 to Franco. The computation of Jones's equity in the new partnership is:

Partnership capital before Jones is admitted ($230,000 + $150,000)	$380,000
Jones's investment in the partnership	100,000
Partnership capital after Jones is admitted	$480,000
Jones's capital in the partnership ($480,000 × 1/3)	$160,000
Bonus to the new partner ($160,000 − $100,000)	$ 60,000

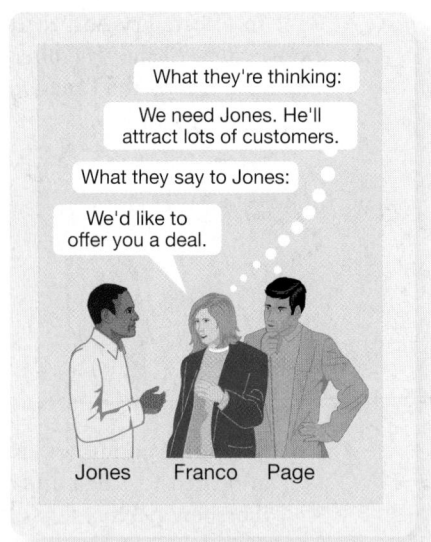

In this case, Jones entered the partnership at a price ($100,000) below the book value of his equity ($160,000). The bonus of $60,000 went to Jones from the other partners so their capital accounts are debited for the bonus. The old partners share this decrease in capital as though it were a loss, on the basis of their profit-and-loss ratio. The entry to record Jones's investment is:

Aug. 24	Cash		100,000	
	Page, Capital ($60,000 × 2/3)		40,000	
	Franco, Capital ($60,000 × 1/2)		20,000	
		Jones, Capital		160,000
	To admit T. Jones as a partner.			

The new partnership's balance sheet reports these amounts:

Cash		Total liabilities	$120,000
($140,000 + $100,000)	$240,000	Page, capital	
Other assets	360,000	($230,000 − $40,000)	190,000
		Franco, capital	
		($150,000 − $20,000)	130,000
		Jones, capital	160,000
Total assets	$600,000	Total liabilities and capital	$600,000

Now let's see how to account for the withdrawal of a partner from the firm.

Withdrawal of a Partner

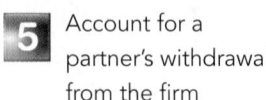

Account for a partner's withdrawal from the firm

A partner may leave the business for many reasons, including retirement or a dispute. The withdrawal of a partner dissolves the old partnership. The agreement should specify how to settle up with a withdrawing partner.

In the simplest case, a partner may sell his or her interest to another party in a personal transaction. This is the same as admitting a new person who purchases an existing partner's interest, as we saw earlier. The journal entry simply debits the withdrawing partner's capital account and credits the new partner's capital. The dollar amount is the old partner's capital balance, as illustrated for Fisher and Holt on page 604.

Often, however, the withdrawal is more complex, as we shall see next.

Revaluation of Assets

The withdrawing partner may receive assets other than cash. Then the question is what value to assign the assets—book value or current market value? The settlement procedure often specifies an independent appraisal to determine current market value because market values may have changed. In that case the partnership must revalue its assets. The partners share any market-value changes in their profit-and-loss ratio.

Suppose Keith Jackson retires from the partnership of Green, Henry, and Jackson.

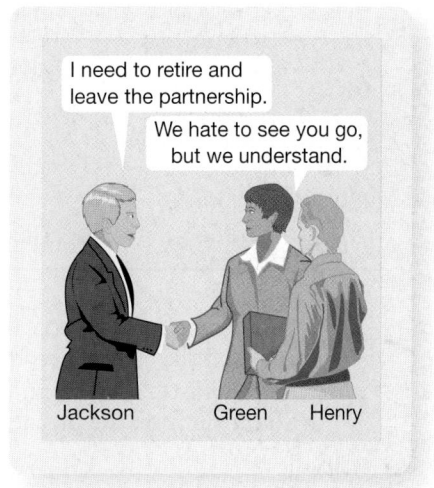

Before any asset appraisal, the partnership balance sheet reports the following:

Cash		$ 70,000	Total liabilities	$ 80,000
Inventory		40,000	Green, capital	50,000
Land		50,000	Henry, capital	40,000
Building	$90,000		Jackson, capital	20,000
Less Accum. depr.	(60,000)	30,000	Total liabilities and	
Total assets		$190,000	capital	$190,000

An independent appraiser revalues the inventory at $34,000 (down from $40,000) and the land at $100,000 (up from $50,000). The partners share the differences between market value and book value on the basis of their profit-and-loss ratio.

The partnership agreement allocates 1/4 of the profits to Green, 1/2 to Henry, and 1/4 to Jackson. (This ratio may be written 1:2:1 for one part to Green, two parts to Henry, and one part to Jackson.) For each share that Green or Jackson has, Henry gets two. The entries to record the revaluation of the inventory and land are:

July 31	Green, Capital ($6,000 × 1/4)		1,500	
	Henry, Capital ($6,000 × 1/2)		3,000	
	Jackson, Capital ($6,000 × 1/4)		1,500	
	Inventory ($40,000 − $34,000)			6,000
	To revalue the inventory.			
31	Land ($100,0000 − $50,000)		50,000	
	Green, Capital ($50,000 × 1/4)			12,500
	Henry, Capital ($50,000 × 1/2)			25,000
	Jackson, Capital ($50,000 × 1/4)			12,500
	To revalue the land.			

After the revaluations, the partnership balance sheet reports the following:

Cash		$ 70,000	Total liabilities.......................................	$ 80,000
Inventory		34,000	Green, capital ($50,000 − $1,500 + $12,500)......	61,000
Land		100,000	Henry, capital ($40,000 − $3,000 + $25,000)	62,000
Building	$90,000		Jackson, capital ($20,000 − $1,500 + $12,500)...	31,000
Less Accum. depr. ...	(60,000)	30,000		
Total assets		$234,000	Total liabilities and capital	$234,000

The books now carry the assets at market value, which becomes the new book value, and the capital accounts are up-to-date. As the balance sheet shows, Jackson has a claim to $31,000 in partnership assets. Now we can account for Jackson's withdrawal from the business.

Withdrawal at Book Value

If Jackson withdraws by receiving cash for his book value, the entry will be:

July 31	Jackson, Capital		31,000	
	Cash			31,000
	To record withdrawal of Jackson.			

Withdrawal at Less Than Book Value

The withdrawing partner may be so eager to depart that he will take less than full equity. Assume that Jackson withdraws from the business and agrees to receive cash of $10,000 and the new partnership's $15,000 note payable. This $25,000 settlement is $6,000 less than Jackson's $31,000 equity. The remaining partners share this $6,000 difference—a bonus to them—according to their profit-and-loss ratio.

Because Jackson has withdrawn from the partnership, a new agreement—and a new profit-and-loss ratio—is needed. In forming a new partnership, Henry and Green may decide on any ratio they wish. Let's assume they agree that Henry will get 2/3 of the profits and losses and Green 1/3. The entry to record Jackson's withdrawal at less than his book value is:

July 31	Jackson, Capital	31,000	
	Cash		10,000
	Note Payable to K. Jackson		15,000
	Green, Capital ($6,000 × 1/3)		2,000
	Henry, Capital ($6,000 × 2/3)		4,000
	To record withdrawal of Jackson.		

Jackson's account is closed, and Henry and Green may or may not continue the partnership.

Withdrawal at More Than Book Value

A withdrawing partner may receive assets worth more than the book value of his or her equity. This situation creates:

- A bonus to the withdrawing partner
- A decrease in the remaining partners' capital accounts, shared in their profit-and-loss ratio

The accounting for this situation follows the pattern illustrated above for withdrawal at less than book value—with one exception. The remaining partners' capital accounts are debited because they are paying a bonus to the withdrawing partner.

Death of a Partner

The death of a partner dissolves a partnership. The accounts are adjusted to measure net income or loss for the period up to the date of death. Then the accounts are closed to determine all partners' capital balances on that date. Settlement with the deceased partner's estate is based on the partnership agreement. There may or may not be an asset revaluation. The estate commonly receives assets equal to the partner's capital balance.

Suppose Susan Green (of the partnership on page 610) dies, and her capital balance is $61,000. Green's estate may request cash for her final share of the business's assets. The partnership's journal entry is:

Aug. 1	Green, Capital	61,000	
	Cash		61,000
	To record withdrawal of Green.		

Alternatively, a remaining partner may purchase the deceased partner's equity. The deceased partner's capital account is debited, and the purchaser's capital is credited. The journal entry to record this transaction follows the pattern given on page 604 for the transfer of Fisher's equity to Holt. The amount of this entry is the ending capital balance of the deceased partner.

Liquidation of a Partnership

Account for the liquidation of a partnership

As we've seen, the admission or withdrawal of a partner dissolves the partnership. However, it may continue operating with no apparent change to outsiders. In contrast, **liquidation** shuts down the firm by selling its assets and paying its liabilities.

The final step in liquidation is to *distribute any remaining cash to the owners.* Before a business is liquidated, its books should be adjusted and closed. Liquidation includes three steps:

1. Sell the assets. Allocate the gain or loss to the partners' capital accounts based on the profit-and-loss ratio.

2. Pay all partnership liabilities.

3. Pay the remaining cash to the partners based on their capital balances.

The liquidation of a business can stretch over weeks or months—a year or longer for a big company. To avoid excessive detail in our illustrations, we include only two asset categories—Cash and Noncash Assets—and a single liability—Liabilities. Our examples assume that the business sells the assets in a single transaction and then pays the liabilities at once.

Akers, Bloch, and Crane have shared profits and losses in the ratio of 3:1:1. (This ratio is equal to 3/5, 1/5, 1/5, or 60%, 20%, 20%, respectively.) The partners decide to liquidate. After the books are adjusted and closed, these accounts remain.

Cash	$ 10,000	Liabilities	$ 30,000
Noncash assets	90,000	Akers, capital	40,000
		Bloch, capital	20,000
		Crane, capital	10,000
Total assets	$100,000	Total liabilities and capital	$100,000

Sale of Assets at a Gain

Assume that Akers, Bloch, and Crane sell the noncash assets for $150,000 (book value, $90,000). The partnership realizes a gain of $60,000, allocated to the partners based on their profit-and-loss ratio. The entry to record this sale and allocate the gain is:

Oct. 31	Cash	150,000	
	Noncash Assets		90,000
	Akers, Capital ($60,000 × 0.60)		36,000
	Bloch, Capital ($60,000 × 0.20)		12,000
	Crane, Capital ($60,000 × 0.20)		12,000
	To sell assets.		

Now the partner capital accounts have the balances shown.

Akers, Capital		Bloch, Capital		Crane, Capital	
	40,000		20,000		10,000
	36,000		12,000		12,000
	76,000		32,000		22,000

The partnership then pays off its liabilities:

Oct. 31	Liabilities	30,000	
	Cash		30,000
	To pay liabilities.		

The final liquidation transaction pays all remaining cash to the partners *according to their capital balances.*

The amount of cash left in the partnership is $130,000, as follows:

Cash			
Beg. bal.	10,000	Payment of liabilities	30,000
Sale of assets	150,000		
End. bal.	130,000		

The partners divide the remaining cash according to their capital balances:

Oct. 31	Akers, Capital	76,000	
	Bloch, Capital	32,000	
	Crane, Capital	22,000	
	Cash		130,000
	To pay cash in liquidation.		

A convenient way to summarize the transactions in a partnership liquidation is given in Exhibit 12-5. Remember:

- Upon liquidation, gains and losses on the sale of assets are divided according to the *profit-and-loss ratio.*
- The final cash payment to the partners is based on *capital balances.*

EXHIBIT 12-5   **Partnership Liquidation—Sale of Assets at a Gain**

					Capital		
	Cash +	Noncash Assets	= Liabilities +	Akers (60%) +	Bloch (20%) +	Crane (20%)
Balance before sale of assets.............	$ 10,000	$90,000	$30,000	$40,000	$20,000	$10,000
Sale of assets and sharing of gain......	150,000	(90,000)		36,000	12,000	12,000
Balances..	160,000	0	30,000	76,000	32,000	22,000
Payment of liabilities...........................	(30,000)		(30,000)			
Balances..	130,000	0	0	76,000	32,000	22,000
Payment of cash to partners.............	(130,000)			(76,000)	(32,000)	(22,000)
Final balances....................................	$ 0	$ 0	$ 0	$ 0	$ 0	$ 0

After the payment of cash to the partners, the business has no assets, liabilities, or equity. All final balances are zero.

Sale of Assets at a Loss

Liquidation of a business often includes the sale of assets at a loss. When a loss occurs, the partner capital accounts are debited based on the profit-and-loss ratio. Otherwise, the accounting follows the pattern illustrated for the sale at a gain.

Partnership Financial Statements

7 Prepare partnership financial statements

Partnership financial statements are much like the statements of a proprietorship, but with the following differences:

- A partnership income statement shows the division of net income to the partners. For example, the partnership of Gray & Hayward can report its income statement as shown in Exhibit 12-6. All amounts are assumed.
- A partnership balance sheet reports a separate capital account for each partner, as shown in Exhibit 12-6.

EXHIBIT 12-6 Financial Statements of a Partnership

GRAY & HAYWARD
Income Statement
Year Ended December 31, 2008

Revenues	$470,000
Expenses	270,000
Net income	$200,000
Allocation of net income:	
To Gray	$120,000
To Hayward	80,000
Total net income	$200,000

GRAY & HAYWARD
Balance Sheet
December 31, 2008

Assets		
Cash and other assets		$800,000
Liabilities		
Accounts payable and other liabilities		$300,000
Owners' Equity		
Gray, capital		400,000
Hayward, capital		100,000
Total capital		500,000
Total liabilities and owners' equity		$800,000

Now turn to the Decision Guidelines for a summary of the accounting for partnerships.

Decision Guidelines

Suppose you have a friend who's a biology major. He has achieved amazing success growing plants hydroponically (in water). He knows plants but has no sense for business, so the two of you form a partnership to take advantage of your respective skills. How do you organize? What decisions must you make? Consider these decision guidelines.

Decision	Guidelines
How to organize the business?	A partnership offers both advantages and disadvantages in comparison with proprietorships and corporations. (Exhibit 12-2, page 598)
On what matters should the partners agree?	See "The Written Agreement" on page 596.
At what value does the partnership record assets and liabilities?	Current market value on the date of acquisition, because the partnership is buying its assets at their current market value.

How are partnership profits and losses shared among the partners?	• Equally if there is no profit-and-loss-sharing agreement.
	• As provided in the partnership agreement. Can be based on the partners'
	  a. Stated fractions
	  b. Capital contributions
	  c. Service to the partnership
	  d. Any combination of the above.

What happens when a partner withdraws from the firm?	The old partnership dissolves. The remaining partners may or may not form a new partnership.
How are new partners admitted to the partnership?	• *Purchase a partners inte rest.* The old partnership is dissolved. The remaining partners may admit the new partner to the partnership. If not, the new partner gets no voice in management but shares in the profits and losses. Close the withdrawing partner's Capital account, and open a Capital account for the new partner. Carry over the old partner's Capital balance to the Capital account of the new partner. • *Invest in the partnership.* Buying in at book value creates no bonus to any partner. Buying in at a price above book value creates a bonus to the old partners. Buying in at a price below book value creates a bonus for the new partner.

How to account for the withdrawal of a partner from the business?	• First, adjust and close the books up to the date of the partner's withdrawal from the business.
	• Second, appraise the assets and liabilities at current market value.
	• Third, account for the partner's withdrawal.
	  a. At book value (no change in remaining partners' Capital balances)
	  b. At less than book value (increase the remaining partners' Capital balances)
	  c. At more than book value (decrease the remaining partners' Capital balances)

continued . . .

Decision

What happens if the partnership goes out of business?

Guidelines

Liquidate the partnership, as follows:
   a. Adjust and close the books up to the date of liquidation.
   b. Sell the partnership's assets. Allocate gain or loss to the partners based on their profit-and-loss ratio.
   c. Pay the partnership liabilities.
   d. Pay any remaining cash to the partners based on their Capital balances.

Summary Problem

The partnership of Uno & Dos admits Tres as a partner on January 1, 2008. The partnership has these balances on that date:

Cash	$ 9,000	Total liablilities	$ 50,000
Other assets	110,000	Uno, capital	45,000
		Dos, capital	24,000
Total assets	$119,000	Total liabilities and capital	$119,000

Uno's share of profits and losses is 60%, and Dos gets 40%.

Requirements (Items 1 and 2 are independent)
1. Suppose Tres pays Dos $30,000 to buy out Dos. Uno approves Tres as a partner.
   a. Record the transfer of equity on the partnership books.
   b. Prepare the partnership balance sheet immediately after Tres is admitted as a partner.

2. Suppose Tres becomes a partner by investing $31,000 cash to acquire a one-fourth interest in the business.
   a. Compute Tres's capital balance, and determine whether there's any bonus. If so, who gets the bonus?
   b. Record Tres's investment in the business.
   c. Prepare the partnership balance sheet immediately after Tres is admitted as a partner. Include the heading.

Solution

Requirement 1
a.

Jan. 1	Dos, Capital	24,000	
	Tres, Capital		24,000
	To transfer Dos's equity to Tres.		

b. The balance sheet for the partnership of Uno and Tres is identical to the balance sheet given for Uno and Dos in the problem, except that Tres replaces Dos in the title and in the listing of Capital accounts.

Requirement 2
a. Computation of Tres's capital balance.

Partnership capital before Tres is admitted ($45,000 + $24,000)....	$ 69,000
Tres's investment in the partnership...	31,000
Partnership capital after Tres is admitted.......................................	$100,000
Tres's capital in the partnership ($100,000 × 1/4)...........................	$ 25,000
Bonus to the old partners ($31,000 − $25,000).............................	$ 6,000

continued . . .

b. Journal entry to record Tres's investment:

Jan. 1	Cash	31,000	
	Tres, Capital		25,000
	Uno, Capital ($6,000 × 0.60)		3,600
	Dos, Capital ($60,000 × 0.40)		2,400
	To admit Tres as a partner.		

c. New partnership balance sheet:

UNO, DOS, & TRES
Balance Sheet
January 1, 2008

Cash ($9,000 + $31,000)	$ 40,000	Total liabilities	$ 50,000
Other assets	110,000	Uno, capital	
		($45,000 + $3,600)	48,600
		Dos, capital	
		($24,000 + $2,400)	26,400
		Tres, capital	25,000
Total assets	$150,000	Total liabilities and capital	$150,000

Review *Partnerships*

Accounting Vocabulary

Articles of Partnership
The contract between partners that specifies such items as the name, location, and nature of the business; the name, capital investment, and duties of each partner; and the method of sharing profits and losses among the partners. Also called **partnership agreement**.

Dissolution
Ending of a partnership.

General Partnership
A form of partnership in which each partner is an owner of the business with all the privileges and risks of ownership.

Limited Liability Partnership
A form of partnership in which each partner's personal liability for the business's debts is limited to a certain amount. Also called **LLPs**.

Limited Partnership
A partnership with at least two classes of partners: a general partner and limited partners.

Liquidation
The process of going out of business by selling the entity's assets and paying its liabilities. The final step in liquidation is the distribution of any remaining cash to the owner(s).

LLPs
A form of partnership in which each partner's personal liability for the business's debts is limited to a certain amount. Also called **limited liability partnership**.

Mutual Agency
Every partner can bind the business to a contract within the scope of the partnership's regular business operations.

Partnership
An association of two or more persons who co-own a business for profit.

Partnership Agreement
The contract between partners that specifies such items as the name, location, and nature of the business; the name, capital investment, and duties of each partner; and the method of sharing profits and losses among the partners. Also called **articles of partnership**.

S Corporation
A corporation taxed in the same way as a partnership.

Unlimited Personal Liability
When a partnership (or a proprietorship) cannot pay its debts with business assets, the partners (or the proprietor) must use personal assets to meet the debt.

Quick Check

1. How does a partnership get started?
    a. The partners reach an agreement and begin operations.
    b. The partners get a charter from the state.
    c. The partners register under the Uniform Partnership Act.
    d. All of the above.

2. Which characteristic identifies a partnership?
    a. Unlimited life
    b. No business income tax
    c. Limited personal liability
    d. All of the above

3. An S corporation is taxed like a
    a. Corporation
    b. Partnership
    c. Either a or b, depending on the stockholders' decision
    d. None of the above

4. The partnership of Abbot and Brown splits profits 2/3 to Abbot and 1/3 to Brown. There is no provision for losses. The partnership has a net loss of $150,000. What is Brown's share of the loss?
    a. $150,000
    b. $100,000
    c. $50,000
    d. Cannot be determined because the loss-sharing ratio is not given.

5. Partner drawings
    a. Increase partnership liabilities
    b. Decrease partnership net income
    c. Increase partnership capital
    d. Decrease partnership capital

6. Malcolm pays $50,000 to Lloyd to acquire Lloyd's $25,000 interest in a partnership. The journal entry to record this transaction is
    a. Lloyd, Capital............ 75,000
        Malcolm, Capital....   75,000
    b. Lloyd, Capital............ 50,000
        Malcolm, Capital....   50,000
    c. Lloyd, Capital............ 25,000
        Malcolm, Capital....   25,000
    d. Malcolm, Capital........ 25,000
        Lloyd, Capital.........   25,000

7. Clark and Douglas admit Evans to their partnership, with Evans paying $50,000 more than the book value of her equity in the new business. Clark and Douglas have no formal profit-and-loss agreement. What effect does admitting Evans to the partnership have on the capital balances of Clark and Douglas?

   a. Cannot be determined because there's no profit-and-loss ratio

   b. Credit the Clark and Douglas capital accounts for $25,000 each

   c. Credit the Clark and Douglas capital accounts for $50,000 each

   d. Debit the Clark and Douglas capital accounts for $25,000 each

8. Tate retires from the partnership of Roberts, Smith, and Tate. The partners share profits and losses in the ratio of 4:3:3. Tate's capital balance is $40,000, and he receives $47,000 in final settlement. What is the effect on the capital accounts of Roberts and Smith?

   a. Smith's capital decreases by $7,000.

   b. Roberts' capital decreases by $7,000.

   c. Roberts' capital increases by $4,000.

   d. Roberts' capital decreases by $4,000.

9. The book value of the assets of the KLM partnership is $100,000. In liquidation, the partnership sells the assets for $130,000. How should the partnership account for the sale of the assets?

   a. Credit the assets for $100,000

   b. Debit cash for $130,000

   c. Increase the partners' capital accounts

   d. All of the above

10. Partnership financial statements report

   a. Revenues on the income statement

   b. Liabilities on the income statement

   c. Net income on the balance sheet

   d. Expenses on the balance sheet

   Answers are given after Apply Your Knowledge (p. 635).

Assess Your Progress

Short Exercises

Partnership characteristics

S12-1 Study the characteristics of a partnership. Then, in your own words, write two short paragraphs, as follows:

1. Explain the *advantages* of a partnership over a proprietorship and a corporation. (pp. 597–598)

2. Explain the *disadvantages* of a partnership compared to a proprietorship and a corporation. (pp. 597–598)

A partner's investment in a partnership

S12-2 Marty Stubbs invests land in a partnership with Lee Dix. Stubbs purchased the land in 2007 for $200,000. A real estate appraiser now values the land at $500,000. Stubbs wants $400,000 capital in the new partnership, but Dix objects. Dix believes that Stubbs' capital investment should be measured by the book value of his land.

Dix and Stubbs seek your advice. Which value of the land is appropriate for measuring Stubbs' capital—book value or current market value? State the reason for your answer. Give the partnership's journal entry to record Stubbs' investment in the business. (pp. 600–601)

Investments by partners

S12-3 Joe Brown and Chris White are forming a partnership to develop a theme park near Panama City, Florida. Brown invests cash of $1 million and land valued at $10 million. When Brown purchased the land in 2007, its cost was $8 million. The partnership will assume Brown's $3 million note payable on the land. White invests cash of $3 million and equipment worth $7 million.

1. Journalize the partnership's receipt of assets and liabilities from Brown and from White. (p. 601)

2. Compute the partnership's total assets, total liabilities, and total owners' equity immediately after organizing. (p. 602)

Partners' profits, losses, and capital balances

S12-4 Abel and Baker had beginning capital balances of $20,000 and 16,000, respectively. The two partners fail to agree on a profit-and-loss ratio. For the first month (June 2008), the partnership lost $8,000.

1. How much of this loss goes to Abel? How much goes to Baker? (p. 602)

2. The partners withdrew no assets during June. What is each partner's capital balance at June 30? Prepare a T-account for each partner's capital. (p. 602)

Dividing partnership profits based on capital contributions and service
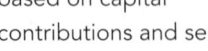

S12-5 Lee, Muse, and Nall have capital balances of $20,000, $30,000, and $50,000, respectively. The partners share profits and losses as follows:

a. The first $40,000 is divided based on the partners' capital balances. (pp. 602–603)

b. The next $40,000 is based on service, shared equally by Lee and Nall.

c. The remainder is divided equally. (pp. 602–603)

Compute each partner's share of the $92,000 net income for the year.

Admitting a partner who purchases an existing partner's interest
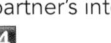

S12-6 Ann Todd has a capital balance of $30,000; Vic Carlson's balance is $25,000. Claire Reynaldo pays $100,000 to purchase Carlson's interest in the Todd & Carlson partnership. Carlson gets the full $100,000.

1. Journalize the partnership's transaction to admit Reynaldo to the partnership. (pp. 604–605)

2. Must Todd accept Reynaldo as a full partner? What right does Reynaldo have after purchasing Carlson's interest in the partnership? (pp. 604–605)

Admitting a partner who invests in the business

S12-7 The partnership of Ecru and Falcon has these capital balances:

- Ecru $60,000
- Falcon $80,000

Joan Gray invests cash of $70,000 to acquire a 1/3 interest in the partnership.

1. Does Gray's investment in the firm provide a bonus to the partners? Show your work. (pp. 605–606)
2. Journalize the partnership's receipt of the $70,000 from Gray. (pp. 605–606)

Admitting a new partner; bonus situation

S12-8 Bo and Go have partner capital balances of $250,000 and $150,000, respectively. Bo gets 60% of profits and losses, and Go gets 40%. Assume Mo invests $100,000 to acquire a 25% interest in the new partnership of Bogomo.

1. Is there a bonus? If so, who gets it?
2. Journalize the partnership's receipt of cash from Mo. (pp. 605–606)

Withdrawal of a partner

S12-9 Adam, Eve, and Cain each have a $100,000 capital balance. They share profits and losses as follows: 25% to Adam, 50% to Eve, and 25% to Cain. Suppose Cain is withdrawing from the business, and the partners agree that no appraisal of assets is needed. How much in assets can Cain take from the partnership? Give the reason for your answer. What role does the profit-and-loss ratio play in this situation? (pp. 610–611)

Withdrawal of a partner; asset revaluation

S12-10 Abraham, Isaac, and Jacob each have a $50,000 capital balance. Abraham is very old and is retiring from the business. The partners agree to revalue the assets at current market value. A real-estate appraiser values the land at $140,000 (book value is $100,000). The profit-and-loss ratio is 1:2:1. Journalize (a) the revaluation of the land on July 31 and (b) payment of $60,000 to Abraham upon his retirement the same day. (pp. 608–611)

Liquidation of a partnership at a loss

S12-11 Use the data in Exhibit 12-5, page 613. Suppose the partnership of Akers, Bloch, and Crane liquidates by selling all noncash assets for $80,000. Complete the liquidation schedule as shown in Exhibit 12-5. (p. 613)

Liquidation of a partnership

S12-12 This exercise builds on the solution to Short Exercise 12-11. After completing the liquidation schedule in Short Exercise 12-11, journalize the partnership's (a) sale of noncash assets for $80,000 (use a single account for Noncash Assets), (b) payment of liabilities, and (c) payment of cash to the partners. Include an explanation with each entry. (pp. 613–614)

S12-13 The partnership of Bush and Carter had these balances at September 30, 2007:

Cash	$20,000	Service revenue	$145,000
Liabilities	40,000	Bush, capital	30,000
Carter, capital	10,000	Total expenses	85,000
Other assets	60,000		

Partnership income statement

Bush gets 60% of profits and losses, and Carter 40%. Prepare the partnership's income statement for the year ended September 30, 2007. (pp. 613–614)

Exercises

Organizing a partnership

E12-14 Monique Coty, a friend from college, asks you to form a partnership to import fragrances. Since graduating, Coty has worked for the French Embassy, developing important contacts among government officials. Coty believes she is in a unique position to capitalize on an important market. With expertise in accounting, you would have responsibility for the partnership's accounting and finance.

Requirements
Discuss the advantages and disadvantages of organizing the business as a partnership rather than a proprietorship. Comment on how partnership income is taxed and how your taxes would change if you organized as a limited-liability company (LLC) or an S corporation. (pp. 597–599)

Recording a partner's investment

E12-15 Nan Fuentes has been operating an apartment-locator service as a proprietorship. She and Misti Fulmer have decided to form a partnership. Fuentes's investment consists of cash, $8,000; accounts receivable, $10,000; furniture, $1,000; a building, $55,000; and a note payable, $10,000.

To determine Funtes's equity in the partnership, she and Fulmer hire an independent appraiser. The appraiser values all the assets and liabilities at their book value except the building, which has a current market value of $90,000. Also there are accounts payable of $3,000.

Requirement
Make the entry on the partnership books to record Fuentes's investment. (pp. 600–601)

Computing partners' shares of net income and net loss

E12-16 Bob Fultz and Jack Hardie form a partnership, investing $40,000 and $80,000, respectively. Determine their shares of net income or net loss for each of the following situations:

a. Net loss is $90,000 and the partners have no written partnership agreement. (p. 602)

b. Net income is $60,000, and the partnership agreement states that the partners share profits and losses on the basis of their capital balances. (pp. 602–603)

c. Net income is $100,000. The first $60,000 is shared on the basis of partner capital balances. The next $30,000 is based on partner service, with Fultz getting 40% and Hardie 60%. The remainder is shared equally. (pp. 602–603)

Computing partners' capital balances

E12-17 Bob Fultz and Jack Hardie each withdrew cash of $40,000 for personal use during the year. Using the data from situation (c) in Exercise 12-16, journalize the entries to close (1) net income to the partners and (2) the partners' drawing accounts. Explanations are not required. What was the overall effect of these events on partnership capital? (pp. 602–603)

Admitting a new partner
4

E12-18 Heather Hollis is admitted to the partnership of Rose & Novak. Prior to her admission, the partnership books show Ginny Rose's capital balance at $100,000 and Chris Novak's at $50,000. Compute each partner's equity on the books of the new partnership under the following plans:

   a. Hollis pays $70,000 for Novak's equity. Hollis pays Novak directly. (pp. 603–605)

   b. Hollis invests $50,000 to acquire a 1/4 interest in the partnership. (pp. 605–606)

   c. Hollis invests $90,000 to acquire a 1/4 interest in the partnership. (pp. 605–606)

Admitting a new partner
4

E12-19 Make the partnership journal entry to record the admission of Hollis under plans (a), (b), and (c) in Exercise 12-18. Explanations are not required. (pp. 603–606)

Withdrawal of a partner
5

E12-20 The O'Brien and Pope partnership balance sheet reports capital of $60,000 for O'Brien and $90,000 for Pope. O'Brien is withdrawing from the firm. The partners agree to write partnership assets up by $30,000. They have shared profits and losses in the ratio of 1/3 to O'Brien and 2/3 to Pope. The partnership agreement states that a withdrawing partner will receive assets equal to the book value of his owner's equity.

   1. How much will O'Brien receive? (pp. 609–610)

   2. Pope will continue to operate the business as a proprietorship. What is Pope's beginning capital on the books of his new proprietorship? (pp. 609–610)

Withdrawal of a partner
5

E12-21 On May 31, Sam retires from the partnership of Sam, Bob, and Tim. The partner capital balances are Sam, $36,000; Bob, $51,000; and Tim, $22,000. The partners have the assets revalued to current market values. The appraiser reports that the value of the inventory should be decreased by $12,000, and the land should be increased by $32,000. The profit-and-loss ratio has been 4:3:3 for Sam, Bob, and Tim, respectively. In retiring from the firm, Sam receives $60,000 cash.

   Requirement
   Journalize (a) the asset revaluations and (b) Sam's withdrawal from the firm. (pp. 608–611)

Liquidation of a partnership
6

E12-22 Ray, Scott, and Van are liquidating their partnership. Before selling the assets and paying the liabilities, the capital balances are Ray $33,000; Scott, $28,000; and Van, $19,000. The partnership agreement specifies no division of profits and losses.

   Requirements
   1. After selling the assets and paying the liabilities, the partnership has cash of $80,000. How much cash will each partner receive in final liquidation? (pp. 612–613)

   2. After selling the assets and paying the liabilities, the partnership has cash of $50,000. How much cash will each partner receive in final liquidation? (pp. 612–614)

E12-23 Prior to liquidation, the accounting records of Boyd, Carl, and Dove included the following balances and profit-and-loss percentages:

	Cash	+	Noncash Assets	=	Liabilities	+	Boyd (40%)	+	Carl (30%)	+	Dove (30%)
							Capital				
Balances before sale of assets.........	$9,000		$57,000		$20,000		$20,000		$15,000		$11,000

The partnership sold the noncash assets for $77,000, paid the liabilities, and gave the remaining cash to the partners. Complete the summary of transactions in the liquidation of the partnership. Use the format illustrated in Exhibit 12-5, page 613.

E12-24 The partnership of Dodd, Gage, and Hamm is liquidating. Business assets, liabilities, and partners' capital balances prior to liquidation follow. The partners share profits and losses as follows: Dodd, 20%; Gage, 30%; and Hamm, 50%.

DODD, GAGE, & HAMM
Sale of Noncash Assets
(for $140,000)

Cash	Noncash Assets	Liabilities	Dodd Capital	Gage Capital	Hamm Capital
$ 6,000	$126,000	$77,000	$12,000	$37,000	$6,000
140,000	(126,000)		?	?	?
$146,000	$ 0	$77,000	$?	$?	$?

Requirement
Create a spreadsheet or solve manually—as directed by your instructor—to compute the ending balances in all accounts after the noncash assets are sold for $140,000. (pp. 613–614)

E12-25 On December 31, 2008, Dana Farrell and Lou Flores agree to combine their proprietorships as a partnership. Their balance sheets on December 31 are shown on this and the next page.

Requirement
Prepare the partnership balance sheet at December 31, 2008. (pp. 600–601)

	Farrell's Business		Flores's Business	
	Book Value	Current Market Value	Book Value	Current Market Value
Assets				
Cash..	$ 10,000	$ 10,000	$ 4,000	$ 4,000
Accounts receivable...................	22,000	20,000	8,000	6,000
Inventory	51,000	45,000	35,000	35,000
Plant assets (net)	121,000	103,000	53,000	57,000
Total assets..............................	$204,000	$178,000	$100,000	$102,000

continued . . .

	Farrell's Business		Flores's Business	
	Book Value	Current Market Value	Book Value	Current Market Value
Liabilities and Capital				
Accounts payable......................	$ 25,000	$ 25,000	$ 10,000	$ 10,000
Accrued expenses payable.........	9,000	9,000		
Notes payable	56,000	56,000		
Farrell, capital...........................	114,000	?		
Flores, capital............................			90,000	?
Total liabilities and capital	$204,000	$178,000	$100,000	$102,000

Problems (Group A)

Writing a partnership agreement

P12-26A Gina Romero and Carlo Ponti are forming a partnership, Italian Leather Goods, to import from Italy. Romero is especially artistic and will travel to Italy to buy the merchandise. Ponti is a super salesman and has already lined up several department stores to sell the leather goods.

Requirement
Write a partnership agreement to cover all elements essential for the business to operate smoothly. Make up names, amounts, profit-and-loss percentages, and so on as needed. (pp. 596–598)

Investments by partners

P12-27A Nicole LeBlanc and Keith Rollins formed a partnership on March 15. The partners agreed to invest equal amounts of capital. LeBlanc invested her proprietorship's assets and liabilities (credit balances in parentheses). See the table that follows.

	LeBlanc's Book Values	Current Market Values
Accounts receivable.........................	$12,000	$10,000
Inventory...	43,000	31,000
Prepaid expenses	3,700	3,000
Store equipment	36,000	26,000
Accounts payable	(20,000)	(20,000)

On March 15, Rollins invested cash in an amount equal to the current market value of LeBlanc's partnership capital. The partners decided that LeBlanc will earn 70% of partnership profits because she will manage the business. Rollins agreed to accept 30% of the profits. During the period ended December 31, the partnership earned net income of $70,000. LeBlanc's drawings were $41,000, and Rollins's drawings totaled $27,000.

continued . . .

Requirements

1. Journalize the partners' initial investments. (pp. 600–601)

2. Prepare the partnership balance sheet immediately after its formation on March 15. (p. 601)

Admitting a new partner

P12-28A Hasselback, Krooch & Kinney, a partnership, is considering admitting Ken Rosenzweig as a new partner. On July 31 of the current year, the capital accounts of the three existing partners and their shares of profits and losses are as follows:

	Capital	Profit-and-Loss %
Hasselback	$40,000	20
Krooch	60,000	25
Kinney....................	80,000	55

Requirements

Journalize the admission of Rosenzweig as a partner on July 31 for each of the following independent situations:

1. Rosenzweig pays Kinney $110,000 cash to purchase Kinney's interest. (pp. 603–605)

2. Rosenzweig invests $60,000 in the partnership, acquiring a 1/4 interest in the business. (pp. 605–606)

3. Rosenzweig invests $60,000 in the partnership, acquiring a 1/6 interest in the business. (pp. 605–606)

Computing partners' shares of net income and net loss; preparing the partnership income statement

P12-29A Evans, Furr, and Good formed the EF&G partnership. Evans invested $20,000; Furr, $40,000; and Good, $60,000. Evans will manage the store; Furr will work in the store three-quarters of the time; and Good will not work.

Requirements

1. Compute the partners' shares of profits and losses under each of the following plans:

   a. Net loss is $40,000, and the partnership agreement allocates 45% of profits to Evans, 35% to Furr, and 20% to Good. The agreement does not discuss the sharing of losses. (pp. 601–602)

   b. Net income for the year ended September 30, 2009, is $90,000. The first $30,000 is allocated on the basis of partner capital balances. The next $30,000 is based on service, with $20,000 going to Evans and $10,000 going to Furr. Any remainder is shared equally. (pp. 602–603)

2. Revenues for the year ended September 30, 2009, were $190,000, and expenses were $100,000. Under plan (b) above, prepare the partnership income statement for the year. (p. 614)

P12-30A Ho-Kim-Li Oriental Design is a partnership owned by three individuals. The partners share profits and losses in the ratio of 30% to Ho, 40% to Kim, and 30% to Li. At December 31, 2008, the firm has this balance sheet:

Cash		$ 13,000	Total liabilities	$105,000
Accounts receivable	$16,000			
Less allowance for uncollectibles	(1,000)	15,000		
Inventory		92,000		
Equipment	130,000		Ho, capital	30,000
Less accumulated			Kim, capital	45,000
depreciation	(30,000)	100,000	Li, capital	40,000
Total assets		$220,000	Total liabilities and capital	$220,000

Ho withdraws from the partnership on this date.

Requirements

Record Ho's withdrawal from the partnership under the following plans:

1. In a personal transaction, Ho sells her equity to Win, who pays Ho $75,000 for her interest. Kim and Li agree to accept Win as a partner. (pp. 608–610)

2. The partnership pays Ho cash of $10,000 and gives her a note payable for the remainder of her book equity in settlement of her partnership interest. (pp. 608–611)

3. The partnership pays Ho $44,000 for her book equity. (p. 611)

4. The partners agree that the equipment is worth $160,000 and that accumulated depreciation should remain at $30,000. After the revaluation, the partnership settles with Ho by giving her cash of $5,000 and inventory for the remainder of her book equity. (pp. 608–610)

P12-31A The partnership of King, Queen, & Page has experienced operating losses for three consecutive years. The partners—who have shared profits and losses in the ratio of King, 15%; Queen, 60%; and Page, 25%—are liquidating the business. They ask you to analyze the effects of liquidation. They present the following condensed partnership balance sheet at December 31, end of the current year:

Cash	$ 7,000	Liabilities	$ 63,000
Noncash assets	163,000	King, capital	24,000
		Queen, capital	66,000
		Page, capital	17,000
Total assets	$170,000	Total liabilities and capital	$170,000

Requirements

1. Prepare a summary of liquidation transactions (as illustrated in Exhibit 12-5). The noncash assets are sold for $103,000. (p. 613)

2. Journalize the liquidation transactions. (pp. 613–614)

Capital amounts for the
balance sheet of a
partnership

P12-32A ABACUS is a partnership owned by Allen, Bacon, and Cush, who share profits and losses in the ratio of 1:3:4. The account balances of the partnership at June 30 follow.

ABACUS Adjusted Trial Balance June 30, 2009		
Account Title	**Debit**	**Credit**
Cash	$ 20,000	
Noncash assets	110,000	
Liabilities		$ 30,000
Allen, capital		20,000
Bacon, capital		40,000
Cush, capital		50,000
Allen, drawing	10,000	
Bacon, drawing	30,000	
Cush, drawing	50,000	
Revenues		160,000
Expenses	80,000	
Totals	$300,000	$300,000

Requirements

1. Prepare the June 30 entries to close the revenue, expense, income summary, and drawing accounts. (pp. 205, 602, 603)

2. Insert the opening capital balances in the partners' capital accounts, post the closing entries to their accounts, and determine each partner's ending capital. (p. 602)

Problems (Group B)

P12-33B Dave Clinton and Andi Groff are forming a partnership, Compass Web Designs, to create Web sites for clients. Clinton can create designs that draw large sales volumes. Groff is a super salesperson and has already lined up several clients.

Requirement

Write a partnership agreement to cover all elements essential for Compass Web Designs to operate smoothly. Make up names, amounts, profit-and-loss percentages, and so on as needed. (pp. 596–598)

P12-34B On June 30, Allie Hayes and Mandy McKay formed a partnership. The women agree to invest equal amounts of capital. Hayes invests her proprietorship's assets and liabilities (credit balances in parentheses), as follows:

continued . . .

	Hayes's Book Values	Current Market Values
Accounts receivable..........................	$ 7,200	$ 7,000
Inventory...	22,000	24,000
Prepaid expenses	1,700	1,000
Office equipment.............................	45,000	27,000
Accounts payable	(19,000)	(19,000)

On June 30, McKay invests cash in an amount equal to the current market value of Hayes' partnership capital. The partners decide that Hayes will earn two-thirds of partnership profits because she will manage the business. McKay agrees to accept one-third of the profits. During the remainder of the year, the partnership earns net income of $90,000. Hayes' drawings are $39,000, and McKay's drawings are $31,000.

Requirements
1. Journalize the partners' initial investments. (pp. 600–601)
2. Prepare the partnership balance sheet immediately after its formation on June 30. (p. 601)

Admitting a new partner

P12-35B Pike, Quinn, and Reed are considering adding Shipp as a new partner. On March 31 of the current year, the capital accounts of the three existing partners and their shares of profits and losses are as follows:

	Capital	Profit-and-Loss %
Pike......................	$ 50,000	20%
Quinn	100,000	30%
Reed......................	150,000	50%

Requirements
Journalize the admission of Shipp as a partner on March 31 for each of the following independent situations:
1. Shipp pays Reed $200,000 cash to purchase Reed's interest in the partnership. (pp. 603–605)
2. Shipp invests $100,000 in the partnership, acquiring a one-fourth interest in the business. (pp. 605–606)
3. Shipp invests $80,000 in the partnership, acquiring a one-fourth interest in the business. (pp. 607–608)

Computing partners' shares of net income and net loss; preparing the partnership income statement

P12-36B Beau, Cole, and Drake formed a partnership. Beau invested $15,000, Cole $20,000, and Drake $25,000. Beau will manage the store; Cole will work in the store half-time; and Drake will not work in the business.

Requirements
1. Compute the partners' shares of profits and losses under each of the following plans:
   a. Net loss is $50,000, and the partnership agreement allocates 40% of profits to Beau, 25% to Cole, and 35% to Drake. The agreement does not specify the sharing of losses. (pp. 601–602)

continued . . .

b. Net income for the year ended January 31, 2009, is $177,000. The first $75,000 is allocated based on partner capital balances, and the next $36,000 is based on service, with Beau receiving $28,000 and Cole receiving $8,000. Any remainder is shared equally. (pp. 602–603)

2. Revenues for the year ended January 31, 2009, were $507,000, and expenses were $330,000. Under plan (b) above, prepare the partnership income statement for the year. (p. 614)

Withdrawal of a partner

P12-37B El Paso Physicians is a partnership of three doctors. The partners share profits and losses in the ratio of 20% to Juan Hernandez, 40% to Rosa Garcia, and 40% to Eva Cahill. At December 31, 2008, the firm has the following balance sheet:

Cash		$ 12,000	Total liabilities	$ 75,000
Accounts receivable	$22,000			
Less allowance for uncollectibles	(4,000)	18,000		
Building	$310,000		Hernandez, capital	83,000
Less accumulated depreciation	(70,000)	240,000	Garcia, capital	50,000
			Cahill, capital	62,000
Total assets		$270,000	Total liabilities and capital	$270,000

Garcia withdraws from the partnership on December 31, 2008, to establish her own medical practice.

Requirements
Record Garcia's withdrawal from the partnership under the following plans:

1. In a personal transaction, Garcia sells her equity to Maria Martinez, who pays Garcia $100,000 for her interest. Hernandez and Cahill accept Martinez as a partner. (pp. 608–610)

2. The partnership pays Garcia cash of $20,000 and gives her a note payable for the remainder of her book equity in settlement of her partnership interest. (pp. 608–611)

3. The partnership pays Garcia cash of $80,000. (pp. 610–611)

4. The partners agree that the building is worth only $250,000 and that its accumulated depreciation should remain at $70,000. After the revaluation, the partnership settles with Garcia by giving her cash of $10,000 and a note payable for the remainder of her book equity. (pp. 608–611)

Liquidation of a partnership

P12-38B The partnership of Donald, Healey & Jaguar has experienced operating losses. The partners—who have shared profits and losses in the ratio of Donald, 10%; Healey, 30%; and Jaguar, 60%—are liquidating the business. They ask you to analyze the effects of liquidation and present the following partnership balance sheet at December 31, end of the current year:

continued . . .

Cash	$ 27,000	Liabilities	$131,000
Noncash assets	202,000	Donald, capital	21,000
		Healey, capital	39,000
		Jaguar, capital	38,000
Total assets	$229,000	Total liabilities and capital	$229,000

Requirements

1. Prepare a summary of liquidation transactions (as illustrated in Exhibit 12-5). The noncash assets are sold for $192,000. (p. 613)

2. Journalize the liquidation transactions. (pp. 613–614)

Capital amounts for the balance sheet of a partnership

P12-39B LM&N is a partnership owned by Lee, Mah, and Nguyen, who share profits and losses in the ratio of 5:3:2. The account balances of the partnership at September 30 follow.

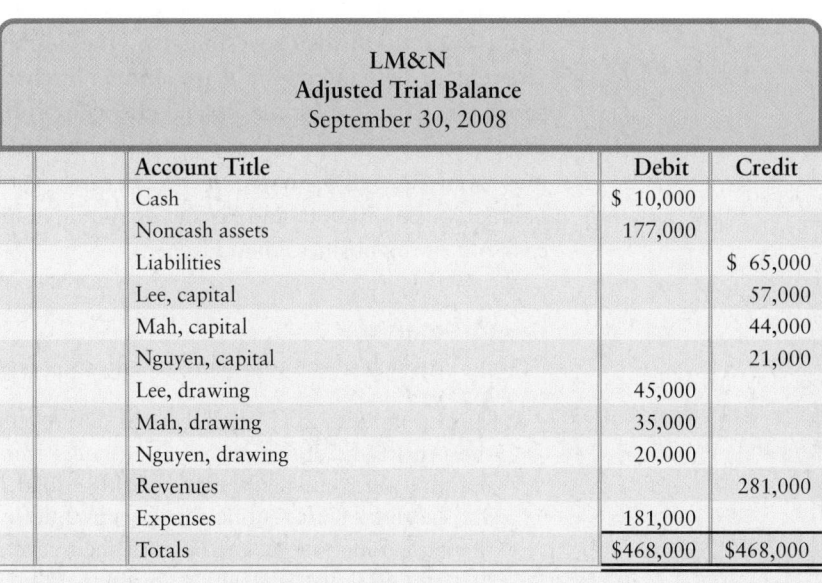

LM&N Adjusted Trial Balance September 30, 2008		
Account Title	**Debit**	**Credit**
Cash	$ 10,000	
Noncash assets	177,000	
Liabilities		$ 65,000
Lee, capital		57,000
Mah, capital		44,000
Nguyen, capital		21,000
Lee, drawing	45,000	
Mah, drawing	35,000	
Nguyen, drawing	20,000	
Revenues		281,000
Expenses	181,000	
Totals	$468,000	$468,000

Requirements

1. Prepare the September 30 entries to close the revenue, expense, income summary, and drawing accounts. (pp. 205, 602, 603)

2. Insert the opening capital balances in the partners' capital accounts, post the closing entries to their accounts, and determine each partner's ending capital. (p. 602)

for 24/7 practice, visit
www.MyAccountingLab.com

Apply Your Knowledge

Decision Cases

Partnership issues
1 5

Case 1. The following questions relate to issues faced by partnerships.

1. The text states that a written partnership agreement should be drawn up between the partners. One benefit of an agreement is that it provides a mechanism for resolving disputes between the partners. List five areas of dispute that might be resolved by a partnership agreement.

2. The statement has been made that "if you must take on a partner, make sure the partner is richer than you are." Why is this statement valid?

3. Loomis & Nelson is a law partnership. Don Loomis is planning to retire from the partnership and move to Canada. What options are available to Loomis to enable him to convert his share of the partnership assets to cash?

Settling disagreements among partners
3

Case 2. Jana Bell invested $20,000 and Matt Fischer $10,000 in a public relations firm that has operated for 10 years. Bell and Fischer have shared profits and losses in the 2:1 ratio of their investments in the business. Bell manages the office, supervises employees, and does the accounting. Fischer, the moderator of a television talk show, is responsible for marketing. His high profile generates important revenue for the business. During the year ended December 2006, the partnership earned net income of $220,000, shared in the 2:1 ratio. On December 31, 2006, Bell's capital balance was $150,000, and Fischer's capital balance was $100,000. (Bell drew more cash out of the business than Fischer.)

Requirements

Respond to each of the following situations.

1. During January 2007, Bell learned that revenues of $60,000 were omitted from the reported 2006 income. She brings this omission to Fischer's attention, pointing out that Bell's share of this added income is two-thirds, or $40,000, and Fischer's share is one-third, or $20,000. Fischer believes they should share this added income on the basis of their capital balances—60%, or $36,000, to Bell and 40%, or $24,000, to himself. Which partner is correct? Why?

2. Assume that the 2006 omission of $60,000 was an account payable for an operating expense. On what basis would the partners share this amount?

Ethical Issue

Hart Nance and Jason Symington operate gift boutiques in shopping malls. The partners split profits and losses equally, and each takes an annual drawing of $80,000. To even out the workload, Nance travels around the country inspecting their properties. Symington manages the business and serves as the accountant. From time to time, they use small amounts of store merchandise for personal use. In preparing for his daughter's wedding, Symington took inventory that cost $10,000. He recorded the transaction as follows:

Cost of Goods Sold	10,000	
Inventory		10,000

1. How should Symington have recorded this transaction?

2. Discuss the ethical aspects of Symington's action.

Team Project

Visit a business partnership in your area and interview one or more of the partners. Obtain answers to the following questions and ask your instructor for directions. As directed by your instructor, either (a) prepare a written report of your findings or (b) make a presentation to your class.

Requirements

1. Why did you organize the business as a partnership? What advantages does the partnership form of organization offer the business? What are the disadvantages of the partnership form of organization?

2. Is the business a general partnership or a limited partnership?

3. Do the partners have a written partnership agreement? What does the agreement cover? Obtain a copy if possible.

4. Who manages the business? Do all partners participate in day-to-day management, or is management the responsibility of only certain partners?

5. If there is no written agreement, what is the mechanism for making key decisions?

6. Has the business ever admitted a new partner? If so, when? What are the partnership's procedures for admitting a new partner?

7. Has a partner ever withdrawn from the business? If so, when? What are the partnership's procedures for settling up with a withdrawing partner?

8. If possible, learn how the partnership divides profits and losses among the partners.

9. Ask for any additional insights the partner you interview can provide about the business.

For Internet Exercises, Excel in Practice, and additional online activities, go to the Web site www.prenhall.com/horngren.

Quick Check Answers

1. *a*   2. *b*   3. *b*   4. *c*   5. *d*   6. *c*   7. *b*   8. *d*   9. *d*   10. *a*

13 Corporations: Paid-In Capital and the Balance Sheet

Learning Objectives

1 Identify the characteristics of a corporation

2 Record the issuance of stock

3 Prepare the stockholders' equity section of a corporation balance sheet

4 Account for cash dividends

5 Use different stock values in decision making

6 Evaluate return on assets and return on stockholders' equity

7 Account for the income tax of a corporation

t's 6 A.M. and you've pulled an all-nighter studying for a history exam. Crammed full of facts, you need a break. Besides that you're hungry. Where can you get a cup of coffee and a quick bite? Many college students go to IHOP near the campus.

You probably never thought of the business aspect of IHOP. The company started as the International House of Pancakes in Toluca Lake, California. In 2001 IHOP opened its 1,000th restaurant. Like Amazon.com and Coca-Cola, IHOP is a corporation. From here on we'll focus on corporations, so this chapter marks a turning point. ■

We begin with the start-up of a corporation and also cover the corporate balance sheet. Fortunately, most of the accounting you've learned thus far also applies to corporations. First, however, let's take an overview of corporations with IHOP as the focus company.

Corporations: An Overview

Corporations dominate business activity in the United States. Proprietorships and partnerships are more numerous, but corporations do much more business and are larger. Most well-known companies, such as UPS and Intel, are corporations. Their full names include *Corporation* or *Incorporated* (abbreviated *Corp.* and *Inc.*) to show that they are corporations—for example, Intel Corporation and NIKE, Inc.

Characteristics of a Corporation

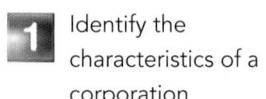
Identify the characteristics of a corporation

What makes the corporate form of organization so attractive? Several things. We now discuss corporations' advantages and disadvantages.

Separate Legal Entity

A corporation is a separate legal entity formed under the laws of a particular state. For example, the state of New York may grant a **charter**, a document that gives the owners permission to form a corporation. Neither a proprietorship nor a partnership requires a state charter, because in the eyes of the law they are the same as their owner(s). A corporation's owners are called **stockholders** or **shareholders**.

A corporation has many of the rights of a person. For example, a corporation may buy, own, and sell property. The assets and liabilities of IHOP belong to the corporation, not to its owners. The corporation may enter into contracts, sue, and be sued, just like an individual.

Continuous Life and Transferability of Ownership

The owners' equity of a corporation is divided into shares of **stock**. A corporation has a *continuous life* regardless of who owns the stock. By contrast, proprietorships and partnerships end when their ownership changes. Stockholders may sell or trade stock to another person, give it away, or bequeath it in a will. Transfer of the stock does not affect the continuity of the corporation.

No Mutual Agency

Mutual agency means that all the owners act as agents of the business. A contract signed by one owner is binding for the whole company. Mutual agency operates in partnerships but *not* in corporations. A stockholder of IHOP cannot commit IHOP to a contract (unless the person is also an officer of the company).

Limited Stockholder Liability

Stockholders have **limited liability** for corporation debts. That means they have no personal obligation for the corporation's liabilities. The most a stockholder can lose on an investment in a corporation is the amount invested. In contrast, proprietors and partners are personally liable for all the debts of their businesses, unless the partnership is a limited liability partnership (LLP).

The combination of limited liability and no mutual agency means that persons can invest in a corporation without fear of losing all their personal wealth if the business fails. This feature enables a corporation to raise more money than proprietorships and partnerships.

Separation of Ownership and Management

Stockholders own a corporation, but a *board of directors*—elected by the stockholders—appoints the officers to manage the business. Stockholders may invest $1,000 or $1 million without having to manage the company.

Corporate Taxation

Corporations are separate taxable entities. They pay several taxes not borne by proprietorships or partnerships, including an annual franchise tax levied by the state. The franchise tax keeps the corporate charter in force. Corporations also pay federal and state income taxes just as individuals do.

Corporate earnings are subject to **double taxation**.

* First, corporations pay income taxes on corporate income.
* Then the stockholders pay personal income tax on the cash dividends they receive from corporations.

Proprietorships and partnerships pay no business income tax. Instead, the tax falls solely on the owners.

Government Regulation

Because of stockholders' limited liability, outsiders can look no further than the corporation for payment of its debts. To protect persons who do business with corporations, government agencies monitor corporations. This *government regulation* can be expensive.

Exhibit 13-1 summarizes the advantages and disadvantages of corporations.

EXHIBIT 13-1 | Advantages and Disadvantages of a Corporation

Advantages	Disadvantages
1. Corporations can raise more money than a proprietorship or partnership.	1. Ownership and management are separated.
2. Corporation has continuous life.	2. Double taxation.
3. The transfer of corporate ownership is easy.	3. Government regulation is expensive.
4. There's no mutual agency among the stockholders.	
5. Stockholders have limited liability.	

Organizing a Corporation

Organizing a corporation begins when the *incorporators* obtain a charter from the state. The charter **authorizes** the corporation to issue a certain number of shares of stock. The incorporators pay fees, sign the charter, and file documents; then the corporation becomes a legal entity. The stockholders agree to a set of **bylaws**, which act as their constitution.

Ultimate control of the corporation rests with the stockholders as they vote their shares of stock. Each share of stock carries one vote. The stockholders elect the **board of directors**, which:

- sets policy
- elects a **chairperson**, who is the most powerful person in the company
- appoints the **president**, who is in charge of day-to-day operations

Most corporations also have vice presidents. Exhibit 13-2 shows the authority structure in a corporation.

EXHIBIT 13-2   **Structure of a Corporation**

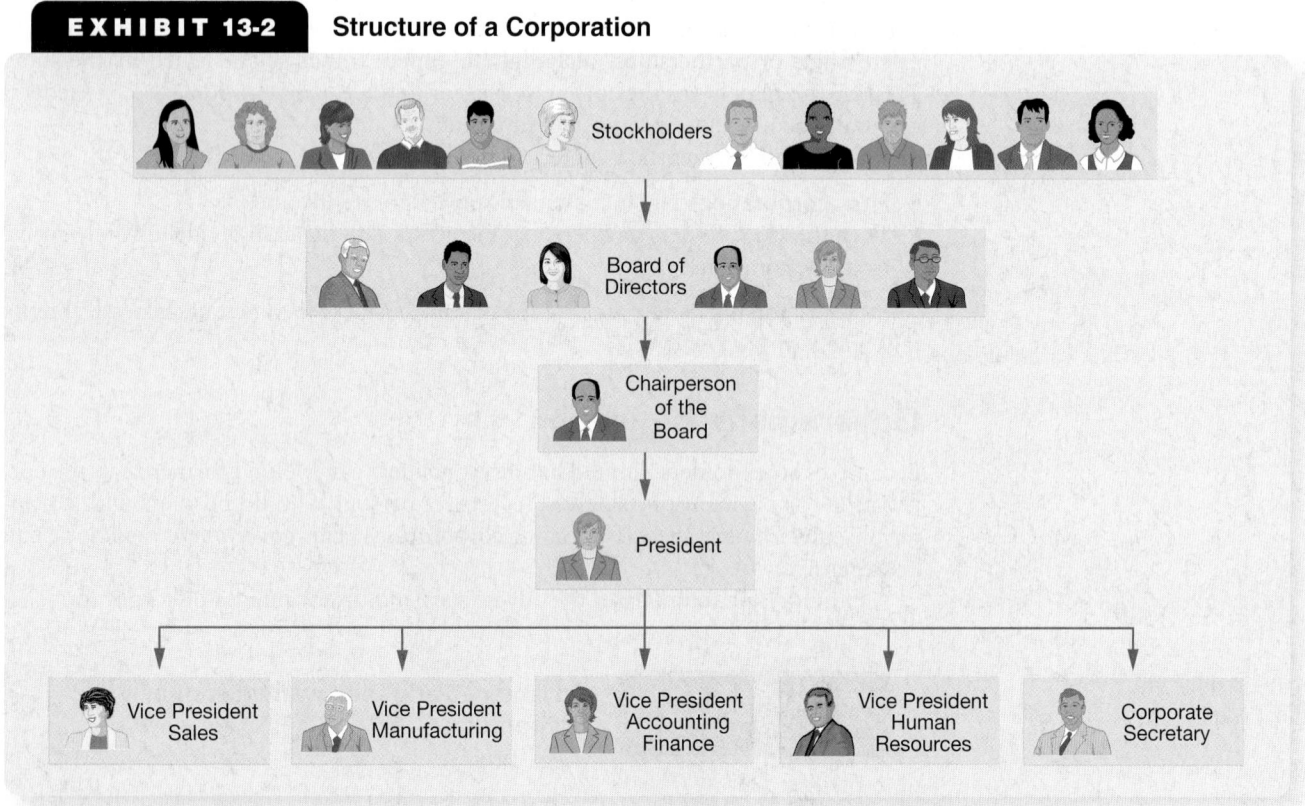

Capital Stock

A corporation issues *stock certificates* to the stockholders when they buy the stock. The stock represents the corporation's capital, so it is called *capital stock*. The basic unit of stock is a *share*. A corporation may issue a stock certificate for any number of shares. Exhibit 13-3 shows a stock certificate for 288 shares of Central Jersey Bancorp common stock. The certificate shows the:

- company name
- stockholder name
- number of shares owned by the stockholder

Stock that is held by the stockholders is said to be **outstanding**. The outstanding stock of a corporation represents 100% of its ownership.

EXHIBIT 13-3 Stock Certificate

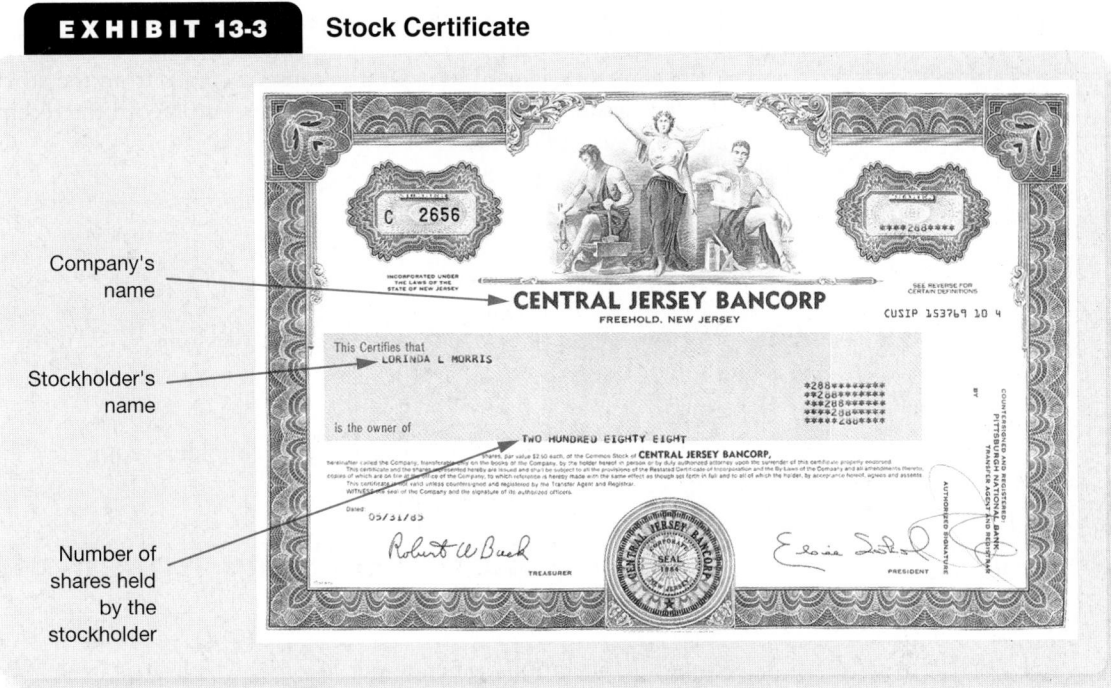

Company's name

Stockholder's name

Number of shares held by the stockholder

Stockholders' Equity Basics

A corporation reports assets and liabilities exactly as for a proprietorship or a partnership. But the owners' equity of a corporation—called **stockholders' equity**—is reported differently. State laws require corporations to report their sources of capital because some of the capital must be maintained by the company. There are two basic sources:

- **Paid-in capital** (also called **contributed capital**) represents amounts received from the stockholders. Common stock is the main source of paid-in capital.
- **Retained earnings** is capital earned by profitable operations.

Exhibit 13-4 outlines a summarized version of the stockholders' equity of IHOP Corporation (amounts in millions):

EXHIBIT 13-4 Stockholders' Equity of IHOP Corporation (Adapted, with amounts in millions)

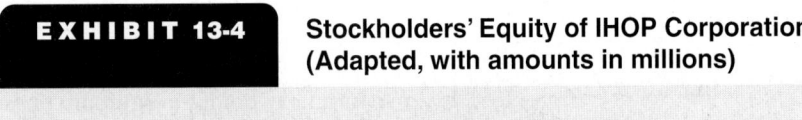

Stockholders' Equity	
Paid-in capital:	
Common stock	$ 32
Retained earnings	308
Total stockholders' equity	340

Paid-In Capital Comes from the Stockholders

Common stock is paid-in capital because it comes from the stockholders. Suppose IHOP is issuing common stock. IHOP's entry to record the receipt of $20,000 cash and the issuance of stock is:

Oct. 20	Cash		20,000	
	Common Stock			20,000
	Issued stock.			

Issuing stock increases both assets and stockholders' equity.

Retained Earnings Come from Profitable Operations

Profitable operations generate net income, which increases equity through a separate account called Retained Earnings.

Some people think of Retained Earnings as a fund of cash. It is not, because Retained Earnings is not an asset; it's an element of stockholders' equity. Retained Earnings has no particular relationship to cash or any other asset.

As we've just seen, a corporation needs at least two capital accounts:

- Common Stock
- Retained Earnings

Corporations close their revenues and expenses into Income Summary, and then they close net income to Retained Earnings. Let's assume IHOP's revenues were $500,000 and expenses totaled $400,000 for December. The closing entries would be:

Dec. 31	Sales Revenue		500,000	
	Income Summary			500,000
	To close sales revenue.			
31	Income Summary		400,000	
	Expenses (detailed)			400,000
	To close expenses.			

Now, Income Summary holds revenues, expenses, and net income.

Income Summary			
Expenses	400,000	Revenues	500,000
		Balance (net income)	100,000

Finally, Income Summary's balance is closed to Retained Earnings.

Dec. 31	Income Summary	100,000	
	Retained Earnings		100,000
	To close net income to Retained Earnings.		

This closing entry completes the closing process. Income Summary is zeroed out, and Retained Earnings now holds net income, as follows:

Income Summary			
Expenses	400,000	Revenues	500,000
Closing	100,000	Net income	100,000

Retained Earnings	
	Closing
	(net income) 100,000

If IHOP has a net *loss,* Income Summary will have a debit balance, as follows:

Income Summary			
Expenses	460,000	Revenues	400,000
Net loss	60,000		

To close this $60,000 loss, the final closing entry credits Income Summary and debits Retained Earnings as follows:

Dec. 31	Retained Earnings	60,000	
	Income Summary		60,000
	To close net loss *to Retained Earnings.*		

The accounts now have their final balances.

Income Summary			
Expenses	460,000	Revenues	400,000
Net loss	60,000	Closing	60,000

Retained Earnings	
Closing (net loss) 60,000	

A Retained Earnings Deficit

A loss may cause a debit balance in Retained Earnings. This condition—called a Retained Earnings **deficit**—is reported as a negative amount in stockholders' equity. HAL, Inc., which owns Hawaiian Airlines, Inc., reported this deficit:

Stockholders' Equity	(In millions)
Paid-in capital:	
Common stock........................	$ 50
Deficit..	(193)
Total stockholders' equity..........	$(143)

A Corporation May Pay Dividends to the Stockholders

A profitable corporation may distribute cash to the stockholders. Such distributions are called **dividends**. Dividends are similar to a proprietor's withdrawals. Dividends decrease both assets and retained earnings. Most states prohibit using paid-in capital for dividends. Accountants, therefore, use the term *legal capital* to refer to the portion of stockholders' equity that cannot be used for dividends.

Stockholders' Rights

A stockholder has four basic rights, unless a right is withheld by contract:

1. **Vote.** Stockholders participate in management by voting on corporate matters. This is a stockholder's sole right to manage the corporation. Each share of stock carries one vote.

2. **Dividends.** Stockholders receive a proportionate part of any dividend. Each share of stock receives an equal dividend.

3. **Liquidation.** Stockholders receive their proportionate share of any assets remaining after the corporation pays its debts and liquidates (goes out of business).

A fourth right is usually withheld because it is rarely exercised.

4. **Preemption.** Stockholders can maintain their proportionate ownership in the corporation. Suppose you own 5% of a corporation's stock. If the corporation issues 100,000 new shares of stock, it must offer you the opportunity to buy 5% (5,000) of the new shares.

Classes of Stock

Corporations can issue different classes of stock. The stock of a corporation may be either:

- common or preferred
- par or no-par

Common Stock and Preferred Stock

Every corporation issues **common stock,** which represents the basic ownership of the corporation. The owners are the common stockholders. Some companies issue Class A common stock, which carries the right to vote. They may also issue Class B common stock, which may be nonvoting. There is a separate account for each class of stock.

Preferred stock gives its owners certain advantages over common. Most notably, preferred stockholders receive dividends before the common stockholders, and preferred receives assets before common if the corporation liquidates. Corporations pay a fixed dividend on preferred stock. Investors usually buy preferred stock to earn those fixed dividends. With these advantages, preferred stockholders take less investment risk than common stockholders.

Owners of preferred stock also have the four basic stockholder rights, unless a right is withheld. The right to vote is sometimes withheld from preferred stock. Companies may issue different series of preferred stock (Series A and Series B, for example). Each series is recorded in a separate account. Preferred stock is rarer than you might think. A recent survey of 600 corporations revealed that only 16% had some preferred stock outstanding (Exhibit 13-5).

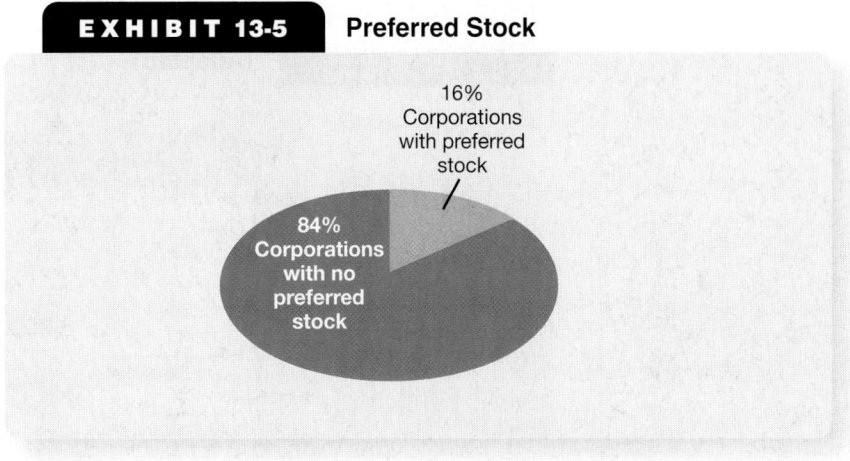

EXHIBIT 13-5 Preferred Stock

Par Value, Stated Value, and No-Par Stock

Stock may carry a par value or it may be no-par stock. **Par value** is an arbitrary amount assigned by a company to a share of its stock. Most companies set par value low to avoid legal difficulties from issuing their stock below par. Companies maintain a minimum amount of stockholders' equity for the protection of creditors, and this minimum represents the corporation's legal capital. **Legal capital** is usually the par value of the shares issued.

The par value of IHOP's common stock is $0.01 (1 cent) per share. Deere & Co., which makes John Deere tractors, and Whirlpool, the appliance company, have common stock with a par value of $1 per share. Par value of preferred stock can be higher—$25 or $100. Par value is used to compute dividends on preferred stock, as we shall see.

No-par stock does not have par value. Pfizer, the pharmaceutical company, has preferred stock with no par value. But some no-par stock has a **stated value**, which makes it similar to par-value stock. The stated value is an arbitrary amount similar to par value.

Issuing Stock

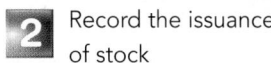 Record the issuance of stock

Corporations such as IHOP and Coca-Cola need huge quantities of money. They cannot finance all their operations through borrowing, so they raise capital by issuing stock. A company can sell its stock directly to stockholders or it can use the services of an *underwriter,* such as the brokerage firms Merrill Lynch and Morgan Stanley, Dean Witter. An underwriter usually agrees to buy all the stock it cannot sell to its clients.

The price that the corporation receives from issuing stock is called the *issue price.* Usually, the issue price exceeds par value because par value is quite low. In the following sections, we use IHOP to show how to account for the issuance of stock.

Issuing Common Stock

The Wall Street Journal is the most popular medium for advertising stock. The ads are called *tombstones.* Exhibit 13-6 reproduces IHOP's tombstone, which appeared in *The Wall Street Journal.*

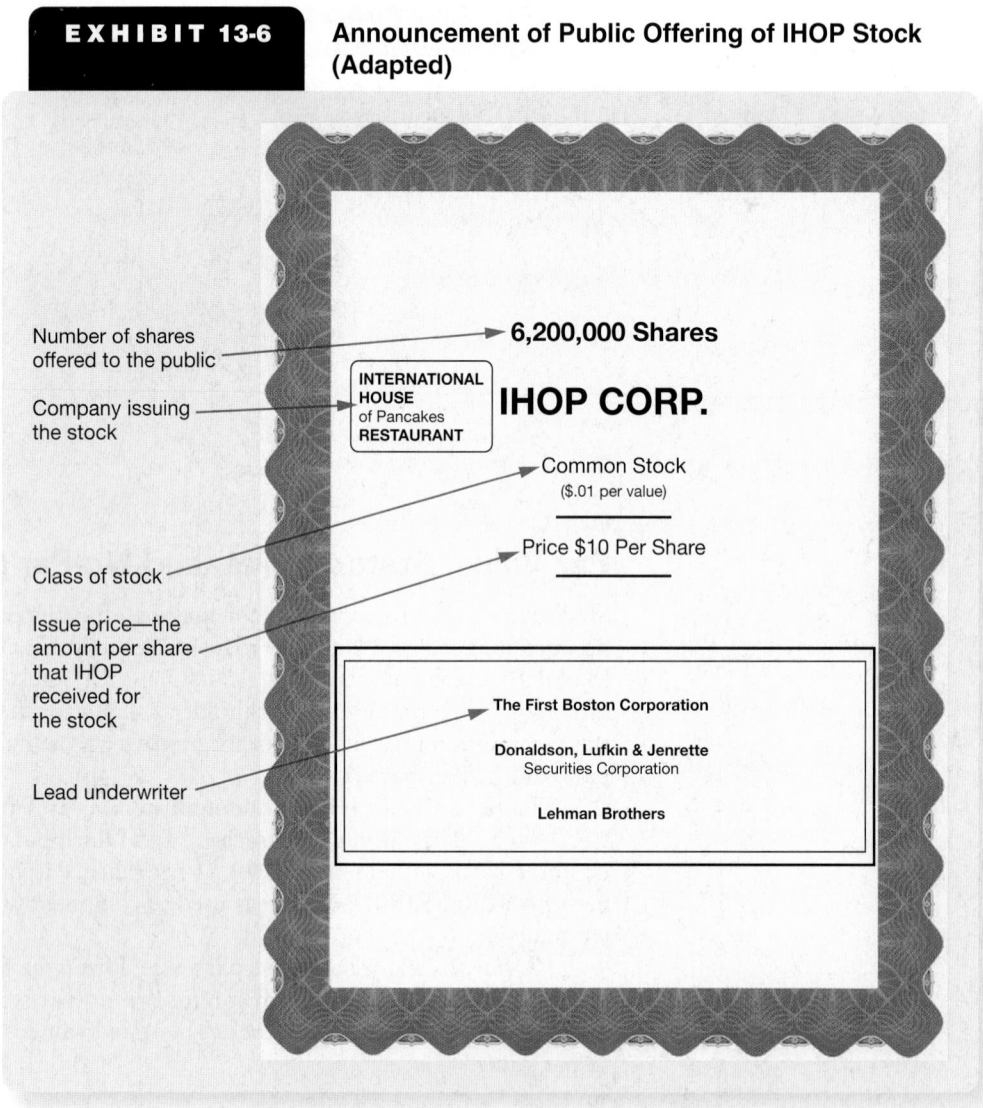

EXHIBIT 13-6 Announcement of Public Offering of IHOP Stock (Adapted)

IHOP's tombstone shows that IHOP hoped to raise approximately $62 million of capital (6,200,000 shares × $10 per share). But in the final analysis, IHOP issued only 3.2 million of the shares and received cash of approximately $32 million.

Issuing Common Stock at Par

Suppose IHOP's common stock carried a par value of $10 per share. The stock issuance entry of 3.2 million shares would be:

Jan. 31	Cash (3,200,000 × $10)	32,000,000	
	Common Stock		32,000,000
	Issued common stock at par.		

Issuing Common Stock at a Premium

Most corporations set par value low and issue common stock for a price above par. The amount above par is called a *premium*. IHOP's common stock has an actual par value of $0.01 (1 cent) per share. The $9.99 difference between the issue price ($10) and par value ($0.01) is a premium. Let's see how to account for the issuance of IHOP stock at a premium.

A premium on the sale of stock is not a gain, income, or profit for the corporation because the company is dealing with its own stockholders. This situation illustrates one of the fundamentals of accounting: *A company can have no profit or loss when buying or selling its own stock.*

With a par value of $0.01, IHOP's entry to record the issuance of its stock at $10 per share is:

Jul. 31	Cash (3,200,000 shares × $10 issue price)	32,000,000	
	Common Stock (3,200,000 shares × $0.01 par value)		32,000
	Paid-In Capital in Excess of Par—		
	Common (3,200,000 shares × $9.99 premium)		31,968,000
	Issued common stock at a premium.		

Paid-In Capital in Excess of Par is also called *Additional Paid-In Capital.*

IHOP Corp. would report stockholders' equity on its balance sheet as follows, assuming that its charter authorizes 40,000,000 shares of common stock and the balance of retained earnings is $308,000,000.

STOCKHOLDERS' EQUITY	
Paid-in capital:	
Common stock; $0.01 par; 40,000,000 shares authorized; 3,200,000 shares issued	$ 32,000
Paid-in capital in excess of par	31,968,000
Total paid-in capital	32,000,000
Retained earnings..	308,000,000
Total stockholders' equity	$340,000,000

The balances of the Common Stock account and of Paid-In Capital in Excess of Par are computed as follows:

$$\text{Common stock balance} = \text{Number of shares issued} \times \text{Par value per share}$$

$$\$32,000 = 3,200,000 \times \$0.01$$

Paid-In Capital in Excess of Par is the total amount received from issuing the common stock minus its par value, as follows:

$$\text{Paid-In Capital in Excess of Par} = \text{Number of Shares issued} \times \text{Premium per share}$$

$$\$31,968,000 = 3,200,000 \times \$9.99$$

Altogether, total paid-in capital is the sum of:

$$\text{Total paid-in capital} = \text{Common stock} + \text{Paid-In Capital in Excess of Par}$$

$$\$32,000,000 = \$32,000 + \$31,968,000$$

Issuing No-Par Stock

When a company issues no-par stock, it debits the asset received and credits the stock account. For no-par stock there can be no paid-in capital in excess of par.

Assume Rocky Mountain Corporation, which manufactures ski equipment, issues 4,000 shares of no-par common stock for $20 per share. The stock-issuance entry is:

Aug. 14	Cash (4,000 × $20)	80,000	
	Common Stock		80,000
	Issued no-par common stock.		

Regardless of the stock's price, Cash is debited and Common Stock is credited for the cash received.

Rocky Mountain's charter authorizes 10,000 shares of no-par stock, and the company has $150,000 in retained earnings. Rocky Mountain reports stockholders' equity on its balance sheet as follows:

STOCKHOLDERS' EQUITY	
Paid-in capital:	
Common stock, no par, 10,000 shares authorized, 4,000 shares issued	$ 80,000
Retained earnings..	150,000
Total stockholders' equity	$230,000

Issuing No-Par Stock with a Stated Value

Accounting for no-par stock with a stated value is identical to accounting for par-value stock. No-par stock with a stated value uses an account titled Paid-In Capital in Excess of *Stated* Value.

Issuing Stock for Assets Other Than Cash

A corporation may issue stock for assets other than cash. It records the assets received at their current market value and credits the stock accounts accordingly. The assets' prior book value is irrelevant. Kahn Corporation issued 10,000 shares of its $1 par common stock for equipment worth $4,000 and a building worth $120,000. Kahn's entry is:

Nov. 30	Equipment	4,000	
	Building	120,000	
	Common Stock (10,000 × $1)		10,000
	Paid-In Capital in Excess of Par—		
	Common ($124,000 – $10,000)		114,000
	Issued common stock in exchange for equipment and a building.		

Issuing Preferred Stock

Accounting for preferred stock follows the pattern illustrated for common stock. Chiquita Brands, famous for bananas, has some preferred stock outstanding. Assume Chiquita issued 10,000 shares of preferred stock at par value of $10 per share. The issuance entry is:

July 31	Cash	100,000	
	Preferred Stock (10,000 shares × $10)		100,000
	Issued preferred stock.		

Most preferred stock is issued at par value. Therefore, Paid-In Capital in Excess of Par is rare for preferred stock. For this reason, we do not cover it in this book.

Ethical Considerations

Issuance of stock for *cash* poses no ethical challenge because the value of the asset received is clearly understood. Issuing stock for assets other than cash can pose a challenge. The company issuing the stock wants to look successful—record a large amount for the asset received and the stock issued. Why? Because large asset and equity amounts make the business look prosperous. The desire to look good can motivate a company to record a high amount for the assets.

A company is supposed to record an asset received at its current market value. But one person's evaluation of a building can differ from another's. One person may appraise the building at a market value of $4 million. Another may honestly believe the building is worth only $3 million. A company receiving the building in exchange for its stock must decide whether to record the building at $3 million, $4 million, or some other amount.

The ethical course of action is to record the asset at its current market value, as determined by independent appraisers. Corporations are rarely found guilty of *understating* their assets, but companies have been sued for *overstating* assets.

Review of Accounting for Paid-In Capital

3 Prepare the stockholders' equity section of a corporation balance sheet

Let's review the first half of this chapter by showing the stockholders' equity section of MedTech Corporation's balance sheet in Exhibit 13-7.

Observe the order of the equity accounts:

- Preferred stock
- Common stock at par value
- Paid-in capital in excess of par (belongs to the common stockholders)
- Retained earnings (after the paid-in capital accounts)

Many companies label Paid-In Capital in Excess of Par as **Additional Paid-In Capital** on the balance sheet. This amount is part of common equity, not preferred equity.

EXHIBIT 13-7   **Part of MedTech.com Corporation's Balance Sheet**

Stockholder's Equity	
Paid-in capital:	
Preferred stock, 5%, $100 par, 5,000 shares authorized 400 shares issued	$ 40,000
Common stock, $10 par, 20,000 shares authorized, 5,000 shares issued	50,000
Paid-in capital in excess of par—common	70,000
Total paid-in capital	160,000
Retained earnings	90,000
Total stockholders' equity	$250,000

The Decision Guidelines will solidify your understanding of stockholders' equity.

Decision Guidelines

THE STOCKHOLDERS' EQUITY OF A CORPORATION

Suppose you are interested in investing in stock. The following guidelines are relevant to your decision.

Decision	Guidelines
What are the two main segments of stockholders' equity?	• Paid-in capital • Retained earnings
Which is more permanent, paid-in capital or retained earnings?	Paid-in capital is more permanent because corporations can use retained earnings for dividends, which decreases the size of the company.

How are paid-in capital and retained earnings
• Similar?
• Different?
	• Both represent stockholders' equity (ownership) of the corporation.
	• Paid-in capital and retained earnings come from different sources:
	  a. *Paid-in capital* comes from the stockholders.
	  b. *Retained earnings* comes from profitable operations.

What are the main categories of paid-in capital?	• Preferred stock • Common stock, plus paid-in capital in excess of par

Summary Problem 1

1. Is each of the following statements true or false?

   a. A stockholder may bind the corporation to a contract.

   b. The policy-making body in a corporation is called the board of directors.

   c. The owner of 100 shares of preferred stock has greater voting rights than the owner of 100 shares of common stock.

   d. Par-value stock is more valuable than no-par stock.

   e. Issuance of 1,000 shares of $5 par-value stock at $12 increases paid-in capital by $7,000.

   f. The issuance of no-par stock with a stated value is fundamentally different from issuing par-value stock.

   g. A corporation issues its preferred stock in exchange for land and a building with a combined market value of $200,000. This transaction increases the corporation's owners' equity by $200,000 regardless of the assets' prior book value.

2. Delphian Corporation has two classes of common stock. The company's balance sheet includes the following:

STOCKHOLDERS' EQUITY	
Paid-in capital:	
Class A common stock, voting, $1 par value, authorized and issued 1,200,000 shares	$ 1,200,000
Additional paid-in capital—Class A common	2,000,000
Class B common stock, nonvoting, no par value, authorized and issued 11,000,000 shares	55,000,000
	58,200,000
Retained earnings	800,000,000
Total stockholders' equity..	$858,200,000

Requirements

a. Record the issuance of the Class A common stock.

b. Record the issuance of the Class B common stock.

c. What is the total paid-in capital of the company?

d. What was the average issue price of each share of Class B common stock?

Solution

1. Answers to true/false statements:
   - a. False
   - b. True
   - c. False
   - d. False
   - e. False
   - f. False
   - g. True

2.

a.	Cash	3,200,000	
	Class A Common Stock		1,200,000
	Additional Paid-In Capital		2,000,000
	To record issuance of Class A common stock.		
b.	Cash	55,000,000	
	Class B Common Stock		55,000,000
	To record issuance of Class B common stock.		
c.	Total paid-in capital is $58,200,000		
	($1,200,000 + $2,000,000 + $55,000,000).		
d.	Average issue price = $5 ($55,000,000/11,000,000 shares)		

Now let's see how to account for dividends.

Accounting for Cash Dividends

Corporations share their wealth with the stockholders through dividends. Corporations declare dividends from retained earnings and then pay with cash.

Dividend Dates

A corporation declares a dividend before paying it. Three dividend dates are relevant.

1. **Declaration date.** On the declaration date—say, May 1—the board of directors announces the intention to pay the dividend. The declaration of a cash dividend creates a liability for the corporation.

2. **Date of record.** Those stockholders holding the stock on the date of record—a week or two after declaration, say, May 15—will receive the dividend.

3. **Payment date.** Payment of the dividend usually follows the record date by a week or two—say, May 30.

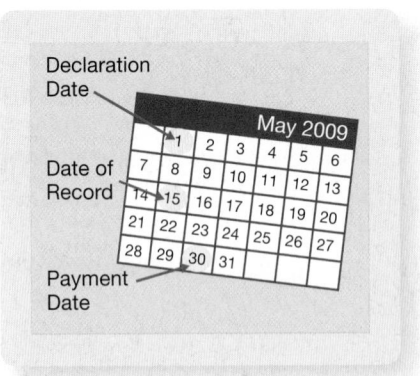

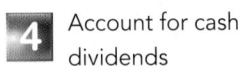 Account for cash dividends

Declaring and Paying Dividends

The cash dividend rate on *preferred stock* is often expressed as a percentage of the preferred-stock par value, such as 6%. But sometimes cash dividends on preferred stock are expressed as a dollar amount per share, such as $2 per share. Therefore, preferred dividends are computed two ways, depending on how the preferred-stock cash-dividend rate is expressed. Here are the two ways to compute preferred dividends, using new figures made up for this illustration:

1. **Par value of the preferred stock × Preferred dividend rate = Preferred dividend**

    Example: $100,000   ×   6% (.06)   = $6,000

2.   **Number of shares of**   **Preferred**
    preferred stock outstanding × dividend rate = Preferred dividend

    Example: 4,000 shares   × $2 per share = $8,000

Cash dividends on *common stock* are computed the second way because cash dividends are not expressed as a percentage.

To account for the declaration of a cash dividend we debit Retained Earnings and credit Dividends Payable, as follows (amount assumed):[1]

May 1	Retained Earnings	20,000	
	Dividends Payable		20,000
	Declared a cash dividend.		

To pay the dividend, debit Dividends Payable and credit Cash.

May 30	Dividends Payable	20,000	
	Cash		20,000
	Paid the cash dividend.		

Dividends Payable is a current liability. When a company has issued both preferred and common, the preferred stockholders get their dividends first. The common stockholders receive dividends only if the total dividend is large enough to satisfy the preferred requirement. Let's see how dividends are divided between preferred and common.

Dividing Dividends Between Preferred and Common

Sierra Corp. has common stock plus 10,000 shares of preferred stock outstanding. The annual preferred dividend rate is $2 per share. Therefore, Sierra's annual dividend must exceed $20,000 for the common stockholders to get anything. Exhibit 13-8 shows the division of dividends between preferred and common for two situations.

EXHIBIT 13-8 **Dividing a Dividend Between Preferred Stock and Common Stock**

Case A: Total dividend of $8,000:	
Preferred dividend (the full $8,000 goes to preferred because the annual preferred dividend is $20,000)	$ 8,000
Common dividend (none because the total dividend did not cover the preferred dividend for the year)	0
Total dividend	$ 8,000
Case B: Total dividend of $50,000:	
Preferred dividend (10,000 shares × $2 per share)	$20,000
Common dividend ($50,000 − $20,000)	30,000
Total dividend	$50,000

If Sierra's dividend is large enough to cover the preferred dividend (Case B), the preferred stockholders get their regular dividend, and the common stockholders get

---

[1]Some accountants debit a Dividends account, which is closed to Retained Earnings. But most businesses debit Retained Earnings directly, as shown here.

the remainder. But if the year's dividend falls below the annual preferred amount (Case A), the preferred stockholders receive the entire dividend, and the common stockholders get nothing that year.

Dividends on Cumulative and Noncumulative Preferred

Preferred stock can be either:

- Cumulative or
- Noncumulative

Preferred is cumulative unless it's specifically designated as noncumulative. Most preferred stock is cumulative. Let's see how this plays out.

A corporation may fail to pay the preferred dividend. This is called *passing the dividend,* and the dividends are said to be *in arrears.* **Cumulative preferred** must receive all dividends in arrears before the common stockholders get a dividend.

The preferred stock of Sierra Corp. mentioned on page 655 is cumulative. How do we know this? Because preferred is not labeled as noncumulative.

Suppose Sierra passed the 2006 preferred dividend of $20,000. Before paying any common dividend in 2007, Sierra must first pay preferred dividends of $20,000 for 2006 and $20,000 for 2007, a total of $40,000. In 2007, Sierra declares a $50,000 dividend. How much of this dividend goes to preferred? How much goes to common? The allocation of this $50,000 dividend is:

Total dividend		$50,000
Preferred gets		
2006: 10,000 shares × $2 per share	$20,000	
2007: 10,000 shares × $2 per share	20,000	
Total to preferred		40,000
Common gets the remainder.		$10,000

Sierra's entry to record the declaration of this dividend is

2007			
Sep. 6	Retained Earnings	50,000	
	Dividends Payable, Preferred ($20,000 × 2)		40,000
	Dividends Payable Common ($50,000 − $40,000)		10,000
	Declared a cash dividend.		

If the preferred stock is *noncumulative,* the corporation need not pay any dividends in arrears. Suppose Sierra's preferred stock was noncumulative and the company passed the 2006 dividend. The preferred stockholders would lose the 2006 dividend forever. Then, before paying any common dividends in 2007, Sierra would have to pay only the 2007 preferred dividend of $20,000.

Dividends in arrears are *not* a liability. A liability for dividends arises only after the board of directors declares the dividend. But a corporation reports cumulative preferred dividends in arrears in notes to the financial statements. This shows the common stockholders how much it will take for them to get any dividends.

Different Values of Stock

5 Use different stock values in decision making

There are several different *stock values* in addition to par value. Market value and book value are used for decision making.

Market Value

Market value, or *market price,* is the price for which a person can buy or sell a share of stock. The corporation's net income and general economic conditions affect market value. The Internet and most newspapers report stock prices. Log on to any company's Web site to track its stock price. *In almost all cases, stockholders are more concerned about the market value of a stock than about any other value.*

When IHOP went public, its stock had a market price of $10 when it was issued. Shortly thereafter, IHOP's stock shot up to $36 per share. The purchase of 100 shares of IHOP stock at $36 would cost you $3,600 ($36 × 100), plus a commission. If you were selling 100 shares of IHOP stock, you would receive cash of $3,600 less a commission. The commission is the fee a stockbroker charges for buying or selling the stock. The price of a share of IHOP stock has fluctuated from $10 at issuance to a recent high of $50.50.

Book Value

Book value is the amount of owners' equity on the company's books for each share of its stock. If the company has only common stock outstanding, you can divide total stockholders' equity by the number of shares *outstanding*. A company with equity of $150,000 and 5,000 shares of common stock has a book value of $30 per share ($150,000/5,000 shares).

If the company has both preferred and common outstanding, preferred has first claim to the equity. Therefore, we subtract preferred equity from total equity to compute book value per share of common. To illustrate, Lille Corporation reports the following amounts:

STOCKHOLDERS' EQUITY	
Paid in capital:	
Preferred stock, 6%, $10 par, 5,000 shares issued	$ 50,000
Common stock, $1 par, 20,000 shares authorized, 10,000 shares issued	10,000
Paid-in capital in excess of par—common	170,000
Total paid-in capital	230,000
Retained earnings..	420,000
Total stockholders' equity	$650,000

Last year's and this year's preferred dividends are in arrears.

Book value per share of common is computed as follows:

Preferred equity:	
Par value..	$ 50,000
Cumulative dividends for two years: ($50,000 × .06 × 2)	6,000
Preferred equity	$ 56,000
Common equity:	
Total stockholders' equity..	$650,000
Less preferred equity..	−56,000
Common equity	$594,000
Book value per share of common ($594,000/10,000 shares).............	$59.40

Book value may figure into the price to pay for a closely-held company, whose stock is not publicly traded. Also, a company may buy out a stockholder by paying the book value of the person's stock. This recently occurred for a friend of the coauthor of this book. The president retired, and his company bought him out at book value.

Some investors compare the book value of a stock with its market value. The idea is that a stock selling below book value is a good buy. But the book value/market value relationship is far from clear. Other investors believe that a stock selling below book value means the company must be having problems.

Exhibit 13-9 contrasts the book values and market values for the stocks of three well-known companies. In all three cases, market price far exceeds book value—a sign of success.

EXHIBIT 13-9   **Book Value and Market Value for Three Well-Known Companies**

	Book Value Per Share	Recent Stock Price
IHOP Corp.	$17.02	$40.98
Coca-Cola	6.61	43.81
Dell	2.61	35.20

Evaluating Operations

Investors are constantly comparing companies' profits. IHOP's net income isn't comparable with that of a new company because IHOP is established and the other company is just getting started. To compare companies, we need some standard profitability measures. Two important ratios are return on assets and return on common stockholders' equity.

Rate of Return on Total Assets

6 Evaluate return on assets and return on stockholders' equity

The **rate of return on total assets,** or simply **return on assets,** measures a company's success in using assets to earn income. Two groups invest money to finance a corporation:

- Stockholders
- Creditors

Net income and interest expense are the returns to these two groups. The stockholders earn the corporation's net income, and the creditors get its interest expense.

The sum of net income plus interest expense is the numerator of the return-on-assets ratio. The denominator is average total assets. Return on assets is computed as follows, using data from the 2004 annual report of IHOP Corp. (dollar amounts in millions):

$$\frac{\text{Rate of Return}}{\text{on Total Assets}} = \frac{\text{Net Income} + \text{Interest Expense}}{\text{Average Total Assets}}$$

$$= \frac{\$33 + \$22}{(\$843 + \$822) / 2} = \frac{\$55}{\$832.5} = 0.066$$

Net income and interest expense are taken from the income statement. Average total assets comes from the beginning and ending balance sheets.

What is a good rate of return on total assets? There is no single answer because rates of return vary widely by industry. In most industries, a 10% return on assets is considered good.

Rate of Return on Common Stockholders' Equity

Rate of return on common stockholders' equity, often shortened to **return on equity,** shows the relationship between net income available to the common stockholders and their average common equity. The numerator is net income minus preferred dividends. Preferred dividends are subtracted because the preferred stockholders have first claim to any dividends. The denominator is average *common stockholders' equity*—total equity minus preferred equity. IHOP's rate of return on common stockholders' equity for 2004 is computed as follows (amounts in millions):

$$\frac{\text{Rate of Return on Common}}{\text{Stockholders' Equity}} = \frac{\text{Net Income} - \text{Preferred Dividends}}{\text{Average Common Stockholders' Equity}}$$

$$= \frac{\$33 - \$0}{(\$340 + \$382) / 2} = \frac{\$33}{\$361} = 0.091$$

IHOP has no preferred stock, so preferred dividends are zero.

IHOP's rates of return carry both bad news and good news.

- The bad news is that these rates of return are low. Most companies strive for return on equity of 15% or higher. IHOP's 9.1% is disappointing.

- The good news is that return on equity exceeds return on assets. That means IHOP is earning more for its stockholders than it's paying for interest expense, and that's a healthy sign.

    If return on assets ever exceeds return on equity, the company is in trouble. Why? Because the company's interest expense is greater than its return on equity. In that case, no investor would buy the company's stock. Return on assets should always be significantly lower than return on equity.

Accounting for Income Taxes by Corporations

7 Account for the income tax of a corporation

Corporations pay income tax just as individuals do, but not at the same rates. At this writing, the federal tax rate on most corporate income is 35%. Most states also levy a corporate income tax, so most corporations pay a combined federal and state income tax rate of approximately 40%.

To account for income tax, a corporation measures two income tax amounts:

- Income tax expense
- Income tax payable

In general, income tax expense and income tax payable can be computed as follows:[2]

$$\begin{array}{ccccc} \text{Income} & & \text{Income before tax} & & \text{Income} \\ \text{tax} & = & \text{from the} & \times & \text{tax} \\ \textit{expense} & & \text{income statement} & & \text{rate} \end{array}$$

$$\begin{array}{ccccc} \text{Income} & & \text{Taxable income} & & \text{Income} \\ \text{tax} & = & \text{from the tax return} & \times & \text{tax} \\ \textit{payable} & & \text{filed with the IRS} & & \text{rate} \end{array}$$

The income statement and the income tax return are entirely separate documents. You've been studying the income statement throughout this course. The tax return is new. It reports taxes to the IRS.

For most companies, income tax expense and income tax payable differ. The most important difference occurs when a corporation uses straight-line depreciation for the income statement and accelerated depreciation for the tax return.

Continuing with the IHOP illustration, suppose for 2008 that IHOP Corp. has

- Income before income tax of $55 million (This comes from the income statement.)
- Taxable income of $40 million (This comes from the tax return.)

IHOP will record income tax for 2008 as follows (dollar amounts in millions and assume an income tax rate of 40%):

2008			
Dec. 31	Income Tax Expense ($55 × 0.40)	22	
	Income Tax Payable ($40 × 0.40)		16
	Deferred Tax Liability		6
	Recorded income tax for the year.		

IHOP will pay the $16 million of Income Tax Payable within a few months. The Deferred Tax Liability account is long-term, so IHOP will pay this debt over a num-

---

[2]The authors thank Jean Marie Hudson for suggesting this presentation.

ber of years. For this situation IHOP's 2008 financial statements would report these figures (in millions):

Income Statement		Balance Sheet	
Income before income tax	$55	Current liabilities:	
Income tax expense	(22)	Income tax payable	$16
Net income	$33	Long-term liabilities:	
		Deferred tax liability	6*

* Assumes the beginning balance of Deferred tax liability was zero.

Decision Guidelines

DIVIDENDS, STOCK VALUES, EVALUATING OPERATIONS, AND CORPORATE INCOME TAX

Suppose you are considering buying some IHOP stock. You are naturally interested in how well the company is doing. Does IHOP pay dividends? What are IHOP's stock values? What are the rates of return on IHOP's assets and equity? The Decision Guidelines will help you evaluate the company.

Decision	Guidelines
Dividends	
Whether to declare a cash dividend?	• Must have enough retained earnings to declare the dividend.
	• Must have enough cash to pay the dividend.
What happens with a dividend?	• The IHOP board of directors declares the dividend. Then the dividend becomes a liability for IHOP.
	• The date of record fixes who will receive the dividend.
	• Payment of the dividend occurs later.
Who receives the dividend?	• Preferred stockholders get their dividends first. Preferred dividends have a specified rate.
	• Common stockholders receive the remainder.
Stock Values	
How much to pay for a stock?	Its market value.
How is book value used in decision making?	Can measure the value of a stock that is not traded on a stock exchange.
Evaluating Operations	
How to evaluate the operations of a corporation?	Two measures:
	• Rate of return on total assets (return on assets)
	• Rate of return on common equity (return on equity)
	For a healthy company, return on equity should exceed return on assets by a wide margin.
Accounting for Income Tax	
What are the three main tax accounts?	• Income tax expense
	• Income tax payable, a current liability
	• Deferred tax liability, usually long-term
How to measure	
• Income tax expense?	Income before income tax (from the income statement) × Income tax rate
• Income tax payable?	Taxable income (from the income tax return filed with the Internal Revenue Service) × Income tax rate
• Deferred tax liability?	Difference between income tax expense and income tax payable

Summary Problem 2

Use the following accounts and related balances to prepare the classified balance sheet of Fiesta, Inc., at September 30, 2007. Use the account format of the balance sheet.

Common stock, $1 par,			Long-term note payable	$ 70,000
50,000 shares authorized,			Inventory	85,000
20,000 shares issued	$20,000		Property, plant, and	
Salary payable	3,000		equipment, net	205,000
Cash	15,000		Accounts receivable, net	25,000
Accounts payable	20,000		Preferred stock, $2.50, no-par,	
Retained earnings	80,000		10,000 shares authorized,	
Paid-in capital in excess of			2,000 shares issued	50,000
par—common	75,000		Income tax payable	12,000

Solution

FIESTA, INC.
Balance Sheet
September 30, 2007

Assets			Liabilities		
Current:			**Current:**		
Cash	$ 15,000		Accounts payable		$ 20,000
Accounts receivable,			Salary payable		3,000
net	25,000		Income tax payable		12,000
Inventory	85,000		Total current liabilities		35,000
Total current			Long-term note payable		70,000
assets	125,000		Total liabilities		105,000
Property, plant, and					
equipment, net	205,000		**Stockholders' Equity**		
			Preferred stock, $2.50, no-par,		
			10,000 shares authorized,		
			2,000 shares issued	$ 50,000	
			Common stock, $1 par,		
			50,000 shares authorized,		
			20,000 shares issued	20,000	
			Paid-in capital in excess of		
			par—common	75,000	
			Total paid-in capital	145,000	
			Retained earnings	80,000	
			Total stockholders' equity		225,000
			Total liabilities and		
Total assets	$330,000		stockholders' equity		$330,000

Compute the book value per share of Fiesta's common stock. No preferred dividends are in arrears, and Fiesta has not declared the current-year dividend.

continued . . .

Preferred equity:	
Carrying value	$ 50,000
Cumulative dividend for the current year (2,000 shares × $2.50).....	5,000
Prefered equity..	$ 55,000
Common:	
Total stockholders' equity	$225,000
Less preferred equity...	55,000)
Common equity	$170,000
Book value per share of common ($170,000/20,000 shares).............	$ 8.50

Review *Corporations: Paid-In Capital and the Balance Sheet*

Accounting Vocabulary

Additional Paid-In Capital
The paid-in capital in excess of par, common plus other accounts combined for reporting on the balance sheet.

Authorization of Stock
Provision in a corporate charter that gives the state's permission for the corporation to issue—that is, to sell—a certain number of shares of stock.

Board of Directors
Group elected by the stockholders to set policy and to appoint the officers.

Book Value
Amount of owners' equity on the company's books for each share of its stock.

Bylaws
Constitution for governing a corporation.

Chairperson
Elected by a corporation's board of directors, the most powerful person in the corporation.

Charter
Document that gives the state's permission to form a corporation.

Common Stock
The class of stock that represents the basic ownership of the corporation.

Contributed Capital
Capital from investment by the stockholders. Also called **paid-in capital**.

Cumulative Preferred Stock
Preferred stock whose owners must receive all dividends in arrears before the corporation pays dividends to the common stockholders.

Deficit
Debit balance in the Retained Earnings account.

Dividends
Distributions by a corporation to its stockholders.

Double Taxation
Corporations pay their own income taxes on corporate income. Then the stockholders pay personal income tax on the cash dividends they receive from corporations.

Legal Capital
The portion of stockholders' equity that cannot be used for dividends.

Limited Liability
No personal obligation of a stockholder for corporation debts. A stockholder can lose no more on an investment in a corporation's stock than the cost of the investment.

Market Value
Price for which a person could buy or sell a share of stock.

Outstanding Stock
Stock in the hands of stockholders.

Paid-in Capital
Capital from investment by the stockholders. Also called **contributed capital**.

Par Value
Arbitrary amount assigned to a share of stock.

Preferred Stock
Stock that gives its owners certain advantages over common stockholders, such as the right to receive dividends before the common stockholders and the right to receive assets before the common stockholders if the corporation liquidates.

President
Chief operating officer in charge of managing the day-to-day operations of a corporation.

Rate of Return on Common Stockholders' Equity
Net income minus preferred dividends, divided by average common stockholders' equity. A measure of profitability. Also called **return on equity**.

Rate of Return on Total Assets
The sum of net income plus interest expense divided by average total assets. Measures the success a company has in using its assets to earn income for those financing the business. Also called **return on assets**.

Retained Earnings
Capital earned through profitable operation of the business.

Return on Assets
The sum of net income plus interest expense divided by average total assets. Measures the success a company has in using its assets to earn income for those financing the business. Also called **rate of return on total assets**.

Return on Equity
Net income minus preferred dividends, divided by average common stockholders' equity. A measure of profitability. Also called **rate of return on common stockholders' equity**.

Shareholder
A person who owns the stock of a corporation. Also called **stockholder**.

Stated Value
An arbitrary amount that accountants treat as though it were par value.

Stock
Shares into which the owners' equity of a corporation is divided.

Stockholder
A person who owns the stock of a corporation. Also called **shareholder**.

Stockholders' Equity
Owners' equity of a corporation.

Quick Check

1. Which characteristic of a corporation is most attractive?
   a. Double taxation
   b. Mutual agency
   c. Limited liability
   d. All of the above

2. Which corporate characteristic is a disadvantage?
   a. Double taxation
   b. Mutual agency
   c. Limited liability
   d. None of the above

3. The two basic sources of corporate capital are
   a. Paid-in capital and retained earnings
   b. Assets and equity
   c. Preferred and common
   d. Retained earnings and dividends

4. Which class of stockholders takes the greater investment risk?
   a. Common
   b. Preferred
   c. Neither; bondholders take the most risk
   d. Both preferred and common take equal risk

5. Suppose Pier 1 Imports issued 100,000 shares of $0.05 par common stock at $1 per share. Which journal entry correctly records the issuance of this stock?

   a. Cash 100,000
       Common Stock 100,000

   b. Common Stock.................................... 100,000
       Cash... 5,000
       Paid-In Capital in Excess of Par 95,000

   c. Common Stock.................................... 100,000
       Cash... 100,000

   d. Cash 100,000
       Common Stock 5,000
       Paid-In Capital in Excess of Par 95,000

6. Suppose IHOP issues common stock to purchase a building. IHOP should record the building at
   a. The par value of the stock given
   b. A value assigned by the board of directors
   c. Its market value
   d. Its book value

7. Chewning Corporation has 10,000 shares of 5%, $10 par preferred stock and 50,000 shares of common stock outstanding. Chewning declared no dividends in 2008. In 2009, Chewning declares a total dividend of $50,000. How much of the dividends go to the common stockholders?

a. $50,000

b. $40,000

c. $10,000

d. None; it all goes to preferred

8. Connor Health Foods has 10,000 shares of $1 par common stock outstanding, which was issued at $10 per share. Connor also has retained earnings of $80,000. How much is Connor's total stockholders' equity?

a. $10,000

b. $90,000

c. $100,000

d. $180,000

9. Dale Corporation has the following data:

Net income	$22,000	Average total assets	$300,000
Interest expense	8,000	Average common equity	100,000
Preferred dividends	10,000		

Dale's return on assets is

a. 15%

b. 12%

c. 10%

d. 4%

10. A corporation's income tax payable is computed as:

a. Income before tax × Income tax rate

b. Taxable income × Income tax rate

c. Net income × Income tax rate

d. Return on equity × Income tax rate

Answers are given after Apply Your Knowledge (p. 687).

Assess Your Progress

Short Exercises

Authority structure in a corporation

S13-1 Answer these questions about corporations. (p. 640)

1. Who is the most powerful person in the corporation?
2. What group holds the ultimate power?
3. Who is in charge of day-to-day operations?
4. Who is in charge of accounting?

The balance sheets of a corporation and a proprietorship

S13-2 How does a proprietorship balance sheet differ from a corporation's balance sheet? How are the two balance sheets similar? (pp. 642–643)

Issuing stock

S13-3 Colorado Corporation has two classes of stock: Common, $1 par: Preferred, $20 par. Journalize Colorado's issuance of

a. 1,000 shares of common stock for $10 per share

b. 1,000 shares of preferred stock for a total of $20,000

Explanations are not required. (pp. 646–647, 648–649)

Effect of a stock issuance

S13-4 IHOP issued common stock and received $32,000,000. The par value of the IHOP stock was only $32,000. Is the excess amount of $31,968,000 a profit to IHOP? Does the excess affect net income? If not, what was it? (pp. 646–647)

Issuing stock and interpreting stockholders' equity

S13-5 Smartpages.com issued stock during 2008 and reported the following on its balance sheet at December 31, 2008:

Common stock, $0.25 par value	
Authorized: 5,000 shares	
Issued: 3,000 shares	$ 750
Paid-in capital in excess of par.........	3,850
Retained earnings	24,500

Journalize the company's issuance of the stock for cash. (pp. 646–647)

Preparing the stockholders' equity section of a balance sheet

S13-6 Hillcrest Corporation reported the following accounts:

Cost of goods sold	$58,800	Accounts payable	$ 6,000
Paid-in capital in excess of par	17,000	Retained earnings	16,000
Common stock, $1 par,		Unearned revenue	5,200
40,000 shares issued	40,000	Total assets	?
Cash	24,000	Long-term note payable	7,600

continued . . .

Prepare the stockholders' equity section of the Hillcrest balance sheet. (pp. 646–647)

Using stockholders' equity data

S13-7 Use the Hillcrest Corporation data in Short Exercise 13-6 to compute Hillcrest's

a. Total liabilities (pp. 144–145)

b. Total assets (p. 11)

Accounting for cash dividends

S13-8 Java Company earned net income of $85,000 during the year ended December 31, 2008. On December 15, Java declared the annual cash dividend on its 4% preferred stock (par value, $100,000) and a $0.50 per share cash dividend on its common stock (50,000 shares). Java then paid the dividends on January 4, 2009.

Journalize for Java:

a. Declaring the cash dividends on December 15, 2008. (pp. 653–656)

b. Paying the cash dividends on January 4, 2009. (pp. 653–655)

Dividing cash dividends between preferred and common stock

S13-9 Sterling Trust has the following stockholders' equity:

Paid-in capital:	
Preferred stock, 5%, $10 par, 5,000 shares authorized, 4,000 shares issued....................................	$ 40,000
Common stock, $0.10 par, 1,000,000 shares authorized and issued...................................	100,000
Paid-in capital in excess of par—common	300,000
Total paid-in capital..	440,000
Retained earnings..	260,000
Total stockholders' equity	$700,000

Answer these questions about Sterling's dividends:

1. Is Sterling's preferred stock cumulative or noncumulative? How can you tell? (pp. 655–656)

2. Sterling declares cash dividends of $15,000 for 2006. How much of the dividends goes to preferred? How much goes to common? (pp. 655–656)

3. Sterling passed the preferred dividend in 2007 and 2008. In 2009 the company declares cash dividends of $15,000. How much of the dividend goes to preferred? How much goes to common? (p. 656)

Book value per share of common stock

S13-10 Refer to the stockholders' equity of Sterling Trust in Short Exercise 13-9. Sterling has not declared preferred dividends for 5 years (including the current year). Compute the book value per share of Sterling's common stock. (p. 657)

Computing return on assets
and return on equity for a
leading company

 6

S13-11 Coca-Cola's 2004 financial statements reported the following items—with 2005 figures given for comparison (adapted, in millions):

	2004	2003
Balance sheet		
Total assets..	$31,327	$27,342
Total liabilities...	$15,392	$13,252
Total stockholders' equity (all common)...........	15,935	14,090
Total liabilities and equity	$31,327	$27,342
Income statement		
Net sales..	$21,962	
Cost of goods sold..	7,638	
Gross profit..	14,324	
Selling, administrative, and general expenses.....	8,146	
Interest expense...	196	
All other expenses	1,135	
Net income..	$ 4,847	

Compute Coca-Cola's rate of return on total assets and rate of return on common stockholders' equity for 2004. Do these rates of return look high or low? (pp. 658–660)

S13-12 Foxey Flowers had income before income tax of $80,000 and taxable income of $70,000 for 2007, the company's first year of operations. The income tax rate is 40%.

1. Make the entry to record Foxey's income taxes for 2007. (pp. 661–662)

2. Show what Foxey Flowers will report on its 2007 income statement, starting with income before income tax. (pp. 661–662)

Exercises

E13-13 Jack and Judy Myers are opening Parties on Demand. To buy stage props and other equipment they need outside capital, so they plan to organize the business as a corporation. They come to you for advice. Write a memorandum informing them of the steps in forming a corporation. Identify specific documents used in this process, and name the different parties involved in the ownership and management of a corporation. (pp. 639–640)

E13-14 Mustang Properties completed the following stock issuance transactions:

June 19	Issued 1,000 shares of $1 par common stock for cash of $8 per share.
July 3	Sold 300 shares of $4.50, no-par preferred stock for $15,000 cash.
11	Received equipment with market value of $20,000. Issued 3,000 shares of the $1 par common stock.

continued . . .

Requirements

1. Journalize the transactions. Explanations are not required. (pp. 646–649)

2. How much paid-in capital did these transactions generate for Mustang Properties? (p. 647)

Recording issuance of no-par stock

E13-15 Manor House Restaurants issued 5,000 shares of no-par common stock for $6 per share. Record issuance of the stock if the stock (a) is true no-par stock and (b) has stated value of $2 per share. Which type of stock results in more total paid-in capital? (pp. 646–647)

Issuing stock to finance the purchase of assets

E13-16 This exercise shows the similarity and the difference between two ways for Mane Event Styling Salons, Inc., to acquire plant assets.

Case A—Issue stock and buy the assets in separate transactions:

Mane Event issued 10,000 shares of its $10 par common stock for cash of $700,000. In a separate transaction, Mane Event purchased a building for $500,000 and equipment for $200,000. Journalize the two transactions.

Case B—Issue stock to acquire the assets:

Mane Event issued 10,000 shares of its $10 par common stock to acquire a building valued at $500,000 and equipment worth $200,000. Journalize this single transaction.

Compare the balances in all accounts after making both sets of entries. Are the account balances similar or different? (pp. 646–649)

Issuing stock and preparing the stockholders' equity section of the balance sheet

2 3

E13-17 The charter for KXAS-TV authorizes the company to issue 100,000 shares of $3, no-par preferred stock and 500,000 shares of common stock with $1 par value. During its start-up phase, KXAS completed the following transactions:

Aug. 6   Issued 500 shares of common stock to the stockholders who organized the corporation, receiving cash of $13,000.

12   Issued 300 shares of preferred stock for cash of $20,000.

14   Issued 1,000 shares of common stock in exchange for land valued at $26,000.

31   Closed net income of $40,000 into Retained Earnings.

Requirements

1. Record the transactions in the general journal. (pp. 646–647, 643–644)

2. Prepare the stockholders' equity section of the KXAS-TV balance sheet at August 31. (p. 649)

Stockholders' equity section of a balance sheet

E13-18 The charter of Maple Leaf Capital Corporation authorizes the issuance of 1,000 shares of preferred stock and 10,000 shares of common stock.

continued . . .

During a two-month period, Maple Leaf completed these stock-issuance transactions:

Nov. 23	Issued 2,000 shares of $1 par common stock for cash of $12.50 per share.
Dec. 12	Received inventory valued at $25,000 and equipment with market value of $16,000 for 3,000 shares of the $1 par common stock.
17	Issued 1,000 shares of 5%, $50 par preferred stock for $50 per share.

Requirement

Prepare the stockholders' equity section of the Maple Leaf Capital balance sheet for the transactions given in this exercise. Retained Earnings has a balance of $70,000. (pp. 649–650)

Paid-in capital for a corporation

2

E13-19 Ariba Corp. recently organized. The company issued common stock to an inventor in exchange for a patent with a market value of $50,000. In addition, Ariba received cash both for 2,000 shares of its $10 par preferred stock at par value and for 6,000 shares of its no-par common stock at $20 per share. Without making journal entries, determine the total *paid-in capital* created by these transactions. (pp. 649–650)

Stockholders' equity section of a balance sheet

3

E13-20 International Publishing Company has the following selected account balances at June 30, 2007. Prepare the stockholders' equity section of International's balance sheet. (pp. 649–650)

Inventory	$112,000	Common stock, no par	
Machinery and equipment	109,000	with $1 stated value,	
Preferred stock, 5%, 10 par,		100,000 shares authorized	
20,000 shares authorized,		and issued	$100,000
5,000 shares issued	50,000	Accumulated depreciation—	
Paid-in capital in excess of		machinery and equipment	62,000
stated value—common	90,000	Retained earnings	110,0000
Cost of goods sold	81,000		

E13-21 Waddell & Reed, Inc., has the following stockholders' equity:

Paid-in capital:	
Preferred stock, 8%, $10 par, 100,000 shares authorized, 20,000 shares issued................................	$ 200,000
Common stock, $0.50 par, 500,000 shares authorized, 300,000 shares issued.............................	150,000
Paid-in capital in excess of par—common	600,000
Total paid-in capital...	950,000
Retained earnings...	150,000
Total stockholders' equity	$1,100,000

Dividing dividends between preferred and common stock

4

continued . . .

First, determine whether preferred stock is cumulative or noncumulative. Then compute the amount of dividends to preferred and to common for 2007 and 2008 if total dividends are $10,000 in 2007 and $50,000 in 2008. (pp. 655–656)

Computing dividends on preferred and common stock
4

E13-22 The following elements of stockholders' equity are adapted from the balance sheet of Volvo Marketing Corp.

Stockholders' Equity	
Preferred stock, 5% cumulative, $2 par, 50,000 shares issued..	$100,000
Common stock, $0.10 par, 9,000,000 shares issued.............	900,000

Volvo paid no preferred dividends in 2008.

Requirement

Compute the dividends to preferred and common for 2009 if total dividends are $150,000. (p. 656)

Book value per share of common stock
5

E13-23 The balance sheet of Mark Todd Wireless, Inc., reported the following:

Preferred stock, $50 par value, 6%, 1,000 shares issued and outstanding..	$ 50,000
Common stock, no par value, 10,000 shares authorized; 5,000 shares issued...	222,000
Total stockholders' equity	$277,000

Assume that Todd has paid preferred dividends for the current year and all prior years (no dividends in arrears). Compute the book value per share of the common stock. (p. 658)

Book value per share of common stock; preferred dividends in arrears
5

E13-24 Refer to Exercise 13-23. Compute the book value per share of Todd's common stock if three years' preferred dividends (including dividends for the current year) are in arrears. (p. 658)

Evaluating profitability
6

E13-25 La Salle Exploration Company reported these figures for 2008 and 2007:

	2008	2007
Income statement:		
Interest expense	$ 12,400,000	$ 17,100,000
Net income.......................................	18,000,000	18,700,000

continued . . .

	2008	2007
Balance sheet:		
Total assets	$326,000,000	$317,000,000
Preferred stock, $2, no-par, 100,000 shares issued and outstanding...........................	2,500,000	2,500,000
Common stockholders' equity.............	184,000,000	176,000,000
Total stockholders' equity	186,500,000	178,500,000

Compute rate of return on total assets and rate of return on common stockholders' equity for 2008. Do these rates of return suggest strength or weakness? Give your reason. (pp. 658–660)

Accounting for income tax by a corporation

7

E13-26 The income statement of eBay, Inc., reported income before income tax of $400 million (rounded) during a recent year. Assume eBay's taxable income for the year was $344 million. The company's income tax rate was close to 37.5%.

1. Journalize eBay's entry to record income tax for the year. (pp. 661–662)

2. Show how eBay would report income tax expense on its income statement and income tax liabilities on its balance sheet. Complete the income statement, starting with income before tax. For the balance sheet, assume all beginning balances were zero. (pp. 661–662)

Problems (Group A)

Organizing a corporation

1

P13-27A Lance Lot and Arthur King are opening a FedEx Kinko's store. There are no competing copy shops in the area. Their fundamental decision is how to organize the business. Lot thinks the partnership form is best for their business. King favors the corporate form of organization. They seek your advice. (pp. 638–640)

Requirement

Write a memo to Lot and King to make them aware of the advantages and disadvantages of organizing the business as a corporation. Use the following format:

Date: _____

To: Lance Lot and Arthur King

From: Student Name

Subject: Advantages and disadvantages of the corporate form of business organization

Journalizing corporation
transactions and preparing
the stockholders' equity
section of the balance sheet

P13-28A A-Mobile Wireless needed additional capital to expand, so the business incorporated. The charter from the state of Georgia authorizes A-Mobile to issue 50,000 shares of 6%, $100-par preferred stock and 100,000 shares of no-par common stock. A-Mobile completed the following transactions:

Dec. 2	Issued 20,000 shares of common stock for equipment with market value of $100,000.
6	Issued 500 shares of preferred stock to acquire a patent with a market value of $50,000.
9	Issued 12,000 shares of common stock for cash of $60,000.

Requirements

1. Record the transactions in the general journal. (pp. 647–649)

2. Prepare the stockholders' equity section of the A-Mobile Wireless balance sheet at December 31. The ending balance of Retained Earnings is $90,000. (pp. 649–650)

Issuing stock and preparing
the stockholders' equity
section of the balance sheet.

P13-29A Lockridge-Priest, Inc., was organized in 2008. At December 31, 2008, the Lockridge-Priest balance sheet reported the following stockholders' equity:

Paid-in capital:	
Preferred stock, 6%, $50 par, 100,000 shares authorized, none issued..	$ —
Common stock, $1 par, 500,000 shares authorized, 60,000 shares issued	60,000
Paid-in capital in excess of par—common	40,000
Total paid-in capital..	100,000
Retained earnings...	25,000
Total stockholders' equity	$125,000

Requirements

1. During 2009, the company completed the following selected transactions. Journalize each transaction. Explanations are not required.

   a. Issued for cash 1,000 shares of preferred stock at par value. (pp. 648–649)

   b. Issued for cash 2,000 shares of common stock at a price of $3 per share. (pp. 646–647)

   c. Net income for the year was $75,000, and the company declared no dividends. Make the closing entry for net income. (pp. 643–644)

2. Prepare the stockholders' equity section of the Lockridge-Priest balance sheet at December 31, 2009. (pp. 649–650)

P13-30A The following summaries for Centroplex Service, Inc., and Jacobs-Cathey Co. provide the information needed to prepare the stockholders' equity section of each company's balance sheet. The two companies are independent.

- *Centroplex Service, Inc.* Centroplex is authorized to issue 40,000 shares of $1 par common stock. All the stock was issued at $10 per share. The company incurred net losses of $50,000 in 2004 and $14,000 in 2005. It earned net income of $28,000 in 2006 and $176,000 in 2007. The company declared no dividends during the four-year period.

- *Jacobs-Cathey Co.* Jacobs-Cathey's charter authorizes the issuance of 50,000 shares of 5%, $15 par preferred stock and 500,000 shares of no-par common stock. Jacobs-Cathey issued 1,000 shares of the preferred stock at $15 per share. It issued 100,000 shares of the common stock for $200,000. The company's retained earnings balance at the beginning of 2007 was $120,000. Net income for 2007 was $90,000, and the company declared the specified preferred dividend for 2007. Preferred dividends for 2006 were in arrears.

Requirements

For each company, prepare the stockholders' equity section of its balance sheet at December 31, 2007. Show the computation of all amounts. Entries are not required. (pp. 649–650, 655–656)

P13-31A Trane Comfort Specialists, Inc., reported the following stockholders' equity on its balance sheet at June 30, 2008.

Stockholders' Equity	
Paid-in capital:	
Preferred stock, 6%—Authorized 600,000 shares; issued 200,000 shares	$ 1,000,000
Common stock—$1 par value—Authorized 5,000,000 shares; issued 1,300,000	1,300,000
Additional paid-in capital, common	2,400,000
Total paid-in capital	4,700,000
Retained earnings	11,900,000
Total stockholders' equity	$16,600,000

Requirements

1. Identify the different issues of stock that Trane has outstanding. (pp. 651–653)

2. What is the par value per share of Trane's preferred stock?

3. Make two summary journal entries to record issuance of all the Trane stock for cash. Explanations are not required. (pp. 646–649)

4. No preferred dividends are in arrears. Journalize the declaration of a $500,000 dividend at June 30, 2008. Use separate Dividends Payable accounts for Preferred and Common. An explanation is not required. (pp. 653–655)

Preparing a corporation
balance sheet; measuring
profitability

 6

P13-32A The following accounts and December 31, 2006, balances of New York
Optical Corporation are arranged in no particular order.

Retained earnings	$145,000	Common stock, $5 par	
Inventory	101,000	100,000 shares authorized,	
Property, plant, and		22,000 shares issued	$110,000
equipment, net	278,000	Dividends payable	3,000
Prepaid expenses	13,000	Paid-in capital in excess	
Goodwill	63,000	of par—common	140,000
Accrued liabilities payable	17,000	Accounts payable	31,000
Long-term note payable	104,000	Preferred stock, 4%, $10, no-par	
Accounts receivable, net	102,000	25,000 shares authorized,	
Cash	43,000	5,000 shares issued	50,000

Requirements

1. Prepare the company's classified balance sheet in account format at
   December 31, 2006 (pp. 663–664)

2. Compute New York Optical's rate of return on total assets and rate
   of return on common stockholders' equity for the year ended
   December 31, 2006. For the rates of return, you will need these data:
   (pp. 658–660)

Total assets, Dec. 31, 2005	$502,000
Common equity, Dec. 31, 2005	305,000
Net income, 2006	47,000
Interest expense, 2006	3,000

3. Do these rates of return suggest strength or weakness? Give your reason. (pp. 659–660)

Computing dividends on
preferred and common stock

4

P13-33A Vogue Skincare has 5,000 shares of 5%, $20 par value preferred stock
and 100,000 shares of $1.50 par common stock outstanding. During a
three-year period, Vogue declared and paid cash dividends as follows:
2006, $4,000; 2007, $10,000; and 2008, $20,000.

Requirements

1. Compute the total dividends to preferred and to common for each of
   the three years if

   a. Preferred is noncumulative. (p. 519)

   b. Preferred is cumulative. (p. 519)

2. For case l.b., journalize the declaration of the 2008 dividends on
   December 22, 2008, and payment on January 14, 2009. Use
   separate Dividends Payable accounts for Preferred and Common.
   (p. 519)

Analyzing the stockholders' equity of a corporation

P13-34A The balance sheet of Beechcraft, Inc., reported the following:

Stockholders' Equity	
Paid-in capital:	
Preferred stock, $5 par, 6%, 1,000 shares authorized and issued	$ 5,000
Common stock, $1 par, 40,000 shares authorized; 16,000 shares issued	16,000
Additional paid-in capital—common...............................	214,000
	235,000
Retained earnings..	70,000
Total stockholders' equity	$305,000

Preferred dividends are in arrears for two years, including the current year. On the balance sheet date, the market value of the Beechcraft common stock was $30 per share.

Requirements

1. Is the preferred stock cumulative or noncumulative? How can you tell? (p. 656)
2. What is the total paid-in capital of the company? (pp. 649–650)
3. What was the total market value of the common stock? (p. 657)
4. Compute the book value per share of the common stock. (p. 656)

Computing and recording a corporation's income tax

P13-35A The accounting records of Reflection Redwood Corporation provide income statement data for 2007.

Total revenue....................	$930,000
Total expenses	700,000
Income before tax.............	$230,000

Total expenses include depreciation of $50,000 computed on the straight-line method. In calculating taxable income on the tax return, Reflection Redwood uses the modified accelerated cost recovery system (MACRS). MACRS depreciation was $80,000 for 2007. The corporate income tax rate is 40%.

Requirements

1. Compute taxable income for the year. For this computation, substitute MACRS depreciation in place of straight-line depreciation. (pp. 661–662)
2. Journalize the corporation's income tax for 2007. (pp. 661–662)
3. Show how to report the two income tax liabilities on Redwood's classified balance sheet. (pp. 661–662)

Problems (Group B)

continued . . .

Organizing a corporation

P13-36B Sherry Taft and Laura Sims are opening Bank Compliance Consultants. The area is growing, and no competitors are located nearby. Their basic decision is how to organize the business. Taft thinks the partnership form is best. Sims favors the corporate form of organization. They seek your advice. (pp. 638–640)

Requirement
Write a memo to Taft and Sims to show them the advantages and disadvantages of organizing the business as a corporation. Use the following format for your memo:

Date: _____

To: Sherry Taft and Laura Sims

From: Student Name

Subject: Advantages and disadvantages of the corporate form of business organization

---

Journalizing corporation transactions and preparing the stockholders' equity section of the balance sheet.

P13-37B Mailmax Direct is incorporated in the state of Arizona. The charter authorizes Mailmax to issue 1,000 shares of 6%, $100 par preferred stock and 250,000 shares of $10-par common stock. In its first month, Mailmax completed these transactions:

Jan. 3	Issued 9,000 shares of common stock for equipment with market value of $90,000.
	12	Issued 500 shares of preferred stock to acquire a patent with a market value of $50,000.
	28	Issued 1,500 shares of common stock for $11 cash per share.

Requirements
1. Record the transactions in the general journal. (pp. 646–649)
2. Prepare the stockholders' equity section of the Mailmax Direct, Inc., balance sheet at January 31. The ending balance of Retained Earnings is $43,500. (pp. 649–650)

Issuing stock and preparing the stockholders' equity section of the balance sheet

P13-38B Lieberman Corporation was organized in 2007. At December 31, 2007, Lieberman's balance sheet reported the following stockholders' equity:

Paid-in capital:		
Preferred stock, 5%, $10 par, 50,000 shares authorized, none issued	$ —
Common stock, $2 par, 100,000 shares authorized, 10,000 shares issued	20,000
Paid-in capital in excess of par—common	30,000
Total paid-in capital	50,000

continued . . .

Retained earnings (Deficit)... (5,000)

Total stockholders' equity $45,000

Requirements

1. During 2008, Lieberman completed the following selected trans-actions. Journalize each transaction. Explanations are not required.

   a. Issued for cash 5,000 shares of preferred stock at par value. (pp. 648–649)

   b. Issued for cash 1,000 shares of common stock at a price of $7 per share. (pp. 646–647)

   c. Net income for the year was $100,000, and the company declared no dividends. Make the closing entry for net income. (pp. 643–644)

2. Prepare the stockholders' equity section of the Lieberman Corporation balance sheet at December 31, 2008. (pp. 649–650)

Stockholders' equity section of the balance sheet

P13-39B Stockholders' equity information for two independent companies, Monterrey Enterprises, Inc., and Guadalupe Corp., follow.

- *Monterrey Enterprises, Inc.* Monterrey is authorized to issue 60,000 shares of $5 par common stock. All the stock was issued at $12 per share. The company incurred a net loss of $40,000 in 2006. It earned net income of $30,000 in 2007 and $90,000 in 2008. The company declared no dividends during the three-year period.

- *Guadalupe Corp.* Guadalupe's charter authorizes the company to issue 10,000 shares of $2.50 preferred stock with par value of $50 and 120,000 shares of no-par common stock. *Guadalupe* issued 1,000 shares of the preferred stock at par. It issued 40,000 shares of the common stock for a total of $220,000. The company's Retained Earnings balance at the beginning of 2008 was $65,000, and net income for the year was $90,000. During 2008, the company declared the specified dividend on preferred and a $0.50 per share dividend on common. Preferred dividends for 2007 were in arrears.

Requirements

For each company, prepare the stockholders' equity section of its balance sheet at December 31, 2008. Show the computation of all amounts. Entries are not required. (pp. 649–650)

Analyzing the stockholders' equity of a corporation

P13-40B Crawford-Austin Properties included the following stockholders' equity on its year-end balance sheet at December 31, 2006.

Stockholders' Equity	
Paid-in capital:	
Preferred stock, 6%...	$ 65,000
Common stock—par value $1 per share; 650,000 shares authorized, 230,000 shares issued..................	230,000
Paid-in capital in excess of par—common	70,000
Total paid-in capital..	365,000

continued . . .

Retained earnings..	2,000,000
Total stockholders' equity	$2,365,000

Requirements

1. Identify the different issues of stock that Crawford-Austin has outstanding. (pp. 644–645)

2. Is the preferred stock cumulative or noncumulative? How can you tell? (p. 656)

3. Give two summary journal entries to record issuance of all the Crawford-Austin stock. All the stock was issued for cash. Explanations are not required. (pp. 646–649)

4. Preferred dividends are in arrears for 2005 and 2006. Record the declaration of a $50,000 cash dividend on December 30, 2007. Use separate Dividends Payable accounts for Preferred and Common. An explanation is not required. (pp. 653–656)

P13-41B The accounts and June 30, 2007, balances of Cromwell Company are arranged in no particular order:

Preparing a corporation balance sheet; measuring profitability

Requirements

1. Prepare the company's classified balance sheet in account format at June 30, 2007. (pp. 663–664)

Accounts receivable, net	$46,000	Property, plant, and	
Paid-in capital in excess of		equipment, net	$231,000
par—common	19,000	Common stock, $1 par,	
Accrued liabilities payable	26,000	500,000 shares authorized,	
Long-term note payable	12,000	236,000 shares issued	236,000
Inventory	81,000	Dividends payable	9,000
Prepaid expenses	10,000	Retained earnings	42,000
Cash	10,000	Preferred stock, $0.10, no-par,	
Accounts payable	31,000	10,000 shares authorized	
Trademark, net	22,000	and issued	25,000

2. Compute Cromwell's rate of return on total assets and rate of return on common stockholders' equity for the year ended June 30, 2007. For the rates of return, you will need these data: (pp. 658–660)

Total assets, June 30, 2006	$404,000
Common equity, June 30, 2006	303,000
Net income, fiscal year 2007	31,000
Interest expense, fiscal year 2007.......	6,000

3. Do these rates of return suggest strength or weakness? Give your reason. (pp. 659–660)

Computing dividends on
preferred and common stock

P13-42B FHA Loan Company has 10,000 shares of $3.50, no-par preferred stock and 50,000 shares of no-par common stock outstanding. FHA declared and paid the following dividends during a three-year period: 2006, $20,000; 2007, $100,000; and 2008, $150,000.

Requirements

1. Compute the total dividends to preferred stock and to common stock for each of the three years if

   a. Preferred is noncumulative. (p. 657)

   b. Preferred is cumulative. (p. 656)

2. For case 1.b., journalize the declaration of the 2008 dividends on December 28, 2008, and the payment on January 17, 2009. Use separate Dividends Payable accounts for Preferred and Common. (p. 656)

Analyzing the stockholders'
equity of a corporation
4 5

P13-43B The balance sheet of Creative Communications, Inc., reported the following:

Stockholders' Equity	
Paid-in capital:	
Preferred stock; nonvoting; no par, $3; 8,000 shares issued	$320,000
Common stock; $1.50 par; 40,000 shares issued	60,000
Additional paid-in capital—common..............................	240,000
	620,000
Retained earnings...	130,000
Total stockholders' equity	$750,000

Preferred dividends are in arrears for three years including the current year. On the balance sheet date, the market value of the Creative Communications common stock is $14 per share.

Requirements

1. Is the preferred stock cumulative or noncumulative? How can you tell? (p. 656)

2. Which class of stockholders controls the company? Give your reason. (pp. 645–655)

3. What is the total paid-in capital of the company? (pp. 649–650)

4. What was the total market value of the common stock? (p. 657)

5. Compute the book value per share of the common stock. (p. 656)

Computing and recording a
corporation's income tax
7

P13-44B The accounting records of Dwyer Minerals Corporation provide income statement data for 2008.

Total revenue	$680,000
Total expenses	460,000
Income before tax.................	$220,000

continued . . .

Total expenses include depreciation of $50,000 computed under the straight-line method. In calculating taxable income on the tax return, Dwyer uses MACRS. MACRS depreciation was $70,000 for 2008. The corporate income tax rate is 35%.

Requirements

1. Compute Dwyer's taxable income for the year. For this computation, substitute MACRS depreciation expense in place of straight-line depreciation. (pp. 661–662)

2. Journalize the corporation's income tax for 2008. (pp. 661–662)

3. Show how to report the two income tax liabilities on Dwyer's classified balance sheet. (pp. 661–662)

**for 24/7 practice, visit
www.MyAccountingLab.com**

Apply Your Knowledge

Decision Cases

Evaluating alternative ways to raise capital

Case 1. Lena Esteé and Kathy Lauder have a patent on a new line of cosmetics. They need additional capital to market the products, and they plan to incorporate the business. They are considering the capital structure for the corporation. Their primary goal is to raise as much capital as possible without giving up control of the business. Esteé and Lauder plan to invest the patent in the company and receive 100,000 shares of the corporation's common stock. They've been offered $100,000 for the patent.

The corporation's plans for a charter include an authorization to issue 5,000 shares of preferred stock and 500,000 shares of $1 par common stock. Esteé and Lauder are uncertain about the most desirable features for the preferred stock. Prior to incorporating, they are discussing their plans with two investment groups. The corporation can obtain capital from outside investors under either of the following plans:

- *Plan 1.* Group 1 will invest $150,000 to acquire 1,500 shares of 6%, $100 par nonvoting, noncumulative preferred stock.

- *Plan 2.* Group 2 will invest $100,000 to acquire 1,000 shares of $5, no-par preferred stock and $70,000 to acquire 70,000 shares of common stock. Each preferred share receives 50 votes on matters that come before the stockholders.

Requirements

Assume that the corporation is chartered.

1. Journalize the issuance of common stock to Esteé and Lauder. Explanations are not required.

2. Journalize the issuance of stock to the outsiders under both plans. Explanations are not required.

3. Net income for the first year is $180,000 and total dividends are $30,000. Prepare the stockholders' equity section of the corporation's balance sheet under both plans.

4. Recommend one of the plans to Esteé and Lauder. Give your reasons.

Characteristics of corporations' capital stock

Case 2. Answering the following questions will enhance your understanding of the capital stock of corporations. Consider each question independently of the others.

1. Why are capital stock and retained earnings shown separately in the shareholders' equity section of the balance sheet?

2. Preferred shares have advantages with respect to dividends and corporate liquidation. Why would investors buy common stock when preferred stock is available?

3. Manuel Chavez, major shareholder of MC, Inc., proposes to sell some land he owns to the company for common shares in MC, Inc. What problem does MC, Inc., face in recording the transaction?

4. If you owned 100 shares of stock in Coca-Cola Company and someone offered to buy the stock for its book value, would you accept the offer? Why or why not?

Ethical Issue

Note: This case is based on an actual situation.

Stan Sewell paid $50,000 for a franchise that entitled him to market software programs in the countries of the European Union. Sewell intended to sell individual franchises for the major language groups of western Europe—German, French, English, Spanish, and Italian. Naturally, investors considering buying a franchise from Sewell asked to see the financial statements of his business.

Believing the value of the franchise to be greater than $50,000, Sewell sought to capitalize his own franchise at $500,000. The law firm of St. Charles & LaDue helped Sewell form a corporation chartered to issue 500,000 shares of common stock with par value of $1 per share. Attorneys suggested the following chain of transactions:

a. A third party borrows $500,000 and purchases the franchise from Sewell.

b. Sewell pays the corporation $500,000 to acquire all its stock.

c. The corporation buys the franchise from the third party, who repays the loan.

In the final analysis, the third party is debt-free and out of the picture. Sewell owns all the corporation's stock, and the corporation owns the franchise. The corporation's balance sheet lists a franchise acquired at a cost of $500,000. This balance sheet is Sewell's most valuable marketing tool.

Requirements

1. What is unethical about this situation?

2. Who can be harmed? How can they be harmed? What role does accounting play?

Financial Statement Case

Analyzing stockholders'
equity

The Amazon.com financial statements appear in Appendix A at the end of this book. Answer the following questions about Amazon's stock. The Accumulated Deficit account is Retained Earnings with a negative balance.

Requirements

1. How much of Amazon's preferred stock was outstanding at December 31, 2005? How can you tell?

2. Examine Amazon.com's balance sheet. Which stockholders' equity account increased the most during 2005? What caused this increase? The statement of operations (income statement) helps to answer this question.

3. Use par value and the number of shares to show how to compute the balances in Amazon.com's Common Stock account at the end of both 2005 and 2004.

4. Would it be meaningful to compute Amazon.com's return on equity? Explain your answer.

Team Project

Competitive pressures are the norm in business. Lexus automobiles (made in Japan) have cut into the sales of Mercedes Benz (a German company), Jaguar (now a division of Ford), General Motors' Cadillac Division, and Ford's Lincoln Division. Dell, Gateway, and Compaq computers have siphoned business away from IBM. Foreign steelmakers have reduced the once-massive U.S. steel industry to a fraction of its former size.

Indeed, corporate downsizing has occurred on a massive scale. During the past few years, companies mentioned here have pared down their plant and equipment, laid off employees, or restructured operations.

Requirements

1. Identify all the stakeholders of a corporation and the stake each group has in the company. A *stakeholder* is a person or a group who has an interest (that is, a stake) in the success of the organization.

2. Identify several measures by which a corporation may be considered deficient and which may indicate the need for downsizing. How can downsizing help to solve this problem? Discuss how each measure can indicate the need for downsizing.

3. Debate the downsizing issue. One group of students takes the perspective of the company and its stockholders, and another group of students takes the perspective of other stakeholders of the company.

For Internet exercises, Excel in Practice, and additional online activities, go to the Web site www.prenhall.com/horngren.

Quick Check Answers

1. *c*   2. *a*   3. *a*   4. *a*   5. *d*   6. *c*   7. *b*   8. *d*   9. *c*   10. *b*

14 Corporations: Retained Earnings and the Income Statement

Learning Objectives

1 Account for stock dividends

2 Distinguish stock splits from stock dividends

3 Account for treasury stock

4 Report restrictions on retained earnings

5 Analyze a corporate income statement

Chapter 13 introduced corporations and covered the basics of stockholders' equity. Our feature company was IHOP, the restaurant chain. We saw that a corporation's balance sheet is the same as for a proprietorship or a partnership, except for owners' equity. Chapter 13 began with IHOP's issuance of common stock and also covered the declaration and payment of cash dividends.

This chapter takes corporate equity a few steps further, as follows:

Chapter 13 Covered	Chapter 14 Covers
Paid-in capital	Retained earnings
Issuing stock	Buying back a corporation's stock (treasury stock)
Cash dividends	Stock dividends and stock splits
Corporate balance sheet	Corporate income statement

Chapter 14 completes our discussion of corporate equity. It begins with *stock dividends* and *stock splits*—terms you've probably heard. Let's see what these terms mean.

Retained Earnings, Stock Dividends, and Stock Splits

We've seen that the owners' equity of a corporation is called *stockholders' equity* or *shareholders' equity*. Paid-in capital and retained earnings make up stockholders' equity. We studied paid-in capital in Chapter 13. Now let's focus on retained earnings.

Retained Earnings

Retained Earnings carries the balance of the business's accumulated lifetime net income less all net losses and less all dividends. A debit balance in Retained Earnings is called a *deficit*. Retained earnings deficits are rare because these companies go out of business. When you see a balance sheet, remember this about Retained Earnings:

1. **Credits to Retained Earnings arise only from net income.** Retained Earnings shows how much net income a corporation has earned and retained over its entire lifetime.

2. **The Retained Earnings account is not a reservoir of cash.** Retained Earnings represents no asset in particular. In fact, the corporation may have a large balance in Retained Earnings but insufficient cash to pay a dividend.

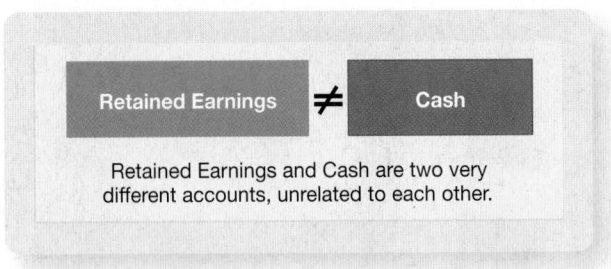

Retained Earnings and Cash are two very different accounts, unrelated to each other.

3. Retained Earnings' ending balance is computed as follows (amounts assumed):

Beginning balance	$ 70,000
Add: Net income for the year	80,000
Less: Net loss (none this year)	
Dividends for the year	(50,000)
Ending balance	$100,000

Stock Dividends

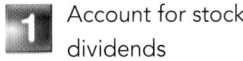

Account for stock
dividends

A **stock dividend** is a distribution of a corporation's own stock to its stockholders. Unlike cash dividends, stock dividends do not give any assets to the stockholders. Stock dividends:

- Affect *only* stockholders' equity accounts (including Retained Earnings and Common Stock)
- Have *no* effect on total stockholders' equity
- Have *no* effect on assets or liabilities

As Exhibit 14-1 shows, a stock dividend decreases Retained Earnings and increases Common Stock. A stock dividend is a transfer from Retained Earnings to Common Stock. Total equity is unchanged.

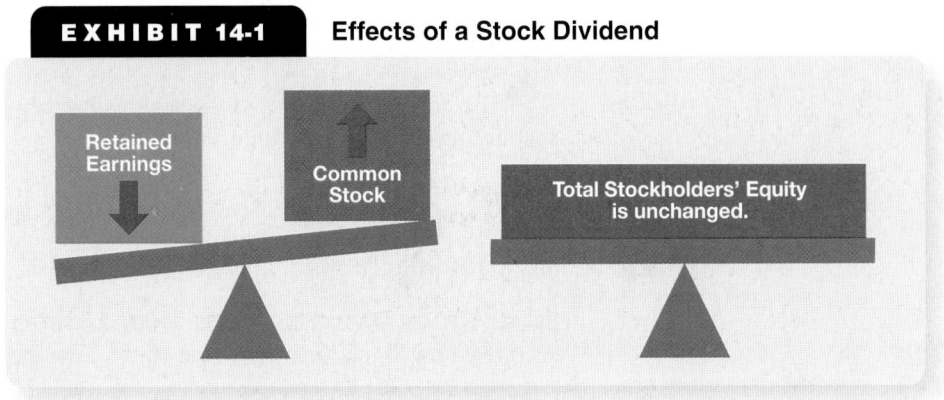

EXHIBIT 14-1 Effects of a Stock Dividend

The corporation distributes stock dividends to stockholders in proportion to the number of shares they already own. Suppose you own 300 shares of IHOP common stock. If IHOP distributes a 10% stock dividend, you would receive 30 (300 × 0.10) additional shares. You would now own 330 shares of the stock. All other IHOP stockholders also receive additional shares equal to 10% of their holdings, so you are all in the same relative position after the dividend as before.

Why Issue Stock Dividends?

A company issues stock dividends for several reasons:

1. **To continue dividends but conserve cash.** A company may wish to continue dividends but need to keep its cash.

2. **To reduce the market price of its stock.** A stock dividend may cause the company's stock price to fall because of the increased supply of the stock. A share of IHOP stock has traded at $50 recently. Doubling the shares outstanding by issuing a stock dividend would drop IHOP's stock price to $25 per share. The objective is to make the stock less expensive and, thus, more attractive to investors.

Recording Stock Dividends

As with a cash dividend, there are three dates for a stock dividend:

- Declaration date
- Record date
- Distribution (payment) date

The board of directors announces the stock dividend on the declaration date. The date of record and the distribution date then follow.

The declaration of a stock dividend does *not* create a liability because the corporation is not obligated to pay assets. (Recall that a liability is a claim on *assets*.) With a stock dividend, the corporation has declared its intention to distribute its stock. Assume that IHOP has the following stockholders' equity prior to a stock dividend:

IHOP CORP. STOCKHOLDERS' EQUITY (ADAPTED, IN THOUSANDS)	
Paid-in capital:	
Common stock, $1 par, 1,000 shares authorized, 200 shares issued ..	$ 200
Paid-in capital in excess of par	31,800
Total paid-in capital	32,000
Retained earnings...	308,000
Total stockholders' equity	$340,000

The entry to record a stock dividend depends on its size. Generally accepted accounting principles distinguish between

- A *small* stock dividend (less than 20% to 25% of issued stock)
- A *large* stock dividend (25% or more of issued stock)

Stock dividends between 20% and 25% are rare.

SMALL STOCK DIVIDENDS—LESS THAN 20% TO 25%   Small stock dividends are accounted for at their market value. Here's how the various accounts are affected:

- Retained Earnings is debited for the market value of the dividend shares.
- Common Stock is credited for the dividend stock's par value.
- Paid-In Capital in Excess of Par is credited for the remainder.

Assume IHOP distributes a stock dividend when the market value of IHOP common stock is $50 per share. Exhibit 14-2 illustrates the accounting for a 10% stock dividend.[1]

EXHIBIT 14-2   **Accounting for a Stock Dividend**

Small Stock Dividend—For Example, 10% (Amounts in thousands)		
Retained Earnings		
(200 × 0.10 × $50 market value)	1,000	
Common Stock		
(200 × 0.10 × $1 par)		20
Paid-In Capital in Excess of Par		980

A stock dividend does not affect assets, liabilities, or *total* stockholders' equity. A stock dividend merely rearranges the equity accounts, leaving total equity unchanged. Exhibit 14-3 shows IHOP's stockholders' equity after the stock dividend.

---

[1]A stock dividend can be recorded with two journal entries—for (1) the declaration and (2) the stock distribution. But most companies record stock dividends with a single entry on the date of distribution, as we illustrate here.

EXHIBIT 14-3	Stockholders' Equity after a Stock Dividend— IHOP Corporation

IHOP Corporation Stockholders' Equity (Adapted, in Thousands)	
Paid-in capital:	
Common stock, $1 par, 1,000 shares authorized,	
220 shares issued ($200 + $20)	$ 220
Paid-in capital in excess of par ($31,800 + $980)	32,780
Total paid-in capital	33,000
Retained earnings ($308,000 – $1,000)	307,000
Total stockholders' equity	$340,000

Observe that total stockholders equity stays at $340,000.

LARGE STOCK DIVIDENDS—25% OR MORE Large stock dividends are rare, so we do not illustrate them. Instead of large stock dividends, companies split their stock, as we illustrate next.

Stock Splits

A **stock split** is fundamentally different from a stock dividend. A stock split increases the number of authorized, issued, and outstanding shares of stock. A stock split also decreases par value per share. For example, if IHOP splits its stock 2 for 1, the number of outstanding shares is doubled and par value per share is cut in half. A stock split also decreases the market price of the stock.

The market price of a share of IHOP common stock has been approximately $50. Assume that IHOP wishes to decrease the market price to approximately $25. IHOP can split its stock 2 for 1, and market price will drop to around $25. A 2-for-1 stock split means that IHOP will have twice as many shares of stock outstanding after the split as before, and each share's par value is cut in half. Assume that IHOP had issued 200,000 shares of $1 par common stock before the split. Exhibit 14-4 shows how a 2-for-1 split affects IHOP's equity.

EXHIBIT 14-4	A 2-for-1 Stock Split

IHOP Stockholders' Equity (Adapted, in Thousands)					
Before 2-for-1 Stock Split			After 2-for-1 Stock Split		
Paid-in capital:			Paid-in capital:		
Common stock, $1.00 par,			Common stock, $0.50 par,		
1,000 shares authorized,			2,000 shares authorized,		
200 shares issued	$ 200		400 shares issued	$ 200	
Paid-in capital in excess			Paid-in capital in excess		
of par	31,800		of par	31,800	
Total paid-in capital	32,000		Total paid-in capital	32,000	
Retained earnings	308,000		Retained earnings	308,000	
Total stockholders' equity	$340,000		Total stockholders' equity	$340,000	

Study the exhibit and you'll see that a 2-for-1 stock split:

- Cuts par value per share in half
- Doubles the shares of stock authorized and issued
- Leaves all account balances and total equity unchanged

Because the stock split affects no account balances, no formal journal entry is needed. Instead, the split is recorded in a *memorandum entry* such as the following:

Aug. 19	Split the common stock 2 for 1. Called in the $1.00 par common stock and distributed two shares of $0.50 par common stock for each old share. Now 400 shares are outstanding.

Stock Dividends and Stock Splits Compared

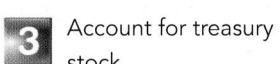 Distinguish stock splits from stock dividends

Stock dividends and stock splits have some similarities and differences. Exhibit 14-5 summarizes their effects on stockholders' equity. For completeness, it also covers cash dividends.

EXHIBIT 14-5 **Effects of Dividends and Stock Splits**

Event	Common Stock	Paid-In Capital in Excess of Par	Retained Earnings	Total Stockholders' Equity
Cash dividend	No effect	No effect	Decrease	Decrease
Stock dividend	Increase	Increase	Decrease	No effect
Stock split	No effect	No effect	No effect	No effect

Treasury Stock

Account for treasury stock

A company's own stock that it has issued and later reacquired is called **treasury stock**.[2] In effect, the corporation holds the stock in its treasury. A corporation such as IHOP may purchase treasury stock for several reasons:

1. Management wants to increase net assets by buying low and selling high.

2. Management wants to support the company's stock price.

3. Management wants to avoid a takeover by an outside party.

Treasury stock transactions are common among corporations. A recent survey of 600 companies showed that 66% held treasury stock. Now let's see how to account for treasury stock.

Purchase of Treasury Stock

Jupiter Cable Company had the following stockholders' equity before purchasing treasury stock:

---

[2]We illustrate the *cost* method of accounting for treasury stock because it is used most widely. Intermediate accounting courses also cover an alternative method.

JUPITER CABLE COMPANY Stockholders' Equity [*Before* Purchase of Treasury Stock]	
Paid-in capital:	
Common stock, $1 par, 10,000 shares authorized and issued	$10,000
Paid-in capital in excess of par	12,000
Total paid-in capital	22,000
Retained earnings	23,000
Total stockholders' equity	$45,000

On March 31, Jupiter purchased 1,000 shares of treasury stock, paying $5 per share. Debit Treasury Stock and credit Cash as follows:

Mar. 31	Treasury Stock (1,000 × $5)	5,000	
	Cash		5,000
	Purchased treasury stock.		

Treasury Stock

5,000	

Treasury Stock Basics

Here are the basics of accounting for treasury stock:

- The Treasury Stock account has a debit balance, which is the opposite of the other equity accounts. Therefore, *Treasury Stock* is *contra equity*.
- Treasury stock is recorded at cost, without reference to par value.
- The Treasury Stock account is reported beneath Retained Earnings on the balance sheet, subtracted as follows:

JUPITER CABLE COMPANY Stockholders' Equity [*After* Purchase of Treasury Stock]	
Paid-in capital:	
Common stock, $1 par, 10,000 shares authorized and issued	$10,000
Paid-in capital in excess of par	12,000
Total paid-in capital	22,000
Retained earnings	23,000
Subtotal	45,000
Less: Treasury stock, 1,000 shares at cost	(5,000)
Total stockholders' equity	$40,000

Treasury stock decreases the company's stock that's outstanding, that is, held by the stockholders. We compute outstanding stock as follows:

$$\frac{\text{Outstanding}}{\text{stock}} = \frac{\text{Issued}}{\text{stock}} - \frac{\text{Treasury}}{\text{stock}}$$

Outstanding shares are important because only outstanding shares have voting rights and receive cash dividends. Treasury stock doesn't carry a vote, and it gets no dividends.

Sale of Treasury Stock

Companies buy their treasury stock with a view toward reselling it. A company may sell treasury stock at its cost, above cost, or below cost.

Sale at Cost

If treasury stock is sold for cost—the same price the corporation paid for it—then debit Cash and credit Treasury Stock for the same amount.

Sale Above Cost

If treasury stock is sold for more than cost, the difference is credited to a new account, Paid-In Capital from Treasury Stock Transactions. This excess is additional paid-in capital because it came from the company's stockholders. It has no effect on net income. Suppose Jupiter Cable Company resold its treasury shares for $9 per share (cost was $5). The entry to sell treasury stock for a price above cost is:

Dec. 7	Cash (1,000 × $9)	9,000	
	Treasury Stock (1,000 × $5 cost)		5,000
	Paid-In Capital from Treasury Stock Transactions		4,000
	Sold treasury stock.		

Treasury Stock	
5,000	5,000
0	

Paid-In Capital from Treasury Stock Transactions is reported with the other paid-in capital accounts on the balance sheet, beneath Common Stock and Paid-In Capital in Excess of Par, as shown here:

JUPITER CABLE COMPANY Stockholders' Equity [*After* Purchase and Sale of Treasury Stock]	
Paid-in capital:	
Common stock, $1 par, 10,000 shares authorized and issued	$10,000
Paid-in capital in excess of par	12,000
Paid-in capital from treasury stock transactions	4,000
Total paid-in capital	26,000
Retained earnings	23,000
Total stockholders' equity	$49,000

Exhibit 14-6 tracks stockholders' equity to show how treasury stock transactions affect corporate equity.

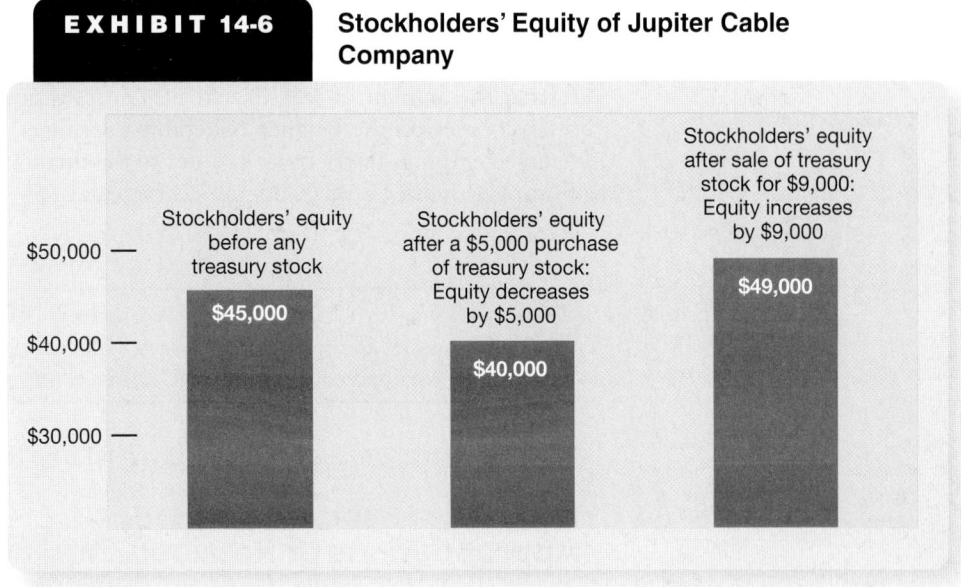

EXHIBIT 14-6 Stockholders' Equity of Jupiter Cable Company

Sale Below Cost

The resale price of treasury stock can be less than cost. The shortfall is debited first to Paid-In Capital from Treasury Stock Transactions. If this account's balance is too small, then debit Retained Earnings for the remaining amount. We illustrate this situation in Summary Problem 1 on page 701.

Other Stockholders' Equity Issues

Companies may retire their stock, restrict retained earnings, and report stockholders' equity in a variety of ways. This section covers these reporting issues.

Retirement of Stock

Not all companies purchase their stock to hold it in the treasury. A corporation may retire its stock by canceling the stock certificates. Retired stock cannot be reissued.

Retirements of preferred stock are common as companies seek to avoid paying the preferred dividends. To purchase stock for retirement, debit the stock account—for example, Preferred Stock—and credit cash. That removes the retired stock from the company's books.

Restrictions on Retained Earnings

4 Report restrictions on retained earnings

Dividends and treasury stock purchases require a cash payment. These outlays leave fewer resources to pay liabilities. A bank may agree to loan $50,000 only if Jupiter Cable Company limits its payment of dividends and its purchases of treasury stock.

Limits on Dividends and Treasury Stock Purchases

To ensure that a corporation maintains a minimum level of equity, lenders may restrict the amount of treasury stock a corporation may purchase. The restriction often focuses on the balance of retained earnings. Companies usually report their retained earnings restrictions in notes to the financial statements. The following disclosure by Jupiter Cable Company is typical:

NOTES TO THE FINANCIAL STATEMENTS
Note F—Long-Term Debt   The . . . Company's loan agreements . . . restrict cash dividends and treasury stock purchases. Under the most restrictive of these provisions, retained earnings of $18,000 were unrestricted at December 31, 2006.

With this restriction, the maximum dividend that Jupiter can pay is $18,000.

Appropriations of Retained Earnings

Appropriations are Retained Earnings restrictions recorded by formal journal entries. A corporation may *appropriate*—that is, segregate in a separate account—a portion of Retained Earnings for a specific use. For example, the board of directors may appropriate part of Retained Earnings for expansion. Appropriated Retained Earnings can be reported as shown near the bottom of Exhibit 14-7.

Variations in Reporting Stockholders' Equity

Companies can report their stockholders' equity in ways that differ from our examples. They assume that investors understand the details. One of the most important skills you will learn in this course is how to read the financial statements of real companies. In Exhibit 14-7, we present a side-by-side comparison of our teaching format and the format you are likely to encounter. Note the following points in the real-world format:

1. The heading Paid-In Capital does not appear. It is commonly understood that Preferred Stock, Common Stock, and Additional Paid-In Capital are elements of paid-in capital.

2. For presentation in the financial statements, all additional paid-in capital accounts are combined and reported as a single amount labeled Additional Paid-In Capital. Additional Paid-In Capital belongs to the common stockholders; therefore, it follows Common Stock in the real-world format.

Retained earnings appropriations are rare. Most companies report retained earnings restrictions in the notes to the financial statements, as shown for Jupiter Cable Company and in the real-world format of Exhibit 14-7.

EXHIBIT 14-7   Formats for Reporting Stockholders' Equity

Teaching Format		Real-World Format	
Stockholders' equity		Stockholders' equity	
Paid-in capital:			
Preferred stock, 8%, $10 par,		Preferred stock, 8%, $10 par,	
30,000 shares authorized and issued	$ 300,000	30,0000 shares authorized and issued	$ 300,000
Common stock, $1 par,		Common stock, $1 par,	
100,000 shares authorized,		100,000 shares authorized, 60,000 shares issued	60,000
60,000 shares issued	60,000	Additional paid-in capital	2,170,000
Paid-in capital in excess of par—common	2,150,000	Retained earnings (Note 7)	1,500,000
Paid-in capital from treasury stock transactions	20,000	Less: Treasury stock, common	
Total paid-in capital	2,530,000	(1,000 shares at cost)	(30,000)
Retained earnings appropriated		Total stockholders' equity	$4,000,000
for contingencies	500,000		
Retained earnings—unappropriated	1,000,000	Note 7—*Restriction on retained earnings.*	
Total retained earnings	1,500,000	At December 31, 2009, $500,000 of retained	
Subtotal	4,030,000	earnings is restricted for contingencies.	
Less: Treasury stock, common		Accordingly, dividends are limited to a	
(1,000 shares at cost)	(30,000)	maximum of $1,000,000.	
Total stockholders' equity	$4,000,000		

Review the first half of the chapter by studying the Decision Guidelines.

Decision Guidelines

ACCOUNTING FOR RETAINED EARNINGS, DIVIDENDS, AND TREASURY STOCK

Retained earnings, dividends, and treasury stock can affect a corporation's equity. The Decision Guidelines will help you understand their effects.

Decision

How to record:

• Distribution of a small stock dividend (20% to 25%)?

• Stock split?

What are the effects of stock dividends and stock splits on:

• Number of shares issued?
• Shares outstanding?
• Par value per share?
• Total assets, total liabilities, and total equity?
• Common Stock?
• Retained Earnings?

How to record:

1. Purchase of treasury stock?
   Sale of treasury stock?
2. At cost? (Amount received = Cost)

3. Above cost?

4. Below cost?

What are the effects of the purchase and sale of treasury stock on:

• Total assets?

• Total stockholders' equity?

Guidelines

Retained Earnings..............	Market value	
Common Stock............		Par value
Paid-In Capital		
in Excess of Par........		Excess

Memorandum only: Split the common stock 2-for-1. Called in the outstanding $10 par common stock and distributed two shares of $5 par for each old share outstanding (amounts assumed).

Effects of Stock

Dividend	Split
Increase	Increase
Increase	Increase
No effect	Decrease
No effect	No effect
Increase	No effect
Decrease	No effect

1. Treasury Stock	Cost	
Cash		Cost
2. Cash	Amt.received	
Treasury Stock		Cost
3. Cash	Amt.received	
Treasury Stock		Cost
Paid-In Capital from		
Treasury Stock		
Transactions...................		Excess
4. Cash	Amt. received	
Paid-In Capital from Treasury		
Stock Transactions	Amt. up to prior bal.	
Retained Earnings..............	Excess	
Treasury Stock		Cost

Effects of

Purchase	Sale
Decrease total assets by full amount of payment	Increase total assets by full amount of cash receipt
Decrease total equity by full amount of payment	Increase total equity by full amount of cash receipt

Summary Problem 1

Simplicity Graphics, creator of magazine designs, reported shareholders' equity:

Shareholders' Equity	
Preferred stock, $10.00 par value	
Authorized—10,000 shares; Issued—None	$ —
Common Stock, $1 par value...	
Authorized 30,000 shares; Issued 15,000 shares	15,000
Capital in excess of par value..	45,000
Retained earnings	90,000
	150,000
Less: Treasury stock, at cost (2,000 common shares)	(16,000)
	$134,000

Requirements

1. What was the average issue price per share of the common stock?

2. Journalize the issuance of 1,000 shares of common stock at $4 per share. Use Simplicity's account titles.

3. How many shares of Simplicity's common stock are outstanding?

4. How many shares of common stock would be outstanding after Simplicity split its common stock 3 for 1?

5. Using Simplicity account titles, journalize the distribution of a 10% stock dividend when the market price of Simplicity common stock is $5 per share. Simplicity distributes the common stock dividend on the shares outstanding, which were computed in requirement 3.

6. Journalize the following treasury stock transactions, which occur in the order given:
   a. Simplicity purchases 500 shares of treasury stock at $8 per share.
   b. Simplicity sells 100 shares of treasury stock for $9 per share.
   c. Simplicity sells 200 shares of treasury stocks for $6 per share.

Solution

1.	Average issue price of common stock was $4 per share [(15,000 + $45,000)/15,000 shares = $4]		
2.	Cash (1,000 × $4)	4,000	
	Common Stock (1,000 × $1)		1,000
	Capital in Excess of Par Value		3,000
	Issued common stock.		
3.	Shares outstanding = 13,000 (15,000 shares issued minus 2,000 shares of treasury stock).		
4.	Shares outstanding after a 3-for-1 stock split = 39,000 (13,000 shares outstanding × 3).		
5.	Retained Earnings (13,000 × 0.10 × $5)	6,500	
	Common Stock (13,000 × 0.10 × $1)		1,300
	Capital in Excess of Par Value		5,200
	Distributed a 10% common stock dividend.		
6.	a. Treasury Stock (500 × $8)	4,000	
	Cash		4,000
	Purchased treasury stock.		
	b. Cash (100 × $9)	900	
	Treasury Stock (100 × $8)		800
	Paid-in Capital from Treasury Stock Transactions		100
	Sold treasury stock.		
	c. Cash (200 × $6)	1,200	
	Paid-in Capital from Treasury Stock Transactions (from entry *b.*)	100	
	Retained Earnings	300	
	Treasury Stock (200 × $8)		1,600
	Sold treasury stock.		

The Corporate Income Statement

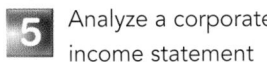

Analyze a corporate income statement

As we have seen, the stockholders' equity of a corporation is more complex than the capital of a proprietorship or a partnership. Also, a corporation's income statement includes some twists and turns that don't often apply to a smaller business. Most of the income statements you will see belong to corporations. Why not proprietorships or partnerships? Because they are privately held, proprietorships and partnerships don't have to publish their financial statements. But public corporations do, so we turn now to the corporate income statement.

Suppose you are considering investing in the stock of IHOP, Coca-Cola, or Pier 1 Imports. You would examine these companies' income statements. Of particular interest is the amount of net income they can expect to earn year after year. To understand net income, let's examine Exhibit 14-8, the income statement of Allied Electronics Corporation, a small manufacturer of precision instruments. New items are in color for emphasis.

Continuing Operations

In Exhibit 14-8, the topmost section reports continuing operations. This part of the business should continue from period to period. Income from continuing operations, therefore, helps investors make predictions about future earnings. We may use this information to predict that Allied Electronics Corporation will earn approximately $54,000 next year.

The continuing operations of Allied Electronics include two items needing explanation:

- Allied had a gain on the sale of machinery, which is outside the company's core business of selling electronics products. This is why the gain is reported in the "other" category—separately from Allied's sales revenue, cost of goods sold, and gross profit.
- Income tax expense ($36,000) is subtracted to arrive at income from continuing operations. Allied Electronics' income tax rate is 40% ($90,000 $\times$ 0.40 = $36,000).

Special Items

After continuing operations, an income statement may include two distinctly different gains and losses:

- Discontinued operations
- Extraordinary gains and losses

Discontinued Operations

Most corporations engage in several lines of business. For example, IHOP is best known for its restaurants. But at one time IHOP owned Golden Oaks Retirement Homes, United Rent-Alls, and even a business college. Sears, Roebuck & Co. is best known for its retail stores, but Sears also has a real-estate company (Homart) and an insurance company (Allstate).

Each identifiable division of a company is called a **segment of the business**. Allstate is the insurance segment of Sears. A company may sell a segment of its business. For example, IHOP sold its retirement homes, United Rent-Alls, and its business college. These were discontinued operations for IHOP.

EXHIBIT 14-8 Income Statement in Multi-Step Format—Allied Electronics Corporation

ALLIED ELECTRONICS CORPORATION
Income Statement
Year Ended December 31, 2008

Net sales revenue	$500,000
Cost of goods sold	240,000
Gross profit	260,000
Operating expenses (detailed)	181,000
Operating income	79,000
Other gains (losses):	
Gain on sale of machinery	11,000
Income from continuing operations before income tax	90,000
Income tax expense	36,000
Income from continuing operations	54,000
Discontinued operations, income of $35,000,	
less income tax of $14,000	21,000
Income before extraordinary item	75,000
Extraordinary flood loss, $20,000,	
less income tax saving of $8,000	(12,000)
Net income	$ 63,000
Earnings per share of common stock	
(20,000 shares outstanding):	
Income from continuing operations	$2.70
Income from discontinued operations	1.05
Income before extraordinary item	3.75
Extraordinary loss	(0.60)
Net income	$3.15

Continuing Operations (bracket covering Net sales revenue through Income from continuing operations)

Special Items (bracket covering Discontinued operations through Net income)

Earnings Per Share (bracket covering Earnings per share section)

Financial analysts are always keeping tabs on companies they follow. They predict companies' net income, and most analysts don't include discontinued operations because the discontinued segments won't be around in the future. The income statement reports information on the segments that have been sold under the heading Discontinued operations. Income from discontinued operations ($35,000) is taxed at 40% and reported as shown in Exhibit 14-8. A loss on discontinued operations is reported similarly, but with a subtraction for the income tax *savings* on the loss.

Gains and losses on the sale of plant assets are *not* reported as discontinued operations. Gains and losses on the sale of plant assets are reported as "Other gains (losses)" up among continuing operations because companies dispose of old plant and equipment all the time.

Extraordinary Gains and Losses (Extraordinary Items)

Extraordinary gains and losses, also called **extraordinary items**, are both unusual and infrequent. Losses from natural disasters (floods, earthquakes, and tornadoes) and the taking of company assets by a foreign government (expropriation) are extraordinary items.

Extraordinary items are reported along with their income tax effect. During 2008, Allied Electronics Corporation lost $20,000 of inventory in a flood. This flood loss reduced both Allied's income and its income tax. The tax effect decreases

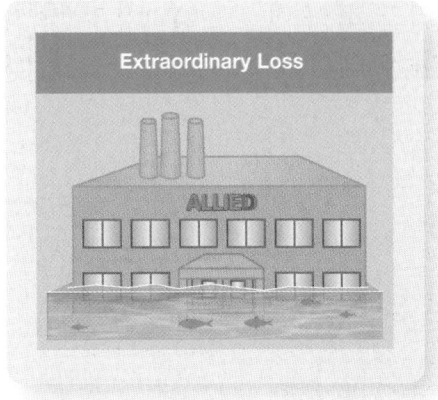

the net amount of Allied's loss the same way income tax reduces net income. An extraordinary loss can be reported along with its tax effect, as follows:

Extraordinary flood loss.....................................	$(20,000)
Less: Income tax saving.....................................	8,000
Extraordinary flood loss, net of tax....................	$(12,000)

Trace this item to the income statement in Exhibit 14-8. An extraordinary gain is reported the same as a loss, net of the income tax.

The following items do *not* qualify as extraordinary:

- Gains and losses on the sale of plant assets
- Losses due to lawsuits
- Losses due to employee labor strikes

These gains and losses fall outside the business's central operations, so they are reported on the income statement as other gains and losses. Examples include the gain on sale of machinery reported up in the Other gains (losses) section of Exhibit 14-8. The two graphics on this page illustrate an extraordinary loss and an "other" gain (loss).

Earnings per Share

The final segment of a corporate income statement reports the company's earnings per share, abbreviated as EPS. EPS is the most widely used of all business statistics.

Earnings per share (EPS) reports the amount of net income for each share of the company's *outstanding common stock*. Recall that:

$$\frac{\text{Outstanding}}{\text{stock}} = \frac{\text{Issued}}{\text{stock}} - \frac{\text{Treasury}}{\text{stock}}$$

For example, Allied Electronics has issued 25,000 shares of its common stock and holds 5,000 shares as treasury stock. Allied, therefore, has 20,000 shares of common stock outstanding, and so we use 20,000 shares to compute EPS.

EPS is a key measure of success in business. EPS is computed as follows:

$$\text{Earnings per share} = \frac{\text{Net income} - \text{Preferred dividends}}{\text{Average number of common shares outstanding}}$$

Corporations report a separate EPS figure for each element of income. Allied Electronics Corporation's EPS calculations follow.

Earnings per share of common stock	
(20,000 shares outstanding):	
Income from continuing operations ($54,000/20,000)	$2.70
Income from discontinued operations ($21,000/20,000)	1.05
Income before extraordinary item ($75,000/20,000)	3.75
Extraordinary loss ($12,000/20,000)	(0.60)
Net income ($63,000/20,000)	$3.15

The final section of Exhibit 14-8 reports the EPS figures for Allied Electronics.

Effect of Preferred Dividends on Earnings per Share

Preferred dividends also affect EPS. Recall that EPS is earnings per share of *common* stock. Recall also that dividends on preferred stock are paid first. Therefore, preferred dividends must be subtracted from income to compute EPS.

Suppose Allied Electronics had 10,000 shares of preferred stock outstanding, each share paying a $1.00 dividend. The annual preferred dividend would be $10,000 (10,000 × $1.00). The $10,000 is subtracted from each of the income subtotals (lines 1, 3, and 5), resulting in the following EPS computations for Allied:

	Earnings per share of common stock (20,000 shares outstanding):	
1	Income from continuing operations ($54,000 − $10,000)/20,000	$2.20
2	Income from discontinued operations ($21,000/20,000)	1.05
3	Income before extraordinary item ($75,000 − $10,000)/20,000	3.25
4	Extraordinary loss ($12,000/20,000)..	(0.60)
5	Net income ($63,000 − $10,000)/20,000	$2.65

Basic and Diluted Earnings per Share

Some corporations must report two sets of EPS figures, as follows:

- EPS based on outstanding common shares (*basic* EPS).
- EPS based on outstanding common plus the additional shares of common stock that would arise from conversion of the preferred stock into common (*diluted* EPS). Diluted EPS is always lower than basic EPS.

Statement of Retained Earnings

The statement of retained earnings reports how the company moved from its beginning balance of retained earnings to its ending balance during the period. This statement is not altogether new; it's essentially the same as the statement of owner's equity for a proprietorship—but adapted to a corporation.

Exhibit 14-9 shows the statement of retained earnings of Allied Electronics for 2008. Notice that corporate dividends take the place of withdrawals in a proprietorship. Allied's net income comes from the income statement in Exhibit 14-8, page 704. All other data are assumed.

EXHIBIT 14-9 Statement of Retained Earnings— Allied Electronics Corporation

ALLIED ELECTRONICS CORPORATION
Statement of Retained Earnings
Year Ended December 31, 2008

Retained earnings, December 31, 2007	$130,000
Add: Net income for 2008	63,000
	193,000
Less: Dividends for 2008	(53,000)
Retained earnings, December 31, 2008	$140,000

Combined Statement of Income and Retained Earnings

Companies can report income and retained earnings on a single statement. Exhibit 14-10 illustrates how Allied Electronics would combine its income statement and its statement of retained earnings.

EXHIBIT 14-10 Combined Statement of Income and Retained Earnings— Allied Electronics Corporation

ALLIED ELECTRONICS CORPORATION
Combined Statement of Income and Retained Earnings
Year Ended December 31, 2008

Income Statement	Sales revenue	$500,000
	Cost of goods sold	240,000
	Gross profit	260,000
	Expenses (listed individually)	197,000
Statement of retained earnings	Net income for 2008	$ 63,000
	Retained earnings, December 31, 2007	130,000
		193,000
	Dividends for 2008	(53,000)
	Retained earnings, December 31, 2008	$140,000

Prior-Period Adjustments

A company may make an accounting error. After the books are closed, Retained Earnings holds the error, and its balance is wrong until corrected. Corrections to Retained Earnings for errors of an earlier period are called **prior-period adjustments**. The prior-period adjustment either increases or decreases the beginning balance of Retained Earnings and appears on that statement.

In recent years there have been more prior-period adjustments than in the 20 previous years combined. Many companies have restated their net income to correct accounting errors. To illustrate, assume De Graff Corporation recorded $30,000 of income tax expense for 2007. The correct amount of income tax was $40,000. This error:

- Understated income tax expense by $10,000
- Overstated net income by $10,000

In 2008 De Graff paid the extra $10,000 in taxes for the prior year. De Graff's prior-period adjustment will decrease retained earnings as follows (all amounts are assumed).

DE GRAFF CORPORATION Statement of Retained Earnings Year Ended December 31, 2008	
Retained earnings, December 31, 2007, as originally reported	$390,000
Prior-period adjustment—To correct error in 2007	(10,000)
Retained earnings, December 31, 2007, as adjusted	380,000
Net income for 2008	100,000
	480,000
Dividends for 2008	(40,000)
Retained earnings, December 31, 2008	$440,000

Reporting Comprehensive Income

As we've seen, all companies report net income or net loss on the income statement. There is another income figure. **Comprehensive income** is the company's change in total stockholders' equity from all sources other than from its owners. Comprehensive income includes net income plus some specific gains and losses, as follows:

- Unrealized gains or losses on certain investments
- Foreign-currency translation adjustments

These items do not enter into the determination of net income but instead are reported as other comprehensive income, as shown in Exhibit 14-11. Assumed figures are used for all items.

Earnings per share apply only to net income and its components, as discussed earlier. Earnings per share are *not* reported for other comprehensive income.

EXHIBIT 14-11   Reporting Comprehensive Income

NATIONAL EXPRESS COMPANY
Income Statement
Year Ended December 31, 2009

Revenues	$10,000
Expenses (summarized)	6,000
Net income	4,000
Other comprehensive income:	
Unrealized gain on investments	1,000
Comprehensive income	$ 5,000

Decision Guidelines

Three years out of college, you've saved $5,000 and are ready to start investing. Where do you start? You might begin by analyzing the income statements of IHOP, Coca-Cola, and Pier 1 Imports. These Decision Guidelines will help you analyze a corporate income statement.

Decision	Guidelines
What are the main sections of the income statement? See Exhibit 14-8 for an example.	**Continuing operations** { • Continuing operations, including other gains and losses and less income tax expense
	Special items { • Discontinued operations— gain or loss—less the income tax effect • Extraordinary gain or loss, less the income tax effect • Net income (or net loss) • Other comprehensive income (Exhibit 14-11)
What earnings-per-share (EPS) figures must a corporation report?	**Earnings per share** { • Earnings per share—applies only to net income (or net loss), not to other comprehensive income Separate EPS figures for: • Income from continuing operations • Discontinued operations • Income before extraordinary item • Extraordinary gain or loss • Net income (or net loss)
How to compute EPS for net income?	$$EPS = \frac{\text{Net income} - \text{Preferred dividends}}{\text{Average number of common shares outstanding}}$$

Summary Problem 2

The following information was taken from the ledger of Calenergy Corporation at December 31, 2008.

Common stock, no-par,		Discontinued operations,	
45,000 shares issued	$180,000	income	$20,000
Sales revenue	620,000	Prior-period adjustment—	
Extraordinary gain	26,000	credit to Retained Earnings	5,000
Loss due to lawsuit	11,000	Gain on sale of plant assets	21,000
General expenses	62,000	Income tax expense (saving):	
Preferred stock 8%	50,000	Continuing operations	32,000
Selling expenses	108,000	Discontinued operations	8,000
Retained earnings, beginning,		Extraordinary gain	10,000
as originally reported	103,000	Treasury stock, common	
Dividends	14,000	(5,000 shares)	25,000
Cost of goods sold	380,000		

Requirements

Prepare a single-step income statement and a statement of retained earnings for Calenergy Corporation for the year ended December 31, 2008. Include the EPS presentation and show your computations. Calenergy had no changes in its stock accounts during the year.

Solution

CALENERGY CORPORATION Income Statement Year Ended December 31, 2008		
Revenue and gains:		
Sales revenue		$620,000
Gain on sale of plant assets		21,000
Total revenues and gains		641,000
Expenses and losses:		
Cost of goods sold	$380,000	
Selling expenses	108,000	
General expenses	62,000	
Loss due to lawsuit	11,000	
Income tax expense	32,000	
Total expenses and losses		593,000
Income from continuing operations		48,000
Discontinued operations, income of $20,000,		
less income tax of $8,000		12,000
Income before extraordinary item		60,000
Extraordinary gain, $26,000, less income tax, $10,000		16,000
Net income		$ 76,000
Earnings per share:		
Income from continuing operations		
[($48,000 – $4,000) / 40,000 shares]		$1.10
Income from discontinued operations		
($12,000 / $40,000 shares)		0.30
Income before extraordinary item		
[($60,000 – $4,000) / 40,000 shares]		1.40
Extraordinary gain ($16,000 / 40,000 shares)		0.40
Net income [($76,000 – $4,000) / 40,000 shares]		$1.80

Computations:

$$\text{EPS} = \frac{\text{Income} - \text{Preferred dividends}}{\text{Common shares outstanding}}$$

Preferred dividends: $50,000 \times 0.08 = \$4,000$

Common shares outstanding:
   45,000 shares issued − 5,000 treasury shares = 40,000 shares outstanding

CALENERGY CORPORATION Statement of Retained Earnings Year Ended December 31, 2008	
Retained earnings balance, beginning, as originally reported	$103,000
Prior-period adjustment—credit	5,000
Retained earnings balance, beginning, as adjusted	108,000
Net income	76,000
	184,000
Dividends	(14,000)
Retained earnings balance, ending	$170,000

Review
Retained Earnings, Treasury Stock, and the Income Statement

Accounting Vocabulary

Appropriation of Retained Earnings
Restriction of retained earnings that is recorded by a formal journal entry.

Comprehensive Income
Company's change in total stockholders' equity from all sources other than from the owners.

Earnings per Share (EPS)
Amount of a company's net income for each share of its outstanding stock.

Extraordinary Gains and Losses
A gain or loss that is both unusual for the company and infrequent. Also called **extraordinary items**.

Extraordinary Item
A gain or loss that is both unusual for the company and infrequent. Also called **extraordinary gains and losses**.

Prior-Period Adjustment
A correction to retained earnings for an error of an earlier period.

Segment of the Business
One of various separate divisions of a company.

Stock Dividend
A distribution by a corporation of its own to stockholders.

Stock Split
An increase in the number of outstanding shares of stock coupled with a proportionate reduction in the value of the stock.

Treasury Stock
A corporation's own stock that it has issued and later reacquired.

Quick Check

1. A company's own stock that it has issued and repurchased is called
   a. Issued stock
   b. Outstanding stock
   c. Treasury stock
   d. Dividend stock

2. A stock dividend
   a. Decreases Common Stock
   b. Increases Retained Earnings
   c. Has no effect on total equity
   d. All of the above

3. In a small stock dividend,
   a. Common stock is debited for the par value of the shares issued.
   b. Retained Earnings is debited for the market value of the shares issued.
   c. Paid-In Capital in Excess of Par is debited for the difference between the debits to Retained Earnings and to Common Stock.
   d. Net income is always decreased.

4. Stock splits
   a. Decrease par value per share
   b. Increase the number of shares of stock issued
   c. Both a and b
   d. None of the above

5. Assume that IHOP paid $10 per share to purchase 1,000 of its $1 par common as treasury stock. The purchase of treasury stock
   a. Decreased total equity by $10,000
   b. Increased total equity by $1,000
   c. Decreased total equity by $1,000
   d. Increased total equity by $10,000

6. Assume that IHOP sold all 1,000 shares of its treasury stock for $15 per share. The sale of treasury stock
   a. Decreased total equity by $15,000
   b. Increased total equity by $5,000
   c. Decreased total equity by $5,000
   d. Increased total equity by $15,000

7. Allied Electronics in Exhibit 14-8, page 704, is most likely to earn net income of $x next year. How much is $x?
   a. $90,000
   b. $79,000
   c. $75,000
   d. $54,000

8. Which of the following events would be an extraordinary loss?
   a. Loss due to an earthquake
   b. Loss on the sale of equipment
   c. Loss on discontinued operations
   d. All of the above are extraordinary items

9. What is the most widely followed statistic in business?
   a. Gross profit
   b. Earnings per share
   c. Retained earnings
   d. Dividends

10. Earnings per share is *not* computed for
    a. Net income
    b. Comprehensive income
    c. Discontinued operations
    d. Extraordinary items

Answers are given after Apply Your Knowledge (p. 731).

Assess Your Progress

Short Exercises

Recording a small stock dividend

1

S14-1 Crestview Pool Supply has 10,000 shares of $1 par common stock outstanding. Crestview distributes a 10% stock dividend when the market value of its stock is $15 per share.

1. Journalize Crestview's distribution of the stock dividend on September 30. An explanation is not required. (pp. 692–693)
2. What is the overall effect of the stock dividend on Crestview's total assets? On total stockholders' equity? (pp. 692–693)

Comparing and contrasting cash dividends and stock dividends

1

S14-2 Compare and contrast the accounting for cash dividends and stock dividends. In the space provided, insert either "Cash dividends," "Stock dividends," or "Both cash dividends and stock dividends" to complete each of the following statements:

1. _____ decrease Retained Earnings. (p. 694)
2. _____ have no effect on a liability. (pp. 692–693)
3. _____ increase paid-in capital by the same amount that they decrease Retained Earnings. (p. 694)
4. _____ decrease both total assets and total stockholders' equity, resulting in a decrease in the size of the company. (p. 694)

Accounting for a stock split

2

S14-3 Pier 1 Imports recently reported the following stockholders' equity (adapted and in millions except par value per share):

Paid-in capital:	
Common stock, $1 par,	
500 shares authorized	
101 shares issued.............................	$101
Paid-in capital in excess of par.............	142
Total paid-in capital............................	243
Retained earnings.....................................	656
Other equity..	(235)
Total stockholders' equity........................	$664

Suppose Pier 1 split its common stock 2 for 1 in order to decrease the market price of its stock. The company's stock was trading at $20 immediately before the split.

1. Prepare the stockholders' equity section of Pier 1 Imports' balance sheet after the stock split. (p. 694)
2. Which account balances changed after the stock split? Which account balances were unchanged? (p. 694)

Accounting for the purchase and sale of treasury stock (above cost)

3

S14-4 True Discount Furniture, Inc., completed the following treasury stock transactions:

a. Purchased 1,000 shares of the company's $1 par common stock as treasury stock, paying cash of $5 per share. (p. 696)
b. Sold 500 shares of the treasury stock for cash of $8 per share. (p. 696)

continued . . .

Journalize these transactions. Explanations are not required. Show how True Discount will report treasury stock on its December 31, 2008, balance sheet after completing the two transactions. In reporting the treasury stock, report only on the Treasury Stock account. You may ignore all other accounts. (p. 696)

Interpreting a restriction of
retained earnings

4

S14-5 MG Corporation reported the following stockholders' equity:

Paid-in capital:	
Preferred stock, $1.50, no par, 10,000 shares authorized; none issued	$ —
Common stock, $1 par, 500,000 shares authorized, 150,000 shares issued	150,000
Paid-in capital in excess of par-common..........................	350,000
Total paid-in capital	500,000
Retained earnings	400,000
Less: Treasury stock, 5,000 shares at cost	(30,000)
Total stockholders' equity	$870,000

1. MG Corporation's agreement with its bank lender restricts MG's dividend payments for the cost of treasury stock the company holds. How much in dividends can MG declare? (pp. 698–699)
2. Why would a bank lender restrict a corporation's dividend payments and treasury stock purchases? (pp. 697–698)

Preparing a corporate
income statement

5

S14-6 List the major parts of a complex corporate income statement for WRS Athletic Clubs, Inc., for the year ended December 31, 2007. Include all the major parts of the income statement, starting with net sales revenue and ending with net income (net loss). You may ignore dollar amounts and earnings per share. (p. 703)

Explaining the items on a
corporate income statement

5

S14-7 Answer these questions about a corporate income statement:
1. How do you measure gross profit? (p. 703)
2. What is the title of those items that are both unusual and infrequent?
3. Which income number is the best predictor of future net income? (pp. 701–703)
4. What's the "bottom line?" (p. 703)
5. What does *EPS* abbreviate? (p. 706)

Preparing a corporate
income statement

5

S14-8 PWC Corp. accounting records include the following items, listed in no particular order, at December 31, 2008:

Other gains (losses)	$ (20,000)	Extraordinary loss	$ (5,000)
Net sales revenue	180,000	Cost of goods sold	70,000
Gain on discontinued operations	15,000	Operating expenses	60,000
Accounts receivable	19,000		

continued . . .

Income tax of 40% applies to all items.

Prepare PWC's income statement for the year ended December 31, 2008. Omit earnings per share. (p. 703)

S14-9 Return to the PWC Corp. data in Short Exercise 14-8. PWC had 10,000 shares of common stock outstanding during 2008. PWC declared and paid preferred dividends of $4,000 during 2008.

Show how PWC reported EPS data on its 2008 income statement. (p. 706)

S14-10 Owens-Illinois, Inc. has preferred stock outstanding.

1. Give the basic equation to compute earnings per share of common stock for net income. (p. 706)

2. List all the income items for which Owens-Illinois must report EPS data. (p. 706)

S14-11 Use the PWC Corp. data in Short Exercise 14-8. In addition, PWC had unrealized gains of $4,000 on investments during 2008. Start with PWC's net income from Short Exercise 14-8 and show how the company could report other comprehensive income on its 2008 income statement.

Should PWC Corp. report earnings per share for other comprehensive income? (pp. 707–708)

S14-12 Statistical Research Service, Inc. (SRSI) ended 2008 with retained earnings of $75,000. During 2009 SRSI earned net income of $90,000 and declared dividends of $30,000. Also during 2009, SRSI got a $20,000 tax refund from the Internal Revenue Service. A tax audit revealed that SRSI paid too much income tax back in 2007.

Prepare Statistical Research Service, Inc.'s statement of retained earnings for the year ended December 31, 2009, to report the prior-period adjustment. (pp. 707–708)

Exercises

E14-13 The stockholders' equity of Lakewood Occupational Therapy, Inc., on December 31, 2009, follows.

STOCKHOLDERS' EQUITY

Paid-in capital:

Common stock, $1 par, 100,000 shares authorized, 50,000 shares issued	$ 50,000
Paid-in capital in excess of par	200,000
Total paid-in capital	250,000
Retained earnings	120,000
Total stockholders' equity	$370,000

On April 30, 2010, the market price of Lakewood's common stock was $14 per share and the company distributed a 10% stock dividend.

continued . . .

Requirements

1. Journalize the distribution of the stock dividend. (pp. 692–693)
2. Prepare the stockholders' equity section of the balance sheet after the stock dividend. (p. 693)

Journalizing cash and stock dividends

E14-14 Martial Arts Schools, Inc., is authorized to issue 500,000 shares of $1 par common stock. The company issued 80,000 shares at $4 per share. When the market price of common stock was $6 per share, Martial Arts distributed a 10% stock dividend. Later, Martial Arts declared and paid a $0.30 per share cash dividend.

Requirements

1. Journalize the distribution of the stock dividend. (pp. 692–693)
2. Journalize both the declaration and the payment of the cash dividend. (pp. 653–655)

Reporting stockholders' equity after a stock split

E14-15 Cobra Golf Club Corp. had the following stockholders' equity at December 31, 2007:

Paid-in capital:	
Common stock, $1 par, 200,000 shares authorized, 50,000 shares issued	$ 50,000
Paid-in capital in excess of par	100,000
Total paid-in capital	150,000
Retained earnings	200,000
Total stockholders' equity	$350,000

On June 30, 2008, Cobra split its common stock 2 for 1. Make the memorandum entry to record the stock split, and prepare the stockholders' equity section of the balance sheet immediately after the split. (p. 694)

Effects of stock dividends, stock splits, and treasury stock transactions

E14-16 Identify the effects of the following transactions on total stockholders' equity. Each transaction is independent.

a. A 10% stock dividend. Before the dividend, 500,000 shares of $1 par common stock were outstanding; market value was $6 at the time of the dividend. (p. 694)

b. A 2-for-1 stock split. Prior to the split, 60,000 shares of $4 par common were outstanding. (p. 694)

c. Purchase of 1,000 shares of treasury stock (par value $0.50) at $5 per share. (pp. 694–695, 697–698)

d. Sale of 600 shares of $1 par treasury stock for $5 per share. Cost of the treasury stock was $2 per share. (pp. 696, 697–698)

Journalizing treasury stock transactions

E14-17 Journalize the following transactions of Austin Driving School, Inc.:

Feb.	4	Issued 20,000 shares of 1 par common stock at $10 per share. (pp. 646–647)
Apr.	22	Purchased 1,000 shares of treasury stock at $14 per share. (pp. 694–695)
Aug.	22	Sold 600 shares of treasury stock at $20 per share. (p. 696)

Journalizing treasury stock transactions and reporting stockholders' equity

E14-18 Mid America Amusements Corporation had the following stockholders' equity on November 30:

STOCKHOLDERS' EQUITY

Common stock, $5 par, 500,000 shares authorized, 50,000 shares issued	$250,000
Paid-in capital in excess of par	150,000
Retained earnings	490,000
Total stockholders' equity	$890,000

On December 30, Mid America purchased 10,000 shares of treasury stock at $9 per share.

1. Journalize the purchase of the treasury stock, and prepare the stockholders' equity section of the balance sheet at December 31. (pp. 694–695)
2. How many shares of common stock are outstanding after the purchase of treasury stock?

Reporting a retained earnings restriction

E14-19 The agreement under which Toshiba Printers issued its long-term debt requires the restriction of $100,000 of the company's retained earnings balance. Total retained earnings is $250,000, and common stock, no-par, has a balance of $50,000.

Requirements

Report stockholders' equity on Toshiba's balance sheet, assuming the following:

a. Toshiba discloses the restriction in a note. Write the note. (pp. 698–700)
b. Toshiba appropriates retained earnings in the amount of the restriction and includes no note in its statements. Follow the Teaching Format on page 699.

Preparing a multistep income statement

E14-20 Cannon Photographic Supplies, Inc., accounting records include the following for 2008:

Income tax saving— extraordinary loss	$ 6,000	Sales revenue	$430,000
Income tax saving—loss on discontinued operations	20,000	Operating expenses (including income tax)	120,000
		Cost of goods sold	240,000
Extraordinary loss	15,000	Loss on discontinued operations	50,000

Requirement

Prepare Cannon's multistep income statement for 2008. Omit earnings per share. (p. 703)

Computing earnings per share

E14-21 Palestine Corp. earned net income of $108,000 for 2007. Palestine's books include the following figures:

Preferred stock, 6%, $50 par, 1,000 shares issued and outstanding	$ 50,000
Common stock, $10 par, 52,000 shares issued	520,000
Paid-in capital in excess of par	480,000
Treasury stock, common, 2,000 shares at cost	40,000

continued . . .

Requirement

Compute Palestine's EPS for the year. (p. 706)

Computing earnings per share

5

E14-22 Athens Academy Surplus had 50,000 shares of common stock and 10,000 shares of 5%, $10 par preferred stock outstanding through December 31, 2008. Income from continuing operations of 2008 was $110,000, and loss on discontinued operations (net of income tax saving) was $8,000. Athens also had an extraordinary gain (net of tax) of $20,000.

Requirement

Compute Athens' EPS amounts for 2008, starting with income from continuing operations. (p. 706)

Preparing a combined statement of income and retained earnings

5

E14-23 Good Times Express Company had retained earnings of $160 million at December 31, 2006. The company reported these figures for 2007:

	($ Millions)
Net income	$140
Cash dividends—preferred......................	2
common	98

Requirement

Beginning with net income, prepare a combined statement of income and retained earnings for Good Times Express Company for the year ended December 31, 2007. (pp. 706–708)

Preparing a statement of retained earnings with a prior-period adjustment

5

E14-24 Sarah Lou Bakery, Inc., reported a prior-period adjustment in 2008. An accounting error caused net income of prior years to be overstated by $5,000. Retained earnings at December 31, 2007, as previously reported, stood at $39,000. Net income for 2008 was $70,000, and dividends were $24,000.

Requirement

Prepare the company's statement of retained earnings for the year ended December 31, 2008. (pp. 706–708)

Computing comprehensive income and reporting earnings per share

5

E14-25 During 2009, Newfoundland Corp. earned income from continuing operations of $135,000. The company also sold a segment of the business (discontinued operations) at a loss of $30,000 and had an extraordinary gain of $10,000. At year-end, Newfoundland had an unrealized loss on investments of $5,000.

1. Compute Newfoundland's net income and comprehensive income for 2009. All amounts are net of income taxes. (pp. 706–708)

2. What final EPS figure should Newfoundland report for 2009? Name the item and show its amount. Newfoundland had 57,500 shares of common stock (and no preferred stock) outstanding. (pp. 706–708)

Problems (Group A)

Journalizing stockholders'
equity transactions

P14-26A Dearborn Manufacturing Co. completed the following transactions during 2009.

Jan. 16	Declared a cash dividend on the 4%, $100 par preferred stock (1,000 shares outstanding). Declared a $0.35 per share dividend on the 100,000 shares of common stock outstanding. The date of record is January 31 and the payment date is February 15. (pp. 653–655)
Feb. 15	Paid the cash dividends. (pp. 653–655)
June 10	Split common stock 2 for 1. Before the split, Dearborn had 100,000 shares of $2 par common stock outstanding. (p. 694)
July 30	Distributed a 5% stock dividend on the common stock. The market value of the common stock was $10 per share. (pp. 692–693)
Oct. 26	Purchased 2,000 shares of treasury stock at $11 per share. (pp. 694–695)
Nov. 8	Sold 1,000 shares of treasury stock for $17 per share. (p. 696)

Requirement

Record the transactions in Dearborn's general journal.

Journalizing dividend and
treasury stock transactions
and reporting stockholders'
equity

P14-27A The balance sheet of Lennox Health Foods, at December 31, 2007, reported 100,000 shares of no-par common stock authorized, with 30,000 shares issued and a Common Stock balance of $180,000. Retained Earnings had a balance of $140,000. During 2008, the company completed the following selected transactions:

Mar. 15	Purchased 5,000 shares of treasury stock at $7 per share. (pp. 694–695)
Apr. 30	Distributed a 20% stock dividend on the 25,000 shares of *outstanding* common stock. The market value of Lennox common stock was $9 per share. (pp. 692–693)
Dec. 31	Earned net income of $110,000 during the year. Closed net income to Retained Earnings. (pp. 643–644)

Requirements

1. Record the transactions in the general journal. Explanations are not required.

2. Prepare the stockholders' equity section of Lennox Health Foods' balance sheet at December 31, 2008. (pp. 693, 694–695)

Using dividends to fight off
a takeover of the
corporation

P14-28A Jennifer Vera, Inc., is the only company with a distribution network for its imported goods. The company does a brisk business with specialty stores such as Neiman Marcus, Saks Fifth Avenue, and Nordstrom. Vera's recent success has made the company a prime target for a

continued . . .

takeover. Against the wishes of Vera's board of directors, an investment group from France is attempting to buy 51% of Vera's outstanding stock. Board members are convinced that the French investors would sell off the most desirable pieces of the business and leave little of value.

At the most recent board meeting, several suggestions were advanced to fight off the hostile takeover bid. One suggestion is to increase the stock outstanding by distributing a 100% stock dividend. The intent is to spread the company's ownership in order to make it harder for the French group to buy a controlling interest.

Requirement

As a significant stockholder of Jennifer Vera, Inc., write a short memo to explain to the board whether distributing the stock dividend would make it difficult for the investor group to take over the company. Include in your memo a discussion of the effect that the stock dividend would have on assets, liabilities, and total stockholders' equity—that is, the dividend's effect on the size of the corporation. (pp. 690–691)

Journalizing dividend and treasury stock transactions; reporting retained earnings and stockholders' equity

1 **3**

P14-29A The balance sheet of Morrisey Management Consulting, Inc., at December 31, 2007, reported the following stockholders' equity:

Paid in capital:	
Common stock, $10 par, 100,000 shares authorized, 20,000 shares issued	$200,000
Paid-in capital in excess of par..	300,000
Total paid-in capital...	500,000
Retained earnings..	160,000
Total stockholders' equity	$660,000

During 2008, Morrisey completed the following selected transactions:

Feb.	6	Distributed a 10% stock dividend on the common stock. The market value of Morrisey's stock was $25 per share. (pp. 692–693)
July	29	Purchased 2,000 shares of treasury stock at $25 per share. (pp. 694–695)
Nov.	27	Declared a $0.30 per share cash dividend on the 20,000 shares of common stock outstanding. The date of record is December 17, and the payment date is January 7, 2009. (pp. 653–655)
Dec.	31	Closed the $86,000 net income to Retained Earnings. (pp. 643–644)

Requirements

1. Record the transactions in the general journal.
2. Prepare a retained earnings statement for the year ended December 31, 2008. (p. 707)
3. Prepare the stockholders' equity section of the balance sheet at December 31, 2008. (pp. 693, 694–695)

P14-30A The following information was taken from the records of Mobile Motorsports, Inc., at September 30, 2008.

General expenses	$133,000	Cost of goods sold	$435,000
Preferred stock, $2, no-par,		Retained earnings, beginning	88,000
5,000 shares issued	200,000	Selling expenses	121,000
Common stock, $10 par, 25,000		Income from discontinued	
shares authorized and issued	250,000	operations	8,000
Net sales revenue	837,000	Income tax expense:	
Treasury stock, common		Continuing operations	72,000
(1,000 shares)	11,000	Income from discontinued	
		operations	2,000

Requirement

Prepare a multistep income statement for Mobile Motorsports, Inc., for the fiscal year ended September 30, 2008. Include earnings per share. (p. 703)

Preparing a corrected
combined statement of
income and retained
earnings

P14-31A Lisa Sheraton, accountant for Chase Home Finance, was injured in a boating accident. Another employee prepared the accompanying income statement for the year ended December 31, 2008.

The individual *amounts* listed on the income statement are correct. However, some accounts are reported incorrectly, and two items don't belong on the income statement at all. Also, income tax has *not* been applied to all appropriate figures. The income tax rate on discontinued operations was 40%. Chase Home Finance issued 52,000 shares of common stock in 2006 and held 2,000 shares as treasury stock during 2008. Retained earnings at December 31, 2007 was $167,000.

CHASE HOME FINANCE
Income Statement
Year Ended December 31, 2008

Revenue and gains:		
Sales		$362,000
Paid-in capital in excess of par—common		90,000
Total revenues and gains		452,000
Expenses and losses:		
Cost of goods sold	$105,000	
Selling expenses	67,000	
General expenses	61,000	
Dividends	17,000	
Sales returns	11,000	
Sales discounts	6,000	
Income tax expense	20,000	
Total expenses and losses		287,000
Income from operations		165,000
Other gains and losses:		
Gain on discontinued operations		5,000
Net income		$170,000
Earnings per share		$ 3.40

continued . . .

Requirement

Prepare a corrected combined statement of income and retained earnings for 2008, including earnings per share. Prepare the income statement in single-step format. (pp. 269–271, 703, 706–708)

Computing earnings per share and reporting a retained earnings restriction

P14-32A The capital structure of Knightsbridge, Inc., at December 31, 2006, included 20,000 shares of $1.25 preferred stock and 40,000 shares of common stock. Common stock outstanding during 2007 totaled 40,000 shares. Income from continuing operations during 2007 was $105,000. The company discontinued a segment of the business at a gain of $20,000, and also had an extraordinary gain of $10,000. The Knightsbridge board of directors restricts $100,000 of retained earnings for contingencies.

Requirement

1. Compute Knightsbridge's earnings per share for 2007. Start with income from continuing operations. All income and loss amounts are net of income tax. (p. 706)

2. Show two ways of reporting Knightsbridge's retained earnings restriction. Retained earnings at December 31, 2006, was $100,000, and the company declared preferred dividends of $25,000 during 2007. (pp. 698–700)

Problems (Group B)

Journalizing stockholders' equity transactions

1 2 3

P14-33B Maxfli Hot Air Balloons, Inc., completed the following selected transactions during 2009:

Feb.	9	Declared a cash dividend on the 10,000 shares of $1.50, no-par preferred stock. Declared a $0.20 per share dividend on the 10,000 shares of common stock outstanding. The date of record is February 16, and the payment date is February 28. (pp. 653–655)
Feb.	28	Paid the cash dividends. (pp. 653–655)
Mar.	21	Split common stock 2 for 1. Before the split, Maxfli had 10,000 shares of $10 par common stock outstanding. (p. 694)
Apr.	18	Distributed a 10% stock dividend on the common stock. The market value of the common stock was $27 per share. (pp. 692–693)
June	18	Purchased 2,000 shares of treasury stock at $25 per share. (pp. 694–695)
Dec.	22	Sold 1,000 shares of treasury stock for $28 per share. (p. 696)

Requirement

Record the transactions in the general journal.

Journalizing dividend and
treasury stock transactions
and reporting stockholders'
equity

P14-34B The balance sheet of Banc One Corp. at December 31, 2007, reported 500,000 shares of $1 par common stock authorized with 100,000 shares issued. Paid-In Capital in Excess of Par had a balance of $300,000. Retained Earnings had a balance of $101,000. During 2008 the company completed the following selected transactions:

Jan. 12	Purchased 10,000 shares of the treasury stock at $4 per share. (pp. 694–695)
Sep. 28	Distributed a 10% stock dividend on the 90,000 shares of *outstanding* common stock. The market value of Banc One's common stock was $5 per share. (pp. 692–693)
Dec. 31	Earned net income of $73,000 during the year. Closed net income to Retained Earnings. (pp. 643–644)

Requirements

1. Record the transactions in the general journal. Explanations are not required.
2. Prepare the stockholders' equity section of the balance sheet at December 31, 2008. (pp. 693, 694–695)

Purchasing treasury stock to
fight off a takeover of the
corporation

P14-35B Guatemalan Imports is the only company with reliable sources for its imported gifts. The company does a brisk business with specialty stores such as Pier 1 Imports. Guatemalan Imports' recent success has made the company a prime target for a takeover. An investment group from Mexico City is attempting to buy 51% of Guatemalan Imports' outstanding stock against the wishes of the company's board of directors. Board members are convinced that the Mexico City investors would sell the most desirable pieces of the business and leave little of value.

At the most recent board meeting, several suggestions were advanced to fight off the hostile takeover bid. The suggestion with the most promise is to purchase a huge quantity of treasury stock. Guatemalan Imports has the cash to carry out this plan.

Requirements

1. As a significant stockholder of Guatemalan Imports, write a memorandum to explain to the board how the purchase of treasury stock would make it difficult for the Mexico City group to take over the company. Include a discussion of the effect that purchasing treasury stock would have on stock outstanding and on the size of the corporation. (pp. 694–695)
2. Suppose Guatemalan Imports is successful in fighting off the takeover bid and later sells the treasury stock at prices greater than the purchase price. Explain what effect these sales will have on assets, stockholders' equity, and net income. (p. 696)

Journalizing dividend and
treasury stock transactions;
reporting retained earnings
and stockholders' equity

P14-36B The balance sheet of Oriental Rug Company at December 31, 2008, included the following stockholders' equity:

Paid-in capital:	
Common stock, $1 par, 250,000 shares authorized,	
50,000 shares issued	$ 50,000

continued . . .

Paid-in capital in excess of par..	350,000	
Total paid-in capital...	400,000	
Retained earnings...	100,000	
Total stockholders' equity	$500,000	

During 2009, Oriental Rug completed the following selected transactions:

Mar. 29	Distributed a 10% stock dividend on the common stock. The market value of Oriental common stock was $8 per share. (pp. 692–693)
July 13	Purchased 10,000 shares of treasury stock at $8 per share. (pp. 694–695)
Dec. 10	Declared a $0.20 per share cash dividend on the 45,000 shares of common stock outstanding. The date of record is December 17, and the payment date is January 2. (pp. 653–655)
31	Closed the $79,000 net income to Retained Earnings. (pp. 643–644)

Requirements

1. Record the transactions in the general journal.

2. Prepare the retained earnings statement for the year ended December 31, 2009. (p. 707)

3. Prepare the stockholders' equity section of the balance sheet at December 31, 2009. (p. 693)

Preparing a detailed income statement

P14-37B The following information was taken from the records of Underwood Company at June 30, 2007:

Selling expenses	$120,000	Common stock, no-par, 22,000	
General expenses	75,000	shares authorized and issued	$350,000
Gain on discontinued operations	5,000	Preferred stock, 6%, $25 par,	
Retained earnings, beginning	63,000	4,000 shares issued	100,000
Cost of goods sold	275,000	Income tax expense:	
Treasury stock, common		Continuing operations	28,000
(2,000 shares)	28,000	Gain on discontinued	
Net sales revenue	565,000	operations	2,000

Requirement

Prepare a multistep income statement for Underwood Company for the fiscal year ended June 30, 2007. Include earnings per share. (p. 703)

Preparing a corrected combined statement of income and retained earnings

P14-38B Jeremy Hawk, accountant for Rainbow International Corp., was injured in an auto accident. Another employee prepared the following income statement for the year ended December 31, 2007:

continued . . .

RAINBOW INTERNATIONAL CORP.
Income Statement
December 31, 2007

Revenue and gains:		
Sales		$733,000
Paid-in capital in excess of par—common		111,000
Total revenues and gains		844,000
Expenses and losses:		
Cost of goods sold	$383,000	
Selling expenses	103,000	
General expenses	91,000	
Sales returns	22,000	
Sales discounts	10,000	
Dividends	15,000	
Income tax expense	32,000	
Total expenses and losses		656,000
Income from operations		188,000
Other gains and losses:		
Loss on discontinued operations		(15,000)
Net income		$173,000
Earnings per share		$ 17.30

The individual *amounts* listed on the income statement are correct. However, some accounts are reported incorrectly, and two items don't belong on the income statement at all. Also, income tax has *not* been applied to all appropriate figures. The income tax rate on discontinued operations is 40%. Rainbow issued 14,000 shares of common stock in 2004 and held 4,000 shares as treasury stock during fiscal year 2007. Retained earnings at June 30, 2006, was $117,000.

Requirements
Prepare a corrected combined statement of income and retained earnings for the fiscal year ended December 31, 2007. Prepare the income statement in single-step format, and include earnings per share. (pp. 269–271, 703, 706–708)

P14-39B The capital structure of Audiology Associates, Inc., at December 31, 2007, included 5,000 shares of $2 preferred stock and 100,000 shares of common stock. Common shares outstanding during 2008 were 100,000. Income from continuing operations during 2008 was $370,000. The company discontinued a segment of the business at a gain of $60,000 and also had an extraordinary gain of $30,000. Audiology Associates' board of directors has restricted $250,000 of retained earnings for expansion of the company's office facilities.

Requirements
1. Compute Audiology Associates' earnings per share for 2008. Start with income from continuing operations. Income and loss amounts are net of income tax. (p. 706)
2. Show two ways of reporting Audiology Associates' retained earnings restriction. Retained Earnings at December 31, 2007, was $160,000, and the company declared cash dividends of $100,000 during 2008. (pp. 698–700)

Computing earnings per share and reporting a retained earnings restriction

for 24/7 practice, visit www.MyAccountingLab.com

Apply Your Knowledge

Decision Cases

Analyzing cash dividends
and stock dividends

Case 1. Valley Mills Construction, Inc., had the following stockholders' equity on June 30, 2008:

Common stock, no-par, 100,000 shares issued	$250,000
Retained earnings	190,000
Total stockholders' equity..	$440,000

In the past, Valley Mills has paid an annual cash dividend of $1 per share. Despite the large retained earnings balance, the board of directors wished to conserve cash for expansion. The board delayed the payment of cash dividends and in July distributed a 5% stock dividend. During August, the company's cash position improved. The board then declared and paid a cash dividend of $0.9524 per share in September.

Suppose you owned 1,000 shares of Valley Mills common stock, acquired three years ago, prior to the 50% stock dividend. The market price of the stock was $30 per share before any of these dividends.

Requirements

1. What amount of cash dividends did you receive last year—before the stock dividend? What amount of cash dividends will you receive after the stock dividend?

2. How does the stock dividend affect your proportionate ownership in Valley Mills Construction, Inc.? Explain.

3. Immediately after the stock dividend was distributed, the market value of Valley Mills stock decreased from $30 per share to $28.571 per share. Does this decrease represent a loss to you? Explain.

Reporting special items

Case 2. The following accounting issues have arisen at T-Shirts Plus, Inc.:

1. Corporations sometimes purchase their own stock. When asked why they do so, T-Shirts Plus management responds that the stock is undervalued. What advantage would T-Shirts Plus gain by buying and selling its own undervalued stock?

2. T-Shirts Plus earned a significant profit in the year ended December 31, 2008, because land that it held was purchased by the State of Nebraska for a new highway. The company proposes to treat the sale of land as operating revenue. Why do you think the company is proposing this plan? Is this disclosure appropriate?

3. The treasurer of T-Shirts Plus wants to report a large loss as an extraordinary item because the company produced too much product and cannot sell it. Why do you think the treasurer wants to report the loss as extraordinary? Would that be acceptable?

Ethical Issue

Bobby's Bagels just landed a contract to open 100 new stores in shopping malls across the country. The new business should triple the company's profits. Prior to

continued . . .

disclosing the new contract to the public, top managers of the company quietly bought most of Bobby's Bagels stock for themselves. After the discovery was announced, Bobby's Bagels stock price shot up from $7 to $52.

Requirements

1. Did Bobby's Bagels managers behave ethically? Explain your answer.

2. Identify the accounting principle relevant to this situation. Review Chapter 6 if necessary.

3. Who was helped and who was harmed by management's action?

Financial Statement Case

Corporate income statement, earnings per share

5

Use the Amazon.com financial statements in Appendix A at the end of this book to answer the following questions.

Requirements

1. Show how Amazon.com computed basic earnings per share of $0.87 for 2005.

2. Prepare a T-account to show the beginning and ending balances and all activity in Retained Earnings (Accumulated Deficit) for 2005.

3. How much in cash dividends did Amazon declare during 2005? Explain your answer.

4. How much treasury stock did Amazon have at December 31, 2005? Explain.

Team Project

Requirements

Obtain the annual reports (or annual report data) of five well-known companies. You can get the reports either from the companies' Web sites, your college library, or by mailing a request directly to the company (allow two weeks for delivery). Or you can visit the Web site for this book (http://www.prenhall.com/horngren) or the SEC EDGAR database, which includes the financial reports of most well-known companies.

1. After selecting five companies, examine their income statements to search for the following items:
   a. Income from continuing operations
   b. Discontinued operations
   c. Extraordinary gains and losses
   d. Net income or net loss
   e. Earnings-per-share data

2. Study the companies' balance sheets to see
   a. What classes of stock each company has issued.
   b. Which item carries a larger balance—the Common Stock account or Paid-In Capital in Excess of Par (also labeled Additional Paid-In Capital).

continued . . .

c. What percentage of each company's total stockholders' equity is made up of retained earnings.

d. Whether the company has treasury stock. If so, how many shares and how much is the cost?

3. Examine each company's statement of stockholders' equity for evidence of

a. Cash dividends

b. Stock dividends (Some companies use the term *stock split* to refer to a large stock dividend.)

c. Treasury stock purchases and sales

4. As directed by your instructor, either write a report or present your findings to your class. You may be unable to understand *everything* you find, but neither can the Wall Street analysts! You will be amazed at how much you have learned.

For Internet exercises, Excel in Practice, and additional online activities, go to the Web site www.prenhall.com/horngren.

Quick Check Answers

1. *c*   2. *c*   3. *b*   4. *c*   5. *a*   6. *d*   7. *d*   8. *a*   9. *b*   10. *b*

15 Long-Term Liabilities

Learning Objectives

1 Account for bonds payable

2 Measure interest expense by the straight-line amortization method

3 Account for retirement and conversion of bonds payable

4 Report liabilities on the balance sheet

5 Show the advantages and disadvantages of borrowing

n earlier chapters of this book you were adventuresome and operated In Motion T-Shirts while in college. You continued with the business after graduation and expanded to several locations. Suppose you grew In Motion to a good-size company and then sold it at a nice profit. What will you do with the cash you received from selling out?

You've noticed that discount airlines Jet Blue and Virgin Airways have done quite well. So you decide to take the plunge and start an airline. You get a charter, issue stock, and raise $5 million. Air West Airlines is up and running.

Needing more cash you must borrow. This will require Air West to issue long-term notes payable or bonds payable. Virtually all companies—both large and small—have borrowed this way.

In this chapter we show how to account for long-term liabilities—notes payable and bonds payable. The chapter appendix includes some related topics that your instructor may or may not wish to cover.

Notes payable and bonds payable are accounted for similarly. Since we covered notes payable back in Chapter 11, we focus on bonds payable here. Before launching into bonds payable, let's compare bonds with stock, which you learned about in Chapters 13 and 14. The following chart shows how stocks and bonds differ.

Stocks	Bonds
1. Stock represents the *ownership* of a corporation. Each stockholder is an *owner*.	1. Bonds represent a *liability* of the corporation. Each bondholder is a *creditor*.
2. The corporation is *not* obligated to repay the stock.	2. The corporation *must* repay the bonds.
3. The corporation *may* or *may not* pay dividends on the stock. Dividends are *not* an expense.	3. The corporation *must* pay interest on the bonds. Interest is an expense.

Bonds: An Introduction

Large companies such as Blockbuster and American Airlines need large amounts of money to finance operations. They may issue bonds payable to the public. **Bonds payable** are groups of notes payable issued to multiple lenders, called bondholders. By issuing bonds payable, Blockbuster can borrow millions of dollars from thousands of investors. Each investor can buy a selected amount of Blockbuster bonds.

Each bondholder gets a bond certificate, which shows the name of the company that borrowed the money, exactly like a note payable. The certificate states the *principal*, which is the amount the company has borrowed. The bonds' principal amount is also called *maturity value*, or *par value*. The company must then pay each bondholder the principal amount at a specific future date, called the maturity date. In Chapter 11 we saw how to account for short-term notes payable. There's a lot of similarity between the accounting for short-term notes payable and long-term notes payable.

People buy bonds to earn interest. The bond certificate states the interest rate that the company will pay and the dates the interest is due (generally twice a year). Exhibit 15-1 shows a bond certificate issued by Air West Airlines, Inc.

Review these bond fundamentals in Exhibit 15-1.

- **Principal amount** (also called **maturity value**, or **par value**)   The amount the borrower must pay back to the bondholders.
- **Maturity date**   The date on which the borrower must pay the principal amount to the bondholders.
- **Stated interest rate**   The annual rate of interest that the borrower pays the bondholders.

Types of Bonds

There are various types of bonds, including the following.

- **Term bonds** all mature at the same time.
- **Serial bonds** mature in installments at regular intervals. For example, a $500,000, 5-year serial bond may mature in $100,000 annual installments over a 5-year period.

EXHIBIT 15-1   **Bond Certificate**

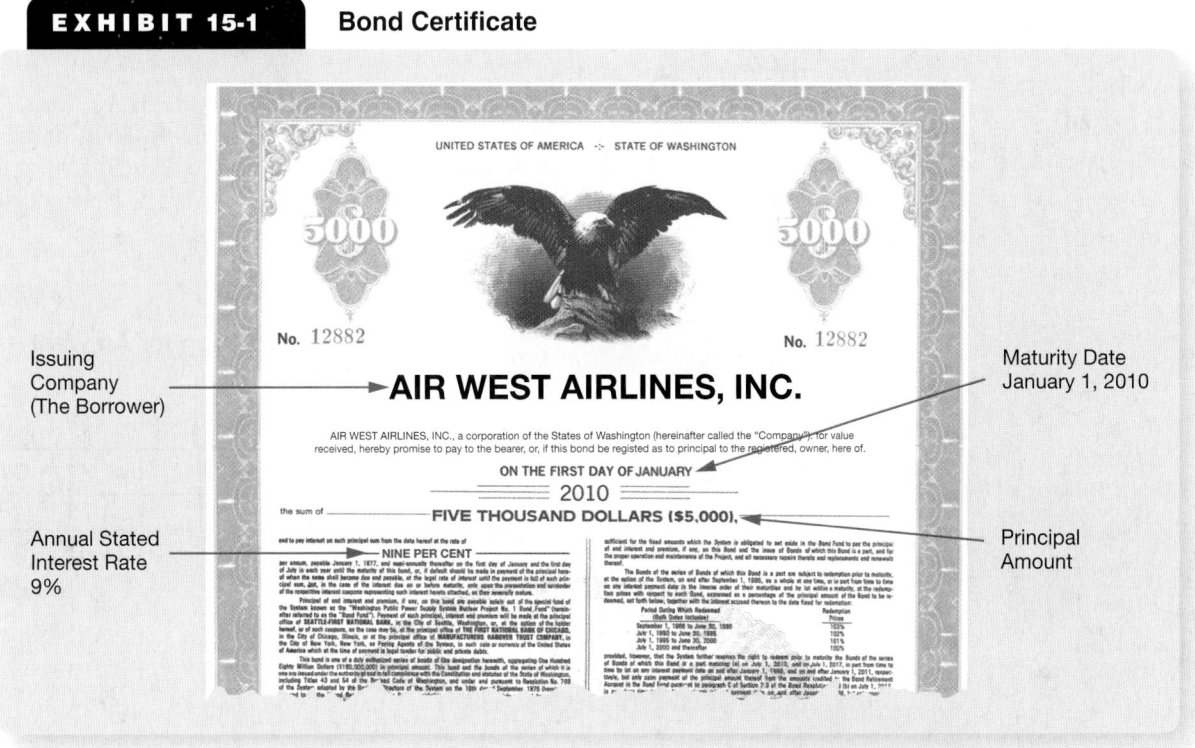

Issuing Company (The Borrower)

Annual Stated Interest Rate 9%

Maturity Date January 1, 2010

Principal Amount

- **Secured bonds** give the bondholder the right to take specified assets of the issuer if the issuer fails to pay principal or interest. A **mortgage** is an example of a secured bond.
- **Debentures** are unsecured bonds backed only by the good faith of the issuer.

Bond Prices

A bond can be issued at any price agreed upon by the issuer and the bondholders. There are three basic categories of bond prices. A bond can be issued at:

- **Maturity (par) value.** Example: A $1,000 bond issued for $1,000. A bond issued at par has no discount or premium.
- **Discount,** a price below maturity (par) value. Example: A $1,000 bond issued for $980. The discount is $20 ($1,000 − $980).
- **Premium,** a price above maturity (par) value. Example: A $1,000 bond issued for $1,015. The premium is $15 ($1,015 − $1,000).

The issue price of a bond does not affect the required payment at maturity. In all cases the company must pay the maturity value of the bonds when they mature.

As a bond approaches maturity, its market price moves toward maturity value. On the maturity date, the market value of a bond exactly equals maturity value because the company pays that amount to retire the bond.

After a bond is issued, investors may buy and sell it through the bond market just as they buy and sell stocks through the stock market. The most famous bond market is the New York Exchange, which lists several thousand bonds.

Bond prices are quoted at a percentage of maturity value. For example,

- A $1,000 bond quoted at 100 is bought or sold for 100% of maturity value ($1,000).
- A $1,000 bond quoted at 101.5 has a price of $1,015 ($1,000 × 1.015).
- A $1,000 bond quoted at 88.375 has a price of $883.75 ($1,000 × .88375).

The issue price of a bond determines the amount of cash the company receives when it issues the bond. In all cases, the company must pay the bonds' maturity value to retire them at maturity.

Exhibit 15-2 shows price information for the bonds of Air West Airlines. On this particular day, 12 of Air West's 9% bonds maturing in 2012 (indicated by 12) were traded. The bonds' highest price on this day was $795 ($1,000 × 0.795). The lowest price of the day was $784.50 ($1,000 × 0.7845). The closing price (last sale of the day) was $795.

EXHIBIT 15-2   **Bond Price Information for Air West Airlines (AirW)**

Bonds	Volume	High	Low	Close
AirW 9% of 12	12	79.5	78.45	79.5

Present Value

Money earns income over time, a fact called the *time value of money*. Appendix 15A covers time value of money in detail, starting on page 771.

Let's see how the time value of money affects bond prices. Assume that a $1,000 bond reaches maturity three years from now and carries no interest. Would you pay $1,000 to purchase this bond? No, because paying $1,000 today to receive $1,000 later yields no income on your investment. How much would you pay today in order to receive $1,000 in three years? The answer is some amount *less* than $1,000. Suppose $750 is a fair price. By investing $750 now to receive $1,000 later, you will earn $250 over the three years. The diagram that follows illustrates the relationship between a bond's price (present value) and its maturity amount (future value).

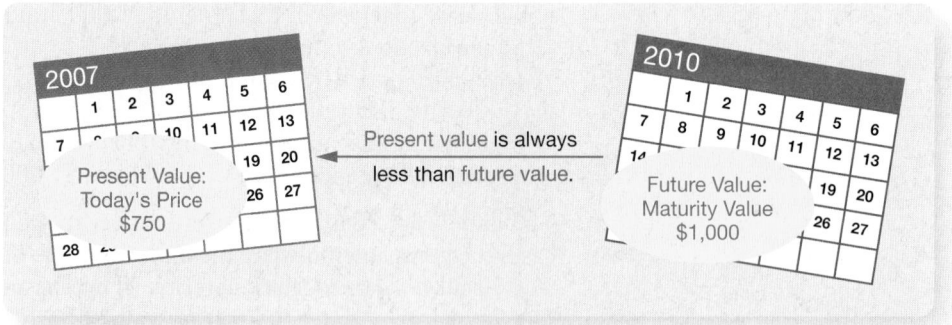

The amount that a person would invest *at the present time* is called the **present value**. The present value is the bond's market price. In our example, $750 is the present value (bond price), and the $1,000 maturity value to be received in three years is the future amount. We show how to compute present value Appendix 15A, page 771.

Bond Interest Rates

Bonds are sold at their market price, which is the bonds' present value. Two interest rates work together to set the price of a bond:

- The **stated interest rate** determines the amount of cash interest the borrower pays each year. The stated interest rate is printed on the bond and *does not change*. For example, Air West Airlines' 9% bonds payable have a stated interest rate of 9% (Exhibit 15-1). Thus, Air West pays $900 of interest annually on each $10,000 bond.

- The **market interest rate** (also known as the **effective interest rate**) is the interest rate that investors demand to earn for loaning their money. The market interest rate *varies* daily. A company may issue bonds with a stated interest rate that differs from the market interest rate.

Air West Airlines may issue its 9% bonds when the market rate has risen to 10%. Will the Air West bonds attract investors in this market? No, because investors can earn 10% on other bonds. Therefore, investors will purchase Air West bonds only at a price less than maturity value. The difference between the lower price and the bonds' maturity value is a *discount*.

Conversely, if the market interest rate is 8%, Air West's 9% bonds will be so attractive that investors will pay more than maturity value for them. The difference between the higher price and maturity value is a *premium*. Exhibit 15-3 shows how the stated interest rate and the market interest rate work together to determine the price of a bond.

EXHIBIT 15-3	**Interaction of the Stated Interest Rate and the Market Interest Rate to Determine the Price of a Bond**

Example: Bond with a Stated Interest Rate of 9%

Bond's Stated Interest Rate		Market Interest Rate		Issue Price of Bonds Payable
9%	=	9%	→	Maturity value of the bond
9%	<	10%	→	Discount (price below maturity value)
9%	>	8%	→	Premium (price above maturity value)

Issuing Bonds Payable to Borrow Money

The basic journal entry to record the issuance of bonds payable debits Cash and credits Bonds Payable. The company may issue bonds for three different bond prices:

- At *maturity (par)* value
- At a *discount*
- At a *premium*

We begin with the simplest case: issuing bonds payable at maturity (par) value.

Issuing Bonds Payable at Maturity (Par) Value

1 Account for bonds payable

Air West Airlines has $50,000 of 8% bonds payable that mature in 5 years. Air West issued these bonds at maturity (par) value on January 1, 2008. The issuance entry is:

2008				
Jan. 1	Cash		50,000	
	Bonds Payable			50,000
	Issued bonds.			

Air West, the borrower, makes this one-time journal entry to record the receipt of cash and issuance of bonds payable. Interest payments occur each January 1 and July 1. Air West's first semiannual interest payment is journalized as follows:

2008				
Jan. 1	Interest Expense ($50,000 × 0.08 × 6/12)		2,000	
	Cash			2,000
	Paid semiannual interest.			

Each semiannual interest payment follows this same pattern.

At maturity, Air West will record payment of the bonds as follows:

2013				
Jan. 1	Bonds Payable		50,000	
	Cash			50,000
	Paid off bonds at maturity.			

Now let's see how to issue bonds payable at a discount. This is one of the most common situations.

Issuing Bonds Payable at a Discount

We know that market conditions may force a company such as Air West Airlines to accept a discount price for its bonds. Suppose Air West issues $100,000 of its 9%, five-year bonds when the market interest rate is 9 1/2%. The market price of the bonds drops to 98, which means 98% of par value. Air West receives $98,000 ($100,000 × 0.98) at issuance and makes the following journal entry:

2008				
Jan. 1	Cash ($100,000 × 0.98)		98,000	
	Discount on Bonds Payable		2,000	
	Bonds Payable			100,000
	Issued bonds at a discount.			

After posting, the bond accounts have these balances:

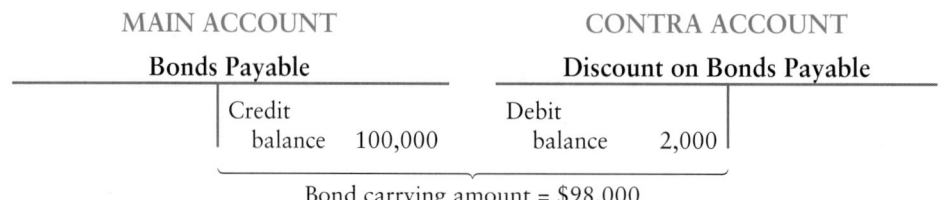

MAIN ACCOUNT	CONTRA ACCOUNT
Bonds Payable	**Discount on Bonds Payable**
Credit	Debit
balance 100,000	balance 2,000

Bond carrying amount = $98,000

Discount on Bonds Payable is a contra account to Bonds Payable. Bonds Payable *minus* the discount gives the carrying amount of the bonds. Air West would report these bonds payable as follows immediately after issuance.

Long-term liabilities:		
Bonds payable...............................	$100,000	
Less: Discount on bonds payable	(2,000)	$98,000

Interest Expense on Bonds Payable with a Discount

We saw that a bond's stated interest rate may differ from the market interest rate. The market rate was 9 1/2% when Air West issued its 9% bonds. The 1/2% interest-rate difference created the $2,000 discount on the bonds. Investors were willing to pay only $98,000 for a $100,000, 9% bond when they could earn 9 1/2% on other bonds.

Air West borrowed $98,000 but must pay $100,000 when the bonds mature five years later. What happens to the $2,000 discount? The discount is additional interest expense to Air West. The discount raises Air West's interest expense on the bonds to the market interest rate of 9 1/2%. The discount becomes interest expense for Air West through a process called *amortization,* the gradual reduction of an item over time.

Straight-Line Amortization of Bond Discount

We can amortize a bond discount by dividing it into equal amounts for each interest period. This method is called *straight-line amortization.* In our example, the initial discount is $2,000, and there are 10 semiannual interest periods during the bonds' 5-year life.

2 Measure interest expense by the straight-line amortization method

Therefore 1/10 of the $2,000 bond discount ($200) is amortized each interest period. Air West's first semiannual interest entry is:[1]

2008			
July 1	Interest Expense	4,700	
	Cash ($100,000 × 0.09 × 6/12)		4,500
	Discount on Bonds Payable ($2,000/10)		200
	Paid interest and amortized discount.		

Interest expense of $4,700 for each six-month period is the sum of

- The stated interest ($4,500, which is paid in cash)
- *Plus* the amortization of discount ($200).

---

[1]You can record the payment of interest and the amortization of bond discount in two separate entries, as follows:

2008			
July 1	Interest Expense	4,500	
	Cash ($100,000 × 0.09 × 6/12)		4,500
	Paid semiannual interest.		
July 1	Interest Expense	200	
	Discount on Bonds Payable ($2,000/10)		200
	Amortized discount on bonds payable.		

These two entries record the same amount of interest expense ($4,700) as the single entry shown above.

Discount on Bonds Payable has a debit balance. Therefore we credit the Discount account to amortize its balance. Ten amortization entries will decrease the Discount to zero. Then the carrying amount of the bonds payable will be $100,000 at maturity.

Finally, the entry to pay off the bonds at maturity is:

2013				
Jan. 1	Bonds Payable		100,000	
	Cash			100,000
	Paid off bonds at maturity.			

Decision Guidelines

Air West Airlines has borrowed some money by issuing bonds payable. What type of bonds did Air West issue? How much cash must Air West pay each interest period?

How much cash must Air West pay at maturity? The Decision Guidelines address these and other questions.

Decision

a. When will you pay off the bonds?

- At maturity? ⟶
- In installments? ⟶

b. Are the bonds secured?

- Yes ⟶
- No ⟶

How are bond prices

- Quoted? ⟶

- Determined? ⟶

What are the two interest rates used for bonds? ⟶

What causes a bond to be priced at

- Maturity (par) value? ⟶

- A discount? ⟶

- A premium? ⟶

How to report bonds payable on the balance sheet? ⟶

What is the relationship between interest expense and interest payments when bonds are issued at

- Maturity (par) value? ⟶
- A discount? ⟶
- A premium? ⟶

Guidelines

Types of bonds:

- Term bonds
- Serial bonds

- Mortgage (secured) bonds
- Debenture (unsecured) bonds

- As a percentage of maturity value (Example: A $500,000 bond priced at $510,000 would be quoted at 102 ($510,000 ÷ $500,000 = 1.02)
- Present value of the future principal amount to pay *plus* present value of the future interest payments (see Appendix 15A)
- The *stated interest rate* determines the amount of cash interest the borrower pays. This interest rate does *not* change.
- The *market interest rate* is the rate that investors demand to earn for loaning their money. This interest rate determines the bonds' market price and varies daily.

- The *stated* interest rate on the bond *equals* the *market* interest rate.
- The *stated* interest rate on the bond is *less than* the *market* interest rate.
- The *stated* interest rate on the bond is *greater than* the *market* interest rate.

$$\text{Maturity (par) value} \begin{cases} -\text{Discount on bonds payable} \\ \qquad\quad \text{or} \\ +\text{Premium on bonds payable} \end{cases}$$

- Interest expense *equals* the interest payment.
- Interest expense is *greater than* the interest payment.
- Interest expense is *less than* the interest payment.

Summary Problem 1

West Virginia Power Company has 8% 10-year bonds payable that mature on June 30, 2018. The bonds are issued on June 30, 2008, and West Virginia Power pays interest each June 30 and December 31.

Requirements

1. Will the bonds be issued at par, at a premium, or at a discount if the market interest rate on the date of issuance is 7%? If the market interest rate is 9%?

2. West Virginia Power issued $100,000 of the bonds at 94.

   a. Record issuance of the bonds on June 30, 2008.

   b. Record the payment of interest and amortization of the discount on December 31, 2008. Use the straight-line amortization method.

   c. Compute the bonds' carrying amount at December 31, 2008.

   d. Record the payment of interest and amortization of discount on June 30, 2009.

Solution

Requirement 1

M Market Interest Rate	Bond Price for an 8% Bond
7%	Premium
9%	Discount

Requirement 2

	2008			
a.	June 30	Cash ($100,000 × 0.94)	94,000	
		Discount on Bonds Payable	6,000	
		Bonds Payable		100,000
		Issued bonds at a discount.		
b.	Dec. 31	Interest Expense	4,300	
		Cash ($100,000 × 0.08 × 6/12)		4,000
		Discount on Bonds Payable ($6,000/20)		300
		Paid interest and amortized discount.		
c.		Bond carrying amount at Dec. 31, 2008:		
		$94,300 [$100,000 − ($6,000 − $300)]		
	2009			
d.	June 30	Interest Expense	4,300	
		Cash ($100,000 × 0.08 × 6/12)		4,000
		Discount on Bonds Payable ($6,000/20)		300
		Paid interest and amortized discount.		

Issuing Bonds Payable at a Premium

The issuance of bonds payable at a premium is rare because a premium occurs only when a bond's stated interest rate exceeds the market rate, and companies don't like to pay a stated interest higher than the market rate.

To illustrate a bond premium, let's change the Air West Airlines example. Assume that the market interest rate is 8% when Air West issues its 9%, five-year bonds. These 9% bonds are attractive in an 8% market, and investors will pay a premium to acquire them. Suppose the bonds are priced at 104 (104% of maturity value). In that case, Air West receives $104,000 cash upon issuance. Air West's entry to borrow money and issue these bonds is:

2008			
Jan. 1	Cash ($100,000 × 1.04)	104,000	
	Bonds Payable		100,000
	Premium on Bonds Payable		4,000
	Issued bonds at a premium.		

After posting, the bond accounts have these balances:

MAIN ACCOUNT	COMPANION ACCOUNT
Bonds Payable	**Premium on Bonds Payable**
Credit balance 100,000	Credit balance 4,000

Bond carrying amount $104,000

Bonds Payable and the Premium account each carries a credit balance. The Premium is a companion account to Bonds Payable. Therefore, we add the Premium to Bonds Payable to determine the bond carrying amount. Air West Airlines would report these bonds payable as follows immediately after issuance:

Long-term liabilities:		
Bonds payable	$100,000	
Plus: Premium on bonds payable	4,000	$104,000

Interest Expense on Bonds Payable with a Premium

The 1% difference between the bonds' 9% stated interest rate and the 8% market rate creates the $4,000 premium. Air West borrows $104,000 but must pay back only $100,000 at maturity. The premium is like a saving of interest expense to Air West. The premium cuts Air West's cost of borrowing and reduces interest expense to 8%, the market rate. The amortization of bond premium decreases interest expense over the life of the bonds.

Straight-Line Amortization of Bond Premium

In our example, the beginning premium is $4,000, and there are 10 semiannual interest periods during the bonds' 5-year life. Therefore, 1/10 of the $4,000 ($400) of bond premium is amortized each interest period. Air West's first semiannual interest entry is:[2]

	2008			
	July 1	Interest Expense	4,100	
		Premium on Bonds Payable ($4,000/10)	400	
		Cash ($100,000 × 0.09 × 6/12)		4,500
		Paid interest and amortized premium.		

Interest expense of $4,100 is:

- The stated interest ($4,500, which is paid in cash)
- *Minus* the amortization of the premium ($400)

At July 1, 2008, immediately after amortizing the bond premium, the bonds have this carrying amount:

$$\$103,600 \; [\$100,000 + (\$4,000 - \$400)]$$

At December 31, 2008, the bonds' carrying amount will be:

$$\$103,200 \; [\$100,000 + (\$4,000 - \$400 - \$400)]$$

At maturity on January 1, 2013, the bond premium will have been fully amortized, and the bonds' carrying amount will be $100,000.

Now we move on to some additional bond topics.

Additional Bond Topics

3 Account for retirement and conversion of bonds payable

Companies that issue bonds payable face additional issues, such as:

- Adjusting entries for bonds payable
- Issuance of bonds payable between interest dates
- Retirement of bonds payable
- Convertible bonds payable
- Reporting bonds payable on the balance sheet
- Advantages and disadvantages of issuing bonds versus stock

Adjusting Entries for Bonds Payable

Companies issue bonds payable whenever they need cash. The interest payments seldom occur on December 31, so interest expense must be accrued at year end. The accrual entry should also amortize any bond discount or premium.

---

[2]The payment of interest and the amortization of bond premium can be recorded in separate entries as follows:

	2008			
	July 1	Interest Expense	4,500	
		Cash ($100,000 × 0.09 × 6/12)		4,500
		Paid semiannual interest.		
	July 1	Premium on Bonds Payable ($4,000/10)	400	
		Interest Expense		400
		Amortized premium on bonds payable.		

These two entries record the same amount of interest expense ($4,100) as the single entry shown above.

Suppose Air West Airlines issued $100,000 of 8%, 10-year bonds at a $2,000 discount on October 1, 2009. The interest payments occur on March 31 and September 30 each year. On December 31, Air West accrues interest and amortizes bond discount for three months (October, November, and December) as follows:

2009			
Dec. 31	Interest Expense	2,050	
	Interest Payable ($100,000 × 0.08 × 3/12)		2,000
	Discount on Bonds Payable ($2,000/10 × 3/12)		50
	Accrued interest and amortized discount.		

Interest Payable is credited for three months (October, November, and December). Discount on Bonds Payable must also be amortized for these three months.

The next semiannual interest payment occurs on March 31, 2010, and Air West makes this journal entry:

2010			
Mar. 31	Interest Payable (from Dec. 31)	2,000	
	Interest Expense	2,050	
	Cash ($100,000 × 0.08 × 6/12)		4,000
	Discount on Bonds Payable ($2,000/10 × 3/12)		50
	Paid interest and amortized discount.		

Amortization of a bond premium is similar except that Premium on Bonds Payable is debited.

Issuing Bonds Payable Between Interest Dates

In most of the examples we've seen thus far, Air West Airlines issued bonds payable on an interest date, such as January 1. Corporations can also issue bonds between interest dates. That creates a complication.

Air West Airlines has $100,000 of 8% bonds payable that are dated January 1. That means the interest starts accruing on January 1.

Suppose Air West issues these bonds on April 1. How should we account for the interest for January, February, and March? At issuance on April 1, Air West collects three months' accrued interest from the bondholder and records the issuance of bonds payable as follows:

2008			
April 1	Cash	102,000	
	Bonds Payable		100,000
	Interest Payable ($100,000 × 0.08 × 3/12)		2,000
	Issued bonds two months after the date of the bonds.		

Companies don't split up interest payments. They pay in six-month or annual amounts as stated on the bond certificate.

On the next interest date, Air West will pay six months' interest to whoever owns the bonds at that time. But Air West will have interest expense only for the three months the bonds have been outstanding (April, May, and June). To allocate interest expense to the correct months, Air West makes this entry on July 1 for the customary six-month interest payment:

2008			
July 1	Interest Payable (from April 1)	2,000	
	Interest Expense (for April, May, June)	2,000	
	Cash ($100,000 × 0.08 × 6/12)		4,000
	Paid interest.		

Retirement of Bonds Payable

Normally, companies wait until maturity to pay off, or *retire*, their bonds payable. The basic retirement entry debits Bonds Payable and credits Cash, as we saw earlier. But companies sometimes retire their bonds prior to maturity. The main reason is to relieve the pressure of paying interest.

Some bonds are **callable**, which means the company may *call*, or pay off, the bonds at a specified price. The call price is usually 100 or a few percentage points above par value, perhaps 101 or 102. Callable bonds give the issuer the flexibility to pay off the bonds whenever it is beneficial. An alternative to calling the bonds is to purchase them in the open market at their current market price. Whether the bonds are called or purchased in the open market, the journal entry is the same.

Suppose Air West Airlines has $700,000 of bonds payable outstanding with a remaining discount of $30,000. Lower interest rates have convinced management to pay off these bonds now. These bonds are callable at 100. If the market price of the bonds is 95, will Air West call the bonds at 100 or purchase them in the open market at 95? The market price is lower than the call price, so Air West will pay off the bonds at their market price. Retiring the bonds at 95 results in a gain of $5,000, computed as follows:

Maturity value of bonds being retired	$700,000
Less: Discount..	(30,000)
Carrying amount of bonds payable	670,000
Market price ($700,000 × 0.95) paid to retire the bonds	665,000
Gain on retirement of bonds payable	$ 5,000

The following entry records retirement of the bonds, immediately after an interest date:

June 30	Bonds Payable	700,000	
	Discount on Bonds Payable		30,000
	Cash ($700,000 × 0.95)		665,000
	Gain on Retirement of Bonds Payable		5,000
	Retired bonds payable.		

After posting, the bond accounts have zero balances.

Bonds Payable		Discount on Bonds Payable	
Retirement 700,000	Prior	Prior	Retirement 30,000
	balance 700,000	balance 30,000	

The journal entry removes the bonds from the books and records a gain on retirement. Any existing premium would be removed with a debit. If Air West retired only half of these bonds, it would remove only half the discount or premium. When retiring bonds before maturity, follow these steps:

1. Record partial-period amortization of discount or premium if the retirement date does not fall on an interest date.

2. Write off the portion of Discount or Premium that relates to the bonds being retired.

3. Credit a gain or debit a loss on retirement.

Convertible Bonds Payable

Convertible bonds are popular both with investors and with companies needing to borrow money. **Convertible bonds** may be converted into common stock at the option of the investor. These bonds combine the benefits of interest and principal on the bonds with the opportunity for a gain on the stock. The conversion feature is so attractive that investors accept a lower interest rate than on non-convertible bonds. For example, Amazon.com's convertible bonds payable carry an interest rate of only 4 3/4%. The low interest benefits Amazon.com.

The issuance of convertible bonds payable is recorded like any other debt: Debit Cash and credit Convertible Bonds Payable. Then, if the market price of Amazon's stock rises above the value of the bonds, the bondholders will convert the bonds into stock. The corporation then debits the bond accounts and credits the stock. The carrying amount of the bonds becomes the book value of the newly issued stock. There is no gain or loss.

Assume the Amazon bondholders convert $100,000 of Amazon's bonds payable into 20,000 shares of Amazon's common stock, which has a par value of $0.01 (1 cent) per share. Assume further that the carrying amount of the Amazon bonds is $90,000; thus, there is a bond discount of $10,000. To record the conversion, Amazon would make this journal entry:

May 14	Bonds Payable	100,000	
	Discount on Bonds Payable ($100,000 – $90,000)		10,000
	Common Stock (20,000 × $0.01)		200
	Paid-In Capital in Excess of Par		89,800
	Recorded conversion of bonds payable.		

The entry zeroes out the Bonds Payable account and its related Discount exactly as for a bond retirement. This journal entry transfers the carrying amount of the bonds ($90,000) to stockholders' equity, as follows:

Common Stock	Paid-In Capital in Excess of Par
200	89,800

Total new stockholders' equity = $90,000

Reporting Liabilities on the Balance Sheet

4 Report liabilities on the balance sheet

Companies report their bonds payable and notes payable among the liabilities on the balance sheet. As we have seen throughout, there are two categories of liabilities, current and long-term.

Serial bonds are payable in installments. The portion payable within one year is a current liability, and the remaining debt is long-term. For example, assume that Toys "Я" Us has $500,000 of bonds payable maturing in $100,000 amounts each year for the next 5 years. The portion payable next year is $100,000. This amount is a current liability, and the remaining $400,000 is a long-term liability. Toys "Я" Us would report the following among its liabilities:

Current liabilities:	
Bonds payable, current	$100,000
Long-term liabilities:	
Bonds payable, long-term	400,000

Notes payable are reported in a similar fashion. We show bonds payable with a discount on page 739 and bonds payable with a premium on page 743.

Advantages and Disadvantages of Issuing Bonds Versus Stock

Borrowing by issuing bonds payable carries a risk: The company may be unable to pay off the bonds. Why then do companies borrow so heavily? Because bonds are a cheaper source of money than stock. Borrowing can help a company increase its earnings per share. Companies thus face this decision: How shall we finance a new project—with bonds or with stock?

Suppose Air West Airlines has net income of $300,000 and 100,000 shares of common stock outstanding before the new project. Air West needs $500,000 for the project and the company is considering two plans:

- Plan 1 is to borrow $500,000 at 10% (issue $500,000 of 10% bonds payable).
- Plan 2 is to issue 50,000 shares of common stock for $500,000.

Air West management believes the new cash can be used to earn income of $200,000 before interest and taxes.

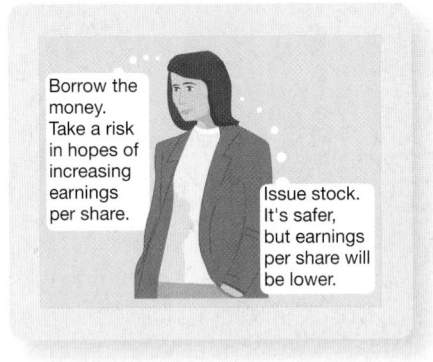

5 Show the advantages and disadvantages of borrowing

Exhibit 15-4 shows the earnings-per-share (EPS) advantage of borrowing.

EXHIBIT 15-4		**Earnings-per-Share Advantage of Borrowing Versus Issuing Stock**		

	Plan 1 Issue $500,000 of 10% Bonds Payable		Plan 2 Issue $500,000 of Common Stock	
Net income before new project		$300,000		$300,000
Expected income on the new project before				
interest and income tax expenses	$200,000		$200,000	
Less: Interest expense ($500,000 × 0.10)	(50,000)		0	
Project income before income tax	150,000		200,000	
Less: Income tax expense (40%)	(60,000)		(80,000)	
Project net income		90,000		120,000
Net income with new project		$390,000		$420,000
Earnings per share with new project:				
Plan 1 ($390,000/100,000 shares)		$3.90		
Plan 2 ($420,000/150,000 shares)				$2.80

EPS is higher if Air West issues bonds. If all goes well, the company can earn more on the new project ($90,000) than the interest it pays on the bonds ($50,000). Earning more income on borrowed money than the related interest expense is called using **leverage**. It is widely used to increase earnings per share of common stock.

Borrowing can increase EPS, but borrowing has its disadvantages. Debts must be paid during bad years as well as good years. Interest expense may be high enough to eliminate net income and even lead to bankruptcy. This happens to lots of ambitious companies.

Now let's wrap up the chapter with some Decision Guidelines.

Decision Guidelines

Suppose Air West Airlines needs $50 million to purchase airplanes. Air West issues bonds payable to finance the purchase and now must account for the bonds payable.

The Decision Guidelines outline some of the issues Air West must decide.

Decision

What happens to the bonds' carrying amount when bonds payable are issued at

- Maturity (par) value? ⟶
- A premium? ⟶
- A discount? ⟶

How to account for the retirement of bonds payable?

How to account for the conversion of convertible bonds payable into common stock? (Assume a bond premium.)

What are the advantages of financing operations with

- Stock? ⟶
- Bonds (or notes) payable? ⟶

Guidelines

- Carrying amount *stays* at maturity (par) value.
- Carrying amount *falls* gradually to maturity value.
- Carrying amount *rises* gradually to maturity value.

At maturity date:

Bonds Payable	Maturity value
Cash	Maturity value

Before maturity date (assume a discount on the bonds and a gain on retirement):

Bonds Payable	Maturity value
Discount on Bonds Payable..................	Balance
Cash	Amount Paid
Gain on Retirement of Bonds Payable...	Excess

Bonds Payable	Maturity value
Premium on Bonds Payable.......................	Balance
Common Stock	Par value
Paid-in Capital in Excess of Par	Excess over par value

- Creates no liability or interest expense. Less risky to the issuing corporation.
- Results in higher earnings per share—under normal conditions.

Summary Problem 2

Trademark, Inc., has outstanding a $100,000 issue of 6% convertible bonds payable that mature in 2026. Suppose the bonds were dated April 1, 2006, and pay interest each April 1 and October 1.

Requirements

Record the following transactions for Trademark:

a. Issuance of the bonds at 104.8 on April 1, 2006.

b. Payment of interest and amortization of premium on October 1, 2006.

c. Accrual of interest and amortization of premium on December 31, 2006.

d. Payment of interest and amortization of premium on April 1, 2007.

e. Conversion of one-half of the bonds payable into no-par common stock on April 1, 2007.

f. Retirement of one-half of the bonds payable on April 1, 2007. Purchase price to retire the bonds was 102.

Solution

	2006			
a.	April 1	Cash ($100,000 × 1.048)	104,800	
		Bonds Payable		100,000
		Premium on Bonds Payable		4,800
		Issued bonds at a premium.		
b.	Oct. 1	Interest Expense	2,880	
		Premium on Bonds Payable ($4,800/40)	120	
		Cash ($100,000 × 0.06 × 6/12)		3,000
		Paid interest and amortized premium.		
c.	Dec. 31	Interest Expense	1,440	
		Premium on Bonds Payable ($4,800/40 × 1/2)	60	
		Interest Payable ($100,000 × 0.06 × 3/12)		1,500
		Accrued interest and amortized premium.		
	2007			
d.	April 1	Interest Payable (from Dec. 31)	1,500	
		Interest Expense	1,440	
		Premium on Bonds Payable ($4,800/40 × 1/2)	60	
		Cash ($100,000 × 0.06 × 6/12)		3,000
e.	April 1	Bonds Payable ($100,000 × 1/2)	50,000	
		Premium on Bonds Payable		
		[($4,800 – $120 – $60 – $60) × 1/2]	2,280	
		Common Stock		52,280
		Recorded conversion of bonds payable.		
f.	April 1	Bonds Payable ($100,000 × 1/2)	50,000	
		Premium on Bonds Payable		
		[($4,800 – $120 – $60 – $60) × 1/2]	2,280	
		Cash ($50,000 × 1.02)		51,000
		Gain on Retirement of Bonds Payable		1,280
		Retired bonds payable.		

Review *Long-Term Liabilities*

Accounting Vocabulary

Bond Discount
Excess of a bond's maturity value over its issue price. Also called a **discount (on a bond)**.

Bond Premium
Excess of a bond's issue price over its maturity value. Also called a **premium**.

Bonds Payable
Groups of notes payable issued to multiple lenders called bondholders.

Callable Bonds
Bonds that the issuer may call or pay off at a specified price whenever the issuer wants.

Convertible Bonds
Bonds that may be converted into the common stock of the issuing company at the option of the investor.

Debentures
Unsecured bonds backed only by the good faith of the borrower.

Discount (on a bond)
Excess of a bond's maturity value over its issue price. Also called a **bond discount.**

Effective Interest Rate
Interest rate that investors demand in order to loan their money. Also called the **market interest rate**.

Leverage
Earning more income on borrowed money than the related interest expense, thereby increasing the earnings for the owners of the business.

Market Interest Rate
Interest rate that investors demand in order to loan their money. Also called the **effective interest rate**.

Maturity (par) value
A bond issued at par has no discount on premium.

Mortgage
Borrower's promise to transfer the legal title to certain assets to the lender if the debt is not paid on schedule.

Par Value
Another name for the maturity value of a bond.

Premium
Excess of a bond's issue price over its maturity value. Also called **bond premium.**

Present Value
Amount a person would invest now to receive a greater amount in the future.

Secured Bonds
Bonds that give bondholders the right to take specified assets of the issuer if the issuer fails to pay principal or interest.

Serial Bonds
Bonds that mature in installments over a period of time.

Stated Interest Rate
Interest rate that determines the amount of cash interest the borrower pays and the investor receives each year.

Term Bonds
Bonds that all mature at the same time for a particular lease.

Quick Check

1. Which type of bond is unsecured?
   a. Common bond
   b. Mortgage bond
   c. Serial bond
   d. Debenture bond

2. A $100,000 bond priced at 103.5 can be bought or sold for
   a. $100,000 + interest
   b. $103,500
   c. $3,500
   d. $10,350

3. Which interest rate on a bond determines the amount of the semiannual interest payment?
   a. Market rate
   b. Effective rate
   c. Stated rate
   d. Semiannual rate

4. The final journal entry to record for bonds payable is
   a. Bonds Payable xxx
      Cash xxx
   b. Cash xxx
      Bonds Payable xxx
   c. Interest Expense............................ xxx
      Cash xxx
   d. Discount on Bonds Payable xxx
      Interest Expense xxx

5. Lafferty Corporation's bonds payable carry a stated interest rate of 7%, and the market rate of interest is 8%. The price of the Lafferty bonds will be at
   a. Par value
   b. Maturity value
   c. Premium
   d. Discount

6. Bonds issued at a premium always have
   a. Interest expense equal to the interest payments
   b. Interest expense greater than the interest payments
   c. Interest expense less than the interest payments
   d. None of the above

7. Galena Park Fitness Gym has $500,000 of 10-year bonds payable outstanding. These bonds had a discount of $40,000 at issuance, which was 5 years ago. The company uses the straight-line amortization method. The carrying amount of these bonds payable is

a. $480,000

b. $460,000

c. $500,000

d. $540,000

8. Nick Spanos Antiques issued its 8%, 10-year bonds payable at a price of $440,000 (maturity value is $500,000). The company uses the straight-line amortization method for the bonds. Interest expense for each year is

a. $35,200

b. $46,000

c. $44,000

d. $50,000

9. Spice Inc. issued bonds payable on December 31. Spice's bonds were dated July 31. Which statement is true of Spice's journal entry to record issuance of the bonds payable?

a. Spice must pay one month's accrued interest.

b. Spice will collect one month's accrued interest in advance.

c. Spice will collect five months' accrued interest in advance.

d. Spice will pay five months' interest in advance.

10. Bull & Bear, Inc., retired $100,000 of its bonds payable, paying cash of $103,000. On the retirement date, the bonds payable had a premium of $2,000. The bond retirement created a

a. Loss of $1,000

b. Loss of $3,000

c. Gain of $5,000

d. Loss of $5,000

Answers are given after Apply Your Knowledge (p. 770).

Assess Your Progress

Short Exercises

Determining bond prices at par, discount, or premium

S15-1 Determine whether the following bonds payable will be issued at maturity value, at a premium, or at a discount: (pp. 734–735)

  a. The market interest rate is 7%. Denver Corp. issues bonds payable with a stated rate of 6 1/2%. (pp. 734–735)

  b. Houston, Inc., issued 7% bonds payable when the market rate was 6 3/4%.

  c. Cincinnati Corporation issued 8% bonds when the market interest rate was 8%.

  d. Miami Company issued bonds payable that pay stated interest of 7%. At issuance, the market interest rate was 8 1/4%.

Pricing bonds

S15-2 Compute the price of the following 7% bonds of Allied Telecom. (pp. 736–737)

  a. $100,000 issued at 77.75

  b. $100,000 issued at 103.8

  c. $100,000 issued at 92.6

  d. $100,000 issued at 102.5

Maturity value of a bond

S15-3 For which bond payable in Short Exercise 15-2 will Allied Telecom have to pay the most at maturity? Explain your answer. (pp. 735–736)

Journalizing basic bond payable transactions

S15-4 Hunter Corporation issued a $100,000, 6 1/2%, 10-year bond payable. Journalize the following transactions for Hunter. Include an explanation for each entry.

  a. Issuance of the bond payable at par on January 1, 2008. (pp. 737–738)

  b. Payment of semiannual cash interest on July 1, 2008. (pp. 737–738)

  c. Payment of the bond payable at maturity. (Give the date.) (pp. 737–738)

Determining bonds payable amounts

S15-5 Sonic Drive-Ins borrowed money by issuing $1,000,000 of 6% bonds payable at 96.5.

  1. How much cash did Sonic receive when it issued the bonds payable? (pp. 740, 743)

  2. How much must Sonic pay back at maturity? (pp. 740, 743)

  3. How much cash interest will Sonic pay each six months? (pp. 740, 743)

Bond interest rates

S15-6 A 7%, 10-year bond was issued at a price of 93. Was the market interest rate at the date of issuance closest to 6%, 7%, or 8%? Explain. (pp. 734–735, 738–739)

Issuing bonds payable at a discount; paying interest and amortizing discount by the straight-line method

S15-7 Ogden, Inc., issued a $50,000, 8%, 10-year bond payable at a price of 90 on January 1, 2006. Journalize the following transactions for Ogden. Include an explanation for each entry.

  a. Issuance of the bond payable on January 1, 2006. (pp. 738–739)

  b. Payment of semiannual interest and amortization of bond discount on July 1, 2006. Ogden uses the straight-line method to amortize bond discount. (pp. 740, 743)

Issuing bonds payable at a premium; paying interest and amortizing premium by the straight-line method

S15-8 Washington Mutual Insurance Company issued an $80,000, 7%, 10-year bond payable at a price of 110 on January 1, 2009. Journalize the following transactions for Washington. Include an explanation for each entry.

a. Issuance of the bond payable on January 1, 2009. (pp. 744–745)

b. Payment of semiannual interest and amortization of bond premium on July 1, 2009. Washington uses the straight-line method to amortize the premium. (pp. 744–745)

Issuing bonds payable and accruing interest

S15-9 Onstar Communication issued $100,000 of 6%, 10-year bonds payable on October 1, 2008, at par value. Onstar's accounting year ends on December 31. Journalize the following transactions. Include an explanation for each entry.

a. Issuance of the bonds on October 1, 2008. (pp. 737–738)

b. Accrual of interest expense on December 31, 2008. (pp. 744–745)

c. Payment of the first semiannual interest amount on April 1, 2009. (pp. 744–745)

Issuing bonds payable between interest dates and then paying the interest

S15-10 Simons Realty issued $250,000 of 6%, 10-year bonds payable at par value on May 1, 2006, four months after the bond's original issue date of January 1, 2006. Journalize the following transactions. Include an explanation for each entry.

a. Issuance of the bonds payable on May 1, 2006. (pp. 744–745)

b. Payment of the first semiannual interest amount on July 1, 2006. (p. 746)

Accounting for the retirement of bonds payable

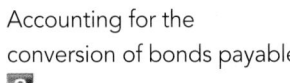

S15-11 On January 1, 2007, Pacifica, Inc., issued $100,000 of 9%, 5-year bonds payable at 104. Pacifica has extra cash and wishes to retire the bonds payable on January 1, 2008, immediately after making the second semiannual interest payment. To retire the bonds, Pacifica pays the market price of 98.

1. What is Pacifica's carrying amount of the bonds payable on the retirement date? (p. 746)

2. How much cash must Pacifica pay to retire the bonds payable? (p. 746)

3. Compute Pacifica's gain or loss on the retirement of the bonds payable. (p. 746)

Accounting for the conversion of bonds payable

S15-12 Newmarket Corp. has $1,000,000 of convertible bonds payable outstanding, with a bond premium of $20,000 also on the books. The bondholders have notified Newmarket that they wish to convert the bonds into stock. Specifically, the bonds may be converted into 400,000 shares of Newmarket's $1 par common stock.

1. What is Newmarket's carrying amount of its convertible bonds payable prior to the conversion? (p. 747)

2. Journalize Newmarket's conversion of the bonds payable into common stock. No explanation is required. (p. 747)

S15-13 Master Suites Hotels includes the following selected accounts in its general ledger at December 31, 2008:

Notes payable, long-term	$100,000	Accounts payable	$32,000
Bonds payable	200,000	Discount on bonds payable	6,000
Interest payable (due next year)	1,000		

Prepare the liabilities section of Master Suites' balance sheet at December 31, 2008, to show how the company would report these items. Report a total for current liabilities. (pp. 568, 748–749)

Earnings-per-share effects of financing with bonds versus stock

5

S15-14 Speegleville Marina needs to raise $1 million to expand. Speegleville's president is considering two plans:

- Plan A: Issue $1,000,000 of 8% bonds payable to borrow the money
- Plan B: Issue 100,000 shares of common stock at $10 per share

Before any new financing, the company expects to earn net income of $300,000, and the company already has 100,000 shares of common stock outstanding. Speegleville believes the expansion will increase income before interest and income tax by $200,000. The income tax rate is 35%.

Prepare an analysis similar to Exhibit 15-4 to determine which plan is likely to result in higher earnings per share. Which financing plan would you recommend? (p. 748–749)

Exercises

Determining whether the bond price will be at par, at a discount, or at a premium

1

E15-15 Havens Corp. is planning to issue long-term bonds payable to borrow for a major expansion. The chief executive, Richie Havens, asks your advice on some related matters, as follows:

a. At what type of bond price will Havens have total interest expense equal to the cash interest payments? (pp. 737–738)

b. Under which type of bond price will Havens's total interest expense be greater than the cash interest payments? (p. 740)

c. The stated interest rate on the bonds is 7%, and the market interest rate is 8%. What type of bond price can Havens expect for the bonds? (pp. 734–735)

d. Havens could raise the stated interest rate on the bonds to 9% (market rate is 8%). In that case, what type of price can Havens expect for the bonds? (pp. 734–735)

Issuing bonds payable, paying interest, and amortizing discount by the straight-line method

E15-16 On January 1, Deutsch Limited issues 8%, 20-year bonds payable with a maturity value of $100,000. The bonds sell at 97 and pay interest on January 1 and July 1. Deutsch amortizes bond discount by the straight-line method. Record (a) issuance of the bonds on January 1, and (b) the semiannual interest payment and amortization of bond discount on July 1. (pp. 738–743)

Issuing bonds payable, paying and accruing interest

1

E15-17 Pluto Corporation issued $400,000 of 7%, 20-year bonds payable on March 31, 2006. The bonds were issued at 100 and pay interest on March 31 and September 30. Record (a) issuance of the bonds on March 31, 2006, (b) payment of interest on September 30, (c) accrual of interest on December 31, and (d) payment of interest on March 31, 2007. (pp. 737–738)

Bond transactions at par, at a discount, and at a premium

1 **2**

E15-18 Columbus, Inc., issued $50,000 of 10-year, 6% bonds payable on January 1, 2006. Columbus pays interest each January 1 and July 1 and amortizes discount or premium by the straight-line method. The company can issue its bonds payable under various conditions:

a. Issuance at par (maturity) value (pp. 737–738)

b. Issuance at a price of 95 (pp. 737–740)

c. Issuance at a price of 105 (pp. 744–745)

Requirements

1. Journalize Columbus's issuance of the bonds and first semiannual interest payment for each situation. Explanations are not required.

2. Which bond price results in the most interest expense for Columbus? Explain in detail. (pp. 740, 744–745)

Issuing bonds, accruing interest, and paying interest

1

E15-19 Fleetwood Homebuilders issued $200,000 of 6%, 10-year bonds at par on August 31. Fleetwood pays semiannual interest on February 28 and August 31. Journalize for Fleetwood:

a. Issuance of the bonds payable on August 31, 2007. (pp. 737–738)

b. Accrual of interest on December 31, 2007. (pp. 744–745)

c. Payment of semiannual interest on February 28, 2008. (pp. 744–745)

Issuing bonds between interest dates

1

E15-20 Saturn Corporation issued $400,000 of 6% bonds payable on June 30. The bonds were dated April 30, and the semiannual interest dates are April 30 and October 31.

1. How much cash will Saturn receive upon issuance of the bonds on June 30? (pp. 744–745)

2. How much cash interest will Saturn pay on October 31, the first semiannual interest date? (p. 746)

Issuing bonds between interest dates and paying interest

1

E15-21 Lakewood Co. issues $100,000 of 6%, 20-year bonds payable that are dated April 30. Record (a) issuance of bonds at par on May 31 and (b) the next semiannual interest payment on October 31.

Recording retirement of bonds payable

3

E15-22 Virtuoso Transportation issued $600,000 of 8% bonds payable at 97 on October 1, 2010. These bonds are callable at 100 and mature on October 1, 2018. Virtuoso pays interest each April 1 and October 1. On October 1, 2015, when the bonds' market price is 99, Virtuoso retires the bonds in the most economical way available.

continued . . .

Requirement

Record the payment of the interest and amortization of bond discount at October 1, 2015, and the retirement of the bonds on that date. Virtuoso uses the straight-line amortization method.

Recording conversion of bonds payable

E15-23 Worldview Magazine, Inc., issued $700,000 of 15-year, 8 1/2% convertible bonds payable on July 31, 2006, at a price of 98. Each $1,000 maturity amount of the bonds is convertible into 50 shares of $5 par stock. On July 31, 2009, bondholders converted the bonds into common stock.

Requirements

1. What would cause the bondholders to convert their bonds into common stock?
2. Without making journal entries, compute the carrying amount of the bonds payable at July 31, 2009. The company uses the straight-line method to amortize bond discount.
3. All amortization has been recorded properly. Journalize the conversion transaction at July 31, 2009. No explanation is required.

Recording early retirement and conversion of bonds payable

E15-24 Superhero Industries reported the following at September 30:

Long-term liabilities:		
Convertible bonds payable	$200,000	
Less: Discount on bonds payable	(12,000)	$188,000

Requirements

1. Record retirement of half of the bonds on October 1 at the call price of 101.
2. Record conversion of the remainder of the bonds into 10,000 shares of Superhero Industries $1 par common stock on October 1. What would cause the bondholders to convert their bonds into stock?

Reporting liabilities

E15-25 At December 31, MediShare Precision Instruments owes $50,000 on accounts payable, plus salary payable of $10,000 and income tax payable of $8,000. MediShare also has $200,000 of bonds payable that require payment of a $20,000 installment next year and the remainder in later years. The bonds payable require an annual interest payment of $7,000, and MediShare still owes this interest for the current year.

Report MediShare's liabilities on its classified balance sheet. List the current liabilities in descending order (largest first, and so on), and show the total of current liabilities. (pp. 568, 748–749)

Analyzing alternative plans for raising money

E15-26 MC Electronics is considering two plans for raising $1,000,000 to expand operations. Plan A is to issue 9% bonds payable, and plan B is to issue 100,000 shares of common stock. Before any new financing, MC has net income of $300,000 and 100,000 shares of common stock outstanding. Management believes the company can use the new funds to earn additional income of $420,000 before interest and taxes. The income tax rate is 40%.

Requirement

Analyze MC Electronics' situation to determine which plan will result in higher earnings per share. Use Exhibit 15-4 as a guide. (pp. 748–749)

E15-27 This (partial and adapted) advertisement appeared in *The Wall Street Journal*.

New Issue

$300,000,000

HEWITT CORPORATION

10.5% Subordinated Debentures due March 31, 2015
interest payable March 31 and September 30

Price 98.50%   **March 31, 2005**

A *subordinated* debenture gives rights to the bondholder that are more restricted than the rights of other bondholders.

Requirements

Answer these questions about Hewitt Corporation's debenture bonds payable:

1. Hewitt issued these bonds payable at their offering price on March 31, 2005. Describe the transaction in detail, indicating who received cash, who paid cash, and how much.
2. Why is the stated interest rate on these bonds so high?
3. Compute Hewitt's annual cash interest payment on the bonds.
4. Compute Hewitt's annual interest expense under the straight-line amortization method.

E15-28 Refer to the bond situation of Hewitt Corporation in Exercise 15-27. Hewitt issued the bonds at the advertised price. The company uses the straight-line amortization method and reports financial statements on a calendar-year basis.

Requirements

1. Journalize the following bond transactions of Hewitt Corporation. Explanations are not required.

2005

Mar. 31   Issuance of the bonds.

Sep. 30   Payment of interest expense and amortization of discount on bonds payable.

---

continued . . .

2. What is Hewitt's carrying amount of the bonds payable at
   a. September 30, 2005?
   b. March 31, 2006?

Problems (Group A)

Analyzing bonds, recording bonds at par, and reporting on the financial statements
1 **4**

P15-29A Environmental Concerns Limited (ECL) issued $500,000 of 10-year, 6% bonds payable at maturity (par) value on May 1, 2008. The bonds pay interest each April 30 and October 31, and the company ends its accounting year on December 31.

Requirements

1. Fill in the blanks to complete these statements: (pp. 736–737)
   a. ECL's bonds are priced at (express the price as a percentage) _____. (pp. 736–737)
   b. When ECL issued its bonds, the market interest rate was _____%. (pp. 734–735)
   c. The amount of bond discount or premium for ECL to account for is $ _____ because the bonds were issued at _____. (pp. 737–738)

2. Journalize for ECL
   a. Issuance of the bonds payable on May 1, 2008. (pp. 737–738)
   b. Payment of interest on October 31, 2008. (pp. 737–738)
   c. Accrual of interest at December 31, 2008. (pp. 744–745)
   d. Payment of interest on April 30, 2009. (pp. 737–738)
   Explanations are not required.

3. Show what ECL will report on its income statement for 2008 and on its classified balance sheet at December 31, 2008. (pp. 748–749)

Issuing bonds and amortizing discount by the straight-line method
1 **2**

P15-30A On March 1, 2007, Educators Credit Union (ECU) issued 6%, 20-year bonds payable with maturity value of $300,000. The bonds pay interest on February 28 and August 31. ECU amortizes bond premium and discount by the straight-line method.

Requirements

1. If the market interest rate is 5% when ECU issues its bonds, will the bonds be priced at maturity (par) value, at a premium, or at a discount? Explain. (p. 739)

2. If the market interest rate is 7% when ECU issues its bonds, will the bonds be priced at par, at a premium, or at a discount? Explain. (p. 736)

3. The issue price of the bonds is 98. Journalize the following bond transactions:
   a. Issuance of the bonds on March 1, 2007. (pp. 744–745)
   b. Payment of interest and amortization of discount on August 31, 2007. (pp. 744–745)
   c. Accrual of interest and amortization of discount on December 31, 2007. (pp. 744–745)
   d. Payment of interest and amortization of discount on February 28, 2008. (pp. 744–745)

Determining bond price,
recording bond transactions
by the straight-line
amortization method

P15-31A El Conquistador, Inc., finances operations with both bonds and stock. Suppose El Conquistador issued $500,000 of 10-year, 8% bonds payable under various market conditions. Match each market interest rate with the appropriate bond price, as follows. The three possible bond prices are $467,000; $500,000; and $536,000.

Market Interest Rate	Bond Price
7%	?
8%	?
9%	?

El Conquistador pays annual interest each December 31.

After determining the respective bond prices, make the following journal entries for the bond discount situation (explanations are not required):

Dec. 31, 2006	Issuance of the bonds at a discount. (pp. 738–739)
Dec. 31, 2007	Payment of interest and amortization of bond discount by the straight-line method. (pp. 740, 743)
Dec. 31, 2016	Payment of interest and amortization of bond discount by the straight-line method. (pp. 740, 743)
Dec. 31, 2016	Final payment of the bonds payable. (pp. 740, 743)

How much total interest expense will El Conquistador have during the 10-year life of these bonds?

Analyzing a company's long-
term debt and journalizing
its transactions

P15-32A Captain Billy Whizbang Hamburgers, Inc., issued 6%, 10-year bonds payable at 95 on December 31, 2005. At December 31, 2007, Captain Billy reported the bonds payable as follows:

Long-Term Debt:		
Bonds payable..................	$200,000	
Less: Discount..................	(8,000)	192,000

Captain Billy uses the straight-line amortization method and pays semi-annual interest each June 30 and December 31.

Requirements

1. Answer the following questions about Captain Billy Whizbang's bonds payable:

   a. What is the maturity value of the bonds? (pp. 738–739)

   b. What is the carrying amount of the bonds at December 31, 2007? (pp. 738–739)

   c. What is the annual cash interest payment on the bonds? (pp. 740, 743)

   d. How much interest expense should the company record each year? (pp. 740, 743)

2. Record the June 30, 2008, semiannual interest payment and amortization of discount. (pp. 740, 743)

3. What will be the carrying amount of the bonds at December 31, 2008? (pp. 740, 743)

P15-33A The board of directors of Changing Seasons Health Spa authorizes the issuance of $600,000 of 7%, 10-year bonds payable. The semiannual interest dates are May 31 and November 30. The bonds are issued on July 31, 2008, at par plus accrued interest.

Requirements
1. Journalize the following transactions:
   a. Issuance of the bonds on July 31, 2008.
   b. Payment of interest on November 30, 2008.
   c. Accrual of interest on December 31, 2008.
   d. Payment of interest on May 31, 2009.
2. Report interest payable and bonds payable as they would appear on the Changing Seasons balance sheet at December 31, 2008.

P15-34A The accounting records of Earthlink Wireless include the following:

Mortgage note payable, long-term	$77,000	Salary payable	$	9,000
		Bonds payable, long-term		160,000
Accounts payable	74,000	Premium on bonds payable		
Bonds payable, current installment	20,000	(all long-term)		13,000
		Unearned service revenue		3,000
Interest payable	14,000	Common stock, no par		100,000

Requirements
Report these liabilities on the Earthlink Wireless balance sheet, including headings and totals for current liabilities and long-term liabilities. (pp. 568, 738–739, 748–749)

Financing operations with debt or with stock

P15-35A Two businesses are considering how to raise $5 million.

Buchanan Corporation is having its best year since it began operations in 1998. For each of the past 10 years, earnings per share have increased by at least 15%. The outlook for the future is equally bright, with new markets opening up and competitors unable to manufacture products of Buchanan's quality. Buchanan Corporation is planning a large-scale expansion.

Garfield Company has fallen on hard times. Net income has been flat for the last 6 years, with this year falling by 10% from last year's level of profits. Top management has experienced turnover, and the company lacks leadership. To become competitive again, Garfield desperately needs $5 million for expansion.

Requirements
1. As an independent consultant, propose a plan for each company to raise the needed cash. Which company should issue bonds payable? Which company should issue stock? Consider the advantages and the disadvantages of raising money by issuing bonds and by issuing stock, and discuss them in your answer. Use the following memorandum headings to report your plans for the two companies. (pp. 748–749)
   • Plan for Buchanan Corporation to raise $5 million
   • Plan for Garfield Company to raise $5 million

continued . . .

Set up your memo as follows:

```
Date: _____

  To: Managements of Buchanan Corporation and Garfield Company

From: (Student Name)

Subject: Plan for each company to raise $5 million
_____

• Plan for Buchanan Corporation to raise $5 million

• Plan for Garfield Company to raise $5 million
```

2. How will what you learned in this problem help you manage a business?

Problems (Group B)

Analyzing bonds, recording bonds at par, and reporting on the financial statements

P15-36B Total Placement Service (TPS) issued $600,000 of 20-year, 7% bonds payable at maturity (par) value on February 1, 2008. The bonds pay interest each January 31 and July 31, and the company ends its accounting year on December 31.

1. Fill in the blanks to complete these statements:
    a. TPS's bonds are priced at (express the price as a percentage) _____. (pp. 736–737)
    b. When TPS issued its bonds, the market interest rate was _____ %. (pp. 734–735)
    c. The amount of bond discount or premium for TPS to account for is $_____ because the bonds were issued at _____. (pp. 737–738)

2. Journalize for TPS
    a. Issuance of the bonds payable on February 1, 2008. (pp. 737–738)
    b. Payment of interest on July 31, 2008. (pp. 737–738)
    c. Accrual of interest at December 31, 2008. (pp. 744–745)
    d. Payment of interest on January 31, 2009. (pp. 737–738)
    Explanations are not required.

3. Show what TPS will report on its income statement for the year ended December 31, 2008, and on its classified balance sheet at December 31, 2008. (pp. 748–749)

Issuing notes payable and amortizing premium by the straight-line method

P15-37B On April 1, 2006, US Ultracom issued 7%, 10-year bonds payable with maturity value of $400,000. The bonds pay interest on March 31 and September 30, and US Ultracom amortizes premium and discount by the straight-line method.

continued . . .

Requirements

1. If the market interest rate is 6 1/2% when US Ultracom issues its bonds, will the bonds be priced at maturity (par) value, at a premium, or at a discount? Explain. (pp. 735–736)

2. If the market interest rate is 8% when US Ultracom issues its bonds, will the bonds be priced at par, at a premium, or at a discount? Explain. (pp. 735–736)

3. Assume that the issue price of the bonds is 101. Journalize the following bonds payable transactions:

    a. Issuance of the bonds on April 1, 2006. (pp. 744–745)

    b. Payment of interest and amortization of premium on September 30, 2006. (pp. 744–745)

    c. Accrual of interest and amortization of premium on December 31, 2006. (pp. 744–745)

    d. Payment of interest and amortization of premium on March 31, 2007. (pp. 744–745)

Determining bond price; recording bond transactions by the straight-line amortization method

P15-38B Tristate Recreation Park (TRP) finances operations with both bonds and stock. Suppose TRP issued $200,000 of 10-year, 6% bonds payable under various market conditions. Match each market interest rate with the appropriate bond price, as follows. The three possible bond prices are $216,000; $200,000; and $186,000.

Market Interest Rate	Bond Price
7%	?
6%	?
5%	?

TRP pays annual interest each December 31.

After determining the respective bond prices, make the following journal entries for the bond premium situation (explanations are not required):

Dec. 31, 2008	Issuance of the bonds at a premium. (pp. 744–745)
Dec. 31, 2009	Payment of interest and amortization of bond premium by the straight-line method. (pp. 744–745)
Dec. 31, 2018	Payment of interest and amortization of bond premium by the straight-line method. (pp. 744–745)
Dec. 31, 2018	Final payment of the bonds payable. (pp. 740, 743)

How much total interest expense will TRP have during the 10-year life of these bonds?

Analyzing a company's long-term debt and journalizing its transactions

P15-39B Holze Music Co. issued 5%, 10-year bonds payable at 75 on December 31, 2006. At December 31, 2009, Holze reported the bonds payable as follows:

Long-Term Debt:		
Bonds payable..................	$200,000	
Less: Discount..................	(35,000)	$165,000

Holze uses the straight-line amortization method.

continued . . .

Requirements

1. Answer the following questions about Holze's bonds payable:

    a. What is the maturity value of the bonds? (pp. 738–739)

    b. What is the carrying amount of the bonds at December 31, 2009? (pp. 738–739)

    c. What is Holze's annual cash interest payment on the bonds? (pp. 740, 743)

    d. How much interest expense should Holze record each year? (pp. 740, 743)

2. Holze pays annual interest for these bonds each year on December 31. Record the December 31, 2010, annual interest payment and amortization of discount. (pp. 740, 743)

3. What will be the carrying amount of the bonds at December 31, 2010? (pp. 740, 743)

Recording bonds (at par) and reporting bonds payable on the balance sheet—bonds issued between interest dates

P15-40B The board of directors of Beta North America, Inc., authorizes the issuance of $1 million of 9%, 20-year bonds payable. The semiannual interest dates are March 31 and September 30. The bonds are issued on April 30, 2007, at par plus accrued interest.

Requirements

1. Journalize the following transactions:

    a. Issuance of the bonds on April 30, 2007. (pp. 744–745)

    b. Payment of interest on September 30, 2007. (p. 746)

    c. Accrual of interest on December 31, 2007. (pp. 744–745)

    d. Payment of interest on March 31, 2008. (pp. 744–745)

2. Report interest payable and bonds payable as they would appear on the Beta balance sheet at December 31, 2007. (pp. 748–749)

Reporting liabilities on the balance sheet

P15-41B The accounting records of Compass Bookstores, Inc., include the following:

Accounts payable	$ 68,000	Salary payable	$32,000
Mortgage note payable—		Bonds payable, current portion	25,000
long-term	110,000	Discount on all bonds payable	
Interest payable	19,000	(all long-term)	10,000
Bonds payable, long-term	300,000	Income tax payable	16,000
Common stock, no par	155,000		

Requirement

Report these liabilities on Compass Bookstores' balance sheet, including headings and totals for current liabilities and long-term liabilities. (pp. 568, 738–739, 748–749)

Financing operations with debt or with stock

P15-42B Brigadier Homebuilders is embarking on a massive expansion. Plans call for building 100 homes within the next two years. Management estimates that the expansion will cost $15 million. The board of directors is considering obtaining the $15 million through issuing either bonds payable or common stock.

continued . . .

Requirements

1. Write a memo to company management. Discuss the advantages and disadvantages of issuing bonds and of issuing common stock to raise the needed cash. Use the following format for your memo (pp. 748–749):

Date: _____

To: Management of Brigadier Homebuilders

From: (Student Name) _____

Subject: Advantages and disadvantages of issuing bonds and of issuing stock to raise $15 million for expansion

---

Advantages and disadvantages of issuing bonds:

Advantages and disadvantages of issuing stock:

for 24-7 practice, visit
www.MyAccountingLab.com

2. How will what you learned in this problem help you manage a business?

Apply Your Knowledge

Decision Cases

Questions about long-term debt

Case 1. The following questions are not related.

1. Duncan Brooks Co. needs to borrow $500,000 to open new stores. Brooks can borrow $500,000 by issuing 5%, 10-year bonds at a price of 96. How much will Brooks actually be borrowing under this arrangement? How much must Brooks pay back at maturity? How will Brooks account for the difference between the amount borrowed and the amount paid back? (pp. 738–739, 740, 743)

2. Brooks prefers to borrow for longer periods when interest rates are low and for shorter periods when interest rates are high. Why is this a good business strategy? (Challenge)

Analyzing alternative ways of raising $4 million

5

Case 2. Business is going well for Email Designers. The board of directors of this family-owned company believes that Email Designers could earn an additional $1,000,000 income before interest and taxes by expanding into new markets. However, the $4,000,000 the business needs for growth cannot be raised within the family. The directors, who strongly wish to retain family control of the company, must issue securities to outsiders. They are considering three financing plans.

Plan A is to borrow at 6%. Plan B is to issue 100,000 shares of common stock. Plan C is to issue 100,000 shares of nonvoting, $2.50 preferred stock ($2.50 is the annual cash dividend for each share of preferred stock). Email Designers currently has net income of $1,200,000 and 400,000 shares of common stock outstanding. The company's income tax rate is 40%.

Requirements

1. Prepare an analysis similar to Exhibit 15-4 to determine which plan will result in the highest earnings per share of common stock. (pp. 748–749)

2. Recommend one plan to the board of directors. Give your reasons.

Ethical Issue

Axiom Sports Co. owes $5 million on notes payable that will come due for payment in $2.5 million annual installments, starting next year. Cash is scarce, and Axiom management doesn't know where next year's note payment will come from. Axiom has prepared its balance sheet as follows:

Liabilities	
Current:	
Accounts payable	$1,900,000
Salary payable and other accrued liabilities	300,000
Unearned revenue collected in advance	500,000
Income tax payable	200,000
Total current liabilities	2,900,000
Long-term:	
Notes payable	5,000,000

What is wrong with the way Axiom reported its liabilities? Why did Axiom report its liabilities this way? What is unethical about this way of reporting *these* liabilities? Who can be harmed as a result?

Financial Statement Case

Analyzing long-term debt

1 **2**

The Amazon.com balance sheet, income statement (statement of operations), and Note 4 in Appendix A at the end of this book provide details about the company's long-term debt. Use those data to answer the following questions.

Requirements

1. How much did Amazon.com owe on long-term debt at December 31, 2005? How much of this debt was payable in the coming year?

2. Journalize in a single entry Amazon's interest expense for 2005. Amazon paid cash of $105 million for interest.

3. Refer to Note 4 and compute the annual interest on Amazon's 4.75% convertible subordinated notes. Round to the nearest $1 thousand.

Team Project

Each member of the team should select a large corporation and go to its Web site. Surf around until you find the company's balance sheet. Often the appropriate tab is labeled as

- Investor Relations

- About the Company

- Financial Reports

- 10-K Report

From the company's balance sheet scroll down until you find the liabilities.

Requirements

1. List all the company's liabilities—both current and long-term—along with each amount.

2. Read the company's notes to the financial statements and include any details that help you identify the amount of a liability.

3. Compute the company's current ratio and debt ratio. (p. 210)

4. Bring your findings to your team meeting, compare your results with those of your team members, and prepare either a written report or an oral report, as directed by your instructor.

For Internet exercises, Excel in Practice, and additional online activities, go to the Web site www.prenhall.com/horngren.

Quick Check Answers

1. *d* 2. *b* 3. *c* 4. *a* 5. *d* 6. *c* 7. *a* 8. *b* 9. *c* 10. *a*

The Time Value of Money: Present Value of a Bond and Effective-Interest Amortization

The term *time value of money* refers to the fact that money earns interest over time. Interest is the cost of using money. To borrowers, interest is the expense of renting money. To lenders, interest is the revenue earned from lending. In this chapter we focus on the borrower, who owes money on the bonds payable.

Present Value

Often a person knows a future amount, such as the maturity value of a bond, and needs to know the bond's present value. The present value of the bond measures its price and tells an investor how much to pay for the bond.

Present Value of 1

Suppose an investment promises you $5,000 at the *end* of one year. How much would you pay *now* to acquire this investment? You would be willing to pay the present value of the $5,000 future amount.

Present value depends on three factors:

1. the amount to be received in the future

2. the time span between your investment and your future receipt

3. the interest rate

Computing a present value is called *discounting* because the present value is *always less* than the future value.

In our example, the future receipt is $5,000. The investment period is one year. Assume that you demand an annual interest rate of 10% on your investment. The following diagram shows that the present value of $5,000 at 10% for one year is $4,545.

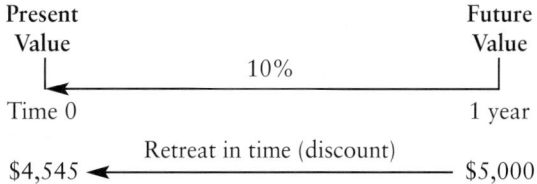

You can compute the present value of $5,000 at 10% for one year, as follows:

$$\frac{\text{Future value}}{(1 + \text{Interest rate})} = \frac{\$5,000}{1.10} = \$4,545$$

If the $5,000 is to be received two years from now, you will pay only $4,132 for the investment, as follows:

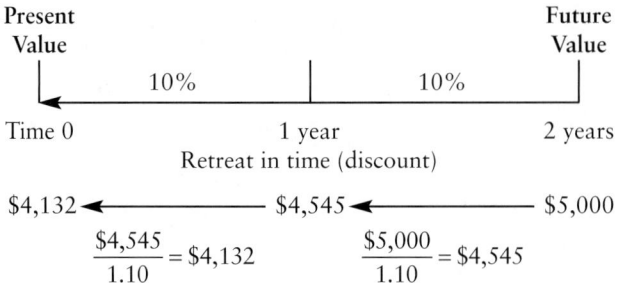

$$\frac{\$4,545}{1.10} = \$4,132 \qquad \frac{\$5,000}{1.10} = \$4,545$$

Present-Value Tables

We have shown how to compute a present value. But that computation is burdensome for an investment that spans many years. Present-value tables ease our work. Let's reexamine our examples of present value by using Exhibit 15A-1, Present Value of $1.

EXHIBIT 15A-1   Present Value of $1

Present Value of $1

Period	4%	5%	6%	7%	8%	10%	12%	14%	16%
1	0.962	0.952	0.943	0.935	0.926	0.909	0.893	0.877	0.862
2	0.925	0.907	0.890	0.873	0.857	0.826	0.797	0.769	0.743
3	0.889	0.864	0.840	0.816	0.794	0.751	0.712	0.675	0.641
4	0.855	0.823	0.792	0.763	0.735	0.683	0.636	0.592	0.552
5	0.822	0.784	0.747	0.713	0.681	0.621	0.567	0.519	0.476
6	0.790	0.746	0.705	0.666	0.630	0.564	0.507	0.456	0.410
7	0.760	0.711	0.665	0.623	0.583	0.513	0.452	0.400	0.354
8	0.731	0.677	0.627	0.582	0.540	0.467	0.404	0.351	0.305
9	0.703	0.645	0.592	0.544	0.500	0.424	0.361	0.308	0.263
10	0.676	0.614	0.558	0.508	0.463	0.386	0.322	0.270	0.227
11	0.650	0.585	0.527	0.475	0.429	0.350	0.287	0.237	0.195
12	0.625	0.557	0.497	0.444	0.397	0.319	0.257	0.208	0.168
13	0.601	0.530	0.469	0.415	0.368	0.290	0.229	0.182	0.145
14	0.577	0.505	0.442	0.388	0.340	0.263	0.205	0.160	0.125
15	0.555	0.481	0.417	0.362	0.315	0.239	0.183	0.140	0.108
16	0.534	0.458	0.394	0.339	0.292	0.218	0.163	0.123	0.093
17	0.513	0.436	0.371	0.317	0.270	0.198	0.146	0.108	0.080
18	0.494	0.416	0.350	0.296	0.250	0.180	0.130	0.095	0.069
19	0.475	0.396	0.331	0.277	0.232	0.164	0.116	0.083	0.060
20	0.456	0.377	0.312	0.258	0.215	0.149	0.104	0.073	0.051

For the 10% investment for one year, we find the junction in the 10% column and across from 1 in the Period column. The figure 0.909 is computed as follows: 1/1.10 = 0.909. This work has been done for us and all the present values are given in the table. The heading in Exhibit 15A-1 states $1. To figure present value for $5,000, we multiply $5,000 by 0.909. The result is $4,545, which matches the result we obtained by hand.

For the two-year investment, we read down the 10% column and across the Period 2 row. We multiply 0.826 (computed as 0.909/1.10 = 0.826) by $5,000 and get $4,130, which confirms our earlier computation of $4,132 (the difference is due to rounding in the present-value table). Using the table, we can compute the present value of any single future amount.

Present Value of an Annuity

Let's return to the investment example that provided a single future receipt ($5,000 at the end of two years). Annuity investments provide multiple receipts of an equal amount at fixed intervals.

Consider an investment that promises *annual* cash receipts of $10,000 to be received at the end of each of three years. Assume that you demand a 12% return on your investment. What is the investment's present value? The present value determines how much you would pay today to acquire the investment. The investment spans three periods, and you would pay the sum of three present values. The computation follows.

The present value of this annuity is $24,020. By paying $24,020 today, you will receive $10,000 at the end of each of the three years while earning 12% on your investment.

Year	Annual Cash Receipt	×	Present Value of $1 at 12% (Exhibit 15A-1)	=	Present Value of Annual Cash Receipt
1	$10,000	×	0.893	=	$ 8,930
2	10,000	×	0.797	=	7,970
3	10,000	×	0.712	=	7,120
		Total present value of investment		=	$24,020

The example illustrates repetitive computations of the three future amounts. One way to ease the computational burden is to add the three present values of $1 (0.893 + 0.797 + 0.712) and multiply their sum (2.402) by the annual cash receipt ($10,000) to obtain the present value of the annuity ($10,000 × 2.402 = $24,020).

An easier approach is to use a present value of an annuity table. Exhibit 15A-2 on the next page shows the present value of $1 to be received at the end of each period for a given number of periods. The present value of a three-period annuity at 12% is 2.402 (the junction of the Period 3 row and the 12% column). Thus, $10,000 received annually at the end of each of three years, discounted at 12%, is $24,020 ($10,000 × 2.402), which is the present value.

Present Value of Bonds Payable

The present value of a bond—its market price—is the sum of

- the present value of the principal amount to be received at maturity—a single amount (present value of $1) *plus*
- the present value of the future stated interest amounts—an annuity because it occurs periodically (present value of annuity of $1).

Present Value of Annuity of $1

Period	4%	5%	6%	7%	8%	10%	12%	14%	16%
1	0.962	0.952	0.943	0.935	0.926	0.909	0.893	0.877	0.862
2	1.886	1.859	1.833	1.808	1.783	1.736	1.690	1.647	1.605
3	2.775	2.723	2.673	2.624	2.577	2.487	2.402	2.322	2.246
4	3.630	3.546	3.465	3.387	3.312	3.170	3.037	2.914	2.798
5	4.452	4.329	4.212	4.100	3.993	3.791	3.605	3.433	3.274
6	5.242	5.076	4.917	4.767	4.623	4.355	4.111	3.889	3.685
7	6.002	5.786	5.582	5.389	5.206	4.868	4.564	4.288	4.039
8	6.733	6.463	6.210	5.971	5.747	5.335	4.968	4.639	4.344
9	7.435	7.108	6.802	6.515	6.247	5.759	5.328	4.946	4.607
10	8.111	7.722	7.360	7.024	6.710	6.145	5.650	5.216	4.833
11	8.760	8.306	7.887	7.499	7.139	6.495	5.938	5.453	5.029
12	9.385	8.863	8.384	7.943	7.536	6.814	6.194	5.660	5.197
13	9.986	9.394	8.853	8.358	7.904	7.103	6.424	5.842	5.342
14	10.563	9.899	9.295	8.745	8.244	7.367	6.628	6.002	5.468
15	11.118	10.380	9.712	9.108	8.559	7.606	6.811	6.142	5.575
16	11.652	10.838	10.106	9.447	8.851	7.824	6.974	6.265	5.669
17	12.166	11.274	10.477	9.763	9.122	8.022	7.120	6.373	5.749
18	12.659	11.690	10.828	10.059	9.372	8.201	7.250	6.467	5.818
19	13.134	12.085	11.158	10.336	9.604	8.365	7.366	6.550	5.877
20	13.590	12.462	11.470	10.594	9.818	8.514	7.469	6.623	5.929

Discount Price

Let's compute the present value of the 9%, five-year bonds of Air West Airlines. The maturity value of the bonds is $100,000 and they pay 4 1/2% stated interest semi-annually. At issuance, the annual market interest rate is 10% (5% semiannually). Therefore, the market interest rate for each of the 10 semiannual periods is 5%. We use 5% to compute the present value (PV) of the maturity and the present value (PV) of the stated interest. The market price of these bonds is $96,149, as follows:

AIR WEST BONDS—DISCOUNT PRICE $96,149

	Effective Annual Interest Rate ÷ 2	Number of Semiannual Interest Payments	
PV of principal:			
$100,000 × PV of single amount at 5%		for 10 periods	
($100,000 × 0.614—Exhibit 15A-1)			$61,400
PV of stated interest:			
($100,000 × 0.045) × PV of annuity at 5%		for 10 periods	
($4,500 × 7.722—Exhibit 15A-2)			34,749
PV (market price) of bonds			$96,149

The market price of the Air West bonds shows a discount because the stated interest rate on the bonds (9%) is less than the market interest rate (10%). We discuss these bonds in more detail in the next section of this appendix.

Premium Price

Let's consider a premium price for the Air West bonds. Now suppose the market interest rate is 8% at issuance (4% for each of the 10 semiannual periods):

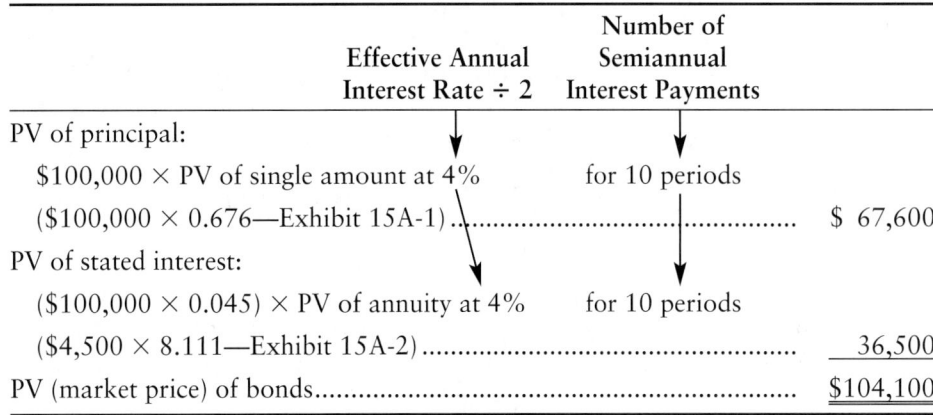

AIR WEST BONDS—PREMIUM PRICE $104,100

	Effective Annual Interest Rate ÷ 2	Number of Semiannual Interest Payments	
PV of principal:			
$100,000 × PV of single amount at 4%		for 10 periods	
($100,000 × 0.676—Exhibit 15A-1)			$ 67,600
PV of stated interest:			
($100,000 × 0.045) × PV of annuity at 4%		for 10 periods	
($4,500 × 8.111—Exhibit 15A-2)			36,500
PV (market price) of bonds			$104,100

We discuss accounting for these bonds in the next section.

Effective-Interest Method of Amortization

We began this chapter with straight-line amortization to introduce the concept of amortizing bonds. A more precise way of amortizing bonds is used in practice, and it's called the **effective-interest method**. That method uses the present-value concepts covered in this appendix.

Generally accepted accounting principles require that interest expense be measured using the *effective-interest method* unless the straight-line amounts are similar. In that case, either method is permitted. Total interest expense over the life of the bonds is the same under both methods. We now show how the effective-interest method works.

Effective-Interest Amortization for a Bond Discount

Assume that Air West Airlines issues $100,000 of 9% bonds at a time when the market rate of interest is 10%. These bonds mature in 5 years and pay interest semiannually, so there are 10 semiannual interest payments. As we just saw, the issue price of the bonds is $96,149,[3] and the discount on these bonds is $3,851 ($100,000 − $96,149). Exhibit 15-A3 shows how to measure interest expense by the effective-interest method. (You will need an amortization table to account for bonds by the effective-interest method.)

EXHIBIT 15A-3   **Effective-Interest Amortization of a Bond Discount**

PANEL A—Bond Data

Maturity value—$100,000
Stated interest rate—9%
Interest paid—4 1/2% semiannually, $4,500 ($100,000 × 0.045)
Market interest rate at time of issue—10% annually, 5% semiannually
Issue price—$96,149 on January 1, 2008

PANEL B—Amortization Table

End of Semiannual Interest Period	A Interest Payment (4 1/2% of maturity value)	B Interest *Expense* (5% of preceding bond carrying amount)	C Discount Amortization (B – A)	D Discount Balance (D – C)	E Bond Carrying Amount ($100,000 – D)
Jan. 1, 2008				$3,851	$ 96,149
July 1	$4,500	$4,807	$307	3,544	96,456
Jan. 1, 2009	4,500	4,823	323	3,221	96,779
July 1	4,500	4,839	339	2,882	97,118
Jan. 1, 2010	4,500	4,856	356	2,526	97,474
July 1	4,500	4,874	374	2,152	97,848
Jan. 1, 2011	4,500	4,892	392	1,760	98,240
July 1	4,500	4,912	412	1,348	98,652
Jan. 1, 2012	4,500	4,933	433	915	99,085
July 1	4,500	4,954	454	461	99,539
Jan. 1, 2013	4,500	4,961*	461	0	100,000

*Adjusted for effect of rounding.

Notes
• *Column A* The interest payments are constant.
• *Column B* The interest expense each period is the preceding bond carrying amount multiplied by the market interest rate.
• *Column C* The excess of interest expense (B) over interest payment (A) is the discount amortization.
• *Column D* The discount decreases by the amount of amortization for the period (C).
• *Column E* The bonds' carrying amount increases from $96,149 at issuance to $100,000 at maturity.

The *accounts* debited and credited under the effective-interest method and the straight-line method are the same. Only the *amounts* differ.

---

[3]We compute this present value on page 774.

Exhibit 15-A3 gives the amounts for all the bond transactions of Air West Airlines. Let's begin with issuance of the bonds payable on January 1, 2008, and the first interest payment on July 1. Entries follow, using amounts from the respective lines of Exhibit 15-A3.

2008			
Jan. 1	Cash (column E)	96,149	
	Discount on Bonds Payable (column D)	3,851	
	Bonds Payable (maturity value)		100,000
	Issued bonds at a discount.		

2008			
July 1	Interest Expense (column B)	4,807	
	Discount on Bonds Payable (column C)		307
	Cash (column A)		4,500
	Paid interest and amortized discount.		

Effective-Interest Amortization of a Bond Premium

Air West Airlines may issue its bonds payable at a premium. Assume that Air West issues $100,000 of 5-year, 9% bonds when the market interest rate is 8%. The bonds' issue price is $104,100,[4] and the premium is $4,100.

Exhibit 15-A4 provides the data for all the bond transactions of Air West Airlines. Let's begin with issuance of the bonds on January 1, 2008, and the first interest payment on July 1. These entries follow.

2008			
Jan. 1	Cash (column E)	104,100	
	Bonds Payable (maturity value)		100,000
	Premium on Bonds Payable (column D)		
	Issued bonds at a premium.		4,100

2008			
July 1	Interest Expense (column B)	4,164	
	Premium on Bonds Payable (column C)	336	
	Cash (column A)		4,500
	Paid interest and amortized premium.		

---

[4]Again, we compute the present value of the bonds on page 775.

PANEL A—Bond Data

Maturity value—$100,000

Stated interest rate—9%

Interest paid—4 1/2% semiannually, $4,500 ($100,000 × 0.045)

Market interest rate at time of issue—8% annually, 4% semiannually

Issue price—$104,100 on January 1, 2008

PANEL B—Amortization Table

	A	B	C	D	E
		Interest *Expense*			
	Interest	(4% of			
	Payment	preceding			Bond
End of	(4 1/2% of	bond	Premium	Premium	Carrying
Semiannual	maturity	carrying	Amortization	Balance	Amount
Interest Period	value)	amount)	(B – A)	(D – C)	($100,000 + D)
Jan. 1, 2008				$4,100	$104,100
July 1	$4,500	$4,164	$336	3,764	103,764
Jan. 1, 2009	4,500	4,151	349	3,415	103,415
July 1	4,500	4,137	363	3,052	103,052
Jan. 1, 2010	4,500	4,122	378	2,674	102,674
July 1	4,500	4,107	393	2,281	102,281
Jan. 1, 2011	4,500	4,091	409	1,872	101,872
July 1	4,500	4,075	425	1,447	101,447
Jan. 1, 2012	4,500	4,058	442	1,005	101,005
July 1	4,500	4,040	460	545	100,545
Jan. 1, 2013	4,500	3,955*	545	0	100,000

*Adjusted for effect of rounding.

Notes
- *Column A* The interest payments are constant.
- *Column B* The interest expense each period is the preceding bond carrying amount multiplied by the market interest rate.
- *Column C* The excess of interest payment (A) over interest expense (B) is the premium amortization.
- *Column D* The premium balance decreases by the amount of amortization for the period.
- *Column E* The bonds' carrying amount decreases from $104,100 at issuance to $100,000 at maturity.

Appendix 15A Assignments

Problems

Computing present-value
amounts

P15A-1 Exxel, Inc., needs new manufacturing equipment. Two companies can
provide similar equipment but under different payment plans:

    a. General Electric (GE) offers to let Exxel pay $60,000 each year for
five years. The payments include interest at 12% per year. What is
the present value of the payments? (pp. 773–774, 775)

continued . . .

b. Westinghouse will let Exxel make a single payment of $400,000 at the end of five years. This payment includes both principal and interest at 12%. What is the present value of this payment? (pp. 771, 772)

c. Exxel will purchase the equipment that costs the least, as measured by present value. Which equipment should Exxel select? Why? (Challenge)

Computing the present values of bonds

P15A-2 Determine the present value of the following bonds (pp. 744–745):

a. Ten-year bonds payable with maturity value of $88,000 and stated interest rate of 12%, paid semiannually. The market rate of interest is 12% at issuance.

b. Same bonds payable as in a, but the market interest rate is 14%.

c. Same bonds payable as in a, but the market interest rate is 10%.

Recording bond transactions; straight-line amortization

P15A-3 For each bond in Problem 15A-2, journalize issuance of the bond and the first semiannual interest payment. The company amortizes bond premium and discount by the straight-line method. Explanations are not required. (pp. 738–739, 740, 743, 744–745)

Issuing bonds payable and amortizing discount by the effective-interest method

P15A-4 IMAX, Inc., issued $600,000 of 7%, 10-year bonds payable at a price of 90 on March 31, 2008. The market interest rate at the date of issuance was 9%, and the bonds pay interest semiannually.

1. How much cash did IMAX receive upon issuance of the bonds payable? (p. 776)

2. Prepare an effective-interest amortization table for the bond discount, through the first two interest payments. Use Exhibit 15-A3 as a guide, and round amounts to the nearest dollar. (p. 776)

3. Record IMAX's issuance of the bonds on March 31, 2008, and on September 30, 2008, payment of the first semiannual interest amount and amortization of the bond discount. Explanations are not required. (p. 777)

Issuing bonds payable and amortizing premium by the effective-interest method

P15A-5 Jon Spelman Co. issued $200,000 of 8%, 10-year bonds payable at a price of 110 on May 31, 2008. The market interest rate at the date of issuance was 6%, and the Spelman bonds pay interest semiannually.

1. How much cash did Spelman receive upon issuance of the bonds payable? (p. 777)

2. Prepare an effective-interest amortization table for the bond premium, through the first two interest payments. Use Exhibit 15-A4 as a guide, and round amounts to the nearest dollar. (p. 777)

3. Record Spelman's issuance of the bonds on May 31, 2008, and, on November 30, 2008, payment of the first semiannual interest amount and amortization of the bond premium. Explanations are not required. (p. 777)

Effective-interest method for bond discount: recording interest payments and interest expense

P15A-6 Serenity, Inc., is authorized to issue 7%, 10-year bonds payable. On January 2, 2007, when the market interest rate is 8%, the company issues $300,000 of the bonds and receives cash of $279,600. Serenity amortizes bond discount by the effective-interest method. Interest dates are January 2 and July 2.

continued . . .

Requirements

1. Prepare an amortization table for the first two semiannual interest periods. Follow the format of Exhibit 15-A3, page 776.

2. Record issuance of the bonds payable and the first semiannual interest payment on July 2. (p. 776)

Debt payment and discount amortization schedule

P15A-7 Neiderhoffer Corp. issued $500,000 of 8 3/8% (0.08375), five-year bonds payable when the market interest rate was 9 1/2% (0.095). Neiderhoffer pays interest annually at year-end. The issue price of the bonds was $478,402.

Requirement

Create a spreadsheet model to prepare a schedule to measure interest expense on these bonds. Use the effective-interest method of amortization. Round to the nearest dollar, and format your answer as follows. (p. 776)

	A	B	C	D	E	F
1						
2						Bond
3		Interest	Interest	Discount	Discount	Carrying
4	Date	Payment	Expense	Amortization	Balance	Amount
5	1-1-01				$ ☐	$478,402
6	12-31-01	$ ☐	$ ☐	$ ☐		☐
7	12-31-02					
8	12-31-03					
9	12-31-04					
10	12-31-05					
		500000*.08375	+F5*.095	+C6−B6	500000−F5	+F5+D6

Computing a bond's present value, recording its issuance, interest payments, and amortization by the effective-interest method

P15A-8 On December 31, 2008, when the market interest rate is 8%, Willis Realty Co. issues $400,000 of 7.25%, 10-year bonds payable. The bonds pay interest semiannually.

Requirements

1. Determine the present value of the bonds at issuance. (pp. 744–745)

2. Assume that the bonds are issued at the price computed in requirement 1. Prepare an effective-interest method amortization table for the first two semiannual interest periods. (p. 776)

3. Using the amortization table prepared in requirement 2, journalize issuance of the bonds and the first two interest payments. (p. 777)

Comprehensive Problem for Chapters 13 - 15

Apache Motors' Corporate Transactions

Apache Motors' corporate charter authorizes the company to issue 1 million shares of $1 par-value common stock and 200,000 shares of no-par preferred stock. During the first quarter of operations, Apache completed the following selected transactions:

Oct.	1	Issued 50,000 shares of $1-par common stock for cash of $6 per share. (pp. 646–647)
	1	Issued $200,000 of 9%, 10-year bonds payable at 90. (pp. 738–739)
	5	Issued 2,000 shares of no-par preferred stock, receiving cash of $100,000. (pp. 648–649)
Nov.	2	Purchased 11,000 shares of Apache common stock for the treasury at $5 per share. (pp. 694–695)
	19	Experienced a $16,000 extraordinary flood loss of inventory that cost $20,000. Cash received from the insurance company was $4,000. There is no income tax effect from this loss. (pp. 704–705)
Dec.	1	Sold 1,000 shares of the treasury stock for cash of $6.25 per share. (p. 696)
	30	Sold merchandise on account, $700,000. Cost of goods sold was $400,000. Operating expenses totaled $170,000, with $160,000 of this amount paid in cash. Apache uses a perpetual inventory system. (pp. 261–262, 72–73)
	31	Accrued interest and amortized discount (straight-line method) on the bonds payable issued on October 1. (pp. 744–745)
	31	Accrued income tax expense of $35,000. (pp. 661–662)
	31	Closed all revenues, expenses, and losses to Income Summary in a single closing entry. (pp. 641–644)
	31	Declared a quarterly cash dividend of $1.00 per share on the preferred stock. Record date is January 11, with payment scheduled for January 19. (pp. 653–655)

Requirements

1. Record these transactions in the general journal. Explanations are not required.

2. Prepare a multistep income statement, including earnings per share, for the quarter ended December 31. Apache had 40,000 shares of common stock outstanding. (pp. 703–706)

16 The Statement of Cash Flows

Learning Objectives

1 Identify the purposes of the statement of cash flows

2 Distinguish among operating, investing, and financing cash flows

3 Prepare the statement of cash flows by the indirect method

4 Prepare the statement of cash flows by the direct method (Appendix 16A)

Why is cash so important? You can probably answer that question from your own experience: It takes cash to pay the bills. You have some income, you have expenses, and these events create cash receipts and payments.

Businesses, including eBay, work the same way. Net income is a good thing, but eBay needs enough cash to pay the bills and run its operations. Lots of dot.coms have come and gone, but eBay is going strong. One reason is that eBay is cash-rich. In 2004, eBay's operations provided more than $1.3 billion of cash. Having plenty of cash helps eBay fight off competition from Google and others.

This chapter covers cash flows—cash receipts and cash payments. We'll see how to prepare the statement of cash flows, starting with the format used by the vast majority of companies; it's called the *indirect approach*. Chapter Appendix 16A covers the alternate format of the statement of cash flows, the *direct approach*.

The chapter has four distinct sections:

- Introduction: The Statement of Cash Flows
- Preparing the Statement of Cash Flows by the Indirect Method
- Chapter Appendix 16A: Preparing the Statement of Cash Flows by the Direct Method
- Chapter Appendix 16B: Preparing the Statement of Cash Flows Using a Spreadsheet

The introduction applies to both methods. To concentrate on the indirect method, instructors can cover the first two sections. For the direct method, you can cover the introduction and the chapter's Appendix 16A, starting on page 828. The focus company throughout the chapter is Anchor Corporation, which imports auto parts for Jaguars, Porches, and other European cars.

Chapter Appendix 16B shows how to use a spreadsheet to prepare the statement of cash flows. This appendix presents the indirect-method spreadsheet first, and the direct-method spreadsheet last—in the same order that these topics are covered in the chapter.

Introduction: The Statement of Cash Flows

The balance sheet reports financial position, and balance sheets for two periods show whether cash increased or decreased. For example, Anchor Corporation's comparative balance sheet reported the following:

	2008	2007	Increase (Decrease)
Cash	$22,000	$42,000	$(20,000)

Anchor's cash decreased by $20,000 during 2008. But the balance sheet doesn't show *why* cash decreased. We need the cash-flow statement for that.

The **statement of cash flows** reports **cash flows**—cash receipts and cash payments. It

- shows where cash came from (receipts) and how cash was spent (payments)
- reports why cash increased or decreased during the period
- covers a span of time and is dated "Year Ended December 31, 2008," same as the income statement

Exhibit 16-1—on the next page—illustrates the relationships among the balance sheet, the income statement, and the statement of cash flows.

1 Identify the purposes of the statement of cash flows

How do people use cash-flow information? The statement of cash flows helps

1. **predict future cash flows.** Past cash receipts and payments help predict future cash flows.

2. **evaluate management decisions.** Wise investment decisions help the business prosper. Unwise decisions cause problems. Investors and creditors use cash-flow information to evaluate managers' decisions.

3. **predict ability to pay debts and dividends.** Lenders want to know whether they'll collect on their loans. Stockholders want dividends on their investments. The statement of cash flows helps make these predictions.

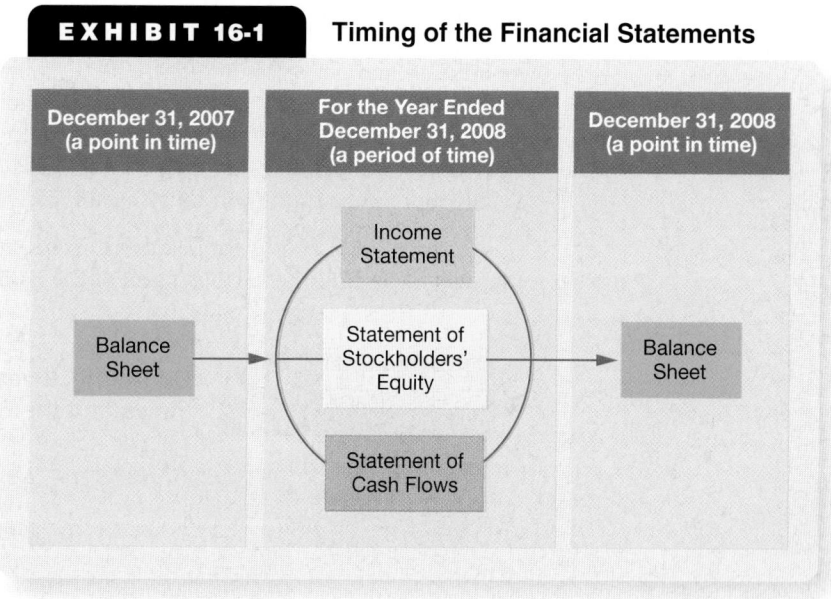

EXHIBIT 16-1 Timing of the Financial Statements

December 31, 2007 (a point in time)	For the Year Ended December 31, 2008 (a period of time)	December 31, 2008 (a point in time)
Balance Sheet	Income Statement / Statement of Stockholders' Equity / Statement of Cash Flows	Balance Sheet

Cash Equivalents

On a statement of cash flows, *Cash* means more than cash on hand and cash in the bank. *Cash* includes **cash equivalents**, which are highly liquid investments that can be converted into cash quickly. Examples of cash equivalents are money-market accounts and investments in U.S. government securities. Throughout this chapter, the term *cash* refers to cash and cash equivalents.

Operating, Investing, and Financing Activities

2 Distinguish among operating, investing, and financing cash flows

There are three basic types of cash-flow activities:

- Operating activities
- Investing activities
- Financing activities

The statement of cash flows has a section for each category of cash flows. Let's see what each section reports.

Operating Activities

- Create revenues, expenses, gains, and losses
- Affect net income on the income statement
- Affect current assets and current liabilities on the balance sheet
- Are the most important category of cash flows because they reflect the day-to-day operations that determine the future of an organization

Investing Activities

- Increase and decrease long-term assets, such as computers, software, land, buildings, and equipment
- Include purchases and sales of these assets, plus loans to others and collections of loans
- Are next-most important after operating activities

Financing activities

- Increase and decrease long-term liabilities and owners' equity
- Include issuing stock, paying dividends, and buying and selling treasury stock
- Include borrowing money and paying off loans
- Are least important of all the activities because what a company invests in is usually more important than how the company finances the purchase

Exhibit 16-2 shows the relationship between operating, investing, and financing cash flows and the various parts of the balance sheet.

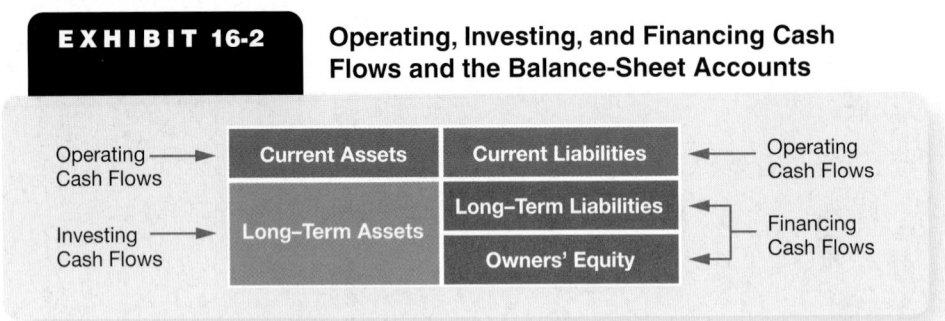

EXHIBIT 16-2 **Operating, Investing, and Financing Cash Flows and the Balance-Sheet Accounts**

As you can see, operating cash flows affect the current accounts. Investing cash flows affect the long-term assets. Financing cash flows affect long-term liabilities and owners' equity.

Two Formats for Operating Activities

There are two ways to format operating activities on the statement of cash flows:

- **Indirect method,** which reconciles from net income to net cash provided by operating activities
- **Direct method,** which reports all the cash receipts and all the cash payments from operating activities

The indirect and direct methods

- use different computations but produce the same amount of cash flow from operations
- have no effect on investing activities or financing activities

The following illustration shows how to compute cash flows from operating activities by the two methods. All amounts are assumed.

Indirect Method	Direct Method
Cash flows from operating activities:	Cash flows from operating activities:
Net income $300	Collections from customers $900
Adjustments:	*Deductions:*
Depreciation, etc. .... <u>100</u>	Payments to suppliers, etc. ..... <u>(500)</u>
Net cash provided by operating activities $400	Net cash provided by operating activities $400

Let's begin with the indirect method because 99% of public companies use it. To focus on the direct method, go to chapter Appendix 16A, page 828.

Preparing the Statement of Cash Flows by the Indirect Method

To prepare the statement of cash flows, you need the income statement and both the beginning and the ending balance sheets. Consider Anchor Corporation, an importer of parts for European cars. To prepare the statement of cash flows by the indirect method,

3 Prepare the statement of cash flows by the indirect method

STEP 1 Lay out the statement format as shown in Exhibit 16-3. Steps 2 to 4 will complete the statement of cash flows.

EXHIBIT 16-3	**Format of the Statement of Cash Flows: Indirect Method**

ANCHOR CORPORATION
Statement of Cash Flows
Year Ended December 31, 2008

Cash flows from operating activities:		
Net income		
Adjustments to reconcile net income to net cash provided by operating activities:		
+ Depreciation / amortization expense		
+ Loss on sale of long-term assets		
– Gain on sale of long-term assets		
– Increases in current assets other than cash		
+ Decreases in current assets other than cash		
+ Increases in current liabilities		
– Decreases in current liabilities		
Net cash provided by operating activities		
± Cash flows from investing activities:		
Sales of long-term assets (investments, land, building, equipment, and so on)		
– Purchases of long-term assets		
Net cash provided by (used for) investing activities		
± Cash flows from financing activities:		
Issuance of stock		
+ Sale of treasury stock		
– Purchase of treasury stock		
+ Issuance of notes or bonds payable (borrowing)		
– Payment of notes or bonds payable		
– Payment of dividends		
Net cash provided by (used for) financing activities		
= Net increase (decrease) in cash during the year		
+ Cash at December 31, 2007		
= Cash at December 31, 2008		

STEP 2 Compute the change in cash from the comparative balance sheet. The change in cash is the "check figure" for the statement of cash flows. Exhibit 16-4 is the comparative balance sheet of Anchor Corporation, where the top line shows that cash decreased by $20,000 during 2008.

EXHIBIT 16-4   Comparative Balance Sheet

ANCHOR CORPORATION
Comparative Balance Sheet
December 31, 2008 and 2007

(In thousands)	2008	2007	Increase (Decrease)	
Assets				
Current:				
Cash	$ 22	$ 42	$ (20)	
Accounts receivable	90	73	17	Operating **D**
Inventory	143	145	(2)	
Plant assets, net	460	210	250	Investing
Total	$715	$470	$ 245	
Liabilities				
Current:				
Accounts payable	$ 90	$ 50	$ 40	
Accrued liabilities	5	10	(5)	Operating **D**
Long-term notes payable	160	80	80	
Stockholders' Equity				Financing
Common stock	350	250	100	
Retained earnings	110	80	30	Net income—Operating Otherwise Financing
Total	$715	$470	$ 245	

STEP 3   Take net income, depreciation, and any gains or losses from the income statement. Exhibit 16-5 gives the 2008 income statement of Anchor Corporation, with the relevant items highlighted.

STEP 4   Complete the statement of cash flows, using data from the income statement and the balance sheet. The statement is complete only after you have explained all the year-to-year changes in all the accounts on the balance sheet.

Let's apply these steps to show the operating activities of Anchor Corporation. Exhibit 16-6 gives the operating activities section of the statement of cash flows. All items are highlighted for emphasis. That makes it easy to trace the data from one statement to the other.

Cash Flows from Operating Activities

Operating cash flows begin with net income, taken from the income statement.

A Net Income

The statement of cash flows—indirect method—begins with net income because revenues and expenses, which affect net income, produce cash receipts and cash payments. Revenues bring in cash receipts and expenses must be paid. But the cash flows don't always equal the revenues and the expenses. For example, sales *on account* are revenues that increase net income, but the company hasn't yet collected cash from those sales. Accrued expenses decrease your net income, but you haven't paid cash *if the expenses are accrued*.

To go from net income to cash flow from operations, we must make some adjustments to net income on the statement of cash flows. These additions and subtractions follow net income and are labeled *Adjustments to reconcile net income to net cash provided by operating activities*, as explained on page 790.

EXHIBIT 16-5   Income Statement

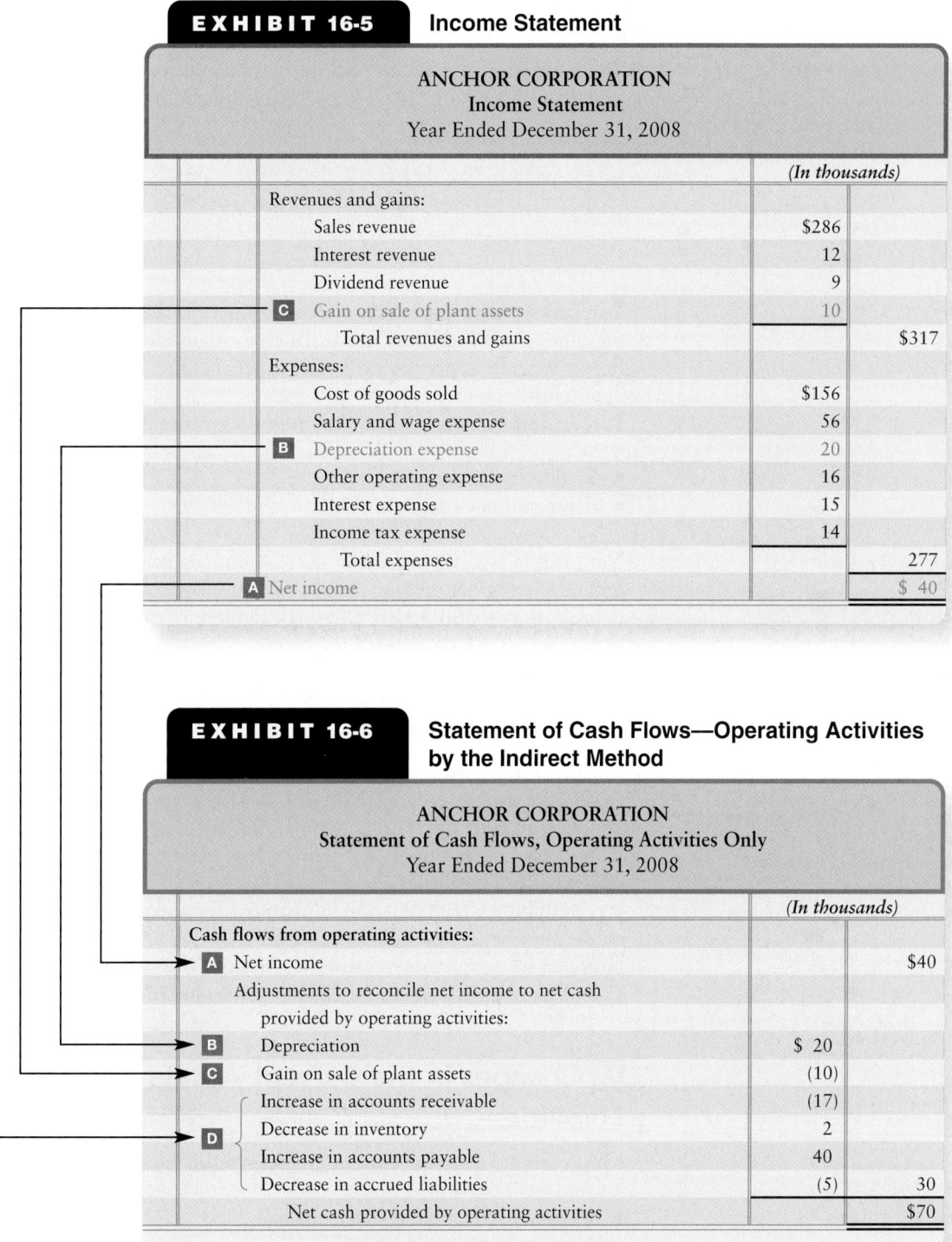

ANCHOR CORPORATION
Income Statement
Year Ended December 31, 2008

		(In thousands)	
Revenues and gains:			
Sales revenue	$286	
Interest revenue	12	
Dividend revenue	9	
C Gain on sale of plant assets	10	
Total revenues and gains		$317
Expenses:		
Cost of goods sold	$156	
Salary and wage expense	56	
B Depreciation expense	20	
Other operating expense	16	
Interest expense	15	
Income tax expense	14	
Total expenses		277
A Net income		$ 40

EXHIBIT 16-6   Statement of Cash Flows—Operating Activities
by the Indirect Method

ANCHOR CORPORATION
Statement of Cash Flows, Operating Activities Only
Year Ended December 31, 2008

		(In thousands)	
Cash flows from operating activities:		
A Net income		$40
Adjustments to reconcile net income to net cash		
provided by operating activities:		
B Depreciation	$ 20	
C Gain on sale of plant assets	(10)	
Increase in accounts receivable	(17)	
D Decrease in inventory	2	
Increase in accounts payable	40	
Decrease in accrued liabilities	(5)	30
Net cash provided by operating activities		$70

A **B** **C** **D** are explained on pages 788 – 790 as noted there.

B Depreciation, Depletion, and Amortization Expenses

These expenses are added back to net income to reconcile from net income to cash flow from operations. Let's see why. Depreciation is recorded as follows:

Depreciation Expense	20,000	
Accumulated Depreciation		20,000

You can see that depreciation does not affect cash. However, depreciation, like all the other expenses, decreases net income. Therefore, to go from net income to cash flows, we add depreciation back to net income. The add-back cancels the earlier deduction.

Example: Suppose you had only two transactions during the period:

- $1,000 cash sale
- depreciation expense of $300

Net income is $700 ($1,000 − $300). But cash flow from operations is $1,000. To reconcile from net income ($700) to cash flow from operations ($1,000), add back depreciation ($300). Also add back depletion and amortization expenses because they're similar to depreciation.

C Gains and Losses on the Sale of Assets

Sales of long-term assets such as land and buildings are investing activities, and these sales usually create a gain or a loss. The gain or loss is included in net income, which is part of operations. Gains and losses require an adjustment to cash flow from operating activities: The gain or loss must be adjusted out of net income on the statement of cash flows.

Exhibit 16-6 includes an adjustment for a gain (item C). During 2008 Anchor sold equipment, and there was a gain of $8,000 on the sale. The gain must be removed from operating cash flows because the gain itself is not cash. A loss on the sale of plant assets would be added back to net income.

D Changes in the Current Assets and the Current Liabilities

Most current assets and current liabilities result from operating activities. For example,

- accounts receivable result from sales,
- inventory relates to cost of goods sold, and so on.

Changes in the current accounts create adjustments to net income on the cash-flow statement, as follows:

↑ **Current assets** ⇒ ↓ **Cash**

1. **An increase in a current asset other than cash causes a decrease in cash.** It takes cash to acquire assets. If Accounts Receivable, Inventory, or Prepaid Expenses increased, cash decreased. Therefore, subtract the increase in the current asset from net income to get cash flow from operations.

↓ **Current assets** ⇒ ↑ **Cash**

2. **A decrease in a current asset other than cash causes an increase in cash.** Suppose Anchor's Accounts Receivable decreased by $4,000. What caused the

decrease? Anchor must have collected the Accounts Receivable, and cash increased. Therefore, add decreases in Accounts Receivable and the other current assets to net income.

↓ **Current liabilities** ⇒ ↓ **Cash**

3. **A decrease in a current liability causes a decrease in cash.** The payment of a current liability decreases cash. Therefore, we subtract decreases in current liabilities from net income to get cash flow from operations.

↑ **Current liabilities** ⇒ ↑ **Cash**

4. **An increase in a current liability causes an increase in cash.** Anchor's Accounts Payable increased. This means that cash was *not* spent to pay the liability, so Anchor has more cash on hand. Thus, an increase in a current liability is *added* to net income.

Evaluating Cash Flows from Operating Activities

During 2008, Anchor Corporation's operations provided net cash flow of $70,000. This amount exceeds net income, as it should because of the add-back of depreciation. However, to fully evaluate a company's cash flows, we must also examine Anchor's investing and financing activities. Let's see how to report investing and financing cash flows, as shown in Exhibit 16-7, which gives Anchor's full-blown statement of cash flows.

EXHIBIT 16-7   Statement of Cash Flows—Indirect Method

ANCHOR CORPORATION
Statement of Cash Flows
Year Ended December 31, 2008

	(In thousands)	
Cash flows from operating activities:		
A Net income		$ 40
Adjustments to reconcile net income to net cash		
provided by operating activities:		
Depreciation	$ 20	
Gain on sale of plant assets	(10)	
Increase in accounts receivable	(17)	
Decrease in inventory	2	
Increase in accounts payable	40	
Decrease in accrued liabilities	(5)	30
Net cash provided by operating activities		70
Cash flows from investing activities:		
Acquisition of plant assets	$(310)	
Cash receipt from sale of plant assets	50	
Net cash used for investing activities		(260)
Cash flows from financing activities:		
Cash receipt from issuance of common stock	$ 100	
Cash receipt from issuance of notes payable	90	
Payment of notes payable	(10)	
Payment of dividends	(10)	
Net cash provided by financing activities		170
Net decrease in cash		$(20)
Cash balance, December 31, 2007		42
Cash balance, December 31, 2008		$ 22

Cash Flows from Investing Activities

Investing activities affect long-term assets, such as Plant Assets and Investments. Let's see how to compute the investing cash flows.

Computing Acquisitions and Sales of Plant Assets

Companies keep a separate account for each asset. But for computing investing cash flows, it is helpful to combine all the plant assets into a single Plant Assets account. And we subtract accumulated depreciation from the assets' cost in order to work with a single net figure for plant assets, such as Plant assets, net . . . $460,000. This simplifies the computations.

To illustrate, observe that Anchor Corporation's

- balance sheet reports 2007 plant assets, net of depreciation, of $460,000 at the end of 2008 and $210,000 at the end of 2007 (Exhibit 16-4).
- income statement shows depreciation expense of $20,000 and a $10,000 gain on sale of plant assets (Exhibit 16-5).

Anchor's acquisitions of plant assets during 2008 totaled $310,000 (Exhibit 16-7). Anchor also sold some older plant assets. How much cash did Anchor receive from the sale of plant assets? Cash received from selling plant assets can be computed as follows:

$$\text{Cash receipt} = \text{Book value of plant asset sold} \begin{cases} + \text{Gain} \\ \quad \text{or} \\ - \text{Loss} \end{cases}$$

The book-value information comes from the Plant Assets (Net) account on the balance sheet. The gain or loss comes from the income statement. First, we must compute the book value of plant assets sold, as follows (item to be computed is in color):

Plant Assets (Net)

Beginning balance	+	Acquisitions	−	Depreciation expense	−	Book value of assets sold	=	Ending balance
$210,000	+	$310,000	−	$20,000	−	$40,000	=	$460,000

Now we can compute the cash receipt from the sale as follows (item computed in color):

Cash receipt from sale	=	Book value of assets sold	+	Gain	−	Loss
$50,000	=	$40,000	+	$10,000	−	$0

Trace the cash receipt of $50,000 to the statement of cash flows in Exhibit 16-7.

If the sale resulted in a loss of $5,000, the cash receipt would be $45,000 ($50,000 − $5,000), and the statement of cash flows would report $45,000 as a cash receipt from this investing activity.

The Plant Assets T-account provides another look at the computation of the book value of the assets sold.

Plant Assets (Net)

Beginning balance	210,000	Depreciation	20,000
Acquisitions	310,000	Book value of assets sold	40,000
Ending balance	460,000		

Exhibit 16-8 summarizes the computation of the investing cash flows. Items to be computed are shown in color.

Computing Cash Flows from Investing Activities

Cash Receipts

| From sale of plant assets | Beginning plant assets (net) | + | Acquisition | − | Depreciation Expense | − | Book value of assets sold | = | Ending plant assets (net) |

$$\text{Cash receipt} = \text{Book value of assets sold} \begin{cases} + & \text{Gain on sale} \\ \text{or} & \\ - & \text{Loss on sale} \end{cases}$$

Cash Payments

| For acquisition of plant assets | Beginning plant assets (net) | + | Acquisition | − | Depreciation Expense | − | Book value of assets sold | = | Ending plant assets (net) |

Cash Flows from Financing Activities

Financing activities affect the liability and owners' equity accounts, such as Long-Term Notes Payable, Bonds Payable, Common Stock, and Retained Earnings.

Computing Issuances and Payments of Long-Term Notes Payable

The beginning and ending balances of Notes Payable or Bonds Payable are taken from the balance sheet. If either the amount of new issuances or payments is known, the other amount can be computed. For Anchor Corporation, new issuances of notes payable total $90,000 (Exhibit 16-7). The computation of note payments uses the Long-Term Notes Payable account, with amounts from Anchor Corporation's balance sheet in Exhibit 16-4:

Formula Approach:

Long-Term Notes Payable

Beginning balance	+	Cash receipt from issuance of notes payable	−	Payment of notes payable	=	Ending balance
$80,000	+	$90,000	−	$10,000	=	$160,000

T-Account Approach:

Long-Term Notes Payable

	Beginning balance	80,000
Payments 10,000	Issuance of notes payable	90,000
	Ending balance	160,000

Computing Issuances of Stock and Purchases of Treasury Stock

Cash flows for these financing activities can be determined by analyzing the stock accounts. For example, the amount of a new issuance of common stock is determined from Common Stock. Using data from Exhibits 16-4 and 16-7:

Formula Approach:

Common Stock				
Beginning balance	+	Cash receipt from issuance of common stock	=	Ending balance
$250,000	+	$100,000	=	$350,000

T-Account Approach:

Common Stock	
	Beginning balance 250,000
	Issuance of stock 100,000
	Ending balance 350,000

Apart from the Anchor Corporation example, cash flows affecting Treasury Stock can be analyzed as follows:

Formula Approach:

Treasury Stock (Amounts assumed for illustration only)				
Beginning balance	+	Purchase of treasury stock	=	Ending balance
$10,000	+	$5,000	=	$15,000

T-Account Approach:

Treasury Stock	
Beginning balance 10,000	
Purchase of treasury stock 5,000	
Ending balance 15,000	

Computing Dividend Payments

The amount of dividend payments can be computed by analyzing Retained Earnings.

Formula Approach:

Retained Earnings						
Beginning balance	+	Net income	−	Dividends	=	Ending balance
$80,000	+	$40,000	−	$10,000	=	$110,000

T-Account Approach:

Retained Earnings			
		Beginning balance	80,000
Dividends	10,000	Net income	40,000
		Ending balance	110,000

A stock dividend has *no* effect on Cash and is *not* reported on the cash-flow statement. Exhibit 16-9 summarizes the computation of cash flows from financing activities, highlighted in color.

EXHIBIT 16-9 **Computing Cash Flows from Financing Activities**

Cash Receipts

From issuance of notes payable: Beginning notes payable + Cash receipt from issuance of notes payable − Payment of notes payable = Ending notes payable

From issuance of stock: Beginning stock = Cash receipt from issuance of new stock = Ending stock

Cash Payments

Of notes payable: Beginning notes payable + Cash receipt from issuance of notes payable − Payment of notes payable = Ending notes payable

To purchase treasury stock: Beginning treasury stock + Cost of treasury stock purchased = Ending treasury stock

Of dividends: Beginning retained earnings + Net income − Dividends = Ending retained earnings

Noncash Investing and Financing Activities

Companies make investments that do not require cash. They also obtain financing other than cash. Our examples thus far have included none of these transactions. Now suppose Anchor Corporation issued common stock of $300,000 to acquire a building. Anchor would record the purchase as follows:

Building	300,000	
Common Stock		300,000

This transaction would not be reported on the cash-flow statement because Anchor paid no cash. But the building and the common stock are important.

The purchase of the building is an investing activity. The issuance of common stock is a financing activity. Taken together, this transaction is a *noncash investing and financing activity.*

Noncash investing and financing activities can be reported in a separate schedule that accompanies the statement of cash flows. Exhibit 16-10 illustrates noncash investing and financing activities (all amounts are assumed). This information follows the cash-flow statement or can be disclosed in a note.

EXHIBIT 16-10	Noncash Investing and Financing Activities (Amounts assumed)

	(Thousands)
Noncash investing and financing activities:	
Acquisition of building by issuing common stock	$300
Acquisition of land by issuing note payable	70
Payment of note payable by issuing common stock	100
Total noncash investing and financing activities	$470

Measuring Cash Adequacy: Free Cash Flow

Throughout we have focused on cash flows from operating, investing, and financing activities. Some investors want to know how much cash a company can "free up" for new opportunities. **Free cash flow** is the amount of cash available from operations after paying for planned investments in long-term assets. Free cash flow can be computed as follows:

$$\text{Free cash flow} = \begin{matrix}\text{Net cash provided} \\ \text{by operating} \\ \text{activities}\end{matrix} - \begin{matrix}\text{Cash payments planned for} \\ \text{investments in plant, equipment,} \\ \text{and other long-term assets}\end{matrix}$$

PepsiCo, Inc. uses free cash flow to manage its operations. Suppose PepsiCo expects net cash provided by operations of $2.3 billion. Assume PepsiCo plans to spend $1.9 billion to modernize its bottling plants. In this case, PepsiCo's free cash flow would be $0.4 billion ($2.3 billion − $1.9 billion). If a good investment opportunity comes along, PepsiCo should have $0.4 billion to invest in the other company. Shell Oil Company also uses free-cash-flow analysis. A large amount of free cash flow is preferable because it means a lot of cash is available for new investments.

Now let's put into practice what you have learned about the statement of cash flows prepared by the indirect method.

Decision Guidelines

USING CASH-FLOW AND RELATED INFORMATION TO EVALUATE INVESTMENTS

Ann Browning is a private investor. Through the years, she has devised some guidelines for evaluating investments. Here are some of her guidelines.

Question	Financial Statement	What to Look For
Where is most of the company's cash coming from?	Statement of cash flows	Operating activities ⟶ Good sign Investing activities ⟶ Bad sign Financing activities ⟶ Okay sign
Do high sales and profits translate into more cash?	Statement of cash flows	Usually, but cash flows from *operating* activities must be the main source of cash for long-term success.
If sales and profits are low, how is the company generating cash?	Statement of cash flows	If *investing* activities are generating the cash, the business may be in trouble because it is selling off its long-term assets. If *financing* activities are generating the cash, that cannot go on forever. Sooner or later, investors will demand cash flow from operating activities.
Is the cash balance large enough to provide for expansion?	Balance sheet	The cash balance should be growing over time. If not, the company may be in trouble.
Can the business pay its debts?	Income statement	Increasing trend of net income.
	Statement of cash flows	Cash flows from operating activities should be the main source of cash.
	Balance sheet	Current ratio, debt ratio.

Summary Problem

Robins Corporation reported the following income statement and comparative balance sheet for 2009 and 2008, along with transaction data for 2009:

ROBINS CORPORATION
Income Statement
Year Ended December 31, 2009

Sales revenue		$662,000
Cost of goods sold		560,000
Gross profit		102,000
Operating expenses:		
Salary expense	$46,000	
Depreciation expense	10,000	
Rent expense	2,000	
Total operating expenses		58,000
Income from operations		44,000
Other items:		
Loss on sale of equipment		(2,000)
Income before income tax		42,000
Income tax expense		16,000
Net income		$ 26,000

ROBINS CORPORATION
Balance Sheet
December 31, 2009 and 2008

Assets	2009	2008	Liabilities	2009	2008
Current:			Current:		
Cash and equivalents	$ 22,000	$ 3,000	Accounts payable	$ 35,000	$ 26,000
Accounts receivable	22,000	23,000	Accrued liabilities	7,000	9,000
Inventories	35,000	34,000	Income tax payable	10,000	10,000
Total current assets	79,000	60,000	Total current liabilities	52,000	45,000
Equipment, net	126,000	72,000	Bonds payable	84,000	53,000
			Owner's Equity		
			Common stock	52,000	20,000
			Retained earnings	27,000	19,000
			Less: Treasury stock	(10,000)	(5,000)
Total assets	$205,000	$132,000	Total liabilities and equity	$205,000	$132,000

Transaction Data for 2009:

Purchase of equipment	$140,000
Payment of dividends	18,000
Issuance of common stock to retire bonds payable	13,000
Issuance of bonds payable to borrow cash	44,000
Cash receipt from issuance of common stock	19,000
Cash receipt from sale of equipment (book value, $76,000)	74,000
Purchase of treasury stock	5,000

Requirements

Prepare Robins Corporation's statement of cash flows for the year ended December 31, 2009. Format operating cash flows by the indirect method. Follow the four steps outlined below.

STEP 1 Lay out the format of the statement of cash flows.

STEP 2 From the comparative balance sheet, compute the increase in cash during the year, $19,000.

STEP 3 From the income statement, take net income, depreciation, and the loss on sale of equipment to the statement of cash flows.

STEP 4 Complete the statement of cash flows. Account for the year-to-year change in each balance sheet account. Prepare a T-account to show the transaction activity in each long-term balance-sheet account.

Solution

ROBINS CORPORATION Statement of Cash Flows Year Ended December 31, 2009			
Cash flows from operating activities:			
Net income			$26,000
Adjustments to reconcile net income to net cash			
provided by operating activities:			
Depreciation		$ 10,000	
Loss on sale of equipment		2,000	
Decrease in accounts receivable		1,000	
Increase in inventories		(1,000)	
Increase in accounts payable		9,000	
Decrease in accrued liabilities		(2,000)	19,000
Net cash provided by operating activities			45,000
Cash flows from investing activities:			
Purchase of equipment		$(140,000)	
Sale of equipment		74,000	
Net cash used for investing activities			(66,000)
Cash flows from financing activities:			
Issuance of common stock		$ 19,000	
Payment of dividends		(18,000)	
Issuance of bonds payable		44,000	
Purchase of treasury stock		(5,000)	
Net cash provided by financing activities			40,000
Net increase in cash			$19,000
Cash balance, December 31, 2008			3,000
Cash balance, December 31, 2009			$22,000
Noncash investing and financing activities:			
Issuance of common stock to retire bonds payable			$13,000
Total noncash investing and financing activities			$13,000

Relevant T-Accounts:

Equipment, Net			
Bal.	72,000		
	140,000	10,000	
		76,000	
Bal.	126,000		

Bonds Payable			
		Bal.	53,000
	13,000		44,000
		Bal.	84,000

Common Stock			
		Bal.	20,000
			13,000
			19,000
		Bal.	52,000

Retained Earnings			
		Bal.	19,000
	18,000		26,000
		Bal.	27,000

Treasury Stock			
Bal.	5,000		
	5,000		
Bal.	10,000		

Review *The Statement of Cash Flows*

Accounting Vocabulary

Cash Equivalents
Highly liquid short-term investments that can be readily converted into cash.

Cash Flows
Cash receipts and cash payments.

Direct Method
Format of the operating activities section of the statement of cash flows; lists the major categories of operating cash receipts and cash payments.

Financing Activities
Activities that obtain the cash needed to launch and sustain the business; a section of the statement of cash flows.

Free Cash Flow
The amount of cash available from operations after paying for planned investments in plant, equipment, and other long-term assets.

Indirect Method
Format of the operating activities section of the statement of cash flows; starts with net income and reconciles to net cash provided by operating activities.

Investing Activities
Activities that increase or decrease long-term assets; a section of the statement of cash flows.

Operating Activities
Activities that create revenue or expense in the entity's major line of business; a section of the statement of cash flows. Operating activities affect the income statement.

Statement of Cash Flows
Reports cash receipts and cash payments during the period.

Quick Check

1. The main categories of cash-flow activities are
   a. Operating, investing, and financing
   b. Direct and indirect
   c. Noncash investing and financing
   d. Current and long-term

2. The purposes of the cash-flow statement are to
   a. Predict future cash flows
   b. Evaluate management decisions
   c. Determine ability to pay liabilities and dividends
   d. All of the above

3. Operating activities are most closely related to
   a. Current assets and current liabilities
   b. Long-term assets
   c. Long-term liabilities and owners' equity
   d. Dividends and treasury stock

4. Which item does *not* appear on a statement of cash flows prepared by the indirect method?
   a. Net income
   b. Collections from customers
   c. Depreciation
   d. Gain on sale of land

5. Source Today earned net income of $60,000 after deducting depreciation of $4,000 and all other expenses. Current assets decreased by $3,000, and current liabilities increased by $5,000. How much was Source Today's cash provided by operations (indirect method)?
   a. $48,000
   b. $50,000
   c. $72,000
   d. $66,000

6. The Plant Assets account of Star Media shows the following:

Plant Assets, Net			
Beg.	100,000	Depr.	30,000
Purchase	400,000	Sale	50,000
End.	420,000		

Star Media sold plant assets at a $10,000 loss. Where on the statement of cash flows should Star Media report the sale of plant assets? How much should Star Media report for the sale?
   a. Investing cash flows—cash receipt of $40,000
   b. Investing cash flows—cash receipt of $50,000
   c. Investing cash flows—cash receipt of $60,000
   d. Financing cash flows—cash receipt of $60,000

7. Round Rock Corp. borrowed $35,000, issued common stock of $10,000, and paid dividends of $25,000. What was Round Rock's net cash provided (used) by financing activities?

a. $0

b. $20,000

c. $(25,000)

d. $70,000

8. Which item appears on a statement of cash flows prepared by the indirect method?

a. Payments to suppliers

b. Payments of income tax

c. Depreciation

d. Collections from customers

Appendix 16A: Direct Method

9. Peppertree Copy Center had accounts receivable of $20,000 at the beginning of the year and $50,000 at year-end. Revenue for the year totaled $110,000. How much cash did Peppertree collect from customers?

a. $180,000

b. $140,000

c. $130,000

d. $80,000

10. Pilot Company had operating expense of $40,000. At the beginning of the year, Pilot owed $8,000 on accrued liabilities. At year-end, accrued liabilities were $4,000. How much cash did Pilot pay for operating expenses?

a. $32,000

b. $36,000

c. $44,000

d. $45,000

Answers are given after Apply Your Knowledge (p. 827).

Assess Your Progress

Short Exercises

Purposes of the statement
of cash flows

1

S16-1 Describe how the statement of cash flows helps investors and creditors perform each of the following functions (p. 785):

1. Predict future cash flows
2. Evaluate management decisions
3. Predict the ability to make debt payments to lenders and pay dividends to stockholders

Classifying cash-flow items

1

S16-2 Answer these questions about the statement of cash flows:

a. List the categories of cash flows in order of importance. (pp. 785–786)

b. What is the "check figure" for the statement of cash flows? Where do you get this check figure? (pp. 786–788)

c. What is the first dollar amount to report for the indirect method? (pp. 786–788)

Identifying items for
reporting cash flows from
operations—indirect
method

2

S16-3 Triumph Corporation is preparing its statement of cash flows by the *indirect* method. Triumph has the following items for you to consider in preparing the statement. Identify each item as an

- Operating activity—addition to net income (O+), or subtraction from net income (O−)
- Investing activity (I)
- Financing activity (F)
- Activity that is not used to prepare the cash-flow statement (N)

Answer by placing the appropriate symbol in the blank space. (pp. 787–788)

_____ a. Increase in accounts payable   _____ g. Depreciation expense

_____ b. Payment of dividends   _____ h. Increase in inventory

_____ c. Decrease in accrued liabilities   _____ i. Decrease in accounts
                                                  receivable
_____ d. Issuance of common stock

_____ e. Gain on sale of building   _____ j. Purchase of
                                                  equipment
_____ f. Loss on sale of land

Computing cash flows from
operating activities—
indirect method

3

S16-4 DVR Equipment, Inc., reported these data for 2007:

Income Statement	
Net income	$42,000
Depreciation	8,000
Balance sheet	
Increase in Accounts Receivable.......	6,000
Decrease in Accounts Payable	4,000

Compute DVR's net cash provided by operating activities—indirect method. (pp. 788–789)

S16-5 (Short Exercise 16-6 is an alternate.) One Way Cellular accountants have assembled the following data for the year ended June 30, 2008.

Cash receipt from sale of land	$30,000	Net income	$60,000
Depreciation expense	15,000	Purchase of equipment	40,000
Payment of dividends	6,000	Decrease in current liabilities	5,000
Cash receipt from issuance of		Increase in current assets	
common stock	20,000	other than cash	12,000

Prepare the *operating* activities section of One Way Cellular's statement of cash flows for the year ended June 30, 2008. One Way uses the *indirect* method for operating cash flows. (pp. 788–789)

S16-6 Use the data in Short Exercise 16-5 to prepare One Way Cellular's statement of cash flows for the year ended June 30, 2008. One Way Cellular uses the *indirect* method for operating activities. Use Exhibit 16-7 as a guide, but you may stop after determining the net increase (or decrease) in cash. (pp. 791–792)

S16-7 Sun West Media Corporation had the following income statement and balance sheet for 2009:

SUN WEST MEDIA CORPORATION
Income Statement
Year Ended December 31, 2009

Service revenue	$80,000
Depreciation expense	6,000
Other expenses	54,000
Net income	$20,000

SUN WEST MEDIA CORPORATION
Comparative Balance Sheet
December 31, 2009 and 2008

Assets	2009	2008	Liabilities	2009	2008
Current:			Current:		
Cash	$ 5,000	$ 4,000	Accounts payable	$ 8,000	$ 6,000
Accounts receivable	10,000	6,000	Long-term notes payable	10,000	12,000
Equipment, net	75,000	70,000			
			Owners' Equity		
			Common stock	22,000	20,000
			Retained earnings	50,000	42,000
	$90,000	$80,000		$90,000	$80,000

continued . . .

Compute for Sun West during 2009:

a. Acquisition of equipment. Sun West sold no equipment during the year. (pp. 792–793)

b. Payment of a long-term note payable. During the year Sun West issued a $5,000 note payable. (p. 793)

Preparing the statement of cash flows—indirect method

S16-8 Use the Sun West Media Corporation data in Short Exercise S16-7 to prepare Sun West's statement of cash flows—indirect method—for the year ended December 31, 2009. (pp. 791–792)

Computing a cash increase or decrease—indirect method

S16-9 JoAnn's Bridal Shops earned net income of $80,000, which included depreciation of $15,000. JoAnn's paid $120,000 for a building and borrowed $60,000 on a long-term note payable. How much did JoAnn's cash balance increase or decrease during the year? (pp. 792–796)

Free cash flow

S16-10 Anita Maxwell Company expects the following for 2007:

- Net cash provided by operating activities of $150,000
- Net cash provided by financing activities of $60,000
- Net cash used for investing activities of $80,000 (no sales of long-term assets)

How much free cash flow does Maxwell expect for 2007? (p. 796)

Appendix 16A: Direct Method

Preparing a statement of cash flows—direct method

S16-11 Chocolate Inc. began 2007 with cash of $55,000. During the year Chocolate Inc. earned revenue of $600,000 and collected $620,000 from customers. Expenses for the year totaled $420,000, of which Chocolate paid $410,000 in cash to suppliers and employees. Chocolate also paid $140,000 to purchase equipment and a cash dividend of $50,000 to its stockholders during 2007.

Prepare the company's statement of cash flows for the year ended December 31, 2007. Format operating activities by the direct method. (Exhibit 16A-3, p. 830)

Computing operating cash flows—direct method

S16-12 (Short Exercise 16-13 is an alternate.) Little People Learning Center (LPLC) has assembled the following data for the year ended June 30, 2005.

Payments to suppliers	$110,000
Purchase of equipment	40,000
Payments to employees	70,000
Payment of note payable	30,000
Payment of dividends	6,000
Cash receipt from issuance of stock	20,000
Collections from customers	200,000
Cash receipt from sale of land	60,000

Prepare the *operating* activities section of LPLC's statement of cash flows for the year ended June 30, 2005. LPLC uses the direct method for operating cash flows. (Exhibit 16A-3, p. 830)

Preparing a statement of
cash flows—direct method

Computing operating cash
flows—direct method

S16-13 Use the data in Short Exercise 16-12 to prepare Little People Learning Center's (LPLC) statement of cash flows for the year ended June 30, 2005. LPLC uses the *direct* method for operating activities. Use Exhibit 16A-3, page 830, as a guide, but you may stop after determining the net increase (or decrease) in cash.

S16-14 Lagos Toy Company reported the following comparative balance sheet:

LAGOS TOY COMPANY
Comparative Balance Sheet
December 31, 2009 and 2008

Assets	2009	2008	Liabilities	2009	2008
Current:			Current:		
Cash	$ 19,000	$ 16,000	Accounts payable	$ 47,000	$ 42,000
Accounts receivable	54,000	48,000	Salary payable	23,000	21,000
Inventory	80,000	84,000	Accrued liabilities	8,000	11,000
Prepaid expenses	3,000	2,000	Long-term notes payable	66,000	68,000
Long-term investments	75,000	90,000	**Stockholders' Equity**		
Plant assets, net	225,000	185,000	Common stock	40,000	37,000
			Retained earnings	272,000	246,000
Total	$456,000	$425,000	Total	$456,000	$425,000

Compute for Lagos:

a. Collections from customers during 2009. Sales totaled $140,000. (p. 834)

b. Payments for inventory during 2009. Cost of goods sold was $80,000. (p. 834)

Exercises

Identifying the purposes of
the statement of cash flows

E16-15 SmartPages Media Corp. has experienced 10 years of growth in net income. Nevertheless, the business is facing bankruptcy. Creditors are calling all of SmartPages' loans for immediate payment, and the cash is simply not available. Where did SmartPages go wrong? Managers placed too much emphasis on net income and gave too little attention to cash flows.

Requirement
Write a brief memo, in your own words, to explain to the managers of SmartPages Media the purposes of the statement of cash flows. (p. 785)

Identifying activities for the
statement of cash flows—
indirect method

E16-16 Identify each of the following transactions as
- Operating activity (O)
- Investing activity (I)
- Financing activity (F)
- Noncash investing and financing activity (NIF)
- Transaction that is not reported on the statement of cash flows (N)

continued . . .

For each cash flow, indicate whether the item increases (+) or decreases (−) cash. The *indirect* method is used to report cash flows from operating activities. (pp. 787–788, 795)

_____ **a.** Loss on sale of land		_____ **i.** Cash sale of land	
_____ **b.** Acquisition of equipment by issuance of note payable		_____ **j.** Issuance of long-term note payable to borrow cash	
_____ **c.** Payment of long-term debt		_____ **k.** Depreciation	
_____ **d.** Acquisition of building by issuance of common stock		_____ **l.** Purchase of treasury stock	
_____ **e.** Accrual of salary expense		_____ **m.** Issuance of common stock	
_____ **f.** Decrease in inventory		_____ **n.** Increase in accounts payable	
_____ **g.** Increase in prepaid expenses		_____ **o.** Net income	
_____ **h.** Decrease in accrued liabilities		_____ **p.** Payment of cash dividend	

Classifying transactions for the statement of cash flows—indirect method

2

E16-17 Indicate whether each of the following transactions would result in an operating activity, an investing activity, or a financing activity for a statement of cash flows prepared by the *indirect* method and the accompanying schedule of noncash investing and financing activities. (Exhibit 16-3, p. 787; p. 795)

a. Cash	81,000		g. Land	18,000	
Common Stock		81,000	Cash		18,000
b. Treasury Stock	13,000		h. Cash	7,200	
Cash		13,000	Equipment		7,200
c. Cash	60,000		i. Bonds Payable	45,000	
Sales Revenue		60,000	Cash		45,000
d. Land	87,700		j. Building	164,000	
Cash		87,700	Note Payable, Long-Term		164,000
e. Depreciation Expense	9,000		k. Loss on Disposal of Equipment	1,400	
Accumulated Depreciation		9,000	Equipment Net		1,400
f. Dividends Payable	16,500				
Cash		16,500			

Computing cash flows from operating activities—indirect method

3

E16-18 The records of Paramount Color Engraving reveal the following:

Net income	$40,000	Depreciation	$12,000
Sales revenue	9,000	Decrease in current liabilities	20,000
Loss on sale of land	5,000	Increase in current assets	
Acquisition of land	37,000	other than cash	7,000

continued . . .

Compute cash flows from operating activities by the indirect method. Use the format of the operating activities section of Exhibit 16-7. Also evaluate the operating cash flow of Paramount Color Engraving. Give the reason for your evaluation. (pp. 788–798, 785–786)

Computing cash flows from operating activities— indirect method

3

E16-19 The accounting records of DVD Sales, Inc., include these accounts:

Cash		
Mar. 1	5,000	
Mar. 31	4,000	

Accounts Receivable		
Mar. 1	18,000	
Mar. 31	14,000	

Inventory		
Mar. 1	19,000	
Mar. 31	21,000	

Accounts Payable		
	Mar. 1	14,000
	Mar. 31	19,000

Accumulated Depreciation— Equipment		
	Mar. 1	52,000
	Depreciation	3,000
	Mar. 31	55,000

Retained Earnings			
Dividend	18,000	Mar. 1	64,000
		Net income	81,000
		Mar. 31	127,000

Compute DVD's net cash provided by (used for) operating activities during March. Use the indirect method. (pp. 788–789)

Preparing the statement of cash flows—indirect method

3

E16-20 The income statement and additional data of Vitamins Plus, Inc., follow:

VITAMINS PLUS, INC.
Income Statement
Year Ended June 30, 2006

Revenues:		
Service revenue		$237,000
Expenses:		
Cost of goods sold	$98,000	
Salary expense	58,000	
Depreciation expense	29,000	
Income tax expense	9,000	194,000
Net income		$ 43,000

Additional data:
a. Acquisition of plant assets is $116,000. Of this amount, $101,000 is paid in cash and $15,000 by signing a note payable.
b. Cash receipt from sale of land totals $24,000. There was no gain or loss.

continued . . .

c. Cash receipts from issuance of common stock total $30,000.

d. Payment of note payable is $15,000.

e. Payment of dividends is $11,000.

f. From the balance sheet:

	June 30,	
	2006	2005
Current Assets:		
Cash..	$32,000	$20,000
Accounts receivable................	43,000	58,000
Inventory................................	92,000	85,000
Current Liabilities:		
Accounts payable	$35,000	$22,000
Accrued liabilities...................	13,000	21,000

Requirement

Prepare Vitamins Plus, Inc.'s statement of cash flows for the year ended June 30, 2006, using the indirect method. Include a separate section for noncash investing and financing activities. (pp. 791–792, 795)

Computing investing and financing amounts for the statement of cash flows

E16-21 Compute the following items for the statement of cash flows:

a. Beginning and ending Retained Earnings are $45,000 and $70,000, respectively. Net income for the period is $60,000. How much are cash dividends? (p. 794)

b. Beginning and ending Plant Assets, Net, are $103,000 and $107,000, respectively. Depreciation for the period is $16,000, and acquisitions of new plant assets total $27,000. Plant assets were sold at a $4,000 gain. What was the amount of the cash receipt from the sale? (pp. 793–794)

Computing investing cash flows

E16-22 Hawkeye Gymnastics Equipment, Inc., reported the following financial statements for 2006:

HAWKEYE GYMNASTICS EQUIPMENT, INC. Income Statement Year Ended December 31, 2006	
	(In thousands)
Sales revenue	$710
Cost of goods sold	$340
Depreciation expense	50
Other expenses	200
Total expenses	590
Net income	$120

continued . . .

HAWKEYE GYMNASTICS EQUIPMENT, INC.						
Comparative Balance Sheet						
December 31, 2006 and 2005						
(In thousands)						
Assets	**2006**	**2005**	**Liabilities**	**2006**	**2005**
Current:			Current:		
Cash	$ 19	$ 16	Accounts payable	$ 75	$ 73
Accounts receivable	54	48	Salary payable	1	3
Inventory	83	86	Long-term notes payable	60	68
Long-term investments	90	75	**Stockholders' Equity**		
Plant assets, net	225	185	Common stock	45	35
			Retained earnings	290	231
Total	$471	$410	Total	$471	$410

Compute the amount of Hawkeye's acquisition of plant assets. Hawkeye sold no plant assets. (pp. 791–793)

Computing financing cash flows

3

E16-23 Use the Hawkeye Gymnastics data in Exercise 16-22 to compute

   a. New borrowing or payment of long-term notes payable, with Hawkeye having only one long-term note payable transaction during the year (pp. 792–793)

   b. Issuance of common stock, with Hawkeye having only one common stock transaction during the year (p. 794)

   c. Payment of cash dividends (p. 794)

Preparing the statement of cash flows—indirect method

3

E16-24 Use the Hawkeye Gymnastics data in Exercises E16-22 and E16-23 to prepare the company's statement of cash flows—indirect method—for the year ended December 31, 2006. Show all amounts in thousands, as in the exercise. (pp. 791–792)

Appendix 16A: Direct Method

Identifying activities for the statement of cash flows—direct method

4

E16-25 Identify each of the following transactions as

   • Operating activity (O)

   • Investing activity (I)

   • Financing activity (F)

   • Noncash investing and financing activity (NIF)

   • Transaction that is not reported on the statement of cash flows (N)

For each cash flow, indicate whether the item increases (+) or decreases (−) cash. The *direct* method is used for cash flows from operating activities. (pp. 828–829, 831–832)

_____	**a.** Collection of account receivable	_____	**d.** Purchase of treasury stock
_____	**b.** Issuance of note payable to borrow cash	_____	**e.** Issuance of common stock for cash
_____	**c.** Depreciation	_____	**f.** Payment of account payable

continued . . .

_____	**g.** Issuance of preferred stock for cash			_____	**l.**	Acquisition of building by issuance of common stock
_____	**h.** Payment of cash dividend			_____	**m.**	Purchase of equipment
_____	**i.** Sale of land			_____	**n.**	Payment of wages to employees
_____	**j.** Acquisition of equipment by issuance of note payable			_____	**o.**	Collection of cash interest
_____	**k.** Payment of note payable			_____	**p.**	Sale of building

Classifying transactions for the statement of cash flows—direct method

4

E16-26 Indicate where, if at all, each of the following transactions would be reported on a statement of cash flows prepared by the *direct* method and the accompanying schedule of noncash investing and financing activities. (Exhibit 16A-3, p. 830)

a. Land	18,000		g. Salary Expense	4,300	
Cash		18,000	Cash		4,300
b. Cash	7,200		h. Cash	81,000	
Equipment		7,200	Common Stock		81,000
c. Bonds Payable	45,000		i. Treasury Stock	13,000	
Cash		45,000	Cash		13,000
d. Building	164,000		j. Cash	2,000	
Note Payable		164,000	Interest Revenue		2,000
e. Cash	1,400		k. Land	87,700	
Accounts Receivable		1,400	Cash		87,700
f. Dividends Payable	16,500		l. Accounts Payable	8,300	
Cash		16,500	Cash		8,300

Computing cash flows from operating activities—direct method

4

E16-27 The accounting records of Fuzzy Dice Auto Parts reveal the following:

Payment of salaries and wages	$ 34,000	Net income	$22,000
Depreciation	12,000	Payment of income tax	13,000
Payment of interest	16,000	Collection of dividend revenue	7,000
Payment of dividends	7,000	Payment to suppliers	54,000
Collections from customers	112,000		

Requirement

Compute cash flows from operating activities by the *direct* method. Use the format of the operating activities section of Exhibit 16A-3, page 830.

Identifying items for the statement of cash flows— direct method

4

E16-28 Selected accounts of Dimension Networks, Inc., show the following:

Accounts Receivable

Beginning balance	9,000		
Service revenue	40,000	Cash collections	38,000
Ending balance	11,000		

continued . . .

Land

Beginning balance	90,000		
Acquisition	18,000		
Ending balance	108,000		

Long-Term Notes Payable

		Beginning balance	273,000
Payments	69,000	Issuance for cash	83,000
		Ending balance	287,000

Requirements

For each account, identify the item or items that should appear on a statement of cash flows prepared by the *direct* method. Also state each item's amount and where to report the item. (Exhibit 16A-3, p. 830)

Preparing the statement of cash flows—direct method

E16-29 The income statement and additional data of Capitol Hill Corporation follow:

CAPITOL HILL CORPORATION
Income Statement
Year Ended June 30, 2006

Revenues:		
Sales revenue	$229,000	
Dividend revenue	8,000	$237,000
Expenses:		
Cost of goods sold	$103,000	
Salary expense	45,000	
Depreciation expense	28,000	
Advertising expense	12,000	
Interest expense	2,000	
Income tax expense	9,000	199,000
Net income		$ 38,000

Additional data:
a. Collections from customers are $15,000 more than sales.
b. Dividend revenue, interest expense, and income tax expense equal their cash amounts.
c. Payments to suppliers are the sum of cost of goods sold plus advertising expense.
d. Payments to employees are $1,000 more than salary expense.
e. Acquisition of plant assets is $101,000.
f. Cash receipts from sale of land total $24,000.
g. Cash receipts from issuance of common stock total $30,000.
h. Payment of long-term note payable is $15,000.
i. Payment of dividends is $11,000.
j. Cash balance, June 30, 2005, was $20,000; June 30, 2006, was $27,000.

continued . . .

Requirement

Prepare Capitol Hill Corporation's statement of cash flows for the year ended June 30, 2006. Use the *direct* method. Follow the format given in Exhibit 16A-3, page 830.

Computing amounts for the statement of cash flows—direct method

E16-30 Compute the following items for the statement of cash flows:

a. Beginning and ending Accounts Receivable are $22,000 and $18,000, respectively. Credit sales for the period total $60,000. How much are cash collections from customers? (pp. 832–834)

b. Cost of goods sold is $75,000. Beginning Inventory balance is $25,000, and ending Inventory balance is $21,000. Beginning and ending Accounts Payable are $11,000 and $8,000, respectively. How much are cash payments for inventory? (pp. 832–834)

Computing cash-flow amounts—direct method

E16-31 Elite Mobile Homes reported the following in its financial statements for the year ended December 31, 2007 (adapted, in millions):

	2007	2006
Income Statement		
Net sales	$24,623	$21,207
Cost of sales..................................	18,048	15,466
Depreciation	269	230
Other operating expenses...............	4,883	4,248
Income tax expense........................	537	486
Net income	$ 886	$ 777
Balance Sheet		
Cash and equivalents	$ 17	$ 13
Accounts receivable	798	615
Inventories	3,482	2,831
Property and equipment, net..........	4,345	3,428
Accounts payable...........................	1,547	1,364
Accrued liabilities	938	848
Long-term liabilities.......................	478	464
Common stock	676	446
Retained earnings	4,531	3,788

Determine the following for Elite Mobile Homes during 2007:

a. Collections from customers (pp. 832–834)

b. Payments for inventory (pp. 832–834)

c. Payments of operating expenses (pp. 832–834)

d. Acquisitions of property and equipment (no sales during 2007) (pp. 791–792)

e. Borrowing, with Elite paying no long-term liabilities (pp. 792–793, 794)

f. Cash receipt from issuance of common stock (p. 794)

g. Payment of cash dividends (p. 794)

For computing the operating cash flows, follow the approach outlined in Exhibit 16A-6, page 834.

Problems (Group A)

Using cash-flow information to evaluate performance

P16-32A Top managers of Bernard Associates are reviewing company performance for 2009. The income statement reports a 15% increase in net income, which is outstanding. The balance sheet shows modest increases in assets, liabilities, and stockholders' equity. The assets with the largest increases are plant and equipment because the company is halfway through an expansion program. No other assets and no liabilities are increasing dramatically. A summarized version of the cash-flow statement reports the following:

Net cash provided by operating activities	$310,000
Net cash used for investing activities	(290,000)
Net cash provided by financing activities	80,000
Increase in cash during 2009	$100,000

Requirement

Write a memo giving top managers of Bernard Associates your assessment of 2009 operations and your outlook for the future. Focus on the information content of the cash-flow data. (pp. 784–786)

Preparing an income statement, balance sheet, and statement of cash flows—indirect method

P16-33A American Reserve Rare Coins (ARRC) was formed on January 1, 2006, when ARRC issued its common stock for $200,000. Early in January, ARRC made the following cash payments:

a. For store fixtures, $50,000

b. For inventory, $100,000

c. For rent expense on a store building, $10,000

Later in the year, ARRC purchased inventory on account for $240,000. Before year-end, ARRC paid $140,000 of this account payable.

During 2006, ARRC sold 2,500 units of inventory for $200 each. Before year-end, the company collected 90% of this amount. Cost of goods sold for the year was $300,000, and ending inventory totaled $40,000.

The store employs three people. The combined annual payroll is $90,000, of which ARRC still owes $5,000 at year-end. At the end of the year, ARRC paid income tax of $20,000.

Late in 2006, ARRC declared and paid cash dividends of $40,000.

For equipment, ARRC uses the straight-line depreciation method, over 5 years, with zero residual value.

Requirements

1. Prepare American Reserve's income statement for the year ended December 31, 2006. Use the single-step format, with all revenues listed together and all expenses together. (pp. 269–271, 788–789)

2. Prepare American Reserve's balance sheet at December 31, 2006. (pp. 787–788)

3. Prepare American Reserve's statement of cash flows for the year ended December 31, 2006. Format cash flows from operating activities by the *indirect* method. (pp. 791–792)

P16-34A Accountants for Datsun, Inc., have assembled the following data for the year ended December 31, 2007:

	December 31,	
	2007	2006
Current Accounts:		
Current assets:		
Cash and cash equivalents	$49,000	$34,000
Accounts receivable	70,100	73,700
Inventories......................................	90,600	86,600
Current liabilities:		
Accounts payable............................	71,600	67,500
Income tax payable.........................	5,900	6,800

Transaction Data for 2007:

Payment of cash dividends...	$48,000	Depreciation expense.........	$ 30,200
Issuance of note payable		Purchase of equipment.......	69,000
to borrow cash.................	63,000	Acquisition of land by issuing	
Net income.........................	50,500	long-term note payable...	118,000
Issuance of common stock		Payment of note payable....	47,000
for cash...........................	36,000	Gain on sale of building	3,500

Requirement

Prepare Datsun's statement of cash flows using the *indirect* method to report operating activities. Include an accompanying schedule of non-cash investing and financing activities. (pp. 791–792, 795)

P16-35A The comparative balance sheet of Fidelity Medical Supply at December 31, 2008, reported the following:

	December 31,	
	2008	2007
Current Assets:		
Cash and cash equivalents	$32,500	$22,500
Accounts receivable	26,600	29,300
Inventories...................................	54,600	53,000
Current Liabilities:		
Accounts payable.........................	$29,100	$28,000
Accrued liabilities	14,300	16,800

Fidelity's transactions during 2008 included the following:

Purchase of building	$104,000	Payment of cash dividends	$17,000
Net income	31,600	Purchase of equipment	55,000
Issuance of common stock		Issuance of long-term note	
for cash	105,000	payable to borrow cash	32,000
Depreciation expense	17,700		

continued . . .

Requirements

1. Prepare the statement of cash flows of Fidelity Medical Supply for the year ended December 31, 2008. Use the *indirect* method to report cash flows from operating activities. (pp. 791–792)

2. Evaluate Fidelity's cash flows for the year. Mention all three categories of cash flows and give the reason for your evaluation. (pp. 784–786)

Preparing the statement of cash flows—indirect method

P16-36A The 2008 comparative balance sheet and income statement of Digital Subscriptions, Inc., follow.

Digital Subscriptions had no noncash investing and financing transactions during 2008. During the year, there were no sales of land or equipment, no issuances of notes payable, no retirements of stock, and no treasury stock transactions.

Requirements

1. Prepare the 2008 statement of cash flows, formatting operating activities by the *indirect* method. (pp. 791–792)

2. How will what you learned in this problem help you evaluate an investment? (pp. 784–786)

DIGITAL SUBSCRIPTIONS, INC.
Comparative Balance Sheet

	December 31, 2008	December 31, 2007	Increase (Decrease)
Current assets:			
Cash and cash equivalents	$ 26,700	$ 18,700	$ 8,000
Accounts receivable	46,500	43,100	3,400
Inventories	84,300	89,900	(5,600)
Plant assets:			
Land	35,100	10,000	25,100
Equipment, net	100,900	93,700	7,200
Total assets	$293,500	$255,400	$38,100
Current liabilities:			
Accounts payable	$ 31,100	$ 29,800	$ 1,300
Accrued liabilities	18,100	18,700	(600)
Long-term liabilities:			
Notes payable	55,000	65,000	(10,000)
Stockholders' equity:			
Common stock	131,100	122,300	8,800
Retained earnings	58,200	19,600	38,600
Total liabilities and stockholders' equity	$293,500	$255,400	$38,100

continued . . .

DIGITAL SUBSCRIPTIONS, INC.
Income Statement
Year Ended December 31, 2008

Revenues:		
Sales revenue		$438,000
Interest revenue		11,700
Total revenues		449,700
Expenses:		
Cost of goods sold	$205,200	
Salary expense	76,400	
Depreciation expense	15,300	
Other operating expense	49,700	
Interest expense	24,600	
Income tax expense	16,900	
Total expenses		388,100
Net income		$ 61,600

Appendix 16A: Direct Method

Preparing the statement of cash flows—direct method
2 **4**

P16-37A GSK Inc., accountants have developed the following data from the company's accounting records for the year ended November 30, 2005:

a. Purchase of plant assets, $100,000
b. Cash receipt from issuance of notes payable, $44,100
c. Payments of notes payable, $18,800
d. Cash receipt from sale of plant assets, $59,700
e. Cash receipt of dividends, $2,700
f. Payments to suppliers, $574,500
g. Interest expense and payments, $37,000
h. Payments of salaries, $104,000
i. Income tax expense and payments, $56,000
j. Depreciation expense, $27,700
k. Collections from customers, $827,100
l. Cash receipt from issuance of common stock, $66,900
m. Payment of cash dividends, $50,500
n. Cash balance: November 30, 2004–$23,800; November 30, 2005–$83,500

Requirement
Prepare GSK's statement of cash flows for the year ended November 30, 2005. Use the *direct* method for cash flows from operating activities. Follow the format of Exhibit 16A-3, page 830, but do *not* show amounts in thousands.

Preparing an income statement, balance sheet, and statement of cash flows—direct method
2 **4**

P16-38A Use the American Reserve Rare Coins data from Problem 16-33A.

Requirements
1. Prepare American Reserve Rare Coins' income statement for the year ended December 31, 2006. Use the single-step format, with all revenues listed together and all expenses together. (pp. 269–271, 788–789)

continued . . .

2. Prepare American Reserve's balance sheet at December 31, 2006. (pp. 787–788)

3. Prepare American Reserve's statement of cash flows for the year ended December 31, 2006. Format cash flows from operating activities by the *direct* method, as shown in Exhibit 16A-3, page 830.

Preparing the statement of cash flows—direct method

P16-39A Use the Digital Subscriptions, Inc., data from Problem 16-36A.

Requirements

1. Prepare the 2008 statement of cash flows by the *direct* method. Follow the statement format shown in Exhibit 16A-3, page 830.

2. How will what you learned in this problem help you evaluate an investment? (pp. 784–786)

Preparing the statement of cash flows—direct method

P16-40A To prepare the statement of cash flows, accountants for A-Mobile, Inc., you have summarized 2008 activity in the Cash account as follows:

Cash

Beginning balance	87,100	Payments of operating expenses	46,100
Issuance of common stock	60,800	Payments of salaries and wages	67,500
Receipts of interest revenue	14,100	Payment of note payable	80,000
Collections from customers	308,100	Payment of income tax	8,000
		Payments on accounts payable	101,600
		Payment of dividends	1,800
		Payments of interest	21,800
		Purchase of equipment	51,500
Ending balance	91,800		

Requirement

Prepare A-Mobile's statement of cash flows for the year ended December 31, 2008, using the *direct* method to report operating activities. Follow the statement format given in Exhibit 16A-3, page 830.

Problems (Group B)

Using cash-flow information to evaluate performance

P16-41B Top managers of Chase Financial Services are reviewing company performance for 2009. The income statement reports a 20% increase in net income over 2008. However, most of the net-income increase resulted from an extraordinary gain on the sale of equipment. The balance sheet shows a large increase in receivables. The cash-flow statement, in summarized form, reports the following:

Net cash used for operating activities	$(80,000)
Net cash provided by investing activities	40,000
Net cash provided by financing activities............	50,000
Increase in cash during 2009	$ 10,000

Requirement

Write a memo giving the top managers of Chase Financial Services your assessment of 2009 operations and your outlook for the future. Focus on the information content of the cash-flow data. (pp. 784–786)

Preparing an income
statement, balance sheet,
and statement of cash
flows—indirect method

2 **3**

P16-42B Lucenay Interiors, a furniture store, was formed on January 1, 2008, when Lucenay issued common stock for $400,000. Early in January, Lucenay made the following cash payments:

a. $100,000 for equipment

b. $260,000 for inventory

c. $20,000 for 2008 rent expense on a store building

Later in the year, Lucenay purchased inventory on account. Cost of this inventory was $120,000. Before year-end, Lucenay paid $60,000 of this debt.

During 2008, Lucenay sold 2,000 units of inventory for $200 each. Before year end, Lucenay collected 80% of this amount. Cost of goods sold for the year was $260,000 and at year-end the inventory balance was $120,000.

The store employs a salesperson whose annual pay is $45,000, of which Lucenay owes $4,000 at year-end. At the end of the year, Lucenay paid income tax of $10,000.

Late in 2008, Lucenay paid cash dividends of $11,000.

For equipment, Lucenay uses the straight-line depreciation method, over 5 years, with zero residual value.

Requirements

1. Prepare Lucenay Interiors' income statement for the year ended December 31, 2008. Use the single-step format, with all revenues listed together and all expenses together. (pp. 269–271, 788–789)

2. Prepare Lucenay's balance sheet at December 31, 2008. (pp. 787–788)

3. Prepare Lucenay's statement of cash flows for the year ended December 31, 2008. Format cash flows from operating activities by the *indirect* method. (pp. 791–792)

P16-43B Carlson Corporation accountants have assembled the company's data for the year ended December 31, 2007.

Requirement

Prepare Carlson Corporation's statement of cash flows using the *indirect* method to report operating activities. Include an accompanying schedule of noncash investing and financing activities. (pp. 791–792, 795)

	December 31,	
	2007	2006
Current Accounts:		
Current assets:		
Cash and cash equivalents	$50,000	$22,000
Accounts receivable	69,200	64,200
Inventories	80,000	83,000
Current liabilities:		
Accounts payable...........................	$57,800	$55,800
Income tax payable........................	14,700	16,700

continued . . .

Transaction Data for 2007:

Net income	$ 57,000	Purchase of treasury stock	$14,000
Issuance of common stock for cash	41,000	Loss on sale of equipment	11,000
		Payment of cash dividends....	18,000
Depreciation expense	21,000	Issuance of long-term note	
Purchase of building	160,000	payable to borrow cash.....	34,000
Retirement of bonds payable by issuing common stock	65,000	Sale of equipment	58,000

Preparing the statement of cash flows—indirect method

P16-44B The comparative balance sheet of Fitzwater Company at March 31, 2009, reported the following:

	March 31,	
	2009	2008
Current Assets:		
Cash and cash equivalents	$22,200	$15,000
Accounts receivable	14,900	21,700
Inventories	63,200	60,600
Current Liabilities:		
Accounts payable	$30,100	$27,600
Accrued liabilities	10,700	11,100
Income tax payable	8,000	4,700

Fitzwater's transactions during the year ended March 31, 2009, included the following:

Payment of cash dividend	$30,000	Depreciation expense	$17,300
Purchase of equipment	78,700	Purchase of building	47,000
Issuance of note payable to borrow cash	50,000	Net income	75,000
		Issuance of common stock	11,000

Requirements

1. Prepare Fitzwater's statement of cash flows for the year ended March 31, 2009, using the *indirect* method to report cash flows from operating activities. (pp. 791–792)

2. Evaluate Fitzwater's cash flows for the year. Mention all three categories of cash flows and give the reason for your evaluation. (pp. 784–786)

Preparing the statement of cash flows—indirect method

P16-45B The 2005 comparative balance sheet and income statement of Get Wired, Inc., follow on the next page.

Get Wired, Inc., had no noncash investing and financing transactions during 2005. During the year, there were no sales of land or equipment, no issuances of notes payable, no retirements of stock, and no treasury stock transactions.

continued . . .

GET WIRED, INC.
Comparative Balance Sheet

	December 31, 2005	December 31, 2004	Increase (Decrease)
Current assets:			
Cash and cash equivalents	$ 26,700	$ 15,300	$ 11,400
Accounts receivable	25,300	26,900	(1,600)
Inventories	91,800	79,800	12,000
Plant assets:			
Land	69,000	60,000	9,000
Equipment, net	53,500	49,400	4,100
Total assets	$266,300	$231,400	$34,900
Current liabilities:			
Accounts payable	$ 30,900	$ 35,400	$ (4,500)
Accrued liabilities	30,600	28,600	2,000
Long-term liabilities:			
Notes payable	75,000	100,000	(25,000)
Stockholders' equity:			
Common stock	88,300	64,700	23,600
Retained earnings	41,500	2,700	38,800
Total liabilities and stockholders' equity	$266,300	$231,400	$34,900

GET WIRED, INC.
Income Statement
Year Ended December 31, 2005

Revenues:		
Sales revenue		$213,000
Interest revenue		8,600
Total revenues		221,600
Expenses:		
Cost of goods sold	$70,600	
Salary expense	27,800	
Depreciation expense	4,000	
Other operating expense	10,500	
Interest expense	11,600	
Income tax expense	29,100	
Total expenses		153,600
Net income		$ 68,000

Requirements

1. Prepare the 2005 statement of cash flows, formatting operating activities by the *indirect* method. (pp. 791–792)

2. How will what you learned in this problem help you evaluate an investment? (p. 785)

Appendix 16A: Direct Method

P16-46B Accountants for Compass Software have developed the following data from the company's accounting records for the year ended April 30, 2005:

a. Purchase of plant assets, $59,400

b. Cash receipt from issuance of common stock, $8,000

c. Payment of dividends, $48,400

d. Collection of interest, $4,400

e. Payments of salaries, $93,000

f. Cash receipt from sale of plant assets, $22,400

g. Collections from customers, $605,300

h. Cash receipt of dividend revenue, $4,100

i. Payments to suppliers, $370,300

j. Depreciation expense, $59,900

k. Cash receipt from issuance of notes payable, $19,600

l. Payments of notes payable, $50,000

m. Interest expense and payments, $13,000

n. Income tax expense and payments, $37,000

o. Cash balance: April 30, 2004, $39,300; April 30, 2005, $32,000

Requirement

Prepare Compass Software's statement of cash flows for the year ended April 30, 2005. Use the *direct* method for cash flows from operating activities. Follow the format of Exhibit 16A-3, page 830, but do *not* show amounts in thousands.

P16-47B Use the Lucenay Interiors data from Problem 16-42B.

Requirements

1. Prepare Lucenay Interiors' income statement for the year ended December 31, 2008. Use the single-step format, with all revenues listed together and all expenses together. (pp. 269–271, 788–789)

2. Prepare Lucenay's balance sheet at December 31, 2008. (pp. 787–788)

3. Prepare Lucenay's statement of cash flows for the year ended December 31, 2008. Format cash flows from operating activities by the *direct* method, as shown in Exhibit 16A-3, page 830.

P16-48B Use the Get Wired, Inc., data from Problem 16-45B.

Requirements

1. Prepare the 2005 statement of cash flows by the *direct* method. Follow the statement format given in Exhibit 16A-3, page 830.

2. How will what you learned in this problem help you evaluate an investment? (p. 785)

P16-49B To prepare the statement of cash flows, accountants for Toll-Free Calling, Inc., have summarized 2008 activity in the Cash account as follows:

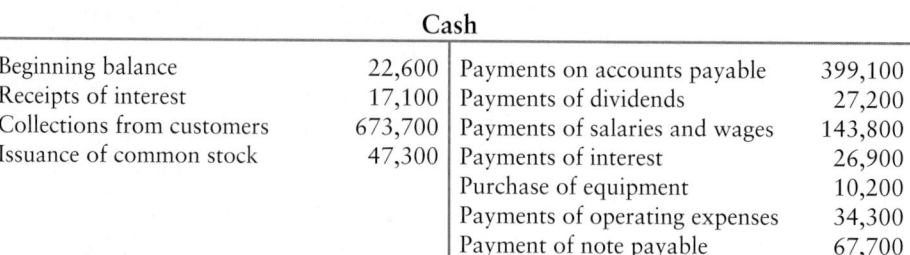

Cash			
Beginning balance	22,600	Payments on accounts payable	399,100
Receipts of interest	17,100	Payments of dividends	27,200
Collections from customers	673,700	Payments of salaries and wages	143,800
Issuance of common stock	47,300	Payments of interest	26,900
		Purchase of equipment	10,200
		Payments of operating expenses	34,300
		Payment of note payable	67,700
		Payment of income tax	18,900
Ending balance	32,600		

Requirement

Prepare the statement of cash flows of Toll-Free Calling, Inc., for the year ended December 31, 2008, using the *direct* method for operating activities. Follow the statement format given in Exhibit 16A-3, page 830.

Apply Your Knowledge

Decision Cases

Preparing and using the
statement of cash flows to
evaluate operations
3

Case 1. The 2008 comparative income statement and the 2008 comparative balance sheet of Golf America, Inc., have just been distributed at a meeting of the company's board of directors. The members of the board of directors raise a fundamental question: Why is the cash balance so low? This question is especially hard to understand because 2008 showed record profits. As the controller of the company, you must answer the question.

GOLF AMERICA, INC.
Comparative Income Statement
Years Ended December 31, 2008 and 2007

(In thousands)	2008	2007
Revenues and gains:		
Sales revenue	$444	$310
Gain on sale of equipment (sale price, $33)	—	18
Total revenues and gains	$444	$328
Expenses and losses:		
Cost of goods sold	$221	$162
Salary expense	48	28
Depreciation expense	46	22
Interest expense	13	20
Amortization expense on patent	11	11
Loss on sale of land (sale price, $61)	—	35
Total expenses and losses	339	278
Net income	$105	$ 50

GOLF AMERICA, INC.
Comparative Balance Sheet
December 31, 2008 and 2007

(In thousands)	2008	2007
Assets		
Cash	$ 25	$ 63
Accounts receivable, net	72	61
Inventories	194	181
Long-term investments	31	0
Property, plant, and equipment, net	125	61
Patents	177	188
Totals	$624	$554
Liabilities and Owners' Equity		
Accounts payable	$ 63	$ 56
Accrued liabilities	12	17
Notes payable, long-term	179	264
Common stock	149	61
Retained earnings	221	156
Totals	$624	$554

continued . . .

Requirements

1. Prepare a statement of cash flows for 2008 in the format that best shows the relationship between net income and operating cash flow. The company sold no plant assets or long-term investments and issued no notes payable during 2008. There were *no* noncash investing and financing transactions during the year. Show all amounts in thousands.

2. Considering net income and the company's cash flows during 2008, was it a good year or a bad year? Give your reasons.

Using cash-flow data to evaluate an investment

Case 2. Showcase Cinemas and Theater by Design are asking you to recommend their stock to your clients. Because Showcase and Theater by Design earn about the same net income and have similar financial positions, your decision depends on their cash-flow statements, summarized as follows:

	Theater by Design		Showcase Cinemas	
Net cash provided by operating activities......	$30,000		$70,000	
Cash provided by (used for) investing activities:				
Purchase of plant assets	$(20,000)		$(100,000)	
Sale of plant assets....................	40,000	20,000	10,000	(90,000)
Cash provided by (used for) financing activities:				
Issuance of common stock	—			30,000
Paying off long-term debt	(40,000)			—
Net increase in cash....................		$10,000		$10,000

Based on their cash flows, which company looks better? Give your reasons.

Ethical Issue

Moss Exports is having a bad year. Net income is only $60,000. Also, two important overseas customers are falling behind in their payments to Moss, and Moss's accounts receivable are ballooning. The company desperately needs a loan. The Moss Exports board of directors is considering ways to put the best face on the company's financial statements. Moss's bank closely examines cash flow from operations. Daniel Peavey, Moss's controller, suggests reclassifying as long-term the receivables from the slow-paying clients. He explains to the board that removing the $80,000 rise in accounts receivable from current assets will increase net cash provided by operations. This approach may help Moss get the loan.

Requirements

1. Using only the amounts given, compute net cash provided by operations, both without and with the reclassification of the receivables. Which reporting makes Moss look better?

2. Under what condition would the reclassification of the receivables be ethical? Unethical?

Financial Statement Case

Using the statement of cash flows
2 3 4

Use the Amazon.com statement of cash flows along with the company's other financial statements, all in Appendix A, at the end of this book, to answer the following questions.

Requirements

1. Which method does Amazon use to report net cash flows from *operating* activities? How can you tell?

2. Amazon earned net income during 2005. Did operations *provide* cash or *use* cash during 2005? Give the amount. How did operating cash during 2005 compare with 2004? Be specific, and state the reason for your answer.

3. Suppose Amazon reported net cash flows from operating activities by the direct method. Compute these amounts for the year ended December 31, 2005:

   a. Collections from customers (Other current assets were $15 million at December 31, 2005, and $12 million at December 31, 2004.)

   b. Payments for inventory

4. Evaluate 2005 in terms of net income, cash flows, balance sheet position, and overall results. Be specific.

Team Projects

Project 1. Each member of the team should obtain the annual report of a different company. Select companies in different industries. Evaluate each company's trend of cash flows for the most recent two years. In your evaluation of the companies' cash flows, you may use any other information that is publicly available—for example, the other financial statements (income statement, balance sheet, statement of stockholders' equity, and the related notes) and news stories from magazines and newspapers. Rank the companies' cash flows from best to worst and write a two-page report on your findings.

Project 2. Select a company and obtain its annual report, including all the financial statements. Focus on the statement of cash flows and, in particular, the cash flows from operating activities. Specify whether the company uses the *direct* method or the *indirect* method to report operating cash flows. As necessary, use the other financial statements (income statement, balance sheet, and statement of stockholders' equity) and the notes to prepare the company's cash flows from operating activities by the *other* method.

For Internet exercises, Excel in Practice, and additional online activities, go to the Web site www.prenhall.com/horngren.

Quick Check Answers

   1. *a*   2. *d*   3. *a*   4. *b*   5. *c*   6. *a*   7. *b*   8. *c*   9. *d*   10. *c*

Preparing the Statement of Cash Flows by the Direct Method

The Financial Accounting Standards Board (FASB) prefers the direct method of reporting cash flows from operating activities. The direct method provides clearer information about the sources and uses of cash. But very few companies use the direct method because it takes more computations than the indirect method. Investing and financing cash flows are unaffected by operating cash flows.

4 Prepare the statement of cash flows by the direct method

To illustrate the statement of cash flows by the direct method, we will be using Anchor Corporation, a dealer in auto parts for European cars. You can prepare the statement of cash flows by the direct method as follows:

STEP 1 Lay out the format of the statement of cash flows by the direct method, as shown in Exhibit 16A-1.

EXHIBIT 16A-1 Format of the Statement of Cash Flows: Direct Method

ANCHOR CORPORATION
Statement of Cash Flows
Year Ended December 31, 2008

Cash flows from operating activities:
  Receipts:
    Collections from customers
    Interest received
    Dividends received on investments
      Total cash receipts
  Payments:
    To suppliers
    To employees
    For interest and income tax
      Total cash payments
  Net cash provided by operating activities
± Cash flows from investing activities:
  Cash receipts from sales of long-term assets (investments,
    land, building, equipment, and so on)
  – Acquisitions of long-term assets
  Net cash provided by (used for) investing activities
± Cash flows from financing activities:
  Cash receipts from issuance of stock
  + Sale of treasury stock
  – Purchase of treasury stock
  + Cash receipts from issuance of notes or bonds payable (borrowing)
  – Payment of notes or bonds payable
  – Payment of dividends
  Net cash provided by (used for) financing activities
= Net increase (decrease) in cash during the year
  + Cash at December 31, 2007
  = Cash at December 31, 2008

STEP 2 Use the comparative balance sheet to determine the increase or decrease in cash during the period. The change in cash is the "check figure" for the statement of cash flows. Anchor's comparative balance sheet shows that cash decreased by $20,000 during 2008. See Exhibit 16A-2.

EXHIBIT 16A-2 Comparative Balance Sheet (Partial)

ANCHOR CORPORATION
Comparative Balance Sheet (Partial)
December 31, 2008 and 2007

(In thousands)	2008	2007	Increase (Decrease)
Assets			
Current:			
Cash	$22	$42	$(20)

STEP 3 Use the available data to prepare the statement of cash flows. Anchor has assembled the following summary of its 2008 cash transactions.

Operating Activities

1. Collections from customers, $269,000
2. Cash receipt of interest revenue, $12,000
3. Cash receipt of dividend revenue, $9,000
4. Payments to suppliers, $135,000
5. Salary expense and payments, $56,000
6. Interest expense and payments, $15,000
7. Income tax expense and payments, $14,000

Investing Activities

8. Cash payments to acquire plant assets, $310,000
9. Cash receipts from sale of plant assets, $50,000

Financing Activities

10. Cash receipts from issuance of common stock, $100,000
11. Cash receipts from issuance of notes payable, $90,000
12. Payment of note payable, $10,000
13. Payment of cash dividends, $10,000

The statement of cash flows reports only transactions with cash effects. Exhibit 16A-3 gives Anchor Corporation's statement of cash flows for 2008. You should trace each item from the list of transactions to the statement of cash flows in Exhibit 16A-3.

Cash Flows from Operating Activities

Operating cash flows are listed first because they are the most important source of cash. Exhibit 16A-3 shows that Anchor is sound; its operating activities were the largest source of cash receipts, $290,000. Let's examine Anchor's operating cash flows.

Cash Collections from Customers

Cash sales bring in cash immediately; collections of accounts receivable take a little longer. Both are reported as "Collections from customers . . . $269,000" in Exhibit 16A-3.

Cash Receipts of Interest

The income statement reports interest revenue. Only the cash receipts of interest appear on the statement of cash flows—$12,000 in Exhibit 16A-3.

ANCHOR CORPORATION
Statement of Cash Flows
Year Ended December 31, 2008

	(In thousands)	
Cash flows from operating activities:		
Receipts:		
Collections from customers	$ 269	
Interest received	12	
Dividends received	9	
Total cash receipts		$290
Payments:		
To suppliers	$(135)	
To employees	(56)	
For interest	(15)	
For income tax	(14)	
Total cash payments		(220)
Net cash provided by operating activities		70
Cash flows from investing activities:		
Acquisition of plant assets	$(310)	
Cash receipts from sale of plant assets	50	
Net cash used for investing activities		(260)
Cash flows from financing activities:		
Cash receipts from issuance of common stock	$ 100	
Cash receipts from issuance of notes payable	90	
Payment of note payable	(10)	
Payment of dividends	(10)	
Net cash provided by financing activities		170
Net decrease in cash		$ (20)
Cash balance, December 31, 2007		42
Cash balance, December 31, 2008		$ 22

Now return to "Cash Flows from Operating Activities" on page 829.

Cash Receipts of Dividends

Dividend revenue is reported on the income statement. Cash received from dividends is reported on the statement of cash flows—$9,000 in Exhibit 16A-3.

Payments to Suppliers

Payments to suppliers include all payments for:

• inventory
• operating expenses except employee compensation, interest, and income taxes.

Suppliers are those entities that provide the business with its inventory and essential services. In Exhibit 16A-3, Anchor Corporation reports payments to suppliers of $135,000.

Payments to Employees

This category includes payments for salaries, wages, and other forms of employee compensation. Accrued amounts are not cash flows because they have not yet been paid. The statement of cash flows in Exhibit 16A-3 reports only the cash payments, $56,000.

Payments for Interest Expense and Income Tax Expense

These cash payments are reported separately from the other expenses. For Anchor Corporation, interest ($15,000) and income tax expenses ($14,000) equal their cash payments amounts.

Depreciation, Depletion, and Amortization Expense

These expenses are *not* reported on the statement of cash flows because they do not affect cash.

Cash Flows from Investing Activities

Investing is critical because a company's investments determine its future. Large purchases of plant assets signal expansion. Low levels of investing show that the business is not replenishing assets.

Purchases of Plant Assets and Investments in Other Companies

These cash payments acquire a long-term asset. The first investing activity reported by Anchor Corporation in Exhibit 16A-3 is the purchase of plant assets ($310,000).

Cash Receipts from the Sale of Plant Assets and Investments

These cash receipts are also investing activities. Exhibit 16A-3 reports that Anchor Corporation received $50,000 cash from the sale of plant assets. For the sale of a long-term asset, the statement of cash flows reports only the amount of cash received from the sale—not the gain or loss on the sale value or the book value of the asset sold.

Investors and creditors are critical of a company that sells large amounts of its plant assets. Selling off lots of plant assets may signal an emergency need for cash.

Cash Flows from Financing Activities

Financing refers to how the business obtains money from outside sources. Cash flows from financing activities include the following:

Cash Receipts from Issuance of Stock and Notes Payable

Investors want to know how the entity obtains its financing. Issuing stock and borrowing money are two ways to finance a business. In Exhibit 16A-3, Anchor Corporation issued common stock and received cash of $100,000. Anchor also received cash when it issued notes payable to borrow $90,000.

Payment of Notes Payable and Purchases of Treasury Stock

The payment of notes payable decreases cash, which is the opposite of borrowing. Anchor Corporation reports note payments of $10,000. Other transactions in this category include the purchase and the sale of treasury stock.

Payment of Cash Dividends

The payment of dividends is a financing activity, as shown by Anchor's $10,000 payment in Exhibit 16A-3. A stock dividend has *no* effect on cash and is *not* reported on the cash-flow statement.

Noncash Investing and Financing Activities

Companies make investments that do not require cash. They also obtain financing other than cash. Our examples thus far have included none of these transactions. Now suppose that Anchor Corporation issued common stock of $300,000 to acquire a building. Anchor would record the purchase as follows:

Building	300,000	
Common Stock		300,000

The purchase of the building is an investing activity. The issuance of common stock is a financing activity. Taken together, this transaction is a *noncash investing and financing activity.* This transaction would not be reported on the cash-flow statement because Anchor paid no cash. But the building and the common stock are important. Noncash investing and financing activities can be reported in a separate schedule that accompanies the statement of cash flows, as follows (all amounts are assumed). This information follows the cash-flow statement or can be disclosed in a note.

	(Thousands)
Noncash investing and financing activities:	
Acquisition of building by issuing common stock	$300
Acquisition of land by issuing note payable	70
Payment of note payable by issuing common stock	100
Total noncash investing and financing activities	$470

Now let's see how to compute the individual operating cash flows for the direct method.

Computing Operating Cash Flows by the Direct Method

How do we compute the operating cash flows for the direct method? We can use Anchor's income statement (Exhibit 16A-4) and the *changes* in the related balance sheet accounts (Exhibit 16A-5).

Exhibit 16A-6 shows how to compute the operating cash flows under the direct method.

Computing Cash Collections from Customers

Collections can be computed by converting sales revenue (an accrual-basis amount) to the cash basis. Anchor Corporation's income statement (Exhibit 16A-4) reports sales of $286,000. But cash collections are different. Exhibit 16A-5 shows that

ANCHOR CORPORATION
Income Statement
Year Ended December 31, 2008

		(In thousands)
Revenues and gains:		
Sales revenue	$286	
Interest revenue	12	
Dividend revenue	9	
Gain on sale of plant assets	10	
Total revenues and gains		$317
Expenses:		
Cost of goods sold	$156	
Salary and wage expense	56	
Depreciation expense	20	
Other operating expense	16	
Interest expense	15	
Income tax expense	14	
Total expenses		277
Net income		$ 40

ANCHOR CORPORATION
Comparative Balance Sheet
December 31, 2008 and 2007

(In thousands)	2008	2007	Increase (Decrease)	
Assets				
Current:				
Cash	$ 22	$ 42	$ (20)	
Accounts receivable	90	73	17	} Operating
Inventory	143	145	(2)	
Plant assets, net	460	210	250	} Investing
Total	$715	$470	$245	
Liabilities				
Current:				
Accounts payable	$ 90	$ 50	$ 40	} Operating
Accrued liabilities	5	10	(5)	
Long-term notes payable	160	80	80	
				} Financing
Stockholders' Equity				
Common stock	350	250	100	
Retained earnings	110	80	30	
Total	$715	$470	$245	

Direct Method: Computing Cash Flows from Operating Activities

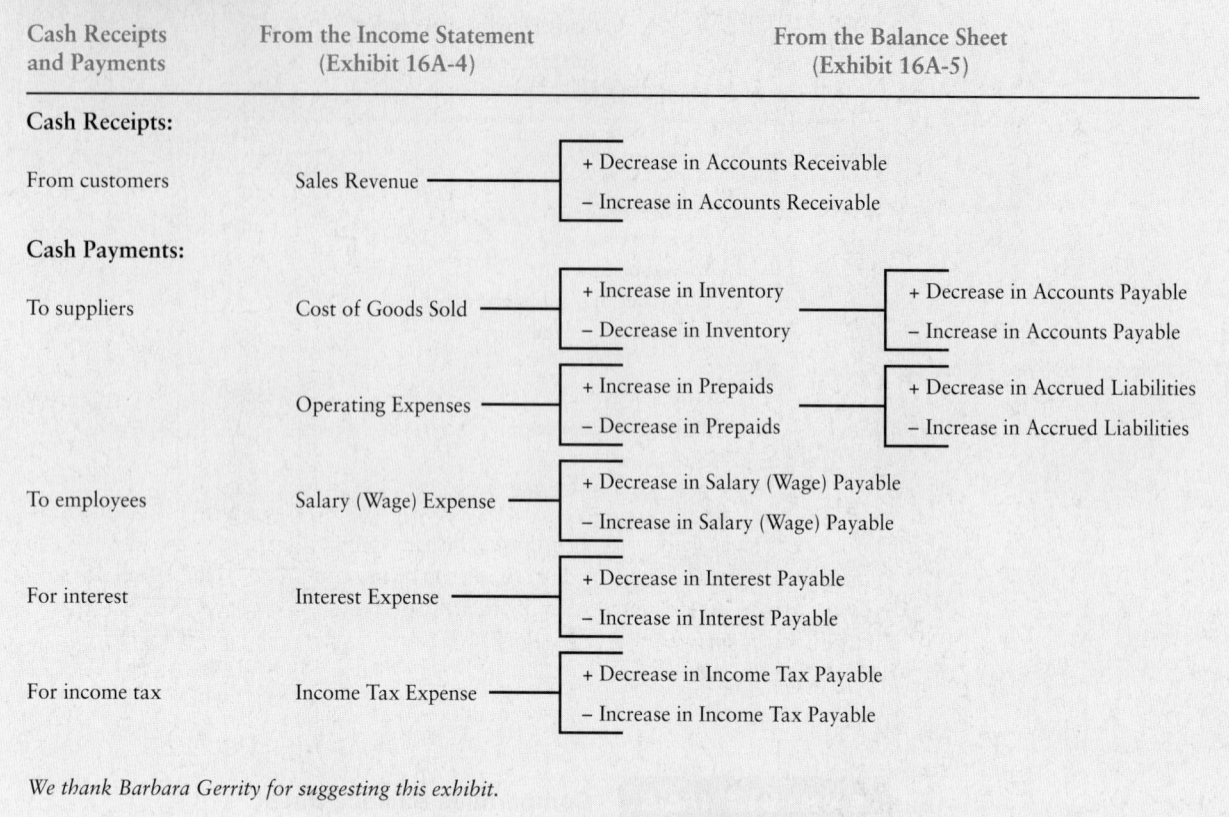

Cash Receipts and Payments	From the Income Statement (Exhibit 16A-4)	From the Balance Sheet (Exhibit 16A-5)
Cash Receipts:		
From customers	Sales Revenue	+ Decrease in Accounts Receivable – Increase in Accounts Receivable
Cash Payments:		
To suppliers	Cost of Goods Sold	+ Increase in Inventory → + Decrease in Accounts Payable – Decrease in Inventory → – Increase in Accounts Payable
	Operating Expenses	+ Increase in Prepaids → + Decrease in Accrued Liabilities – Decrease in Prepaids → – Increase in Accrued Liabilities
To employees	Salary (Wage) Expense	+ Decrease in Salary (Wage) Payable – Increase in Salary (Wage) Payable
For interest	Interest Expense	+ Decrease in Interest Payable – Increase in Interest Payable
For income tax	Income Tax Expense	+ Decrease in Income Tax Payable – Increase in Income Tax Payable

We thank Barbara Gerrity for suggesting this exhibit.

Accounts Receivable increased by $17,000 during the year. Based on those amounts, Cash Collections equal $269,000, as follows:

$$\text{Collections from Customers} = \text{Sales Revenue} - \text{Increase in Accounts Receivable}$$

$$\$269,000 = \$286,000 - \$17,000$$

Computing Payments to Suppliers

This computation has two parts:

- Payments for inventory
- Payments for operating expenses (other than salaries, wages, interest, and income tax)

Payments for inventory are computed by converting cost of goods sold to the cash basis. We must analyze Cost of Goods Sold from the income statement and Inventory and Accounts Payable from the balance sheet, as follows:

$$\text{Payments for Inventory} = \text{Cost of Goods Sold} - \text{Decrease in Inventory} - \text{Increase in Accounts Payable}$$

$$\$114,000 = \$156,000 - \$2,000 - \$40,000$$

Payments for operating expenses use other operating expenses from the income statement and accrued liabilities from the balance sheet. Throughout, all amounts come from Exhibits 16A-4 and 16A-5. Items to be computed are shown in color.

$$\begin{array}{ccc} \text{Payments for} & & \text{Other} & & \text{Decrease in} \\ \text{Operating} & = & \text{Operating} & + & \text{Accrued} \\ \text{Expenses} & & \text{Expense} & & \text{Liabilities} \\ \$21,000 & = & \$16,000 & + & \$5,000 \end{array}$$

$$\begin{array}{ccc} \text{Payments to} & = & \text{Payments for} & + & \text{Payments for} \\ \text{Suppliers} & & \text{Inventory} & & \text{Operating} \\ & & & & \text{Expenses} \\ \$135,000 & = & \$114,000 & + & \$21,000 \end{array}$$

Computing Payments to Employees and Payments for Interest and Income Tax

Anchor Corporation's payments to employees and payments for interest and income tax were the same as the expenses. In this particular case we can take the expense amounts from the income statement to the statement of cash flows. Normally, however, you must adjust the expense amount for any change in the related liability account, as shown in Exhibit 16A-6.

Computing Investing and Financing Cash Flows

The computations of investing and financing cash flows are given on pages 792–795.

Measuring Cash Adequacy: Free Cash Flow

Throughout we have focused on cash flows from operating, investing, and financing activities. Some investors want to know how much cash a company can "free up" for new opportunities. **Free cash flow** is the amount of cash available from operations after paying for planned investments in long-term assets. Free cash flow can be computed as follows:

$$\text{Free cash flow} = \begin{array}{c} \text{Net cash provided} \\ \text{by operating} \\ \text{activities} \end{array} - \begin{array}{c} \text{Cash payments for planned} \\ \text{investments in plant, equipment,} \\ \text{and other long-term assets} \end{array}$$

PepsiCo, Inc. uses free cash flow to manage its operations. Suppose PepsiCo expects net cash provided by operations of $2.3 billion. Assume PepsiCo plans to spend $1.9 billion to modernize its bottling plants. In this case, PepsiCo's free cash flow would be $0.4 billion ($2.3 billion − $1.9 billion). If a good investment opportunity comes along, PepsiCo should have $0.4 billion to invest in the other company. Shell Oil Company also uses free-cash-flow analysis. A large amount of free cash flow is preferable because it means a lot of cash is available for new investments.

Decision Guidelines

USING CASH-FLOW AND RELATED INFORMATION TO EVALUATE INVESTMENTS

Ann Browning is a private investor. Through the years, she has devised some guidelines for evaluating investments. Here are some of her guidelines.

Question	Financial Statement	What to Look For
Where is most of the company's cash coming from?	Statement of cash flows	Operating activities ⟶ Good sign Investing activities ⟶ Bad sign Financing activities ⟶ Okay sign
Do high sales and profits translate into more cash?	Statement of cash flows	Usually, but cash flows from *operating* activities must be the main source of cash for long-term success.
If sales and profits are low, how is the company generating cash?	Statement of cash flows	If *investing* activities are generating the cash, the business may be in trouble because it is selling off its long-term assets. If *financing* activities are generating the cash, that cannot go on forever. Sooner or later, investors will demand cash flow from operating activities.
Is the cash balance large enough to provide for expansion?	Balance sheet	The cash balance should be growing over time. If not, the company may be in trouble.
Can the business pay its debts?	Income statement	Increasing trend of net income.
	Statement of cash flows	Cash flows from operating activities should be the main source of cash.
	Balance sheet	Current ratio, debt ratio.

Summary Problem

Assume that Berkshire Hathaway is considering buying Granite Shoals Corporation. Granite Shoals reported the following comparative balance sheet and income statement for 2009.

GRANITE SHOALS CORPORATION
Balance Sheet
December 31, 2009 and 2008

	2009	2008	Increase (Decrease)
Cash	$ 19,000	$ 3,000	$16,000
Accounts receivable	22,000	23,000	(1,000)
Inventory	34,000	31,000	3,000
Prepaid expenses	1,000	3,000	(2,000)
Equipment (net)	90,000	79,000	11,000
Intangible assets	9,000	9,000	—
	$175,000	$148,000	$27,000
Accounts payable	$ 14,000	$ 9,000	$ 5,000
Accrued liabilities	16,000	19,000	(3,000)
Income tax payable	14,000	12,000	2,000
Long-term note payable	45,000	50,000	(5,000)
Common stock	31,000	20,000	11,000
Retained earnings	64,000	40,000	24,000
Treasury stock	(9,000)	(2,000)	(7,000)
	$175,000	$148,000	$27,000

GRANITE SHOALS CORPORATION
Income Statement
Year Ended December 31, 2009

Sales revenue	$190,000
Gain on sale of equipment	6,000
Total revenue and gains	196,000
Cost of goods sold	$ 85,000
Depreciation expense	19,000
Other operating expenses	36,000
Total expenses	140,000
Income before income tax	56,000
Income tax expense	18,000
Net income	$ 38,000

Requirements

1. Compute the following cash-flow amounts for 2009.

    a. Collections from customers

    b. Payments for inventory

    c. Payments for other operating expenses

    d. Payment of income tax

e. Acquisition of equipment. Granite Shoals sold equipment that had book value of $15,000.

f. Cash receipt from sale of plant assets

g. Issuance of long-term note payable. Granite Shoals paid off $10,000 of long-term notes payable.

h. Issuance of common stock

i. Payment of dividends

j. Purchase of treasury stock

2. Prepare Granite Shoals Corporation's statement of cash flows (*direct* method) for the year ended December 31, 2009. There were no noncash investing and financing activities. Follow the statement format in Exhibit 16A-3, page 830.

Solution

1. Cash-flow amounts:

a. $$\begin{array}{ccccc} \text{Collections} & & & & \text{Decrease in} \\ \text{from} & = & \text{Sales} & + & \text{accounts} \\ \text{customers} & & \text{revenue} & & \text{receivables} \\ \$191{,}000 & = & \$190{,}000 & + & \$1{,}000 \end{array}$$

b. $$\begin{array}{ccccccc} \text{Payments} & & \text{Cost of} & & \text{Increase} & & \text{Increase in} \\ \text{for} & = & \text{goods} & + & \text{in} & - & \text{accounts} \\ \text{inventory} & & \text{sold} & & \text{inventory} & & \text{payable} \\ \$83{,}000 & = & \$85{,}000 & + & \$3{,}000 & - & \$5{,}000 \end{array}$$

c. $$\begin{array}{ccccccc} \text{Payments} & & \text{Other} & & \text{Decrease} & & \text{Decrease in} \\ \text{for other} & = & \text{Operating} & - & \text{in prepaid} & + & \text{accrued} \\ \text{operating expenses} & & \text{expenses} & & \text{expenses} & & \text{liabilities} \\ \$37{,}000 & = & \$36{,}000 & - & \$2{,}000 & + & \$3{,}000 \end{array}$$

d. $$\begin{array}{ccccc} \text{Payment of} & = & \text{Income tax} & - & \text{Increase in} \\ \text{income tax} & & \text{expense} & & \text{income tax payable} \\ \$16{,}000 & = & \$18{,}000 & - & \$2{,}000 \end{array}$$

e. Equipment, Net (let X = Acquisitions)

$$\begin{array}{ccccccccc} \text{Beginning} & + & \text{Acquisitions} & - & \text{Depreciation} & - & \text{Book value} & = & \text{Ending} \\ & & & & \text{expense} & & \text{sold} & & \\ \$79{,}000 & + & X & - & \$19{,}000 & - & \$15{,}000 & = & \$90{,}000 \\ & & X & = & \$45{,}000 & & & & \end{array}$$

f. Sale of plant assets

$$\begin{array}{ccccc} \text{Cash} & = & \text{Book value of} & + & \text{Gain on sale} \\ \text{received} & & \text{assets sold} & & \\ \$21{,}000 & = & \$15{,}000 & + & \$6{,}000 \end{array}$$

g. Long-Term Note Payable (let X = Issuance)

$$\begin{array}{ccccccc} \text{Beginning} & + & \text{Issuance} & - & \text{Payment} & = & \text{Ending} \\ \$50{,}000 & + & X & - & \$10{,}000 & = & \$45{,}000 \\ & & X & = & \$5{,}000 & & \end{array}$$

h. Common Stock (let X = Issuance)

$$\begin{array}{ccccc} \text{Beginning} & + & \text{Issuance} & = & \text{Ending} \\ \$20{,}000 & + & X & = & \$31{,}000 \\ & & X & = & \$11{,}000 \end{array}$$

i. Retained Earnings (let X = Dividends)

Beginning	+	Net income	−	Dividends	=	Ending
$40,000	+	$38,000	−	X	=	$64,000
				X	=	$14,000

j. Treasury Stock (let X = Purchases)

Beginning	+	Purchases	=	Ending
$2000	+	X	=	$9,000
		X	=	$7,000

2.

GRANITE SHOALS CORPORATION
Statement of Cash Flows
Year Ended December 31, 2009

Cash flows from operating activities:		
Receipts:		
Collections from customers	$191,000	
Payments:		
To suppliers ($83,000 + $37,000)	(120,000)	
For income tax	(16,000)	
Net cash provided by operating activities		$55,000
Cash flows from investing activities:		
Acquisition of plant assets	$ (45,000)	
Sale of plant assets ($15,000 + $6,000)	21,000	
Net cash used for investing activities		(24,000)
Cash flows from financing activities:		
Payment of dividends	$ (14,000)	
Issuance of common stock	11,000	
Payment of note payable	(10,000)	
Purchase of treasury stock	(7,000)	
Issuance of note payable	5,000	
Net cash used for financing activities		(15,000)
Net increase in cash		$16,000
Cash balance, December 31, 2008		3,000
Cash balance, December 31, 2009		$19,000

Assignment materials for the *direct* method include:

- Short Exercises 16-11 through 16-14 on pages 806 and 807.
- Exercises 16-25 through 16-31 on pages 811–814.
- Problems 16-37A through 16-40A on pages 818 and 819.
- Problems 16-46B through 16-49B on pages 823 and 824.

Appendix 16B

Preparing the Statement of Cash Flows Using a Spreadsheet

The body of this chapter discusses the uses of the statement of cash flows in decision making and shows how to prepare the statement using T-accounts. The T-account approach works well as a learning device. In practice, however, most companies face complex situations. In these cases, a spreadsheet can help in preparing the statement of cash flows.

The spreadsheet starts with the beginning balance sheet and concludes with the ending balance sheet. Two middle columns—one for debit amounts and the other for credit amounts—complete the spreadsheet. These columns, labeled Transaction Analysis, hold the data for the statement of cash flows. Accountants can prepare the statement directly from the lower part of the spreadsheet. This appendix is based on the Anchor Corporation data used in the chapter. We begin with the indirect method for operating activities.

Preparing the Spreadsheet— Indirect Method for Operating Activities

The *indirect* method reconciles net income to net cash provided by operating activities. Exhibit 16B-1 is the spreadsheet for preparing the statement of cash flows by the *indirect* method. Panel A shows the transaction analysis, and Panel B gives the statement of cash flows.

Transaction Analysis on the Spreadsheet—Indirect Method

Net income, transaction (a), is the first operating cash inflow. Net income is entered on the spreadsheet (Panel B) as a debit to Net Income under Cash flows from operating activities and as a credit to Retained Earnings. Next come the adjustments to net income, starting with depreciation—transaction (b)—which is debited to Depreciation and credited to Plant Assets, Net. Transaction (c) is the sale of plant assets. The $10,000 gain on the sale is entered as a credit to Gain on Sale of Plant Assets—a subtraction from net income—under operating cash flows. This credit removes the $10,000 gain from operations because the cash proceeds from the sale were $50,000, not $10,000. The $50,000 sale amount is then entered on the spreadsheet under investing activities. Entry (c) is completed by crediting the plant assets' book value of $40,000 to the Plant Assets, Net account.

Entries (d) through (g) reconcile net income to cash flows from operations for increases and decreases in the other current assets and for increases and decreases in the current liabilities. Entry (d) debits Accounts Receivable for its $17,000 increase during the year. This amount is credited to Increase in Accounts Receivable under operating cash flows. Entries (e), (f), and (g) adjust for the other current accounts.

EXHIBIT 16B-1 — Spreadsheet for Statement of Cash Flows—Indirect Method

	A	B	C	D	E
1		ANCHOR CORPORATION			
2		Spreadsheet for Statement of Cash Flows (Indirect Method)			
3		Year Ended December 31, 2008			
4	(In thousands)	Balances	Transaction Analysis		Balances
5		Dec. 31, 2007	Debit	Credit	Dec. 31, 2008
6	PANEL A—Balance-Sheet Accounts				
7	Cash	42		(m) 20	22
8	Accounts receivable	73	(d) 17		90
9	Inventory	145		(e) 2	143
10	Plant assets, net	210	(h) 310	(b) 20	
				(c) 40	460
11	Totals	470			715
				(f)	
12	Accounts payable	50	(g)	40	90
13	Accrued liabilities	10	(k) 5	(j)	5
14	Long-term notes payable	80	10	(i) 90	160
15	Common stock	250	(l)	(a) 100	350
16	Retained earnings	80	10	40	110
17	Totals	470	352	352	715
18	PANEL B—Statement of Cash Flows				
19	Cash flows from operating activities:				
20	Net income		(a) 40		
21	Add (subtract) adjustments:				
22	Depreciation		(b) 20		
23	Gain on sale of plant assets			(c) 10	
24	Increase in accounts receivable			(d) 17	
25	Decrease in inventory		(e) 2		
26	Increase in accounts payable		(f) 40		
27	Decrease in accrued liabilities			(g) 5	
28	Cash flows from investing activities:				
29	Acquisition of plant assets			(h) 310	
30	Cash receipt from sale of plant assets		(c) 50		
31	Cash flows from financing activities:				
32	Cash receipts from issuance of common stock		(i) 100		
33	Cash receipts from issuance of note payable		(j) 90		
34	Payment of note payable			(k) 10	
35	Payment of dividends			(l) 10	
36			342	362	
37	Net decrease in cash		(m) 20		
38	Totals		362	362	

Entries (h) through (l) account for the investing and financing transactions. Entry (h) debits Plant Assets, Net for their purchase and credits Acquisition of plant assets under investing cash flows. Entry (i) debits Cash receipts from issuance of common stock under financing cash flows. The offsetting debit is to Common Stock.

The final item in Exhibit 16B-1 is the Net decrease in cash—transaction (m) on the spreadsheet—a credit to Cash and a debit to Net decrease in cash. To prepare the statement of cash flows, the accountant can rewrite Panel B of the spreadsheet, adding subtotals for the three categories of activities.

Noncash Investing and Financing Activities on the Spreadsheet

Noncash investing and financing activities can be analyzed on the spreadsheet. These transactions include both an investing activity and a financing activity, so they require two spreadsheet entries. Suppose Anchor Corporation purchased a building by issuing common stock of $300,000. Exhibit 16B-2 illustrates the analysis of this transaction. Cash is unaffected. Spreadsheet entry (a) records the purchase of the building, and entry (b) records the issuance of the stock. All amounts are assumed for this illustration.

EXHIBIT 16B-2 Noncash Investing and Financing Activities on the SpreadSheet

ANCHOR CORPORATION
Spreadsheet for Statement of Cash Flows
Year Ended December 31, 2008

	Balances Dec. 31, 2007	Transaction Analysis Debit	Transaction Analysis Credit	Balances Dec. 31, 2008
PANEL A—Balance-Sheet Accounts				
Cash				
Building	600,000	(a)300,000		900,000
Common stock	400,000		(b)300,000	700,000
PANEL B—Statement of Cash Flows				
Noncash investing and financing transactions:				
Purchase of building by issuing				
common stock		(b)300,000	(a)300,000	

Preparing the Spreadsheet— Direct Method for Operating Activities

The *direct* method separates operating activities into cash receipts and cash payments. Exhibit 16B-3 is the spreadsheet for the preparation of the statement of cash flows by the *direct* method.

	A	B	C		D		E
1		ANCHOR CORPORATION					
2		Work Sheet for Statement of Cash Flows (Direct Method)					
3		Year Ended December 31, 2008					
				Transaction			
4	(In thousands)	Balances		Analysis			Balances
5		Dec. 31, 2007	Debit		Credit		Dec. 31, 2008
6	PANEL A—Balance-Sheet Accounts						
7	Cash	42				20	22
8	Accounts receivable	73		286	(t)	269	90
9	Inventory	145	(a)	154	(b)	156	143
10	Equipment, net	210	(e)	310	(f)	20	
			(n)		(i)	40	460
11	Totals	470			(o)		715
12	Accounts payable	50		114		154	90
13	Accrued liabilities	10	(g)	21	(e)	16	5
14	Long-term notes payable	80	(m)	10	(j)	90	160
15	Common stock	250	(r)		(q)	100	350
16	Retained earnings	80		156	(p)	286	110
			(f)	56	(a)	12	
			(h)	20	(c)	9	
			(i)	16	(d)	10	
			(j)	15	(o)		
			(k)	14			
			(l)	10			
17	Totals	470	(s)	1,182		1,182	715
18	PANEL B—Statement of Cash Flows						
19	Cash flows from operating activities:						
20	Receipts:						
21	Collections from customers			269			
22	Interest received		(b)	12			
23	Dividends received		(c)	9			
24	Payments:		(d)				
25	To suppliers					114	
					(g)	21	
26	To employees				(m)	56	
27	For interest				(h)	15	
28	For income tax				(k)	14	
29	Cash flows from investing activities:				(l)		
30	Acquisition of plant assets					310	
31	Cash receipt from sale of plant assets			50	(n)		
32	Cash flows from financing activities:		(o)				
33	Cash receipt from issuance of common stock			100			
34	Cash receipt from issuance of note payable		(p)	90			
35	Payment of note payable		(q)			10	
36	Payment of dividends				(r)	10	
				530	(s)	550	
37	Net decrease in cash			20			
38	Totals		(t)	550		550	

Transaction Analysis on the Spreadsheet—Direct Method

For your convenience, we repeat the Anchor Corporation transaction data here.

Operating Activities:

a. Sales on account, $286,000

*b. Collections from customers, $269,000

*c. Cash receipt of interest revenue, $12,000

*d. Cash receipt of dividend revenue, $9,000

e. Purchase of inventory on account, $154,000

f. Cost of goods sold, $156,000

*g. Payments for inventory on account, $114,000

*h. Salary expense and payments, $56,000

i. Depreciation expense, $20,000

j. Accrual of other operating expense, $16,000

*k. Interest expense and payments, $15,000

*l. Income tax expense and payments, $14,000

*m. Payment of accrued liabilities, $21,000

Investing Activities:

*n. Cash payments to acquire plant assets, $310,000

*o. Cash receipt from sale of plant assets, $50,000, including $10,000 gain

Financing Activities:

*p. Cash receipt from issuance of common stock, $100,000

*q. Cash receipt from issuance of note payable, $90,000

*r. Payment of note payable, $10,000

*s. Declaration and payment of cash dividends, $10,000

*Indicates a cash flow to be reported on the statement of cash flows.

The transaction analysis on the spreadsheet includes all the journal entries. Only balance-sheet accounts are used on the spreadsheet. Therefore, revenues are entered as credits to Retained Earnings, and expenses are entered as debits to Retained Earnings. For example, in transaction (a), sales on account are debited to Accounts Receivable and credited to Retained Earnings. Cash is neither debited nor credited because sales on account do not affect cash. But all transactions should be entered on the spreadsheet to identify all the cash effects of the period's transactions. In transaction (c), the collection of cash for interest revenue is entered by debiting Cash and crediting Retained Earnings.

Entries (n) through (s) account for the investing and financing transactions. Entry (n) debits Equipment, Net for their purchase and credits Acquisition of plant assets under investing cash flows. Entry (p) debits cash receipt from issuance of common stock under financing cash flows. The offsetting credit is to Common stock.

The final item in Exhibit 16B-3 is the Net decrease in cash—transaction (t) on the spreadsheet—a credit to cash and a debit to Net decrease in cash. To prepare the statement of cash flows, you can rewrite Panel B of the spreadsheet, adding subtotals for the three categories of activities.

Appendix 16B Assignments

Problems

Preparing the spreadsheet for the statement of cash flows—indirect method

P16B-1 The 2008 comparative balance sheet and income statement of Alden Group, Inc., follow. Alden had no noncash investing and financing transactions during 2008.

ALDEN GROUP, INC.
Comparative Balance Sheet

	December 31, 2008	December 31, 2007	Increase (Decrease)
Current assets:			
Cash and cash equivalents	$ 13,700	$15,600	$ (1,900)
Accounts receivable	41,500	43,100	(1,600)
Inventories	96,600	93,000	3,600
Plant assets:			
Land	35,100	10,000	25,100
Equipment, net	100,900	93,700	7,200
Total assets	$287,800	$255,400	$32,400
Current liabilities:			
Accounts payable	$ 24,800	$ 26,000	$ (1,200)
Accrued liabilities	24,400	22,500	1,900
Long-term liabilities:			
Notes payable	55,000	65,000	(10,000)
Stockholders' equity:			
Common stock	131,100	122,300	8,800
Retained earnings	52,500	19,600	32,900
Total liabilities and stockholders' equity	$287,800	$255,400	$32,400

ALDEN GROUP, INC.
Income Statement
Year Ended December 31, 2008

Revenues:		
Sales revenue		$438,000
Interest revenue		11,700
Total revenues		449,700
Expenses:		
Cost of goods sold	$205,200	
Salary expense	76,400	
Depreciation expense	15,300	
Other operating expense	49,700	
Interest expense	24,600	
Income tax expense	16,900	
Total expenses		388,100
Net income		$ 61,600

Requirement

Prepare the spreadsheet for the 2008 statement of cash flows. Format cash flows from operating activities by the *indirect* method.

Preparing the spreadsheet for the statement of cash flows—direct method

P16B-2 Using the Alden Group, Inc., data from Problem 16B-1, prepare the spreadsheet for Alden's 2008 statement of cash flows. Format cash flows from operating activities by the *direct* method.

17 Financial Statement Analysis

Learning Objectives

1 Perform a horizontal analysis of financial statements

2 Perform a vertical analysis of financial statements

3 Prepare and use common-size financial statements

4 Compute the standard financial ratios

Google was born in 1998. If it were a person, it would have started elementary school in 2004, and today it would have just about finished the first grade.

If Google were a person, it would graduate from high school in 2016. Given a typical life span, it would expect to be around for almost a century [. . .] In the words of its top two executives, "We're just getting started."

Source: Adapted from Google Inc. 2004 Annual Report, Founder's Letter.

You probably use Google's Internet search engine daily, as many others do. The company is an amazing success story. In fact, on November 17, 2005, Google's stock price topped $400—one of only four companies listed on a major U.S. stock exchange with a stock price that high.

To show you how to analyze financial statements, we'll be using Google Inc. in the first half of this chapter. Then in the second part of the chapter we'll shift over to a different type of company—Palisades Furniture—to round out your introduction to financial statement analysis.

To get started, take a look at Google's comparative income statement, which follows.

GOOGLE INC. Income Statement (Adapted) Year Ended December 31,		
(In millions)	**2004**	**2003**
Revenues (same as Net sales)	$3,189	$1,466
Expenses:		
Cost of revenues (same as Cost of goods sold)	1,458	626
Sales and marketing expense	246	120
General and administrative expense	140	57
Research and development expense	225	91
Other expense	470	225
Income before income tax	650	347
Income tax expense	251	241
Net income	$ 399	$ 106

You can see that 2004 was an incredible year for the company. Net income was over three times the net income of 2003, and Wall Street was very happy. ▦

Investors and creditors can't evaluate a company by examining only one year's data. This is why most financial statements cover at least two periods, like the Google Inc. income statement. In fact, most financial analysis covers trends of three to five years. This chapter shows you how to use some of the analytical tools for charting a company's progress through time.

The graphs in Exhibit 17-1 show some important data about Google's progress. They depict a three-year trend of revenues and research and development (R&D). Revenues (sales) and R&D are important drivers of profits.

EXHIBIT 17-1 Financial Data of Google Inc. (Adapted)

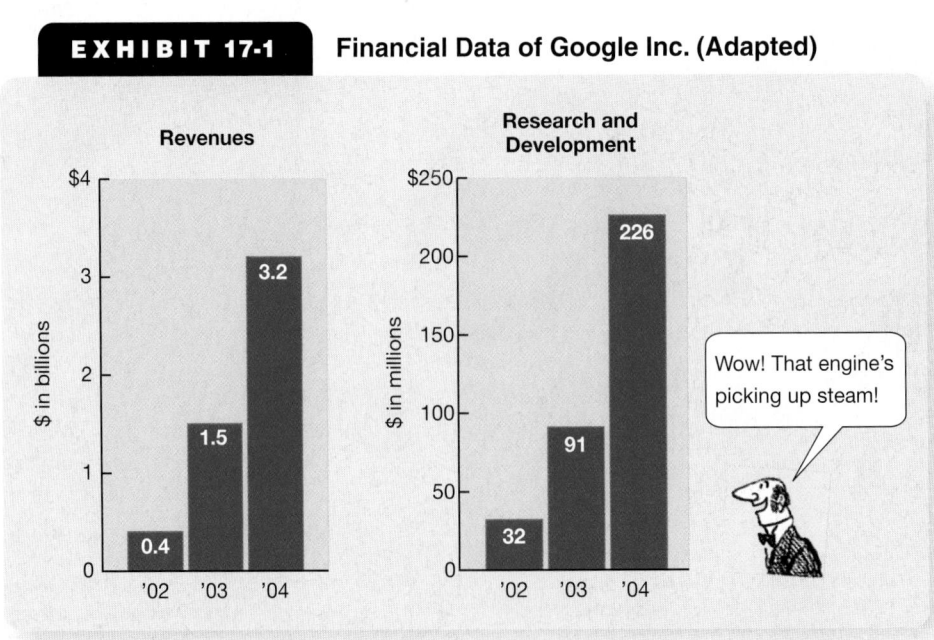

For Google, both revenues and research and development grew dramatically during 2002–2004. These are good signs for the future. But how can we decide what we really think about Google's performance? We need some way to compare a company's performance

- From year to year
- With a competing company, like Yahoo! Inc.
- With the Internet-information industry

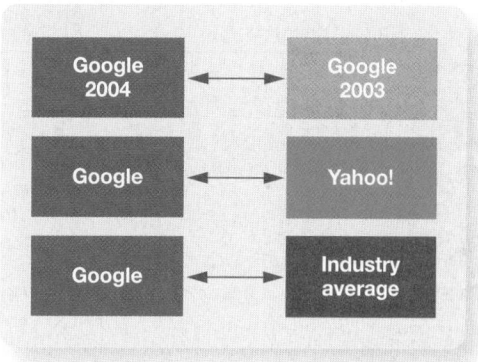

Then we will have a better idea of how to judge Google's present situation and predict what might happen in the near future.

Methods of Analysis

There are two main ways to analyze financial statements.

- Horizontal analysis provides a year-to-year comparison of a company's performance in different periods.
- Another technique, vertical analysis, is the standard way to compare different companies. Let's begin with horizontal analysis.

Horizontal Analysis

1 Perform a horizontal analysis of financial statements

Many decisions hinge on whether the numbers—in sales, expenses, and net income—are increasing or decreasing. Have sales and other revenues risen from last year? By how much? Sales may have increased by $20,000, but considered alone, this fact is not very helpful. The *percentage change* in sales over time is more helpful. It is better to know that sales increased by 20% than to know that sales increased by $20,000.

The study of percentage changes in comparative statements is called **horizontal analysis**. Computing a percentage change in comparative statements requires two steps:

1. Compute the dollar amount of the change from the earlier period to the later period.

2. Divide the dollar amount of change by the earlier period amount. We call the earlier period the base period.

Illustration: Google Inc.

Google reports *revenues*, not sales, because Google sells services rather than a product. You can think of revenues and net sales as the same thing. Horizontal analysis is illustrated for Google Inc. as follows (dollar amounts in millions):

	2004	2003	Increase (Decrease) Amount	Percentage
Revenues (same as net sales)..........	$3,189	$1,466	$1,723	117.5%

Sales increased by an incredible 117.5% during 2004, computed as follows:

Step 1 Compute the dollar amount of change in sales from 2003 to 2004:

$$2004 \quad 2003 \quad \text{Increase}$$
$$\$3,189 - \$1,466 = \$1,723$$

Step 2 Divide the dollar amount of change by the base-period amount. This computes the percentage change for the period:

$$\text{Percentage change} = \frac{\text{Dollar amount of change}}{\text{Base-year amount}}$$

$$= \frac{\$1,723}{\$1,466} = 1.175 = 117.5\%$$

Detailed horizontal analyses of Google's financial statements are shown in:

- Exhibit 17-2 Income Statement
- Exhibit 17-3 Balance Sheet

EXHIBIT 17-2 **Comparative Income Statement—Horizontal Analysis**

GOOGLE INC.
Income Statement (Adapted)
Year Ended December 31, 2004 and 2003

(Dollar amounts in millions)	2004	2003	Increase (Decrease) Amount	Percentage
Revenues	$3,189	$1,466	$1,723	117.5%
Cost of revenues	1,458	626	832	132.9
Gross profit	1,731	840	891	106.1
Operating expenses:				
Sales and marketing expense	246	120	126	105.0
General and administrative expense	140	57	83	145.6
Research and development expense	225	91	134	147.3
Other expense	470	225	245	108.9
Income before income tax	650	347	303	87.3
Income tax expense	251	241	10	4.1
Net income	$ 399	$ 106	$ 293	276.4

| EXHIBIT 17-3 | Comparative Balance Sheet—Horizontal Analysis |

GOOGLE INC.
Balance Sheet (Adapted)
December 31, 2004 and 2003

(Dollar amounts in millions)	2004	2003	Increase (Decrease) Amount	Increase (Decrease) Percentage
Assets				
Current Assets:				
Cash and cash equivalents	$ 427	$149	$ 278	186.6%
Other current assets	2,266	411	1,855	451.3
Total current assets	2,693	560	2,133	380.9
Property, plant and equipment, net	379	188	191	101.6
Intangible assets, net	194	106	88	83.0
Other assets	47	17	30	176.5
Total assets	$3,313	$871	$2,442	280.4
Liabilities				
Current Liabilities:				
Accounts payable	$ 33	$ 46	$ (13)	(28.3)%
Other current liabilities	307	189	118	62.4
Total current liabilities	340	235	105	44.7
Long-term liabilities	44	47	(3)	(6.4)
Total liabilities	384	282	102	36.2
Stockholders' Equity				
Capital stock	1	45	(44)	(97.8)
Retained earnings and other equity	2,928	544	2,384	438.2
Total stockholders' equity	2,929	589	2,340	397.3
Total liabilities and equity	$3,313	$871	$2,442	280.4

Horizontal Analysis of the Income Statement

Google's comparative income statement reveals exceptional growth during 2004. An increase of 100% occurs when an item doubles, so Google's 117.5% increase in revenues means that revenues more than doubled.

The item on Google's income statement with the slowest growth rate is income tax expense. Income taxes increased by 4.1%. On the bottom line, net income grew by an astounding 276.4%. That's real progress!

Horizontal Analysis of the Balance Sheet

Google's comparative balance sheet also shows rapid growth in assets, with total assets increasing by 280.4%. That means total assets almost tripled in one year. Very few companies grow that fast.

Google's liabilities grew more slowly. Total liabilities increased by 36.2%, and Accounts Payable actually decreased, as indicated by the liability figures in parentheses. Here's how to compute the percentage decrease in Google's Accounts Payable:

STEP 1   Increase

(Decrease)	2004	2003
$(13)	= $33	− $46

$$\text{STEP 2} \quad \frac{\text{Percentage}}{\text{Change}} = \frac{\text{Dollar amount of change}}{\text{Base-year amount}}$$

$$(28.3)\% = \frac{\$(13)}{\$46}$$

Trend Percentages

Trend percentages are a form of horizontal analysis. Trends indicate the direction a business is taking. How have sales changed over a five-year period? What trend does net income show? These questions can be answered by trend percentages over a period, such as three to five years.

Trend percentages are computed by selecting a base year. The base-year amounts are set equal to 100%. The amounts for each following year are expressed as a percentage of the base amount. To compute trend percentages, divide each item for following years by the base-year amount.

$$\text{Trend \%} = \frac{\text{Any year \$}}{\text{Base year \$}}$$

Google Inc.'s total revenues were $19 million in 2000 and rose to $3,189 million in 2004. The company's trend of revenues is so dramatic that percentages in the thousands are hard to interpret.

To illustrate trend analysis, we use a more representative company, Caterpillar Inc., which is famous for its CAT earthmoving machinery. Caterpillar's trend of net sales during 2000–2004 follows, with dollars in millions. The base year is 2000, so that year's percentage is set equal to 100.

(in millions)	2004	2003	2002	2001	2000
Net sales..................	$30,251	$22,763	$20,152	$20,450	$20,175
Trend percentages......	150%	113%	99.9%	101%	100%

We want trend percentages for the five-year period 2000 through 2004. Trend percentages are computed by dividing each year's amount by the 2000 amount.

Net sales increased a little in 2001 and took a dip in 2002. The rate of growth increased in 2003 and took off in 2004.

You can perform a trend analysis on any item you consider important. Trend analysis is widely used to predict the future.

Vertical Analysis

2 Perform a vertical analysis of financial statements

As we have seen, horizontal analysis and trend percentages highlight changes in an item over time. But no single technique gives a complete picture of a business, so we also need vertical analysis.

Vertical analysis of a financial statement shows the relationship of each item to its base amount, which is the 100% figure. Every other item on the statement is then reported as a percentage of that base. For an income statement, net sales is the base. Suppose under normal conditions a company's gross profit is 50% of revenues. A drop to 40% may cause the company to suffer a loss. Investors view a large decline in gross profit with alarm.

Illustration: Google Inc.

Exhibit 17-4 shows the vertical analysis of Google's income statement. In this case,

$$\text{Vertical analysis \%} = \frac{\text{Each income-statement item}}{\text{Revenues (net sales)}}$$

EXHIBIT 17-4	Comparative Income Statement—Vertical Analysis

GOOGLE INC.
Income Statement (Adapted)
Year Ended December 31, 2004

(Dollar amounts in millions)	Amount	Percent of Total
Revenues	$3,189	100.0%
Cost of revenues	1,458	45.7
Gross profit	1,731	54.3
Operating expenses:		
Sales and marketing expense	246	7.7
General and administrative expense	140	4.4
Research and development expense	225	7.1
Other expense	470	14.7
Income before income tax	650	20.4
Income tax expense	251	7.9
Net income	$ 399	12.5%

For Google, the vertical-analysis percentage for cost of revenues is 45.7% ($1,458/$3,189 = 0.457). On the bottom line, Google's net income is 12.5% of revenues. That is very good.

Exhibit 17-5 shows the vertical analysis of Google's balance sheet. The base amount (100%) is total assets.

The vertical analysis of Google's balance sheet reveals several interesting things.

- Current assets make up 81.3% of total assets. For most companies this percentage is closer to 30%.
- Property, plant, and equipment make up only 11.4% of total assets. This percentage is low because of the nature of Google's business. Google's Web-based operations don't require lots of buildings and equipment.
- Total liabilities are only 11.6% of total assets, and stockholders' equity makes up 88.4% of total assets. Most of Google's equity is additional paid-in capital and retained earnings—signs of a strong company.

How Do We Compare One Company with Another?

3 Prepare and use common-size financial statements

Horizontal analysis and vertical analysis provide lots of useful data about a company. As we have seen, Google's percentages depict a very successful company. But the Google data apply only to one business.

To compare Google Inc. to another company we can use a common-size statement. A **common-size statement** reports only percentages—the same percentages

EXHIBIT 17-5	Comparative Balance Sheet—Vertical Analysis

GOOGLE INC.
Balance Sheet (Adapted)
December 31, 2004

(Dollar amount in millions)	Amount	Percent of Total
Assets		
Current Assets:		
Cash and cash equivalents	$ 427	12.9%
Other current assets	2,266	68.4
Total current assets	2,693	81.3
Property, plant, and equipment, net	379	11.4
Intangible assets, net	194	5.9
Other assets	47	1.4
Total assets	$3,313	100.0%
Liabilities		
Current Liabilities:		
Accounts payable	$ 33	1.0%
Other current liabilities	307	9.3
Total current liabilities	340	10.3
Long-term liabilities	44	1.3
Total liabilities	384	11.6
Stockholders' Equity		
Common stock	1	0.0
Retained earnings and other equity	2,928	88.4
Total stockholders' equity	2,929	88.4
Total liabilities and equity	$3,313	100.0%

that appear in a vertical analysis. For example, Google's common-size income statement comes directly from the percentages in Exhibit 17-4.

We can use a common-size income statement to compare Google Inc. and Yahoo! Inc. on profitability. Google and Yahoo! compete in the Internet service industry. Which company earns a higher percentage of revenues as profits for its shareholders? Exhibit 17-6 gives both companies' common-size income statements for 2004.

Exhibit 17-6 shows that Yahoo! Inc. is more profitable than Google. Yahoo!'s gross profit percentage is 63.7%, compared to Google's 54.3%. And, most importantly, Yahoo!'s percentage of net income to revenues is 23.5%. That means almost one-fourth of Yahoo!'s revenues ends up as profits for the company's stockholders.

Benchmarking

Benchmarking is the practice of comparing a company with other leading companies. There are two main types of benchmarks in financial statement analysis.

EXHIBIT 17-6 Common-Size Income Statement
Google versus Yahoo!

	Google Inc.	Yahoo! Inc.
GOOGLE INC. Common-Size Income Statement Google Versus YAHOO!		
Revenues	100.0%	100.0%
Cost of revenues	45.7	36.3
Gross profit	54.3	63.7
Sales and marketing expense	7.7	21.8
General and administrative expense	4.4	7.3
Research and development expense	7.1	10.3
Other expense (income)	14.7	(11.5)
Income before income tax	20.4	35.8
Income tax expense	7.9	12.3
Net income	12.5%	23.5%

Benchmarking Against a Key Competitor

Exhibit 17-6 uses a key competitor, Yahoo! Inc., to measure Google's profitability. The two companies compete in the same industry, so Yahoo! serves as an ideal benchmark for Google. The graphs in Exhibit 17-7 highlight the profitability difference between Google and Yahoo!. Focus on the segment of the graphs showing net income. Yahoo! is clearly more profitable than Google.

EXHIBIT 17-7 Graphical Analysis of Common-Size Income Statement
Google Versus Yahoo!

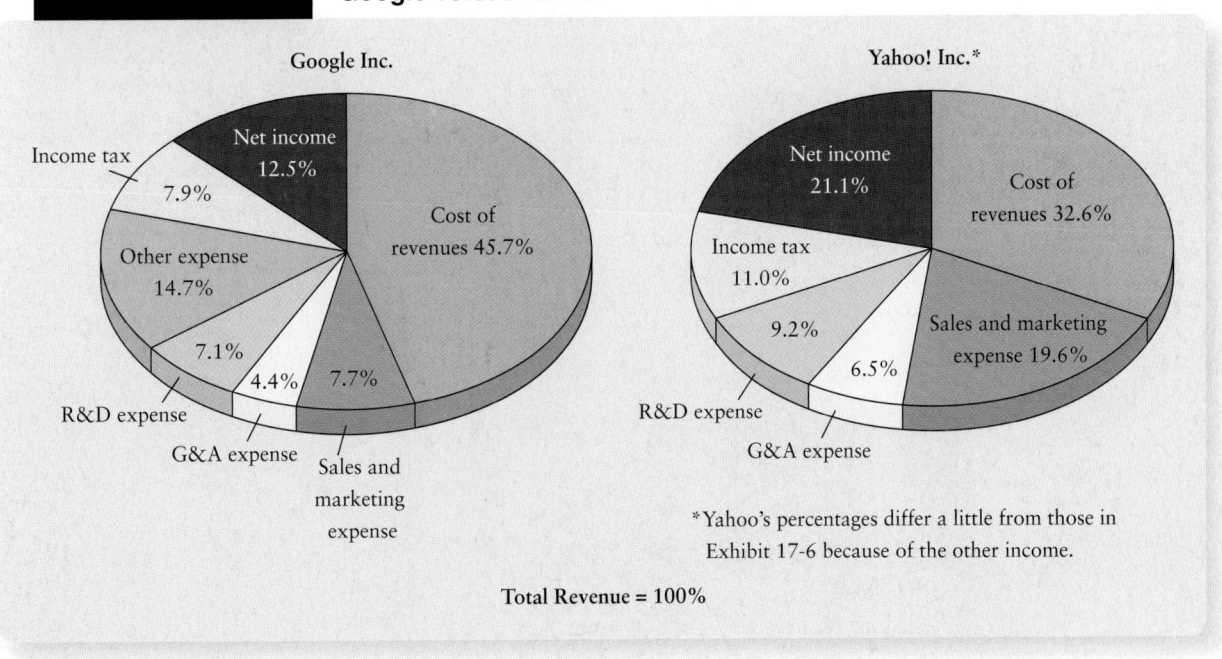

Benchmarking Against the Industry Average

The industry average can also serve as a useful benchmark for evaluating a company. An industry comparison would show how Google is performing alongside the average for its industry. *Annual Statement Studies*, published by The Risk Management Association, provides common-size statements for most industries. To compare Google Inc. to the industry average, simply insert the industry-average common-size income statement in place of Yahoo! Inc. as shown in Exhibit 17-6.

Now let's put your learning to practice. Work the summary problem, which reviews the concepts from the first half of this chapter.

Summary Problem 1

Perform a horizontal analysis and a vertical analysis of the comparative income statement of Kimball Corporation, which makes iPod labels. State whether 2008 was a good year or a bad year, and give your reasons.

KIMBALL CORPORATION Comparative Income Statement Years Ended December 31, 2008 and 2007		
	2008	2007
Net sales	$275,000	$225,000
Expenses:		
Cost of goods sold	$194,000	$165,000
Engineering, selling, and administrative expenses	54,000	48,000
Interest expense	5,000	5,000
Income tax expense	9,000	3,000
Other expense (income)	1,000	(1,000)
Total expenses	263,000	220,000
Net income	$ 12,000	$ 5,000

Solution

KIMBALL CORPORATION Horizontal Analysis of Comparative Income Statement Years Ended December 31, 2008 and 2007				
			Increase (Decrease)	
	2008	2007	Amount	Percent
Net sales	$275,000	$225,000	$50,000	22.2%
Expenses:				
Cost of goods sold	$194,000	$165,000	$29,000	17.6
Engineering, selling, and administrative expenses	54,000	48,000	6,000	12.5
Interest expense	5,000	5,000	—	—
Income tax expense	9,000	3,000	6,000	200.0
Other expense (income)	1,000	(1,000)	2,000	—*
Total expenses	263,000	220,000	43,000	19.5
Net income	$ 12,000	$ 5,000	$ 7,000	140.0%

*Percentage changes are typically not computed for shifts from a negative to a positive amount, and vice versa.

The horizontal analysis shows that total revenues increased 22.2%. Total expenses increased by 19.5%, and net income rose by 140%.

KIMBALL CORPORATION
Vertical Analysis of Comparative Income Statement
Years Ended December 31, 2008 and 2007

	2008 Amount	2008 Percent	2007 Amount	2007 Percent
Net sales	$275,000	100.0%	$225,000	100.0%
Expenses:				
Cost of goods sold	$194,000	70.5	$165,000	73.3
Engineering, selling, and administrative expenses	54,000	19.6	48,000	21.3
Interest expense	5,000	1.8	5,000	2.2
Income tax expense	9,000	3.3	3,000	1.4**
Other expense (income)	1,000	0.4	(1,000)	(0.4)
Total expenses	263,000	95.6	220,000	97.8
Net income	$ 12,000	4.4%	$ 5,000	2.2%

**Number rounded up.

The vertical analysis shows decreases in the percentages of net sales consumed by:

- cost of goods sold (from 73.3% to 70.5%)
- engineering, selling, and administrative expenses (from 21.3% to 19.6%).

These two items are Kimball's largest dollar expenses, so their percentage decreases are important.

2008 net income rose to 4.4% of sales, compared with 2.2% the preceding year. The analysis shows that 2008 was significantly better than 2007.

Using Ratios to Make Decisions

Online financial databases, such as Lexis/Nexis and the Dow Jones News Retrieval Service, provide data on thousands of companies. Suppose you want to compare some companies' recent earnings histories. You might have the computer compare companies' returns on stockholders' equity. The computer could then give you the names of the 20 companies with the highest return on equity. You can use any ratio that is relevant to a particular decision.

The ratios we discuss in this chapter may be classified as follows:

1. Measuring ability to pay current liabilities

2. Measuring ability to sell inventory and collect receivables

3. Measuring ability to pay long-term debt

4. Measuring profitability

5. Analyzing stock as an investment

Measuring Ability to Pay Current Liabilities

4 Compute the standard financial ratios

Working capital is defined as:

$$\text{Working capital} = \text{Current assets} - \text{Current liabilities}$$

Working capital measures the ability to meet short-term obligations with current assets. Two decision tools based on working-capital data are the *current ratio* and the *acid-test ratio*.

Current Ratio

The most widely used ratio is the **current ratio**, which is current assets divided by current liabilities. The current ratio measures ability to pay current liabilities with current assets.

Exhibit 17-8 gives the comparative income statement and balance sheet of Palisades Furniture Co., which we'll be using in the remainder of this chapter.

The current ratios of Palisades Furniture at December 31, 2008 and 2007, follow, along with the average for the retail furniture industry:

	Formula	Palisades' Current Ratio		Industry Average
		2008	2007	
Current ratio =	$\dfrac{\text{Current assets}}{\text{Current liabilities}}$	$\dfrac{\$262,000}{\$142,000} = 1.85$	$\dfrac{\$236,000}{\$126,000} = 1.87$	1.50

A high current ratio indicates that the business has sufficient current assets to maintain normal business operations. Compare Palisades Furniture's current ratio of 1.85 with the industry average of 1.50 and with the current ratios of some well-known companies:

Company	Current Ratio
Walgreen Co	1.90
Amazon.com.....................	1.57
FedEx...............................	1.05

continued after exhibit on page 861 . . .

EXHIBIT 17-8 Comparative Financial Statements

PALISADES FURNITURE CO.
Comparative Income Statement
Years Ended December 31, 2008 and 2007

	2008	2007
Net sales	$858,000	$803,000
Cost of goods sold	513,000	509,000
Gross profit	345,000	294,000
Operating expenses:		
Selling expenses	126,000	114,000
General expenses	118,000	123,000
Total operating expenses	244,000	237,000
Income from operations	101,000	57,000
Interest revenue	4,000	—
Interest (expense)	(24,000)	(14,000)
Income before income taxes	81,000	43,000
Income tax expense	33,000	17,000
Net income	$ 48,000	$ 26,000

PALISADES FURNITURE CO.
Comparative Balance Sheet
December 31, 2008 and 2007

	2008	2007
Assets		
Current Assets:		
Cash	$ 29,000	$ 32,000
Accounts receivable, net	114,000	85,000
Inventories	113,000	111,000
Prepaid expenses	6,000	8,000
Total current assets	262,000	236,000
Long-term investments	18,000	9,000
Property, plant, and equipment, net	507,000	399,000
Total assets	$787,000	$644,000
Liabilities		
Current Liabilities:		
Notes payable	$ 42,000	$ 27,000
Accounts payable	73,000	68,000
Accrued liabilities	27,000	31,000
Total current liabilities	142,000	126,000
Long-term notes payable	289,000	198,000
Total liabilities	431,000	324,000
Stockholders' Equity		
Common stock, no par	186,000	186,000
Retained earnings	170,000	134,000
Total stockholders' equity	356,000	320,000
Total liabilities and equity	$787,000	$644,000

What is an acceptable current ratio? The answer depends on the industry. The norm for companies in most industries is around 1.50, as reported by The Risk Management Association. Palisades Furniture's current ratio of 1.85 is strong. In most industries, a current ratio of 2.0 is very strong.

Acid-Test Ratio

The **acid-test** (or **quick**) **ratio** tells us whether the entity could pay all its current liabilities if they came due immediately. That is, could the company pass this *acid test?*

To compute the acid-test ratio, we add cash, short-term investments, and net current receivables (accounts and notes receivable, net of allowances) and divide this sum by current liabilities. Inventory and prepaid expenses are *not* included in the acid test because they are the least-liquid current assets. Palisades Furniture's acid-test ratios for 2008 and 2007 follow.

Formula	Palisades' Acid-Test Ratio		Industry Average
	2008	2007	
Acid-test ratio $=$ $\dfrac{\text{Cash + Short-term investments + Net current receivables}}{\text{Current liabilities}}$	$\dfrac{\$29,000 + \$0 + \$114,000}{\$142,000} = 1.01$	$\dfrac{\$32,000 + \$0 + \$85,000}{\$126,000} = 0.93$	0.40

The company's acid-test ratio improved during 2008 and is significantly better than the industry average. Palisades' 1.01 acid-test ratio also compares favorably with the acid-test values of some well-known companies.

Company	Acid-Test Ratio
Procter & Gamble....................	0.49
Wal-Mart Stores, Inc................	0.15
General Motors, Inc.................	0.91

The norm for the acid-test ratio ranges from 0.20 for shoe retailers to 1.00 for manufacturers of equipment, as reported by The Risk Management Association. An acid-test ratio of 0.90 to 1.00 is acceptable in most industries.

Measuring Ability to Sell Inventory and Collect Receivables

The ability to sell inventory and collect receivables is fundamental to business. In this section, we discuss three ratios that measure the company's ability to sell inventory and collect receivables.

Inventory Turnover

Inventory turnover measures the number of times a company sells its average level of inventory during a year. A high rate of turnover indicates ease in selling inventory; a low rate indicates difficulty. A value of 6 means that the company sold its average level of inventory six times—every two months—during the year.

To compute inventory turnover, we divide cost of goods sold by the average inventory for the period. We use the cost of goods sold—not sales—because both cost of goods sold and inventory are stated *at cost*. Sales at *retail* are not comparable with inventory at *cost*.

Palisades Furniture's inventory turnover for 2008 is:

Formula	Palisades' Inventory Turnover	Industry Average
Inventory turnover = $\dfrac{\text{Cost of goods sold}}{\text{Average inventory}}$	$\dfrac{\$513,000}{\$112,000} = 4.6$	3.4

Cost of goods sold comes from the income statement (Exhibit 17-8). Average inventory is figured by averaging the beginning inventory ($111,000) and ending inventory ($113,000). (See the balance sheet, Exhibit 17-8.)

Inventory turnover varies widely with the nature of the business. For example, Google has no inventory turnover because the company carries no inventory. Most manufacturers of farm machinery have an inventory turnover close to three times a year. In contrast, companies that remove natural gas from the ground hold their inventory for a very short period of time and have an average turnover of 30. Palisades Furniture's turnover of 4.6 times a year is high for its industry, which has an average turnover of 3.4 times per year.

Accounts Receivable Turnover

Accounts receivable turnover measures the ability to collect cash from credit customers. The higher the ratio, the faster the cash collections. But a receivable turnover that's too high may indicate that credit is too tight, causing the loss of sales to good customers.

To compute accounts receivable turnover, divide net credit sales by average net accounts receivable. Palisades Furniture's accounts receivable turnover ratio for 2008 is computed as follows:

Formula	Palisades' Accounts Receivable Turnover	Industry Average
Accounts receivable turnover = $\dfrac{\text{Net credit sales}}{\begin{array}{c}\text{Average net}\\\text{accounts receivable}\end{array}}$	$\dfrac{\$858,000}{\$99,500} = 8.6$	51.0

Average net accounts receivable is figured by adding the beginning accounts receivable balance ($85,000) and the ending balance ($114,000), then dividing by 2: [($85,000 + $114,000)/2 = $99,500].

Palisades' receivable turnover of 8.6 times per year is much slower than the industry average. Why the difference? Palisades is a hometown store that sells to local people who pay their accounts over time. Many furniture stores sell their receivables to other companies called *factors*. That keeps receivables low and receivable turnover high. Palisades Furniture follows a different strategy.

Days' Sales in Receivables

The **days'-sales-in-receivables** ratio also measures the ability to collect receivables. Days' sales in receivables tell us how many days' sales remain in Accounts Receivable. To compute the ratio, we can follow a logical two-step process:

First, divide net sales by 365 days to figure average sales for one day.

Second, divide this average day's sales amount into average net accounts receivable.

The data to compute this ratio for Palisades Furniture, Inc., for 2008 are taken from the income statement and the balance sheet (Exhibit 17-8):

Formula	Palisades' Days' Sales in Accounts Receivable	Industry Average
Days' Sales in *average* Accounts Receivable:		
1. One day's sales $= \dfrac{\text{Net sales}}{\text{365 days}}$	$\dfrac{\$858,000}{\text{365 days}} = \$2,351$	
2. Days' sales in average accounts receivable $= \dfrac{\text{Average net accounts receivable}}{\text{One day's sales}}$	$\dfrac{\$99,500}{\$2,351} = 42 \text{ days}$	7 days

Average accounts receivable of $99,500 = ($85,000 + $114,000)/2.

Palisades' ratio tells us that 42 average days' sales remain in accounts receivable and need to be collected. Palisades' days'-sales-in-receivables ratio is much higher (worse) than the industry average because Palisades collects its own receivables. Palisades Furniture remains competitive because of its personal relationship with customers. Without their good paying habits, the company's cash flow would suffer.

Measuring Ability to Pay Long-Term Debt

The ratios discussed so far yield insight into current assets and current liabilities. They help us measure ability to sell inventory, collect receivables, and pay current liabilities. Most businesses also have long-term debt. Two key indicators of a business's ability to pay long-term liabilities are the *debt ratio* and the *times-interest-earned ratio*.

Debt Ratio

A loan officer at Metro Bank is evaluating loan applications from two companies. Both companies have asked to borrow $500,000 and have agreed to repay the loan over a 5-year period. The first firm already owes $600,000 to another bank. The second owes only $100,000. Other things equal, you are more likely to lend money to Company 2 because that company owes less than Company 1.

This relationship between total liabilities and total assets—called the **debt ratio**—shows the proportion of assets financed with debt. If the debt ratio is 1, then all the assets are financed with debt. A debt ratio of 0.50 means that debt finances half the assets; the owners of the business have financed the other half. The higher the debt ratio, the higher the company's financial risk.

The debt ratios for Palisades Furniture at the ends of 2008 and 2007 follow.

	Palisades' Debt Ratio		Industry
Formula	2008	2007	Average
Debt ratio $= \dfrac{\text{Total liabilities}}{\text{Total assets}}$	$\dfrac{\$431,000}{\$787,000} = 0.55$	$\dfrac{\$324,000}{\$644,000} = 0.50$	0.64

Palisades Furniture's debt ratio of 0.55 is not very high. The Risk Management Association reports that the average debt ratio for most companies ranges from 0.57 to 0.67, with relatively little variation from company to company. Palisades' debt ratio indicates a fairly low-risk position compared with the industry average debt ratio of 0.64.

Times-Interest-Earned Ratio

The debt ratio says nothing about ability to pay interest expense. Analysts use the **times-interest-earned-ratio** to relate income to interest expense. This ratio is also called the **interest-coverage ratio**. It measures the number of times operating income can cover interest expense. A high interest-coverage ratio indicates ease in paying interest expense; a low ratio suggests difficulty.

To compute this ratio, we divide income from operations (operating income) by interest expense. Calculation of Palisades' times-interest-earned ratio follows.

Formula	Palisades' Times-Interest-Earned Ratio 2008	2007	Industry Average
Times-interest-earned ratio $=\dfrac{\text{Income from operations}}{\text{Interest expense}}$	$\dfrac{\$101,000}{\$24,000}=4.21$	$\dfrac{\$57,000}{\$14,000}=4.07$	2.80

The company's times-interest-earned ratio of around 4.00 is significantly better than the average for furniture retailers. The norm for U.S. business, as reported by The Risk Management Association, falls in the range of 2.0 to 3.0. Based on its debt ratio and its times-interest-earned ratio, Palisades Furniture appears to have little difficulty *servicing its debt*, that is, paying liabilities.

Measuring Profitability

The fundamental goal of business is to earn a profit. Ratios that measure profitability are reported in the business press and discussed on *Money Line*. We examine four profitability measures.

Rate of Return on Net Sales

In business, the term *return* is used broadly as a measure of profitability. Consider a ratio called the **rate of return on net sales**, or simply **return on sales**. (The word *net* is usually omitted for convenience, even though net sales is used to compute the ratio.) This ratio shows the percentage of each sales dollar earned as net income. Palisades Furniture's rate of return on sales follows.

Formula	Palisades' Rate of Return on Sales 2008	2007	Industry Average
Rate of return on sales $=\dfrac{\text{Net income}}{\text{Net sales}}$	$\dfrac{\$48,000}{\$858,000}=0.056$	$\dfrac{\$26,000}{\$803,000}=0.032$	0.008

Companies strive for a high rate of return on sales. The higher the rate of return, the more sales dollars end up as profit. The increase in Palisades Furniture's return on sales is significant and identifies the company as more successful than the average furniture store. Compare Palisades' rate of return on sales to the rates of return for some leading companies in other industries:

Company	Rate of Return on Sales
Google Inc.	0.125
Texas Instruments	0.045
Walgreen	0.036

Rate of Return on Total Assets

The **rate of return on total assets**, or simply **return on assets**, measures success in using assets to earn a profit. Two groups finance a company's assets.

- Creditors have loaned money to the company, and they earn interest.
- Shareholders have invested in stock, and their return is net income.

The sum of interest expense and net income is thus the return to the two groups that have financed the company's assets. Computation of the return-on-assets ratio for Palisades Furniture follows.

Formula	Palisades' 2008 Rate of Return on Total Assets	Industry Average
$\text{Rate of return on assets} = \dfrac{\text{Net income} + \text{Interest expense}}{\text{Average total assets}}$	$\dfrac{\$48{,}000 + \$24{,}000}{\$715{,}500} = 0.101$	0.078

Average total assets is the average of beginning and ending total assets from the comparative balance sheet: ($644,000 + $787,000)/2 = $715,500. Compare Palisades Furniture's rate of return on assets with the rates of some other companies:

Company	Rate of Return on Assets
Amazon.com.................................	0.256
FedEx...	0.056
Procter & Gamble........................	0.136

Rate of Return on Common Stockholders' Equity

A popular measure of profitability is **rate of return on common stockholders' equity**, often shortened to **return on equity**. This ratio shows the relationship between net income and common stockholders' equity—how much income is earned for each $1 invested by the common shareholders.

To compute this ratio, we first subtract preferred dividends from net income to get net income available to the common stockholders. Then divide net income available to common stockholders by average common equity during the year. Common equity is total stockholders' equity minus preferred equity. The 2008 rate of return on common stockholders' equity for Palisades Furniture follows.

Formula	Palisades' 2008 Rate of Return on Common Stockholders' Equity	Industry Average
$\text{Rate of return on common stockholders' equity} = \dfrac{\text{Net income} - \text{Preferred dividends}}{\text{Average common stockholders' equity}}$	$\dfrac{\$48{,}000 - \$0}{\$338{,}000} = 0.142$	0.121

Average equity is the average of the beginning and ending balances [($356,000 + $320,000)/2 = $338,000].

Palisades' return on equity (0.142) is higher than its return on assets (0.101). This difference results from borrowing at one rate—say, 8%—and investing the money to earn a higher rate, such as the firm's 14.2% return on equity. This practice is called **trading on the equity**, or using **leverage**. It is directly related to the debt ratio. The higher the debt ratio, the higher the leverage. Companies that finance operations with debt are said to *leverage* their positions.

During good times, leverage increases profitability. But leverage can have a negative impact on profitability. Therefore, leverage is a double-edged sword, increasing profits during good times but compounding losses during bad times. Compare Palisades Furniture's return on equity with the rates of some leading companies.

Company	Rate of Return on Common Equity
Walgreen..	0.176
Procter & Gamble.........................	0.410
FedEx...	0.109

Palisades Furniture is not as profitable as these leading companies. A return on equity of 15% to 20% year after year is considered good in most industries.

Earnings per Share of Common Stock

Earnings per share of common stock, or simply **earnings per share (EPS)**, is perhaps the most widely quoted of all financial statistics. EPS is the only ratio that must appear on the face of the income statement. EPS is the amount of net income earned for each share of the company's outstanding *common* stock. Recall that:

Outstanding stock = Issued stock − Treasury stock

Earnings per share is computed by dividing net income available to common stockholders by the number of common shares outstanding during the year. Preferred dividends are subtracted from net income because the preferred stockholders have a prior claim to dividends. Palisades Furniture has no preferred stock outstanding and no preferred dividends.

The firm's EPS for 2008 and 2007 follow (Palisades had 10,000 shares of common stock outstanding throughout 2007 and 2008).

		Palisades' Earnings per Share	
	Formula	2008	2007
Earnings per share of common stock	$= \dfrac{\text{Net income} - \text{Preferred dividends}}{\text{Number of shares of common stock outstanding}}$	$\dfrac{\$48{,}000 - \$0}{10{,}000} = \$4.80$	$\dfrac{\$26{,}000 - \$0}{10{,}000} = \$2.60$

Palisades Furniture's EPS increased 85%. Its stockholders should not expect this big a boost in EPS every year. Most companies strive to increase EPS by 10% to 15% annually, and leading companies do so. But even the most successful companies have an occasional bad year.

Analyzing Stock Investments

Investors purchase stock to earn a return on their investment. This return consists of two parts: (1) gains (or losses) from selling the stock at a price above or below purchase price and (2) dividends. The ratios we examine in this section help analysts evaluate stock investments.

Price/Earnings Ratio

The **price/earnings ratio** is the ratio of the market price of a share of common stock to the company's earnings per share. It shows the market price of $1 of earnings. This ratio, abbreviated P/E, appears in *The Wall Street Journal* stock listings.

Calculations for the P/E ratios of Palisades Furniture Co. follow. The market price of its common stock was $60 at the end of 2008 and $35 at the end of 2007.

These prices can be obtained from a financial publication, a stockbroker, or the company's Web site.

	Formula	Palisades' Price/Earnings Ratio	
		2008	2007
P/E ratio =	$\dfrac{\text{Market price per share of common stock}}{\text{Earnings per share}}$	$\dfrac{\$60.00}{\$4.80} = 12.5$	$\dfrac{\$35.00}{\$2.60} = 13.5$

Palisades Furniture's P/E ratio of 12.5 means that the company's stock is selling at 12.5 times earnings. The decline from the 2007 P/E ratio of 13.5 is no cause for alarm because the market price of the stock is not under Palisades Furniture's control. Net income is more controllable, and net income increased during 2008.

Dividend Yield

Dividend yield is the ratio of dividends per share to the stock's market price per share. This ratio measures the percentage of a stock's market value that is returned annually as dividends. *Preferred* stockholders, who invest primarily to receive dividends, pay special attention to dividend yield.

Palisades Furniture paid annual cash dividends of $1.20 per share of common stock in 2008 and $1.00 in 2007, and market prices of the company's common stock were $60 in 2008 and $35 in 2007. The firm's dividend yields on common stock follow.

	Formula	Dividend Yield on Palisades' Common Stock	
		2008	2007
Dividend yield on common stock* =	$\dfrac{\text{Dividend per share of common stock}}{\text{Market price per share of common stock}}$	$\dfrac{\$1.20}{\$60.00} = .020$	$\dfrac{\$1.00}{\$35.00} = .029$

*Dividend yields may also be calculated for preferred stock.

An investor who buys Palisades Furniture common stock for $60 can expect to receive 2% of the investment annually in the form of cash dividends.

Book Value per Share of Common Stock

Book value per share of common stock is common equity divided by the number of common shares outstanding. Common equity equals total stockholders' equity less preferred equity. Palisades Furniture has no preferred stock outstanding. Its book-value-per-share-of-common-stock ratios follow (10,000 shares of common stock were outstanding).

	Formula	Book Value per Share of Palisades' Common Stock	
		2008	2007
Book value per share of common stock =	$\dfrac{\text{Total stockholders' equity} - \text{Preferred equity}}{\text{Number of shares of common stock outstanding}}$	$\dfrac{\$356,000 - \$0}{10,000} = \$35.60$	$\dfrac{\$320,000 - \$0}{10,000} = \$32.00$

Many experts argue that book value is not useful for investment analysis. It bears no relationship to market value and provides little information beyond stockholders' equity reported on the balance sheet. But some investors base their investment decisions on book value. For example, some investors rank stocks on the basis of the ratio of market price to book value. To these investors, the lower the ratio, the more attractive the stock.

Red Flags in Financial Statement Analysis

Analysts look for *red flags* that may signal financial trouble. Recent accounting scandals highlight the importance of these red flags. The following conditions may reveal that the company is too risky.

- **Movement of Sales, Inventory, and Receivables.** Sales, receivables, and inventory generally move together. Increased sales lead to higher receivables and require more inventory to meet demand. Strange movements among sales, inventory, and receivables make the financial statements look suspect.
- **Earnings Problems.** Has net income decreased significantly for several years in a row? Has income turned into a loss? Most companies cannot survive consecutive loss years.
- **Decreased Cash Flow.** Cash flow validates net income. Is cash flow from operations consistently lower than net income? If so, the company is in trouble. Are the sales of plant assets a major source of cash? If so, the company may face a cash shortage.
- **Too Much Debt.** How does the company's debt ratio compare to that of major competitors? If the debt ratio is too high, the company may be unable to pay its debts.
- **Inability to Collect Receivables.** Are days' sales in receivables growing faster than for competitors? A cash shortage may be looming.
- **Buildup of Inventories.** Is inventory turnover too slow? If so, the company may be unable to sell goods, or it may be overstating inventory.

Do any of these red flags apply to Google Inc.? No, Google's financial statements depict a strong and growing company. Will Google continue to grow at its present breakneck pace? Stay tuned. Time will tell.

The Decision Guidelines summarize the most widely used ratios.

Decision Guidelines

USING RATIOS IN FINANCIAL STATEMENT ANALYSIS

Mike and Roberta Robinson operate a financial-services firm. They manage other people's money and do most of their own financial-statement analysis. How do they measure companies' ability to pay bills, sell inventory, collect receivables, and so on? They use the standard ratios discussed in this chapter.

Ratio	Computation	Information Provided
Measuring ability to pay current liabilities:		
1. Current ratio	$\dfrac{\text{Current assets}}{\text{Current liabilities}}$	Measures ability to pay current liabilities with current assets
2. Acid-test (quick) ratio	$\dfrac{\text{Cash} + \dfrac{\text{Short-term}}{\text{investments}} + \dfrac{\text{Net current}}{\text{receivables}}}{\text{Current liabilities}}$	Shows ability to pay all current liabilities if they came due immediately
Measuring ability to sell inventory and collect receivables:		
3. Inventory turnover	$\dfrac{\text{Cost of goods sold}}{\text{Average inventory}}$	Indicates saleability of inventory—the number of times a company sells its average inventory during a year
4. Accounts receivable turnover	$\dfrac{\text{Net credit sales}}{\text{Average net accounts receivable}}$	Measures ability to collect cash from customers
5. Days' sales in receivables	$\dfrac{\text{Average net accounts receivable}}{\text{One day's sales}}$	Shows how many days' sales remain in Accounts Receivable—how many days it takes to collect the average level of receivables
Measuring ability to pay long-term debt:		
6. Debt ratio	$\dfrac{\text{Total liabilities}}{\text{Total assets}}$	Indicates percentage of assets financed with debt
7. Times-interest-earned ratio	$\dfrac{\text{Income from operations}}{\text{Interest expense}}$	Measures the number of times operating income can cover interest expense
Measuring profitability:		
8. Rate of return on net sales	$\dfrac{\text{Net income}}{\text{Net sales}}$	Shows the percentage of each sales dollar earned as net income
9. Rate of return on total assets	$\dfrac{\text{Net income} + \text{Interest expense}}{\text{Average total assets}}$	Measures how profitably a company uses its assets
10. Rate of return on common stockholders' equity	$\dfrac{\text{Net income} - \text{Preferred dividends}}{\text{Average common stockholders' equity}}$	Gauges how much income is earned for each dollar invested by the common shareholders
11. Earnings per share of common stock	$\dfrac{\text{Net income} - \text{Preferred dividends}}{\text{Number of shares of common stock outstanding}}$	Gives the amount of net income earned for each share of the company's common stock

continued . . .

Ratio	Computation	Information Provided
Analyzing stock as an investment:		
12. Price/earnings ratio	$$\frac{\text{Market price per share of common stock}}{\text{Earnings per share}}$$	Indicates the market price of $1 of earnings
13. Dividend yield	$$\frac{\text{Annual dividend per share of common (or preferred) stock}}{\text{Market price per share of common (or preferred) stock}}$$	Shows the percentage of a stock's market value returned as dividends to stockholders each year
14. Book value per share of common stock	$$\frac{\text{Total stockholders' equity} - \text{Preferred equity}}{\text{Number of shares of common stock outstanding}}$$	Indicates the recorded accounting amount for each share of common stock outstanding

Summary Problem 2

JAVA INC. Five-Year Selected Financial Data (adapted) Years Ended January 31,				
Operating Results*	**2007**	**2006**	**2005**	**2004**
Net sales	$13,848	$13,673	$11,635	$ 9,054
Cost of goods sold	9,704	8,599	6,775	5,318
Interest expense	109	75	45	46
Income from operations	338	1,455	1,817	1,333
Net income (net loss)	(8)	877	1,127	824
Cash dividends	76	75	76	77
Financial Position				
Merchandise inventory	1,677	1,904	1,462	1,056
Total assets	7,591	7,012	5,189	3,963
Current ratio	1.48:1	0.95:1	1.25:1	1.20:1
Stockholders' equity	3,010	2,928	2,630	1,574
Average number of shares of common stock outstanding (in thousands)	860	879	895	576

*Dollar amounts are in thousands.

Requirements

Compute the following ratios for 2005 through 2007, and evaluate Java's operating results. Are operating results strong or weak? Did they improve or deteriorate during this period? Your analysis will reveal a clear trend.

1. Gross profit percentage

2. Net income as a percentage of sales

3. Earnings per share

4. Inventory turnover

5. Times-interest-earned ratio

6. Rate of return on stockholders' equity

Solution

	2007	2006	2005
1. Gross profit percentage	$\dfrac{\$13{,}848-\$9{,}704}{\$13{,}848}=29.9\%$	$\dfrac{\$13{,}673-\$8{,}599}{\$13{,}673}=37.1\%$	$\dfrac{\$11{,}635-\$6{,}775}{\$11{,}635}=41.8\%$
2. Net income as a percentage of sales	$\dfrac{\$(8)}{\$13{,}848}=(.06\%)$	$\dfrac{\$877}{\$13{,}673}=6.4\%$	$\dfrac{\$1{,}127}{\$11{,}635}=9.7\%$
3. Earnings per share	$\dfrac{\$(8)}{860}=\$(0.01)$	$\dfrac{\$877}{879}=\$1.00$	$\dfrac{\$1{,}127}{895}=\$1.26$
4. Inventory turnover	$\dfrac{\$9{,}704}{(\$1{,}677+\$1{,}904)/2}=5.4$ times	$\dfrac{\$8{,}599}{(\$1{,}904+\$1{,}462)/2}=5.1$ times	$\dfrac{\$6{,}775}{(\$1{,}462+\$1{,}056)/2}=5.4$ times
5. Times-interest-earned ratio	$\dfrac{\$338}{\$109}=3.1$ times	$\dfrac{\$1{,}455}{\$75}=19.4$ times	$\dfrac{\$1{,}817}{\$45}=40.4$ times
6. Rate of return on stockholders' equity	$\dfrac{\$(8)}{(\$3{,}010+\$2{,}928)/2}=(0.3\%)$	$\dfrac{\$877}{(\$2{,}928+\$2{,}630)/2}=31.6\%$	$\dfrac{\$1{,}127}{(\$2{,}630+\$1{,}574)/2}=53.6\%$

Evaluation: During this period, Java's operating results deteriorated on all these measures except inventory turnover. The gross profit percentage is down sharply, as are the times-interest-earned ratio and return on equity. From these data it is clear that Java could sell its coffee, but not at the markups the company enjoyed in the past. The final result, in 2007, was a net loss for the year.

Review *Financial Statement Analysis*

Accounting Vocabulary

Account Receivable Turnover
Measure a company s ability to collect cash from credit customers. To compute accounts receivable turnover, divide net credit sales by average net accounts receivable.

Acid-Test Ratio
Ratio of the sum of cash plus short-term investments plus net current receivables to total current liabilities. Tells whether the entity can pay all its current liabilities if they come due immediately. Also called the **quick ratio**.

Benchmarking
The practice of comparing a company with other companies that are leaders.

Book Value per Share of Common Stock
Common stockholders' equity divided by the number of shares of common stock outstanding. The recorded amount for each share of common stock outstanding.

Collection Period
Ratio of average net accounts receivable to one day's sale. Indicates how many days' sales remain in Accounts Receivable awaiting collection. Also called the **days' sales in receivables**.

Common-Size Treatment
A financial statement that reports only percentages (no dollar amounts).

Current Ratio
Current assets divided by current liabilities. Measures ability to pay current liabilities with current assets.

Days' Sales in Receivables
Ratio of average net accounts receivable to one day's sale. Indicates how many days' sales remain in Accounts Receivable awaiting collection. Also called the **collection period**.

Debt Ratio
Ratio of total liabilities to total assets. Shows the proportion of a company's assets that is financed with debt.

Dividend Yield
Ratio of dividends per share of stock to the stock's market price per share. Tells the percentage of a stock's market value that the company returns to stockholders annually as dividends.

Earnings per Share (EPS)
Amount of a company's net income for each share of its outstanding common stock.

Horizontal Analysis
Study of percentage changes in comparative financial statements.

Interest-Coverage Ratio
Ratio of income from operations to interest expense. Measure the number of times that operating income can cover interest expense. Also called the **times-interest earned ratio**.

Inventory Turnover
Ratio of cost of goods sold to average inventory. Indicates how rapidly inventory is sold.

Leverage
Earning more income on borrowed money than the related interest expense, thereby increasing the earnings for the owners of the business. Also called **trading on equity**.

Price/Earnings Ratio
Ratio of the market price of a share of common stock to the company's earnings per share. Measures the value that the stock market places on $1 of a company's earnings.

Quick Ratio
Ratio of the sum of cash plus short-term investments plus net current receivables to total current liabilities. Tells whether the entity can pay all its current liabilities if they come due immediately. Also called the **acid-test ratio**.

Rate of Return on Common Stockholders' Equity
Net income minus preferred dividends, divided by average common stockholders' equity. A measure of profitability. Also called **return on equity**.

Rate of Return on Net Sales
Ratio of net income to net sales. A measure of profitability. Also called **return on sales**.

Rate of Return on Total Assets
Net income plus interest expense, divided by average total assets. This ratio measures a company's success in using its assets to earn income for the persons who finance the business. Also called **return on assets**.

Return on Assets

Net income plus interest expense, divided by average total assets. This ratio measure a company's success in using its assets to earn income for the persons who finance the business. Also called **rate of return on total assets**.

Return on Equity

Net income minus preferred dividends, divided by average common stockholders' equity. A measure of profitability. Also called **rate of return on common stockholders' equity**.

Return on Sales

Ratio of net income to net sales. A measure of profitability. Also called **rate of return on net sales**.

Times-Interest-Earned Ratio

Ratio of income from operations to interest expense. Measures the number of times that operating income can cover interest expense. Also called the **interest-coverage ratio**.

Trading on Equity

Earning more income on borrowed money than the related interest expense, thereby increasing the earnings for the owners of the business. Also called **leverage**.

Trend Percentages

A form of horizontal analysis in which percentages are computed by selecting a base year as 100% and expressing amounts for following years as a percentage of the base amount.

Vertical Analysis

Analysis of a financial statement that reveals the relationship of each statement item to a specified base, which is the 100% figure.

Working Capital

Current assets minus current liabilities; measures a business's ability to meet its short-term obligations with its current assets.

Quick Check

Liberty Corporation reported these figures:

	2007	2006		2007
Cash and equivalents	$ 2,345	$ 1,934	Sales	$19,564
Receivables	2,097	1,882	Cost of sales	7,105
Inventory	1,294	1,055	Operating expenses............	7,001
Prepaid expenses...........................	1,616	2,300	Operating income	5,458
Total current assets	7,352	7,171	Interest expense	199
Other assets	17,149	15,246	Other expense.....................	2,209
Total assets	$24,501	$22,417	Net income	$ 3,050
Total current liabilities..................	$ 7,341	$ 8,429		
Long-term liabilities......................	5,360	2,622		
Common equity	11,800	11,366		
Total liabilities and equity.............	$24,501	$22,417		

1. Horizontal analysis of Liberty's balance sheet for 2007 would report
   a. Cash as 9.6% of total assets
   b. 21% increase in Cash
   c. Current ratio of 1.00
   d. Inventory turnover of 6 times

2. Vertical analysis of Liberty's balance sheet for 2007 would report
   a. 21% increase in Cash
   b. Current ratio of 1.00
   c. Cash as 9.6% of total assets
   d. Inventory turnover of 6 times

3. A common-size income statement for Liberty would report (amounts rounded)
   a. Net income of 16%
   b. Cost of sales at 36%
   c. Sales of 100%
   d. All the above

4. Which statement best describes Liberty's acid-test ratio?
   a. Less than 1
   b. Equal to 1
   c. Greater than 1
   d. None of the above

5. Liberty's inventory turnover during 2007 was
   a. 6 times
   b. 7 times
   c. 8 times
   d. Not determinable from the data given

6. During 2005, Liberty's days' sales in receivables ratio was
   a. 39 days
   b. 37 days
   c. 35 days
   d. 30 days

7. Which measure expresses Liberty's times-interest-earned ratio?
   a. 15 times
   b. 27 times
   c. 20 times
   d. 51.8%

8. Liberty's return on common stockholders' equity can be described as
   a. Weak
   b. Normal
   c. Average
   d. Strong

9. The company has 2,500 shares of common stock outstanding. What is Liberty's earnings per share?
   a. 2.04
   b. 3.6 times
   c. $1.22
   d. $3.05

10. Liberty's stock has traded recently around $44 per share. Use your answer to question 9 to measure the company's price/earnings ratio.
    a. 36
    b. 44
    c. 1.00
    d. 69

Answers are given after Apply Your Knowledge (p. 895).

Assess Your Progress

Short Exercises

S17-1 Micatin Corp. reported the following on its comparative income statement:

Horizontal analysis of revenues and gross profit

1

S17-1 Micatin Corp. reported the following on its comparative income statement:

(in millions)	2006	2005	2004
Revenue......................................	$9,993	$9,489	$8,995
Cost of sales	5,905	5,785	5,404

Perform a horizontal analysis of revenues and gross profit—both in dollar amounts and in percentages—for 2006 and 2005. (p. 849)

Trend analysis of revenues and net income

1

S17-2 Micatin Corp. reported the following revenues and net income amounts:

(in millions)	2006	2005	2004	2003
Revenues.......................	$9,993	$9,489	$8,995	$8,777
Net income	634	590	579	451

1. Show Micatin's trend percentages for revenues and net income. Use 2003 as the base year, and round to the nearest percent.
2. Which measure increased faster during 2004–2006? (p. 852)

Vertical analysis of assets

2

S17-3 TriState Optical Company reported the following amounts on its balance sheet at December 31, 2006:

	2006
Cash and receivables..	$ 48,000
Inventory	38,000
Property, plant, and equipment, net................	96,000
Total assets	$182,000

Perform a vertical analysis of TriState assets at the end of 2006. (p. 852)

Common-size income statements of two companies

3

S17-4 Compare Sanchez, Inc., and Alioto Corp. by converting their income statements to common size.

	Sanchez	Alioto
Net sales...........................	$9,489	$19,536
Cost of goods sold.............	5,785	14,101
Other expense	3,114	4,497
Net income........................	$ 590	$ 938

continued . . .

Which company earns more net income? Which company's net income is a higher percentage of its net sales? (pp. 853–854).

S17-5 though S17-9 use the following data for Short Exercises S17-5 through S17-9. Lowe's Companies, the home-improvement-store chain, reported these summarized figures (in billions):

LOWE'S COMPANIES Income Statement (Adapted) Year Ended January 30, 20X4	
Net sales	$30.8
Cost of goods sold	21.2
Interest expense	.2
All other expenses	7.5
Net income	$ 1.9

LOWE'S COMPANIES
Balance Sheet (Adapted)
January 31,

	20X4	20X3		20X4	20X3
Cash	$ 1.4	$ 0.8	Total current liabilities	$ 4.4	$ 3.6
Short-term investments	0.2	0.3	Long-term liabilities	4.3	4.2
Accounts receivable	0.1	0.2	Total liabilities	8.7	7.8
Inventory	4.6	4.0			
Other current assets	0.4	0.3	Common stock	2.6	2.4
Total current assets	6.7	5.6	Retained earnings	7.7	5.9
All other assets	12.3	10.5	Total equity	10.3	8.3
Total assets	$19.0	$16.1	Total liabilities and equity	$19.0	$16.1

Evaluating a company's current ratio

S17-5 Use the foregoing Lowe's Companies data.

1. Compute Lowe's current ratio at December 31, 20X4 and 20X3. (p. 859)

2. Did Lowe's current ratio improve, deteriorate, or hold steady during 2006? (p. 859)

Computing inventory turnover and days' sales in receivables

S17-6 Use the foregoing Lowe's Companies data to compute the following (amounts in billions):

a. The rate of inventory turnover for 20X4. (pp. 861–862)

b. Days' sales in average receivables during 20X4. Round dollar amounts to three decimal places. (p. 862)

Measuring ability to pay liabilities

S17-7 Use the foregoing financial statements of Lowe's Companies.

1. Compute the debt ratio at December 31, 20X4. (p. 863)

2. Is Lowe's ability to pay its liabilities strong or weak? Explain your reasoning. (p. 863)

Measuring profitability

4

S17-8 Use the foregoing financial statements of Lowe's Companies to compute these profitability measures for 20X4.

    a. Rate of return on net sales. (p. 864)

    b. Rate of return on total assets. Interest expense for 20X4 was $0.2 billion. (p. 865)

    c. Rate of return on common stockholders' equity. (p. 865)

    Are these rates of return strong or weak? Explain. (pp. 865–866)

Computing EPS and the
price/earnings ratio

4

S17-9 Use the foregoing financial statements of Lowe's Companies, plus the following items (in billions):

Number of shares of common stock outstanding	0.8

    1. Compute earnings per share (EPS) for Lowe's. Round to the nearest cent. (p. 866)

    2. Compute Lowe's price/earnings ratio. The price of a share of Lowe's stock is $66.50. (pp. 866–867)

Using ratio data to
reconstruct an income
statement

4

S17-10 A skeleton of Heirloom Mills' income statement appears as follows (amounts in thousands):

INCOME STATEMENT

Net sales	$7,200
Cost of goods sold	(a)
Selling and administrative expenses	1,710
Interest expense	(b)
Other expenses	150
Income before taxes	1,000
Income tax expense	(c)
Net income	$ (d)

Use the following ratio data to complete Heirloom Mills' income statement: (pp. 860, 862, 864)

    a. Inventory turnover was 5.5 (beginning inventory was $790; ending inventory was $750).

    b. Rate of return on sales is 0.095.

Using ratio data to
reconstruct a balance sheet

4

S17-11 A skeleton of Heirloom Mills' balance sheet appears as follows (amounts in thousands):

BALANCE SHEET

Cash	$ 50	Total current liabilities	$2,100
Receivables	(a)	Long-term note	
Inventories	750	payable	(e)
Prepaid expenses	(b)	Other long-term	
Total current assets	(c)	liabilities	820
Plant assets, net	(d)	Stockholders' equity	2,400
Other assets	2,150	Total liabilities and	
Total assets	$6,800	equity	$ (f)

continued . . .

Use the following ratio data to complete Heirloom Mills' balance sheet:
(pp. 859, 861)

a. Current ratio is 0.70.

b. Acid-test ratio is 0.30.

Exercises

Computing year-to-year
changes in working capital

1

E17-12 Compute the dollar amount of change and the percentage of change in
Media Enterprises' working capital each year during 2008 and 2009. Is
this trend favorable or unfavorable?

	2009	2008	2007
Total current assets...............	$330,000	$300,000	$280,000
Total current liabilities..........	160,000	150,000	140,000

Horizontal analysis of an
income statement

1

E17-13 Prepare a horizontal analysis of the following comparative income statement of Enchanted Designs, Inc. Round percentage changes to the nearest one-tenth percent (three decimal places) (pp. 850, 851):

ENCHANTED DESIGNS Comparative Income Statement Years Ended December 31, 2007 and 2006		
	2007	2006
Net sales revenue	$430,000	$373,000
Expenses:		
Cost of goods sold	$202,000	$188,000
Selling and general expenses	98,000	93,000
Other expense	7,000	4,000
Total expenses	307,000	285,000
Net income	$123,000	$ 88,000

Why did net income increase by a higher percentage than net sales revenue during 2007? (pp. 850, 851)

Computing trend
percentages

1

E17-14 Compute trend percentages for Thousand Oaks Realty's net revenue and
net income for the following 5-year period, using 2004 as the base year.
Round to the nearest full percent. (p. 852)

(in thousands)	2008	2007	2006	2005	2004
Net revenue	$1,318	$1,187	$1,106	$1,009	$1,043
Net income	122	114	83	71	85

Which grew faster during the period, net revenue or net income?

E17-15 Alpha Graphics, Inc., has requested that you perform a vertical analysis of its balance sheet. (p. 854)

ALPHA GRAPHICS, INC.
Balance Sheet
December 31, 2006

Assets	
Total current assets	$ 42,000
Property, plant, and equipment, net	207,000
Other assets	35,000
Total assets	$284,000
Liabilities	
Total current liabilities	$ 48,000
Long-term debt	108,000
Total liabilities	156,000
Stockholders' Equity	
Total stockholders' equity	128,000
Total liabilities and stockholders' equity	$284,000

E17-16 Prepare a comparative common-size income statement for Enchanted Designs, Inc., using the 2007 and 2006 data of Exercise 17-13 and rounding percentages to one-tenth percent (three decimal places). To an investor, how does 2007 compare with 2006? Explain your reasoning. (pp. 853, 854)

E17-17 The financial statements of Nature's Health Foods include the following items:

	Current Year	Preceding Year
Balance sheet:		
Cash	$ 17,000	$ 22,000
Short-term investments	11,000	26,000
Net receivables	54,000	73,000
Inventory	77,000	71,000
Prepaid expenses	16,000	8,000
Total current assets	$175,000	$200,000
Total current liabilities	$131,000	$ 91,000
Income statement:		
Net credit sales	$464,000	
Cost of goods sold	317,000	

Requirements

Compute the following ratios for the current year:

a. Current ratio (p. 859)

b. Acid-test ratio (p. 861)

c. Inventory turnover (pp. 861–862)

d. Days' sales in average receivables (pp. 862–863)

E17-18 Big Bend Picture Frames has asked you to determine whether the company's ability to pay current liabilities and total liabilities improved or deteriorated during 2007. To answer this question, compute these ratios for 2007 and 2006:

a. Current ratio (p. 859)

b. Acid-test ratio (p. 861)

c. Debt ratio (p. 863)

d. Times-interest-earned ratio (p. 864)

Summarize the results of your analysis in a written report.

	2007	2006
Cash...	$ 61,000	$ 47,000
Short-term investments...............	28,000	—
Net receivables	122,000	116,000
Inventory....................................	237,000	272,000
Total assets.................................	560,000	490,000
Total current liabilities................	275,000	202,000
Long-term note payable..............	40,000	52,000
Income from operations	165,000	158,000
Interest expense	48,000	39,000

E17-19 Compute four ratios that measure the ability to earn profits for Bonaparte, Inc., whose comparative income statement follows. 2004 data are given as needed. (pp. 864–866):

BONAPARTE				
Comparative Income Statement				
Years Ended December 31, 2006 and 2005				
Dollars in Thousands		2006	2005	2004
Net sales		$174,000	$158,000	
Cost of goods sold		$ 93,000	$ 86,000	
Selling and general expenses		46,000	41,000	
Interest expense		9,000	10,000	
Income tax expense		10,000	9,000	
Net income		$ 16,000	$ 12,000	
Additional data:				
Total assets		$204,000	$191,000	$171,000
Common stockholders' equity		$ 96,000	$ 89,000	$ 79,000
Preferred dividends		$ 3,000	$ 3,000	$ 0
Common shares outstanding during				
the year		20,000	20,000	18,000

Did the company's operating performance improve or deteriorate during 2006? (pp. 864–866)

Evaluating a stock as an investment
4

E17-20 Evaluate the common stock of Shamrock State Bank as an investment. Specifically, use the three stock ratios to determine whether the common stock has increased or decreased in attractiveness during the past year. (pp. 866–867)

	2008	2007
Net income	$ 60,000	$ 52,000
Dividends—common...	20,000	20,000
Dividends—preferred	12,000	12,000
Total stockholders' equity at year-end (includes 80,000 shares of common stock)	780,000	600,000
Preferred stock, 6%	200,000	200,000
Market price per share of common stock	$16.50	$13

Using ratio data to reconstruct a company's balance sheet
4

E17-21 The following data (dollar amounts in millions) are adapted from the financial statements of Super Saver Stores, Inc.

Total current assets..........................	$10,500
Accumulated depreciation	$ 2,000
Total liabilities.................................	$15,000
Preferred stock	$ 0
Debt ratio...	60%
Current ratio	1.50

Requirement
Complete Super Saver's condensed balance sheet. (pp. 860, 862)

Current assets..		$?
Property, plant, and equipment	$?	
Less Accumulated depreciation.......................	(?)	?
Total assets..		$?
Current liabilities		$?
Long-term liabilities		?
Stockholders' equity		?
Total liabilities and stockholders' equity.............		$?

Problems (Group A)

Trend percentages, return on common equity, and comparison with the industry
1 **4**

P17-22A Net sales revenue, net income, and common stockholders' equity for Shawnee Mission Corporation, a manufacturer of contact lenses, follow for a four-year period.

(in thousands)	2008	2007	2006	2005
Net sales revenue	$761	$704	$641	$662
Net income	60	40	36	48
Ending common stockholders' equity	366	354	330	296

continued . . .

Requirements

1. Compute trend percentages for each item for 2006 through 2008. Use 2005 as the base year, and round to the nearest whole percent. (p. 852)

2. Compute the rate of return on common stockholders' equity for 2006 through 2008, rounding to three decimal places. (p. 865)

Common-size statements, analysis of profitability, and financial position, and comparison with the industry

2 3 4

P17-23A Todd Department Stores' chief executive officer (CEO) has asked you to compare the company's profit performance and financial position with the average for the industry. The CEO has given you the company's income statement and balance sheet, as well as the industry average data for retailers.

TODD DEPARTMENT STORES, INC. Income Statement Compared with Industry Average Year Ended December 31, 2006		
	Todd	Industry Average
Net sales	$781,000	100.0%
Cost of goods sold	528,000	65.8
Gross profit	253,000	34.2
Operating expenses	163,000	19.7
Operating income	90,000	14.5
Other expenses	5,000	0.4
Net income	$ 85,000	14.1%

TODD DEPARTMENT STORES, INC. Balance Sheet Compared with Industry Average December 31, 2006		
	Todd	Industry Average
Current assets	$305,000	70.9%
Fixed assets, net	119,000	23.6
Intangible assets, net	4,000	0.8
Other assets	22,000	4.7
Total assets	$450,000	100.0%
Current liabilities	$207,000	48.1%
Long-term liabilities	102,000	16.6
Stockholders' equity	141,000	35.3
Total liabilities and stockholders's equity	$450,000	100.0%

Requirements

1. Prepare a common-size income statement and balance sheet for Todd. The first column of each statement should present Todd's

continued . . .

–common-size statement, and the second column, the industry averages. (pp. 853–854, 855)

2. For the profitability analysis, compute Todd's (a) ratio of gross profit to net sales, (b) ratio of operating income to net sales, and (c) ratio of net income to net sales. Compare these figures with the industry averages. Is Todd's profit performance better or worse than the industry average? (pp. 863, 854, 856)

3. For the analysis of financial position, compute Todd's (a) ratio of current assets to total assets and (b) ratio of stockholders' equity to total assets. Compare these ratios with the industry averages. Is Todd's financial position better or worse than the industry averages? (pp. 853, 854, 856)

Effects of business transactions on selected ratios

4

P17-24A Financial statement data of Yankee Traveler Magazine include the following items (dollars in thousands):

Cash	$ 22,000
Accounts receivable, net	82,000
Inventories	149,000
Total assets	637,000
Short-term notes payable	49,000
Accounts payable	103,000
Accrued liabilities	38,000
Long-term liabilities	191,000
Net income	71,000
Common shares outstanding	50,000

Requirements

1. Compute Yankee Traveler's current ratio (p. 859), debt ratio (p. 863), and earnings per share (p. 866). Round all ratios to two decimal places, and use the following format for your answer:

Transaction	Current Ratio	Debt Ratio	Earnings per Share

2. Compute the three ratios after evaluating the effect of each transaction that follows. Consider each transaction *separately*.

a. Purchased inventory on account, $46,000.

b. Borrowed $125,000 on a long-term note payable.

c. Issued 5,000 shares of common stock, receiving cash of $120,000.

d. Received cash on account, $19,000.

Format your answer as follows:

Transaction	Current Ratio	Debt Ratio	Earnings per Share
a.			

P17-25A Comparative financial-statement data of Weinstein, Inc., follow.

WEINSTEIN, INC.
Comparative Income Statement
Years Ended December 31, 2009 and 2008

	2009	2008
Net sales	$462,000	$427,000
Cost of goods sold	240,000	218,000
Gross profit	222,000	209,000
Operating expenses	136,000	134,000
Income from operations	86,000	75,000
Interest expense	11,000	12,000
Income before income tax	75,000	63,000
Income tax expense	25,000	27,000
Net income	$ 50,000	$ 36,000

WEINSTEIN, INC.
Comparative Balance Sheet
December 31, 2009 and 2008

	2009	2008	2007*
Current assets:			
Cash	$ 96,000	$ 97,000	
Current receivables, net	112,000	116,000	$103,000
Inventories	147,000	162,000	207,000
Prepaid expenses	16,000	7,000	
Total current assets	371,000	382,000	
Property, plant, and equipment, net	214,000	178,000	
Total assets	$585,000	$560,000	598,000
Total current liabilities	$226,000	$243,000	
Long-term liabilities	119,000	97,000	
Total liabilities	345,000	340,000	
Preferred stock, 6%	100,000	100,000	
Common stockholders' equity, no par	140,000	120,000	90,000
Total liabilities and stockholders' equity	$585,000	$560,000	

*Selected 2007 amounts.

Other Information:
1. Market price of Weinstein's common stock: $49 at December 31, 2009, and $32.50 at December 31, 2008.

2. Common shares outstanding: 10,000 during 2009 and 9,000 during 2008.

3. All sales on credit.

Requirements
1. Compute the following ratios for 2009 and 2008:
   a. Current ratio (p. 859)
   b. Times-interest-earned ratio (pp. 863–864)
   c. Inventory turnover (pp. 861–862)

continued . . .

d. Return on common stockholders' equity (p. 865)

e. Earnings per share of common stock (p. 866)

f. Price/earnings ratio (pp. 866–867)

2. Decide (a) whether Weinstein's ability to pay debts and to sell inventory improved or deteriorated during 2009 and (b) whether the investment attractiveness of its common stock appears to have increased or decreased.

P17-26A Assume that you are purchasing an investment and have decided to invest in a company in the digital phone business. You have narrowed the choice to Singular Corp. and Very Zone, Inc., and have assembled the following data:

Using ratios to decide between two stock investments

4 **5**

Selected income-statement data for the current year:

	Singular	Very Zone
Net sales (all on credit)	$421,000	$497,000
Cost of goods sold	209,000	258,000
Interest expense......................	—	19,000
Net income	50,000	72,000

Selected balance-sheet data at the *beginning* of the current year:

	Singular	Very Zone
Current receivables, net	$ 40,000	$ 48,000
Inventories..	83,000	88,000
Total assets	259,000	270,000
Common stock, $1 par (10,000 shares)........	10,000	
$1 par (15,000 shares)		15,000

Selected balance-sheet and market-price data at the *end* of the current year:

	Singular	Very Zone
Current assets:		
Cash	$ 26,000	$ 19,000
Short-term investments	40,000	18,000
Current receivables, net	38,000	46,000
Inventories..	67,000	100,000
Prepaid expenses.....................................	2,000	3,000
Total current assets	173,000	186,000
Total assets..	265,000	328,000
Total current liabilities	100,000	98,000
Total liabilities..	100,000	131,000
Common stock, $1 par (10,000 shares).......	10,000	
$1 par (15,000 shares).......		15,000
Total stockholders' equity	157,000	197,000
Market price per share of common stock	$ 80	$ 86.40

continued . . .

Your strategy is to invest in companies that have low price/earnings ratios but appear to be in good shape financially. Assume that you have analyzed all other factors and that your decision depends on the results of ratio analysis.

Requirements

Compute the following ratios for both companies for the current year, and decide which company's stock better fits your investment strategy.

a. Acid-test ratio (p. 861)

b. Inventory turnover (pp. 861–862)

c. Days' sales in average receivables (pp. 862–863)

d. Debt ratio (p. 863)

e. Earnings per share of common stock (p. 866)

f. Price/earnings ratio (pp. 866–867)

Analyzing two companies based on their ratios

P17-27A Take the role of an investment analyst at Prudential Bache. It is your job to recommend investments for your clients. The only information you have are some ratio values for two companies in the pharmaceuticals industry.

Ratio	Healthtime Inc.	Mocek Corp.
Return on equity (pp. 863–864)	21.5%	32.3%
Return on assets (p. 862)	16.4%	17.1%
Days' sales in receivables (pp. 853–854)	42	36
Inventory turnover (pp. 853–854)	8	6
Gross profit percentage (pp. 864–866)	51%	53%
Net income as a percentage of sales (pp. 864–866)	8.3%	7.2%
Times-interest-earned (pp. 864–866)	9	16

Write a report to Prudential Bache's investment committee. Recommend one company's stock over the other. State the reasons for your recommendation.

Problems (Group B)

Trend percentages, return on sales, and comparison with the industry
1 4

P17-28B Net sales, net income, and total assets for Azbell Electronics for a four-year period follow.

(in thousands)	2008	2007	2006	2005
Net sales	$307	$313	$266	$281
Net income	9	21	11	18
Total assets	266	254	209	197

continued . . .

Requirements

1. Compute trend percentages for each item for 2006 through 2008. Use 2005 as the base year and round to the nearest whole percentage. (p. 852)

2. Compute the rate of return on net sales for 2006 through 2008, rounding to three decimal places. (p. 864)

Common-size statements, analysis of profitability, and financial position, and comparison with the industry

2 3 4

P17-29B Top managers of Crescent City Music Company have asked your help in comparing the company's profit performance and financial position with the average for the industry. The accountant has given you the company's income statement and balance sheet and also the following data for the industry:

			Crescent City	Industry Average
CRESCENT CITY MUSIC COMPANY				
Income Statement Compared with Industry Average				
Year Ended December 31, 2008				
	Net sales		$957,000	100.0%
	Cost of goods sold		613,000	65.9
	Gross profit		344,000	34.1
	Operating expenses		204,000	28.1
	Operating income		140,000	6.0
	Other expenses		10,000	0.4
	Net income		$130,000	5.6%

	Crescent City	Industry Average
CRESCENT CITY MUSIC COMPANY		
Balance Sheet Compared with Industry Average		
December 31, 2008		
Current assets	$486,000	74.4%
Fixed assets, net	117,000	20.0
Intangible assets, net	24,000	0.6
Other assets	3,000	5.0
Total assets	$630,000	100.0%
Current liabilities	$246,000	45.6%
Long-term liabilities	136,000	19.0
Stockholders' equity	248,000	35.4
Total liabilities and stockholders' equity	$630,000	100.0%

continued . . .

Requirements

1. Prepare a common-size income statement and balance sheet for Crescent City Music Company. The first column of each statement should present Crescent City's common-size statement, and the second column should show the industry averages. (pp. 853–854)

2. For the profitability analysis, compute Crescent City's (a) ratio of gross profit to net sales, (b) ratio of operating income to net sales, and (c) ratio of net income to net sales. Compare these figures with the industry averages. Is Crescent City's profit performance better or worse than the average for the industry? (pp. 853, 856)

3. For the analysis of financial position, compute Crescent City's (a) ratios of current assets and current liabilities to total assets and (b) ratio of stockholders' equity to total assets. Compare these ratios with the industry averages. Is Crescent City's financial position better or worse than average for the industry? (pp. 853, 856)

Effects of business transactions on selected ratios

4

P17-30B Financial statement data on I70 RV Park include the following:

Cash	$ 47,000	Accounts payable	$ 96,000
Accounts receivable, net	123,000	Accrued liabilities	50,000
Inventories	189,000	Long-term liabilities	224,000
Total assets	833,000	Net income	110,000
Short-term notes payable	72,000	Common shares outstanding	20,000

Requirements

1. Compute I70 RV Park's current ratio (p. 859), debt ratio (p. 863), and earnings per share (p. 866). Round all ratios to two decimal places, and use the following format for your answer:

Transaction Letter	Current Ratio	Debt Ratio	Earnings per Share

2. Compute the three ratios after evaluating the effect of each transaction that follows. Consider each transaction *separately*.

 a. Borrowed $27,000 on a long-term note payable.

 b. Issued 10,000 shares of common stock, receiving cash of $108,000.

 c. Purchased inventory of $48,000 on account.

 d. Received cash on account, $6,000.

Format your answer as follows:

Transaction	Current Ratio	Debt Ratio	Earnings per Share
a.			

P17-31B Comparative financial statement data of Banfield DVDs, Inc., follow:

BANFIELD DVDs, INC.
Comparative Income Statement
Years Ended December 31, 2006 and 2005

	2006	2005
Net sales	$667,000	$599,000
Cost of goods sold	378,000	283,000
Gross profit	289,000	316,000
Operating expenses	129,000	147,000
Income from operations	160,000	169,000
Interest expense	37,000	51,000
Income before income tax	123,000	118,000
Income tax expense	34,000	53,000
Net income	$ 89,000	$ 65,000

BANFIELD DVDs INC.
Comparative Balance Sheet
December 31, 2006 and 2005

	2006	2005	2004*
Current assets:			
Cash	$ 37,000	$ 40,000	
Current receivables, net	208,000	151,000	$138,000
Inventories	298,000	286,000	184,000
Prepaid expenses	5,000	20,000	
Total current assets	548,000	497,000	
Property, plant, and equipment, net	287,000	276,000	
Total assets	$835,000	$773,000	707,000
Total current liabilities	$286,000	$267,000	
Long-term liabilities	245,000	235,000	
Total liabilities	531,000	502,000	
Preferred stock, 4%	50,000	50,000	
Common stockholders' equity, no par	308,000	221,000	198,000
Total liabilities and stockholders' equity	$889,000	$773,000	

*Selected 2004 amounts.

Other Information:
1. Market price of Banfield's common stock: $92.80 at December 31, 2006, and $67.50 at December 31, 2005.

2. Common shares outstanding: 15,000 during 2006 and 14,000 during 2005.

3. All sales on credit.

Requirements
1. Compute the following ratios for 2006 and 2005:
   a. Current ratio (p. 859)
   b. Times-interest-earned ratio (p. 864)

continued . . .

c. Inventory turnover (pp. 861–862)

d. Return on common stockholders' equity (p. 865)

e. Earnings per share of common stock (p. 866)

f. Price/earnings ratio (pp. 866–867)

Decide whether (a) Banfield's ability to pay its debts and to sell inventory improved or deteriorated during 2006 and (b) the investment attractiveness of its common stock appears to have increased or decreased.

Using ratios to decide between two stock investments

P17-32B Assume that you are considering purchasing stock in a company in the music industry. You have narrowed the choice to Minnesota Music Makers (MMM), and Carolina Sound and have assembled the following data:

Selected income-statement data for the current year:

	MMM	Carolina
Net sales (all on credit)...........	$603,000	$519,000
Cost of goods sold..................	484,000	387,000
Interest expense......................	—	8,000
Net income...........................	75,000	38,000

Selected balance-sheet and market-price data at the *end* of the current year:

	MMM	Carolina
Current assets:		
Cash..	$ 45,000	$ 39,000
Short-term investments................................	76,000	13,000
Current receivables, net	99,000	164,000
Inventories..	211,000	183,000
Prepaid expenses..	19,000	15,000
Total current assets.....................................	450,000	414,000
Total assets..	974,000	938,000
Total current liabilities	306,000	338,000
Total liabilities	667,000	691,000
Common stock, $1 par (150,000 shares).......	150,000	
$5 par (20,000 shares).........		100,000
Total stockholders' equity	307,000	247,000
Market price per share of common stock	$ 8	$ 41.80

Selected balance-sheet data at the *beginning* of the current year:

	MMM	Carolina
Current receivables, net	$102,000	$193,000
Inventories...	209,000	197,000
Total assets	842,000	909,000
Common stock, $1 par (150,000 shares)	150,000	
$5 par (20,000 shares)		100,000

continued . . .

Your strategy is to invest in companies that have low price/earnings ratios but appear to be in good shape financially. Assume that you have analyzed all other factors and that your decision depends on the results of ratio analysis.

Requirements

Compute the following ratios for both companies for the current year and decide which company's stock better fits your investment strategy.

a. Acid-test ratio (p. 861)

b. Inventory turnover (pp. 861–862)

c. Days' sales in average receivables (pp. 862–863)

d. Debt ratio (p. 863)

e. Earnings per share of common stock (p. 866)

f. Price/earnings ratio (pp. 866–867)

Analyzing two companies based on their ratios

P17-33B Take the role of an investment analyst at A. G. Edwards. It is your job to recommend investments for your client. The only information you have are the ratio values for two companies in the graphics software industry.

Ratio	Hourglass Software Company	PC Tech, Inc.
Return on equity (p. 865)	36%	29%
Return on assets (p. 865)	21%	20%
Days' sales in receivables (p. 863)	43	51
Inventory turnover (pp. 861–862)	8	9
Gross profit percentage (p. 853)	71%	62%
Net income as a percent of sales (p. 853)	14%	16%
Times-interest earned (p. 864)	18	12

Write a report to the A. G. Edwards investment committee. Recommend one company's stock over the other. State the reasons for your recommendation.

for 24/7 practice, visit www.MyAccountingLab.com

Apply Your Knowledge

Decision Cases

Assessing the effects of transactions on a company

Case 1. General Motors, Inc., and Ford Motor Company both had a bad year in 2005; the companies' auto units suffered net losses. The loss pushed some return measures into the negative column, and the companies' ratios deteriorated. Assume top management of GM and Ford are pondering ways to improve their ratios. In particular, management is considering the following transactions:

1. Borrow $100 million on long-term debt.

2. Purchase treasury stock for $500 million cash.

3. Expense one-fourth of the goodwill carried on the books.

4. Create a new auto-design division at a cash cost of $300 million.

5. Purchase patents from DaimlerChrysler, paying $20 million cash.

Requirements

Top management wants to know the effects of these transactions (increase, decrease, or no effect) on the following ratios:

a. Current ratio (p. 859)

b. Debt ratio (p. 863)

c. Return on equity (pp. 865–866)

Understanding the components of accounting ratios

Case 2. Lance Berkman is the controller of Saturn, a dance club whose year-end is December 31. Berkman prepares checks for suppliers in December and posts them to the appropriate accounts in that month. However, he holds on to the checks and mails them to the suppliers in January. What financial ratio(s) are most affected by the action? What is Berkman's purpose in undertaking this activity? (Challenge)

Ethical Issue

Betsy Ross Flag Company's long-term debt agreements make certain demands on the business. For example, Ross may not purchase treasury stock in excess of the balance of retained earnings. Also, long-term debt may not exceed stockholders' equity, and the current ratio may not fall below 1.50. If Ross fails to meet any of these requirements, the company's lenders have the authority to take over management of the company.

Changes in consumer demand have made it hard for Ross to attract customers. Current liabilities have mounted faster than current assets, causing the current ratio to fall to 1.47. Before releasing financial statements, Ross management is scrambling to improve the current ratio. The controller points out that an investment can be classified as either long-term or short-term, depending on management's intention. By deciding to convert an investment to cash within one year, Ross can classify the investment as short-term—a current asset. On the controller's recommendation, Ross's board of directors votes to reclassify long-term investments as short-term.

Requirements

1. What effect will reclassifying the investments have on the current ratio? Is Ross's true financial position stronger as a result of reclassifying the investments?

2. Shortly after the financial statements are released, sales improve; so, too, does the current ratio. As a result, Ross management decides not to sell the investments it had reclassified as short-term. Accordingly, the company reclassifies the investments as long-term. Has management behaved unethically? Give the reasoning underlying your answer.

Financial Statement Case

Analyzing a balance sheet and measuring profitability

4

Amazon.com's financial statements in Appendix A at the end of this book reveal some interesting relationships. Answer these questions about Amazon.com:

1. What is most unusual about the balance sheet?

2. Compute trend percentages for net sales and net income. Use 2003 as the base year. Which trend percentage looks strange? Explain your answer.

3. Compute inventory turnover for 2005 and 2004. The inventory balance at December 31, 2003, was $294 million. Do the trend of net income from 2004 to 2005 and the change in the rate of inventory turnover tell the same story or a different story? Explain your answer.

Team Projects

Project 1. Select an industry you are interested in, and use the leading company in that industry as the benchmark. Then select two other companies in the same industry. For each category of ratios in the Decision Guidelines on pp. 869–870, compute all the ratios for the three companies. Write a two-page report that compares the two companies with the benchmark company.

Project 2. Select a company and obtain its financial statements. Convert the income statement and the balance sheet to common size, and compare the company you selected to the industry average. The Risk Management Association's *Annual Statement Studies*, Dun & Bradstreet's *Industry Norms & Key Business Ratios*, and Prentice Hall's *Almanac of Business and Industrial Financial Ratios*, by Leo Troy, publish common-size statements for most industries.

For Internet exercises, Excel in Practice, and additional online activities, go to the Web site www.prenhall.com/horngren.

Quick Check Answers

1. *b*   2. *c*   3. *d*   4. *a*   5. *a*   6. *b*   7. *b*   8. *d*   9. *c*   10. *a*

Comprehensive Problem for Chapters 16 and 17

Analyzing a Company for Its Investment Potential

In its annual report, WRS Athletic Supply includes the following five-year financial summary. Analyze the company's financial summary for the fiscal years 2001 through 2005 to decide whether to invest in the common stock of WRS.

WRS ATHLETIC SUPPLY, INC. 5-Year Financial Summary (Partial; adapted)						
(Dollar Amounts in Thousands Except per Share Data)	2005	2004	2003	2002	2001	2000
Net sales	$244,524	$217,799	$191,329	$165,013	$137,634	
Net sales increase	12%	14%	16%	20%	17%	
Domestic comparative store sales increase	5%	6%	5%	8%	9%	
Other income—net	2,001	1,873	1,787	1,615	1,391	
Cost of sales	191,838	171,562	150,255	129,664	108,725	
Operating, selling, and general and administrative expenses	41,043	36,173	31,550	27,040	22,363	
Interest costs:						
Debt	1,063	1,357	1,383	1,045	803	
Interest income	(138)	(171)	(188)	(204)	(189)	
Income tax expense	4,487	3,897	3,692	3,338	2,740	
Net income	8,039	6,671	6,295	5,377	4,430	
Per share of common stock:						
Net income	1.81	1.49	1.41	1.21	0.99	
Dividends	0.30	0.28	0.24	0.20	0.16	
Financial Position						
Current assets	$ 30,483	$ 27,878	$ 26,555	$ 24,356	$ 21,132	
Inventories at LIFO cost	24,891	22,614	21,442	19,793	17,076	$16,497
Net property, plant, and equipment	51,904	45,750	40,934	35,969	25,973	
Total assets	94,685	83,527	78,130	70,349	49,996	
Current liabilities	32,617	27,282	28,949	25,803	16,762	
Long-term debt	19,608	18,732	15,655	16,674	9,607	
Shareholders' equity	39,337	35,102	31,343	25,834	21,112	
Financial Ratios						
Current ratio	0.9	1.0	0.9	0.9	1.3	
Return on assets	9.2%	8.5%	8.7%	9.5%	9.6%	
Return on shareholders' equity	21.6%	20.1%	22.0%	22.9%	22.4%	

Include the following sections in your analysis, and fully explain your final decision.

1. Trend analysis for net sales and net income (use 2001 as the base year)

2. Profitability analysis

3. Measuring ability to sell inventory (WRS uses the LIFO method)

4. Measuring ability to pay debts

5. Measuring dividends

18 Introduction to Management Accounting

Learning Objectives

1 Distinguish management accounting from financial accounting

2 Identify trends in the business environment and the role of management accountability

3 Classify costs and prepare an income statement for a service company

4 Classify costs and prepare an income statement for a merchandising company

5 Classify costs and prepare an income statement for a manufacturing company

6 Use reasonable standards to make ethical judgments

You got a 40% discount on your new Regal sport boat, and you're relaxing after a day on the lake. As you sit there, you wonder how Regal was able to sell the boat at such a low price. Management accounting information helped Regal design the boat to maximize performance while holding down costs. Managing costs helps a company sell the right product for the right price. ▪

Chapters 1 through 17 of this book laid your foundation in the building blocks of accounting:

- Accounts in the ledger for accumulating information
- Journals for recording transactions
- Financial statements for reporting operating results, financial position, and cash flows

What you've learned so far is called *financial accounting* because its main products are the financial statements.

This chapter shifts the focus to the accounting tools that managers use to run a business. As you can imagine, it's called *management accounting*. If you've ever dreamed of having your own business, you'll find management accounting fascinating.

As a college student, one of the authors of this book learned some of these tools in an accounting class. He then applied them to his father's laundry business. Dad quickly learned that some parts of the business weren't earning enough profit. The result? Dad closed a location, saved some energy, and kept the same level of income. Hopefully, you'll find management accounting equally helpful.

Before launching into how managers use accounting, let's see some of the groups to whom managers must answer. We call these groups the stakeholders of the company because each group has a stake in the business.

Management Accountability

Accountability is responsibility for one's actions. **Management accountability** is the manager's responsibility to the various stakeholders of the company. Many different stakeholders have an interest in an organization, as shown in Exhibit 18-1. Keep in mind that managers are merely the employees of the owners.

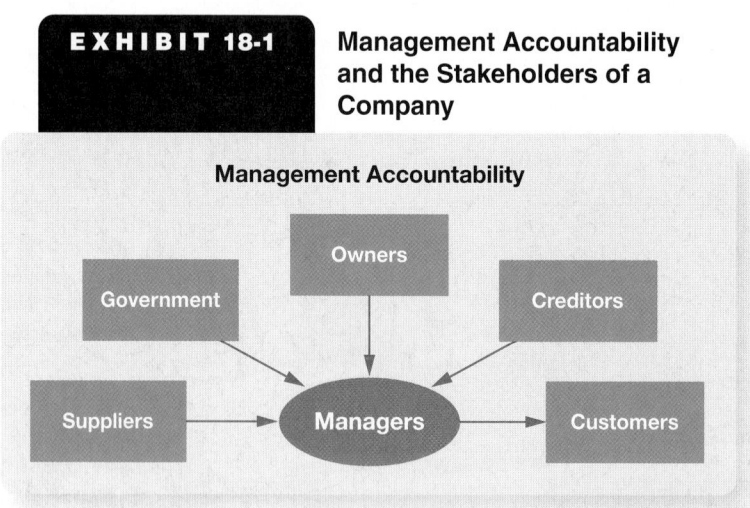

EXHIBIT 18-1 Management Accountability and the Stakeholders of a Company

Exhibit 18-2 shows the links between management and the various stakeholders of a company. The exhibit is organized by the three main categories of cash-flow activities: operating, investing, and financing. For each activity we list the stakeholders and what they provide to the organization. The far-right column then shows how managers are accountable to the stakeholders.

	EXHIBIT 18-2	Management Accountability to Stakeholders

Stakeholders	Provide and	Management is accountable for
Operating activities		
Suppliers	Products and services	Using the goods and services to earn a profit
Employees	Time and expertise	Providing a safe and productive work environment
Customers	Cash	Providing products and services for a reasonable price
Investing activities		
Suppliers	Long-term assets (equipment, buildings, land)	Purchasing the most productive assets
Financing activities		
Owners	Cash or other assets	Providing a return on the owners' investment
Creditors	Cash	Repaying principal and interest
Actions that affect society		
Governments	Permission to operate	Obeying laws and paying taxes
Communities	Human and physical resources	Providing jobs and operating in an ethical manner to support the community

To earn the stakeholders' trust, managers provide information about their decisions and the results of those decisions. Thus, management accountability requires two forms of accounting:

- Financial accounting for *external* reporting
- Management accounting for *internal* planning and control

This chapter launches your study of management accounting.

Financial accounting provides financial statements that report results of operations, financial position, and cash flows both to managers and to external stakeholders: owners, creditors, suppliers, customers, the government, and society. Financial accounting satisfies management's accountability to:

- Owners and creditors for their investment decisions
- Regulatory agencies, such as the Securities Exchange Commission, the Federal Trade Commission, and the Internal Revenue Service
- Customers and society to ensure that the company acts responsibly

The financial statements that you studied in chapters 1 through 17 report on the company as a whole.

Management accounting provides information to help managers plan and control operations as they lead the business. This includes managing the company's plant, equipment, and human resources. Management accounting often requires forward-looking information because of the futuristic nature of business decisions.

Managers are responsible to external stakeholders, so they must plan and control operations carefully.

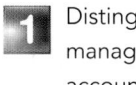 Distinguish management accounting from financial accounting

- **Planning** means choosing goals and deciding how to achieve them. For example, a common goal is to increase operating income (profits). To achieve this goal, managers may raise selling prices or advertise more in the hope of increasing sales. The **budget** is a quantitative expression of the plan that managers use to coordinate the business's activities. The budget shows the expected financial impact of decisions and helps identify the resources needed to achieve goals.
- **Controlling** means implementing the plans and evaluating operations by comparing actual results to the budget. For example, managers can compare actual costs to budgeted costs to evaluate their performance. If actual costs fall below budgeted costs, that is good news. But if actual costs exceed the budget, managers may need to make changes. Cost data help managers make these types of decisions.

Exhibit 18-3 highlights the differences between management accounting and financial accounting. Both management accounting and financial accounting use the accrual basis of accounting. But management accounting is required to meet no external reporting requirements, such as generally accepted accounting principles. Therefore, managers have more leeway in preparing management accounting reports, as you can see in points 1 through 4 of the exhibit.

Managers tailor their management accounting system to help them make wise decisions. Managers weigh the *benefits* of the system (better information leads to higher profits) against the *costs* to develop and run the system. Weighing the costs against benefits is called **cost/benefit analysis**. To remain in service, a management accounting system's benefits must exceed its costs.

EXHIBIT 18-3 **Management Accounting Versus Financial Accounting**

	Management Accounting	Financial Accounting
1. Primary users	Internal—the company's managers	External—investors, creditors, and government authorities
2. Purpose of information	Help managers plan and control operations	Help investors and creditors make investment and credit decisions
3. Focus and time dimension of the information	Relevance of the information and focus on the future—example: 2009 budget prepared in 2008	Relevance and reliability of the information and focus on the past—example: 2009 actual performance reported in 2010
4. Type of report	Internal reports are restricted only by cost/benefit analysis; no audit required	Financial statements are restricted by GAAP and audited by independent CPAs
5. Scope of information	Detailed reports on parts of the company (products, departments, territories), often on a daily or weekly basis	Summary reports primarily on the company as a whole, usually on a quarterly or annual basis
6. Behavioral	Concern about how reports will affect employee behavior	Concern about adequacy of disclosures; behavioral implications are secondary

Point 5 indicates that management accounting provides more detailed and timely information than does financial accounting. On a day-to-day basis, managers identify ways to cut costs, set prices, and evaluate employee performance. Company Intranets and handheld computers provide this information with the click of a mouse.

Point 6 reminds us that management accounting reports affect people's behavior. "You get what you measure," so employees perform well on the parts of their jobs that the accounting system measures. For example, if a manufacturing company evaluates a plant manager based only on costs, the manager may use cheaper materials or hire less experienced workers. These actions will cut costs, but they can hurt profits if product quality drops and sales fall as a result. Therefore, managers must consider how their decisions will motivate company employees.

Today's Business Environment

Today's business environment affects everyone. Managers of both large corporations and mom-and-pop businesses must consider recent trends, such as the following.

2 Identify trends in the business environment and the role of management accountability.

- **Shift Toward a Service Economy**   Service companies provide health-care, communication, banking, and other important benefits to society. FedEx, Google, and Citibank don't sell products; they sell their services. In the last century, many developed economies shifted their focus from manufacturing to service, and now service companies employ more than 55% of the workforce. The U.S. Census Bureau expects services, such as technology and health care, to grow especially fast.
- **Global Competition**   To be competitive, many companies are moving operations to other countries to be closer to new markets. Other companies are partnering with foreign companies to meet local needs. For example, Ford, General Motors, and DaimlerChrysler all built plants in Brazil to feed Brazil's car-hungry middle class.
- **Time-Based Competition**   The Internet, electronic commerce (e-commerce), and express delivery speed the pace of business. Customers who instant message around the world won't wait two weeks to receive DVDs purchased on Amazon.com. Time is the new competitive turf for world-class business. To compete, companies have developed the following:

    Advanced Information Systems   Many companies use **enterprise resource planning (ERP) systems** to integrate all their worldwide functions, departments, and data. ERP systems help to streamline operations, and that enables companies to respond quickly to changes in the marketplace.

    E-Commerce   Companies use the Internet in everyday operations of selling and customer service. For example, a sales clerk can sell to thousands of customers around the world by providing every product the company offers 24-7.

    Just-in-time Management   Inventory held too long becomes obsolete. Storing goods takes space that costs money. The just-in-time philosophy helps managers cut costs by speeding the transformation of raw materials into finished products. **Just-in-time (JIT)** means producing *just in time* to satisfy needs. Ideally, suppliers deliver materials for today's production in exactly the right quantities *just in time* to begin production, and finished units are completed *just in time* for delivery to customers.

- **Total Quality Management**   Companies must deliver high-quality goods and services to stay alive. **Total quality management (TQM)** is a philosophy designed to provide customers with superior products and services. Companies achieve this goal by continuously improving quality and reducing or eliminating defects and waste. In TQM, each business function sets higher and higher goals. With TQM, General Motors was able to cut warranty cost from $1,600 to $1,000 per vehicle.

Now let's see how different types of companies use management accounting.

- Service companies
- Merchandising companies
- Manufacturing companies

Service Companies, Merchandising Companies, and Manufacturing Companies

3 Classify costs and prepare an income statement for a service company

In this section we compare and contrast the accounting by three different types of businesses. We begin with service companies.

Service companies, such as eBay (online auction), H&R Block (tax-return preparation), and Randstad (temporary personnel services), sell services. As with other types of businesses, service companies seek to provide three things:

- Quality services
- At a reasonable price
- In a timely manner

Management is accountable to owners to generate a profit and provide a reasonable return on the owner's investment in the company.

Service companies have the simplest accounting. Service companies carry no inventories of products for sale. All of their costs are period costs. **Period costs** are those costs that are incurred and expensed in the same accounting period.

To illustrate the differences in accounting for service companies, merchandisers, and manufacturers, we use three separate companies:

- Service — Joe's Delivery Service delivers for Maria's Birthday Cakes.
- Merchandising — Maria's Birthday Cakes buys the cakes—ready for delivery—from Roberto's Bakery.
- Manufacturing — Roberto's Bakery makes the cakes for sale to Maria's.

We now take you through the accounting for these three businesses. Let's look first at Joe's Delivery Service. Joe Baca's college friend, Maria Schenk, started a business that delivers birthday cakes and a birthday card to college students. Maria's customers are the students' parents. For a small price, she delivers a cake and a birthday card, including the parents' signatures, to their student on his or her birthday. Maria pays Joe to deliver the cakes from her business to the student dorm rooms.

Here is the income statement for Joe's Delivery Service for the year ended December 31, 2009.

EXHIBIT 18-4 **Income Statement for a Service Company**

JOE'S DELIVERY SERVICE
Income Statement
Year Ended December 31, 2009

Service revenue	$ 36,000	100%
Expenses:		
Salary expense	15,000	42%
Fuel expense	3,000	8%
Depreciation expense—truck	6,000	17%
	24,000	67%
Operating income	$ 12,000	33%

The delivery service has no inventory, so Joe's income statement has no Cost of Goods Sold. The largest expense is for the salaries of drivers who deliver the birthday cakes. Salary expense eats up 42% of Joe's revenue. Joe's Delivery Service had a 33% profit margin for 2009.

Service companies need to know which services are most profitable, and that means evaluating both revenues and costs. Knowing the cost per service helps managers set the price of each service and then to calculate operating income. In 2009, Joe delivered 12,000 cakes. What is the cost per cake delivered? Use the following formula to calculate the unit cost for a service:

Unit cost
per service = Total service costs ÷ Total number of services provided
       = $24,000   ÷   12,000 cakes delivered   = $2 per cake delivered

Merchandising Companies

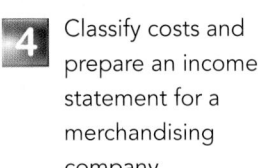

4 Classify costs and prepare an income statement for a merchandising company

Merchandising companies, such as Amazon.com, Wal-Mart, and Footlocker, resell products they buy from suppliers. Merchandisers keep an inventory of products, and managers are accountable for the purchasing, storage, and sale of the products.

In contrast with service companies, merchandisers' income statements report Cost of Goods Sold as the major expense. The cost-of-goods-sold section of the income statement shows the flow of the product costs through the inventory. These product costs are **inventoriable product costs** because the products are held in inventory until sold. For *external reporting*, Generally Accepted Accounting Principles (GAAP) require companies to treat inventoriable product costs as an asset until the product is sold, at which time the costs are expensed.

Merchandising companies' inventoriable product costs include *only* the goods' purchase cost plus freight in. The activity in the Inventory account provides the information for the cost-of-goods-sold section of the income statement as shown in the following formula:

Beginning Inventory + Purchases + Freight In − Ending Inventory = Cost of Goods Sold

To highlight the roles of beginning inventory, purchases, and ending inventory, we use the periodic inventory system. However, the concepts in this chapter apply equally to companies that use perpetual inventory systems.

In management accounting we distinguish inventoriable product costs from period costs. **Period costs** are those operating costs that are expensed in the period in which they are incurred. Therefore, period costs are the expenses that are not part of inventoriable product cost.

Let's continue with Maria Schenk's business. Exhibit 18-5 shows the income statement of Maria's Birthday Cakes for the year ended December 31, 2009.

The beginning inventory of cakes cost $300, which is the cost of the cakes still on hand at December 31, 2008. During 2009, Maria purchased additional cakes from Roberto's Bakery. The total cost to purchase and receive the cakes was $72,100. At the end of 2009, Maria's ending inventory included cakes costing $400. Of the $72,400 available for sale, the cost of cakes sold in 2009 was $72,000. Other operating expenses include the $36,000 paid to Joe's Delivery Service. This amount agrees to the service revenue shown on the income statement for Joe's Delivery Service (page 904).

Notice that cost of goods sold is 40% of sales. Managers watch the gross profit % (60% for Maria's) to make sure it doesn't change too much. A large decrease in the gross profit percentage may indicate that the company has a problem with inventory theft or shrinkage (waste). The company's profit margin is 21% for the year ended December 31, 2009.

| EXHIBIT 18-5 | Income Statement for a Merchandising Company |

MARIA'S BIRTHDAY CAKES
Income Statement
Year Ended December 31, 2009

Sales revenue		$180,000		100%
Cost of goods sold:				
Beginning inventory	$ 300			
Purchases and freight in	72,100			
Cost of goods available for sale	72,400			
Ending inventory	(400)			
Cost of goods sold		72,000		40%
Gross profit		108,000		60%
Operating expenses:				
Delivery expense	$36,000		20%	
Advertising expense	18,000		10	
Salary expense	10,000		6	
Rent expense	6,000		3	
Total operating expenses		70,000		39
Operating income		$ 38,000		21%

Merchandising companies need to know which products are most profitable. Knowing the unit cost per product helps managers set selling prices. During the year Maria sold 12,000 cakes. What is the cost of each cake she sold? Use the following formula to calculate the unit cost per cake:

Unit cost per cake = Total cost of goods sold ÷ Total number of cakes sold
              = $72,000   ÷   12,000   = $6 per cake

Now practice what you've learned by solving Summary Problem 1.

Summary Problem 1

Jackson, Inc., a retail distributor of futons, provided the following information for 2009:

Merchandise inventory, January 1	$ 20,000
Merchandise inventory, December 31	30,000
Selling expense	50,000
Delivery expense	18,000
Purchases of futons	265,000
Rent expense	15,000
Utilities expense	3,000
Freight in	15,000
Administrative expense	64,000
Sales revenue	500,000
Units sold during the year	2,500 futons

Requirements

1. Calculate cost of goods sold. What is the cost per futon sold?

2. Calculate the total period costs.

3. Prepare Jackson, Inc.'s income statement for the year ended December 31, 2009. What is the gross profit percentage? The profit margin percentage?

Solution

1. Cost of goods sold = Beginning inventory + Purchases + Freight-in − Ending inventory

   $270,000 = $20,000 + $265,000 + $15,000 − $30,000

   The cost per futon sold = Cost of goods sold ÷ number of futons sold

   $108 = $270,000 ÷ 2,500 futons

2. Total period costs include all expenses not included in inventory:

Selling expense	$ 50,000
Delivery expense	18,000
Rent expense	15,000
Utilities expense	3,000
Administrative expense	64,000
Total period costs	$150,000

3. Income Statement

<table>
<tr><td colspan="5" align="center">**JACKSON, INC.**
Income Statement
Year Ended December 31, 2009</td></tr>
<tr><td>Sales revenue</td><td></td><td></td><td>$500,000</td><td>100%</td></tr>
<tr><td>Cost of goods sold:</td><td></td><td></td><td></td><td></td></tr>
<tr><td>   Merchandise inventory, January 1</td><td>$ 20,000</td><td></td><td></td><td></td></tr>
<tr><td>   Purchases and freight in ($265,000 + $15,000)</td><td>280,000</td><td></td><td></td><td></td></tr>
<tr><td>   Cost of goods available for sale</td><td>300,000</td><td></td><td></td><td></td></tr>
<tr><td>   Merchandise inventory, December 31</td><td>30,000</td><td></td><td></td><td></td></tr>
<tr><td>Cost of goods sold</td><td></td><td></td><td>270,000</td><td>54%</td></tr>
<tr><td>Gross profit</td><td></td><td></td><td>230,000</td><td>46%</td></tr>
<tr><td>Operating expenses:</td><td></td><td></td><td></td><td></td></tr>
<tr><td>   Administrative expense</td><td>$ 64,000</td><td></td><td></td><td></td></tr>
<tr><td>   Selling expense</td><td>50,000</td><td></td><td></td><td></td></tr>
<tr><td>   Delivery expense</td><td>18,000</td><td></td><td></td><td></td></tr>
<tr><td>   Rent expense</td><td>15,000</td><td></td><td></td><td></td></tr>
<tr><td>   Utilities expense</td><td>3,000</td><td>150,000</td><td></td><td>30%</td></tr>
<tr><td>Operating income</td><td></td><td></td><td>$ 80,000</td><td>16%</td></tr>
</table>

Gross profit % = $230,000 / $500,000 = 46%

Profit margin % = $80,000 / $500,000 = 16%

Manufacturing Companies

5 Classify costs and prepare an income statement for a manufacturing company

Manufacturing companies use labor, equipment, supplies, and facilities to convert raw materials into finished products. Managers in manufacturing companies must use these resources to create a product that customers want. They are responsible for generating profits and maintaining positive cash flows.

In contrast with service and merchandising companies, manufacturing companies have a broad range of production activities. That requires tracking costs in three kinds of inventory:

1. **Materials inventory:** *Raw materials used in making a product.* For example, a baker's raw materials include flour, sugar, and eggs. Materials to manufacture a boat include fiberglass, plywood, wiring, glass, and upholstery fabric.

2. **Work in process inventory:** *Goods that are in the manufacturing process but not yet complete.* Some production activities have transformed the raw materials, but the product is not yet ready for sale. A baker's work in process inventory includes dough ready for cooking. A boat manufacturer's work in process could include a hull without an engine or seats.

3. **Finished goods inventory:** *Completed goods that have not yet been sold.* Finished goods are the products that the manufacturer sells to a merchandiser (or to other customers).

Inventoriable Product Costs

The completed product in finished goods inventory is an **inventoriable product cost.** The inventoriable product cost includes three components of manufacturing costs:

- Direct materials
- Direct labor
- Manufacturing overhead

Direct materials and direct labor are examples of direct costs. A **direct cost** is a cost that can be directly traced to a cost object, such as a product. A **cost object** is anything for which managers want a separate measurement of cost. Managers may want to know the cost of a product or a department, a sales territory, or an activity. Costs that cannot be traced directly to a cost object are **indirect costs.** In manufacturing companies, product costs include direct costs (direct materials and direct labor) and indirect costs (manufacturing overhead).

- **Direct materials** become a physical part of the finished product. The cost of direct materials (purchase cost plus freight in) can be traced directly to the finished product.
- **Direct labor** is the labor of employees who convert materials into the company's products. The cost of direct labor can be traced *directly* to the finished products.
- **Manufacturing overhead** includes all manufacturing costs other than direct materials and direct labor. These costs are created by all of the supporting production activities, including storing materials, setting up machines, and cleaning the work areas. These activities incur costs of indirect materials, indirect labor, repair and maintenance, utilities, rent, insurance, property taxes, and depreciation on manufacturing plant buildings and equipment. Manufacturing overhead is also called **factory overhead** or **indirect manufacturing cost.**

Exhibit 18-6 summarizes a manufacturer's inventoriable product costs.

EXHIBIT 18-6 Manufacturer's Inventoriable Product Costs

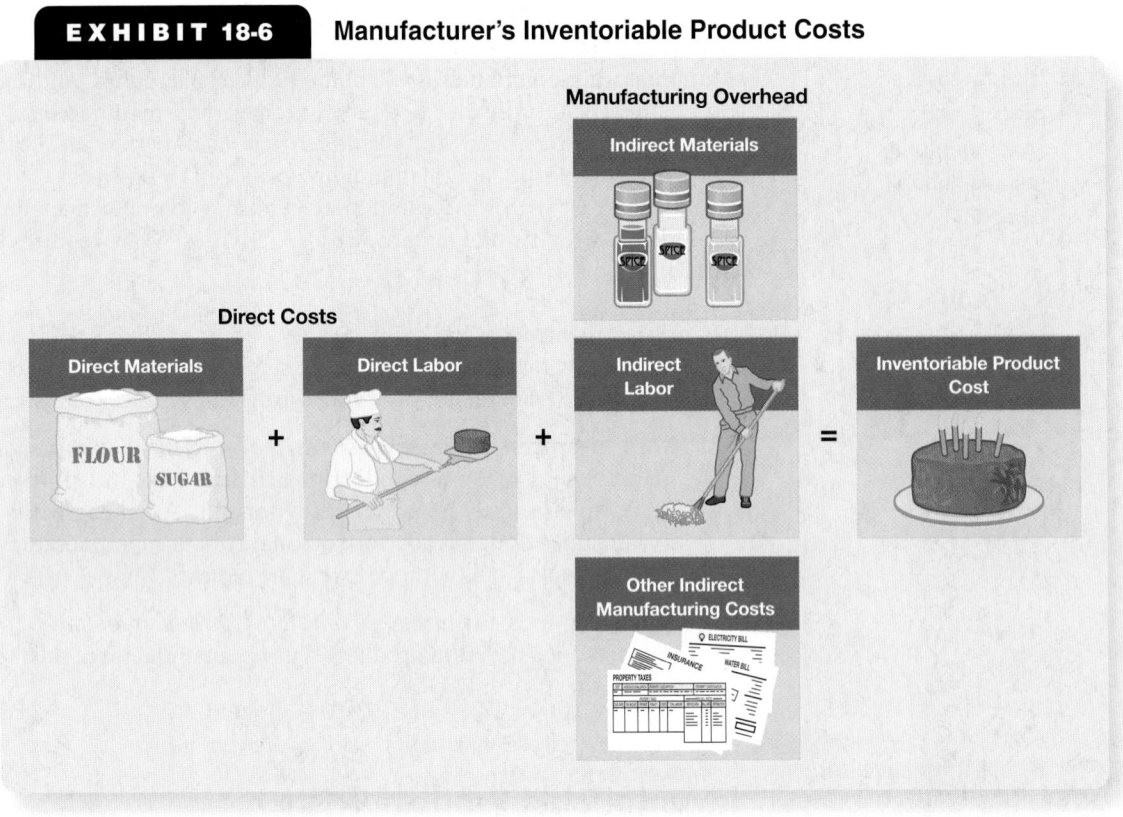

A Closer Look at Manufacturing Overhead

- *Manufacturing overhead includes only those indirect costs that are related to the manufacturing operation.* Insurance and depreciation on the *manufacturing plant's* building and equipment are indirect manufacturing costs, so they are part of manufacturing overhead. In contrast, depreciation on *delivery trucks* is not part of manufacturing overhead. Instead, depreciation on delivery trucks is a cost of moving the product to the customer. Its cost is delivery expense (a period cost), not an inventoriable product cost. Similarly, the cost of auto insurance for the sales force is marketing expense (a period cost), not manufacturing overhead.

- *Manufacturing overhead includes indirect materials and indirect labor.* The spices used in cakes become physical parts of the finished product. But these costs are minor compared with flour and sugar for the cake. Since those low-priced materials' costs can't conveniently be traced to a particular cake, these costs are called **indirect materials** and become part of manufacturing overhead.

  Like indirect materials, **indirect labor** is difficult to trace to specific products so it is part of manufacturing overhead. Examples include the pay of forklift operators, janitors, and plant managers.

Now let's look at the income statement for Roberto's Bakery for the year ended December 31, 2009, given in Exhibit 18-7. Roberto's only customer is Maria Schenk, who buys the birthday cakes and then delivers them to students.

Roberto's cost of goods sold represents 61% of his sales revenue. This is the inventoriable product cost of the goods that Roberto sold to Maria's Birthday Cakes. Roberto's balance sheet at December 31, 2009, reports the inventoriable product costs of the finished birthday cakes that are still on hand at the end of that year. The cost of the ending inventory ($600) will become the beginning inventory of

EXHIBIT 18-7	Income Statement for a Manufacturing Company

ROBERTO'S BAKERY
Income Statement
Year Ended December 31, 2009

Sales revenue		$60,000	100%
Cost of goods sold:			
Beginning finished goods inventory	$ 300		
Cost of goods manufactured*	36,900		
Cost of goods available for sale	37,200		
Ending finished goods inventory	(600)		
Cost of goods sold		36,600	61%
Gross profit		23,400	39%
Operating expenses:			
Salary expense	$ 3,000		
Depreciation expense	400	3,400	6%
Operating income		$20,000	33%

*From the Schedule of Cost of Goods Manufactured in Exhibit 18-10.

next year and will then be included as part of the Cost of Goods Sold on Roberto's income statement next year. The operating expenses, which represent 6% of sales revenue, are period costs.

Exhibit 18-8 summarizes the differences between inventoriable product costs and period costs for service, merchandising, and manufacturing companies.

EXHIBIT 18-8	Inventoriable Product Costs and Period Costs for Service, Merchandising, and Manufacturing Companies

Type of Company	Inventoriable Product Costs—Initially an asset (Inventory), and expensed (Cost of Goods Sold) when the inventory is sold	Period Costs—Expensed in the period incurred; never considered an asset
Service company	None	Salaries, depreciation, utilities, insurance, property taxes, advertising expenses
Merchandising company	Purchases plus freight in	Salaries, depreciation, utilities, insurance, property taxes, advertising, delivery expenses
Manufacturing company	Direct materials, direct labor, and manufacturing overhead (including indirect materials; indirect labor; depreciation on the manufacturing plant and equipment; plant insurance, utilities, and property taxes)	Delivery expense; depreciation expense, utilities, insurance, and property taxes on executive headquarters (separate from the manufacturing plant); advertising; CEO's salary

Let's compare Roberto's income statement in Exhibit 18-7 with Maria's income statement in Exhibit 18-5. The only difference is that the merchandiser (Maria) uses *purchases* in computing cost of goods sold, while the manufacturer (Roberto's) uses the *cost of goods manufactured*. Notice that the term **cost of goods manufactured** is in the past tense. It is the manufacturing cost of the goods that Roberto's *completed during 2009*. Here's the difference between a manufacturer and a merchandiser:

- The manufacturer *made* the product that it later sold.
- The merchandiser *purchased* a pre-manufactured product that was complete and ready for sale.

CALCULATING THE COST OF GOODS MANUFACTURED The cost of goods manufactured summarizes the activities and the costs that take place in a manufacturing plant over the period. Let's begin by reviewing these activities. Exhibit 18-9 reminds us that the manufacturer starts by buying materials. Then the manufacturer uses direct labor and manufacturing plant and equipment (overhead) to transform these materials into work in process inventory. When inventory is completed, it becomes finished goods inventory. These are all inventoriable product costs because they are related to the inventory production process.

EXHIBIT 18-9 **Manufacturing Company: Inventoriable Product Costs and Period Costs**

*Examples: Indirect labor, plant supplies, plant insurance, and depreciation. When insurance and depreciation relate to manufacturing, they are inventoriable; when they relate to nonmanufacturing functions, they are operating expenses (period costs).

Finished goods are the only category of inventory that's ready to sell. The cost of the finished goods that the manufacturer sells becomes its cost of goods sold on the income statement. Costs the manufacturer incurs in nonmanufacturing activities, such as sales salaries, are operating expenses—period costs—that are expensed in the period incurred. Exhibit 18-9 shows that these operating costs are deducted from gross profit to compute operating income.

You now have a clear understanding of the flow of activities and costs in the plant, and you're ready to figure the cost of goods manufactured. Exhibit 18-10 shows how Roberto's computes its cost of goods manufactured. This is the cost of the 12,300 cakes that Roberto *finished* during 2009.

Cost of goods manufactured summarizes the activities and related costs incurred to produce inventory during the year. As of December 31, 2008, Roberto had spent a

EXHIBIT 18-10   Schedule of Cost of Goods Manufactured

ROBERTO'S BAKERY
Schedule of Cost of Goods Manufactured
Year Ended December 31, 2009

Beginning work in process inventory			$ 800
Add: Direct materials used			
Beginning materials inventory	$ 150		
Purchases of direct materials plus freight in	10,800		
Available for use	10,950		
Ending materials inventory	(50)		
Direct materials used		$10,900	
Direct labor		12,100	
Manufacturing overhead:			
Indirect materials	$3,600		
Indirect labor	3,000		
Depreciation—plant and equipment	6,000		
Plant utilities, insurance, and property taxes	600		
		13,200	
Total manufacturing costs incurred during year			36,200
Total manufacturing costs to account for			37,000
Less: Ending work in process inventory			(100)
Costs of goods manufactured			$36,900

total of $800 to partially complete the cakes still being made. This 2008 ending work in process inventory became the beginning work in process inventory for 2009.

Exhibit 18-10 shows that during the year, Roberto's Bakery used $10,900 of direct materials, $12,100 of direct labor, and $13,200 of manufacturing overhead.

Total manufacturing costs incurred during the year are the sum of these three amounts:

TOTAL MANUFACTURING COSTS	
Direct materials used	$10,900
Direct labor	12,100
Manufacturing overhead	13,200
Total manufacturing costs incurred...........	$36,200

Adding total manufacturing cost ($36,200) to the beginning Work in Process Inventory of $800 gives the total manufacturing cost to account for, $37,000. At December 31, 2009, unfinished cakes costing only $100 remained in Work in Process (WIP) Inventory. The bakery finished 12,300 cakes and sent them to Finished Goods (FG) Inventory. Cost of goods manufactured for the year was $36,900. Here's the computation of cost of goods manufactured:

Beginning WIP	+	Direct materials used	+	Direct labor	+	Manufacturing overhead	−	Ending WIP	=	Cost of goods manufactured
$800	+	$10,900	+	$12,100	+	$13,200	−	$100	=	$36,900

FLOW OF COSTS THROUGH THE INVENTORY ACCOUNTS Exhibit 18-11 diagrams the flow of costs through Roberto's inventory accounts. The format is the same for all three stages:

- Direct materials
- Work in process
- Finished goods

The final amount at each stage flows into the next stage. Take time to see how the schedule of cost of goods manufactured in Exhibit 18-11 uses the flows of the direct materials and work in process stages. Then examine the income statement for Maria's Birthday Cakes in Exhibit 18-5. Maria, the merchandiser, uses only a single Inventory account.

EXHIBIT 18-11   Flow of Costs Through a Manufacturer's Inventory Accounts

Direct Materials Inventory		Work in Process Inventory		Finished Goods Inventory	
Beginning inventory	$ 150	Beginning inventory	$ 800	Beginning inventory	$ 300
+ Purchases and freight in	10,800	+ Direct materials used	$10,900	+ Cost of goods	
		+ Direct labor	12,100	manufactured	36,900
		+ Manufacturing overhead	13,200		
		Total manufacturing costs			
		incurred during the year	36,200		
= Direct materials available		= Total manufacturing costs		= Cost of goods available	
for use	10,950	to account for	37,000	for sale	37,200
− Ending inventory	(50)	− Ending inventory	(100)	− Ending inventory	(600)
= Direct materials used	$10,900	= Cost of goods manufactured	$36,900	= Cost of goods sold	$36,600

Source: The authors are indebted to Judith Cassidy for this presentation.

Calculating Unit Product Cost

Manufacturing companies need to know which products are most profitable. Knowing the unit product cost helps managers decide on the prices to charge for each product. They can then measure operating income and determine the cost of finished goods inventory. Roberto produced 12,300 cakes during 2009. What did it cost Roberto to make each cake?

Unit product cost = Cost of goods manufactured ÷ Total units produced

= $36,900 ÷ 12,300 cakes = $3 per cake

During 2009, Roberto sold 12,200 cakes, and he knows each cake cost $3 to produce. With this information Roberto can compute his cost of goods sold as a manager would, as follows:

$$\frac{\text{Cost of}}{\text{goods sold}} = \frac{\text{Number of}}{\text{units sold}} \times \frac{\text{Unit product}}{\text{cost}}$$

= 12,200 × $3 = $36,600

Ethical Standards

6 Use reasonable standards to make ethical judgments

The WorldCom and Enron scandals underscore that ethical behavior is a critical component of quality. Unfortunately, the ethical path is not always clear. You may want to act ethically and do the right thing, but the consequences can make it difficult to decide what to do. Consider the following examples:

- Sarah Baker is examining the expense reports of her staff, who counted inventory at Top-Flight's warehouses in Arizona. She discovers that Mike Flinders has claimed travel expenses of $1,000 for hotel bills. Flinders could not show the paid receipts. Another staff member, who also claimed $1,000, did attach hotel receipts. When asked about the receipt, Mike admits that he stayed with an old friend, not in the hotel, but he believes he deserves the money he saved. After all, the company would have paid his hotel bill.
- As the accountant of Casey Computer Co., you are aware of Casey's weak financial condition. Casey is close to signing a lucrative contract that should ensure its future. To do so, the controller states that the company *must* report a profit this year. He suggests: "Two customers have placed orders that are to be shipped in early January. Ask production to fill and ship those orders on December 31, so we can record them in this year's sales."

These situations pose ethical challenges for a manager. The Institute of Management Accountants (IMA) has developed standards to help management accountants meet the ethical challenge. The IMA standards remind us that society expects professional accountants to exhibit the highest level of ethical behavior. An excerpt from the *Standards of Ethical Conduct for Management Accountants* appears in Exhibit 18-12. These standards require management accountants to:

- Maintain their professional competence
- Preserve the confidentiality of the information they handle
- Act with integrity and objectivity

EXHIBIT 18-12 IMA Standards of Ethical Conduct for Management Accountants (excerpt)

Management accountants have an obligation to maintain the highest standards of ethical conduct. These standards include the following:
Competence
- Maintain professional competence by ongoing development of knowledge and skills
- Perform professional duties in accordance with relevant laws, regulations, and technical standards
Confidentiality
- Refrain from disclosing confidential information acquired in the course of work except when authorized, unless legally obligated to do so
Integrity
- Avoid actual or apparent conflicts of interest and advise all appropriate parties of any potential conflict
- Refuse any gift, favor, or hospitality that would influence or would appear to influence actions
- Communicate unfavorable as well as favorable information and professional judgments or opinions
Objectivity
- Communicate information fairly and objectively

Source: Adapted from Institute of Management Accountants, *Standards of Ethical Conduct for Management Accountants* (Montvale, N.J.).

To resolve ethical dilemmas, the IMA also suggests discussing ethical situations with your immediate supervisor, or with an objective adviser.

Let's return to the two ethical dilemmas. By asking to be reimbursed for hotel expenses he did not incur, Mike Flinders violated the IMA's integrity standards (conflict of interest in which he tried to enrich himself at the company's expense). Because Sarah Baker discovered the inflated expense report, she would not be fulfilling her ethical responsibilities (integrity and objectivity) if she allowed the reimbursement and did not take disciplinary action.

The second dilemma, in which the controller asked you to accelerate the shipments, is less clear-cut. You should discuss the available alternatives and their consequences with others. Many people believe that following the controller's suggestion to manipulate the company's income would violate the standards of competence, integrity, and objectivity. Others would argue that because Casy Computer already has the customer order, shipping the goods and recording the sale in December is still ethical behavior. If you refuse to ship the goods in December and you simply resign without attempting to find an alternative solution, you might only hurt yourself and your family.

Decision Guidelines

Hewlett-Packard (HP) engages in *manufacturing* when it assembles its computers, *merchandising* when it sells them on its Web site, and support *services* such as start-up and implementation services. HP had to make the following decisions in designing its management accounting system to provide managers with the information they need to run the manufacturing, merchandising, and service operations efficiently and effectively.

Decision	Guidelines
What information should management accountants provide? What is the primary focus of management accounting?	Management accounting provides information that helps managers make better decisions; it has a • Focus on *relevance* to business decisions • *Future* orientation
How do you decide on a company's management accounting system, which is not regulated by GAAP?	Use cost/benefit analysis: Design the management accounting system so that benefits (from helping managers make wise decisions) outweigh the costs of the system.
How do you distinguish among service, merchandising, and manufacturing companies? How do their balance sheets differ?	*Service companies:* • Provide customers with intangible services • Have no inventories on the balance sheet *Merchandising companies:* • Resell tangible products purchased ready-made from suppliers • Have only one category of inventory *Manufacturing companies:* • Use labor, plant, and equipment to transform raw materials into new finished products • Have three categories of inventory: Materials inventory Work in process inventory Finished goods inventory
How do you compute cost of goods sold?	• *Service companies:* No cost of goods sold, because they don't sell tangible goods • *Merchandising companies:* Beginning *merchandise* inventory + Purchases and freight in – Ending *merchandise* inventory = Cost of goods sold • *Manufacturing companies:* Beginning *finished goods* inventory + Cost of goods manufactured – Ending *finished goods* inventory = Cost of goods sold

Decision	Guidelines
How do you compute the cost of goods manufactured for a manufacturer?	Beginning *work in process* inventory + Current period manufacturing costs (direct materials used + direct labor + manufacturing overhead) – Ending *work in process* inventory = Cost of goods manufactured
Which costs are initially treated as assets for external reporting? When are these costs expensed?	*Inventoriable product costs* are initially treated as assets (Inventory); these costs are expensed (as Cost of Goods Sold) when the products are sold.
What costs are inventoriable under GAAP?	• *Service companies:* No inventoriable product costs • *Merchandising companies:* Purchases and freight in • *Manufacturing companies:* Direct materials used, direct labor, and manufacturing overhead
Which costs are never inventoriable product costs?	Period costs. These are never assets. They're always expenses.

Summary Problem 2

Requirements

1. For a manufacturing company, identify the following as either an inventoriable product cost or a period cost:

   a. Depreciation on plant equipment

   b. Depreciation on salespersons' automobiles

   c. Insurance on plant building

   d. Marketing manager's salary

   e. Raw materials

   f. Manufacturing overhead

   g. Electricity bill for home office

   h. Production employee wages

2. Show how to compute cost of goods manufactured. Use the following amounts: direct materials used ($24,000); direct labor ($9,000); manufacturing overhead ($17,000); beginning work in process inventory ($5,000); and ending work in process inventory ($4,000).

Solution

1. Inventoriable product cost: a, c, e, f, h
   Period cost: b, d, g

2. Cost of goods manufactured:

Beginning work in process inventory......................................		$ 5,000
Add: Direct materials used	$24,000	
Direct labor	9,000	
Manufacturing overhead	17,000	
Total manufacturing costs incurred during the period ..		50,000
Total manufacturing costs to account for		55,000
Less: Ending work in process inventory		(4,000)
Cost of goods manufactured		$51,000

Review *Introduction to Management Accounting*

Accounting Vocabulary

Controlling
Implementing plans and evaluating the results of business operations by comparing the actual results to the budget.

Cost/Benefit Analysis
Weighing costs against benefits to help make decisions.

Cost Object
Anything for which managers want a separate measurement of cost.

Cost of Goods Manufactured
The manufacturing or plant-related costs of the goods that finished the production process this period.

Direct Cost
A cost that can be traced to a cost object.

Direct Labor
The compensation of employees who physically convert materials into finished products.

Direct Materials
Materials that become a physical part of a finished product and whose costs are traceable to the finished product.

Enterprise Resource Planning (ERP)
Software systems that can integrate all of a company's worldwide functions, departments, and data into a single system.

Factory Overhead
All manufacturing costs other than direct materials and direct labor. Also called **manufacturing overhead** or **indirect manufacturing costs**.

Finished Goods Inventory
Completed goods that have not yet been sold.

Indirect Cost
A cost that cannot be traced to a cost object.

Indirect Labor
Labor costs that are difficult to trace to specific products.

Indirect Manufacturing Cost
All manufacturing costs other than direct materials and direct labor. Also called **factory overhead** or **manufacturing overhead**.

Indirect Materials
Materials whose costs cannot conveniently be directly traced to particular finished products.

Inventoriable Product Costs
All costs of a product that GAAP requires companies to treat as an asset for external financial reporting. These costs are not expensed until the product is sold.

Just-in-Time (JIT)
A system in which a company produces just in time to satisfy needs. Suppliers deliver materials just in time to begin production and finished units are completed just in time for delivery to the customer.

Management Accountability
The manager's fiduciary responsibility to manage the resources of an organization.

Management Accounting
The branch of accounting that focuses on information for internal decision makers of a business.

Manufacturing Company
A company that uses labor, plant, and equipment to convert raw materials into new finished products.

Manufacturing Overhead
All manufacturing costs other than direct materials and direct labor. Also called **factory overhead** or **indirect manufacturing costs**.

Materials Inventory
Raw materials for use in manufacturing.

Merchandising Company
A company that resells products previously bought from suppliers.

Period Costs
Operating costs that are expensed in the period in which they are incurred.

Planning
Choosing goals and deciding how to achieve them.

Service Company
A company that sells intangible services, rather than tangible products.

Total Manufacturing Costs
Costs that include direct materials, direct labor, and manufacturing overhead.

Total Quality Management (TQM)
A philosophy of delighting customers by providing them with superior products and services. Requires improving quality and eliminating defects and waste throughout the value chain.

Work in Process Inventory
Goods that are partway through the manufacturing process but not yet complete.

Quick Check

1. Which is *not* a characteristic of management accounting information?
   a. Emphasizes the external financial statements
   b. Focuses on the future
   c. Provides detailed information about individual parts of the company
   d. Emphasizes relevance

2. World-class businesses must compete based on time. To compete effectively many companies have developed
   a. Enterprise resource planning
   b. Cost standards
   c. Just-in-time management
   d. All of the above

3. Today's business environment is characterized by
   a. Shift toward a service economy
   b. Global competition
   c. Time-based competition
   d. All of the above

4. Which account does PepsiCo, but not FedEx (a service company) have?
   a. Advertising expense
   b. Cost of goods sold
   c. Salary payable
   d. Retained earnings

5. Which is a direct cost of manufacturing a sportboat?
   a. Cost of boat engine
   b. Depreciation on plant and equipment
   c. Salary of engineer who rearranges plant layout
   d. Cost of customer hotline

6. Which of the following is *not* part of manufacturing overhead for producing a computer?
   a. Insurance on plant and equipment
   b. Manufacturing plant property taxes
   c. Depreciation on delivery trucks
   d. Manufacturing plant utilities

7. In computing cost of goods sold, which of the following is the manufacturer's counterpart to the merchandiser's purchases?
   a. Direct materials used
   b. Cost of goods manufactured
   c. Total manufacturing costs to account for
   d. Total manufacturing costs incurred during the period

Questions 8 and 9 use the data that follow. Suppose a bakery reports this information (in thousands of dollars):

Beginning materials inventory	$ 6
Ending materials inventory	5
Beginning work in process inventory	2
Ending work in process inventory	1
Beginning finished goods inventory	3
Ending finished goods inventory	5
Direct labor	30
Purchases of direct materials	100
Manufacturing overhead	20

8. If the cost of direct materials used is $101, what is cost of goods manufactured?
   a. $152
   b. $151
   c. $150
   d. $149

9. If the cost of goods manufactured is $152, what is cost of goods sold?
   a. $154
   b. $153
   c. $152
   d. $150

10. A management accountant who avoids conflicts of interest meets the ethical standard of
   a. Objectivity
   b. Confidentiality
   c. Competence
   d. Integrity

Answers are given after Apply Your Knowledge (p. 941).

Assess Your Progress

Short Exercises

Business trends terminology

2

S18-1 Match the term with the definition below. (pp. 920–921)

    a. ERP

    b. Just-in-time (JIT)

    c. E-commerce

    d. Total quality management

    _____ 1. A philosophy of delighting customers by providing them with superior products and services. Requires improving quality and eliminating defects and waste.

    _____ 2. Use of the Internet for such business functions as sales and customer service. Enables companies to reach thousands of customers around the world.

    _____ 3. Software systems that integrate all of a company's worldwide functions, departments, and data into a single system.

    _____ 4. A system in which a company produces just in time to satisfy needs. Suppliers deliver materials just in time to begin production, and finished units are completed just in time for delivery to customers.

Management accountability and the stakeholders

2

S18-2 Management has the responsibility to manage the resources of an organization in a responsible manner. For each of the following management responsibilities, indicate the primary stakeholder group to whom management is responsible. In the space provided, write the letter corresponding to the appropriate stakeholder group. (pp. 900–902).

    _____ 1. Providing high-quality, reliable products/services for a reasonable price in a timely manner

    _____ 2. Paying taxes in a timely manner

    _____ 3. Providing a safe, productive work environment

    _____ 4. Generating a profit

    _____ 5. Repaying principal plus interest in a timely manner

    a. Owners

    b. Creditors

    c. Suppliers

    d. Employees

    e. Customers

    f. Government

    g. Community

Management accounting vs. financial accounting

1

S18-3 For each of the following, indicate whether the statement relates to management accounting (MA) or financial accounting (FA): (pp. 901–902)

    _____ 1. Helps investors make investment decisions

    _____ 2. Provides detailed reports on parts of the company

    _____ 3. Helps in planning and controlling operations

    _____ 4. Reports can influence employee behavior

continued . . .

_____ **5.** Reports must following Generally Accepted Accounting Principles (GAAP)

_____ **6.** Reports audited annually by independent certified public accountants

Calculating income and cost per unit for a service organization

3

S18-4 Duncan and Noble provides hair cutting services in the local community. In August, Carol Duncan, the owner, incurred the following operating costs to cut the hair of 200 clients:

Hair supplies expense....................	$ 700
Building rent expense	1,100
Utilities	150
Depreciation on equipment...........	50

Duncan and Noble earned $5,000 in revenues from haircuts for the month of August. What is the net operating income for the month? What is the cost of one haircut? (pp. 903–905)

Computing cost of goods sold

4

S18-5 The Glass Doctor, a retail merchandiser of auto windshields, has the following information.

Web site maintenance	$ 7,000
Delivery expenses	1,000
Freight in	3,000
Purchases...............................	40,000
Ending inventory	5,000
Revenues	60,000
Marketing expenses................	10,000
Beginning inventory................	8,000

Compute The Glass Doctor's cost of goods sold. (pp. 905–906)

Computing cost of goods sold

4

S18-6 Compute the missing amounts.

	Company A	Company B
Sales...	$100,000	(d)
Cost of goods sold		
Beginning inventory.............................	(a)	$ 30,000
Purchases and freight in.......................	59,000	(e)
Cost of goods available for sale	(b)	90,000
Ending inventory	2,000	2,000
Cost of goods sold	60,000	(f)
Gross margin...	$ 40,000	$112,000
Selling and administrative expenses.........	(c)	85,000
Operating income....................................	$ 12,000	(g)

Match type of company with product and period costs
3 4 5

S18-7 For each of the following costs, indicate if the cost would be found on the income statement of a service company (S), a merchandising company (Mer), and/or a manufacturing company (Man). Some costs can be found on the income statements of more than one type of company. (pp. 903–914)

S, Mer, Man Example: Advertising costs

_____ 1. Cost of goods manufactured

_____ 2. The CEO's salary

_____ 3. Cost of goods sold

_____ 4. Building rent expense

_____ 5. Customer service expense

Computing direct materials used
5

S18-8 You are a new accounting intern at Cookies By Design. Your boss gives you the following information:

Purchases of direct materials	$6,500
Freight in	200
Property taxes	1,000
Ending inventory of direct materials	1,500
Beginning inventory of direct materials	4,000

Compute direct materials used. (p. 909)

Distinguishing between direct and indirect costs
5

S18-9 Consider Hallmark Cards' manufacturing plant. Match one of the following terms with each example of a manufacturing cost given below:

1. Direct materials
2. Direct labor
3. Indirect materials
4. Indirect labor
5. Other manufacturing overhead

Examples of manufacturing costs: (p. 910)

_____ a. Artists' wages

_____ b. Wages of warehouse workers

_____ c. Paper

_____ d. Depreciation on equipment

_____ e. Manufacturing plant manager's salary

_____ f. Property taxes on manufacturing plant

_____ g. Glue for envelopes

Computing manufacturing overhead
5

S18-10 Polo Company manufactures sunglasses. Suppose the company's March records include the following items.

Glue for frames	$ 250	Company president's salary	$25,000
Depreciation expense on company cars used by sales force	3,000	Plant foreman's salary	4,000
		Plant janitor's wages	1,000
Plant depreciation expense	7,000	Oil for manufacturing equipment	50
Interest expense	2,000	Lenses	50,000

continued . . .

List the items and amounts that are manufacturing overhead costs. Calculate Polo's total manufacturing overhead cost in March. (pp. 912–913)

Compute cost of goods manufactured

S18-11 Max-Fli Golf Company had the following inventory data for the year ended December 31, 2008:

Direct materials used......................	$12,000
Manufacturing overhead	18,000
Work in process inventory:	
Beginning....................................	7,000
Ending	5,000
Direct labor....................................	9,000
Finished goods inventory.................	10,000

Compute Max-Fli's cost of goods manufactured for 2008. (pp. 912–913)

Inventoriable product costs vs. period costs

S18-12 Classify each of a paper manufacturer's costs as an inventoriable product cost or a period cost: (pp. 909–912)

a. Salaries of scientists studying ways to speed forest growth

b. Cost of computer software to track inventory

c. Cost of electricity at a paper mill

d. Salaries of the company's top executives

e. Cost of chemicals to treat paper

f. Cost of TV ads

g. Depreciation on the gypsum board plant

h. Cost of lumber to be cut into boards

i. Life insurance on CEO

Ethical decisions

S18-13 The Institute of Management Accountants' *Standards of Ethical Conduct for Management Accountants* (Exhibit 18-12, page 915) require management accountants to meet standards regarding:

- Competence
- Confidentiality
- Integrity
- Objectivity

Consider the following situations. Which guidelines are violated in each situation? (pp. 915–916)

a. You tell your brother that your company will report earnings significantly above financial analysts' estimates.

b. You see that others take home office supplies for personal use. As an intern, you do the same thing, assuming that this is a "perk."

c. At a conference on e-commerce, you skip the afternoon session and go sightseeing.

d. You failed to read the detailed specifications of a new general ledger package that you asked your company to purchase. After it is

continued . . .

installed, you are surprised that it is incompatible with some of your company's older accounting software.

e. You do not provide top management with the detailed job descriptions they requested because you fear they may use this information to cut a position from your department.

Exercises

Understanding today's business environment

2

E18-14 Complete the following statements with one of the terms listed here.

E-commerce	Just-in-time (JIT) manufacturing
Enterprise Resource Planning (ERP)	Total quality management (TQM)

a. _____ is a management philosophy that focuses on producing products as needed by the customer.

b. The goal of _____ is to please customers by providing them with superior products and services by eliminating defects and waste.

c. _____ can integrate all of a company's worldwide functions, departments, and data.

d. Firms adopt _____ to conduct business on the Internet.

Management vs. financial accounting and managers' use of information

1

E18-15 Complete the following statements with one of the terms listed here. You may use a term more than once, and some terms may not be used at all. (p. 901)

Budget	Creditors	Managers	Planning
Controlling	Financial accounting	Management accounting	Shareholders

a. Companies must follow GAAP in their _____ systems.

b. Financial accounting develops reports for external parties, such as _____ and _____.

c. When managers compare the company's actual results to the plan, they are performing the _____ role of management.

d. _____ are decision makers inside a company.

e. _____ provides information on a company's past performance.

f. _____ systems are not restricted by GAAP but are chosen by comparing the costs versus the benefits of the system.

g. Choosing goals and the means to achieve them is the _____ function of management.

Calculating income and cost per unit for a service company

3

E18-16 Fido Grooming provides grooming services in the local community. In July, John Conway, owner, incurred the following operating costs to groom 600 dogs:

Wages	$4,800
Grooming supplies expense	1,200
Building rent expense	1,000
Utilities	250
Depreciation on equipment	100

continued . . .

Fido Grooming earned $15,000 in revenues from grooming for the month of July.

Requirement

What is Fido's net operating income for July? What is the cost to groom one dog? (pp. 904–905)

Preparing an income statement and computing the unit cost for a service company

E18-17 Gloria's Grooming is a competitor of Fido Grooming. Gloria Stanley, owner, incurred the following operating costs to groom 2,000 dogs for the first quarter of 2009 (January, February, and March):

Wages	$16,000
Grooming supplies expense	4,000
Building rent expense	2,500
Utilities	1,000
Depreciation on furniture and equipment	500

Gloria's Grooming earned $45,000 in revenues for the first quarter of 2009.

Requirements

1. Prepare an income statement for the first quarter of 2009. Compute the ratio of operating expense to total revenue and operating income to total revenue. (pp. 904–905)
2. Compute Gloria's unit cost to groom one dog. (pp. 905–906)

Preparing an income statement and computing the unit cost for a merchandising company

E18-18 Kingston Brush Company sells standard hair brushes. The following information summarizes Kingston's operating activities for 2009:

Selling and administrative expenses	$ 45,000
Purchases	63,000
Sales revenue	125,000
Merchandise inventory, January 1, 2009	7,000
Merchandise inventory, December 31, 2009	5,000

Requirements

1. Prepare an income statement for 2009. Compute the ratio of operating expense to total revenue and operating income to total revenue. (pp. 905–906)
2. Kingston sold 5,800 brushes in 2009. Compute the unit cost for one brush. (pp. 905–906)

Service, merchandising, and manufacturing companies and their inventories

E18-19 Complete the following statements with one of the terms listed here. You may use a term more than once, and some terms may not be used at all. (pp. 904–909)

Finished goods inventory	Merchandise inventory	Service companies
Manufacturing companies	Merchandising companies	Work in process inventory
Materials inventory		

continued . . .

a. _____ produce their own inventory.

b. _____ typically have a single category of inventory.

c. _____ do not have tangible products intended for sale.

d. _____ resell products they previously purchased ready-made from suppliers.

e. _____ use their workforce and equipment to transform raw materials into new finished products.

f. Swaim, a company based in North Carolina, makes furniture. Partially completed sofas are _____. Completed sofas that remain unsold in the warehouse are _____. Fabric and wood are _____.

g. For Kellogg's, corn, cardboard boxes, and waxed-paper liners are classified as _____.

Cost terminology
3 4 5

E18-20 Match one of the following terms with each definition below. (pp. 909–910)

a. Direct labor   e. Inventoriable product costs

b. Direct materials   f. Manufacturing overhead

c. Indirect labor   g. Period costs

d. Indirect materials

_____ 1. Operating costs that are expensed in the period in which they are incurred.

_____ 2. Materials that become a physical part of a finished product and whose costs are traceable to the finished product.

_____ 3. All manufacturing costs other than direct materials and direct labor.

_____ 4. Labor costs that are difficult to trace to specific products.

_____ 5. Materials whose costs cannot conveniently be directly traced to particular finished products.

_____ 6. Product costs included in inventory, as required by GAAP.

_____ 7. The compensation of employees who physically convert materials into the company's products; labor costs that are directly traceable to finished products.

Computing cost of goods manufactured
5

E18-21 Compute the missing amounts. (pp. 912–913)

	Company X	Company Y	Company Z
Beginning work in process inventory....	(a)	$40,000	$2,000
Direct materials used...........................	$14,000	35,000	(g)
Direct labor.......................................	10,000	20,000	1,000
Manufacturing overhead.....................	(b)	10,000	500
Total manufacturing costs incurred during year	44,000	(d)	(h)
Total manufacturing costs to account for	$54,000	(e)	$6,500
Less: Ending work in process inventory	(c)	25,000	2,500
Costs of goods manufactured..............	$50,000	(f)	(i)

Preparing a statement of
cost of goods manufactured

E18-22 Snyder Corp., a lamp manufacturer, provided the following information for the year ended December 31, 2008.

Inventories:	Beginning	Ending
Materials	$ 50,000	$ 25,000
Work in process	100,000	65,000
Finished goods	40,000	43,000

Other information:

Depreciation: plant building and equipment	$ 15,000	Repairs and maintenance— plant	$ 5,000
Materials purchases	155,000	Indirect labor	30,000
Insurance on plant	20,000	Direct labor	120,000
Sales salaries expense	48,000	Administrative expenses	52,000

Requirements

1. Prepare a schedule of cost of goods manufactured. (pp. 912–913)
2. What is the unit product cost if Snyder manufactured 3,000 lamps for the year? (p. 914)

Flow of costs through a
manufacturer's inventory
accounts

E18-23 Compute cost of goods manufactured and cost of goods sold from the following amounts: (p. 914)

	Beginning of Year	End of Year
Direct materials inventory..............	$22,000	$26,000
Work in process inventory..............	38,000	30,000
Finished goods inventory................	18,000	23,000
Purchases of direct materials		75,000
Direct labor..................................		82,000
Manufacturing overhead................		39,000

Ethical decisions

E18-24 Mary Gonzales is the controller at Automax, a car dealership. Cory Loftus recently has been hired as bookkeeper. Cory wanted to attend a class on Excel spreadsheets, so Mary temporarily took over Cory's duties, including overseeing a fund for topping-off a car's gas before a test drive. Mary found a shortage in this fund and confronted Cory when he returned to work. Cory admitted that he occasionally uses this fund to pay for his own gas. Mary estimated that the amount involved is close to $300.

Requirements (pp. 915–916)

1. What should Mary Gonzales do?
2. Would you change your answer to the previous question if Mary Gonzales was the one recently hired as controller and Cory Loftus was a well-liked longtime employee who indicated that he always eventually repaid the fund?

Problems (Group A) ──────────────────────────────

Calculating income and
cost per unit for a service
company

3

P18-25A The Tree Doctors provide tree-spraying services in the company's home
county. Fergus McNabb, owner, incurred the following operating costs
for the month of May 2008:

Salaries and wages	$8,000
Chemicals	4,500
Depreciation on buildings and equipment...........	700
Depreciation on truck	300
Supplies expense	500
Gasoline and utilities	1,000

The Tree Doctors earned $20,000 in revenues for the month of May by
spraying trees totaling 30,000 feet in height.

Requirements

1. Prepare an income statement for the month of May. Compute the
   ratio of total operating expense to total revenue and operating
   income to total revenue. (p. 905)

2. Compute the unit operating cost of spraying one foot of tree height.
   (pp. 905–906)

Preparing an income
statement for a
merchandising company

4

P18-26A In 2007 Clyde Blackstock opened Clyde's Pets, a small retail shop selling
pet supplies. On December 31, 2007, Clyde's accounting records showed
the following:

Inventory on December 31, 2007.............	$10,250
Inventory on January 1, 2007	15,000
Sales revenue...	54,000
Utilities for shop	3,000
Rent for shop...	4,000
Sales commissions	2,250
Purchases of merchandise........................	27,000

Requirement

Prepare an income statement for Clyde's Pets, a merchandiser, for the
year ended December 31, 2007. (pp. 904–905)

Preparing cost of goods
manufactured schedule and
income statement for a
manufacturing company

5

P18-27A Clyde's Pets succeeded so well that Clyde decided to manufacture his
own brand of chewing bone—Denim Bones. At the end of December
2009, his accounting records showed the following:

Inventories:	Beginning	Ending
Materials	$13,500	$ 9,000
Work in process	0	1,250
Finished goods	0	5,700

continued . . .

Other information:

Direct material purchases	$ 31,000	Utilities for plant	$ 4,500
Plant janitorial services	1,250	Rent on plant	9,000
Sales salaries expense	5,000	Customer service hotline expense	1,000
Delivery expense	1,500	Direct labor	18,000
Sales revenue	105,000		

Requirements

1. Prepare a schedule of cost of goods manufactured for Denim Bones for the year ended December 31, 2009. (pp. 912–913)

2. Prepare an income statement for Denim Bones for the year ended December 31, 2009. (p. 911)

3. How does the format of the income statement for Denim Bones differ from the income statement of Clyde's Pets? (pp. 905, 911)

4. Denim Bones manufactured 17,500 units of its product in 2009. Compute the company's unit product cost for the year. (p. 914)

Preparing financial statements for a manufacturer

5

P18-28A Certain item descriptions and amounts are missing from the monthly schedule of cost of goods manufactured and the income statement of Tinto Manufacturing Company. Fill in the missing items. (pp. 912–913)

_____ MANUFACTURING COMPANY			
_____ June 30, 2010			
Beginning _____			$ 21,000
Direct _____:			
Beginning materials inventory	$ X		
Purchase of materials	51,000		
_____	78,000		
Ending materials inventory	(23,000)		
Direct _____		$ X	
Direct _____		X	
Manufacturing overhead		40,000	
Total _____ costs _____			166,000
Total _____ costs _____			X
Ending _____			(25,000)
_____			$ X
Sales revenue		$ X	
Cost of goods sold:			
Beginning _____	$115,000		
_____	X		
Cost of goods _____	X		
Ending _____	X		
Cost of goods sold		209,000	
Gross profit		254,000	
_____ expenses:			
Marketing expense	99,000		
Administrative expense	X	154,000	
_____ income		$ X	

P18-29A Bass Shoe Company makes loafers. During the most recent year, Bass incurred total manufacturing costs of $21.4 M. Of this amount, $3.0 M was direct materials used and $13.8 M was direct labor. Beginning balances for the year were Direct Materials Inventory, $.7 M; Work in Process Inventory, $.9 M; and Finished Goods Inventory, $.4 M. At the end of the year, inventory accounts showed these amounts:

	Materials	Direct Labor	Manufacturing Overhead
Direct Materials Inventory........	$.6M	$ −0−	$ −0−
Work in Process Inventory........	.4M	.45M	.15M
Finished Goods Inventory.........	.1M	.15M	.05M

Requirements

Refer to Exhibit 18-11, p. 914. Compute:

1. Bass Shoe Company's cost of goods manufactured for the year.

2. Bass's cost of goods sold for the year.

3. The cost of materials purchased during the year.

Making ethical decisions

P18-30A Lee Reinhardt is the new controller for Night Software, Inc., which develops and sells education software. Shortly before the December 31 fiscal year-end, Richard Oliver, the company president, asks Reinhardt how things look for the year-end numbers. He is not happy to learn that earnings growth may be below 15% for the first time in the company's five-year history. Oliver explains that financial analysts have again predicted a 15% earnings growth for the company and that he does not intend to disappoint them. He suggests that Reinhardt talk to the assistant controller, who can explain how the previous controller dealt with such situations. The assistant controller suggests the following strategies:

a. Persuade suppliers to postpone billing until January 1.

b. Record as sales certain software awaiting sale that is held in a public warehouse.

c. Delay the year-end closing a few days into January of the next year, so that some of next year's sales are included as this year's sales.

d. Reduce the allowance for bad debts (and bad debts expense), given the company's continued strong performance.

e. Postpone routine monthly maintenance expenditures from December to January.

Which of these suggested strategies are inconsistent with IMA standards? What should Reinhardt do if Oliver insists that she follow all of these suggestions? (pp. 915–916)

Problems (Group B)

Calculating income and cost per unit for a service company

P18-31B The Dent Fixer repairs small dents and dings in the doors and other body panels of automobiles. Grant Edwards, owner, incurred the following operating costs in the month of October 2008.

continued . . .

Salary	$4,000
Depreciation on truck	250
Supplies expense	150
Gasoline	250
Utilities	650

The Dent Fixer earned $8,000 in revenue for the month of October, when Edwards repaired 160 automobiles.

Requirements

1. Prepare an income statement for the month of October. Compute the ratio of total operating expense to total revenue and operating income to total revenue. (p. 905)
2. Compute the unit operating cost per automobile repaired. (p. 906)

P18-32B On January 1, 2008, Lindsey Owens opened Picture Perfect, a small retail store that sells picture frames, crafts, and art. On December 31, 2008, her accounting records showed the following:

Store rent	$7,000	Sales revenue	$90,000
Sales salaries	4,500	Store utilities	1,950
Freight in	600	Purchases of merchandise	36,000
Inventory on December 31, 2008	9,600	Inventory on January 1, 2008	12,000
Advertising expense	2,300		

Requirement

Prepare an income statement for Picture Perfect, a merchandiser, for the year ended December 31, 2008. (p. 905)

P18-33B Picture Perfect succeeded so well that Lindsey Owens decided to manufacture her own special brand of picture frames, to be called Always. At the end of December 2009, her accounting records showed the following:

Inventories:	Beginning	Ending
Materials	$ 13,000	$ 8,000
Work in process	0	2,000
Finished goods	0	3,000

Other information:			
Direct material purchases	$ 32,000	Rent on plant	$11,000
Plant janitorial services	750	Customer warranty refunds	1,500
Sales commissions	4,000	Depreciation expense on delivery truck	2,500
Administrative expenses	7,000		
Sales revenue	128,000	Depreciation expense on plant equipment	3,250
Utilities for plant	1,000	Direct labor	20,000

continued . . .

Requirements

1. Prepare a schedule of cost of goods manufactured for Always Manufacturing, for the year ended December 31, 2009. (pp. 912–913)

2. Prepare an income statement for Always Manufacturing, for the year ended December 31, 2009. (p. 911)

3. How does the format of the income statement for Always Manufacturing differ from the income statement of Picture Perfect? (pp. 905, 911)

4. Always Manufacturing made 1,300 picture frames in 2009. Compute the company's unit product cost for the year. (pp. 905–906)

Preparing financial statements for a manufacturer

5

P18-34B Certain item descriptions and amounts are missing from the monthly schedule of cost of goods manufactured and income statement of Lima Manufacturing Company. Fill in the missing items.

_____ MANUFACTURING COMPANY			
_____ April 30, 2009			
_____ work in process inventory			$ 15,000
Direct materials used:			
_____ materials _____	$ X		
_____ of materials	65,000		
_____	75,000		
_____ materials _____	(23,000)		
Direct _____		$ X	
Direct _____		68,000	
Manufacturing overhead		X	
Total _____ costs _____			X
Total _____ costs _____			175,000
_____ work in process inventory			X
_____			$150,000
_____ revenue		$450,000	
_____ :			
Beginning _____	$ X		
_____	X		
Cost of goods _____	X		
Ending _____	(67,000)		
Cost of goods sold		X	
_____		243,000	
_____ expenses:			
Marketing expenses	X		
Administrative expenses	$ 64,000	X	
_____		$ 76,000	

Flow of costs through a manufacturer's inventory accounts

5

P18-35B Wrangler Company makes casual jeans. During the most recent year, Wrangler incurred direct labor cost of $60 M and manufacturing overhead of $75M. The company purchased direct materials of $25.7M. Beginning balances for the year were Direct Materials Inventory, $3.4M;

continued . . .

work in Process Inventory, $3.8M; and Finished Goods Inventory, $7.4M. At year-end, inventory accounts showed these amounts:

	Materials	Direct Labor	Manufacturing Overhead
Direct Materials Inventory........	$ .9M	$ —0—	$ —0—
Work in Process Inventory........	1.5M	2.0M	2.5M
Finished Goods Inventory.........	2.4M	3.2M	4.0M

Requirements

Refer to Exhibit 18-11, p. 914. Compute:

1. Wrangler Company's cost of direct materials used for the year.

2. Wrangler's cost of goods manufactured for the year.

3. The company's cost of goods sold for the year.

Making ethical decisions

6

P18-36B Tom Williams is the new controller for Vance Design, a designer and manufacturer of sportswear. Shortly before the December 31 fiscal year-end, Tenisha Roberts (the company president) asks Tom how things look for the year-end numbers. Tenisha is not happy to learn that earnings growth may be below 10% for the first time in the company's five-year history. Tenisha explains that financial analysts have again predicted a 12% earnings growth for the company and that she does not intend to disappoint them. She suggests that Tom talk to the assistant controller, who can explain how the previous controller dealt with this type of situation. The assistant controller suggests the following strategies:

a. Postpone planned advertising expenditures from December to January.

b. Do not record sales returns and allowances because they are individually immaterial.

c. Persuade retail customers to accelerate January orders to December.

d. Reduce the allowance for bad debts, given the company's continued strong performance.

e. Vance Design ships finished goods to public warehouses across the country for temporary storage, until it receives firm orders from customers. As Vance Design receives orders, it directs the warehouse to ship the goods to the nearby customer. The assistant controller suggests recording goods sent to the public warehouses as sales.

Which of these suggested strategies are inconsistent with IMA standards? What should Tom Williams do if Tenisha Roberts insists that he follow all of these suggestions? (pp. 915–916)

Apply Your Knowledge

Decision Cases

Case 1. PowerSwitch, Inc., designs and manufactures switches used in telecommunications. Serious flooding throughout North Carolina affected PowerSwitch's facilities. Inventory was completely ruined, and the company's computer system, including all accounting records, was destroyed.

Before the disaster recovery specialists clean the buildings, Stephen Plum, the company controller, is anxious to salvage whatever records he can to support an insurance claim for the destroyed inventory. He is standing in what is left of the accounting department with Paul Lopez, the cost accountant.

"I didn't know mud could smell so bad," Paul says. "What should I be looking for?"

"Don't worry about beginning inventory numbers," responds Stephen, "we'll get them from last year's annual report. We need first-quarter cost data."

"I was working on the first-quarter results just before the storm hit," Paul says. "Look, my report's still in my desk drawer. All I can make out is that for the first quarter, material purchases were $476,000 and direct labor, manufacturing overhead, and total manufacturing costs to account for were $505,000, $245,000, and $1,425,000, respectively. Wait, and cost of goods available for sale was $1,340,000."

"Great," says Stephen. "I remember that sales for the period were approximately $1.7 million. Given our gross profit of 30%, that's all you should need."

Paul is not sure about that, but decides to see what he can do with this information. The beginning inventory numbers are

- Direct materials, $113,000

- Work in process, $229,000

- Finished goods, $154,000

He remembers a schedule he learned in college that may help him get started.

Requirements
1. Exhibit 18-11 (p. 914) resembles the schedule Paul has in mind. Use it to determine the ending inventories of direct materials, work in process, and finished goods.

2. Draft an insurance claim letter for the controller, seeking reimbursement for the flood damage to inventory. PowerSwitch's insurance representative is Gary Ogleby, at Industrial Insurance Co., 1122 Main Street, Hartford, CT 06268.

The policy number is #3454340-23. PowerSwitch's address is 5 Research Triangle Way, Raleigh, NC 27698.

Case 2. The IMA's *Standards of Ethical Conduct for Management Accountants* can be applied to more than just management accounting. They are also relevant to college students. Explain at least one situation that shows how each IMA standard in Exhibit 18-12 (p. 915) is relevant to your experiences as a student. For example, the ethical standard of competence would suggest not cutting classes!

Ethical Issue

Hector Valencia recently resigned his position as controller for Shamalay Automotive, a small, struggling foreign car dealer in Austin, Texas. Hector has just started a new job as controller for Mueller Imports, a much larger dealer for the same car manufacturer. Demand for this particular make of car is exploding, and the manufacturer cannot produce enough to satisfy demand. The manufacturer's regional sales managers are each given a certain number of cars. Each sales manager then decides how to divide the cars among the independently owned dealerships in the region. Because most dealerships can sell every car they receive, the key is getting a large number of cars from the manufacturer's regional sales manager.

Hector's former employer, Shamalay Automotive, received only about 25 cars a month. Consequently, the dealership was not very profitable.

Hector is surprised to learn that his new employer, Mueller Imports, receives over 200 cars a month. Hector soon gets another surprise. Every couple of months, a local jeweler bills the dealer $5,000 for "miscellaneous services." Franz Mueller, the owner of the dealership, personally approves payment of these invoices, noting that each invoice is a "selling expense." From casual conversations with a salesperson, Hector learns that Mueller frequently gives Rolex watches to the manufacturer's regional sales manager and other sales executives. Before talking to anyone about this, Hector decides to work through his ethical dilemma using the framework from Chapter 8. Put yourself in Hector's place and complete the framework.

1. What is the ethical issue?

2. What are my options?

3. What are the possible consequences?

4. What shall I do?

Team Project

Search the Internet for a nearby company that also has a Web page. Arrange an interview with a management accountant, a controller, or other accounting/ finance officer of the company. Before you conduct the interview, answer the following questions:

1. Is this a service, merchandising, or manufacturing company? What is its primary product or service?

2. Is the primary purpose of the company's Web site to provide information about the company and its products, to sell online, or to provide financial information for investors?

3. Are parts of the company's Web site restricted so that you need password authorization to enter? What appears to be the purpose of limiting access?

4. Does the Web site provide an e-mail link for contacting the company?

At the interview, begin by clarifying your answers to questions 1 through 4, and ask the following additional questions:

5. If the company sells over the Web, what benefits has the company derived? Did the company perform a cost-benefit analysis before deciding to begin Web sales?

Or

If the company does not sell over the Web, why not? Has the company performed a cost/benefit analysis and decided not to sell over the Web?

6. What is the biggest cost of operating the Web site?

7. Does the company make any purchases over the Internet? What percentage?

8. How has e-commerce affected the company's management accounting system? Have the management accountant's responsibilities become more or less complex? More or less interesting?

9. Does the company use Web-based accounting applications, such as accounts receivable or accounts payable?

10. Does the company use an ERP system? If so, do managers view the system as a success? What have been the benefits? The costs?

For Internet Exercises, Excel in Practice, and additional online activities, go to the Web site www.prenhall.com/horngren

---

Quick Check Answers

1. *a*   2. *c*   3. *d*   4. *b*   5. *a*   6. *c*   7. *b*   8. *a*   9. *d*   10. *d*

19 Job Order Costing

Learning Objectives

1 Distinguish between job order costing and process costing

2 Record materials and labor in a job order costing system

3 Record overhead in a job order costing system

4 Record completion and sales of finished goods and the adjustment for under- or overallocated overhead

5 Calculate unit costs for a service company

Many schools use fundraising events to finance extracurricular events. Let's say that you are responsible for an enchilada dinner to finance a band trip. You have to decide how many dinners you expect to sell, what price to charge, and the ingredients needed. Knowing the cost to prepare an enchilada dinner is important. You want to set a price low enough to draw a crowd and high enough to generate a profit.

This chapter shows how to measure cost in situations similar to the enchilada dinner. This type of cost accounting system is called job order costing because production is arranged by the job. Chapter 20 then covers the other main type of costing system—called process costing.

Businesses face the same situation. They must draw a crowd—sell enough goods and services to earn a profit. So, regardless of the type of business you own or manage, you need to know how much it costs to produce your product or service. This applies whether you plan a career in marketing, engineering, or finance.

Marketing managers must consider their unit product cost in order to set the selling price high enough to cover costs. Engineers study the materials, labor, and overhead that go into a product to pinpoint ways to cut costs. Production managers then decide whether it is more profitable to make the product or to *outsource* it (buy from an outside supplier). The finance department arranges financing for the venture.

You can see that it's important for managers in all areas to know how much it costs to make a product. This chapter and the next shows you how to figure these costs.

How Much Does It Cost to Make a Product? Two Approaches

1 Distinguish between job order costing and process costing

Cost accounting systems accumulate cost information so that managers can measure how much it costs to produce each unit of merchandise. For example, Intel must know how much each processor costs to produce. FedEx knows its cost of flying each pound of freight one mile. These unit costs help managers

- Set selling prices that will lead to profits
- Compute cost of goods sold for the income statement
- Compute the cost of inventory for the balance sheet

If a manager knows the cost to produce each product, then the manager can plan and control the cost of resources needed to create the product and deliver it to the customer. A cost accounting system assigns these costs to the company's product or service.

JOB ORDER COSTING   Some companies manufacture batches of unique products or specialized services. A **job order costing** system accumulates costs for each batch, or job. Law firms, music studios, health-care providers, building contractors, and furniture manufacturers are examples of companies that use job order costing systems. For example, Dell makes personal computers based on customer orders (see the "Customize" button on Dell's Web site).

PROCESS COSTING   Other companies, such as Procter & Gamble and PepsiCo, produce identical units through a series of production steps or processes. A **process costing** system accumulates the costs of each process needed to complete the product. Chevron Texaco and Kraft Foods are examples of companies that use process costing systems.

Both job order and process costing systems:

- Accumulate the costs incurred to make the product
- Assign costs to the products

Accountants use **cost tracing** to assign directly traceable costs, such as direct materials and direct labor, to the product. They use a less precise technique—**cost allocation**—to assign manufacturing overhead and other indirect costs to the product. Let's see how a job order costing system works for a manufacturing company.

Job Order Costing for Manufacturing Products

How Job Costs Flow Through the Accounts: An Overview

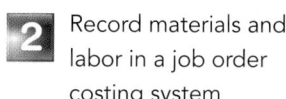 Record materials and labor in a job order costing system

The job order costing system tracks costs as raw materials move from the storeroom to the production floor to finished products. Exhibit 19-1 diagrams the flow of costs through a job order costing system. Let's consider how a manufacturer, Seasons Greeting Cards, uses job order costing. For Seasons Greeting, each customer order is a separate job. Seasons Greeting uses a **job cost record** to accumulate the costs of each job's:

- Direct materials
- Direct labor
- Manufacturing overhead

The company starts the job cost record when work begins on the job. As Seasons Greeting incurs costs, the company adds costs to the job cost record. For jobs started but not yet finished, the job cost records show the Work in Process Inventory. When Seasons Greeting finishes a job, the company totals the costs and transfers costs from Work in Process Inventory to Finished Goods Inventory.

When the job's units are sold, the costing system moves the costs from Finished Goods Inventory to Cost of Goods Sold. Exhibit 19-1 summarizes this sequence.

EXHIBIT 19-1   **Flow of Costs Through the Accounts in a Job Order Costing System**

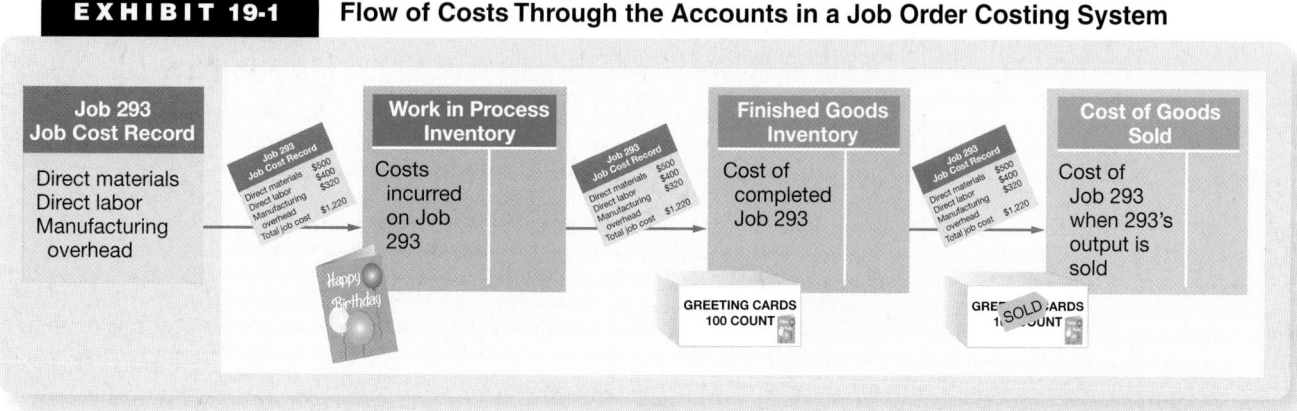

Job Order Costing: Accounting for Materials and Labor

Accounting for Materials

PURCHASING MATERIALS   On January 1, 2009, Seasons Greeting had these inventory balances:

Materials Inventory	Work in Process Inventory	Finished Goods Inventory
4,000	7,000	9,000

During the year, Seasons Greeting purchased paper for $22,000 on account. We record the purchase of materials as follows:

(1) Materials Inventory	22,000	
Accounts Payable		22,000

Materials Inventory

4,000	
22,000	

Materials Inventory is a general ledger account. Seasons Greeting also uses a subsidiary ledger for materials. The subsidiary materials ledger includes a separate record for each type of material, as shown in Exhibit 19-2. The balance of the Materials Inventory account in the general ledger should always equal the sum of the balances in the subsidiary materials ledger.

EXHIBIT 19-2   **Subsidiary Materials Ledger Record**

SUBSIDIARY MATERIALS LEDGER RECORD   *Seasons Greeting*

Item No. B–220   Description   Paper

	Received			Used				Balance		
Date	Units	Cost	Total Cost	Mat. Req. No.	Units	Cost	Total Cost	Units	Cost	Total Cost
2009										
7–20								20	$14	$280
7–23	20	$14	$280					40	14	560
7–24				334	10	$14	$140	30	14	420

USING MATERIALS   Seasons Greeting works on many jobs during the year. In 2009 the company used materials costing $21,000, including paper ($18,000) and ink ($3,000). The paper can be traced to the job, so the paper is a *direct material*. Direct material costs go directly into the Work in Process Inventory account.

By contrast, the cost of ink is difficult to trace to a specific job, so ink is an *indirect material*. The cost of indirect material is recorded first as Manufacturing Overhead. The following journal entry then records the use of materials in production.

(2) Work in Process Inventory (for direct materials)	18,000	
Manufacturing Overhead (for indirect materials)	3,000	
Materials Inventory		21,000

We can summarize the flow of materials costs through the T-accounts as follows:

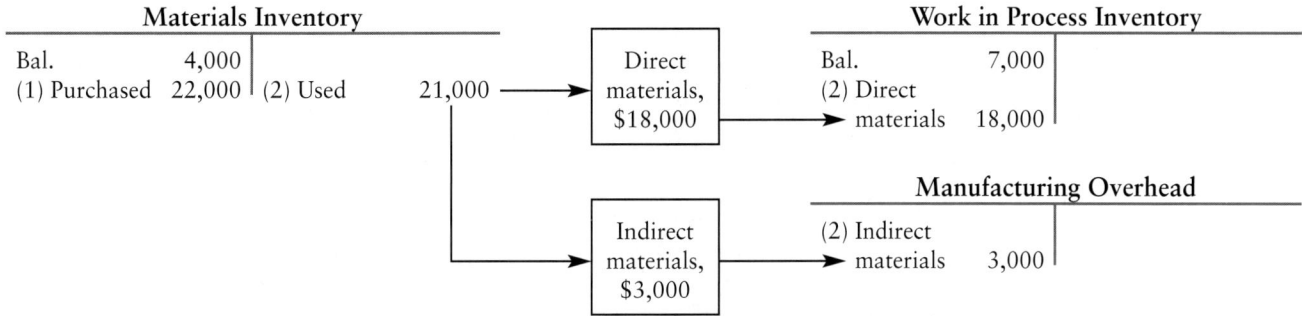

For both direct materials and indirect materials, the production team completes a document called a **materials requisition** to request the transfer of materials to the production floor. Exhibit 19-3 shows Seasons Greeting's materials requisition for the 10 units of paper needed to make 1,000 greeting cards for Job 16.

EXHIBIT 19-3   **Materials Requisition**

MATERIALS REQUISITION NO. 334

Seasons Greeting

Date 7–24–09   Job No. 16

Item	Quantity	Unit cost	Amount
Paper	10	$14	**$140**

Exhibit 19-4 is a job cost record. It assigns the cost of the direct material (paper) to Job 16. Follow the $140 cost of the paper from the materials inventory record (Exhibit 19-2), to the materials requisition (Exhibit 19-3), and to the job cost record in Exhibit 19-4. Notice that all the dollar amounts in these exhibits show Seasons Greeting's *costs*—not the prices at which Seasons Greeting sells its products. Let's see how to account for labor costs.

Accounting for Labor

Seasons Greeting incurred labor costs of $24,000 during 2009. We record manufacturing wages as follows:

(3) Manufacturing Wages	24,000	
Wages Payable		24,000

EXHIBIT 19-4   Direct Materials on Job Cost Record

JOB COST RECORD   *Seasons Greeting*

Job No. __16__
Customer Name and Address Macy's New York City
Job Description 1,000 Birthday Greeting Cards

Date Promised		7–31	Date Started	7–24	Date Completed		
	Direct Materials		Direct Labor		Manufacturing Overhead Allocated		
Date	Requisition Numbers	Amount	Labor Time Record Numbers	Amount	Date	Rate	Amount
7–24	334	$140					
					Overall Cost Summary		
					Direct Materials.......$		
					Direct Labor.............		
					Manufacturing Over-head Allocated		
Totals					Total Job Cost.......$		

This entry includes the costs of both direct labor and indirect labor.

Each employee completes a labor time record for each job he or she works on. The **labor time record** in Exhibit 19-5 identifies the employee (Jay Barlow), the amount of time he spent on Job 16 (5 hours), and the labor cost charged to the job ($60 = 5 hours × $12 per hour).

EXHIBIT 19-5   Labor Time Record

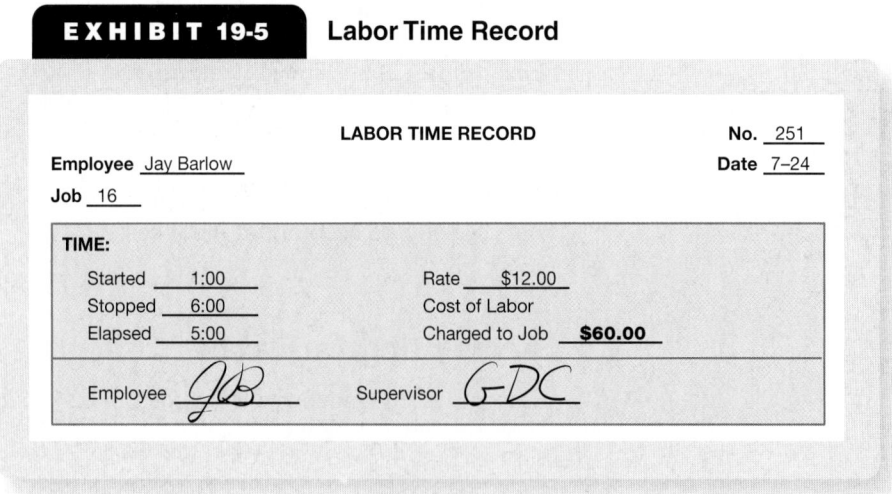

LABOR TIME RECORD   **No.** __251__
Employee Jay Barlow   **Date** __7–24__
Job __16__

TIME:

Started	1:00	Rate	$12.00
Stopped	6:00	Cost of Labor	
Elapsed	5:00	Charged to Job	**$60.00**

Employee _JB_   Supervisor _GDC_

Seasons Greeting totals the labor time records for each job. Exhibit 19-6 shows how Seasons Greeting adds the direct labor cost to the job cost record. The "Labor

EXHIBIT 19-6 Direct Labor on Job Cost Record

JOB COST RECORD

Seasons Greeting

Job No. __16__

Customer Name and Address __Macy's New York City__

Job Description __1,000 Birthday Greeting Cards__

Date Promised	7–31	Date Started	7–24	Date Completed		
Date	Direct Materials		Direct Labor		Manufacturing Overhead Allocated		
	Requisition Numbers	Amount	Labor Time Record Numbers	Amount	Date	Rate	Amount
7–24	334	$140	236, 251, 258	$200			
					Overall Cost Summary		
					Direct Materials..........$		
					Direct Labor.................		
					Manufacturing Overhead Allocated............		
Totals					Total Job Cost..........$		

Time Record Numbers" show that on July 24, three employees worked on Job 16. Labor time record 251 is Jay Barlow's, from Exhibit 19-5. Labor time records 236 and 258 (not shown) indicate that two other employees also worked on Job 16. The job cost record shows that Seasons Greeting assigned Job 16 a total of $200 of direct labor costs for the three employees' work.

During 2009 Seasons Greeting incurred $20,000 for direct labor and $4,000 for indirect labor (overhead). These amounts include the labor costs for Job 16 that we've been working with plus all the company's other jobs as well.

Seasons Greeting's accounting for labor cost requires the company to:

- Assign labor cost to individual jobs, as we saw for Jay Barlow's work on Job 16
- Transfer labor cost out of the Manufacturing Wages account and into Work in Process Inventory (for direct labor) and into Manufacturing Overhead (for indirect labor)

The following journal entry zeroes out the Manufacturing Wages account and shifts the labor cost to Work in Process and the Overhead account.

(4) Work in Process Inventory (for direct labor)	20,000	
Manufacturing Overhead (for indirect labor)	4,000	
Manufacturing Wages		24,000

This entry brings the balance in Manufacturing Wages to zero. Its transferred balance is now divided between Work in Process Inventory ($20,000 of direct labor) and Manufacturing Overhead ($4,000 of indirect labor), as shown in the following T-accounts:

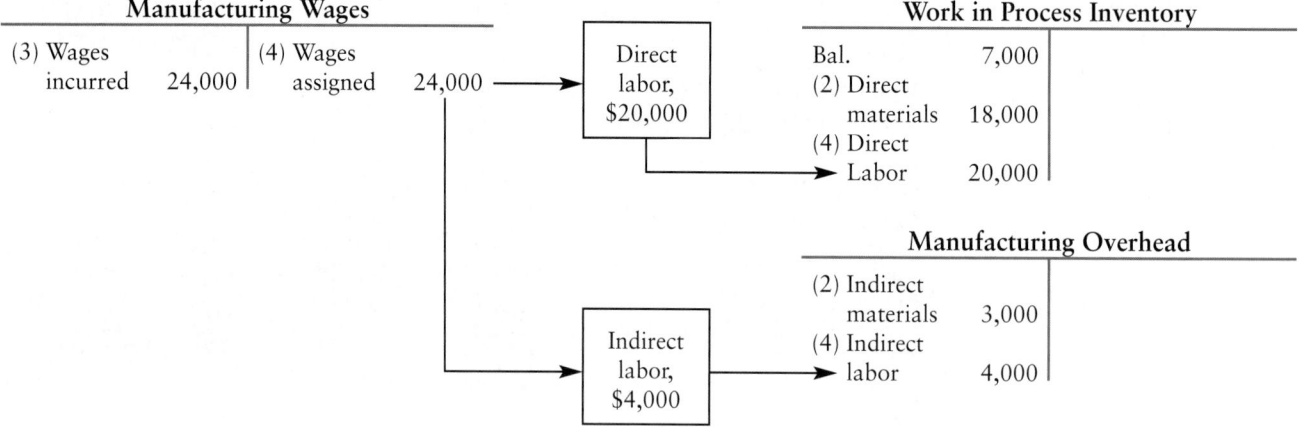

Many companies have automated these accounting procedures.

Study the Decision Guidelines to summarize the first half of the chapter. Then work the summary problem that follows.

Decision Guidelines

TRACING DIRECT MATERIALS AND DIRECT LABOR

Seasons Greeting Cards uses a job order costing system that assigns manufacturing costs to each individual job for greeting cards. These guidelines explain some of the decisions Seasons made in designing its system.

Decision	Guidelines
Should we use job costing or process costing?	Use *job order costing* when the company produces unique products (custom greeting cards) in small batches (usually a "batch" contains a set of seasonal cards). Use *process costing* when the company produces identical products in large batches, often in a continuous flow.

How to record:

- Purchase and use of materials?

Purchase of materials:

Materials Inventory	XX	
Accounts Payable (or Cash)		XX

Use of materials:

Work in Process Inventory (direct materials)	XX	
Manufacturing Overhead (indirect materials)	XX	
Materials Inventory		XX

- Incurrence and assignment of labor to jobs?

Incurrence of labor cost:

Manufacturing Wages	XX	
Wages Payable (or Cash)		XX

Assignment of labor cost to jobs:

Work in Process Inventory (direct labor)	XX	
Manufacturing Overhead (indirect labor)	XX	
Manufacturing Wages		XX

Summary Problem 1

Tom Baker manufactures custom teakwood patio furniture. Suppose Baker has the following transactions:

a. **Purchased raw materials on account, $135,000.**

b. **Materials costing $130,000 were requisitioned (used) for production. Of this total, $30,000 were indirect materials.**

c. **Labor time records show that direct labor of $22,000 and indirect labor of $5,000 were incurred (but not yet paid).**

d. **Assigned labor cost to work in process and manufacturing overhead.**

Requirement

Prepare journal entries for each transaction. Then explain each journal entry in terms of what got increased and what got decreased.

Solution

a.

Materials Inventory	135,000	
Accounts Payable		135,000

When materials are purchased on account:

- Debit (increase) Materials Inventory for the *cost* of the materials purchased.
- Credit (increase) Accounts Payable to record the liability for the cost of the materials.

b.

Work in Process Inventory	100,000	
Manufacturing Overhead	30,000	
Materials Inventory		130,000

When materials are requisitioned (used) in production, we record the movement of materials out of materials inventory and into production, as follows:

- Debit (increase) Work in Process Inventory for the cost of the *direct* materials (in this case, $100,000—the $130,000 total materials requisitioned less the $30,000 indirect materials).
- Debit (increase) Manufacturing Overhead for the cost of the *indirect* materials.
- Credit (decrease) Materials Inventory for the cost of both direct materials and indirect materials moved out of the materials storage area and into production.

c.

Manufacturing Wages ($22,000 + $5,000)	27,000	
Wages Payable		27,000

To record total labor costs actually incurred,

- Debit (increase) Manufacturing Wages.
- Credit (increase) Wages Payable to record the liability for wages incurred, but not paid.

d.

Work in Process Inventory	22,000	
Manufacturing Overhead	5,000	
Manufacturing Wages		27,000

To assign the labor costs,

- Debit (increase) Work in Process Inventory for the cost of the *direct* labor.
- Debit (increase) Manufacturing Overhead for the cost of the *indirect* labor.
- Credit (decrease) Manufacturing Wages to zero out its balance.

Job Order Costing: Allocating Manufacturing Overhead

3 Record overhead in a job order costing system

All manufacturing overhead costs are *accumulated* as debits to a single general ledger account—Manufacturing Overhead. We have already assigned the costs of indirect materials (entry 2, bottom of page 946) and indirect labor (entry 4, bottom of page 949) to manufacturing overhead. In addition to indirect materials and indirect labor, Seasons Greeting incurred the following overhead costs:

- Depreciation on plant and equipment, $7,000
- Plant utilities, $4,000
- Plant insurance, $1,000
- Property taxes on the plant, $2,000

Entries 5 through 8 record these manufacturing overhead costs. The account titles in parentheses indicate the specific records that were debited in the overhead subsidiary ledger.

(5) Manufacturing Overhead (Depreciation—Plant and Equipment)	7,000	
Accumulated Depreciation—Plant and Equipment		7,000
(6) Manufacturing Overhead (Plant Utilities)	4,000	
Cash		4,000
(7) Manufacturing Overhead (Plant Insurance)	1,000	
Prepaid Insurance—Plant		1,000
(8) Manufacturing Overhead (Property Taxes—Plant)	2,000	
Property Taxes Payable		2,000

The actual manufacturing overhead costs (such as indirect materials, indirect labor, plus depreciation, utilities, insurance, and property taxes on the plant) are debited to Manufacturing Overhead as they occur throughout the year. By the end of the year, the Manufacturing Overhead account has accumulated all the actual overhead costs as debits:

Manufacturing Overhead		
(2) Indirect materials	3,000	
(4) Indirect labor	4,000	
(5) Depreciation—plant and equipment	7,000	
(6) Plant utilities	4,000	
(7) Plant insurance	1,000	
(8) Property taxes—plant	2,000	
Total overhead cost	21,000	

Now you have seen how Seasons Greeting *accumulates* overhead costs in the accounting records. But how does Seasons Greeting *assign* overhead costs to individual jobs? As you can see, overhead includes a variety of costs that Seasons Greeting cannot trace to individual jobs. For example, it is impossible to say how much of the cost of plant utilities is related to Job 16. Yet manufacturing overhead costs are as essential as direct materials and direct labor, so Seasons Greeting must find some way to assign overhead costs to specific jobs. Otherwise, each job would not bear its fair share of total cost. Seasons Greeting may then set unrealistic prices for some of its greeting cards and wind up losing money on some of its hard-earned sales.

Allocating Manufacturing Overhead to Jobs

Companies perform two steps in allocating manufacturing overhead:

1. **Compute the predetermined overhead rate.** The **predetermined manufacturing overhead rate** (sometimes called the **budgeted overhead rate**) is computed as follows:

$$\text{Predetermined manufacturing overhead rate} = \frac{\text{Total estimated manufacturing overhead costs}}{\text{Total estimated quantity of the manufacturing overhead allocation base}}$$

The most accurate allocation can be made only when total overhead cost is known—and that's at the end of the year. But managers can't wait that long for product cost information. So the predetermined overhead rate is calculated before the year begins. Then throughout the year, companies use this predetermined rate to allocate overhead cost to individual jobs. The predetermined overhead rate is based on two factors:

- Total *estimated* manufacturing overhead costs for the year
- Total *estimated* quantity of the manufacturing overhead allocation base

The key to assigning indirect manufacturing costs to jobs is to identify a workable manufacturing overhead allocation base. The **allocation base** is a common denominator that links overhead costs to the products. Ideally, the allocation base is the primary cost driver of manufacturing overhead. As the phrase implies, a **cost driver** is the primary factor that causes a cost. Traditionally manufacturing companies have used:

- Direct labor hours (for labor-intensive production environments)
- Direct labor cost (for labor-intensive production environments)
- Machine hours (for machine-intensive production environments)

For simplicity, we'll assume Seasons Greeting uses only one allocation base to assign manufacturing overhead to jobs. Later in the textbook, Chapter 24 relaxes this assumption. There, we'll see how companies use a method called *activity-based costing* to identify different allocation bases that link indirect costs with specific jobs more precisely. First, however, we need to develop a solid understanding of the simpler system that we describe here.

2. **Allocate manufacturing overhead costs to jobs as the company makes its products.** Allocate manufacturing overhead cost to jobs as follows:

$$\text{Allocated manufacturing overhead cost} = \text{\textit{Predetermined} manufacturing overhead rate (from Step 1)} \times \text{\textit{Actual} quantity of the allocation base used by each job}$$

As we have seen, Seasons Greeting traces direct costs directly to each job. Now let's see how it allocates overhead cost to jobs. Recall that indirect manufacturing costs include plant depreciation, utilities, insurance, and property taxes, plus indirect materials and indirect labor.

1. Seasons Greeting uses direct labor cost as the allocation base. In 2008, Seasons Greeting estimated that total overhead costs for 2009 would be $20,000 and direct labor cost would total $25,000. Using this information, we can compute the predetermined manufacturing overhead rate as follows:

$$\text{Predetermined manufacturing overhead rate} = \frac{\text{Total estimated manufacturing overhead costs}}{\text{Total estimated quantity of the manufacturing overhead allocation base}} = \frac{\text{Total estimated manufacturing overhead costs}}{\text{Total estimated direct labor cost}}$$

$$= \frac{\$20,000}{\$25,000} = 0.80, \text{ or } 80\%$$

As jobs are completed in 2009, Seasons Greeting will allocate $0.80 of overhead cost for each $1 of labor cost incurred for the job ($0.80 = 80% × $1). Seasons Greeting uses the same predetermined overhead rate (80% of direct labor cost) to allocate manufacturing overhead to all jobs worked on throughout the year. Now back to Job 16.

2. The total direct labor cost for Job 16 is $200 and the predetermined overhead allocation rate is 80% of direct labor cost. Therefore, Seasons Greeting allocates $160 ($200 × 0.80) of manufacturing overhead to Job 16.

The completed job cost record for the Macy's order (Exhibit 19-7) shows that Job 16 cost Seasons Greeting a total of $500: $140 for direct materials, $200 for direct labor, and $160 of allocated manufacturing overhead. Job 16 produced 1,000 greeting cards, so Seasons Greeting's cost per greeting card is $0.50 ($500 ÷ 1,000).

EXHIBIT 19-7 **Manufacturing Overhead on Job Cost Record**

JOB COST RECORD

Seasons Greeting

Job No. __16__
Customer Name and Address Macy's New York City
Job Description 1,000 Birthday Greeting Cards

Date Promised	7–31	Date Started	7–24	Date Completed	7–29

Date	Direct Materials		Direct Labor		Manufacturing Overhead Allocated		
	Requisition Numbers	Amount	Labor Time Record Numbers	Amount	Date	Rate	Amount
7–24	334	$140	236, 251, 258	$200	7–29	80% of Direct Labor Cost	$160
					Overall Cost Summary		
					Direct Materials $140		
					Direct Labor...................200		
					Manufacturing Overhead Allocated 160		
Totals		$140		$200	Total Job Cost............$500		

Seasons Greeting worked on many jobs, including Job 16, during 2009. The company allocated manufacturing overhead to each of these jobs. Seasons Greeting's direct labor cost for 2009 was $20,000, and total overhead allocated to all jobs is 80% of the $20,000 direct labor cost, or $16,000. The journal entry to allocate manufacturing overhead cost to Work in Process Inventory is

	(9) Work in Process Inventory	16,000	
	Manufacturing Overhead		16,000

The flow of manufacturing overhead through the T-accounts follows:

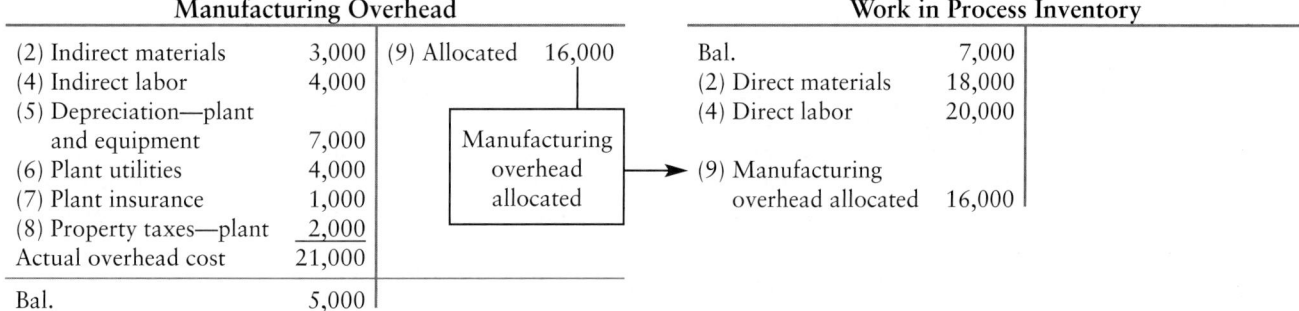

After allocation, a $5,000 debit balance remains in the Manufacturing Overhead account. This means that Seasons Greeting's actual overhead costs ($21,000) exceed the overhead allocated to Work in Process Inventory ($16,000). We say that Seasons Greeting's Manufacturing Overhead is *underallocated*. We'll show how to correct this problem later in the chapter.

Accounting for Completion and Sale of Finished Goods and Adjusting Manufacturing Overhead

Now you know how to accumulate and assign the cost of direct materials, direct labor, and overhead to jobs. To complete the process, we must:

- Account for the completion and sale of finished goods
- Adjust manufacturing overhead at the end of the period

Accounting for the Completion and Sale of Finished Goods

4 Record completion and sales of finished goods and the adjustment for under- or overallocated overhead

Study Exhibit 19-1 on page 945 to review the flow of costs as a job goes from work in process to finished goods to cost of goods sold. Seasons Greeting reported the following inventory balances one year ago, back on December 31, 2008:

Materials Inventory.......................	$4,000
Work in Process Inventory	7,000
Finished Goods Inventory	9,000

The following transactions occurred in 2009:

Cost of goods manufactured	$55,000
Sales on account	85,000
Cost of goods sold	54,000

The $55,000 cost of goods manufactured is the cost of the jobs Seasons Greeting completed during 2009. The cost of goods manufactured goes from Work in Process Inventory to Finished Goods Inventory as completed products move into the finished goods storage area. Seasons Greeting records goods completed in 2009 as follows:

(10) Finished Goods Inventory	55,000	
Work in Process Inventory		55,000

As the greeting cards are sold, Seasons Greeting records sales revenue and accounts receivable, as follows:

(11) Accounts Receivable	85,000	
Sales Revenue		85,000

The goods have been shipped to customers, so Seasons Greeting must also decrease the Finished Goods Inventory account and increase Cost of Goods Sold with the following journal entry:

(11) Cost of Goods Sold	54,000	
Finished Goods Inventory		54,000

The key T-accounts for Seasons Greeting's manufacturing costs now show

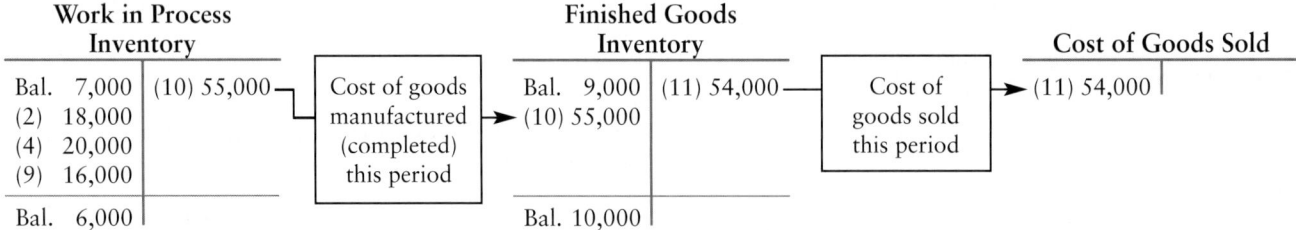

Some jobs are completed, and their costs are transferred out to Finished Goods Inventory ($54,000). We end the period with other jobs started but not finished ($6,000 ending balance of Work in Process Inventory) and jobs completed and not sold ($10,000 ending balance of Finished Goods Inventory).

Adjusting Underallocated or Overallocated Manufacturing Overhead at the End of the Period

During the year, Seasons Greeting:

- Debits Manufacturing Overhead for actual overhead costs
- Credits Manufacturing Overhead for amounts allocated to Work in Process Inventory

The total debits to the Manufacturing Overhead Account rarely equal the total credits. Why? Because Seasons Greeting allocates overhead to jobs using a *predetermined* allocation rate that's based on estimates. The predetermined allocation rate represents the *expected* relation between overhead costs and the allocation base. In our example, the $5,000 debit balance of Manufacturing Overhead shown at the top of page 957 is called **underallocated overhead** because the manufacturing overhead allocated to Work in Process Inventory is *less* than actual overhead cost. (**Overallocated overhead** has a credit balance.)

Accountants adjust underallocated and overallocated overhead at year-end, when closing the Manufacturing Overhead account. When overhead is underallocated, as in our example, a credit to Manufacturing Overhead is needed to bring the account balance to zero. What account should we debit?

Because Seasons Greeting *undercosted* jobs during the year, the correction should increase (debit) Cost of Goods Sold:

(12) Cost of Goods Sold	5,000	
Manufacturing Overhead		5,000

The Manufacturing Overhead balance is now zero and Cost of Goods Sold is up to date.

Manufacturing Overhead				Cost of Goods Sold	
Actual	21,000	Allocated	16,000	54,000	
		Closed	5,000	5,000	
				59,000	

Exhibit 19-8 summarizes the accounting for manufacturing overhead:

- Before the period
- During the period
- At the end of the period

EXHIBIT 19-8 **Summary of Accounting for Manufacturing Overhead**

Before the Period

$$\text{Compute predetermined manufacturing overhead rate} = \frac{\text{Total estimated manufacturing overhead cost}}{\text{Total estimated quantity of allocation base}}$$

During the Period

$$\text{Allocate the overhead} = \text{Actual quantity of the manufacturing overhead allocation base} \times \text{Predetermined manufacturing overhead rate}$$

At the End of the Period

Close the Manufacturing Overhead account:

Jobs are undercosted

If actual > allocated → **Underallocated** manufacturing overhead
Need to *increase* Cost of Goods Sold, as follows:

Cost of Goods Sold	XXX	
Manufacturing Overhead		XXX

Jobs are overcosted

If allocated > actual → **Overallocated** manufacturing overhead
Need to *reduce* Cost of Goods Sold, as follows:

Manufacturing Overhead	XXX	
Cost of Goods sold		XXX

Overview of Job Order Costing in a Manufacturing Company

Exhibit 19-9 provides an overview of Seasons Greeting's job order costing system. Each entry is keyed to 1 of the 12 transactions described on page 961. Study this exhibit carefully.

Now review the flow of costs through Seasons Greeting's general ledger accounts (amounts in thousands):

- Material and labor costs are split between (a) direct costs (traced directly to specific jobs in Work in Process Inventory) and (b) indirect costs (accumulated in Manufacturing Overhead and then allocated to Work in Process Inventory).
- The Work in Process Inventory account summarizes all transactions that occurred on the floor of the manufacturing plant.
- The $55 credit to Work in Process Inventory (debit to Finished Goods Inventory) is the cost of goods manufactured. This is the cost of goods completed and ready for sale, which is the manufacturer's counterpart to merchandise purchases.
- At the end of the period Seasons Greeting closed the $5,000 underallocated Manufacturing Overhead to Cost of Goods Sold.

Job Order Costing in a Service Company

5 Calculate unit costs for a service company

As we have seen, service firms have no inventory. These firms incur only noninventoriable costs. But their managers still need to know the costs of different jobs in order to set prices for their services, as follows (amounts assumed):

Cost of Job 19	$6,000
Add standard markup of 50% ($6,000 × .50).........	3,000
Sale price of Job 19..................................	$9,000

A merchandising company can set the selling price of its products this same way.

We now illustrate how service firms assign costs to jobs. The law firm of Walsh Associates considers each client a separate job. Walsh's most significant cost is direct labor—attorney time spent on clients' cases. How do service firms trace direct labor to individual jobs?

Suppose Walsh's accounting system is not automated. Walsh employees can fill out a weekly **time record**. Software tallies the total time spent on each job. Attorney Lois Fox's time record in Exhibit 19-10 shows that she devoted 14 hours to client 367 during the week of June 10, 2009.

Fox's salary and benefits total $100,000 per year. Assuming a 40-hour workweek and 50 workweeks in each year, Fox has 2,000 available work hours per year (50 weeks × 40 hours per week). Fox's hourly pay rate is

$$\text{Hourly rate to the employer} = \frac{\$100,000 \text{ per year}}{2,000 \text{ hours per year}} = \$50 \text{ per hour}$$

Fox worked 14 hours for client 367, so the direct labor cost traced to client 367 is 14 hours × $50 per hour = $700.

For automated services like Web-site design, employees enter the client number when they start on the client's job. Software records the time elapsed until the employee signs off that job.

EXHIBIT 19-9   **Job Costing—Flow of Costs Through Seasons Greeting's Accounts (amounts in thousands)**

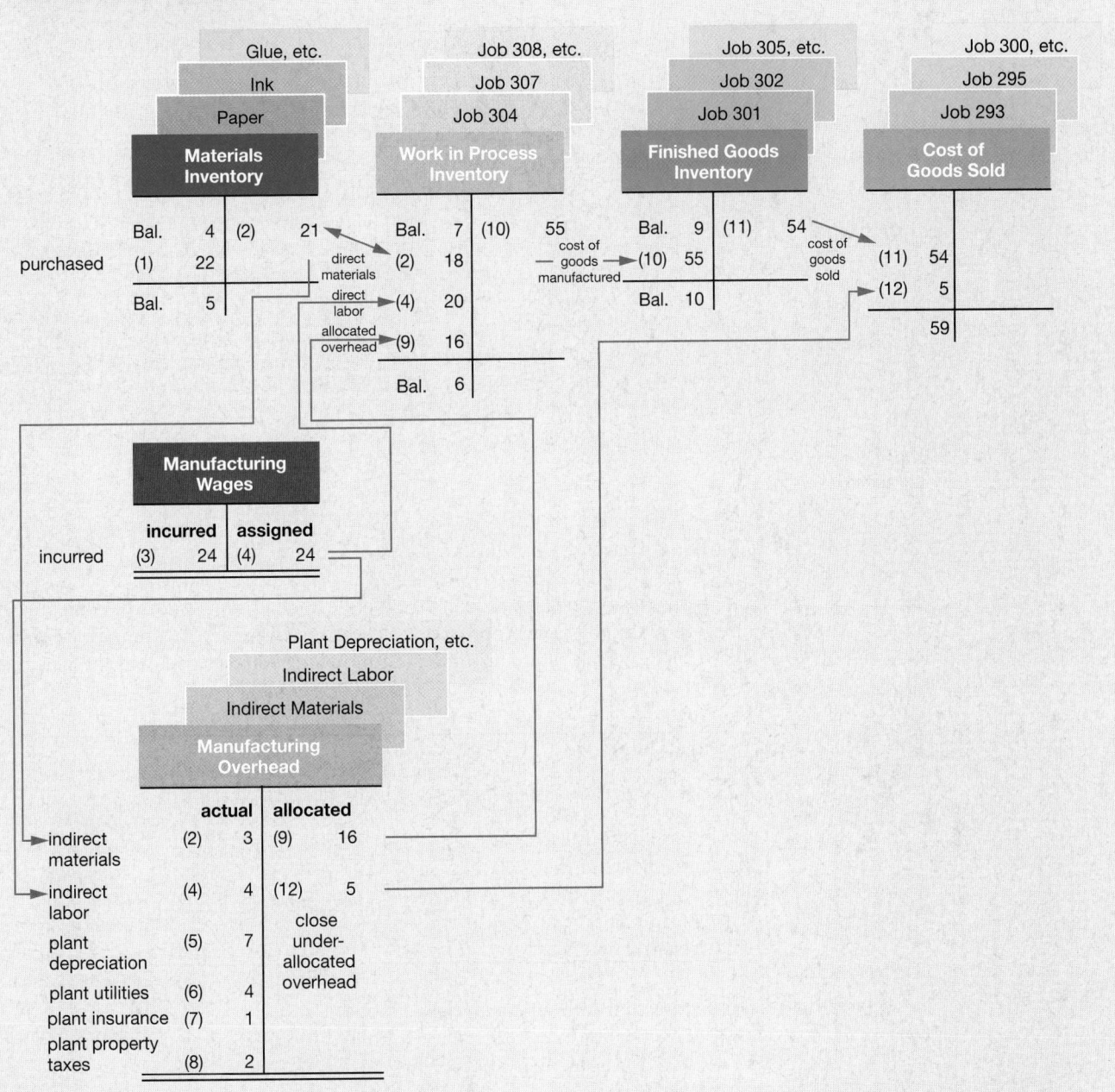

EXHIBIT 19-10 Employee Time Record

Barnett Associates		M	T	W	Th	F
Name _Lois Fox_	8:00 – 8:30	367	520	415	367	415
	8:30 – 9:00					
Employee Time Record	9:00 – 9:30					
Week of _6/10/09_	9:30 – 10:00					
	10:00 – 10:30			367		
Weekly Summary	10:30 – 11:00					
Client # Total hours	11:00 – 11:30	520				
367 14	11:30 – 12:00	520				
415 13	12:00 – 1:00					
520 13	1:00 – 1:30	520	367	415	520	415
	1:30 – 2:00					
	2:00 – 2:30					
	2:30 – 3:00					
	3:00 – 3:30					
	3:30 – 4:00					
	4:00 – 4:30			367		
	4:30 – 5:00					

Founding partner John Walsh wants to know the total cost of serving each client, not just the direct labor cost. Walsh Associates also allocates indirect costs to individual jobs (clients). The law firm develops a predetermined indirect cost allocation rate, following the same approach that Seasons Greeting used on page 955. In December 2008, Walsh estimates that the following indirect costs will be incurred in 2009:

Office rent	$200,000
Office support staff..	70,000
Maintaining and updating law library for case research	25,000
Advertisements in the yellow pages.......................................	3,000
Sponsorship of the symphony	2,000
Total indirect costs...	$300,000

Walsh uses direct labor hours as the allocation base, because direct labor hours are the main driver of indirect costs. He estimates that Walsh attorneys will work 10,000 direct labor hours in 2009.

STEP 1. Compute the predetermined indirect cost allocation rate.

$$\frac{\text{Predetermined indirect cost}}{\text{allocation rate}} = \frac{\$300,000 \text{ expected indirect costs}}{10,000 \text{ expected direct labor hours}}$$

$$= \$30 \text{ per direct labor hour}$$

STEP 2. Allocate indirect costs to jobs by multiplying the predetermined indirect cost rate (Step 1) by the actual quantity of the allocation base used by each job. Client 367 required 14 direct labor hours, so the indirect costs are allocated as follows:

14 direct labor hours × $30/hour = $420

To summarize, the total costs assigned to client 367 are

Direct labor: 14 hours × $50/hour..........	$ 700
Indirect costs: 14 hours × $30/hour........	420
Total costs	$1,120

You have now learned how to use a job order cost system and assign costs to jobs. Review the Decision Guidelines to solidify your understanding.

Decision Guidelines

JOB ORDER COSTING

Companies using a job order costing system treat each job separately. Here are some of the decisions that a company makes when designing its job order costing system:

Decision	Guidelines
Are utilities, insurance, property taxes, and depreciation • Manufacturing overhead? • Or operating expenses?	These costs are part of manufacturing overhead *only* if they are incurred in the manufacturing plant. If unrelated to manufacturing, they are operating expenses. For example, if related to the research lab, they are R&D expenses. If related to executive headquarters, they are administrative expenses. If related to distribution centers, they are selling expenses. These are all operating expenses, not manufacturing overhead.

How to record *actual* manufacturing overhead costs?

Manufacturing Overhead	XXX	
Accumulated Depreciation—		
Plant and Equipment		XX
Prepaid Insurance—Plant & Equip.		XX
Utilities Payable (or Cash)		XX
and so on		XX

How to compute a predetermined manufacturing overhead rate?

$$\frac{\text{Total estimated manufacturing overhead cost}}{\text{Total estimated quantity of allocation base}}$$

How to record allocation of manufacturing overhead?

Work in Process Inventory	XX	
Manufacturing Overhead		XX

What is the *amount* of the allocated manufacturing overhead?

$$\begin{matrix}\text{Actual quantity} \\ \text{of the manufacturing} \\ \text{overhead allocation base}\end{matrix} \times \begin{matrix}\text{Predetermined} \\ \text{manufacturing} \\ \text{overhead rate}\end{matrix}$$

How to close Manufacturing Overhead at the end of the period?

Close directly to Cost of Goods Sold, as follows:

For *underallocated* overhead:

Cost of Goods Sold	XX	
Manufacturing Overhead		XX

For *overallocated* overhead:

Manufacturing Overhead	XX	
Cost of Goods sold		XX

When providing services, how to trace employees' direct labor to individual jobs?

Either automated software directly captures the amount of time employees spend on a client's job, or employees fill out a time record.

Why allocate noninventoriable costs to jobs?

Managers need total product costs for internal decisions (such as setting selling prices).

Summary Problem 2

Skippy Scooters manufactures motor scooters. The company has automated production, so it allocates manufacturing overhead based on machine hours. Skippy expects to incur $240,000 of manufacturing overhead costs and to use 4,000 machine hours during 2009.

At the end of 2008, Skippy reported the following inventories:

Materials Inventory........................	$20,000
Work in Process Inventory	17,000
Finished Goods Inventory	11,000

During January 2009, Skippy actually used 300 machine hours and recorded the following transactions:

a. **Purchased materials on account, $31,000.**

b. **Used direct materials, $39,000.**

c. **Manufacturing wages incurred totaled $40,000.**

d. **Manufacturing labor was 90% direct labor and 10% indirect labor.**

e. **Used indirect materials, $3,000.**

f. **Incurred other manufacturing overhead, $13,000 (credit Accounts Payable).**

g. **Allocated manufacturing overhead for January 2009.**

h. **Cost of completed motor scooters, $100,000.**

i. **Sold motor scooters on account, $175,000; cost of motor scooters sold, $95,000.**

Requirements

1. Compute Skippy's predetermined manufacturing overhead rate for 2009.

2. Record the transactions in the general journal.

3. Enter the beginning balances and then post the transactions to the following accounts:

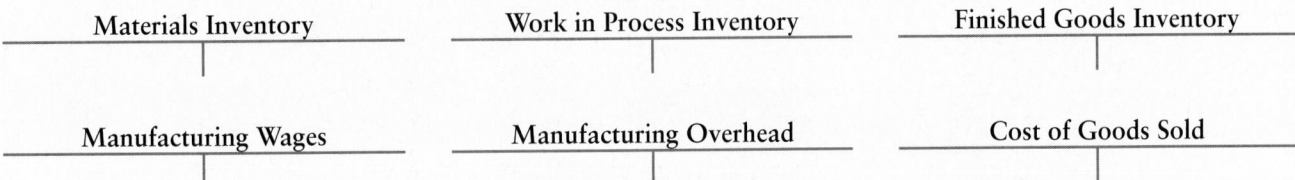

4. Close the ending balance of Manufacturing Overhead. Post your entry to the T-accounts.

5. What are the ending balances in the three inventory accounts and in Cost of Goods Sold?

Solution

Requirement 1

$$\text{Predetermined manufacturing overhead rate} = \frac{\text{Total estimated manufacturing overhead cost}}{\text{Total estimated quantity of allocation base}}$$

$$= \frac{\$240,000}{4,000 \text{ machine hours}}$$

$$= \$60/\text{machine hour}$$

Requirement 2

Journal entries:

a.		Materials Inventory	31,000	
		Accounts Payable		31,000
b.		Work in Process Inventory	39,000	
		Materials Inventory		39,000
c.		Manufacturing Wages	40,000	
		Wages Payable		40,000
d.		Work in Process Inventory ($40,000 × 0.90)	36,000	
		Manufacturing Overhead ($40,000 × 0.10)	4,000	
		Manufacturing Wages		40,000
e.		Manufacturing Overhead	3,000	
		Materials Inventory		3,000
f.		Manufacturing Overhead	13,000	
		Accounts Payable		13,000
g.		Work in Process Inventory (300 × $60)	18,000	
		Manufacturing Overhead		18,000
h.		Finished Goods Inventory	100,000	
		Work in Process Inventory		100,000
i.		Accounts Receivable	175,000	
		Sales Revenue		175,000
j.		Costs of Goods Sold	95,000	
		Finished Goods Inventory		95,000

Requirement 3

Post the transactions:

	Materials Inventory				
Bal.	20,000	(b)	39,000		
(a)	31,000	(e)	3,000		
Bal.	9,000				

	Work in Process Inventory				
Bal.	17,000	(h)	100,000		
(b)	39,000				
(d)	36,000				
(g)	18,000				
Bal.	10,000				

	Finished Goods Inventory				
Bal.	11,000	(j)	95,000		
(h)	100,000				
Bal.	16,000				

	Manufacturing Wages				
(c)	40,000	(d)	40,000		

	Manufacturing Overhead				
(d)	4,000	(g)	18,000		
(e)	3,000				
(f)	13,000				
Bal.	2,000				

	Cost of Goods Sold			
(j)	95,000			

Requirement 4

Close Manufacturing Overhead:

Cost of Goods Sold		2,000	
Manufacturing Overhead			2,000

	Manufacturing Overhead				
(d)	4,000	(g)	18,000		
(e)	3,000		2,000		
(f)	13,000				

	Cost of Goods Sold			
(j)	95,000			
	2,000			
Bal.	97,000			

Requirement 5

Ending Balances:

Materials Inventory (from Requirement 3)......................	$ 9,000
Work in Process Inventory (from Requirement 3)	10,000
Finished Goods Inventory (from Requirement 3)	16,000
Cost of Goods Sold (from Requirement 4).......................	97,000

Review *Job Order Costing*

Accounting Vocabulary

Allocation Base
A common denominator that links indirect costs to cost objects. Ideally, the allocation base is the primary cost driver of the indirect costs.

Cost Allocation
Assigning indirect costs (such as manufacturing overhead) to cost objects (such as jobs or production processes).

Cost Driver
The primary factor that causes a cost.

Cost Tracing
Assigning direct costs (such as direct materials and direct labor) to cost objects (such as jobs or production processes) that used those costs.

Job Cost Record
Document that accumulates the direct materials, direct labor, and manufacturing overhead costs assigned to an individual job.

Job Order Costing
A system that accumulates costs for each job. Law firms, music studios, health-care providers, mail-order catalog companies, building contractors, and custom furniture manufacturers are examples of companies that use job order costing systems.

Labor Time Record
Identifies the employee, the amount of time spent on a particular job, and the labor cost charged to the job; a record used to assign direct labor cost to specific jobs.

Materials Requisition
Request for the transfer of materials to the production floor, prepared by the production team.

Overallocated (manufacturing) Overhead
The manufacturing overhead allocated to Work in Progress Inventory is more than the amount of manufacturing overhead costs actually incurred.

Predetermined Manufacturing Overhead Rate
Estimated manufacturing overhead cost per unit of the allocation base, computed at the beginning of the year.

Process Costing
System for assigning costs to large numbers of identical units that usually proceed in a continuous fashion through a series of uniform productions steps or processes.

Time Record
Source document used to trace direct labor to specific jobs.

Underallocated (manufacturing) Overhead
The manufacturing overhead allocated to Work in Progress Inventory is less than the amount of manufacturing overhead costs actually incurred.

Quick Check

1. Would an advertising agency use job or process costing? What about a paper mill?

   a. Advertising agency—job order costing
      Paper mill—job order costing

   b. Advertising agency—process costing
      Paper mill—job order costing

   c. Advertising agency—job order costing
      Paper mill—process costing

   d. Advertising agency—process costing
      Paper mill—process costing

2. When a manufacturing company *uses* direct materials, it *traces* the cost by debiting:

   a. Materials Inventory

   b. Direct Materials

   c. Work in Process Inventory

   d. Manufacturing Overhead

3. When a manufacturing company *uses* indirect materials, it *assigns* the cost by debiting:

   a. Materials Inventory

   b. Manufacturing Overhead

   c. Indirect Materials

   d. Work in Process Inventory

4. When a manufacturing company *uses* direct labor, it *traces* the cost by debiting:

   a. Work in Process Inventory

   b. Manufacturing Wages

   c. Manufacturing Overhead

   d. Direct Labor

Questions 5, 6, 7, and 8 are based on the following information about Dell Corporation's manufacturing of computers. Assume Dell

- Allocates manufacturing overhead based on machine hours.
- Budgeted 10 million machine hours and $90 million of manufacturing overhead costs.
- Actually used 12 million machine hours and incurred the following actual costs (in millions):

Indirect labor	$10
Depreciation on plant	47
Machinery repair	15
Direct labor	75
Plant supplies	5
Plant utilities	8
Advertising	35
Sales commissions	25

5. What is Dell's predetermined manufacturing overhead rate?

   a. $0.11/machine hour

   b. $0.13/machine hour

   c. $7.50/machine hour

   d. $9.00/machine hour

6. What is Dell's actual manufacturing overhead cost?

   a. $220   c. $120

   b. $160   d. $85

7. How much manufacturing overhead would Dell allocate?

   a. $108   c. $85

   b. $90   d. $220

8. What entry would Dell make to close the manufacturing overhead account?

a.	Manufacturing Overhead	5	
	Costs of Goods Sold		5
b.	Cost of Goods Sold	5	
	Manufacturing Overhead		5
c.	Manufacturing Overhead	23	
	Costs of Goods Sold		23
d.	Cost of Goods Sold	23	
	Manufacturing Overhead		23

9. Dell's management can use product cost information to:

   a. Set prices of its products

   b. Decide which products to emphasize

   c. Identify ways to cut production costs

   d. All of the above

10. For which of the following reasons would John Walsh, owner of the Walsh Associates law firm, want to know the total costs of a job (serving a particular client)?

   a. For inventory valuation

   b. To determine the fees to charge clients

   c. For external reporting

   d. For all of the above

Answers are given after Apply Your Knowledge (p. 991).

Assess Your Progress

Short Exercises

Distinguishing between job costing and process costing

S19-1 Would the following companies use job order costing or process costing? (pp. 944–945)

A manufacturer of plywood

A manufacturer of wakeboards

A manufacturer of luxury yachts

A professional services firm

A landscape contractor

Flow of costs in job order costing

S19-2 For a manufacturer that uses job order costing, show the order of the cost flow through the following accounts, starting with the purchase of materials in the Materials Inventory (1). (p. 945)

   1   **a.** Materials Inventory

_____ **b.** Finished Goods Inventory

_____ **c.** Cost of Goods Sold

_____ **d.** Work in Process Inventory

Accounting for materials

2

S19-3 PackRite manufactures backpacks. Its plant records include the following materials-related transactions:

Purchases of canvas (on account).............	$70,000
Purchases of thread (on account)	1,000
Material requisitions:	
Canvas	63,000
Thread	300

What journal entries record these transactions? Post these transactions to the Materials Inventory account. If the company had $35,000 of Materials Inventory at the beginning of the period, what is the ending balance of Materials Inventory? (pp. 945–947).

Accounting for materials

2

S19-4 Use the following T-accounts to determine direct materials used and indirect materials used. (pp. 945–947)

Materials Inventory		
Bal.	15	
Purchases	230	X
Bal.	25	

Work in Process Inventory			
Bal.	30		
Direct materials	Y	Cost of goods	
Direct labor	300	manufactured	630
Manufacturing overhead	150		
Bal.	50		

Accounting for labor

S19-5 Seattle Crystal reports the following labor-related transactions at its plant in Seattle, Washington.

Plant janitor's wages	600
Furnace operator's wages	900
Glass blowers' wages	75,000

Record the journal entries for the incurrence and assignment of these wages. (pp. 947–950)

Accounting for overhead
3

S19-6 Teak Outdoor Furniture manufactures wood patio furniture. The company reports the following costs for June 2008. What is the balance in the Manufacturing Overhead account? (p. 954)

Wood...	$230,000
Nails, glue, and stain	21,000
Depreciation on saws........................	5,000
Indirect manufacturing labor............	40,000
Depreciation on delivery truck...........	2,200
Assembly-line workers' wages	56,000

Allocating overhead
3

S19-7 Job 303 includes direct materials cost of $500 and direct labor costs of $400. If the manufacturing overhead allocation rate is 70% of direct labor cost, what is the total cost assigned to Job 303? (pp. 955–956)

Accounting for materials, labor, overhead, and completed goods
2 3 4

S19-8 Boston Enterprises produces LCD touch screen products. The company reports the following information at December 31, 2008. Boston began operations on January 30, 2008.

Materials Inventory		Work in Process Inventory		Finished Goods Inventory		Manufacturing Wages		Manufacturing Overhead	
52,000	33,000	30,000	125,000	125,000	110,000	72,000	72,000	3,000	54,000
		60,000						12,000	
		54,000						37,000	

1. What is the cost of direct materials used? The cost of indirect materials used?
2. What is the cost of direct labor? The cost of indirect labor?
3. What is the cost of goods manufactured?
4. What is cost of goods sold (before adjusting for any under- or overallocated manufacturing overhead)? (pp. 957–958)

Allocating overhead
3

S19-9 Refer to S19-8.

1. What is the actual manufacturing overhead of Boston Enterprises? Allocated manufacturing overhead? (pp. 958–959)
2. Is manufacturing overhead underallocated or overallocated? By how much? (pp. 958–959)

S19-10 The T-account showing the manufacturing overhead activity for Brian Corp. for 2007 is as follows:

Manufacturing Overhead

200,000	210,000

1. What is the actual manufacturing overhead? Allocated manufacturing overhead? (p. 958)
2. What is the predetermined manufacturing overhead rate as a percentage of direct labor cost, if actual direct labor costs were $168,000? (p. 945)
3. Is manufacturing overhead underallocated or overallocated? By how much? (pp. 958–959)
4. Is Cost of Goods Sold too high or too low? (pp. 958–959)

S19-11 Refer to S19-10. Make the journal entry to close out Brian Corp.'s Manufacturing Overhead account. (pp. 958–959)

S19-12 Sautter Advertising pays Thomas Tibbs $110,000 per year. Tibbs works 2,000 hours per year.

1. What is the hourly cost to Sautter Advertising of employing Tibbs? (pp. 961–963)
2. What direct labor cost would be traced to client 507 if Tibbs works 14 hours to prepare client 507's magazine ad? (pp. 960–963)

S19-13 Refer to S19-12. Assume that Sautter's advertising agents are expected to work a total of 12,000 direct labor hours in 2009. Sautter's estimated total indirect costs are $240,000.

1. What is Sautter's indirect cost allocation rate? (pp. 960–963)
2. What indirect costs will be allocated to client 507 if Tibbs works 14 hours to prepare the magazine ad? (pp. 960–963)

Exercises

E19-14 Complete the following statements with the term job order costing or process costing. (pp. 944–945)

a. _____ is used by companies that produce small quantities of many different products.
b. Georgia-Pacific pulverizes wood into pulp to manufacture cardboard. The company uses a _____ system.
c. To record costs of maintaining thousands of identical mortgage files, financial institutions like Money Tree use a _____ system.
d. Companies that produce large numbers of identical products use _____ systems for product costing.
e. The computer repair service that visits your home and repairs your computer uses a _____ system.

Accounting for job costs

E19-15 Thrifty Trailers' job cost records yielded the following information:

Job No.	Date			Total Cost of Job at March 31
	Started	Finished	Sold	
1	February 21	March 16	March 17	$ 3,000
2	February 29	March 21	March 26	13,000
3	March 3	April 11	April 13	6,000
4	March 7	March 29	April 1	4,000

Requirements

Using the dates above to identify the status of each job, compute Thrifty's cost of (a) Work in Process Inventory at March 31, (b) Finished Goods Inventory at March 31, and (c) Cost of Goods Sold for March. (pp. 957–958)

Job order costing journal entries

E19-16 Record the following transactions in Sloan's Seats' general journal. (pp. 965–967)

a. Incurred and paid Web site expenses, $3,500.

b. Incurred and paid manufacturing wages, $15,000.

c. Purchased materials on account, $14,000.

d. Used in production: direct materials, $6,000; indirect materials, $4,000.

e. Assigned $15,000 of manufacturing labor to jobs, 60% of which was direct labor and 40% of which was indirect labor.

f. Recorded manufacturing overhead: depreciation on plant, $13,000; plant insurance, $1,000; plant property tax, $4,000 (credit Property Tax Payable).

g. Allocated manufacturing overhead to jobs, 200% of direct labor costs.

h. Completed production, $30,000.

i. Sold inventory on account, $20,000; cost of goods sold, $10,000.

Identifying job order costing journal entries

E19-17 Describe the lettered transactions in the following manufacturing accounts: (pp. 965–967)

Materials Inventory		Work in Process Inventory		Finished Goods Inventory	
(a)	(b)	(b)	(g)	(g)	(h)
		(d)			
		(f)			

Manufacturing Wages		Manufacturing Overhead		Cost of Goods Sold	
(c)	(d)	(b)	(f)	(h)	
		(d)	(i)	(i)	
		(e)			

Using the Work in Process Inventory account

E19-18 September production generated the following activity in Rohr Chassis Company's Work in Process Inventory account:

Work in Process Inventory	
September 1 Bal.	20,000
Direct materials used	30,000
Direct labor assigned to jobs	32,000
Manufacturing overhead allocated to jobs	16,000

continued...

Completed production, not yet recorded, consists of Jobs 142 and 143, with total costs of $40,000 and $38,000, respectively.

Requirements

1. Compute the cost of work in process at September 30. (pp. 965–967)
2. Prepare the journal entry for production completed in September. (pp. 957–958)
3. Prepare the journal entry to record the sale (on credit) of Job 143 for $45,000. Also make the cost-of-goods-sold entry. (pp. 965–967)
4. What is the gross profit on Job 143? What other costs must this gross profit cover?

Allocating manufacturing overhead

E19-19 Selected cost data for Classic Poster Co. are as follows:

Estimated manufacturing overhead cost for the year............	$100,000
Estimated direct labor cost for the year................................	80,000
Actual manufacturing overhead cost for the year.................	83,000
Actual direct labor cost for the year.....................................	64,000

Requirements

1. Compute the predetermined manufacturing overhead rate per direct labor dollar. (p. 955)
2. Prepare the journal entry to allocate overhead cost for the year. (p. 956)
3. Use a T-account to determine the amount of underallocated or over-allocated manufacturing overhead. (pp. 958–959)
4. Prepare the journal entry to close the balance of the Manufacturing Overhead account. (pp. 958–959)

Allocating manufacturing overhead

E19-20 Alba Foundry uses a predetermined manufacturing overhead rate to allocate overhead to individual jobs, based on the machine hours required. At the beginning of 2009, the company expected to incur the following:

Manufacturing overhead costs	$ 600,000
Direct labor cost.................................	1,500,000
Machine hours	60,000

At the end of 2009, the company had actually incurred:

Direct labor cost..	$1,210,000
Depreciation on manufacturing property, plant, and equipment...	480,000
Property taxes on plant	20,000
Sales salaries..	25,000
Delivery drivers' wages...	15,000
Plant janitors' wages...	10,000
Machine hours	55,000 hours

continued...

Requirements

1. Compute Alba's predetermined manufacturing overhead rate. (p. 955)

2. Record the summary journal entry for allocating manufacturing overhead. (p. 956)

3. Post the manufacturing overhead transactions to the Manufacturing Overhead T-account. Is manufacturing overhead underallocated or overallocated? By how much? (pp. 958–959)

4. Close the Manufacturing Overhead account to Cost of Goods Sold. Does your entry increase or decrease cost of goods sold? (pp. 958–959)

Allocating manufacturing
overhead

E19-21 Refer to the data in E19-20. Alba's accountant found an error in her 2009 cost records. Depreciation on manufacturing property, plant, and equipment was actually $530,000, not the $480,000 she originally reported.

Unadjusted balances at the end of 2009 include:

Finished Goods Inventory	$130,000
Cost of Goods Sold	600,000

Requirements

1. Use a T-account to determine whether manufacturing overhead is underallocated or overallocated, and by how much. (pp. 958–959)

2. Record the entry to close out the underallocated or overallocated manufacturing overhead. (pp. 958–959)

3. What is the adjusted ending balance of Cost of Goods Sold? (pp. 958–959)

Job order costing in a
service company

5

E19-22 Martin Realtors, a real estate consulting firm, specializes in advising companies on potential new plant sites. The company uses a job order costing system with a predetermined indirect cost allocation rate, computed as a percentage of direct labor costs.

At the beginning of 2009, managing partner Ken Martin prepared the following budget for the year:

Direct labor hours (professionals)	17,000 hours
Direct labor costs (professionals)..............	$2,550,000
Office rent...	300,000
Support staff salaries	900,000
Utilities...	330,000

Lieberman Manufacturing, Inc., is inviting several consultants to bid for work. Ken Martin estimates that this job will require about 220 direct labor hours.

Requirements

1. Compute Martin Realtors' (a) hourly direct labor cost rate and (b) indirect cost allocation rate. (pp. 960–963)

continued...

2. Compute the predicted cost of the Lieberman Manufacturing job. (pp. 960–963)

3. If Martin wants to earn a profit that equals 50% of the job's cost, how much should he bid for the Lieberman Manufacturing job? (pp. 960–963)

Allocating manufacturing overhead

E19-23 The manufacturing records for Kool Kayaks at the end of the 2008 fiscal year show the following information about manufacturing overhead:

Overhead allocated to production	$405,000
Actual manufacturing overhead costs	$430,250
Overhead allocation rate for the year	$40 per machine hour

Requirements
1. How many machine hours did Kool Kayaks use in 2008? (p. 956)
2. Was manufacturing overhead over- or underallocated for the year? By how much? (pp. 958–959)
3. Record the entry to close out the over- or underallocated overhead. (pp. 958–959)

Problems (Group A)

Analyzing job cost data

P19-24A Hartley Manufacturing makes carrying cases for portable electronic devices. Its job order costing records yield the following information:

Job No.	Date			Total Cost of Job at November 30	Total Manufacturing Costs Added in December
	Started	Finished	Sold		
1	11/3	11/12	11/13	$1,500	
2	11/3	11/30	12/1	2,000	
3	11/17	12/24	12/27	300	$ 700
4	11/29	12/29	1/3	500	1,600
5	12/8	12/12	12/14		750
6	12/23	1/6	1/9		500

Requirements
1. Using the dates above to identify the status of each job, compute Hartley's account balances at November 30 for Work in Process Inventory, Finished Goods Inventory, and Cost of Goods Sold. Compute account balances at December 31 for Work in Process Inventory, Finished Goods Inventory, and Cost of Goods Sold. (pp. 957–958)

2. Record summary journal entries for the transfer of completed units from work in process to finished goods for November and December. (pp. 957–958)

3. Record the sale of Job 3 for $1,500. (pp. 957–958)

4. What is the gross profit for Job 3? What other costs must this gross profit cover?

Accounting for construction
transactions

P19-25A Steinborn Construction, Inc., is a home builder in New Mexico. Steinborn uses a job order costing system in which each house is a job. Because it constructs houses, the company uses accounts titled Construction Wages and Construction Overhead. The following events occurred during August:

a. Purchased materials on account, $480,000.

b. Incurred construction wages of $220,000. Requisitioned direct materials and used direct labor in construction:

	Direct Materials	Direct Labor
House 402	$58,000	$42,000
House 403	69,000	33,000
House 404	68,000	50,000
House 405	85,000	53,000

c. Depreciation of construction equipment, $6,400.

d. Other construction overhead costs incurred on houses 402 through 405:

Indirect labor	$42,000
Equipment rentals paid in cash	37,000
Worker liability insurance expired	7,000

e. Allocated overhead to jobs at the predetermined overhead rate of 40% of direct labor cost.

f. Houses completed: 402, 404.

g. House sold: 404 for $200,000.

Requirements

1. Record the events in the general journal. (p. 956)

2. Open T-accounts for Work in Process Inventory and Finished Goods Inventory. Post the appropriate entries to these accounts, identifying each entry by letter. Determine the ending account balances, assuming that the beginning balances were zero. (pp. 965–967)

3. Add the costs of the unfinished houses, and show that this total amount equals the ending balance in the Work in Process Inventory account. (p. 956)

4. Add the cost of the completed house that has not yet been sold, and show that this equals the ending balance in Finished Goods Inventory. (p. 956)

5. Compute gross profit on the house that was sold. What costs must gross profit cover for Steinborn Construction?

Preparing and using a job
cost record

P19-26A Yu Technology Co. manufactures CDs and DVDs for computer software and entertainment companies. Yu uses job order costing and has a perpetual inventory system.

continued. . .

On November 2, Yu began production of 5,000 DVDs, Job 423, for Cheetah Pictures for $1.10 each. Yu promised to deliver the DVDs to Cheetah by November 5. Yu incurred the following costs:

Date	Labor Time Record No.	Description	Amount
11-2	655	10 hours @ $20	$200
11-3	656	20 hours @ $15	300

Date	Materials Requisition No.	Description	Amount
11-2	63	31 lbs. polycarbonate plastic @ $11	$341
11-2	64	25 lbs. acrylic plastic @ $28	700
11-3	74	3 lbs. refined aluminum @ $48	144

Yu Technology allocates manufacturing overhead to jobs based on the relation between estimated overhead ($540,000) and estimated direct labor costs ($450,000). Job 423 was completed and shipped on November 3.

Requirements

1. Prepare a job cost record similar to Exhibit 19-7 for Job 423. Calculate the predetermined overhead rate, then apply manufacturing overhead to the job. (pp. 955–956)

2. Journalize in summary form the requisition of direct materials and the assignment of direct labor and manufacturing overhead to Job 423. (pp. 945–946, 947–948, 957–958).

3. Journalize completion of the job and the sale of the 5,000 DVDs (pp. 957, 958).

Accounting for manufacturing overhead
3 4

P19-27A Weiters Woods manufactures jewelry boxes. The primary materials (wood, brass, and glass) and direct labor are traced directly to the products. Manufacturing overhead costs are allocated based on machine hours. Data for 2008 follow:

	Budget	Actual
Machine hours..................................	28,000 hours	32,800 hours
Maintenance labor (repairs to equipment).....................................	12,000	22,500
Plant supervisor's salary....................	42,000	44,000
Screws, nails, and glue	23,000	41,000
Plant utilities.....................................	48,000	90,850
Freight out..	35,000	44,500
Depreciation on plant and equipment......................................	85,000	81,000
Advertising expenses..........................	40,000	55,000

Requirements

1. Compute the predetermined manufacturing overhead rate. (p. 955)

2. Post actual and allocated manufacturing overhead to the Manufacturing Overhead T-account. (pp. 957–958)

continued. . .

3. Close the under- or overallocated overhead to Cost of Goods Sold. (pp. 958–959)

4. The predetermined manufacturing overhead rate usually turns out to be inaccurate. Why don't accountants just use the actual manufacturing overhead rate? (p. 955)

Comprehensive accounting for manufacturing transactions

P19-28A Lonyx Telecommunications produces components for telecommunication systems. Initially the company manufactured the parts for its own networks, but it gradually began selling them to other companies as well. Lonyx's trial balance on April 1 follows.

LONYX TELECOMMUNICATIONS
Trial Balance
April 1, 2009

Account Title	Debit	Credit
Cash	$ 18,000	
Accounts receivable	170,000	
Inventories:		
Materials	5,300	
Work in process	41,300	
Finished goods	21,300	
Plant assets	250,000	
Accumulated depreciation		$ 68,000
Accounts payable		129,000
Wages payable		2,800
Common stock		140,000
Retained earnings		166,100
Sales revenue		—
Cost of goods sold	—	
Manufacturing wages	—	
Manufacturing overhead	—	
Marketing and general expenses	—	
	$505,900	$505,900

April 1 balances in the subsidiary ledgers were:

- Materials ledger: glass substrate, $4,800; indirect materials, $500.
- Work in process ledger: Job 120, $41,300.
- Finished goods ledger: fiber optic cable, $9,300; laser diodes, $12,000.

April transactions are summarized as follows:

a. Collections on account, $149,000.

b. Marketing and general expenses incurred and paid, $25,000.

c. Payments on account, $38,000.

d. Materials purchased on credit: glass substrate, $24,500; indirect materials, $4,600.

continued. . .

e. Materials used in production (requisitioned):
   - Job 120: glass substrate, $750.
   - Job 121: glass substrate, $7,800.
   - Indirect materials, $2,000.

f. Manufacturing wages incurred during April, $38,000, of which $36,000 was paid. Wages payable at March 31 were paid during April, $2,800.

g. Labor time records for the month: Job 120, $4,000; Job 121, $18,000; indirect labor, $16,000.

h. Depreciation on plant and equipment, $2,400.

i. Manufacturing overhead was allocated at the predetermined rate of 70% of direct labor cost.

j. Jobs completed during the month: Job 120, 400 fiber optic cables at total cost of $48,850.

k. Credit sales on account: all of Job 120 for $110,000.

l. Closed the Manufacturing Overhead account to Cost of Goods Sold.

Requirements

1. Open T-accounts for the general ledger, the materials ledger, the work in process ledger, and the finished goods ledger. Insert each account balance as given, and use the reference *Bal.* (pp. 965–967)

2. Record the April transactions directly in the accounts, using the letters as references. Lonyx uses a perpetual inventory system. (pp. 965–967)

3. Prepare a trial balance at April 30.

4. Use the Work in Process T-account to prepare a schedule of cost of goods manufactured for the month of April. (You may want to review Exhibit 18-10.)

5. Prepare an income statement for the month of April. To calculate cost of goods sold, you may want to review Exhibit 18-7. (*Hint:* In transaction l you closed any under/overallocated manufacturing overhead to Cost of Goods Sold. In the income statement, show this correction as an adjustment to Cost of Goods Sold. If manufacturing overhead is underallocated, the adjustment will increase Cost of Goods Sold. If overhead is overallocated, the adjustment will decrease Cost of Goods Sold.)

Job order costing in a service company

5

P19-29A Bluebird Design, Inc., is a Web site design and consulting firm. The firm uses a job order costing system, in which each client is a different job. Bluebird Design traces direct labor, licensing costs, and travel costs directly to each job. It allocates indirect costs to jobs based on a predetermined indirect cost allocation rate, computed as a percentage of direct labor costs.

At the beginning of 2009, managing partner Judi Jacquin prepared the following budget:

Direct labor hours (professional)............	6,250 hours
Direct labor costs (professional).............	$1,000,000
Support staff salaries.............................	120,000
Computer leases....................................	45,000
Office supplies.......................................	25,000
Office rent...	60,000

continued. . .

In November 2009, Bluebird Design served several clients. Records for two clients appear here:

	Food Coop	Mesilla Chocolates
Direct labor hours	750 hours	50 hours
Licensing costs.................	$ 2,000	$150
Travel costs......................	14,000	—

Requirements

1. Compute Bluebird Design's predetermined indirect cost allocation rate for 2009. (pp. 960–963)

2. Compute the total cost of each job. (pp. 960–963)

3. If Jacquin wants to earn profits equal to 20% of sales revenue, how much (what fee) should she charge each of these two clients? (pp. 960–963)

4. Why does Bluebird Design assign costs to jobs? (pp. 960–963)

Problems (Group B)

Analyzing job cost data

P19-30B EnginePro, Inc., reconditions engines. Its job order costing records yield the following information. EnginePro uses a perpetual inventory system.

Job No.	Date Started	Date Finished	Date Sold	Total Cost of Job at March 31	Total Manufacturing Costs Added in April
1	2/26	3/7	3/9	$1,400	
2	2/3	3/12	3/13	1,600	
3	3/29	3/31	4/3	1,300	
4	3/31	4/1	4/1	500	$ 400
5	4/8	4/12	4/14		700
6	4/23	5/6	5/9		1,200

Requirements

1. Using the dates above to identify the status of each job, compute EnginePro's account balances at March 31 for Work in Process Inventory, Finished Goods Inventory, and Cost of Goods Sold. Compute account balances at April 30 for Work in Process Inventory, Finished Goods Inventory, and Cost of Goods Sold. (pp. 957–958)

2. Make summary journal entries to record the transfer of completed jobs from Work in Process to Finished Goods for March and April. (pp. 957–958)

3. Record the sale of Job 5 for $1,600. (pp. 957–958)

4. Compute the gross profit for Job 5. What costs must the gross profit cover?

P19-31B Vacation Homes manufactures prefabricated chalets in Utah. The company uses a job order costing system in which each chalet is a job. The following events occurred during May.

a. Purchased materials on account, $405,000.

b. Incurred manufacturing wages of $112,000. Requisitioned direct materials and used direct labor in manufacturing:

	Direct Materials	Direct Labor
Chalet 20	$41,000	$15,000
Chalet 21	56,000	29,000
Chalet 22	62,000	19,000
Chalet 23	66,000	21,000

c. Depreciation of manufacturing equipment, $20,000.

d. Other overhead costs incurred on chalets 20 through 23:

Indirect labor..	$28,000
Equipment rentals paid in cash............	10,400
Plant insurance expired........................	6,000

e. Allocated overhead to jobs at the predetermined rate of 60% of direct labor cost.

f. Chalets completed: 20, 22, and 23.

g. Chalets sold: 20 for $99,000; 23 for $141,900.

Requirements

1. Record the preceding events in the general journal. (p. 966)

2. Open T-accounts for Work in Process Inventory and Finished Goods Inventory. Post the appropriate entries to these accounts, identifying each entry by letter. Determine the ending account balances, assuming that the beginning balances were zero. (pp. 947–948)

3. Add the costs of the unfinished chalet, and show that this equals the ending balance in Work in Process Inventory. (p. 958)

4. Add the cost of the completed chalet that has not yet been sold, and show that this equals the ending balance in Finished Goods Inventory. (p. 956)

5. Compute the gross profit on each chalet that was sold. What costs must the gross profit cover for Vacation Homes?

P19-32B Alamo Co. manufactures tires for all-terrain vehicles. Alamo uses job order costing and has a perpetual inventory system.

On June 22, 2008, Alamo received an order for 100 TX tires from ATV Corporation at a price of $55 each. The job, assigned number 300, was promised for July 10. After purchasing the materials, Alamo began production on June 30 and incurred the following costs in completing the order:

Date	Labor Time Record No.	Description	Amount
6/30	1896	12.5 hours @ $20	$250
7/3	1904	30 hours @ $19	570

continued. . .

Date	Materials Requisition No.	Description	Amount
6/30	437	60 lbs. rubber @ $12	$ 720
7/2	439	40 meters polyester fabric @ $12.50	500
7/3	501	100 meters steel cord @ $10	1,000

Alamo allocates manufacturing overhead to jobs on the basis of the relation between estimated overhead ($400,000) and estimated direct labor cost ($250,000). Job 300 was completed on July 3 and shipped to ATV on July 5.

Requirements

1. Prepare a job cost record similar to Exhibit 19-7 for Job 300. Calculate the predetermined overhead rate, then apply manufacturing overhead to the job. (pp. 955–956)

2. Journalize in summary form the requisition of direct materials and the assignment of direct labor and manufacturing overhead to Job 300. (pp. 945–946, 947–948, 957–958)

3. Journalize completion of the job and sale of the tires. (pp. 957–958)

Accounting for manufacturing overhead
3 **4**

P19-33B Regal Company produces hospital uniforms. The company allocates manufacturing overhead based on the machine hours each job uses. Regal reports the following cost data for 2009:

	Budget	Actual
Machine hours....................................	7,000 hours	6,500 hours
Indirect materials................................	50,000	52,000
Depreciation on trucks used to deliver uniforms to customers	14,000	12,000
Depreciation on plant and equipment	65,000	67,000
Indirect manufacturing labor	40,000	43,000
Customer service hotline.....................	19,000	21,000
Plant utilities......................................	27,000	20,000

Requirements

1. Compute the predetermined manufacturing overhead rate. (p. 955)

2. Post actual and allocated manufacturing overhead to the Manufacturing Overhead T-account. (pp. 957–958)

3. Close the under- or overallocated overhead to Cost of Goods Sold. (pp. 958–959)

4. How can managers use accounting information to help control manufacturing overhead costs? (pp. 955–956)

P19-34B WireComm manufactures specialized components used in wireless communication. Initially, the company manufactured the components for its own use, but it gradually began selling them to other wireless companies as well. The trial balance of WireComm's manufacturing operations on January 1, 2009, is as follows:

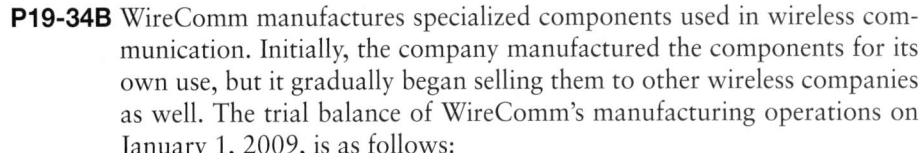

Account Title	Debit	Credit
Cash	$147,000	
Accounts receivable	88,000	
Inventories:		
Materials	17,000	
Work in process	44,000	
Finished goods	61,000	
Plant assets	353,000	
Accumulated depreciation		$157,000
Accounts payable		84,000
Wages payable		5,500
Common stock		225,000
Retained earnings		238,500
Sales revenues		—
Cost of goods sold	—	
Manufacturing wages	—	
Manufacturing overhead	—	
Marketing and general expenses	—	
	$710,000	$710,000

January 1 balances in the subsidiary ledgers were:
- Materials ledger: electronic parts, $15,300; indirect materials, $1,700.
- Work in process ledger: Job 90, $44,000.
- Finished goods ledger: transmitters, $38,000; power supplies, $23,000.

January transactions are summarized as follows:

a. Payments on account, $81,000.

b. Marketing and general expenses incurred and paid, $22,000.

c. Collections on account, $195,000.

d. Materials purchased on credit: electronic parts, $49,000; indirect materials, $6,000.

e. Materials used in production (requisitioned):
- Job 90: electronic parts, $4,000.
- Job 91: electronic parts, $38,000.
- Indirect materials, $7,000.

continued. . .

f. Manufacturing wages incurred during January, $56,000, of which $50,500 was paid. Wages payable at December 31 were paid during January, $5,500.

g. Labor time records for the month: Job 90, $6,000; Job 91, $28,000; indirect labor, $22,000.

h. Depreciation on manufacturing plant and equipment, $7,500.

i. Manufacturing overhead was allocated at the predetermined rate of 120% of direct labor cost.

j. Jobs completed during the month: Job 90, 1,000 transmitters, at total cost of $61,200.

k. Credit sales on account: all of Job 90 for $125,000.

l. Close the Manufacturing Overhead account to Cost of Goods Sold.

Requirements

1. Open T-accounts for the general ledger, the materials ledger, the work in process ledger, and the finished goods ledger. Insert each account balance as given, and use the reference *Bal.* (pp. 965–967)

2. Record the January transactions directly in the accounts, using the letters as references. WireComm uses a perpetual inventory system. (pp. 965–967)

3. Prepare a trial balance at January 31.

4. Use the Work in Process T-account to prepare a schedule of cost of goods manufactured for the month of January. (You may want to review Exhibit 18-10.)

5. Prepare an income statement for the month of January. To calculate cost of goods sold, you may want to review Exhibit 18-7. (*Hint:* In transaction l, you closed any under/overallocated manufacturing overhead to Cost of Goods Sold. In the income statement, show this correction as an adjustment to Cost of Goods Sold. If manufacturing overhead is underallocated, the adjustment will increase Cost of Goods Sold. If overhead is overallocated, the adjustment will decrease Cost of Goods Sold.)

Job order costing in a service company

5

P19-35B Simms Advertising is an Internet advertising agency. The firm uses a job order costing system in which each client is a different job. Simms Advertising traces direct labor, software licensing costs, and travel costs directly to each job. The company allocates indirect costs to jobs based on a predetermined indirect cost allocation rate, computed as a percentage of direct labor costs.

At the beginning of 2008, managing partner Stacy Simms prepared the following budget:

Direct labor hours (professional)............	16,000 hours
Direct labor costs (professional).............	$1,600,000
Support staff salaries.............................	350,000
Rent and utilities...................................	150,000
Supplies...	15,000
Leased computer hardware	285,000

continued. . .

In January 2008, Simms Advertising served several clients. Records for two clients appear here:

	VacationPlan.com	Port Arthur Golf Resort
Direct labor hours......................	450 hours	30 hours
Software licensing costs.............	$1,500	$300
Travel costs	9,000	—

Requirements

1. Compute Simms Advertising's predetermined indirect cost allocation rate for 2008. (pp. 960–963)
2. Compute the total cost of each job. (pp. 960–963)
3. If Simms Advertising wants to earn profits equal to 30% of sales revenue, how much (what fee) should it charge each of these two clients? (pp. 960–963)
4. Why does Simms Advertising assign costs to jobs? (pp. 960–963)

for 24/7 practice, visit www.MyAccountingLab.com

Apply Your Knowledge

Decision Cases

Costing and pricing
identical products

Case 1. Hiebert Chocolate Ltd. is located in Memphis. The company prepares gift boxes of chocolates for private parties and corporate promotions. Each order contains a selection of chocolates determined by the customer, and the box is designed to the customer's specifications. Accordingly, Hiebert uses a job order costing system and allocates manufacturing overhead based on direct labor cost.

One of Hiebert's largest customers is the Goforth and Leos law firm. This organization sends chocolates to its clients each Christmas and also provides them to employees at the firm's gatherings. The law firm's managing partner, Bob Goforth, placed the client gift order in September for 500 boxes of cream-filled dark chocolates. But Goforth and Leos did not place its December staff-party order until the last week of November. This order was for an additional 100 boxes of chocolates identical to the ones to be distributed to clients.

Hiebert budgeted the cost per box for the original 500-box order as follows:

Chocolate, filling, wrappers, box.....................................	$14.00
Employee time to fill and wrap the box (10 min.)	2.00
Manufacturing overhead	1.00
Total manufacturing cost..	$17.00

Ben Hiebert, president of Hiebert Chocolate Ltd., priced the order at $20 per box.

In the past few months, Hiebert has experienced price increases for both dark chocolate and direct labor. All other costs have remained the same. Hiebert budgeted the cost per box for the second order as:

Chocolate, filling, wrappers, box.....................................	$15.00
Employee time to fill and wrap the box (10 min.)	2.20
Manufacturing overhead	1.10
Total manufacturing cost..	$18.30

1. Do you agree with the cost analysis for the second order? Explain your answer. (pp. 945–946, 956–958)

2. Should the two orders be accounted for as one job or two in Hiebert's system? (pp. 945–946)

3. What sale price per box should Ben Hiebert set for the second order? What are the advantages and disadvantages of this price?

Accounting for
manufacturing overhead
3

Case 2. Nature's Own manufactures organic fruit preserves sold primarily through health food stores and on the Web. The company closes for two weeks each December to enable employees to spend time with their families over the holiday season. Nature's Own's manufacturing overhead is mostly straight-line depreciation on its plant and air-conditioning costs for keeping the berries cool during the summer months. The company uses direct labor hours as the manufacturing overhead allocation base. President Cynthia Ortega has just approved new accounting software and is telling Controller Jack Strong about her decision.

"I think this new software will be great," Ortega says. "It will save you time in preparing all those reports."

"Yes, and having so much more information just a click away will help us make better decisions and help control costs," replies Strong. "We need to consider how we can use the new system to improve our business practices."

"And I know just where to start," says Ortega. "You complain each year about having to predict the weather months in advance for estimating air-conditioning costs and direct labor hours for the denominator of the predetermined manufacturing overhead rate, when professional meteorologists can't even get tomorrow's forecast right! I think we should calculate the predetermined overhead rate on a monthly basis."

Controller Strong is not so sure this is a good idea.

Requirements

1. What are the advantages and disadvantages of Ortega's proposal?

2. Should Nature's Own compute its predetermined manufacturing overhead rate on an annual basis or monthly basis? Explain. (p. 955)

Ethical Issue

Ethics

Farley, Inc. is a contract manufacturer that produces customized computer components for several well-known computer-assembly companies. Farley's latest contract with CompWest.com calls for Farley to deliver sound cards that simulate surround sound from two speakers. Farley spent several hundred thousand dollars to design the sound card to meet CompWest.com's specifications.

Farley's president, Bryon Wilson, has stipulated a pricing policy that requires the bid price for a new job to be based on Farley's estimated costs to design, manufacture, distribute, and provide customer service for the job, plus a profit margin. Upon reviewing the contract figures, Farley's controller, Paul York, was startled to find that the cost estimates developed by Farley's cost accountant, Tony Hayes, for the CompWest.com bid were based on only the manufacturing costs. York is upset with Hayes. He is not sure what to do next.

Requirements

1. How did using manufacturing cost only rather than all costs associated with the CompWest.com job affect the amount of Farley's bid for the job?

2. Identify the parties involved in Paul York's ethical dilemma. What are his alternatives? How would each party be affected by each alternative? What should York do next?

Team Project

Major airlines like American, Delta, and Continental are struggling to meet the challenges of budget carriers such as Southwest and JetBlue. Suppose Delta CFO

continued . . .

Comparing job costs across
airlines, evaluating strategic
alternatives

M. Michele Burns has just returned from a meeting on strategies for responding to competition from budget carriers. The vice president of operations suggested doing nothing: "We just need to wait until these new airlines run out of money. They cannot be making money with their low fares." In contrast, the vice president of marketing, not wanting to lose market share, suggests cutting Delta's fares to match the competition. "If JetBlue charges only $75 for that flight from New York, so must we!" Others, including CFO Burns, emphasized the potential for cutting costs. Another possibility is starting a new budget airline within Delta. CEO Leo Mullin cut the meeting short, and directed Burns to "get some hard data."

As a start, Burns decides to collect cost and revenue data for a typical Delta flight, and then compare it to the data for a competitor. Assume she prepares the following schedule:

	Delta	JetBlue
Route: New York to Tampa	Flight 1247	Flight 53
Distance	1,000 miles	1,000 miles
Seats per plane	142	162
One-way ticket price	$80–$621*	$75
Food and beverage	Meal	Snack

*The highest price is first class airfare

Excluding food and beverage, Burns estimates that the cost per available seat mile is 8.4 cents for Delta, compared to 5.3 cents for JetBlue. (That is, the cost of flying a seat for one mile—whether or not the seat is occupied—is 8.4 cents for Delta, and 5.3 cents for JetBlue.) Assume the average cost of food and beverage is $5 per passenger for snacks and $10 for a meal.

Split your team into two groups. Group 1 should prepare its response to Requirement 1 and group 2 should prepare its response to Requirement 2 before the entire team meets to consider Requirements 3 and 4.

Requirements

1. Use the data to determine for Delta:
   a. the total cost of Flight 1247, assuming a full plane (100% load factor)
   b. the revenue generated by Flight 1247, assuming a 100% load factor and average revenue per one-way ticket of $102
   c. the profit per Flight 1247, given the responses to a. and b.

2. Use the data to determine for JetBlue:
   a. the total cost of Flight 53, assuming a full plane (100% load factor)
   b. the revenue generated by Flight 53, assuming a 100% load factor
   c. the profit per Flight 53, given the responses to a. and b.

3. Based on the responses to Requirements 1 and 2, carefully evaluate each of the four alternative strategies discussed in Delta's executive meeting.

continued...

4. The analysis in this project is based on several simplifying assumptions. As a team, brainstorm factors that your quantitative evaluation does not include, but that may affect a comparison of Delta's operations to budget carriers.

For Internet exercises, Excel in Practice, and additional online activities, go to the Web site www.prenhall.com/horngren.

Quick Check Answers

1. *c*   2. *c*   3. *b*   4. *a*   5. *d*   6. *d*   7. *a*   8. *c*   9. *d*   10. *b*

20 Process Costing

Learning Objectives

1 Distinguish between process costing and job order costing

2 Compute equivalent units

3 Use process costing to assign costs to units completed and to units in ending work in process inventory

4 Use the weighted-average method to assign costs to units completed and to units in ending work in process inventory in a second department

What's your favorite crayon color? Purple heart? Caribbean green? Electric lime? Or maybe Laser lemon? Have you ever wondered how they make these crayons? Every day Crayola makes 12 million crayons through five different processes:

- Mixing wax and pigment
- Molding and cooling
- Inspecting
- Labeling
- Packaging

Binney and Smith, the owner of Crayola, needs to know how much it costs to make each batch. That helps Binney and Smith set selling prices and measure profits. The company can also control costs if it knows how the processes are operating. The company uses accounting information to answer these questions.

Crayola mass-produces crayons in a sequence of processes. The company accumulates costs for each *process.* Then Crayola spreads these costs over the processes used to make crayons. This is easier than trying to keep track of the cost of each crayon, especially when the company manufactures 12 million crayons every day! ■

Let's start by contrasting the two basic types of costing systems:

- Job order costing
- Process costing

Process Costing: An Overview

Two Basic Costing Systems: Job Order Costing and Process Costing

1 Distinguish between process costing and job order costing

We saw in Chapter 19 that companies like Dell Computer, Boeing, and PricewaterhouseCoopers, the CPA firm, use job order costing to determine the cost of their custom goods and services. Companies like Seasons Greeting, a manufacturer of handmade greeting cards, create a job order for each customer. In contrast, Shell Oil, Crayola, and Sony use a series of steps (called *processes*) to make large quantities of similar products. Shell, Crayola, and Sony typically use *process costing* systems.

To introduce process costing, we will look at the crayon manufacturing process. Let's combine Crayola's manufacturing into three processes: Mixing, Molding, and Packaging. Crayola accumulates the costs of each process. The company then assigns these costs to the crayons passing through that process.

Suppose Crayola's production costs incurred to make 10,000 crayons and the costs per crayon are:

	Total Costs	Cost per Crayon
Mixing...............	$200	$0.02
Molding..............	100	0.01
Packaging	300	0.03
Total cost.............	$600	$0.06

The total cost to produce 10,000 crayons is the sum of the costs incurred for the three processes. The cost per crayon is the total cost divided by the number of crayons, or $600/10,000 = $.06 per crayon.

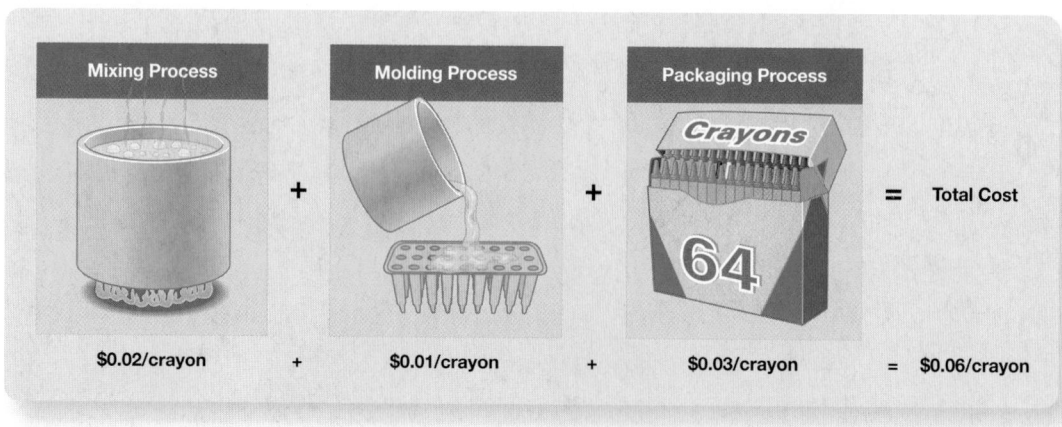

Crayola Company uses the cost per unit of each process to:

- Control costs. The company can find ways to cut the costs where actual process costs are more than planned process costs.
- Set selling prices. The company wants the selling price to cover the costs of making the crayons and also to earn a profit.
- Calculate the ending inventory of crayons for the balance sheet and the cost of goods sold for the income statement.

At any moment, some crayons are in the mixing process, some are in the molding process, and others are in the packaging department. Computing the crayons' cost becomes more complicated when some of the units are still in process. In this chapter, you will learn how to use process costing to calculate the cost of homogeneous products, such as crayons, gasoline, and breakfast cereal.

How Does the Flow of Costs Differ Between Job and Process Costing?

Exhibit 20-1 compares cost flows in:

- A job order costing system for Dell Computer
- A process costing system for Crayola

Panel A shows that Dell's job order costing system has a single Work in Process Inventory control account. Keep in mind that the Work in Process Inventory account in the general ledger is supported by an individual subsidiary cost record for each job (for example, each custom-built computer). The job order system assigns direct materials, direct labor, and manufacturing overhead to individual jobs, as discussed in Chapter 19.

In contrast, Crayola uses a series of *manufacturing processes* to produce crayons. Exhibit 20-2 shows the following:

- Mixing process: Crayola uses labor and heated tanks to mix wax and pigments.
- Molding process: Crayola uses labor and crayon molds to shape the crayons.
- Packaging process: Crayola uses labor, roller presses, cardboard containers, and labels to package crayons.

Exhibit 20-1, Panel B summarizes the flow of costs through this process costing system. Study the exhibit carefully, focusing on the following key points.

1. Each process (Mixing, Molding, and Packaging) is a separate department and each department has its own Work in Process Inventory account.

2. Direct materials, direct labor, and manufacturing overhead are assigned to Work in Process Inventory for each process, as shown in these T-accounts:

	Work in Process Inventory Mixing		Work in Process Inventory Molding		Work in Process Inventory Packaging	
Direct materials	Wax & Pigment		None		Boxes & Labels	
Direct labor	Mixing operators' wages		Molding operators' wages		Packaging operators' wages	
Manufacturing overhead	Depreciation of mixing tanks		Depreciation of molds		Depreciation of roller presses	

continued on page 997 . . .

EXHIBIT 20-1 Comparison of Job Order Costing and Process Costing

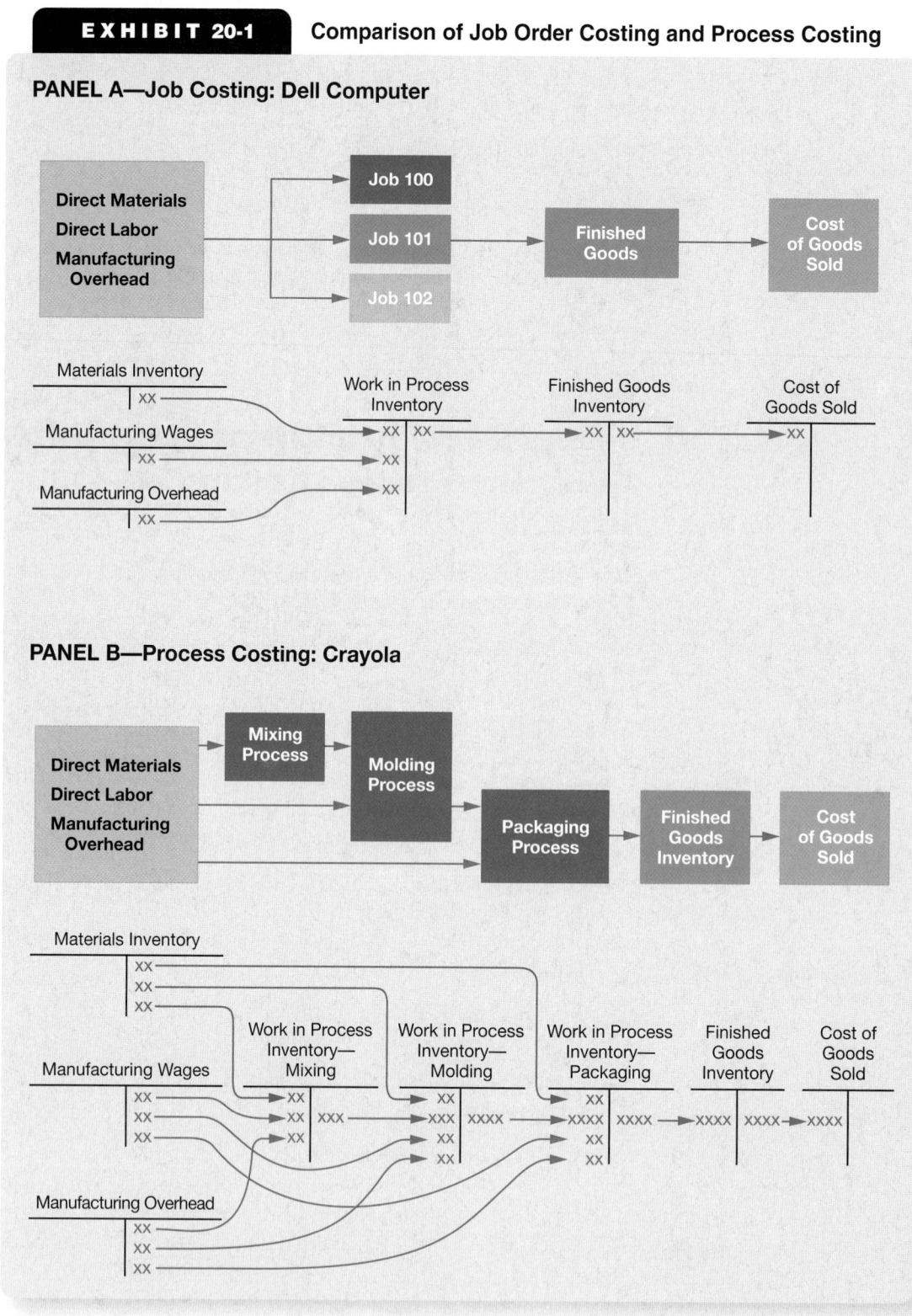

PANEL A—Job Costing: Dell Computer

PANEL B—Process Costing: Crayola

EXHIBIT 20-2   **Flow of Costs in Production of Crayons**

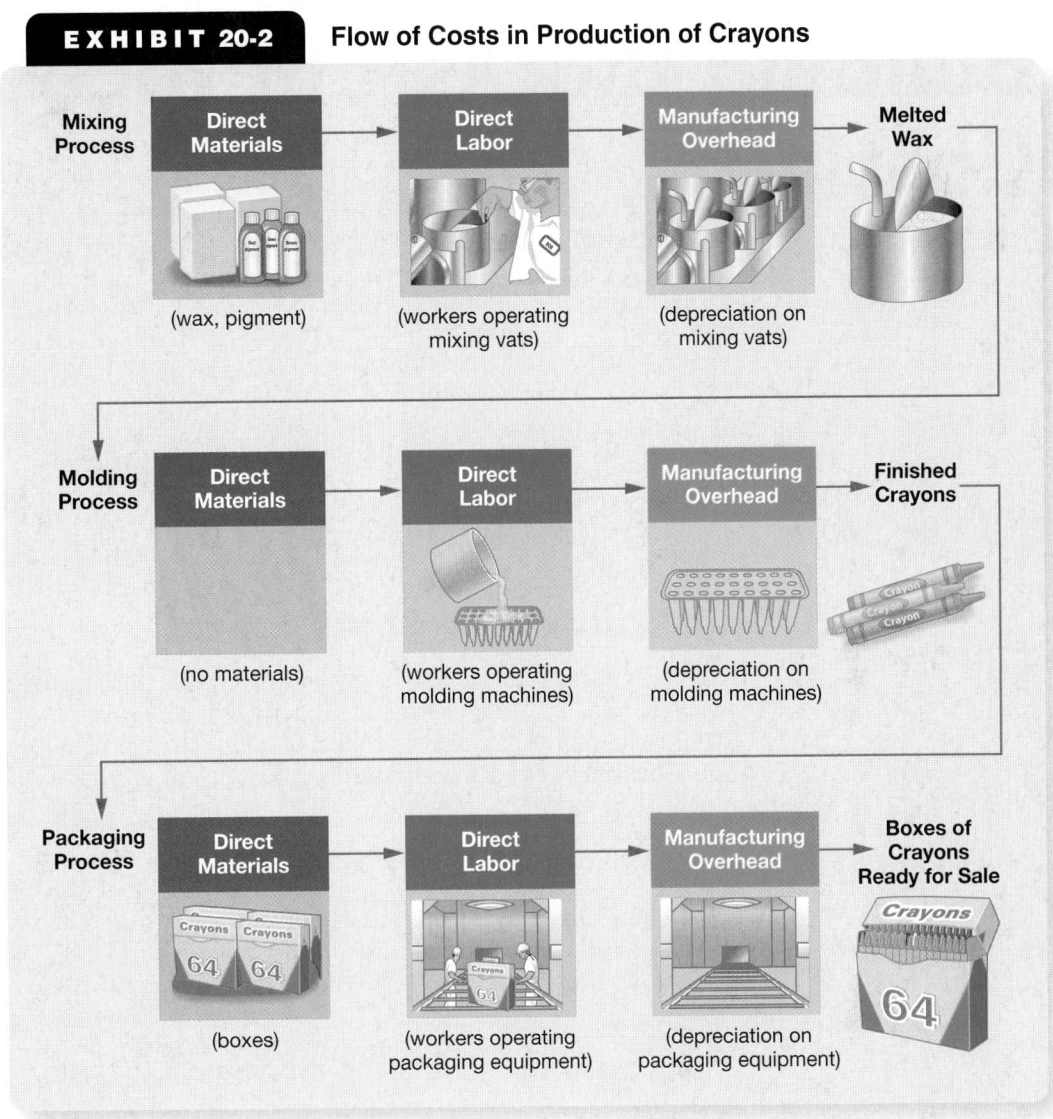

3. When the Mixing Department's process is complete, the wax moves out of mixing and into the Molding Department. The Mixing Department's cost is also transferred out of Work in Process Inventory—Mixing into Work in Process Inventory—Molding.

4. When the Molding Department's process is complete, the finished crayons move from molding into the Packaging Department. The cost of the crayons flows out of Work in Process Inventory—Molding into Work in Process Inventory—Packaging.

5. When production is complete, the boxes of crayons go into finished goods storage. The combined costs from all departments then flow into Finished Goods Inventory. In process costing, *costs flow into Finished Goods Inventory only from the Work in Process Inventory account of the **last** manufacturing process.*

Building Blocks of Process Costing

Process costing is more complex than job costing. For example, Panel B of Exhibit 20-1 shows that we need to determine an amount of the total costs incurred in the Mixing Department to be assigned to:

- The wax that was transferred out of the Mixing Department
- The ending inventory in the Mixing Department

To do this, we use two building blocks of process costing:

- Conversion costs
- Equivalent units of production

Conversion Costs

Chapter 18 introduced three kinds of manufacturing costs: direct materials, direct labor, and manufacturing overhead. Companies like Hewlett Packard and Harley-Davidson use automated production processes. For many companies direct labor is a small part of total manufacturing costs. Such companies often use only two categories:

- Direct materials
- **Conversion costs** (direct labor plus manufacturing overhead)

Combining direct labor and manufacturing overhead in a single category simplifies the accounting. We call this category *conversion costs* because it is the cost (direct labor plus manufacturing overhead) to *convert* raw materials into finished products.

Equivalent Units of Production

2 Compute equivalent units

Completing most products takes time, so the Crayola Company may have work in process inventories for crayons that are partially completed. Accountants have developed the concept of equivalent units to measure the amount of work done during a period. **Equivalent units** express the amount of work done during a period in terms of fully complete units of output. Assume Crayola's production plant has 10,000 crayons in ending work in process inventory. Each crayon is 80% complete. If conversion costs are incurred evenly throughout the process, then getting 10,000 crayons 80% of the way through production takes about the same amount of work as completing 8,000 crayons (10,000 × 80%). Thus, ending work in process inventory has 8,000 equivalent units.

Here's how to compute equivalent units for costs that are incurred evenly throughout the production process, using our 80% example:

$$\begin{array}{ccc} \text{Number of} \\ \text{partially complete units} \end{array} \times \begin{array}{c} \text{Percentage of} \\ \text{process completed} \end{array} = \begin{array}{c} \text{Number of} \\ \text{equivalent units} \end{array}$$

$$10{,}000 \quad \times \quad 80\% \quad = \quad 8{,}000$$

Use this formula when costs are incurred evenly throughout production. This is usually true for conversion costs (direct labor and manufacturing overhead). However, direct materials are often added at a particular point in the process. For example, Crayola's wax is added at the beginning of production, and packaging materials are added at the end. How many equivalent units of wax, conversion costs, and packaging materials are in the ending inventory of 10,000 crayons?

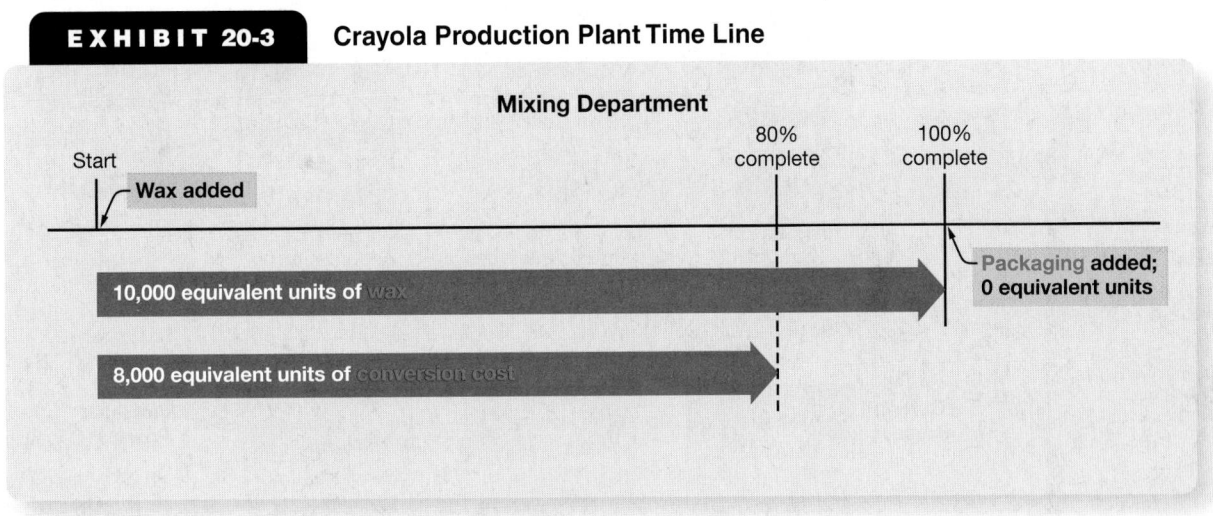

EXHIBIT 20-3 Crayola Production Plant Time Line

Look at the time line in Exhibit 20-3. The 10,000 crayons in ending work in process inventory have:

- 10,000 equivalent units of wax (10,000 × 100% have the wax material)
- 0 equivalent units of packaging materials (The crayons have not been packaged yet.)
- 8,000 equivalent units of conversion costs (10,000 × 80% complete in conversion costs)

This example illustrates an important point:

> We must compute separate equivalent units for:
> - Materials
> - Conversion costs

Process Costing in the First Department with No Beginning Inventory

3 Use process costing to assign costs to units completed and to units in ending work in process inventory

To illustrate process costing, we will use Puzzle Me, a company that recycles calendars into jigsaw puzzles. Exhibit 20-4 illustrates the two major production processes:

- The Assembly Department applies the glue to cardboard and then presses a calendar page onto the cardboard.
- The Cutting Department cuts the calendar board into puzzle pieces and packages the puzzles in a box. The box is then moved to finished goods storage.

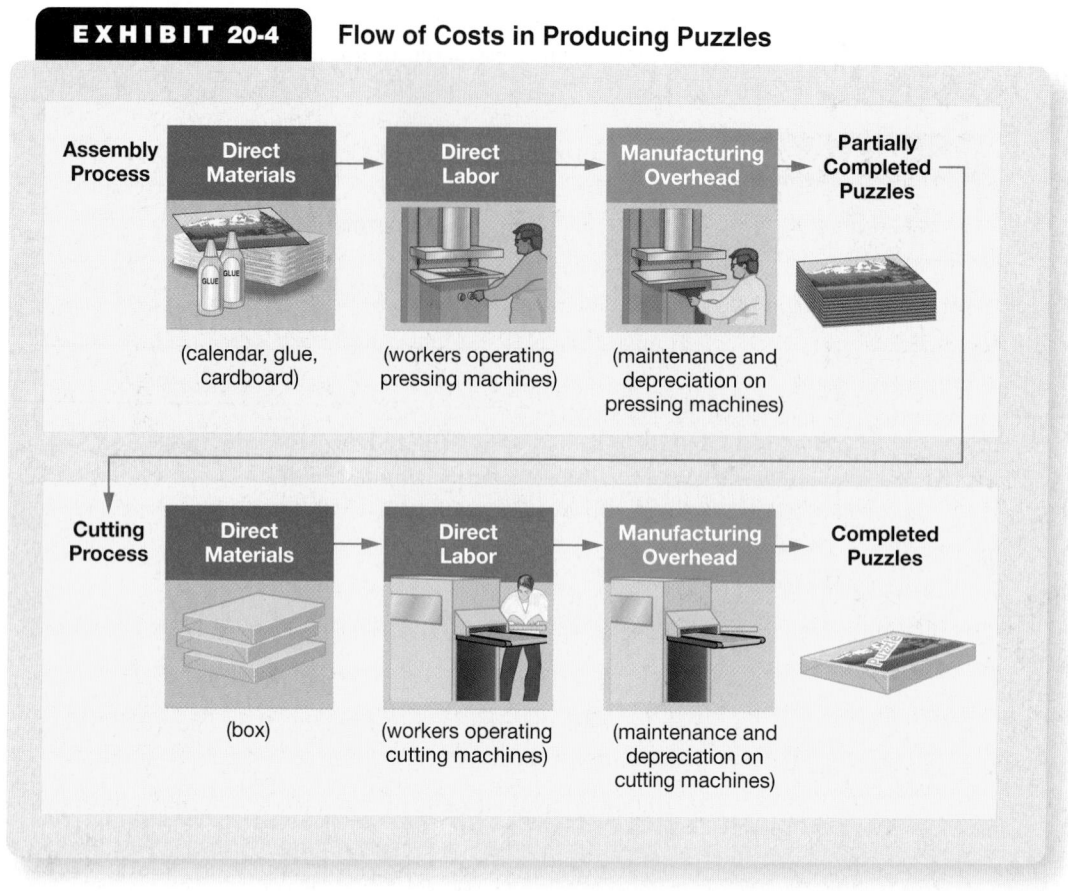

EXHIBIT 20-4 Flow of Costs in Producing Puzzles

The production process uses materials, machines, and human resources in both departments, as shown in the two Work in Process Inventory accounts:

Where Costs Are Added in the Manufacture of Calendars

	Work in Process Inventory Assembly	Work in Process Inventory Cutting
Direct materials	Calendar, cardboard, glue	Package
Direct labor	Assembly/pressing operators' wages	Cutting/packaging operators' wages
Manufacturing overhead	Depreciation on pressing machine	Depreciation on cutting/packaging machine
	Machine maintenance	Machine maintenance
	Supervisor salary	Supervisor salary

Now, let's see how Puzzle Me uses process costing to measure its cost to produce puzzles. During July, the Assembly Department incurred the following costs to make 50,000 puzzle boards:

Direct materials..............................		$140,000
Conversion costs:		
Direct labor	$20,000	
Manufacturing overhead	48,000	
Total conversion costs.................		68,000
Costs to account for		$208,000

The accounting period ends before all of the puzzle boards are made. Therefore, the Assembly Department must allocate some of its costs to

- 40,000 puzzle boards completed and transferred to the Cutting Department
- 10,000 puzzle boards still in the Assembly Department at the end of the accounting period

Suppose at the end of July the Assembly Department still has 10,000 puzzle boards that are only 25% complete. We split the $208,000 cost between

- 40,000 completed puzzle boards that have been transferred to the Cutting Department
- 10,000 partially completed puzzle boards remaining in the Assembly Department's work in process inventory on July 31

Process costing can be performed in four steps:

- Step 1: Summarize the flow of physical units.
- Step 2: Compute output in terms of equivalent units.
- Step 3: Compute the cost per equivalent unit.
- Step 4: Assign costs to units completed and to units still in ending work in process inventory.

Step 1: Summarize the Flow of Physical Units

Let's assume that Puzzle Me has no work in process on July 1. During July, Puzzle Me started 50,000 puzzle boards. It is helpful to separate the "units to account for" from the "units accounted for."

- "Units to account for" include the number of puzzle boards still in process at the beginning of July plus the number of puzzle boards started during July. We want to know the costs incurred during the accounting period to manufacture these puzzle boards.
- "Units accounted for" shows what happened to the puzzle boards in process during July. We want to take the July costs incurred in each department and allocate them to the puzzle boards completed and to the puzzle boards still in process at the end of July.

We use the following formula:

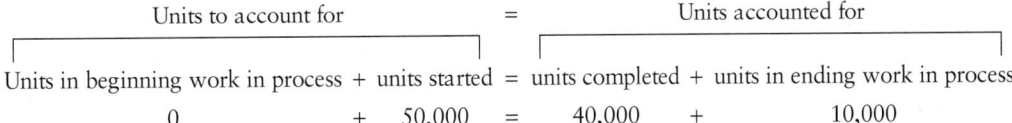

Units to account for		=		Units accounted for	
Units in beginning work in process	+ units started	=	units completed	+	units in ending work in process
0	+ 50,000	=	40,000	+	10,000

Of the 50,000 puzzle boards started by the Assembly Department in July, 40,000 were completed and transferred out to the Cutting Department. The remaining 10,000 are only partially completed. These partially complete units are the Assembly Department's ending work in process inventory on July 31. The following T-account shows the physical flow of production in units.

Work in Process Inventory—Assembly
(in Physical Units)

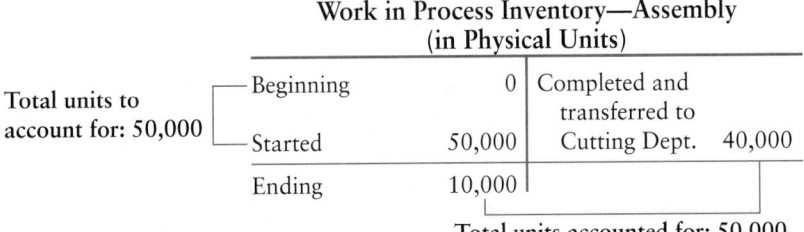

Total units to account for: 50,000	Beginning	0	Completed and transferred to
	Started	50,000	Cutting Dept. 40,000
	Ending	10,000	

Total units accounted for: 50,000

The remaining steps will help us assign the costs of direct materials, direct labor, and manufacturing overhead to production. We need to assign these three product cost elements to each puzzle so that we can compute the cost of

- Puzzles that have passed through the Assembly Department during July
- Puzzle boards still in the Assembly Department production process at the end of July

Step 2: Compute Output in Terms of Equivalent Units

The Assembly Department time line in Exhibit 20-5 shows that all direct materials are added at the beginning of the process. In contrast, conversion costs are incurred evenly throughout the process. This is because labor and overhead production activities occur daily. Thus, we must compute equivalent units separately for:

- Direct materials
- Conversion costs

EXHIBIT 20-5   Puzzle Me's Assembly Department Time Line

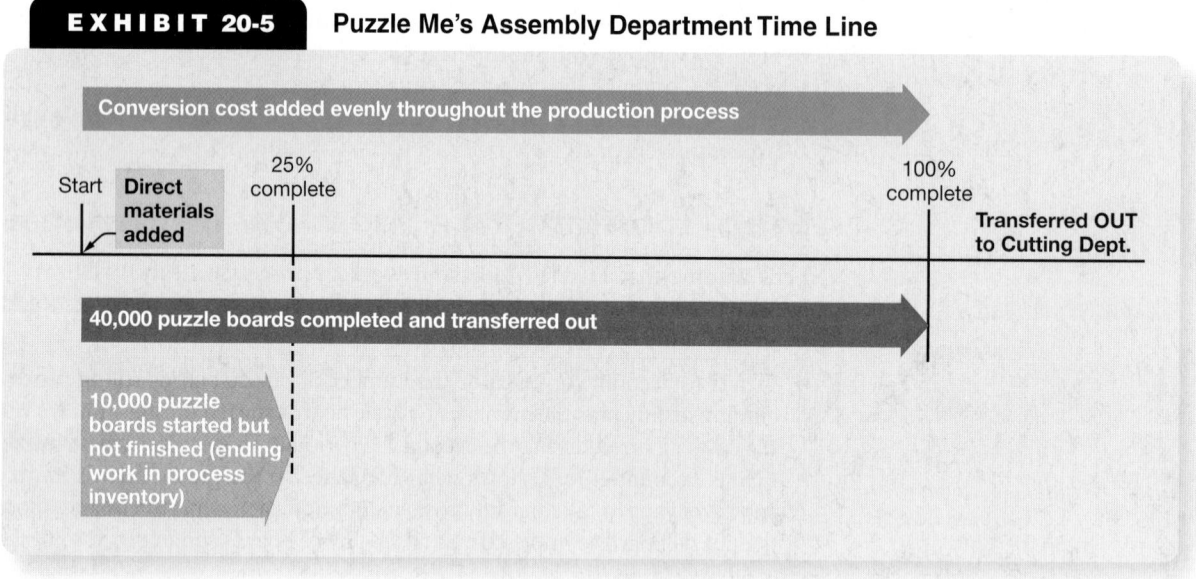

The Assembly Department worked on 50,000 puzzle boards during July. As Exhibit 20-5 shows, 40,000 puzzles boards are now complete for both materials and conversion costs. Another 10,000 puzzle boards are only 25% complete. How many equivalent units did Assembly produce during July?

EQUIVALENT UNITS FOR MATERIALS Equivalent units for materials total 50,000 because all the direct materials have been added to all 50,000 units worked on during July.

$$\begin{aligned} \text{Equivalent units} \atop \text{for materials} &= 40{,}000 + 10{,}000 \\ &= 50{,}000 \end{aligned}$$

EQUIVALENT UNITS FOR CONVERSION COSTS Equivalent units for conversion costs total 42,500. Conversion costs are complete for the 40,000 puzzle boards completed and transferred out. But only 25% of the conversion work has been done on the 10,000 puzzle boards in ending work in process inventory. Therefore, ending inventory represents only 2,500 equivalent units for conversion costs.

$$\begin{aligned} \text{Equivalent units} \atop \text{for conversion costs} &= 40{,}000 + 10{,}000\,(.25) \\ &= 42{,}500 \end{aligned}$$

Exhibit 20-6 summarizes steps 1 and 2.

EXHIBIT 20-6	Step 1: Summarize the Flow of Physical Units; Step 2: Compute Output in Terms of Equivalent Units

PUZZLE ME ASSEMBLY DEPARTMENT
Month Ended July 31, 2008

	Step 1	Step 2: Equivalent Units	
Flow of Production	Flow of Physical Units	Direct Materials	Conversion Costs
Units to account for:			
Beginning work in process, June 30	—		
Started in production during July	50,000		
Total physical units to account for	50,000		
Units accounted for:			
Completed and transferred out during July	40,000	40,000	40,000
Ending work in process, July 31	10,000	10,000	2,500*
Total physical units accounted for	50,000		
Equivalent units		50,000	42,500

*10,000 units each 25% complete = 2,500 equivalent units

Step 3: Compute the Cost per Equivalent Unit

The cost per equivalent unit requires information about total costs and equivalent units. The computations are

$$\text{Cost per equivalent unit for direct materials} = \frac{\text{Total direct materials cost}}{\text{Equivalent units of materials}}$$

$$\text{Cost per equivalent unit for conversion costs} = \frac{\text{Total conversion cost}}{\text{Equivalent units for conversion}}$$

Exhibit 20-7 summarizes the total costs to account for in the Assembly Department (cost data are from the bottom of page 1000).

EXHIBIT 20-7	Summary of Total Costs to Account For

PUZZLE ME ASSEMBLY DEPARTMENT
Work in Process Inventory—Assembly
Month Ended July 31, 2008

	Physical Units	Dollars		Physical Units	Dollars
Beginning inventory, June 30	0	$ 0	Transferred out	40,000	$?
Production started:	50,000				
Direct materials		140,000			
Conversion costs:					
Direct labor		20,000			
Manufacturing overhead		48,000			
Total to account for	50,000	$208,000			
			Ending inventory	10,000	$?

The Assembly Department has 50,000 physical units and $208,000 of costs to account for. Our next task is to split these costs between:

- 40,000 puzzle boards transferred out to the Cutting Department
- 10,000 partially complete puzzle boards that remain in the Assembly Department's ending work in process inventory

In Exhibit 20-6, we computed equivalent units for direct materials (50,000) and conversion costs (42,500). Because the equivalent units differ, we must compute a separate cost per unit for direct materials and for conversion costs. Exhibit 20-7 shows that the direct materials costs are $140,000. Conversion costs are $68,000, which is the sum of direct labor ($20,000) and manufacturing overhead ($48,000).

The cost per equivalent unit of material is $2.80, and the cost per equivalent unit of conversion cost is $1.60, as shown in Exhibit 20-8.

EXHIBIT 20-8 Step 3: Compute the Cost per Equivalent Unit

PUZZLE ME ASSEMBLY DEPARTMENT
Month Ended July 31, 2008

	Direct Materials	Conversion Costs
Beginning work in process, June 30	$ 0	$ 0
Costs added during July (from Exhibit 20-7)	$140,000	$ 68,000
Divide by equivalent units (from Exhibit 20-6)	÷ 50,000	÷ 42,500
Cost per equivalent unit	$ 2.80	$ 1.60

Step 4: Assign Costs to Units Completed and to Units in Ending Work in Process Inventory

We must determine how much of the $208,000 total costs to be accounted for by the Assembly Department should be assigned to:

- 40,000 completed puzzle boards that have been transferred out to the Cutting Department
- 10,000 partially completed puzzle boards remaining in the Assembly Department's ending work in process inventory

Exhibit 20-9 shows how to assign costs.

The total cost of completed puzzle boards for the Assembly Department is 40,000 × ($2.80 + $1.60) = $176,000, as shown in Exhibit 20-9. The cost of the 10,000 partially completed puzzle boards in ending work in process inventory is $32,000, which is the sum of direct material costs ($28,000) and conversion costs ($4,000).

Exhibit 20-9 has accomplished our goal of splitting the $208,000 total cost between:

The 40,000 puzzles completed and transferred out to the Cutting Department	$176,000
The 10,000 puzzles remaining in the Assembly Department's ending work in process inventory on July 31 ($28,000 + $4,000)......	32,000
Total costs of the Assembly Department...	$208,000

EXHIBIT 20-9	Step 4: Assign Costs to Units Completed and to Units in Ending Work in Process Inventory

PUZZLE ME ASSEMBLY DEPARTMENT
Month Ended July 31, 2008

	Direct Materials	Conversion Costs	Total
Completed and transferred out (40,000)	[40,000 × ($2.80 + $1.60)]		= $176,000
Ending work in process inventory (10,000):			
Direct materials	[10,000 × $2.80]		= 28,000
Conversion costs		[2,500 × $1.60]	= 4,000
Total cost of ending inventory			32,000
Total costs accounted for			$208,000

Journal entries to record July production in the Assembly Department follow (data from Exhibit 20-7):

Work in Process Inventory—Assembly	208,000	
Materials Inventory		140,000
Manufacturing Wages		20,000
Manufacturing Overhead		48,000
To assign materials, labor, and overhead cost to Assembly.		

The entry to transfer the cost of the 40,000 completed puzzles out of the Assembly Department and into the Cutting Department follows (data from Exhibit 20-9):

Work in Process Inventory—Cutting	176,000	
Work in Process Inventory—Assembly		176,000
To transfer costs from Assembly to Cutting.		

After these entries are posted, the Work in Process Inventory—Assembly account appears as follows:

Work in Process Inventory—Assembly

Balance, June 30	—	Transferred to Cutting	176,000
Direct materials	140,000		
Direct labor	20,000		
Manufacturing overhead	48,000		
Balance, July 31	32,000		

Decision Guidelines

Here are some of the key decisions Puzzle Me made in setting up its process costing system.

Decision	Guidelines
How do costs flow from Work in Process Inventory to Finished Goods Inventory in Puzzle Me's process costing system?	In Puzzle Me's process costing system, costs flow from: Work in Process Inventory — Assembly ↓ Work in Process Inventory — Cutting ↓ Finished Goods Inventory Costs flow from one Work in Process Inventory account to the next until they flow into Finished Goods Inventory.
How many Work in Process Inventory accounts does Puzzle Me's process costing system have?	Puzzle Me uses a separate Work in Process Inventory account for each process, Assembly and Cutting.
How do we account for partially completed products?	Use equivalent units. Puzzle Me computes equivalent units separately for materials and conversion costs because materials are added at a particular point in the production process, but conversion costs are added evenly throughout the process.
How are equivalent units computed?	Puzzle Me's *conversion costs* are incurred evenly throughout the production process, so the equivalent units are computed as follows: $$\text{Equivalent units} = \begin{array}{c}\text{Number of} \\ \text{partially} \\ \text{complete} \\ \text{units}\end{array} \times \begin{array}{c}\text{Percentage} \\ \text{of} \\ \text{process} \\ \text{completed}\end{array}$$ Puzzle Me's equivalent units for *materials* are computed as follows: • If materials are added to physical units at the beginning of the process, then equivalent units of materials = total of physical units worked on. • If materials are added at the end of the process, then equivalent units of materials = 0.
How is the cost per equivalent unit computed?	Divide the cost by the number of equivalent units.
How are the costs of the Assembly process split between • Puzzles completed and transferred out? • Partially complete puzzles in ending work in process inventory?	Multiply the cost per equivalent unit by • Number of equivalent units of work completed and transferred out • Number of equivalent units of work in the ending work in process inventory

Summary Problem 1

Use the four steps of process costing to identify the missing amounts X for the cost of units completed and transferred out and Y for the cost of ending work in process in the following report prepared by Santa Fe Paints for September.

MIXING DEPARTMENT
Month Ended September 30, 2008

	Physical Units	Total Costs
Beginning work in process, August 31	—	$ —
Started in production during September	18,000	38,000*
Total to account for	18,000	$38,000
Completed and transferred to Finishing Department during September	14,000	$ X
Ending work in process, September 30 (25% complete as to direct materials, 50% complete as to conversion cost)	4,000	Y
Total accounted for	18,000	$38,000

*Includes direct materials of $6,000 and conversion costs of $32,000

Solution

STEP 1 Summarize the flow of physical units.

STEP 2 Compute output in terms of equivalent units.

MIXING DEPARTMENT
Month Ended September 30, 2008

	Step 1	Step 2: Equivalent Units	
Flow of Production	Flow of Physical Units	Direct Materials	Conversion Costs
Units to account for:			
Beginning work in process, August 31	—		
Started in production during September	18,000		
Total physical units to account for	18,000		
Units accounted for:			
Completed and transferred out in September	14,000	14,000	14,000
Ending work in process, September 30	4,000	1,000*	2,000*
Total physical units accounted for	18,000		
Equivalent units		15,000	16,000

*Direct materials: 4,000 units each 25% complete = 1,000 equivalent units
 Conversion costs: 4,000 units each 50% complete = 2,000 equivalent units

STEP 3 Compute the cost per equivalent unit.

Summary of total costs to account for. This supports the computation of cost per equivalent unit.

MIXING DEPARTMENT
Month Ended September 30, 2008

	Direct Materials	Conversion Costs	Total
Beginning work in process, August 31	$ 0	$ 0	$ 0
Costs added during September	6,000	32,000	38,000
Total costs to account for	$6,000	$32,000	$38,000

MIXING DEPARTMENT
Month Ended September 30, 2008

	Direct Materials	Conversion Costs
Beginning work in process, August 31	$ —	$ —
Costs added during September	$6,000	$32,000
Divide by equivalent units	÷15,000	÷16,000
Cost per equivalent unit	$ 0.40	$ 2.00

STEP 4 Assign costs to units completed and to units in ending work in process inventory.

MIXING DEPARTMENT
Month Ended September 30, 2008

	Direct Materials	Conversion Costs	Total
X: Units completed and transferred out (14,000)	[14,000 × ($0.40 + $2.00)]		= $33,600
Units in ending work in process inventory (4,000)			
Direct materials	[1,000 × $0.40]		= $ 400
Conversion costs		[2,000 × $2.00]	= 4,000
Y: Total costs of ending work in process inventory			4,400
Total costs accounted for			$38,000

Process Costing in a Second Department

4 Use the weighted-average method to assign costs to units completed and to units in ending work in process inventory in a second department

Most products require a series of processing steps. In this section, we consider a second department—Puzzle Me's Cutting Department—to complete the picture of process costing.

The Cutting Department receives the puzzle boards and cuts the board into puzzle pieces before inserting the pieces into the boxes at the end of the process. Exhibit 20-10 shows the following:

- Glued puzzle boards are transferred in from the Assembly Department at the beginning of the Cutting Department's process.
- The Cutting Department's conversion costs are added evenly throughout the process.
- The Cutting Department's direct materials (box) are added at the end of the process.

Keep in mind that *direct materials* in the Cutting Department refers to the boxes added *in that department* and not to the materials (calendars, cardboard, and glue) added in the Assembly Department. Likewise, *conversion costs* in the Cutting Department refers to the direct labor and manufacturing overhead costs incurred only in the Cutting Department.

EXHIBIT 20-10   **Puzzle Me's Cutting Department Time Line**

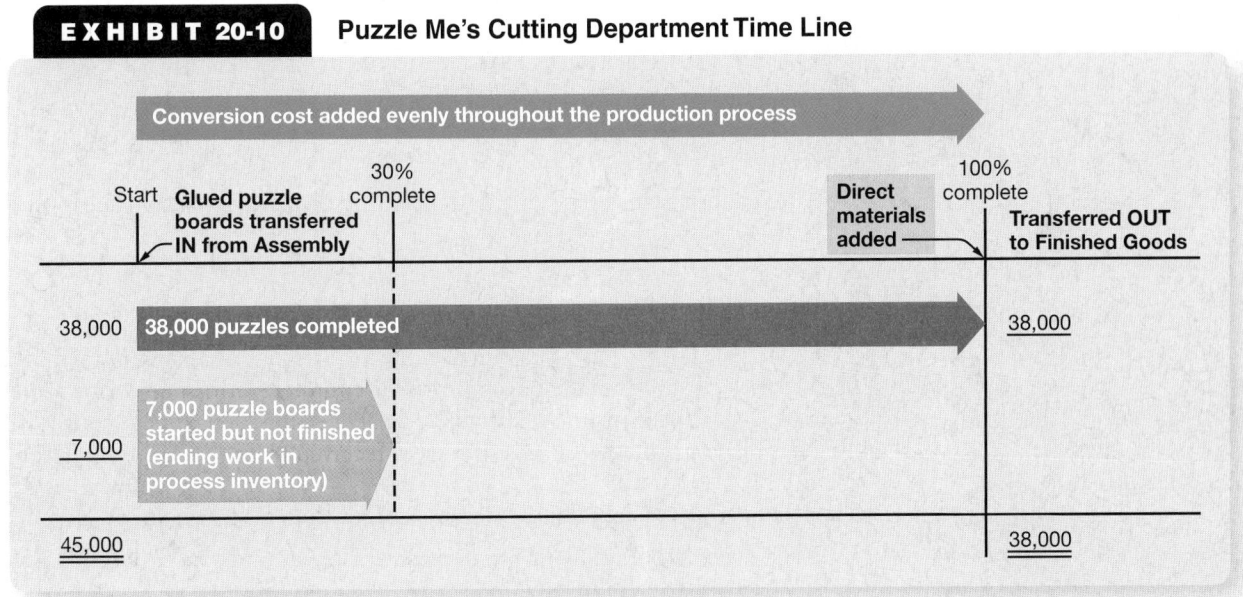

The Weighted-Average Process Costing Method

As you saw in earlier chapters, companies may use different inventory methods. For manufacturing companies, two methods are commonly used for process costing:

- Weighted-average
- FIFO (first-in, first-out)

The difference in the two methods involves the treatment of the costs of beginning inventory. Here we illustrate the weighted-average method of accounting for process costs because it is easier and the differences between the two methods' results are usually insignificant. The appendix to this chapter covers the FIFO method.

Exhibit 20-11 lists July information for Puzzle Me's Cutting Department. Study this information carefully. We'll be using these data in the remainder of the chapter.

EXHIBIT 20-11	Puzzle Me's Cutting Department Data for July

Units:		
Beginning work in process, June 30 (0% complete as to direct materials, 60% complete as to conversion costs)		5,000 puzzle boards
Transferred in from Assembly Department during July (Exhibit 20-6)		40,000 puzzle boards
Completed and transferred out to Finished Goods Inventory during July		38,000 puzzles
Ending work in process, July 31 (0% complete as to direct materials, 30% complete as to conversion work)		7,000 puzzles
Costs:		
Beginning work in process, June 30 (transferred-in costs, $22,000; conversion costs, $1,200)		$ 23,200
Transferred in from Assembly Department during July (from Exhibit 20-9)		$176,000
Direct materials added during July in Cutting Department		$ 19,000
Conversion costs added during July in Cutting Department:		
Direct labor	$ 3,840	
Manufacturing overhead	11,000	$ 14,840

Remember that work in process inventory at the close of business on June 30 is both:

- Ending inventory for June
- Beginning inventory for July

Exhibit 20-11 shows that Puzzle Me's Cutting Department started the July period with 5,000 puzzle boards partially completed through work done in the Cutting Department in June. During July, the Cutting Department started work on 40,000 additional puzzle boards that were received from the Assembly Department.

The weighted-average method combines the Cutting Department's:

- Work done last month—in June—to start the Cutting process on the 5,000 puzzle boards that were in beginning work in process inventory
- Work done in July to complete the 5,000 puzzle boards in beginning inventory and to work on the 40,000 additional puzzle boards that were transferred in from the Assembly Department during July

Thus, the **weighted-average process costing method** determines the average cost of all the Cutting Department's equivalent units of work on these 45,000 puzzle boards (5,000 beginning work in process inventory + 40,000 transferred in).

Just as we did for the Assembly Department, our goal is to split the total cost in the Cutting Department between:

- 38,000 puzzles that the Cutting Department completed and transferred out to finished goods inventory
- 7,000 partially completed puzzles remaining in the Cutting Department's ending work in process inventory at the end of July

We use the same four-step costing procedure that we used for the Assembly Department.

Steps 1 and 2: Summarize the Flow of Physical Units and Compute Output in Terms of Equivalent Units

Summarize the Flow of Physical Units

Using the following formula, let's account for July production, as follows:

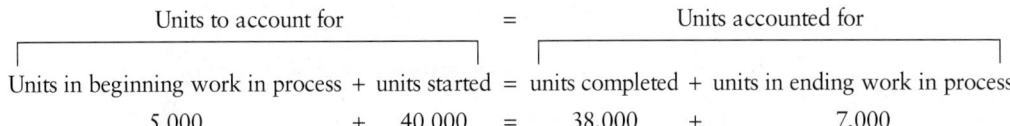

Units to account for		=	Units accounted for	
Units in beginning work in process	+ units started	= units completed	+ units in ending work in process	
5,000	+ 40,000	= 38,000	+ 7,000	

We must account for these 45,000 units (beginning inventory of 5,000 plus 40,000 started). Exhibit 20-12 shows that of the 45,000 units to account for, Puzzle Me completed and transferred out 38,000 units. That left 7,000 units as ending work in process in the Cutting Department on July 31. The following T-account illustrates the physical flow in units for the Cutting Department.

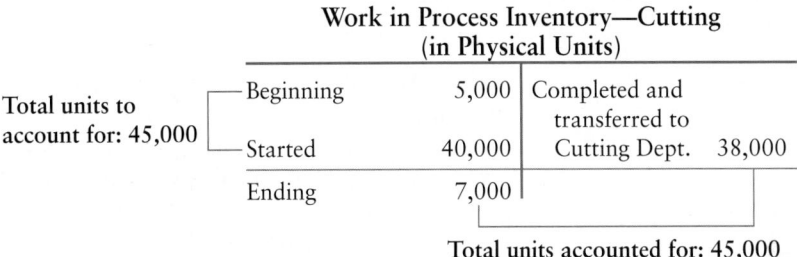

Work in Process Inventory—Cutting
(in Physical Units)

Total units to account for: 45,000

Beginning	5,000	Completed and transferred to		
Started	40,000	Cutting Dept.	38,000	
Ending	7,000			

Total units accounted for: 45,000

Steps 2 and 3 will help us determine the costs of these units.

Compute Equivalent Units

Exhibit 20-12 computes the Cutting Department's equivalent units of work. Under the weighted-average method, Puzzle Me computes the equivalent units for the total work done to date. This includes all the work done in the current period (July), plus the work done last period (June) on the beginning work in process inventory.

We can see in Exhibit 20-12 that the total equivalent units with respect to:

- Transferred-in costs include all 45,000 units because they are complete with respect to work done in the Assembly Department.
- Direct materials include only the 38,000 finished puzzles because Cutting Department materials are added at the end.
- Conversion costs include the 38,000 finished puzzles plus the 2,100 puzzles (7,000 puzzle boards × 30%) that are still in process at the end of the month. Conversion work occurs evenly throughout the cutting process.

The Cutting Department has three categories of equivalent units:

- Equivalent Units for Transferred-In Costs: The equivalent units for transferred-in costs will always be 100% of the units to account for, because these units must be 100% complete on previous work before coming to the Cutting Department.

EXHIBIT 20-12	Step 1: Summarize the Flow of Physical Units; Step 2: Compute Output in Terms of Equivalent Units

PUZZLE ME CUTTING DEPARTMENT
Month Ended July 31, 2008

Flow of Production	Step 1 Flow of Physical Units	Step 2: Equivalent Units		
		Transferred In	Direct Materials	Conversion Costs
Units to account for:				
Beginning work in process, June 30	5,000			
Transferred in during July	40,000			
Total physical units to account for	45,000			
Units accounted for:				
Completed and transferred out during July	38,000	38,000	38,000*	38,000*
Ending work in process, July 31	7,000	7,000	—†	2,100†
Total physical units accounted for	45,000			
Equivalent units		45,000	38,000	40,100

In the Cutting Department:
*Units completed and transferred out
    Direct materials: 38,000 units each 100% completed = 38,000 equivalent units
    Conversion costs: 38,000 units each 100% completed = 38,000 equivalent units
†Ending inventory
    Direct materials: 7,000 units each 0% completed = 0 equivalent units
    Conversion costs: 7,000 units each 30% completed = 2,100 equivalent units

- Equivalent Units for Direct Materials: The equivalent units of materials include only the units transferred out because these are the only units ready to be placed in a box for transfer to the Finished Goods Inventory.
- Equivalent Units for Conversion Costs: The computation of equivalent units for conversion costs is similar to our computation of equivalent units in the Assembly Department. Equivalent units include 100% of the units transferred out and 30% of the units in the Cutting Department's ending work in process inventory.

Step 3: Summarize Total Costs to Account For and Compute the Cost per Equivalent Unit

Exhibit 20-13 accumulates the Cutting Department's total costs to account for. In addition to direct material and conversion costs, the Cutting Department must account for transferred-in costs. **Transferred-in costs** are those costs that were incurred in a previous process (the Assembly Department, in the Puzzle Me example) and brought into a later process (the Cutting Department) as part of the product's cost.

Exhibit 20-13 shows that the Cutting Department's total cost to account for ($233,040) is the sum of:

- The cost incurred in June to start the Cutting process on the 5,000 puzzles in Cutting's beginning work in process inventory ($23,200)
- The costs added to Work in Process Inventory—Cutting during July ($209,840 = $176,000 transferred in from the Assembly Department + $19,000 direct materials incurred in the Cutting Department + $14,840 conversion costs incurred in the Cutting Department)

EXHIBIT 20-13 **Step 3: Compute the Cost per Equivalent Unit**

PUZZLE ME CUTTING DEPARTMENT
Month Ended July 31, 2008

	Transferred In	Direct Materials	Conversion Costs	Total
Beginning work in process, June 30 (from Exhibit 20-11)	$ 22,000	$ —	$ 1,200	$ 23,200
Costs added during July (from Exhibit 20-11)	176,000	19,000	14,840	209,840
Total costs	$198,000	$ 19,000	$ 16,040	
Divide by equivalent units (from Exhibit 20-12)	÷ 45,000	÷ 38,000	÷ 40,100	
Cost per equivalent unit	$ 4.40	$ 0.50	$ 0.40	
Total costs to account for				$233,040

Exhibit 20-13 also shows the cost per equivalent unit. For each cost category, we divide total cost by the number of equivalent units. Perform this computation for all cost categories: transferred-in costs, direct materials, and conversion costs. In this illustration the total cost per equivalent unit is $5.30 ($4.40 + $0.50 + $0.40).

Step 4: Assign Total Costs to Units Completed and to Units in Ending Work in Process Inventory

Exhibit 20-14 shows how Puzzle Me assigns the total Cutting Department costs ($233,040, from Exhibit 20-13) to

- Units completed and transferred out to finished goods inventory ($201,400)
- Units remaining in the Cutting Department's ending work in process inventory ($31,640)

We use the same approach as we used for the Assembly Department in Exhibit 20-9. Multiply the number of equivalent units from step 2 (Exhibit 20-12) by the cost per equivalent unit from step 3 (Exhibit 20-13).

EXHIBIT 20-14 **Step 4: Assign Total Costs to Completed Units and to Units in Ending Work in Process Inventory**

PUZZLE ME CUTTING DEPARTMENT
Month Ended July 31, 2008

	Transferred In	Direct Materials	Conversion Costs	Total
Units completed and transferred out to				
Finished goods inventory		[38,000 × ($4.40 + $0.50 + $0.40)]		= $201,400
Ending work in process, July 31:				
Transferred-in costs	[7,000 × $4.40]			= 30,800
Direct materials		—		—
Conversion costs			[2,100 × $0.40]	= 840
Total ending work in process, July 31				31,640
Total costs accounted for				$233,040

Exhibit 20-15 shows how Exhibit 20-14 assigns the Cutting Department's costs.

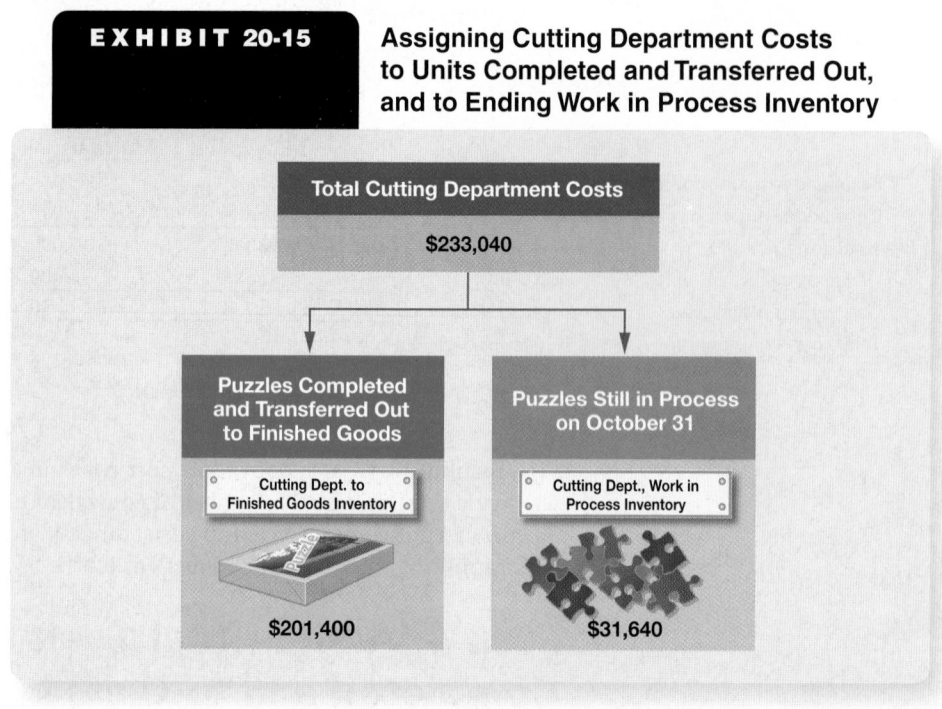

EXHIBIT 20-15   **Assigning Cutting Department Costs to Units Completed and Transferred Out, and to Ending Work in Process Inventory**

The Cutting Department's journal entries are similar to those of the Assembly Department. First, recall the entry previously made to transfer the cost of puzzle boards into the Cutting Department (page 1005):

Work in Process Inventory—Cutting	176,000	
Work in Process Inventory—Assembly		176,000
To transfer costs from Assembly to Cutting.		

The following entry records the Cutting Department other costs during July (data from Exhibit 20-11):

Work in Process Inventory—Cutting	33,840	
Materials Inventory		19,000
Manufacturing Wages		3,840
Manufacturing Overhead		11,000
To assign materials and conversion costs to the		
Cutting Department.		

The entry to transfer the cost of completed puzzles out of the Cutting Department and into Finished Goods Inventory is based on the dollar amount in Exhibit 20-14:

Finished Goods Inventory	201,400	
Work in Process Inventory—Cutting		201,400
To transfer costs from Cutting to Finished Goods.		

After posting, the key accounts appear as follows:

Work in Process Inventory—Assembly

(Exhibit 20-7)		(Exhibit 20-9)	
Balance, June 30	—	Transferred to Cutting	176,000
Direct materials	140,000		
Direct labor	20,000		
Manufacturing overhead	48,000		
Balance, July 31	32,000		

Work in Process Inventory—Cutting

(Exhibit 20-11)		(Exhibit 20-14)	
Balance, June 30	23,200	Transferred to Finished	
Transferred in from Assembly	176,000	Goods Inventory	201,400
Direct materials	19,000		
Direct labor	3,840		
Manufacturing overhead	11,000		
Balance, July 31	31,640		

Finished Goods Inventory

Balance, June 30	
Transferred in from Cutting	201,400

How Managers Use a Production Cost Report

As we saw in Chapter 19, accountants prepare cost reports to help production managers evaluate the efficiency of their manufacturing operations. Both job order and process costing are similar in that they:

- *Accumulate* costs as the product moves through production
- *Assign* costs to the units (such as gallons of gasoline or number of crayons) passing through that process

The difference between job order costing and process costing lies in the way costs are accumulated. Job order costing uses a *job cost sheet* and process costing uses a *production cost report*.

The **production cost report** in Exhibit 20-16 summarizes Puzzle Me's Cutting Department operations during July. The report combines the costs to account for and the cost per equivalent unit (Exhibit 20-13). It shows how those costs were assigned to the puzzles completed and transferred out of the Cutting Department ($201,400) and to ending work in process inventory ($31,640).

How do managers use the production cost report?

- Controlling cost: Puzzle Me uses product cost data to reduce costs. For materials the company may need to change suppliers or a certain component. Labor may need different employee job requirements. New production equipment may help save on labor cost.
- Evaluating performance: Managers are often rewarded based on how well they meet the budget. Puzzle Me compares the actual direct materials and conversion costs with expected amounts. If actual unit costs are too high, managers look for ways to cut. If actual costs are less than expected, the Cutting Department's managers may receive a pay raise.
- Pricing products: Puzzle Me must set its selling price high enough to cover the manufacturing cost of each puzzle ($5.30 = $4.40 + $0.50 + $0.40 in Exhibit 20-13) plus marketing and distribution costs.

EXHIBIT 20-16 Production Cost Report (Weighted-Average)

PUZZLE ME CUTTING DEPARTMENT
Production Cost Report (Weighted-Average Method)
Month Ended July 31, 2008

	Transferred In	Direct Materials	Conversion Costs	Total
Costs to account for:				
Beginning work in process, June 30	$ 22,000	$ —	$ 1,200	$ 23,200
Costs added during July	176,000	19,000	14,840	209,840
Total costs to account for	$198,000	$19,000	$16,040	$233,040
Costs accounted for:				
Equivalent units	÷ 45,000	÷ 38,000	÷ 40,100	
Cost per equivalent unit	$ 0.40	$ 0.50	$ 0.40	
Assignment of total costs:				
Units completed during July	[38,000 × ($4.40 + $ 0.50 + $ 0.40)]			$201,400
Ending work in process, July 31				
Transferred-in costs	[7,000 × $4.40]			30,800
Direct materials		—		—
Conversion costs			[2,100 × $ 0.40]	840
Total ending work in process, July 31				31,640
Total costs accounted for				$233,040

- Identifying the most profitable products: Selling price and cost data help managers figure out which products are most profitable. They can then promote the most profitable products.
- Preparing the financial statements: Finally, the production cost report aids financial reporting. It provides inventory data for the balance sheet and cost of goods sold for the income statement.

Decision Guidelines

PROCESS COSTING—SECOND PROCESS

Process costing is more complicated in second (or later) department because of units and costs transferred in from previous departments. Let's use Puzzle Me's Cutting Department to review some of the key process costing decisions that arise in a second (or later) process that has beginning inventory.

Decision	Guidelines
At what point in the Cutting process are transferred-in costs (from the Assembly process) incurred?	Transferred-in costs are incurred at the *beginning* of the Cutting process. The puzzles must be completely assembled before cutting begins.
How do we compute equivalent units using the weighted-average method?	Weighted-average equivalent units equal • All work done on units completed and transferred out this period (whether work was done this period or last period), plus • Work done to *start* the ending inventory
What checks and balances does the four-step process costing procedure provide?	The four-step procedure provides two important checks: 1. The units to account for (beginning inventory + units started or transferred in) must equal the units accounted for (units completed and transferred out + units in ending inventory). 2. The total costs to account for (cost of beginning inventory + costs incurred in the current period) must equal the costs accounted for (cost of units completed and transferred out + cost of ending work in process inventory).
What is the main goal of the Cutting Department's process costing?	The main goal is to split total costs between • Puzzles completed and transferred out to finished goods inventory • Puzzles that remain in the Cutting Department's ending work in process inventory
For what kinds of decisions do Puzzle Me's managers use the Cutting Department's production cost report?	Managers use the cost per equivalent unit for (1) Controlling cost (2) Evaluating performance (3) Pricing products (4) Identifying the financial statements (5) Preparing the financial statements

Summary Problem 2

This problem extends Summary Problem 1 to a second department, Finishing. During September, Santa Fe Paints reports the following in its Finishing Department:

FINISHING DEPARTMENT DATA FOR SEPTEMBER 2008

Units:

Beginning work in process, August 31 (20% complete as to direct materials, 70% complete as to conversion work)...........	4,000 units
Transferred in from Mixing Department during September.........	14,000 units
Completed and transferred out to Finished Goods Inventory during September.................	15,000 units
Ending work in process, September 30 (30% complete as to direct materials, 80% complete as to conversion work).......	3,000 units

Costs:

Work in process, August 31 (transferred-in costs, $11,400; direct materials costs, $1,000; conversion costs, $1,800).........	$14,200
Transferred in from Mixing Department during September (bottom of page 1008).............	33,600
Finishing direct materials added during September.....................	5,360
Finishing conversion costs added during September	24,300

Requirement

Assign the Finishing Department's September total costs to units completed and to units in ending work in process inventory, using the weighted-average method.

Hint: Don't confuse the Finishing Department with finished goods inventory. The Finishing Department is Santa Fe Paint's second process. The paint does not become part of finished goods inventory until Santa Fe has completed the second process, which is the Finishing Department.

Solution

STEPS 1 AND 2 Summarize the flow of physical units; compute output in terms of equivalent units.

FINISHING DEPARTMENT
Month Ended September 30, 2008

| | Step 1 | Step 2: Equivalent Units | | |
| | Flow of | Transferred | Direct | Conversion |
Flow of Production	Physical Units	In	Materials	Costs
Units to account for:				
Beginning work in process, August 31	4,000			
Transferred in from Mixing during September	14,000			
Total physical units to account for	18,000			
Units accounted for:				
Completed and transferred out during				
September	15,000	15,000	15,000	15,000
Ending work in process, September 30	3,000	3,000	900*	2,400*
Total physical units accounted for	18,000			
Equivalent units		18,000	15,900	17,400

*Ending inventory
  Direct materials: 3,000 units each 30% completed = 900 equivalent units
  Conversion costs: 3,000 units each 80% completed = 2,400 equivalent units

STEP 3 Summarize total costs to account for; compute the cost per equivalent unit.

FINISHING DEPARTMENT
Month Ended September 30, 2008

	Transferred In	Direct Materials	Conversion Costs	Total
Beginning work in process, August 31	$11,400	$ 1,000	$ 1,800	$14,200
Costs added during September	33,600	5,360	24,300	63,260
Total costs	$45,000	$ 6,360	26,100	
Divide by equivalent units	÷18,000	÷15,900	÷17,400	
Cost per equivalent unit	$ 2.50	$ 0.40	$ 1.50	
Total costs to account for				$77,460

STEP 4 Assign costs to units completed and to units in ending work in process inventory.

FINISHING DEPARTMENT
Month Ended September 30, 2008

	Transferred In	Direct Materials	Conversion Costs	Total
Units completed and transferred out to				
Finished Goods Inventory		[15,000 × $2.50 + $0.40 + $1.50)]		$66,000
Ending work in process, September 30:				
Transferred-in costs	[3,000 × $2.50}			7,500
Direct materials		[900 × $0.40]		360
Conversion costs			[2,400 × $1.50]	3,600
Total ending work in process, September 30				11,460
Total costs accounted for				$77,460

Review *Process Costing*

Accounting Vocabulary

Conversion Costs
Direct labor plus manufacturing overhead.

Equivalent Units
Express the amount of work done during a period in terms of fully complete units of output.

Production Cost Report
Summarizes a processing department's operations for a period.

Transferred-in Costs
Costs incurred in a previous process that are carried forward as part of the product's cost when it moves to the next process.

Weighted-Average Process Costing Method
A process costing method that costs all equivalent units of work with a weighted average of the previous period's and the current period's cost per equivalent unit.

Quick Check

1. Which of these companies would use process costing?
   a. Saatchi & Saatchi advertising firm
   b. Accenture management consultants
   c. Pace Foods, producer of Pace picante sauce
   d. Amazon.com

2. Which of the following statements describes Puzzle Me's process costing system? (p. 1000)
   a. Direct materials and direct labor are traced to each specific order.
   b. Costs flow through a sequence of Work in Process Inventory accounts and then into Finished Goods Inventory from the final Work in Process Inventory account.
   c. Costs flow directly from a single Work in Process Inventory account to Finished Goods Inventory.
   d. The subsidiary Work in Process Inventory accounts consist of separate records for each individual order, detailing the materials, labor, and overhead assigned to that order.

Use the following data to answer questions 3 through 7. Suppose Chupa Chups, a candy manufacturer, uses a mixing process that adds sugar at the beginning and flavorings 75% of the way through the mixing process. Conversion costs are incurred evenly throughout the mixing process, and mixing had no beginning inventory. The company started making 10,000 lollipops, completed mixing for 8,000 lollipops, and in ending work in process inventory has 2,000 lollipops that are 60% through the mixing process.

3. Compute the equivalent units of *sugar* used.
   a. 8,000
   b. 8,700
   c. 9,200
   d. 10,000

4. How many equivalent units of *flavorings* did Chupa Chups use?
   a. 8,000
   b. 8,700
   c. 9,200
   d. 10,000

5. What are the equivalent units of *conversion costs?*
   a. 8,000
   b. 8,700
   c. 9,200
   d. 10,000

6. If the cost per equivalent unit is $0.50 for sugar, $1.00 for flavorings, and $0.40 for conversion costs, what is the cost assigned to the Mixing Department's *ending work in process inventory?*
   a. $1,480
   b. $1,800
   c. $2,520
   d. $3,800

7. Suppose Chupa Chup's second process, Shaping, starts out with 3,000 lollipops in its beginning work in process inventory. During the month 8,000 units came to Shaping from Mixing. At the end of the period Shaping has 1,500 lollipops 70% through the process. Compute the number of equivalent units of *transferred-in* costs that the Shaping process will use to compute its cost per equivalent unit.

   a. 6,500

   b. 8,000

   c. 9,500

   d. 11,000

8. The cost of the Shaping Department's beginning work in process inventory included $20 of transferred-in cost. Transferred-in costs of Shaping added $200. Use the equivalent units for transferred-in costs that you computed for question 7 to determine Shaping's cost per equivalent unit for transferred-in costs.

   a. $0.02

   b. $0.12

   c. $0.20

   d. $2.00

9. In general, transferred-in costs include:

   a. Costs incurred in the previous period

   b. Costs incurred in all prior processes

   c. Costs incurred in only the previous process

   d. Costs incurred in all prior periods

10. A production cost report shows

   a. Costs to account for

   b. Cost of units completed

   c. Cost of ending work in process inventory

   d. All the above

Answers are given after Apply Your Knowledge (p. 1041).

Assess Your Progress

Short Exercises

Distinguishing between the flow of costs in job order costing and process costing

1

S20-1 Use Exhibit 20-1 to help you describe, in your own words, the major difference in the flow of costs between a job order costing system and a process costing system. (pp. 995–957)

Comparison of job order costing and process costing

1

S20-2 Indicate whether each of the following statements is true or false. (pp. 955–957)

_____ 1. Job order costing accumulates the costs of each process.

_____ 2. Companies that manufacture cell phones use process costing.

_____ 3. After the product moves through the final stage of the manufacturing process, its cost moves to finished goods inventory.

_____ 4. Production reports summarize the costs of each job completed in a job order costing system.

Calculate conversion costs

1

S20-3 Florida Orange manufactures orange juice. Last month's total manufacturing costs for the Saratoga operation included:

Direct materials	$400,000
Direct labor	35,000
Manufacturing overhead	125,000

What was the conversion cost for Florida Orange's Saratoga operation last month? (pp. 998–999)

Compute equivalent units

2

S20-4 LG manufactures cell phones. The conversion costs to produce cell phones for November are added evenly throughout the process in the assembly department. For each of the following separate assumptions, calculate the equivalent units of conversion costs in the ending work in process inventory for the assembly department:

1. 12,000 cell phones were 80% complete (pp. 998–999)

2. 22,000 cell phones were 20% complete (pp. 998–999)

Compute equivalent units

2

S20-5 FritoLay makes potato chips. At the end of the month, the ending work in process included 6,000 units in the Mixing Department. All materials are added at the beginning of the mixing process. What are the equivalent units of direct materials cost in ending work in process for the Mixing Department? (pp. 998–999)

Calculate conversion costs and unit cost

1 **3**

S20-6 China Spring produces premium bottled water. China Spring purchases artesian water, stores the water in large tanks, and then runs the water through two processes: filtration and bottling.

During February, the filtration process incurred the following costs in processing 200,000 liters:

Wages of workers operating the filtration equipment	$ 23,950
Manufacturing overhead allocated to filtration	24,050
Water	120,000

continued . . .

China Spring had no beginning inventory in the Filtration Department in February.

1. Compute the February conversion costs in the Filtration Department. (pp. 998–999)
2. The Filtration Department completely processed 200,000 liters in February. What was the filtration cost per liter? (pp. 1003–1004)

Drawing a time line; computing equivalent units
2

S20-7 Refer to S20-6. At China Spring, water is added at the beginning of the filtration process. Conversion costs are added evenly throughout the process. Now assume that in February, 150,000 liters were completed and transferred out of the Filtration Department into the Bottling Department. The 50,000 units remaining in Filtration's ending work in process inventory were 80% of the way through the filtration process. Recall that China Spring has no beginning inventories.

1. Draw a time line for the filtration process. (pp. 1002–1003)
2. Compute the equivalent units of direct materials and conversion costs for the Filtration Department. (p. 1003)

Computing equivalent units
2

S20-8 The Mixing Department of Healthy Foods had 40,000 units to account for in October. Of the 40,000 units, 30,000 units were completed and transferred to the next department, and 10,000 units were 30% complete. All of the materials are added at the beginning of the process. Conversion costs are added equally throughout the process. Compute the total equivalent units of direct materials and conversion costs. (p. 1003)

Computing the cost per equivalent unit
3

S20-9 Refer to S20-8. The Mixing Department of Healthy Foods has 40,000 equivalent units of materials and 33,000 equivalent units of conversion costs for October. The direct materials costs are $30,000 and the conversion costs are $16,500. Compute the cost per equivalent unit for direct materials and for conversion costs. (pp. 1004–1005)

Computing cost of units transferred out and units in ending work in process
3

S20-10 Refer to S20-8 and S20-9. Healthy Foods' costs per equivalent unit are $0.75 for direct materials and $0.50 for conversion costs. Calculate the cost of (1) the 30,000 units completed and transferred out and (2) the 10,000 units, 30% complete, in the ending work in process inventory. (pp. 1004–1005)

Compute the physical flow
3

S20-11 The Baking Department at Rainbow Bakery had no loaves in beginning inventory, started 15,000 loaves of bread, and completed 10,000 loaves during January.

Requirements
1. What are the total loaves to account for? (pp. 1002–1003)
2. How many loaves are in ending Baking Department work in process inventory on January 31? (pp. 1002–1003)
3. What are the total loaves accounted for? (pp. 1002–1003)

Compute the physical flow
3

S20-12 The Baking Department at Rainbow Baker had a beginning work in process inventory of 6,000 cakes, completed 10,000 cakes, and had 5,000 cakes in ending work in process inventory in February.

Requirements
1. How many cakes were started in February? (pp. 1002–1003)
2. What are the total cakes to account for? (pp. 1002–1003)
3. What are the total cakes accounted for? (pp. 1002–1003)

S20-13 Calculate the missing items for each of the following flows of physical units. (pp. 1002–1003)

Units to account for:	Dept. A	Dept. 33	Dept. Z17
Beginning work in process	100	(3)	50
Started in production during month	250	105	(7)
Total physical units to account for	350	170	(6)
Units accounted for:			
Completed and transferred out during month	(2)	120	120
Ending work in process	120	(4)	30
Total physical units accounted for	(1)	170	(5)

Exercises

Diagramming flows through a process costing system

E20-14 Pule produces kitchen cabinets in a two-stage process of milling and assembling. Direct materials are added in the Milling Department. Direct labor and overhead are incurred in both departments. The company's general ledger includes the following accounts:

Cost of Goods Sold	Materials Inventory
Manufacturing Wages	Finished Goods Inventory
Work in Process Inventory—Milling	Manufacturing Overhead
Work in Process Inventory—Assembling	

Outline the flow of costs through the company's accounts, including a brief description of each flow. Include a T-account for each account title given. (pp. 955–957)

Journalizing process costing transactions

E20-15 Record the following process costing transactions in the general journal: (pp. 1013–1015)

a. Requisition of direct materials by the Milling Department, $4,000.

b. Assignment of conversion costs to the Assembling Department:

Direct labor, $4,700

Manufacturing overhead, $2,900

c. Cost of goods completed and transferred out of Milling and into Assembling, $10,250.

d. Cost of goods completed and transferred out of the Assembling Department into Finished Goods Inventory, $15,600.

Drawing a time line, computing equivalent units, and assigning cost to completed units and ending work in process; no beginning inventory or cost transferred in

E20-16 Paint My World prepares and packages paint products. Paint My World has two departments: (1) Blending and (2) Packaging. Direct materials are added at the beginning of the blending process (dyes) and at the end of the packaging process (cans). Conversion costs are added evenly throughout each process. Data from the month of May for the Blending Department are as follows:

continued . . .

Gallons:	
Beginning work in process inventory	0
Started production	8,000 gallons
Completed and transferred out to Packaging in May	6,000 gallons
Ending work in process inventory (30% of the way through blending process)	2,000 gallons
Costs:	
Beginning work in process inventory	$ 0
Costs added during May:	
Direct materials	4,800
Direct labor	800
Manufacturing overhead	2,170
Total costs added during May	$ 7,770

Requirements

1. Draw a time line for the Blending Department. (pp. 1003–1004)
2. Use the time line to help you compute the Blending Department's equivalent units for direct materials and for conversion costs. (p. 1003)
3. Compute the total costs of the units (gallons)
   a. Completed and transferred out to the Packaging Department (pp. 1004–1005)
   b. In the Blending Department ending work in process inventory (pp. 1004–1005)

E20-17 Refer to E20-16.

Preparing journal entries and posting to work in process T-account

Requirements

1. Present the journal entries to record the assignment of direct materials and direct labor and the allocation of manufacturing overhead to the Blending Department. Also, give the journal entry to record the costs of the gallons completed and transferred out to the Packaging Department. (pp. 1004–1005)
2. Post the journal entries to the Work in Process Inventory—Blending T-account. What is the ending balance? (p. 1005)
3. What is the average cost per gallon transferred out of Blending into Packaging? Why would Paint My World's managers want to know this cost?

Computing equivalent units; assigning cost to goods completed and ending work in process inventory; first department, no beginning inventory

E20-18 The following information was taken from the ledger of Riley Co. Ending inventory is 60% complete as to direct materials but 30% complete as to conversion work.

WORK IN PROCESS—FORMING

	Physical Units	Dollars		Physical Units	Dollars
Beginning inventory, June 30	-0-	$ -0-	Transferred to Finishing	72,000	$?
Production started:	80,000				
Direct materials		$215,040			
Conversion costs		148,800			
Ending Inventory, July 31	8,000	?			

continued . . .

Requirements

1. Compute the equivalent units for direct materials and conversion costs. (p. 1003)

2. Compute the cost per equivalent unit. (pp. 1004–1005)

3. Assign the costs to units completed and transferred out and ending work in process inventory. (pp. 1004–1005)

Computing equivalent units; assigning cost to goods completed and ending work in process inventory; first department, no beginning inventory

E20-19 The Assembly Department of Audio Manufacturers began June with no work in process inventory. During the month, production that cost $41,200 (direct materials, $9,100, and conversion costs, $32,100) was started on 23,000 units. The Assembly Department completed and transferred to the Testing Department a total of 15,000 units. The ending work in process inventory was 40% complete as to direct materials and 80% complete as to conversion work.

Requirements

1. Compute the equivalent units for direct materials and conversion costs. (p. 1003)

2. Compute the cost per equivalent unit. (pp. 1004–1005)

3. Assign the costs to units completed and transferred out and ending work in process inventory. (pp. 1004–1005)

4. Record the journal entry for the costs transferred out of Assembly into Testing. (p. 1005)

5. Post all the transactions in the Work in Process Inventory—Assembly Department T-account. What is the ending balance? (p. 1005)

Drawing a time line; computing equivalent units; assigning costs to completed units and ending work in process; no beginning inventory or cost transferred in

E20-20 Anderson Winery in Napa Valley, California, has two departments: Fermenting and Packaging. Direct materials are added at the beginning of the fermenting process (grapes) and at the end of the packaging process (bottles). Conversion costs are added evenly throughout each process. Data from the month of March for the Fermenting Department are as follows:

Gallons:	
Beginning work in process inventory	0
Started production	8,000 gallons
Completed and transferred out to Packaging in March	6,550 gallons
Ending work in process inventory (80% of the way through the fermenting process)	1,450 gallons
Costs:	
Beginning work in process inventory	$ 0
Costs added during March:	
Direct materials	10,400
Direct labor	2,400
Manufacturing overhead	4,539
Total costs added during March	$17,339

continued . . .

Requirements

1. Draw a time line for the Fermenting Department. (pp. 1003–1004)
2. Use the time line to help you compute the equivalent units for direct materials and for conversion costs. (p. 1003)
3. Compute the total costs of the units (gallons)
   a. Completed and transferred out to the Packaging Department (pp. 1004–1005)
   b. In the Fermenting Department ending work in process inventory (pp. 1004–1005)

Preparing journal entries and posting to work in process T-account

1 **3**

E20-21 Refer to E20-20.

Requirements

1. Present the journal entries to record the assignment of direct materials and direct labor and the allocation of manufacturing overhead to the Fermenting Department. Also give the journal entry to record the cost of the gallons completed and transferred out to the Packaging Department. (pp. 1004–1005)
2. Post the journal entries to the Work in Process Inventory— Fermenting T-account. What is the ending balance? (p. 1005)
3. What is the average cost per gallon transferred out of Fermenting into Packaging? Why would Anderson Winery's managers want to know this cost?

Computing equivalent units, two departments; weighted-average method

4

E20-22 Selected production and cost data of Kristi's Divinity Co. follow for May 2008.

| | Flow of Physical Units | |
| | Mixing Department | Heating Department |
Flow of Production		
Units to account for:		
Beginning work in process, April 30	20,000	6,000
Started during May	70,000	
Transferred in during May		80,000
Total physical units to account for	90,000	86,000
Units accounted for:		
Completed and transferred out during May	80,000	74,000
Ending work in process, May 31	10,000	12,000
Total physical units accounted for	90,000	86,000

On May 31, the Mixing Department ending work in process inventory was 70% complete as to materials and 20% complete as to conversion costs. The Heating Department ending work in process inventory was 65% complete as to materials and 55% complete as to conversion costs. Kristi's uses weighted-average costing.

continued . . .

Requirements

1. Compute the equivalent units for direct materials and for conversion costs for the Mixing Department. (p. 1003)

2. Compute the equivalent units for transferred-in costs, direct materials, and conversion costs for the Heating Department. (pp. 1011–1012)

Drawing a time line; computing equivalent units; computing cost per equivalent unit; assigning costs; journalizing; second department, weighted-average method

E20-23 Clear Spring Company produces premium bottled water. In the second department, the Bottling Department, conversion costs are incurred evenly throughout the bottling process, but packaging materials are not added until the end of the process. Costs in beginning work in process inventory include transferred in costs of $1,760, direct labor of $600, and manufacturing overhead of $520. February data for the Bottling Department follow:

CLEAR SPRING COMPANY
Work in Process Inventory—Bottling
Month Ended February 28, 2009

	Physical Units	Dollars		Physical Units	Dollars
Beginning inventory,					
January 31 (40% complete)	8,000	$ 2,880	Transferred out	154,000	$?
Production started:					
Transferred in	160,000	136,000			
Direct materials		30,800			
Conversion costs:					
Direct labor		33,726			
Manufacturing overhead		22,484			
Total to account for	168,000	$225,890			
Ending inventory, February 28					
(70% complete)	14,000	$?			

Requirements

1. Draw a time line. (pp. 1009–1011)

2. Compute the Bottling Department equivalent units for the month of February. Use the weighted-average method. (pp. 1011–1012)

3. Compute the cost per equivalent unit for February. (pp. 1012–1013)

4. Assign the costs to units completed and transferred out and to ending inventory. (p. 1013)

5. Prepare the journal entry to record the cost of units completed and transferred out. (p. 1015)

6. Post all transactions to the Work in Process Inventory—Bottling Department T-account. What is the ending balance? (p. 1015)

Problems (Group A)

Computing equivalent units and assigning costs to completed units and ending work in process; no beginning inventory or cost transferred in

P20-24A Dee Electronics makes CD players in three processes: assembly, programming, and packaging. Direct materials are added at the beginning of the assembly process. Conversion costs are incurred evenly throughout the process. The Assembly Department had no work in process on May 30. In mid-June, Dee Electronics started production on 100,000 CD players. Of this number, 76,400 CD players were assembled during June and transferred out to the Programming Department. The June 30 work in process in the Assembly Department was 40% of the way through the assembly process. Direct materials costing $375,000 were placed in production in Assembly during June, and direct labor of $157,248 and manufacturing overhead of $100,272 were assigned to that department.

Requirements

1. Draw a time line for the Assembly Department. (pp. 1002–1003)

2. Use the time line to help you compute the number of equivalent units (p. 1003) and the cost per equivalent unit in the Assembly Department for June. (pp. 1004–1005)

3. Assign total costs in the Assembly Department to (a) units completed and transferred to Programming during June and (b) units still in process at June 30. (pp. 1004–1005)

4. Prepare a T-account for Work in Process Inventory—Assembly to show its activity during June, including the June 30 balance. (p. 1005)

Computing equivalent units; assigning costs to completed units and ending work in process; journalizing transactions; no beginning inventory or cost of goods transferred in

P20-25A Reed Paper Co. produces the paper used by wallpaper manufacturers. Reed's four-stage process includes mixing, cooking, rolling, and cutting. During August, the Mixing Department started and completed mixing for 4,500 rolls of paper. The department started but did not finish the mixing for an additional 500 rolls, which were 20% complete with respect to both direct materials and conversion work at the end of August. Direct materials and conversion costs are incurred evenly throughout the mixing process. The Mixing Department incurred the following costs during August:

Work in Process Inventory—Mixing		
Balance, Aug. 1	0	
Direct materials	5,520	
Direct labor	580	
Manufacturing overhead	5,860	

Requirements

1. Draw a time line for the Mixing Department. (pp. 1002–1003)

2. Use the time line to help you compute the number of equivalent units and the cost per equivalent unit in the Mixing Department for August. (pp. 1003–1004)

continued . . .

3. Show that the sum of (a) cost of goods transferred out of the Mixing Department and (b) ending Work in Process Inventory—Mixing equals the total cost accumulated in the department during August. (pp. 1004–1005)

4. Journalize all transactions affecting the company's mixing process during August, including those already posted. (pp. 1004–1005)

Computing equivalent units and assigning costs to completed units and ending WIP inventory; two materials, added at different points; no beginning inventory or cost transferred in

P20-26A Hall's Exteriors produces exterior siding for homes. The Preparation Department begins with wood, which is chopped into small bits. At the end of the process, an adhesive is added. Then the wood/adhesive mixture goes on to the Compression Department, where the wood is compressed into sheets. Conversion costs are added evenly throughout the preparation process. January data for the Preparation Department are as follows (in millions):

Sheets		Costs	
Beginning work in process inventory	0 sheets	Beginning work in process inventory	$ 0
Started production	3,000 sheets	Costs added during January:	
Completed and transferred out to		Wood	2,700
Compression in January	1,950 sheets	Adhesives	1,365
Ending work in process inventory (40%		Direct labor	629
of the way through the preparation		Manufacturing overhead	2,452
process)	1,050 sheets	Total costs	7,146

Requirements

1. Draw a time line for the Preparation Department. (pp. 1002–1003)

2. Use the time line to help you compute the equivalent units for direct materials and for conversion costs. (*Hint:* Each direct material added at a different point in the production process requires its own equivalent-unit computation.) (p. 1003)

3. Compute the total costs of the units (sheets)

   a. Completed and transferred out to the Compression Department (pp. 1004–1005)

   b. In the Preparation Department's ending work in process inventory (pp. 1004–1005)

4. Prepare the journal entry to record the cost of the sheets completed and transferred out to the Compression Department. (p. 1005)

5. Post the journal entries to the Work in Process Inventory— Preparation T-account. What is the ending balance? (p. 1005)

Computing equivalent units for a second department with beginning inventory; preparing a production cost report and recording transactions on the basis of the report's information; weighted-average method

P20-27A Casey Carpet manufactures broadloom carpet in seven processes: spinning, dyeing, plying, spooling, tufting, latexing, and shearing. In the Dyeing Department, direct materials (dye) are added at the beginning of the process. Conversion costs are incurred evenly throughout the process. Casey uses weighted-average process costing. Information for March 2007 follows:

continued . . .

Units:	
Beginning work in process	75 rolls
Transferred in from Spinning Department during March	560 rolls
Completed during March	500 rolls
Ending work in process (80% complete as to conversion work)	135 rolls
Costs:	
Beginning work in process (transferred-in costs, $4,400; materials cost, $1,575; conversion costs, $5,199)	$11,174
Transferred in from Spinning Department during March	21,000
Materials costs added during March	11,760
Conversion costs added during March (manufacturing wages, $8,445; manufacturing overhead, $43,508)	51,953

Requirements

1. Prepare a time line for Casey's Dyeing Department. (pp. 1009–1010)
2. Use the time line to help you compute the equivalent units, cost per equivalent unit, and total costs to account for in Casey's Dyeing Department for March. (pp. 1012–1015)
3. Prepare the March production cost report for Casey's Dyeing Department. (pp. 1015–1016)
4. Journalize all transactions affecting Casey's Dyeing Department during March, including the entries that have already been posted. (pp. 1013–1015)

Computing equivalent units for a second department with beginning inventory; assigning costs to completed units and ending work in process; weighted-average method

P20-28A SeaWorthy uses three processes to manufacture lifts for personal watercraft: forming a lift's parts from galvanized steel, assembling the lift, and testing the completed lifts. The lifts are transferred to finished goods before shipment to marinas across the country.

SeaWorthy's Testing Department requires no direct materials. Conversion costs are incurred evenly throughout the testing process. Other information follows:

Units:	
Beginning work in process	2,000 units
Transferred in from the Assembling Department during the period	7,000 units
Completed during the period	4,000 units
Ending work in process (40% complete as to conversion work)	5,000 units
Costs:	
Beginning work in process (transferred-in costs, $93,000; conversion costs, $18,000)	$111,000
Transferred in from the Assembling Department during the period	672,000
Conversion costs added during the period	54,000

continued . . .

The cost transferred into Finished Goods Inventory is the cost of the lifts transferred out of the Testing Department. SeaWorthy uses weighted-average process costing.

Requirements

1. Draw a time line for the Testing Department. (pp. 1009–1010)

2. Use the time line to compute the number of equivalent units of work performed by the Testing Department during the period. (pp. 1011–1012)

3. Compute SeaWorthy's transferred-in and conversion costs per equivalent unit. Use the unit costs to assign total costs to (a) units completed and transferred out of Testing and (b) units in Testing's ending work in process inventory. (pp. 1012–1013)

4. Compute the cost per unit for lifts completed and transferred out to Finished Goods Inventory. Why would management be interested in this cost? (p. 1013)

Problems (Group B)

Computing equivalent units and assigning costs to completed units and ending work in process; no beginning inventory or cost transferred in

P20-29B Great Lips produces women's lipstick, which is manufactured in a single processing department. Direct materials are added at the beginning of the process, and conversion costs are incurred evenly throughout the process. No lipstick was in process on September 30. Great Lips started production on 20,400 lipstick tubes during October 2008. Completed production for October totaled 15,200 units. The October 31 work in process was 75% of the way through the production process. Direct materials costing $4,080 were placed in production during October, and direct labor of $3,315 and manufacturing overhead of $2,415 were assigned to the process.

Requirements

1. Draw a time line for Great Lips. (pp. 1002–1003)

2. Use the time line to help you compute the number of equivalent units (p. 1002) and the cost per equivalent unit for October. (pp. 1004–1005)

3. Assign total costs to (a) units completed and transferred to finished goods and (b) units still in process at October 31. (pp. 1004–1005)

4. Prepare a T-account for Work in Process Inventory to show activity during October, including the October 31 balance. (p. 1005)

Computing equivalent units; assigning costs to completed units and ending work in process; journalizing transactions; no beginning inventory or cost of goods transferred in

P20-30B The Great Southern Furniture Company produces dining tables in a three-stage process: cutting, assembly, and staining. Direct materials (lumber) are added at the beginning of the cutting process, and conversion costs are incurred evenly throughout the process. September 2009 activity in the Cutting Department included cutting 11,000 meters of lumber, which were transferred to the Assembly Department. Also, work began on 1,000 meters of lumber, which on September 30 were 70% of the way through the cutting process.

continued . . .

Costs incurred in the Cutting Department during September are summarized as follows:

Work in Process Inventory—Cutting

Balance, Sept. 1	0
Direct materials	1,860,000
Direct labor	139,100
Manufacturing overhead	165,100

Requirements

1. Draw a time line for the Cutting Department. (pp. 1002–1003)

2. Use the time line to help you compute the number of equivalent units and the cost per equivalent unit in the Cutting Department for September. (pp. 1003–1004)

3. Show that the sum of (a) cost of goods transferred out of the Cutting Department and (b) ending Work in Process Inventory—Cutting equals the total cost accumulated in the department during September. (pp. 1004–1005)

4. Journalize all transactions affecting the company's cutting process during September, including those already posted. (pp. 1004–1005)

Computing equivalent units and assigning costs to completed units and ending WIP inventory; two materials, added at different points; no beginning inventory or cost transferred in

P20-31B Jolly Giant produces canned Italian green beans. The green beans move through three departments: (1) Mixing, (2) Retort (sterilization), and (3) Packing. In the Mixing Department, green beans are added at the beginning of the process, the mixture is partly cooked, then chopped red peppers are added at the end of the process. Conversion costs are added evenly throughout the mixing process. April 2008 data from the Mixing Department are as follows:

Gallons		Costs	
Beginning work in process inventory	0 gallons	Beginning work in process inventory	$ 0
Started production	15,000 gallons	Costs added during April:	
Completed and transferred out to		Green beans	16,500
Retort in April	12,900 gallons	Red peppers	11,610
		Conversion costs (direct labor,	
Ending work in process inventory (60%		$11,108; manufacturing	
of the way through the mixing		overhead, $17,212)	28,320
process)	2,100 gallons	Total costs	$56,430

Requirements

1. Draw a time line for the Mixing Department. (pp. 1002–1003)

2. Use the time line to help you compute the equivalent units. (*Hint:* Each direct material added at a different point in the production process requires its own equivalent-unit computation.) (p. 1003)

continued . . .

3. Compute the total costs of the units (gallons)

   a. Completed and transferred out to the Retort Department (pp. 1004–1005)

   b. In the Mixing Department's ending work in process inventory (pp. 1004–1005)

4. Prepare the journal entry to record the cost of the gallons completed and transferred out to the Retort Department. (p. 1005)

5. Post the transactions to the Work in Process Inventory—Mixing T-account. What is the ending balance? (p. 1005)

6. What is the primary purpose of the work required in steps 1 through 3?

Computing equivalent units for a second department with beginning inventory; preparing a production cost report and recording transactions on the basis of the report's information; weighted-average method

P20-32B Chrome Accessories manufactures chrome bumpers for classic cars in a two-stage process that includes molding and plating. The direct materials (chrome) are added at the end of the plating process. Conversion costs are incurred evenly throughout the process. Chrome Accessories uses weighted-average process costing. At March 31, 2009, before recording the transfer of cost to Finished Goods Inventory, Chrome Accessories' records included the following data for the Plating Department:

Units:	
Beginning work in process	600 bumpers
Transferred in from the Molding Department during March	3,000 bumpers
Completed during March	2,200 bumpers
Ending work in process (50% complete as to conversion work)	1,400 bumpers
Costs:	
Beginning work in process (transferred-in cost, $18,000; conversion costs, $12,480)	$30,480
Transferred in from the Molding Department during March	36,000
Materials cost added during March	24,200
Conversion costs added during March (manufacturing wages, $21,732; manufacturing overhead, $38,288)	60,020

Requirements

1. Draw a time line for the Plating Department. (pp. 1009–1011)

2. Use the time line to help you compute the equivalent units, cost per equivalent unit, and total costs to account for in the Plating Department for March. (pp. 1012–1015)

3. Prepare the March production cost report for the Plating Department. (pp. 1015–1016)

4. Journalize all transactions affecting the Plating Department during March, including the entries that have already been posted. (pp. 1013–1015)

P20-33B Goldman Company uses three departments to produce handles for kitchen cabinets. Forming the handles requires mixing the raw materials, molding, and drying.

continued . . .

Computing equivalent units for a second department with beginning inventory; assigning costs to completed units and ending work in process; weighted-average method

Goldman's Drying Department requires no direct materials. Conversion costs are incurred evenly throughout the drying process. Other information follows:

Units:	
Beginning work in process	7,000 units
Transferred in from the Molding Department during the period	28,000 units
Completed during the period	16,000 units
Ending work in process (20% complete as to conversion work)	19,000 units
Costs:	
Beginning work in process (transferred-in cost, $140; conversion cost, $231)	$ 371
Transferred in from the Molding Department during the period	4,760
Conversion costs added during the period	2,937

After the drying process, the handles are packaged for shipment to retail outlets. Goldman uses weighted-average process costing.

Requirements

1. Draw a time line of the Drying Department's process for the period. (pp. 1009–1011)

2. Use the time line to compute the number of equivalent units of work performed by the Drying Department during the period. (pp. 1011–1012)

3. Compute Goldman's transferred-in and conversion costs per equivalent unit. Use the unit costs to assign total costs to (a) units completed and transferred to the assembly operation and (b) units in the Drying Department's ending work in process inventory. (pp. 1012–1013)

Apply Your Knowledge

Decision Case

Billy Davidson operates Billy's Worm Farm in Mississippi. Davidson raises worms for fishing. He sells a box of 20 worms for $12.60 per box. Davidson has invested $400,000 in the worm farm. He had hoped to earn a 24% annual rate of return (net income divided by total assets), which works out to a 2% monthly return on his investment. After looking at the farm's bank balance, Davidson fears he is not achieving this return. To evaluate the farm's performance, he prepared the following process-costing reports. The finished goods inventory is zero because the worms ship out as soon as they reach the required size. Monthly operating expenses total $2,000 (in addition to the costs below).

BILLY'S WORM FARM
Brooding Department
Month Ended June 30, 2007

| | | Equivalent Units | | |
Flow of Production	Flow of Physical Units	Transferred In	Direct Materials	Conversion Costs
Units to account for:				
Beginning work in process inventory	9,000			
Transferred in during June	21,000			
Total units to account for	30,000			
Units accounted for:				
Completed and shipped out during June	20,000	20,000	20,000	20,000
Ending work in process, June 30	10,000	10,000	6,000	3,600
Total physical units accounted for	30,000			
Equivalent units		30,000	26,000	23,600

BILLY'S WORM FARM
Brooding Department
Production Cost Report (Weighted-Average Method)
Month Ended June 30, 2007

	Transferred In	Direct Materials	Conversion Costs	Total
Units costs:				
Beginning work in process, May 31	$21,000	$ 39,940	$ 5,020	$ 65,960
Costs added during June	46,200	152,460	56,340	255,000
Total costs to account for	$67,200	$192,400	$61,360	$320,960
Divide by equivalent units	÷30,000	÷26,000	÷23,600	
Cost per equivalent unit	$ 2.24	$ 7.40	$ 2.60	
Assignment of total cost:				
Units completed and shipped out during June	[20,000 × ($2.24 + $7.40 + $2.60)]			$244,800
Ending work in process, June 30:				
Transferred-in costs	[10,000 × $2.24]			22,400
Direct materials		[6,000 × $7.40]		44,400
Conversion costs			[3,600 × $2.60]	9,360
Total ending work in progress, June 30				76,160
Total cost accounted for				$320,960

Requirements

Billy Davidson has the following questions about the farm's performance during June.

1. What is the cost per box of worms sold? (*Hint:* This is the unit cost of the boxes completed and shipped out of brooding.) (p. 1013)

2. What is the gross profit per box?

3. How much operating income did Billy's Worm Farm make in June?

4. What is the return on Davidson's investment of $400,000 for the month of June? (Compute this as June's operating income divided by Davidson's $400,000 investment, expressed as a percentage.)

5. What monthly operating income would provide a 2% monthly rate of return? What price per box would Billy's Worm Farm have had to charge in June to achieve a 2% monthly rate of return?

Ethical Issue

Rick Pines and Joe Lopez are the plant managers for High Mountain Lumber's particle board division. High Mountain Lumber has adopted a just-in-time management philosophy. Each plant combines wood chips with chemical adhesives to produce particle board to order, and all production is sold as soon as it is completed. Laura Green is High Mountain Lumber's regional controller. All of High Mountain Lumber's plants and divisions send Green their production and cost information. While reviewing the numbers of the two particle board plants, she is surprised to find that both plants estimate their ending work in process inventories at 75% complete, which is higher than usual. Green calls Lopez, whom she has known for some time. He admits that to ensure their division would meet its profit goal and that both he and Pines would make their bonus (which is based on division profit), they agreed to inflate the percentage completion. Lopez explains, "Determining the percent complete always requires judgment. Whatever the percent complete, we'll finish the work in process inventory first thing next year."

Requirements

1. How would inflating the percentage completion of ending work in process inventory help Pines and Lopez get their bonus?

2. The particle board division is the largest of High Mountain Lumber's divisions. If Green does not correct the percentage completion of this year's ending work in process inventory, how will the misstatement affect High Mountain Lumber's financial statements?

3. Evaluate Lopez's justification, including the effect, if any, on next year's financial statements.

4. Address the following: What is the ethical issue? What are the options? What are the potential consequences? What should Green do?

Team Project

Idaho Food Processors processes potatoes into french fries. Production requires two processes: cutting and cooking. Direct materials are added at the beginning of the cutting process (potatoes) and at the end of the cooking process (boxes). Conversion costs are incurred evenly throughout each process. Idaho uses the weighted-average method of process costing.

Assume that McDonald's offers Idaho $0.40 per pound to supply restaurants in the Far East. If Idaho accepts McDonald's offer, the cost (per equivalent unit) that Idaho will incur to fill the McDonald's order equals the April cost per equivalent unit. M. A. Keltner, manager of the cooking process, must prepare a report recommending whether Idaho should accept the offer. Keltner gathers the following information from April's cooking operations:

IDAHO FOOD PROCESSORS
Cooking Department
April 2008 Activity and Costs

Beginning work in process inventory	12,000 pounds
Raw shoestring fries transferred in during April	129,000 pounds
French fries completed and transferred out	130,000 pounds
Ending work in process inventory (30% of way through process)	11,000 pounds
Conversion costs *within* the Cooking Dept. to start the 12,000 pounds	
of beginning work in process inventory in March	$ 576
Costs added during April:	
Direct materials	9,100
Conversion costs	15,420

Rita Mendez manages the cutting process. She reports the following data for her department's April operations.

IDAHO FOOD PROCESSORS
Cooking Department
April 2008 Activity and Costs

Beginning work in process inventory	21,000 pounds
Potatoes started in April	121,000 pounds
Raw shoestring fries completed and transferred out	129,000 pounds
Ending work in process inventory (60% of way through process)	13,000 pounds
Costs to start the 21,000 pounds of beginning work in process	
inventory in March ($1,260 for direct materials; $840 for	
conversion costs)	$ 2,100
Costs added during April:	
Direct materials	7,260
Conversion costs	12,840

Split your team into two groups. Each group should meet separately before a meeting of the entire team.

Requirements

1. The first group takes the role of M.A. Keltner, manager of the cooking production process. Before meeting with the entire team, determine the maximum transferred-in cost per pound of raw shoestring fries the Cooking Department can incur from the Cutting Department if Idaho is to make a profit on the McDonald's order. (*Hint:* You may find it helpful to prepare a time line as a guide to your analysis.) (pp. 1009–1011, 1012–1015)

2. The second group takes the role of Rita Mendez, manager of the cutting process. Before meeting with the entire team, determine the April cost per pound of raw shoestring fries in the cutting process. (*Hint:* You may find it helpful to prepare a time line as a guide to your analysis.)

3. After each group meets, the entire team should meet to decide whether Idaho should accept or reject McDonald's offer.

For Internet Exercises, Excel in Practice, and additional online activities, go to the Web site www.prenhall.com/horngren.

Quick Check Answers

1. *c*   2. *b*   3. *d*   4. *a*   5. *c*   6. *a*   7. *d*   8. *a*   9. *b*   10. *d*

The FIFO Process Costing Method

The cost per equivalent unit often changes over time. In the second half of the chapter, we used the weighted-average process costing method in Puzzle Me's Cutting Department. The weighted-average method values both beginning inventory and current production at the same cost per equivalent unit. That cost is a weighted average of last period's and this period's costs.

In contrast, the **first-in, first-out (FIFO) method** of process costing values each equivalent unit of work at the cost per equivalent unit in effect during the period the work is done. Therefore, FIFO requires us to keep the beginning inventory units and costs (which were incurred *last period*) completely separate from current-period production and costs.[1]

Let's see how Puzzle Me could use FIFO process costing in its Cutting Department. Consider a batch of puzzles transferred out of the Assembly Department and into Cutting at the end of June. These puzzles did not make it completely through the Cutting Department during June, so the puzzles are in the Cutting Department's ending (work in process) inventory at the end of June. The puzzles are not completed until July. Under FIFO, when these puzzles are completed in July, the total Cutting Department cost of these puzzles is the sum of

- June's equivalent units of Cutting's work on these puzzles, costed at June's cost per equivalent unit, *plus*
- July's equivalent units of Cutting's work on these puzzles, costed at July's cost per equivalent unit

Steps 1 and 2: Summarize the Flow of Physical Units and Compute Output in Terms of Equivalent Units

SUMMARIZE THE FLOW OF PHYSICAL UNITS Exhibit 20A gives the July data for Puzzle Me's Cutting Department.

---

[1] The FIFO and weighted-average process costing methods differ only in how they treat beginning inventory. Because Puzzle Me's first department, Assembly, had no beginning work in process inventory, we did not need to specify which method that department used.

EXHIBIT 20A-1   Puzzle Me's Cutting Department Time Line (FIFO)

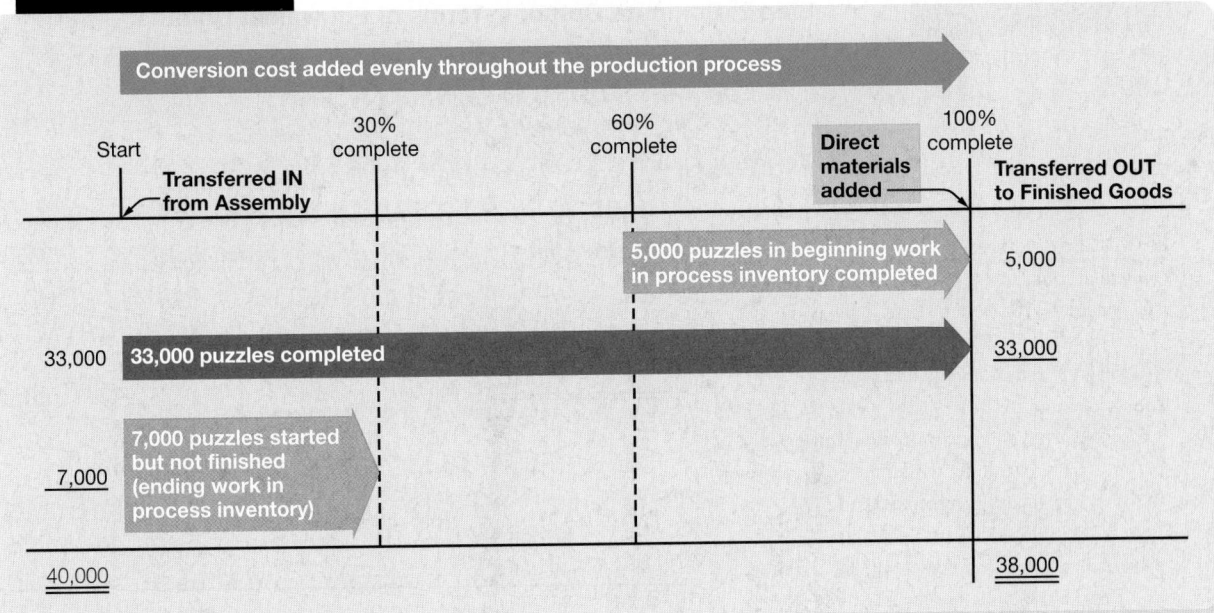

The time line in Exhibit 20A-1 shows that glued puzzles are transferred in from Assembly at the beginning of Cutting's process, but Cutting's direct materials (boxes) are not added until the end of the process.

The FIFO time line that diagrams the Cutting Department's flow of physical units (step 1) is more complex than the weighted-average time line in Exhibit 20-10. Why? Because FIFO costs each equivalent unit of work at the cost per equivalent unit in effect at the time the work was done. Under FIFO, we must separate the work done last period (June) from the work done this period (July). Exhibit 20A-1 identifies work that Cutting performed during *July.*

Start with the 38,000 puzzles completed and transferred out of the Cutting Department and into finished goods inventory during July. The time line in Exhibit 20A-1 shows that these include:

- 5,000 puzzles that were the Cutting Department's beginning work in process inventory. These puzzles were *completed* (but not started) in July.
- 33,000 puzzles that Cutting both *started* and *completed* during July. This number is computed as:

38,000	puzzles completed and transferred out of the Cutting Department in July
(5,000)	puzzles completed from Cutting's beginning inventory
33,000	puzzles *started and completed during July*

The time line also shows that the 40,000 puzzles *transferred into* Cutting from Assembly during July also fall into two categories: (1) 33,000 puzzles *started and completed* in the Cutting Department during July, plus (2) 7,000 puzzles *started* in Cutting but not completed in July.

Exhibit 20A-2 summarizes the flow of physical units diagrammed in the time line. The Cutting Department starts July with 5,000 puzzles in beginning inventory and begins work on 40,000 more transferred in from Assembly during the month.

PUZZLE ME CUTTING DEPARTMENT
Month Ended July 31, 2008

| | Step 1 | Step 2: Equivalent Units | | |
Flow of Production	Flow of Physical Units	Transferred In	Direct Materials	Conversion Costs
Units to account for:				
Beginning work in process, June 30	5,000			
Transferred in during July	40,000			
Total physical units to account for	45,000			
Units accounted for:				
Completed and transferred out during July:				
From beginning work in process inventory	5,000	—	5,000*	2,000*
Started and completed during July				
(38,000 – 5,000)	33,000	33,000	33,000	33,000
Ending work in process, July 31	7,000	7,000	—†	2,100†
Total physical units accounted for	45,000			
Equivalent units		40,000	38,000	37,100

During July in the Cutting Department:
*Finish beginning inventory
  Direct materials: 5,000 units each 100% completed = 5,000 equivalent units
  Conversion costs: 5,000 units each 40% completed = 2,000 equivalent units
†Start ending inventory
  Direct materials: 7,000 units each 0% completed = 0 equivalent units
  Conversion costs: 7,000 units each 30% completed = 2,100 equivalent units

Cutting thus must account for 45,000 puzzles (5,000 + 40,000). Where did these 45,000 puzzles go? Exhibit 20A-2 shows that 38,000 were completed and transferred out to finished goods inventory (the 5,000 from beginning inventory + 33,000 started and completed during July). The remaining 7,000 puzzles are still in the Cutting Department's ending inventory.

COMPUTE EQUIVALENT UNITS The Cutting Department has three categories of equivalent units. In addition to direct materials (boxes) and conversion costs added in the Cutting Department, Puzzle Me must also compute equivalent units for the glued puzzles that are *transferred in* from the Assembly Department. (All second and later departments must account for units (and costs) transferred in from preceding departments.) Exhibit 20A-1 shows that these transferred-in costs (from Assembly) act like costs that are added at the very beginning of the Cutting process.

To figure out how many equivalent units of work the Cutting Department completed *during July,* look at the time line in Exhibit 20A-1 and add the number of equivalent units of work performed to:

• *Complete* the 5,000 puzzles in beginning inventory that were started in June,
• *Start and complete* an additional 33,000 puzzles, and
• *Start* (but not complete) the 7,000 puzzles that make up the department's work in process inventory at the end of July.

Repeat these computations for each of the three cost categories.

EQUIVALENT UNITS TRANSFERRED IN Keep in mind that our goal is to figure the number of equivalent units of work performed *during July.* Also recall that transferred-in costs (from Assembly) act like costs that are added at the very beginning of the Cutting process. The time line in Exhibit 20A-1 shows that the 5,000 units in Cutting's beginning inventory were *not* transferred in from Assembly *this* month.

Look at the time line again—it shows that the 33,000 puzzles Cutting started and completed during July and the 7,000 puzzles in Cutting's ending inventory *were* transferred in during July. Exhibit 20A-2 shows that the total transferred-in equivalent units during July is 40,000 (33,000 + 7,000).

EQUIVALENT UNITS OF DIRECT MATERIALS The time line in Exhibit 20A-1 shows that the Cutting Department's direct materials (boxes) are not added until the end of the process. Exhibit 20A-1 shows that during July the 5,000 units in beginning inventory were completed, so they reached the end of the production process, where the boxes are added. The 33,000 units started and completed also reached the end of the process. However, ending inventory has not yet reached the point where workers insert boxes. Thus, Exhibit 20A-2 shows that Cutting added 5,000 + 33,000 = 38,000 equivalent units of materials (boxes) during July.

EQUIVALENT UNITS OF CONVERSION COSTS The time line shows that beginning inventory was 60% complete at the beginning of July. To complete these units during July, these 5,000 puzzles from the Cutting Department's beginning inventory went through the final 40% of the Cutting process. This yields $5,000 \times 0.40 = 2,000$ equivalent units of conversion work during July. The 33,000 puzzles started and completed during July went through the entire process during July. The 7,000 puzzles in ending inventory that were *started* in Cutting during July made it 30% of the way through the process by July 31. Cutting performed $7,000 \times 0.30 = 2,100$ equivalent units of conversion work on this ending inventory during July. Thus, Exhibit 20A-2 shows that the total conversion work performed in Cutting during July includes:

2,000	units to *complete* the beginning inventory ($5,000 \times (100\% - 60\%)$)
33,000	units from puzzles started *and* completed during July ($33,000 \times 100\%$)
2,100	units to *start* the ending inventory ($7,000 \times 30\%$ complete)
37,100	total equivalent units of conversion costs during July

Step 3: Summarize Total Costs to Account for and Compute the Cost per Equivalent Unit

Exhibit 20A-3 accumulates the Cutting Department's July costs from Exhibit 20-11. *Under FIFO, the July cost per equivalent unit equals the costs incurred in July divided by the equivalent units of work performed in July.* The $24,000 cost of the beginning inventory is kept separate and is not included in the cost per equivalent unit for work done in July. Why? Because Cutting incurred this $24,000 in *June* to start the 5,000 puzzles in process on July 1.

FIFO, Steps 3 and 4: Summarize Total Costs to Account for and Compute the Cost per Equivalent Unit

PUZZLE ME CUTTING DEPARTMENT
Month Ended July 31, 2008

	Transferred In	Direct Materials	Conversion Costs	Total
Beginning work in process, June 30 (Exhibit 20-11)				$ 23,200
Costs added during July (Exhibit 20-11)	$176,000	$19,000	$14,840	209,840
Divide by equivalent units (Exhibit 20A-2)	÷40,000	÷38,000	÷37,100	
Cost per equivalent unit	$4.40	$0.50	$0.40	
Total costs to account for				$233,040

Step 4: Assign Total Costs to Units Completed and to Units in Ending Work in Process Inventory

Exhibit 20A-4 shows that the Cutting Department uses the same approach as we have used previously to assign its total cost ($233,040 from Exhibit 20A-3) to:

- Units completed and transferred out to Finished Goods Inventory
- Units still in Cutting's ending work in process inventory

Multiply the number of equivalent units from step 2 (Exhibit 20A-2) by the cost per equivalent unit from step 4 (Exhibit 20A-3).

Exhibit 20A-4 shows that when computing the cost of puzzles completed and transferred out of Cutting, we must remember to include the costs of the beginning inventory:

- $23,200 of Cutting Department beginning inventory costs (incurred in June)
- $3,300 of costs to complete that beginning inventory in July [(5,000 equivalent units of materials added × $0.50) + (2,000 equivalent units of conversion costs added × $0.40)]

The entry to transfer the cost of completed puzzles out of the Cutting Department and into Finished Goods Inventory is based on the dollar amount computed in Exhibit 20A-4:

Finished Goods Inventory	201,400	
Work in Process Inventory—Cutting		201,400

PUZZLE ME CUTTING DEPARTMENT
Month Ended July 31, 2008

	Transferred In	Direct Materials	Conversion Costs	Total
Units completed and transferred out to Finished Goods Inventory:				
From beginning work in process, June 30				$ 23,200
Costs added during July:				
Direct materials		[5,000 × $0.50]		2,500
Conversion costs			[2,000 × $0.40]	800
Total completed from beginning inventory				26,500
Units started and completed during July		[33,000 × ($4.40 + $0.50 + $0.40)]		174,900
Total costs transferred out				$201,400
Ending work in process, July 31:				
Transferred-in costs	[7,000 × $4.40]			30,800
Direct materials		—		—
Conversion costs			[2,100 × $0.40]	840
Total ending work in process, July 31				31,640
Total costs accounted for				$233,040

Many companies combine Exhibits 20A-3 and 20A-4 to form a FIFO-based production cost report. (This report is the FIFO-based counterpart to the weighted-average-based production cost report in Exhibit 20-16.)

Appendix 20A Assignments

Short Exercises

Drawing a time line; computing equivalent units; FIFO method

S20A-34 Refer to the Clear Spring bottling process in E20-23.

1. Draw a time line for the Bottling Department under FIFO process costing. Your time line should be similar to Exhibit 20A-1. (p. 1043)

2. Use the time line to help you compute the Bottling Department's equivalent units using the FIFO method. (p. 1044)

Computing costs per equivalent unit; FIFO method

S20A-35 Refer to E20-23 and S20A-34. Compute the costs per equivalent unit using FIFO.

Assigning costs; FIFO method

S20A-36 Use the information about Clear Spring's Bottling Department in E20-23, S20A-34, and S20A-35 to assign the costs to units completed and transferred out and to ending inventory under FIFO.

Appendix Exercise

Computing equivalent units;
FIFO method

E20A-37 Donnie's Frozen Pizzas uses FIFO process costing. Selected production and cost data follow for April 2009.

	Flow of Physical Units	
Flow of Production	Mixing Department	Heating Department
Units to account for:		
Beginning work in process, March 31	20,000	6,000
Transferred in during April	70,000	80,000
Total physical units to account for	90,000	86,000
Units accounted for:		
Completed and transferred out during April		
From beginning work in process inventory	20,000	6,000
Started and completed during April	60,000	70,000
Ending work in process, April 30	10,000	10,000
Total physical units accounted for	90,000	86,000

Requirements

1. a. On March 31, the Mixing Department beginning work in process inventory was 60% complete as to materials and 75% complete as to conversion costs. This means that for the beginning inventory _____% of the materials and _____% of the conversion costs were added during April.

   b. On April 30, the Mixing Department ending work in process inventory was 70% complete as to materials and 20% complete as to conversion costs. This means that for the ending inventory _____% of the materials and _____% of the conversion costs were added during April.

   c. On March 31, the Cooking Department beginning work in process inventory was 60% complete as to materials and 80% complete as to conversion costs. This means that for the beginning inventory _____% of the materials and _____% of the conversion costs were added during April.

   d. On April 30, the Cooking Department ending work in process inventory was 65% complete as to materials and 55% complete as to conversion costs. This means that for the ending inventory _____% of the materials and _____% of the conversion costs were added during April.

2. Use the information in the Flow of Physical Units table and the information in Requirement 1 to compute the equivalent units for transferred-in costs, direct materials, and conversion costs for both the Mixing and the Cooking Departments.

Appendix Problems

P20A-38 Viva, Inc., manufactures tire tubes in a two-stage process that includes assembly and sealing. The Sealing Department tests the tubes and adds a puncture-resistant coating to each tube to prevent air leaks.

Drawing a time line;
computing equivalent units;
assigning costs;
journalizing; FIFO method

The direct materials (coating) are added at the end of the sealing process. Conversion costs are incurred evenly throughout the process. Work in process of the Sealing Department on February 28, 2008, consisted of 700 tubes that were 30% of the way through the production process. During March, 3,600 tubes were transferred in from the Assembly Department. The Sealing Department transferred 3,100 tubes to Finished Goods Inventory in March, and 1,200 were still in process on March 31. This ending inventory was 50% of the way through the sealing process. Viva uses FIFO process costing.

At March 31, before recording the transfer of costs from the Sealing Department to Finished Goods Inventory, the Viva general ledger included the following account:

Work in Process Inventory—Sealing

Balance, Feb. 28	28,100
Transferred in from Assembly	36,000
Direct materials	24,800
Direct labor	25,340
Manufacturing overhead	33,990

Requirements

1. Draw a time line for the Sealing Department. (p. 1043)

2. Use the time line to help you compute (a) the equivalent units, (b) cost per equivalent unit, and (c) total costs to account for in the Sealing Department for March. (pp. 1044–1046)

3. Assign total Sealing Department costs to (a) goods transferred out of the Sealing Department and (b) Work in Process Inventory—Sealing on March 31. (p. 1047)

4. Journalize all transactions affecting the Sealing Department during March, including the entries that have already been posted. (pp. 1013, 1015)

Computing equivalent units
for a second department
with beginning inventory;
assigning costs; FIFO
method

P20A-39 Work P20-33B, using the FIFO method. The Drying Department beginning work in process of 7,000 units is 30% complete as to conversion costs. Round equivalent unit costs to three decimal places.

21 Cost-Volume-Profit Analysis

Learning Objectives

1 Identify how changes in volume affect costs

2 Use CVP analysis to compute breakeven points

3 Use CVP analysis for profit planning, and graph the CVP relations

4 Use CVP methods to perform sensitivity analyses

5 Calculate the breakeven point for multiple product lines or services

Remember when you were 15 and ready to drive? Before you received your license, you needed training and practice. Many of us took driving courses to prepare for the driving tests. Do you think driving schools are profitable? How many students do they need to cover the costs of a training facility, instructors, and a fleet of cars? What happens to income if the business adds a new Honda to its fleet? ■

This chapter will look at cost behavior and you will learn how cost-volume-profit (CVP) analysis is used to manage a business. **Cost-volume-profit (CVP) analysis** expresses the relationships among costs, volume, and profit or loss. It's a wonderful management tool and easy to understand. You can take this material home and apply it to your family's business—immediately!

Cost Behavior

Some costs increase as the volume of activity increases. Other costs are not affected by volume changes. Managers need to know how a business's costs are affected by changes in its volume of activity. Let's look at the three different types of **costs.**

- Variable costs
- Fixed costs
- Mixed costs

Variable Costs

1 Identify how changes in volume affect costs

Total variable costs change in direct proportion to changes in the volume of activity. For our purposes, an activity is a business action that affects costs. Those activities include selling, producing, driving, and calling. These activities can be measured by units sold, units produced, miles driven, and the number of phone calls placed. So variable costs are those costs that increase or decrease in total as the volume of activity increases or decreases.

For example, Mi Tierra Driving School offers classroom and driving instruction. For each student taking driving lessons, the school spends $15 per month for gasoline. Mi Tierra can provide driving lessons for 15 to 30 students. To calculate total variable costs Ms. Lopez, the office manager, would show:

Number of Students per Month	Gasoline Cost per Student	Total Gasoline Cost per Month
15	$15	$225
20	$15	$300
30	$15	$450

As you can see, the total variable cost of gasoline increases as the number of students increases. But the gasoline cost per student does not change. Exhibit 21-1 graphs total variable costs for gasoline as the number of students increase from 0 to 30.

If there are no students, Mi Tierra incurs no gasoline costs, so the total variable cost line begins at the bottom left corner. This point is called the *origin,* and it represents zero volume and zero cost. The *slope* of the variable cost line is the change in gasoline cost (on the vertical axis) divided by the change in the number of students (on the horizontal axis). The slope of the graph equals the variable cost per unit. In Exhibit 21-1, the slope of the variable cost line is $15 because the driving school spends $15 on gas for each student.

If the driving school signs 15 students for the month, it will spend a total of $225 (15 students × $15 each) for gasoline. Follow this total variable cost line to the right to see that doubling the number of students to 30 likewise doubles the total variable cost to $450 (30 × $15 = $450). Exhibit 21-1 shows how the *total variable cost* of gasoline varies with the number of students. *But note that the per-person cost remains constant* at $15 per student.

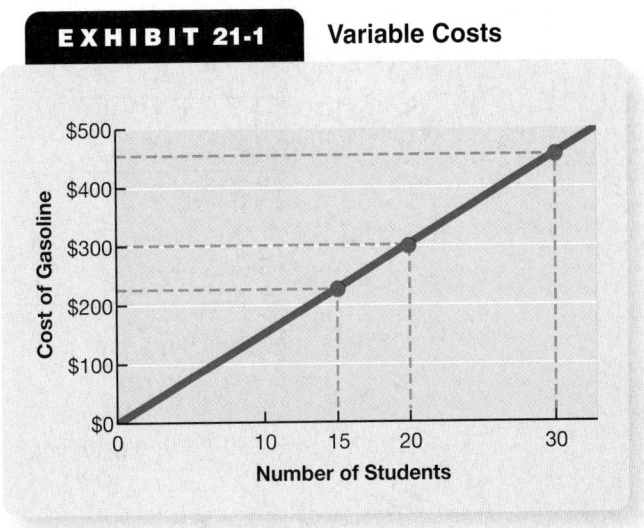

EXHIBIT 21-1 **Variable Costs**

Remember this important fact about **variable costs:**

> Total variable costs fluctuate with changes in volume,
> but the variable cost per unit remains constant.

Fixed Costs

In contrast, **total fixed costs** are costs that do not change over wide ranges of volume. Mi Tierra's fixed costs include depreciation on the cars, as well as the salaries of the driving instructors. Mi Tierra has these fixed costs regardless of the number of students—15, 20, or 30.

Suppose Mi Tierra incurs $12,000 of fixed costs each month, and the number of students enrolled is between 15 and 30 students. Exhibit 21-2 graphs total fixed costs as a flat line that intersects the cost axis at $12,000, because Mi Tierra will incur the same $12,000 of fixed costs regardless of the number of students.

Total fixed cost doesn't change, as shown in Exhibit 21-2. But the *fixed cost per student* depends on the number of students. If Mi Tierra teaches 15 students, the fixed cost per student is $800 ($12,000 ÷ 15 students). If the number of students doubles to 30, the fixed cost per student is cut in half to $400 ($12,000 ÷ 30 students).

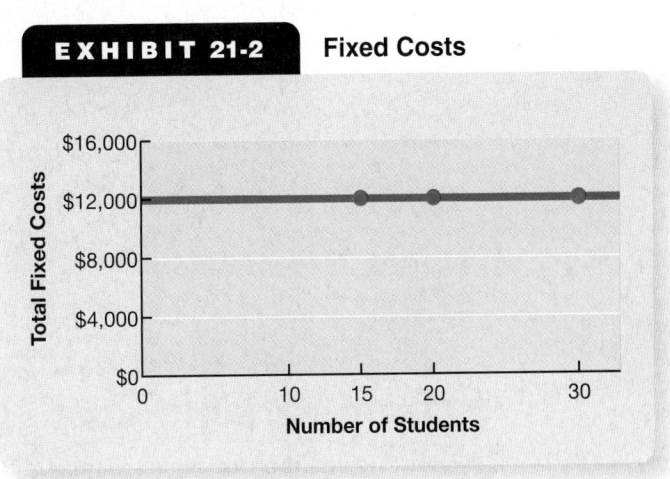

EXHIBIT 21-2 **Fixed Costs**

Thus, the fixed cost per student is *inversely* proportional to the number of students, as shown here.

Total Fixed Costs	Number of Students	Fixed Cost per Student
$12,000	15	$800
$12,000	20	$600
$12,000	30	$400

Remember this important fact about **fixed costs**:

Total fixed costs remain constant,
but fixed cost per unit is inversely proportional to volume.

Mixed Costs

Costs that have both variable and fixed components are called **mixed costs**. For example, Mi Tierra's cell-phone company may charge $10 a month to provide the service and $0.15 for each minute you talk. If you talk for 100 minutes, the company will bill you $25 [$10 + (100 × $0.15)].

Exhibit 21-3 shows how you can separate your cell-phone bill into fixed and variable components. The $10 monthly charge is a fixed cost because it is the same no matter how many minutes you use the cell phone. The $0.15-per-minute charge is a variable cost that increases in direct proportion to the number of minutes you talk. If you talk for 100 minutes, your total variable cost is $15 (100 × $0.15). If you double your talking to 200 minutes, total variable cost also doubles to $30 (200 × $0.15), and your total bill rises to $40 ($10 + $30).

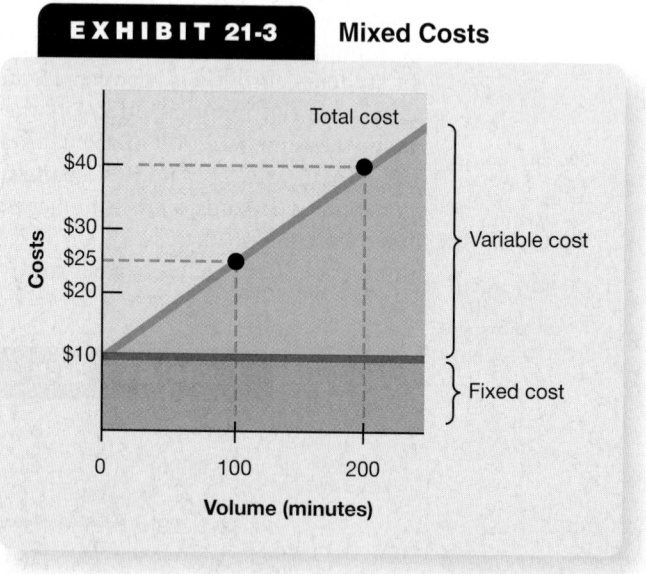

EXHIBIT 21-3 **Mixed Costs**

High-Low Method to Separate Fixed Cost from Variable Cost

An easy method to separate mixed costs into variable and fixed components is the **high-low method**. This method requires you to identify the highest and lowest levels of activity over a period of time. Using this information, you complete three steps:

STEP 1. Calculate the variable cost per unit.

Variable cost per unit = Change in total cost ÷ Change in volume of activity

STEP 2. Calculate total fixed costs.

Total fixed cost = Total mixed cost − Total variable cost

STEP 3. Create and use an equation to show the behavior of a mixed cost.

Total mixed cost = (Variable cost per unit × number of units) + Total fixed costs

Let's revisit the Mi Tierra Driving School illustration. A summary of Mi Tierra's auto maintenance costs for the past year shows these costs for each quarter:

	Student Driving Hours	Total Maintenance Cost	
1st Quarter	360	$1,720	
2nd Quarter	415	1,830	
3rd Quarter	480	1,960	◄——— Highest Volume and Cost
4th Quarter	240	1,480	◄——— Lowest Volume and Cost

The highest volume is 480 student-driving hours in the 3rd quarter of the year, and the lowest volume is 240 student-driving hours. We can use the high-low method to identify Mi Tierra's fixed and variable costs of auto maintenance.

STEP 1. Calculate the variable cost per unit.

Variable cost per unit = Change in total cost ÷ Change in volume of activity
= ($1,960 − $1,480) ÷ (480 hours − 240 hours)
= $480 ÷ 240 hours
= $2 per student-driving hour

STEP 2. Calculate total fixed costs.

Total fixed cost = Total mixed cost − Total variable cost
= $1,960 − ($2 × 480)
= $1,960 − $960
= $1,000

This example uses the highest cost and volume to calculate total fixed costs, but you can use any volume and calculate the same $1,000 total fixed cost.

STEP 3. Create and use an equation to show the behavior of a mixed cost.

Total mixed cost = (Variable cost per unit × number of units) + Total fixed costs
Total car maintenance cost = $2 per student-driver hour + $1,000

Using this equation, the estimated car maintenance cost for 400 student-driver hours would be:

$$(\$2 \times 400 \text{ student-driver hours}) + \$1,000 = \$1,800$$

This method provides a rough estimate of fixed and variable costs for cost-volume-profit analysis. The high and low volumes become the relevant range, which we discuss in the next section. Managers find the high-low method to be quick and easy, but regression analysis provides the most accurate estimates and is discussed in cost accounting textbooks.

Relevant Range

The **relevant range** is the band of volume where total fixed costs remain constant and the variable cost *per unit* remains constant. To estimate costs, managers need to know the relevant range. Why? Because:

- Total "fixed" costs can differ from one relevant range to another
- The variable cost *per unit* can differ in various relevant ranges

Exhibit 21-4 shows fixed costs for Mi Tierra Driving School over three different relevant ranges. If the school expects to offer 15,000 student-driving hours next year, the relevant range is between 10,000 and 20,000 student-driving hours, and managers budget fixed costs of $80,000.

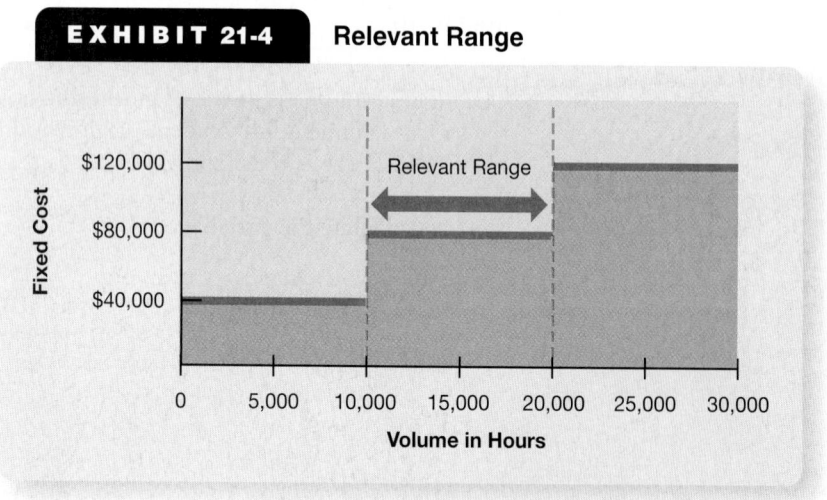

EXHIBIT 21-4 **Relevant Range**

To offer 22,000 student-driving hours, Mi Tierra will have to expand the school. This will increase total fixed costs for added rent cost. Exhibit 21-4 shows that total fixed costs increase to $120,000 as the relevant range shifts to this higher band of volume. Conversely, if Mi Tierra expects to offer only 8,000 student-driving hours, the school will budget only $40,000 of fixed costs. Managers will have to lay off employees or take other actions to cut fixed costs.

Variable cost per unit can also change outside the relevant range. For example, Mi Tierra Driving School may get a quantity discount for training materials if it can provide more than 20,000 student-driving hours.

We have now covered the basics of CVP analysis. Let's apply CVP analysis to answer some interesting management questions.

Basic CVP Analysis: What Must We Sell to Break Even?

2 Use CVP analysis to compute breakeven points

Kim Chan is considering starting an e-tail business to sell art posters on the Internet. Chan plans to be a "virtual retailer" and carry no inventory. Chan's software will total customer orders each day and automatically order posters from a wholesaler. Chan buys only what she needs to fulfill yesterday's sales orders. Here are Chan's basic CVP data:

Selling price per poster	$ 35
Variable cost per poster	$ 21
Fixed costs for server leasing, software, and office rental	$7,000

Chan faces several important questions:

- How many posters must Chan sell to break even?
- What will profits be if sales double?
- How will changes in selling price, variable costs, or fixed costs affect profits?

Before getting started, let's review the assumptions required for CVP analysis to be accurate.

Assumptions

CVP analysis assumes that:

1. Managers can classify each cost as either variable or fixed.

2. The only factor that affects costs is change in volume. Fixed costs don't change.

Chan's business meets these assumptions.

1. The $21 purchase cost for each poster is a variable cost. Thus, Chan's *total variable cost* increases directly with the number of posters she sells (an extra $21 in cost for each poster sold). The $7,000 monthly server, software, and office rentals are fixed costs and don't change regardless of the number of posters she sells.

2. Sales volume is the only factor that affects Chan's costs.

Most business conditions don't perfectly meet these assumptions, so managers regard CVP analysis as approximate, not exact.

How Much Must Chan Sell to Break Even? Three Approaches

Virtually all businesses want to know their breakeven point. The **breakeven point** is the sales level at which operating income is zero: Total revenues equal total costs. Sales below the breakeven point result in a loss. Sales above breakeven provide a profit. Chan needs to know how many posters she must sell to break even, and that will help her plan her profits.

There are several ways to figure the breakeven point, including the

- Income statement approach
- Contribution margin approach

We start with the income statement approach because it is the easiest method to remember. You are already familiar with the income statement.

The Income Statement Approach

Start by expressing income in equation form:

$$\text{Sales revenue} - \underbrace{\text{Total costs}} = \text{Operating income}$$

$$\text{Sales revenue} - \text{Variable costs} - \text{Fixed costs} = \text{Operating income}$$

Sales revenue equals the unit sale price ($35 per poster in this case) multiplied by the number of units (posters) sold. Variable costs equal variable cost per unit ($21 in this case) times the number of units sold. Chan's fixed costs total $7,000. At the breakeven point, operating income is zero. We use this information to solve the income statement equation for the number of posters Chan must sell to break even.

SALES REVENUE	−	VARIABLE COSTS	− FIXED COSTS	= OPERATING INCOME
$\left(\dfrac{\text{Sale price}}{\text{per unit}} \times \text{Units sold}\right)$	−	$\left(\dfrac{\text{Variable cost}}{\text{per unit}} \times \text{Units sold}\right)$	− Fixed costs =	Operating income
($35 × Units sold)	−	($21 × Units sold) −	$7,000 =	$0
($35	−	$21) × Units sold −	$7,000 =	$0
		$14 × Units sold	=	$7,000
		Units sold	=	$7,000/$14
		Breakeven sales in units	=	500 posters

Kim Chan must sell 500 posters to break even. Her breakeven sales level in dollars is $17,500 (500 posters × $35).

Be sure to check your calculations. "Prove" the breakeven point by substituting the breakeven number of units into the income statement. Then check to ensure that this level of sales results in zero profit.

$$\text{Proof:} \quad (\$35 \times 500) - (\$21 \times 500) - \$7,000 = \$0$$
$$\$17,500 \;-\; \$10,500 \;-\; \$7,000 = \$0$$

The Contribution Margin Approach: A Shortcut

This shortcut method of computing the breakeven point uses Chan's contribution margin. **Contribution margin** is sales revenue minus variable costs. It is called the *contribution margin* because the excess of sales revenue over variable costs contributes to covering fixed costs and then to providing operating income. We can refer to contribution margin on a total basis or on a per-unit basis, as follows:

$$\text{Total contribution margin} \;=\; \text{Total sales revenue} \;-\; \text{Total variable costs}$$
$$\text{Contribution margin per unit} \;=\; \text{Sales revenue per unit} \;-\; \text{Variable cost per unit}$$

The **contribution margin income statement** shows costs by cost behavior—variable costs and fixed costs—and highlights the contribution margin. The format shows:

> Sales revenue
> − Variable costs
> = Contribution margin
> − Fixed costs
> = Operating income

Now let's rearrange the income statement and use the contribution margin to develop a shortcut method for finding the number of posters Chan must sell to break even.

$$\text{Sales revenue} \quad - \quad \text{Variable costs} \quad - \text{Fixed costs} = \text{Operating income}$$

$$\left(\frac{\text{Sale price}}{\text{per unit}} \times \text{Units sold}\right) - \left(\frac{\text{Variable cost}}{\text{per unit}} \times \text{Units sold}\right) - \text{Fixed costs} = \text{Operating income}$$

$$\underbrace{\left(\frac{\text{Sale price}}{\text{per unit}} - \frac{\text{Variable cost}}{\text{per unit}}\right) \times \text{Units sold}}_{} = \frac{\text{Fixed}}{\text{costs}} + \frac{\text{Operating}}{\text{income}}$$

$$\text{Contribution margin per unit} \times \text{Units sold} = \frac{\text{Fixed}}{\text{costs}} + \frac{\text{Operating}}{\text{income}}$$

Dividing both sides of the equation by contribution margin per unit yields the cost-volume-profit equation:

$$\text{Units sold} = \frac{\text{Fixed costs} + \text{Operating income}}{\text{Contribution margin per unit}}$$

Kim Chan can use this contribution margin approach to find her breakeven point. Her fixed costs total $7,000. Operating income is zero at breakeven. Her contribution margin per poster is $14 ($35 sale price − $21 variable cost). Chan's breakeven computation is:

$$\text{BREAKEVEN SALES IN UNITS} = \frac{\$7,000}{\$14}$$
$$= 500 \text{ posters}$$

Why does this shortcut method work? Each poster Chan sells provides $14 of contribution margin. To break even, Chan must generate enough contribution margin to cover $7,000 of fixed costs. At the rate of $14 per poster, Chan must sell 500 posters ($7,000/$14) to cover her fixed costs. You can see that the contribution margin approach simply rearranges the income statement equation, so the breakeven point is the same under both methods.

To "prove" the breakeven point, you can also use the contribution margin income statement format:

Proof:

Sales revenue ($35 × 500 posters)	$17,500
Less: Variable costs ($21 × 500 posters)	(10,500)
Contribution margin ($14 × 500 posters)	7,000
Less: Fixed costs	(7,000)
Operating income	$ 0

Using the Contribution Margin Ratio to Compute the Breakeven Point in Sales Dollars

Companies can use the contribution margin ratio to compute their breakeven point in terms of *sales dollars*. The **contribution margin ratio** is the ratio of contribution margin to sales revenue. For Kim Chan's poster business, we have:

$$\text{Contribution margin ratio} = \frac{\text{Contribution margin}}{\text{Sales revenue}} = \frac{\$14}{\$35} = 40\%$$

The 40% contribution margin ratio means that each dollar of sales revenue contributes $0.40 toward fixed costs and profit, as shown in Exhibit 21-5.

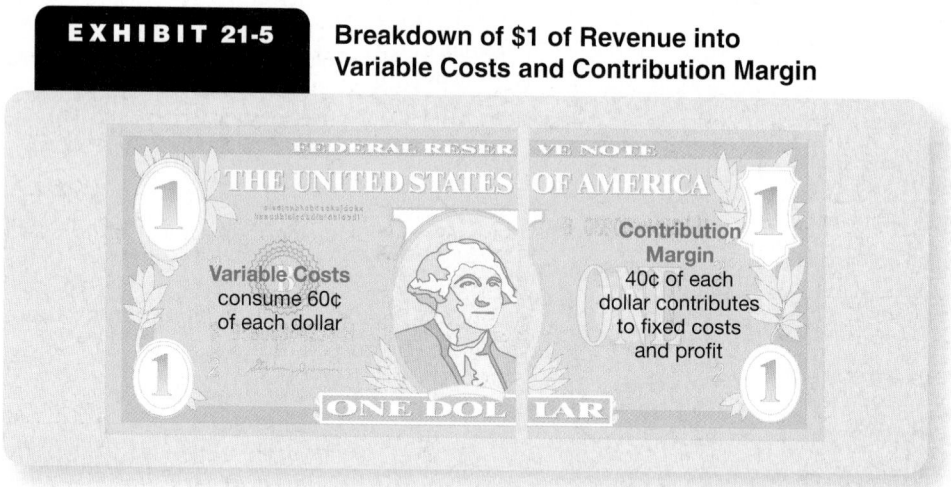

EXHIBIT 21-5 Breakdown of $1 of Revenue into Variable Costs and Contribution Margin

Variable Costs consume 60¢ of each dollar

Contribution Margin 40¢ of each dollar contributes to fixed costs and profit

The contribution margin *ratio* approach differs from the shortcut contribution margin approach we've just seen in only one way: Here we use the contribution margin *ratio* rather than the dollar amount of the contribution margin:

$$\text{BREAKEVEN SALES IN DOLLARS} = \frac{\text{Fixed costs}}{\text{Contribution margin ratio}}$$

Using this ratio formula, Kim Chan's breakeven point in sales dollars is

$$\text{BREAKEVEN SALES IN DOLLARS} = \frac{\$7,000}{0.40}$$
$$= \$17,500$$

This is the same breakeven sales revenue as shown in the proof at the bottom of page 1059.

Why does the contribution margin ratio formula work? Each dollar of Kim Chan's sales contributes 40% of each dollar of sales to fixed costs and profit. To break even, she must generate enough contribution margin at the rate of 40% of sales to cover the $7,000 fixed costs ($7,000 ÷ 0.40 = $17,500).

Now, we've seen how companies use *contribution margin* to estimate breakeven points in CVP analysis. But managers use the contribution margin for other purposes too, such as motivating the sales force. Salespeople who know the contribution margin of each product can generate more profit by emphasizing high-margin products. This is why many companies base sales commissions on the contribution margins produced by sales rather than on sales revenue alone.

Using CVP to Plan Profits

3 Use CVP analysis for profit planning, and graph the CVP relations

For established products and services, managers are more interested in the sales level needed to earn a target profit than in the breakeven point. Managers of new business ventures are also interested in the profits they can expect to earn. For example, now that Kim Chan knows she must sell 500 posters to break even, she wants to know how many more posters she must sell to earn a monthly operating profit of $4,900.

How Much Must Chan Sell to Earn a Profit?

What is the only difference from our prior analysis? Here, Chan wants to know how many posters she must sell to earn a $4,900 profit. We can use the income statement approach or the shortcut contribution margin approach to find the answer. Let's start with the income statement approach.

SALES REVENUE − VARIABLE COSTS − FIXED COSTS = OPERATING INCOME

($35 × Units sold) − ($21 × Units sold) −	$7,000	=	$4,900
($35 − $21) × Units sold −	$7,000	=	$4,900
$14 × Units sold		=	$11,900
	Units sold	=	$11,900/$14
	Units sold	=	850 posters

Proof:

($35 × 850)	− ($21 × 850)	− $7,000	=	$4,900
$29,750	− $17,850	− $7,000	=	$4,900

This analysis shows that Chan must sell 850 posters each month to earn an operating profit of $4,900. This is 850 − 500 = 350 more posters than the breakeven sales level (500 posters).

The proof shows that Chan needs sales revenues of $29,750 to earn a profit of $4,900. Alternatively, we can compute the dollar sales necessary to earn a $4,900 profit directly, using the contribution margin ratio form of the CVP formula:

$$\text{TARGET SALES IN DOLLARS} = \frac{\text{Fixed costs} + \text{Operating income}}{\text{Contribution margin ratio}}$$

$$= \frac{\$7,000 + \$4,900}{0.40}$$

$$= \frac{\$11,900}{0.40}$$

$$= \$29,750$$

Graphing Cost-Volume-Profit Relations

Kim Chan can graph the CVP relations for her proposed business. A graph provides a picture that shows how changes in the levels of sales will affect profits. As in the variable-, fixed-, and mixed-cost graphs of Exhibits 21-1, 2, and 3, Chan shows the volume of units (posters) on the horizontal axis and dollars on the vertical axis.

Then she follows four steps to graph the CVP relations for her business, as illustrated in Exhibit 21-6.

STEP 1 Choose a sales volume, such as 1,000 posters. Plot the point for total sales revenue at that volume: 1,000 posters × $35 per poster = sales of $35,000. Draw the *sales revenue line* from the origin (0) through the $35,000 point. Why start at the origin? If Chan sells no posters, there's no revenue.

STEP 2 Draw the *fixed cost line,* a horizontal line that intersects the dollars axis at $7,000. The fixed cost line is flat because fixed costs are the same ($7,000) no matter how many posters Chan sells.

STEP 3 Draw the *total cost line.* Total cost is the sum of variable cost plus fixed cost. Thus, total cost is *mixed.* So the total cost line follows the form of the mixed cost line in Exhibit 21-3. Begin by computing variable cost at the chosen sales volume: 1,000 posters × $21 per poster = variable cost of $21,000. Add variable cost to fixed cost: $21,000 + $7,000 = $28,000. Plot the total cost point ($28,000) for 1,000 units. Then draw a line through this point from the $7,000 fixed cost intercept on the dollars vertical axis. This is the *total cost line.* The total cost line starts at the fixed cost line because even if Chan sells no posters, she still incurs the $7,000 fixed cost.

STEP 4 Identify the *breakeven point* and the areas of operating income and loss. The breakeven point is where the sales revenue line intersects the total cost line. This is where revenue exactly equals total costs—at 500 posters, or $17,500 in sales.

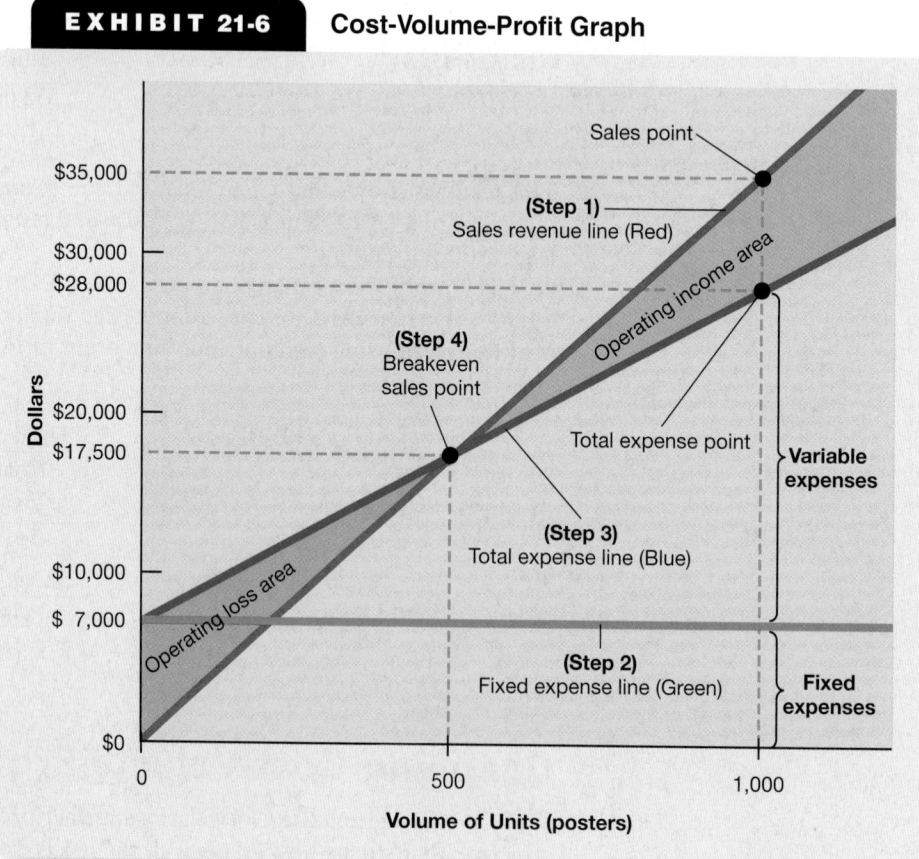

EXHIBIT 21-6 **Cost-Volume-Profit Graph**

Mark the *operating income* and the *operating loss* areas on the graph. To the left of the breakeven point, total costs exceed sales revenue—leading to an operating loss, indicated by the red zone.

To the right of the breakeven point, the business earns a profit because sales revenue exceeds total cost, as shown by the green zone.

Why bother with a graph? Why not just use the income statement approach or the shortcut contribution margin approach? Graphs like Exhibit 21-6 help managers quickly estimate the profit or loss earned at different levels of sales. The income statement and contribution margin approaches indicate income or loss for only a single sales amount.

Summary Problem 1

Happy Feet buys hiking socks for $6 a pair and sells them for $10. Management budgets monthly fixed costs of $10,000 for sales volumes between 0 and 12,000 pairs.

Requirements

1. Use both the income statement approach and the shortcut contribution margin approach to compute the company's monthly breakeven sales in units.

2. Use the contribution margin ratio approach to compute the breakeven point in sales dollars.

3. Compute the monthly sales level (in units) required to earn a target operating income of $6,000. Use either the income statement approach or the shortcut contribution margin approach.

4. Prepare a graph of Happy Feet's CVP relationships, similar to Exhibit 21-6. Draw the sales revenue line, the fixed cost line, and the total cost line. Label the axes, the breakeven point, the operating income area, and the operating loss area.

Solution

Requirement 1

Income statement approach:

$$\text{Sales revenue} - \text{Variable costs} - \frac{\text{Fixed}}{\text{costs}} = \frac{\text{Operating}}{\text{income}}$$

$$\left(\frac{\text{Sale price}}{\text{per unit}} \times \frac{\text{Units}}{\text{sold}}\right) - \left(\frac{\text{Variable}}{\text{cost per unit}} \times \frac{\text{Units}}{\text{sold}}\right) - \frac{\text{Fixed}}{\text{costs}} = \frac{\text{Operating}}{\text{income}}$$

$$
\begin{aligned}
(\$10 \times \text{Units sold}) - (\$6 \times \text{Units sold}) \quad -\$10,000 &= \$0 \\
(\$10 - \$6) \times \text{Units sold} &= \$10,000 \\
\$4 \times \text{Units sold} &= \$10,000 \\
\text{Units sold} &= \$10,000 \div \$4 \\
\text{Breakeven sales in units} &= 2,500 \text{ units}
\end{aligned}
$$

Shortcut contribution margin approach:

$$\text{Units sold} = \frac{\text{Fixed costs} + \text{Operating income}}{\text{Contribution margin per unit}}$$

$$
\begin{aligned}
\text{Breakeven sales in units} &= \frac{\$10,000 + \$0}{\$10 - \$6} \\
&= \frac{\$10,000}{\$4} \\
&= 2,500 \text{ units}
\end{aligned}
$$

Requirement 2

$$\text{Breakeven sales in dollars} = \frac{\text{Fixed costs} + \text{Operating income}}{\text{Contribution margin ratio}}$$

$$
\begin{aligned}
&= \frac{\$10,000 + \$0}{0.40^*} \\
&= \$25,000
\end{aligned}
$$

$$^*\text{Contribution margin ratio} = \frac{\text{Contribution margin per unit}}{\text{Sale price per unit}} = \frac{\$4}{\$10} = 0.40$$

Requirement 3

Income statement equation approach:

$$\text{Sales revenue} \quad - \quad \text{Variable costs} \quad - \quad \begin{array}{c}\text{Fixed}\\\text{costs}\end{array} = \begin{array}{c}\text{Operating}\\\text{income}\end{array}$$

$$\left(\begin{array}{c}\text{Sale price}\\\text{per unit}\end{array} \times \begin{array}{c}\text{Units}\\\text{sold}\end{array}\right) - \left(\begin{array}{c}\text{Variable}\\\text{cost per unit}\end{array} \times \begin{array}{c}\text{Units}\\\text{sold}\end{array}\right) - \begin{array}{c}\text{Fixed}\\\text{costs}\end{array} = \begin{array}{c}\text{Operating}\\\text{income}\end{array}$$

($10 × Units sold) − ($6 × Units sold) − $10,000	= $6,000
($10 − $6) × Units sold	= $10,000 + $6,000
$4 × Units sold	= $16,000
Units sold	= $16,000 ÷ $4
Units sold	= 4,000 units

Shortcut contribution margin approach:

$$\text{Units sold} = \frac{\text{Fixed costs} + \text{Operating income}}{\text{Contribution margin per unit}}$$

$$= \frac{\$10,000 + \$6,000}{(\$10 - \$6)}$$

$$= \frac{\$16,000}{\$4}$$

$$= 4,000 \text{ units}$$

Requirement 4

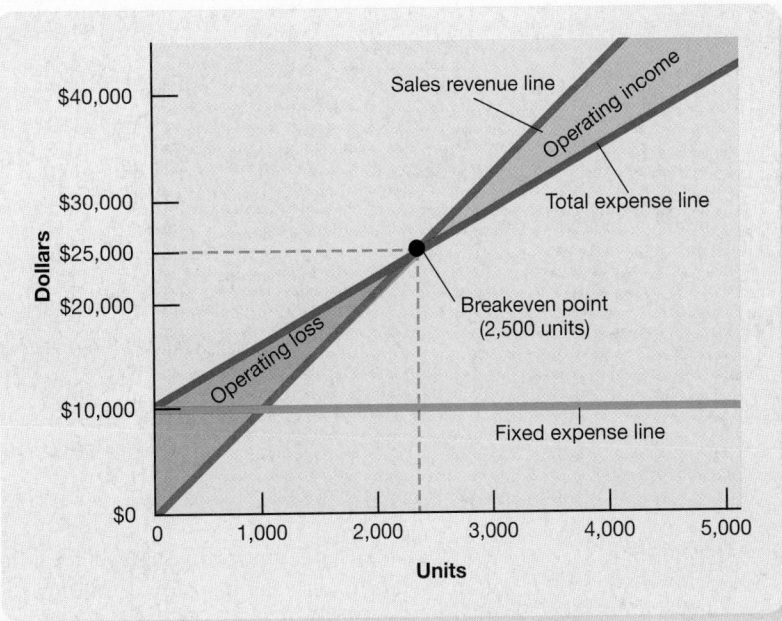

Using CVP for Sensitivity Analysis

Managers often want to predict how changes in sale price, costs, or volume affect their profits. Managers can use CVP relationships to conduct sensitivity analysis. **Sensitivity analysis** is a "what if" technique that asks what results are likely if selling price or costs change, or if an underlying assumption changes. Let's see how Kim Chan can use CVP analysis to estimate the effects of some changes in her business environment.

Changing the Selling Price

Competition in the art poster business is so fierce that Kim Chan believes she must cut the selling price to $31 per poster to maintain her market share. Suppose Chan's variable costs remain $21 per poster and her fixed costs stay at $7,000. How will the lower sale price affect her breakeven point?

Using the income statement approach:

SALES REVENUE − VARIABLE COSTS − FIXED COSTS = OPERATING INCOME

$$(\$31 \times \text{Units sold}) - (\$21 \times \text{Units sold}) - \$7,000 = \$0$$
$$(\$31 - \$21) \times \text{Units sold} - \$7,000 = \$0$$
$$\$10 \times \text{Units sold} = \$7,000$$
$$\text{Units sold} = \$7,000/\$10$$
$$\text{Units sold} = 700 \text{ posters}$$

Proof:

Sales revenue (700 × $31)	$21,700
Less: Variable costs (700 × $21)	(14,700)
Contribution margin (700 × $10)	7,000
Less: Fixed costs	(7,000)
Operating income	$ 0

With the original $35 sale price, Chan's breakeven point was 500 posters (page 1059). With the new lower sale price of $31 per poster, her breakeven point increases to 700 posters. The lower sale price means that each poster contributes less toward fixed costs, so Chan must sell 200 more posters to break even.

Changing Variable Costs

Return to Kim Chan's original data on page 1057. Chan's supplier raises his prices, which increases her purchase cost for each poster to $28 (instead of the original $21). Chan can't pass this increase on to her customers, so she holds her sale price at the original $35 per poster. Her fixed costs remain at $7,000. How many posters must Chan sell to break even after her supplier raises his prices?

Using the income statement approach:

SALES REVENUE	− VARIABLE COSTS	− FIXED COSTS	= OPERATING INCOME
($35 × Units sold)	− ($28 × Units sold)	− $7,000	= $0
($35 − $28) × Units sold		− $7,000	= $0
	$7 × Units sold		= $7,000
		Breakeven units sold	= $7,000/$7
		Breakeven units sold	= 1,000 posters

Higher variable costs per poster reduce Chan's per-unit contribution margin from $14 per poster to $7 per poster. As a result, Chan must sell more posters to break even—1,000 rather than the original 500 posters. This analysis shows why managers are particularly concerned with controlling costs during an economic downturn. Increases in cost raise the breakeven point, and a higher breakeven point can lead to problems if demand falls due to a recession.

Of course, a decrease in variable costs would have the opposite effect. Lower variable costs increase the contribution margin on each poster and, therefore, lower the breakeven point.

Changing Fixed Costs

Return to Kim Chan's original data on page 1057. Kim is considering spending an additional $3,500 on Web site banner ads. This would increase her fixed costs from $7,000 to $10,500. If she sells the posters at the original price of $35 each and her variable costs remain at $21 per poster, what is her new breakeven point?

Using the income statement approach:

SALES REVENUE	− VARIABLE COSTS	− FIXED COSTS	= OPERATING INCOME
($35 × Units sold)	− ($21 × Units sold)	− $10,500	= $0
($35 − $21) × Units sold		− $10,500	= $0
	$14 × Units sold		= $10,500
		Breakeven units sold	= $10,500/$14
		Breakeven units sold	= 750 posters

Higher fixed costs increase the total contribution margin required to break even. In this case, increasing the fixed costs from $7,000 to $10,500 increases the breakeven point to 750 posters (from the original 500 posters).

Managers usually prefer a lower breakeven point to a higher one. But don't overemphasize this one aspect of CVP analysis. Even though investing in the Web banner ads increases Chan's breakeven point, Chan should pay the extra $3,500 if that would increase both her sales and profits.

Exhibit 21-7 on the next page shows how all of these changes affect the contribution margin and breakeven.

Margin of Safety

The **margin of safety** is the excess of expected sales over breakeven sales. The margin of safety is therefore the "cushion" or drop in sales that the company can absorb without incurring a loss.

> The higher the margin of safety $\Rightarrow$ The greater the cushion against loss $\Rightarrow$ The less risky the business plan

EXHIBIT 21-7	How Changes in Selling Price, Variable Costs, and Fixed Costs Affect the Contribution Margin per Unit and the Breakeven Point

Cause	Effect	Result
Change	Contribution Margin per Unit	Breakeven Point
Selling Price per Unit Increases	Increases	Decreases
Selling Price per Unit Decreases	Decreases	Increases
Variable Cost per Unit Increases	Decreases	Increases
Variable Cost per Unit Decreases	Increases	Decreases
Total Fixed Cost Increases	Is not affected	Increases
Total Fixed Cost Decreases	Is not affected	Decreases

Managers use the margin of safety to evaluate the risk of both their current operations and their plans for the future. Let's apply the margin of safety to Kim Chan's poster business.

Kim Chan's original breakeven point was 500 posters. Suppose Chan expects to sell 900 posters. Her margin of safety is:

MARGIN OF SAFETY IN UNITS = EXPECTED SALES IN UNITS − BREAKEVEN SALES IN UNITS

$$= 900 \text{ posters} \quad - 500 \text{ posters}$$
$$= 400 \text{ posters}$$

MARGIN OF SAFETY IN DOLLARS = MARGIN OF SAFETY IN UNITS × SALE PRICE PER UNIT

$$= 400 \text{ posters} \quad \times \$35$$
$$= \$14,000$$

Sales can drop by 400 posters, or $14,000, before Chan incurs a loss. This margin of safety (400 posters) is 44.4% of expected sales (900 posters). That's a comfortable margin of safety.

Information Technology and Sensitivity Analysis

Information technology allows managers to perform lots of sensitivity analyses before launching a new product or shutting down a plant. Excel spreadsheets are useful for sensitivity analyses like those we just did for Kim Chan. Spreadsheets can show how one change (or several changes simultaneously) affects operations. Managers can plot basic CVP data to show profit-planning graphs similar to Exhibit 21-6.

Large companies use enterprise resource planning software—SAP, Oracle, and Peoplesoft—for their CVP analysis. For example, after Sears stores lock their doors at 9:00 P.M., records for each individual transaction flow into a massive database. From a Diehard battery sold in California to a Trader Bay polo shirt sold in New Hampshire, the system compiles an average of 1.5 million transactions a day. With the click of a mouse, managers can conduct breakeven or profit planning analysis on any product they choose.

Effect of Sales Mix on CVP Analysis

5 Calculate the breakeven point for multiple product lines or services

Most companies sell more than one product. Selling price and variable costs differ for each product, so each product line makes a different contribution to profits. The same CVP formulas we used earlier apply to a company with multiple products.

To calculate breakeven for each product line, we must compute the *weighted-average contribution margin* of all the company's products. The sales mix provides the weights. **Sales mix** is the combination of products that make up total sales. For example, Fat Cat Furniture sold 6,000 cat beds and 4,000 scratching posts during the past year. The sales mix of 6,000 beds and 4,000 posts creates a ratio of 3:2 or a percentage of 60% for the beds and 40% for the posts. For every 3 cat beds, Fat Cat expects to sell 2 scratching posts, so Fat Cat expects 3/5 of the sales to be cat beds and 2/5 to be scratching posts.

Fat Cat's total fixed costs are $40,000. The cat bed's unit selling price is $44 and variable costs per bed are $24. The scratching post's unit selling price is $100 and variable cost per post is $30. To compute breakeven sales in units for both product lines, Fat Cat completes three steps.

STEP 1. Calculate the weighted-average contribution margin per unit, as follows:

		Cat Beds	Scratching Posts	Total
Sale price per unit		$44	$100	
Deduct: Variable cost per unit		(24)	(30)	
Contribution margin per unit		$20	$ 70	
Sales mix in units		× 3	× 2	5
Contribution margin		$60	$140	$200
Weighted-average contribution margin per unit ($200/5)				$ 40

STEP 2. Calculate the breakeven point in units for the "package" of products:

$$\text{BREAKEVEN SALES IN TOTAL UNITS} = \frac{\text{Fixed costs} + \text{Operating income}}{\text{Weighted-average contribution margin per unit}}$$

$$= \frac{\$40,000 + \$0}{\$40}$$

$$= 1,000 \text{ items}$$

STEP 3. Calculate the breakeven point in units for each product line. Multiply the "package" breakeven point in units by each product line's proportion of the sales mix.

Breakeven sales of cat beds (1,000 × 3/5)		600 cat beds
Breakeven sales of scratching posts (1,000 × 2/5)		400 scratching posts

In this example the calculations yield round numbers. When the calculations don't yield round numbers, round your answer up to the next whole number.

The overall breakeven point in sales dollars is $66,400:

600 cat beds at $44 selling price each	$26,400
400 scratching posts at $100 selling price each	40,000
Total revenues	$66,400

We can prove this breakeven point by preparing a contribution margin income statement:

	Cat Beds	Scratching Posts	Total
Sales revenue:			
Cat beds (600 × $44)	$26,400		
Scratching posts (400 × $100)		$40,000	$66,400
Variable costs:			
Cat beds (600 × $24)	14,400		
Scratching posts (400 × $30)		12,000	26,400
Contribution margin	$12,000	$28,000	$40,000
Fixed costs			(40,000)
Operating income			$ 0

If the sales mix changes, then Fat Cat can repeat this analysis using new sales mix information to find the breakeven points for each product line.

In addition to finding the breakeven point, Fat Cat can also estimate the sales needed to generate a certain level of operating profit. Suppose Fat Cat would like to earn operating income of $20,000. How many units of each product must Fat Cat now sell?

$$\text{BREAKEVEN SALES IN TOTAL UNITS} = \frac{\text{Fixed costs} + \text{Operating income}}{\text{Weighted-average contribution margin per unit}}$$

$$= \frac{\$40,000 + \$20,000}{\$40}$$

$$= 1,500 \text{ items}$$

Breakeven sales of cat beds (1,500 × 3/5)	900 cat beds
Breakeven sales of scratching posts (1,500 × 2/5)	600 scratching posts

We can prove this planned profit level by preparing a contribution margin income statement:

	Cat Beds	Scratching Posts	Total
Sales revenue:			
Cat beds (900 × $44)	$39,600		
Scratching posts (600 × $100)		$60,000	$99,600
Variable costs:			
Cat beds (900 × $24)	21,600		
Scratching posts (600 × $30)		18,000	39,600
Contribution margin	$18,000	$42,000	$60,000
Fixed costs			(40,000)
Operating income			$20,000

You have learned how to use CVP analysis as a managerial tool. Review the CVP Analysis Decision Guidelines to make sure you understand these basic concepts.

Decision Guidelines

COST-VOLUME-PROFIT ANALYSIS

As a manager, you will find CVP very useful. Here are some questions you will ask, and guidelines for answering them.

Decision	Guidelines

How do changes in volume of activity affect

- total costs?

Total *variable* costs → Change in proportion to changes in volume (number of products or services sold)

Total *fixed* costs → No change

- cost per unit?

Variable cost per unit → No change

Fixed cost per unit:

- Decreases when volume rises (Fixed costs are spread over *more* units)
- Increases when volume drops (Fixed costs are spread over *fewer* units)

How do I calculate the sales needed to break even or earn a target operating income

- in units?

Income Statement Method:

$$\text{Sales revenue} - \text{Variable costs} - \text{Fixed costs} = \text{Operating income}$$

$$\left(\frac{\text{Sale price}}{\text{per unit}} \times \frac{\text{Units}}{\text{sold}}\right) - \left(\frac{\text{Variable cost}}{\text{per unit}} \times \frac{\text{Units}}{\text{sold}}\right) - \frac{\text{Fixed}}{\text{costs}} = \text{Operating income}$$

$$\left(\frac{\text{Sale price}}{\text{per unit}} - \frac{\text{Variable cost}}{\text{per unit}}\right) \times \frac{\text{Units}}{\text{sold}} = \frac{\text{Fixed}}{\text{costs}} + \frac{\text{Operating}}{\text{income}}$$

$$\text{Contribution margin per unit} \times \frac{\text{Units}}{\text{sold}} = \frac{\text{Fixed}}{\text{costs}} + \frac{\text{Operating}}{\text{income}}$$

$$\frac{\text{Units}}{\text{sold}} = \frac{\text{Fixed costs} + \text{Operating income}}{\text{Contribution margin per unit}}$$

Shortcut Contribution Margin Method:

$$\frac{\text{Fixed costs} + \text{Operating income}}{\text{Contribution margin per unit}}$$

- in dollars?

Shortcut Contribution Margin Ratio Method:

$$\frac{\text{Fixed costs} + \text{Operating income}}{\text{Contribution margin ratio}}$$

How will changes in sale price or variable or fixed costs, affect the breakeven point?

Cause	Effect	Result
Change	Contribution Margin per Unit	Breakeven Point
Selling Price per Unit Increases	Increases	Decreases
Selling Price per Unit Decreases	Decreases	Increases
Variable Cost per Unit Increases	Decreases	Increases
Variable Cost per Unit Decreases	Increases	Decreases
Total Fixed Cost Increases	Is not affected	Increases
Total Fixed Cost Decreases	Is not affected	Decreases

Decision	Guidelines
How do I use CVP analysis to measure risk?	Margin of safety = Expected sales − Breakeven sales
How do I calculate my breakeven point when I sell more than one product or service?	**STEP 1.** Compute the weighted-averaged contribution margin per unit as on page 1069. **STEP 2.** Calculate the breakeven point in units for the "package" of products. **STEP 3.** Calculate breakeven point in units for each product line. Multiply the "package" breakeven point in units by each product line's proportion of the sales mix.

Summary Problem 2

Happy Feet buys hiking socks for $6 a pair and sells them for $10. Management budgets monthly fixed costs of $12,000 for sales volumes between 0 and 12,000 pairs.

Requirements

Consider each of the following questions separately by using the foregoing information each time.

1. Calculate the breakeven point in units.

2. Happy Feet reduces its selling price from $10 a pair to $8 a pair. Calculate the new breakeven point in units.

3. Happy Feet finds a new supplier for the socks. Variable costs will decrease by $1 a pair. Calculate the new breakeven point in units.

4. Happy Feet plans to advertise in hiking magazines. The advertising campaign will increase total fixed costs by $2,000 per month. Calculate the new breakeven point in units.

5. In addition to selling hiking socks, Happy Feet would like to start selling sports socks. Happy Feet expects to sell 1 pair of hiking socks for every 3 pair of sports socks. Happy Feet will buy the sports socks for $4 a pair and sell them for $8 a pair. Total fixed costs will stay at $12,000 per month. Calculate the breakeven point in units for both hiking socks and sports socks.

Solution

Requirement 1

$$\text{Units sold} = \frac{\text{Fixed costs}}{\text{Contribution margin per unit}}$$

$$\text{Breakeven sales in units} = \frac{\$12,000}{\$10 - \$6}$$

$$= \frac{\$12,000}{\$4}$$

$$= 3,000 \text{ units}$$

Requirement 2

$$\text{Units sold} = \frac{\text{Fixed costs}}{\text{Contribution margin per unit}}$$

$$\text{Breakeven sales in units} = \frac{\$12,000}{\$8 - \$6}$$

$$= \frac{\$12,000}{\$2}$$

$$= 6,000 \text{ units}$$

Requirement 3

$$\text{Units sold} = \frac{\text{Fixed costs}}{\text{Contribution margin per unit}}$$

$$\text{Breakeven sales in units} = \frac{\$12,000}{\$10 - \$5}$$

$$= \frac{\$12,000}{\$5}$$

$$= 2,400 \text{ units}$$

Requirement 4

$$\text{Units sold} = \frac{\text{Fixed costs}}{\text{Contribution margin per unit}}$$

$$\text{Breakeven sales in units} = \frac{\$14,000}{\$10 - \$6}$$

$$= \frac{\$14,000}{\$4}$$

$$= 3,500 \text{ units}$$

Requirement 5

STEP 1 Calculate the Weighted-Average Contribution Margin:

	Hiking	Sports	
Sales price per unit	$ 10.00	$ 8.00	
Variable expenses per unit	6.00	4.00	
Contribution margin per unit	$ 4.00	$ 4.00	
Sales mix in units	× 1	× 3	4
Contribution margin per unit	$ 4.00	$ 12.00	$ 16.00
Weighted-average CM ($16/4)			$ 4.00

STEP 2 Calculate breakeven point for "package" of products:

$$\text{BREAKEVEN SALES IN UNITS} = \frac{\text{Fixed costs}}{\text{Contribution margin per unit}}$$

$$= \frac{\$12,000}{\$4}$$

$$= 3,000 \text{ units}$$

STEP 3 Calculate breakeven point for each product line:

Number of hiking socks (3,000 × (1/4))	750
Number of sport socks (3,000 × (3/4))	2,250

Review Cost-Volume-Profit Analysis

Accounting Vocabulary

Absorption Costing
The costing method that assigns both variable and fixed manufacturing costs to products.

Breakeven Point
The sales level at which operating income is zero: Total revenues equal total expenses.

Contribution Margin
Sales revenue minus variable expenses.

Contribution Margin Income Statement
Income statement that groups costs by behavior—variable costs or fixed costs—and highlights the contribution margin.

Contribution Margin Ratio
Ratio of contribution margin to sales revenue.

Cost Behavior
Describes how costs change as volume changes.

Cost-Volume-Profit (CVP) Analysis
Expresses the relationships among costs, volume, and profit or loss.

Fixed Costs
Costs that tend to remain the same in amount, regardless of variations in level of activity.

High-Low Method
A method used to separate mixed costs into variable and fixed components, using the highest and lowest total cost.

Margin of Safety
Excess of expected sales over breakeven sales. Drop in sales a company can absorb without incurring an operating loss.

Mixed Costs
Costs that have both variable and fixed components.

Relevant Range
The band of volume where total fixed costs remain constant and the variable cost per unit remains constant.

Sales Mix
Combination of products that make up total sales.

Sensitivity Analysis
A "what if" technique that asks what results will be if actual prices or costs change, or if an underlying assumption changes.

Total Fixed Costs
Costs that do not change in total despite wide changes in volume.

Total Variable Costs
Costs that change in total in direct proportion to changes in volume.

Variable Costing
The costing method that assigns only variable manufacturing costs to products.

Quick Check

1. For Mi Tierra's Driving School, straight-line depreciation on the cars is:
   a. Variable cost
   b. Fixed cost
   c. Mixed cost
   d. None of the above

2. Assume Telluride Railway is considering hiring a reservations agency to handle passenger reservations. The agency would charge a flat fee of $10,000 per month, plus $1 per passenger reservation. What is the total reservation cost if 100,000 passengers take the trip next month?
   a. $1.10
   b. $10,000
   c. $100,000
   d. $110,000

3. If Telluride Railway's fixed costs total $50,000 per month, the variable cost per passenger is $10, and tickets sell for $60, what is the breakeven point in units?
   a. 1,000 passengers
   b. 833 passengers
   c. 714 passengers
   d. 100 passengers

4. Suppose Telluride Railway's total revenues are $3 million, its variable costs are $1.8 million, and its fixed costs are $0.6 million. Compute the breakeven point in dollars.
   a. $1.2 million
   b. $1.5 million
   c. $2.0 million
   d. $2.5 million

5. If Telluride Railway's fixed costs total $50,000 per month, the variable cost per passenger is $36, and tickets sell for $60, how much revenue must the Railway have to earn $100,000 in operating income per month?
   a. $60,000
   b. $150,000
   c. $250,000
   d. $375,000

6. On a CVP graph, the total cost line intersects the vertical (dollars) axis at:
   a. The level of the fixed costs
   b. The level of the variable costs
   c. The breakeven point
   d. The origin

7. If a company increases its selling price per unit for Product A, then the new breakeven point will

   a. Increase

   b. Decrease

   c. Remain the same

8. If a company increases its fixed costs for Product B, then the contribution margin per unit will

   a. Increase

   b. Decrease

   c. Remain the same

9. Telluride Railway had the following revenue over the past 5 years:

2003	$ 600,000
2004	700,000
2005	900,000
2006	800,000
2007	1,000,000

   To predict revenues for 2008, Telluride uses the average for the past 5 years. The company's breakeven revenue is $800,000 per year. What is Telluride's margin of safety?

   a. $0

   b. $50,000

   c. $100,000

   d. $110,000

10. Telluride Railway sells half of its tickets for the regular price of $60. The other half go to senior citizens and children for the discounted price of $40. Variable cost per passenger is $10 for both groups, and fixed costs total $50,000 per month. What is Telluride's breakeven point in total passengers? regular passengers? discount passengers?

    a. 600/300/300

    b. 1,000/500/500

    c. 1,250/625/625

    d. 1,500/750/750

    Answers are given after Apply Your Knowledge (p. 1092).

Assess Your Progress

Short Exercises

Variable and fixed costs

1

S21-1 Chicago Acoustics builds innovative loudspeakers for music and home theater. Identify the following costs as variable or fixed. Indicate V for variable costs and F for fixed costs. (pp. 1052–1054)

    _____ 1. Depreciation on routers used to cut wood enclosures

    _____ 2. Wood for speaker enclosures

    _____ 3. Patents on crossover relays

    _____ 4. Crossover relays

    _____ 5. Grill cloth

    _____ 6. Glue

    _____ 7. Quality inspector's salary

Variable and fixed costs

1

S21-2 Sally's DayCare has been in operation for several years. She needs your help to classify the following as variable costs or fixed costs. Indicate V for variable costs and F for fixed costs. (pp. 1052–1054)

    _____ 1. Building rent

    _____ 2. Toys

    _____ 3. Playground equipment

    _____ 4. Afternoon snacks

    _____ 5. Sally's salary

    _____ 6. Wages of after school employees

    _____ 7. Drawing paper

    _____ 8. Tables and chairs

Mixed costs

1

S21-3 Suppose Global-Link offers an international calling plan that charges $5.00 per month plus $0.35 per minute for calls outside the United States. (pp. 1054–1056)

1. Under this plan, what is your monthly international long-distance cost if you call Europe for

    a. 20 minutes?

    b. 40 minutes?

    c. 80 minutes?

2. Draw a graph illustrating your total cost under this plan. Label the axes, and show your costs at 20, 40, and 80 minutes.

Mixed costs

1

S21-4 Mike owns a machine shop. In reviewing his utility bill for the last 12 months he found that his highest bill ($2,400) occurred in August when his machines worked 1,000 machine hours. His lowest utility bill of $2,200 occurred in December when his machines worked 500 machine hours. Calculate (1) the variable rate per machine hour and (2) Mike's total fixed utility cost. (pp. 1054–1056)

Computing breakeven point in sales units

2

S21-5 Playtime Park competes with DisneyWorld by providing a variety of rides. Playtime sells tickets at $60 per person as a one-day entrance fee. Variable costs are $20 per person, and fixed costs are $275,000 per month. Compute the number of tickets Playtime must sell to break even. Perform a numerical proof to show that your answer is correct. (pp. 1057–1061)

Computing breakeven point in sales dollars

S21-6 Refer to Short Exercise S21-5.

1. Compute Playtime Park's contribution margin ratio. Carry your computation to five decimal places. (p. 1060)
2. Use the contribution margin ratio CVP formula to determine the sales revenue Playtime Park needs to break even. (p. 1060)

Sensitivity analysis of changing sale price and variable costs on breakeven point

S21-7 Refer to Short Exercise S21-5.

1. Suppose Playtime Park cuts its ticket price from $60 to $50 to increase the number of tickets sold. Compute the new breakeven point in tickets and in sales dollars. Carry your computations to five decimal places. (p. 1060)
2. Ignore the information in part 1 above. Instead, assume that Playtime Park reduces the variable cost from $20 to $15 per ticket. Compute the new breakeven point in tickets and in dollars. Carry your computations to five decimal places. (p. 1060)

Sensitivity analysis of changing fixed cost on breakeven point

S21-8 Refer to Short Exercise S21-5. Suppose Playtime Park reduces fixed costs from $275,000 per month to $200,000 per month. Compute the new breakeven point in tickets and in sales dollars. (pp. 1058, 1060)

Computing margin of safety

S21-9 Refer to Short Exercise S21-5. If Playtime Park expects to sell 7,000 tickets, compute the margin of safety in tickets and in sales dollars. (pp. 1058, 1060)

Computing contribution margin, breakeven point, and units to achieve operating income

S21-10 Complete the calculations using the information provided for each scenario. (pp. 1058–1061)

	A	B	C
Number of units	1,000	3,000	8,000
Sale price per unit	$ 10	$ 16	$ 30
Variable costs per unit	6	8	21
Total fixed costs	50,000	21,000	180,000
Target operating income	50,000	70,000	90,000
Calculate:			
Contribution margin per unit	_____	_____	_____
Contribution margin ratio	_____	_____	_____
Breakeven point in units	_____	_____	_____
Breakeven point in sales dollars	_____	_____	_____
Units to achieve target operating income	_____	_____	_____

Calculating weighted-average contribution margin

S21-11 WetNWild Swim Park sells individual and family tickets, which include a meal, 3 beverages, and unlimited use of the swimming pools. WetNWild has the following ticket prices and variable costs for 2008:

	Individual	Family
Sale price per ticket..................	$25	$75
Variable cost per ticket	15	60

WetNWild expects to sell 1 individual ticket for every 3 family tickets. Compute the weighted-average contribution margin per ticket. (p. 1070)

S21-12 Refer to Short Exercise S21-11. For 2009, WetNWild expects a sales mix of 2 individual tickets for every 3 family tickets. In this mix, the weighted-average contribution margin per ticket is $13. WetNWild's total fixed costs are $39,000. Calculate

1. The total number of tickets WetNWild must sell to break even. (p. 1070)

2. The number of individual tickets and the number of family tickets the company must sell to break even. (p. 1070)

Exercises _____

E21-13 Match the term with the definition.

   a. Breakeven

   b. Contribution margin

   c. Cost behavior

   d. Margin of safety

   e. Relevant range

   f. Sales mix

   g. Fixed costs

   h. Variable costs

   _____ 1. Costs that do not change in total despite wide changes in volume (pp. 1053–1054)

   _____ 2. The sales level at which operating income is zero: total revenues equal total costs (p. 1057)

   _____ 3. Drop in sales a company can absorb without incurring an operating loss (pp. 1067–1068)

   _____ 4. Combination of products that make up total sales (p. 1069)

   _____ 5. Sales revenue minus variable costs (p. 1058)

   _____ 6. Describes how costs change as volume changes (p. 1052)

   _____ 7. Costs that change in total in direct proportion to changes in volume (p. 1052)

   _____ 8. The band of volume where total fixed costs remain constant and the variable cost *per unit* remains constant (p. 1056)

E21-14 LubeNGo provides several services, including oil changes. LubeNGo operates in a building with space for the service work and a waiting room for customers. Classify each of the following as a variable cost (V) or a fixed cost (F). (pp. 1052–1054)

   _____ 1. Oil filter

   _____ 2. Building rent

   _____ 3. Oil

   _____ 4. Wages of maintenance worker

   _____ 5. Television

   _____ 6. Manager's salary

   _____ 7. Cash register

   _____ 8. Equipment

E21-15 Graph these cost behavior patterns over a relevant range of 0–10,000 units:

   a. Variable costs of $8 per unit (p. 1052)

   b. Mixed costs made up of fixed costs of $20,000 and variable costs of $3 per unit (p. 1054)

   c. Fixed costs of $15,000 (pp. 1053–1054)

E21-16 The manager of Quik Car Inspection reviewed his monthly operating costs for the past year. His costs ranged from $4,000 for 1,000 inspections to $3,600 for 600 inspections.

Requirements

1. Calculate the variable cost per inspection. (p. 1055)

2. Calculate the total fixed costs. (p. 1055)

3. Write the equation and calculate the operating costs for 900 inspections. (pp. 1055–1056)

Preparing contribution
margin income statements
and calculating breakeven
sales

E21-17 For its top managers, Aussie Travel formats its income statement as follows:

AUSSIE TRAVEL Contribution Margin Income Statement Three Months Ended March 31, 2007	
Sales revenue	$312,500
Variable costs	125,000
Contribution margin	187,500
Fixed costs	170,000
Operating income	$ 17,500

Aussie's relevant range is between sales of $250,000 and $360,000.

Requirements

1. Calculate the contribution margin ratio. (p. 1060)

2. Prepare two contribution margin income statements: one at the $250,000 level and one at the $360,000 level. (*Hint:* The proportion of each sales dollar that goes toward variable costs is constant within the relevant range. The proportion of each sales dollar that goes toward contribution margin also is constant within the relevant range.) (pp. 1059–1060)

3. Compute breakeven sales in dollars. (p. 1060)

Computing breakeven sales
by the contribution margin
approach

E21-18 Hang Ten Co. produces sports socks. The company has fixed costs of $85,000 and variable costs of $0.85 per package. Each package sells for $1.70.

Requirements

1. Compute the contribution margin per package and the contribution margin ratio. (pp. 1058–1060)

2. Find the breakeven point in units and in dollars, using the contribution margin approach. (pp. 1058–1060)

Computing a change in
breakeven sales

E21-19 Owner Shan Lo is considering franchising her Noodles restaurant concept. She believes people will pay $5 for a large bowl of noodles. Variable costs are $1.50 per bowl. Lo estimates monthly fixed costs for a franchise at $8,400.

Requirements

1. Use the contribution margin ratio approach to find a franchise's breakeven sales in dollars. (p. 1060)
2. Lo believes most locations could generate $25,000 in monthly sales. Is franchising a good idea for Lo if franchisees want a minimum monthly operating income of $8,750? (p. 1061)

Computing breakeven sales
and operating income or
loss under different
conditions

E21-20 Gordon's Steel Parts produces parts for the automobile industry. The company has monthly fixed costs of $640,000 and a contribution margin of 80% of revenues.

Requirements

1. Compute Gordon's monthly breakeven sales in dollars. Use the contribution margin ratio approach. (p. 1060)
2. Use contribution margin income statements to compute Gordon's monthly operating income or operating loss if revenues are $500,000 and if they are $1,000,000. (p. 1058)
3. Do the results in Requirement 2 make sense given the breakeven sales you computed in Requirement 1? Explain.

Analyzing a cost-volume-
profit graph

E21-21 Zac Hill is considering starting a Web-based educational business, e-Prep MBA. He plans to offer a short-course review of accounting for students entering MBA programs. The materials would be available on a password-protected Web site; students would complete the course through self-study. Hill would have to grade the course assignments, but most of the work is in developing the course materials, setting up the site, and marketing. Unfortunately, Hill's hard drive crashed before he finished his financial analysis. However, he did recover the following partial CVP chart:

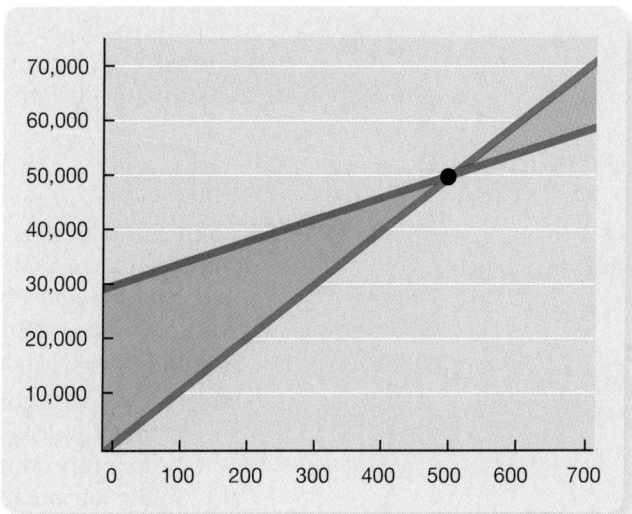

continued . . .

Requirements

1. Label each axis, the sales revenue line, the total costs line, the fixed costs, the operating income area, and the breakeven point. (p. 1062)

2. If Hill attracts 400 students to take the course, will the venture be profitable? (p. 1062)

3. What are the breakeven sales in students and dollars? (pp. 1058–1060)

Impact on breakeven point if sale price, variable costs, and fixed costs change

E21-22 Mi Tierra Driving School charges $200 per student to prepare and administer written and driving tests. Variable costs of $120 per student include trainers' wages, study materials, and gasoline. Annual fixed costs of $50,000 include the training facility and fleet of cars. For each of the following independent situations, calculate the contribution margin per unit and the breakeven point in units:

1. Breakeven point with no change in information. (p. 1058)

2. Decrease sale price to $180 per student. (p. 1066)

3. Decrease variable costs to $110 per student. (pp. 1066–1067)

4. Decrease fixed costs to $40,000. (p. 1067)

Compare the impact of changes in the sale price, variable costs, and fixed costs on the contribution margin per unit and the breakeven point in units.

Computing breakeven and the margin of safety

E21-23 Robbie's Repair Shop has a monthly target operating income of $12,000. Variable costs are 70% of sales, and monthly fixed costs are $9,000.

Requirements

1. Compute the monthly margin of safety in dollars if the shop achieves its income goal. (pp. 1067–1068)

2. Express Robbie's margin of safety as a percentage of target sales.

Calculating breakeven point for two product lines

E21-24 Scotty's Scooters plans to sell a standard scooter for $54 and a chrome scooter for $78. Scotty purchases the standard scooter for $36 and the chrome scooter for $50. Scotty expects to sell two standard scooters for every three chrome scooters. His monthly fixed costs are $12,000. How many of each type of scooter must Scotty sell each month to break even? To earn $6,600? (pp. 1058–1060, 1061)

Problems (Group A)

Contribution margin; sensitivity analysis; margin of safety

P21-25A Fox Club Clothiers is managed as traditionally as the button-down shirts that have made it famous. Arch Fox founded the business in 1972 and has directed operations "by the seat of his pants" ever since. Approaching retirement, he must turn over the business to his son, Ralph. Recently Arch and Ralph had this conversation:

Ralph: Dad, I am convinced that we can increase sales by advertising. I think we can spend $600 monthly on advertising and increase monthly sales by $6,000. With our contribution margin, operating income should increase by $3,000.

Arch: You know how I feel about advertising. We've never needed it in the past. Why now?

continued . . .

Ralph: Two new shops have opened near us this year, and those guys are getting lots of business. I've noticed our profit margin slipping as the year has unfolded. Our margin of safety is at its lowest point ever.

Arch: Profit margin I understand, but what is the contribution margin that you mentioned? And what is this "margin of safety"?

Requirement

Explain for Arch Fox the contribution margin approach to decision making. Show how Ralph Fox computed the $3,000. (Advertising is a fixed cost.) Also, describe what Ralph means by margin of safety, and explain why the business's situation is critical. (pp. 1058–1059, 1067)

Calculating cost-volume-profit elements

P21-26A The budgets of four companies yield the following information:

		Company			
		North	East	South	West
Target sales		$703,000	$ (4)	$600,000	$ (10)
Variable costs		(1)	150,000	280,000	156,000
Fixed costs		(2)	123,000	138,000	(11)
Operating income (loss)		$ 27,200	$ (5)	$ (7)	$ 35,000
Units sold		190,000	10,000	(8)	(12)
Contribution margin per unit		$ 1.48	$ (6)	$ 100	$ 12
Contribution margin ratio		(3)	0.20	(9)	.20

Fill in the blanks for each company. Which company has the lowest breakeven point in sales dollars? What causes the low breakeven point? (pp. 1058–1060, 1061)

BE sales and sales to earn a target operating income; contribution margin income statement

P21-27A British Productions performs London shows. The average show sells 1,000 tickets at $60 per ticket. There are 120 shows a year. The average show has a cast of 60, each earning an average of $320 per show. The cast is paid after each show. The other variable cost is program-printing cost of $8 per guest. Annual fixed costs total $459,200.

Requirements

1. Compute revenue and variable costs for each show. (pp. 1052, 1053)

2. Use the income statement equation approach to compute the number of shows British Productions must perform each year to break even. (p. 1058)

3. Use the contribution margin approach to compute the number of shows needed each year to earn a profit of $4,264,000. Is this profit goal realistic? Give your reason. (pp. 1058–1059)

4. Prepare British Productions' contribution margin income statement for 120 shows for 2007. Report only two categories of costs: variable and fixed. (pp. 1059, 1060)

P21-28A Kincaid company sells flags with team logos. Kincaid has fixed costs of $639,600 per year plus variable costs of $4.20 per flag. Each flag sells for $12.00.

Requirements

1. Use the income statement equation approach to compute the number of flags Kincaid must sell each year to break even. (p. 1058)

2. Use the contribution margin ratio CVP formula to compute the dollar sales Kincaid needs to earn $32,500 in operating income for 2007. (p. 1060)

3. Prepare Kincaid's contribution margin income statement for the year ended December 31, 2007, for sales of 70,000 flags. Cost of goods sold is 60% of variable costs. Operating costs make up the rest of variable costs and all of fixed costs. (pp. 1059, 1060)

4. The company is considering an expansion that will increase fixed costs by 20% and variable costs by 30 cents per flag. Compute the new breakeven point in units and in dollars. Should Kincaid undertake the expansion? Give your reason. (pp. 1066, 1067)

P21-29A Big Time Investment Group is opening an office in Dallas. Fixed monthly costs are office rent ($8,100), depreciation on office furniture ($1,700), utilities ($2,000), special telephone lines ($1,000), a connection with an online brokerage service ($2,000), and the salary of a financial planner ($4,800). Variable costs include payments to the financial planner (9% of revenue), advertising (12% of revenue), supplies and postage (4% of revenue), and usage fees for the telephone lines and computerized brokerage service (5% of revenue).

Requirements

1. Use the contribution margin ratio CVP formula to compute Big Time's breakeven revenue in dollars. If the average trade leads to $700 in revenue for Big Time, how many trades must be made to break even? (pp. 1058–1059)

2. Use the income statement equation approach to compute the dollar revenues needed to earn a target monthly operating income of $9,800. (p. 1058)

3. Graph Big Time's CVP relationships. Assume that an average trade leads to $700 in revenue for Big Time. Show the breakeven point, the sales revenue line, the fixed cost line, the total cost line, the operating loss area, the operating income area, and the sales in units (trades) and dollars when monthly operating income of $9,800 is earned. The graph should range from 0 to 80 units. (pp. 1061–1067)

4. Suppose that the average revenue Big Time earns increases to $800 per trade. Compute the new breakeven point in trades. How does this affect the breakeven point? (p. 1066)

Calculating breakeven point
for two product lines;
margin of safety

P21-30A The contribution margin income statement of Krazy Kustard Donuts for March 2008 follows:

KRAZY KUSTARD DONUTS
Contribution Margin Income Statement
For the Month of March 2008

Sales revenue		$128,000
Variable costs:		
Costs of goods sold	$32,560	
Marketing costs	17,280	
General and administrative cost	5,402	55,242
Contribution margin		72,758
Fixed costs:		
Marketing cost	38,880	
General and administrative cost	4,320	43,200
Operating income		$ 29,558

Krazy Kustard sells 2 dozen plain donuts for every dozen custard-filled donuts. A dozen plain donuts sells for $6, with a variable cost of $2 per dozen. A dozen custard-filled donuts sells for $7, with a variable cost of $4.20 per dozen.

Requirements

1. Determine Krazy Kustard's monthly breakeven point in dozens of plain donuts and custard-filled donuts. Prove your answer by preparing a summary contribution margin income statement at the breakeven level of sales. Show only two categories of costs: variable and fixed. (pp. 1069–1071)
2. Compute Krazy Kustard's margin of safety in dollars for March 2008. (p. 1058)
3. If Krazy Kustard can increase monthly sales volume by 10%, what will operating income be? (The sales mix remains unchanged.) (p. 1061)

Problems (Group B)

Variable costs; fixed costs;
BEP

P21-31B Saffron Restaurant Supply is opening early next year. The owner is considering two plans for paying her employees. Plan 1 calls for paying employees straight salaries. Under plan 2, Saffron would pay employees low salaries but give them a big part of their pay in commissions on sales. Discuss the effects of the two plans on variable costs, fixed costs, breakeven sales, and likely profits for a new business in the start-up stage. Indicate which plan you favor for Saffron.

P21-32B The budgets of four companies yield the following information:

		Company			
		J	K	L	M
Target sales		$810,000	$300,000	$190,000	$ (10)
Variable costs		270,000	(4)	(7)	260,000
Fixed costs		(1)	56,000	100,000	(11)
Operating income (loss)		$ 66,000)	$ (5)	$ (8)	$ 80,000
Units sold		(2)	40,000	12,000	16,000
Contribution margin per unit		$ 6	$ (6)	$ 9.50	$ 40
Contribution margin ratio		(3)	0.40	(9)	(12)

Fill in the blanks for each company. Which company has the lowest breakeven point in sales dollars? What causes the low breakeven point? (pp. 1058–1060, 1061)

BE sales and sales to earn a
target operating income;
contribution margin income
statement

P21-33B Broadway Shows is a traveling production company that coordinates New York Broadway productions each year. The average show sells 800 tickets at $50 per ticket. There are 100 shows each year. Each show has a cast of 40, each actor earning an average of $260 per show. The cast is paid after each show. The other variable cost is program printing cost of $6 per guest. Annual fixed costs total $892,800.

Requirements

1. Compute revenue and variable costs for each show. (p. 1052)

2. Use the income statement equation approach to compute the number of shows needed annually to break even. (p. 1058)

3. Use the contribution margin approach to compute the number of shows needed annually to earn a profit of $1,438,400. Is this goal realistic? Give your reason. (p. 1058)

4. Prepare the contribution margin income statement for 100 shows performed in 2008. Report only two categories of costs: variable and fixed. (pp. 1059, 1060)

P21-34B Go Spirit imprints calendars with college names. The company has fixed costs of $1,104,000 each month plus variable costs of $3.60 per carton of calendars. Go Spirit sells each carton of calendars for $10.50.

Requirements

1. Use the income statement equation approach to compute the number of cartons of calendars Go Spirit must sell each month to break even. (p. 1058)

2. Use the contribution margin ratio CVP formula to compute the dollar amount of monthly sales Go Spirit needs to earn $285,000 in operating income. (Round the contribution margin ratio to 2 decimal places.) (p. 1060)

3. Prepare Go Spirit's contribution margin income statement for June 2009 for sales of 450,000 cartons of calendars. Cost of goods sold is

continued . . .

70% of variable costs. Operating costs make up the rest of the variable costs and all of the fixed costs. (pp. 1059–1060)

4. The company is considering an expansion that will increase fixed costs by 40% and variable costs by one-fourth. Compute the new breakeven point in units and in dollars. How would this expansion affect Go Spirit's risk? Should Go Spirit expand? (pp. 1066, 1067)

Computing breakeven sales and sales needed to earn a target operating income; graphing CVP relationships; sensitivity analysis

P21-35B Retirement Investors is opening an office in Denver. Fixed monthly costs are office rent ($2,500), depreciation on office furniture ($260), utilities ($380), special telephone lines ($500), a connection with an online brokerage service ($640), and the salary of a financial planner ($3,400). Variable costs include payments to the financial planner (10% of revenue), advertising (5% of revenue), supplies and postage (2% of revenue), and usage fees for the telephone lines and computerized brokerage service (3% of revenue).

Requirements

1. Use the contribution margin ratio CVP formula to compute the investment firm's breakeven revenue in dollars. If the average trade yields $400 in revenue for Retirement Investors, how many trades must be made to break even? (p. 1060)

2. Use the income statement equation approach to compute dollar revenues needed to earn monthly operating income of $3,840. (p. 1058)

3. Graph Retirement Investors' CVP relationships. Assume that an average trade yields $400 in revenue for the firm. Show the breakeven point, the sales revenue line, the fixed cost line, the total cost line, the operating loss area, the operating income area, and the sales in units (trades) and dollars when monthly operating income of $3,840 is earned. The graph should range from 0 to 40 units. (pp. 1061–1063)

4. Suppose that the average revenue Retirement Investors earns decreases to $320 per trade. How does this affect the breakeven point in number of trades? (p. 1060)

Calculating breakeven point for two product lines; margin of safety

P21-36B The contribution margin income statement of Cosmo Coffee for February 2009 follows:

COSMO COFFEE Contribution Margin Income Statement For the Month of February 2009		
Sales revenue		$90,000
Variable costs:		
Costs of goods sold	$32,000	
Marketing costs	10,000	
General and administrative cost	3,000	45,000
Contribution margin		45,000
Fixed costs:		
Marketing cost	16,500	
General and administrative cost	3,500	20,000
Operating income		$25,000

continued . . .

Cosmo Coffee sells three small coffees for every large coffee. A small coffee sells for $2, with a variable cost of $1. A large coffee sells for $4, with a variable cost of $2.

Requirements

1. Determine Cosmo Coffee's monthly breakeven point in the numbers of small coffees and large coffees. Prove your answer by preparing a summary contribution margin income statement at the breakeven level of sales. Show only two categories of costs: variable and fixed. (pp. 1069, 1070)

2. Compute Cosmo Coffee's margin of safety in dollars for February 2009. (p. 1058)

3. If Cosmo Coffee can increase monthly sales volume by 10%, what will operating income be? (The sales mix remains unchanged.) (pp. 1060, 1061, 1069)

**for 24/7 practice, visit
www.MyAccountingLab.com**

Apply Your Knowledge

Decision Cases

Case 1. Steve and Linda Hom live in Bartlesville, Oklahoma. Two years ago, they visited Thailand. Linda, a professional chef, was impressed with the cooking methods and the spices used in the Thai food. Bartlesville does not have a Thai restaurant, and the Homs are contemplating opening one. Linda would supervise the cooking, and Steve would leave his current job to be the maitre d'. The restaurant would serve dinner Tuesday through Saturday.

Steve has noticed a restaurant for lease. The restaurant has seven tables, each of which can seat four. Tables can be moved together for a large party. Linda is planning two seatings per evening, and the restaurant will be open 50 weeks per year.

The Homs have drawn up the following estimates:

Average revenue, including beverages and dessert	$ 45 per meal
Average cost of food	$ 15 per meal
Chef's and dishwasher's salaries	$ 61,200 per *year*
Rent (premises, equipment)	$4,000 per month
Cleaning (linen and premises)	$ 800 per month
Replacement of dishes, cutlery, glasses	$ 300 per month
Utilities, advertising, telephone	$2,300 per month

Requirements

Compute the *annual* breakeven number of meals and sales revenue for the restaurant. Also compute the number of meals and the amount of sales revenue needed to earn operating income of $75,600 for the year. How many meals must the Homs serve each night to earn their target income of $75,600? Should the couple open the restaurant?

Ethical Issue

You have just begun your summer internship at Omni Instruments. The company supplies sterilized surgical instruments for physicians. To expand sales, Omni is considering paying a commission to its sales force. The controller, Matthew Barnhill, asks you to compute (1) the new breakeven sales figure and (2) the operating profit if sales increase 15% under the new sales commission plan. He thinks you can handle this task because you learned CVP analysis in your accounting class.

You spend the next day collecting information from the accounting records, performing the analysis, and writing a memo to explain the results. The company president is pleased with your memo. You report that the new sales commission plan will lead to a significant increase in operating income and only a small increase in breakeven sales.

The following week, you realize that you made an error in the CVP analysis. You overlooked the sales personnel's $2,800 monthly salaries and you did not include this fixed marketing cost in your computations. You are not sure what to do. If you tell Matthew Barnhill of your mistake, he will have to tell the president. In this case, you are afraid Omni might not offer you permanent employment after your internship.

Requirements

1. How would your error affect breakeven sales and operating income under the proposed sales commission plan? Could this cause the president to reject the sales commission proposal?

2. Consider your ethical responsibilities. Is there a difference between (a) initially making an error and (b) subsequently failing to inform the controller?

3. Suppose you tell Matthew Barnhill of the error in your analysis. Why might the consequences not be as bad as you fear? Should Barnhill take any responsibility for your error? What could Barnhill have done differently?

4. After considering all the factors, should you inform Barnhill or simply keep quiet?

For Internet Exercises, Excel in Practice, and additional online activities, go to the Web site, www.prenhall.com/horngren.

Quick Check Answers

1. *b*   2. *d*   3. *a*   4. *b*   5. *d*   6. *a*   7. *b*   8. *c*   9. *a*   10. *c*

Appendix 21A

Variable Costing and Absorption Costing

Up to this point, we've focused on the income statements that companies report to the public under GAAP. GAAP requires that we assign both variable and fixed manufacturing costs to products. This approach is called **absorption costing** because products absorb both fixed and variable manufacturing costs. Supporters of absorption costing argue that companies cannot produce products without incurring fixed costs, so these costs are an important part of product costs. Financial accountants usually prefer absorption costing.

The alternate method is called variable costing. **Variable costing** assigns only variable manufacturing costs to products. Fixed costs are considered *period costs* and are *expensed immediately* because the company incurs these fixed costs whether or not it produces any products or services. In variable costing, fixed costs are not product costs. Management accountants often prefer variable costing for their planning and control decisions.

The key difference between absorption costing and variable costing is that:

- Absorption costing considers fixed manufacturing costs as inventoriable product costs
- Variable costing considers fixed manufacturing costs as period costs (expenses)

All other costs are treated the same way under both absorption and variable costing:

- Variable manufacturing costs are inventoriable products costs.
- All nonmanufacturing costs—both fixed and variable—are period costs and are expensed immediately when incurred.

Exhibit 21A-1 summarizes the difference between variable and absorption costing, with the differences shown in color.

| EXHIBIT 21A-1 | Differences Between Absorption Costing and Variable Costing |

Type of Cost	Absorption Costing	Variable Costing
Product Costs (Capitalized as Inventory until expensed as Cost of Goods Sold)	Direct materials Direct labor Variable manufacturing overhead Fixed manufacturing overhead	Direct materials Direct labor Variable manufacturing overhead
Period Costs (Expensed in period incurred)	Variable nonmanufacturing costs Fixed nonmanufacturing costs	Fixed manufacturing overhead Variable nonmanufacturing costs Fixed nonmanufacturing costs
Income Statement Format	Conventional income statement, as in Chapters 1–17	Contribution margin income statement

Applying Variable Costing Versus Absorption Costing: Limonade

To see how absorption costing and variable costing differ, let's consider the following example. Limonade incurs the following costs for its powdered sports beverage mix in March 2009.

Direct materials cost per case	$ 8.00
Direct labor cost per case	$ 3.00
Variable manufacturing overhead cost per case	$ 2.00
Total fixed manufacturing overhead costs	$50,000
Total fixed selling and administrative costs	$25,000
Cases of powdered mix produced	10,000
Cases of powdered mix sold	8,000
Sale price per case of powdered mix	$ 25

There were no beginning inventories, so Limonade has 2,000 cases of powdered mix in ending inventory (10,000 cases produced − 8,000 cases sold).

What is Limonade's inventoriable product cost per case under absorption costing and variable costing?

	Absorption Costing	Variable Costing
Direct materials	$ 8.00	$ 8.00
Direct labor	3.00	3.00
Variable manufacturing overhead	2.00	2.00
Fixed manufacturing overhead ($50,000/10,000 cases)	5.00	
Total cost per case	$18.00	$13.00

The only difference between absorption and variable costing is that fixed manufacturing overhead is a product cost under absorption costing, but a period cost under variable costing. This is why the cost per case is $5 higher under absorption (total cost of $18) than under variable costing ($13).

Exhibit 21A-2 shows the income statements using absorption costing and variable costing. The exhibit also shows the calculation for ending inventory at March 31, 2009.

Absorption costing income is higher because of the differing treatments of fixed manufacturing cost. Look at the two ending inventory amounts:

- $36,000 under absorption costing
- $26,000 under variable costing

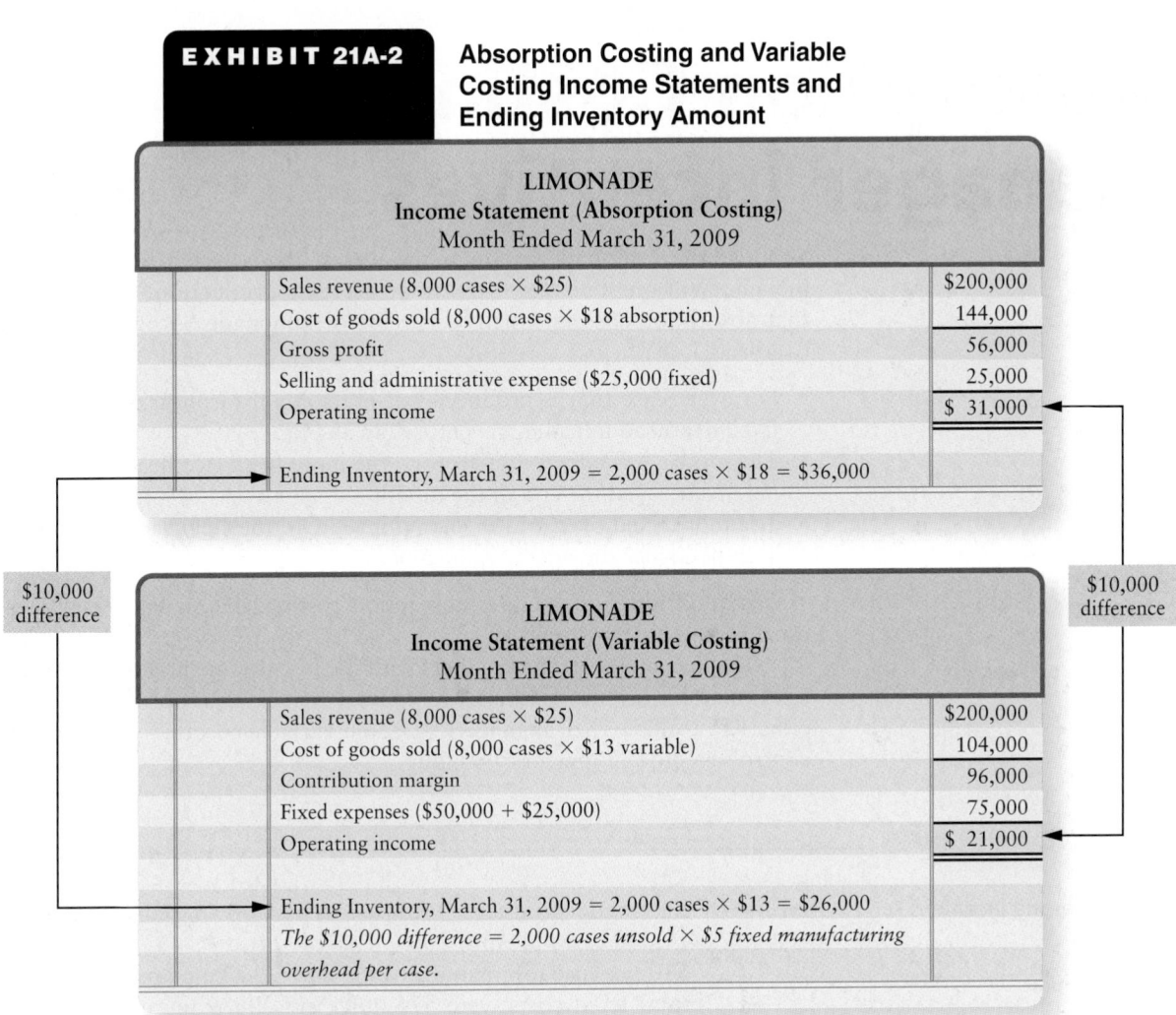

EXHIBIT 21A-2 Absorption Costing and Variable Costing Income Statements and Ending Inventory Amount

LIMONADE
Income Statement (Absorption Costing)
Month Ended March 31, 2009

Sales revenue (8,000 cases × $25)	$200,000
Cost of goods sold (8,000 cases × $18 absorption)	144,000
Gross profit	56,000
Selling and administrative expense ($25,000 fixed)	25,000
Operating income	$ 31,000

Ending Inventory, March 31, 2009 = 2,000 cases × $18 = $36,000

$10,000 difference

$10,000 difference

LIMONADE
Income Statement (Variable Costing)
Month Ended March 31, 2009

Sales revenue (8,000 cases × $25)	$200,000
Cost of goods sold (8,000 cases × $13 variable)	104,000
Contribution margin	96,000
Fixed expenses ($50,000 + $25,000)	75,000
Operating income	$ 21,000

Ending Inventory, March 31, 2009 = 2,000 cases × $13 = $26,000
The $10,000 difference = 2,000 cases unsold × $5 fixed manufacturing overhead per case.

This $10,000 difference results because ending inventory under absorption costing holds $10,000 of fixed manufacturing cost that got expensed under variable costing, as follows:

Units of ending finished goods inventory		Fixed manufacturing cost per unit		Difference in ending inventory
2,000	×	$5	=	$10,000

PRODUCTION EXCEEDS SALES   Limonade produced 10,000 units and sold only 8,000 units, leaving 2,000 units in ending inventory. Whenever production exceeds sales, as for Limonade, absorption costing will produce more reported income.

SALES EXCEED PRODUCTION   Companies sometimes sell more units of inventory than they produced that period. How can they do that? By drawing down inventories built up in prior periods. In these situations, inventory quantities decrease, and fixed costs in the earlier inventory get expensed under variable costing. That leads to the opposite result: Variable costing will produce more reported income whenever sales exceed production.

Absorption Costing and Manager Incentives

Suppose the Limonade manager receives a bonus based on absorption costing income. Will the manager increase or decrease production? The manager knows that absorption costing assigns each case of Limonade $5 of fixed manufacturing overhead.

- For every case that is produced but not sold, absorption costing "hides" $5 of fixed overhead in ending inventory (an asset).
- The more cases added to inventory, the more fixed overhead is "hidden" in ending inventory at the end of the month.
- The more fixed overhead in ending inventory, the smaller the cost of goods sold and the higher the operating income.

To maximize the bonus under absorption costing, the manager may increase production to build up inventory.

This incentive directly conflicts with the just-in-time philosophy, which emphasizes minimal inventory levels. Companies that have adopted just-in-time should either (1) evaluate their managers based on variable costing income or (2) use strict controls to prevent inventory buildup.

Short Exercises

Variable costing income statement

S21A-37 Limonade produced 11,000 cases of powdered drink mix and sold 10,000 cases in April 2009. The sale price was $25, variable costs were $10 per case ($8 manufacturing and $2 selling and administrative), and total fixed costs were $75,000 ($55,000 manufacturing and $20,000 selling and administrative). The company had no beginning inventory. Prepare the April income statement using variable costing. (p. 1095)

Absorption costing income statement; reconciling incomes

S21A-38 Refer to Short Exercise S21A-37.
1. Prepare the April income statement under absorption costing. (p. 1095)
2. Is absorption costing income higher or lower than variable costing income? Explain why. (p. 1095)

Exercise

Variable and absorption costing; reconciling incomes

E21A-39 The 2008 data that follow pertain to Seams Company, a manufacturer of swimming goggles. (Seams had no beginning inventories in January 2008.)

Sale price	$35	Fixed manufacturing overhead	$2,000,000
Variable manufacturing cost		Fixed operating costs	300,000
per unit	15	Number of goggles produced	200,000
Sales commission cost per unit	5	Number of goggles sold	185,000

continued . . .

Requirements

1. Prepare both conventional (absorption costing) and contribution margin (variable costing) income statements for Seams for the year ended December 31, 2008. (p. 1095)

2. Which statement shows the higher operating income? Why? (p. 1095)

3. Seams' marketing vice president believes a new sales promotion that costs $150,000 would increase sales to 200,000 goggles. Should the company go ahead with the promotion? Give your reason. (p. 1095)

Problems

Variable and absorption costing; reconciling incomes; production exceeds sales

P21A-40 Gia's Foods produces frozen meals, which it sells for $8 each. The company computes a new monthly fixed manufacturing overhead rate based on the planned number of meals to be produced that month. All costs and production levels are exactly as planned. The following data are from Gia's Foods' first month in business.

		January 2007
Sales		1,000 meals
Production		1,400 meals
Variable manufacturing cost per meal		$ 4
Sales commission cost per meal		$ 1
Total fixed manufacturing overhead		$700
Total fixed marketing and administrative costs		$600

Requirements

1. Compute the product cost per meal produced under absorption costing and under variable costing. (p. 1094)

2. Prepare income statements for January 2007 using
   a. Absorption costing (p. 1095)
   b. Variable costing (p. 1095)

3. Is operating income higher under absorption costing or variable costing in January? (p. 1095)

Variable and absorption costing; reconciling incomes; sales exceed production

P21A-41 Video King manufactures video games, which it sells for $40 each. The company uses a fixed manufacturing overhead rate of $4 per game. All costs and production levels are exactly as planned. The following data are from Video King's first two months in business during 2008:

		October	November
Sales		2,000 units	3,000 units
Production		2,500 units	2,500 units
Variable manufacturing cost per game		$ 15	$ 15
Sales commission per game		$ 8	$ 8
Total fixed manufacturing overhead		$10,000	$10,000
Total fixed marketing and administrative costs		$ 9,000	$ 9,000

continued . . .

Requirements

1. Compute the product cost per game produced under absorption costing and under variable costing. (p. 1094)
2. Prepare monthly income statements for November, using
   a. Absorption costing (p. 1095)
   b. Variable costing (p. 1095)
3. Is operating income higher under absorption costing or variable costing in November? Explain the pattern of differences in operating income based on absorption costing versus variable costing. (p. 1095)

Team Project

FASTPACK Manufacturing produces filament packaging tape. In 2007, FASTPACK produced and sold 15 million rolls of tape. The company has recently expanded its capacity, so it now can produce up to 30 million rolls per year. FASTPACK's accounting records show the following results from 2007:

Sale price per roll	$ 3.00
Variable manufacturing costs per roll	$ 2.00
Variable marketing and administrative costs per roll	$ 0.50
Total fixed manufacturing overhead costs	$8,400,000
Total fixed marketing and administrative costs	$1,100,000
Sales	15 million rolls
Production	15 million rolls

There were no beginning or ending inventories in 2007.

In January 2008, FASTPACK hired a new president, Kevin McDaniel. McDaniel has a one-year contract that specifies he will be paid 10% of FASTPACK's 2008 absorption costing operating income, instead of a salary. In 2008, McDaniel must make two major decisions:

- Should FASTPACK undertake a major advertising campaign? This campaign would raise sales to 24 million rolls. This is the maximum level of sales FAST-PACK can expect to make in the near future. The ad campaign would add an additional $2.3 million in fixed marketing and administrative costs. Without the campaign, sales will be 15 million rolls.

- How many rolls of tape will FASTPACK produce?

At the end of the year, FASTPACK Manufacturing's Board of Directors will evaluate McDaniel's performance and decide whether to offer him a contract for the following year.

Requirements

Within your group, form two subgroups. The first subgroup assumes the role of Kevin McDaniel, FASTPACK Manufacturing's new president. The second subgroup assumes the role of FASTPACK Manufacturing's Board of Directors. McDaniel will meet with the Board of Directors shortly after the end of 2008 to decide whether he

continued . . .

will remain at FASTPACK. Most of your effort should be devoted to advance preparation for this meeting. Each subgroup should meet separately to prepare for the meeting between the Board and McDaniel. [*Hint:* Keep computations (other than per-unit amounts) in millions.]

Kevin McDaniel should:

1. Compute FASTPACK Manufacturing's 2007 operating income.

2. Decide whether to adopt the advertising campaign. Prepare a memo to the Board of Directors explaining this decision. Give this memo to the Board of Directors as soon as possible (before the joint meeting).

3. Assume FASTPACK adopts the advertising campaign. Decide how many rolls of tape to produce in 2008.

4. Given your response to Requirement 3, prepare an absorption costing income statement for the year ended December 31, 2008, ending with operating income before bonus. Then compute your bonus separately. The variable cost per unit and the total fixed costs (with the exception of the advertising campaign) remain the same as in 2007. Give this income statement and your bonus computation to the Board of Directors as soon as possible (before your meeting with the Board).

5. Decide whether you wish to remain at FASTPACK for another year. You currently have an offer from another company. The contract with the other company is identical to the one you currently have with FASTPACK—you will be paid 10% of absorption costing operating income instead of a salary.

The Board of Directors should:

1. Compute FASTPACK's 2007 operating income.

2. Determine whether FASTPACK should adopt the advertising campaign.

3. Determine how many rolls of tape FASTPACK should produce in 2008.

4. Evaluate McDaniel's performance, based on his decisions and the information he provided the Board. (*Hint:* You may want to prepare a variable costing income statement.)

5. Evaluate the contract's bonus provision. Are you satisfied with this provision? If so, explain why. If not, recommend how it should be changed.

After McDaniel has given the Board his memo and income statement, and after the Board has had a chance to evaluate McDaniel's performance, McDaniel and the Board should meet. The purpose of the meeting is to decide whether it is in their mutual interest for McDaniel to remain with FASTPACK, and if so, the terms of the contract FASTPACK will offer McDaniel.

22 The Master Budget and Responsibility Accounting

Learning Objectives

1 Learn how to use a budget

2 Prepare an operating budget

3 Prepare a financial budget

4 Prepare performance reports for responsibility centers

Have you ever prepared a budget to ensure that you have enough cash to pay your expenses? You should. A budget helps you plan your cash receipts and payments. If your cash receipts are less than your cash payments, you need help. You can either

- Increase your cash inflows or
- Cut your payments

How can you increase your cash receipts? You can get a job—or a better job—or take out a student loan.

How can you cut your payments? Get a cheaper car, eat less-expensive food, move in with your parents—that sort of thing.

A budget forces you to plan for the future. It can also help you control expenses. To stay within your grocery budget, you can buy chicken instead of shrimp. Suppose your bank balance is less than expected. You can compare actual cash receipts and payments to your budget to see why your cash balance is down. A budget will help you take corrective action. ◼

Budgeting is for everyone, from individuals like you to complex international organizations like Amazon.com and Procter & Gamble. Careful budgeting helps both individuals and businesses stay out of trouble by reducing the risk that they will spend more than they earn.

Why Managers Use Budgets

Let's see how a small service business develops a simple budget. Suppose you begin an online service to provide travel itineraries for clients. You need to earn operating income of $550 a month to help with college expenses. You expect to sell 20 itineraries each month at a price of $30 each. Over the past six months, you paid your Internet service provider $25 a month, and you spent an additional $25 on travel materials. You expect these monthly costs to remain about the same. Finally, you spend 5% of your sales revenue for banner ads on other travel Web sites.

Exhibit 22-1 shows how you can budget for the operating income of your travel business. You must compute your budgeted revenues and then subtract your budgeted expenses to arrive at budgeted operating income.

EXHIBIT 22-1	Service Company Budget

CUSTOM TRAVEL ITINERARIES
Budget for May 2009

Budgeted revenues:		
Service revenue (30 itineraries at $20 each)		$600
Budgeted expenses:		
Internet service	$25	
Travel materials	25	
Advertising ($600 × .05)	30	
Total expenses		80
Budgeted operating income		$520

If business goes according to plan, you will not meet your goal of earning operating income of $550 per month. You will have to increase revenue (perhaps through word-of-mouth advertising) or cut expenses (perhaps by finding a less-expensive Internet service provider). It's much better to know this now rather than later when you find yourself in a cash bind.

Using Budgets to Plan and Control

1 Learn how to use a budget.

Large international companies like Procter & Gamble and nonprofit organizations like Habitat for Humanity use budgets for the same reasons you do. Everyone needs to plan and control his or her actions and the related revenues and expenses.

Exhibit 22-2 shows how managers use a budget.

- First, they develop strategies, such as Procter & Gamble's goal to expand its international operations. Start with the top box, "Develop Strategy."
- Then companies plan ways to achieve those goals.

- The next step is to act. Procter & Gamble develops new products and works with suppliers to cut costs.
- After acting, managers compare actual results with the budget.

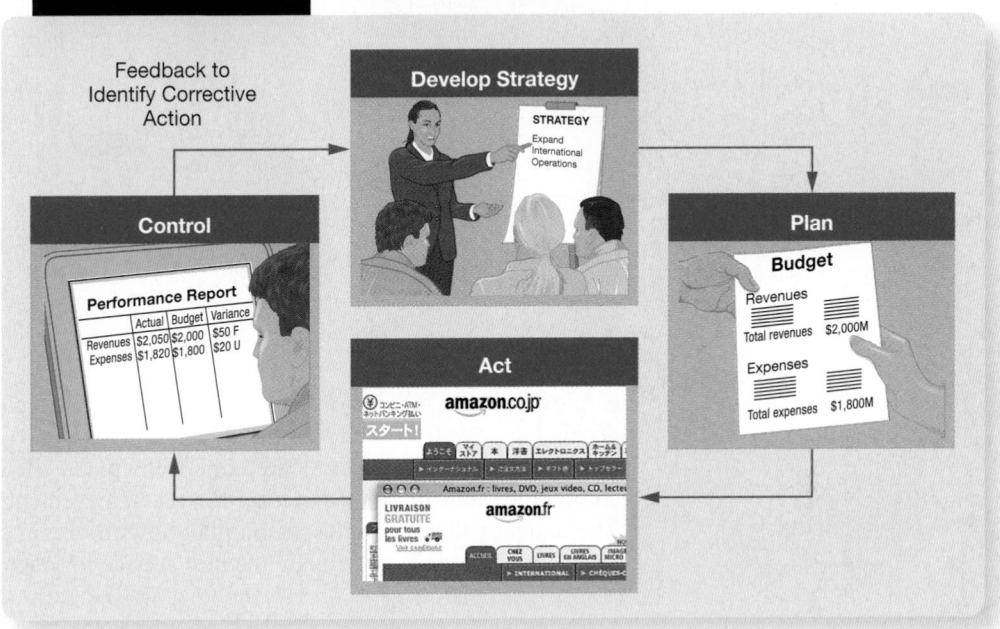

EXHIBIT 22-2   **Managers Use Budgets to Plan and Control Business Activities**

Feedback helps managers improve operations. For example, if Procter & Gamble spent too much on new products, managers must cut other costs or increase revenues.

Companies use different types of budgets.

- Most companies, including Procter & Gamble, budget cash flows monthly, weekly, and even daily to ensure they have enough cash.
- They budget revenues and expenses—and thus operating income—for months, quarters, and years.

This chapter focuses on budgets of one year or less. Chapter 25 explains how companies budget for major expenditures on property, plant, and equipment.

The Benefits of Budgeting

Exhibit 22-3 summarizes three key benefits of budgeting. Budgeting:

- Forces managers to plan for the future
- Promotes coordination and communication within the organization
- Provides a benchmark for evaluating performance

Planning

Exhibit 22-1 shows your expected income from the online travel business ($520) which falls short of the target ($550). The sooner you see this, the better you can plan how to increase revenues or cut expenses. The better your plan, the more likely you can meet your target.

Coordination and Communication

Companies have limited resources. Budgets require managers to coordinate activities so as to focus on achieving the goals of the organization. Knowledgeable

Budgets force managers to plan.

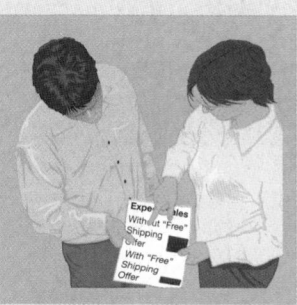

Budgets promote coordination and communication.

Budgets provide a benchmark that helps managers evaluate performance.

employees and a reliable online system are valuable resources. The budget helps you decide how much to spend on these items.

Budgets also communicate consistent plans throughout the company. This communication provides direction for the achievement of the organization's goals. The budget will help a salesperson plan how to obtain customers. It helps the office manager assign jobs to provide the best service for clients.

Benchmarking

Budgets provide a benchmark—a performance target—that motivates employees and helps managers evaluate actual results. Companies compare their actual results to the budget. The managers are motivated to beat their budgeted figures. The budgeted expenses for your travel business encourage employees to find less-expensive technology for the online system.

To illustrate benchmarking, suppose you compare your actual results to your budget. The comparison leads to the performance report in Exhibit 22-4.

EXHIBIT 22-4 **Summary Performance Report**

	Actual	Budget	Income Variance (Actual – Budget)
Sales revenue	$550	$600	$(50)
Total expenses	90	80	(10)
Operating income	$460	$520	$(60)

Operating income is only $460. This report should prompt you to investigate why operating income is less than budgeted ($460 versus $520). There are several possibilities:

- You sold less than you planned.
- You spent more to operate the business than you planned.

- The budget was unrealistic (you overestimated your sales and/or you underestimated expenses).
- Uncontrollable factors (such as a sluggish economy) reduced sales.

You need to answer these kinds of questions to get your business back on track. The budget doesn't automatically solve all your problems, but it helps identify ways to improve the business. Now that you know *why* managers develop budgets, let's see how to prepare a budget.

Preparing the Master Budget

The overall budget for an organization is called the master budget and has several components.

Components of the Master Budget

The **master budget** is the financial plan for the entire organization. It includes budgeted financial statements and supporting schedules. Exhibit 22-5 shows the order in which managers prepare the components of the master budget for a merchandiser.

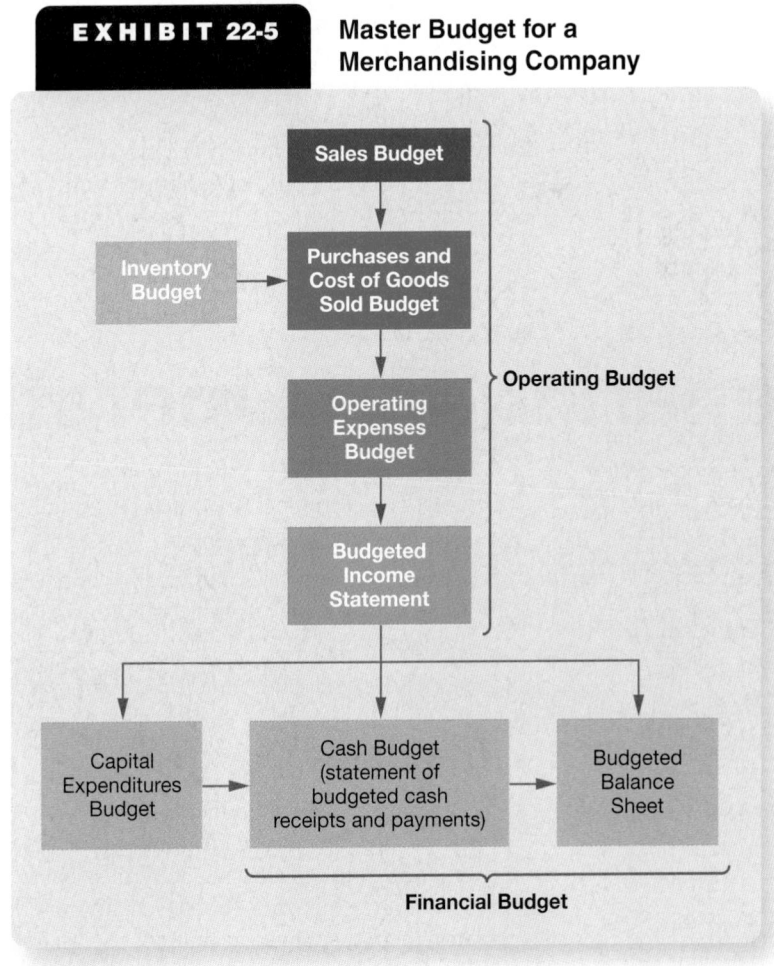

EXHIBIT 22-5 **Master Budget for a Merchandising Company**

The master budget includes three types of budgets:

- The operating budget
- The capital expenditures budget
- The financial budget

In this chapter we cover the operating budget and the financial budget. Chapter 25 explains how to budget for capital expenditures.

The first component of the **operating budget** is the sales budget, which forms the cornerstone. Why? Because sales affect everything. After projecting sales revenue, cost of goods sold, and operating expenses, management prepares the budgeted income statement. This document provides the organization's goal for net income.

The second type of budget is the **capital expenditures budget**. This budget presents the company's plan for purchases of property, plant, and equipment.

The third type is the **financial budget**, which includes the:

- Cash budget
- Budgeted balance sheet

The cash budget combines figures from the budgeted income statement, the capital expenditures budget, and plans for raising cash and paying debts. The cash budget projects cash receipts and payments and feeds into the budgeted balance sheet. The budgeted balance sheet looks exactly like an ordinary balance sheet. The only difference is that it lists budgeted (projected) figures rather than actual amounts.

In this chapter, you'll learn how to prepare an operating budget and a financial budget. Let's assume you manage Pete's Pet Shop, Store Number 4, which carries pet products for dogs, cats, and fish. You are to prepare the store's master budget for April, May, and June, the main selling season. Your division manager and the head of the Accounting Department will come from company headquarters to review the budget with you.

It is exciting to realize that you are developing the store's operating and financial plan for the next three months. These plans will aid decisions you'll make. You must think carefully about pricing, product lines, job assignments, the need for additional equipment, and negotiations with banks. A budget forces you to sit back and consider the whole organization in one broad view.

Preparing the Operating Budget

2 Prepare an operating budget

The budgeted income statement shows planned revenues and expenses for a future period. The components of the operating budget are:

- Sales budget (Exhibit 22-6)
- Inventory, purchases, and cost of goods sold budget (Exhibit 22-7)
- Operating expenses budget (Exhibit 22-8)
- Budgeted income statement (Exhibit 22-9)

We consider each component of the operating budget in turn.

The Sales Budget

We begin the master budget with the sales budget. The **sales budget** is the detailed plan for sales revenue in a future period. Sales managers use this information to plan their selling and advertising activities. The operations manager uses this information to plan for purchasing goods, scheduling employees, and renting space. Sales information helps accountants anticipate cash collections for the cash budget. You can see the critical nature of the sales budget. It drives almost everything in the organization.

Budgeted total sales for each product is computed as follows:

$$\begin{array}{c} \text{Budgeted sales} \\ \text{for each product} \end{array} = \begin{array}{c} \text{Sale price} \\ \text{per unit} \end{array} \times \begin{array}{c} \text{Expected number of} \\ \text{units to be sold} \end{array}$$

The estimated sale price may be the current price, or it may change to meet competition. A sales forecast projects the sales demand, or estimated sales, based on external and internal factors. External factors include the condition of the economy and competitors' products and prices. Internal factors may include the prior year's sales and your company's credit policies.

Exhibit 22-6 shows the sales budget for Pete's Pet Shop. Pete's normally makes 60% of its sales for cash and 40% on credit. The sales manager predicts these monthly sales totals for April, May, and June:

April	$60,000
May	$80,000
June	$70,000

EXHIBIT 22-6 Sales Budget

PETE'S PET SHOP #4
Sales Budget

	April	May	June	April–June Total
Cash sales, 60%	$36,000	$48,000	$42,000	
Credit sales, 40%	24,000	32,000	28,000	
Total sales, 100%	$60,000	$80,000	$70,000	$210,000

The overall sales budget in Exhibit 22-6 includes all the company's products. Trace the April through June total sales ($210,000) to the budgeted income statement in Exhibit 22-9.

The Inventory, Purchases, and Cost of Goods Sold Budget

Once we know budgeted sales, we can prepare the budget for

- Cost of goods sold on the budgeted income statement
- Ending inventory on the budgeted balance sheet
- Purchases of inventory

This information guides the purchase and the management of inventory.

The familiar cost of goods sold model shows the relations among these items:

$$\begin{array}{c} \text{Beginning} \\ \text{inventory} \end{array} + \text{Purchases} - \begin{array}{c} \text{Ending} \\ \text{inventory} \end{array} = \begin{array}{c} \text{Cost of} \\ \text{goods sold} \end{array}$$

Beginning inventory is known from last month's balance sheet; budgeted cost of goods sold is 70% of sales in this illustration; and budgeted ending inventory is a target amount set by management. You must solve for the budgeted purchases figure. To do this, rearrange the cost of goods sold model to isolate purchases on the left side:

$$\text{Purchases} = \frac{\text{Cost of}}{\text{goods sold}} + \frac{\text{Ending}}{\text{inventory}} - \frac{\text{Beginning}}{\text{inventory}}$$

This equation makes sense. How much must Pete's Pet Shop purchase to meet its target? Enough to cover sales and the desired level of ending inventory, less the amount of beginning inventory already on hand at the start of the period.

Pete's Pet Shop expects to maintain the following relationships among inventory, cost of goods sold, and purchases for the three months of April, May, and June:

- March 31 (our beginning) inventory was $53,600.
- June 30 (our ending) target inventory is $53,600.
- Target inventory at the end of each month = $20,000 + 80% of cost of goods sold for the next month.
- Cost of goods sold averages 70% of sales.

Pete's question is this:

> How much inventory must we purchase each month (April, May, and June) to keep operations within the budget?

Exhibit 22-7 shows Pete's Pet Shop's inventory, purchases, and cost of goods sold budget. Let's begin by showing how Pete's determined its inventory balance of $53,600 at March 31.

$$
\begin{aligned}
\text{March 31 inventory} &= \$20,000 + 0.80 \times (\text{Cost of goods sold for April}) \\
&= \$20,000 + 0.80 \times (0.70 \times \text{April sales of } \$60,000) \\
&= \$20,000 + (0.80 \times \$42,000) \\
&= \$20,000 + \$33,600 = \$53,600
\end{aligned}
$$

EXHIBIT 22-7 **Inventory, Purchases, and Cost of Goods Sold Budget**

PETE'S PET SHOP #4
Inventory, Purchases, and Cost of Goods Sold Budget

	April	May	June	April–June Total
Cost of goods sold (0.70 × sales, from Sales Budget in Exhibit 22-6)	$42,000	$56,000	$49,000	$147,000
+ Desired ending inventory ($20,000 + 0.80 × Cost of goods sold for the next month)	64,800*	59,200	53,600‡	
= Total inventory required	106,800	115,200	102,600	
− Beginning inventory	(53,600)†	(64,800)	(59,200)	
= Purchases	$53,200	$50,400	$43,400	$147,000

*$20,000 + (0.80 × $56,000) = $64,800.
†Balance at March 31 given.
‡Amount given.

Remember that the desired ending inventory for one month becomes the beginning inventory for the next month. Trace the total budgeted cost of goods sold from

Exhibit 22-7 ($147,000) to the budgeted income statement in Exhibit 22-9. We will use the budgeted inventory and purchases amounts later.

The Operating Expenses Budget

In addition to managing the purchases of inventory, Pete's must estimate its operating expenses. Pete plans to pay a salary and sales commissions to employees. Monthly payroll has two parts: a salary of $2,500 plus sales commissions equal to 15% of sales. The company pays all of this amount during the month the employees work. Other budgeted expenses include:

Rent expense	$2,000, paid as incurred
Depreciation expense	500
Insurance expense	200
Miscellaneous expenses	5% of sales, paid as incurred

Exhibit 22-8 shows the operating expenses budget. Study each expense to make sure you know how it's computed. For example, sales commissions fluctuate with sales. Other expenses, such as rent and insurance, are the same each month (fixed).

EXHIBIT 22-8   **Operating Expenses Budget**

PETE'S PET SHOP #4
Operating Expenses Budget

	April	May	June	April–June Total
Salary, fixed amount	$ 2,500	$ 2,500	$ 2,500	
Commission, 15% of sales from				
Sales Budget (Exhibit 22-6)	9,000	12,000	10,500	
Total salary and commissions	11,500	14,500	13,000	$39,000
Rent expense, fixed amount	2,000	2,000	2,000	6,000
Depreciation expense, fixed amount	500	500	500	1,500
Insurance expense, fixed amount	200	200	200	600
Miscellaneous, expenses, 5% of sales from				
Sales Budget (Exhibit 22-6)	3,000	4,000	3,500	10,500
Total operating expenses	$17,200	$21,200	$19,200	$57,600

Trace the April through June totals of $57,600 from the operating expenses budget in Exhibit 22-8 to the budgeted income statement in Exhibit 22-9.

The Budgeted Income Statement

Use the sales budget (Exhibit 22-6); the inventory, purchases, and cost of goods sold budget (Exhibit 22-7); and the operating expenses budget (Exhibit 22-8) to prepare the budgeted income statement in Exhibit 22-9. (We'll explain the computation of interest expense as part of the cash budget. For now, take interest expense as a given amount, $30.)

EXHIBIT 22-9   Budgeted Income Statement

PETE'S PET SHOP #4
Budgeted Income Statement
Three Months Ending June 30, 2009

	Amount	Source
Sales revenue	$210,000	Sales Budget (Exhibit 22-6)
Cost of goods sold	147,000	Inventory, Purchases, and Cost of Goods
		Sold Budget (Exhibit 22-7)
Gross profit	63,000	
Operating expenses	57,600	Operating Expenses Budget (Exhibit 22-8)
Operating income	5,400	
Interest expense	30	Amount given
Net income	$ 5,370	

Take this opportunity to solidify your understanding of operating budgets by carefully working Summary Problem 1.

Summary Problem 1

Review the Pete's Pet Shop example. The sales manager believes June and July sales will each be $80,000 instead of the projected $70,000 in Exhibit 22-6. You want to see how this change in sales affects the operating budget.

Requirement

Revise the sales budget (Exhibit 22-6), the inventory, purchases, and cost of goods sold budget (Exhibit 22-7), and the operating expenses budget (Exhibit 22-8). Prepare a revised budgeted income statement for the three months ended June 30, 2009. Interest expense is $30.

Note: You need not repeat the parts of the revised schedules that do not change.

Solution

Although not required, this solution repeats the budgeted amounts for April and May. Revised June figures appear in color for emphasis. This will help you to see which items were affected on each budget.

PETE'S PET SHOP #4
Sales Budget — Revised

	April	May	June	April–June Total
Cash sales, 60%	$36,000	$48,000	$48,000	
Credit sales, 40%	24,000	32,000	32,000	
Total sales, 100%	$60,000	$80,000	$80,000	$220,000

PETE'S PET SHOP #4
Inventory, Purchases, and Cost of Goods Sold Budget — Revised

	April	May	June	April–June Total
Cost of goods sold (0.70 × sales, from Sales Budget—Revised)	$42,000	$56,000	$56,000	$154,000
+ Desired ending inventory ($20,000 + 0.80 × Cost of goods sold for the next month)	64,800*	59,200	64,800*	
= Total inventory required	106,800	115,200	120,800	
− Beginning inventory	(53,600)†	(64,800)	(59,200)	
= Purchases	$53,200	$50,400	$61,600	

*$20,000 + (0.80 × $56,000) = $64,800.
†Balance at March 31 given (Exhibit 22-7).

PETE'S PET SHOP #4
Operating Expenses Budget—Revised

	April	May	June	April–June Total
Salary, fixed amount	$ 2,500	$ 2,500	$ 2,500	
Commission, 15% of sales from				
Sales Budget	9,000	12,000	12,000	
Total salary and commissions	11,500	14,500	14,500	$40,500
Rent expense, fixed amount	2,000	2,000	2,000	6,000
Depreciation expense, fixed amount	500	500	500	1,500
Insurance expense, fixed amount	200	200	200	600
Miscellaneous expenses, 5% of sales from				
Sales Budget—Revised	3,000	4,000	4,000	11,000
Total operating expenses	$17,200	$21,200	$21,200	$59,600

PETE'S PET SHOP #4
Budgeted Income Statement—Revised
Three Months Ending June 30, 2009

	Amount	Source
Sales revenue	$220,000	Sales Budget—Revised
Cost of goods sold	154,000	Inventory, Purchases, and Cost of Goods
		Sold Budget—Revised
Gross profit	66,000	
Operating expenses	59,600	Operating Expenses Budget—Revised
Operating income	6,400	
Interest expense	30	Amount given
Net income	$ 6,370	

Preparing the Financial Budget

3 Prepare a financial budget

You should now have a clear understanding of Pete's operating budget. With this knowledge you can prepare the financial budget. Exhibit 22-5, page 1105, shows that the financial budget includes the cash budget and the budgeted balance sheet. We start with the cash budget.

Preparing the Cash Budget

The **cash budget** is also called the **statement of budgeted cash receipts and payments.** The cash budget details how the business expects to go from its beginning cash balance to the desired ending balance. The cash budget has four major parts:

- Cash collections from customers (Exhibit 22-10)
- Cash payments for purchases (Exhibit 22-11)
- Cash payments for operating expenses (Exhibit 22-12)
- Cash payments for capital expenditures (Pete's Pet Shop will pay $5,800 in April and $2,800 in May to acquire equipment, a total of $8,600.)

Cash collections and payments depend on revenues and expenses, which appear in the operating budget. This is why the operating budget comes before the cash budget.

Budgeted Cash Collections from Customers

Pete's sales include cash sales and credit sales. Sales are 60% cash and 40% on credit. Pete's Pet Shop collects all credit sales during the month after the sale. Exhibit 22-10 shows that April's budgeted cash collections consist of two parts: (1) April's cash sales from the sales budget in Exhibit 22-6 ($36,000) plus (2) collections of the March 31 accounts receivable balance of $16,000 (amount assumed). Uncollectible accounts are insignificant. Trace April's $52,000 ($36,000 + $16,000) total cash collections to the cash budget in Exhibit 22-13.

EXHIBIT 22-10 Budgeted Cash Collections

PETE'S PET SHOP #4
Budgeted Cash Collections from Customers

	April	May	June	April–June Total
Cash sales from Sales Budget (Exhibit 22-6)	$36,000	$48,000	$42,000	
Collections of last month's credit sales, from Sales Budget (Exhibit 22-6)	16,000*	24,000	32,000	
Total collections	$52,000	$72,000	$74,000	$198,000

*Assume March 31 accounts receivable were $16,000.

Budgeted Cash Payments for Purchases

Pete's Pet Shop pays for inventory as follows:

- 50% during the month of purchase
- 50% during the next month

Accounts payable consists of inventory purchases only and was $16,800 on March 31. Exhibit 22-11 uses this information and the inventory, purchases, and cost of goods sold budget from Exhibit 22-7 to budget cash payments for inventory.

EXHIBIT 22-11   Budgeted Cash Payments for Purchases

PETE'S PET SHOP #4
Budgeted Cash Payments for Inventory Purchases

	April	May	June	Total
50% of last month's purchases of inventory (Exhibit 22-7)	$16,800*	$26,600	$25,200	
50% of this month's purchases of inventory (Exhibit 22-7)	26,600	25,200	21,700	
Total payments for purchases	$43,400	$51,800	$46,900	$142,100

*Assume March 31 accounts payable were $16,800.

April's cash payments for purchases consist of two parts:

1. Payment of the March 31 accounts payable ($16,800) plus

2. Payment for 50% of April's purchases ($26,600 = 50% × $53,200 from Exhibit 22-7)

Trace April's payment of $43,400 ($16,800 + $26,600) to the cash budget in Exhibit 22-13.

Budgeted Cash Payments for Operating Expenses

The cash budget shows all budgeted cash receipts and payments—including payments for operating expenses. We use the operating expenses budget (Exhibit 22-8) to compute the related cash payments.

EXHIBIT 22-12   Budgeted Cash Payments for Operating Expenses

PETE'S PET SHOP #4
Budgeted Cash Payments for Operating Expenses

	April	May	June
Salary, fixed amount	$ 2,500	$ 2,500	$ 2,500
Commission, 15% of sales from			
Sales Budget (Exhibit 22-6)	9,000	12,000	10,500
Total salary and commissions	11,500	14,500	13,000
Rent expense, fixed amount	2,000	2,000	2,000
Insurance expense, fixed amount	200	200	200
Miscellaneous expenses, 5% of sales from			
Sales Budget (Exhibit 22-7)	3,000	4,000	3,500
Total operating expenses	$16,700	$20,700	$18,700

The budgeted cash payments do not include depreciation expense. Why? Because depreciation is a noncash expense, it isn't a current-period payment of cash. Trace April's cash payments of $16,700 for operating expenses to the cash budget in Exhibit 22-13.

The Cash Budget

The **cash budget** projects cash receipts and payments for a future period. For most companies,

Cash receipts include:

- Cash collected from customers
- Cash received from the sale of long-term assets, such as equipment, land, and buildings
- Cash received from borrowing
- Cash received from owners of the business

Cash payments include:

- Cash payments for inventory purchases
- Cash payments for operating expenses
- Cash payments to purchase long-term assets, such as equipment, land, and buildings
- Cash payments on loans
- Cash payments to the owners of the business

The following T-account for cash gives one view of the steps to prepare a cash budget:

Step 1: Calculate cash available = beginning cash + cash receipts

Step 2: Calculate ending cash balance before financing = beginning cash + cash receipts − cash payments

Step 3: Determine financing needs.
* Excess (deficiency) = ending cash balance before financing − minimum cash balance desired.
* If deficiency, then borrow to cover.

Cash	
Beginning balance	
Cash receipts	Cash payments
Ending balance before financing	
Borrow if necessary	Repay principal Pay interest
Ending balance	

Step 4: Calculate ending cash balance = ending cash before financing +/− total effects of financing

The following format will be used to prepare the cash budget for Pete's Pet Shop:

		Beginning cash balance
	+	Cash receipts
STEP 1	=	Cash available
	−	Cash payments
		Purchases of inventory

continued . . .

	Operating expenses	
	Purchase of equipment	
	Total cash payments	
STEP 2	= Ending cash balance before financing (a)	
	− Minimum cash balance desired	
	= Cash excess (deficiency)	
	Financing	
STEP 3	Borrowing	
	Principal payments	
	Interest expense	
	Total effects of financing (b)	
STEP 4	Ending cash balance (a) + (b)	

In addition to Pete's sales, purchases, and operating expenses, the business has these additional plans:

- Pete plans to purchase equipment in April and May.
- Pete wants to maintain a minimum cash balance of $10,000 at the end of each month. The store can borrow money on short-term notes payable of $1,000 each at an annual interest rate of 12%. Management borrows only the amount needed to maintain the $10,000 minimum. Borrowing and all principal and interest payments occur at the end of the month.
- The March 31 cash balance was $25,000.

EXHIBIT 22-13   **Cash Budget**

PETE'S PET SHOP #4
Cash Budget
Three Months Ending June 30, 2009

		April	May	June
	Beginning cash balance	$25,000[a]	$11,100	$10,800
	Cash collections (Exhibit 22-10)	52,000	72,000	74,000
	Cash available	$77,000	$83,100	$84,800
	Cash payments:			
	Purchases of inventory (Exhibit 22-11)	$43,400	$51,800	$46,900
	Operating expenses (Exhibit 22-12)	16,700	20,700	18,700
	Purchase of equipment	5,800	2,800	—
	Total cash payments	65,900	75,300	65,600
(a)	Ending cash balance before financing	11,100	7,800	19,200
	Less: Minimum cash balance desired	(10,000)	(10,000)	(10,000)
	Cash excess (deficiency)	$ 1,100	$ (2,200)	$ 9,200
	Financing of cash deficiency (see notes b–d):			
	Borrowing (at end of month)		$ 3,000	
	Principal payments (at end of month)			$ (3,000)[c]
	Interest expense (at 12% annually)			(30)[d]
(b)	Total effects of financing	0	3,000	(3,030)
	Ending cash balance (a) + (b)	$11,100	$10,800	$16,170

[a]Assume the March 31 cash balance was $25,000.
[b]Borrowing occurs in multiples of $1,000 and only for the amount needed to maintain a minimum cash balance of $10,000.
[c]Repayment of loan occurs as quickly as possible without going below the minimum cash balance of $10,000.
[d]Interest expense paid in June: $3,000 × 0.12 × 1/12 = $30.

Now we can prepare the cash budget. Exhibit 22-13 starts with the beginning cash balance and adds the budgeted cash collections (Exhibit 22-10) to determine the cash available for use in the business. Then subtract cash payments for inventory purchases (Exhibit 22-11), operating expenses (Exhibit 22-12), and any capital expenditures ($8,600 for the equipment). This yields the ending cash balance before financing. Pete's Pet shop needs a minimum cash balance of $10,000 to stay out of financial trouble.

At the end of April, Pete's expects to have cash of $11,100. This is well above the minimum. But in May, cash is expected to drop to $7,800. This will require Pete to borrow in order to maintain a minimum balance of $10,000. Recall that Pete borrows in round $1,000 amounts. Therefore, Pete will borrow $3,000, as shown near the bottom of Exhibit 22-13.

Fortunately, the cash balance should increase in June. Pete expects to have excess cash and will pay off the $3,000 note payable plus $30 of interest expense ($3,000 × 0.12 × 1/12 = $30).

After all cash receipts and cash payments, Pete's Pet Shop expects to end June with cash of $16,170. This cash balance appears on the budgeted balance sheet in Exhibit 22-14.

The Budgeted Balance Sheet

The budgeted balance sheet brings together the final effects of all the expected revenues, expenses, cash receipts, and payments.

EXHIBIT 22-14   **Budgeted Balance Sheet**

PETE'S PET SHOP #4
Budgeted Balance Sheet
June 30, 2009

Assets			Source
Current assets:			
Cash		$ 16,170	Cash Budget (Exhibit 22-13)
Accounts receivable		28,000	$16,000 + Sales of $210,000 (Exhibit 22-6)
			− Collections of $198,000 (Exhibit 22-10)
Inventory		53,600	Inventory Budget (Exhibit 22-7)
Plant assets:			
Equipment	$35,000		$26,400* + $8,600 (Cash Budget, Exhibit 22-13)
Less: Accumulated			
depreciation	(14,300)	20,700	$12,800* + $1,500 (Operating Expenses Budget, Exhibit 22-8)
Total assets		$118,470	
Liabilities			
Current liabilities:			
Accounts payable		$ 21,700	June inventory purchases of $43,400
			(Purchases Budget, Exhibit 22-7) − June payments of $21,700
			for inventory purchases (Exhibit 22-11)
Note payable		0	Paid off in June (Exhibit 22-13)
Total liabilities		21,700	
Owner's Equity			
Owner's equity		96,770	$91,400* + net income of $5,370 (Budgeted Income Statement,
Total liabilities and			Exhibit 22-9)
owner's equity		$118,470	

*These amounts are assumed for this illustration.

To prepare the budgeted balance sheet of Pete's Pet Shop at June 30, 2009, we need three additional pieces of data at March 31, which was the beginning of our budget period:

- Accounts receivable were $16,000.
- Equipment cost $26,400, with accumulated depreciation of $12,800.
- Owner's equity was $91,400.

Now we can prepare Pete's budgeted balance sheet at June 30, 2009. Exhibit 22-14 gives references so you can see where all the balance sheet data come from.

Exhibit 22-15 provides a summary of all the budgeted transactions. You may find it helpful for organizing the data. For example, the bottom line of the summary gives the ending amounts for the budgeted balance sheet. But the summary is not a required part of the budgeting process.

EXHIBIT 22-15 Summary of Budgeted Transactions

	Cash	+ Accounts Receivable	+ Inventory	+ Equipment	+ Accum. Depr.	= Accounts Payable	+ Notes Payable	+ Owner's Equity
			ASSETS			**LIABILITIES**		**EQUITY**
March 31 balance	$ 25,000	$ 16,000	$ 53,600	$ 26,400	$(12,800)	$ 16,800	$ 0	$ 91,400
Sales (Exhibit 22-6)		210,000						210,000
Purchases (Exhibit 22-7)			147,000			147,000		
Cost of goods sold (Exhibit 22-7)			(147,000)					(147,000)
Operating expenses (Exhibits 22-12 and 22-8)	(56,100)				(1,500)			(57,600)
Cash collections (Exhibit 22-10)	198,000	(198,000)						
Payments for inventory (Exhibit 22-11)	(142,100)					(142,100)		
Purchase of equipment (Exhibit 22-13)	(8,600)			8,600				
Borrowing (Exhibit 22-13)	3,000						3,000	
Payments on note payable (Exhibit 22-13)	(3,000)						(3,000)	
Payment of interest expense (Exhibit 22-13)	(30)							(30)
June 30 balance	$ 16,170	+ $ 28,000	+ $ 53,600	+ $ 35,000	+ $(14,300)	= $ 21,700	+ $ 0	+ $ 96,770

$118,470   = $118,470

Getting Employees to Accept the Budget

What is the most important part of the budgeting system of Pete's Pet Shop? It's getting managers and employees to accept the budget.

Few people enjoy having their work monitored and evaluated. Therefore, managers must first motivate employees to accept the budget's goals. Here's how managers sell the budget to the workers:

- Managers must support the budget themselves, or no one else will.
- Show employees how budgets can help them achieve better results.
- Have employees participate in developing the budget.

But these principles alone are not enough. As the manager of Store Number 4, your performance is evaluated by comparing actual results to budget. When you develop your own budget, you may be tempted to build in *slack*. For example, you might want to budget fewer sales than you expect. This increases the chance that your performance will look better than the budget and give you a good evaluation. But adding slack into the budget makes it less accurate—and less useful for planning and control. When the division manager and the head of the Accounting Department arrive from headquarters next week, they will scour your budget to weed out any slack you may have inserted.

Using Information Technology for Sensitivity Analysis and Rolling Up Unit Budgets

Exhibits 22-6 through 22-14 show that the manager must prepare many calculations to develop the master budget for just one store. No wonder managers embrace information technology to help prepare budgets! Let's see how advances in technology make it more cost-effective for managers to:

- Conduct sensitivity analysis on their own part of the business
- Roll up individual unit budgets to create the companywide budget

Sensitivity Analysis

The master budget models the company's *planned* activities. Top managers pay special attention to ensure that the budgeted income statement, the cash budget, and the budgeted balance sheet support key strategies.

But actual results often differ from plans, so executives want to know how budgeted figures would change if key assumptions turned out to be incorrect. Chapter 21 defined *sensitivity analysis* as a *what-if* technique that asks *what* a result will be *if* a predicted amount is not achieved or *if* an underlying assumption changes. *What* will Pete's Pet Shop's cash balance be on June 30 *if* sales are 45% cash, not 60% cash? Will the company have to borrow? How much must Pete borrow?

Most companies use spreadsheet programs (or special budget software) to prepare the master budget. In fact, one of the earliest spreadsheets was developed by business students who realized that computers could take the drudgery out of budgeting. Today, managers answer what-if questions simply by changing a number. At the press of a key, the computer screen flashes a revised budget that includes all the effects of the change.

Rolling Up Individual Unit Budgets into the Companywide Budget

Pete's Pet Shop Store Number 4 is just one of many Pete's stores. As Exhibit 22-16 shows, Pete's headquarters must roll up the budget data from Store Number 4, along with budgets for all the other stores, to prepare the companywide master budget.

This roll-up can be difficult for companies that prepare their budgets with different spreadsheets.

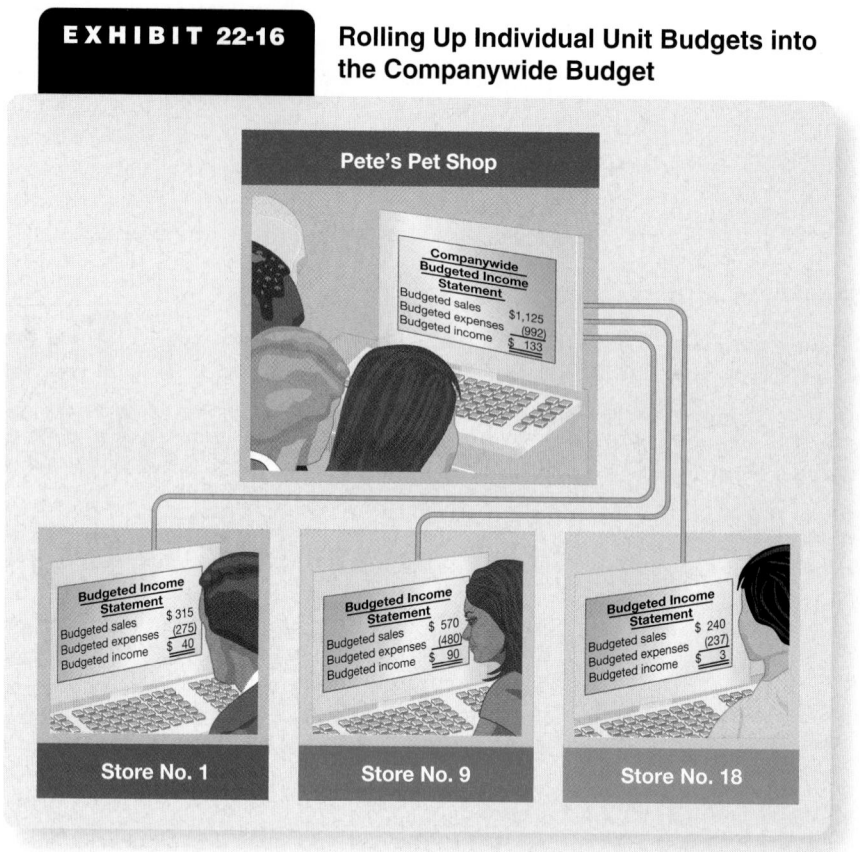

EXHIBIT 22-16 Rolling Up Individual Unit Budgets into the Companywide Budget

Companies like Intel often turn to budget-management software to solve this problem. The company's Enterprise Resource Planning (ERP) system (or data warehouse) should include software to help managers develop and analyze budgets.

Across the globe, managers sit at their desks, log onto the company's system, and enter their numbers. The software allows them to analyze their unit's data. When the manager is satisfied with her unit budget, she can enter it in the companywide budget with the click of a mouse. The unit's budget automatically rolls up with the budgets from all other company units around the world.

Responsibility Accounting

You've now seen how managers set strategic goals and then budget resources to reach those goals. Let's look more closely at how managers *use* budgets to control operations.

Each manager is responsible for planning and controlling some part of the firm. A **responsibility center** is a part of an organization whose manager is accountable for its activities. Lower-level managers are often responsible for budgeting and controlling the costs of a single function. For example, one manager of Pete's Pet Shop is responsible for planning and controlling the *purchasing* of toys for the pet stores. Another manager is responsible for planning and controlling the *marketing* of the product to customers. Lower-level managers report to higher-level managers, who have broader responsibilities. Managers in charge of purchasing and marketing report to senior managers who are responsible for the profits earned by the entire product line.

Four Types of Responsibility Centers

Responsibility accounting is a system for evaluating the performance of each responsibility center and its manager. As we have seen, managers use performance reports to compare plans (budgets) with actions (actual results) for each center. Superiors then evaluate how well each manager:

- Used his or her budgeted resources to achieve the responsibility center's goals
- Controlled the operations for which he or she was responsible

Exhibit 22-17 illustrates four types of responsibility centers.

1. **In a cost center, managers are accountable for costs (expenses) only.** Manufacturing operations like the production lines that make fluffy dog beds are cost centers. The line foreman controls costs by ensuring that employees work efficiently. The foreman is *not* responsible for generating revenues, because he is not involved in selling the product. The plant manager evaluates the foreman on his ability to control *costs* by comparing actual costs to budgeted costs. The foreman is likely to receive a more favorable evaluation if actual costs are less than budgeted costs and if product quality stays high.

EXHIBIT 22-17   **Four Types of Responsibility Centers**

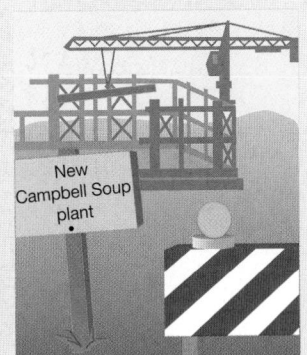

In a **cost center**, such as a production line for dog beds, managers are responsible for costs.

In a **revenue center**, such as the Sears appliance department, managers are responsible for generating sales revenue.

In a **profit center**, such as a line of products, managers are responsible for generating income.

In an **investment center**, such as Campbell Soups and Sauces division, managers are responsible for income and invested capital.

2. **In a revenue center, managers are primarily accountable for revenues.** Examples of revenue centers include the appliance department of a Sears store and a McDonald's restaurant. For these businesses, cost is largely set by company policy. Therefore, these managers are responsible mainly for generating revenue. A salesperson can be viewed as a revenue center. The manager of a revenue center is likely to receive a more-favorable evaluation if actual revenues exceed the budget.

3. **In a profit center, managers are accountable for both revenues and expenses and, therefore, profits.** The higher-level manager responsible for all Pete's Pet Shops in Pennsylvania would be accountable both for increasing sales *and* for controlling costs to achieve the company's profit goals. Profit center reports include both revenues and expenses to show the profit center's income. Superiors evaluate the managers' performance by comparing revenues, expenses, and profits to the budget. The manager is likely to receive a better evaluation if actual profits exceed the budget.

4. **In an investment center, managers are accountable for investments, revenues, and costs.** Examples include the Saturn Division of General Motors and the North American Sauces and Beverages Division of Campbell Soup Company. Managers of investment centers are responsible for:
   - Generating sales
   - Controlling expenses
   - Managing the amount of investment required to earn the target operating income

Bell South Corp considers its information technology (IT) department an investment center. Managers are responsible both for keeping IT costs within the budget and for company assets to generate revenue from e-business operations.

Top management often evaluates investment center managers based on return on investment (ROI). When evaluating a division, the return on investment can be computed as:

$$ROI = \frac{\text{Division's operating income}}{\text{Division's average total assets}}$$

The manager of an investment center will receive a better evaluation if the division's actual return on investment exceeds the budgeted return on investment.

Responsibility Accounting Performance Reports

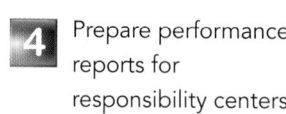
4 Prepare performance reports for responsibility centers

Exhibit 22-18 shows how an organization like Campbell Soup Company, the parent company of Pace Foods, may assign responsibility. At the top level, the CEO oversees all four company divisions. Each division is managed by a vice president. Most companies consider divisions as *investment centers*.

Each vice president (VP) supervises all the product lines in that division. Exhibit 22-18 shows that the VP of North American Sauces and Beverages oversees the Prego Italian sauces, Pace Mexican sauces, and V8 juice. Product lines are generally considered *profit centers*. Thus, the manager of the Pace product line is responsible for evaluating lower-level managers of both:

- *Cost centers,* such as the plants that make Pace products
- *Revenue centers,* such as the managers responsible for selling Pace products

Exhibit 22-19 on page 1124 illustrates a responsibility accounting performance report. Exhibit 22-19 uses assumed numbers to illustrate reports like those:

- The CEO may use to evaluate divisions
- The divisional VPs may use to evaluate individual product lines
- The product-line managers may use to evaluate the production and distribution of their products

EXHIBIT 22-18   **Partial Organization Chart**

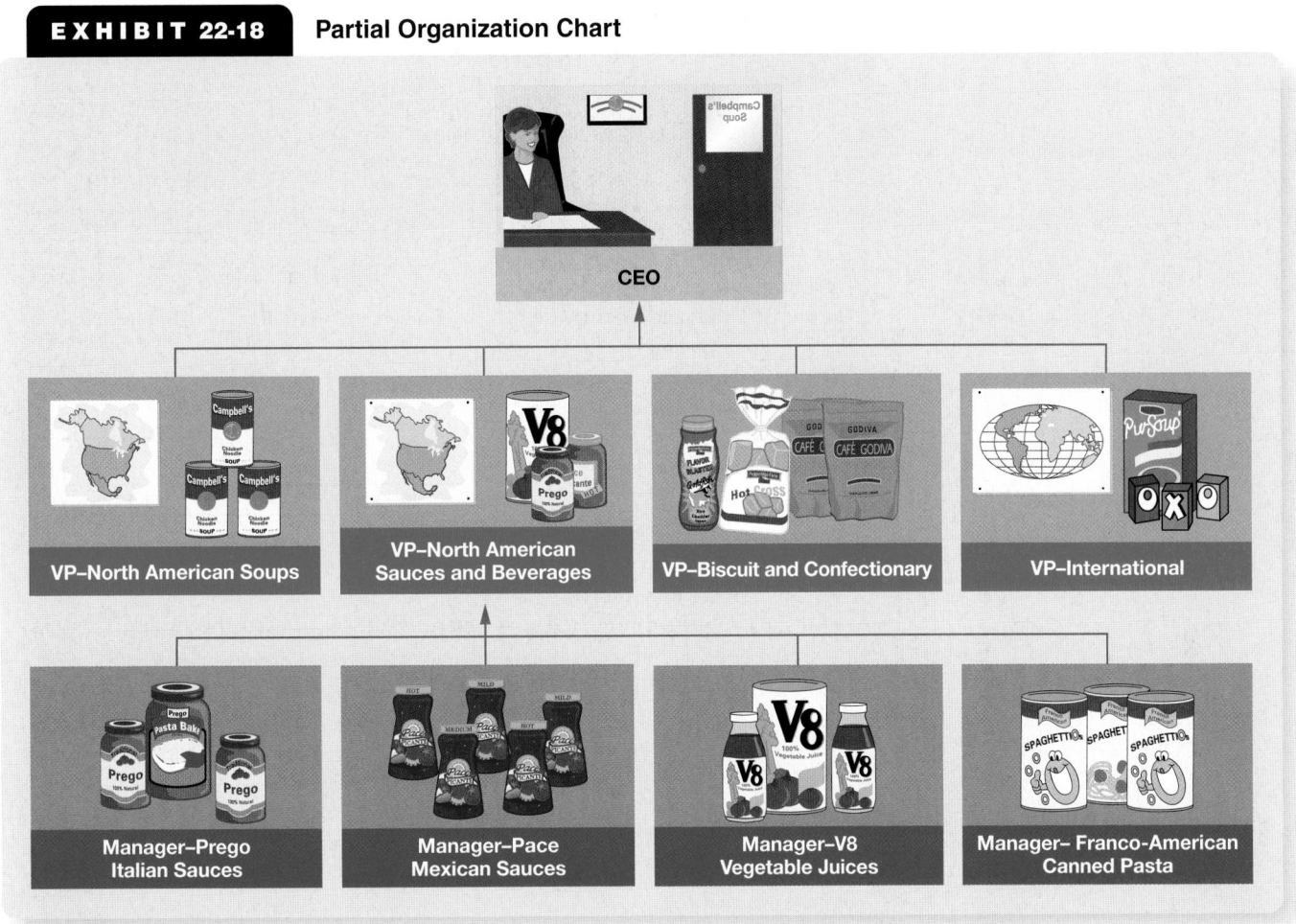

At each level, the reports compare actual results with the budget.

Start with the lowest level of Exhibit 22-19 and move to the top. Follow the $25 million budgeted operating income from Mexican sauces to the report evaluated by the VP–North American Sauces and Beverages. Then trace the $70 million budgeted operating income from the VP's report to the CEO. The CEO gets the summary of each division's budgeted and actual profits. The CEO is responsible for the whole company.

Management by Exception

The variances reported in Exhibit 22-19 aid **management by exception.** This is a management technique that directs attention to important differences between actual and budgeted amounts. Look at the CEO's report. The International Soups and Sauces Division's actual operating income of $34 million is very close to the budgeted $35 million. Unless there are other signs of trouble, the CEO will not waste time investigating such a small variance.

In contrast, the North American Sauces and Beverages Division earned much more profit than budgeted. The CEO will want to know why. Suppose the VP of the division believes a major sales promotion was especially effective. That promotion may be used by other divisions. Managers investigate large favorable variances (not just large unfavorable ones). They want to identify the reason for exceptional results, so that other parts of the organization may also benefit.

EXHIBIT 22-19 Responsibility Accounting Performance Reports

Responsibility Accounting Performance Reports at Various Levels
(in Millions of Dollars)

CEO

Operating Income of Divisions and Corporate Headquarters Expense	CEO'S Quarterly Responsibility Report		
	Budget	Actual	Variance Favorable/ (Unfavorable)
North American Soups	$218	$209	$ (9)
North American Sauces and Beverages	70	84	14
Biscuits and Confectionary	79	87	8
International Soups and Sauces	35	34	(1)
Corporate Headquarters Expense	(33)	(29)	4
Operating Income	$369	$385	$16

VP—North American Sauces and Beverages

Operating Income of Product Lines	VP—North American Sauces and Beverages Quarterly Responsibility Report		
	Budget	Actual	Variance Favorable/ (Unfavorable)
Italian Sauces	$20	$18	$ (2)
Mexican Sauces	25	38	13
Vegetable Juices	10	15	5
Canned Pastas	15	13	(2)
Operating Income	$70	$84	$14

Mexican Sauces

Revenues and Expenses	Manager—Mexican Sauces Quarterly Responsibility Report		
	Budget	Actual	Variance Favorable/ (Unfavorable)
Sales revenue	$80	$84	$ 4
Cost of goods sold	(36)	(30)	6
Gross profit	44	54	10
Marketing expenses	(12)	(9)	3
Research and development expenses	(2)	(3)	(1)
Other expenses	(5)	(4)	1
Operating income	$25	$38	$13

A CEO who received the report at the top of Exhibit 22-19 would likely concentrate on improving the North American Soups Division, because its actual income fell $9 million below budget. The CEO will want to see which product lines caused the shortfall, so that he or she and the VP of the division can work together to correct any problems.

Exhibit 22-19 also shows how summarized data may hide problems. Although the North American Sauces and Beverages Division as a whole performed well,

Italian sauces and canned pasta did not. If the CEO received only the condensed report at the top of the exhibit, a division manager could hide problems in individual product lines.

Not a Question of Blame

Responsibility accounting holds managers accountable for their actions. It also provides a way to evaluate their unit's performance. But superiors should not merely find fault or place blame. The question is not "Who is to blame for an unfavorable variance?" Instead, the question is "Who can best explain why a specific variance occurred?"

Consider the North American Soups Division in Exhibit 22-19. Suppose a tornado devastated the production plant. The remaining plants may have operated efficiently, and this efficiency kept the income variance down to $9 million. If so, the North American Soups Division and its VP may have done a good job.

The following Decision Guidelines review how managers use budgets in responsibility accounting. Study these guidelines before working the summary problem 2, which ends the chapter.

Decision Guidelines

Without a budget, spending can get out of control. Here are decisions that you could make as you set up a budgeting process for your business.

Decision	Guidelines
What benefits can I expect to obtain from developing a budget for my company?	A budget • Requires managers to *plan* how to increase sales and cut costs. • Promotes *coordination and communication* within the organization. • Provides a *benchmark* for measuring performance and motivating employees.
In what order do I prepare the components of the master budget for a merchandising operation?	Begin with the *operating budget*. • Start with the *sales budget*. • The sales budget drives the *inventory, purchases, and cost of goods sold budget*. • The *operating expense budget* lists all the operating expenses and their amount. • Prepare the budgeted income statement. Next, prepare the *capital expenditures budget*. Finally, prepare the other *financial budget*. • Start with the *cash budget*, which details the expected sources and uses of cash. • Prepare the budgeted balance sheet.
How do I compute budgeted purchases?	$$\frac{\text{Beginning}}{\text{inventory}} + \text{Purchases} - \frac{\text{Ending}}{\text{inventory}} = \frac{\text{Cost of}}{\text{goods sold}}$$ so $$\text{Purchases} = \frac{\text{Cost of}}{\text{goods sold}} + \frac{\text{Ending}}{\text{inventory}} - \frac{\text{Beginning}}{\text{inventory}}$$
How do I use a budget to evaluate performance?	$$\frac{\text{Actual}}{\text{results}} - \frac{\text{Budgeted}}{\text{amount}} = \frac{\text{Budget}}{\text{variance}}$$
How can I handle the uncertainty of sales forecasts?	Prepare a *sensitivity analysis* and project budgeted results at different sales levels.
What responsibility centers can I use to manage my company?	Cost center: Costs only Revenue center: Revenues only Profit center: Profits (both revenues and expenses) Investment center: Revenues, expenses, and the amount of investment required to earn the income.
How can I evaluate managers?	Compare actual performance with the budget for the manager's responsibility center. *Management by exception* focuses on large differences between budgeted and actual results.

Summary Problem 2

Continue the revised Pete's Pet Shop illustration from summary problem 1, page 1111. Now that you think June sales will be $80,000 instead of $70,000, as projected in the revised sales budget on page 1111, how will this affect the financial budget?

Requirement

Prepare a revised schedule of budgeted cash collections (Exhibit 22-10), a revised schedule of budgeted cash payments for purchases (Exhibit 22-11), and a revised schedule of budgeted cash payments for operating expenses (Exhibit 22-12). Then prepare a revised cash budget and a revised budgeted balance sheet at June 30, 2009. *Note:* You need not repeat the parts of the revised schedule that do not change.

Solution

Although not required, this solution repeats the budgeted amounts for April and May. Revised June figures appear in color for emphasis.

PETE'S PET SHOP #4
Budgeted Cash Collections from Customers—Revised

	April	May	June	April–June Total
Cash sales, from Revised Sales Budget (page 1111)	$36,000	$48,000	$48,000	
Collections of last month's credit sales, from				
Revised Sales Budget (page 1111)	16,000*	24,000	32,000	
Total collections	$52,000	$72,000	$80,000	$204,000

*Assume March 31 accounts receivable were $16,000.

PETE'S PET SHOP #4
Budgeted Cash Payments for Inventory Purchases—Revised

	April	May	June
50% of last month's purchases of inventory,			
from Revised Inventory, Purchases,			
and Cost of Goods Sold Budget (page 1111)	$16,800*	$26,600	$25,200
50% of this month's purchases, from Revised			
Inventory, Purchases, and Cost of Goods			
Sold Budget (page 1111)	26,600	25,200	30,800
Total payments for purchases	$43,400	$51,800	$56,000

*Assume March 31 accounts payable were $16,800.

PETE'S PET SHOP #4
Budgeted Cash Payments for Operating Expenses—Revised

	April	May	June
Salary, fixed amount	$ 2,500	$ 2,500	$ 2,500
Commission, 15% of sales from Revised			
Sales Budget	9,000	12,000	12,000
Total salary and commissions	11,500	14,500	14,500
Rent expense, fixed amount	2,000	2,000	2,000
Insurance expense, fixed amount	200	200	200
Miscellaneous, expenses, 5% of sales from			
Revised Sales Budget	3,000	4,000	4,000
Total operating expenses	$16,700	$20,700	$20,700

PETE'S PET SHOP #4
Cash Budget—Revised
Three Months Ending June 30, 2009

		April	May	June
	Beginning cash balance	$25,000[a]	$11,100	$10,800
	Cash collections (Revised)	52,000	72,000	80,000
	Cash available	$77,000	$83,100	$90,800
	Cash payments:			
	Purchases of inventory (Revised)	$43,400	$51,800	$56,000
	Operating expenses (Revised)	16,700	20,700	20,700
	Purchase of equipment	5,800	2,800	—
	Total cash payments	65,900	75,300	76,700
(a)	Ending cash balance before financing	11,100	7,800	14,100
	Less: Minimum cash balance desired	(10,000)	(10,000)	(10,000)
	Cash excess (deficiency)	$ 1,100	$ (2,200)	$ 4,100
	Financing of cash deficiency (see notes b–d):			
	Borrowing (at end of month)		$ 3,000	
	Principal payments (at end of month)			$ (3,000)
	Interest expense (at 12% annually)			(30)
(b)	Total effects of financing	0	3,000	(3,030)
	Ending cash balance (a) + (b)	$11,100	$10,800	$11,070

[a]Assume the March 31 cash balance was $25,000.
[b]Borrowing occurs in multiples of $1,000 and only for the amount needed to maintain a minimum cash balance of $10,000.
[c]Repayment of loan occurs as quickly as possible without going below the minimum cash balance of $10,000.
[d]Interest expense paid in June: $3,000 × 0.12 × 1/12 = $30.

			PETE'S PET SHOP #4 Budgeted Balance Sheet—Revised June 30, 2009
Assets			**Source**
Current assets:			
Cash		$ 11,070	Cash Budget—revised (bottom of page 1128)
Accounts receivable		32,000	$16,000 + Sales of $220,000 (Sales Budget—revised, page 1111) – Collections of $204,000 (Budgeted Cash Collections—revised, page 1127)
Inventory		64,800	Inventory Budget—revised (page 1111)
Plant assets:			
Equipment	$35,000		$26,400 + $8,600 (Cash Budget—revised, page 1128)
Less: Accumulated			
depreciation	(14,300)	20,700	$12,800 + $1,500 (Operating Expenses Budget—
Total assets		$128,570	revised, page 1112)
Liabilities			
Current liabilities:		$ 30,800	June inventory purchases of $61,600 (Purchases Budget—
Accounts payable			revised, page 1111) – June payments for June purchases of $30,800 (Budgeted payments for purchases—revised, page 1127)
Note payable		0	Paid off in June (Cash Budget—revised, page 1128)
Total liabilities		30,800	
Owner's Equity			
Owner's equity		97,770	$91,400 + net income of $6,370 (Budgeted
Total liabilities and			Income Statement—revised, page 1112)
owner's equity		$128,570	

Review The Master Budget and Responsibility Accounting

Accounting Vocabulary

Capital Expenditures Budget

A company's plan for purchases of property, plant, equipment, and other long-term assets.

Cash Budget

Details how the business expects to go from the beginning cash balance to the desired ending balance. Also called the **statement of budgeted cash receipts and payments.**

Financial Budget

The cash budget (cash inflows and outflows), the budgeted period-end balance sheet, and the budgeted statement of cash flows.

Management by Exception

Directs management's attention to important differences between actual and budgeted amounts.

Master Budget

The set of budgeted financial statements and supporting schedules for the entire organization. Includes the operating budget, the capital expenditures budget, and the financial budget.

Operating Budget

Projects sales revenue, cost of goods sold, and operating expenses, leading to the budgeted income statement that projects operating income for the period.

Responsibility Accounting

A system for evaluating the performance of each responsibility center and its manager.

Responsibility Center

A part or subunit of an organization whose manager is accountable for specific activities.

Sales Budget

A detailed plan that shows the estimated sales revenue for a future period.

Statement of Budgeted Cash Receipts and Payments

Details how the business expects to go from the beginning cash balance to the desired ending balance. Also called the **cash budget.**

Quick Check

1. Which of the following is a benefit of the budgeting process?
   a. The planning budgets helps managers foresee and avoid potential problems before they occur.
   b. The budget helps motivate employees to achieve the company's sales growth and cost-reduction goals.
   c. The budget provides managers with a benchmark against which to compare actual results for performance evaluation.
   d. All of the above.

2. Which of the following is the starting point of the master budget?
   a. The operating expenses budget
   b. The inventory budget
   c. The purchases and cost of goods sold budget
   d. The sales budget

3. The balance sheet is part of which element of the master budget?
   a. The operating budget
   b. The financial budget
   c. The capital expenditures budget
   d. None of the above

Use the following information to answer questions 4 through 6. Suppose Amazon.com sells 1 million hardback books a day at an average price of $30. Assume that Amazon's purchase price for the books is 60% of the selling price it charges customers. Amazon has no beginning inventory, but for ending inventory Amazon wants to have a three-day supply. Assume that operating expenses are $1 million per day.

4. Compute Amazon's budgeted sales for the next (seven-day) week.
   a. $52.5 million
   b. $210 million
   c. $220.5 million
   d. $367.5 million

5. Determine Amazon's budgeted purchases for Amazon's first (seven-day) week.
   a. $126 million
   b. $180 million
   c. $210 million
   d. $54 million

6. What is Amazon.com's budgeted operating income for a (seven-day) week?
   a. $52.5 million
   b. $56 million
   c. $77 million
   d. $147 million

7. Which of the following expenses would *not* appear in a cash budget?

   a. Marketing expense

   b. Wages expense

   c. Interest expense

   d. Depreciation expense

8. Information technology has made it easier for managers to perform all of the following tasks *except*:

   a. Sensitivity analyses

   b. Rolling up individual units' budgets into the companywide budget

   c. Removing slack from the budget

   d. Preparing responsibility center performance reports that identify variances between actual and budgeted revenues and costs

9. Which of the following managers is at the highest level of the organization?

   a. Investment center manager

   b. Revenue center manager

   c. Profit center manager

   d. Cost center manager

10. Suppose a company budgets $5 million for customer service costs but actually spends $4 million.

   a. Because this $1 million variance is favorable, management does not need to investigate further.

   b. Management will investigate this $1 million unfavorable variance to try to identify and then correct the problem that led to the unfavorable variance.

   c. Management will investigate this $1 million favorable variance to ensure that the cost savings do not reflect skimping on customer service.

   d. Management should focus its investigation on unfavorable variances.

   Answers are given after Apply Your Knowledge (p. 1149).

Assess Your Progress

Short Exercises

Preparing a summary
performance report
1

S22-1 Petra prepared a budget for her summer break. She planned to earn $3,000 working for 3 months in a restaurant in Vail, Colorado. She planned to spend $2,700 on housing, food, and other expenses. At the end of the summer, she reviewed her bank account and found that she earned $4,200 and incurred $3,200 in expenses. Prepare a summary performance report including actual costs, budgeted costs, and variance (actual − budget). Should she be concerned that she spent too much money? (pp. 1102–1103)

Components of the
operating budget
2

S22-2 Identify the order in which you would prepare the following components of the operating budget. Number from 1 to 4 to indicate first to last in preparation. (p. 1105)

_____ a. Budgeted income statement
_____ b. Operating expenses budget
_____ c. Sales budget
_____ d. Inventory, purchases, and cost of goods sold budget

Ordering components of
the master budget
2 **3**

S22-3 Identify the order in which you would prepare the following components of the master budget. Number from 1 to 6 to indicate first to last in preparation. (p. 1105)

_____ a. Budgeted balance sheet
_____ b. Sales budget
_____ c. Capital expenditures budget
_____ d. Budgeted income statement
_____ e. Cash budget
_____ f. Inventory, purchases, and cost of goods sold budget

Preparing a sales budget
2

S22-4 Eagle Outfitters expects to sell 5,000 water bottles in January and 6,000 water bottles in February for $10 each. Prepare the sales budget for January and February. (pp. 1106–1108)

Preparing an inventory,
purchases, and cost of
goods sold budget
2

S22-5 Eagle Outfitters expects revenue of $2,000 in June, $1,500 in July, and $1,800 in August for sales of hiking socks. Suppose the cost of goods sold averages 40% of sales. Beginning inventory in June is expected to be $100. Ending inventory is 50% of next month's cost of goods sold. Prepare an inventory, purchases, and cost of goods sold budget for June and July. (pp. 1108–1109)

Preparing a sales budget
2

S22-6 Eagle Outfitter's store in Butte, Montana, is projecting sales as follows: January, $50,000; February, $80,000; March, $40,000; April, $50,000. Cash sales are 60% of total sales; credit sales are 40%. Prepare the sales budget showing the portion of total sales estimated as cash sales and credit sales. (pp. 1106–1107)

Preparing an inventory,
purchases, and cost of
goods sold budget
2

S22-7 Refer to the information in S22-6. Suppose cost of goods sold averages 75% of sales. Ending inventory is $20,000 plus 80% of cost of goods sold for next month. January 1 inventory balance is $48,000. Prepare the Butte store's inventory, purchases, and cost of goods sold budget for January and February. (p. 1107)

S22-8 Waterking sells crystal vases. Budgeted sales are $40,000 for March and $50,000 for April. Sales are planned to be 80% cash and 20% on credit. The balance of Accounts Receivable on February 28 is $9,000. Credit sales are collected in the following month. Prepare a sales budget and the budgeted cash collections for March and April. (pp. 1107, 1113)

S22-9 Waterking sells crystal vases. Budgeted purchases are $25,000 for May and $30,000 for June. Waterking pays for 60% of inventory purchases in the month of the purchase and 40% in the next month. The balance of Accounts Payable on April 30 is $8,000. Prepare the budgeted cash payments for purchases of inventory for May and June. (pp. 1113, 1114)

S22-10 Petra is preparing a budget for her first semester in college. She has saved $2,000 from her summer job. She will receive $5,000 in scholarships and $2,500 from the university as a work study. Her dorm will cost $3,500; food, $1,200; and transportation, $1,000. Prepare a cash budget for Petra. (pp. 1115–1117)

S22-11 Coles has $8,300 cash on hand on January 1. The company requires a minimum cash balance of $7,500. Budgeted January cash collections are $548,330. Total cash payments for January are expected to be $563,200. Prepare a cash budget for January. Will Coles need to borrow cash by the end of January? (pp. 1115–1117)

S22-12 Fill in the blanks with the letter of the phrase that best completes the sentence. (pp. 1121–1122)

    a. A cost center

    b. An investment center

    c. A profit center

    d. A responsibility center

    e. A revenue center

    f. Lower

    g. Higher

1. The Maintenance Department at the San Diego Zoo is _____.

2. The concession stand at the San Diego Zoo is _____.

3. The Menswear Department at Bloomingdale's, which is responsible for buying and selling merchandise, is _____.

4. A production line at a Palm Pilot plant is _____.

5. _____ is any segment of the business whose manager is accountable for specific activities.

6. Gatorade, a division of Quaker Oats, is _____.

7. The sales manager in charge of NIKE's northwest sales territory oversees _____.

8. Managers of cost and revenue centers are at _____ levels of the organization than managers of profit and investment centers.

Exercises

Budgeting and performance
evaluation

E22-13 Daniel Garcia owns a chain of travel goods stores. Last year, his sales staff sold 10,000 suitcases at an average sale price of $150. Variable expenses were 80% of sales revenue, and the total fixed expense was $120,000. This year the chain sold more-expensive product lines. Sales were 8,000 suitcases at an average price of $200. The variable expense percentage and the total fixed expense were the same both years. Garcia evaluates the chain manager by comparing this year's income with last year's income.

  Prepare a performance report for this year, similar to Exhibit 22-4. How would you improve Garcia's performance evaluation system to better analyze this year's results? (p. 1104)

Budgeting inventory,
purchases, and cost of
goods sold

E22-14 Spencer Inc. sells tire rims. Its sales budget for the nine months ended September 30, 2008, follows:

| | Quarter Ended | | | Nine-Month |
	March 31	June 30	Sept. 30	Total
Cash sales, 30%	$ 30,000	$ 45,000	$ 37,500	$112,500
Credit sales, 70%	70,000	105,000	87,500	262,500
Total sales, 100%	$100,000	$150,000	$125,000	$375,000

In the past, cost of goods sold has been 60% of total sales. The director of marketing and the financial vice president agree that each quarter's ending inventory should not be below $20,000 plus 10% of cost of goods sold for the following quarter. The marketing director expects sales of $200,000 during the fourth quarter. The January 1 inventory was $19,000.

  Prepare an inventory, purchases, and cost of goods sold budget for each of the first three quarters of the year. Compute cost of goods sold for the entire nine-month period. (pp. 1108–1109)

Budgeting quarterly income
for a year

E22-15 Olivas International, Inc., is an exotic car dealership. Suppose that its Los Angeles office projects that 2007 quarterly sales will increase by 3% in quarter 1, by 4% in quarter 2, by 6% in quarter 3, and by 5% in quarter 4. Management expects operating expenses to be 80% of revenues during each of the first two quarters, 79% of revenues during the third quarter, and 81% during the fourth. The office manager expects to borrow $100,000 on July 1, with quarterly principal payments of $10,000 beginning on September 30 and interest paid at an annual rate of 13%. Assume that fourth-quarter 2006 sales were $4,000,000.

  Prepare a budgeted income statement for each of the four quarters of 2007 and for the entire year. Present the 2007 budget as follows: (pp. 1109–1110)

Quarter 1	Quarter 2	Quarter 3	Quarter 4	Full Year

E22-16 Agua Olé is a distributor of bottled water. For each of items a through c, compute the amount of cash receipts or payments Agua Olé will budget for September. The solution to one item may depend on the answer to an earlier item.

    a. Management expects to sell equipment that cost $16,000 at a gain of $2,000. Accumulated depreciation on this equipment is $7,000. (p. 1115)

    b. Management expects to sell 7,500 cases of water in August and 9,200 in September. Each case sells for $12. Cash sales average 30% of total sales, and credit sales make up the rest. Three-fourths of credit sales are collected in the month of sale, with the balance collected the following month. (p. 1113)

    c. The company pays rent and property taxes of $4,200 each month. Commissions and other selling expenses average 25% of sales. Agua Olé pays two-thirds of commissions and other selling expenses in the month incurred, with the balance paid in the following month. (p. 1114)

E22-17 Lim Auto Parts, a family-owned auto parts store, began January with $10,500 cash. Management forecasts that collections from credit customers will be $11,000 in January and $15,000 in February. The store is scheduled to receive $6,000 cash on a business note receivable in January. Projected cash payments include inventory purchases ($13,000 in January and $13,900 in February) and operating expenses ($3,000 each month).

    Lim Auto Parts' bank requires a $10,000 minimum balance in the store's checking account. At the end of any month when the account balance dips below $10,000, the bank automatically extends credit to the store in multiples of $1,000. Lim Auto Parts borrows as little as possible and pays back loans in quarterly installments of $2,000, plus 4% interest on the entire unpaid principal. The first payment occurs three months after the loan.

Requirements

1. Prepare Lim Auto Parts' cash budget for January and February. (pp. 1115–1117)

2. How much cash will Lim Auto Parts borrow in February if collections from customers that month total $13,500 instead of $15,000?

E22-18 You recently began a job as an accounting intern at Regis Golf Park. Your first task was to help prepare the cash budget for April and May. Unfortunately, the computer with the budget file crashed, and you did not have a backup. You ran a program to salvage bits of data from the budget file. After entering the following data in the budget, you have just enough information to reconstruct the budget.

    Regis Golf Park eliminates any cash deficiency by borrowing the exact amount needed from State Street Bank, where the current interest rate is 8%. Regis Golf Park pays interest on its outstanding debt at the end of each month. The company also repays all borrowed amounts at the end of the month, as cash becomes available.

    Complete the following cash budget: (pp. 1115–1117)

continued . . .

	April	May
	REGIS GOLF PARK Cash Budget April and May	
Beginning cash balance	$ 16,900	$?
Cash collections	?	79,600
Cash from sale of plant assets	0	1,800
Cash available	106,900	?
Cash payments:		
Purchase of inventory	$?	$41,000
Operating expenses	47,200	?
Total payments	98,000	?
(1) Ending cash balance before financing	?	22,100
Minimum cash balance desired	20,000	20,000
Cash excess (deficiency)	$?	$?
Financing of cash deficiency:		
Borrowing (at end of month)	?	?
Principal repayments (at end of month)	?	?
Interest expense	?	?
(2) Total effects of financing	?	?
Ending cash balance (1) + (2)	$?	$?

Preparing a budgeted balance sheet

3

E22-19 Use the following March operating information and February 28 account balances to prepare a budgeted balance sheet for Oleanders at March 31, 2008.

March operating activity information

Budgeted sales, $12,200, all on credit

Cost of goods sold, 60% of sales

March depreciation expense, $600

Cash payments for March expenses, including income tax, total $5,000

Cash collected from customers on account, $14,300

Cash payments for inventory, $4,600

Cash payments of accounts payable, $8,200

Worksheet including February 28 account balances:

	Cash	+	Accounts Receivable	+	Inventory	+	Equipment	+	(Accumulated Depreciation)	=	Accounts Payable	+	Owner's Equity
February 28 balance	$11,400	+	$5,150	+	$17,720	+	$34,800	+	$(29,870)	=	$10,500	+	$28,700
Sales on credit													
Cost of goods sold													
Depreciation expense													
Operating expenses													
Collections on Account													
Payments for Inventory													
Payments on Account													
March 31 balance		+		+		+		+		=		+	

continued . . .

Requirements

1. Complete the worksheet using the planned March operating activity and cash transactions. (p. 1118)
2. Prepare a budgeted balance sheet for Oleanders as of March 31, 2008. (p. 1117)

Identifying different types of responsibility centers

E22-20 Identify each responsibility center as a cost center (C), a revenue center (R), a profit center (P) , or an investment center (I). (pp. 1121–1122)

a. The bakery department of an Albertson's supermarket reports income for the current year.

b. Pace Foods is a subsidiary of Campbell Soup Company.

c. The personnel department of USAA Life Insurance Company prepares its budget and subsequent performance report on the basis of its expected expenses for the year.

d. The shopping section of Burpee.com reports both revenues and expenses.

e. Burpee.com's investor relations Web site provides operating and financial information to investors and other interested parties.

f. The manager of a car service station is evaluated based on the station's revenues and expenses.

g. A charter airline records revenues and expenses for each airplane each month. The airplane's performance report shows its ratio of operating income to average book value.

h. The manager of the Southwest sales territory is evaluated based on a comparison of current period sales against budgeted sales.

Using responsibility accounting to evaluate profit centers

E22-21 WebTouch is a Fresno company that sells cell phones and PDAs on the Web. WebTouch has assistant managers for its digital and video cell phone operations. These assistant managers report to the manager of the total cell phone product line, who with the manager of PDAs reports to the manager for sales of all handheld devices, Monica Beasley. Monica received the following data for September 2009 operations:

	Cell Phones		PDAs
	Digital	**Video**	**PDAs**
Revenues, budget............	$204,000	$800,000	$400,000
Expenses, budget	140,000	390,000	275,000
Revenues, actual.............	214,000	840,000	390,000
Expenses, actual	135,000	400,000	270,000

Arrange the data in a performance report similar to Exhibit 22-19 on p. 1124. Show September results, in thousands of dollars, for digital cell phones, for the total cell phone product line, and for all handheld devices. Should Monica investigate the performance of digital cell phone operations?

E22-22 24/7, Inc. is an international company that provides customer call services to the United States, Great Britain, and Canada. The following

continued . . .

reports have been partially completed. Calculate the amounts for items
(a) through (g). (p. 1122–1123)

CEO of 24/7, Inc.			
Operating Income by Country	**Budget**	**Actual**	**Variance Favorable/ (Unfavorable)**
China	$ 60	$ 25	$(35)
India	(a)	113	8
Operating income	$165	$138	(b)

VP—India Operations			
Operating Income by City	**Budget**	**Actual**	**Variance Favorable/ (Unfavorable)**
Bangalore	$ 70	$ 85	$15
Delhi	(c)	28	(e)
Operating income	$105	(d)	$8

Manager—Bangalore			
Revenues and Expenses	**Budget**	**Actual**	**Variance Favorable/ (Unfavorable)**
Revenues	$120	$130	(f)
Expenses	50	45	5
Operating income	(g)	$ 85	$15

Problems (Group A)

P22-23A Representatives of the various departments of Go Cycles have assembled
the following data. As the business manager, you must prepare the budgeted income statements for August and September 2008.

Sales budget information: Sales in July were $196,000. You fore-
cast that monthly sales will increase 3% in August and 2% in
September.

Inventory, purchases, and cost of goods sold budget information: Go
Cycles tries to maintain inventory of $50,000 plus 20% of the sales
revenue budgeted for the following month. Monthly purchases average 60% of sales revenue in that same month. Actual inventory on
July 31 is $90,000. Sales budgeted for October are $220,000.

Operating expense budget information:

a. Monthly salaries amount to $15,000. Sales commissions equal 6%
of sales for that month. Combine salaries and commissions into a
single figure.

continued . . .

b. Other monthly expenses are

Rent expense	$13,000, paid as incurred
Depreciation expense	$ 4,000
Insurance expense	$ 1,000, expiration of prepaid amount

Requirements

1. Prepare the inventory, purchases, and cost of goods sold budget, and the operating expenses budget for August and September. (pp. 1109–1110)

2. Prepare Go Cycles' budgeted income statements for August and September. Round *all* amounts to the nearest $1,000. For example, budgeted August sales are $202,000 ($196,000 × 1.03) and September sales are $206,000 ($202,000 × 1.02). (p. 1110)

Budgeting cash receipts and cash payments

P22-24A Refer to P22-23A. You have gathered information to complete the cash budget for Go Cycles.

Budgeted cash collections information: Sales are 50% cash and 50% credit. (Use sales on the last two lines of P22-23A, Req. 2.) Credit sales are collected in the month after the sale.

Budgeted cash payments for purchases information: Inventory purchases are paid 60% in the month of purchase and 40% the following month.

Cash payments for operating expenses information: All cash expenses are paid in the month incurred.

The July 31, 2008 balance sheet showed a cash balance of $22,000 and an accounts payable balance of $52,000.

Requirements

1. Prepare schedules of budgeted cash collections from customers (p. 1113) and budgeted cash payments for purchases (p. 1112). Show amounts for each month and totals for August and September. Round your computations to the *nearest dollar.*

2. Prepare a cash budget similar to Exhibit 22-13 (p. 1115).

Preparing a cash budget and budgeted balance sheet

P22-25A The Pottery Store has applied for a loan. First Central Bank has requested a budgeted balance sheet at June 30, 2009, and a budgeted statement of cash flows for June. As the controller (chief accounting officer) of The Pottery Store, you have assembled the following information:

May 31 balance sheet information: Cash, $50,200; Accounts Receivable, $15,300; Inventory balance, $11,900; Equipment, $80,800; Accumulated Depreciation, $12,400; Accounts Payable, $8,300; Accrued Liabilities, $0; Owners' Equity, $137,500

Planned June operating activity information:

a. Purchase inventory costing $48,200, paying $20,000 in cash and $28,200 on credit

b. Sales, $85,000, 40% of which is for cash. The remaining 60% is credit sales.

c. Cost of goods sold, 50% of sales

continued . . .

d. June depreciation expense, $400

e. Other June operating expenses, including income tax, total $34,000, 75% of which will be paid in cash and the remainder accrued at June 30

Planned June cash information:

a. Collect $40,800 from customers on account

b. Pay $26,900 to creditors and suppliers on account

c. Pay cash for equipment costing $16,400

Requirements

1. Use the accounting equation on page 11 to prepare a worksheet with columns for each asset, liability, and owner's equity item. Enter the May 31 balance sheet information in the first row. Record the information above into the worksheet. Calculate the June 30 balances by adding the numbers in each column.

2. Prepare the cash budget for June. (p. 1118)

3. Prepare the budgeted balance sheet for The Pottery Store at June 30, 2009. (pp. 1115–1117)

Preparing a profit center performance report for management by exception; benefits of budgeting

1 5

P22-26A EStore is a chain of home electronics stores. Each store has a manager who answers to a city manager, who in turn reports to a statewide manager. The actual income statements of Store No. 23, all stores in the Phoenix area (including Store No. 23), and all stores in the state of Arizona (including all Phoenix stores) are summarized as follows for October:

	Store No. 23	Phoenix	State of Arizona
Sales revenue	$43,300	$486,000	$3,228,500
Expenses:			
City/state manager's office expenses	$ —	$ 18,000	$ 44,000
Cost of goods sold	15,000	171,300	1,256,800
Salary expense	4,000	37,500	409,700
Other operating expenses	6,300	49,000	751,600
Total expenses	25,300	275,800	2,462,100
Operating income	$18,000	$210,200	$ 766,400

Budgeted amounts for October were as follows:

	Store No. 23	Phoenix	State of Arizona
Sales revenue	$39,000	$470,000	$3,129,000
Expenses:			
City/state manager's office expenses	$ —	$ 19,000	$ 145,000
Cost of goods sold	12,100	160,800	1,209,000
Salary expense	6,000	37,900	412,000
Other operating expenses	4,900	54,100	741,000
Total expenses	23,000	271,800	2,407,000
Operating income	$16,000	$198,200	$ 722,000

continued . . .

Requirements

1. Prepare a report for October that shows the performance of Store No. 23, all the stores in the Phoenix area, and all the stores in Arizona. Follow the format of Exhibit 22-19 on page 1124.

2. As the city manager of the Phoenix area stores, would you investigate Store No. 23 on the basis of this report? Why or why not? (p. 1124)

3. Briefly discuss the benefits of budgeting. Base your discussion on Estore's performance report. (pp. 1103–1105)

Distinguishing among different types of responsibility centers

P22-27A Is each of the following most likely a cost center, a revenue center, a profit center, or an investment center? (pp. 1121–1122)

a. Purchasing Department of Milliken, a textile manufacturer

b. Quality Control Department of Mayfield Dairies

c. European subsidiary of Coca-Cola

d. Payroll Department of the University of Illinois

e. Lighting Department in a Sears store

f. Children's nursery in a church or synagogue

g. Personnel Department of E* Trade, the online broker

h. igourmet.com, an e-tailer of gourmet cheeses

i. Service Department of an automobile dealership

j. Customer Service Department of Procter & Gamble Co.

k. Proposed new office of Deutsche Bank

l. Southwest region of Pizza Inns, Inc.

m. Delta Air Lines, Inc.

n. Order-Taking Department at Lands' End mail-order company

o. Editorial Department of The Wall Street Journal

p. A Ford Motor Company production plant

q. Police Department of Boston

r. Century 21 Real Estate Co.

s. A small pet grooming business

t. Northeast sales territory for Boise-Cascade

u. Different product lines of Broyhill, a furniture manufacturer

v. McDonald's restaurants under the supervision of a regional manager

w. Job superintendents of a home builder

Problems (Group B)

Budgeting income for two months

2

P22-28B The budget committee of Omaha Office Supply Co. has assembled the following data. As the business manager, you must prepare the budgeted income statements for May and June 2008.

Sales budget information: Sales in April were $42,100. You forecast that monthly sales will increase 2.0% in May and 2.4% in June.

Inventory, purchases, and cost of goods sold budget information: Omaha maintains inventory of $9,000 plus 25% of the sales revenue budgeted for the following month. Monthly purchases average 50% of sales revenue in that same month. Actual inventory on April 30 is $14,000. Sales budgeted for July are $42,400.

continued . . .

Operating expense budget information:

a. Monthly salaries amount to $4,000. Sales commissions equal 4% of sales for that month. Combine salaries and commissions into a single figure.

b. Other monthly expenses are:

Rent expense	$3,000, paid as incurred
Depreciation expense	$ 600
Insurance expense	$ 200, expiration of prepaid amount

Requirements

1. Prepare the inventory, purchases, and cost of goods sold budget, and the operating expenses budget for May and June. (pp. 1109–1110)
2. Prepare Omaha's budgeted income statements for May and June. Round *all* amounts to the nearest $100. (Round amounts ending in $50 or more upward, and amounts ending in less than $50 downward.) For example, budgeted May sales are $42,900 ($42,100 × 1.02), and June sales are $43,900 ($42,900 × 1.024). (p. 1112)

Budgeting cash receipts and cash payments

3

P22-29B Refer to P22-28B. You have gathered the following information to complete the cash budget for Omaha Office Supply.

Budgeted cash collections information: Sales are 70% cash and 30% credit. (Use the rounded sales on the last two lines of P22-28B, Req. 2.) Credit sales are collected in the month after sale.

Budgeted cash payments for purchases information: Inventory purchases are paid 50% in the month of purchase and 50% the following month.

Cash payments for operating expenses information: Salaries and sales commissions are paid half in the month earned and half the next month.

The April 30, 2008, balance sheet showed the following balances:

Cash	$15,000
Accounts payable	7,400
Salary and commissions payable	2,850

Requirements

1. Prepare schedules of budgeted cash collections from customers (p. 1113) and budgeted cash payments for purchases (p. 1112). Show amounts for each month and totals for May and June. Round your computations to the nearest dollar.
2. Prepare a cash budget similar to Exhibit 22-13 on p. 1115.

P22-30B Greely Printing of Albany has applied for a loan. Bank of America has requested a budgeted balance sheet at April 30, 2009, and a budgeted statement of cash flows for April. As Greely's controller, you have assembled the following information:

> *March 31 balance sheet information:* Cash, $45,600; Accounts Receivable, $29,700; Inventory, $29,600; Equipment, $52,400; Accumulated Depreciation, $41,300; Accounts Payable, $17,300; Accrued Liabilities, $0; Owner's Equity, $98,700.

> *Planned April operating activity information:*

> a. Purchase inventory costing $46,800, paying $10,000 in cash and $36,800 on credit.

> b. Sales, $90,000, 70% of which is for cash. The remaining 30% is credit sales.

> c. Cost of goods sold, 60% of sales

> d. April depreciation expense, $900

> e. Other April operating expenses, including income tax, total $13,200, 25% of which will be paid in cash and the remainder accrued at April 30.

> *Planned April cash information:*

> a. Collect $43,200 from customers on account.

> b. Pay $35,700 to creditors and suppliers.

> c. Pay cash for equipment costing $42,800.

Requirements

1. Use the accounting equation on page 11 to prepare a worksheet with columns for each asset, liability, and owner's equity item. Enter the March 31 balance sheet information in the first row. Record the information above into the worksheet. Calculate the April 30 balances by adding the numbers in each column.

2. Prepare the cash budget for April. (pp. 1115–1117)

3. Prepare the budgeted balance sheet for Greely Printing at April 30, 2009. (p. 1117)

Preparing a profit center
performance report for
management by exception;
benefits of budgeting

 5

P22-31B Doggy World operates a chain of pet stores in the South. The manager of each store reports to the region manager, who in turn reports to headquarters in Atlanta, Georgia. The actual income statements for the Miami store, the Florida region (including the Miami store), and the company as a whole (including the Florida region) for July 2008 are:

	Miami	Florida	Companywide
Revenue	$148,900	$1,647,000	$4,200,000
Expenses:			
Region manager/headquarters office	$ —	$ 60,000	$ 116,000
Cost of materials	81,100	871,900	1,807,000
Salary expense	38,300	415,100	1,119,000
Other operating expenses	13,600	171,900	873,000
Total expenses	133,000	1,518,900	3,915,000
Operating income	$ 15,900	$ 128,100	$ 285,000

continued . . .

Budgeted amounts for July were as follows:

	Miami	Florida	Companywide
Revenue	$162,400	$1,769,700	$4,450,000
Expenses:			
Region manager/headquarters office	$ —	$ 65,600	$ 118,000
Cost of materials	86,400	963,400	1,972,000
Salary expense	38,800	442,000	1,095,000
Other operating expenses	15,200	174,500	894,000
Total expenses	140,400	1,645,500	4,079,000
Operating income	$ 22,000	$ 124,200	$ 371,000

Requirements

1. Prepare a report for July 2008 that shows the performance of the Miami store, the Florida region, and the company as a whole. Follow the format of Exhibit 22-19 on page 1124.

2. As the Florida region manager, would you investigate the Miami store on the basis of this report? Why or why not? (p. 1124)

3. Briefly discuss the benefits of budgeting. Base your discussion on Doggy World's performance report. (pp. 1103–1105)

Distinguishing among different types of responsibility centers

4

P22-32B Is each of the following most likely a cost center, a revenue center, a profit center, or an investment center?

a. Shipping department of Amazon.com

b. Eastern district of a salesperson's territory

c. Hurricane victims relief activities of a church or synagogue

d. Catering operation of Sonny's BBQ restaurant

e. Executive headquarters of the United Way

f. Accounts payable section of the Accounting Department at Home Depot

g. Proposed new office of Coldwell Banker, a real-estate firm

h. Disneyland

i. The Empire State Building in New York City

j. Branch warehouse of Dalton Carpets

k. Information systems department of Habitat for Humanity

l. Service Department of Audio Forest stereo shop

m. Investments Department of Citibank

n. Assembly-line department at a Dell Computer plant

o. American subsidiary of a Japanese manufacturer

p. Surgery unit of a privately owned hospital

q. Research and Development Department of Cisco Systems

r. Childrenswear department at a Target store

s. Typesetting Department of Northend Press, a printing company

t. Prescription Filling Department of Drugstore.com

u. Order Taking Department at L.L.Bean

v. Personnel Department of Goodyear Tire and Rubber Company

w. Grounds maintenance department at Augusta National golf course

Apply Your Knowledge

Decision Cases

Using a budgeted income statement

Case 1. Donna Scribner has recently accepted the position of assistant manager at Cycle City, a bicycle store in Austin, Texas. She has just finished her accounting courses. Cycle City's manager and owner, Jeff Towry, asks Donna to prepare a budgeted income statement for 2009 based on the information he has collected. Scribner's budget follows:

CYCLE CITY
Budgeted Income Statement
For the Year Ended July 31, 2009

Sales revenue		$244,000
Cost of goods sold		177,000
Gross profit		67,000
Operating expenses:		
Salary and commission expense	$50,000	
Rent expense	8,000	
Depreciation expense	2,000	
Insurance expense	800	
Miscellaneous expenses	12,000	72,800
Operating loss		(5,800)
Interest expense		225
Net loss		$ (6,025)

Requirement

Scribner does not want to give Towry this budget without making constructive suggestions for steps Towry could take to improve expected performance. Write a memo to Towry outlining your suggestions (pp. 1103–1104). Your memo should take the following form:

Date: _____

  To: Mr. Jeff Towry, Manager
       Cycle City

From: Donna Scribner

Subject: Cycle City's 2009 budgeted income statement

Budgeting cash flows and financial statements to analyze alternatives

Case 2. Each autumn, as a hobby, Suzanne Aker weaves cotton placemats to sell through a local craft shop. The mats sell for $20 per set of four. The shop charges a 10% commission and remits the net proceeds to Aker at the end of December. Aker has woven and sold 25 sets each of the last two years. She has enough cotton in inventory to make another 25 sets. She paid $7 per set for the cotton. Aker uses a four-harness loom that she purchased for cash exactly two years ago. It is depreci-

ated at the rate of $10 per month. The accounts payable relate to the cotton inventory and are payable by September 30.

Aker is considering buying an eight-harness loom so that she can weave more-intricate patterns in linen. The new loom costs $1,000; it would be depreciated at $20 per month. Her bank has agreed to lend her $1,000 at 18% interest, with $200 principal plus accrued interest payable each December 31. Aker believes she can weave 15 linen placemat sets in time for the Christmas rush if she does not weave any cotton mats. She predicts that each linen set will sell for $50. Linen costs $18 per set. Aker's supplier will sell her linen on credit, payable December 31.

Aker plans to keep her old loom whether or not she buys the new loom. The balance sheet for her weaving business at August 31, 2007, is as follows:

SUZANNE AKER, WEAVER
Balance Sheet
August 31, 2007

Assets		Liabilities	
Current assets:		Current liabilities:	
Cash	$125	Accounts payable	$ 74
Inventory of cotton	175		
	300		
Fixed assets:			
Loom	500	**Owner's Equity**	
Accumulated depreciation	(240)	Owner's equity	486
	260		
Total assets	$560	Total liabilities and owners' equity	$560

Requirements

1. Prepare a cash budget for the four months ending December 31, 2007, for two alternatives: weaving the placemats in cotton using the existing loom, and weaving the placemats in linen using the new loom. (pp. 1115–1117) For each alternative, prepare a budgeted income statement for the four months ending December 31, 2007, (p. 1110) and a budgeted balance sheet at December 31, 2007. (p. 1117)

2. On the basis of financial considerations only, what should Aker do? Give your reason.

3. What nonfinancial factors might Aker consider in her decision?

Ethical Issue

Budget slack

Homewood Suites operates a regional hotel chain. Each hotel is operated by a manager and an assistant manager/controller. Many of the staff who run the front desk, clean the rooms, and prepare the breakfast buffet work part-time or have a second job, so turnover is high.

Assistant manager/controller Terry Peake asked the new bookkeeper to help prepare the hotel's master budget. The master budget is prepared once a year and submitted to company headquarters for approval. Once approved, the master budget is used to evaluate the hotel's performance. These performance evaluations affect hotel managers' bonuses and they also affect company decisions on which hotels deserve extra funds for capital improvements.

When the budget was almost complete, Peake asked the bookkeeper to increase the amounts budgeted for labor and supplies by 15%. When asked why, Peake responded that hotel manager Clay Hipp told him to do this when he began working at the hotel. Hipp explained that this budgetary cushion gave him flexibility in running the hotel. For example, since company headquarters tightly controls capital improvement funds, Hipp can use the extra money budgeted for labor and supplies to replace broken televisions or pay "bonuses" to keep valued employees. Peake initially accepted this explanation because he had observed similar behavior at the hotel where he worked previously.

Put yourself in Peake's position. Use the ethical judgment decision guidelines in Chapter 8 (page 433) to decide how Peake should deal with the situation.

Team Project

Responsibility accounting, return on investment

Zianet provides e-commerce software for the pharmaceuticals industry. Zianet is organized into several divisions. A companywide planning committee sets general strategy and goals for the company and its divisions, but each division develops its own budget.

Rick Watson is the new division manager of wireless communications software. His division has two departments: Development and Sales. Carrie Pronai manages the 20 or so programmers and systems specialists typically employed in Development to create and update the division's software applications. Liz Smith manages the Sales Department.

Zianet considers the divisions to be investment centers. To earn his bonus next year, Watson must achieve a 30% return on the $3 million invested in his division. Within the Wireless Division, Development is a cost center and Sales is a revenue center.

Budgeting is in progress. Carrie Pronai met with her staff and is now struggling with two sets of numbers. Alternative A is her best estimate of next year's costs. However, unexpected problems can arise when writing software, and finding competent programmers is an ongoing challenge. She knows that Watson was a programmer before he earned an MBA, so he should be sensitive to this uncertainty. Consequently, she is thinking of increasing her budgeted costs (Alternative B). Her department's bonuses largely depend on whether the department meets its budgeted costs.

ZIANET
Wireless Division
Development Budget 2008

	Alternative A	Alternative B
Salaries (including overtime and part-time)	$2,400,000	$2,640,000
Software costs	120,000	132,000
Travel costs	65,000	71,500
Depreciation	255,000	255,000
Miscellaneous costs	100,000	110,000
Total costs	$2,940,000	$3,208,500

Liz Smith also is struggling with her sales budget. Companies have made their initial investments in communications software, so it is harder to win new customers. If things go well, she believes her sales team can maintain the level of growth achieved over the last few years. This is Alternative A in the Sales Budget. However, if Smith is too optimistic, sales may fall short of the budget. If this happens, her team will not receive bonuses. Smith therefore is considering reducing the sales numbers and submitting Alternative B.

ZIANET Wireless Division Sales Budget 2008		
	Alternative A	Alternative B
Sales revenue	$5,000,000	$4,500,000
Salaries	360,000	360,000
Travel costs	240,000	210,500

Split your team into three groups. Each group should meet separately before the entire team meets.

Requirements

1. The first group plays the role of Development Manager Carrie Pronai. Before meeting with the entire team, determine which set of budget numbers you are going to present to Rick Watson. Write a memo supporting your decision. Use the format shown in Decision Case 1. Give this memo to the third group before the team meeting.

2. The second group plays the role of Sales Manager Liz Smith. Before meeting with the entire team, determine which set of budget numbers you are going to present to Rick Watson. Write a memo supporting your decision. Use the format shown in Decision Case 1. Give this memo to the third group before the team meeting.

3. The third group plays the role of Division Manager Rick Watson. Before meeting with the entire team, use the memos that Pronai and Smith provided you to prepare a division budget based on the development and sales budgets. Your divisional overhead costs (additional costs beyond those incurred by the Development and Sales Departments) are approximately $400,000. Determine whether the Wireless Division can meet its targeted 30% return on assets given the budget alternatives submitted by your department managers.

During the meeting of the entire team, the group playing Watson presents the division budget and considers its implications. Each group should take turns discussing its concerns with the proposed budget. The team as a whole should consider whether the division budget must be revised. The team should prepare a report that includes the division budget and a summary of the issues covered in the team meeting.

For Internet Exercises, Excel in Practice, and additional online activities, go to the Web site www.prenhall.com/horngren.

Quick Check

1. *d*   2. *d*   3. *b*   4. *b*   5. *b*   6. *c*   7. *d*   8. *c*   9. *a*   10. *c*

Appendix 22A

Departmental Accounting

Responsibility centers are often called *departments*. Consider a retailer such as Macy's, Dillards, or Nordstrom. Top managers of a department store want more information than just the net income of the store as a whole. They want to know each department's gross profit (sales minus cost of goods sold). They also usually want to know each department's operating income. These data can help identify the most profitable departments.

It is easy to measure gross profit because each department records sales and cost of goods sold. It is more difficult to measure a department's operating income (gross profit minus operating expenses). Why? Many operating expenses are indirect costs that are not directly traced to the department.

Allocating Indirect Costs

Chapter 19 explained how indirect costs are allocated to *products*. Indirect costs are allocated to *departments* or responsibility centers using a similar process.

- Choose an allocation base for the indirect cost
- Compute an indirect cost allocation rate:

$$\text{Indirect cost allocation rate} = \frac{\text{Total indirect costs}}{\text{Total quantity of allocation base}}$$

- Allocate the indirect cost to the department:

$$\text{Allocation of indirect costs} = \frac{\text{Quantity of allocation}}{\text{base used by department}} \times \frac{\text{Indirect cost}}{\text{allocation rate}}$$

As we noted in Chapter 20, the ideal cost allocation base is the cost driver. Suppose Macy's decides that its receiving costs are driven by the number of orders placed to purchase inventory. If 15% of the orders are for the Shoe Department and 20% are for the Menswear Department, then Macy's will allocate 15% of the Receiving Department costs to the Shoe Department and 20% to the Menswear Department. (The remaining Receiving Department costs will be allocated to other departments in proportion to the number of orders each issued.)

Exhibit 22A-1 lists common allocation bases for different indirect costs. Managers use their experience and judgment to choose these bases, but there is no single "correct" allocation base for each indirect cost.

Cost or Expense	Base for Allocating Cost
Supervisors' salaries	Time spent, or number of employees, in each department
Equipment depreciation	Separately traced, or hours used by each department
Building depreciation, property taxes	Square feet of space
Janitorial services	Square feet of space
Advertising	Separately traced if possible; otherwise, in proportion to sales
Materials handling	Number or weight of items handled for each department
Personnel Department	Number of employees in each department
Purchasing Department	Number of purchase orders placed for each department

How to Allocate Indirect Costs to Departments: An Example

Exhibit 22A-2 shows a departmental income statement for HomePC, a retail computer store. Let's see how the company assigns operating expenses to the store's two departments: Hardware and Software.

EXHIBIT 22A-2 Departmental Income Statement

HOMEPC
Departmental Income Statement
Year Ended December 31, 2009

		Department	
(In Thousands)	Total	Hardware	Software
Sales revenue	$10,000	$7,000	$3,000
Cost of goods sold	6,500	4,500	2,000
Gross profit	3,500	2,500	1,000
Operating expenses:			
Salaries and wages expense	1,400	660	740
Rent expense	600	480	120
Purchasing department expense	48	36	12
Total operating expenses	2,048	1,176	872
Operating income	$ 1,452	$1,324	$ 128

SALARIES AND WAGES HomePC traces salespersons' salaries and department managers' salaries directly to each department.

RENT HomePC allocates the $600,000 rent expense based on the square feet each department occupies. The Hardware and Software departments occupy 20,000 square feet and 5,000 square feet, respectively, so HomePC allocates rent as follows:

Rent for entire store	$600,000
Total square feet (20,000 + 5,000)	÷ 25,000
Rent per square foot	$ 24
Hardware Department:	20,000 square feet × $24 per square foot = $480,000
Software Department:	5,000 square feet × $24 per square foot = 120,000
Total rent expense	= $600,000

PURCHASING DEPARTMENT HomePC found that it takes just as long to complete a purchase order for inexpensive modems as for expensive notebook computers. Consequently, the company allocates the $48,000 costs of the Purchasing Department based on the number of purchase orders processed. Hardware had 300 purchase orders, and Software had 100.

Purchasing Department costs	$48,000
Total number of purchase orders (300 + 100)	÷ 400
Cost per purchase order	$ 120
Hardware Department:	300 purchase orders × $120 per purchase order = $36,000
Software Department:	100 purchase orders × $120 per purchase order = 12,000
Total Purchasing Department cost	$48,000

HomePC's top executives can use the departmental income statements in Exhibit 22A-2 to evaluate how well each department and its manager performed in 2009. Hardware was more profitable than Software. Hardware's profit margin (income divided by sales) was $1,324 ÷ $7,000 = 18.9%, while Software's profit margin was only $128 ÷ $3,000 = 4.3%. However, it is better to compare a department's actual results to its budget rather than to another department's results. For example, if HomePC has just added the Software Department, performance may have exceeded expectations.

Appendix 22A Assignments

Short Exercises

Identifying indirect cost allocation bases

S22A-33 Match the most likely cost driver to each of the costs below. (pp. 1150–1152)

a. Number of loads of materials moved

b. Number of purchase orders

c. Number of shipments received

continued . . .

d. Number of customer complaints

e. Number of machine hours

f. Number of column inches

g. Number of pages

h. Number of employees

i. Number of square feet

_____ 1. Photocopying Department costs

_____ 2. Maintenance Department costs

_____ 3. Receiving Department costs

_____ 4. Customer Service Department costs

_____ 5. Purchasing Department costs

_____ 6. Material handling costs

_____ 7. Personnel Department costs

_____ 8. Building rent and utilities

_____ 9. Newspaper advertising costs

Allocating indirect costs to
departments

S22A-34 Suppose HomePC's rent expense for the entire store is $900,000. The Hardware Department occupies 20,000 square feet and the Software Department occupies 10,000 square feet. How much of the $900,000 rent expense would be allocated to each department? (pp. 1150–1152)

Exercises

Allocating indirect expenses
to departments

E22A-35 Fox Manufacturing incurred the following indirect costs in May:

Indirect labor cost	$24,000
Equipment depreciation cost	24,000
Marketing cost	25,200

Data for cost allocations:

	Department		
	Priming	Welding	Custom Orders
Sales revenue	$60,000	$30,000	$90,000
Indirect labor hours	500	700	300
Machine hours	550	525	125
Building square feet	11,000	3,500	1,000
Marketing cost—allocated to departments in proportion to sales.			

Requirements

1. Allocate Fox Manufacturing's May indirect costs to the three departments. (pp. 1150–1152)

2. Compute total indirect costs for each department. (p. 1152)

E22A-36 PlayAlong sells chrome and plastic harmonicas. It has two departments: Chrome and Plastic. The company's income statement for 2008 appears as follows:

Sales revenue	$372,000
Cost of goods sold	154,000
Gross profit	218,000
Operating expenses:	
Salaries expense	$ 78,000
Depreciation expense	40,000
Advertising expense	6,000
Other expenses	12,000
Total operating expenses	136,000
Operating income	$ 82,000

PlayAlong's sales revenues totaled $206,000 for chrome harmonicas and $166,000 for plastic harmonicas. Cost of goods sold is distributed $68,000 to Chrome and $86,000 to Plastic. Salaries are traced directly to departments: Chrome, $36,000; and Plastic, $42,000. The Chrome Department accounts for 70% of advertising. Depreciation is allocated based on the warehouse square footage occupied by each department: Chrome has 20,000 square feet and Plastic has 30,000 square feet. Other expenses are allocated based on the number of employees. The Chrome Department currently employs 55% of PlayAlong's employees.

Requirements

1. Prepare departmental income statements that show revenues, expenses, and operating income for each of the two departments. (p. 1152)
2. Which of the expenses in the departmental performance report are the most important for evaluating PlayAlong's department managers? Give your reason.

Problem

P22A-37 The Hyatt Club, an exclusive "hotel within a hotel," provides an even more luxurious atmosphere than the hotel's regular accommodations. Access is limited to guests residing on the hotel's top floors. The Club's private lounge serves complimentary continental breakfast, afternoon snacks, and evening cocktails and chocolates. The Club has its own concierge staff that provides personal service to Club guests. Guests staying in regular accommodations do not receive complimentary snacks and beverages, nor do they have a private concierge.

Hyatt Club floors are considered one department, and regular accommodations are considered a separate department.

Suppose the general manager of the new Hyatt hotel in Bermuda, an island in the Atlantic Ocean, wants to know the costs of her hotel's Club

continued . . .

Accommodations Department and Regular Accommodations Department. Housekeeping costs are allocated based on the number of occupied room-nights, utilities are allocated based on the number of cubic feet, and building depreciation is allocated based on the number of square feet. Assume each department reports the following information for March:

	Club Accommodations	Regular Accommodations
Number of occupied room-nights	540	7,560
Cubic feet	192,000	1,440,000
Square feet	16,000	144,000

Requirements

1. Given the following total costs, what are the costs assigned to the Club Accommodations and the Regular Accommodations Departments? (pp. 1150–1152)

Food and beverage expense	$ 12,000
Housekeeping expense	194,400
Utilities expense	97,920
Building depreciation expense	480,000
Concierge staff salaries	18,240
Total	$802,560

2. What is the cost per occupied room in Club Accommodations? In Regular Accommodations? (p. 1150)

3. Why might the general manager want to know the cost per occupied room for the Club Accommodations and the Regular Accommodations? (p. 1152)

23 Flexible Budgets and Standard Costs

Learning Objectives

1 Prepare a flexible budget for the income statement

2 Prepare an income statement performance report

3 Identify the benefits of standard costs and learn how to set standards

4 Compute standard cost variances for direct materials and direct labor

5 Analyze manufacturing overhead in a standard cost system

6 Record transactions at standard cost and prepare a standard cost income statement

Suppose you bought soft drinks for a party. Your budget was $30, but you actually spent $35. You need to stay within your budget in the future. It would be helpful to know *why* you spent more than the $30 budget. Here are some possibilities.

1. If each case of drinks costs more than the budget, then you might:

   - Find a cheaper price at a place like Costco, or wait for the drinks to go on sale.
   - Buy less-expensive store-brand drinks.

2. If you bought a larger quantity of soft drinks than you budgeted, why did you need this larger quantity?

   - If too many folks came to the party, next time you can restrict the invitation list.
   - If each guest drank more than you budgeted, perhaps you can cut per-guest consumption. Start the party later or end it earlier, or reduce the salty snacks.

3. If the budget for soft drinks was too low, you may need to increase the budget. ■

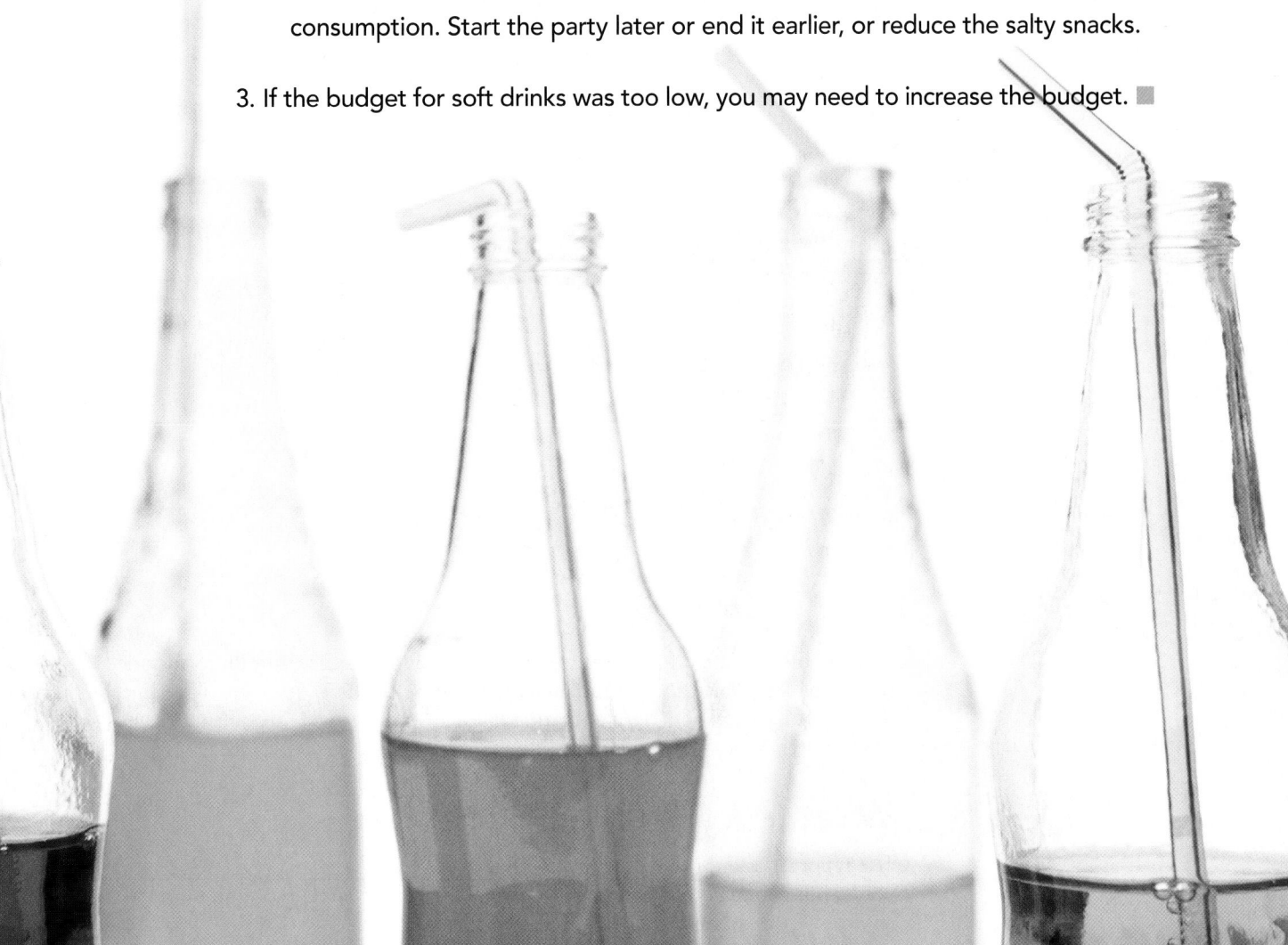

This chapter builds on your knowledge of budgeting from Chapter 22. You'll recall that a budget variance is the difference between an actual amount and a budgeted figure. This chapter shows how managers use variances to operate a business. It's important to know *why* actual costs differ from the budget. That will enable you to identify problems and decide what action to take.

In this chapter, you'll learn how to figure out *why* actual results differ from your budget. This is the first step in correcting problems. You'll also learn to use another management tool—standard costing.

How Managers Use Flexible Budgets

1 Prepare a flexible budget for the income statement

Pluto Pools installs swimming pools. At the beginning of the year, Pluto managers prepared a master budget like the one in Chapter 22. The master budget is a **static budget,** which means that it's prepared for only *one* level of sales volume. The static budget doesn't change after it's developed.

Exhibit 23-1 shows that Pluto's actual operating income is $16,000. This is $4,000 higher than expected from the static budget. This is a $4,000 favorable variance for June operating income. A **variance** is the difference between an actual amount and the budget. The variances in the third column of Exhibit 23-1 are:

- Favorable (F) if an actual amount increases operating income
- Unfavorable (U) if an actual amount decreases operating income

EXHIBIT 23-1   **Actual Results Versus Static Budget**

PLUTO POOLS
Comparison of Actual Results with Static Budget
Month Ended June 30, 2009

	Actual Results	Static Budget	Variance
Output units (pools installed)	10	8	2 F
Sales revenue	$121,000	$96,000	$25,000 F
Cost	(105,000)	(84,000)	(21,000) U
Operating income	$ 16,000	$12,000	$ 4,000 F

Pluto Pools' variance for operating income is favorable because Pluto installed 10 rather than 8 pools during June. But there's more to this story. Pluto Pools needs a flexible budget to show *why* operating income was favorable during June. Let's see how to prepare and use a flexible budget.

What Is a Flexible Budget?

The report in Exhibit 23-1 is hard to analyze because the static budget is based on 8 pools, but actual results are for 10 pools. This report raises more questions than it answers—for example:

- Why did the $21,000 unfavorable cost variance occur?
- Did workers waste materials?
- Did the cost of materials suddenly increase?
- How much of the additional cost arose because Pluto installed 10 rather than 8 pools?

We need a flexible budget to help answer these questions.

A **flexible budget** summarizes costs and revenues for several different volume levels within a relevant range. Flexible budgets separate variable costs from fixed costs; it is the variable costs that put the "flex" in the flexible budget. To create a flexible budget, you need to know your:

- Budgeted selling price per unit
- Variable cost per unit
- Total fixed costs
- Different volume levels within the relevant range

Exhibit 23-2 is a flexible budget for Pluto's revenues and costs to show what will happen if sales reach 5, 8, or 10 pools during June. The budgeted sale price per pool is $12,000. Budgeted variable costs (such as direct materials and direct labor) are $8,000 per pool, and budgeted fixed costs total $20,000. The formula for total cost is:

$$\text{Total cost} = \left(\begin{array}{c} \text{Number of} \\ \text{output units} \end{array} \times \begin{array}{c} \text{Variable cost} \\ \text{per output unit} \end{array} \right) + \text{Total fixed cost}$$

EXHIBIT 23-2   **Flexible Budget**

PLUTO POOLS
Flexible Budget
Month Ended June 30, 2009

			Flexible Budget per Output Unit	Outputs Units (Pools Installed)		
				5	8	10
		Sales revenue	$12,000	$60,000	$96,000	$120,000
		Variable costs	8,000	40,000	64,000	80,000
		Fixed costs*		20,000	20,000	20,000
		Total costs		60,000	84,000	100,000
		Operating income		$ 0	$12,000	$ 20,000

*Fixed costs are usually given as a total amount rather than as a cost per unit.

Notice in Exhibit 23-2 that sales revenue and variable costs increase as more pools are installed. But fixed costs remain constant regardless of the number of pools installed within the relevant range of 5 to 10 pools. Remember: *The cost formula applies only to a specific relevant range.* Why? Because fixed costs and the variable cost per pool may change outside this range. In our example, Pluto's relevant range is 5 to 10 pools. If the company installs 12 pools, it will have to rent additional equipment, so fixed costs will exceed $20,000. Pluto will also have to pay workers for overtime pay, so the variable cost per pool will be more than $8,000.

Using the Flexible Budget: Why Do Actual Results Differ from the Static Budget?

2 Prepare an income statement performance report

It's not enough to know that a variance occurred. That's like knowing you have a fever. The doctor needs to know *why* your temperature is above normal.

Managers must know *why* a variance occurred—to pinpoint problems and take corrective action. As you can see in Exhibit 23-1, the static budget underestimated both sales and total costs. The variance in Exhibit 23-1 is called a static budget variance because actual activity differed from what was expected in the static budget. To develop more useful information, managers divide the static budget variance into two broad categories:

- **Sales volume variance**—arises because the number of units actually sold differed from the number of units on which the static budget was based.
- **Flexible budget variance**—arises because the company had more or less revenue, or more or less cost, than expected for the *actual* level of output.

Exhibit 23-3 diagrams these variances.

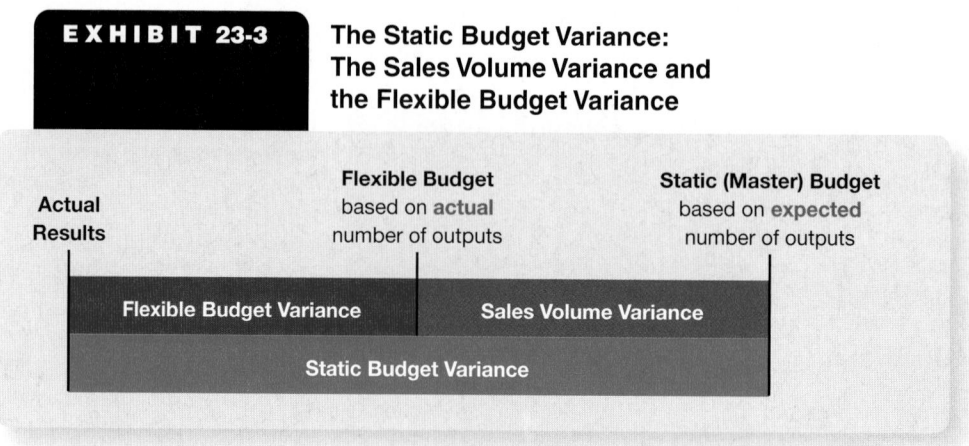

EXHIBIT 23-3 The Static Budget Variance: The Sales Volume Variance and the Flexible Budget Variance

Actual Results	Flexible Budget based on **actual** number of outputs	Static (Master) Budget based on **expected** number of outputs
Flexible Budget Variance	Sales Volume Variance	
Static Budget Variance		

Here's how to compute the two variances:

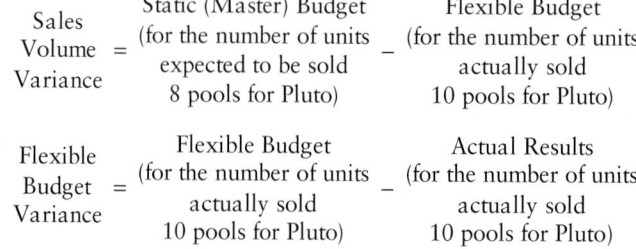

$$\begin{matrix} \text{Sales} \\ \text{Volume} \\ \text{Variance} \end{matrix} = \begin{matrix} \text{Static (Master) Budget} \\ \text{(for the number of units} \\ \text{expected to be sold} \\ \text{8 pools for Pluto)} \end{matrix} - \begin{matrix} \text{Flexible Budget} \\ \text{(for the number of units} \\ \text{actually sold} \\ \text{10 pools for Pluto)} \end{matrix}$$

$$\begin{matrix} \text{Flexible} \\ \text{Budget} \\ \text{Variance} \end{matrix} = \begin{matrix} \text{Flexible Budget} \\ \text{(for the number of units} \\ \text{actually sold} \\ \text{10 pools for Pluto)} \end{matrix} - \begin{matrix} \text{Actual Results} \\ \text{(for the number of units} \\ \text{actually sold} \\ \text{10 pools for Pluto)} \end{matrix}$$

We've seen that Pluto Pools budgeted for 8 pools during June. Actual production was 10 pools. We will need to compute a sales volume variance for Pluto, and there may also be a flexible budget variance. Exhibit 23-4 is Pluto's income statement performance report for June.

EXHIBIT 23-4 Income Statement Performance Report

PLUTO POOLS
Income Statement Performance Report
Month Ended June 30, 2009

	1 Actual Results at Actual Prices	2 (1) – (3) Flexible Budget Variance	3 Flexible Budget for Actual Number of Output Units*	4 (3) – (5) Sales Volume Variance	5 Static (Master) Budget*
Output Units (pools installed)	10	0	10	2 F	8
Sales revenue	$121,000	$1,000 F	$120,000	$24,000 F	$96,000
Variable costs	83,000	3,000 U	80,000	16,000 U	64,000
Fixed costs	22,000	2,000 U	20,000	0	20,000
Total costs	105,000	5,000 U	100,000	16,000 U	84,000
Operating income	$ 16,000	$4,000 U	$ 20,000	$ 8,000 F	$12,000
	Flexible budget variance, *$4,000 U*			*Sales volume variance,* *$8,000 F*	
	Static budget variance, $4,000 F				

*Budgeted sale price is $12,000 per pool, budgeted variable cost is $8,000 per pool, and budgeted total monthly fixed costs are $20,000.

Column 1 of the performance report shows actual results—based on the 10 pools installed. Operating income was $16,000 for June.

Column 3 is Pluto's flexible budget for the 10 pools actually installed. Operating income should have been $20,000.

Column 5 gives the static budget for the 8 pools expected for June. Pluto hoped to earn $12,000.

The budget variances appear in columns 2 and 4 of the exhibit. Let's begin with the static budget in column 5. These data come from Exhibit 23-2.

The flexible budget for 10 units is in column 3. The differences between the static budget and the flexible budget—column 4—arise only because Pluto installed 10 pools rather than 8 during June. Column 4 shows the sales volume variances. Operating income is favorable by $8,000 because Pluto installed 10 pools rather than 8.

Column 1 of Exhibit 23-4 gives the actual results for June—10 pools and operating income of $16,000. OOPS! Operating income is $4,000 less than Pluto would have expected for 10 pools. Why did operating income not measure up to the flexible budget?

- It wasn't because the selling price of swimming pools took a dive. Sales revenue was $1,000 more than expected for 10 pools.
- Variable costs were $3,000 too high for 10 pools.
- Fixed costs were $2,000 too high for 10 pools.

Overall, expenses rose by $5,000 above the flexible budget, while sales revenue was only $1,000 more than the budget. That's why operating income didn't measure up.

The static budget is developed *before* the period. The performance report in Exhibit 23-4 is not developed until the *end* of the period. Why? Because *flexible budgets used in performance reports are based on the actual number of outputs, and the actual outputs aren't known until the end of the period.*

Decision Guidelines

You and your roommate have started a business that prints T-shirts (for example, for school and student organizations). How can you use flexible budgets to plan and control your costs?

Decision	Guidelines
How to estimate sales revenue, costs, and profits over your relevant range?	Prepare a set of flexible budgets for different sales levels.
How to prepare a flexible budget for total costs?	$$\text{Total cost} = \left(\begin{array}{c} \text{Number} \\ \text{of T-shirts} \end{array} \times \begin{array}{c} \text{Variable cost} \\ \text{per T-shirt} \end{array} \right) + \begin{array}{c} \text{Fixed} \\ \text{cost} \end{array}$$
How to use budgets to help control costs?	Prepare an income statement performance report, as in Exhibit 23-4.
On which output level is the budget based?	Static (master) budget—*expected* number of T-shirts, estimated before the period Flexible budget—*actual* number of T-shirts, not known until the end of the period
Why does your actual income differ from budgeted income?	Prepare an income statement performance report comparing actual results, flexible budget for actual number of T-shirts sold, and static (master) budget, as in Exhibit 23-4.
• How much of the difference arises because the actual number of T-shirts sold doesn't equal budgeted sales?	Compute the sales volume variance (SVV) by comparing the flexible budget with the static budget. • Favorable SVV—Actual number of T-shirts sold > Expected number of T-shirts sold • Unfavorable SVV—Actual number of T-shirts sold < Expected number of T-shirts sold

• How much of the difference occurs because revenues and costs are not what they should have been for the actual number of T-shirts sold?	Compute the flexible budget variance (FBV) by comparing actual results with the flexible budget.
	• Favorable FBV—Actual sales revenue > Flexible budget sales revenue
	      Actual costs < Flexible budget costs
	• Unfavorable FBV—Actual sales revenue < Flexible budget sales revenue
	      Actual costs > Flexible budget costs

What actions can you take to avoid an unfavorable sales volume variance?	• Design more attractive T-shirts to increase demand. • Provide marketing incentives to increase number of T-shirts sold.
What actions can you take to avoid an unfavorable flexible budget variance?	• Avoid an unfavorable flexible budget variance for *sales revenue* by maintaining (not discounting) your selling price. • Avoid an unfavorable flexible budget variance for *costs* by controlling variable costs, such as the cost of the T-shirts, dye, and labor, and by controlling fixed costs.

Summary Problem 1

Exhibit 23-4 shows that Pluto Pools installed 10 swimming pools during June. Now assume that Pluto installed 7 pools (instead of 10) and that the actual sale price averaged $12,500 per pool. Actual variable costs were $57,400, and actual fixed costs were $19,000.

Requirements

1. Prepare a revised income statement performance report using Exhibit 23-4 as a guide.

2. As the company owner, which employees would you praise or criticize after you analyze this performance report?

Solution

Requirement 1

PLUTO POOLS
Income Statement Performance Report—Revised
Month Ended June 30, 2009

	1 Actual Results at Actual Prices	2 (1) – (3) Flexible Budget Variance	3 Flexible Budget for Actual Number of Output Units	4 (3) – (5) Sales Volume Variance	5 Static (Master) Budget
Output Units (pools installed)	7	0	7	1 U	8
Sales revenue	$87,500	$3,500 F	$84,000	$12,000 U	$96,000
Variable costs	57,400	1,400 U	56,000	8,000 F	64,000
Fixed costs	19,000	1,000 F	20,000	—	20,000
Total costs	76,400	400 U	76,000	8,000 F	84,000
Operating income	$11,100	$3,100 F	$ 8,000	$ 4,000 U	$12,000

Flexible budget variance, $3,100 F

Sales volume variance, $4,000 U

Static budget variance, $900 U

Requirement 2

As the company owner, you should determine the *causes* of the variances before praising or criticizing employees. It is especially important to determine whether the variance is due to factors the manager can control. For example,

- The unfavorable sales volume variance could be due to an ineffective sales staff. Or it could be due to a long period of rain that brought work to a standstill.
- The $1,000 favorable flexible budget variance for fixed costs could be due to an employee finding less expensive equipment. Or the savings might have come from delaying a needed overhaul of equipment that could decrease the company's costs in the long run.

Smart managers use variances to raise questions and direct attention, not to fix blame.

Standard Costing

3 Identify the benefits of standard costs and learn how to set standards

Most companies use **standard costs** to develop their flexible budgets. Think of a standard cost as a budget for a single unit. For example, Pluto Pools' standard variable cost is $8,000 per pool (Exhibit 23-2). This $8,000 variable cost includes the standard cost of inputs like the direct materials, direct labor, and variable overhead needed for one pool.

In a standard cost system, each input has both a quantity standard and a price standard. Pluto Pools has a standard for the following:

- Amount of gunite—a concrete derivative—used per pool (this determines the quantity standard)
- Price it pays per cubic foot of gunite (this determines the price standard)

Let's see how managers set these price and quantity standards.

Price Standards

The price standard for direct materials starts with the base purchase cost of each unit of inventory. Accountants help managers set a price standard for materials after considering early-pay discounts, freight in, and receiving costs.

World-class businesses demand continuous reductions in costs. This can be achieved several ways. You can work with suppliers to cut their costs. You can use the Internet to solicit price quotes from suppliers around the world, and you can share information.

For direct labor, accountants work with human resource managers to determine standard labor rates. They must consider basic pay rates, payroll taxes, and fringe benefits. Job descriptions reveal the level of experience needed for each task.

Accountants work with production managers to estimate manufacturing overhead costs. Production managers identify an appropriate allocation base such as direct labor hours or direct labor cost, as you learned in Chapter 19. Accountants then compute the standard overhead rates. Exhibit 23-5 summarizes the setting of standard costs.

EXHIBIT 23-5   Summary of Standard Setting Issues

	Price Standard	Quality Standard
Direct Materials	Responsibility: Purchasing manager Factors: Purchase price, discounts, delivery requirements, credit policy	Responsibility: Production manager and engineers Factors: Product specifications, spoilage, production scheduling
Direct Labor	Responsibility: Human resource managers Factors: Wage rate based on experience requirements, payroll taxes, fringe benefits	Responsibility: Production manager and engineers Factors: Time requirements for the production level of experience needed
Manufacturing Overhead	Responsibility: Production managers Factors: Nature and amount of resources needed for support activities (e.g., moving materials, maintaining equipment, and inspecting output)	

Application

Let's see how Pluto Pools might determine its cost standards for materials, labor, and overhead.

The manager in charge of purchasing for Pluto Pools indicates that the purchase price, net of discounts, is $1.90 per cubic foot of gunite. Delivery, receiving, and inspection add an average of $0.10 per cubic foot. Pluto's hourly wage for workers is $8 and payroll taxes and fringe benefits total $2.50 per direct labor hour. Variable and fixed overhead will total $6,400 and $9,600, respectively, and overhead is allocated based on 3,200 estimated direct labor hours.

Requirement

Compute Pluto Pools' cost standards for direct materials, direct labor, and overhead.

Answer

Direct materials price standard for gunite:

Purchase price, net of discounts	$1.90 per cubic foot
Delivery, receiving, and inspection	0.10 per cubic foot
Total standard cost per cubic foot of gunite	$2.00 per cubic foot

Direct labor price (or rate) standard:

Hourly wage	$ 8.00 per direct labor hour
Payroll taxes and fringe benefits..............................	2.50 per direct labor hour
Total standard cost per direct labor hour	$10.50 per direct labor hour

Variable overhead price (or rate) standard:

$$\frac{\text{Estimated variable overhead cost}}{\text{Estimated quantity of allocation base}} = \frac{\$6,400}{3,200 \text{ direct labor hours}}$$

$$= \$2.00 \text{ per direct labor hour}$$

Fixed overhead price (or rate) standard:

$$\frac{\text{Estimated fixed overhead cost}}{\text{Estimated quantity of allocation base}} = \frac{\$9,600}{3,200 \text{ direct labor hours}}$$

$$= \$3.00 \text{ per direct labor hour}$$

Quantity Standards

Production managers and engineers set direct material and direct labor *quantity standards*. To set its labor standards, Westinghouse Air Brake's Chicago plant analyzed every moment in the production of the brakes.

To eliminate unnecessary work, Westinghouse rearranged machines in tight U-shaped cells so that work could flow better. Workers no longer had to move parts all over the plant floor, as illustrated in this diagram.

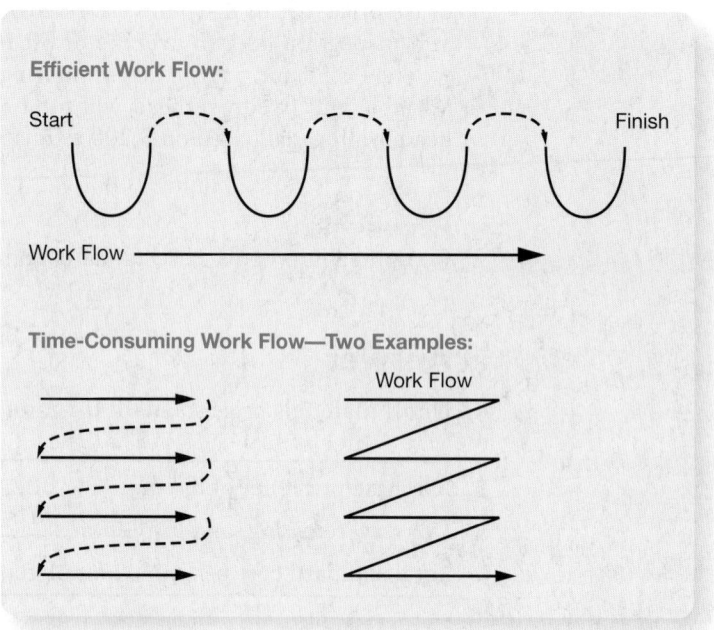

Westinghouse conducted time-and-motion studies to streamline various tasks. For example, the plant installed a conveyer at waist height to minimize bending and lifting. The result? Workers slashed one element of standard time by 90%.

Companies from Ritz-Carlton to Federal Express develop quantity standards based on "best practices." This is often called **benchmarking.** The *best practice* may be an internal benchmark from other plants or divisions within the company or it may be an external benchmark from other companies. Internal benchmarks are easy to obtain, but managers can also purchase external benchmark data. For example, Riverside Hospital in Columbus, Ohio, can compare its cost of performing an appendectomy with the "best practice" cost developed by a consulting firm that compares many different hospitals' costs for the same procedure.

Why Do Companies Use Standard Costs?

U.S. surveys show that more than 80% of responding companies use standard costing. Over half of responding companies in the United Kingdom, Ireland, Sweden, and Japan use standard costing. Why? Standard costing help managers:

- Prepare the budget
- Set target levels of performance
- Identify performance standards
- Set sales prices of products and services
- Decrease accounting costs

Standard cost systems might appear to be expensive. Indeed, the company must invest up front to develop the standards. But standards can save accounting costs. It is cheaper to value inventories at standard rather than actual costs. With standard costs, accountants avoid the LIFO, FIFO, or average-cost computations.

Variance Analysis

Once we establish standard costs, we can use the standards to assign costs to production. At least once a year, we will compare our actual production costs to the standards to locate variances. Exhibit 23-6 shows how to separate total variances for materials and labor into price and efficiency (quantity) variances. Study this exhibit carefully. It's used for the materials variances and the labor variances.

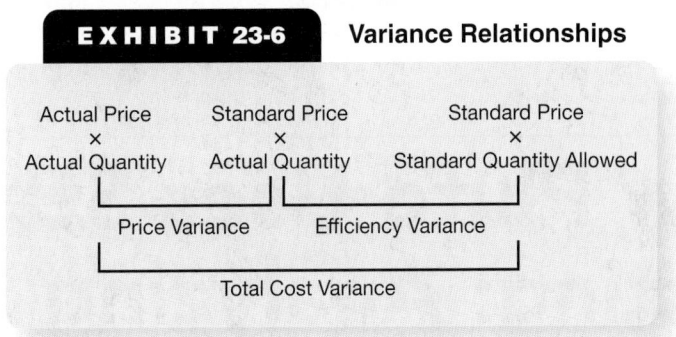

EXHIBIT 23-6   **Variance Relationships**

A **price variance** measures how well the business keeps unit prices of material and labor inputs within standards. As the name suggests, the price variance is the *difference in prices* (actual price per unit – standard price per unit) of an input, multiplied by the *actual quantity* of the input:

$$\text{Price Variance} = (\text{Actual Price} \times \text{Actual Quantity}) - (\text{Standard Price} \times \text{Actual Quantity})$$

$$\text{Or, Price Variance} = (\text{Actual Price} - \text{Standard Price}) \times \text{Actual Quantity}$$

$$= \quad (AP \quad - \quad SP) \quad \times \quad AQ$$

An **efficiency** or **quantity variance** measures how well the business uses its materials or human resources. The efficiency variance is the difference in quantities (actual quantity of input used – standard quantity of input allowed for the actual number of outputs) multiplied by the standard price per unit of the input:

$$\text{Efficiency Variance} = (\text{Standard Price} \times \text{Actual Quantity}) - (\text{Standard Price} \times \text{Standard Quantity})$$

$$\text{Or, Efficiency Variance} = (\text{Actual Quantity} - \text{Standard Quantity}) \times \text{Standard Price}$$

$$= \quad (AQ \quad - \quad SQ) \quad \times \quad SP$$

Exhibit 23-7 illustrates these variances and emphasizes two points.

- First, the price and efficiency variances sum to the flexible budget variance.
- Second, static budgets like column 5 of Exhibit 23-4 play no role in the price and efficiency variances.

The static budget is used only to compute the sales volume variance—never to compute the flexible budget variance or the price and efficiency cost variances for materials and labor.

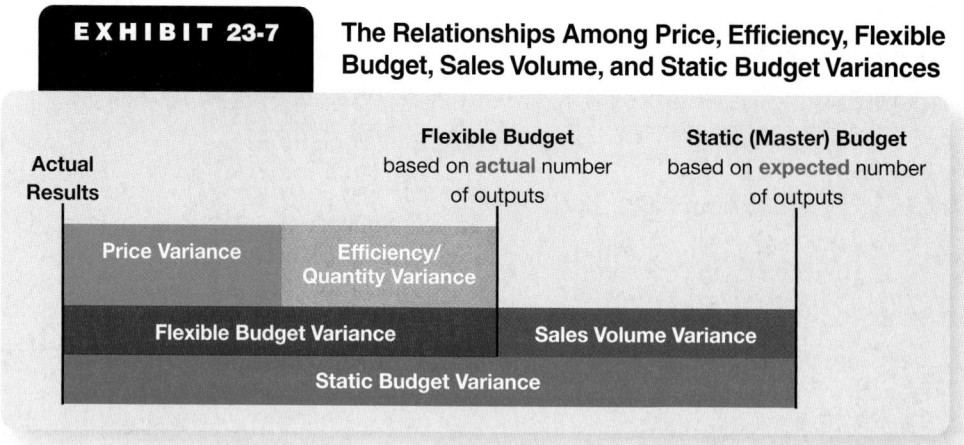

EXHIBIT 23-7 The Relationships Among Price, Efficiency, Flexible Budget, Sales Volume, and Static Budget Variances

How Pluto Uses Standard Costing: Analyzing the Flexible Budget Variance

4 Compute standard cost variances for direct materials and direct labor

Let's return to our Pluto Pools example. Exhibit 23-4 showed that the main cause for concern at Pluto is the $4,000 unfavorable flexible budget variance for total costs. The first step in identifying the causes of the cost variance is to identify the variable and fixed costs, as shown in Panel A of Exhibit 23-8.

Study Exhibit 23-8 carefully. Panel B shows how to compute the flexible budget amounts. Panel C shows how to compute actual materials and labor costs. Trace the following:

- Flexible budget amounts from Panel B to column (2) of Panel A
- Actual costs from Panel C to column (1) of Panel A

Column 3 of Panel A gives the flexible budget variances for direct materials and direct labor. For now, focus on materials and labor. We'll cover overhead later.

Direct Material Variances

Direct Materials Price Variance

Let's investigate the $2,800 unfavorable variance for direct materials. Recall that the direct materials standard price was $2.00 per cubic foot, and 10,000 cubic feet are needed for 10 pools (1,000 cubic feet per pool × 10 pools). The actual price of materials was $1.90 per cubic foot, and 12,000 cubic feet were actually used to make 10 pools. Using the formula, the **materials price variance** is $1,200 favorable. The calculation follows.

$$
\begin{aligned}
\text{Materials Price Variance} &= (\text{AP} - \text{SP}) \times \text{AQ} \\
&= (\$1.90 \text{ per cubic foot} - \$2.00 \text{ per cubic foot}) \times 12,000 \text{ cubic feet} \\
&= -\$0.10 \text{ per cubic foot} \times 12,000 \text{ cubic feet} \\
&= \$1,200 \text{ F}
\end{aligned}
$$

EXHIBIT 23-8 **Data for Standard Costing Example**

PANEL A—Comparison of Actual Results with Flexible Budget for 10 Swimming Pools

PLUTO POOLS
Data for Standard Costing Example
Month Ended June 30, 2009

	Actual Results at Actual Prices	Flexible Budget for 10 Pools	Flexible Budget Variance
Variable costs:			
Direct materials	$ 22,800*	$20,000†	$ 2,800 U
Direct labor	41,800*	42,000†	200 F
Variable overhead	9,000	8,000†	1,000 U
Marketing and administrative costs	9,400	10,000	600 F
Total variable costs	83,000	80,000	3,000 U
Fixed costs:			
Fixed overhead	12,300	9,600‡	2,700 U
Marketing and administrative expense	9,700	10,400	700 F
Total fixed costs	22,000	20,000	2,000 U
Total costs	$105,000	$100,000	$5,000 U

*See Panel C.
†See Panel B.
‡Fixed overhead was budgeted at $9,600 per month (Application Answer on page 1165).

PANEL B—Computation of Flexible Budget for Direct Materials, Direct Labor, and Variable Overhead for 7 Swimming Pools—Based on Standard Costs

	(1) Standard Quantity of Inputs Allowed for 10 Pools	(2) Standard Price per Unit of Input	(3) (1) × (2) Flexible Budget for 10 Pools
Direct materials	1,000 cubic feet per pool × 10 pools = 10,000 cubic feet	$ 2.00	$20,000
Direct labor	400 hours per pool × 10 pools = 4,000 hours	$10.50	42,000
Variable overhead	400 hours per pool × 10 pools = 4,000 hours	$ 2.00	8,000

PANEL C—Computation of Actual Costs for Direct Materials and Direct Labor for 10 Swimming Pools

	(1) Actual Quantity of Inputs Used for 10 Pools	(2) Actual Price per Unit of Input	(3) (1) × (2) Actual Cost for 10 Pools
Direct materials	12,000 cubic feet actually used	$1.90 actual cost/cubic foot	$22,800
Direct labor	3,800 hours actually used	$11.00 actual cost/hour	41,800

The $1,200 direct materials price variance is *favorable*, because the purchasing manager spent $0.10 *less* per cubic foot of gunite than budgeted ($1.90 actual price − $2.00 standard price). A negative amount means that the variance is favorable. A positive variance is unfavorable.

Direct Materials Efficiency Variance

Now let's see what portion of the unfavorable materials variance was due to the quantity used.

The standard quantity of inputs is the *quantity that should have been used* for the actual output. For Pluto, the *standard quantity of inputs (gunite) that workers should have used for the actual number of outputs* (10 pools) is:

1,000 cubic feet of gunite per pool × 10 pools installed = 10,000 cubic feet of gunite

Thus, the **direct materials efficiency variance** is:

$$
\begin{aligned}
\text{Direct Materials Efficiency Variance} &= (\text{AQ} - \text{SQ}) \times \text{SP} \\
&= (12{,}000 \text{ cubic feet} - 10{,}000 \text{ cubic feet}) \times \$2.00 \text{ per cubic foot} \\
&= +2{,}000 \text{ cubic feet} \times \$2.00 \text{ per cubic foot} \\
&= \$4{,}000 \text{ U}
\end{aligned}
$$

The $4,000 direct materials efficiency variance is *unfavorable*, because workers used 2,000 *more* cubic feet of gunite than they should have used on 10 pools. A positive amount means that the variance is unfavorable.

SUMMARY OF DIRECT MATERIAL VARIANCES Exhibit 23-9 summarizes how Pluto splits the $2,800 unfavorable direct materials flexible budget variance into price and efficiency effects.

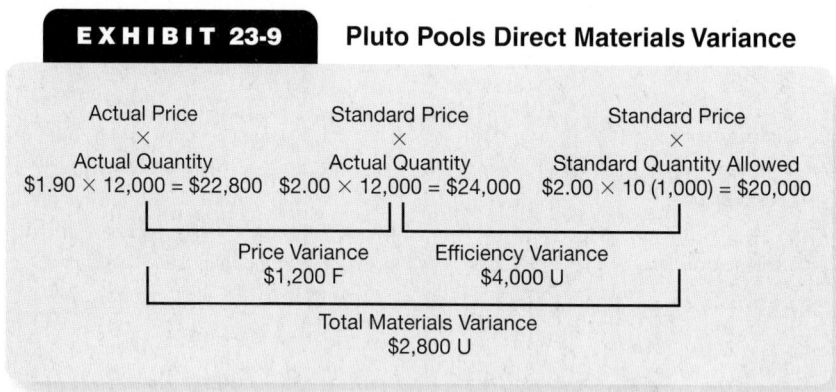

EXHIBIT 23-9 **Pluto Pools Direct Materials Variance**

In summary, Pluto spent $2,800 more than it should have for gunite because:

- A good price for the gunite increased profits by $1,200, but
- Inefficient use of the gunite reduced profits by $4,000.

Let's review who is responsible for each of these variances and consider why each variance may have occurred.

1. The purchasing manager is in the best position to explain the favorable price variance. Pluto's purchasing manager may have negotiated a good price for gunite.

2. The manager in charge of installing pools can explain why workers used so much gunite to install the 10 pools. Was the gunite of lower quality? Did workers waste materials? Did their equipment malfunction? Pluto's top management needs this information to decide what corrective action to take.

These variances raise questions that can help pinpoint problems. But be careful! A favorable variance doesn't always mean that a manager did a good job, nor does an unfavorable variance mean that a manager did a bad job. Perhaps Pluto's purchasing manager got a lower price by purchasing inferior-quality materials. This would lead to waste and spoilage. If so, the purchasing manager's decision hurt the company. This illustrates why good managers:

- Use variances as a guide for investigation rather than merely to assign blame
- Investigate favorable as well as unfavorable variances

Direct Labor Variances

Pluto uses a similar approach to analyze the direct labor flexible budget variance. Exhibit 23-10 shows how Pluto computes labor variances.

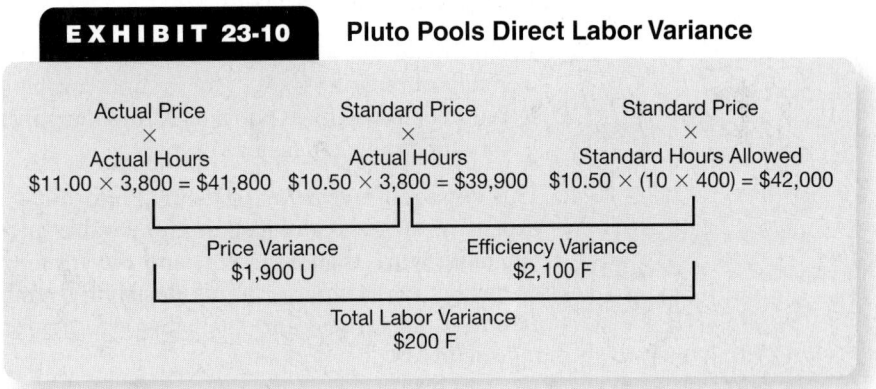

EXHIBIT 23-10   Pluto Pools Direct Labor Variance

Why did Pluto spend $200 less on labor than it should have used for 10 pools? To answer this question, Pluto computes the labor price and efficiency variances, in exactly the same way as it did for direct materials. Recall that the standard price for direct labor is $10.50 per hour, and 4,000 hours were budgeted for 10 pools (400 hours per pool × 10 pools). But actual direct labor cost was $11.00 per hour, and it took 3,800 hours to install 10 pools.

Direct Labor Price Variance

Using the formula, the **direct labor price variance** was $1,900 unfavorable. The calculation follows.

$$\text{Direct Labor Price Variance} = (AP - SP) \times AH$$
$$= (\$11.00 - \$10.50) \times 3,800 \text{ hours}$$
$$= \$1,900 \text{ U}$$

The $1,900 direct labor price variance is *unfavorable* because Pluto paid workers $0.50 *more* per hour than budgeted ($11.00 actual price − $10.50 standard price). The positive amount indicates an unfavorable variance.

DIRECT LABOR EFFICIENCY VARIANCE   Now let's see how efficiently Pluto used its labor. The *standard quantity of direct labor hours that workers should have used to install 10 pools* is:

400 direct labor hours per pool × 10 pools installed = 4,000 direct labor hours

Thus, the **direct labor efficiency variance** is:

$$
\begin{aligned}
\text{Direct Labor Efficiency Variance} &= (\text{AH} - \text{SH}) \times \text{SP} \\
&= (3{,}800 \text{ hours} - 4{,}000 \text{ hours}) \times \$10.50 \text{ per hour} \\
&= -200 \text{ hours} \times \$10.50 \\
&= -\$2{,}100 \text{ F}
\end{aligned}
$$

The \$2,100 direct labor efficiency variance is *favorable* because installers actually worked 200 *fewer* hours than the budget called for. If the calculation results in a negative amount, the variance is favorable.

SUMMARY OF DIRECT LABOR VARIANCES Exhibit 23-10 summarizes how Pluto computes the labor price and efficiency variances.

The \$200 favorable direct labor variance suggests that labor costs were close to expectations. But to manage Pluto Pools' labor costs, we need to "peel the onion" to gain more insight:

- Pluto paid its employees an average of \$11.00 per hour in June instead of the standard rate of \$10.50—for an unfavorable price variance.
- Workers installed 10 pools in 3,800 hours instead of the budgeted 4,000 hours— for a favorable efficiency variance.

This situation reveals a trade-off. Pluto hired more experienced (and thus more expensive) workers and had an unfavorable price variance. But the installers turned out more work than expected, and the strategy was successful. The overall effect on profits was favorable. This possibility reminds us that managers should take care in using variances to evaluate performance. Go slow. Analyze the data. Then take action.

Manufacturing Overhead Variances

5 Analyze manufacturing overhead in a standard cost system

In this section of the chapter we use the terms *manufacturing overhead* and *overhead* interchangeably. The total overhead variance is the difference between:

Actual overhead cost	and	Standard overhead allocated to production

Exhibit 23-8 shows that Pluto actually incurred \$21,300 of overhead: \$9,000 variable and \$12,300 fixed. The next step is to see how Pluto allocates overhead in a standard cost system.

Allocating Overhead in a Standard Cost System

In a standard costing system, the manufacturing overhead allocated to production is:

$$
\begin{array}{c}
\text{Overhead} \\
\text{allocated to production}
\end{array}
=
\begin{array}{c}
\text{Standard (predetermined)} \\
\text{overhead rate}
\end{array}
\times
\begin{array}{c}
\text{Standard quantity of} \\
\text{the allocation base} \\
\text{allowed for } \textit{actual} \\
\text{output}
\end{array}
$$

Let's begin by computing Pluto's standard overhead rate, as follows (data from page 1165):

$$\begin{aligned}\text{Standard overhead rate} &= \frac{\text{Budgeted manufacturing overhead cost}}{\text{Budgeted direct labor hours}} \\[6pt] &= \frac{\text{Variable overhead} + \text{Fixed overhead}}{\text{Budgeted direct labor hours}} \\[6pt] &= \frac{\$6,400 + \$9,600}{3,200 \text{ direct labor hours}} \\[6pt] &= \frac{\$6,400}{3,200} + \frac{\$9,600}{3,200} \\[6pt] &= \$2.00 \text{ variable} + \$3.00 \text{ fixed} \\[6pt] &= \$5.00 \text{ per direct labor hour}\end{aligned}$$

Now let's determine the standard quantity of direct labor hours that Pluto allowed for actual output (10 pools), as follows (data from Exhibit 23-8, Panel B):

$$\begin{aligned}\text{Standard quantity of direct labor hours for actual output} &= 400 \text{ hours per pool} \times 10 \text{ pools} \\[6pt] &= 4,000 \text{ direct labor hours}\end{aligned}$$

Thus, Pluto allocates the cost of overhead to production based on standard costs as follows:

$$\begin{aligned}\text{\textit{Standard} overhead allocated to production} &= \textit{Standard} \text{ overhead rate} \times \begin{array}{c}\textit{Standard} \text{ quantity of} \\ \text{the allocation base} \\ \text{allowed for \textit{actual} output}\end{array} \\[6pt] &= \$5.00 \text{ per hour} \quad \times 4,000 \text{ hours} \\[6pt] &= \$20,000\end{aligned}$$

Pluto computes its total overhead cost variance as follows:

$$\begin{aligned}\begin{array}{c}\text{Total overhead} \\ \text{variance}\end{array} &= \begin{array}{c}\text{Actual overhead cost} \\ \text{(Exhibit 23-8, Panel A)}\end{array} - \begin{array}{c}\text{Standard overhead allocated to production} \\ (\$4,000 \text{ hours} \times \$5.00 \text{ per hour})\end{array} \\[6pt] &= \qquad \$21,300^{*} \qquad - \qquad\qquad \$20,000 \\[6pt] &= \qquad \$1,300 \text{ U}\end{aligned}$$

*Variable ($9,000) + fixed ($12,300) = $21,300.

Pluto actually spent $1,300 more on overhead than it allocated to production. To see why this unfavorable variance occurred, Pluto "drills down" by splitting the total overhead variance into two components:

- The overhead flexible budget variance
- The production volume variance

Exhibit 23-11 shows the computation of the overhead variances, and the discussion that follows explains them.

Overhead Flexible Budget Variance

The **overhead flexible budget variance** tells how well managers controlled overhead costs. Pluto actually spent $21,300 on overhead ($9,000 variable + $12,300 fixed) to install the 10 pools. The flexible budget for 10 pools called for overhead of only

EXHIBIT 23-11	Manufacturing Overhead Variances

PLUTO POOLS
Manufacturing Overhead Variances
Month Ended June 30, 2009

	(1) Actual Overhead Cost (Exhibit 23-8)	(2) (1) – (3) Flexible Budget Overhead for Actual Output (Exhibit 23-8)	(3) Standard Overhead Allocated to Production for Actual Output (Rates from page 1173)
Variable overhead	$ 9,000	$ 8,000	$2.00 × 4,000 direct labor hours = $ 8,000
Fixed overhead	12,300	9,600	$3.00 × 4,000 direct labor hours = $12,000
Total overhead	$21,300	$17,600	$5.00 × 4,000 direct labor hours = $20,000
	Flexible budget variance, $3,700 U		*Production volume variance, $2,400 F*
	Total manufacturing overhead variance, $1,300 U		

$17,600 ($8,000 variable + $9,600 fixed). So Pluto's **overhead flexible budget variance** is computed as follows:

$$
\begin{aligned}
\text{Overhead Flexible} \atop \text{Budget Variance} &= \text{Actual overhead} \atop \text{cost} - \text{Flexible budget overhead} \atop \text{for actual output} \\
&= \quad \$21,300 \qquad\qquad \$17,600 \\
&= \quad \$3,700\,U
\end{aligned}
$$

Why did Pluto spend $3,700 more on overhead than it should have spent to install the 10 pools in June? You can see from Exhibit 23-11 that $1,000 ($9,000 − $8,000) of the variance is due to higher-than-expected spending on *variable* overhead. The remaining $2,700 ($12,300 − $9,600) is due to higher spending on *fixed* overhead. Pluto will investigate the reason for each of these variances.

Overhead Production Volume Variance

The second component of the total overhead variance is the **overhead production volume variance**. This variance arises when actual production differs from expected production. Pluto expected to install 8 pools during June, but actually installed 10. The **overhead production volume variance** is computed as follows:

$$
\begin{aligned}
\text{Overhead Production} \atop \text{Volume Variance} &= \text{Flexible budget overhead for} \atop \text{actual output (10 pools)} - \text{Standard overhead allocated to} \atop \text{(actual) production} \\
&= \quad \$17,600 \qquad\qquad\qquad \$20,000 \\
&\quad \text{(Exhibit 23-11, column 2)} \qquad \text{(Exhibit 23-11, column 3)} \\
&= \quad \$2,400\,F
\end{aligned}
$$

The production volume variance is favorable because Pluto's actual output (10 pools) exceeded expected output (8 pools). By installing 10 pools Pluto used its production capacity more fully than originally planned. If Pluto had installed 7 or fewer pools, the production volume variance would have been unfavorable because the company would have had unused production capacity.

Summary of Overhead Variances

Most companies compile cost information for the individual items of overhead, such as indirect materials, indirect labor, and utilities. Managers drill down by comparing actual to budgeted costs for each item. For example, Pluto's analysis might reveal that variable overhead costs were higher than expected because water rates increased or because workers used more water than expected. Perhaps spending on fixed overhead increased because Pluto purchased new equipment and its depreciation increased.

Standard Cost Accounting Systems

6 Record transactions at standard cost and prepare a standard cost income statement

Journal Entries

We use Pluto Pools' June transactions to demonstrate standard costing in a job costing context. Management needs to know about variances to address each problem. Therefore, Pluto records variances from standards as soon as possible. This means that Pluto records direct materials price variances when materials are purchased. It also means that Work in Process Inventory is debited (swimming pools are costed) at standard input quantities and standard prices. June's entries follow.

Purchase of direct materials

1.	Materials Inventory (12,000 cubic feet × $2.00)	24,000	
	Direct Materials Price Variance		1,200
	Accounts Payable (12,000 × $1.90)		22,800
	To record purchase of direct materials.		

The credit to Accounts Payable is for the *actual quantity* of gunite purchased (12,000 cubic feet) at the *actual price* ($1.90 per cubic foot). In contrast, the debit to Materials Inventory is recorded at the *standard price* ($2 per cubic foot). Maintaining Materials Inventory at the *standard price* ($2.00) allows Pluto to record the direct materials price variance at time of purchase. Recall that Pluto's direct materials price variance was $1,200 favorable (p. 1168). A favorable variance has a credit balance and is a contra expense. An unfavorable variance means extra expense and has a debit balance.

Use of direct materials

2.	Work in Process Inventory (10,000 cubic feet × $2.00)	20,000	
	Direct Materials Efficiency Variance	4,000	
	Materials Inventory (12,000 × $2.00)		24,000
	To record use of direct materials.		

Pluto debits Work in Process Inventory for the *standard cost* of the 10,000 cubic feet of direct materials that should have been used to install 10 pools. This maintains Work in Process Inventory at standard cost. Materials Inventory is credited for the *actual quantity* of materials put into production (12,000 cubic feet) costed at the *standard price*.

Pluto's direct materials efficiency variance was $4,000 unfavorable (page 1170). An unfavorable variance has a debit balance, which increases expense and decreases profits.

Direct labor cost incurred

3.	Manufacturing Wages (3,800 hours × $10.50)	39,900	
	Direct Labor Price Variance	1,900	
	Wages Payable (3,800 × $11.00)		41,800
	To record direct labor costs incurred.		

Manufacturing Wages is debited for the *standard price* ($10.50) of direct labor hours actually used (3,800). Wages Payable is credited for the *actual cost* (the *actual* hours worked at the *actual* wage rate) because this is the amount Pluto must pay the workers. The direct labor price variance is $1,900 unfavorable (page 1171), a debit amount.

Direct labor cost allocated to production

4.	Work in Process Inventory (4,000 hours × $10.50)	42,000	
	Direct Labor Efficiency Variance		2,100
	Manufacturing Wages (3,800 × $10.50)		39,900
	To allocate direct labor cost to production.		

Pluto debits Work in Process Inventory for the standard cost per direct labor hour ($10.50) that should have been used for 10 pools (4,000 hours), like direct materials entry 2. Manufacturing Wages is credited to close its prior debit balance. The direct labor efficiency variance is credited for the $2,100 favorable variance (page 1172). This maintains Work in Process Inventory at standard cost.

Actual overhead cost incurred

5.	Manufacturing Overhead (actual cost)	21,300	
	Accounts Payable, Accumulated		
	Depreciation, etc.		21,300
	To record actual overhead costs incurred (Exhibit 23-11).		

This entry records Pluto's actual overhead cost for June.

Overhead allocated to production

6.	Work in Process Inventory (4,000 hours × $5.00)	20,000	
	Manufacturing Overhead		20,000
	To allocate overhead to production (See Exhibit 23-11).		

In standard costing, the overhead allocated to Work in Process Inventory is computed as the standard overhead rate ($5.00 per hour) × standard quantity of the allocation base allowed for actual output (4,000 hours for 10 pools).

Completion of production

7.	Finished Goods Inventory	82,000	
	Work in Process Inventory		82,000
	To record completion of 10 pools ($20,000 of materials +		
	$42,000 of labor + $20,000 of manufacturing overhead),		
	all at standard cost.		

This entry transfers the standard cost of the 10 pools completed during June from Work in Process to Finished Goods.

Cost of sales

	8.	Cost of Goods Sold	82,000	
		Finished Goods Inventory		82,000
		To record the cost of sales of 10 pools, at standard cost.		

Close the overhead account

	9.	Overhead Flexible Budget Variance	3,700	
		Overhead Production Volume Variance		2,400
		Manufacturing Overhead		1,300
		To record overhead variances and close the Manufacturing		
		Overhead account. (Exhibit 23-11)		

Entry 9 closes the Manufacturing Overhead account and records the overhead variances. Exhibit 23-12 shows the relevant Pluto accounts after posting these entries.

EXHIBIT 23-12 **Pluto Pools' Flow of Costs in a Standard Costing System**

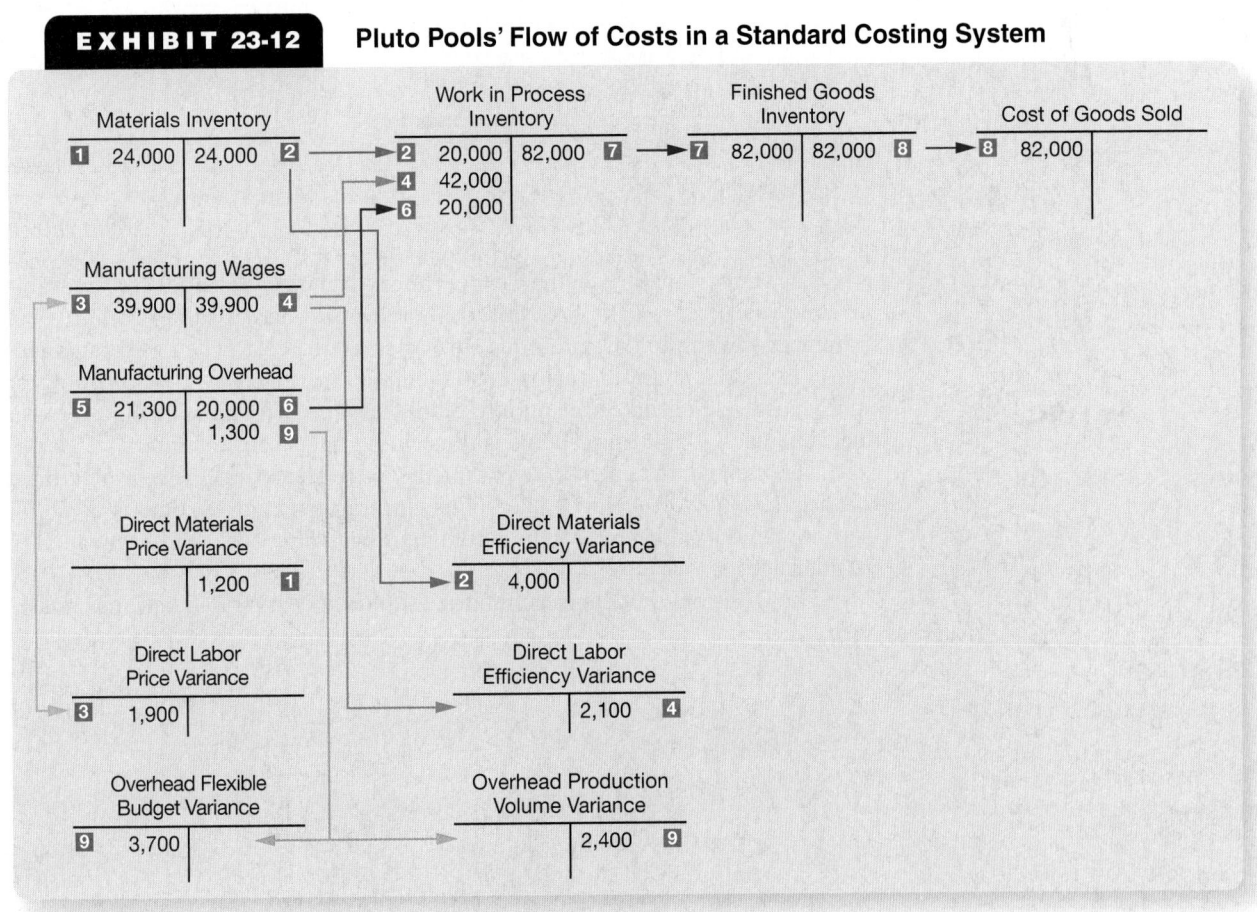

Standard Cost Income Statement for Management

Pluto Pools' top management needs to know about the company's cost variances. Exhibit 23-13 shows a standard cost income statement that highlights the variances for management.

EXHIBIT 23-13   **Standard Cost Income Statement**

PLUTO POOLS
Standard Cost Income Statement
Month Ended June 30, 2009

Sales revenue at standard (10 × $12,000)			$120,000
Sales revenue variance			1,000
Sales revenue at actual			121,000
Cost of goods sold at standard cost		$82,000	
Manufacturing cost variances (parentheses denote a credit balance):			
Direct materials price variance	$(1,200)		
Direct materials efficiency variance	4,000		
Direct labor rate variance	1,900		
Direct labor efficiency variance	(2,100)		
Overhead flexible budget variance	3,700		
Overhead production volume variance	(2,400)		
Total manufacturing variance		3,900	
Cost of goods sold at actual cost			85,900
Gross profit			35,100
Marketing and administrative expense*			(19,100)
Operating income			$ 16,000

*$9,400 + $9,700 from Exhibit 23-8, Panel A.

The statement starts with sales revenue at standard and adds the favorable sales revenue variance of $1,000 (Exhibit 23-4) to yield actual sales revenue. Next, the statement shows the cost of goods sold at standard cost. Then the statement separately lists each manufacturing cost variance, followed by cost of goods sold at actual cost. At the end of the period, all the variance accounts are closed to zero out their balances. Operating income is thus closed to Income Summary.

The income statement shows that the net effect of all the manufacturing cost variances is $3,900 unfavorable. Thus, June's operating income is $3,900 lower than it would have been if all the actual manufacturing costs had been equal to their standard costs.

The Decision Guidelines summarize standard costing and variance analysis.

Decision Guidelines

Now you've seen how managers use standard costs and variances to identify potential problems. Variances help managers see *why* actual costs differ from the budget.

This is the first step in determining how to correct problems. Let's review how Pluto Pools made some key decisions in setting up and using its standard cost system.

Decision	Guidelines
How to set standards?	Historical performance data
	Engineering analysis/time-and-motion studies
	Continuous improvement standards
	Benchmarking
How to compute a price variance for materials or labor?	$\text{Price variance} = \left(\begin{array}{c} \text{Actual price} \\ \text{per input unit} \end{array} - \begin{array}{c} \text{Standard price} \\ \text{per input unit} \end{array} \right) \times \begin{array}{c} \text{Actual} \\ \text{quantity} \\ \text{of input} \end{array}$
How to compute an efficiency variance for materials or labor?	$\text{Efficiency variance} = \left(\begin{array}{c} \text{Actual} \\ \text{quantity} \\ \text{of input} \end{array} - \begin{array}{c} \text{Standard quantity} \\ \text{of input for actual} \\ \text{output} \end{array} \right) \times \begin{array}{c} \text{Standard} \\ \text{price per} \\ \text{input unit} \end{array}$
Who is best able to explain a	
Sales volume variance?	Marketing Department
Sales revenue variance?	Marketing Department
Direct material price variance?	Purchasing Department
Direct material efficiency variance?	Production Department
Direct labor price variance?	Human Resources Department
Direct labor efficiency variance?	Production Department
How to allocate manufacturing overhead in a standard costing system?	$\begin{array}{c} \text{Manufacturing} \\ \text{overhead} \\ \text{allocated} \end{array} = \left(\begin{array}{c} \text{Standard} \\ \text{overhead rate} \end{array} \right) \times \left(\begin{array}{c} \text{Standard quantity of} \\ \text{allocation base allowed} \\ \text{for actual output} \end{array} \right)$
How to analyze over- or underallocated overhead?	Split over- or underallocated overhead into
	$\begin{array}{c} \text{Flexible} \\ \text{budget} \\ \text{variance} \end{array} = \begin{array}{c} \text{Actual} \\ \text{overhead} \end{array} - \begin{array}{c} \text{Flexible budget} \\ \text{overhead for} \\ \text{actual output} \end{array}$
	$\begin{array}{c} \text{Production} \\ \text{volume} \\ \text{variance} \end{array} = \begin{array}{c} \text{Flexible budget} \\ \text{overhead for} \\ \text{actual output} \end{array} - \begin{array}{c} \text{Standard overhead} \\ \text{allocated to} \\ \text{actual output} \end{array}$
How to record standard costs in the accounts?	Materials Inventory: Actual quantity at standard price
	Work in Process Inventory (and Finished Goods Inventory and Cost of Goods Sold): Standard quantity of inputs allowed for actual outputs, at standard price of inputs
How to analyze cost variances?	Debit balance → more expense
	Credit balance → less expense

Summary Problem 2

Exhibit 23-8 indicates that Pluto Pools installed 10 swimming pools in June. Suppose Pluto had installed 7 pools instead of 10 and that *actual costs* were

Direct materials (gunite).............	7,400 cubic feet @ $2.00 per cubic foot
Direct labor...............................	2,740 hours @ $10.00 per hour
Variable overhead.......................	$5,400
Fixed overhead...........................	$11,900

Requirements

1. Given these new data, prepare an exhibit similar to Exhibit 23-8. Ignore marketing and administrative expense.

2. Compute price and efficiency variances for direct materials and direct labor.

3. Compute the total variance, the flexible budget variance, and the production volume variance for manufacturing overhead. Standard total overhead allocated to production is $5.00 per direct labor hour.

Solution

Requirement 1

PANEL A—Comparison of Actual Results with Flexible Budget for 7 Swimming Pools

PLUTO POOLS
Revised Data for Standard Costing Example
Month Ended June 30, 2009

	Actual Results at Actual Prices	Flexible Budget for 7 Pools	Flexible Budget Variance
Variable costs:			
Direct materials	$14,800*	$14,000†	$ 800 U
Direct labor	27,400*	29,400†	2,000 F
Variable overhead	5,400	5,600†	200 F
Total variable costs	47,600	49,000	1,400 F
Fixed costs:			
Fixed overhead	11,900	9,600‡	2,300 U
Total costs	$59,500	$58,600	$ 900 U

*See Panel C.
†See Panel B.
‡Fixed overhead was budgeted at $9,600 per month

PANEL B—Computation of Flexible Budget for Direct Materials, Direct Labor, and Variable Overhead for 7 Swimming Pools—Based on Standard Costs

	(1) Standard Quantity of Inputs Allowed for 7 Pools	(2) Standard Price per Unit of Input	(3) (1) × (2) Flexible Budget for 10 Pools
Direct materials	1,000 cubic feet per pool × 7 pools = 7,000 cubic feet	$ 2.00	$14,000
Direct labor	400 hours per pool × 7 pools = 2,800 hours	$10.50	29,400
Variable overhead	400 hours per pool × 7 pools = 2,800 hours	$ 2.00	5,600

PANEL C—Computation of Actual Costs for Direct Materials and Direct Labor for 7 Swimming Pools

	(1) Actual Quantity of Inputs Used for 7 Pools	(2) Actual Price per Unit of Input	(3) (1) × (2) Actual Cost for 7 Pools
Direct materials	7,400 cubic feet actually used	$2.00 actual cost/cubic foot	$14,800
Direct labor	2,740 hours actually used	$10.00 actual cost/hour	27,400

Requirement 2

$$\text{Price variance} = \left(\begin{array}{c} \text{Actual price} \\ \text{per input unit} \end{array} - \begin{array}{c} \text{Standard price} \\ \text{per input unit} \end{array} \right) \times \begin{array}{c} \text{Actual quantity} \\ \text{of input} \end{array}$$

Direct materials:

$$\text{Price variance} = (\$2.00 - \$2.00) \times 7,400 \text{ cubic feet} = \$0$$

Direct labor:

$$\text{Rate variance} = (\$10.00 - \$10.50) \times 2,740 \text{ hours} = \$1,370 \text{ F}$$

$$\text{Efficiency variance} = \left(\begin{array}{c} \text{Actual quantity} \\ \text{of input} \end{array} - \begin{array}{c} \text{Standard quantity} \\ \text{of input} \end{array} \right) \times \begin{array}{c} \text{Standard price per} \\ \text{input unit} \end{array}$$

Direct materials:

$$\text{Efficiency variance} = \left(\begin{array}{c} 7,400 \\ \text{cubic feet} \end{array} - \begin{array}{c} 7,000 \\ \text{cubic feet} \end{array} \right) \times \begin{array}{c} \$2.00 \text{ per} \\ \text{cubic foot} \end{array} = \$800 \text{ U}$$

Direct labor:

$$\text{Efficiency variance} = \left(\begin{array}{c} 2,740 \\ \text{hours} \end{array} - \begin{array}{c} 2,800 \\ \text{hours} \end{array} \right) \times \begin{array}{c} \$10.50 \text{ per} \\ \text{hours} \end{array} = \$630 \text{ F}$$

Requirement 3

Total overhead variance:	
Actual overhead cost ($5,400 variable + $11,900 fixed)...............	$17,300
Standard overhead allocated to actual output (2,800 standard direct labor hours × $5.00)	14,000
Total overhead variance...	$ 3,300 U
Overhead flexible budget variance:	
Actual overhead cost ($5,400 + $11,900).....................................	$17,300
Flexible budget overhead for actual output ($5,600 + $9,600)........	15,200
Overhead flexible budget variance...	$ 2,100 U
Overhead production volume variance:	
Flexible budget overhead for actual output ($5,600 + $9,600)........	$15,200
Standard overhead allocated to actual output (2,800 standard direct labor hours × $5.00)	14,000
Overhead production volume variance	$ 1,200 U

Review Flexible Budgets and Standard Costs

Accounting Vocabulary

Benchmarking

Using standards based on "best practice." Best practice may be an internal benchmark or an external benchmark from other companies.

Efficiency (quantity) Variance

Measure whether the quantity of materials or labor use to make the actual number of outputs is within the standard allowed for that number of outputs. This is computed as the difference in quantities (actual quantity of input used minus standard quantity of input allowed for the actual number of outputs) multiplied by the standard price per unit of the input.

Flexible Budget

A summarized budget that managers can easily compute for several different volume levels. Flexible budgets separate variable costs from fixed costs; it is the variable costs that put the "flex" in the flexible budget.

Flexible Budget Variance

The difference arising because the company actually earned more or less revenue, or incurred more or less cost, than expected for the actual level of output. This equals the difference between the actual amount and a flexible budget amount.

Master Budget

The budget prepared for only one level of sales volume. Also called the **static budget**.

Overhead Flexible Budget Variance

Shows how well management has controlled overhead costs. It is the difference between the actual overhead cost and the flexible budget overhead for the actual number of outputs.

Price (rate) Variance

Measures how well the business keeps unit prices of material and labor inputs within standards. This is computed as the difference in prices (actual price per unit minus standard price per unit) of an input multiplied by the actual quantity of the input.

Production Volume Variance

Arises when actual production differs from expected production. It is the difference between (1) the manufacturing overhead cost in the flexible budget or actual outputs and (2) the standard overhead allocated to production.

Sales Volume Variance

The difference arising only because the number of units actually sold differs from the static budget units. This equals the difference between a static budget amount and a flexible budget amount.

Standard Cost

A budget for a single unit.

Static Budget

The budget prepared for only one level of sales volume. Also called the **master budget**.

Variance

The difference between an actual amount and the budget. A variance is labeled as favorable if it increases operating income and unfavorable if it decreases operating income.

Quick Check _____

Questions 1 through 4 rely on the following data. ProNet Systems is a start-up company that makes connectors for high-speed Internet connections. The company has budgeted variable costs of $130 for each connector and fixed costs of $8,000 per month.

ProNet's static budget predicted production and sales of 100 connectors in August, but the company actually produced and sold only 75 connectors at a total cost of $23,000.

1. ProNet's total flexible budget cost for 75 connectors per month is
   a. $8,130
   b. $9,750
   c. $13,000
   d. $17,750

2. ProNet's sales volume variance for total costs is
   a. $5,250 F
   b. $3,250 F
   c. $3,250 U
   d. $5,250 U

3. ProNet's flexible budget variance for total costs is
   a. $5,250 U
   b. $5,250 F
   c. $3,250 U
   d. $3,250 F

4. ProNet Systems' managers could set direct labor standards based on:
   a. Past actual performance
   b. Continuous improvement
   c. Benchmarking
   d. Time-and-motion studies
   e. Any of the above

Questions 5 through 7 rely on the following data. ProNet Systems has budgeted 3 hours of direct labor per connector, at a standard cost of $15 per hour. During January, technicians actually worked 210 hours completing the 75 connectors. ProNet paid the technicians $15.50 per hour.

5. What is ProNet's direct labor price variance for August?
   a. $37.50 U
   b. $112.50 U
   c. $105.00 U
   d. $120.00 U

6. What is ProNet's direct labor efficiency variance for August?
   a. $75.00 F
   b. $232.50 F
   c. $225.00 F
   d. $1,350.00 F

7. The journal entry to record ProNet's *use* of direct labor in August is
    a. Manufacturing Wages
       Direct Labor Efficiency Variance
          Work in Process Inventory
    b. Manufacturing Wages
          Direct Labor Efficiency Variance
       Work in Process Inventory
    c. Work in Process Inventory
       Direct Labor Efficiency Variance
          Manufacturing Wages
    d. Work in Process Inventory
          Direct Labor Efficiency Variance
          Manufacturing Wages

8. ProNet Systems allocates manufacturing overhead based on machine hours. Each connector should require 10 machine hours. According to the static budget, ProNet expected to incur:

    1,000 machine hours per month (100 connectors × 10 machine hours per connector)

    $5,250 in variable manufacturing overhead costs

    $8,000 in fixed manufacturing overhead costs

    During August, ProNet actually used 825 machine hours to make the 75 connectors. ProNet's predetermined standard *total* manufacturing overhead rate is
    a. $5.25 per machine hour
    b. $13.25 per machine hour
    c. $8.00 per machine hour
    d. $16.06 per machine hour

9. The total manufacturing overhead variance is composed of:
    a. Flexible budget variance and production volume variance
    b. Price variance and production volume variance
    c. Efficiency variance and production volume variance
    d. Price variance and efficiency variance

10. When ProNet *uses* direct materials, the amount of the debit to Work in Process Inventory is based on:
    a. Standard quantity of the materials allowed for actual production × Standard price per unit of the materials
    b. Standard quantity of the materials allowed for actual production × Actual price per unit of the materials
    c. Actual quantity of the materials used × Actual price per unit of the materials
    d. Actual quantity of the materials used × Standard price per unit of the materials

    Answers are given after Apply Your Knowledge (p. 1201).

Assess Your Progress

Short Exercises

Matching terms
1

S23-1 Match each of the following terms to the definitions below.

a. Flexible Budget

b. Flexible Budget Variance

c. Sales Volume Variance

d. Static Budget

e. Variance

_____ 1. The budget prepared for only one level of sales volume. (p. 1158)

_____ 2. The difference between an actual amount and the budget. (p. 1158)

_____ 3. A summarized budget for several levels of volume that separates variable costs from fixed costs. (p. 1159)

_____ 4. The difference arising only because the number of units actually sold differs from the static budget units. (p. 1160)

_____ 5. The difference arising because the company actually earned more or less revenue, or incurred more or less cost, than expected for the actual level of output. (p. 1160)

Matching terms
2

S23-2 Match each of the following terms to the definitions below.

a. Benchmarking

b. Efficiency Variance

c. Overhead Flexible Budget Variance

d. Price Variance

e. Production Volume Variance

f. Standard Cost

_____ 1. A budget for a single unit. (p. 1164)

_____ 2. Using standards based on "best practice." (p. 1166)

_____ 3. Measures how well the business keeps unit prices of material and labor inputs within standards. (p. 1167)

_____ 4. Measures whether the quantity of materials or labor used to make the actual number of outputs is within the standard allowed for that number of outputs. (p. 1167)

_____ 5. Shows how well management has controlled overhead costs. (p. 1173)

_____ 6. Arises when actual production differs from expected production. (p. 1174)

Flexible budget preparation
1

S23-3 Boje, Inc. manufactures travel locks. The budgeted selling price is $15 per lock, the variable cost is $10 per lock, and budgeted fixed costs are $15,000. Prepare a flexible budget for output levels of 4,000 locks and 6,000 locks for the month ended April 30, 2007. (p. 1159)

Flexible budget variance
2

S23-4 Complete the flexible budget variance analysis for Boje, Inc. by filling in the blanks in the following partial Income Statement Performance Report for 5,000 travel locks. (p. 1161)

continued . . .

BOJE, INC. Income Statement Performance Report Month Ended April 30, 2007			
	Actual Results at Actual Prices	**Flexible Budget Variance**	**Flexible Budget for Actual Number of Output Units**
Output units	5,000	_____	5,000
Sales revenue	$80,000	_____	$75,000
Variable costs	52,000	_____	50,000
Fixed costs	16,000	_____	15,000
Total costs	68,000	_____	65,000
Operating income	$12,000	_____	$10,000

Static budgets and flexible budgets

1 **2**

S23-5 Fill in the blanks with the phrase that best completes the sentence.

Actual number of outputs	Beginning of the period	Static budget variance
Expected number of outputs	End of the period	
Sales volume variance	Flexible budget variance	

a. The static budget is developed at the _____. (p. 1158)

b. The flexible budget used in an income statement performance report is based on the _____. (pp. 1159, 1160)

c. The master budget is based on the _____. (p. 1158)

d. The flexible budget used in an income statement performance report is developed at the _____. (pp. 1160, 1161)

e. The difference between actual costs and the costs that should have been incurred for the actual number of outputs is the _____. (p. 1160)

Calculate materials variances

4

S23-6 Longman, Inc. is a manufacturer of lead crystal glasses. The standard materials quantity is 1 pound per glass at a price of $0.40 per pound. The actual results for the production of 7,000 glasses was 1.1 pound per glass, at a price of $0.50 per pound. Calculate the materials price variance and the materials efficiency variance. (pp. 1168–1170)

Calculate labor variances

4

S23-7 Longman, Inc. manufactures lead crystal glasses. The standard direct labor time is 1/5 hour per glass, at a price of $14 per hour. The actual results for the production of 7,000 glasses was 1/4 hour, at a price of $13 per hour. Calculate the labor price variance and the labor efficiency variance. (pp. 1171–1172)

Interpreting material and labor variances

4

S23-8 Refer to S23-6 and S23-7. For each variance, who in Longman's organization is most likely responsible? Interpret the direct materials and direct labor variances for Longman's management. (pp. 1168–1172)

S23-9 Longman, Inc. manufactures lead crystal glasses. The following information relates to the company's overhead costs:

Static budget variable overhead	$7,000
Static budget fixed overhead	$3,000
Static budget direct labor hours	1,000 hours
Static budget number of glasses	5,000

Longman allocates manufacturing overhead to production based on standard direct labor hours. Last month, Longman reported the following actual results for the production of 7,000 glasses: actual variable overhead, $10,400; actual fixed overhead, $2,800. Compute the standard variable overhead rate and the standard fixed overhead rate. (p. 1174)

S23-10 Refer to the Longman data in S23-9. Compute the overhead variances. (Use Exhibit 23-11 on p. 1174 as a guide.)

S23-11 The following materials variance analysis was performed for Longman. Record Longman's direct materials journal entries. (p. 1175)

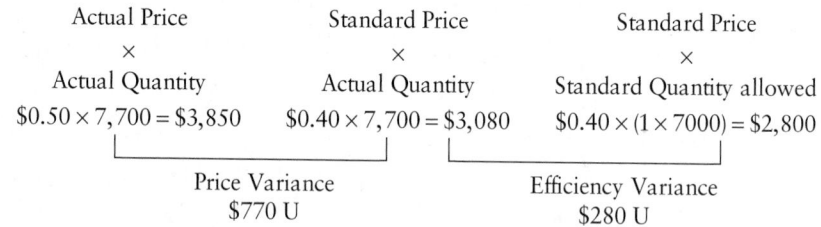

S23-12 The following labor variance analysis was performed for Longman. Record Longman's direct labor journal entries. (p. 1176)

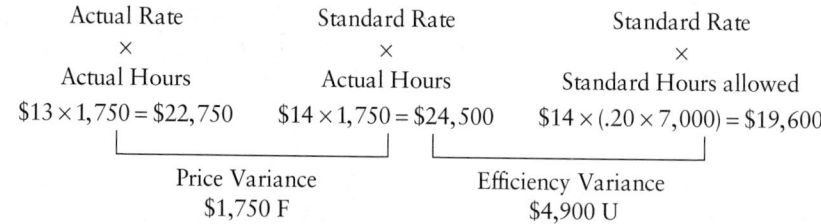

S23-13 Longman completed 70,000 glasses in 2008, at a standard cost of $364,000. The company sold all of them on account at a sale price of $8.00 each. There were no beginning or ending inventories of any kind. Record the journal entries for the completion and sale of the 70,000 glasses. (p. 1176)

S23-14 Use the following information to prepare a standard cost income statement for Longman, using Exhibit 23-13 on page 1178 as a guide. Remember that unfavorable variances are added to cost of goods sold.

Cost of goods sold $364,000

Direct labor price variance $48,000 U

Direct materials efficiency variance $2,800 U

Overhead flexible budget variance $3,000 U

continued . . .

Direct labor efficiency
variance $17,500 F

Sales Revenue $560,000

Marketing and administrative
costs were $75,000

Direct materials price
variance $7,700 U

Production volume
variance $12,000 F

Exercises

Prepare a flexible budget

E23-15 ErgoNow sells its main product, ergonomic mouse pads, for $11 each. Its variable cost is $5.20 per pad. Fixed costs are $200,000 per month for volumes up to 60,000 pads. Above 60,000 pads, monthly fixed costs are $250,000. Prepare a monthly flexible budget for the product, showing sales revenue, variable costs, fixed costs, and operating income for volume levels of 40,000, 50,000, and 70,000 pads. (p. 1159)

Prepare an income statement
performance report

2

E23-16 Ranger Pro Company managers received the following incomplete performance report: (p. 1161)

RANGER PRO COMPANY
Income Statement Performance Report
Year Ended July 31, 2009

	Actual Results at Actual Prices	Flexible Budget Variance	Flexible Budget for Actual Number of Output Units	Sales Volume Variance	Static (Master) Budget
Output units	36,000	——	36,000	4,000 F	——
Sales revenue	$216,000	——	$216,000	$24,000 F	——
Variable costs	84,000	——	80,000	9,000 U	——
Fixed costs	106,000	——	100,000	0	——
Total costs	190,000	——	180,000	9,000 U	——
Operating income	$ 26,000	——	$ 36,000	$15,000 F	——

Complete the performance report. Identify the employee group that may deserve praise and the group that may be subject to criticism. Give your reasons.

Prepare an income statement
performance report

2

E23-17 Top managers of Kyler Industries predicted 2008 sales of 14,500 units of its product at a unit price of $8. Actual sales for the year were 14,000 units at $9.50 each. Variable costs were budgeted at $2.20 per unit, and actual variable costs were $2.30 per unit. Actual fixed costs of $42,000 exceeded budgeted fixed costs by $2,000. Prepare Kyler's income statement performance report in a format similar to that of Exercise E23-16. What variance contributed most to the year's favorable results? What caused this variance? (p. 1161)

Calculate materials and
labor variances

E23-18 Urieta, Inc. produced 1,000 units of the company's product in 2009. The standard quantity of materials was 3 yards of cloth per unit at a standard price of $1 per yard. The accounting records showed that 2,800 yards of

continued . . .

cloth were used and the company paid $1.10 per yard. Standard time was 2 direct labor hours per unit at a standard rate of $5 per direct labor hour. Employees worked 1,500 hours and were paid $4.75 per hour. Calculate the materials price variance and the materials efficiency variance, as well as the labor price and efficiency variances. (pp. 1168, 1170–1172)

E23-19 The following direct materials variance computations are incomplete:

Calculate materials variances
4

$$\text{Price variance} = (\$? - \$10) \times 9{,}600 \text{ pounds} = \$4{,}800 \text{ U}$$
$$\text{Efficiency variance} = (? - 10{,}400 \text{ pounds}) \times \$10 = ? \text{ F}$$
$$\text{Flexible budget variance} = \$?$$

Fill in the missing values, and identify the flexible budget variance as favorable or unfavorable. (pp. 1168, 1170)

Calculate materials and labor variances
4

E23-20 Great Fender, which uses a standard cost accounting system, manufactured 20,000 boat fenders during the year, using 145,000 feet of extruded vinyl purchased at $1.05 per foot. Production required 450 direct labor hours that cost $14.00 per hour. The materials standard was 7 feet of vinyl per fender, at a standard cost of $1.10 per foot. The labor standard was 0.025 direct labor hour per fender, at a standard price of $13.00 per hour. Compute the price and efficiency variances for direct materials and direct labor. Does the pattern of variances suggest Great Fender's managers have been making trade-offs? Explain. (pp. 1168, 1170, 1172)

Prepare journal entries
6

E23-21 Make the journal entries to record the purchase and use of direct materials and direct labor in E23-20. (pp. 1175, 1176)

Prepare a standard cost income statement
6

E23-22 The managers of Ennis DVD Co., a contract manufacturer of DVD drives, are seeking explanations for the variances in the following report. Explain the meaning of each of Ennis's materials, labor, and overhead variances. (p. 1178)

ENNIS DVD CO. Standard Cost Income Statement Year Ended December 31, 2007		
Sales revenue		$1,200,000
Cost of goods sold at standard cost		700,000
Manufacturing cost variances:		
Direct materials price variance	$10,000 F	
Direct materials efficiency variance	32,000 U	
Direct labor price variance	24,000 F	
Direct labor efficiency variance	10,000 U	
Overhead flexible budget variance	28,000 U	
Production volume variance	8,000 F	
Total manufacturing variances		28,000
Cost of goods sold at actual cost		728,000
Gross profit		472,000
Marketing and administrative costs		418,000
Operating income		$ 54,000

Compute overhead variances

5

E23-23 Tulsa Paint Company's budgeted production volume for the month was 30,000 gallons of paint. The standard overhead cost included $0.50 variable overhead per gallon and fixed overhead costs of $30,000.

Tulsa Paint actually produced 33,000 gallons of paint. Actual variable overhead was $16,200, and fixed overhead was $31,000. Compute the total overhead variance, the overhead flexible budget variance, and the production volume variance. (pp. 1173, 1174)

Prepare a standard cost income statement

5

E23-24 The May 2008 revenue and cost information for Odessa Outfitters, Inc., follows:

Sales revenue	$560,000
Cost of goods sold (standard)	342,000
Direct materials price variance	1,000 F
Direct materials efficiency variance	6,000 F
Direct labor price variance	4,000 U
Direct labor efficiency variance	2,000 F
Overhead flexible budget variance	3,500 U
Production volume variance	8,000 F

Prepare a standard cost income statement for management through gross profit. (p. 1178) Report all standard cost variances for management's use. Has management done a good or poor job of controlling costs? Explain.

Problems (Group A)

Prepare an income statement performance report

2

P23-25A Cellular Technologies manufactures capacitors for cellular base stations and other communications applications. The company's March 2009 flexible budget income statements show output levels of 7,500, 9,000, and 11,000 units. The static budget was based on expected sales of 9,000 units.

CELLULAR TECHNOLOGIES
Flexible Budget Income Statement
Month Ended March 31, 2009

	Flexible Budget per Output Unit	Output Units (Capacitors)		
		7,500	9,000	11,000
Sales revenue	23	$172,500	$207,000	$253,000
Variable costs	12	90,000	108,000	132,000
Fixed costs		54,000	54,000	54,000
Total costs		144,000	162,000	186,000
Operating income		$ 28,500	$ 45,000	$ 67,000

continued . . .

The company sold 11,000 units during March, and its actual operating income was as follows:

CELLULAR TECHNOLOGIES
Income Statement
Month Ended March 31, 2009

Sales revenue	$257,000
Variable costs	134,250
Fixed costs	55,575
Total costs	189,825
Operating income	$ 67,175

Requirements

1. Prepare an income statement performance report for March. (p. 1161)

2. What was the effect on Cellular Technologies' operating income of selling 2,000 units more than the static budget level of sales? (p. 1159)

3. What is Cellular Technologies' static budget variance? (p. 1158) Explain why the income statement performance report provides more useful information to Cellular Technologies' managers than the simple static budget variance. (p. 1161) What insights can Cellular Technologies' managers draw from this performance report?

Preparing a flexible budget and computing standard cost variances

P23-26A Rocky Recliners manufactures leather recliners and uses flexible budgeting and a standard cost system. Rocky allocates overhead based on yards of direct materials. The company's performance report includes the following selected data:

	Static Budget (1,000 recliners)	Actual Results (980 recliners)
Sales (1,000 recliners × $500)	$500,000	
(980 recliners × $490)		$480,200
Variable manufacturing costs:		
Direct materials (6,000 yds. × $8.90)	53,400	
(6,150 yds. × $8.70)		53,505
Direct labor (10,000 hrs. × $9.00)	90,000	
(9,600 hrs. × $9.15)		87,840
Variable overhead (6,000 yds. × $5.00)	30,000	
(6,150 yds. × $6.40)		39,360
Fixed manufacturing costs:		
Fixed overhead	60,000	62,000
Total cost of goods sold	233,400	242,705
Gross profit	$266,600	$237,495

continued . . .

1. Prepare a flexible budget based on the actual number of recliners sold. (p. 1159)

2. Compute the price variance and the efficiency variance for direct materials and for direct labor. (pp. 1168, 1170) For manufacturing overhead, compute the total variance, the flexible budget variance, and the production volume variance. (pp. 1173–1174)

3. Have Rocky's managers done a good job or a poor job controlling materials and labor costs? Why?

4. Describe how Rocky's managers can benefit from the standard costing system. (p. 1166)

Using incomplete cost and variance information to determine the number of direct labor hours worked

P23-27A Samantha's Shades manufactures lamp shades. Samantha Sanders, the manager, uses standard costs to judge performance. Recently, a clerk mistakenly threw away some of the records, and Sanders has only partial data for October. She knows that the direct labor flexible budget variance for the month was $1,050 U, the standard labor rate was $9 per hour, and the actual labor rate was $9.50 per hour. The standard direct labor hours for the actual October output were 4,475.

Requirements

1. Find the actual number of direct labor hours worked during October. First, calculate the standard labor cost. Next, calculate the actual labor cost by adding the unfavorable flexible budget variance of $1,050 to the standard labor cost. Finally, divide the actual labor cost by the actual labor rate per hour. (p. 1171)

2. Compute the direct labor price and efficiency variances. Do these variances suggest the manager may have made a trade-off? Explain. (pp. 1171–1172)

Computing and journalizing standard cost variances

P23-28A Bria manufactures coffee mugs that it sells to other companies for customizing with their own logos. Bria prepares flexible budgets and uses a standard cost system to control manufacturing costs. The standard unit cost of a coffee mug is based on static budget volume of 60,000 coffee mugs per month:

Direct materials (0.2 lbs. @ $0.25 per lb.)		$0.05
Direct labor (3 minutes @ $0.12 per minute)		0.36
Manufacturing overhead:		
Variable (3 minutes @ $0.06 per minute)	$0.18	
Fixed (3 minutes @ $0.14 per minute)	0.42	0.60
Total cost per coffee mug		$1.01

Actual cost and production information for July:

a. Actual production and sales were 62,700 coffee mugs.

b. Actual direct materials usage was 12,000 lbs., at an actual price of $0.18 per lb.

continued . . .

c. Actual direct labor usage of 200,000 minutes at a total cost of $30,000.

d. Actual overhead cost was $40,800.

Requirements

1. Compute the price and efficiency variances for direct materials and direct labor. (pp. 1168, 1170)

2. Journalize the usage of direct materials and the assignment of direct labor, including the related variances. (pp. 1175–1177)

3. For manufacturing overhead, compute the total variance, the flexible budget variance, and the production volume variance. (*Hint:* Remember that the fixed overhead in the flexible budget equals the fixed overhead in the static budget.) (pp. 1173–1174)

4. Bria intentionally hired more-skilled workers during July. How did this decision affect the cost variances? Overall, was the decision wise? (p. 1170)

Computing standard cost
variances and reporting to
management

P23-29A HeadSmart manufactures headphone cases. During September 2008, the company produced and sold 106,000 cases and recorded the following cost data:

Standard Cost Information:

	Quantity	Price
Direct materials	2 parts	$0.16 per part
Direct labor	0.02 hours	$8.00 per hour
Variable manufacturing overhead	0.02 hours	$10.00 per hour

Fixed manufacturing overhead ($32,000 for static budget volume of 100,000 units and 2,000 hours, or $16 per hour).

Actual Information:

Direct materials (220,000 parts @ $0.21 per part = $46,200)

Direct labor (1,700 hrs. @ $8.10 per hr. = $13,770)

Manufacturing overhead $60,500

Requirements

1. Compute the price and efficiency variances for direct materials and direct labor. (pp. 1168, 1170)

2. For manufacturing overhead, compute the total variance, the flexible budget variance, and the production volume variance. (pp. 1173, 1174)

3. Prepare a standard cost income statement through gross profit to report all variances to management. Sale price of the headset cases was $1.50 each. (p. 1178)

4. HeadSmart's management used more-experienced workers during September. Discuss the trade-off between the two direct labor variances. (pp. 1170, 1171)

Problems (Group B)

Prepare an income statement performance report

2

P23-30B Nambe Clay, Inc., produces clay products for art in elementary school art programs. The company's flexible budget income statement for January 2009 shows output levels of 55,000, 60,000, and 65,000 clay kits. The static budget was based on 55,000 units.

NAMBE CLAY, INC.
Flexible Budget Income Statement
Month Ended January 31, 2009

	Flexible Budget per Output Unit	Output Units (kits)		
		55,000	60,000	65,000
Sales revenue	$3.00	$165,000	$180,000	$195,000
Variable costs	1.50	82,500	90,000	97,500
Fixed costs		70,000	70,000	70,000
Total costs		152,500	160,000	167,500
Operating income		$ 12,500	$ 20,000	$ 27,500

The company sold 60,000 clay kits during January 2009. Its actual operating income was as follows:

NAMBE CLAY, INC.
Income Statement
Month Ended January 31, 2009

Sales revenue	$185,000
Variable costs	$ 95,000
Fixed costs	69,000
Total costs	164,000
Operating income	$ 21,000

Requirements

1. Prepare an income statement performance report for January 2009. (p. 1161)
2. What accounts for most of the difference between actual operating income and static budget operating income? (p. 1159)
3. What is Nambe's static budget variance? (p. 1158) Explain why the income statement performance report provides Nambe's managers with more useful information than the simple static budget variance. (p. 1160) What insights can Nambe's managers draw from this performance report?

Preparing a flexible budget
and computing standard
cost variances

P23-31B Dawkins Co. assembles PCs and uses flexible budgeting and a standard cost system. Dawkins allocates overhead based on the number of direct materials parts. The company's performance report includes the following selected data:

	Static Budget (20,000 PCs)	Actual Results (22,000 PCs)
Sales (20,000 PCs × $400)	$8,000,000	
(22,000 PCs × $420)		$9,240,000
Variable manufacturing costs:		
Direct materials (200,000 parts @ $10.00)	2,000,000	
(214,200 parts @ $9.80)		2,099,160
Direct labor (40,000 hrs. @ $14.00)	560,000	
(41,000 hrs. @ $14.60)		598,600
Variable overhead (200,000 parts @ $4.00)	800,000	
(214,200 parts @ $4.10)		878,220
Fixed manufacturing costs:		
Fixed overhead	900,000	930,000
Total cost of goods sold	4,260,000	4,505,980
Gross profit	$3,740,000	$4,734,020

Requirements

1. Prepare a flexible budget based on the actual number of PCs sold. (p. 1159)

2. Compute the price variance and the efficiency variance for direct materials and for direct labor. (pp. 1168, 1170) For manufacturing overhead, compute the total variance, the flexible budget variance, and the production volume variance. (pp. 1173, 1174)

3. Have Dawkins's managers done a good job or a poor job controlling materials and labor costs? Why?

4. Describe how Dawkins's managers can benefit from the standard costing system. (p. 1166)

Using incomplete cost and
variance information to
determine the number of
direct labor hours worked

4

P23-32B Petra's Music manufactures harmonicas. Petra uses standard costs to judge performance. Recently, a clerk mistakenly threw away some of the records, and Petra has only partial data for October. She knows that the direct labor flexible budget variance for the month was $2,050 F and that the standard labor rate was $10 per hour. The actual labor rate was $9.50 per hour. The standard direct labor hours for actual October output were 6,000.

Requirements

1. Find the actual number of direct labor hours worked during October. First, calculate the standard labor cost. Next, calculate the actual labor cost by subtracting the favorable flexible budget variance of $2,050 from the standard labor cost. Finally, divide the actual labor cost by the actual labor rate per hour. (p. 1172)

2. Compute the direct labor price and efficiency variances. Do these variances suggest the manager may have made a trade-off? Explain. (pp. 1171–1172)

Computing and journalizing
standard cost variances

P23-33B Mancini manufactures embroidered jackets. The company prepares flexible budgets and uses a standard cost system to control manufacturing costs. The standard unit cost of a jacket is based on static budget volume of 14,000 jackets per month:

Direct materials (3.0 sq. ft @ $4.00 per sq. ft)		$12.00
Direct labor (2 hours @ $9.40 per hour)		18.80
Manufacturing overhead:		
Variable (2 hours @ $0.65 per hour)	$1.30	
Fixed (2 hours @ $2.20 per hour)	4.40	5.70
Total cost per jacket		$36.50

Actual cost and production information:

a. Actual production was 13,600 jackets.

b. Actual direct materials usage was 2.8 square feet per jacket, at an actual price of $4.10 per square foot.

c. Actual direct labor usage of 25,000 hours at a total cost of $237,500.

d. Total actual overhead cost was $79,000.

Requirements

1. Compute the price and efficiency variances for direct materials and direct labor. (pp. 1168, 1170)

2. Journalize the usage of direct materials and the assignment of direct labor, including the related variances. (pp. 1175, 1177)

3. For manufacturing overhead, compute the total variance, the flexible budget variance, and the production volume variance. (*Hint:* Remember that the fixed overhead in the flexible budget equals the fixed overhead in the static budget.) (pp. 1173, 1174)

4. Mancini's management intentionally purchased superior materials for November production. How did this decision affect the cost variances? Overall, was the decision wise? (p. 1171)

Computing standard cost
variances and reporting to
management

P23-34B Pecos Pecan Pads makes pressed pecan wood covers to prevent weed growth. During July 2009, the company produced and sold 44,000 rolls and recorded the following cost data:

STANDARD COST INFORMATION:

	Quantity	Price
Direct materials	3 lbs.	$1.10 per lb.
Direct labor	0.10 hours	$9.00 per hour
Variable manufacturing overhead	0.10 hours	$18.00 per hour
Fixed manufacturing overhead ($96,000 for static budget volume of 40,000 units and 4,000 hours, or $24 per hour)		

continued . . .

ACTUAL INFORMATION:

Direct materials (135,000 lbs. @ $1.00 per lb. = $135,000)

Direct labor (4,500 hrs. @ $8.75 per hr. = $39,375)

Manufacturing overhead $168,800

Requirements

1. Compute the price and efficiency variances for direct materials and direct labor. (pp. 1168, 1170)

2. For manufacturing overhead, compute the total variance, the flexible budget variance, and the production volume variance. (pp. 1173, 1174)

3. Prepare a standard cost income statement through gross profit to report all variances to management. Sale price was $10.60 per roll. (p. 1178)

4. Pecos intentionally purchased cheaper materials during July. Was the decision wise? Discuss the trade-off between the two materials variances. (p. 1170)

Apply Your Knowledge

Decision Cases

Prepare an income statement performance report

2

Case 1. Movies Galore distributes DVDs to movie retailers, including dot.coms. Movies Galore's top management meets monthly to evaluate the company's performance. Controller Allen Walsh prepared the following performance report for the meeting.

MOVIES GALORE
Income Statement Performance Report
Month Ended July 31, 2008

	Actual Results	Static Budget	Variance
Sales revenue	$1,640,000	$1,960,000	$320,000 U
Variable costs:			
Cost of goods sold	775,000	980,000	205,000 F
Sales commisions	77,000	107,800	30,800 F
Shipping cost	43,000	53,900	10,900 F
Fixed costs:			
Salary cost	311,000	300,500	10,500 U
Depreciation cost	209,000	214,000	5,000 F
Rent cost	129,000	108,250	20,750 U
Advertising cost	81,000	68,500	12,500 U
Total costs	1,625,000	1,832,950	207,950 F
Operating income	$ 15,000	$ 127,050	$112,050 U

Walsh also revealed that the actual sale price of $20 per movie was equal to the budgeted sale price and that there were no changes in inventories for the month.

Management is disappointed by the operating income results. CEO Jilinda Robinson exclaims, "How can actual operating income be roughly 12% of the static budget amount when there are so many favorable variances?"

Requirements

1. Prepare a more informative performance report. Be sure to include a flexible budget for the actual number of DVDs bought and sold. (p. 1161)

2. As a member of Movies Galore's management team, which variances would you want investigated? Why?

3. Robinson believes that many consumers are postponing purchases of new movies until after the introduction of a new format for recordable DVD players. In light of this information, how would you rate the company's performance?

Compute standard cost variances for direct materials and direct labor

4

Case 2. Suppose you manage the local Scoopy's ice cream parlor. In addition to selling ice cream cones, you make large batches of a few flavors of milk shakes to sell throughout the day. Your parlor is chosen to test the company's "Made-for-You" system. This new system enables patrons to customize their milk shakes by choosing different flavors.

Customers like the new system and your staff appears to be adapting, but you wonder whether this new made-to-order system is as efficient as the old system in which you just made a few large batches. Efficiency is a special concern because your performance is evaluated in part on the restaurant's efficient use of materials and labor. Your superiors consider efficiency variances greater than 5% to be unacceptable.

You decide to look at your sales for a typical day. You find that the parlor used 390 lbs. of ice cream and 72 hours of direct labor to produce and sell 2,000 shakes. The standard quantity allowed for a shake is 0.2 pounds of ice cream and 0.03 hours (1.8 minutes) of direct labor. The standard prices are $1.50 per pound for ice cream and $8 an hour for labor.

Requirements

1. Compute the efficiency variances for direct labor and direct materials. (pp. 1168–1170, 1171–1172)

2. Provide likely explanations for the variances. Do you have reason to be concerned about your performance evaluation? Explain.

3. Write a memo to Scoopy's national office explaining your concern and suggesting a remedy. Your memo should take the following form:

Date: _____

To: Scoopy's National Office

From: _____

Subject: "Made-for-You" System

Ethical Issues

Rita Lane is the accountant for Outdoor Living, a manufacturer of outdoor furniture that is sold through specialty stores and Internet companies. Lane is responsible for reviewing the standard costs. While reviewing the standards for the coming year, two ethical issues arise. Use the IMA's ethical guidelines, page xx, to identify the ethical dilemma in each situation. Identify the relevant factors in each situation and suggest what Lane should recommend to the controller.

Issue 1. Lane has been approached by Casey Henderson, a former colleague who worked with Lane when they were both employed by a public accounting firm. Henderson has recently started his own firm, Henderson Benchmarking Associates, which collects and sells data on industry benchmarks. He offers to provide Lane with benchmarks for the outdoor furniture industry free of charge if she will provide him with the last three years of Outdoor Living's standard and actual costs. Henderson explains that this is how he obtains most of his firm's benchmarking data. Lane always has a difficult time with the standard-setting process and believes that the benchmark data would be very useful.

Issue 2. Outdoor Living's management is starting a continuous improvement policy that requires a 10% reduction in standard costs each year for the next three years. Dan Jacobs, manufacturing foreman of the Teak furniture line, asks Lane to set loose standard costs this year before the continuous improvement policy is implemented. Jacobs argues that there is no other way to meet the tightening standards while maintaining the high quality of the Teak line.

Team Project

Lynx Corp. manufactures wood windows and doors. Lynx has been using a standard cost system that bases price and quantity standards on Lynx's historical long-run average performance. Suppose Lynx's controller has engaged your team of management consultants to advise her whether Lynx should use some basis other than historical performance for setting standards.

1. List the types of variances you recommend that Lynx compute (for example, direct materials price variance for glass). (pp. 1168, 1170, 1173–1174) For each variance, what specific standards would Lynx need to develop? (pp. 1164–1167) In addition to cost standards, do you recommend that Lynx develop any nonfinancial standards?

2. There are many approaches to setting standards other than simply using long-run average historical prices and quantities.
   a. List three alternative approaches that Lynx could use to set standards, and explain how Lynx could implement each alternative. (pp. 1165–1166)
   b. Evaluate each alternative method of setting standards, including the pros and cons of each method.
   c. Write a memo to Lynx's controller detailing your recommendations. First, should Lynx retain its historical data-based standard cost approach? If not, which of the alternative approaches should it adopt? Use the following format for your memo:

Date: _____

To: Controller, Lynx Corporation

From: _____ , Management Consultants

Subject: Standard Costs

For Internet Exercises, Excel in Practice, and additional online activities, go to the Web site, www.prenhall.com/horngren.

Quick Check

1. *d*   2. *b*   3. *a*   4. *e*   5. *c*   6. *c*   7. *d*   8. *b*   9. *a*   10. *a*

24 Activity-Based Costing and Other Cost Management Tools

Learning Objectives

1 Develop activity-based costs (ABC)

2 Use activity-based management (ABM) to achieve target costs

3 Describe a just-in-time (JIT) production system, and record its transactions

4 Use the four types of quality costs to make decisions

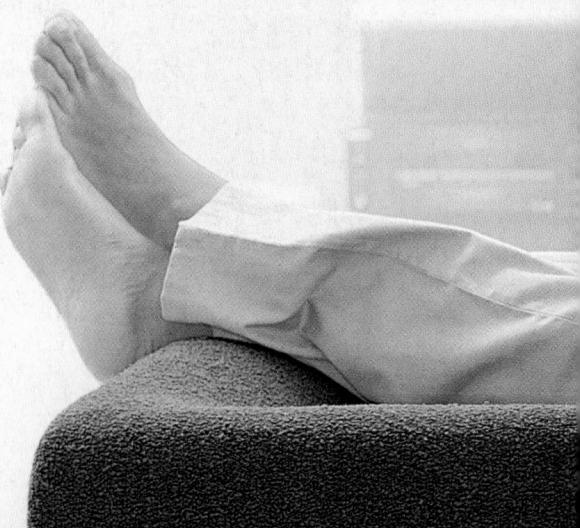

David Larimer, Matt Sewell, and Brian Jobe are college friends who share an apartment. They split the following monthly costs equally:

Rent and utilities	$570
Cable TV	50
High-speed Internet access	40
Groceries	240
Total monthly costs	$900

Each roommate's share is $300 ($900/3).

Things go smoothly the first few months. But then David calls a meeting. "Since I started having dinner at Amy's, I shouldn't have to pay a full share for the groceries." Matt then pipes in: "I'm so busy surfing the Net that I never have time to watch TV. I don't want to pay for the cable TV any more. And Brian, since your friend Jennifer eats here most evenings, you should pay a double share of the grocery bill." Brian retorts, "Matt, then you should pay for the Internet access, since you're the only one around here who uses it!"

What happened? The friends originally shared the costs equally. But they are not participating equally in eating, watching TV, and surfing the Net. Splitting these costs equally isn't the best arrangement.

The roommates could better match their costs with the people who participate in each activity. This means splitting cable TV between David and Brian,

letting Matt pay for Internet access, and allocating the grocery bill 1/3 to Matt and 2/3 to Brian. Exhibit 24-1 compares the results of this refined system with the original system.

| **EXHIBIT 24-1** | **More-Refined Versus Less-Refined Cost Allocation System** |

	David	Matt	Brian
More-refined cost allocation system:			
Rent and utilities	$190	$190	$190
Cable TV	25	—	25
High-speed Internet access	—	40	—
Groceries	—	80	160
Total costs allocated	$215	$310	$375
Original cost allocation system	$300	$300	$300
Difference	$ (85)	$ 10	$ 75

No wonder David called the meeting! The original system cost him $300 a month, but under the refined system David pays only $215. ▪

Fedex, PepsiCo, and Intel face situations like this every day. What's the best way to allocate our costs to the things we do? The stakes are high—friendships for David, Matt, and Brian and profits and losses for companies.

Refining Cost Systems

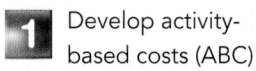

1 Develop activity-based costs (ABC)

Sharpening the Focus: Assigning Costs Based on the Activities That Caused the Costs

Let's illustrate cost refinement by looking at Dell, the computer company. In today's competitive market, Dell needs to know what it costs to make a laptop. The cost information helps Dell set a selling price to cover costs and provide a profit. To remain competitive with Gateway and HP, Dell must hold costs down.

We've seen that direct costs (materials and labor) are easy to assign to products. But indirect costs (utilities, supervisor salaries, and plant depreciation) are another story. It's the indirect costs—and they are significant—that cause the headaches. One way to manage costs is to refine the way indirect costs are allocated. Exhibit 24-2 provides an example. The first column of Exhibit 24-2 starts with Dell's production function—making the computers. Production is where most companies begin refining their cost systems.

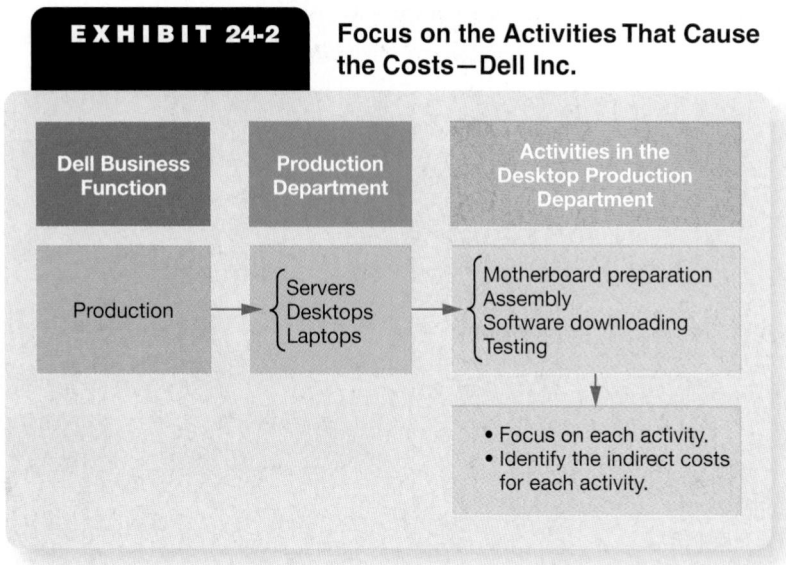

EXHIBIT 24-2 Focus on the Activities That Cause the Costs—Dell Inc.

Before business got so competitive, managers could limit their focus to a broad business function such as production, and use a single plantwide rate to allocate manufacturing overhead cost to their inventory.

But today's environment calls for more refined cost accounting. Managers need better data to set prices and identify the most profitable products. They drill down to focus on the costs incurred by each activity within the production function, as shown in the lower right of Exhibit 24-2. This has led to a better way to allocate indirect cost to production, and it's called activity-based costing.

Activity-Based Costing

Activity-based costing (ABC) focuses on *activities*. The costs of those activities become the building blocks for measuring the costs of products and services. Companies like Dell, Coca-Cola, and American Express use ABC.

Each activity has its own (usually unique) cost driver. For example, Dell allocates indirect assembly costs to computers based on the number of times a worker touches the computer as it moves through assembly. Computers that require more touches cost more to manufacture. Exhibit 24-3 shows some representative activities and cost drivers for Dell.

Developing an Activity-Based Costing System

The main difference between ABC and traditional systems is that ABC uses a separate allocation rate for each activity. ABC requires four steps, as outlined in Exhibit 24-4.

The first step in developing an activity-based costing system is to identify the activities. Analyzing all the activities required for a product or service forces managers to think about how each activity might be improved—or whether it's necessary at all.

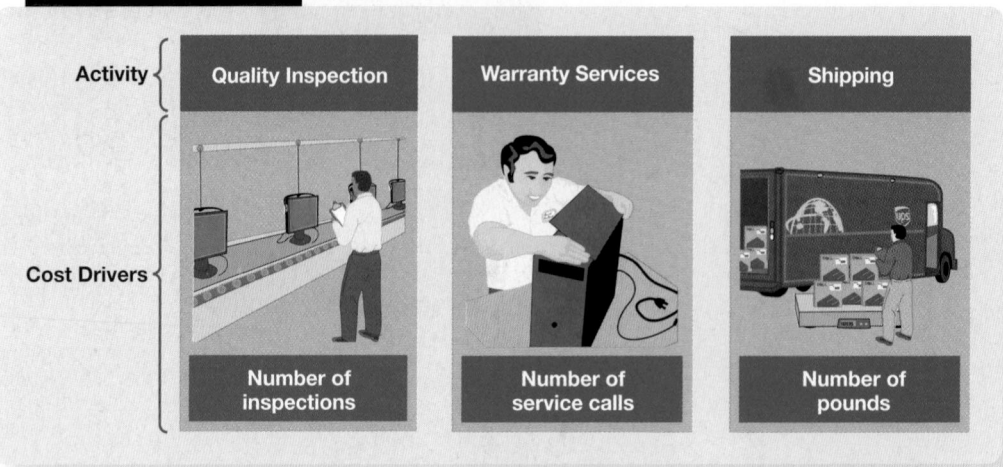

EXHIBIT 24-3   Activities and Cost Drivers

Activity: Quality Inspection | Warranty Services | Shipping

Cost Drivers: Number of inspections | Number of service calls | Number of pounds

EXHIBIT 24-4   Activity-Based Costing in Four Easy Steps

ABC Step	Application
1. Identify each activity and estimate its total indirect cost.	Activity Customer service Estimated total indirect cost per year $60,000
2. Identify the cost driver for each activity and estimate the total quantity of each drivers allocation base.	Cost driver for customer service Phone calls Estimated total number of customer- service phone calls each year 40,000
3. Compute the cost allocation rate for each activity. $$\text{Cost allocation rate} = \frac{\text{Estimated total indirect cost}}{\text{Estimated total quantity of the allocation base}}$$	$$\text{Cost allocation rate} = \frac{\$60,000}{40,000 \text{ calls}} = \$1.50 \text{ per call}$$
4. Allocate indirect costs to the cost object— in this case, all the customer-service calls during April. $$\text{Allocated activity cost} = \text{Cost allocation rate} \times \text{Actual quantity of the allocation base}$$	$$\text{Cost of customer service for April} = \$1.50 \text{ per call} \times \frac{3,000 \text{ calls}}{\text{during April}}$$ $$= \underline{\$4,500}$$

Traditional Versus Activity-Based Costing Systems: Fischer Chemical Company

To illustrate an ABC system, we use Fischer Chemical Company. Fischer produces hundreds of different chemicals, including mass quantities of "commodity" chemicals for large companies such as Xerox and Goodyear, and small quantities of "specialty" chemicals for others.

We begin with a traditional cost system to show its weakness. The ABC system that follows is clearly superior.

A Traditional Cost System

Fischer Chemical's cost system allocates all manufacturing overhead the traditional way—based on a single allocation rate: 200% of direct labor cost. Fischer's controller, Martha Wise, gathered data for two of the company's products:

- Aldehyde—a *commodity* chemical used in a wide range of plastics
- Phenylephrine hydrochloride (PH)—a *specialty* chemical (A single customer uses PH in blood-pressure medications.)

Based on Fischer's traditional cost system, Wise computed each product's gross profit as shown in Exhibit 24-5.

EXHIBIT 24-5 Fischer's Traditional Cost System— Manufacturing Cost and Gross Profit

	Aldehyde	PH
Sale price per pound	$12.00	$70.00
Less: Manufacturing cost per pound:		
Direct materials	5.00	14.00
Direct labor	1.00	12.00
Manufacturing overhead		
(at 200% of direct labor cost)	2.00	24.00
Total manufacturing cost per pound	8.00	50.00
Gross profit per pound	$4.00	$20.00

The gross profit for the PH chemical is $20 per pound—5 times as high as the gross profit for the aldehyde ($4). Fischer CEO Randy Smith is surprised that PH appears so much more profitable. He asks Wise to check this out. Wise confirms that the gross profit per pound is 5 times as high for PH. Smith wonders whether Fischer should produce more PH chemicals.

Smith

Based on recent activity, here's how Fischer Chemicals allocated overhead cost to each pound of product:

Aldehyde (7,500 pounds @ $2 per pound)	$15,000
PH (5 pounds @ $24 per pound)	$ 120

Key Point: Because direct labor cost is the single allocation base for all products, Fischer allocates far more total overhead cost to aldehyde than to PH. This costing is accurate only if direct labor really is the overhead cost driver, and only if aldehyde really does cause more overhead than PH.

CEO Smith calls a meeting with production foreman Steve Pronai and controller Wise. Smith is perplexed: The accounting numbers show that PH is much more profitable (on a per-pound basis) than aldehyde. He expected aldehyde to be more efficient because it's produced in a few large batches. By contrast, PH is produced in many small batches.

Wise fears that the problem could be Fischer's cost accounting system. Wise suggests that foreman Pronai work with her to develop a pilot ABC system. Exhibit 24-6 compares the traditional single-allocation-base system (Panel A) to the new ABC system that Wise's team developed (Panel B).

EXHIBIT 24-6 Overview of Fischer's Traditional and ABC Systems

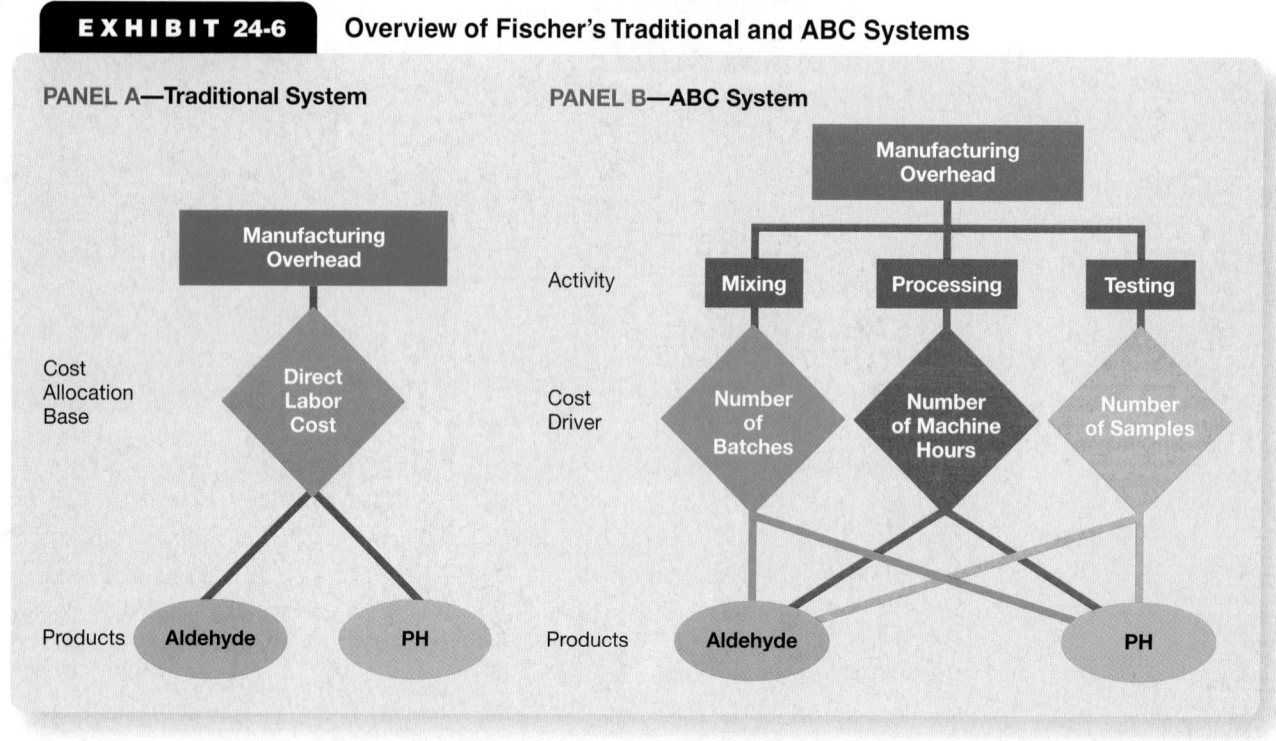

Activity-Based Cost System

Panel B of Exhibit 24-6 shows that Fischer's ABC team identifies three activities: mixing, processing, and testing. Each activity has its own cost driver. But exactly how does ABC work? The ABC team develops the new system by following the four steps described in Exhibit 24-4.

Let's see how an ABC system works, with a focus on the mixing activity. Exhibit 24-7 develops Fischer's ABC system. Follow the details of each step. Make sure you understand exactly how each ABC step applies to Fischer's mixing process.

Controller Wise then uses the ABC costs allocated to aldehyde and to PH (from Exhibit 24-7) to recompute manufacturing overhead costs, as shown in Exhibit 24-8. For each product, Wise adds the total costs of mixing, processing, and testing. She then divides each product's total manufacturing overhead cost by the number of pounds produced to get the overhead cost per pound.

EXHIBIT 24-7 Fischer's ABC System

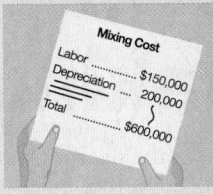

Step 1: Identify activities and estimate their total indirect costs.

Controller Wise's team identifies all the manufacturing activities. Focus on Mixing.

Foreman Pronai estimates total Mixing cost at $600,000.

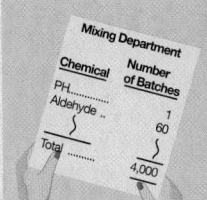

Step 2: Identify the cost driver for each activity.
Then estimate the total quantity of each driver's allocation base.

The allocation base for each activity should be its cost driver. The number of batches drive Mixing costs.

Wise and Pronai estimate the Mixing Department will produce 4,000 batches.

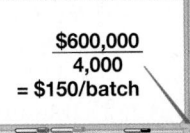

Step 3: Compute the allocation rate for each activity.

Wise computes the allocation rate for Mixing as follows:

$$\text{Cost allocation rate} = \frac{\$600,000}{4,000 \text{ batches}} = \$150 \text{ per batch}$$

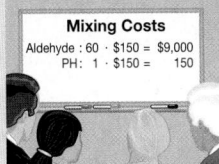

Step 4: Allocate indirect costs to the cost object—batches of chemicals in this case.

Wise allocates Mixing costs as follows:

Aldehyde:	60 batches × $150 per batch	= $9,000
PH:	1 batch × $150 per batch	= $ 150

Activity-based costs are more accurate because ABC considers the resources each product actually uses. Focus on the bottom line of Exhibit 24-8. Manufacturing overhead cost of:

- Aldehyde is $1.68 per pound, which is less than the $2.00 cost under the old system (shown in color in Exhibit 24-5).
- PH is $110 per pound, which far exceeds the $24 cost under the old system (shown in color in Exhibit 24-5).

EXHIBIT 24-8 Fischer's Manufacturing Overhead Costs Under ABC

Manufacturing Overhead Costs	Aldehyde	PH
Mixing (from Exhibit 24-7)	$ 9,000	$150
Processing (amounts assumed)	1,600	170
Testing (amounts assumed)	2,000	230
Total manufacturing overhead cost	$12,600	$550
Divide by number of pounds (bottom of page 1207)	÷ 7,500 lb	÷ 5 lb
Manufacturing overhead cost per pound	$ 1.68/lb	$110/lb

Now that we know the indirect costs of aldehyde and PH under ABC, let's see how Fischer's managers *use* the ABC cost information to make better decisions.

Activity-Based Management: Using ABC for Decision Making

2 Use activity-based management (ABM) to achieve target costs

Activity-based management (ABM) uses activity-based costs to make decisions that increase profits while meeting customer needs. We show how Fischer can use ABC in two kinds of decisions:

1. Pricing and product mix
2. Cost cutting

Pricing and Product Mix Decisions

Controller Wise now knows the ABC manufacturing overhead cost per pound (Exhibit 24-8). To determine which products are the most profitable, she recomputes each product's total manufacturing cost and gross profit. Panel A of Exhibit 24-9 shows that the total manufacturing cost per pound of aldehyde is $7.68 under the ABC system. Contrast this with the $8.00 cost per pound under Fischer's traditional cost system, as shown in Panel B. More important, the ABC data in Panel A show that PH costs $130 per pound, rather than the $50 per pound indicated by the old system (Panel B). Fischer has been losing $60 on each pound of PH—and this is *before* R&D, marketing, and distribution expenses! It seems that PH chemicals are dragging the company down.

EXHIBIT 24-9   **Comparison of Fischer's Manufacturing Product Costs Under ABC and Traditional Systems**

PANEL A—Total Manufacturing Cost and Gross Profit Under ABC

	Aldehyde	PH
Sale price per pound	$12.00	$ 70.00
Less: Manufacturing cost per pound:		
Direct materials	$ 5.00	$ 15.00
Direct labor	1.00	5.00
Manufacturing overhead (from Exhibit 24-8)	1.68	110.00
Total manufacturing cost	7.68	130.00
Gross profit (loss) per pound	$ 4.32	$(60.00)

PANEL B—Total Manufacturing Cost and Gross Profit Under the Traditional Cost System (Exhibit 24-5)

	Aldehyde	PH
Sale price per pound	$12.00	$70.00
Less: Manufacturing cost per pound	8.00	50.00
Gross profit per pound	$ 4.00	$20.00

This illustration shows that ABC is often the best way to measure the cost of manufacturing a product. ABC therefore helps businesses set the selling prices of their products. The selling price must cover *all* costs—both manufacturing costs and operating expenses—plus provide a profit.

As you'll see in the next section, Fischer may be able to use ABC to cut costs. If Fischer can't cut costs enough to earn a profit on PH, then Fischer may have to raise the sale price. If customers won't pay more, Fischer may have to drop PH. *This is the exact opposite of the strategy suggested by cost data from the traditional system. That system favored PH.*

Cutting Costs

Most companies adopt ABC to get better product costs for pricing and product-mix decisions. But they often benefit more by cutting costs. ABC and value engineering can work together. **Value engineering** means reevaluating activities to reduce costs. It requires these cross-functional teams:

- Marketers to identify customer needs
- Engineers to design more efficient products
- Accountants to estimate costs

Why are managers turning to value engineering? Because it gets results. Companies like General Motors and Carrier Corporation are following Japanese automakers Toyota and Nissan and setting sale prices based on **target prices**—what customers are willing to pay for the product or service. Exhibit 24-10 provides an example. Study each column separately.

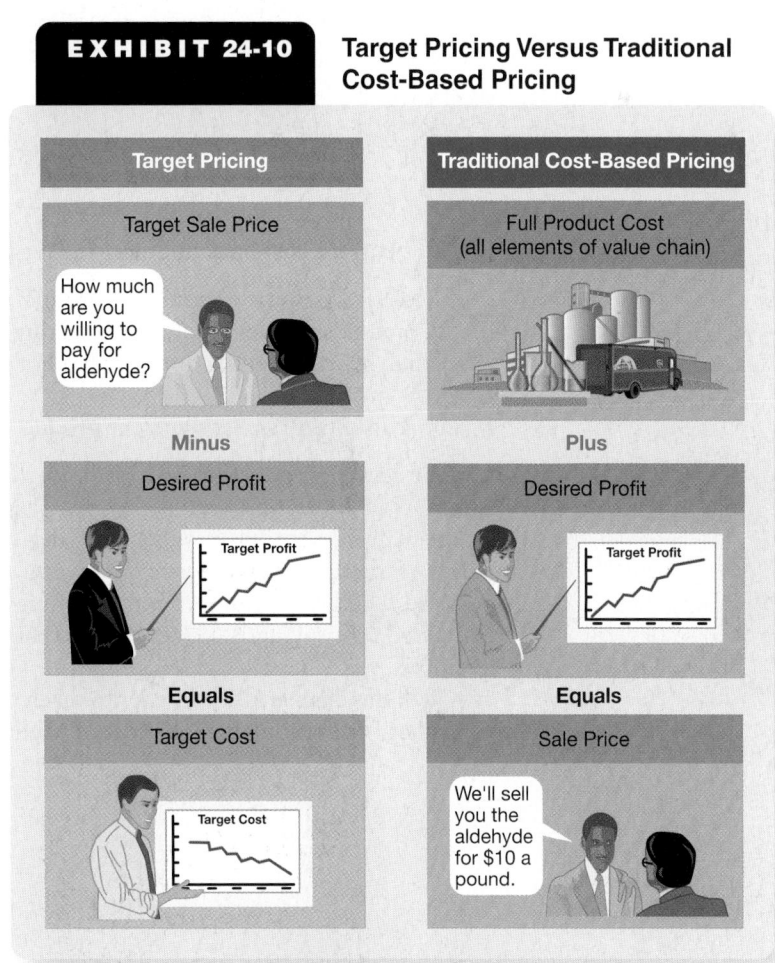

EXHIBIT 24-10 | **Target Pricing Versus Traditional Cost-Based Pricing**

Instead of starting with product cost and then adding a profit to determine the sale price (right column of the exhibit), target pricing (left column) does just the opposite. Target pricing starts with the price that customers are willing to pay and then subtracts the company's desired profit to determine the **target cost**. Then the company works backward to develop the product at the target cost. The target cost is a goal the company must shoot for.

Let's return to our Fischer Chemical illustration. The ABC analysis in Exhibit 24-9, Panel A, prompts CEO Smith to push aldehyde because it appears that PH is losing money. The marketing department says the selling price of aldehyde is likely to fall to $9.50 per pound. Smith wants to earn a profit equal to 20% of the sale price.

What is Fischer's target full-product cost per pound of aldehyde? Here's the computation:

Target sale price per pound of aldehyde	$9.50
– Desired profit ($9.50 × 20%)	(1.90)
= Target cost per pound of aldehyde	$7.60

Does Fischer's current full-product cost meet this target? Let's see.

Current total manufacturing cost per pound of aldehyde (Exhibit 24-9)	$7.68
Nonmanufacturing costs (operating expenses)	0.50
Current full-product cost per pound of aldehyde	$8.18

Fischer's current cost does not meet the target cost.

Because Fischer's current full-product cost ($8.18) exceeds the target cost of $7.60, Smith assembles a value-engineering team to identify ways to cut costs. The team analyzes each production activity. For each activity, the team considers how to

- Cut costs given Fischer's current production process
- Redesign the production process to further cut costs

Of the team's several proposals, Smith decides to

Redesign Mixing to reduce the mixing cost per batch. Group raw materials that are used together to reduce the time required to assemble the materials for mixing. Estimated cost saving is $160,000, and the number of batches remains unchanged at 4,000.

Will this change allow Fischer to reach the target cost? Exhibit 24-11 shows how controller Wise recomputes the cost of Mixing based on the value-engineering study.

EXHIBIT 24-11 Recomputing Activity Costs After a Value-Engineering Study

| | Manufacturing Overhead | | | |
	Mixing	Processing	Testing	Total Cost
Estimated total indirect costs of activity:				
Mixing ($600,000 − $160,000)	$440,000			
Estimated total quantity of each allocation base	4,000 batches			
Compute the cost allocation rate for each activity:				
(Divide estimated indirect cost by estimated	$440,000	Amounts	Amounts	
quantity of the allocation base)	÷ 4,000 batches	assumed	assumed	
Cost allocation rate for each activity	=$110.00/batch			
Actual quantity of each allocation base used				
by aldehyde:				
Mixing	× 60 batches			
Allocate the costs to aldehyde:				
Mixing (60 batches × $110.00)	= $6,600	+ $1,400	+ $1,100	= $9,100

Exhibit 24-11 shows that value engineering cuts total manufacturing overhead cost of aldehyde to $9,100 from $12,600 (in Exhibit 24-8). Spread over 7,500 pounds of aldehyde, overhead costs $1.21 per pound ($9,100 ÷ 7,500). Now Wise totals the revised cost estimates for aldehyde:

Direct materials (from Exhibit 24-9)................	$5.00
Direct labor (from Exhibit 24-9).....................	1.00
Manufacturing overhead.................................	1.21
Total manufacturing cost of aldehyde..............	$7.21

Cost of $7.21 is quite an improvement from the prior manufacturing cost of $7.68 per pound (Exhibit 24-9, Panel A). Value engineering worked. Now Fischer can meet the $7.60 target cost.

Decision Guidelines

Several years ago Dell refined its cost system. Starting with an Excel spreadsheet, Dell developed a simple ABC system to focus on its 10 most critical activities. Here are some of the decisions Dell faced as it began refining its cost system.

Decision	Guidelines
How to develop an ABC system?	1. Identify each activity and estimate its total indirect costs. 2. Identify the cost driver for each activity. Then estimate the total quantity of each driver's allocation base. 3. Compute the cost allocation rate for each activity. 4. Allocate indirect costs to the cost object.
How to compute a cost allocation rate for an activity?	$$\frac{\text{Estimated total indirect cost of the activity}}{\text{Estimated total quantity of the allocation base}}$$
How to allocate an activity's cost to the cost object?	$$\begin{array}{c}\text{Cost allocation rate} \\ \text{for the activity}\end{array} \times \begin{array}{c}\text{Actual quantity of the allocation} \\ \text{base used by the cost object}\end{array}$$
For what kinds of decisions do managers use ABC?	Managers use ABC data to decide on • Pricing and product mix • Cost cutting
How to set target costs?	Target sale price (based on market research) − Desired profit = Target cost
How to achieve target costs?	Use value engineering to cut costs by improving product design and production processes.
What are the main benefits of ABC?	• More accurate product cost information. • More detailed information on the costs of activities and their cost drivers helps managers control costs.

Summary Problem 1

Indianapolis Auto Parts (IAP) has a Seat Manufacturing Department that uses activity-based costing. IAP's system has the following features:

Activity	Allocation Base	Cost Allocation Rate
Purchasing	Number of purchase orders	$50.00 per purchase order
Assembling	Number of parts	$0.50 per part
Packaging	Number of finished seats	$1.00 per finished seat

Each auto seat has 20 parts. Direct materials cost per seat is $11. Suppose Ford has asked IAP for a bid on 50,000 built-in baby seats that would be installed as an option on some Ford SUVs. IAP will use a total of 200 purchase orders if Ford accepts IAP's bid.

Requirements

1. Compute the total cost IAP will incur to (a) purchase the needed materials and then (b) assemble and (c) package 50,000 baby seats. Also compute the average cost per seat.

2. For bidding, IAP adds a 30% markup to total cost. What total price will IAP bid for the entire Ford order?

3. Suppose that instead of an ABC system, IAP has a traditional product costing system that allocates all costs other than direct materials at the rate of $65 per direct labor hour. The baby-seat order will require 10,000 direct labor hours. What price will IAP bid using this system's total cost?

4. Use your answers to Requirements 2 and 3 to explain how ABC can help IAP make a better decision about the bid price to offer Ford.

Solution

Requirement 1
Total Cost of Order and Average Cost per Seat:

Direct materials, 50,000 × $11.00	$ 550,000
Activity costs:	
Purchasing, 200 × $50.00	10,000
Assembling, 50,000 × 20 × $0.50	500,000
Packaging, 50,000 × $1.00	50,000
Total cost of order	$1,110,000
Divide by number of seats	÷ 50,000
Average cost per seat	$ 22.20

Requirement 2
Bid Price (ABC System):

Bid price ($1,110,000 × 130%) $1,443,000

Requirement 3

Bid Price (Traditional System):

Direct materials, 50,000 × $11.00		$ 550,000
Other product costs, 10,000 × $65		650,000
Total cost of order		$1,200,000
Bid price ($1,200,000 × 130%)		$1,560,000

Requirement 4

IAP's bid would be $117,000 higher using the traditional system than using ABC ($1,560,000 − $1,443,000). Assuming the ABC system more accurately captures the costs caused by the order, the traditional system overcosts the order. This leads to a higher bid price and reduces IAP's chance of winning the bid. The ABC system can increase IAP's chance of getting the order by bidding a lower price.

Just-in-Time (JIT) Systems

Competition is fierce, especially in manufacturing and technology-related services. Chinese and Indian companies are producing high-quality goods at very low costs. As we saw in the discussion of activity-based costing, there's a never-ending quest to cut costs.

The cost of buying, storing, and moving inventory can be significant for Home Depot, Toyota, and Dell. To lower inventory costs, many companies use a just-in-time (JIT) system.

3 Describe a just-in-time production system, and record its transactions

Companies with **JIT systems** buy materials and complete finished goods *just in time* for delivery to customers. Production is completed in self-contained work cells as shown in Exhibit 24-12. Each cell includes the machinery and labor resources to manufacture a product. Employees work in a team and are empowered to complete the work without supervision. Workers complete a small batch of units and are responsible for inspecting for quality throughout the process. As the completed product moves out of the work cell, the suppliers deliver more materials just in time to keep production moving along.

By contrast, traditional production systems separate manufacturing into various processing departments that focus on a single activity. Work in process moves from one department to another, and that wastes time.

Under JIT, a customer's order—customer demand—triggers manufacturing. The sales order "pulls" materials, labor, and overhead into production. This "demand–pull" system extends back to the suppliers of materials. Suppliers make frequent deliveries of defect-free materials *just in time* for production. Purchasing only what customers demand reduces inventory. Less inventory frees floor space for more productive use. Thus, JIT systems help to reduce waste. Exhibit 24-12 shows a traditional production system in Panel B. The traditional system requires more inventory, more workers, and usually costs more to operate than a JIT system.

Companies like Toyota, Carrier, and Dell credit JIT for saving them millions. But JIT systems are not without problems. With no inventory buffers, JIT users lose sales when they can't get materials on time, or when poor-quality materials arrive just in time. There's no way to make up for lost time. As a result, many JIT companies still maintain small inventories of critical materials.

Just-in-Time Costing

JIT costing leads many companies to simplify their accounting. **Just-in-time costing**, sometimes called **backflush costing**, seems to work backwards. JIT costing starts with output that has been completed and then assigns manufacturing costs to units sold and to inventories. There are three major differences between JIT costing and traditional standard costing as shown in Exhibit 24-13.

1. JIT systems do not track the cost of products from raw materials inventory to work in process inventory to finished goods inventory. Instead, JIT costing waits until the units are completed to record the cost of production.

2. JIT systems combine raw materials and work in process inventories into a single account called Raw and In-Process Inventory.

3. Under the JIT philosophy, workers perform many tasks. Most companies using JIT combine labor and manufacturing overhead costs into a single account called Conversion Costs. Conversion Costs is a temporary account

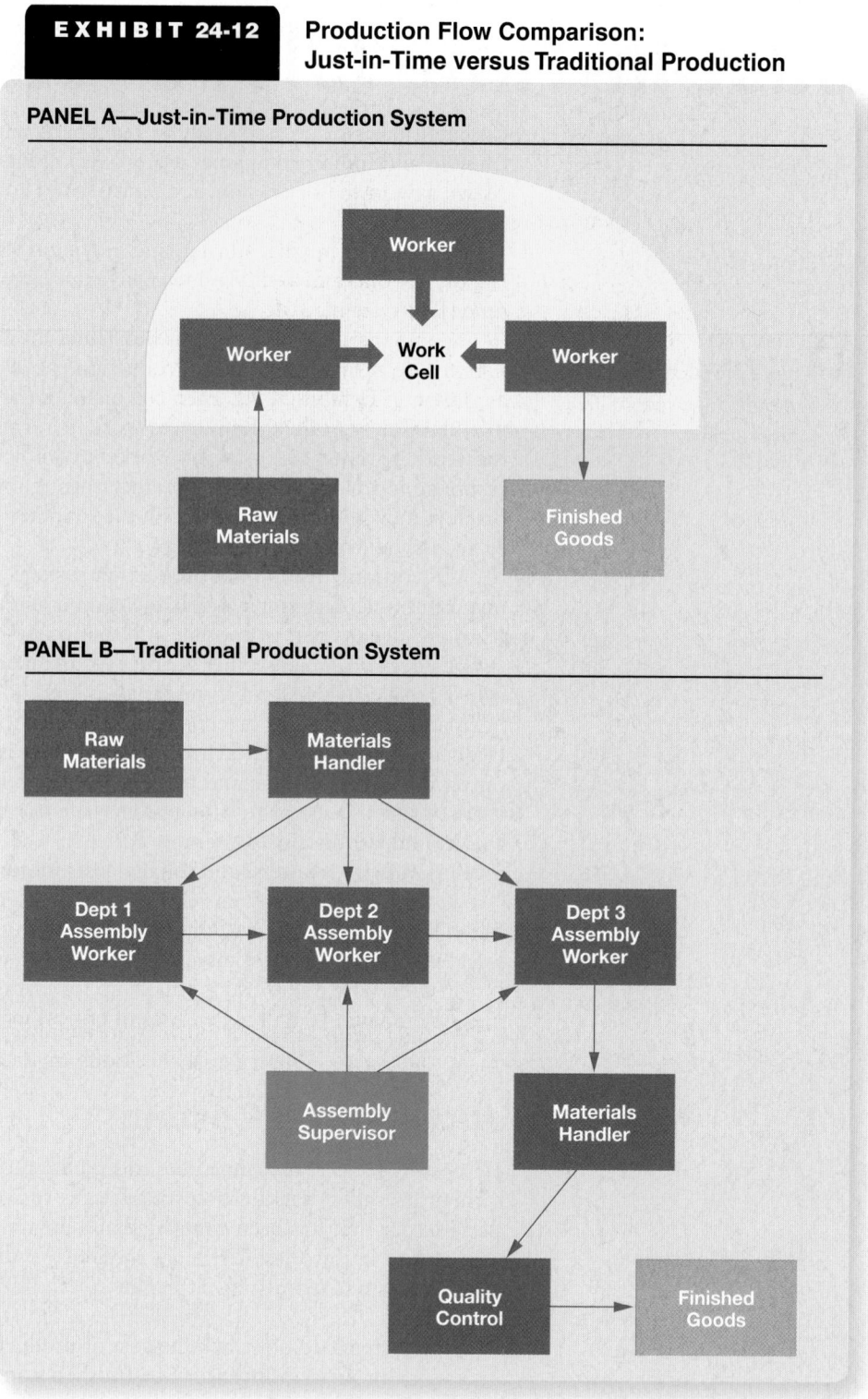

EXHIBIT 24-12 Production Flow Comparison: Just-in-Time versus Traditional Production

PANEL A—Just-in-Time Production System

PANEL B—Traditional Production System

that works just like the Manufacturing Overhead account. Actual conversion costs accumulate as debits in the Conversion Cost account. This account is credited when conversion costs are allocated to completed units. Accountants close any under- or overallocated conversion costs to Cost of Goods Sold at the end of the year, just like they do for under- or overallocated manufacturing overhead.

EXHIBIT 24-13	Comparison of Traditional and Just-in-Time Costing

	Traditional	Just-in-Time
Recording production activity	Build the costs of products as they move from raw materials into work in process and on to finished goods inventory	Record the costs of products when units are completed
Inventory accounts	Materials Inventory Work in Process Inventory Finished Goods Inventory	Raw and In-Process Inventory Finished Goods Inventory
Manufacturing costs	Direct Materials Direct Labor Manufacturing Overhead	Direct Materials Conversion Costs

Now, back to JIT Costing on page 1217.

JIT Costing Illustrated: Mintel Company

To illustrate JIT costing, consider Mintel Company, which converts silicon wafers into integrated circuits for computers. Mintel has only one direct material cost: silicon wafers. This cost is recorded in the Raw and In-Process Inventory account. All other manufacturing costs, including labor, various materials, and overhead, are indirect costs of converting the "raw" silicon wafers into finished goods (integrated circuits). All these indirect costs are collected in the "Conversion Costs" account.

JIT does not use a separate Work in Process Inventory account. Instead, it uses only two inventory accounts:

- Raw and In-Process Inventory, which combines direct materials with work in process
- Finished Goods Inventory

At July 31, Mintel had $100,000 of beginning Raw and In-Process Inventory and $900,000 of beginning Finished Goods Inventory. During August, Mintel uses JIT costing to record the following transactions.

1. Mintel purchased $3,020,000 of direct materials (silicon wafers) on account.

1.		Raw and In-Process Inventory	3,020,000	
		Accounts Payable		3,020,000
		Purchased direct materials on account.		

2. Mintel spent $18,540,000 on labor and overhead.

2.		Conversion Costs	18,540,000	
		Wages Payable, Accumulated Depreciation, etc.		18,540,000
		Incurred conversion costs.		

3. Mintel completed 3,000,000 circuits that it moved to finished goods. The standard cost of each circuit is $7 ($1 direct materials + $6 conversion cost). The debit (increase) to Finished Goods Inventory is standard cost of $21,000,000

(3,000,000 completed circuits × $7). There is no work in process inventory in JIT costing, so Mintel credits:
- Raw and In-Process Inventory for the silicon wafers, $3,000,000 (3,000,000 completed circuits × $1 standard raw material cost per circuit)
- Conversion Costs for the labor and other indirect costs allocated to the finished circuits, $18,000,000 (3,000,000 completed circuits × $6 standard conversion cost per circuit)

3.	Finished Goods Inventory (3,000,000 × $7)	21,000,000	
	Raw and In-Process Inventory (3,000,000 × $1)		3,000,000
	Conversion Costs (3,000,000 × $6)		18,000,000
	Completed production.		

This is the essence of JIT costing. The system does not track costs as the circuits move through manufacturing. Instead, *completion* of the circuits triggers the accounting system to go back and pull costs from Raw and In-Process Inventory and to allocate conversion costs to the finished products.

4. Mintel sold 2,900,000 circuits (2,900,000 circuits × cost of $7 per circuit = $20,300,000). The cost of goods sold entry is:

4.	Cost of Goods Sold	20,300,000	
	Finished Goods Inventory		20,300,000
	Cost of sales.		

Exhibit 24-14 shows Mintel's relevant accounts. Combining raw materials with work in process to form the single Raw and In-Process Inventory account eliminates detail.

EXHIBIT 24-14 **Mintel's JIT Costing Accounts**

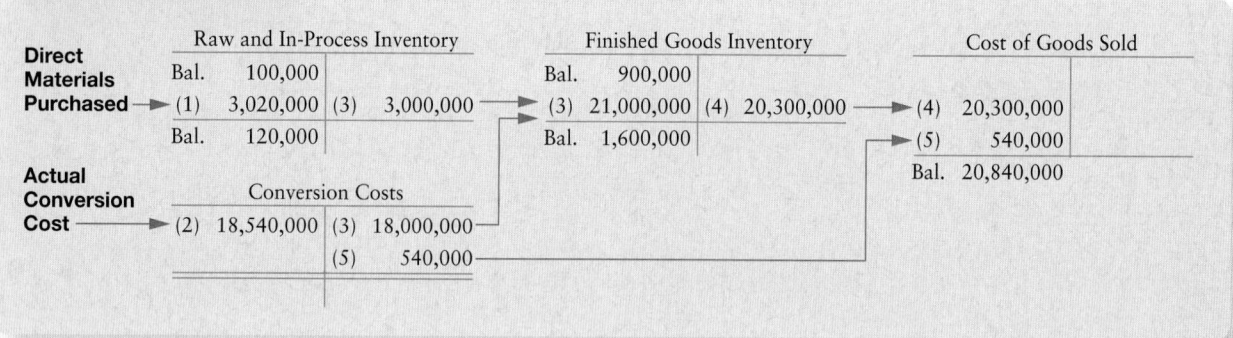

5. You can see from Exhibit 24-14 that conversion costs are underallocated by $540,000 (actual cost of: $18,540,000 − applied cost of $18,000,000). Under- and overallocated conversion costs are treated just like under- and over-

allocated manufacturing overhead and closed to Cost of Goods Sold, as follows for Mintel:

5.	Cost of Goods Sold	540,000	
	Conversion Costs		540,000
	Closed conversion costs account.		

In the final analysis, cost of goods sold for August is $20,840,000, as shown in the T-account on page 1220.

Continuous Improvement and the Management of Quality

 Use the four types of quality costs to make decisions

Companies using just-in-time production systems strive for high-quality production. Poor-quality materials or defective products shut down production, and that runs counter to the JIT philosophy.

To meet this challenge, many companies adopt *total quality management (TQM)*. The goal of TQM is to provide customers with superior products and services. Each business function monitors its activities to improve quality and eliminate defects and waste. Continuous improvement is the goal. Take a break, or miss a beat, and a Chinese manufacturer will put you out of business.

Well-designed products reduce inspections, rework, and warranty claims. Investing in research and development (R&D) can generate savings in marketing and customer service. World-class companies like Toyota and Dell *design* and *build* quality into their products rather than having to *inspect* and *repair* later. Let's see how they achieve the goal of high quality.

The Four Types of Quality Costs

The four types of quality-related costs include:

1. **Prevention costs** *avoid* poor-quality goods or services.

2. **Appraisal costs** *detect* poor-quality goods or services.

3. **Internal failure costs** avoid poor-quality goods or services *before* delivery to customers.

4. **External failure costs** occur when the company *delivers poor-quality goods or services* to customers and then has to make things right with the customer.

Exhibit 24-15 gives examples of the four types of quality costs. Most prevention costs occur in the R&D stage of the value chain. In contrast, most appraisal and internal failure costs occur in production. External failure occurs in customer service or, worse, they result from lost sales due to an unhappy customer. Prevention is much cheaper than external failure. One expert estimates that 8¢ spent on prevention saves $1 in failure costs.

EXHIBIT 24-15 Four Types of Quality Costs

Prevention Costs	Appraisal Costs
Training personnel	Inspection at various stages of production
Improved materials	Inspection of final products or services
Preventive maintenance	Product testing

Internal Failure Costs	External Failure Costs
Production loss caused by downtime	Lost profits due to unhappy customers
Rework	Warranty costs
Rejected product units	Service costs at customer sites
	Sales returns due to product defects

Deciding Whether to Adopt a New Quality Program

Let's revisit Fischer Chemical Company. CEO Randy Smith is considering spending the following on a new quality program to:

Inspect raw materials	$100,000
Reengineer to improve product quality	750,000
Inspect finished goods	150,000
Preventive maintenance of equipment	100,000

Fischer expects this quality program to reduce costs by the following amounts:

Avoid lost profits due to unhappy customers	$800,000
Fewer sales returns	50,000
Decrease the cost of rework	250,000
Lower warranty costs	100,000

Smith asks controller Wise to

1. Classify each cost into one of the four categories (prevention, appraisal, internal failure, external failure). Total the estimated cost for each category.

2. Recommend whether Fischer should undertake the quality program. Wise uses Exhibit 24-16 to compare the costs to:
   • Undertake the quality program, or
   • Do not undertake the quality program.

EXHIBIT 24-16	Analysis of Fischer's Proposed Quality Program

Undertake the Quality Program		Do Not Undertake the Quality Program	
Prevention		**Internal Failure**	
Reengineer to improve product quality	$ 750,000	Cost of rework	$ 250,000
Preventive maintenance of equipment	100,000	Total internal failure costs	$ 250,000
Total prevention costs	$ 850,000		
		External Failure	
		Lost profits due to unhappy customers	$ 800,000
Appraisal		Sales returns	50,000
Inspect raw materials	$ 100,000	Warranty costs	100,000
Inspect finished goods	150,000	Total external failure costs	$ 950,000
Total appraisal costs	$ 250,000	**Total costs of not undertaking the**	
Total costs of the quality program	$1,100,000	**quality program**	$1,200,000

Decision: Undertake the Quality Program and Save $100,000.

These estimates suggest that Fischer would save $100,000 ($1,200,000 − $1,100,000) by undertaking the quality program.

Quality costs can be hard to measure. For example, it's very hard to measure external failure costs. Lost profits due to unhappy customers do not appear in the accounting records! Therefore, total quality management uses lots of nonfinancial measures such as the number of customer complaints and the volume of incoming customer-service phone calls.

Decision Guidelines

Dell Computer is famous for using just-in-time production and total quality management. Dell's managers made the following decisions.

Decision	**Guidelines**

How to change from traditional production to JIT?

Traditional	JIT
Similar machines grouped together	Production cells
Larger batches	Smaller batches
Higher inventories	Lower inventories
Each worker does a few tasks	Each worker does a wide range of tasks
Many suppliers	Fewer, but well-coordinated suppliers

How does costing work under JIT?

Under JIT costing,

1. Raw materials and work in process are combined into a single Raw and In-Process Inventory account.
2. Labor and overhead are combined into a Conversion Cost account.
3. Summary journal entries are recorded *after* units are completed.

What are the four types of quality costs?

Prevention
Appraisal
Internal failure
External failure

How to manage the four types of quality costs?

Invest up front in prevention and appraisal to reduce internal and external failure costs.

Summary Problem 2

Flores Company manufactures cell phones and uses JIT costing. The standard unit cost is $30: $20 direct materials and $10 conversion costs. Direct materials purchased on account during June totaled $2,500,000. Actual conversion costs totaled $1,100,000. Flores completed 100,000 cell phones in June and sold 98,000.

Requirements

1. Journalize these transactions.

2. Were conversion costs under- or overallocated? Explain your answer and then make the entry to close the Conversion Costs account.

3. How much cost of goods sold did Flores have in June?

Solutions

Requirement 1

Raw and In-Process Inventory	2,500,000	
Accounts Payable		2,500,000
Conversion Costs	1,100,000	
Wages Payable, Accumulated Depreciation, etc.		1,000,000
Finished Goods Inventory	3,000,000	
Raw and In-Process Inventory (100,000 × $20)		2,000,000
Conversion Costs (100,000 × $10)		1,000,000
Cost of Goods Sold (98,000 × $30)	2,940,000	
Finished Goods Inventory		2,940,000

Requirement 2

Conversion costs were underallocated. Actual costs ($1,100,000) exceeded the cost allocated to inventory ($1,000,000).		
Cost of Goods Sold	100,000	
Conversion Costs		100,000

Requirement 3
COGS = $3,040,000 ($2,940,000 + $100,000)

Review Activity-Based Costing and Other Cost Management Tools

Accounting Vocabulary

Activity-Based Costing (ABC)

Focuses on activities as the fundamental cost objects. The costs of those activities become building blocks for compiling the indirect costs of products, services, and customers.

Activity-Based Management (ABM)

Using activity-based cost information to make decisions that increase profits while satisfying customers needs.

Appraisal Costs

Costs incurred to detect poor-quality goods or services.

Backflush Costing

A standard costing system that starts with output completed and then assigns manufacturing costs to units sold and to inventories. Also called **just-in-time costing**.

External Failure Costs

Costs incurred when the company does not detect poor-quality goods or services until after delivery to customers.

Internal Failure Costs

Costs incurred when the company detects and corrects poor-quality goods or services before delivery to customers.

Just-in-Time (JIT) Costing

A standard costing system that starts with output completed and then assigns manufacturing costs to units sold and to inventories. Also called **backflush costing**.

Prevention Costs

Costs incurred to avoid poor-quality goods or services.

Target Cost

Allowable cost to develop, produce, and deliver the product or service. Equals target price minus desired profit.

Target Price

What customers are willing to pay for the product or service.

Value Engineering

Reevaluating activities to reduce costs while satisfying customer needs.

Quick Check

1. Which statement is *false*?

    a. ABC focuses on indirect costs.

    b. Information technology makes it feasible for most companies to adopt ABC.

    c. An ABC system is more refined than one that uses a companywide overhead rate.

    d. ABC is primarily for manufacturing companies.

Use the following for questions 2 through 4. Two of Dell's production activities are *kitting* (assembling the raw materials needed for each computer in one kit) and *boxing* the completed products for shipment to customers. Assume that Dell spends $5 million a month on kitting and $10 million a month on boxing. Dell allocates

   • Kitting costs based on the number of parts used in the computer
   • Boxing costs based on the cubic feet of space the computer requires

Suppose Dell estimates it will use 500 million parts a month and ship products with a total volume of 20 million cubic feet.

   Assume that each desktop computer requires 100 parts and has a volume of 5 cubic feet.

2. What is the activity cost allocation rate for:

	Kitting	Boxing
a.	$0.0125/part	$0.25/cubic foot
b.	$0.01/part	$0.50/cubic foot
c.	$0.25/part	$0.20/cubic foot
d.	$160/part	$2/cubic foot

3. What are the kitting and boxing costs assigned to one desktop computer?

	Kitting	Boxing
a.	$0.9375	$3.50
b.	$0.625	$2.00
c.	$1.25	$1.25
d.	$1.00	$2.50

4. Dell contracts with its suppliers to pre-kit certain component parts before delivering them to Dell. Assume this saves $1.5 million of the kitting cost and reduces the total number of parts by 400 million (because Dell considers each pre-kit as one part). If a desktop now uses 80 parts, what is the new kitting cost assigned to one desktop?

    a. $2.80

    b. $0.70

    c. $0.9375

    d. $1.00

5. Dell can use ABC information for what decisions?

    a. Pricing

    b. Cost cutting

    c. Product mix

    d. All of the above

6. Which of the following is true for Dell, the computer company?

    a. Most of Dell's costs are for direct materials and direct labor. Indirect costs are a small proportion of total costs.

    b. Dell uses only a few activities, so a companywide overhead allocation rate would serve Dell quite well.

    c. ABC helps Dell keep costs low and remain competitive.

    d. All the above are true.

7. Dell enjoys many benefits from using JIT. Which is *not* a benefit of adopting JIT?

    a. Ability to continue production despite disruptions in deliveries of raw materials

    b. More space available for production

    c. Ability to respond quickly to changes in customer demand

    d. Lower inventory carrying costs

8. Which account is *not* used in JIT costing?

    a. Work in process inventory

    b. Conversion costs

    c. Raw and in-process inventory

    d. Finished goods inventory

9. The cost of lost future sales after a customer finds a defect in a product is which type of quality cost?

    a. Internal failure cost

    b. External failure cost

    c. Appraisal cost

    d. Prevention cost

10. Dell's spending on testing its computers before shipment to customers is which type of quality cost?

    a. Prevention cost

    b. Appraisal cost

    c. External failure cost

    d. None of the above

Answers are given after Apply Your Knowledge (p. 1249).

Assess Your Progress

Short Exercises

Activity-based costing

1

S24-1 Activity-based costing requires four steps. Rank the following steps in the order they would be completed. Number the first step as "1" until you have ranked all four steps. (p. 1206)

_____ **a.** Compute the cost allocation rate for each activity

_____ **b.** Identify the cost driver for each activity and estimate the total quantity of each driver's allocation base

_____ **c.** Allocate indirect costs to the cost object

_____ **d.** Identify each activity and estimate its total indirect cost

Calculating costs using ABC

1

S24-2 Bubba and Roscoe are college friends planning a skiing trip to Aspen before the new year. They estimated the following costs for the trip:

	Estimated Costs	Cost Driver	Activity Allocation	
			Bubba	Roscoe
Food	$ 500	Pounds of food eaten	20	30
Skiing	300	# of lift tickets	3	0
Lodging	300	# of nights	2	2
	$1,100			

1. Bubba suggests that the costs be shared equally. Calculate the amount each person would pay. (p. 1204)

2. Roscoe doesn't like the idea because he plans to stay in the room rather than ski. Roscoe suggests that each type of cost be allocated to each person based on the cost driver listed above. Using the activity allocation for each person, calculate the amount that each person would pay based on his own consumption of the activity. (p. 1204)

Computing indirect manufacturing costs per unit

1

S24-3 Daily Corp. is considering the use of activity-based costing. The following information is provided for the production of two product lines:

Activity	Cost	Cost Driver
Setup	$100,000	Number of setups
Machine maintenance	50,000	Machine hours
Total indirect manufacturing costs	$150,000	

	Product A	Product B	Total
Direct labor hours	6,000	4,000	10,000
Number of setups	30	70	100
Number of machine hours	1,250	3,750	5,000

Daily plans to produce 200 units of Product A and 200 units of Product B.

Compute the ABC indirect manufacturing cost per unit for each product. (pp. 1209, 1210)

S24-4 The following information is provided for the Astro Antenna Corp.,
which manufactures two products: low-gain antennas, and high-gain
antennas for use in remote areas.

Activity	Cost	Cost Driver
Setup	$50,000	Number of setups
Machine maintenance	30,000	Machine hours
Total indirect costs	$80,000	

	Lo-Gain	Hi-Gain	Total
Direct labor hours	1,500	2,500	4,000
Number of setups	20	20	40
Number of machine hours	1,800	1,200	3,000

Astro plans to produce 100 Lo-Gain antennas and 200 Hi-Gain antennas.

1. Compute the ABC indirect manufacturing cost per unit for each
   product. (pp. 1209, 1210)
2. Compute the indirect manufacturing cost per unit using direct labor
   hours from the single-allocation-base system. (p. 1207)

S24-5 Weekly Corp. makes two products: C and D. The following data have
been summarized:

	Product C	Product D
Direct materials cost per unit	$700	$1,800
Direct labor cost per unit	300	200
Indirect manufacturing cost per unit	?	?

Indirect manufacturing cost information includes:

		Allocation Base Units	
Activity	Allocation Rate	Product C	Product D
Setup	$1,200	30	70
Machine maintenance	$ 10	1,250	3,750

The company plans to manufacture 200 units of each product.

Calculate the product cost per unit for Products C and D using
activity-based costing. (pp. 1209, 1210)

S24-6 Johnstone Corp. manufactures mid-fi and hi-fi stereo receivers. The following data have been summarized:

	Mid-Fi	Hi-Fi
Direct materials cost per unit	$800	$1,000
Direct labor cost per unit	200	300
Indirect manufacturing cost per unit	?	?

continued . . .

Indirect manufacturing cost information includes:

| Activity | Allocation Rate | Allocation Base Units | |
		Mid-Fi	Hi-Fi
Setup	$1,200	20	20
Inspections	$ 600	40	10
Machine maintenance	$ 10	1,800	1,200

The company plans to manufacture 100 units of the mid-fi receivers and 200 units of the hi-fi receivers.

Calculate the product cost per unit for both products using activity-based costing. (pp. 1209, 1210)

Allocating indirect costs and computing income

S24-7 Alamo, Inc., is a technology consulting firm focused on Web site development and integration of Internet business applications. The president of the company expects to incur $706,000 of indirect costs this year, and she expects her firm to work 5,000 direct labor hours. Alamo's systems consultants earn $350 per hour. Clients are billed at 150% of direct labor cost. Last month Alamo's consultants spent 100 hours on Crockett's engagement.

1. Compute Alamo's indirect cost allocation rate per direct labor hour. (p. 1209)

2. Compute the total cost assigned to the Crockett engagement. (p. 1209)

3. Compute the operating income from the Crockett engagement. (p. 1209)

Computing ABC allocation rates

S24-8 Refer to Short Exercise S24-7. The president of Alamo, Inc. suspects that her allocation of indirect costs could be giving misleading results, so she decides to develop an ABC system. She identifies three activities: documentation preparation, information technology support, and training. The president figures that documentation costs are driven by the number of pages, information technology support costs are driven by the number of software applications used, and training costs are most closely associated with the number of direct labor hours worked. Estimates of the costs and quantities of the allocation bases follow:

Activity	Estimated Cost	Allocation Base	Estimated Quantity of Allocation Base
Documentation preparation	$100,000	Pages	3,125 pages
Information technology support	156,000	Applications used	780 applications
		Direct labor hours	5,000 hours
Training	450,000		
Total indirect costs	$706,000		

Compute the cost allocation rate for each activity. (p. 1209)

S24-9 Refer to Short Exercises S24-7 and S24-8. Suppose Alamo's direct labor rate was $350 per hour, the documentation cost was $32 per page, the information technology support cost was $100 per application, and training costs were $90 per direct labor hour. The Crockett engagement used the following resources last month:

Cost Driver	Crockett
Direct labor hours	100
Pages	300
Applications used	78

1. Compute the cost assigned to the Crockett engagement, using the ABC system. (pp. 1209, 1210)
2. Compute the operating income from the Crockett engagement, using the ABC system. (p. 1210)

S24-10 Indicate whether each of the following is characteristic of a JIT production system or a traditional production system. (pp. 1217–1221)

a. Products produced in large batches.
b. Large stocks of finished goods protect against lost sales if customer demand is higher than expected.
c. Suppliers make frequent deliveries of small quantities of raw materials.
d. Long setup times.
e. Employees do a variety of jobs, including maintenance and setups as well as operating machines.
f. Machines are grouped into self-contained production cells or production lines.
g. Machines are grouped according to function. For example, all cutting machines are located in one area.
h. Suppliers can access the company's intranet.
i. The final operation in the production sequence "pulls" parts from the preceding operation.
j. Each employee is responsible for inspecting his or her own work.
k. Management works with suppliers to ensure defect-free raw materials.

S24-11 Xeno Products uses a JIT system to manufacture trading pins for the 2008 Olympic Games in China. The standard cost per pin is $2 for raw materials and $3 for conversion costs. Last month Xeno recorded the following data:

Number of pins completed	4,000 pins	Raw material purchases	$ 9,000
Number of pins sold	3,500 pins	Conversion costs	$13,000

Use JIT costing to prepare journal entries for the month, including the entry to close the Conversion Costs account. (pp. 1219–1220)

Matching cost-of-quality
examples to categories

S24-12 Harry, Inc., manufactures motor scooters. For each of the following examples of quality costs, indicate the quality cost category it represents. (pp. 1221)

P   Prevention costs   IF   Internal failure costs

A   Appraisal costs   EF   External failure costs

_____ **1.** Preventive maintenance on machinery

_____ **2.** Direct materials, direct labor, and manufacturing overhead costs incurred to rework a defective scooter that is detected in-house through inspection

_____ **3.** Lost profits from lost sales if company's reputation was hurt because customers previously purchased a poor-quality scooter

_____ **4.** Costs of inspecting raw materials, such as chassis and wheels

_____ **5.** Working with suppliers to achieve on-time delivery of defect-free raw materials.

_____ **6.** Cost of warranty repairs on a scooter that malfunctions at customer's location

_____ **7.** Costs of testing durability of vinyl

_____ **8.** Cost to re-inspect reworked scooters

Exercises

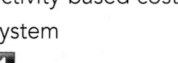

Product costing in an
activity-based costing
system

E24-13 Frederick, Inc., uses activity-based costing to account for its chrome bumper manufacturing process. Company managers have identified four manufacturing activities: materials handling, machine setup, insertion of parts, and finishing. The budgeted activity costs for 2009 and their allocation bases are as follows:

Activity	Total Budgeted Cost	Allocation Base
Materials handling	$ 9,000	Number of parts
Machine setup	3,400	Number of setups
Insertion of parts	48,000	Number of parts
Finishing	80,000	Finishing direct labor hours
Total	$140,400	

Frederick, Inc., expects to produce 1,000 chrome bumpers during the year. The bumpers are expected to use 3,000 parts, require 10 setups, and consume 2,000 hours of finishing time.

Requirements

1. Compute the cost allocation rate for each activity. (p. 1209)

2. Compute the indirect manufacturing cost of each bumper. (p. 1209)

Product costing in an
activity-based costing
system

E24-14 Turbo Champs Corp. uses activity-based costing to account for its 4-wheeler manufacturing process. Company managers have identified three supporting manufacturing activities: inspection, machine setup, and machine

continued . . .

maintenance. The budgeted activity costs for 2008 and their allocation bases are as follows:

Activity	Total Budgeted Cost	Allocation Base
Inspection	$ 6,000	Number of inspections
Machine setup	24,000	Number of setups
Machine maintenance	2,000	Maintenance hours
Total	$32,000	

Turbo Champs expects to produce 10 custom-built 4-wheelers for the year. The 4-wheelers are expected to require 30 inspections, 20 setups, and 100 maintenance hours.

Requirements
1. Compute the cost allocation rate for each activity. (p. 1209)
2. Compute the indirect manufacturing cost of each 4-wheeler. (p. 1209)

Product costing in an activity-based costing system

E24-15 Eason Company manufactures wheel rims. The controller budgeted the following ABC allocation rates for 2009:

Activity	Allocation Base	Cost Allocation Rate
Materials handling	Number of parts	$ 3.00 per part
Machine setup	Number of setups	300.00 per setup
Insertion of parts	Number of parts	24.00 per part
Finishing	Finishing direct labor hours	50.00 per hour

The number of parts is now a feasible allocation base because Eason recently purchased bar coding technology. Eason produces two wheel rim models: standard and deluxe. Budgeted data for 2009 are as follows:

	Standard	Deluxe
Parts per rim	4.0	6.0
Setups per 1,000 rims	15.0	15.0
Finishing direct labor hours per rim	1.0	2.5
Total direct labor hours per rim	2.0	3.0

The company's managers expect to produce 1,000 units of each model during the year.

Requirements
1. Compute the total budgeted indirect manufacturing cost for 2009. (p. 1209)
2. Compute the ABC indirect manufacturing cost per unit of each model. Carry each cost to the nearest cent. (p. 1209)
3. Prior to 2009, Eason used a direct labor hour single-allocation-base system. Compute the (single) allocation rate based on direct labor hours for 2009. Use this rate to determine the indirect manufacturing cost per wheel rim for each model, to the nearest cent. (p. 1209)

E24-16 Refer to Exercise E24-15. For 2010, Eason's managers have decided to use the same indirect manufacturing costs per wheel rim that they computed in 2009. In addition to the unit indirect manufacturing costs, the following data are budgeted for the company's standard and deluxe models for 2010:

	Standard	Deluxe
Sale price	$300.00	$440.00
Direct materials	30.00	46.00
Direct labor	45.00	50.00

Because of limited machine-hour capacity, Eason can produce *either* 2,000 standard rims *or* 2,000 deluxe rims.

Requirements
1. If Eason's managers rely on the ABC unit cost data computed in E24-15, which model will they produce? Carry each cost to the nearest cent. (All nonmanufacturing costs are the same for both models.) (p. 1210)
2. If the managers rely on the single-allocation-base cost data, which model will they produce? (p. 1210)
3. Which course of action will yield more income for Eason?

E24-17 Refer to Exercises E24-15 and E24-16. Controller Matthew Barnhill is surprised by the increase in cost of the deluxe model under ABC. Market research shows that for the deluxe rim to provide a reasonable profit, Eason will have to meet a target manufacturing cost of $350 per rim. A value engineering study by Eason's employees suggests that modifications to the finishing process could cut finishing cost from $50 to $40 per hour and reduce the finishing direct labor hours per deluxe rim from 2.5 hours to 2 hours. Direct materials would remain unchanged at $46 per rim, as would direct labor at $50 per rim. The materials handling, machine setup, and insertion of parts activity costs also would remain the same. Would implementing the value engineering recommendation enable Eason to achieve its target cost for the deluxe rim? (pp. 1211–1213)

E24-18 Daisy Dog Collars uses activity-based costing. Daisy's system has the following features:

Activity	Allocation Base	Cost Allocation Rate
Purchasing	Number of purchase orders	$60.00 per purchase order
Assembling	Number of parts	0.40 per part
Packaging	Number of finished collars	0.20 per collar

Each collar has 3 parts; direct materials cost per collar is $8. Suppose PetSmart has asked for a bid on 30,000 dog collars. Daisy will issue a total of 100 purchase orders if PetSmart accepts Daisy's bid.

continued . . .

Requirements

1. Compute the total cost Daisy will incur to purchase the needed materials and then assemble and package 30,000 dog collars. Also compute the cost per collar. (p. 1209)

2. For bidding, Daisy adds a 30% markup to total cost. What total price will the company bid for the entire PetSmart order? (p. 1210)

3. Suppose that instead of an ABC system, Daisy has a traditional product costing system that allocates all costs other than direct materials at the rate of $9.50 per direct labor hour. The dog collar order will require 10,000 direct labor hours. What total price will Daisy bid using this system's total cost? (p. 1210)

4. Use your answers to Requirements 2 and 3 to explain how ABC can help Daisy make a better decision about the bid price it will offer PetSmart. (p. 1210)

Recording manufacturing costs in a JIT costing system

3

E24-19 Luxor, Inc., produces universal remote controls. Luxor uses a JIT costing system. One of the company's products has a standard direct materials cost of $8 per unit and a standard conversion cost of $32 per unit.

During January 2007, Luxor produced 500 units and sold 480. It purchased $4,400 of direct materials and incurred actual conversion costs totaling $15,280.

Requirements

1. Prepare summary journal entries for January. (pp. 1219–1220)

2. The January 1, 2007, balance of the Raw and In-Process Inventory account was $80. Use a T-account to find the January 31 balance. (p. 1220)

3. Use a T-account to determine whether conversion cost is over- or underallocated for the month. By how much? Give the journal entry to close the Conversion Costs account. (p. 1220)

Recording manufacturing costs in a JIT costing system

4

E24-20 Cameron produces electronic calculators. Suppose Cameron's standard cost per calculator is $24 for materials and $64 for conversion costs. The following data apply to July production:

Materials purchased	$ 6,500	
Conversion costs incurred	$14,840	
Number of cameras completed		200 cameras
Number of cameras sold		196 cameras

Cameron uses JIT costing.

Requirements

1. Prepare summary journal entries for July, including the entry to close the Conversion Costs account. (pp. 1219, 1220)

2. The beginning balance of Finished Goods Inventory was $1,000. Use a T-account to find the ending balance of Finished Goods Inventory. (p. 1220)

E24-21 Millan & Co. makes electronic components. Mike Millan, the president, recently instructed vice president Steve Bensen to develop a total quality control program. "If we don't at least match the quality improvements our competitors are making," he told Bensen, "we'll soon be out of business." Bensen began by listing various "costs of quality" that Millan incurs. The first six items that came to mind were:

a. Costs incurred by Millan customer representatives traveling to customer sites to repair defective products

b. Lost profits from lost sales due to reputation for less-than-perfect products

c. Costs of inspecting components in one of Millan's production processes

d. Salaries of engineers who are designing components to withstand electrical overloads

e. Costs of reworking defective components after discovery by company inspectors

f. Costs of electronic components returned by customers

Requirements

Classify each item as a prevention cost, an appraisal cost, an internal failure cost, or an external failure cost. (p. 1221)

Classifying quality costs and using these costs to make decisions

4

E24-22 Clason, Inc., manufactures door panels. Suppose Clason is considering spending the following amounts on a new total quality management (TQM) program:

Strength-testing one item from each batch of panels	$70,000
Training employees in TQM	30,000
Training suppliers in TQM	40,000
Identifying preferred suppliers who commit to on-time delivery of perfect-quality materials	60,000

Clason expects the new program would save costs through the following:

Avoid lost profits from lost sales due to disappointed customers	$90,000
Avoid rework and spoilage	60,000
Avoid inspection of raw materials	50,000
Avoid warranty costs	15,000

Requirements

1. Classify each item as a prevention cost, an appraisal cost, an internal failure cost, or an external failure cost. (p. 1221)

2. Should Clason implement the new quality program? Give your reason. (p. 1222)

E24-23 Keaton manufactures high-quality speakers. Suppose Keaton is considering spending the following amounts on a new quality program:

Additional 20 minutes of testing for each speaker	$ 600,000
Negotiating with and training suppliers to obtain higher-quality materials and on-time delivery	400,000
Redesigning the speakers to make them easier to manufacture	1,400,000

Keaton expects this quality program to save costs, as follows:

Reduce warranty repair costs	$200,000
Avoid inspection of raw materials	500,000
Avoid rework because of fewer defective units	750,000

It also expects this program to avoid lost profits from:

Lost sales due to disappointed customers	$850,000
Lost production time due to rework	300,000

Requirements

1. Classify each of these costs into one of the four categories of quality costs (prevention, appraisal, internal failure, external failure). (p. 1221)
2. Should Keaton implement the quality program? Give your reasons. (p. 1222)

Problems (Group A)

P24-24A The Niehbur Manufacturing Company in Hondo, Texas, assembles and tests electronic components used in handheld video phones. Consider the following data regarding component T24:

Direct materials cost	$81.00
Activity costs allocated	?
Manufacturing product cost	?

The activities required to build the component follow.

Activity	Allocation Base	Cost Allocated to Each Unit
Start station	Number of raw component chassis	2 × $ 1.30 = $ 2.60
Dip insertion	Number of dip insertions	? × $ 0.40 = 12.00
Manual insertion	Number of manual insertions	12 × $ 0.80 = ?
Wave solder	Number of components soldered	1 × $ 1.60 = 1.60
Backload	Number of backload insertions	7 × $? = 4.20
Test	Testing hours	0.40 × $80.00 = ?
Defect analysis	Defect analysis hours	0.10 × $? = 5.00
Total		$?

continued . . .

Requirements

1. Fill in the blanks in both the opening schedule and the list of activities. (p. 1209)

2. How is labor cost assigned to products under this ABC product costing system?

3. Why might managers favor this ABC system instead of Niehbur's older system, which allocated all conversion costs on the basis of direct labor? (pp. 1209–1210)

Product costing in an ABC system

P24-25A Lawton, Inc., manufactures bookcases and uses an activity-based costing system. Lawton's activity areas and related data follow.

Activity	Budgeted Cost of Activity	Allocation Base	Cost Allocation Rate
Materials handling	$ 200,000	Number of parts	$ 0.80
Assembling	3,000,000	Direct labor hours	15.00
Finishing	160,000	Number of finished units	3.90

Lawton produced two styles of bookcases in April: the standard bookcase and an unfinished bookcase, which has fewer parts and requires no finishing. The totals for quantities, direct materials costs, and other data follow.

Product	Total Units Produced	Total Direct Materials Costs	Total Number of Parts	Total Assembling Direct Labor Hours
Standard bookcase	3,000	$29,300	80,000	3,000
Unfinished bookcase	3,600	28,800	84,000	2,000

Requirements

1. Compute the manufacturing product cost per unit of each type of bookcase. (pp. 1209, 1210)

2. Suppose that premanufacturing activities, such as product design, were assigned to the standard bookcases at $4 each and to the unfinished bookcases at $3 each. Similar analyses were conducted of postmanufacturing activities such as distribution, marketing, and customer service. The postmanufacturing costs were $20 per standard bookcase and $15 per unfinished bookcase. Compute the full product costs per unit. (p. 1213)

3. Which product costs are reported in the external financial statements? Which costs are used for management decision making? Explain the difference.

4. What price should Lawton's managers set for unfinished bookcases to earn a unit profit of $16? (p. 1210)

P24-26A Hampton Pharmaceuticals manufactures an over-the-counter allergy medication. The company sells both large commercial containers of 1,000 capsules to health-care facilities and travel packs of 20 capsules to shops in airports, train stations, and hotels. The following information has been developed to determine if an activity-based costing system would be beneficial:

Activity	Estimated Indirect Activity Costs	Allocation Base	Estimated Quantity of Allocation Base
Materials handling	$ 95,000	Kilos...........................	19,000 kilos
Packaging.......................	200,000	Machine hours	2,000 hours
Quality assurance............	112,500	Samples	1,875 samples
Total indirect costs	$407,500		

Other production information includes:

	Commercial Containers	Travel Packs
Units produced	2,000 containers	40,000 packs
Weight in kilos	8,000	6,000
Machine hours	1,200	400
Number of samples	200	300

Requirements

1. Compute the cost allocation rate for each activity. (p. 1209)

2. Use the activity-based cost allocation rates to compute the activity costs per unit of the commercial containers and the travel packs. (*Hint*: First compute the total activity costs allocated to each product line, and then compute the cost per unit.) (pp. 1209, 1210)

3. Hampton's original single-allocation-base costing system allocated indirect costs to products at $150 per machine hour. Compute the total indirect costs allocated to the commercial containers and to the travel packs under the original system. Then compute the indirect cost per unit for each product. (p. 1207)

4. Compare the activity-based costs per unit to the costs from the single-allocation-base system. How have the unit costs changed? Explain why the costs changed as they did. (pp. 1209, 1210)

P24-27A High Range produces fleece jackets. The company uses JIT costing for its JIT production system.

High Range has two inventory accounts: Raw and In-Process Inventory and Finished Goods Inventory. On February 1, 2009, the account balances were Raw and In-Process Inventory, $6,000; Finished Goods Inventory, $1,000.

continued . . .

The standard cost of a jacket is $40—$15 direct materials plus $25 conversion costs. Data for February's activity follow.

| Number of jackets completed | 18,000 | Direct materials purchased | $265,000 |
| Number of jackets sold | 17,600 | Conversion costs incurred | 551,000 |

Requirements

1. What are the major features of a JIT production system such as that of High Range? (pp. 1217–1221)

2. Prepare summary journal entries for February. Under- or over-allocated conversion costs are closed to Cost of Goods Sold monthly. (pp. 1219, 1220)

3. Use a T-account to determine the February 28, 2009, balance of Raw and In-Process Inventory. (p. 1220)

Analyzing costs of quality

4

P24-28A Roxi, Inc., is using a costs-of-quality approach to evaluate design engineering efforts for a new wakeboard. Roxi's senior managers expect the engineering work to reduce appraisal, internal failure, and external failure activities. The predicted reductions in activities over the 2-year life of the wakeboards follow. Also shown are the cost allocation rates for each activity.

Activity	Predicted Reduction in Activity Units	Activity Cost Allocation Rate per Unit
Inspection of incoming materials........	400	$ 40
Inspection of work in process.............	400	20
Number of defective units discovered in-house	1,100	50
Number of defective units discovered by customers	300	70
Lost sales to dissatisfied customers.....	100	100

Requirements

1. Calculate the predicted quality cost savings from the design engineering work. (p. 1222)

2. Roxi spent $106,000 on design engineering for the new wakeboard. What is the net benefit of this "preventive" quality activity? (p. 1222)

3. What major difficulty would Roxi's managers have in implementing this costs-of-quality approach? What alternative approach could they use to measure quality improvement? (pp. 1222–1223)

Problems (Group B)

Product costing in an ABC system

P24-29B Abram Technology's Assembly Department, which assembles and tests digital processors, reports the following data regarding processor G27:

Direct materials cost	$56.00
Activity costs allocated	?
Manufacturing product cost	$?

The activities required to build the processors are as follows:

Activity	Allocation Base	Cost Allocated to Each Board
Start station	Number of processor boards	1 × $ 0.90 = $0.90
Dip insertion	Number of dip insertions	20 × $ 0.25 = ?
Manual insertion	Number of manual insertions	5 × $? = 2.00
Wave solder	Number of processor boards soldered	1 × $ 6.80 = 6.80
Backload	Number of backload insertions	? × $ 0.70 = 2.80
Test	Testing hours	0.15 × $90.00 = ?
Defect analysis	Defect analysis hours	0.16 × $? = 8.00
Total		$?

Requirements

1. Fill in the blanks in both the opening schedule and the list of activities. (p. 1209)

2. How is labor cost assigned to products under this ABC product costing system?

3. Why might managers favor this ABC system instead of Abram's older system that allocated all conversion costs on the basis of direct labor? (pp. 1209–1210)

Product costing in an ABC system

P24-30B Woodway Furniture manufactures computer desks. The company uses activity-based costing. Its activities and related data follow.

Activity	Budgeted Cost of Activity	Allocation Base	Cost Allocation Rate
Materials handling	$ 300,000	Number of parts	$ 0.60
Assembling	2,500,000	Direct labor hours	15.00
Painting	170,000	Number of painted desks	5.00

continued . . .

Woodway produced two styles of desks in April: the standard desk and an unpainted desk. Data for each follow:

Product	Total Units Produced	Total Direct Materials Costs	Total Number of Parts	Total Assembling Direct Labor Hours
Standard desk	6,000	$102,000	120,000	6,000
Unpainted desk	1,500	22,500	30,000	900

Requirements

1. Compute the per-unit manufacturing product cost of standard desks and unpainted desks. (pp. 1209, 1210)

2. Premanufacturing activities, such as product design, were assigned to the standard desks at $5 each and to the unpainted desks at $3 each. Similar analyses were conducted of postmanufacturing activities such as distribution, marketing, and customer service. The post-manufacturing costs were $25 per standard desk and $22 per unpainted desk. Compute the full product costs per desk. (p. 1213)

3. Which product costs are reported in the external financial statements? Which costs are used for management decision making? Explain the difference.

4. What price should Woodway's managers set for standard desks to earn a $42.00 profit per desk? (p. 1210)

Comparing costs from ABC and single-rate systems

[1]

P24-31B Wallace, Inc., develops software for Internet applications. The market is very competitive. Wallace offers a wide variety of different software—from simple programs that enable new users to create personal Web pages (called Personal-Page), to complex commercial search engines (called Hi-Secure). The company's managers know they need accurate product-cost data. They have developed the following information to determine if an activity-based costing system would be beneficial.

Activity	Estimated Indirect Activity Costs	Allocation Base	Estimated Quantity of Allocation Base
Applications development........	$ 800,000	New applications	4 new applications
Content production..................	1,200,000	Lines of code	12 million lines
Testing	288,000	Testing hours	1,800 testing hours
Total indirect costs..................	$2,288,000		

Other production information for Personal-Page and Hi-Secure includes:

	Personal-Page	Hi-Secure
Units produced..............................	20,000	10
Number of new applications	1	1
Lines of code.................................	500,000	7,500,000
Hours of testing	100	600

continued . . .

1. Compute the cost allocation rate for each activity. Carry each cost to the nearest cent. (p. 1209)

2. Use the activity-based cost allocation rates to compute the activity costs per unit of Personal-Page and Hi-Secure. (*Hint:* First compute the total activity costs allocated to each product line, and then compute the cost per unit.) (pp. 1209, 1210)

3. Wallace's original single-allocation-base costing system allocated indirect costs to products at $50 per programmer hour. Personal-Page requires 10,000 programmer hours; Hi-Secure requires 15,000 programmer hours. Compute the total indirect costs allocated to Personal-Page and Hi-Secure under the original system. Then compute the indirect cost per unit for each product. (p. 1207)

4. Compare the activity-based costs per unit to the costs from the single-allocation-base system. How have the unit costs changed? Explain why the costs changed as they did. (pp. 1209, 1210)

Recording manufacturing costs for a JIT costing system

3

P24-32B Timekeepers produces sports watches. The company has a JIT production system and uses JIT costing.

Timekeepers has two inventory accounts: Raw and In-Process Inventory and Finished Goods Inventory. On August 1, 2007, the account balances were Raw and In-Process Inventory, $12,000; Finished Goods Inventory, $2,000.

Timekeepers's standard cost per watch is $50: $30 direct materials plus $20 conversion costs. The following data pertain to August manufacturing and sales:

| Number of watches completed | 9,000 watches | Raw materials purchased | $300,000 |
| Number of watches sold | 8,800 watches | Conversion costs incurred | $100,000 |

Requirements

1. What are the major features of a JIT production system such as that of Timekeepers? (pp. 1219, 1220)

2. Prepare summary journal entries for August. Under- and overallocated conversion costs are closed to Cost of Goods Sold at the end of each month. (pp. 1219, 1220)

3. Use a T-account to determine the August 31, 2007, balance of Raw and In-Process Inventory. (p. 1220)

Analyzing costs of quality

4

P24-33B Largo Toys is using a costs-of-quality approach to evaluate design engineering efforts for a new toy robot. The company's senior managers expect the engineering work to reduce appraisal, internal failure, and external failure activities. The predicted reductions in activities over the 2-year life of the toy robot follow. Also shown are the cost allocation rates for each activity.

continued . . .

Activity	Predicted Reduction in Activity Units	Activity Cost Allocation Rate Per Unit
Inspection of incoming materials........	300	$20
Inspection of finished goods...............	300	30
Number of defective units discovered in-house	3,200	15
Number of defective units discovered by customers	900	40
Lost sales to dissatisfied customers.....	300	60

Requirements

1. Calculate the predicted quality cost savings from the design engineering work. (p. 1222)

2. Largo Toys spent $60,000 on design engineering for the new toy robot. What is the net benefit of this "preventive" quality activity? (p. 1222)

3. What major difficulty would Largo Toys' managers have in implementing this costs-of-quality approach? What alternative approach could they use to measure quality improvement? (pp. 1222, 1223)

Apply Your Knowledge

Decision Cases

Comparing costs from ABC
and single-rate systems;
activity-based management
1 2

Case 1. Harris Systems specializes in servers for workgroup, e-commerce, and ERP applications. The company's original job costing system has two direct cost categories: direct materials and direct labor. Overhead is allocated to jobs at the single rate of $22 per direct labor hour.

A task force headed by Harris's CFO recently designed an ABC system with four activities. The ABC system retains the current system's two direct cost categories. Thus, it budgets only overhead costs for each activity. Pertinent data follow.

Activity	Allocation Base	Cost Allocation Rate
Materials handling	Number of parts	$ 0.85
Machine setup	Number of setups	500.00
Assembling	Assembling hours	80.00
Shipping	Number of shipments	1,500.00

Harris Systems has been awarded two new contracts, which will be produced as Job A and Job B. Budget data relating to the contracts follow.

	Job A	Job B
Number of parts...............................	15,000	2,000
Number of setups..............................	6	4
Number of assembling hours..............	1,500	200
Number of shipments........................	1	1
Total direct labor hours.....................	8,000	600
Number of output units	100	10
Direct materials cost.........................	$220,000	$30,000
Direct labor cost...............................	$160,000	$12,000

Requirements

1. Compute the product cost per unit for each job, using the original costing system (with two direct cost categories and a single overhead allocation rate). (p. 1207)

2. Suppose Harris Systems adopts the ABC system. Compute the product cost per unit for each job using ABC. (pp. 1209, 1210)

3. Which costing system more accurately assigns to jobs the costs of the resources consumed to produce them? Explain. (p. 1208)

4. A dependable company has offered to produce both jobs for Harris for $5,400 per output unit. Harris may outsource (buy from the outside company) either Job A only, Job B only, or both jobs. Which course of action will Harris's managers take if they base their decision on (a) the original system? (b) ABC system costs? Which course of action will yield more income? Explain.

Use activity-based
management to achieve
target costs
2

Case 2. To remain competitive, Harris Systems' management believes the company must produce Job B–type servers (from Decision Case 1) at a target cost of $5,400. Harris Systems has just joined a B2B e-market site that management believes will enable the firm to cut direct materials costs by 10%. Harris's management also believes that a value-engineering team can reduce assembly time.

Compute the assembling cost savings per Job B–type server required to meet the $5,400 target cost. (*Hint:* Begin by calculating the direct materials, direct labor, and allocated activity costs per server.) (p. 1213)

Ethical Issue

Cassidy Manning is assistant controller at LeMar Packaging, Inc., a manufacturer of cardboard boxes and other packaging materials. Manning has just returned from a packaging industry conference on activity-based costing. She realizes that ABC may help LeMar meet its goal of reducing costs by 5% over each of the next three years.

LeMar Packaging's Order Department is a likely candidate for ABC. While orders are entered into a computer that updates the accounting records, clerks manually check customers' credit history and hand-deliver orders to shipping. This process occurs whether the sales order is for a dozen specialty boxes worth $80, or 10,000 basic boxes worth $8,000.

Manning believes that identifying the cost of processing a sales order would justify (1) further computerization of the order process and (2) changing the way the company processes small orders. However, the significant cost savings would arise from elimination of two positions in the Order Department. The company's sales order clerks have been with the company many years. Manning is uncomfortable with the prospect of proposing a change that will likely result in terminating these employees.

Requirements
Use the IMA's ethical standards to consider Manning's responsibility when cost savings come at the expense of employees' jobs.

Team Project

Bronson Shrimp Farms, in Alabama, has a Processing Department that processes raw shrimp into two products:

- Headless shrimp

- Peeled and deveined shrimp

Bronson recently submitted bids for two orders: (1) headless shrimp for a cruise line and (2) peeled and deveined shrimp for a restaurant chain. Bronson won the first bid, but lost the second. The production and sales managers are upset. They believe that Bronson's state-of-the-art equipment should have given the company an edge in the peeled and deveined market. Consequently, production managers are starting to keep their own sets of product cost records.

Bronson is reexamining both its production process and its costing system. The existing costing system has been in place since 1991. It allocates all indirect costs based on direct labor hours. Bronson is considering adopting activity-based costing. Controller Heather Barefield and a team of production managers performed a preliminary study. The team identified six activities, with the following (department-wide) estimated indirect costs and cost drivers for 2008:

Activity	Estimated Total Cost of Activity	Allocation Base
Redesign of production process (costs of changing process and equipment)..............	$ 5,000	Number of design changes
Production scheduling (production scheduler's salary)........................	6,000	Number of batches
Chilling (depreciation on refrigerators)..............................	1,500	Weight (in pounds)
Processing (utilities and depreciation on equipment).........	20,675	Number of cuts
Packaging (indirect labor and depreciation on equipment).........	1,425	Cubic feet of surface exposed
Order filling (order-takers' and shipping clerks' wages)...............	7,000	Number of orders
Total indirect costs for the entire department.................................	$41,600	

The raw shrimp are chilled and then cut. For headless shrimp, employees remove the heads, then rinse the shrimp. For peeled and deveined shrimp, the headless shrimp are further processed—the shells are removed and the backs are slit for deveining. Both headless shrimp and peeled and deveined shrimp are packaged in foam trays and covered with shrink wrap. Order-filling personnel assemble orders of headless shrimp as well as peeled and deveined shrimp.

Barefield estimates that Bronson will produce 10,000 packages of headless shrimp and 50,000 packages of peeled and deveined shrimp in 2008. The two products incur the following costs per package:

	Costs per Package	
	Headless Shrimp	Peeled and Deveined Shrimp
Shrimp......................................	$3.50	$4.50
Foam trays................................	$0.05	$0.05
Shrink wrap..............................	$0.05	$0.02
Number of cuts.........................	12 cuts	48 cuts
Cubic feet of exposed surface....	1 cubic foot	0.75 cubic foot
Weight (in pounds)	2.5 pounds	1 pound
Direct labor hours.....................	0.01 hour	0.05 hour

Bronson pays direct laborers $20 per hour. Barefield estimates that each product line also will require the following *total* resources:

	Headless Shrimp		Peeled and Deveined Shrimp	
Design changes	1 change	for all	4 changes	for all
Batches	40 batches	10,000	20 batches	50,000
Sales orders	90 orders	packages	110 orders	packages

Requirements

Form groups of four students. All group members should work together to develop the group's answers to the three requirements.

(Carry all computations to at least four decimal places.)

1. Using the original costing system with the single indirect cost allocation base (direct labor hours), compute the total budgeted cost per package for the headless shrimp and then for the peeled and deveined shrimp. (*Hint:* First, compute the indirect cost allocation rate—that is, the predetermined overhead rate. Then, compute the total budgeted cost per package for each product.) (p. 1207)

2. Use activity-based costing to recompute the total budgeted cost per package for the headless shrimp and then for the peeled and deveined shrimp. (*Hint:* First, calculate the budgeted cost allocation rate for each activity. Then, calculate the total indirect costs of (a) the entire headless shrimp product line and (b) the entire peeled and deveined shrimp product line. Next, compute the indirect cost per package of each product. Finally, calculate the total cost per package of each product.) (pp. 1209–1210)

3. Write a memo to Bronson CEO Gary Pololu explaining the results of the ABC study. Compare the costs reported by the ABC system with the costs reported by the original system. Point out whether the ABC system shifted costs toward headless shrimp or toward peeled and deveined shrimp, and explain why. Finally, explain whether Pololu should feel more comfortable making decisions using cost data from the original system or from the new ABC system.

For Internet Exercises, Excel in Practice, and additional online activities, go to the Web site www.prenhall.com/horngren.

Quick Check Answers

1. *d*   2. *b*   3. *d*   4. *a*   5. *d*   6. *c*   7. *a*   8. *a*   9. *b*   10. *b*

25 Special Decisions and Capital Budgeting

Learning Objectives

1 Identify the relevant information for a special business decision

2 Make five types of short-term special decisions

3 Use payback and accounting rate of return to make longer-term capital budgeting decisions

4 Use discounted cash-flow models to make longer-term capital budgeting decisions

5 Compare and contrast the four capital budgeting methods

We make many decisions. As a student you decide where to attend college, where to live, and whether to cook or eat out. You make time to study, work, and have some fun.

As you launch your career and start earning more, you will consider how to invest your money. Like many, you may invest in a house or buy mutual funds. These decisions require information. By focusing on the relevant factors for your decision, you can clear away unnecessary data. ◼

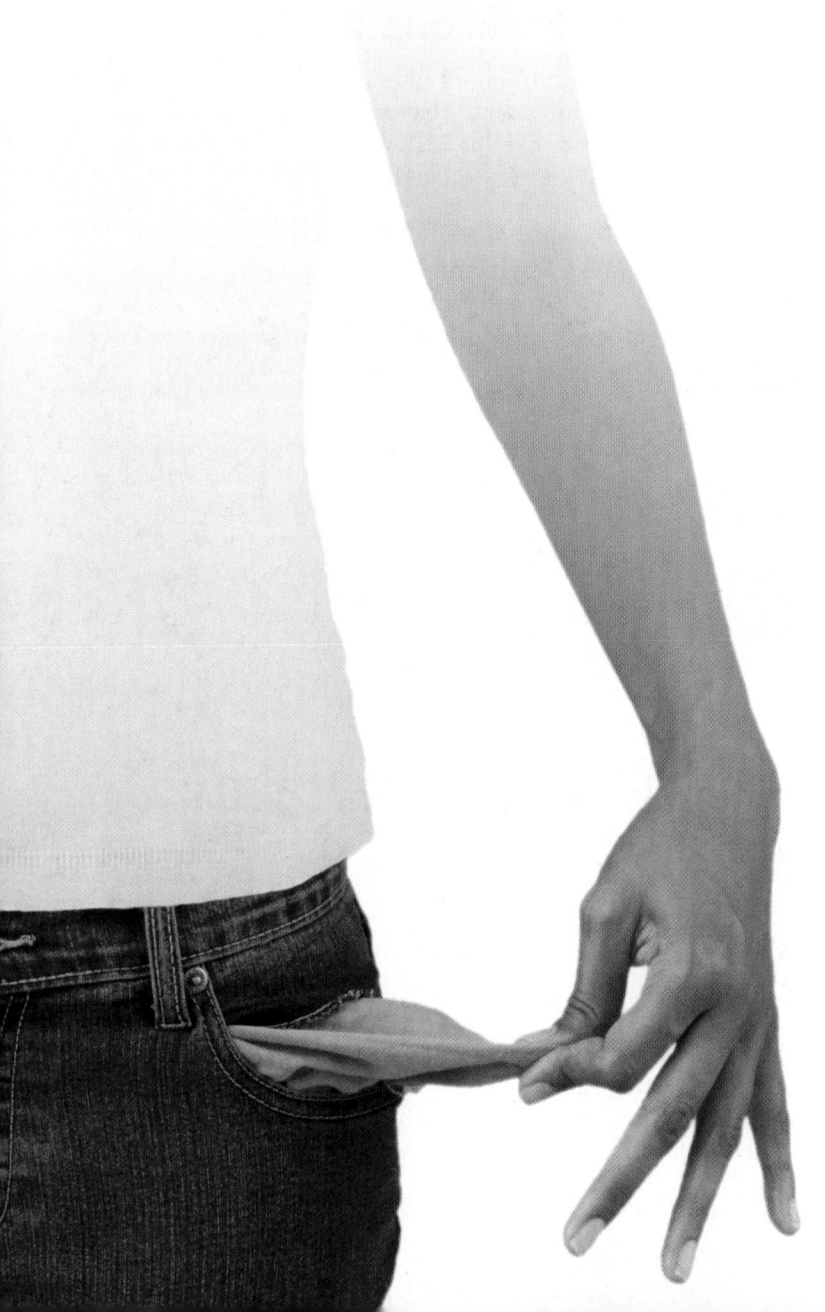

Just as you make personal decisions, companies develop strategies and make decisions that will affect the future. Business decisions use human, financial, and physical resources, and they affect whole communities. In this chapter, you will learn some ways to make both short-term and long-term business decisions.

We begin with some very interesting short-term decisions. Then, in the second half of the chapter, we'll see how companies decide on long-term investments that will tie up the company's resources for years. First, let's get a handle on separating relevant information from the irrelevant.

Relevant Information

The goal of business is to maximize profits. In this chapter, you'll see how managers use information to guide important decisions toward that goal.

How Managers Make Decisions

Exhibit 25-1 illustrates how managers decide among alternative courses of action. Management accountants help with all three steps. The key is to focus on information that's *relevant* to the decision at hand. Exhibit 25-1 shows the steps that managers take to make a decision.

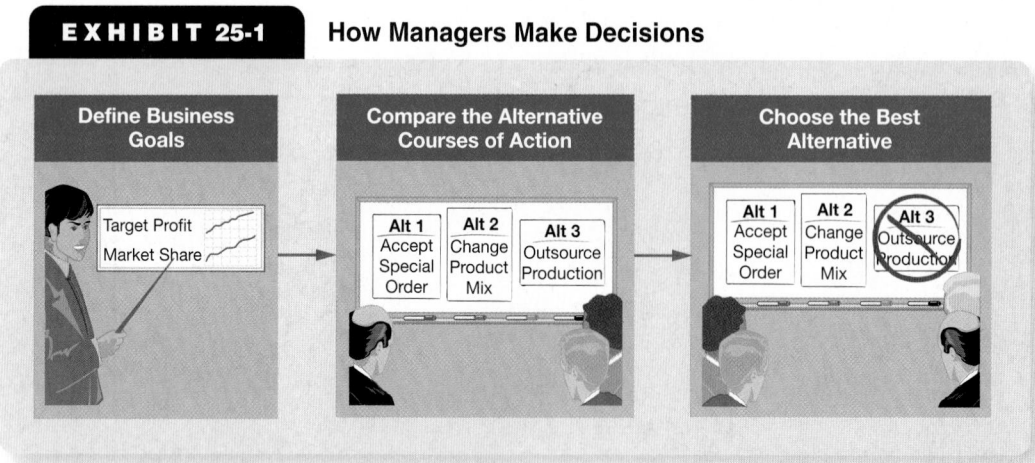

EXHIBIT 25-1   **How Managers Make Decisions**

What Information Is Relevant to a Special Business Decision?

1 Identify the relevant information for a special business decision

Relevant information makes a difference to a decision and has two distinguishing characteristics. Relevant information:

- Affects the future, and
- Differs among your alternative courses of action.

Let's apply this principle to a decision you may have faced.

Suppose you're deciding whether to buy a new or used car. The cost of the car, the insurance premium, and the fuel economy are all relevant because these costs will:

- *Affect your future*, and
- *Differ between the alternatives.*

Costs that were incurred in the past and costs that don't differ between the alternatives are *irrelevant*. For example, a campus parking sticker costs the same whether you buy the new or the used car, so that cost is irrelevant to your decision. If the two cars' fuel economy is the same, then gas mileage is irrelevant. The same distinction applies to all situations—*only relevant data affect decisions*.

How to Make Short-Term Special Decisions

2 Make five types of short-term special decisions

Our approach to making short-term decisions is called the *relevant information approach*, or the *incremental approach*. Under this approach, we consider only the information that's relevant to the decision. To be **relevant**, the **information** must make a difference to a decision. We'll show you how to make five kinds of decisions:

- Special sales orders
- Dropping a business segment (a product, a department, or a territory)
- Product mix: which product to emphasize
- Outsourcing—make or buy the product
- Selling as-is or processing further

As you study these decisions, keep in mind the two keys in analyzing short-term special decisions shown in Exhibit 25-2. We'll use these two keys for each decision.

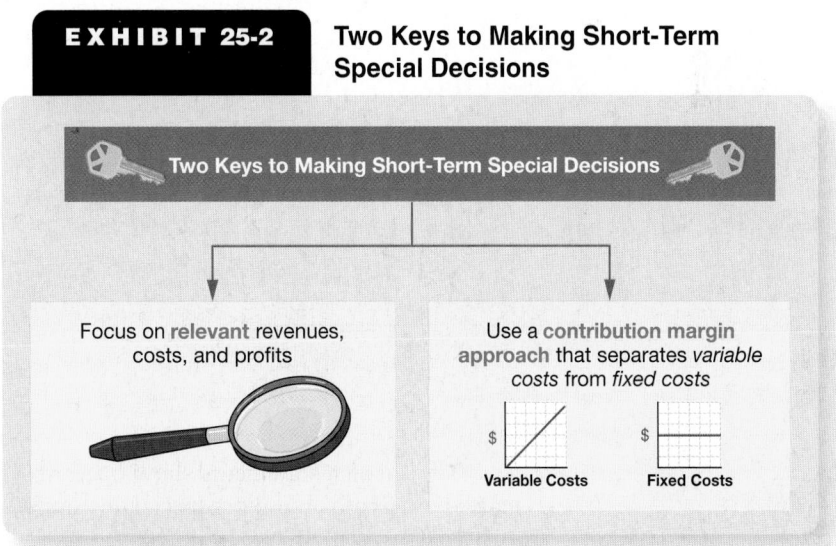

EXHIBIT 25-2   **Two Keys to Making Short-Term Special Decisions**

Exhibit 25-2 shows that the distinction between variable costs and fixed costs is important for special decisions. Why? Because the variable costs will differ among your alternative courses of action. That makes the variable costs relevant. By contrast, the fixed costs usually don't change, and that makes fixed costs irrelevant.

Special Sales Order

A potential customer may approach Timex to buy some wristwatches at a sale price lower than the regular price. Timex must decide whether to accept the special sales order. One of the factors in making the decision is whether the special order will increase net income. To answer this question Timex compares the increase in additional revenue to the increase in additional cost. If the additional revenue exceeds the additional cost, then net income will increase. In that case, Timex should accept the order. But if the additional revenue is less than the additional cost, then net income will decrease, and Timex will reject the order.

To illustrate this decision, suppose Seasons Greeting sells Christmas ornaments for $3.20 each to its customers in the United States. A Canadian company has offered Seasons Greeting $3,500 for 2,000 ornaments. The offer works out to a price of $1.75 per ornament ($3,500 ÷ 2,000 = $1.75). This special sale will not affect Seasons Greeting's regular business, and it:

- Will not change fixed costs
- Will not require any additional marketing and administrative expenses
- Will use manufacturing capacity that would otherwise lie idle

Suppose Seasons Greeting made and sold 25,000 ornaments before considering the special order. Cost of goods sold was $50,000, so the manufacturing cost per unit is $2 ($50,000 ÷ 25,000). Exhibit 25-3 shows Seasons Greeting's conventional income statement in the left column.

EXHIBIT 25-3 **Conventional Income Statement and Contribution Margin Income Statements**

SEASONS GREETING
Income Statement
Year Ended December 31, 2008

Conventional Format (Sales = 25,000 units)		Contribution Margin Format (Sales = 25,000 units)		
Sales revenue	$80,000	Sales revenue		$80,000
Less Cost of goods sold (25,000 units × $2)	50,000	Less variable expenses:		
Gross profit	30,000	Manufacturing	$30,000	
Less Marketing and administrative expenses	20,000	Marketing and administrative	7,500	37,500
		Contribution margin		42,500
		Less fixed expenses:		
		Manufacturing	$20,000	
		Marketing and administrative	12,500	32,500
Operating income	$10,000	Operating income		$10,000

Both income statements show operating income of $10,000, but they are formatted differently. For most special decisions, the contribution margin income statement is more helpful. Let's see why.

The conventional income statement suggests that Seasons Greeting should *not* accept the special order at a sale price of $1.75, because each ornament costs $2 to manufacture. But appearances can be deceiving!

The right-hand side of Exhibit 25-3 shows the contribution margin income statement that separates variable costs from fixed costs. This format is more useful for management decisions because it shows how sales volume affects costs and income. The contribution margin income statement reveals that the *variable* manufacturing cost per unit is only $1.20 ($30,000 ÷ 25,000 units).

Now let's reconsider Seasons Greeting's decision: How would the special sale affect operating income? The correct analysis in Exhibit 25-4 is an incremental approach that follows the two key guidelines:

1. Focus on relevant revenues, costs, and profits.
2. Use a contribution margin approach.

EXHIBIT 25-4   Analysis of Special Sales Order

Increase in revenues—Sale of 2,000 ornaments × $1.75 each	$ 3,500
Increase in expenses—variable manufacturing costs:	
2,000 ornaments × $1.20 each	(2,400)
Increase in operating income	$ 1,100

Exhibit 25-4 shows that this special sale increases revenues by $3,500 (2,000 × $1.75). The only cost that will differ between the alternatives is the variable manufacturing cost, which is expected to increase by $2,400 (2,000 × $1.20). All the other costs are irrelevant because they don't change. Variable marketing and administrative expenses will be the same because no special efforts were made to get this sale. Fixed expenses are unchanged because Seasons Greeting has enough idle capacity to produce 2,000 extra ornaments without adding more facilities.

Seasons Greeting compares the additional revenues with the additional expenses. In this case the increase in revenues exceeds the increase in expenses, so the sale adds $1,100 to profits. Seasons Greeting should accept the special order.

Here's the decision rule for a special sales order:

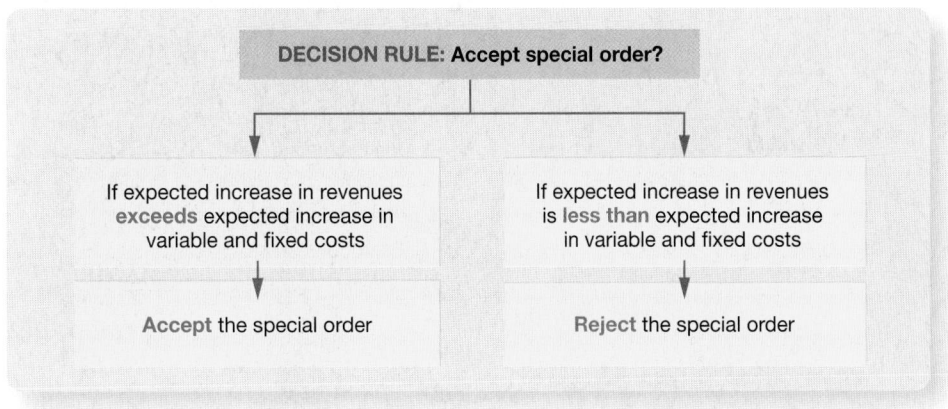

Our special sales order analyzed only the short-term effect on operating income. We must also consider long-term factors. Will accepting the order at $1.75 hurt Seasons Greeting's ability to sell the ornament at the regular price of $3.20? Will regular customers find out about the special price and balk at paying more? Will this sale start a price war?

If the sales manager believes these disadvantages outweigh the extra profit from accepting the order, he should reject the special order. The company is better off passing up $1,100 now to protect its long-term market position and customer relations.

This same approach to analyzing changes in revenues and costs also applies to the remaining short-term special decisions.

Dropping a Business Segment (a Product, a Department, or a Territory)

Some of a company's product lines, departments, or sales territories may be unprofitable. Managers need to eliminate the unprofitable business segments. Can the manager find ways to reduce costs or increase revenues? Dropping the segment may improve the company's profits. To make this decision, calculate the change in net income if the segment is dropped. Then,

- Keep the segment if its revenues are more than its relevant costs.
- Drop the segment if its revenues are less than the relevant costs.

To continue with our illustration, assume that Seasons Greeting is selling 35,000 units, as shown in Exhibit 25-5. Suppose the company is now considering *dropping* the scented candle product line. Exhibit 25-5 shows Seasons Greeting's contribution margin income statement by product line.

EXHIBIT 25-5	**Contribution Margin Income Statement by Product Line**

	Product Line	
	Ornaments (25,000 units)	Scented Candles (10,000 units)
Sales revenue	$80,000	$10,000
Variable expenses	50,000	7,500
Contribution margin	30,000	2,500
Fixed expenses:		
Manufacturing	12,500	5,000
Marketing and administrative	6,250	2,500
Total fixed expenses	18,750	7,500
Operating income (loss)	$11,250	$ (5,000)

Scented candles appear to be losing $5,000. Should Seasons Greeting drop the scented candle product line? We shall see. The answer depends on whether or not fixed costs change.

Fixed Costs Do Not Change

As in the special sales order example, we follow the two key guidelines for special decisions: (1) focus on relevant data, and (2) use a contribution margin approach. The relevant items are still the changes in revenues and expenses, but now we are considering a *decrease* in volume rather than an increase. If fixed costs remain the same whether or not scented candles are dropped, the fixed costs are irrelevant to the decision. In that case, only the revenues and variable expenses are relevant.

Exhibit 25-5 shows that scented candles provide a positive contribution margin of $2,500. If this product line is dropped, Seasons Greeting will forgo this $2,500. The company will have $2,500 less contribution margin available to cover fixed costs, and operating income will drop by $2,500. Exhibit 25-6 suggests that management should *not* drop scented candles.

EXHIBIT 25-6   Analysis for Dropping a Product—
Fixed Costs Do Not Change

Decrease in income if scented candles are dropped:	
Decrease in sales	$10,000
Decrease in variable expenses	7,500
Decrease in operating income	$ 2,500

Fixed Costs Change

Don't jump to the conclusion that fixed costs never change and are always irrelevant. Seasons Greeting employs a part-time foreman to oversee the scented candle product line. The foreman's $13,000 salary can be avoided if the company stops producing scented candles.

Exhibit 25-7 shows that in this situation, operating income will increase by $10,500 if Seasons Greeting drops scented candles. The elimination of the manager's salary expense is an example of a "*fixed*" cost that *is* relevant, so managers must consider the change in the cost.

EXHIBIT 25-7   Analysis for Dropping a Product—
Fixed Costs Change

Increase in income if scented candles are dropped:		
Decrease in sales		$10,000
Decreases in expenses:		
Variable expenses	$ 7,500	
Fixed expenses—no foreman salary to pay	13,000	
Expected decrease in total expenses		20,500
Increase in operating income		$10,500

Special decisions should take into account all costs that are affected by the decision. Managers must ask: What total costs—variable *and* fixed—will change? As Exhibits 25-6 and 25-7 show, the key to deciding whether to drop a business segment is to compare the lost revenue with the costs that can be saved from dropping the segment.

The decision rule for dropping a business segment is this:

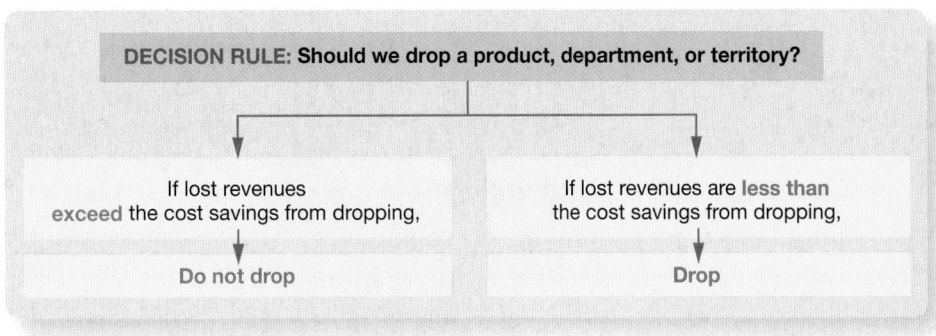

DECISION RULE: Should we drop a product, department, or territory?

If lost revenues exceed the cost savings from dropping,	If lost revenues are less than the cost savings from dropping,
Do not drop	Drop

Product Mix: Which Product to Emphasize

Companies—even Intel, Toyota, and Verizon—have limited resources. **Constraints** restrict the production or sale of a product, and these constraints vary from company to company. For a manufacturer, the constraint may be labor hours, machine hours, or available materials. For a merchandiser, the primary constraint is cubic feet of display space. Most companies are constrained by sales. The market may be very competitive, which may limit the number of units the company can sell.

To manage production constraints, managers must decide which products to make first. Once again, managers want to maximize profits in the short run, so the most profitable products will be manufactured first.

This product-mix decision requires two steps:

1. Compute the contribution margin per unit for each product line.

2. Convert the contribution margin per unit into the contribution margin per constrained resource.

Lead off with the product line with the highest contribution margin per constrained resource.

Consider Ryder, a manufacturer of shirts and slacks. Exhibit 25-8 shows that shirts have a higher contribution margin per unit than slacks (see Step 1). However, an important piece of information is missing—it takes twice as much time to make a shirt. Ryder can produce either 20 pairs of slacks *or* 10 shirts per machine hour.

EXHIBIT 25-8   **Product Mix—Which Product to Emphasize**

			Shirts	Slacks
		Sale price	$ 30	$ 60
		Variable costs	12	48
	Step 1.	Contribution margin per unit	$ 18	$ 12
		Units that can be produced each hour	× 10	× 20
	Step 2.	Contribution margin per hour	$ 180	$ 240
		Capacity—number of hours	×2,000	×2,000
		Total contribution margin at full capacity	$360,000	$480,000

Ryder can sell all the shirts and slacks it produces and has 2,000 machine hours of capacity. Which product should Ryder manufacture first—shirts or slacks? Machine hours are the constraint, so Ryder should produce the product with the highest contribution margin per machine hour.

Exhibit 25-8, Step 2 shows that slacks have a higher contribution margin per machine hour ($240) than shirts ($180). Ryder will therefore earn more profit by producing slacks. The bottom line of the exhibit shows that Ryder can earn $480,000 of contribution margin by producing slacks, but only $360,000 by producing shirts.

Notice that the analysis again follows the two guidelines for special business decisions:

• Focus on relevant data
(contribution margin per machine hour in this example) and

• Use a contribution margin approach

The decision rule for a product-mix decision is this:

> **DECISION RULE: Which product to emphasize?**
>
> ↓
>
> Emphasize the product with the **highest contribution margin per unit of the constraint.**

Outsourcing—Make or Buy the Product

To compete in global markets companies identify their core competencies—what they do best—and focus on these activities. For example, Esteé Lauder may decide it's not very good at making a component part (say, the nozzle) of a spray can of cologne. Esteé Lauder then must decide whether to continue making the nozzle or to buy the nozzles from an outside supplier. This is a classic make-or-buy decision, and it may lead Esteé Lauder to **outsource** the manufacture of the nozzles, that is, buy the nozzles from an outside supplier.

As with the other decisions, managers want to know if outsourcing is more expensive than producing in-house. The goal is to minimize costs and maximize profits. The decision process involves comparing the relevant costs to make the item with the relevant costs to outsource. If the cost to make is less than the cost to outsource (buy), a company will continue making the product. But if the costs to make exceeds the cost to outsource, a company will buy from the outside supplier.

Let's see how to make an outsourcing decision. Alto, a manufacturer of hand-painted dishware, has an offer from Dolly's Design to hand-paint 2,000 dinner plates. Alto's cost to paint 2,000 dinner plates is $18,000, as follows:

To Paint the Plates Alto Needs	Total Cost (2,000 plates)
Direct materials—paint	$ 400
Direct labor	11,000
Variable overhead	1,600
Fixed overhead	5,000
Total manufactuing cost	$18,000
Cost to paint each plate ($18,000 ÷ 2,000)	$ 9

Dolly's Design offers to paint the plates for $8 per plate. Should Alto paint the plates or outsource the painting to Dolly's Design? Alto's $9 cost per plate is $1 higher than Dolly's offer of $8, so it appears that Alto should outsource the painting. But the decision is not that simple.

To make the best decision, you must compare the difference in expected future costs between the alternatives. Which costs will differ if Alto paints the plates or outsources the painting?

Alto can avoid all variable manufacturing costs and reduce fixed overhead by $1,000 if Dolly does the painting. (Fixed overhead will decrease to $4,000.) Exhibit 25-9 shows the differences in costs between the make and buy alternatives. The costs that differ are also called *incremental* costs.

EXHIBIT 25-9 Analysis for Outsourcing (Make or Buy) Decision

Costs to Paint 2,000 Plates	Paint Plates	Outsource Painting	Difference
Direct materials—paint	$ 400	$ —	$ 400
Direct labor	11,000	—	11,000
Variable overhead	1,600	—	1,600
Fixed overhead	5,000	4,000	1,000
Purchase cost from Dolly's Design (2,000 × $8)	—	16,000	(16,000)
Total cost to paint the plates	18,000	20,000	(2,000)
Cost per unit—Divide by 2,000 plates	$ 9	$ 10	$ (1)

The decision rule is:

- Outsource if the incremental costs of making the item are *more than* the incremental costs of outsourcing (buying) the item.
- Make the item (do not outsource) if the incremental costs of making the item are *less than* the incremental costs of outsourcing (buying) the item.

Exhibit 25-9 shows that it would cost Alto less to paint the plates in-house than to outsource the painting to Dolly's Design. The net savings from painting 2,000 plates is $2,000, or $1 per plate.

This example shows that *fixed costs are relevant to a special decision when those fixed costs differ between alternatives.*

The analysis in Exhibit 25-9 assumes that Alto can't use the production facilities freed up if Alto outsources the painting. But suppose Alto can make more plates and earn extra profit of $3,000. Let's see how Alto's managers decide among three alternatives:

1. Paint the plates in-house.

2. Outsource the painting and leave facilities idle.

3. Outsource the painting and make more plates.

The alternative with the lowest *net* cost is the best use of Alto's facilities because it will generate the most profit. Exhibit 25-10 compares the three alternatives.

EXHIBIT 25-10 Best Use of Facilities

	Paint Plates	Outsource Painting Facilities Idle	Outsource Painting Make More Plates
Total cost to paint 2,000 plates (Exhibit 25-9)	$18,000	$20,000	$20,000
Profit from selling additional plates	—	—	(3,000)
Net cost to paint 2,000 plates	$18,000	$20,000	$17,000

In this case, Alto should outsource the painting and use its facilities to make more plates. If Alto paints the plates, or if it outsources the plates but leaves its production facilities idle, it will forgo the opportunity to earn $3,000.

This make-or-buy decision illustrates the concept of opportunity cost. An **opportunity cost** is the cost of forgoing a course of action. We normally use the term *opportunity cost* to describe a good deal that we passed up for one reason or another. For example, Alto's opportunity cost of outsourcing the painting and leaving the plant idle is the $3,000 of additional revenue from making additional plates.

There are qualitative factors—not just the revenues and costs—to consider in making these decisions. Alto should continue painting the plates if Alto can do a better job than Dolly's Designs. Alto may also be concerned about employee morale if Alto lays off workers. In addition, the community may suffer economically due to the layoffs. These decisions affect human beings and can give managers ulcers.

Outsourcing decisions are increasingly important in today's global economy. In the past, make-or-buy decisions often ended up as "make" because it was inconvenient to buy from outside suppliers. Now companies can use the Web to locate suppliers around the world, and UPS and DHL can deliver parts tomorrow. As a result, companies focus on their core competencies and outsource more and more other functions.

Sell As-Is or Process Further

Shell Oil Company refines crude oil into gasoline. After producing regular gas, should Shell sell the regular gas as-is, or should Shell spend more to process the gas into premium grade? Suppose Shell spent $48,000 to produce 50,000 gallons of regular gasoline, as shown in Exhibit 25-11. Assume Shell can sell this regular gas for $60,000. Alternatively, Shell can further process this regular gas into premium. Suppose the additional processing cost is $5,500. Assume the sale price of this premium gasoline is $70,000. Should Shell leave the regular gas as-is, or should Shell process further into premium?

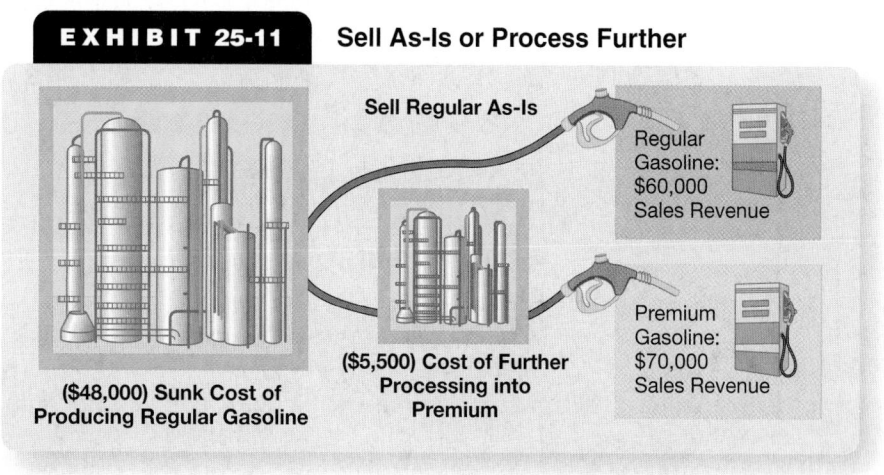

EXHIBIT 25-11 Sell As-Is or Process Further

Sell Regular As-Is

Regular Gasoline: $60,000 Sales Revenue

Premium Gasoline: $70,000 Sales Revenue

($48,000) Sunk Cost of Producing Regular Gasoline

($5,500) Cost of Further Processing into Premium

Which items are relevant to the sell-or-process-further decision? The $48,000 cost of the regular gasoline is *not* relevant. It is a **sunk cost**—a past cost that cannot be changed regardless of which future action Shell takes. The $48,000 has been incurred whether Shell sells the regular gas as-is or processes it into premium.

Exhibit 25-12 shows that the relevant items that differ between Shell's (1) sell as-is and (2) process further alternatives are:

- Expected revenues
- Expected costs of processing further

EXHIBIT 25-12   Sell As-Is or Process Further

	Sell As-Is	Process Further	Difference
Expected revenue from selling regular gas	$60,000		
Expected revenue from selling premium gas		$70,000	$10,000
Additional costs to process regular gas into premium		(5,500)	(5,500)
Total net revenue	$60,000	$64,500	
Difference in net revenue— Advantage of processing further			$ 4,500

The $10,000 extra revenue ($70,000 − $60,000) outweighs the $5,500 cost of the extra processing, so Shell should process the gasoline into the premium grade.

Thus, the decision rule is:

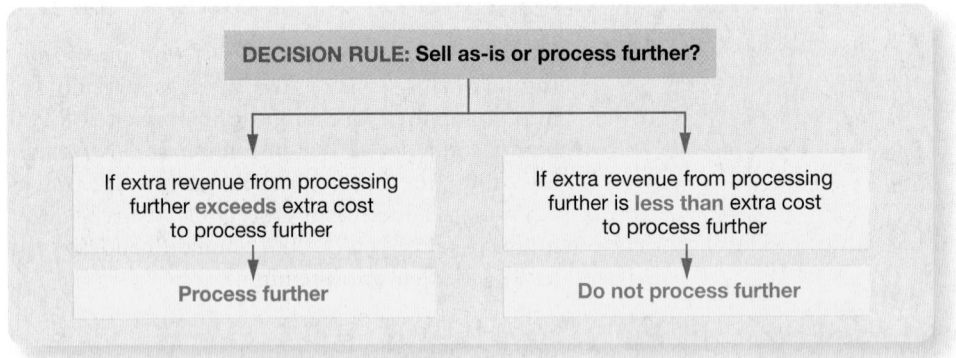

DECISION RULE: Sell as-is or process further?

If extra revenue from processing further **exceeds** extra cost to process further → **Process further**

If extra revenue from processing further is **less than** extra cost to process further → **Do not process further**

How Do Short-Term and Long-Term Special Decisions Differ?

The special decisions we reviewed pertain to short periods of time, such as a year or less. In this time frame

- Many costs are fixed and do not vary with the volume of goods or services produced. This is why short-term special decisions use the contribution margin approach, which distinguishes variable from fixed costs.
- There is no need to worry about the time value of money. Managers don't bother computing present values of revenues and expenses for these decisions because the time period is so short.

In the remainder of the chapter, we turn to longer-term decisions. For long-term decisions

- Few if any costs are fixed.
- Managers often take into account the time value of money.

The approach to long-term decisions will reflect these differences. But before moving on to long-term special decisions, stop for a moment to review the Decision Guidelines that summarize our short-term decisions. Then work Summary Problem 1.

Decision Guidelines

The following analysis of a short-term decision's immediate effect on profits is a good starting point. Here are some guidelines to follow in making these decisions.

Decision	Guidelines
What information is relevant to a short-term special decision?	Relevant data have two characteristics: 1. Affect the *future* 2. *Differ* between alternatives
What are two key guidelines in making short-term special decisions?	Key guidelines: 1. Focus on the *relevant* data 2. Use a *contribution margin* approach that separates variable costs from fixed costs
When should you accept a special sales order?	If the revenue from the order exceeds the extra variable and fixed costs, then accept the order and you'll increase operating income.
When should you drop a business segment?	If the cost savings exceed the lost revenues from dropping the business segment, then drop the segment and increase your operating income.
Which products should be made first when resource constraints exist?	Focus on selling the products with the highest contribution margin per unit of the constraint.
When should you outsource?	If the incremental cost to make the product exceeds the cost of outsourcing, then outsource, and you'll increase operating income.
How to decide whether to sell a product as-is or process further?	Process further only if the extra sales revenue less additional costs exceeds the revenue from selling as-is.

Summary Problem 1

1. Sunguard, Inc., produces standard and deluxe sunglasses:

	Per Pair	
	Standard	Deluxe
Sale price	$20	$30
Variable expenses	15	19

The company has 10,000 machine hours available. In one machine hour, Sunguard can produce either 70 pairs of the standard model or 30 pairs of the deluxe model. Which should Sunguard emphasize?

2. Sock It To Me incurs the following costs for 20,000 pairs of its high-tech hiking socks:

Direct materials	$ 20,000
Direct labor	60,000
Variable overhead	40,000
Fixed overhead	80,000
Total manufacturing cost	$200,000
Cost per pair ($200,000 ÷ 20,000)	$ 10

Another manufacturer has offered to sell Sock It To Me similar socks for $9, a total purchase cost of $180,000. If Sock It To Me outsources *and* leaves its plant idle, it can save $50,000 of fixed overhead cost. Or, the company can use the released facilities to make other products that will contribute $70,000 to profits. Analyze the alternatives. What is Sock It To Me's best course of action?

Solution

Requirement 1

	Style of Sunglasses	
	Standard	Deluxe
Sale price per pair	$ 20	$ 30
Variable expense per pair	(15)	(19)
Contribution margin per pair	$ 5	$ 11
Units produced each machine hour	× 70	× 30
Contribution margin per machine hour	$ 350	$ 330
Capacity—number of machine hours	×10,000	×10,000
Total contribution margin at full capacity	$3,500,000	$3,300,000

Decision:

Produce the standard model first because it has the higher contribution margin per unit of the constraint—machine hours.

Requirement 2

	Make Socks	Buy Socks	
		Facilities Idle	Make Other Products
Relevant costs:			
Direct materials	$ 20,000	—	
Direct labor	60,000	—	
Variable overhead	40,000	—	
Fixed overhead	80,000	$ 30,000	$ 80,000
Purchase cost from outsider (20,000 × $9)	—	180,000	180,000
Total cost of obtaining socks	200,000	210,000	260,000
Profit from other products	—	—	(70,000)
Net cost of obtaining 20,000 pairs of socks	$200,000	$210,000	$190,000

Decision:

Sock It To Me should buy the socks from the outside supplier and use the vacated facilities to make other products.

Using Payback and Accounting Rate of Return to Make Capital Budgeting Decisions

3 Use payback and accounting rate of return to make longer-term capital budgeting decisions

Business expansion usually requires the purchase of additional plant and equipment. Managers must evaluate various investments, and that leads to what we call capital budgeting. **Capital budgeting** is budgeting for the acquisition of *capital assets*—assets used for the long term—several years. We use the word *capital* here in the sense of capital expenditures on long-term assets as explained in Chapter 10. In this context, *capital* does not refer to common stock or owners' equity as used in the early chapters of this book.

Capital budgeting is not exact. The calculations may appear precise, but they are based on predictions about an uncertain future. Managers must consider many unknown factors, such as changing consumer preferences, competition, and inflation. The further into the future the decision goes, the more likely that actual results will differ from predictions. Long-term decisions become riskier than short-term decisions.

We now discuss four popular capital budgeting models (or decision methods):

- Payback
- Accounting rate of return
- Net present value
- Internal rate of return

Three of these models compare the *net cash inflows from operations* that each alternative generates. Generally accepted accounting principles are based on accrual accounting, but capital budgeting focuses on cash flows. An asset's desirability depends on its ability to generate net cash inflows—that is, inflows in excess of outflows—over the asset's useful life.

In capital budgeting, we use the terms:

- cash inflows
- cash outflows

Cash inflows have the same effect as *cash receipts*, which you've seen in previous chapters. But cash inflows are broader than cash receipts because cash inflows include cost savings, which also increase your cash. *Cash outflows* are similar to *cash payments*.

Payback Period

Payback is the length of time it takes to recover, in net cash inflows, the dollars of an investment in a long-term asset. The payback model measures how quickly managers expect to recover their investment dollars. The shorter the payback period, the more attractive the asset, all else being equal.

Mojo Motors, which makes electric motors, is considering investing $240,000 in software to develop a business-to-business (B2B) electronic model. Mojo Motors expects the B2B model to save $60,000 a year—a net cash inflow—for the six years of its useful life. The savings will arise from lower prices on the goods and services purchased.

When net cash receipts are equal each year, managers compute the payback period as follows:

$$\text{Payback period} = \frac{\text{Amount invested in the asset}}{\text{Expected annual net cash inflow}}$$

Net cash inflows arise from an increase in revenues or a decrease in expenses or both. In Mojo's case, the net cash inflows result from lower expenses. Mojo computes the investment's payback as follows:

$$\text{Payback period for B2B model} = \frac{\$240,000}{\$60,000} = 4 \text{ years}$$

Exhibit 25-13 verifies that Mojo expects to recoup the $240,000 investment in the B2B model by the end of year 4, when the accumulated net cash inflows (cost savings) total $240,000.

EXHIBIT 25-13   **Payback—Equal Annual Net Cash Inflows**

| | | Net Cash Receipts | | | |
| | | B2B Model | | Web Site Development | |
Year	Amount Invested	Annual Net Cash Inflows	Accumulated Net Cash Inflows	Annual Net Cash Inflows	Accumulated Net Cash Inflows
0	$240,000				
1	—	$60,000	$ 60,000	$80,000	$ 80,000
2	—	60,000	120,000	80,000	160,000
3	—	60,000	180,000	80,000	240,000
4	—	60,000	240,000		
5	—	60,000	300,000		
6	—	60,000	360,000		

(B2B Model: Useful life 6 years; Web Site Development: Useful life 3 years)

As an alternative investment, Mojo Motors is also considering investing $240,000 to develop a Web site. The company expects the Web site to generate $80,000 in net cash inflows each year of its three-year life. The Web site's payback period is computed as follows:

$$\text{Payback period for Web site development} = \frac{\$240,000}{\$80,000} = 3 \text{ years}$$

Exhibit 25-13 shows that Mojo Motors will recoup the $240,000 investment for Web site development by the end of year 3, when the accumulated net cash inflows total $240,000. The payback model therefore favors Web site development because it recovers the investment more quickly. Do we need to take a closer look?

Let's consider this decision more carefully. Is the Web site investment really better for Mojo than the B2B model? Here are some factors to consider:

- The Web site recovers its investment more quickly, but has only a three-year life. It will provide no profit for Mojo Motors.
- The B2B model takes four years to recover its investment but has a six-year life. The B2B model should generate two years of profits.

These considerations highlight a weakness of the payback decision model: Payback ignores profitability.

Here's the decision rule for the payback model:

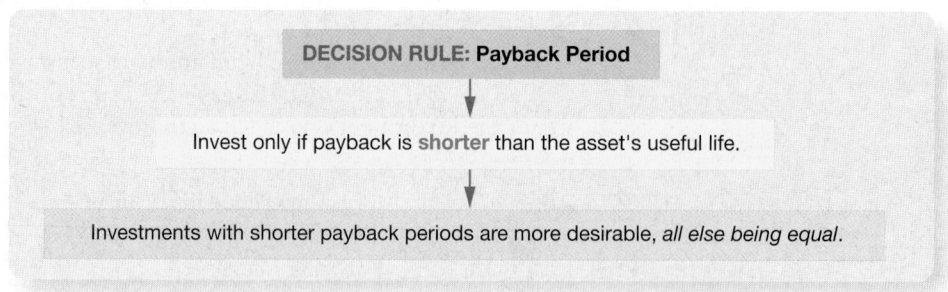

Managers use the payback method to eliminate proposals that are too risky—those with long payback periods. However, because payback ignores profitability, managers also use other decision models.

Accounting Rate of Return

Companies operate to earn profits. One measure of profitability is the **accounting rate of return** on an asset or other investment. Accounting rate of return measures the *average* rate of return over the asset's entire life, computed as follows.

$$\frac{\text{Accounting}}{\text{rate of return}} = \frac{\text{Average annual operating income from the asset}}{\text{Average amount invested in the asset}}$$

Let's examine the accounting rate of return in detail.

1. Consider the average annual operating income in the numerator. If operating income varies by year, add up the *total* operating income over the asset's life. Then divide by the asset's useful life to find *average* annual operating income from the asset.

2. Consider the average amount invested in the denominator. The book value of the asset decreases as it's used and depreciated. Thus, the company's investment in the asset declines over time. The *average* investment is the amount invested halfway through the asset's useful life. To find the average amount invested, we divide by 2. If the asset's residual value is zero, the average investment is half the asset's cost. Exhibit 25-14 shows that the average amount invested in Mojo's B2B model from the original payback example is $120,000 ($240,000 ÷ 2).

The accounting rate of return focuses on the operating income an asset can earn. Operating income can be computed either of two ways, depending on the available data—as:

• Net cash inflows from the asset minus depreciation on the asset, or
• Revenue minus operating expenses, including depreciation on the asset

Exhibit 25-14 computes the accounting rate of return for Mojo Motors's B2B model in the original payback example. Recall that Mojo expects the model to generate annual net cash inflows of $60,000. The model costs $240,000, and it has a useful life of six years with no residual value. Annual straight-line depreciation is $40,000 ($240,000 ÷ 6 years). Exhibit 25-14 shows that Mojo expects the model to generate average annual operating income of $20,000 ($60,000 − $40,000).

EXHIBIT 25-14 **Accounting Rate of Return**

$$\text{Accounting rate of return} = \frac{\text{Average annual operating income from the asset}}{\text{Average amount invested in the asset}}$$

$$= \frac{\begin{array}{c}\text{Annual net cash inflow} \\ \text{from the asset}\end{array} - \begin{array}{c}\text{Annual depreciation} \\ \text{on the asset}\end{array}}{(\text{Amount invested in the asset} + \text{Residual value}) \div 2}$$

$$= \frac{\$60,000 - \$40,000^*}{(\$240,000 + \$0) \div 2}$$

$$= \frac{\$20,000}{\$120,000} = 0.167 = 16.7\%$$

$$^*\$40,000 = \frac{\$240,000}{6 \text{ years}}$$

If the asset's residual value is not zero, the average amount invested is greater than half the asset's cost. For example, assume the residual value of the B2B model's technology is $30,000. Then annual depreciation declines to $35,000 [($240,000 − $30,000)/6]. The accounting rate of return becomes

$$\begin{array}{c}\text{Accounting} \\ \text{rate of return}\end{array} = \frac{\$60,000 - \$35,000}{(\$240,000 + \$30,000)/2} = \frac{\$25,000}{\$135,000} = 0.185 = 18.5\%$$

Companies compare the accounting rate of return to their minimum required rate of return and use this decision rule:

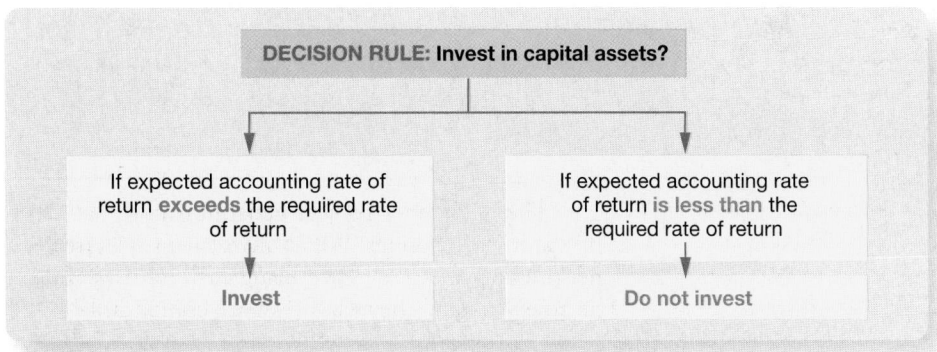

Now let's turn to the best capital budgeting decision models.

Using Discounted Cash-Flow Models for Capital Budgeting

A dollar received today is worth more than a dollar to be received in the future. Why? Because you can invest today's dollar and start earning extra income immediately. If you receive $1 today and deposit it in a bank that pays 6% interest, a year

Use discounted cash-flow models to make longer-term capital budgeting decisions.

from today you will have $1.06 (the original $1 plus $0.06 interest). Therefore, you would rather receive the $1 now because it will grow to $1.06 a year from today, rather than wait a year to receive $1. The fact that money can be invested to earn income over time is called the **time value of money**, and this explains why we prefer to receive cash sooner rather than later.

The time value of money makes the timing of net cash flows important. Consider two $10,000 investments that each promises a future cash receipt of $12,000.

- Investment 1 will bring in cash of $6,000 at the end of each of the next two years.
- Investment 2 will return the full $12,000 at the end of the second year.

Which investment do you prefer? Investment 1 is better, because it brings in cash sooner. Its $6,000 net cash inflow at the end of the first year can be reinvested right away to earn additional returns.

Neither the payback period nor the accounting rate of return recognizes the time value of money. That is, these models fail to consider the *timing* of the net cash flows an asset generates. *Discounted cash-flow models*— the net present value and the internal rate of return—overcome this weakness. Over 85% of large firms in the United States use discounted cash-flow methods to make their capital budgeting decisions.

Net Present Value

Midland Media Corporation is considering producing CD players and VCRs. The products require different specialized machines that each cost $1 million. Each machine has a 5-year life and zero residual value. CDs and VCRs have different patterns of predicted net cash inflows:

Year	Annual Net Cash Inflows	
	CD Players	**VCRs**
1	$ 305,000	$ 500,000
2	305,000	350,000
3	305,000	300,000
4	305,000	250,000
5	305,000	40,000
Total	$1,525,000	$1,440,000

The CD-player project generates more net cash inflows. But the VCR project brings in cash sooner. Which investment is better? To answer this question, we use **net present value (NPV)** to bring cash inflows and outflows back to the same point in time. Then all the cash flows are comparable.

We *discount* these expected future cash flows to their present value, using Midland's minimum desired rate of return on the investment, which is also called the **discount rate**. Synonyms are **hurdle rate, required rate of return**, and **cost of capital**. The discount rate depends on the riskiness of the investments. The higher the risk, the higher the discount rate. Midland's discount rate for these investments is 14%, which indicates they are fairly risky.

Net Present Value with Equal Periodic Cash Flows (An Annuity)

Midland expects the CD-player project to generate $305,000 of net cash inflows each year. This stream of equal periodic cash flows is called an **annuity**. The present value of an annuity is:

$$\text{Present Value of an Annuity} = \text{Periodic Cash Flow} \times \frac{\text{Present Value of an Annuity of \$1}}{\text{(Exhibit 25-15 and Appendix C-2)}}$$

EXHIBIT 25-15   Present Value of Annuity of $1

Present Value of Annuity of $1

Period	4%	6%	8%	10%	12%	14%	16%
1	0.962	0.943	0.926	0.909	0.893	0.877	0.862
2	1.886	1.833	1.783	1.736	1.690	1.647	1.605
3	2.775	2.673	2.577	2.487	2.402	2.322	2.246
4	3.630	3.465	3.312	3.170	3.037	2.914	2.798
5	4.452	4.212	3.993	3.791	3.605	3.433	3.274
6	5.242	4.917	4.623	4.355	4.111	3.889	3.685
7	6.002	5.582	5.206	4.868	4.564	4.288	4.039
8	6.733	6.210	5.747	5.335	4.968	4.639	4.344
9	7.435	6.802	6.247	5.759	5.328	4.946	4.607
10	8.111	7.360	6.710	6.145	5.650	5.216	4.833

Appendix C-2 provides a more comprehensive table for the present value of an annuity of $1.

Exhibit 25-15 shows the present value of annuity factors for various interest rates and numbers of periods. (This is an excerpt from the more comprehensive table in Appendix C-2.) The present value of an annuity of $1 received each year for five years, discounted at 14% per year, is $3.433. That is, the value today of receiving $1 at the end of each year for the next five years, discounted at 14%, is $3.433. Another way to think about this is that if Midland invested $3.433 today to earn a 14% annual interest rate, there would be just enough money to pay out $1 at the end of each year for the next five years.

The present value of the net cash inflows from Midland 's CD-player project is:

$$\text{Present Value} = \text{Periodic Cash Flow} \times \text{Present Value of an Annuity of \$1}$$
$$= \quad \$305,000 \quad \times \quad 3.433$$
$$= \quad \$1,047,065$$

After subtracting the $1,000,000 investment, the net present value of the CD-player project is $47,065, as shown in Exhibit 25-16.

EXHIBIT 25-16   Net Present Value with Equal Cash Flows—
CD-Player Project

	Present Value at 14%	Net Cash Inflow	Total Present Value
Present value of annuity of equal annual net cash inflows for 5 years at 14%	3.433* ×	$305,000 per year =	$ 1,047,065
− Investment			(1,000,000)
= Net present value of the CD-player project			$ 47,065

*Present value of an annuity of $1 for 5 years at 14%.

A positive net present value means that the project earns more than the required rate of return. A negative net present value means that the project fails to earn the required rate of return. This leads to the following decision rule:

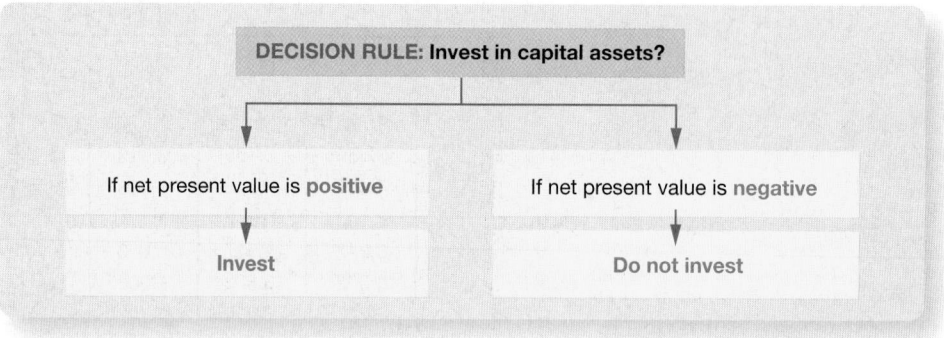

In Midland's case, the $47,065 positive net present value means that the CD-player project earns more than Midland target 14% rate of return. The project is an attractive investment.

Net Present Value with Unequal Periodic Cash Flows

In contrast to the CD-player project, the net cash inflows of the VCR project are unequal—$500,000 in year 1, $350,000 in year 2, and so on. Because these amounts vary by year, Midland's managers cannot use the annuity table in Exhibit 25-15 to compute the present value of the VCR project. They must compute the present value of each individual year's cash flows separately, using the present value of $1 table in Exhibit 25-17 (which is an excerpt from the more comprehensive table in Appendix C-1).

EXHIBIT 25-17   Present Value of $1

Present Value of $1							
Period	4%	6%	8%	10%	12%	14%	16%
1	0.962	0.943	0.926	0.909	0.893	0.877	0.862
2	0.925	0.890	0.857	0.826	0.797	0.769	0.743
3	0.889	0.840	0.794	0.751	0.712	0.675	0.641
4	0.855	0.792	0.735	0.683	0.636	0.592	0.552
5	0.822	0.747	0.681	0.621	0.567	0.519	0.476
6	0.790	0.705	0.630	0.564	0.507	0.456	0.410
7	0.760	0.665	0.583	0.513	0.452	0.400	0.354
8	0.731	0.627	0.540	0.467	0.404	0.351	0.305
9	0.703	0.592	0.500	0.424	0.361	0.308	0.263
10	0.676	0.558	0.463	0.386	0.322	0.270	0.227

Appendix C-1 provides a more comprehensive table for the present value of $1.

Exhibit 25-18—on the next page—shows that the total present value of the VCR project's net cash inflows is $1,078,910. After subtracting the $1,000,000 investment, the VCR project has a net present value of $78,910. That means Midland expects the VCR project to earn more than the 14% target rate of return, so the VCRs are an attractive investment.

EXHIBIT 25-18	Net Present Value with Unequal Cash Flows— VCR Project

	Present Value of $1 from Exhibit 25-17, 14% Column	Net Cash Inflow	Present Value of Net Cash Inflow
Present value of each year's net cash inflows discounted at 14%:			
Year 1	0.877 ×	$500,000 =	$ 438,500
Year 2	0.769 ×	350,000 =	269,150
Year 3	0.675 ×	300,000 =	202,500
Year 4	0.592 ×	250,000 =	148,000
Year 5	0.519 ×	40,000 =	20,760
Total present value of net cash inflows			1,078,910
− Investment			(1,000,000)
= Net present value of the VCR project			$ 78,910

*Present value of $1 in 1 year, 2 years, 3 years, and so on, at 14%, from Exhibit 25-17.

Exhibits 25-16 and 25-18 show that both projects have positive net present values. Therefore, both are attractive investments. If Midland wants to pursue only one project, the net present value analysis favors the VCR. This project should earn an additional $78,910 beyond the 14% required rate of return, while the CD-player project returns only an additional $47,065.

This example illustrates an important point. The CD-player project promises more *total* net cash inflows. But the *timing* of the VCR cash flows—loaded near the beginning of the project—gives VCRs a higher net present value. The VCR project is therefore more attractive because of the time value of money. Its dollars, which are received sooner, are worth more now than the more distant dollars of the CD project.

Sensitivity Analysis

Capital budgeting decisions affect cash flows far into the future. Midland's managers might want to know whether their decision would be affected by any of their major assumptions. For example:

- Changing the discount rate from 14% to 12% or to 16%
- Changing the net cash flows each year

After entering the net present value data into a spreadsheet, you can perform sensitivity analysis with a few keystrokes. The software quickly recalculates and displays the results.

Internal Rate of Return

Another discounted cash-flow model for capital budgeting is the internal rate of return. The **internal rate of return (IRR)** is the rate of return (based on discounted cash flows) a company can expect to earn by investing in the project. It is the discount rate that makes the net present value of the project's cash flows equal to zero. The higher the IRR, the more attractive the project.

For projects with equal cash flows each period, like Midland's CD-player project, use the following three steps to compute the IRR:

1. Identify the expected net cash inflow ($305,000 each year for five years) exactly as we did for the net present value method.

2. Find the discount rate that makes the total present value of the net cash inflows equal to the present value of the cash outflows. Work backward to find the discount rate that makes the present value of the annuity of net cash inflows equal to the amount of the investment by solving for the annuity present value (PV) factor, as follows:

$$\text{Investment} = \text{Expected annual net cash flow} \times \text{Annuity PV factor}$$

$$\text{Annuity PV factor} = \frac{\text{Investment}}{\text{Expected annual net cash flow}}$$

$$= \frac{\$1,000,000}{\$305,000}$$

$$= 3.279$$

3. Turn to the table for the present value of an annuity of $1 (Exhibit 25-15). Scan the row corresponding to the project's expected life—period 5, in our example. Choose the column with the number closest to the annuity PV factor you calculated in step 2. The 3.279 annuity factor is very close to 3.274 in the 16% column. Therefore, the IRR of the CD-player project is approximately 16%. Midland expects the project to earn an annual rate of return of 16% over its life. Exhibit 25-19 confirms this result.

EXHIBIT 25-19   Internal Rate of Return, CD-Player Project

	Present Value at 16%	Net Cash Inflow	Present Value of Net Cash Inflow
Present value of annuity of equal annual net cash inflows for 5 years at 16%	3.279* ×	$305,000 =	$1,000,095
– Investment			(1,000,000)
= Net present value of the CD-player project			$ 95†

*Present value of annuity of $1 for 5 years at 16% (Exhibit 25-15) is 3.274.
†The near-zero difference proves that the IRR is very close to 16%.

To decide whether the project is acceptable, compare the IRR with your minimum desired rate of return. The IRR decision rule is:

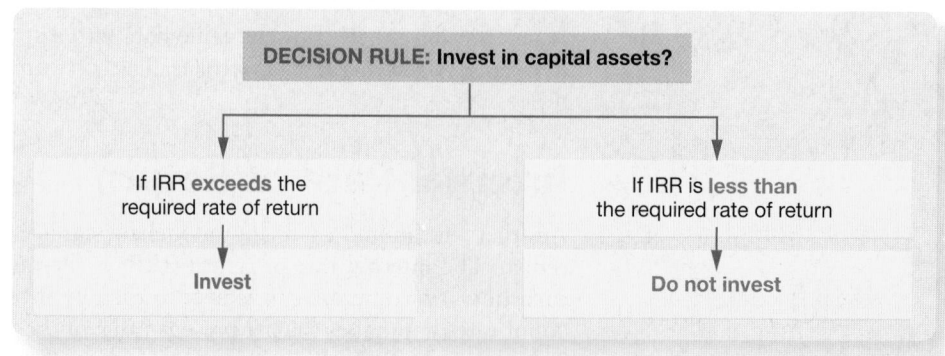

DECISION RULE: Invest in capital assets?

If IRR **exceeds** the required rate of return → **Invest**

If IRR is **less than** the required rate of return → **Do not invest**

Comparing Capital Budgeting Methods

5 Compare and contrast the four capital budgeting methods

Only net present value and internal rate of return consider both profitability and the time value of money, and that makes these methods superior. How do the net present value and IRR approaches compare? Net present value indicates the amount of the excess (or deficiency) of a project's present value of net cash inflows over (or under) its cost—at a specified discount rate. But net present value does not show the project's unique rate of return. The internal rate of return shows the project's rate but does not indicate the dollar difference between the project's present value and its cost. In most cases, the two discounted cash-flow methods lead to the same investment decision.

Exhibit 25-20 summarizes the strengths and weaknesses of payback, accounting rate of return, and the discounted cash-flow methods. Managers often use more than one method to gain different perspectives on risks and returns. For example, Dell's managers may invest in projects with positive net present values, provided that those projects have a payback of four years or less.

EXHIBIT 25-20   **Capital Budgeting Methods**

Method	Strengths	Weaknesses
Payback	Easy to understand Based on cash flows Highlights risks	Ignores profitability and the time value of money
Accounting rate of return	Based on profitability	Ignores the time value of money
Discounted cash flow: Net present value Internal rate of return	Based on cash flows, profitability, and the time value of money	It may be difficult to determine the appropriate discount rate

Decision Guidelines

CAPITAL BUDGETING

Here are some guidelines managers can use to make capital budgeting decisions.

Decision	**Guidelines**
Should we make a long-term investment in plant and equipment?	Investment may be worthwhile if: • Payback period is shorter than the asset's useful life. • Expected accounting rate of return is more than your required rate of return. • Discounted cash-flow methods: Net present value (NPV) is positive. Internal rate of return (IRR) is more than your required rate of return.
How to compute the payback period?	$$\text{Payback period} = \frac{\text{Amount invested in the asset}}{\text{Expected annual net cash inflow (from cost savings)}}$$
How to compute the accounting rate of return?	$$\frac{\text{Accounting}}{\text{rate of return}} = \frac{\text{Average annual operating income (or cost savings) from the asset}}{\text{Average amount invested in the asset}}$$ $$= \frac{\text{Average annual net cash inflow from the asset} - \text{Annual depreciation on the asset}}{(\text{Amount invested in the asset} + \text{Residual value})/2}$$
How to compute net present value with • Equal annual cash flows?	$$\frac{\text{Present value of }\textit{annuity}}{\text{of \$1 (Exhibit 25-15)}} \times \frac{\text{Annual net cash}}{\text{inflow or outflow}}$$
• Unequal annual cash flows?	Compute the present value of each year's net cash inflow or outflow (present value of \$1 from Exhibit 25-17 × net cash receipts) and add up the yearly present values.
How to compute internal rate of return?	$$\frac{\text{Annuity PV factor}}{\text{(Use Exhibit 25-15)}} = \frac{\text{Investment in the asset}}{\text{Expected annual net cash inflow}}$$
Which capital budgeting methods are best?	Discounted cash-flow methods (net present value and IRR) are best because they incorporate both profitability and the time value of money.

Summary Problem 2

Leggs is considering buying a new bar-coding machine for its Reno plant. The data for the machine follow.

Cost of machine	$48,000
Estimated residual value	$ 0
Estimated annual net cash inflow (for 5 years)	$12,000
Estimated useful life	5 years
Required rate of return	12%

Requirements

1. Compute the bar-coding machine's payback period.

2. Compute the bar-coding machine's accounting rate of return.

3. Compute the bar-coding machine's net present value.

4. Would you buy the bar-coding machine? Why?

Solution

Requirement 1

$$\text{Payback period} = \frac{\text{Amount invested}}{\text{Expected annual net cash inflow}} = \frac{\$48,000}{\$12,000} = 4 \text{ years}$$

Requirement 2

$$\text{Accounting rate of return} = \frac{\text{Average annual operating income from asset}}{\text{Average amount invested in asset}}$$

$$= \frac{\begin{array}{c}\text{Average annual net cash} \\ \text{inflow from asset}\end{array} - \begin{array}{c}\text{Annual} \\ \text{depreciation on asset}\end{array}}{(\text{Amount invested in asset} + \text{Residual value})/2}$$

$$= \frac{\$12,000 - \$9,600^*}{(\$48,000 + \$0)/2}$$

$$= \frac{\$2,400}{\$24,000}$$

$$= 0.10$$

$$= 10\%$$

$$^*\frac{\$48,000}{5 \text{ years}} = \$9,600$$

Requirement 3

Present value of annuity of equal annual net cash inflow at 12% ($12,000 × 3.605†)	$ 43,260
− Investment	(48,000)
= Net present value	$ (4,740)

†Present value of annuity of $1 for 5 years at 12%, from Exhibit 25-15.

Requirement 4

Decision: Do not buy the bar-coding machine because it has a negative net present value. The net present value model considers profitability and the time value of money. The other models ignore at least one of those factors.

Review *Special Decisions and Capital Budgeting*

Accounting Vocabulary _____

Accounting Rate of Return
A measure of profitability computed by dividing the average annual operating income from an asset by the average amount invested in the asset.

Annuity
A stream of equal periodic cash flows.

Capital Budgeting
Budgeting for the acquisition of capital assets—assets used for a long period of time.

Constraint
A constraint restricts production or sale of a product and may vary from company to company.

Cost of Capital
Management's minimum desired rate of return on an investment. Also called the **hurdle rate, required rate of return**, and **discount rate**.

Discount Rate
Management's minimum desired rate of return on an investment. Also called the **hurdle rate, required rate of return**, and **cost of capital**.

Hurdle Rate
Management's minimum desired rate of return on an investment. Also called the **discount rate, required rate of return**, and **cost of capital**.

Internal Rate of Return (IRR)
The rate of return (based on discounted cash flows) that a company can expect to earn by investing in the project. The discount rate that makes the net present value of the project's cash flows equal to zero.

Net Present Value (NPV)
The decision model that brings cash inflows an outflows back to a common time period by discounting these expected future cash flows to their present value, using a minimum desired rate of return.

Opportunity Cost
The benefit forgone by not choosing an alternative course of action.

Outsourcing
A make-or-buy decision: managers decide whether to buy a component product or service or produce it in-house.

Payback
The length of time it takes to recover, in net cash inflows, the dollars of a capital outlay.

Relevant Information
Expected future data that differs among alternatives.

Required Rate of Return
Management's minimum desired rate of return on an investment. Also called the **hurdle rate, discount rate**, and **cost of capital**.

Sunk Cost
A past cost that cannot be changed regardless of which future action is taken.

Time Value of Money
The fact that money can be invested to earn income over time.

Quick Check

1. In making *short-term* special decisions, you should:
   a. Separate variable from fixed costs
   b. Focus on total costs
   c. Use a conventional income statement approach
   d. Discount cash flows to their present values

2. Which of the following is relevant to Amazon.com's decision to accept a large special order at a lower sale price from a customer in China?
   a. The cost of warehouses in the United States
   b. The cost of shipping the order to the customer
   c. Investment in its Web site
   d. Company president's salary

3. In deciding whether to drop its electronics product line, Best Buy's managers would consider:
   a. The revenues it would lose from dropping the product line
   b. The costs it could save by dropping the product line
   c. How dropping the electronics product line would affect sales of its other products like CDs
   d. All of the above

4. In deciding which product lines to emphasize, a company's managers should focus on the product line that has the highest:
   a. Profit per unit of product
   b. Contribution margin per unit of the constraining factor
   c. Contribution margin ratio
   d. Contribution margin per unit of product

5. Suppose a restaurant is considering whether to (1) bake bread in-house or (2) buy the bread from a local bakery. The chef estimates that variable costs for each loaf include $0.50 of ingredients and $1.00 of direct labor for in-house baking. Allocating fixed overhead (depreciation on the kitchen equipment) based on direct labor assigns $1.00 of fixed overhead per loaf. The local bakery charges $1.75 per loaf. Which statement helps the restaurant decide whether to bake the bread in-house or buy from the local bakery?
   a. There is a $0.25 per loaf advantage to buying the bread from the local bakery.
   b. There is a $1.25 per loaf advantage to baking the bread in-house.
   c. There is a $0.25 per loaf advantage to baking the bread in-house.
   d. There is a $0.75 per loaf advantage to buying the bread from the local bakery.

6. In computing the accounting rate of return for a business expansion, the company's managers would consider all of the following *except*:
   a. Present value factors
   b. The cost of the expansion
   c. Depreciation on the assets built in the expansion
   d. Predicted net cash inflows over the life of the expansion

7. Suppose a company is deciding whether to purchase new software. The payback period for the $30,000 software package is 4 years, and the software's expected life is 6 years. What are the expected annual net cash savings from the new software?

   a. $5,000

   b. $130

   c. $200

   d. $7,500

8. In computing the net present value of the Snow Park Lodge expansion, managers would consider all of the following *except*:

   a. Predicted net cash inflows over the life of the expansion

   b. The cost of the expansion

   c. Depreciation on the assets built in the expansion

   d. The company's required rate of return on investments

9. Suppose Prentice Hall is considering investing in warehouse-management software that costs $500,000 and should lead to cost savings of $120,000 a year for its 5-year life. If Prentice Hall has a 12% required rate of return, what is the net present value of the software investment?

   a. ($67,400)

   b. ($88,040)

   c. $411,960

   d. $432,600

10. Which of the following is the most reliable method for making capital budgeting decisions?

   a. Incremental method

   b. Accounting rate of return method

   c. Payback method

   d. Net present value method

Answers are given after Apply Your Knowledge (p. 1297).

Assess Your Progress

Short Exercises

Identifying relevant data

S25-1 You are trying to decide whether or not to trade in your old printer for a new model. Your usage pattern will remain unchanged, but the old and new printers use different ink cartridges. Are the following items relevant or irrelevant to your decision? (p. 1252)

a. The price of the new printer

b. The price you paid for the old printer

c. The trade-in value of the old printer

d. Paper costs

e. The difference between ink cartridges' costs

Accepting or rejecting a special sales order

S25-2 Jones received a special order for 1,000 units of the XB4 engine part at a selling price of $20 per unit. Excess capacity exists to make this order. No additional selling costs will be incurred. Unit costs to make and sell this product include:

Direct materials	$ 7
Direct labor	3
Variable manufacturing overhead	9
Fixed manufacturing overhead	4
Variable selling costs	2
	$25

List the relevant costs. What will be the change in operating income if Jones accepts the special order? Should Jones accept the order? (pp. 1254–1255)

Dropping a department

S25-3 Gila Fashions operates three departments: Men's, Women's, and Accessories. Gila Fashions allocates fixed expenses (building depreciation and utilities) based on the square feet occupied by each department. Departmental operating income data for the third quarter of 2009 are as follows:

	Department			Total
	Men's	Women's	Accessories	
Sales revenue	$ 105,000	$ 54,000	$ 100,000	$ 259,000
Variable expenses	60,000	30,000	90,000	180,000
Fixed expenses	25,000	20,000	25,000	70,000
Total expenses	85,000	50,000	115,000	250,000
Operating income (loss)	$ 20,000	$ 4,000	$ (15,000)	$ 9,000

Should Gila Fashions drop any of the departments? Give your reason. (The store will remain in the same building regardless of the decision.) (pp. 1256–1257)

S25-4 Consider Gila Fashions from S25-3. Assume that the fixed expenses assigned to each department include only:

- Salary of the department's manager
- Cost of advertising directly related to that department

Gila Fashions will not incur these fixed expenses for any department that is dropped. Under these circumstances, should Gila Fashions drop any of the departments? Give your reason. (pp. 1256–1257)

S25-5 TreadLight, Inc., produces two types of exercise treadmills: Deluxe and Regular.

The exercise craze is such that TreadLight could use all its available machine hours producing either model. The two models are processed through the same production departments.

What is the constraint? Which model should TreadLight produce? If both models should be produced, compute the mix that will maximize operating income. (p. 1258)

		Per Unit	
		Deluxe	Regular
Sale price		$1,000	$540
Costs:			
	Direct materials	$290	$100
	Direct labor	80	180
	Variable manufacturing overhead*	240	80
	Fixed manufactuing overhead*	120	40
	Variable operating expenses	115	65
	Total cost	845	465
Operating income		$155	$75

*Allocated on the basis of machine hours.

S25-6 Rita Riley manages a fleet of 200 delivery trucks for Greely Corp. Riley must decide if the company should outsource the fleet management function. If she outsources to Fleet Management Services (FMS), FMS will be responsible for maintenance and scheduling activities. This alternative would require Riley to lay off her five employees. However, her own job would be secure; she would be Greely's liaison with FMS. If she continues to manage the fleet, she will need fleet-management software. Rita gathers the following information:

Book value of 200 delivery trucks, with an estimated 5-year life	$3,500,000
Annual leasing fee for new fleet-management software	8,000
Annual maintenance of trucks	145,000
Riley's annual salary	60,000
Total annual salaries of five other fleet-management employees	150,000

continued . . .

Suppose that FMS offers to manage this fleet for an annual fee of $280,000. What will be the impact on operating income if Greely out-sources the fleet-management services to FMS? (pp. 1259–1261)

Outsourcing decision for services

S25-7 Refer to S25-6. What qualitative factors should Riley consider before making her final decision? (p. 1261)

Deciding whether to sell as-is or process further

S25-8 Car Components, Inc., has an inventory of 500 obsolete remote-entry keys that are carried in inventory at a manufacturing cost of $80,000. Production supervisor Leo George must decide whether to:

- Process the inventory further at a cost of $20,000, with the expectation of selling it for $28,000, or
- Scrap the inventory for a sale price of $5,000

What should George do? Present figures to support your decision. (p. 1262)

Computing payback period

S25-9 Rico buys a new treadmill for his training facility. The treadmill costs $5,000 and will generate annual cash flows of $2,000. What is the payback period? (p. 1267)

Computing payback period

S25-10 José Munoz, owner of a water park, is considering adding a 50-foot waterslide. The waterslide will cost $20,000. José estimates that the waterslide will generate annual cash flows of $4,000. What is the payback period? (p. 1267)

Computing accounting rate of return

S25-11 The Hampton Corporation bought a new machine costing $50,000 with a 5-year useful life and no residual value. The company plans to generate annual cash inflows of $15,000. Calculate the accounting rate of return. (p. 1269)

Computing accounting rate of return

S25-12 To begin new operations in Chicago, the Serna Corporation bought a new building costing $500,000. The corporation expects the new facility to generate $25,000 in income annually. Calculate the accounting rate of return. (p. 1269)

Computing net present value

S25-13 Leo Franco owns a bowling alley. He wants to add a video arcade that would cost $30,000 and would have a 3-year life and no residual value. Franco expects the video arcade to generate $11,000 in annual cash inflows. The discount rate is 10%. Calculate the net present value of this investment. Should Franco make the investment? (pp. 1271, 1272)

Computing net present value

S25-14 Tom Higgins, a snow plowing service in Minnesota, bought a snowplow for $125,000. The snowplow will have a 6-year useful life and no residual value. Tom expects the snowplow to generate $30,000 in annual cash inflows. The discount rate is 10%. Calculate the net present value of this investment.

Exercises

E25-15 FreeStyle manufactures a variety of recreational foot bags. FreeStyle's total production cost is $4 per HackySack foot bag, as follows:

Variable costs:	
Direct materials	$0.50
Direct labor	0.95
Variable overhead	1.30
Fixed overhead	1.25
Total cost	$4.00

Alba Athletics offers to buy 5,000 HackySack foot bags for $3.00 per bag. FreeStyle has enough excess capacity to handle the special order.

Requirements

1. Prepare an incremental analysis to determine the impact on operating income if FreeStyle accepts the special sales order from Alba Athletics. Should FreeStyle accept the special order? (pp. 1254–1255)

2. Now suppose that Alba wants FreeStyle to replace the hand-woven fabric with a three-panel design made of leather. FreeStyle will spend an additional $.40 per bag to replace the fabric with leather. What will be the impact on operating income if FreeStyle increases its costs for this special order? Should FreeStyle accept the special order under these circumstances? (pp. 1254–1255)

E25-16 Challenger inflatable kayaks sell for $65 per kayak. The average cost for an inflatable kayak is $42, as follows:

Direct materials	$20
Direct labor	6
Variable manufacturing overhead	4
Variable marketing expenses	2
Fixed manufacturing overhead	10*
Total costs	$42

*$10,000 total fixed manufacturing overhead ÷ 1,000 kayaks

Challenger has enough idle capacity to accept a one-time-only special order from Alaska Adventures for 100 kayaks at $40 per kayak. Challenger will not incur any additional variable marketing expenses for the order.

Requirements

1. How would accepting the order affect Challenger's operating income? In addition to the special order's effect on profits, what

continued . . .

other (longer-term, qualitative) factors should Challenger's managers consider in deciding whether to accept the order? (pp. 1254–1255)

2. Challenger's marketing manager, Eva Winan, argues against accepting the special order because the offer price of $40 is less than Challenger's $42 cost to make the kayaks. Explain whether her analysis is correct. (p. 1255)

Keeping or dropping a product line (fixed costs unchanged)

1 **2**

E25-17 Top managers at CalPaks are considering dropping the rolling backpacks product line. Company accountants have prepared the following analysis to help make this decision:

	Total	Day Packs	Rolling Backpacks
Sales revenue	$420,000	$300,000	$120,000
Variable expenses	240,000	150,000	90,000
Contribution margin	180,000	150,000	30,000
Fixed expenses:			
Manufacturing	125,000	70,000	55,000
Marketing and administrative	70,000	55,000	15,000
Total fixed expenses	195,000	125,000	70,000
Operating income (loss)	$ (15,000)	$ 25,000	$ (40,000)

Total fixed expenses will not change if the company stops selling rolling backpacks.

Prepare an incremental analysis to show the impact on operating income if CalPaks drops the rolling backpacks line. Should CalPaks drop the product line? Will dropping the rolling backpacks line add $40,000 to operating income? Explain. (pp. 1256–1257)

Keeping or dropping a product line (fixed costs change)

1 **2**

E25-18 Refer to E25-17. Assume that CalPaks can avoid $40,000 of fixed expenses by dropping the rolling backpacks product line. Prepare an incremental analysis to show the impact on operating income if CalPaks drops the rolling backpacks line. Should CalPaks drop the product line? (p. 1258)

Determining product mix

1 **2**

E25-19 Johnson Company sells both designer and moderately priced jewelry. Top management is deciding which product line to emphasize. Accountants have provided the following data:

	Per Item	
	Designer	Moderately Priced
Average sale price	$ 200	$ 84
Average variable expenses	85	24
Average contribution margin	115	60
Average fixed expenses (allocated)	20	10
Average operating income	$ 95	$ 50

continued . . .

The Johnson store in Boise, Idaho, has 10,000 square feet of floor space. If it emphasizes moderately priced goods, 700 items can be displayed in the store. If it emphasizes designer wear, only 300 designer items can be displayed. These numbers also are the average monthly sales in units.

Prepare an analysis to show which product line to emphasize. (p. 1258)

Outsourcing decision

E25-20 Riva Snowboards manufactures fiberglass snowboards. The Z120 fiberglass snowboard has the following manufacturing costs per unit:

Direct materials	$18
Direct labor	6
Variable overhead	11
Fixed overhead	3
Manufacturing product cost	$38

Lima, Inc. has offered to make the Z120 snowboard for $34 per snowboard. If Riva buys the snowboard from the outside supplier, the manufacturing facilities that will be idled cannot be used for any other purpose. Should Riva make or buy the Z120 snowboard? (pp. 1259–1261)

Determining best use of facilities

E25-21 Refer to E25-20. Riva Snowboards needs 10,000 Z120 fiberglass snowboards. By outsourcing them, Riva can use its idle facilities to manufacture another product that will contribute $30,000 to operating income. Identify the incremental costs that Riva will incur to acquire 10,000 snowboards under three alternative plans: make, buy and leave facilities idle, or buy and use facilities for other product. Which plan makes the best use of Riva's facilities? Support your answer. (p. 1261)

Sell as-is or process further

E25-22 Concert Sounds has damaged some custom speakers that cost the company $10,000 to manufacture. Owner Jim Buffett is considering two options for disposing of this inventory. One plan is to sell the speakers as damaged inventory for $2,500. The alternative is to spend an additional $500 to repair the damage and expect to sell the speakers for $3,200. What should Buffett do? Support your answer with an analysis that shows expected net revenue under each alternative. (p. 1262)

Computing payback

E25-23 Hoek Co. is considering the purchase of a new machine. The purchase price is $120,000. The owners believe the machine will generate net cash inflows of $25,000 annually. It will have to be replaced in 6 years. Compute the payback period of the machine. Does the payback method support purchase of the machine? (p. 1267)

Determining accounting rate of return

E25-24 The managers of Car Design are considering two investments in equipment. Equipment manufactured by Ward, Inc., costs $1,000,000 and will last for 5 years, with no residual value. The Ward equipment is expected to generate annual cash inflows of $250,000. Equipment manu-

continued . . .

factured by Vargas Co. is priced at $1,200,000 and will last six years. It promises annual operating cash inflows of $240,500, and its expected residual value is $100,000. Car Design depreciates equipment using the straight-line method.

Which equipment offers the higher accounting rate of return? (p. 1269)

Computing net present value

4

E25-25 Use the net present value method to determine whether Stuebs Products should invest in the following projects:

- *Project A*: Costs $275,000 and offers eight annual net cash inflows of $55,000. Stuebs Products requires an annual return of 14% on projects like A.

- *Project B*: Costs $380,000 and offers nine annual net cash inflows of $72,000. Stuebs Products demands an annual return of 12% on investments of this nature.

What is the net present value of each project? What is the maximum acceptable price to pay for each project? (pp. 1271, 1272)

Computing internal rate of return

4

E25-26 Refer to Exercise E25-25. Compute the internal rate of return of each project, and use this information to identify the better investment. (p. 1274)

Problems (Group A)

Accepting or rejecting a special sales order

1 **2**

P25-27A The Hat Man's contribution margin income statement follows:

Sales in units	360,000
Sales revenue	$432,000
Variable expenses:	
Manufacturing	$108,000
Marketing and administrative	53,000
Total variable expenses	161,000
Contribution margin	271,000
Fixed expenses:	
Manufacturing	156,000
Marketing and administrative	40,000
Total fixed expenses	196,000
Operating income	$ 75,000

Sports King has offered to purchase 5,000 beanie caps for $0.70 per cap, which is considerably below the normal sale price of $1.20. Acceptance of the order will not increase any of The Hat Man's marketing and administrative expenses. The Hat Man's plant has enough unused capacity to manufacture the additional boxes.

Requirements

1. Prepare an incremental analysis to determine the impact on The Hat Man's operating income if the special sales order is accepted. Should The Hat Man accept the special order? (pp. 1254–1255)

2. Identify long-term factors that The Hat Man should consider in deciding whether to accept the special sales order. (p. 1255)

P25-28A The following operating income data of Sam's Sportswear highlight the losses of the T-shirts product line:

| | Total | Product Line | |
		T-shirts	Sweatshirts
Sales revenue	$730,000	$190,000	$540,000
Cost of goods sold:			
Variable	$138,000	$ 44,000	$ 94,000
Fixed	61,000	20,000	41,000
Total cost of goods sold	199,000	64,000	135,000
Gross profit	531,000	126,000	405,000
Marketing and administrative expenses:			
Variable	223,000	98,000	125,000
Fixed	93,000	38,000	55,000
Total marketing and administrative expenses	316,000	136,000	180,000
Operating income (loss)	$215,000	$ (10,000)	$225,000

Sam is considering discontinuing the T-shirts product line. The company's accountants estimate that dropping the T-shirts line will decrease the fixed cost of goods sold (fixed manufacturing expenses) by $16,000 and decrease fixed marketing and administrative expenses by $12,000.

Requirements

1. Prepare an incremental analysis to show the impact on operating income if Sam drops the T-shirts product line. Should Sam drop the T-shirts line? (p. 1258)

2. Prepare contribution margin income statements to compare Sam's total operating income (a) with the T-shirts product line, and (b) without it. Compare the *difference* between the two alternatives' income numbers to your answer to Requirement 1. What have you learned from this comparison? (p. 1256)

P25-29A Outdoor Living specializes in outdoor furniture and spas. Owner Cheryl Homberg is expanding the store. She is deciding which product line to emphasize. To make this decision, she assembles the following data:

| | Per Unit | |
	Spas	Patio Sets
Sale price	$1,000	$ 800
Variable expenses	480	440
Contribution margin	$ 520	$ 360
Contribution margin ratio	52%	45%

After renovation, the store will have 8,000 square feet of floor space. By devoting the new floor space to patio sets, Outdoor Living can display 50 patio sets. Alternatively, Outdoor Living could display 30 spas. Homberg expects monthly sales to equal the maximum number of units displayed.

continued . . .

Requirements
1. Identify the constraining factor for Outdoor Living. (p. 1258)
2. Prepare an analysis to show which product line to emphasize. (p. 1258)

Outsourcing; best use of facilities

P25-30A Healthy Grain, Inc., makes organic cereal. Cost data for producing 140,000 boxes of cereal each year are as follows:

Direct materials	$ 220,000
Direct labor	140,000
Variable overhead	60,000
Fixed overhead	430,000
Total manufacturing costs	$ 850,000

Suppose General Mills will make the cereal and sell it to Healthy Grain for $4 a box. Healthy Grain also would pay $0.20 a box to transport the cereal from General Mills to Healthy Grain's warehouse.

Requirements
1. Healthy Grain's accountants predict that purchasing the cereal from General Mills will enable the company to avoid $130,000 of fixed overhead. Prepare an analysis to show whether Healthy Grain should make or buy the cereal. (pp. 1259–1261)
2. Assume that the Healthy Grain's facilities freed up by purchasing the cereal from General Mills can be used to manufacture cereal bars that will contribute $180,000 to profit. Total fixed costs will be the same as if Healthy Grain used the plant to make cereal. Prepare an analysis to show which alternative makes the best use of Healthy Grain's facilities: (a) make cereal, (b) buy cereal and leave facilities idle, or (c) buy cereal and make cereal bars. (p. 1261)

Deciding whether to sell as-is or process further

P25-31A Seminole Petroleum has spent $200,000 to refine 60,000 gallons of petroleum distillate. Suppose Seminole can sell the distillate for $6 a gallon. Alternatively, it can process the distillate further and produce 55,000 gallons of cleaner fluid. The additional processing will cost another $1.75 *per gallon of distillate*. The cleaner fluid can be sold for $9 a gallon. To sell cleaner fluid, Seminole must pay a sales commission of $0.10 a gallon and a transportation charge of $0.15 a gallon.

Requirements
1. Diagram Seminole's alternatives, using Exhibit 25-11 as a guide. (p. 1261)
2. Identify the sunk cost. Is the sunk cost relevant to Seminole's decision? (p. 1261)
3. Prepare an analysis to indicate whether Seminole should sell the distillate or process it into cleaner fluid. Show the expected net revenue difference between the two alternatives. (p. 1262)

Capital budgeting

P25-32A Jasso Co. manufactures motorized wheelchairs. The company is considering an expansion. The plan calls for a construction cost of $5,200,000. The expansion will generate annual net cash inflows of $700,000 for 10 years.

continued . . .

Engineers estimate that the new facilities will remain useful for 10 years and have a residual value of $500,000. The company uses straight-line depreciation, and its stockholders demand an annual return of 10% on investments of this nature.

Requirements

1. Compute the payback period (p. 1267), the accounting rate of return (p. 1269), and the net present value (pp. 1271–1272) of this investment.
2. Make a recommendation whether the company should invest in this project. (p. 1272)

Capital budgeting

P25-33A Milagro Café is considering two alternative expansion plans. Plan A is to open four cafés at a total cost of $2,090,000. Expected annual net cash inflows are $400,000, with residual value of $300,000 at the end of six years. Under plan B, Milagro Café would open six cafés at a total cost of $2,100,000. This investment is expected to generate net cash inflows of $500,000 each year for six years, which is the estimated useful life of the properties. Estimated residual value of the plan B cafés is zero. Milagro Café uses straight-line depreciation and requires an annual return of 10%.

Requirements

1. Compute the payback period (p. 1267), the accounting rate of return (p. 1269), and the net present value (pp. 1270–1273) of each plan. Use the residual value when calculating the accounting rate of return for plan A, but *assume a zero residual value when calculating its net present value*. What are the strengths and weaknesses of these capital budgeting models? (pp. 1275–1276)
2. Which expansion plan should Milagro Café adopt? Why? (p. 1273)
3. Estimate the internal rate of return (IRR) for plan B. How does plan B's IRR compare with Milagro Café's required rate of return? (p. 1274)

Problems (Group B)

Accepting or rejecting a special sales order

25-34B LMS, Inc. manufactures stadium seat cushions. LMS's contribution margin income statement for the most recent month contains the following data:

Sales in units	31,000
Sales revenue	$434,000
Variable expenses:	
Manufacturing	$ 93,000
Marketing and administrative	107,000
Total variable expenses	200,000
Contribution margin	234,000
Fixed expenses:	
Manufacturing	126,000
Marketing and administrative	90,000
Total fixed expenses	216,000
Operating income	$ 18,000

continued . . .

Underwood Company has offered $9 per unit for 5,000 stadium seat cushions, which is below the normal sale price of $14. Acceptance of the order will not increase any of LMS's marketing and administrative expenses. The LMS plant has enough unused capacity to manufacture the additional cushions.

Requirements

1. Prepare an incremental analysis to determine the change in operating income if LMS accepts the special sales order. Should LMS accept the order? (pp. 1253–1254)

2. Identify long-term factors LMS should consider in deciding whether to accept the special sales order. (p. 1255)

Keeping or dropping a product line

P25-35B Members of the board of directors of Solid Security, Inc., have received the following operating income data for the year just ended.

| | Product Line | | |
	Home Systems	Business Systems	Total
Sales revenue	$300,000	$310,000	$610,000
Cost of goods sold:			
Variable	$ 38,000	$ 42,000	$ 80,000
Fixed	210,000	69,000	279,000
Total cost of goods sold	248,000	111,000	359,000
Gross profit	52,000	199,000	251,000
Marketing and administrative expenses:			
Variable	66,000	71,000	137,000
Fixed	40,000	22,000	62,000
Total marketing and administrative expenses	106,000	93,000	199,000
Operating income (loss)	$ (54,000)	$106,000	$ 52,000

Members of the board are surprised that the Home Systems product line is losing money. They commission a study to determine whether the company should drop the line. Company accountants estimate that dropping Home Systems will decrease the fixed cost of goods sold (fixed manufacturing expenses) by $80,000 and decrease the fixed marketing and administrative expenses by $14,000.

Requirements

1. Prepare an incremental analysis to calculate the change in operating income if the Home Systems product line is dropped. Should Solid Security drop the Home Systems product line? (p. 1258)

2. Prepare contribution margin income statements to show Solid Security's total operating income under the two alternatives: (a) with the Home Systems line, and (b) without the line. Compare the *difference* between the two alternatives' income numbers to your answer to Requirement 1. What have you learned from this comparison? (p. 1256)

P25-36B IPond Corp. produces two lines of MP3 players: 512MB and 1GB. Because IPond can sell all the MP3 players it can produce, the owners are expanding the plant. They are deciding which product line to emphasize. To make this decision, they assemble the following data:

		Per Unit	
		IPond 1 GB	IPond 512 MB
Sale price		$90	$48
Variable expenses		20	18
Contribution margin		$70	$30
Contribution margin ratio		77.8%	62.5%

After expansion, the factory will have a production capacity of 4,500 machine hours per month. The plant can manufacture either 24 IPond 1 GB players or 60 IPond 512 MB players per machine hour.

Requirements
1. Identify the constraining factor for IPond. (p. 1258)
2. Prepare an analysis to show which product line to emphasize. (p. 1258)

P25-37B Weekenders manufactures wooden decks. The costs to make 1,800 7-ply decks from maple wood are:

Direct materials	$17,520
Direct labor	3,100
Variable overhead	2,080
Fixed overhead	6,800
Total manufacturing costs for 1,800 decks	$29,500

Suppose Weekenders can purchase 7-ply decks from Lancaster Company for $14 each. Weekenders would pay $1 per unit to transport the decks to its manufacturing plant, where it would add its own logo at a cost of $0.50 per deck.

Requirements
1. Weekenders's accountants predict that purchasing the decks from Lancaster would enable the company to avoid $2,200 of fixed overhead. Prepare an analysis to show whether Weekenders should make or buy the decks. (pp. 1259–1261)
2. The facilities freed by purchasing decks from Lancaster can be used to manufacture another product that will contribute $3,100 to profit. Total fixed costs will be the same as if Weekenders had produced the decks. Show which alternative makes the best use of Weekenders's facilities: (a) make decks, (b) buy decks and leave facilities idle, or (c) buy decks and make the other product. (p. 1261)

Deciding whether to sell
as-is or process further

P25-38B Castillo Chemical Corporation has spent $240,000 to refine 72,000 gallons of acetone, which can be sold for $2.50 a gallon. Alternatively, Castillo can process the acetone further. This processing will yield a total of 60,000 gallons of lacquer thinner that can be sold for $3.00 a gallon. The additional processing will cost $0.53 *per gallon of lacquer thinner*. To sell the lacquer thinner, Castillo must pay shipping of $0.22 a gallon and administrative expenses of $0.10 a gallon on the thinner.

Requirements

1. Diagram Castillo's decision, using Exhibit 25-11 as a guide. (p. 1261)
2. Identify the sunk cost. Is the sunk cost relevant to Castillo's decision? (p. 1261)
3. Should Castillo sell the acetone or process it into lacquer thinner? Show the expected net revenue difference between the two alternatives. (p. 1262)

Capital budgeting

P25-39B Playtime, Inc. is considering purchasing an amusement park in El Paso, Texas, for $2,000,000. The new facility will generate annual net cash inflows of $520,000 for eight years. Engineers estimate that the facility will remain useful for eight years and have a residual value of $200,000. The company uses straight-line depreciation, and its stockholders demand an annual return of 12% on investments of this nature.

Requirements

1. Compute the payback period (p. 1267), the accounting rate of return (p. 1269), and the net present value (pp. 1270–1273) of this investment.
2. Make a recommendation whether the company should invest in this project. (p. 1262)

Capital budgeting

P25-40B Qwizmo operates a chain of sandwich shops. The company is considering two alternative expansion plans. Plan A is to open two smaller shops at a total cost of $844,000. Expected annual net cash inflows are $150,000, with zero residual value at the end of 10 years. Under plan B, Qwizmo would open one larger shop at a cost of $834,000. This plan is expected to generate net cash inflows of $90,000 per year for 10 years, the estimated life of the shop. Estimated residual value is $100,000. Qwizmo uses straight-line depreciation and requires an annual return of 8%.

Requirements

1. Compute the payback period (p. 1267), the accounting rate of return (p. 1269), and the net present value (pp. 1270–1273) of these two plans. Use the residual value when calculating the accounting rate of return for plan B, but *assume a residual value of zero when calculating its net present value*. What are the strengths and weaknesses of these capital budgeting models? (pp. 1275–1276)
2. Which expansion plan should Qwizmo choose? Why? (p. 1273)
3. Estimate plan A's internal rate of return (IRR). How does the IRR compare with the company's required rate of return? (p. 1273)

Apply Your Knowledge

Decision Cases

Case 1. Rye Financial Services provides banks access to sophisticated financial information and analysis systems over the Web. The company combines these tools with access to benchmarking data, including e-mail and wireless communications, so that banks can instantly evaluate individual loan applications and entire loan portfolios.

Rye Financial Services' CEO Jon Wise is happy with the company's growth. To better focus on client service, Wise is considering outsourcing some functions. CFO Jenny Lee suggests that the company's e-mail may be the place to start. She recently attended a conference and learned that many companies were outsourcing their e-mail function. Wise asks Lee to identify costs related to Rye Financial Services' in-house Microsoft Exchange e-mail application, which has 2,300 mailboxes. This information follows:

Variable costs:	
E-mail license	$ 7 per mailbox per month
Virus protection license	$ 1 per mailbox per month
Other variable costs	$ 4 per mailbox per month
Fixed costs:	
Computer hardware costs	$ 94,300 per month
$8,050 monthly salary for two information technology staff members who work only on e-mail	$ 16,100 per month

Requirements

1. Compute the total cost per mailbox per month of Rye Financial Services' current e-mail function.

2. Suppose Mail.com, a leading provider of Internet-messaging outsourcing services, offers to host Rye Financial Services' e-mail function for $9 per mailbox per month. If Rye Financial Services outsources its e-mail to Mail.com, Rye Financial Services will still need the virus protection license, its computer hardware, and one information technology staff member, who would be responsible for maintaining virus protection, quarantining suspicious e-mail, and managing content (e.g., screening e-mail for objectionable content). Should CEO Wise accept Mail.com's offer?

3. Suppose for an additional $5 per mailbox per month, Mail.com also will provide virus protection, quarantine, and content-management services. Outsourcing these additional functions would mean that Rye Financial Services would not need either an e-mail information technology staff member or the separate virus protection license. Should CEO Wise outsource these additional services to Mail.com?

Case 2. Ted Robertson, a second-year business student at the University of Florida, will graduate in two years with an accounting major and a Spanish minor. Robertson is trying to decide where to work this summer. He has two choices: work full-time for a bottling plant or work part-time in the Accounting Department of a meat-packing plant. He probably will work at the same place next summer as well. He is able to work 12 weeks during the summer.

The bottling plant will pay Robertson $380 per week this year and 7% more next year. At the meat-packing plant, he could work 20 hours per week at $9 per hour. By working only part-time, he could take two accounting courses this summer. Tuition is $225 per hour for each of the four-hour courses. Robertson believes that the experience he gains this summer will qualify him for a full-time accounting position with the meat-packing plant next year. That position will pay $550 per week.

Robertson sees two additional benefits of working part-time this summer. First, he could reduce his workload during the fall and spring semesters by one course each term. Second, he would have the time to work as a grader in the university's Accounting Department during the 15-week fall term. Grading pays $50 per week.

Requirements

1. Suppose that Ted Robertson ignores the time value of money in decisions that cover this short a time period. Suppose also that his sole goal is to make as much money as possible between now and the end of next summer. What should he do? What would *you* do if you were faced with these alternatives?

2. Now suppose that Robertson considers the time value of money for all cash flows that he expects to receive one year or more in the future. Which alternative does this consideration favor? Why?

Ethical Issue

Linda Peters is the controller for Long Associates, a property management company in Portland, Oregon. Each year Peters and payroll clerk Toby Stock meet with the external auditors about payroll accounting. This year, the auditors suggest that Peters consider outsourcing Long Associates' payroll accounting to a company specializing in payroll processing services. This would enable Peters and her staff to focus on their primary responsibility: accounting for the properties under management. At present, payroll requires 1.5 employee positions—payroll clerk Toby Stock and a bookkeeper who spends half her time entering payroll data in the system.

Peters considers this suggestion. She lists the following items relating to outsourcing payroll accounting:

a. The current payroll software that was purchased for $4,000 three years ago would not be needed if payroll processing were outsourced.

b. Long's bookkeeper would spend half her time preparing the weekly payroll input form that is given to the payroll processing service. She is paid $450 a week.

c. Long Associates would no longer need payroll clerk Toby Stock, whose annual salary is $42,000.

d. The payroll processing service would charge $2,000 a month.

Requirements
1. Would outsourcing the payroll function increase or decrease Long Associates' operating income?

2. Peters believes that outsourcing payroll would simplify her job, but she does not like the prospect of having to lay off Toby Stock, who has become a close personal friend. She does not believe there is another position available for Stock at his current salary. Can you think of other factors that might support keeping Stock, rather than outsourcing payroll processing? How should each of the factors affect Peters's decision if she wants to act ethically and do what is best for the company?

Team Project

John Abel is the founder and sole owner of Abel, Inc. Analysts have estimated that his chain of home improvement stores scattered around nine midwestern states generates about $3 billion in annual sales. But how can Abel compete with giant Lowe's?

Suppose Abel is trying to decide whether to invest $45 million in a state-of-the-art manufacturing plant in Kansas City. Abel expects the plant would operate for 15 years, after which it would have no residual value. The plant would produce Abel's own line of Formica countertops, cabinets, and picnic tables.

Abel would incur the following unit costs in producing its own product lines:

	Per Unit		
	Countertops	Cabinets	Picnic Tables
Direct materials	$15	$10	$25
Direct labor	10	5	15
Variable manufacturing overhead	5	2	6

Rather than making these products, Abel could buy them from outside suppliers. Suppliers would charge Abel $40 per countertop, $25 per cabinet, and $65 per picnic table.

Whether Abel makes or buys the products, he expects the following annual sales:

- Countertops—487,200 at $130 each

- Picnic tables—100,000 at $225 each

- Cabinets—150,000 at $75 each

If "making" is sufficiently more profitable than outsourcing, Abel will build the new plant. He has asked your consulting group for a recommendation. Abel uses a 14% discount rate and the straight-line depreciation method.

Requirements

1. Are the following items relevant or irrelevant in Abel's decision to build a new plant to manufacture his own products?

   a. The unit sale prices of the countertops, cabinets, and picnic tables (the sale prices that Abel charges its customers)

   b. The prices outside suppliers would charge Abel for the three products, if Abel decides to outsource the products rather than make them

   c. The $45 million to build the new plant

   d. The direct materials, direct labor, and variable overhead Abel would incur to manufacture the three product lines

   e. Abel's salary

2. Determine whether Abel should make or outsource the countertops, cabinets, and picnic tables, *assuming that the company already has built the plant and therefore has the manufacturing capacity to produce these products*. In other words, what is the annual difference in cash flows if Abel decides to make rather than outsource each of these three products?

3. In Requirement 2, you computed the annual difference in cash flows if Abel decides to make rather than buy the three products. To analyze the investment in the plant relative to the alternative of outsourcing the products, use this *difference* in annual cash flows to compute the following for the investment in the new plant:

   a. Payback period

   b. Accounting rate of return

   c. Net present value

   d. Internal rate of return

   (*Hint*: Base the benefit side of your computations on the *difference* in annual cash flows you computed in Requirement 2, *not* the total expected cash flows from building the plant. Use the present value tables in Appendix C.)

4. Write a memo giving your recommendation to John Abel. The memo should clearly state your recommendation, along with a brief summary of the reasons for your recommendation.

For Internet Exercises, Excel in Practice, and additional online activities, go to the Web site, www.prenhall.com/horngren.

Quick Check

1. *a*   2. *b*   3. *d*   4. *b*   5. *c*   6. *a*   7. *d*   8. *c*   9. *a*   10. *d*

Appendix A

2 0 0 5

ANNUAL REPORT

REPORT OF ERNST & YOUNG LLP
INDEPENDENT REGISTERED PUBLIC ACCOUNTING FIRM

The Board of Directors and Stockholders
Amazon.com, Inc.

We have audited the accompanying consolidated balance sheets of Amazon.com, Inc. as of December 31, 2005 and 2004, and the related consolidated statements of operations, stockholders' equity (deficit), and cash flows for each of the three years in the period ended December 31, 2005. Our audits also included the financial statement schedule listed in the Index at Item 15(a)(2). These financial statements and schedule are the responsibility of the Company's management. Our responsibility is to express an opinion on these financial statements and schedule based on our audits.

We conducted our audits in accordance with the standards of the Public Company Accounting Oversight Board (United States). Those standards require that we plan and perform the audit to obtain reasonable assurance about whether the financial statements are free of material misstatement. An audit includes examining, on a test basis, evidence supporting the amounts and disclosures in the financial statements. An audit also includes assessing the accounting principles used and significant estimates made by management, as well as evaluating the overall financial statement presentation. We believe that our audits provide a reasonable basis for our opinion.

In our opinion, the financial statements referred to above present fairly, in all material respects, the consolidated financial position of Amazon.com, Inc. at December 31, 2005 and 2004, and the consolidated results of its operations and its cash flows for each of the three years in the period ended December 31, 2005, in conformity with U.S. generally accepted accounting principles. Also, in our opinion, the related financial statement schedule, when considered in relation to the basic financial statements taken as a whole, presents fairly in all material respects the information set forth therein.

As discussed in Note 1 to the consolidated financial statements, the Company adopted Statement of Financial Accounting Standards No. 123 (revised 2004), Share-Based Payment, effective January 1, 2005.

We also have audited, in accordance with the standards of the Public Company Accounting Oversight Board (United States), the effectiveness of Amazon.com, Inc.'s internal control over financial reporting as of December 31, 2005, based on criteria established in Internal Control-Integrated Framework issued by the Committee of Sponsoring Organizations of the Treadway Commission and our report dated February 16, 2006 expressed an unqualified opinion thereon.

/s/ ERNST & YOUNG LLP

Seattle, Washington
February 16, 2006

AMAZON.COM, INC.

CONSOLIDATED STATEMENTS OF CASH FLOWS
(in millions)

	Year Ended December 31,		
	2005	**2004**	**2003**
CASH AND CASH EQUIVALENTS, BEGINNING OF PERIOD	$ 1,303	$ 1,102	$ 738
OPERATING ACTIVITIES:			
Net income	359	588	35
Adjustments to reconcile net income to net cash provided by operating activities:			
Depreciation of fixed assets, including internal-use software and website development, and other amortization	121	76	76
Stock-based compensation	87	58	88
Other operating expense (income)	7	(8)	3
Gains on sales of marketable securities, net	(1)	(1)	(10)
Remeasurements and other	(42)	1	130
Non-cash interest expense and other	5	5	13
Deferred income taxes	70	(257)	1
Cumulative effect of change in accounting principle	(26)	—	—
Changes in operating assets and liabilities:			
Inventories	(104)	(169)	(77)
Accounts receivable, net and other current assets	(84)	(2)	2
Accounts payable	274	286	168
Accrued expenses and other current liabilities	60	(14)	(26)
Additions to unearned revenue	156	110	102
Amortization of previously unearned revenue	(149)	(107)	(112)
Net cash provided by operating activities	733	566	393
INVESTING ACTIVITIES:			
Purchases of fixed assets, including internal-use software and website development	(204)	(89)	(46)
Acquisitions, net of cash acquired	(24)	(71)	—
Sales and maturities of marketable securities and other investments	836	1,427	813
Purchases of marketable securities	(1,386)	(1,584)	(536)
Proceeds from sale of subsidiary	—	—	5
Net cash (used in) provided by investing activities	(778)	(317)	236
FINANCING ACTIVITIES:			
Proceeds from exercises of stock options and other	66	60	163
Proceeds from long-term debt and other	11	—	—
Repayments of long-term debt and capital lease obligations	(270)	(157)	(495)
Net cash used in financing activities	(193)	(97)	(332)
Foreign-currency effect on cash and cash equivalents	(52)	49	67
Net (decrease) increase in cash and cash equivalents	(290)	201	364
CASH AND CASH EQUIVALENTS, END OF PERIOD	$ 1,013	$ 1,303	$1,102
SUPPLEMENTAL CASH FLOW INFORMATION:			
Cash paid for interest	$ 105	$ 108	$ 120
Cash paid for income taxes	12	4	2

See accompanying notes to consolidated financial statements.

AMAZON.COM, INC.

CONSOLIDATED STATEMENTS OF OPERATIONS
(in millions, except per share data)

| | Year Ended December 31, | | |
	2005	2004	2003
Net sales	$8,490	$6,921	$5,264
Cost of sales	6,451	5,319	4,007
Gross profit	2,039	1,602	1,257
Operating expenses (1):			
Fulfillment	745	601	495
Marketing	198	162	128
Technology and content	451	283	257
General and administrative	166	124	104
Other operating expense (income)	47	(8)	3
Total operating expenses	1,607	1,162	987
Income from operations	432	440	270
Interest income	44	28	22
Interest expense	(92)	(107)	(130)
Other income (expense), net	2	(5)	7
Remeasurements and other	42	(1)	(130)
Total non-operating expense	(4)	(85)	(231)
Income before income taxes	428	355	39
Provision for income taxes	95	(233)	4
Income before change in accounting principle	333	588	35
Cumulative effect of change in accounting principle	26	—	—
Net income	$ 359	$ 588	$ 35
Basic earnings per share:			
Prior to cumulative effect of change in accounting principle	$ 0.81	$ 1.45	$ 0.09
Cumulative effect of change in accounting principle	0.06	—	—
	$ 0.87	$ 1.45	$ 0.09
Diluted earnings per share:			
Prior to cumulative effect of change in accounting principle	$ 0.78	$ 1.39	$ 0.08
Cumulative effect of change in accounting principle	0.06	—	—
	$ 0.84	$ 1.39	$ 0.08
Weighted average shares used in computation of earnings per share:			
Basic	412	406	395
Diluted	426	425	419

---

(1) Includes stock-based compensation as follows:

Fulfillment	$16	$10	$18
Marketing	6	4	5
Technology and content	45	32	50
General and administrative	20	12	15
Total stock-based compensation expense	$87	$58	$88

See accompanying notes to consolidated financial statements.

AMAZON.COM, INC.

CONSOLIDATED BALANCE SHEETS
(in millions, except per share data)

	December 31,	
	2005	2004
ASSETS		
Current assets:		
Cash and cash equivalents	$ 1,013	$ 1,303
Marketable securities	987	476
Cash, cash equivalents, and marketable securities	2,000	1,779
Inventories	566	480
Deferred tax assets, current portion	89	81
Accounts receivable, net and other current assets	274	199
Total current assets	2,929	2,539
Fixed assets, net	348	246
Deferred tax assets, long-term portion	223	282
Goodwill	159	139
Other assets	37	42
Total assets	$ 3,696	$ 3,248
LIABILITIES AND STOCKHOLDERS' EQUITY (DEFICIT)		
Current liabilities:		
Accounts payable	$ 1,366	$ 1,142
Accrued expenses and other current liabilities	563	478
Total current liabilities	1,929	1,620
Long-term debt and other	1,521	1,855
Commitments and contingencies		
Stockholders' equity (deficit):		
Preferred stock, $0.01 par value:		
Authorized shares—500		
Issued and outstanding shares—none	—	—
Common stock, $0.01 par value:		
Authorized shares—5,000		
Issued and outstanding shares—416 and 410 shares	4	4
Additional paid-in capital	2,263	2,123
Accumulated other comprehensive income	6	32
Accumulated deficit	(2,027)	(2,386)
Total stockholders' equity (deficit)	246	(227)
Total liabilities and stockholders' equity (deficit)	$ 3,696	$ 3,248

See accompanying notes to consolidated financial statements.

AMAZON.COM, INC.

CONSOLIDATED STATEMENTS OF STOCKHOLDERS' EQUITY (DEFICIT)

(in millions)

	Common Stock Shares	Common Stock Amount	Additional Paid-In Capital	Accumulated Other Comprehensive Income	Accumulated Deficit	Total Stockholders' Equity (Deficit)
Balance at December 31, 2002	388	$ 4	$1,643	$ 10	$(3,009)	$(1,352)
Net income	—	—	—	—	35	35
Foreign currency translation gains, net	—	—	—	15	—	15
Increase of net unrealized gains on available-for-sale securities	—	—	—	2	—	2
Net activity of terminated Euro Currency Swap	—	—	—	11	—	11
Comprehensive income						63
Exercise of common stock options, net and vesting of restricted stock	15	—	163	—	—	163
Income tax benefit on stock awards	—	—	2	—	—	2
Deferred stock-based compensation, net	—	—	4	—	—	4
Issuance of common stock – employee benefit plan	—	—	1	—	—	1
Stock compensation – restricted stock units	—	—	31	—	—	31
Stock compensation – variable accounting	—	—	52	—	—	52
Balance at December 31, 2003	403	4	1,896	38	(2,974)	(1,036)
Net income	—	—	—	—	588	588
Foreign currency translation losses, net	—	—	—	(1)	—	(1)
Decline of unrealized gains on available-for-sale securities, net of tax effect	—	—	—	(11)	—	(11)
Amortization of unrealized loss on terminated Euro Currency Swap, net of tax	—	—	—	6	—	6
Comprehensive income						582
Exercise of common stock options, net and vesting of restricted stock	6	—	60	—	—	60
Income tax benefit on stock awards	—	—	107	—	—	107
Deferred stock-based compensation, net	—	—	3	—	—	3
Issuance of common stock – employee benefit plan	1	—	3	—	—	3
Stock compensation – restricted stock units	—	—	49	—	—	49
Stock compensation – variable accounting	—	—	5	—	—	5
Balance at December 31, 2004	410	4	2,123	32	(2,386)	(227)
Net income	—	—	—	—	359	359
Foreign currency translation losses, net	—	—	—	(15)	—	(15)
Decline of unrealized gains on available-for-sale securities, net of tax effect	—	—	—	(14)	—	(14)
Amortization of unrealized loss on terminated Euro Currency Swap, net of tax	—	—	—	3	—	3
Comprehensive income						333
Exercise of common stock options, net and vesting of restricted stock	6	—	58	—	—	58
Change in accounting principle	—	—	(26)	—	—	(26)
Income tax benefit on stock awards	—	—	10	—	—	10
Issuance of common stock – employee benefit plan	—	—	4	—	—	4
Stock-based compensation	—	—	94	—	—	94
Balance at December 31, 2005	416	$ 4	$2,263	$ 6	$(2,027)	$ 246

See accompanying notes to consolidated financial statements.

AMAZON.COM, INC.

NOTES TO CONSOLIDATED FINANCIAL STATEMENTS (Excerpts)

Note 1—DESCRIPTION OF BUSINESS AND ACCOUNTING POLICIES

Description of Business

Amazon.com, Inc., a Fortune 500 company, opened its virtual doors on the World Wide Web in July 1995 and today offers Earth's Biggest Selection. We seek to be Earth's most customer-centric company, where customers can find and discover anything they might want to buy online, and endeavor to offer customers the lowest possible prices.

Amazon.com and its affiliates operate retail websites, including: *www.amazon.com, www.amazon.co.uk, www.amazon.de, www.amazon.co.jp, www.amazon.fr, www.amazon.ca,* and *www.joyo.com.* We have organized our operations into two principal segments: North America and International. The North America segment includes the operating results of *www.amazon.com* and *www.amazon.ca.* The International segment includes the operating results of *www.amazon.co.uk, www.amazon.de, www.amazon.fr, www.amazon.co.jp,* and *www.joyo.com.* In addition, we operate other websites, including *www.a9.com* and *www.alexa.com* that enable search and navigation; *www.imdb.com,* a comprehensive movie database; and Amazon Mechanical Turk at *www.mturk.com* which provides a web service for computers to integrate a network of humans directly into their processes.

Principles of Consolidation

The consolidated financial statements include the accounts of the Company, its wholly-owned subsidiaries, and those entities (relating to *www.joyo.com*) in which we have a variable interest. Intercompany balances and transactions have been eliminated.

Use of Estimates

The preparation of financial statements in conformity with GAAP requires estimates and assumptions that affect the reported amounts of assets and liabilities, revenues and expenses, and related disclosures of contingent liabilities in the consolidated financial statements and accompanying notes. Estimates are used for, but not limited to, valuation of investments, receivables valuation, sales returns, incentive discount offers, inventory valuation, depreciable lives of fixed assets, internally-developed software, valuation of acquired intangibles, deferred tax assets and liabilities, stock-based compensation, restructuring-related liabilities, and contingencies. Actual results could differ materially from those estimates.

Business Acquisitions

We acquired certain companies during 2005 for an aggregate cash purchase price of $29 million. Acquired intangibles totaled $10 million and have estimated useful lives of between one and three years. The excess of purchase price over the fair value of the net assets acquired was $19 million and is classified as "Goodwill" on our consolidated balance sheets. The results of operations of each of the acquired businesses have been included in our consolidated results from each transaction closing date forward. The effect of these acquisitions on consolidated net sales and operating income during 2005 was not significant.

In 2004, we acquired all of the outstanding shares of Joyo.com Limited, a British Virgin Islands company that operates an Internet retail website in the People's Republic of China ("PRC") in cooperation with a PRC subsidiary and PRC affiliates, at a purchase price of $75 million, including a cash payment of $71 million (net of cash acquired), the assumption of employee stock options, and transaction-related costs. Acquired intangibles were $6 million with estimated useful lives of between one and four years. The excess of purchase price over the fair value of the net assets acquired was $70 million and is classified as "Goodwill" on the consolidated balance sheets. The results of operations of Joyo.com have been included in our consolidated results from the acquisition date forward.

AMAZON.COM, INC.

NOTES TO CONSOLIDATED FINANCIAL STATEMENTS—(Continued)

The PRC regulates Joyo.com's business through regulations and license requirements restricting (i) the scope of foreign investment in the Internet, retail and delivery sectors, (ii) Internet content and (iii) the sale of certain media products. In order to meet the PRC local ownership and regulatory licensing requirements, Joyo.com's business is operated through a PRC subsidiary which acts in cooperation with PRC companies owned by nominee shareholders who are PRC nationals.

Joyo.com does not own any capital stock of the PRC affiliates, but is the primary beneficiary of future losses or profits through contractual rights. As a result, we consolidate the results of the PRC affiliates in accordance with FIN 46R, "Consolidation of Variable Interest Entities." The net assets and operating results for the PRC affiliates were not significant.

Accounting Change

As of January 1, 2005, we adopted SFAS No. 123(R) using the modified prospective method, which requires measurement of compensation cost for all stock-based awards at fair value on date of grant and recognition of compensation over the service period for awards expected to vest. The adoption of SFAS 123(R) resulted in a cumulative benefit from accounting change of $26 million, which reflects the net cumulative impact of estimating future forfeitures in the determination of period expense, rather than recording forfeitures when they occur as previously permitted. See "Note 1—Description of Business and Accounting Policies—Stock-based Compensation."

Cash and Cash Equivalents

We classify all highly liquid instruments, including money market funds that comply with Rule 2a-7 of the Investment Company Act of 1940, with a remaining maturity of three months or less at the time of purchase as cash equivalents.

Inventories

Inventories, consisting of products available for sale, are accounted for using the FIFO method, and are valued at the lower of cost or market value. This valuation requires us to make judgments, based on currently-available information, about the likely method of disposition, such as through sales to individual customers, returns to product vendors, or liquidations, and expected recoverable values of each disposition category. Based on this evaluation, we adjust the carrying amount of our inventories to lower of cost or market value.

We provide fulfillment-related services in connection with certain of our third parties and Amazon Enterprise Solutions programs. In those arrangements, as well as all other product sales by third parties, the third party maintains ownership of the related products.

Accounts Receivable, Net and Other Current Assets

Included in "Accounts receivable, net and other current assets" are prepaid expenses of $15 million and $12 million at December 31, 2005 and 2004, representing advance payments for insurance, licenses, and other miscellaneous expenses.

Allowance for Doubtful Accounts

We estimate losses on receivables based on known troubled accounts, if any, and historical experience of losses incurred. The allowance for doubtful accounts receivable was $43 million and $23 million at December 31, 2005 and 2004.

AMAZON.COM, INC.

NOTES TO CONSOLIDATED FINANCIAL STATEMENTS—(Continued)

Internal-use Software and Website Development

Costs incurred to develop software for internal use are required to be capitalized and amortized over the estimated useful life of the software in accordance with Statement of Position (SOP) 98-1, *Accounting for the Costs of Computer Software Developed or Obtained for Internal Use.* Costs related to design or maintenance of internal-use software are expensed as incurred. For the years ended 2005, 2004, and 2003, we capitalized $90 million (including $11 million of stock-based compensation), $44 million, and $30 million of costs associated with internal-use software and website development, which are partially offset by amortization of previously capitalized amounts of $50 million, $30 million, and $24 million.

Depreciation of Fixed Assets

Fixed assets include assets such as furniture and fixtures, heavy equipment, technology infrastructure, internal-use software and website development, and our DVD rental library. Depreciation is recorded on a straight-line basis over the estimated useful lives of the assets (generally two years or less for assets such as internal-use software and our DVD rental library, three years for our technology infrastructure, five years for furniture and fixtures, and ten years for heavy equipment). Depreciation expense is generally classified within the corresponding operating expense categories on the consolidated statements of operations, and certain assets, such as our DVD rental library, are amortized as "Cost of sales."

Leases and Asset Retirement Obligations

We account for our lease agreements pursuant to SFAS No 13, *Accounting for Leases*, which categorizes leases at their inception as either operating or capital leases depending on certain defined criteria. On certain of our lease agreements, we may receive rent holidays and other incentives. We recognize lease costs on a straight-line basis without regard to deferred payment terms, such as rent holidays that defer the commencement date of required payments. Additionally, incentives we receive are treated as a reduction of our costs over the term of the agreement. Leasehold improvements are capitalized at cost and amortized over the lesser of their expected useful life or the life of the lease, without assuming renewal features, if any, are exercised.

In accordance with Statement of Financial Accounting Standards (SFAS) No. 143, *Accounting for Asset Retirement Obligations,* we establish assets and liabilities for the present value of estimated future costs to return certain of our leased facilities to their original condition. Such assets are depreciated over the lease period into operating expense, and the recorded liabilities are accreted to the future value of the estimated restoration costs.

Goodwill

We evaluate goodwill for impairment, at a minimum, on an annual basis and whenever events and changes in circumstances suggest that the carrying amount may not be recoverable. Impairment of goodwill is tested at the reporting unit level by comparing the reporting unit's carrying amount, including goodwill, to the fair value of the reporting unit. The fair values of the reporting units are estimated using discounted projected cash flows. If the carrying amount of the reporting unit exceeds its fair value, goodwill is considered impaired and a second step is performed to measure the amount of impairment loss, if any. We conduct our annual impairment test as of October 1 of each year, and have determined there to be no impairment in 2005 or 2004. There were no events or circumstances from the date of our assessment through December 31, 2005 that would impact this assessment.

At December 31, 2005 and December 31, 2004, approximately 71% and 72% of our acquired goodwill was assigned to our International segment, the majority of which relates to our acquisition of Joyo.com in 2004.

AMAZON.COM, INC.

NOTES TO CONSOLIDATED FINANCIAL STATEMENTS—(Continued)

Unearned Revenue

Unearned revenue is recorded when payments are received in advance of performing our service obligations and is recognized ratably over the service period. Unearned revenue was $48 million and $41 million at December 31, 2005 and 2004. These amounts are included in "Accrued expenses and other current liabilities" on the consolidated balance sheets.

Note 3—FIXED ASSETS(partial)

Fixed assets, at cost, consist of the following (in millions):

	December 31,	
	2005	**2004**
Gross Fixed Assets (1):		
Fulfillment and customer service (2)	$309	$263
Technology infrastructure	69	38
Internal-use software, content, and website development	138	79
Other corporate assets	55	43
Gross fixed assets	571	423
Accumulated Depreciation (1):		
Fulfillment and customer service	123	106
Technology infrastructure	27	15
Internal-use software, content, and website development	51	32
Other corporate assets	22	24
Total accumulated depreciation	223	177
Total fixed assets, net	$348	$246

Depreciation expense on fixed assets was $113 million [for 2005] and $75 million [for 2004] . . .

Note 4—LONG-TERM DEBT AND OTHER

Our long-term debt and other long-term liabilities are summarized as follows:

	December 31,	
	2005	**2004**
	(in millions)	
4.75% Convertible Subordinated Notes due February 2009	$ 900	$ 900
6.875% PEACS due February 2010	580	935
Other long-term debt and capital lease obligations	44	22
	1,524	1,857
Less current portion of other long-term debt and capital lease obligations	(3)	(2)
Total long-term debt and other	$1,521	$1,855

Appendix B

Investments and International Operations

Investments in stock can be a few shares or the acquisition of an entire company. In Chapters 13 through 15 we discussed the stocks and bonds that companies issued to finance their operations. Here we examine stocks and bonds for the investor who bought them.

Stock Investments

Some Basics

The owner of the stock in a corporation is the *investor*. The corporation that issued the stock is the *investee*. If you own shares of McDonald's stock, you are the investor and McDonald's is the investee.

Classifying Investments

An investment is an asset to the investor. The investment may be short-term or long-term.

- **Short-term investments**—sometimes called **marketable securities**—are current assets. Short-term investments are liquid (readily convertible to cash), and the investor intends to convert them to cash within one year.
- **Long-term investments** are all investments that are not short-term. Long-term investments include stocks and bonds that the investor expects to hold longer than one year or that are not readily marketable—for instance, real estate held for sale.

Exhibit B-1 shows the positions of short-term and long-term investments on the balance sheet.

EXHIBIT B-1 Reporting Investments on the Balance Sheet

Assets		
Current Assets		
Cash	$X	
Short-term investments	X	
Accounts receivable	X	
Inventories	X	
Prepaid expenses	X	
Total current assets		$X
Long-term investments (or simply Investments)		X
Property, plant, and equipment		X
Intangible assets		X
Other assets		X

The balance sheet reports assets by order of liquidity, starting with cash. Short-term investments are the second-most-liquid asset. Long-term investments are less liquid than current assets but more liquid than property, plant, and equipment.

Trading and Available-for-Sale Investments

We begin stock investments with situations in which the investor owns less than 20% of the investee company. These investments in stock are classified as trading investments or as available-for-sale investments.

- **Trading investments** are to be sold in the very near future—days, weeks, or only a few months—with the intent of generating a profit on a quick sale. Trading investments are short-term.
- **Available-for-sale investments** are all less-than-20% investments other than trading investments. Available-for-sale investments are current assets if the business expects to sell them within the next year or within the operating cycle if longer than a year. All other available-for-sale investments are long-term.

The investor accounts for trading investments and available-for-sale investments separately. Let's begin with trading investments.

Trading Investments

The **market-value method** is used to account for trading investments because they will be sold in the near future at their current market value. Cost is the initial amount for a trading investment. Assume McDonald's Corporation has excess cash to invest. Suppose McDonald's buys 500 shares of Ford Motor Company stock for $50 per share on October 23, 2008. Assume further that McDonald's management plans to sell this stock within three months. This is a trading investment, which McDonald's records as follows:

2008			
Oct. 23	Short-Term Investment (500 × $50)	25,000	
	Cash		25,000
	Purchased investment.		

Short-Term Investment

25,000	

Ford pays cash dividends, so McDonald's would receive a dividend on the investment. McDonald's entry to record receipt of a $2-per-share cash dividend is

2008			
Nov. 14	Cash (500 × $2.00)	1,000	
	Dividend Revenue		1,000
	Received cash dividend.		

Trading investments are reported on the balance sheet at current market value, not at cost. This requires a year-end adjustment of the trading investment to current market value. Assume that the Ford stock has decreased in value, and at December 31,

2008, McDonald's investment in Ford stock is worth $20,000 ($5,000 less than the purchase price). At year-end, McDonald's would make the following adjustment:

2008			
Dec. 31	Loss on Trading Investment ($25,000 – $20,000)	5,000	
	Short-Term Investment		5,000
	Adjusted trading investment to market value.		

Short-Term Investment

25,000	5,000
20,000	

Reporting Trading Investments

The T-account shows the $20,000 balance of Short-Term Investment. McDonald's would report its trading investment on the balance sheet at December 31, 2008, and the loss on trading investment on the 2008 income statement, as follows:

Balance Sheet (Partial):	**Income Statement (Partial):**
ASSETS	Other gains and losses:
Current assets:	Gain (loss) on trading
Short-term investments, at market value $20,000	investment .... $(5,000)

If the investment's market value had risen above $25,000, McDonald's would have debited Short-Term Investment and credited Gain on Trading Investment.

Selling a Trading Investment

When a company sells a trading investment, the gain or loss on the sale is the difference between the sale proceeds and the last carrying amount. If McDonald's sells the Ford stock for $18,000, McDonald's would record the sale as follows:

2009			
Jan. 19	Cash	18,000	
	Loss on Sale of Investment	2,000	
	Short-Term Investment		20,000
	Sold investment.		

Short-Term Investment

25,000	5,000
20,000	20,000

For reporting on the income statement, McDonald's could combine all gains and losses ($5,000 loss + $2,000 loss) on short-term investments and report a single net amount under Other gains (losses). . . . $(7,000).

Long-Term Available-for-Sale Investments

The **market-value method** is used to account for available-for-sale investments because the company expects to resell the stock at its market value. Available-for-sale investments therefore are reported on the balance sheet at their *current market value*, just like trading investments.

Suppose Dell Corporation purchases 1,000 shares of Coca-Cola common stock at the market price of $33. Dell plans to hold this stock for longer than a year and classifies it as a long-term available-for-sale investment. Dell's entry to record the investment is

2008			
Feb. 23	Long-Term Available-for-Sale Investment (1,000 × $33)	33,000	
	Cash		33,000
	Purchased investment.		

Assume that Dell receives a $0.60 per share cash dividend on the Coca-Cola stock. Dell's entry for receipt of the dividend is

2008			
July 14	Cash (1,000 × $0.60)	600	
	Dividend Revenue		600
	Received dividend.		

Available-for-sale investments are accounted for at market value. This requires an adjustment to current market value. Assume that the market value of Dell's investment in Coca-Cola stock has risen to $36,000 on December 31, 2008. In this case, Dell makes the following adjustment:

2008			
Dec. 31	Allowance to Adjust Investment to		
	Market ($36,000 – $33,000)	3,000	
	Unrealized Gain on Investment		3,000
	Adjusted investment to market value.		

Allowance to Adjust Investment to Market is a companion account to Long-Term Investment. The Allowance account brings the investment to current market value. Cost ($33,000) plus the Allowance ($3,000) equals the investment carrying amount ($36,000).

Long-Term Available-for-Sale Investment	Allowance to Adjust Investment to Market
33,000	3,000

Investment carrying amount = Market value of $36,000

Observe that the Long-Term Available-for-Sale account is carried at cost, not at market value. It takes the allowance account to adjust the investment carrying amount to market value.

Here the Allowance has a debit balance because the investment has increased in value. If the investment's value declines, the Allowance is credited. In that case, the investment carrying amount is cost *minus* the Allowance. The Allowance with a credit balance becomes a contra account.

Reporting Available-for-Sale Investments

The other side of the December 31 adjustment credits Unrealized Gain on Investment. If the investment declines, the company debits an Unrealized Loss. *Unrealized* means that the gain or loss resulted from a change in market value, not from a sale of the investment. A gain or loss on the sale of an investment is said to be *realized* when the company receives cash. For available-for-sale investments, the Unrealized Gain (or Loss) account is reported on the balance sheet as part of stockholders' equity, as shown here.

BALANCE SHEET (PARTIAL)			
Assets		**Stockholders' Equity**	
Total current assets............................	$ XXX	Common stock	$ XXX
Long-term available-for-sale investments—at market value........	36,000	Retained earnings ...	XXX
		Unrealized gain	
Property, plant, and equipment, net	XXX	on investments	3,000

Selling an Available-for-Sale Investment

The sale of an available-for-sale investment usually results in a *realized* gain or loss. Suppose Dell Corporation sells its investment in Coca-Cola stock for $32,000 during 2009. Dell would record the sale as follows:

2009			
May 19	Cash	32,000	
	Loss on Sale of Investment	1,000	
	Long-Term Available-for-Sale Investment (cost)		33,000
	Sold investment.		

Dell would report the Loss on Sale of Investment as an "Other gain or loss" on the income statement.

Equity-Method Investments

An investor with a stock holding between 20% and 50% of the investee's voting stock can *significantly influence* the investee's decisions. For this reason, investments in the range of 20% to 50% are common. For example, General Motors owns nearly 40% of Isuzu Motors. We use the **equity method** to account for 20% to 50% investments.

Recording the Initial Investment

Investments accounted for by the equity method are recorded initially at cost. Suppose Walgreen Co. pays $400,000 to purchase 20% of the common stock of

Drugstore.com. Walgreen then refers to Drugstore.com as an *affiliated company*. Walgreen's entry to record the purchase of this investment follows.

2008			
Jan. 6	Long-Term Equity-Method Investment	400,000	
	Cash		400,000
	Purchased equity-method investment.		

Adjusting the Investment Account for Investee Net Income

Under the equity method, the investor applies its percentage of ownership to record its share of the investee's net income. The investor debits the Investment account and credits Investment Revenue when the investee reports income. As the investee's equity increases, so does the Investment account on the investor's books.

Suppose Drugstore.com reported net income of $250,000 for the year. Walgreen would record 20% of this amount as an increase in the investment account, as follows:

2008			
Dec. 31	Long-Term Equity-Method Investment ($250,000 × 0.20)	50,000	
	Equity-Method Investment Revenue		50,000
	Recorded investment revenue.		

Receiving Dividends on an Equity-Method Investment

Walgreen records its proportionate part of cash dividends received from Drugstore.com. Suppose Drugstore.com declares and pays a cash dividend of $100,000. Walgreen receives 20% of this dividend and makes the following journal entry:

2009			
Jan. 17	Cash ($100,000 × 0.20)	20,000	
	Long-Term Equity-Method Investment		20,000
	Received dividend on equity-method investment.		

The Investment account is credited for the receipt of a dividend on an equity-method investment. Why? Because the dividend *decreases* the investee's equity. It also decreases the investor's investment.

Reporting Equity-Method Investments

After the preceding entries are posted, Walgreen's Investment account shows its equity in the net assets of Drugstore.com:

Long-Term Equity-Method Investment

2008			2009		
Jan. 6	Purchase	400,000	Jan. 17	Dividends received	20,000
Dec. 31	Net income	50,000			
2009					
Jan. 17	Balance	430,000			

Walgreen can report the long-term investment on the balance sheet and the revenue on the income statement as follows:

Balance Sheet (Partial):		Income Statement (Partial):	
ASSETS		Income from operations	$ XXX
Total current assets...........	$ XXX	Other revenue:	
Long-term equity-method		Equity-method investment	
investments	430,000	revenue	50,000
Property, plant, and		Net income.........................	$ XXX
equipment, net	XXX		

Selling an Equity-Method Investment

There is usually a gain or a loss on the sale of an equity-method investment. The gain or loss is the difference between the sale proceeds and the investment carrying amount. Suppose Walgreen sells one-tenth of the Drugstore.com common stock for $40,000. The sale is recorded as follows:

Feb. 13	Cash	40,000	
	Loss on Sale of Investment	3,000	
	Long-Term Equity-Method Investment		
	($430,000 × 1/10)		43,000
	Sold investment.		

The following T-account summarizes the accounting for equity-method investments:

Long-Term Equity-Method Investment	
Cost	Share of losses
Share of income	Share of dividend received

Joint Ventures

A *joint venture* is a separate entity owned by a group of companies. Joint ventures are common in international business. Companies such as ExxonMobil, British Telecom, and Toyota partner with companies in other countries. A participant in a joint venture accounts for its investment by the equity method.

Consolidated Subsidiaries

Most large corporations own controlling interests in other companies. A **controlling (or majority) interest** is more than 50% of the investee's voting stock. A greater-than-50% investment enables the investor to elect a majority of the board of directors and thereby control the investee. The corporation that controls the other company is called the **parent company**, and the company that is controlled by another corporation is called the **subsidiary**. A well-known example is Saturn Corporation, which is a subsidiary of General Motors, the parent company. Because GM owns Saturn Corporation, the stockholders of GM control Saturn. Exhibit B-2 shows some of the subsidiaries of three large automakers.

EXHIBIT B-2 Selected Subsidiaries of Three Large Automobile Manufacturers

Parent Company	Selected Subsidiaries
General Motors Corporation	Saturn Corporation
	Hughes Aircraft Company
Ford Motor Company	Ford Aerospace Corporation
	Jaguar, Ltd.
DaimlerChrysler Corporation	Jeep/Eagle Corporation
	DaimlerChrysler Rail Systems

Consolidation Accounting

Consolidation accounting is the way to combine the financial statements of two or more companies that have the same owners. Most published financial reports include consolidated statements. **Consolidated statements** combine the balance sheets, income statements, and cash-flow statements of the parent company plus those of its majority-owned subsidiaries. The final outcome is a single set of statements as if the parent and its subsidiaries were the same entity.

In consolidation accounting, the assets, liabilities, revenues, and expenses of each subsidiary are added to the parent's accounts. For example, Saturn's cash balance is added to the cash balance of General Motors, and the overall sum is reported on GM's balance sheet. The consolidated financial statements bear only the name of the parent company, in this case General Motors Corporation.

Exhibit B-3 summarizes the accounting for investments in stock by showing which accounting method is used for each type of investment.

EXHIBIT B-3

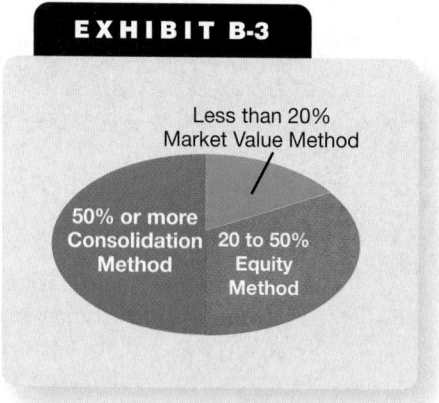

Accounting Methods for Stock Investments by Percentage of Ownership

Goodwill and Minority Interest

Goodwill is an intangible asset that is recorded in the consolidation process. Goodwill is reported on the parent company's consolidated balance sheet. As we saw in Chapter 10, **goodwill** is the excess of the cost to acquire another company over the sum of the market value of its net assets.

A parent company may purchase less than 100% of a subsidiary company. For example, Nokia, the cellular telephone company, has a minority interest in (owns less than 100% of) several other companies. **Minority interest** is the portion (less than 50%) of a subsidiary's stock owned by outside stockholders. Nokia Corporation, the parent company, therefore reports on its consolidated balance sheet an account titled Minority Interest.

Bond Investments

The relationship between the issuing corporation (the debtor that borrowed money) and the bondholders (investors who own the bonds) may be diagrammed as follows:

Issuing Corporation Has		Bondholder Has
Bonds payable	⟷	Investment in bonds
Interest expense	⟷	Interest revenue

The dollar amount of a bond transaction is the same for both the issuing corporation and the bondholder because money passes from one to the other. However, the accounts debited and credited differ. For example, the corporation has bonds payable; the bondholder has an investment. The corporation has interest expense, and the bondholder has interest revenue. Chapter 15 covers bonds payable.

Virtually all investments in bonds are long-term. These are called **held-to-maturity investments.** Bond investments are recorded at cost. At maturity, the bondholders will receive the bonds' full face value. We must amortize any discount or premium, as we did for bonds payable in Chapter 15. Held-to-maturity investments are reported at their *amortized cost.*

Suppose an investor purchases $10,000 of 6% CBS bonds at a price of 94 (94% of maturity value) on July 1, 2008. The investor intends to hold the bonds as a long-term investment until their maturity. Interest dates are June 30 and December 31. These bonds mature on July 1, 2010, so they will be outstanding for 60 months. Let's amortize the discount by the straight-line method. The bondholder's entries for this investment follow.

	2008			
	July 1	Long-Term Investment in Bonds ($10,000 × 0.94)	9,400	
		Cash		9,400
		Purchased bond investment.		

At December 31, the year-end entries are

	Dec. 31	Cash ($10,000 × 0.06 × 6/12)	300	
		Interest Revenue		300
		Received interest.		
	Dec. 31	Long-Term Investment in Bonds		
		[($10,000 − $9,400)/5 × 6/12]	60	
		Interest Revenue		60
		Amortized discount on bond investment.		

Reporting Bond Investments

The financial statements at December 31, 2008, report the following for this investment in bonds:

Balance sheet at December 31, 2008:	
Long-term investments in bonds ($9,400 + $ 60)......................	$9,460

Income statement for 2008:	
Other revenues:	
Interest revenue ($300 + $60).......	$ 360

Decision Guidelines

ACCOUNTING FOR LONG-TERM INVESTMENTS

Suppose you work for Bank of America. Your duties include accounting for the bank's investments. The following Decision Guidelines can serve as your checklist for using the appropriate method to account for each type of investment.

Decision

INVESTMENT TYPE

Short-Term Investment
   Trading investment

Long-Term Investment
   Investor owns less than 20% of investee stock (available-for-sale investment)

Investor owns between 20% and 50% of investee stock

Investor owns more than 50% of investee stock

Long-term investment in bonds (held-to-maturity investment)

Guidelines

ACCOUNTING METHOD

Market value—report all gains (losses) on the income statement

Market value—report *unrealized* gains (losses) on the balance sheet

   —report *realized* gains (losses) from sale of the investment on the income statement

Equity

Consolidation

Amortized cost

Summary Problem 1

1. Identify the appropriate accounting method for each of the following situations:

   a. Investment in 25% of investee company's stock.

   b. Available-for-sale investment in stock.

   c. Investment in more than 50% of investee company's stock.

2. At what amount should the following available-for-sale investment portfolio be reported on the December 31 balance sheet? All the investments are less than 5% of the investee's stock.

Stock	Investment Cost	Current Market Value
Amazon.com	$ 5,000	$ 5,500
Intelysis	61,200	53,000
Procter & Gamble	3,680	6,230

Journalize any adjusting entry required by these data.

3. Investor paid $67,900 to acquire a 40% equity-method investment in the common stock of Investee. At the end of the first year, Investee's net income was $80,000, and Investee declared and paid cash dividends of $55,000. Journalize Investor's (a) purchase of the investment, (b) share of Investee's net income, (c) receipt of dividends from Investee, and (d) sale of Investee stock for $80,100.

Solutions

1. (a) Equity (b) Market value (c) Consolidation

2. Report the investments at market value, $64,730, as follows:

Stock	Investment Cost	Current Market Value
Amazon.com	$ 5,000	$ 5,500
Intelysis	61,200	53,000
Procter & Gamble	3,680	6,230
Totals	$69,880	$64,730

Adjusting entry:

Unrealized Loss on Investments ($69,880 − $64,730)	5,150	
Allowance to Adjust Investment to Market		5,150
To adjust investments to current market value.		

3. a.	Long-Term Equity-Method Investment		67,900	
	Cash			67,900
	Purchased equity-method investment.			
b.	Long-Term Equity-Method Investment ($80,000 × 0.40)		32,000	
	Equity-Method Investment Revenue			32,000
	Recorded investment revenue.			
c.	Cash ($55,000 × 0.40)		22,000	
	Long-Term Equity-Method Investment			22,000
	Received dividend on equity-method investment.			
d.	Cash		80,100	
	Long-Term Equity-Method Investment			77,900
	($67,900 + $32,000 – $22,000)			
	Gain on Sale of Investment			2,200
	Sold investment.			

Accounting for International Operations

Accounting across national boundaries is called *international accounting*. Did you know that Coca-Cola, IBM, and Bank of America earn most of their revenue outside the United States? It is common for U.S. companies to do a large part of their business abroad. McDonald's and AMR (American Airlines) are also very active in other countries. Exhibit B-4 shows the percentages of international sales for three leading companies.

EXHIBIT B-4   **Extent of International Business**

Company	Percentage of International Sales
McDonald's	65%
IBM	63%
AMR (American Airlines)	35%

Foreign Currencies and Foreign-Currency Exchange Rates

If Boeing, a U.S. company, sells a 747 jet to Air France, will Boeing receive U.S. dollars or euros? If the transaction is stated in dollars, Air France must buy dollars to pay Boeing in U.S. currency. If the transaction is in euros, Boeing will collect euros. To get dollars, Boeing must sell euros. In either case, a step has been added to the transaction: One company must convert domestic currency into foreign currency, or vice versa.

One nation's currency can be stated in terms of another's monetary unit. The price of a foreign currency is called the **foreign-currency exchange rate**. In Exhibit B-5, the U.S. dollar value of a European euro is $1.28. This means that one euro can be bought for $1.28. Other currencies are also listed in Exhibit B-5.

EXHIBIT B-5   **Foreign-Currency Exchange Rates**

Country	Monetary Unit	U.S Dollar Value	Country	Monetary Unit	U.S Dollar Value
Canada	Dollar	$0.90	Japan	Yen	$0.009
European Common Market	European currency unit	1.28	Mexico	Peso	0.090
Great Britain	Pound	1.90	Russia	Ruble	0.037

Source: The Wall Street Journal, Sept. 26, 2006, p. C11.

We use the exchange rate to *translate* the price of an item stated in one currency to its price in a second currency. Suppose an item costs 200 Canadian dollars. To compute its cost in U.S. dollars, we multiply the amount in Canadian dollars by the translation rate: 200 Canadian dollars × $0.90 = $180.

Currencies are described as "strong" or "weak." The exchange rate of a **strong currency** is rising relative to other nations' currencies. The exchange rate of a **weak currency** is falling relative to other currencies.

Foreign-Currency Transactions

Many companies conduct transactions in foreign currencies. D. E. Shipp Belting of Waco, Texas, provides an example. Shipp makes conveyor belts for several industries, including M&M Mars, which makes Snickers candy bars. Farmers along the Texas–Mexico border use Shipp conveyor belts to process vegetables. Shipp Belting conducts some of its business in pesos, the Mexican monetary unit.

Collecting Cash in a Foreign Currency

Consider Shipp Belting's sale of conveyor belts to Artes de Mexico, a vegetable grower in Matamoros. Suppose Artes orders conveyor belts valued at 1,000 pesos (approximately $90), and Artes will pay in pesos. Shipp will need to convert the pesos to dollars. Let's see how to account for this transaction.

Shipp Belting sells goods to Artes de Mexico for a price of 1,000 pesos on June 2. On that date, a peso was worth $0.090. One month later, on July 2, the peso has strengthened against the dollar and a peso is worth $0.100. Shipp still receives 1,000 pesos from Artes because that was the agreed price. Now the dollar value of Shipp's cash receipt is $10 more than the original amount, so Shipp ends up earning $10 more than expected. The following journal entries account for these transactions of Shipp Belting:

June 2	Accounts Receivable—Artes (1,000 pesos × $0.090)	90	
	Sales Revenue		90
	Sale on account.		

July 2	Cash (1,000 pesos × $0.100)	100	
	Accounts Receivable—Artes		90
	Foreign-Currency Gain		10
	Collection on account.		

Paying Cash in a Foreign Currency

Shipp Belting buys inventory from Gesellschaft Ltd., a Swiss company. The two companies decide on a price of 10,000 Swiss francs. On August 10, when Shipp receives the goods, the Swiss franc is priced at $0.72. When Shipp pays two weeks later, the Swiss franc has strengthened against the dollar and is now worth $0.78. This works to Shipp's disadvantage. Shipp would record the purchase and payment as follows:

Aug. 10	Inventory (10,000 Swiss francs × $0.72)	7,200	
	Accounts Payable—Gesellschaft Ltd.		7,200
	Purchase on account.		
Aug. 24	Accounts Payable—Gesellschaft Ltd.	7,200	
	Foreign-Currency Loss	600	
	Cash (10,000 Swiss francs × $0.78)		7,800
	Payment on account.		

In this case, the strengthening of the Swiss franc gave Shipp a foreign-currency loss.

Reporting Foreign-Currency Gains and Losses on the Income Statement

The Foreign-Currency Gain (Loss) account reports gains and losses on foreign-currency transactions. The company reports the *net amount* of these two accounts on the income statement as Other gains (losses). For example, Shipp Belting would combine the $600 foreign-currency loss and the $10 gain and report the net loss of $590 on the income statement, as follows:

Other gains (losses):
Foreign-currency gain (loss), net ($600 − $10) .... $(590)

These gains and losses fall into the "Other" category because they arise from outside activities. Buying and selling foreign currencies are not Shipp Belting's main business.

International Accounting Standards

In this text, we focus on generally accepted accounting principles in the United States. Most accounting methods are consistent throughout the world. Double-entry, the accrual system, and the basic financial statements (balance sheet, income statement, and so on) are used worldwide. But some differences exist among countries, as shown in Exhibit B-6.

EXHIBIT B-6　Some International Accounting Differences

Country	Inventories	Goodwill	Research and Development Costs
United States	Specific unit cost, FIFO, LIFO, weighted-average.	Written down when current value decreases.	Expensed as incurred.
Germany	LIFO is unacceptable for tax purposes and is not widely used.	Amortized over 5 years.	Expensed as incurred.
Japan	Similar to U.S.	Amortized over 5 years.	May be capitalized and amortized over 5 years.
United Kingdom (Great Britain)	LIFO is unacceptable for tax purposes and is not widely used.	Amortized over useful life or not amortized if life is indefinite.	Expense research costs. Some development costs may be capitalized.

The International Accounting Standards Committee (IASC), headquartered in London, operates much as the Financial Accounting Standards Board in the United States. It has the support of the accounting professions in many countries. However, the IASC has no authority to require compliance and must rely on cooperation by the various national accounting professions.

Decision Guidelines

You've just opened a boutique to import clothing manufactured in China. Should you transact business in Chinese *renminbi* (the official currency unit), or in U.S. dollars? What foreign-currency gains or losses might occur? The Decision Guidelines will help you address these questions.

Decision	Guidelines
When to record a	
• Foreign-currency gain?	• When you receive foreign currency worth *more* U.S. dollars than the receivable on your books
	• When you pay foreign currency that costs *fewer* U.S. dollars than the payable on your books
• Foreign-currency loss?	• When you receive foreign currency worth *fewer* U.S. dollars than the receivable on your books
	• When you pay foreign currency that costs *more* U.S. dollars than the payable on your books

Summary Problem 2

Journalize the following transactions of American Corp. Explanations are not required.

2008

Nov. 16   Purchased equipment on account for 40,000 Swiss francs when the exchange rate was $0.73 per Swiss franc.

     27   Sold merchandise on account to a Belgian company for 7,000 euros. Each euro is worth $1.10.

Dec. 22   Paid the Swiss company when the franc's exchange rate was $0.725.

     31   Adjusted for the change in the exchange rate of the euro. Its current exchange rate is $1.08.

2009

Jan.   4   Collected from the Belgian company. The euro exchange rate is $1.12.

Solution

Entries for transactions stated in foreign currencies:

2008			
Nov. 16	Equipment (40,000 × $0.73)	29,200	
	Accounts Payable		29,200
27	Accounts Receivable (7,000 × $1.10)	7,700	
	Sales Revenue		7,700
Dec. 22	Accounts Payable	29,200	
	Cash (40,000 × $0.725)		29,000
	Foreign-Currency Gain		200
31	Foreign-Currency Loss		
	[7,000 × ($1.10 − $1.08)]	140	
	Accounts Receivable		140
2009			
Jan. 4	Cash (7,000 × $1.12)	7,840	
	Accounts Receivable ($7,700 − $140)		7,560
	Foreign-Currency Gain		280

Exercises

Accounting for a trading
investment

EB-1 Boston Today Publishers completed the following trading-investment transactions during 2007 and 2008:

2007	
Dec. 6	Purchased 1,000 shares of Subaru stock at a price of $52.25 per share, intending to sell the investment next month.
23	Received a cash dividend of $1.10 per share on the Subaru stock.
31	Adjusted the investment to its market value of $50 per share.
2008	
Jan. 27	Sold the Subaru stock for $48 per share.

Journalize Boston Today Publishers' investment transactions. Explanations are not required. (pp. B-2–B-3)

Accounting for an available-
for-sale investment

EB-2 Raider Investments completed these long-term available-for-sale investment transactions during 2007:

2007	
Jan. 14	Purchased 300 shares of Fossil stock, paying $44 per share. Raider intends to hold the investment for the indefinite future.
Aug. 22	Received a cash dividend of $0.60 per share on the Fossil stock.
Dec. 31	Adjusted the Fossil investment to its current market value of $12,000.

1. Journalize Raider's investment transactions. Explanations are not required. (pp. B-4–B-5)
2. Show how to report the investment and any unrealized gain or loss on Raider's balance sheet at December 31, 2007. (p. B-5)

Accounting for the sale of
an available-for-sale
investment

EB-3 Use the data given in Exercise EB-2. On August 4, 2008, Raider Investments sold its investment in Fossil stock for $45 per share.

1. Journalize the sale. No explanation is required. (p. B-5)
2. How does the gain or loss that you recorded differ from the gain or loss that was recorded at December 31, 2007 (in Exercise EB-2)? (p. B-5)

Accounting for a 40%
investment in another
company

EB-4 Suppose on January 6, 2008, General Motors paid $500 million for its 40% investment in Isuzu. Assume Isuzu earned net income of $60 million and paid cash dividends of $50 million during 2008.

1. What method should General Motors use to account for the investment in Isuzu? Give your reason. (p. B-5)
2. Journalize these three transactions on the books of General Motors. Show all amounts in millions of dollars and include an explanation for each entry. (pp. B-5–B-6)
3. Post to the Long-Term Equity-Method Investment T-account. What is its balance after all the transactions are posted? (pp. B-5–B-6)

EB-5 Smith Barney & Co. owns vast amounts of corporate bonds. Suppose Smith Barney buys $1,000,000 of Primo Corp. bonds at a price of 98. The Primo bonds pay stated interest at the annual rate of 8% and mature within five years.

1. How much did Smith Barney pay to purchase the bond investment? How much will Smith Barney collect when the bond investment matures? (pp. B-9–B-10)

2. How much cash interest will Smith Barney receive each year from Primo? (pp. B-9–B-10)

3. Compute Smith Barney's annual interest revenue on this bond investment. Use the straight-line method to amortize the discount on the investment. (pp. B-9–B-10)

EB-6 Return to Exercise EB-5, the Smith Barney investment in Primo Corp. bonds. Journalize on Smith Barney's books, along with an explanation for each entry:

a. Purchase of the bond investment on January 2, 2007. Smith Barney expects to hold the investment to maturity. (pp. B-9–B-10)

b. Receipt of annual cash interest on December 31, 2007. (pp. B-9–B-10)

c. Amortization of discount on December 31, 2007. (pp. B-9–B-10)

d. Collection of the investment's face value at its maturity date on January 2, 2012. (Challenge) (Interest and amortization of discount for 2011 have already been recorded, so you may ignore these entries.)

EB-7 Suppose Wilson & Co. sells athletic shoes to a Russian company on March 14. Wilson agrees to accept 2,000,000 Russian rubles. On the date of sale, the ruble is quoted at $0.030. Wilson collects half the receivable on April 19, when the ruble is worth $0.028. Then, on May 10, when the price of the ruble is $0.036, Wilson collects the final amount.

Journalize these three transactions for Wilson; include an explanation. Overall, how well did Wilson come out in terms of a net foreign-currency gain or loss? (pp. B-5–B-7)

Problems

PB-8 Jetway Corporation generated excess cash and invested in securities, as follows:

July 2	Purchased 3,500 shares of common stock as a trading investment, paying $12 per share.
Aug. 21	Received cash dividend of $0.40 per share on the trading investment.
Sep. 16	Sold the trading investment for $13.50 per share.
Oct. 8	Purchased trading investments for $136,000.
Dec. 31	Adjusted the trading securities to market value of $133,000.

continued . . .

Requirements

1. Record the transactions in the journal of Jetway Corporation. Explanations are not required. (pp. B-2–B-3)

2. Post to the Short-Term Investments account, and show how to report the short-term investments on Jetway's balance sheet at December 31, 2007. (p. B-3)

Accounting for available-for-sale and equity-method investments

PB-9 The beginning balance sheet of Media Source Co. included the following:

Long-Term Equity-Method Investments	$600,000

During the year Media Source completed these investment transactions:

Mar. 3	Purchased 5,000 shares of Flothru Software common stock as a long-term available-for-sale investment, paying $9 per share.
May 14	Received cash dividend of $0.80 per share on the Flothru investment.
Dec. 15	Received cash dividend of $80,000 from equity-method investments.
31	Received annual reports from equity-method investee companies. Their total net income for the year was $600,000. Of this amount, Media Source's proportion is 25%.
31	Adjusted the available-for-sale investment to market value of $44,000.

Requirements

1. Record the transactions in the journal of Media Source Co. (pp. B-4–B-7)

2. Post entries to T-accounts for Long-Term Available-for-Sale Investments and Allowance to Adjust Investment to Market. Then determine their balances at December 31.

   Post to a T-account for Long-Term Equity-Method Investment, and determine its December 31 balance. (pp. B-5–B-6)

3. Show how to report the Long-Term Available-for-Sale Investment and the Long-Term Equity-Method Investments on Media Source's balance sheet at December 31. (pp. B-5–B-7)

Accounting for a bond investment; amortizing discount by the straight-line method

PB-10 Financial institutions hold large quantities of bond investments. Suppose Solomon Brothers purchases $800,000 of 6% bonds of Buster Brown Corporation for 92 on January 1, 2004. These bonds pay interest on June 30 and December 31 each year. They mature on January 1, 2009.

Requirements

1. Journalize Solomon Brothers' purchase of the bonds as a long-term investment on January 1, 2004 (to be held to maturity). Then record the receipt of cash interest and amortization of discount on June 30 and December 31, 2004. The straight-line method is appropriate for amortizing discount. (pp. B-9–B-10)

2. Show how to report this long-term bond investment on Solomon Brothers' balance sheet at December 31, 2004. (pp. B-9–B-10)

Recording foreign-currency
transactions and reporting
the foreign-currency gain
or loss

PB-11 Suppose Tommy Hilfiger completed the following transactions:

May	4	Sold clothing on account to a Mexican department store for $70,000. The customer agrees to pay in dollars.
	13	Purchased inventory on account from a Canadian company at a price of Canadian $60,000. The exchange rate of the Canadian dollar is $0.85, and payment will be in Canadian dollars.
	20	Sold goods on account to an English firm for 80,000 British pounds. Collection will be in pounds, and the exchange rate of the pound is $1.80.
	27	Collected from the Mexican company.
June	21	Paid the Canadian company. The exchange rate of the Canadian dollar is $0.82.
July	17	Collected from the English firm. The exchange rate of the British pound is $1.77.

Requirements

1. Record these transactions in Tommy Hilfiger's journal, and show how to report the net foreign-currency gain or loss on the income statement. Explanations are not required. (pp. B-5–B-7)

2. How will what you learned in this problem help you structure international transactions? (Challenge)

Appendix C

Present Value Tables

This appendix provides present value tables and future value tables (more complete than those in the Chapter 15 appendix and in Chapter 26).

EXHIBIT C·1 **Present Value of $1**

						Present Value						
Periods	1%	2%	3%	4%	5%	6%	7%	8%	9%	10%	12%
1	0.990	0.980	0.971	0.962	0.952	0.943	0.935	0.926	0.917	0.909	0.893
2	0.980	0.961	0.943	0.925	0.907	0.890	0.873	0.857	0.842	0.826	0.797
3	0.971	0.942	0.915	0.889	0.864	0.840	0.816	0.794	0.772	0.751	0.712
4	0.961	0.924	0.888	0.855	0.823	0.792	0.763	0.735	0.708	0.683	0.636
5	0.951	0.906	0.883	0.822	0.784	0.747	0.713	0.681	0.650	0.621	0.567
6	0.942	0.888	0.837	0.790	0.746	0.705	0.666	0.630	0.596	0.564	0.507
7	0.933	0.871	0.813	0.760	0.711	0.665	0.623	0.583	0.547	0.513	0.452
8	0.923	0.853	0.789	0.731	0.677	0.627	0.582	0.540	0.502	0.467	0.404
9	0.914	0.837	0.766	0.703	0.645	0.592	0.544	0.500	0.460	0.424	0.361
10	0.905	0.820	0.744	0.676	0.614	0.558	0.508	0.463	0.422	0.386	0.322
11	0.896	0.804	0.722	0.650	0.585	0.527	0.475	0.429	0.388	0.350	0.287
12	0.887	0.788	0.701	0.625	0.557	0.497	0.444	0.397	0.356	0.319	0.257
13	0.879	0.773	0.681	0.601	0.530	0.469	0.415	0.368	0.326	0.290	0.229
14	0.870	0.758	0.661	0.577	0.505	0.442	0.388	0.340	0.299	0.263	0.205
15	0.861	0.743	0.642	0.555	0.481	0.417	0.362	0.315	0.275	0.239	0.183
16	0.853	0.728	0.623	0.534	0.458	0.394	0.339	0.292	0.252	0.218	0.163
17	0.844	0.714	0.605	0.513	0.436	0.371	0.317	0.270	0.231	0.198	0.146
18	0.836	0.700	0.587	0.494	0.416	0.350	0.296	0.250	0.212	0.180	0.130
19	0.828	0.686	0.570	0.475	0.396	0.331	0.277	0.232	0.194	0.164	0.116
20	0.820	0.673	0.554	0.456	0.377	0.312	0.258	0.215	0.178	0.149	0.104
21	0.811	0.660	0.538	0.439	0.359	0.294	0.242	0.199	0.164	0.135	0.093
22	0.803	0.647	0.522	0.422	0.342	0.278	0.226	0.184	0.150	0.123	0.083
23	0.795	0.634	0.507	0.406	0.326	0.262	0.211	0.170	0.138	0.112	0.074
24	0.788	0.622	0.492	0.390	0.310	0.247	0.197	0.158	0.126	0.102	0.066
25	0.780	0.610	0.478	0.375	0.295	0.233	0.184	0.146	0.116	0.092	0.059
26	0.772	0.598	0.464	0.361	0.281	0.220	0.172	0.135	0.106	0.084	0.053
27	0.764	0.586	0.450	0.347	0.268	0.207	0.161	0.125	0.098	0.076	0.047
28	0.757	0.574	0.437	0.333	0.255	0.196	0.150	0.116	0.090	0.069	0.042
29	0.749	0.563	0.424	0.321	0.243	0.185	0.141	0.107	0.082	0.063	0.037
30	0.742	0.552	0.412	0.308	0.231	0.174	0.131	0.099	0.075	0.057	0.033
40	0.672	0.453	0.307	0.208	0.142	0.097	0.067	0.046	0.032	0.022	0.011
50	0.608	0.372	0.228	0.141	0.087	0.054	0.034	0.021	0.013	0.009	0.003

EXHIBIT C-1 Present Value of $1 (con't)

					Present Value							
14%	15%	16%	18%	20%	25%	30%	35%	40%	45%	50%	Periods
0.877	0.870	0.862	0.847	0.833	0.800	0.769	0.741	0.714	0.690	0.667	1
0.769	0.756	0.743	0.718	0.694	0.640	0.592	0.549	0.510	0.476	0.444	2
0.675	0.658	0.641	0.609	0.579	0.512	0.455	0.406	0.364	0.328	0.296	3
0.592	0.572	0.552	0.516	0.482	0.410	0.350	0.301	0.260	0.226	0.198	4
0.519	0.497	0.476	0.437	0.402	0.328	0.269	0.223	0.186	0.156	0.132	5
0.456	0.432	0.410	0.370	0.335	0.262	0.207	0.165	0.133	0.108	0.088	6
0.400	0.376	0.354	0.314	0.279	0.210	0.159	0.122	0.095	0.074	0.059	7
0.351	0.327	0.305	0.266	0.233	0.168	0.123	0.091	0.068	0.051	0.039	8
0.308	0.284	0.263	0.225	0.194	0.134	0.094	0.067	0.048	0.035	0.026	9
0.270	0.247	0.227	0.191	0.162	0.107	0.073	0.050	0.035	0.024	0.017	10
0.237	0.215	0.195	0.162	0.135	0.086	0.056	0.037	0.025	0.017	0.012	11
0.208	0.187	0.168	0.137	0.112	0.069	0.043	0.027	0.018	0.012	0.008	12
0.182	0.163	0.145	0.116	0.093	0.055	0.033	0.020	0.013	0.008	0.005	13
0.160	0.141	0.125	0.099	0.078	0.044	0.025	0.015	0.009	0.006	0.003	14
0.140	0.123	0.108	0.084	0.065	0.035	0.020	0.011	0.006	0.004	0.002	15
0.123	0.107	0.093	0.071	0.054	0.028	0.015	0.008	0.005	0.003	0.002	16
0.108	0.093	0.080	0.060	0.045	0.023	0.012	0.006	0.003	0.002	0.001	17
0.095	0.081	0.069	0.051	0.038	0.018	0.009	0.005	0.002	0.001	0.001	18
0.083	0.070	0.060	0.043	0.031	0.014	0.007	0.003	0.002	0.001		19
0.073	0.061	0.051	0.037	0.026	0.012	0.005	0.002	0.001	0.001		20
0.064	0.053	0.044	0.031	0.022	0.009	0.004	0.002	0.001			21
0.056	0.046	0.038	0.026	0.018	0.007	0.003	0.001	0.001			22
0.049	0.040	0.033	0.022	0.015	0.006	0.002	0.001				23
0.043	0.035	0.028	0.019	0.013	0.005	0.002	0.001				24
0.038	0.030	0.024	0.016	0.010	0.004	0.001	0.001				25
0.033	0.026	0.021	0.014	0.009	0.003	0.001					26
0.029	0.023	0.018	0.011	0.007	0.002	0.001					27
0.026	0.020	0.016	0.010	0.006	0.002	0.001					28
0.022	0.017	0.014	0.008	0.005	0.002						29
0.020	0.015	0.012	0.007	0.004	0.001						30
0.005	0.004	0.003	0.001	0.001							40
0.001	0.001	0.001									50

EXHIBIT C-2   Present Value of Annuity of $1

					Present Value					
Periods	1%	2%	3%	4%	5%	6%	7%	8%	9%	10%	12%
1	0.990	0.980	0.971	0.962	0.952	0.943	0.935	0.926	0.917	0.909	0.893
2	1.970	1.942	1.913	1.886	1.859	1.833	1.808	1.783	1.759	1.736	1.690
3	2.941	2.884	2.829	2.775	2.723	2.673	2.624	2.577	2.531	2.487	2.402
4	3.902	3.808	3.717	3.630	3.546	3.465	3.387	3.312	3.240	3.170	3.037
5	4.853	4.713	4.580	4.452	4.329	4.212	4.100	3.993	3.890	3.791	3.605
6	5.795	5.601	5.417	5.242	5.076	4.917	4.767	4.623	4.486	4.355	4.111
7	6.728	6.472	6.230	6.002	5.786	5.582	5.389	5.206	5.033	4.868	4.564
8	7.652	7.325	7.020	6.733	6.463	6.210	5.971	5.747	5.535	5.335	4.968
9	8.566	8.162	7.786	7.435	7.108	6.802	6.515	6.247	5.995	5.759	5.328
10	9.471	8.983	8.530	8.111	7.722	7.360	7.024	6.710	6.418	6.145	5.650
11	10.368	9.787	9.253	8.760	8.306	7.887	7.499	7.139	6.805	6.495	5.938
12	11.255	10.575	9.954	9.385	8.863	8.384	7.943	7.536	7.161	6.814	6.194
13	12.134	11.348	10.635	9.986	9.394	8.853	8.358	7.904	7.487	7.103	6.424
14	13.004	12.106	11.296	10.563	9.899	9.295	8.745	8.244	7.786	7.367	6.628
15	13.865	12.849	11.938	11.118	10.380	9.712	9.108	8.559	8.061	7.606	6.811
16	14.718	13.578	12.561	11.652	10.838	10.106	9.447	8.851	8.313	7.824	6.974
17	15.562	14.292	13.166	12.166	11.274	10.477	9.763	9.122	8.544	8.022	7.120
18	16.398	14.992	13.754	12.659	11.690	10.828	10.059	9.372	8.756	8.201	7.250
19	17.226	15.678	14.324	13.134	12.085	11.158	10.336	9.604	8.950	8.365	7.366
20	18.046	16.351	14.878	13.590	12.462	11.470	10.594	9.818	9.129	8.514	7.469
21	18.857	17.011	15.415	14.029	12.821	11.764	10.836	10.017	9.292	8.649	7.562
22	19.660	17.658	15.937	14.451	13.163	12.042	11.061	10.201	9.442	8.772	7.645
23	20.456	18.292	16.444	14.857	13.489	12.303	11.272	10.371	9.580	8.883	7.718
24	21.243	18.914	16.936	15.247	13.799	12.550	11.469	10.529	9.707	8.985	7.784
25	22.023	19.523	17.413	15.622	14.094	12.783	11.654	10.675	9.823	9.077	7.843
26	22.795	20.121	17.877	15.983	14.375	13.003	11.826	10.810	9.929	9.161	7.896
27	23.560	20.707	18.327	16.330	14.643	13.211	11.987	10.935	10.027	9.237	7.943
28	24.316	21.281	18.764	16.663	14.898	13.406	12.137	11.051	10.116	9.307	7.984
29	25.066	21.844	19.189	16.984	15.141	13.591	12.278	11.158	10.198	9.370	8.022
30	25.808	22.396	19.600	17.292	15.373	13.765	12.409	11.258	10.274	9.427	8.055
40	32.835	27.355	23.115	19.793	17.159	15.046	13.332	11.925	10.757	9.779	8.244
50	39.196	31.424	25.730	21.482	18.256	15.762	13.801	12.234	10.962	9.915	8.305

EXHIBIT C-2   Present Value of Annuity of $1 (con't)

Present Value

14%	15%	16%	18%	20%	25%	30%	35%	40%	45%	50%	Periods
0.877	0.870	0.862	0.847	0.833	0.800	0.769	0.741	0.714	0.690	0.667	1
1.647	1.626	1.605	1.566	1.528	1.440	1.361	1.289	1.224	1.165	1.111	2
2.322	2.283	2.246	2.174	2.106	1.952	1.816	1.696	1.589	1.493	1.407	3
2.914	2.855	2.798	2.690	2.589	2.362	2.166	1.997	1.849	1.720	1.605	4
3.433	3.352	3.274	3.127	2.991	2.689	2.436	2.220	2.035	1.876	1.737	5
3.889	3.784	3.685	3.498	3.326	2.951	2.643	2.385	2.168	1.983	1.824	6
4.288	4.160	4.039	3.812	3.605	3.161	2.802	2.508	2.263	2.057	1.883	7
4.639	4.487	4.344	4.078	3.837	3.329	2.925	2.598	2.331	2.109	1.922	8
4.946	4.772	4.607	4.303	4.031	3.463	3.019	2.665	2.379	2.144	1.948	9
5.216	5.019	4.833	4.494	4.192	3.571	3.092	2.715	2.414	2.168	1.965	10
5.553	5.234	5.029	4.656	4.327	3.656	3.147	2.752	2.438	2.185	1.977	11
5.660	5.421	5.197	4.793	4.439	3.725	3.190	2.779	2.456	2.197	1.985	12
5.842	5.583	5.342	4.910	4.533	3.780	3.223	2.799	2.469	2.204	1.990	13
6.002	5.724	5.468	5.008	4.611	3.824	3.249	2.814	2.478	2.210	1.993	14
6.142	5.847	5.575	5.092	4.675	3.859	3.268	2.825	2.484	2.214	1.995	15
6.265	5.954	5.669	5.162	4.730	3.887	3.283	2.834	2.489	2.216	1.997	16
6.373	6.047	5.749	5.222	4.775	3.910	3.295	2.840	2.492	2.218	1.998	17
6.467	6.128	5.818	5.273	4.812	3.928	3.304	2.844	2.494	2.219	1.999	18
6.550	6.198	5.877	5.316	4.844	3.942	3.311	2.848	2.496	2.220	1.999	19
6.623	6.259	5.929	5.353	4.870	3.954	3.316	2.850	2.497	2.221	1.999	20
6.687	6.312	5.973	5.384	4.891	3.963	3.320	2.852	2.498	2.221	2.000	21
6.743	6.359	6.011	5.410	4.909	3.970	3.323	2.853	2.498	2.222	2.000	22
6.792	6.399	6.044	5.432	4.925	3.976	3.325	2.854	2.499	2.222	2.000	23
6.835	6.434	6.073	5.451	4.937	3.981	3.327	2.855	2.499	2.222	2.000	24
6.873	6.464	6.097	5.467	4.948	3.985	3.329	2.856	2.499	2.222	2.000	25
6.906	6.491	6.118	5.480	4.956	3.988	3.330	2.856	2.500	2.222	2.000	26
6.935	6.514	6.136	5.492	4.964	3.990	3.331	2.856	2.500	2.222	2.000	27
6.961	6.534	6.152	5.502	4.970	3.992	3.331	2.857	2.500	2.222	2.000	28
6.983	6.551	6.166	5.510	4.975	3.994	3.332	2.857	2.500	2.222	2.000	29
7.003	6.566	6.177	5.517	4.979	3.995	3.332	2.857	2.500	2.222	2.000	30
7.105	6.642	6.234	5.548	4.997	3.999	3.333	2.857	2.500	2.222	2.000	40
7.133	6.661	6.246	5.554	4.999	4.000	3.333	2.857	2.500	2.222	2.000	50

EXHIBIT C-3   Future Value of $1

							Future Value						
Periods	1%	2%	3%	4%	5%	6%	7%	8%	9%	10%	12%	14%	15%
1	1.010	1.020	1.030	1.040	1.050	1.060	1.070	1.080	1.090	1.100	1.120	1.140	1.150
2	1.020	1.040	1.061	1.082	1.103	1.124	1.145	1.166	1.188	1.210	1.254	1.300	1.323
3	1.030	1.061	1.093	1.125	1.158	1.191	1.225	1.260	1.295	1.331	1.405	1.482	1.521
4	1.041	1.082	1.126	1.170	1.216	1.262	1.311	1.360	1.412	1.464	1.574	1.689	1.749
5	1.051	1.104	1.159	1.217	1.276	1.338	1.403	1.469	1.539	1.611	1.762	1.925	2.011
6	1.062	1.126	1.194	1.265	1.340	1.419	1.501	1.587	1.677	1.772	1.974	2.195	2.313
7	1.072	1.149	1.230	1.316	1.407	1.504	1.606	1.714	1.828	1.949	2.211	2.502	2.660
8	1.083	1.172	1.267	1.369	1.477	1.594	1.718	1.851	1.993	2.144	2.476	2.853	3.059
9	1.094	1.195	1.305	1.423	1.551	1.689	1.838	1.999	2.172	2.358	2.773	3.252	3.518
10	1.105	1.219	1.344	1.480	1.629	1.791	1.967	2.159	2.367	2.594	3.106	3.707	4.046
11	1.116	1.243	1.384	1.539	1.710	1.898	2.105	2.332	2.580	2.853	3.479	4.226	4.652
12	1.127	1.268	1.426	1.601	1.796	2.012	2.252	2.518	2.813	3.138	3.896	4.818	5.350
13	1.138	1.294	1.469	1.665	1.886	2.133	2.410	2.720	3.066	3.452	4.363	5.492	6.153
14	1.149	1.319	1.513	1.732	1.980	2.261	2.579	2.937	3.342	3.798	4.887	6.261	7.076
15	1.161	1.346	1.558	1.801	2.079	2.397	2.759	3.172	3.642	4.177	5.474	7.138	8.137
16	1.173	1.373	1.605	1.873	2.183	2.540	2.952	3.426	3.970	4.595	6.130	8.137	9.358
17	1.184	1.400	1.653	1.948	2.292	2.693	3.159	3.700	4.328	5.054	6.866	9.276	10.76
18	1.196	1.428	1.702	2.026	2.407	2.854	3.380	3.996	4.717	5.560	7.690	10.58	12.38
19	1.208	1.457	1.754	2.107	2.527	3.026	3.617	4.316	5.142	6.116	8.613	12.06	14.23
20	1.220	1.486	1.806	2.191	2.653	3.207	3.870	4.661	5.604	6.728	9.646	13.74	16.37
21	1.232	1.516	1.860	2.279	2.786	3.400	4.141	5.034	6.109	7.400	10.80	15.67	18.82
22	1.245	1.546	1.916	2.370	2.925	3.604	4.430	5.437	6.659	8.140	12.10	17.86	21.64
23	1.257	1.577	1.974	2.465	3.072	3.820	4.741	5.871	7.258	8.954	13.55	20.36	24.89
24	1.270	1.608	2.033	2.563	3.225	4.049	5.072	6.341	7.911	9.850	15.18	23.21	28.63
25	1.282	1.641	2.094	2.666	3.386	4.292	5.427	6.848	8.623	10.83	17.00	26.46	32.92
26	1.295	1.673	2.157	2.772	3.556	4.549	5.807	7.396	9.399	11.92	19.04	30.17	37.86
27	1.308	1.707	2.221	2.883	3.733	4.822	6.214	7.988	10.25	13.11	21.32	34.39	43.54
28	1.321	1.741	2.288	2.999	3.920	5.112	6.649	8.627	11.17	14.42	23.88	39.20	50.07
29	1.335	1.776	2.357	3.119	4.116	5.418	7.114	9.317	12.17	15.86	26.75	44.69	57.58
30	1.348	1.811	2.427	3.243	4.322	5.743	7.612	10.06	13.27	17.45	29.96	50.95	66.21
40	1.489	2.208	3.262	4.801	7.040	10.29	14.97	21.72	31.41	45.26	93.05	188.9	267.9
50	1.645	2.692	4.384	7.107	11.47	18.42	29.46	46.90	74.36	117.4	289.0	700.2	1,084

EXHIBIT C-4   Future Value of Annuity $1

Future Value

Periods	1%	2%	3%	4%	5%	6%	7%	8%	9%	10%	12%	14%	15%
1	1.000	1.000	1.000	1.000	1.000	1.000	1.000	1.000	1.000	1.000	1.000	1.000	1.000
2	2.010	2.020	2.030	2.040	2.050	2.060	2.070	2.080	2.090	2.100	2.120	2.140	2.150
3	3.030	3.060	3.091	3.122	3.153	3.184	3.215	3.246	3.278	3.310	3.374	3.440	3.473
4	4.060	4.122	4.184	4.246	4.310	4.375	4.440	4.506	4.573	4.641	4.779	4.921	4.993
5	5.101	5.204	5.309	5.416	5.526	5.637	5.751	5.867	5.985	6.105	6.353	6.610	6.742
6	6.152	6.308	6.468	6.633	6.802	6.975	7.153	7.336	7.523	7.716	8.115	8.536	8.754
7	7.214	7.434	7.662	7.898	8.142	8.394	8.654	8.923	9.200	9.487	10.09	10.73	11.07
8	8.286	8.583	8.892	9.214	9.549	9.897	10.26	10.64	11.03	11.44	12.30	13.23	13.73
9	9.369	9.755	10.16	10.58	11.03	11.49	11.98	12.49	13.02	13.58	14.78	16.09	16.79
10	10.46	10.95	11.46	12.01	12.58	13.18	13.82	14.49	15.19	15.94	17.55	19.34	20.30
11	11.57	12.17	12.81	13.49	14.21	14.97	15.78	16.65	17.56	18.53	20.65	23.04	24.35
12	12.68	13.41	14.19	15.03	15.92	16.87	17.89	18.98	20.14	21.38	24.13	27.27	29.00
13	13.81	14.68	15.62	16.63	17.71	18.88	20.14	21.50	22.95	24.52	28.03	32.09	34.35
14	14.95	15.97	17.09	18.29	19.60	21.02	22.55	24.21	26.02	27.98	32.39	37.58	40.50
15	16.10	17.29	18.60	20.02	21.58	23.28	25.13	27.15	29.36	31.77	37.28	43.84	47.58
16	17.26	18.64	20.16	21.82	23.66	25.67	27.89	30.32	33.00	35.95	42.75	50.98	55.72
17	18.43	20.01	21.76	23.70	25.84	28.21	30.84	33.75	36.97	40.54	48.88	59.12	65.08
18	19.61	21.41	23.41	25.65	28.13	30.91	34.00	37.45	41.30	45.60	55.75	68.39	75.84
19	20.81	22.84	25.12	27.67	30.54	33.76	37.38	41.45	46.02	51.16	63.44	78.97	88.21
20	22.02	24.30	26.87	29.78	33.07	36.79	41.00	45.76	51.16	57.28	72.05	91.02	102.4
21	23.24	25.78	28.68	31.97	35.72	39.99	44.87	50.42	56.76	64.00	81.70	104.8	118.8
22	24.47	27.30	30.54	34.25	38.51	43.39	49.01	55.46	62.87	71.40	92.50	120.4	137.6
23	25.72	28.85	32.45	36.62	41.43	47.00	53.44	60.89	69.53	79.54	104.6	138.3	159.3
24	26.97	30.42	34.43	39.08	44.50	50.82	58.18	66.76	76.79	88.50	118.2	158.7	184.2
25	28.24	32.03	36.46	41.65	47.73	54.86	63.25	73.11	84.70	98.35	133.3	181.9	212.8
26	29.53	33.67	38.55	44.31	51.11	59.16	68.68	79.95	93.32	109.2	150.3	208.3	245.7
27	30.82	35.34	40.71	47.08	54.67	63.71	74.48	87.35	102.7	121.1	169.4	238.5	283.6
28	32.13	37.05	42.93	49.97	58.40	68.53	80.70	95.34	113.0	134.2	190.7	272.9	327.1
29	33.45	38.79	45.22	52.97	62.32	73.64	87.35	104.0	124.1	148.6	214.6	312.1	377.2
30	34.78	40.57	47.58	56.08	66.44	79.06	94.46	113.3	136.3	164.5	241.3	356.8	434.7
40	48.89	60.40	75.40	95.03	120.8	154.8	199.6	259.1	337.9	442.6	767.1	1,342	1,779
50	64.46	84.58	112.8	152.7	209.3	290.3	406.5	573.8	815.1	1,164	2,400	4,995	7,218

Appendix D

(NCF = No check figure)*

Chapter 1

Quick Check   1 d; 2 a; 3 d; 4 c; 5 c; 6 b; 7 d; 8 a; 9 b; 10 c

S1-1	NCF
S1-2	NCF
S1-3	NCF
S1-4	NCF
S1-5	Owner, Capital $2,000
S1-6	Craven, Capital $4,000
S1-7	NCF
S1-8	Total assets $3,000
S1-9	NCF
S1-10	Owner, Capital: (a) $300 (b) −$200
S1-11	Total assets $35,400
S1-12	NCF
S1-13	Net income $30,000
E1-14	NCF
E1-15	NCF
E1-16	NCF
E1-17	NCF
E1-18	Benbrook Exxon Owner's Equity $21,000
E1-19	1. Increase in equity $4,000
E1-20	Net income: 1. $13,000; 2. $20,000; 3. $19,000
E1-21	NCF
E1-22	Total assets $49,500
E1-23	2. Net income $1,300
E1-24	1. Total assets $24,000
E1-25	1. Net income $62,100 2. Capital, ending $27,100
E1-26	1. Net income $3 billion 2. Owner equity, ending $16 billion
E1-27	Net income $55,000
P1-28A	2. a. Total assets $68,000 d. Net income $4,000
P1-29A	1. Total assets $30,900 2. Net income $2,700
P1-30A	NCF
P1-31A	a. Net income $51,000 b. M. A. Thomas, capital $61,000 c. Total assets $97,000
P1-32A	1. Net income $75,000 2. Andrew Stryker, capital $185,000 3. Total assets $240,000
P1-33A	1. Total assets $122,000
P1-34A	1. Total assets $94,000

P1-35B	2. a. Total assets $106,000 d. Net income $1,500
P1-36B	1. Total assets $39,980 2. Net income $4,300
P1-37B	NCF
P1-38B	a. Net income $41,000 b. Mike Magid capital, $75,000 c. Total assets $93,000
P1-39B	1. Net income $39,000 2. Kevin Kobelsky, capital $50,000 3. Total assets $94,000
P1-40B	1. Total assets $115,000
P1-41B	Total assets $49,300
P1-42	2. Net income $1,800 3. Carl Redmon, capital $11,800 4. Total assets $15,700
Case 1	1. DeFilippo $13,000 3. Sherman $8,000
Case 2	2. Total assets $200,000
Financial Statement Case	2. Total assets Dec. 31, 2005 $3,696 mil. 4. Net sales increased $1,569 mil.

Chapter 2

Quick Check   1 a; 2 c; 3 b; 4 c; 5 d; 6 a; 7 d; 8 a; 9 c; 10 b

S2-1	NCF
S2-2	NCF
S2-3	NCF
S2-4	NCF
S2-5	NCF
S2-6	2. Accounts Payable bal. $500
S2-7	NCF
S2-8	3. a. Earned $5,000 b. Total assets $5,000
S2-9	3. Trial bal. total $47,000
S2-10	Trial bal. total $74,000
S2-11	Incorrect Trial bal. total debits $68,800
S2-12	Incorrect Trial bal. total debits $37,000
E2-13	NCF
E2-14	NCF
E2-15	1. Owners' equity $80,000 2. Net income $40,000
E2-16	NCF
E2-17	Total debits $40,600
E2-18	NCF
E2-19	2. Trial bal. total $65,200
E2-20	4. Trial bal. total $22,600
E2-21	NCF
E2-22	Trial bal. total $49,400
E2-23	Trial bal. total $199,000
E2-24	Cash bal. $4,300

E2-25	Trial bal. total $26,300
E2-26	Trial bal. total $34,600
E2-27	NCF
E2-28	b. Cash paid $55,000 c. Cash collected $73,000
E2-29	NCF
P2-30A	1. Total assets $74,000 Net income $62,000
P2-31A	NCF
P2-32A	3. Trial bal. total $32,300
P2-33A	3. Trial bal. total $42,500
P2-34A	4. Trial bal. total $63,600
P2-35A	1. Net income $2,800 2. Maury Wills, capital Dec. 31, 2008 $52,800 3. Total assets $54,700
P2-36A	Trial bal. total $101,000
P2-37B	1. Total assets $147,000 Net income $59,000
P2-38B	NCF
P2-39B	3. Trial bal. total $41,500
P2-40B	3. Trial bal. total $32,400
P2-41B	3. Trial bal. total $64,600
P2-42B	1. Net income $700 2. Vince Serrano, capital Jan. 31, 2007 $58,100 3. Total assets $58,600
P2-43B	Trial bal. total $83,700
P2-44	4. Trial bal. total $16,400
Case 1	3. Trial bal. total $19,500 4. Net income $5,600
Case 2	NCF
Financial Statement Case	Dec. 1 Debit Cash $60,000; Credit Sales Revenue $60,000

Chapter 3

Quick Check   1 c; 2 d; 3 d; 4 a; 5 b; 6 b; 7 c; 8 a; 9 c; 10 d

S3-1	Service revenue: Cash basis $600; Accrual basis $1,100
S3-2	a. Expense $5,000 b. Asset $5,000
S3-3	NCF
S3-4	Prepaid Rent $900 Rent Expense $2,700
S3-5	Prepaid Rent bal. $2,500 Rent Expense bal. $500
S3-6	NCF
S3-7	2. Book value $35,000
S3-8	2. Interest Payable bal. at Dec. 31 $700
S3-9	NCF
S3-10	Adjusted Trial Bal. total $23,300
S3-11	Net income $6,300
S3-12	Total assets $15,600

E3-13 NCF
E3-14 NCF
E3-15 NCF
E3-16 a. Rent Expense $1,200
c. Total to account for $1,800
E3-17 NCF
E3-18 Overall, net income is overstated by $9,300
E3-19 NCF
E3-20 Service Revenue bal. $5,500
E3-21 Adjusted Trial Bal. total $36,500
E3-22 NCF
E3-23 a. Net income $11,500;
b. Total assets $18,100
E3-24 Adjusted Trial Bal. total $50,500
E3-25 NCF
E3-26 Net income $4,800
Total assets $24,900
E3-27 1. Net income $70,000
E3-28 Cynthia Norcross, capital Dec. 31, 2005 $119,000
E3-29 Supplies expense $5,000
Salary expense $45,500
Service revenue $83,000
P3-30A NCF
P3-31A 2. Net income $2,050
P3-32A a. Salary Expense $1,000
P3-33A 2. Service Revenue bal. $17,300; Rent Expense bal. $2,000
3. Adjusted Trial Bal. total $66,800
c. Supplies Expense $6,400
P3-34A NCF
P3-35A 1. Net income $41,000;
d. Brooks capital Dec. 31, 2008 $13,000; Total assets $37,000
P3-36A 2. Net income $7,500; Ben Hummer, capital, Oct. 31, 2007 $76,900; Total assets $79,900
P3-37B NCF
P3-38B 2. Net income $14,500
P3-39B a. Insurance Expense $2,500
d. Supplies Expense $5,000
P3-40B 3. Adjusted Trial Bal. total $449,000
P3-41B Service Revenue $900; Supplies Expense $700; Rent Expense $800
P3-42B 1. Net income $40,800; Dot Snyder, capital Dec. 31, 2007 $14,800; Total assets $19,900
P3-43B 2. Net income $12,200; Spike Martin, capital, July 31, 2007 $47,300; Total assets $50,900
P3-44 7. Net income $1,690
Carl Redmon, capital $10,090
Total assets $14,790
Case 1 1. Your highest price $114,000
2. Nicholas's lowest price $112,100

Case 2 Net income $33,000
Financial Statement Case 3. Account balances: Accum. Depr. $223 mil.; Accounts Payable $1,366 mil.; Other Assets $37 mil

Chapter Appendix 3A

E3A-1 Supplies bal. $800
E3A-2 Unearned Service Revenue bal. $3,700
P3A-1 3. Prepaid Rent bal. $1,500;
Unearned Service Revenue bal. $2,400

Chapter 4

Quick Check 1 d; 2 a; 3 c; 4 c; 5 c; 6 a; 7 d; 8 d; 9 b; 10 d
S4-1 NCF
S4-2 NCF
S4-3 NCF
S4-4 d. Credit Brett Kaufman, Capital $8,000
S4-5 2. Brett Kaufman, Capital bal. $27,000
S4-6 NCF
S4-7 Income Summary credit bal. $2,200
S4-8 Trial bal. total $7,200 mil.
S4-9 NCF
S4-10 a. $800
b. $700
c. $2,000
S4-11 Current ratio 2.00
Debt ratio 0.63
S4-12 NCF
E4-13 Net income $1,900
E4-14 Nov. 30 Close net income of $1,900 to Charles Voss, Capital
E4-15 Charles Voss, Capital bal. $35,900
E4-16 Trial bal. total $43,400
E4-17 Prepaid Rent bal. $600
E4-18 Ending balances of Rent Expense and Service Revenue are zero
E4-19 Pablo Pikasso, Capital bal. $38,100
E4-20 2. Roland Poe, Capital bal. $66,000
E4-21 Rhonda Fleet, Capital, Dec. 31, 2007 $272,000
E4-22 2. Net income $10,700
E4-23 1. Total assets $63,700
2. Current year: current ratio 1.92; debit ratio 0.22
E4-24 Net income $48,000
P4-25A Net income $11,200
P4-26A 2. Net income $86,000; S. Paladdin, capital $60,000; Total assets $131,000

P4-27A 3. Credit Maggie Glenn, Capital $63,300
P4-28A Net income $63,300
P4-29A 3. Net income $16,400; Total assets $33,100
5. Postclosing trial bal. total $46,200
P4-30A 1. Total assets $164,600
2. Debt ratio 2007 0.41
P4-31A a. Overall, net income is overstated by $3,500
P4-32B Net income $16,100
P4-33B 2. Net income $40,000; Tom Fritz, Capital $27,000; Total assets $84,000
P4-34B 3. Credit Jen Weaver, Capital $45,600
P4-35B Net income $45,600
P4-36B 3. Net income $17,210
Total assets $50,000
5. Postclosing trial bal. total $53,650
P4-37B 1. Total assets $90,000
2. Debt ratio 2008 0.48
P4-38B a. Overall, net income is understated by $1,900
P4-39 2. Total assets $14,790
Carl Redmon, capital $10,090
3. Net income $1,690
Case Net income $52,000
Financial Statement Case 3. Current ratio at Dec. 31, 2005 1.52
5. Book value $348 mil.
Team Project 1. Net income $3,000
2. Total assets $3,200

Chapter Appendix 4A

P4A-1 All balances are the same for both situations.
Comprehensive Problem 4. Net income $29,400;
Total assets $16,300
7. Totals $16,350

Chapter 5

Quick Check 1 d; 2 d; 3 a; 4 c; 5 c; 6 b; 7 a; 8 b; 9 d; 10 b
S5-1 NCF
S5-2 a. $90,000
b. $87,300
S5-3 c. Credit Cash for $87,300
S5-4 Cost of inventory $58,800
S5-5 c. Debit Cash for $58,800
S5-6 c. Debit Cash for $8,820
S5-7 b. Gross profit $3,420
S5-8 Debit Cost of Good Sold $1,100
S5-9 c. Credit J. Hayes, Capital for $276,000
S5-10 Net income $1,500
S5-11 Total assets $10,700
S5-12 Gross profit % 20%
Invy. turnover 57.1 times

S5-13	Cost of goods sold $82,000
E5-14	May 22 Credit Cash for $902.84
E5-15	May 14 Credit Cash for $4,850
E5-16	May 14 Debit Cash for $4,850
E5-17	Feb. 23 Debit Cash for $2,522
E5-18	2. Gross profit $43,200
E5-19	d. $60,300;
	f. $115,100;
	g. $112,100
E5-20	2. Jackson, Capital bal. $10,750
E5-21	Net income $71,000
E5-22	Net income $71,000
E5-23	1. Net income $68,000
	2. Invy. turnover—current year 4.2 times
E5-24	Net income $68,000
	Gross profit %—current year 56.3%
E5-25	Gross profit % 49.2%
	Invy. turnover 9.4 times
E5-26	Gross profit $78,000
P5-27A	NCF
P5-28A	Oct. 27 Debit Cash for $1,100
P5-29A	May 28 Debit Cash for $2,940
P5-30A	1. Net income $28,300
P5-31A	1. Net income $20,000
	2. Total assets $184,500
P5-32A	1. Net income $70,000
	2. Total assets $184,500
P5-33A	1. Dec. 31 Credit Big Daddy, Capital for $60,500
	2. Gross profit % 2008 53.9%
	3. Cost of goods sold $82,000
P5-34A	Net income $57,000
P5-35A	2. J. Harley, Capital bal. $68,000
P5-36B	NCF
P5-37B	Aug. 26 Debit Cash for $500
P5-38B	Sept. 23 Debit Cash for $6,860
P5-39B	1. Net income $60,000
P5-40B	1. Net income $40,000
	2. Total assets $154,100
P5-41B	1. Net income $40,000
	2. Total assets $154,100
P5-42B	1. Dec. 31 Credit B. Bonds, Capital for $56,600
	2. Gross profit % 2009 46.1%
	3. Cost of goods sold $101,000
P5-43B	Net income $43,400
P5-44B	2. Andrea Sulak, Capital bal. $65,100
P5-45	4. Net income $4,800
Case 1	Net income $73,600
Case 2	Net income: Hildebrand plan $97,000
	Nordhaus plan $102,000
Financial Statement Case	Dec. 31 Credit Income Summary for total revenues of $8,604 mil. Then debit Income Summary for total expenses of $8,245 mil. Finally, credit Income Summary for net income of $359 mil.

Chapter Appendix 5B

E5B-1	May 14 Credit Cash for $6,790
E5B-2	May 14 Debit Cash for $6,790
P5B-1	Nov. 27 Walgreen credits Cash for $2,300. Providence debits Cash for $2,300.
Comprehensive Problem	
	3. Net income $29,400; Total assets $283,610

Chapter 6

Quick Check   1 a; 2 c; 3 a; 4 b; 5 d; 6 c; 7 b; 8 c; 9 a; 10 d

S6-1	End. Inventory $400
S6-2	End. Inventory $350
S6-3	End. Inventory $383
S6-4	June 30 COGS $1,900
S6-5	NCF
S6-6	NCF
S6-7	Report Inventory at $400
S6-8	Debit COGS for $40
S6-9	COGS $28,000; GP $22,000
S6-10	COGS overstated by $1,000 GP understated by $1,000
S6-11	Ending invy. $200,000
S6-12	Estimated cost of ending invy. $75,000
E6-13	End. Invy. $237; COGS $903
E6-14	May 17 COGS $298
E6-15	End. Invy. $219; COGS $921
E6-16	End. Invy. $232; COGS $908
E6-17	2. Gross profit $34,000
E6-18	End. Invy.: FIFO $60; LIFO $48
E6-19	COGS: FIFO $210; LIFO $222
E6-20	Gross profit: FIFO $750; LIFO $630; Avg. $686
E6-21	a. $64,000; c. $24,000; d. $30,000; f. $35,000
E6-22	Report inventory at $13,000
E6-23	Gross profit $67,000
E6-24	Gross profit is $13,000 with invy. overstated; $19,000 with invy. understated
E6-25	Net income: 2008 $45,000; 2007 $33,000
E6-26	Estimated cost of invy. destroyed $350,000
E6-27	Estimated cost of end. invy. $41,000
P6-28A	1. COGS $4,640; End. Invy. $1,360
P6-29A	1. COGS $7,675; End. Invy. $275
P6-30A	1. COGS $7,606; End. Invy. $344
	2. Net Income $1,044
P6-31A	Report Invy. at $75,000; COGS at $625,000
P6-32A	1. Net income: 2008 $53,000; 2007 $43,000; 2006 $31,000

P6-33A	1. Estimated cost of end. invy. $830,000
	2. Gross profit $3,200,000
P6-34B	1. COGS $6,000; End. Invy. $1,200
P6-35B	1. COGS $6,022; End. Invy. $1,178
	2. Net income $2,178
P6-36B	1. COGS $1,425; End. Invy. $315
	3. Gross profit $1,255
P6-37B	Report Invy. at $75,000; COGS at $415,000
P6-38B	1. Net income: 2008 $20,000; 2007 $22,000; 2006 $42,000
P6-39B	1. Estimated cost of end. invy. $400,000
	2. Gross profit $1,870,000
Case 1	NCF
Case 2	NCF
Financial Statement Case	3. Purchases $6,537 mil.

Chapter Appendix 6A

E6A-1	End. Invy.: Avg. $529; FIFO $590; LIFO $480 COGS: Avg. $1,191; FIFO $1,130; LIFO $1,240
E6A-2	C.4. Credit COGS for $1,130
P6A-1	2. Gross profit: Avg. $13,800; FIFO $14,260; LIFO $13,300

Chapter 7

Quick Check   1 a; 2 d; 3 b; 4 c; 5 b; 6 d; 7 d; 8 a; 9 c; 10 b

S7-1	NCF
S7-2	NCF
S7-3	NCF
S7-4	NCF
S7-5	NCF
S7-6	NCF
S7-7	NCF
S7-8	NCF
S7-9	2. Decrease in Accounts Receivable $1,235
S7-10	2. Credit Cash for $2,876
S7-11	1. Total purchases on account $2,876
S7-12	2. Net sales revenue $7,456
E7-13	NCF
E7-14	Total assets $81,500; Owner's equity $25,600
E7-15	NCF
E7-16	NCF
E7-17	Total debit to Cash $530
E7-18	NCF
E7-19	NCF
E7-20	Purchases journal: Total credit to Accounts Payable $8,110
E7-21	3. Total bals. in Accounts Payable $3,270
E7-22	Total credit to Cash $11,550

E7-23	Stevens Dec. 19: Credit Cash for $1,058
E7-24	Gross profit $3,935
P7-25A	NCF
P7-26A	1. Cash receipts journal: Total debit to Cash $35,982
P7-27A	3. Corrected cash receipts journal: Total debit to Cash $6,730
P7-28A	1. Cash payments journal: Total credit to Cash $15,931
P7-29A	6. Total Accounts Receivable $2,900 Total Accounts Payable $2,692
P7-30B	NCF
P7-31B	1. Cash receipts journal: Total debit to Cash $40,576
P7-32B	3. Corrected cash receipts journal: Total debit to Cash $10,302
P7-33B	1. Cash payments journal: Total credit to Cash $12,634
P7-34B	6. Total Accounts Receivable $1,800 Total Accounts Payable $2,925
Case 1	Cash receipts journal: Total debit to Cash $6,449
Case 2	NCF
Comprehensive Problem	2. Cash receipts journal: Total debit to Cash $8,309 Cash payments journal: Total credit to Cash $10,806 4. Net income $2,064

Chapter 8

Quick Check   1 c; 2 d; 3 c; 4 d; 5 c; 6 d; 7 c; 8 b; 9 b; 10 d

S8-1	NCF
S8-2	NCF
S8-3	NCF
S8-4	NCF
S8-5	NCF
S8-6	Adjusted balance $3,100
S8-7	NCF
S8-8	NCF
S8-9	NCF
S8-10	NCF
S8-11	April 30 Credit Cash Short & Over for $6
S8-12	NCF
E8-13	NCF
E8-14	NCF
E8-15	NCF
E8-16	NCF
E8-17	Adjusted balance $1,290
E8-18	Adjusted balance $2,221
E8-19	NCF
E8-20	NCF
E8-21	NCF
E8-22	Debit Cash Short & Over for $3
E8-23	3. Petty Cash balance $100
E8-24	NCF

P8-25A	NCF
P8-26A	NCF
P8-27A	Adjusted balance $6,901
P8-28A	1. Adjusted balance $12,047
P8-29A	NCF
P8-30A	3. Apr. 30 Credit Cash Short & Over for $3
P8-31A	NCF
P8-32B	NCF
P8-33B	NCF
P8-34B	Adjusted balance $14,660
P8-35B	1. Adjusted balance $2,046
P8-36B	NCF
P8-37B	3. June 30 Debit Cash Short & Over for $2
P8-38B	NCF
Case 1	NCF
Case 2	NCF
Case 3	Cashier stole $500
Financial Statement Case	5. Cash decreased by $290 mil.

Chapter 9

Quick Check   1 d; 2 d; 3 a; 4 b; 5 a; 6 d; 7 c; 8 b; 9 b; 10 c

S9-1	NCF
S9-2	NCF
S9-3	Accts. Rec., net $33,000
S9-4	4. Uncollectible-Account Expense $8,000
S9-5	Allowance for Uncollectible Accts. bal. $2,200
S9-6	1. Uncollectible-Account Expense $2,000 2. Accts. Rec. at June 30 $13,000
S9-7	NCF
S9-8	Debit Cash for $7,880
S9-9	Note 1 $1,250 Note 2 $150
S9-10	b. Debit Cash for $102,500
S9-11	1. Net income $1,600 2. Accts. Rec., net $2,460
S9-12	a. 1.09 b. 31 days
S9-13	a. 1.61 b. 0.55 c. 0.45 d. 6.9 times
E9-14	NCF
E9-15	2. Accts. Rec., net $53,800
E9-16	2. Accts. Rec. bal. $55,600
E9-17	2. Accts. Rec., net $288,500
E9-18	NCF
E9-19	1. Interest for: 2007 $4,800 2008 $2,400 3. Payoff total of $84,200
E9-20	June 30 Debit Interest Receivable for $260
E9-21	Aug. 1, 2009 Debit Cash for $22,400

E9-22	Dec. 31 Debit Cash for $15,250
E9-23	1. 2009 0.76 2. 30 days
E9-24	1. 25 days
P9-25A	NCF
P9-26A	Uncollectible-Acct. Expense: 1. $8,200 2. $7,000
P9-27A	3. Accts. Rec., net $51,850
P9-28A	3. Accts. Rec., net $159,200
P9-29A	1. Note 1 $13,080; Note 2 $11,330; Note 3 $15,125 3. Debit Cash for $13,080
P9-30A	Jan. 20, 2008 Debit Cash for $4,433 Dec. 14, 2008 Debit Cash for $6,195
P9-31A	Dec. 31, 2007 Debit Uncollectible-Acct. Expense for $1,700
P9-32A	1. Ratios for 2008: a. 1.52 b. 0.58 c. 24 days
P9-33B	NCF
P9-34B	Uncollectible-Acct. Expense: 1. $11,200 2. $8,000
P9-35B	3. Accts. rec., net $158,400
P9-36B	3. Accts. rec., net $133,200
P9-37B	1. Note 1 $14,170; Note 2 $12,720; Note 3 $9,150 3. Debit Cash for $14,170
P9-38B	Feb. 17, 2008 Debit Cash for $5,100 Dec. 1, 2008 Debit Cash for $10,550
P9-39B	Dec. 31, 2007 Debit Uncollectible-Acct. Expense for $3,100
P9-40B	1. Ratios for 2009: a. 1.59 b. 0.88 c. 17 days
Case 1	Net income: Without bankcards $75,000; With bankcards $94,300
Case 2	2. Expected amount to collect $11,900
Financial Statement Case	2. b. Expect to collect $274 mil. c. Expect not to collect $43 mil. 3. Acid-test ratio for 2005 1.18

Chapter Appendix 9A

E9A-1	Dec. 1 Debit Interest Expense for $200
P9A-1	2. Note 1 $8,081; Note 2 $8,979; Note 3 $6,056

Chapter 10

Quick Check   1 a; 2 c; 3 a; 4 b; 5 a;
6 c; 7 d; 8 d; 9 b; 10 c

S10-1	NCF
S10-2	Land $75,000; Building $56,250; Equipment $18,750
S10-3	2. Net income overstated by $250,000
S10-4	2. Book value $29,000,000
S10-5	2nd-year depreciation: b. UOP $7,500,000; DDB $8,400,000
S10-6	2. Extra tax deduction with DDB $8,000,000
S10-7	$10,800
S10-8	Depreciation Expense $15,000
S10-9	Gain on Sale $7,000
S10-10	Debit Equipment (new) for $3,300
S10-11	2. Depletion Expense $5 bil.
S10-12	Goodwill $190,000
S10-13	Net income $248,000
E10-14	Land $390,000; Land improvements $66,000; Building $500,000
E10-15	Lot 1 $41,700; Lot 2 $49,950; Lot 3 $58,350
E10-16	NCF
E10-17	NCF
E10-18	NCF
E10-19	2010 Depreciation: SL $3,000; UOP $2,400; DDB $375
E10-20	Extra depreciation with DDB $30,400
E10-21	Depreciation for Year 16 $25,000
E10-22	Gain on Sale $2,000
E10-23	Debit Office Fixtures (new) 1. $115,000 2. $110,000
E10-24	Cost of new truck $270,000
E10-25	c. Depletion Expense $75,000
E10-26	2. Amortization Expense for year 5 $150,000
E10-27	Goodwill $3,000,000
P10-28A	2. Depreciation: Land Improvements $9,300; Building $2,100; Furniture $600
P10-29A	Dec. 31 Depreciation Expense: Comm. Equip. $1,200; Office Equip. $4,500
P10-30A	NCF
P10-31A	1. Book value at Dec. 31, 2010: SL $23,500; UOP $22,012; DDB $14,200
P10-32A	1. Depletion Expense $980,000 2. Net income $320,000
P10-33A	1. Goodwill $340,000
P10-34A	1. Book value $9 bil.; 2. Owners' equity $8 bil.; 3. Net income $1 bil.
P10-35B	2. Depreciation: Land Improvements $2,400; Building $7,500; Furniture $10,000
P10-36B	Dec. 31 Depreciation Expense: Equip. $15,000; Buildings $1,250
P10-37B	NCF
P10-38B	1. Book value at Dec. 31, 2010: SL $64,000; UOP $53,000; DDB $31,104
P10-39B	1. Depletion Expense $300,000 2. Net income $140,000
P10-40B	1. Goodwill $300,000
P10-41B	1. Book value $8 bil.; 2. Owners' equity $14 bil.; 3. Net income $4 bil.
Case	1. Net income: Woods $49,000; Mickelson $11,700

Financial Statement Case
2. Depreciation expense $113 million
3. Purchases of fixed assets $204 mil.

Chapter 11

Quick Check   1 c; 2 a; 3 c; 4 b; 5 d;
6 d; 7 d; 8 a; 9 a; 10 b

S11-1	b. Credit Cash for $8,720
S11-2	Interest Expense $360
S11-3	2. Estimated Warranty Payable bal. $4,000
S11-4	NCF
S11-5	NCF
S11-6	2. Net pay $721.60
S11-7	Total expense $1,065.96
S11-8	a. Salary Payable $721.60
S11-9	Net pay $4,120
S11-10	1. Total salary expense $14,625; 2. Net pay $10,255
S11-11	NCF
S11-12	Total current liabilities $37,640
E11-13	Mar. 31 Debit Cash for $216,000
E11-14	May 1, 2008 Credit Cash for $16,200
E11-15	Unearned sales revenue bal. $100
E11-16	2. Estimated Warranty Payable bal. $2,000
E11-17	Net pay $7,385
E11-18	1. Net pay $451.50
E11-19	Payroll Tax Expense $6,378
E11-20	Salary expense $450,000; Salary payable $8,000
E11-21	2009: Current portion of long-term note payable $100,000; Interest payable $10,000
E11-22	Total current liabilities $49,080
E11-23	Ratios for 2006: Current 1.24; Debt 0.702
E11-24	NCF
P11-25A	NCF
P11-26A	1. b. $23,900
P11-27A	1. Net pay $69,000 2. Total cost $102,300
P11-28A	3. Total liabilities $336,000
P11-29A	1. Total net pay $3,332 3. Credit Cash for $3,332 4. Debit Payroll Tax Expense for $207
P11-30A	a. Est. warranty pay. $1,000
P11-31B	NCF
P11-32B	1. b. $82,000
P11-33B	1. Net pay $68,267 2. Total cost $101,790
P11-34B	3. Total liabilities $148,000
P11-35B	1. Total net pay $2,238 3. Credit Cash for $2,238 4. Debit Payroll Tax Expense for $277
P11-36B	b. Est. warranty pay. $1,100
Case 1	NCF
Case 2	NCF

Financial Statement Case
2. $48 mil.
3. Long-term debt $1,521 mil. Current portion $3 mil.

Comprehensive Problem   Gold Rush net income, revised $356,000

Chapter 12

Quick Check   1 a; 2 b; 3 b; 4 c; 5 d;
6 c; 7 b; 8 d; 9 d; 10 a

S12-1	NCF
S12-2	Debit Land for $500,000
S12-3	2. Total equity $18 mil.
S12-4	2. Abel, Capital $16,000 Baker, Capital $12,000
S12-5	Lee $32,000; Muse $16,000; Nall $44,000
S12-6	NCF
S12-7	Gray, Capital $70,000
S12-8	Credit Mo, Capital $125,000
S12-9	NCF
S12-10	a. Credit Abraham, Capital $10,000; Isaac, Capital $20,000; Jacob, Capital $10,000
S12-11	Pay Akers $34,000; Bloch $18,000; Crane $8,000
S12-12	Final entry: Debit Akers, Capital $34,000; Bloch, Capital $18,000; Crane, Capital $8,000
S12-13	Net income: Bush $36,000; Carter $24,000

E12-14	NCF
E12-15	Credit Fuentes, Capital for $96,000
E12-16	c. Fultz $37,000; Hardie $63,000
E12-17	Partnership capital increased by $20,000
E12-18	c. Hollis, capital $60,000; Rose, capital $115,000; Novak, capital $65,000
E12-19	c. Credit Hollis, Capital for $60,000; Rose, Capital for $15,000; Novak, Capital for $15,000
E12-20	1. O'Brien receives $70,000; 2. Pope's capital $110,000
E12-21	b. Debit Sam, Capital for $44,000; Bob, Capital for $8,000; Tim, Capital for $8,000
E12-22	2. Ray gets $23,000, Scott $18,000, and Van $9,000
E12-23	Pay Boyd $28,000, Carl $21,000, Dove $17,000
E12-24	Selling for $140,000: Dodd, Capital $14,800; Gage, Capital $41,200; Hamm, Capital $13,000
E12-25	Total assets $280,000; Farrell, capital $88,000; Flores, capital $92,000
P12-26A	NCF
P12-27A	2. Total assets $120,000; LeBlanc, capital $50,000; Rollins, capital $50,000
P12-28A	Rosenzweig capital: 2. $60,000; 3. $40,000
P12-29A	1. b. Net income to: Evans $35,000 Furr $30,000 Good $25,000
P12-30A	3. Debit Ho, Capital for $30,000; Kim, Capital for $8,000; Li, Capital for $6,000
P12-31A	1. Pay King $15,000, Queen $30,000, Page $2,000
P12-32A	2. Capital balances: Allen $20,000 Bacon $40,000 Cush $40,000
P12-33B	NCF
P12-34B	2. Total assets $99,000; Hayes, capital $40,000; McKay, capital $40,000
P12-35B	Shipp's capital: 2. $100,000; 3. $95,000
P12-36B	1. b. Net income to: Beau $68,750 Cole $55,000 Drake $53,250
P12-37B	3. Debit Garcia, Capital for $50,000; Hernandez, Capital

	for $10,000; Cahill, Capital for $20,000
P12-38B	1. Pay Donald $20,000; Healey $36,000; Jaguar $32,000
P12-39B	2. Capital balances: Lee $62,000 Mah $39,000 Nguyen $21,000
Case 1	NCF
Case 2	NCF

Chapter 13

Quick Check   1 c; 2 a; 3 a; 4 a; 5 d; 6 c; 7 b; 8 d; 9 c; 10 b

S13-1	NCF
S13-2	NCF
S13-3	NCF
S13-4	NCF
S13-5	1. Paid-in Capital in Excess of Par $3,850
S13-6	Total stockholders' equity $73,000
S13-7	a. Total liabilities $18,800 b. Total assets $91,800
S13-8	NCF
S13-9	3. Preferred gets $6,000; common gets $9,000
S13-10	Book value per share of common $0.65
S13-11	ROA 17.2% ROE 32.3%
S13-12	2. Net income $48,000
E13-13	NCF
E13-14	2. Total paid-in capital $43,000
E13-15	Both plans result in total paid-in capital of $30,000
E13-16	Balances: Building $500,000; Equip. $200,000
E13-17	2. Total stockholders' equity $99,000
E13-18	Total stockholders' equity $186,000
E13-19	Total paid-in capital $190,000
E13-20	Total stockholders' equity $350,000
E13-21	2008: Preferred gets $22,000; common gets $28,000
E13-22	Preferred gets $10,000; Common gets $140,000
E13-23	Book value per share of common $44.40
E13-24	Book value per share of common $43.60
E13-25	ROA 0.095 ROE 0.099
E13-26	2. Net income $250 mil. Deferred tax liability $21 mil.
P13-27A	NCF
P13-28A	2. Total stockholders' equity $300,000
P13-29A	2. Total stockholders' equity $256,000

P13-30A	Total stockholders' equity: Centroplex $540,000; Jacobs-Cathey $423,500
P13-31A	4. Dividends Payable: Preferred $60,000; Common $440,000.
P13-32A	1. Total assets $600,000; Total S/E $445,000 2. ROA 0.091; ROE 0.129
P13-33A	1. b. 2008: Preferred gets $5,000; Common gets $15,000
P13-34A	4. Book value per share of common $18.71
P13-35A	3. Income tax payable $80,000 Deferred tax liability $12,000
P13-36B	NCF
P13-37B	2. Total stockholders' equity $200,000
P13-38B	2. Total stockholders' equity $202,000
P13-39B	Total stockholders' equity: Monterrey $800,000; Guadalupe $400,000
P13-40B	4. Dividends Payable: Preferred $11,700; Common $38,300
P13-41B	1. Total assets $400,000; Total S/E $322,000 2. ROA 0.092; ROE 0.100
P13-42B	1. b. 2008: Preferred gets $35,000; common gets $115,000
P13-43B	5. Book value per share of common $8.95
P13-44B	3. Income tax payable $70,000 Deferred tax liability $7,000
Case 1	3. Total stockholders' equity: Plan 1 $400,000; Plan 2 $420,000
Case 2	NCF
Financial Statement Case	3. At Dec. 31, 2005, Common shares issued $416 mil.; Common Stock balance $4 mil.

Chapter 14

Quick Check   1 c; 2 c; 3 b; 4 c; 5 a; 6 d; 7 d; 8 a; 9 b; 10 b

S14-1	1. Paid-in Capital in Excess of Par $14,000
S14-2	NCF
S14-3	1. Total stockholders' equity $664 mil.
S14-4	Balance sheet reports Treasury stock $(2,500)
S14-5	NCF
S14-6	NCF
S14-7	NCF
S14-8	Net income $24,000
S14-9	EPS for net income $2.00

S14-10	NCF
S14-11	Comprehensive income $28,000
S14-12	Retained earnings Dec. 31, 2009 $155,000
E14-13	2. Total stockholders' equity $370,000
E14-14	1. Paid in Capital in Excess of Par $40,000
E14-15	Total stockholders' equity $350,000
E14-16	d. Increase stockholders' equity by $3,000
E14-17	Aug. 22 Credit Paid-in Capital from Treasury Stock Transactions for $3,600
E14-18	1. Total stockholders' equity $800,000
E14-19	b. Total stockholders' equity $300,000
E14-20	Net income $31,000
E14-21	EPS $2.10
E14-22	EPS for net income $2.34
E14-23	Retained earnings Dec. 31, 2007 $200 mil.
E14-24	Retained earnings Dec. 31, 2008 $80,000
E14-25	1. Comprehensive income $110,000 2. EPS $2.00
P14-26A	Nov. 8 Credit Paid-in Capital from Treasury Stock Transactions for $6,000
P14-27A	2. Total stockholders' equity $395,000
P14-28A	NCF
P14-29A	3. Total stockholders' equity $690,000
P14-30A	Net income $82,000; EPS for net income $3.00
P14-31A	Retained earnings Dec. 31, 2008 $245,000; EPS for net income $1.90
P14-32A	1. EPS for net income $2.75 Dec. 22 Credit Paid-in Capital from Treasury Stock Transactions for $3,000
P14-33B	
P14-34B	2. Total stockholders' equity $534,000
P14-35B	NCF
P14-36B	3. Total stockholders' equity $490,000
P14-37B	Net income $70,000; EPS for net income $3.20
P14-38B	Retained earnings Dec. 31, 2007 $185,000; EPS for net income $8.30
P14-39B	1. EPS for net income $4.50
Case 1	NCF
Case 2	NCF
Financial Statement Case	1. Basic EPS $0.87 2. Accumulated Deficit balance—debit of $2,027 mil.

Chapter 15

Quick Check   1 d; 2 b; 3 c; 4 a; 5 d; 6 c; 7 a; 8 b; 9 c; 10 a

S15-1	NCF
S15-2	a. $77,750 b. $103,800
S15-3	NCF
S15-4	NCF
S15-5	a. $965,000 c. $30,000
S15-6	NCF
S15-7	July 1, 2006 Interest Expense $2,250
S15-8	July 1, 2009 Interest Expense $2,400
S15-9	Dec. 31, 2008 Interest Expense $1,500
S15-10	July 1, 2006 Interest Expense $5,000
S15-11	3. Gain on retirement of bonds $5,200
S15-12	2. Paid-in Capital in Excess of Par $620,000
S15-13	Total current liabilities $33,000; LT bonds payable, net $194,000
S15-14	EPS: Plan A $3.78; Plan B $2.15
E15-15	NCF
E15-16	July 1 Interest Expense $4,075
E15-17	c. Dec. 31 Interest Expense $7,000
E15-18	1. At July 1: b. Credit Discount for $125 c. Debit Premium for $125
E15-19	NCF
E15-20	1. $406,000 2. $12,000
E15-21	b. Oct. 31 Interest Expense $2,500
E15-22	Oct. 1 Loss on Retirement of Bonds $750
E15-23	2. Bond carrying amount July 31, 2009 $688,800
E15-24	2. Oct. 1 Credit Paid-in Capital in Excess of Par for $84,000
E15-25	Total current liab. $95,000 LT liab. $180,000
E15-26	EPS: Plan A $4.98; Plan B $2.76
E15-27	4. Interest expense $31,950
E15-28	2. a. $295,725 b. $295,950
P15-29A	2. Apr. 30, 2009 Interest Expense $10,000; 3. Interest expense for 2008 $20,000; Interest payable $5,000
P15-30A	3. d. Feb. 28, 2008 Interest Expense $3,050
P15-31A	Interest Expense: Dec. 31, 2007 $43,300 Dec. 31, 2016 $43,300

P15-32A	3. Bond carrying amount Dec. 31, 2008 $193,000
P15-33A	1. d. May 31, 2009 Interest Expense $17,500 2. Interest payable at Dec. 31, 2008 $3,500
P15-34A	Total current liabilities $120,000 Total LT liabilities $250,000
P15-35A	NCF
P15-36B	2. Jan. 31, 2009 Interest Expense $3,500 3. Interest expense for 2008 $38,500; Interest payable $17,500
P15-37B	3. d. Mar. 31, 2007 Interest Expense $6,900
P15-38B	Interest Expense: Dec. 31, 2009 $10,400 Dec. 31, 2018 $10,400
P15-39B	3. Bond carrying amount Dec. 31, 2010 $170,000
P15-40B	1. d. Mar 31, 2008 Interest Expense $22,500 2. Interest payable at Dec. 31, 2007 $22,500
P15-41B	Total current liabilities $160,000 Total LT liabilities $400,000
P15-42B	NCF
Case 1	NCF
Case 2	EPS: Plan A $4.14; Plan B $3.60; Plan C $3.88
Financial Statement Case	3. Annual interest $42.75 mil.

Chapter Appendix 15A

P15A-1	Present value: GE $216,300 Westinghouse $226,800
P15A-2	Present value of bonds: a. $88,018 b. $78,640 c. $98,975
P15A-3	Interest expense for bonds issued at: 12% $5,280 14% $5,748 10% $4,731
P15A-4	2. Mar. 31, 2008 Bond carrying amount $546,749
P15A-5	2. May 31, 2009 Bond carrying amount $217,158
P15A-6	1. 1-2-08 Bond carrying amount $280,995
P15A-7	12-31-05 Bond carrying amount $500,000
P15A-8	2. 12-31-09 Bond carrying amount $380,838 3. Dec. 31, 2009 Interest expense $15,205

Comprehensive Problem
    2. Net income $74,000;
    EPS for net income $1.80

Chapter 16

Quick Check 1 a; 2 d; 3 a; 4 b; 5 c;
  6 a; 7 b; 8 c; 9 d; 10 c

S16-1	NCF
S16-2	NCF
S16-3	NCF
S16-4	Net cash from operating $40,000
S16-5	Net cash from operating $58,000
S16-6	Net cash from operating $58,000; Net increase in cash $62,000
S16-7	a. $11,000; b. $7,000
S16-8	Net cash from operating $24,000; investing $(11,000); financing $(12,000)
S16-9	Increase in cash $35,000
S16-10	Free cash flow $70,000
S16-11	Net cash from operating $210,000; investing $(140,000); financing $(50,000)
S16-12	Net cash from operating $20,000
S16-13	Net cash from operating $20,000; investing $20,000; financing $(16,000)
S16-14	a. $134,000 b. $71,000
E16-15	NCF
E16-16	NCF
E16-17	NCF
E16-18	Net cash from operating $30,000
E16-19	Net cash from operating $91,000
E16-20	1. Net cash from operating $85,000; investing $(77,000); financing $4,000
E16-21	a. $35,000 b. $11,000
E16-22	$90,000
E16-23	a. $8,000 b. $10,000 c. $61,000
E16-24	Net cash from operating $167,000; investing $(105,000); financing $(59,000)
E16-25	NCF
E16-26	NCF
E16-27	Net cash from operating $2,000
E16-28	NCF
E16-29	Net cash from operating $80,000; investing $(77,000); financing $4,000
E16-30	a. $64,000 b. $74,000
E16-31	a. $24,440 mil. b. $18,516 mil. c. $4,793 mil. d. $1,186 mil. e. $14 mil. f. $230 mil. g. $143 mil.
P16-32A	NCF
P16-33A	1. Net income $70,000 2. Total assets $335,000 3. Net cash from operating $95,000; Cash bal., Dec. 31, 2006 $205,000
P16-34A	Net cash from operating $80,000; investing $(69,000); financing $4,000; Total non-cash investing and financing $118,000
P16-35A	1. Net cash from operating $49,000; investing $(159,000); financing $120,000
P16-36A	1. Net cash from operating $79,800; investing $(47,600); financing $(24,200)
P16-37A	Net cash from operating $58,300; investing $(40,300); financing $41,700
P16-38A	1. Net income $70,000; 2. Total assets $335,000; 3. Net cash from operating $95,000; Cash balance Dec. 31, 2006 $205,000
P16-39A	1. Net cash from operating $79,800; investing $(47,600); financing $(24,200)
P16-40A	Net cash from operating $77,200; investing $(51,500); financing $(21,000)
P16-41B	NCF
P16-42B	1. Net income $45,000 2. Total assets $498,000 3. Net cash used for operating $(71,000); Cash bal., Dec. 31, 2008 $218,000
P16-43B	Net cash from operating $87,000; investing $(102,000); financing $43,000; Total non-cash investing and financing $65,000
P16-44B	1. Net cash from operating $101,900; investing $(125,700); financing $31,000
P16-45B	1. Net cash from operating $59,100; investing $(17,100); financing $(30,600)
P16-46B	Net cash from operating $100,500; investing $(37,000); financing $(70,800)
P16-47B	1. Net income $45,000 2. Total assets $498,000 3. Net cash used for operating $(71,000); Cash bal., Dec. 31, 2008 $218,000
P16-48B	1. Net cash from operating $59,100; investing $(17,100); financing $(30,600)
P16-49B	Net cash from operating $67,800; investing $(10,200); financing $(47,600)
Case 1	1. Net cash from operating $140,000; investing $(141,000); financing $(37,000)
Case 2	NCF

Financial Statement Case
    3. a. Collections $8,418 mil.
    b. Payments $6,313 mil.

Chapter Appendix 16A

P16A-1	Column totals: Dec. 31, 20X7 $255,400 Dec. 31, 20X8 $287,800
P16A-2	Column totals: Dec. 31, 20X7 $255,400 Dec. 31, 20X8 $287,800

Chapter 17

Quick Check 1 b; 2 c; 3 d; 4 a; 5 a;
  6 b; 7 b; 8 d; 9 c; 10 a

S17-1	2006 Gross profit increase 10.4%
S17-2	1. Trend % for 2006 revenue 114%
S17-3	2006 Cash 26.4% of total assets
S17-4	Net income % of sales: Sanchez 6.2%; Alioto 4.8%
S17-5	1. Current ratio for 2006 0.77
S17-6	a. 4.9 times b. 2 days
S17-7	1. Debt ratio 0.46
S17-8	a. 6.2% b. 12.0% c. 20.4%
S17-9	1. $2.38 2. 28 times
S17-10	d. $684,000
S17-11	a. $580,000 c. $1,470,000 f. $6,800,000
E17-12	2009 Increase in working capital 13.3%
E17-13	Net sales revenue increased 15.3%; Net income increased 39.8%
E17-14	Trend % for 2008: Total revenue 126% Net income 144%
E17-15	Total current assets 14.8%; Long-term debt 38.0%
E17-16	% for 2007: COGS 47.0%; Net income 28.6%

E17-17   a. 1.34
          b. 0.63
          c. 4.28 times
          d. 50 days
E17-18   Ratios for 2007:
          a. 1.63
          b. 0.77
          c. 0.56
          d. 3.44 times
E17-19   Ratios for 2006:
          a. 0.092
          b. 0.127
          c. 0.141
          d. $0.65
E17-20   Ratios for 2008:
          a. 27.5
          b. 0.015
          c. $7.25
E17-21   Total assets $25,000 mil.;
          Current liabilities $7,000 mil.
P17-22A   1. Trend % for 2008: Net
          sales 115%; Net income
          125%; Common equity 124%
          2. Return on equity for 2008
          0.167
P17-23A   1. Gross profit 32.4%; Net
          income 10.9%; Current assets
          67.8%; Stockholders' equity
          31.3%
P17-24A   2. a. Current ratio 1.27; Debt
          ratio 0.63; EPS no effect
P17-25A   1. Ratios for 2009:
          a. 1.64
          b. 7.82
          c. 1.55
          d. 0.338
          e. $4.40
          f. 11.1
P17-26A   1. Singular ratios:
          a. 1.04
          b. 2.79
          c. 34 days
          d. 0.38
          e. $5.00
          f. 16
P17-27A   NCF
P17-28B   1. Trend % for 2008: Net
          sales 109%; Net income 50%;
          Total assets 135%
          2. Return on sales for 2008
          0.029
P17-29B   1. Gross profit 35.9%; Net
          income 13.6%; Current assets
          77.1%; Stockholders' equity
          39.4%
P17-30B   2. a. Current ratio 1.77; Debt
          ratio 0.55; EPS No effect
P17-31B   1. Ratios for 2006:
          a. 1.92   b. 4.32   c. 1.29
          d. 0.329   e. $5.80   f. 16
P17-32B   1. MMM ratios:
          a. 0.72   b. 2.30   c. 61 days
          d. 0.68   e. $0.50   f. 16
P17-33B   NCF

Case 1   NCF
Case 2   NCF
Financial Statement Case
          2. Trend % for 2005:
          Net sales 161.
          Net income 10,257.
          3. Invy. turnover for 2005
          12.3 times.
Comprehensive Problem   All answers
          for 20X5:
          1. Trend of net sales 178%;
          net income 181%
          2. Return on sales 3.3%;
          ROA 9.2%; ROE 21.6%;
          3. Invy. turnover 8.08 times;
          4. Current ratio 0.9; Debt
          ratio 58.5%
          5. Dividends per share $0.30

Chapter 18

Quick Check   1 a; 2 c; 3 d; 4 b; 5 a;
          6 c; 7 b; 8 a; 9 d; 10 d
S18-1   NCF
S18-2   NCF
S18-3   NCF
S18-4   Net operating income $3,000
S18-5   COGS $46,000
S18-6   a. $3,000
          b. $62,000
          c. $28,000
          d. $200,000
          e. $60,000
          f. $88,000
          g. $27,000
S18-7   NCF
S18-8   DM used $9,200
S18-9   NCF
S18-10   Total MOH $12,300
S18-11   COGM $41,000
S18-12   NCF
S18-13   NCF
E18-14   NCF
E18-15   NCF
E18-16   Net operating income $7,650
E18-17   Net operating income
          $21,000
E18-18   1. Operating income
          $15,000
          2. $11.21
E18-19   NCF
E18-20   NCF
E18-21   a. $10,000
          b. $20,000
          c. $4,000
          d. $65,000
          e. $105,000
          f. $80,000
          g. $3,000
          h. $4,500
          i. $4,000
E18-22   COGM $405,000
E18-23   COGM $200,000
          COGS $195,000

E18-24   NCF
P18-25A   1. Net operating income
          $5,000
          2. $0.50/foot
P18-26A   Operating income $13,000
P18-27A   1. COGM $67,000
          2. Operating income $36,200
          4. $3.83/unit
P18-28A   DM used $55,000; COGM
          $162,000; End. FG invy.
          $68,000; Operating income
          $100,000
P18-29A   1. COGM $21.3 M
          2. COGS $21.4 M
          3. DM purchases $2.9 M
P18-30A   NCF
P18-31B   1. Net operating income
          $2,700
          2. $33.12/automobile
P18-32B   Operating income $35,250
P18-33B   1. COGM $71,000
          2. Operating income
          $45,000
          4. $54.62/unit
P18-34B   DM used $52,000; COGM
          $150,000; COG available
          $274,000; Operating income
          $76,000
P18-35B   1. DM used $28.2 M;
          2. COGM $161.0 M;
          3. COGS $158.8 M
P18-36B   NCF
Case 1   End. inventory:
          1. DM $143,000
          2. WIP $239,000;
          3. FG $150,000
Case 2   NCF

Chapter 19

Quick Check   1 c; 2 c; 3 b; 4 a; 5 d;
          6 d; 7 a; 8 c; 9 d; 10 b
S19-1   NCF
S19-2   NCF
S19-3   Ending Materials Inv.,
          $42,700
S19-4   Bals.: Mat. $25; WIP $50
S19-5   NCF
S19-6   MOH bal. $66,000
S19-7   Total cost, $1,180
S19-8   Indirect materials used,
          $3,000; COGM $125,000;
          COGS $110,000
S19-9   3. MOH is $2,000
          overallocated
S19-10   3. MOH is $10,000
          overallocated
S19-11   NCF
S19-12   2. DL for Client 507 $770
S19-13   2. Indirect cost for Client 507
          $280
E19-14   NCF
E19-15   WIP Inv. $6,000; FG Inv.
          $4,000; COGS $16,000

E19-16 MOH allocated $18,000

E19-17 NCF

E19-18 1. End. WIP Inv. $20,000
4. GP $7,000

E19-19 2. MOH allocated $80,000
3. MOH underallocated, $3,000

E19-20 2. MOH allocated $550,000
3. MOH overallocated, $40,000

E19-21 1. MOH underallocated, $10,000
3. Adjusted COGS, $610,000

E19-22 1. b. Indirect cost allocation rate 60%
2. Total predicted cost $52,800

E19-23 1. MH used, 10,125
2. MOH underallocated $25,250

P19-24A 1. c. Nov. COGS $1,500
Dec. COGS $3,750
2. Debit FG in Nov. $3,500
Debit FG in Dec. $3,850
4. GP $500

P19-25A 2. End. WIP Inv. $274,400
FG Inv. $116,800
5. GP $62,000

P19-26A 1. MOH allocated $600
Total job cost $2,285

P19-27A 1. PMOH rate $7.50/MH
3. MOH underallocated $33,350

P19-28A 2. End. WIP Inv. $38,400
FG Inv. $21,300
4. COGM $48,850

P19-29A 2. Food Coop $166,000
3. Mesilla $10,150

P19-30B 1. c. March COGS $3,000
April COGS $2,900
4. GP for Job 5 $900

P19-31B 2. End. WIP Inv. $102,400
FG Inv. $92,400
5. GP for Chalet 23 $42,300

P19-32B 1. MOH allocated $1,312
Total job cost $4,352

P19-33B 1. PMOH rate $25/MH
3. MOH underallocated $13,000

P19-34B 2. End. WIP Inv. $99,600
FG Inv. $61,000
4. COGM $61,200

P19-35B 2. Vacationplan.com $78,000
Port Arthur $4,800

Case 1 NCF

Case 2 NCF

Team Project 1. c. Delta's profit per flight 1247, $1,136
2. c. JetBlue's profit per flight 53 $2,754

Chapter 20

Quick Check 1 c; 2 b; 3 d; 4 a; 5 c; 6 a; 7 d; 8 a; 9 b; 10 d

S20-1 NCF

S20-2 NCF

S20-3 $160,000

S20-4 1. 9,600
2. 4,400

S20-5 6,000

S20-6 1. $48,000
2. $0.84/liter

S20-7 2. EU for DM 200,000; EU for CC 190,000

S20-8 EU for DM 40,000
EU for CC 33,000

S20-9 DM $0.75; CC $0.50

S20-10 1. $37,500
2. $9,000

S20-11 2. 5,000
3. 15,000

S20-12 1. 9,000
2. 15,000
3. 15,000

S20-13 1. 350
2. 230
3. 65
4. 50
5. 150
6. 150
7. 100

E20-14 NCF

E20-15 NCF

E20-16 2. EU of DM 8,000; CC 6,600
3. End. WIP Inv. $1,470

E20-17 2. End. WIP Inv. $1,470
3. Avg. cost/gal. transferred out $1.05

E20-18 1. EU of DM 76,800; CC 74,400
2. DM $2.80; CC $2.00
3. End. WIP Inv. $18,240

E20-19 1. EU of DM 18,200; CC 21,400
5. End. WIP Inv. $11,200

E20-20 3. Cost per EU: DM $1.30; CC $0.90

E20-21 2. WIP Inv. bal. $2,929
3. Costs transferred out, $2.20/gal.

E20-22 EU of TI costs:
1. Mixing 90,000;
2. Heating 86,000

E20-23 2. EU of TI, 168,000
6. End. WIP Inv., $14,910

P20-24A 2. EU of DM 100,000; CC 85,840; CC/EU $3.00
3b. End. WIP Inv. $116,820

P20-25A 2. EU of DM 4,600; CC 4,600
CC/EU $1.40
3b. End. WIP Inv. $260

P20-26A 2. EU of Wood 3,000; CC 2,370
3. CC/EU, $1.30
5. End. WIP Inv. $1,491

P20-27A 2. EU of TI $635; CC 608
TI cost/EU $40; CC/EU $94
3. Costs transferred out $77,500

P20-28A 2. EU of TI 9,000; CC 6,000
3. TI cost/EU $85
3. b. End. WIP Inv. $449,000

P20-29B 2. EU of DM 20,400; CC 19,100
CC/EU $0.30
4. End. WIP Inv. $2,210

P20-30B 2. EU of DM 12,000; CC $11,700
CC/EU $26
3b. End. WIP Inv. $173,200

P20-31B 2. EU of Green Beans 15,000; CC 14,160
3. CC/EU, $2.00
5. End. WIP Inv. $4,830

P20-32B 2. EU of TI $3,600; CC 2,900
TI cost/EU, $15; CC/EU, $25
3. Costs transferred out $112,200

P20-33B 2. EU of TI, 35,000; CC 19,800
3. TI cost/EU $0.14
3b. End. WIP Inv. $3,268

Case 3. Op. inc. $5,200
5. Selling price per box, $12.74

Team Project 1. Cost per EU:
DM $0.07; CC $0.12
2. Cutting Dept. cost/lb., $0.16

Chapter Appendix 20A

S20A-34 2. EU of TI, 160,000; CC, 160,600

S20A-35 DM/EU, $0.20; CC/EU $0.35

S20A-36 End. WIP Inv., $15,330

E20A-37 1a. DM 40%; CC 25%
2. Mixing Dep't. EU of DM 75,000; CC 67,000
Cooking Dep't. EU of DM 78,900; CC 76,700

E20A-38 2 EU of TI 3,600; CC 3,490
3. b. End. WIP Inv. $22,200

P20A-39 2. EU of TI 28,000; CC 17,700
3. TI/EU $0.17; CC/EU $0.166
3. a. Costs transferred out, $4,208

Chapter 21

Quick Check 1 b; 2 d; 3 a; 4 b; 5 d; 6 a; 7 b; 8 c; 9 a; 10 c

S21-1 NCF

S21-2 NCF

S21-3 1c. Total cost $33

S21-4 1. $0.40; 2. $2,000

S21-5 6,875 tickets

S21-6 2. $412,500

S21-7 1. 9,167 tickets; $458,350 (or $458,333)
2. 6,111 tickets; $366,660 (or $366,667)

S21-8 BEP, 5,000 tickets; $300,000

S21-9	a. Margin of safety, 125 tickets
	b. Margin of safety, $7,500
S21-10	BE sales $125,000; Units to
	achieve target 25,000
S21-11	$13.75
S21-12	1. 3,000;
	2. 1,200 individual;
	1,800 family
S21-13	NCF
E21-14	NCF
E21-15	NCF
E21-16	1. $1/unit
	2. $3,000
E21-17	Op. loss when sales are
	$250,000 = $20,000 BEP,
	$283,333
E21-18	1. CM ratio, 50%
	2. BEP, 100,000 packages;
	$170,000
E21-19	1. BEP, $12,000
	2. Sales required to earn target
	$24,500
E21-20	2. Op. loss when sales are
	$500,000 = $240,000
E21-21	3. BEP, 500 students;
	$50,000
E21-22	1. 625
	2. 833
	3. 556
	4. 500
E21-23	1. Margin of safety $40,000
E21-24	BEP 200 Std.;
	300 Chrome; To earn $6,600:
	310 Std.; 465 Chrome
P21-25A	NCF
P21-26A	North CM ratio 0.40
	East CM per unit $3.75
	South CM ratio 0.533
P21-27A	1. VC per show $27,200
	2. BEP 14 shows
	3. Target 144 shows
	4. Op. inc. $3,476,800
P21-28A	1. BEP 82,000 flags
	2. Target sales $1,034,000
	3. Op. loss $93,600
	4. BEP $1,228,032
P21-29A	1. BEP 40 trades
	2. Target sales $42,000
	4. BEP 35 trades
P21-30A	1. BEP 8,000 plain;
	4,000 custard.
	2. $52,000
	3. $36,774
P21-31B	NCF
P21-32B	CM ratio: J 0.67; M 0.60
	K CM/unit $3.00
P21-33B	1. VC per show, $15,200
	2. BEP, 36 shows
	3. Target, 94 shows
	4. Op. inc., $1,587,200
P21-34B	1. BEP 160,000 cartons
	2. Target sales $2,104,545
	3. Op. inc. $2,001,000
	4. BEP $2,704,800

P21-35B	1. BEP 24 trades
	2. Target sales, $14,400
	4. BEP 30 trades
P21-36B	1. BEP 12,000 small;
	4,000 large
	2. $50,000
	3. $29,500
Case	BEP 5,000 meals; $225,000
	To earn target op. inc.
	7,520 meals; $338,400
Team Project	1. Op. loss $2.0 mil.
	2. Adopting ad campaign
	will increase op. inc. by
	$2.2 mil.
	4. Op. inc. $1.88 mil. if
	30 mil. rolls; $0.2 mil.
	if 24 mil. rolls

Chapter Appendix 21A

S21A-37	Op. inc. $75,000
S21A-38	1. Op. inc. $80,000
E21A-39	1. Op. inc.: Absorption
	$625,000; VC $475,000
	3. Increase in op. inc. $75,000
P21A-40	1. Cost/meal: Absorption
	$4.50; VC $4.00
	2. a. Op. inc. $1,900
	b. Op. inc. $1,700
P21A-41	1. Cost/game: Absorption
	$19; VC $15
	2. a. Op. inc. $30,000
	b. Op. inc. $32,000

Chapter 22

Quick Check	1 d; 2 d; 3 b; 4 b; 5 b;
	6 c; 7 d; 8 c; 9 a; 10 c
S22-1	Income variance $700 F
S22-2	NCF
S22-3	NCF
S22-4	Feb. sales $60,000
S22-5	June purchases $1,000
	July purchases $660
S22-6	Feb. cash sales $48,000
S22-7	Feb. purchases $36,000
S22-8	Apr. total cash collections
	$48,000
S22-9	June total cash payments for
	purchases $28,000
S22-10	End. cash bal. $3,800
S22-11	Must borrow $14,070
S22-12	NCF
E22-13	Op. inc. this year, $200,000
E22-14	Purchases, qtr. ended June 30
	$88,500; Sept. 30 $79,500
E22-15	Qtr. 2 NI, $856,960
	Qtr. 3 NI, $950,546
E22-16	b. Sept. cash receipts
	$106,830
E22-17	End. cash bal. Jan. $11,500;
	Feb. $10,600
E22-18	Apr. borrowing $11,100
	May interest exp. $74

E22-19	2. Total assets $30,280
	Owners' equity $27,980
E22-20	NCF
E22-21	Cell phone total Op. inc. var.
	$45,000 F
E22-22	a. $105 M
	b. $(27) M
	c. $ 35 M
	d. $113 M
	e. $ (7) M
	f. $ 10 M
	g. $ 70 M
P22-23A	$86,000 U
	2. Aug. COGS, $120,000
	Aug. Op. inc., $37,000
	Sept. Op. inc., $40,000
P22-24A	1. Aug. total cash collections
	$199,000
	Aug. total cash payments for
	purchases, $124,600
	2. Ending cash bal.: Aug.
	$55,400; Sept. $95,600
P22-25A	2. Ending cash bal. $36,200
	3. Total assets, $163,700
	Owners' equity, $145,600
P22-26A	1. Op. inc. variance: Phoenix
	$12,000; Other Ariz. $31,400
	Total $44,400
P22-27A	NCF
P22-28B	2. May COGS, $15,500
	May Op. inc. $17,900
	June Op. inc. $11,900
P22-29B	1. May total cash collections
	$42,660
	May total cash payments for
	purchases $18,150
	2. Ending cash bal.: May
	$30,610; June $43,460
P22-30B	2. Ending cash bal. $60,000
	3. Total assets $148,900
	Owners' equity $120,600
P22-31B	1. Op. inc. variance: Florida
	stores $3,900; Other regions
	$(91,900)
	Total $(86,000)
P22-32B	NCF
Case 1	NCF
Case 2	1. NI: cotton, $235; linen $225
	Total assets: cotton $721;
	linen $1,511
Team Project	NCF

Chapter Appendix 22A

S22A-33	NCF
S22A-34	Software Dept. $300,000
E22A-35	Marketing cost allocated to
	Welding, $4,200
	Total indirect costs allocated
	to Priming $27,400
E22A-36	1. Chrome Op. inc. $75,200
P22-A1	1. Housekeeping exp.
	$24/room
	Total Club expense $102,720

2. Club cost $190.22/room
Regular cost $92.57/room

Chapter 23

Quick Check 1 d; 2 b; 3 a; 4 e; 5 c;
6 c; 7 d; 8 b; 9 a; 10 a

S23-1	NCF
S23-2	NCF
S23-3	Op. inc. @4,000 units $5,000; @ 6,000 units $15,000
S23-4	FB Var. for Op. inc. $2,000 F
S23-5	NCF
S23-6	DM Price Var. $770 U DM Eff. Var. $280 U
S23-7	DL Price Var. $1,750 F DL Eff. Var. $4,900 U
S23-8	NCF
S23-9	Std. var. OH rate $7/DLH Std. fixed OH rate $3/DLH
S23-10	OH FB Var. $400 U OH PV Var. $1,200 F
S23-11	Dr. DM Price Var. $770 Dr. DM Eff. Var. $280
S23-12	Cr. DL Price Var. $1,750 Dr. DL Eff. Var. $4,900
S23-13	COGS $364,000
S23-14	Op. inc. $89,000
E23-15	Op. inc. at 40,000 units $32,000; 70,000 units, $156,000
E23-16	Total FB Var. $10,000 U; Static Budget Op. inc. $10,000
E23-17	Sales Revenue FB Var. $21,000 F; Static Budget Op. inc. $44,100
E23-18	DM Price Var. $280 U DM Eff. Var. $200 F DL Price Var. $375 F DL Eff. Var. $2,500 U
E23-19	Actual price $10.50 Eff. Var. $8,000 F FB Var. $3,200 F
E23-20	DM Price Var. $7,250 F DM Eff. Var. $5,500 U DL Price Var. $450 U DL Eff. Var. $650 F
E23-21	Cr. DM Price Var. $7,250 Dr. DM Eff. Var. $5,500 Dr. DL Price Var. $450 Cr. DL Eff. Var. $650
E23-22	NCF
E23-23	Total OH Var. $2,300 F OH FB Var. $700 U OH PV Var. $3,000 F
E23-24	GP $227,500
P23-25A	1. Op. Inc. FB Var. $175 U; SV Var. $22,000 F
P23-26A	1. FB Gross profit $260,068 2. DM Price Var. $1,230 F; DM Eff. Var. $2,403 U; DL Price Var. $1,440 U DL Eff. Var. $1,800 F OH FB Var. $11,960 U

	OH PV Var. $1,200 U
P23-27A	1. DL hrs. worked, 4,350 2. DL Price Var. $2,175 U; Eff. Var. $1,125 F
P23-28A	DM Price Var. $840 F DM Eff. Var. $135 F 1. DL Price Var. $6,000 U; DL Eff. Var. $1,428 U 3. OH FB Var. $4,314 U OH PV Var. $1,134 F
P23-29A	1. DM Price Var. $11,000 U DM Eff. Var. $1,280 U DL Price Var. $170 U DL Eff. Var. $3,360 F 2. OH FB Var. $7,300 U OH PV Var. $1,920 F 3. GP $38,530
P23-30B	1. Op. inc. FB Var. $1,000 F; SV Var. $7,500 F
P23-31B	1. FB Gross profit $4,204,000 2. DM Price Var. $42,840 F; DM Eff. Var. $58,000 F; DL Price Var. $24,600 U DL Eff. Var. $42,000 F OH FB Var. $28,220 U OH PV Var. $90,000 F
P23-32B	1. DL hrs. worked 6,100 2. DL Price Var. $3,050 F; Eff. Var. $1,000 U DM Price Var. $3,808 U DM Eff. Var. $10,880 F
P23-33B	1. DL Price Var. $2,500 U; DL Eff. Var. $20,680 F 3. OH FB Var. $280 F OH PV Var. $1,760 U
P23-34B	1. DM Price Var. $13,500 F DM Eff. Var. $3,300 U DL Price Var. $1,125 F DL Eff. Var. $900 U 2. OH FB Var. $6,400 F OH PV Var. $9,600 F 3. GP $123,225
Case 1	Total FB Var. $21,550 F Total SVV, $133,600 U 51. DM Eff. Var. $15 F
Case 2	1. DM Eff Var. $15 F DL Eff. Var. $96 U
Team Project	NCF

Chapter 24

Quick Check 1 d; 2 b; 3 d; 4 a; 5 d;
6 c; 7 a; 8 a; 9 b; 10 b

S24-1	NCF
S24-2	1. $550 2. Bubba $650; Roscoe $450
S24-3	A $212.50 B $537.50
S24-4	1. Lo-Gain $430; Hi-Gain $185 2. Lo-Gain $300; Hi-Gain $250
S24-5	C $1,242.50 D $2,607.50

S24-6	Mid-Fi $1,660; Hi-Fi $1,510
S24-7	1. $141.20/hour 3. Op. inc. $3,380
S24-8	Doc. prep. $32/page; IT support $200/appl.; Training $90/hour
S24-9	1. $61,400 2. Op. loss $(8,900)
S24-10	NCF
S24-11	CC are $1,000 underallocated
S24-12	NCF
E24-13	1. Mat. Handling, $3/part 2. Total ind. mfg. cost/bumper $140.40
E24-14	2. Total ind. cost $3,200
E24-15	1. $454,000 2. Std. $162.50; Deluxe $291.50 3. Std. $181.60; Deluxe $272.40
E24-16	1. GP/unit: Std. $62.50; Deluxe $52.50 2. GP/unit: Std. $43.40; Deluxe $71.60
E24-17	New total cost/deluxe rim $342.50
E24-18	1. Cost/collar $9.60 2. Bid $374,400 3. Bid $435,500
E24-19	2. RIP Inv. bal. $480 3. CC are $720 overallocated
E24-20	1. CC are $2,040 underallocated 2. FG Inv. bal. $1,352
E24-21	NCF
E24-22	2. Cost saving from new program $15,000
E24-23	2. Cost saving from new program $200,000
P24-24A	Mfg. product cost, $148.00
P24-25A	1. Mfg. cost/unit: Std. $50; Unfinished $35 2. Full product cost/unit: Std. $74; Unfinished $53 4. Sale price $69/unit
P24-26A	2. Commercial indirect cost $86/unit 3. Travel pack indirect cost $1.50/unit
P24-27A	2. CC, $101,000 underallocated 3. RIP Inv. bal. $1,000
P24-28A	2. Net benefit $4,000
P24-29B	Mfg. product cost $95
P24-30B	1. Mfg. product cost/unit: Std. $49; Unpainted $36 2. Full product cost/unit: Std. $79; Unpainted $61 4. Sale price $121/unit
P24-31B	2. Personal-Page indirect cost $13.30/unit 3. Personal-Page indirect cost $25/unit

P24-32B	2. CC, $80,000 overallocated 3. RIP Inv. bal. $42,000
P24-33B	2. Net benefit $57,000
Case 1	1. Original system cost/unit Job A $5,560; B $5,520 2. ABC cost/unit: Job A $5,172.50; B $6,320
Case 2	Savings required $620/unit
Team Project	1. Total cost Headless shrimp $3.96/pkg. 3. Total cost Headless shrimp $4.7934/pkg.

Chapter 25

Quick Check 1 a; 2 b; 3 d; 4 b; 5 c;
6 a; 7 d; 8 c; 9 a; 10 d

S25-1	NCF
S25-2	Expected increase in op. inc. $1,000
S25-3	NCF
S25-4	Drop Accessories & increase op. inc. $15,000
S25-5	CM for equivalent MH: Deluxe $275; Regular $345
S25-6	Advantage to outsourcing $23,000
S25-7	NCF
S25-8	Advantage to processing fur- ther $3,000
S25-9	Payback period 2.5 years
S25-10	Payback period 5 years
S25-11	ARR 20%
S25-12	ARR 10%
S25-13	NPV $(2,643)
S25-14	NPV $5,650
E25-15	1. Increase in op. inc. $1,250 2. Decrease in op. inc. $(750)
E25-16	1. Increase in op. inc. $1,000
E25-17	Decrease in op. inc. $30,000
E25-18	Increase in op. inc. $10,000
E25-19	Total CM: Designer $34,500; Mod. $42,000
E25-20	Advantage to buying $1/unit
E25-21	Cost: Buy and leave idle $340,000, Buy and use facili- ties for other product $310,000

E25-22	Advantage to processing fur- ther $200
E25-23	Payback 4.8 years
E25-24	ARR Ward 10%; Vargas 8.8%
E25-25	NPV: A $(19,855); B $3,616
E25-26	IRR Project A between 10% and 12%
P25-27A	1. Increase in op. inc. $2,000
P25-28A	1. Decrease in op. inc. $20,000 2. b. Op. inc. $195,000
P25-29A	2. Spas: CM, $1.95/sq. ft.; Total CM at capacity $15,600
P25-30A	1. Advantage to making $38,000 2. Net cost to buy cereal and make cereal bars $838,000
P25-31A	1. Cost of processing further $118,750 3. Advantage to process fur- ther $16,250
P25-32A	1. Payback 7.43 years; ARR 8.1%; NPV $(705,500)
P25-33A	1. Payback: a. 5.2 years; b. 4.2 years ARR: a. 8.5%; b. 14.3% NPV: a. $(348,000); b. $77,500
P25-34B	1. Increase in Op. inc. $30,000
P25-35B	1. Decrease in Op. inc. $102,000 2b. Op. (loss) $(50,000)
P25-36B	2. 512 MB CM $1,800/MH; Total CM at capacity $8,100,000
P25-37B	1. Advantage to making $3,000 2. Net cost to buy decks and make another product $31,600
P25-38B	1. Cost of further processing $51,000 3. Advantage to selling as-is $21,000
P25-39B	1. Payback 3.85 years; ARR 26.8%; NPV, $664,160

P25-40B	1. Payback: a. 5.63 years; b. 9.27 years ARR: a. 15.5%; b. 3.6% NPV: a. $162,500; b. $(230,100)
Case 1	1. Total cost/mailbox $60 2. Total advantage to out- sourcing $12,650 3. Advantage to insourcing extra services $1,150
Case 2	1. Total earnings if he chooses bottling $9,439; meat packing $9,510
Team Project	2. Annual cost savings advantage to making $7,972,000 3a. Payback 5.64 years; b. ARR, 22.1%; c. NPV, $3,964,024

Appendix B

EB-1	Jan. 27, 2008 Loss on Sale $2,000
EB-2	2. Unrealized loss $(1,200)
EB-3	1. Gain on Sale $300
EB-4	3. LT Equity-Method Investment bal. $504 mil.
EB-5	3. Annual interest revenue $84,000
EB-6	b. Interest Revenue $80,000 c. Interest Revenue $4,000
EB-7	Overall net foreign-currency gain $4,000
PB-8	1. Dec. 31 Loss on Trading Investment $3,000 2. ST Investments bal. $133,000
PB-9	3. LT available-for-sale invest- ment $44,000; LT equity- method investments $670,000
PB-10	2. LT investments in bonds $748,800
PB-11	Income statement reports Foreign-currency loss, net $(600)

Photo Credits

Chapter 1, *Pages 2–3,* Courtesy of www.istockphoto.com. iStock Photo International/Royalty Free.

Chapter 2, *Pages 68–69,* © Gary Houlder/CORBIS. All Rights Reserved.

Chapter 3, *Pages 124–125,* Courtesy of PhotoEdit Inc.

Chapter 4, *Pages 194–195,* Courtesy of Howard Koby Photography.

Chapter 5, *Pages 252–253,* Courtesy of Getty Images–Stockbyte.

Chapter 6, *Pages 310–311,* Courtesy of Corbis Royalty Free.

Chapter 7, *Pages 354–355,* Courtesy of Masterfile Stock Image Library.

Chapter 8, *Pages 406–407,* Courtesy of Corbis Royalty Free.

Chapter 9, *Pages 454–455,* Courtesy of Getty Images–Stockbyte.

Chapter 10, *Pages 504–505,* Courtesy of The Image Works.

Chapter 11, *Pages 548–549,* Courtesy of Getty Images–Stockbyte.

Chapter 12, *Pages 594–595,* Courtesy of Getty Images/Digital Vision.

Chapter 13, *Pages 636–637,* Courtesy of PhotoEdit Inc.

Chapter 14, *Pages 688–689,* Courtesy of Joel Gordon Photography.

Chapter 15, *Pages 732–733,* Courtesy of www.istockphoto.com. iStock Photo International/Royalty Free.

Chapter 16, *Pages 782–783,* Courtesy of Getty Images, Inc.

Chapter 17, *Pages 846–847,* Courtesy of Alamy Images.

Chapter 18, *Pages 898–899,* Courtesy of www.istockphoto.com. iStock Photo International/Royalty Free.

Chapter 19, *Pages 942–943,* Courtesy of Corbis Royalty Free.

Chapter 20, *Pages 992–993,* Courtesy of Corbis Royalty Free.

Chapter 21, *Pages 1050–1051,* Courtesy of PhotoEdit Inc.

Chapter 22, *Pages 1100–1101,* Courtesy of Getty Images–Stockbyte.

Chapter 23, *Pages 1156–1157,* Courtesy of Corbis Royalty Free.

Chapter 24, *Pages 1202–1203,* Courtesy of Getty Images–Stockbyte.

Chapter 25, *Pages 1250–1251,* Courtesy of Corbis Royalty Free.

Glindex

A Combined Glossary/Subject Index

A

Absorption costing. The costing method that assigns both variable and fixed manufacturing costs to products, 1093
  applying, *vs.* variable costing, 1094–1095, 1095E21A-2
  exercises, 1096–1097
  and manager incentives, 1096
  problems, 1097–1098
  team project, 1098–1099
  vs. variable costing, 1094–1095, 1093E21A-1, 1095E21A-2

Accelerated depreciation method. A depreciation method that writes off more of the asset's cost near the start of its useful life than the straight-line method does, 513

Account. The detailed record of the changes in a particular asset, liability, or owner's equity during a period. The basic summary device of accounting, 60

Account form, 208

Accounting. The information system that measures business activities, processes that information into reports, and communicates the results to decision makers, 4
  concepts and principles of, 9–10
  financial *vs.* management, 5, 5E1-2
  role of, in business, 4
  users of, 4–5, 4E1-1

Accounting, and the business environment
  accounting equation, using, 11–12
  accounting vocabulary, 28–29
  applying your knowledge
    decision cases, 45–46
    ethical issues, 46–47
    financial statement case, 47
    team projects, 47–48
  assessing your progress
    exercises, 30–35
    problems, 36–44
  business organizations, types of, 8–9, 9E1-4
  concepts and principles of, 9–10
  language of, 4–5
  major business decisions, guidelines for, 22
  profession of, 6–7
  review questions (quick check), 26–27
  summary problem, 23–25
  transactions in
    analyzing, 13–17, 23–25
    demo docs, 49–57
    evaluating, user perspective of, 17–19, 18E1-7
    and financial statements used, 19–21, 20E1-8

Accounting concepts and principles
  in the adjusting process, 126–130
  in the business environment, 9–10

Accounting cycle. Process by which companies produce their financial statements for a specific period, 195
  explained, 196, 196E4-1

Accounting cycle, completing
  accounting ratios, 209–210
  accounting vocabulary, 216
  adjusting entries, recording, 203, 203E4-8
  applying your knowledge
    decision case, 236
    ethical issue, 236–237
    financial statement case, 237
    team project, 237–238
  assessing your progress
    exercises, 219–225
    problems, 225–234
  assets and liabilities, classifying, 207–208
  balance sheet
    classifying, 208
    forms, 208, 209E4-12–E4-13
  closing the accounts, 204–206, 204E4-9
    net income, 205–206, 205E4-10
    net loss, 206
  decision guidelines, 211
  financial statements, preparing, 203
  review questions (quick check), 217–218
  work sheet, 197–201, 197E4-2–5, 198E4-2, 199E4-6
    closing a net income, 205–206, 205E4-10
    closing a net loss, 206
    closing entries (demo doc), 244–251
    closing the accounts, 204, 204E4-9
    financial statements, preparing, 202E4-7, 203
    postclosing trial balance, 206, 207E4-11
    recording the adjusting entries, 203, 203E4-8
    summary problems, 200–201, 212–215

Accounting data, flow of, 69, 70E2-10

Accounting equation. The basic tool of accounting, measuring the resources of the business and the claims to those resources: Assets = Liabilities + Owner's Equity, 11–12, 11E1-5
  revenues and expenses, 68E2-6
  rules of debit and credit, 65, 65E2-3, 66E2-4

Accounting information systems
  accounting vocabulary, 378
  applying your knowledge
    decision cases, 401
    ethical issue, 402
    team projects, 402
  assessing your progress
    exercises, 381–388
    problems, 389–400
  computerized *vs.* manual, 355–359
  effective, 354–355

  journals
    and control accounts (decision guidelines) for, 373
    general, role of, 370–372
    special, 360–370
  review questions (quick check), 379–380
  summary problems, 374–377

Accounting period, 127–128

Accounting profession, 6–7
  ethics in, 6–7
  governing organizations, 6, 7E1-3
  professional conduct, standards of, 7

Accounting rate of return. A measure of profitability computed by dividing the average annual operating income from an asset by the average amount invested in the asset, 1268–1269, 1269E25-14

Accounting ratios, 209–210

Accounts, adjusting, 130–131

Accounts payable. A liability backed by the general reputation and credit standing of the debtor, 11, 61, 550

Accounts receivable. A promise to receive cash from customers to whom the business has sold goods or for whom the business has performed services, 60–61, 456

Accounts receivable turnover. Measure of a company's ability to collect cash from credit customers. To computer accounts receivable turnover, divide net credit sales by average net accounts receivable, 862

Accrual accounting. Accounting that records the impact of a business event as it occurs regardless of whether the transaction affected cash, 126
  ethical issues in, 146
  vs. cash-basis accounting, 126–127, 127E3-1

Accrued expense. An expense that the business has incurred but not yet paid. Also called accrued liability, 136
  accruing interest income, 137, 553
  accruing salary expense, 136–137
  adjustments, 140E3-7

Accrued liability. An expense that the business has not yet paid. Also called accrued expense, 61–62, 553

Accrued revenue. A revenue that has been earned but not yet collected in cash, 138

Accumulated depletion, 525

Accumulated depreciation. The cumulative sum of all depreciation expense recorded for an asset, 134

Acid-test ratio. Ratio of the sum of cash plus short-term investments plus net current receivables, to total current liabilities. Tells whether the entity could pay all its current liabilities if they came due immediately. Also called the quick ratio, 475, 861

Trademarks or Trade names. Assets that represent distinctive identifications of a product or service, 526

Trade receivable. *See* Note receivable

Trading on equity. Earning more income on borrowed money than the related interest expense, thereby increasing the earnings for the owners of the business. Also called leverage, 865

Transaction. An event that affects the financial position of a particular entity and can be recorded reliably, 13

business
 analyzing, 13–17, 23–25
 demo docs, 49–57
 evaluating, user perspective of, 17–21, 18E1-7
 financial statements used in, 19–21, 20E1-8
 personal, 13, 16
Transactions, recording
 account categories used in, 60–64
 accounting data, flow of, 71
 accounting terms used in, 60
 accounting vocabulary, 90
 from actual business documents, 80–82, 80E2-15, 81E2-16
 analyzing
  debit/credit (demo docs), 114–123
  decision guidelines for, 82
 applying your knowledge
  decision cases, 111
  ethical issue, 112
  financial statement case, 112
  team project, 112–113
 assessing your progress
  exercises, 91–100
  problems, 100–110
 double-entry accounting, 64–67
 journals and ledgers, details of, 79–81
 revenues and expenses, 67–71
 review questions (quick check), 88–89
 source documents, 72–78
 summary problem, 84–87
Transferred-in costs. Costs incurred in a previous process that are carried forward as part of the product's cost when it moves to the next process, 1011, 1012

Transposition, 78

Treasurer. In a large company, the person in charge of writing checks, 411

Treasury stock. A corporation's own stock that it has issued and later reacquired, 694
 basics of, 695–696
 purchase of, 694–695
 sale of, 696, 697E14-6
Trend percentages. A form of horizontal analysis in which percentages are computed by selecting a base year as 100% and expressing

amounts for following years as a percentage of the base amount, 852

Trial balance. A list of all accounts with their balances, 60, 76–77, 77E2-12
 errors in, correcting, 78
 summary problem, 83–86
 unadjusted, 130, 130E3-4
 see also Adjusted trial balance

Trojan. A malicious program that hides inside a legitimate program and works like a virus, 414

U

Uncollectibles, accounting for
 estimating, 461–464
  aging-of-accounts-receivable method, 462–463, 463E9-2
  percent-of-sales method, 461–462
  using percent-of-sales and aging methods together, 464, 646E9-3
 writing off, 464–465
  direct write-off method, 465
  recovery of, 465
Uncollectible-account expense. Cost to the seller of extending credit. Arises from the failure to collect from credit customers. Also called doubtful-account expense or bad-debt expense, 460

Underallocated (manufacturing) overhead. The manufacturing overhead allocated to Work in Progress Inventory is less than the amount of manufacturing overhead costs actually incurred, 959

Underwriters, 645

Unearned revenue. A liability created when a business collects cash from customers in advance of doing work. Also called deferred revenue, 138–139, 180, 553
 recorded initially as a revenue, 180–182
Unemployment compensation tax. Payroll tax paid by employers to the government, which uses the money to pay unemployment benefits to people who are out of work, 561

Units-of-production (UOP) depreciation method. Depreciation method by which a fixed amount of depreciation is assigned to each unit of output produced by an asset, 513, 513E10-7
 depreciation schedule, 513E10-7
Unlimited personal liability. When a partnership (or a proprietorship) cannot pay its debts with business assets, the partners (or the proprietor) must use personal assets to meet the debt, 597

V

Value engineering. Reevaluating activities to reduce costs while satisfying customer needs, 1210

Variable costing. The costing method that assigns only variable manufacturing costs to products
 and absorption costing, differences between, 1093, 1093E21A-1
 vs. absorption costing, 1094–1995, 1095E21A-2
 applying, *vs.* absorption costing, 1094–1095, 1095EA-2
 exercises, 1096–1097
 and manager incentives, 1096
 problems, 1097–1098
 team project, 1098–1099
Variance. The difference between an actual amount and the budget. A variance is labeled as favorable if it increases operating income and unfavorable if it decreases operating income, 1158

Vertical analysis. Analysis of a financial statement that reveals the relationship of each statement item to a specified base, which is the 100% figure, 852

Vice presidents (VP), 1122

Vote, 644

Voucher. Instrument authorizing a cash payment, 428

W

Wages, 558

Weighted-average process costing method. A process costing method that costs all equivalent units of work with a weighted average of the previous period's and the current period's cost per equivalent unit, 1009–1011, 1010E20-11

Withdrawals, 16–17, 62

Withheld income tax. Income tax deducted from employees' gross pay, 559

Withholding allowances, 559

Withholding deductions. *See* Payroll withholding deductions

Working capital. Current assets minus current liabilities; measures a business's ability to meet its short-term obligations with its current assets, 859

Work in process inventory. Goods that are partway through the manufacturing process but not yet complete, 909, 913

Work sheet. A columnar document designed to help move data from the trial balance to their financial statements, 197
 for closing entries (demo doc), 244–251
 for completing the accounting cycle, 197–201, 198E4-2, 199E4-6
 summary problem, 200–201
 for merchandising business, 279–280, 279E5A-1
Written agreement, 596

Company Index

Typical Charts of Accounts for Different Types of Businesses

(For Businesses Discussed in Chapters 1–12)

Service Proprietorship

Assets

Cash
Accounts Receivable
Allowance for Uncollectible Accounts
Notes Receivable, Short-Term
Interest Receivable
Supplies
Prepaid Rent
Prepaid Insurance
Notes Receivable, Long-Term
Land
Furniture
Accumulated Depreciation—Furniture
Equipment
Accumulated Depreciation—Equipment
Building
Accumulated Depreciation—Building

Liabilities

Accounts Payable
Notes Payable, Short-Term
Salary Payable
Wage Payable
Employee Income Tax Payable
FICA Tax Payable
State Unemployment Tax Payable
Federal Unemployment Tax Payable
Employee Benefits Payable
Interest Payable
Unearned Service Revenue
Notes Payable, Long-Term

Owner's Equity

Owner, Capital
Owner, Withdrawals

Revenues and Gains

Service Revenue
Interest Revenue
Gain on Sale of Land (or Furniture, Equipment, or Building)

Expenses and Losses

Salary Expense
Payroll Tax Expense
Rent Expense
Insurance Expense
Supplies Expense
Uncollectible-Account Expense
Depreciation Expense—Furniture
Depreciation Expense—Equipment
Depreciation Expense—Building
Property Tax Expense
Interest Expense
Miscellaneous Expense
Loss on Sale of Land (Furniture, Equipment, or Building)

Service Partnership

Same as Service Proprietorship, except for Owners' Equity:

Owners' Equity

Partner 1, Capital
Partner 2, Capital
Partner N, Capital

Partner 1, Drawing
Partner 2, Drawing
Partner N, Drawing